OPM - 37

AH - 90, 359
PB - 89

S0-ACO-221

ECIA · Ch. 2 - 69

The Bowker Annual

The Bowker Annual

of Library

&

Book Trade

Information

29th Edition   1984

Compiled and Edited by
Julia Ehresmann

Consulting Editor
Frank L. Schick

Sponsored by
The Council of National Library and
Information Associations, Inc.

R. R. BOWKER COMPANY
NEW YORK & LONDON

Published by R. R. Bowker Company
205 East Forty-second Street, New York, NY 10017
Copyright © 1984 by Xerox Corporation
All rights reserved
International Standard Book Number 0-8352-1680-2
International Standard Serial Number 0068-0540
Library of Congress Catalog Card Number 55-12434
Printed and bound in the United States of America

No copyright is claimed for articles in this volume prepared by U.S. Government employees as part of their official duties. Such articles are in the public domain and can be reproduced at will.

Contents

Part 2
Legislation, Funding, and Grants

Part 3
Library Education, Placement, and Salaries

Part 4
Research and Statistics

Library Research and Statistics

Book Trade Research and Statistics

Part 5

Reference Information

Bibliographies

Distinguished Books

Part 6
Directory of Organizations

Preface

In the three decades that *The Bowker Annual* has been a presence in the library, book trade, and—more recently—information industry communities, it has achieved the status of a classic. Year after year *The Annual* has been a robust and reliable compilation of data, news, research reports, and reference information. Together, the first 29 editions form a unique cumulative record of the library world.

As *The Annual* approached its thirtieth year, we decided to take a fresh look at its contents and to give it a more contemporary look. Early last summer, we polled 600 former users to try to determine which features are most valued today and what we could do to improve *The Annual*'s usefulness to all of you. The results of the poll were not surprising. You asked for more statistics. You told us that you like the narrative-style reports—but that you rarely read them all the way through. You value our lists of library and literary prizes, and you asked for a more complete calendar of coming events. Emphatically, you rejected a larger book size. Most significantly, you expressed almost equal interest in all three worlds that *The Annual* services: libraries, publishing, and the information industry. We responded by giving you what you asked for.

Special Reports this year include two umbrella articles. The first is a three-part piece that traces funding patterns over the past 30 years and anticipates the fiscal outlook for public, school, and academic libraries. The second examines two aspects of the new technologies—what happens to library organization when technology is introduced, and how learning systems have been adapted to library computer-based systems. In individual Special Reports, Patricia Berger addresses the critical issue of access to federal information, and Katharine Phenix sums up the faltering progress of women in the library profession. In anticipation of the continued importance of copyright and networking developments, these two reports have been placed in the News Reports section of Part 1, where they become annual features.

Where the money comes from receives more space than in recent years with the reinstatement of the Foundation Center's data on funding by private foundations in Part 2. Part 3 gives a many-sided picture of education, the labor market, and job placement in the library world. Research and Statistics (Part 4) is fuller than ever, with more data and research reports that are crucial for libraries and also for all industries that serve libraries.

For reference, there are three impressive current bibliographies in Part 5: for the library, the book trade, and—new this year—on high technology for librarians and library users. We especially want to call attention to Part 6, the Directory of Associations. It continues to be a uniquely rich gathering of many kinds of regional, state, national, foreign, and international organizations, giving officers, committees, committee members, and publications—an invaluable book-within-a-book. We think the new design makes *The Annual* easier to use and reflects its position as a contemporary classic.

To all the contributors and individuals who responded to our requests for articles, data, and advice, we extend our sincere thanks. Once again, consulting editor Frank L. Schick has been a dependable adviser. Filomena Simora performed the manuscript editing and in-house data compilation with her usual meticulous professionalism. Finally, it is high time to acknowledge the contribution of Chandler B. Grannis, who for the greater part of the last 30 years has contributed statistics on output, prices, and sales of the book trade. Having begun "out of blind, stupid willingness," Chandler continues to be an inestimably valuable and cheerful giver.

Julia Ehresmann
Editor, *The Bowker Annual*

Part 1
Reports from the Field

News Reports

LJ News Report, 1983

Karl Nyren

Senior Editor, *Library Journal*

Despite automation, networking, online data bases, and the lure of nonprint materials, the book remained very much the central concern of public libraries and of academic libraries where the lion's share of the acquisitions budget hasn't yet been preempted by journals or online data bases. Few librarians dispute the proposition that one measure of administrative success is the percentage of the budget that can be used for book acquisition, but only one spokesperson for the book argued in 1983 that public libraries should forget about networking and put everything into books (as related under "Networks and Networking" later in this report).

Highlights

- Despite automation, networking, online data bases, and the lure of nonprint materials, the book remained very much the central concern of libraries in 1983.
- There was a perception of a growing divergence between the federal administration and the library community, as well as with many, but not all, publishers.
- Administration friendliness to the private sector was evident in a Request for Proposal for a study of alternative library funding.
- A forecast for employment in the coming decade sees the number of library jobs and new library professionals staying constant or increasing only slightly.
- The third decade of library automation is a period of growing decentralization, with libraries returning to cherished local autonomy.
- Federal aid to libraries seems likely to survive, possibly in an improved form, despite the present administration's trend to cut funding of social services.

Public libraries flaunted their circulation records (10 million in Ames, Iowa, after 78 years); revised their selection policies to reflect the mature version of "demand" buying

Note: Adapted from *Library Journal*, January 1984, where the article was entitled "News in Review, 1983."

(Enoch Pratt, Baltimore); studied their readers' tastes and found that they are pleased with the books provided (at the Queens Borough Public Library, New York City); and devised tactics to entice readers into borrowing more books (Prince George's County [Maryland] Memorial Library did so to help achieve circulation goals; Waterville, Maine, saw the circulation of fictionalized history increase after being shelved with historical fiction). Improving libraries in Idaho translates into buying more books for libraries: Newly introduced legislation for a Public Library Improvement Program asks that most of the funds requested—$500,000—go for new books, with much smaller amounts for automation and networking.

Honoring the book is an activity that is flourishing, with the Center for the Book at the Library of Congress providing a national focus. At the American Antiquarian Society in Massachusetts, a major new study of "The Book in History" promises rather more than veneration; it aims to apply the insights of French historian Lucien LeFebvre to the study of the book in its relation to economic, social, and cultural history. Topping off the many efforts to promote reading is the appearance on the ABC network of "Smart Cat," a Library of Congress–sponsored cartoon creature who aims to make reading respectable for children.

The roots of the book in printing technologies of yesterday are drawing the interest of librarians and their patrons. An exhibit in St. Louis commemorated the invention of movable type, which figured in the city's history as a former printing center.

Many libraries displayed the materials provided by the International Association of Printing House Craftsmen for the commemoration of Printing Week. The New York Public Library proudly put on display a handsome edition of a hitherto unpublished Faulkner manuscript, creating a book with both scholarly and artistic luster.

A great tribute to American books was continued in 1983 with the publication of the Library of America series. The Helena Rubenstein Foundation gave New York libraries $25,000 to supply their readers with copies of the new editions of American classics.

Finally, a new bimonthly published by R. R. Bowker Company, *Small Press: The Magazine of Independent Book Publishing*, was received with unexpected enthusiasm for the work of men and women who have elected to carry on the traditions of fine printing.

Collections

The annual tale of the movement into libraries of precious new resources is a reminder that, in the words of Fred Kilgour, the national library is the nation's libraries, and, despite their often insular behavior, all are "a part of the main." Only a few glimpses of this quiet torrent and library efforts to harness it appear in the library news pages, but they are revealing:

In January, there was word of the Research Libraries Group laying the foundations for a national data base of manuscripts and archival materials.

In February, Radio Canada launched a depository program of music and spoken word records with a gift of 750 recordings to Case Western Reserve; Irving Wallace turned over his papers to Claremont Colleges. Also in February, the University of Texas at Austin dramatically demonstrated the role of scholarly collections with an exhibit of books that trace their origins to treasures in UTA rare book collections.

In May, the Birmingham (Alabama) Public Library received a gift of $250,000 to help it fulfill a role as a center of southern culture; the University of California at Santa Cruz accepted a printing history treasure, the archives of the Trianon Press; and Wisconsin libraries received $25,000 to set up collections of learning toys for children too poor to have them at home.

The big numbers came up in October: The University of North Carolina saluted its three-millionth volume; Stanford celebrated its five-millionth; and Temple University increased its already large newspaper holdings with the archives of the *Philadelphia Evening Bulletin.*

National Information Policy

In 1983 there was a perception of a growing divergence between the administration and the library community as well as with many, but not all, publishers. And there were signs that the traditional rapport between librarians and publishers was beginning to reassert itself after the latter's spell of increased identification with the militant and much smiled-upon private sector. The National Information Policy under the Reagan administration can be defined only in terms of how the government stands on a number of issues that involve information, libraries, and publishers.

Copyright

The Copyright Office, in its report to Congress on the workings of the Copyright Act, sided with those publishers, mainly journal publishers, that renewed the accusation that libraries are abusing photocopying. A rebuttal for libraries was issued by the Association of Research Libraries, which found that the most recent study of photocopying, by King Research, Inc., was not only biased in favor of the private sector, but that its figures belied the conclusions drawn by King and those in the private sector representing the industry position.

The OCLC claim to copyright control over its data base raised new issues regarding the copyright of data and became a sticking point in the negotiations between OCLC and the regional networks that broker OCLC services and products. The Copyright Office's current tilt toward the private sector apparently had no effect here, but it could if the matter goes to court.

A new numbering system, still in the works at year's end, promises to make it easy for a new and more sophisticated generation of copying machines to keep track of the traffic in copies of journal articles. The system is based on the ISBN (International Standard Book Number) and the SAN (Standard Address Number); it aims to provide a unique identification number for each journal article.

[See the copyright update for 1983 in the News Reports section of Part 1—*Ed.*]

Minorities

The administration's attitude toward minorities, as expressed in reductions of social programs of which they are the chief beneficiaries, as well as in the hostility expressed toward minority groups by prominent members of the administration, had little if any impact on library concerns. One shining exception: Literacy is favored by everyone, with the prestige of the vice president's wife supporting literacy and the RIF (Reading Is Fundamental) program.

Late in the year, the National Commission on Libraries and Information Science released the report of its Task Force on Library Service to Cultural Minorities. The report recommended a number of ways in which libraries could contribute to the improvement of the quality of life of members of the main minority groups: blacks, Hispanics, Native Americans, and Asian Americans. Among the recommendations were attention to minority interests by libraries and library schools; recruitment of minority group members to staffs and boards of libraries; encouragement of publication by minorities; and more publications that reflect minority interests and counter the negative images of minority group members. The list was predictable; the response of the National Commission to several of the more important items was not, except as a genuflection to the administration. NCLIS, however, withheld its support for a recommendation that a specific percentage of library aid funds be earmarked for minority interests, for a recommendation that publishers produce more books by minority group members, and for one that recommended the withdrawal by publishers of books with negative stereotypes of minorities. The reasons given were technically correct, but the impression left was of a lack of sympathy for the concerns of minority groups.

Access to Federal Information

The administration's intent to clear away the excess of paper created and handled by government agencies, keeping those that pay their way in sales, has led to a wholesale dumping of publications and sharp increases in prices, both of which have alarmed librarians. On the other hand, reports indicate that the Government Printing Office is doing a good job of cutting costs and improving services, as well as keeping the library community informed of its activities in releases that, for a government agency, are models of clarity and good sense. It is also cutting prices.

The ticklish problem posed by the entrenched, often very highly paid, employees of the federal government appears to have been handled well; a single collective bargaining agreement covering all the unions involved in the GPO was hammered out with little conflict.

At year's end, some of the most important issues surrounding government publications were embodied in the recommendations put forth by the Joint Committee on Printing for the better administration of Title 44, which provides for the dissemination of government documents to the public. Perhaps the most important of these recommendations concerns the inclusion of electronic and other new forms of publication within the scope of depository and archival programs. Most likely to draw the fire of the administration and the private sector are recommendations that would establish controls over agency publications produced by the private sector. The jury is still out on this important aspect of national information policy; the fate of the recommendations by the joint committee should be known early in 1984.

[See the special report on public access to federal information later in Part 1 of this volume—*Ed.*]

Public vs. Private Sector

The administration's intention to cut down the size and power of the federal bureaucracy manifested itself in two areas: the transfer of functions performed by federal employees to private firms and the reduction in the pay of federal employees. The first led to a directive issued by the Office of Management and Budget that put pressure on federal agencies to contract out their library operations to private sector firms. The second, pressed by the

Office of Personnel Management (OPM), would reduce the compensation received by federal librarians by dropping the entry-level requirements for professional positions and thus bring in new librarians at lower salaries.

Administration friendliness to the private sector was evident in a document issued by the Department of Education: a Request for Proposal on a study of alternative library funding. Its language clearly indicated what was wanted: that a case be made for libraries getting their funding from nongovernmental sources, such as user fees.

NEH Criticized

Administration support of the divestiture of federally controlled natural resources was most dramatically embodied by Secretary of the Interior James Watt, but it manifested itself also in pressure on the National Endowment for the Humanities.

Late in the year, a television production supported by the NEH, which examined the impact of strip mining in the West, drew immediate criticism that NEH was engaging in matters inappropriate to its mission. NEH, somewhat shamefacedly, agreed, and the administration marked out still another area where information inimical to its policies can be limited.

International

Many good things happened in 1983 to encourage and facilitate the free flow of information across national and linguistic barriers. A conference on North/South American Information Transfer at the University of Michigan School of Librarianship early in the year focused attention on that area. Taking advantage of the presence at IFLA in Canada of distinguished foreign librarians, Rutgers staged a June 10–12 International Conference on Databases in the Humanities and Social Sciences.

A major communications link was forged by Chemical Abstracts Service and the West German *Fachinformationszentrum Energie, Physik, Mathematik*. They will merge the two systems, utilizing the same software and apportioning to each its specialized area. Access to all resources in the new system will be either through Columbus, Ohio, or Karlsruhe, West Germany.

Linguistic barriers to communication in Chinese, Japanese, and Korean started to crumble with the introduction by both RLIN and OCLC of cataloging in the East Asian vernacular languages. OCLC lifted its eyes and aspirations from the West Coast to the whole Pacific Rim, and changed the name of its Western Service Center to the OCLC Pacific Network.

New bonds with Asian librarians and growing interest in the Pacific regions were strengthened by the meeting at the ALA conference in Los Angeles of two groups, the Asian Pacific American Librarians Association and the Chinese-American Librarians Association. The distinguished roster of speakers testified eloquently to the fact that this is no splinter movement, but evidence of a growing mainline interest.

NTIS, the National Technical Information Service, opened a new window on foreign technology with a weekly newsletter, which contains English-language abstracts of articles in several disciplines. *Foreign Technology Abstracts Newsletter* now provides access to works in progress in some 50 countries.

The Universal Serials and Book Exchange moved to make its resources more accessible to foreign clients by reducing prices and procedures that put a premium on orders coming from outside the United States.

Finally, the cosmopolitanism of student bodies in U.S. colleges and universities, with many foreign students lacking fluency in English, has led to special efforts in library orientation. Programs in 1983 featured speakers or tapes for library use orientation in Chinese, Russian, Arabic, Farsi, French, Japanese, Spanish, and Thai.

Presidential Libraries

The Nixon Presidential Library apparently found a home early in the year at Chapman College in San Clemente. Later in the year, however, things were stalled again over the question of the former president's control over the material.

The Reagan Presidential Library, Museum, and Center for the Study of Public Affairs staked out a home at Stanford, under the sympathetic conservative wing of the Hoover Institution for War and Peace. Immediate opposition came from students and faculty and Stanford's administration balked at giving control to Hoover. This one, too, is still up in the air.

Intellectual Freedom

The climate for intellectual freedom turned frosty in 1983 as the administration revealed itself as an enemy of freedom of information. Executive Order 84, still under debate at this writing, threatens to put a lifetime muzzle on anyone who has access to secret information. The directive was apparently an expression of the White House annoyance at embarrassing leaks; as such, it was comparable to swatting a fly with a hand grenade. It was, however, in keeping with administration behavior in this area.

The Freedom of Information Act came under administration attack, with various procedural and financial barriers threatening to emasculate it. An attempt, which was fortunately unsuccessful, was made to bar from showing two Canadian films in this country, one on U.S.-generated acid rain and another on nuclear peril, unless they were labeled "propaganda."

The military was congratulating itself late in 1983 at its successful barring of the press from the invasion of Grenada, a gambit it copied from the British Falklands war.

The forces of freedom celebrated Banned Books Week again, and enthusiastically; they could point to still another in a series of legislative actions protecting the privacy of library records—this one in Nebraska. John Swan, writing in the September 1 issue of *Library Journal* (*LJ*), made a thoughtful critique of the problems of privacy of circulation records and the increasing number of statutes concerning "Public Records and Library Privacy."

The mini-issue of minors borrowing videotapes of R-rated movies from libraries was raised briefly, but only one case made it into print. Librarians, apparently, are handling the matter quietly in accordance with their policies on access to materials by minors. The New York Library Association disavowed film industry ratings as too much like labeling and having no place in the cataloging or other handling of films and tapes in libraries. Again, that failed to raise much interest, possibly because at the moment videotapes are being bought by libraries primarily in two areas: Hollywood features and educational films.

Buildings

According to the Architectural Issue of *Library Journal* (December), library construction fell to a new low in 1983, in number of projects, total square footage of new and remodeled buildings, and funds committed to both academic and public library construction. The big news in federal funding was the one-year, full funding of the Library Services and Construction Act, Title II; it also promises to be the big news in public library building for 1984.

In 1983, approximately $66 million was spent on public library construction. In 1984, the $50 million in new federal funds will expand up to four times that amount with the addition of matching money (if all the money is spent in fiscal 1984). The requirement that the projects be in areas of high unemployment will improve many library facilities that are most in need of it.

Meanwhile, libraries are increasingly being housed in nontraditional structures: Portables, kiosks (both indoor and out), and metal industrial-type buildings are some of the options for hard-pressed library budgets. A growing number of adaptive reuse projects are turning sows' ears, like abandoned supermarkets, gas stations, and truck terminals, into silk purses.

Energy saving continues to be a concern, with solar construction becoming common: In Mercer County, New Jersey, seven solar branches were built to a single master plan; in San Jose, California, the new public library is 100 percent solar; and at Lehigh University in Pennsylvania, passive solar construction will characterize a new $10.8 million library. Heat pumps were widely reported by libraries, and in almost all sections of the country. Something new under the sun, but not yet found in a library, was noted at the University of Minnesota Civil and Mineral Engineering Building, where an innovative system of mirrors, like a reverse periscope, pipes sunlight into underground rooms.

Better access for the handicapped is a continuing concern, and many of the new LSCA-funded construction projects will feature ramps, elevators, and rest rooms designed for the handicapped. In 1983, many libraries bought elevators and chair lifts for this purpose. Something new in this area is found at the University of New Mexico, where two professors have developed an electronic guidance system to guide blind patrons around the library.

Seattle is taking a long look at alternatives to its present standard configuration of main library and branch library buildings. San Diego is approaching the question with real soul-searching, asking whether the public library should be combined with other types of libraries, whether its main library facilities would be better decentralized, and other questions—before building planning even begins.

Signs of the times, both grim ones, emerged at the new library building projects in Dallas and Orlando, Florida. Orlando's big, new library is going to cost $5 million less than estimated, because Florida builders are so desperate for work. In Dallas, the effect of the current dumping of the mentally ill and destitute was felt in that city's beautiful, new library. The new reading room furniture was vandalized so badly by the street people who moved in that the furniture had to be stored. [See "Library Buildings in 1983" in Part 4 of this volume—*Ed.*]

Archives and Libraries

Archives and libraries drew a little closer in 1983, reflecting a mutual concern for information preservation and for the threat to public access to the National Archives posed by the administration's cutoff of funds for the dissemination of census data. (The census data are available again, but only from a private vendor.)

In January, note was taken of plans made by the Research Libraries Group to establish a new data base for archives and manuscripts.

The rise of interest in fostering state archival programs was exemplified in Texas, where a major conference focused on a vision of a Texas Archival Network, and also in Oklahoma, where a new statewide association will link archivists, librarians, and other curators of historical materials for the better preservation of the state's heritage.

Conservation

The awakened interest in conservation of library materials, with librarians once again making much of their curatorial role, shows no signs of abatement. State and regional planning for conservation, a new proliferation of workshops and other training opportunities, and the creation of new agencies characterized the year of work in conservation. Among these were a workshop on the conservation of photographs in Andover, Massachusetts; a National Endowment for the Humanities grant for a five-state cooperative conservation program based at Southern Illinois University at Carbondale; and the creation of the Ohio Cooperative Conservation Information Office (OCCIO), a new agency, housed by the Ohio State Library, but intended to become a self-supporting provider of conservation services to libraries of all types. Istor Products, of Portland, Oregon, came out with videotape training aids for the conservation of rare books.

An American firm, supported by a grant funneled through the American Library Association, is developing a device for the nondestructive photocopying of books. The December 1 issue of *Library Journal* featured a photograph of a British machine that, according to its maker, Optronics, Inc., of Cambridge, England, already does the job.

Library People in 1983

A sampling of the news of people in the library world reveals a number of interesting job changes:

Lillian Bradshaw, Dallas Public Library director, was on temporary assignment to help reorganize the city's court system.

William DeJohn, director of the foundered Pacific Northwest Bibliographic Center, moved to the University of Washington as head of the Resource Sharing Program.

Wesley Doak is the new state librarian of Oregon; other new state librarians are Virginia Downey in New Mexico and Bridget Lamont in Illinois.

Mary Ghikas left the Chicago Public to head the Universal Serials and Book Exchange.

Kathleen Heim, a faculty member at the Graduate School of Library and Information Science at the University of Illinois, became dean of the Louisiana State University School of Library and Information Science.

Joseph Howard left the Library of Congress's Processing Services to become director of the troubled National Agricultural Library.

James Kennedy, director of the AMIGOS Bibliographic Council, joined OCLC as sales manager for the western United States.

Donald Sager is now city librarian, Milwaukee Public Library.

Claude E. Walston left the corporate ranks of ITT to become dean of the College of Library and Information Services at the University of Maryland.

Louella V. Wetherbee is the new executive director of the AMIGOS Bibliographic Council.

Retiring in 1983 were Alice Ball, director of the Universal Serials and Book Exchange; Lillian Bradshaw, director of the Dallas Public Library; Martin M. Cummings, director of the National Medical Library; Richard Darling, who leaves the Columbia School of Library Service to enter the ministry; Ruth Frame, deputy executive director of ALA; Vivian Hewitt, librarian of the Carnegie Endowment for International Peace; Chris Hoy, conference manager for ALA; Philip J. McNiff, director, Boston Public Library.

Resigning were Stephen R. Salmon, assistant vice president at the University of California; Allan B. Veaner, university librarian, University of California, Santa Barbara; and Julie Virgo, executive director of the Association of College and Research Libraries.

In the obituaries for 1983 were some of the most honored names in librarianship. Among them were Edwin Castagna, Lura Currier, Ernest DeProspo, Theodore Hines, Andrew Horn, Keyes Metcalf, Jens Nyholm, Eli Oboler, Annette Phinazee, and Constance Winchel.

Gravely wounded by a discharged former employee, Gustave Harrer, director of Libraries at the University of Florida, was out of the hospital and home for Christmas. Although he is a quadriplegic, he has already resumed work at home and expects to be in his office on a part-time basis after the first of the year.

Personnel in Libraries

News about the people who operate libraries dealt in 1983 with attempts to reduce the cost of personnel and increase productivity; the roles of other professionals working in libraries; continuing education and staff development; jobs and placement; the threats raised by OPM and OMB; discrimination, mainly against women; unions; volunteers; and efforts by administrators to improve the quality of life for staff members.

At the Library Information and Technology Association (LITA) conference in Baltimore, it was quite clear that library administrators are counting on automation to cut library staffs, despite claims that it will "free them for more professional work." [See "The Impact of New Technology on Library Organization" by Hugh Atkinson in Part 1 of this volume—*Ed.*]

Prince George's County Memorial Library in Maryland increased the work week from 37½ to 40 hours, not, it claims, to increase productivity, but to bring the library in line with other county agencies. PGCML, like many libraries, has steadily reduced staff by attrition.

The Office of Personnel Management aimed at considerable savings on librarians in 1983 by reducing the entrance grade (and thus salary) of professional librarians.

The Office of Management and Budget attacked the cost of librarians in another way: by pressing for the contracting out of libraries and library functions throughout the federal government. Private firms running the libraries of the government would very likely be staffed by people displaced by contracting out, and although the contractors might not save the government money, librarians working for contractors would surely work for lower pay.

The continued operation of a long-standing program to staff libraries with less expensive people was noted in January. This is the Maryland program to train library "associates"—people without a library degree but with a bachelor's in a subject area—to do much the same work as higher paid librarians in many Maryland libraries.

Other Professionals

Consultants are steadily increasing on the library scene, both in-house staff members, with special expertise and major responsibility for an area of operation, and outside consultants, who may be librarians (usually directors) or independent professionals. School library consultants are back in Colorado, after funding became available to the state library to pay them for approved consulting assignments at school libraries asking for aid. In April, ALA's Library Administration and Management Association (LAMA) was advertising for a consultant to design an institute on radio and TV.

There was competition: Top automation and network consultants vied for the assignment of studying the automation future of an upstate New York region; King Research beat out RMG and Richard Boss for the job. But Boss won the network planning assignment for one of Connecticut's multitype circulation and interlibrary loan systems. Boss was also the consultant responsible for the vigorous new marketing effort of the Universal Serials and Book Exchange (USBE).

Perhaps because their numbers are growing so rapidly, consultants will no longer be trained by the Association of Research Libraries (ARL) program for this purpose. The last trainees were chosen in 1983.

Other professionals seen this year in American libraries include social workers doing personnel work at the Brooklyn Public Library and the Spokane Public Library. The Wisconsin state library agency added a school library microcomputer specialist to its staff. The Metropolitan Library System of Oklahoma County put a grants officer on its staff this year, on a part-time, contract basis.

Staff Development

One of the more successful statewide initiatives in staff development has been the Michigan Interorganizational Committee on Continuing Library Education (MICCLE) program, which in 1983 was able to issue some 2,000 certificates to people who had earned CEUs (continuing education units). Michigan librarians also have a new and popular annual series of staff development forums, sponsored by a number of library and library education agencies, where national and professional issues are discussed.

As fewer staff members receive funds to attend conferences, the sharing of information and new ideas by those who do attend becomes more important to the professional growth of the whole staff. Three libraries were noted in 1983 for doing an excellent conference reporting job: Cuyahoga County Library (Cleveland, Ohio); the library at the University of California, Irvine; and the Enoch Pratt Free Library in Baltimore.

Low cost and high tech combined last summer when the microcomputer users group of North Carolina (MUGLNC) ran a "summer camp" for microcomputer users. Low-cost dormitory housing and meals, plenty of hardware, and good instructors made this one both easy on the pocketbook and successful.

With an objective similar to that of the Michigan issues forums noted earlier, planners on the staff of the Los Angeles County Library went on a retreat where they could spend hours and days in intensive discussion. And for the second consecutive year,

Washington's Yakima Valley Library held an all-day forum for all its staff on current library issues.

Jobs and Placements

A forecast for library employment in the coming decade, by King Research, sees the number of library jobs and new library professionals staying constant or increasing only a little. But within those numbers, King predicts that many more librarians will have ALA-accredited graduate degrees and fewer will have school certification. [For a report on the results of the survey conducted by King Research, see "The Library Labor Market: A Study of Supply and Demand" in Part 3 of this volume—*Ed.*]

The new Job Training Partnership Act replaces the Comprehensive Employment and Training Act (CETA), but it will be no ready source for low-paid library staff as CETA was. With Private Industry Councils running the county or multicounty projects, libraries will have trouble even getting in the door; at year's end, no good news had come in on this.

The recruiting of librarians, as indicated by "personnel wanted" classified ads, was on a steadily increasing curve in 1983, as compared to the previous year. The qualifications asked for in candidates also were steadily escalating, although salaries for comparable qualifications appeared not to be increasing.

One large group of librarians, those in rural libraries, was found by a survey to be paid between $10,000 and $15,000 a year and to be predominantly 40 to 45 years in age. Since rural libraries are all those serving populations under 20,000 by the most common definition, this covers a lot of mature, midcareer librarians.

Discrimination

In 1983, the Library of Congress issued its first three-year plan for affirmative action. A report on LC staffing indicated that today part-time library workers tend to be middle level white women; a few years ago they were black men, working in lower level jobs.

Also in 1983, the University of Minnesota agreed to award back pay amounting to $750,000, or about $20,000 each, to women librarians charging discrimination. Librarians in Fairfax County, Virginia, are following suit.

An ambitious library education initiative launched at the University of Washington library school was originally intended to enrich the management skills of women, enabling them to move more rapidly into higher administrative positions. Over a period of time, however, the Career Development and Assessment Center changed its emphasis, which is now toward aiding top administrators to pick the best candidates for managerial positions.

Unions

Union activity was very quiet in 1983, with public employees gaining the right to organize in two states for the first time (Ohio and Illinois).

An interesting study reported in the winter issue of *Minnesota Libraries* concluded that unions in Minnesota do indeed go along with higher pay in libraries. Union librarians also get more sick days and paid holidays and better insurance protection, but not more vacation days. In unionized libraries, staff take up a larger share of the budget, but they provide a more stable work force, with less turnover—findings that indicate that the analysis of the cost/benefit of collective bargaining to the library may be a complex task.

Volunteers

There were many fewer stories in the 1983 news about volunteers, largely because a great many volunteer programs have been launched and are steadily functioning, accepted components of the total library staff.

In her second *LJ* Special Report, "Volunteers in Libraries II," Alice Sizer Warner depicts a much matured movement, with experience amassed over the past years and a body of information and knowledge available to any library approaching the use of volunteers for the first time, a cadre of qualified consultants, sample policies, clerical forms, and other materials useful in volunteer programs.

Staff Health

Both library administrators and library workers show an increased interest in staff health today. Librarians turn up in marathons and other running events; at the Library of Congress, an alternate menu is available in the cafeteria for people who prefer to cut down on cholesterol, salt, sugar, and other substances that may be harmful.

Exercise programs are being made available; one mentioned in 1983 was the lunch-hour exercise period, to the Jane Fonda record, that many Houston Public Library staff members choose instead of lunch.

At the Public Library of Columbus and Franklin County, Ohio, a more healthy life-style is being urged on librarians with the help of a survey that showed that too many of them are in a risky condition because of smoking, excess weight, and especially lack of exercise.

Young staff members, particularly, tend to place greater value on health and the effect on it of conditions of work; libraries may not pay attractive salaries, but they can make working conditions much healthier and more pleasant for their most expensive asset.

Associations

The American Library Association continued its progress toward a federation of semi-independent divisions, marked in 1983 by the first annual conferences of the Public Library Association and the Library and Information Technology Association. The finances of the big association were a matter of concern to both the membership and elected officers, with deficits reported for several months and a sudden surplus, appearing from nowhere, raising suspicion of some lack of control at 50 East Huron Street.

The retirements of Deputy Director Ruth Frame and Conference Manager Chris Hoy, as well as the announcement by Robert Wedgeworth that he would not seek an extension of his contract as executive director, suggest that ALA is ripe for a major overhaul of its staff.

The Special Libraries Association appeared to be thriving in 1983, with membership and income growing steadily and progress being made toward a new home for the association.

The Medical Library Association, perhaps the most professional of the big associations in its makeup, continued to develop its educational and certification programs in 1983.

The regional library associations have steadily grown in strength in recent years, as have the state associations. The Midwest Federation of Library Associations had one of the best library conferences of 1983, because of the "unique strength" of regional associations. They are generally less expensive for participants, yet have the numbers and resources to attract national leaders and lots of exhibits.

Cooperation

Library cooperation is the broader concept of which networking is a subset. Although it is hard to separate the two, cooperation covers a much broader range as a voluntary grass-roots activity instituted and maintained on the pragmatic basis that it works and fills a need.

The most striking initiative toward new cooperative goals was hardly grass roots: The Fred Meyer Charitable Trust gave $3.5 million for a project to create a regional collection, a "Northwest Library" for that part of the country. Meyer supplied the money, but library leaders of the region designed the project and lent their prestige to its success.

Following that bold stroke are many good, smaller ones observed in the past year: The Lincoln Trail Libraries System in Illinois linked its interlibrary loan operation, Continuing Library Service, Inc. (CLSI) circulation, and delivery service to involve its member libraries in a comprehensive collection development effort. Each member library agrees to buy everything worth having in a specific subject area.

Members of LCOMM, the Library Council of Metropolitan Milwaukee, add to their card catalogs blue cards that show the holdings of neighbor libraries; the cards are produced by LCOMM and are acquired on a subscription basis.

In Pasadena, the public library system found a source for medical information in the Veterans Hospital; in turn, the hospital gets backup in reference on nonmedical subjects.

Several Wisconsin libraries with collections of industry standards created a union list and now provide clients with access to their collective holdings.

Five Illinois libraries have pooled their resources to hire a marketing professional to promote the services that all of them offer.

Sarah Lawrence College and the Mount Vernon Public Library, both in New York's Westchester County, share in the development of cultural programs, which are then put on at each facility.

School Libraries

The climate of opinion, if not the financial climate, favors the linking of school libraries with libraries of other types, especially for resource sharing. There were several instances noted in 1983 of imaginative cooperative action:

The Inyo County (California) Free Library and the school district entered into a joint powers agreement for the operation of a joint school library/library branch.

Tucson schools are tapping into OCLC at the Tucson Public Library.

In Santa Fe, New Mexico, the schools, the public library, and the community share a video editing and training facility.

Union catalogs were being planned for the school systems in Halifax, Nova Scotia, and Vancouver, British Columbia; in both cases each school would have its own catalog and also have its holdings included in the catalog of the school system.

New York State, stalled in its plan for new statewide networking legislation, is continuing to fund a variety of innovative cooperation projects for its school libraries and BOCES systems: Collection development, user education, and resource sharing are among them.

The high-water mark for intertype library cooperation involving schools was made in Houston, where the new Carnegie Branch functions as a school library for a middle school and a high school, a public library branch for the area, and a library for the community college that shares the building.

The Big Co-op Agencies

The big agencies, most of them created a couple of decades ago to foster cooperative action, were again showing an aggressive and entrepreneurial spirit. Some that were in the news in 1983:

The Universal Serials and Book Exchange (USBE) launched an aggressive marketing effort early in the year and later opened up new channels of rapid access to its holdings by means of the UTLAS and RLG utilities. After 30 years, during which she guided the evolution of USBE from a post-World War II role of rebuilding war-ravaged libraries to an international agency for resource sharing, Alice Ball handed the baton to Mary Ghikas, who promises to be every bit as vigorous as her predecessor and to add new expertise in technology.

The Center for Research Libraries took on an expanded role in 1983, adding medicine and the humanities to its subject coverage.

The Research Libraries Group will attack the perennial problem of delivery with a new trial of telefacsimile, using the latest generation of equipment.

SUNY/OCLC attempted to solve the delivery problem in 1983, by simply hiring Purolator to carry interlibrary loan materials.

The problem of journal access continues unsolved, except for minor fine tuning of existing mechanisms. There has been no return to the ill-fated concept of a National Periodicals Center, although the British Lending Library continues to do an efficient job, providing the kind of access an NPC could have offered, doing it inexpensively, efficiently, and over a large area of the globe. At year's end, and too early to evaluate, a private-sector initiative in this area was launched by University Microfilms, which is offering prompt mail delivery of article copies from its holdings of some 7,000 journals and may eventually offer electronic delivery.

Networks and Networking

In the April 1 *Library Journal,* Richard De Gennaro surveyed the network scene and pronounced the third decade of library automation a period of growing decentralization, with libraries increasingly returning to their cherished local autonomy, a return made possible by the developing technology. He found the big utilities troubled by their own inflexibility and facing new and vigorous competition, especially from vendors of systems developed to perform specialized functions, such as retrospective conversion, serials management, and acquisitions. As a corollary of the return to local autonomy, De

Gennaro noted the emergence of the open-network concept (which has been tested in the recently concluded Canadian pilot I-net project and was the subject of a California institute last year).

[See the 1983 networking update in the News Reports section of Part 1 of this volume—*Ed.*]

The Utilities and Their Competition

The four major utilities, OCLC, Research Libraries Information Network (RLIN), Washington Library Network (WLN), and the University of Toronto Library Automation System (UTLAS), are facing competition from the smaller networks: at least one of the regional organizations, the developing state networks, and member-dominated special networks set up to cut utility brokerage costs and dedicated to specific member library needs. They are also facing an as yet ill-defined threat from the proprietors of large bibliographic data bases, which are increasingly capable of offering network-type services. One that emerged in 1983 was AutoGraphics, with its AGILE-2 system. The California State Library approved AGILE-2 as a "utility" for California libraries to use for state-assisted bibliographic conversion.

The Regional Networks

SOLINET, the Southeastern Library Information Network, is in direct competition with OCLC for retrospective conversion of bibliographic records, offering 17 cents a record against OCLC's 22 cents. Its LAMBDA project (which uses WLN software) offers an enhancement of OCLC records with capabilities for management of the individual institution's data base, authority control, and subject, keyword, and Boolean searching.

AMIGOS, the Texas-based regional that started as a service agency for a small consortium, has extended its reach from Mexico in the South to Minnesota in the North. It has been the most stable and steadily growing of the regionals under the aggressive direction of James Kennedy. In the past year it broke new ground by taking over direction of the entire automation program of Southwestern University in Los Angeles. Kennedy, meanwhile, was co-opted by OCLC and is now serving as its director of marketing for the western United States.

CLASS resembled a regional network when it started life as the California Library Authority for Systems and Services, a unique joint powers organizational concept that never worked out as planned. Yet it prospered as it developed into an international vendor of systems and services, changing its name in 1983 to California Library Agency for Systems and Services. It brokers Brodart tape-maintenance service and RLIN network access (taking RLIN to Maine in 1983); sells software and hardware; and takes a bellwether role by such projects as its 1983 institute on that (maybe) wave of the future, the open network.

Although the strongest regionals have apparently followed a classic evolution from a small, member-dedicated and member-dominated agency to a large, independent, entrepreneurial suprainstitution, it doesn't always work that way, as the Bibliographic Center for Research (BCR) demonstrated last year. BCR overhauled its governance structure to give members more—not less—say in its development and services. Despite this, BCR expanded its service area in 1983, picking up the pieces of OCLC brokerage left by the demise of MIDLNET and opening a new office in Ames, Iowa, to handle the new business, BCR also expanded, virtually coast-to-coast, with its data base brokering service, acquiring customers from Rensselaer Polytech in upstate New York right across the country.

SUNY/OCLC has been taking what might be called the loyalist tack, declaring its future to be in energetically marketing OCLC services in the New York-Massachusetts area. It is giving the OCLC interloan subsystem new luster with a statewide rapid delivery service for which it contracts with Purolator. Competition for OCLC has emerged in Illinois, where a venerable but still growing Library Circulation System (LCS) is serving an expanding network of libraries with interloan and other network services at very competitive prices.

Copyright of the OCLC Data Base

OCLC drew wary attention from many of its client libraries with the announcement that it was claiming copyright for the data base, despite the origin of most of the records in Library of Congress and client library cataloging, much of it financed by taxpayers. Chief rival RLG announced last summer that it would not seek copyright control over its data base, on the grounds that nothing should restrict the free flow of information. WLN and AutoGraphics also took a pew in the angels' section on this issue.

New OCLC Systems

Something like confusion surrounded OCLC's venture into local automation systems. Its first offering, the Claremont Total Library System developed by Patrick Barkey, was never marketed seriously. Its second, the Local Library System, was to be built from the ground up by OCLC and installed at the Five Colleges in Massachusetts. But long before it was developed, OCLC switched to still another approach, an adaptation of the Integrated Library System developed by the National Library of Medicine and marketed by two Maryland firms run by systems people who had helped develop the NLM system. OCLC contracted with one of these, bought the other, and adapted the NLM system— under the name of the ill-fated Local Library System—for the Five Colleges, where, in December, OCLC reported its installation as an integrated library system that will be linked to OCLC.

At the end of the year, there was evidence of much behind-the-scenes friction as OCLC and the regional networks discussed a new contract. The regionals for the first time took a unified stance, hiring a lawyer who advised them that the contract as proposed by OCLC was unfair and full of liability pitfalls. They have proposed a much altered version of the contract, one which would allocate responsibilities and liabilities in what they see as a more equitable arrangement.

There was additional discomfort in OCLC's announcement that it was raising prices, following the general principle that as activity in a system service grows, its contribution to revenue should grow.

But OCLC was still growing; early in the year the University of Minnesota was the first RLG member library to tapeload its holdings records into the OCLC data base. And on the other end of the scale, several small Wisconsin libraries were trying out an arrangement by which they could access OCLC as a group.

RLG and RLIN

At this writing, the results have not yet been announced on the nine-month, $250,000 study of distributed networking announced in January 1983 by the Research Libraries Group. But growth has been steady here too: The authority files of the Library of Congress and the New York Public Library are now on RLIN. Among the valuable collections to come into RLIN was that of the University of Toronto, with its East Asian collection strengths. By September, RLG was announcing that there were 12 million records in RLIN and small, financially poor but collection-rich libraries were being enticed with an offer of an affordable special membership.

UTLAS: Canadian Salient

The UTLAS system, based at the University of Toronto, showed new signs of life last year. It won new funding that will enable it to upgrade its technology, and it won the contract to automate New York's Westchester Library System. This is a prize contract, since the Westchester Library System, just north of New York City, is directed by Maurice (Mitch) Freedman, who can be counted high among the opinion makers on library automation.

By year's end another Canadian system, Geac, seemed to be winning U.S. library contracts almost daily, the most recent of which are with such notable clients as the Smithsonian Institution and the U.S. army (Europe).

State-Level Networking

The state networking scene was a busy one last year. Wyoming started all over again, after learning that its chosen system, Cincinnati Electronics' CLASSIC, was still in development. Iowa was also starting all over again, following widespread rejection of the IOWANET system blueprint developed for it by Becker & Hayes. The system planning group disbanded, handing responsibility for a new approach to new State Librarian Claudya Muller.

Massachusetts, making a slow start in networking at the state level, appeared bent on avoiding the problems that emerged in Iowa and New York. Its network plan was only introduced after a long and painstaking effort to involve every possible stakeholder in the planning and decision making that will guide network development.

In both Nevada and Connecticut, networks are slowly coalescing as a result of the creation of intrastate regional networks based on automated circulation systems. Nevada's are all CLSI systems—three of them so far—but Connecticut has ahead of it the interfacing of CLSI, DataPhase, and Geac systems. The IRVING libraries of Colorado have already issued a Request for Proposal for a network design that will permit interfacing among its several independent automation systems, each with different hardware and software.

New York State, following a revolt in 1982 against its master plan for a new multitype network architecture and the scuttling of plans to seek funding for it, is continuing pilot projects to link school libraries with public and academic libraries and has accomplished a major network link between its NYSILL (interloan) network and the Regional Medical Library Network. But at the end of the year, New York appeared to be stalemated by the opposition of the public library system directors to a proposed dominant role in the state network for the nine reference and research library systems.

Another cautious, evolutionary approach to network building appeared to be working in West Virginia, where a master plan for statewide networking based on minicomputers and the VTLS (Virginia Tech Library System) in regional centers allows for a large measure of local autonomy in system participation.

In neighboring Virginia, where an IOWANET-like networking plan had been rejected, a similar approach appears to be developing and wide consensus is indicated by the governor's recent signing of legislation for a networking future.

Questioning the Network Vision

Debates in 1983 severely questioned the value of networks, especially their value for public libraries. In one, Tom Ballard, director of the Plainfield, New Jersey, Public Library, debated Brooke Sheldon, dean of the library school at Texas Woman's University and ALA president. Before a Texas Library Association audience much concerned with developing state networking plans, Ballard charged that as far as public libraries go, networks serve only a small elite and are a very expensive way of circulating a small percentage of public library materials. It would be far better, he urged, to spend the money on books. Sheldon responded with an eloquent presentation of the modern librarian's dream of the future library. He supported networking for Texas public libraries, urging that the goal of access for all citizens to all the information in libraries be met by networks that utilize new technology to bring the resources of all types of libraries within everyone's reach.

But as technology increasingly promised a return to yesterday's autonomy, cracks in the network vision were increasing. One of the worst seemed to be the inability to deliver interloan materials rapidly and inexpensively.

Delivery

Attempts to resolve the delivery problem included the SUNY/OCLC use of Purolator delivery service and at least two renewed attempts to use facsimile transmission, this time with the faster RAPICOM equipment, which can do 15 seconds per page. The Metropolitan Library System, based in Pasadena, found that it could fine tune its intrasystem delivery service and get—by staying within its own boundaries—acceptable times and costs for resource sharing. The ADONIS project for digitalized transmission of full text articles was reported in full force early in the year, but by year's end, appeared to have been dropped.

Information On Demand (IOD) is trying a new approach, fulfilling requests generated by OCLC's ILL system by means of its network of retrieval specialists stationed around the country. New York State is trying to improve journal access within the state, studying alternatives to its NYSILL network. Veterans' Hospital Libraries are tackling the problem by building up the holdings, including retrospective journals, of the member libraries in its VALNET. Here, as elsewhere, the vision of instantaneous access throughout the galaxy to everything ever printed is giving way to a practical attempt to work out a fine-tuned balance between local area collection development and sharing.

Automation

The automation of libraries in 1983 saw vigorous jockeying for market share by the big vendors of library turnkey systems: CLSI, DataPhase, Geac, and Gaylord the most prominent. The two long-term leaders, CLSI and DataPhase, were weathering legal battles growing out of their problems in handling large systems. CLSI and Austin, Texas, finally came to a settlement after threatening each other with million-dollar suits.

DataPhase made much of its replacement of top management and rebuilding of staff, but was still struggling with unhappy customers at the Chicago Public Library and the Atlanta Public Library. At year's end, however, DataPhase passed a grueling evaluation test at the Orange County Library in California, a test designed to measure its ability to handle peak circulation loads at the circulation volume projected for five years from now in a system of 26 branches with 100 terminals.

SCI finally cleared up its troubled situation at the Montgomery County library in Maryland, to everyone's relief. Geac came on strong in 1983, picking up several accounts, both large and small, and, so far at least, has run into no serious problems.

Integrated vs. Modular

Beyond track records, choice of a turnkey system in 1983 involved only one basic difference, presented by Gaylord, whose batch-type system is being marketed as the most economical one available, and a particularly good choice for the very large or very small library. Integrated, online systems, led by CLSI's System 23, are the stars of the turnkey automation scene, but Gaylord is pushing hard to promote its modular system approach, which does the job much cheaper, despite its lack of online immediacy.

The turnkey vendors are facing new and sharper competition from library systems originally developed for a single library and then packaged for sale to others. The leader in this area is still the public domain Integrated Library System (ILS) developed for the National Library of Medicine and to date on the market in the form of a pair of clones. Tacoma Public Library's UNIFACE has been installed in several other libraries and is being sold by Midwest Library Service, which bought marketing rights from Tacoma Public Library for $100,000. The Northwestern On-Line Total Integrated System (NOTIS) developed by Northwestern University was adopted by Harvard University this year, and the Virginia Tech Library System presented another formidable bid, as did a newcomer, the Pennsylvania State University LIAS system.

Micros, Micros Everywhere

In his March 15 *Library Journal* article on the state of library automation, Joseph Matthews noted over 30 microcomputer-based systems on the market, forming a third, and fast-growing presence on the library automation scene. These range from inexpensive software to run on the library's Apple or TRS to sophisticated interfaces capable of tapping remote data bases and networks.

The micros are literally sprouting up everywhere. There are an IBM PC doing periodicals work and an Apple handling service to the blind at the Tucson Public Library; an Osborne doing newspaper indexing at the Niagara Falls Public Library; a TRS doing reference standing orders in Lorain, Ohio; and library micro user groups all over, with names like MUGLNC, PAMUG, and even SMUG.

Microcomputers are making conversion of library records inexpensive and fast in projects like Wisconsin's MITINET and REMARC's many conversion jobs. They are moving into action as superior terminals for OCLC, providing teaching support at Texas A&M, helping children with their studies at the Scottsdale, Arizona, Public Library and in North York, Ontario, briefing new users on the library in Providence, Rhode Island, and offering inner city unemployed a new skill to learn in Baltimore. Apple programs can be borrowed by mail in Wenatchee, Washington, and entrepreneurs are offering coin-operated machines that cost the library little or nothing.

Interfacing Systems

A basic bugaboo of the early years of automation was the fear of being caught with a system that would leave one isolated from other systems and bar growth. Today, interface technology is so well advanced that Connecticut and Colorado are proceeding, with no apparent concern, toward the linkage of clusters of libraries using different automation systems. A leader in this technology for the past two years has been Innovative Interfaces, with its now widely adopted INNOVACQ system. Tacoma's UNIFACE is another approach to the problem. Most of all, the micros, as well as interface technology, offer libraries the opportunity of keeping their autonomy and tailoring their services to their (possibly) unique clientele, while still participating in networks and resource sharing.

Data Bases

The growing importance of online data bases was evident in 1983, and access to them became increasingly attractive, especially as simplified search systems made it easier for the library user to handle them.

News of data bases that drew library attention included an Information Access Corporation system combining the full text, on microfiche, of several thousand magazine articles plus access to them by means of IAC's MAGAZINEINDEX, all user-operated. The fear of downloading expressed by many data base proprietors as that capability became widely acquired by users, was confronted by *Chem Abstracts*, which offered users downloading for an annual fee; it also introduced bargain rates for use of its data base in off hours.

Other data base developments: The widely used DIALOG announced new directions in its development. It will deal more in information rather than bibliographic citations. The management of AGELINE, a data base that reflects a growing concern of libraries, was taken over by the National Association of Retired Persons. A poll of academic libraries in New York State indicated that librarians want many more data bases in the humanities as well as the sciences. And at Rutgers last summer, a distinguished international conference dealt with data bases in the humanities.

Writing in the September 15 *Library Journal*, Tina Roose reported on "Online Database Searching in Smaller Public Libraries"; she found that fees drastically cut use; that in libraries where searches up to 15 or 20 minutes long are free, few searches run longer; and that in-library use of some data bases (Bowker's *Books in Print*, in particular) really cuts costs and time spent on acquisitions.

Programs for the Public

The spectrum of programs that American public libraries put on for the amusement, edification, and well-being of their varied publics is a many-colored one. At some public library in 1983 one could discuss national issues, explore the history of the depression, celebrate the birthday of Martin Luther King, play war games, get help in finding a job, listen to a controversial author over a brown bag lunch, discuss Third World fiction, or take part in a straw vote on nuclear war. One could take children to a play warning them about strangers, select toys that will help a preschooler get ready for the big day, listen to Vietnam veterans begin to come to grips with their experiences, or take part in discussions on violence in America.

Deaf people could view a videotape explaining how to use a bank, and inner city children could get homework help at a branch dedicated to their needs or call a teacher on a hot line. Children in trouble, and imprisoned in a juvenile detention center, could read books and popular magazines and see films brought in by a public librarian. Blind people could take out cassettes with readings of classics or of the local newspaper, and five blind non-English-speaking Japanese in Livingston, California, could listen to talking books that originated at a library in Japan.

One might have sought aid at one library's law clinic in Cuyahoga County (Ohio) or referral to a social agency by an I&R program at any one of dozens of libraries. The efforts of the Queens Borough (New York) Public Library to encourage adoption of unwanted children may have found a home for one or more. A single parent in Plainedge, New York, might have received a regular newsletter addressed to his or her special needs.

A business looking for a market could have found the way to a government contract in Toledo. A farm tractor dealer in Clarion County, Pennsylvania, could get up-to-the-minute business guidance on a Meade Data Central terminal at his local library. A weary parent in Arlington Heights, Illinois, could find a helpful book on parenting on a shelf in the children's room, and read it in a rocking chair while the child hunted for his or her own book.

Some libraries were circulating computers, others were lending electronic keyboards; one group of Illinois libraries was trying out dial-up access to their CLSI data base from home or office terminals. At least two libraries were lending portable smoke alarms for travelers, and a great many were lending cameras.

Operating Libraries

More library branches took on the appearance of bookstores in 1983, with face-out shelving, numerous paperbacks, and even comic books. Bookmobiles were being replaced with lighter, more energy efficient vehicles, at least one built on a mobile home chassis. Economy, however, isn't everything. The Edmonton, Alberta, library, which had given up bookmobiles for stationary booktrailers as an economy measure, went back to the real thing in 1983.

Lowell Martin's 1983 Bowker Lecture and article in the January *Library Journal,* "The Public Library: Middle Age Crisis or Old Age," warned urban libraries against dissipating their energies in being all things to all persons; he prescribed concentration, specialization of branches, and surgery where needed.

Some large public library systems were tightening up branch administration to get more uniform service and to encourage greater responsiveness between branch and community. Cuyahoga County (Ohio) appointed 14 new regional librarians to supervise its 27 branches and to improve service, communication, and staff training.

Prince George's County Memorial Library in Maryland provided a role model for the library system that must cut back under fiscal pressure, but seeks to maintain its level of service and even to expand services.

The Atlanta Public Library, the latest urban library to call in Lowell Martin to guide it out of the woods, made a big thing of his upbeat but stern prescription for growth and issued an ambitious plan for doubling the library's budget, building collections and staff, and broadening its funding base.

San Diego Public, as noted under "Buildings" earlier in this report, was reexamining the library's role and its relation to other library and educational facilities, as a first step toward planning new facilities. Two other California libraries set out to create their own funding bases, one by building an endowment and the other by charging for a variety of library services. Walter Johnson, of the Huntington Beach Library, broadcast an offer to serve as a consultant to libraries wanting to learn how to make services pay.

Automation was being trumpeted as one solution to the urban library's fiscal problems at an Urban Libraries Council meeting held at the University of Pittsburgh early this month, where one counsel was for public libraries to follow the lead of businesses, rather than the example of academic libraries, in making use of automation.

Much attention was paid to the cost of library services in 1983. A task force of ALA's Public Library Association was seeking to create a procedure for costing services. Looking at it from another angle, a New York study was announced early in the year on quantifying the economic value of libraries to their communities.

Output measures were the buzzwords in many libraries in 1983. Texas made a major effort to spread the output measures gospel statewide with a series of workshops sponsored by the state library. Also in Texas, a study of interlibrary loans showed a transaction cost of over $10 and climbing, with the primary users identified as middle-class readers.

Illinois drew attention with its new standards for public libraries, an attempt to chart a course between the old prescriptive standards and the new Planning Process approach; the document, *Avenues to Excellence,* promised to make the best of both worlds.

Both use of and criticism of the ALA Planning Process was mounting in 1983. One attack by Mary Jo Detweiler, in the January 1, 1983, *Library Journal,* found the emphasis on data collection, at the expense of a clear statement of mission, a prime fault. Another view found it so poorly conceived and so lacking in logic that one could only hope for planning success in spite of the document.

The high point in public relations and publicity was probably the Onondaga County (New York) Public Library takeover of a discotheque for the celebration of National Library Week. The Louisville Public Library won another prestigious public relations award for its summer reading program publicity. The sentimental favorite, however, has to be the Celebrated Jumping Frog Contest at the public library in Haines, New York.

The managers of libraries found their work cut out for them in the pressures of collection growth on already crowded libraries; the depredations of book thieves; the ever-present dangers of fire and flood; the question of whether to offer fee-based services as well as to recover costs of some services through user fees; the new pressures for coordinated collection development and the new tools for this and other aspects of collection management offered by automation; the need for decisions on how much to invest in automation, network, and utility services as against acquisitions and staff for local service; and what to do about nonresident users.

Book theft made headlines in 1983 as a major problem, draining libraries, possibly of millions of dollars' worth of materials. The arrest and imprisonment of James Shinn helped draw attention to theft, and a conference on theft at Oberlin College (Ohio) laid a burden of blame on librarians for not adopting security measures.

A bookmobile fire in Nebraska, which destroyed the vehicle, its collection, the building, and other vehicles parked there, provided an example of the fire danger. Flood damage and the heroic measures to save damaged materials are apparently so common that incidents rarely make the news pages anymore, but the burst pipe and the backed-up roof drain are on the list of the library manager's potential headaches.

A new concern is rising for how automation will change the way libraries are administered and managed. Two major themes along this line were sounded in 1983. First was Hugh Atkinson's arresting prediction at the Library Information and Technology Association (LITA) conference in Baltimore that the standard hierarchical pattern of library bureaucracy will be broken down by the ease of communication and the access to information made possible by automation. Hierarchy, he said, has been necessary because the information store has been all in one place and regulation of access to it has been a necessity. With a library's information immediately accessible to any staff member and communication among people highly flexible, the old, monolithic administration will give way to small groups—a resurgence, he suggested, of the "primal tribe." When librarians can do this, he said, they will be able to relate better to the subject discipline groupings that are a way of life for an academic faculty, and the library will be able to communicate its needs—in terms of client needs—better than ever before. [See the report by Hugh Atkinson in the Special Reports section of Part 1 of this volume—*Ed.*]

A second, and curiously related, theme is the coming integration of the academic library's information structure with the information structure of its parent institution. Several medical libraries, working with National Library of Medicine grants, are now exploring this new integration pattern. Their successful quest may open new horizons for libraries of all types.

Funding

The funding of libraries, particularly public libraries, was pretty much a story of continued retrenchment through the year, with an apparent upturn and recovery near the end of the year. Both academic and public libraries focused on "productivity" or getting more work from staffs slowly shrinking by attrition. Savings through automation were sought more openly than ever; fund raising became a mainstream concern expressed in workshops, hiring of consultants, and creation of staff positions for the sole purpose of finding alternate sources of money. Libraries were drawn to the promising security of endowments, sought minor relief in fees and other user charges, and engaged in the usual bakesale-type activities. [See the three-part report "Lean Years and Fat Years: Lessons to Be Learned" in the Special Reports section of Part 1—*Ed.*]

Retrenching

Early in the year, Oregon's Multnomah County Library closed for a staff furlough when money ran out; the Ohio State Library cut back on its activities and reorganized; the University of North Carolina cut staff positions 25 percent and all but stopped buying books; New York City public library systems were preparing to close large numbers of branches and further curtail hours; and a study of Massachusetts libraries found that the taxpayer revolt (Proposition 2 1/2) of a couple of years ago had done rather permanent damage. As a result, library funding is down more than 12 percent from projections. The Detroit Public Library, facing a real financial disaster, won a short reprieve of emergency funding and brought in the firm of Touche Ross to help it find new support. At year's end, disaster seemed inevitable in Detroit.

A Turnaround?

But toward the end of the year, things began to brighten up for others, as they did on Wall Street and in smokestack America, if not at the shelters for the homeless and in the homes of the "new poor" created by the recession. Ypsilanti, Michigan, opened the closed doors of its library, having won new funding with the creation of a new library district; Altadena, California, came very close to breaking out of the Proposition 13 financial irons with a 61 percent vote for new funding (but not the 66 2/3 needed for success). Spokane voters granted their library a 30 percent increase; and in the November elections voters were absolutely lavish to the libraries of Pikes Peak (Colorado), Mid-Continent (Missouri), Ames (Iowa), and Charlotte & Mecklenburg County (North Carolina).

New York City found new money for its libraries, and service at branches was increased rather than cut back.

Savings through Technology

The Government Printing Office hailed automation of its printing and binding operations as responsible for dollar savings as well as faster production of publications like the huge *Federal Register*. Dearborn, Michigan, appealed for funds for automation on the grounds that it would save the library money at a time when it was scraping bottom. Salt Lake County, Utah, anticipated $500,000 in savings over a six-year period from the replacement of its phone system with a more efficient one. Book-theft security systems were also justified in terms of the thousands of dollars they would save.

Fund Raising

Fund-raising workshops, seminars, and even courses proliferated in 1983. The Michigan Library Cooperative has been devoting a major share of its efforts to inform Michigan libraries about fund-raising tactics and opportunities.

Research libraries were reported to be turning more to fund raising, gaining the most support for acquisitions and automation. Libraries hired fund-raising firms; one of which really had notable success: Ketcham, Inc., of Dallas, hired by Jacksonville, Texas, to raise $500,000, raised considerably more than that for a new library building.

Ingenuity at getting money from friends reached new heights in 1983. The Salt Lake County Library had an auction with prizes that included a vacation for two. The Northern Virginia Community College ran a Faculty Feet Foto contest, whereby students "voted" for the best-looking feet with donations to the library. Tulsa City-County Library reproduced a mural and sold copies for $5 each. In East Brunswick, New Jersey, librarians played softball against stars of the soap opera "Guiding Light." Students passed the hat in a "bucks for books" drive at home games of Florida State University. But the New York

Public Library upstaged everyone on December 6, with 1,000 diners reveling at a Night of 100 Dinners and the library making $200,000.

Gifts

Early in January 1983, the Chase Manhattan Bank took out a full-page ad in the *New York Times,* urging corporations to come to the aid of libraries. There was some indication that corporate giving is increasing; it certainly has been at the New York Public Library, where the receipts from gifts and also the number of donors have increased. Foundation grants (to all causes) were reported up 21 percent, $1 billion over earlier estimates. [For an analysis of foundation grants to libraries in 1983, see the Foundation Grants section of Part 2 of this volume—*Ed.*]

Endowments were sought with new vigor by academic libraries, where they are familiar fixtures, but also at public libraries, where they have not been seen for a great many years. The University of Illinois library reported the largest gift ever to its endowment fund, $450,000. And the San Diego Public Library has established an endowment fund as one means of diversifying its sources of income.

Fees

Many libraries increased charges of all sorts: overdue fines, room rentals, reserve book fees, charges for lost cards, interlibrary loan fees—whatever users would bear, for the most part. One library took an apparently rational and sophisticated approach to making the user pay a fair share for service. The Countway Medical Library in Boston brought in experts to do a complex analysis of costs and devised a system that assesses charges in relation to what the delivered service actually costs the library. The National Library of Canada, bowing to reality, extended the provision of location information (for interlibrary loan) to libraries that charge for the service.

Reference service for pay is apparently spreading, with libraries soliciting corporate business and developing specialized staff to serve them. The Cleveland Public Library, one of many following this route, reported near year end that it was increasing staff and offering a broader range of services to its paying clients. Users of state film and other audiovisual collections in Nebraska were told this year that they will have to pay for the service, with charges representing about 25 percent of the cost of the service.

Federal and State Aid

Federal aid to libraries seems likely to survive, possibly in an improved form, despite the hostility of the administration to the funding of social services. Appropriately, at a time of looking ahead, Dean Edward Holley of the University of North Carolina library school videotaped a series of oral history interviews with people who were involved in the creation of the Library Services and Construction Act. The videotape provides impressive testimony to the human resources, individual and group, and the relationships among librarians, politicians, and library supporters that made LSCA possible. More than anything, the continuity of relations between the library community and the legislature led to the eventual victories: first, the Library Services Act (LSA), riding on a ground swell of concern for rural America and the loneliness of isolated people, then making the quantum jump to LSCA, with the sudden acceptance of the need to reach out and equalize opportunities for all Americans.

The New LSCA

There is a whole new version of LSCA being hammered out; it will place new emphasis on foreign-language materials, literacy, acquisitions, community information, resource-sharing networks, and multitype library cooperation. In 1983, Title II, funding for library construction, was fully funded at $50 million, its first new money in a decade. This was a kind of fluke, providing a convenient means to direct Jobs Bill money to areas of high unemployment. It will have a real impact, however, with matching funds doubling or quadrupling the money available. There will be many new buildings—in places where they will be welcome—and there will be many less visible improvements, such as elevators, ramps, and other facilities for the handicapped, building repairs, and renovations designed to save energy. At the end, the tally of what $50 million in federal funding can do will be impressive.

LSCA in 1984 will have no more construction money, and it will cut out completely the approximately $2 million a year in books bought for academic libraries. It will leave intact the amounts allocated to library services and library cooperation in LSCA Titles I and III. The National Library of Medicine will get its customary support and a little more, and the National Commission on Libraries and Information Science will be funded at last year's level.

Administration hostility to social services probably accounts for the attempt to bar the use of federal funds for lobbying—and even to bar the use of any funds for lobbying if an agency receives any federal money. New requirements for the auditing of federal grants threaten to make accountability so onerous for small agencies that the ones who need aid most may be cut off from it.

State Funding

There are encouraging signs that the states will take a more active role in library support, and not just in funding outreach and innovation, but basic services that should be available to all regardless of the vicissitudes of local funding and the fading of the property tax as an inexhaustible cornucopia.

California was the bellwether. It had been the first state to let a taxpayer revolt attack its social institutions in a really threatening way, and many of its libraries suffered from Proposition 13. It is also the state that passed SD 358, a measure giving the state a role in the support of basic library services. It was funded this year by Governor Deukmejian, whose conservative policies led to the remark that Californians had by mistake elected the governor of Iowa.

Ohio is moving toward support of public libraries through a state sales tax, which would replace the traditional intangibles tax, and although it threatens some libraries that do well under the old arrangement, it could mean a more stable and equitable funding formula for all libraries.

Mississippi was reported moving toward the eventual takeover of some federally funded library programs, another indication of a healthy concern at the state level for public library service.

Idaho's democratic governor was fighting the Republican-dominated legislature on behalf of both libraries and education; late in the year, legislation was introduced to improve Idaho libraries, especially their book collections.

Massachusetts granted $1.5 million in new state aid to libraries, but lost it in a financial maneuver that earmarked the money for local tax relief rather than adding it to library budgets. Prospects look good there, however, for better state aid to libraries, systems, and the developing networks.

Michigan, with its eroded industrial base, is a bleak place for libraries. In May, it was reported that Governor Blanchard had ordered a $1 million cut in library funding.

Florida libraries—except for those in small- and medium-sized cities—are the beneficiaries of state legislation that gives new support to cooperation and extension of service to the unserved. Disgruntled city librarians, barred from any prospect of aid to their budgets, have formed a new group to speak up for their interests at the state level.

Pennsylvania, with library friend Governor Thornburgh in the state house, continues to improve its state aid to libraries, which in 1983 was up 75 percent over the 1980 level.

Finally, Kansas authorized better funding for its public library systems in 1983, and Maine reported new funding to compensate urban libraries for the services they provide to nonresident walk-in library users.

SLJ News Report, 1983

Bertha M. Cheatham
News and Features Editor, *School Library Journal*

Not since 1957, when the Soviet Union launched the first sputnik in its race with the United States to see which country would get a man on the moon first, has so much serious attention been directed toward education. *A Nation at Risk: The Imperative for Educational Reform*—a critical, cogent, and urgent report compiled by a blue ribbon panel of experts selected in 1981 by Education Secretary Terrel H. Bell—was released in April 1983. It indicates that "a rising tide of mediocrity" threatens to engulf America's schools.

After regional hearings were held with representatives of the education community (few librarians were known to have testified; none was on the commission on which a Nobel Prize winner and several educators served), the report and its recommendations were released to the public. They were snapped up so quickly that the first printing ran out within a month. (The Education Department printed and issued a total of five million copies.)

In July, a Gallup Poll found that education ranked second to unemployment as an issue in the 1984 presidential campaign, but most of those polled said that they disapproved of the way President Reagan is handling education issues. It was a pre-election year and Reagan, who in the past has not been demonstrably supportive of education, got on his campaign soapbox to give the press his interpretation of the 34-page report, including references to tuition tax credits and education vouchers—neither of which was mentioned in the report.

This was a curious turnabout considering that, when he ran for office four years ago, Reagan had vowed to dismantle the Education Department—and abolish Secretary Bell's cabinet position. But whatever his motive, Reagan's attention to the report helped rally the American people in support of education improvements, particularly in areas that would have impact on the rapidly changing, diminishing job market. Automation, foreign

Note: Adapted from *School Library Journal,* December 1983, where the article was entitled "Counting Down to 1984: *SLJ*'s Annual News Roundup."

competition, and developments in technology are all affecting U.S. industry and the preparation of tomorrow's work force.

The report had immediate results—concerned citizens, boards of education, state administrators, representatives from private industries, and library educators and practitioners banded together to come up with "initiatives" leading to excellence in the nation's schools.

Highlights

- A report released in April 1983 indicates that "a rising tide of mediocrity" threatens to engulf America's schools.
- Librarians are rapidly losing their technophobia and assimilating as much information about microcomputer applications as they can get.
- School administrators are realizing that nothing is free as they absorb the hidden costs—the purchase of computer software and a company's maintenance contracts.
- More often than not, school library media specialists found that their budgets did not cover the cost of purchasing one new hardcover book per student.
- According to a recent study, until 1990 jobs in school and academic libraries will decline.
- The widespread practice of taping copyrighted material off-air is under scrutiny in school districts as a result of a recent court judgment.

By midyear, education had become a topic for national discussion and debate. Various organizations publicized critical studies of the American educational system. One by the Carnegie Foundation for the Advancement of Teaching focused on the decline in teachers' salaries—average annual pay $20,531, average starting salary in 1982, $12,689; teacher preparation and accreditation; population shifts; and teacher morale. North Carolina Governor James Hunt's Task Force on Education for Economic Growth concluded that better schools meant a healthier economy and more private-sector financial support.

In his well-received book, *A Place Called School* (McGraw-Hill, 1983), John I. Goodlad claims it is possible that the "whole public education system is nearing collapse." Most of the in-depth studies of education were released or issued close together. Parents who had long advocated a "back to basics" reformation in education gathered forces and many, when polled, indicated they were prepared to pay for quality education; disenchanted teachers found themselves involved in debates over merit pay, student discipline rules, longer school days and school years, tougher high-school graduation requirements, and a reexamination of rationales for the dismissal of teachers.

Individual librarians did not remain silent when they discovered that *A Nation at Risk* failed to acknowledge the significant role libraries have in the educational process, but the American Library Association was almost caught short. Although Secretary Bell sent a last-minute telegram to ALA's June conference to assure librarians that they had not been forgotten, the American Association of School Librarians and ALA's council resolved to respond to the report so that libraries could be involved in the efforts to promote "life-long learning." It's a case of "better late than never."

ALA's response may be just in time since Bell scheduled a national forum, to convene in Indianapolis on December 6–8, 1983, to afford an opportunity for state officials and others to share information about the strategies they are pursuing for the implementation of the commission's recommendations. As of late October 1983, 40 states had appointed state commissions of excellence in education and were upgrading high-school graduation requirements; 36 had begun some action to develop reforms. Many states have redefined college entrance requirements, recommended longer school days or years (still a controversial issue: many say the quality of teaching within the normal school day should be strengthened instead); others are seeking to change teacher education requirements in an effort to get better trained teachers.

California, Florida, Kansas, Illinois, New York, and Colorado have already taken steps designed to improve education or have enacted master teaching programs. California's $800 million school reform law bears watching—its Educational Reform Act of 1983 tightens credential requirements for teachers, includes funds for raising teachers' salaries, allows $4,000 a year extra pay for master teachers, and also contains a provision of $36 million to be spent for textbooks—the first state funding ever allotted in California for buying textbooks—and funds for school counselors. Legislators are waiting to see if this funding bill pays off—one critic, Governor George Deukmejian, vetoed $1.1 million from the second year appropriations, but State School Superintendent William (Bill) Honig predicts a renaissance in California schools. School librarians still have to determine how they fit into the picture.

Bell claims the "critical imperative" is to see what legislation will be drafted in 1984 to back the implementation of state initiatives. He said, "At no time in my long years in education . . . have I seen so much readiness [for change]. We must not lose this opportunity."

The critical imperative for librarians is also clear—to achieve public recognition of the qualitative difference well-run, well-stocked libraries provide to the measure of quality education.

The Age of Technology

Librarians are rapidly losing their technophobia and assimilating as much information about microcomputer applications as they can get. They fill every conference meeting that deals with microcomputers and sign up in droves for trips to local demonstration sites. Yet school media specialists are not in the forefront of this technology—in many school districts, teachers and unit heads are in charge of computer centers, and librarians, unless they supervise microcomputers in the library, are not directly involved.

In 1983, educators and librarians debated futuristic predictions made by Jim Naisbitt in his 1982 bestseller *Megatrends* (Warner Books). American society has shifted from an industrial to an information society, he asserts. The number of information occupations has increased over the last 30 years: about 60 percent of the population is now employed in information jobs, says Naisbitt.

The exchange of information is what library service is all about—the rush to master computer technology is on. To date, 14 states have passed legislation relating to computer use in schools; Tennessee and the District of Columbia have made computer literacy a requirement for graduation; 23 states have established statewide committees on computers; about 25 states have organized task forces to make recommendations on computer use in schools. Arkansas has begun a million-dollar, one-year project in which pilot schools will be given 24 computers each, with software, for pupil instruction and use.

The Scottsdale (Arizona) Public Library was one of many that organized free computer literacy projects—for ages 3–13. Its goal was to cash in on the "fun" part of computer use to encourage the improvement of reading and math skills. Its Computer Literacy Center was serious business with the young patrons who completed the user orientation before using the equipment alone.

More schools are becoming involved in networks as they realize the benefits to be derived from them (and as costs decrease). In Pennsylvania, the Penn Link System "interfaces" with more than 100 subscribers, from school districts of all sizes, to small colleges and universities, to the Carnegie Library in Pittsburgh. The system provides high-school students with access to information about careers and job opportunities; school administrators can use it to develop budgets and monitor school supplies; classrooms can access legislative reports and statewide news via the *Pennsylvania Today* information/news service. An electronic mail service and a bulletin board service are also included. Penn Link is under the direction of the Bureau of Press and Communication of the Pennsylvania Department of Education.

Computers are big business—manufacturers know that children remember brand names and in time will become computer owners. With the donation of about 9,200 Apple computers in Apple's Kids Can't Wait program, California schoolchildren were a step ahead of all others. And in San Jose, the Hewlett Packard Company donated systems worth $51,000 to each of two schools. IBM has also publicized the donation of its hardware to schools . . . and so it goes. School administrators are realizing that nothing is free as they absorb the hidden costs—the purchase of computer software and a company's maintenance contracts.

Programs are underway to keep librarians abreast of the technology. Taking their cue from children's computer camps, the Microcomputer Users Group for Libraries in North Carolina held a unique micro summer camp for librarians. Sixty-eight attended the sessions at the School of Science and Mathematics in which they were briefed on BASIC programming and acquired skills through hands-on experience.

Also in North Carolina, the State Department of Education has organized a review service to advise educators of recommended software programs. Its *Advisory List of Computer Courseware,* under the direction of Media Evaluation Services (MES), is a model program that will be emulated by other districts to solve the problem of purchasing inferior software. MES also reviews videotapes and has a computer lab to test hardware.

Interestingly, the department reports that some manufacturers have revised their courseware after reading the MES reviews. Assistant State Superintendent of Schools Elsie Brumback foresees national networks in which states will pool reviews of specific content areas and work together to improve microcomputer courseware, but as yet most states are not far enough along in their review procedures to make this feasible.

[For a special report on "Convergence of Computer-Based Library and Learning Systems," see Part 1—*Ed.*]

Library Budgets

School and public librarians serving children and young people shared the concern of educators and parents for the education of children, but they had an equal concern—

where were the funds for building or rebuilding viable library programs? More often than not, school library media specialists found that their budgets did not cover the cost of purchasing one new hardcover book per student; escalating costs for audiovisual equipment and for microcomputer software meant that funds were quickly depleted. School principals and administrators were examining school library media programs to see if they were getting their money's worth; at the same time they were hiring part-timers or nonprofessionals to run elementary school libraries in order to reduce salary costs.

"Expenditures of School Library Media Centers, 1982," the results of a survey published in *School Library Journal* [and reprinted in Part 4 of this volume], revealed how poorly school librarians have fared in terms of budgets, salaries, and administrative assistance at the state level. The survey questionnaire (sent to more than 1,250 school librarians) sought to determine the extent of school library media center expenditures for the 1982 school year. The responses showed that average school library expenditures were barely enough to keep a book collection up-to-date.

Although the average price of a children's book was $10 in 1983, the surveyors (Dr. Marilyn L. Miller and Barbara B. Moran) found that $4.58 per pupil was the average expenditure for books, and the median rate was $3.71—both far below the cost of a replacement copy. The *SLJ* survey also determined that the average salary of an experienced school library media specialist with a graduate degree is a modest $20,000— as educators have already discovered and librarians are discovering, it's difficult to recruit "the best and the brightest" at such salary levels when industry offers inexperienced business and computer science graduates much higher beginner's pay.

[See the special report "Lean Years and Fat Years: Lessons to Be Learned" in Part 1 and the "Price Indexes for School and Academic Library Acquisitions" in Part 4—*Ed.*]

Federal Funding

Spending for education reached about $230 billion this year; elementary and secondary schools are expected to spend $184 billion. The enrollment in elementary schools, 30.8 million, and in high schools, 13.5 million, reflects a continuing decline in the number of school-age children. In the 1980s there will be a continued decline in the number of students in grades 9–12.

For another year, the nation's economy has been in a state of flux. As the year proceeded, the recession worsened, but the economy began to rally in the fall. To avoid a reoccurrence of taxpayer revolts, library trustees and school boards kept library budgets close to last year's levels.

The phrase "block grant" has become familiar to school library practitioners this year. As one of more than 20 discretionary funding programs consolidated under the Education Consolidation and Improvement Act (ECIA), Chapter 2 incorporates the old Titles IV-B and IV-C, both of which supported improvements in school libraries, educational innovations, and special projects. [For a report on ECIA, Chapter 2 funding in 1983, see Part 2 of this volume—*Ed.*] Chapter 2 funds go to state or local agencies, which apportion them to school districts. Since funds can be used for three types of programs—basic skills development, improvement and support services (including library resources and textbooks), and special projects (including those for the gifted and talented)—it is difficult to ascertain exactly how they were expended.

Twenty percent of each state's allocation goes to local education agencies, based on a formula developed by the state's advisory committee. Federal funding for Chapter 2 is expected to remain at the 1983 level of \$479,420,000; not an impressive sum considering that in fiscal year 1980, before consolidation, the appropriation was around \$750,000,000—bearing out the adage "consolidation leads to elimination."

A large part of the state education agencies' allotments of Chapter 2 block-grant funds went to buy microcomputers. Parental pressure and the necessity of preparing children and young people for a technological future were determining factors here.

With the reorganization of the Office of Libraries and Learning Technology (OLLT) to form the new Center for Education Improvement (CEI) in late 1983, school librarians were left without a source to contact at the federal level. When the OLLT was abolished and its staff reassigned to other duties, it was reported that this change was to "reflect the changes in function for OERI [the Office of the Assistant Secretary for Educational Research and Improvement, U.S. Department of Education] caused by the Education Consolidation and Improvement Act of 1981." The new office has four programs (similar to those under the Chapter 2 consolidation): School Library Resources and other Instructional Materials (ESEA Title IV-13); Television and Radio (ESEA Title IV, Section 611); Teacher Corps; and Pre-College Teacher Development in Science. It is now composed of three divisions: CEI links libraries, the National Diffusion Network, and technology.

Directing the Division of Library Programs is Ray Fry; Lee Wickline is director of the Division of National Dissemination Programs; and Frank Withrow is director of the Division of Technology, Resources and Assessment.

This reorganization of the old OLLT sounds great, but library practitioners have expressed concern that there seems to be no one at the federal level who is monitoring school library development or representing practitioners—many have yet to receive any information or communication from CEI.

Library Jobs Getting Scarce?

A recent study indicated both good and bad news for those hoping to get positions in school or public libraries. Until 1990, jobs in school and academic libraries will decline—according to *Library Human Resources: A Study of Supply and Demand,* a report prepared for the U.S. Department of Education. [A summary appears in Part 3 of this volume—Ed.] And it's predicted that more jobs will be found in public and academic libraries than in school libraries. A total of 136,000 librarians were employed in 1982: 48 percent in school libraries, 23 percent in public libraries, 15 percent in academic libraries, and 14 percent in special libraries. Librarians represented 45 percent of those employed in libraries; 5 percent were other professionals; 50 percent were technical, clerical, or other support staff. The report predicts salaries will rise slightly to reflect the rise in inflation, the current decline in the number of master of library science degree programs will level off, and most graduating librarians will be hired to replace those retiring or leaving the profession.

Intellectual Freedom

All was generally quiet on the intellectual freedom front, but this year librarians became aware of new strategies to combat full access by library patrons of all ages.

For example, the Moral Majority is trying a new tactic. Its chief spokesperson, Cal Thomas, vice president for communications, wrote these words on an editorial page of the

New York Times (September 21, 1983): "Book review editors and some librarians are also part of this new wave of censorship. The idea that many of them are neutral because they are liberals is ludicrous." The occasion was the fiftieth anniversary of the Nazi book-burning episodes in Berlin. Thomas said it was "a good time to re-examine censorship and to ask, "Who are the real censors in America?" Moral Majority leader Jerry Falwell claimed that his organization would look in library card catalogs to see what was missing—"if they don't put our books back up, then take the liberal books down, too."

Perhaps the Moral Majority has finally lost its influence on the people who would condemn a book because it does not suit their religious or political views. At year's end, there was no evidence that Thomas's tough words or Falwell's campaign to put conservative titles in libraries have had much impact on library book selectors or on the American public as a whole. But it's a pre-election year and anything can happen.

Librarians, who are all trained as book selectors, will not soon forget the controversy (picked up by the national press) surrounding the folktale *Jake and Honeybunch Go to Heaven* by Margot Zemach (Farrar, Straus & Giroux). It erupted when a private letter to a Farrar editor from Elizabeth Huntoon, coordinator of Children's Services, Chicago Public Library, was published in a news report in the *New York Times.* Huntoon's letter stated that librarians in an orientation activity had discussed the book and questioned its use of stereotypes of blacks, in a Heaven full of celestial fish fries and barbecues. Huntoon said the library had decided "to restrict purchase" to the central and two regional libraries. In response, Michael di Capua, editor in chief of Farrar, Straus & Giroux defended the book as "a positive celebration of, and a tribute to, black American folklore."

Zemach's book received mixed reviews in other large systems—some reviewers recommended its purchase in limited quantities; others defended it as an enjoyable folktale and did not see its resemblance to Marc Connelly's 1930s play, *Green Pastures*.

In the *Times* report, Farrar, Straus & Giroux accused librarians of censorship because they had heard three large library systems weren't buying the book in quantities. But the fuss died down very quickly.

About the time that *Jake and Honeybunch* was publicized, a long-fought censorship case was finally laid to rest. Known as the Island Trees case, this involved a suit against the Island Trees (New York) Union Free School District board, which banned nine titles from the high school library. Those who followed the case up to the Supreme Court decision felt vindicated when, in January, the Island Trees Union Free School District dropped the stipulation that required a student's parents to be notified when one of the controversial books was checked out. This ended the seven-year court lawsuit brought by students after the books were removed because the board considered them "anti-American, anti-Christian, anti-Semetic (sic), and just plain filthy." Lawyers for the New York Civil Liberties Union, which led the fight for students' rights to read, felt that the notification rule would lead to further "stigmatizing" of the controversial books and might be emulated in other school districts.

Potential censors might take note that *Newsday* reported the Island Trees school board is paying $107,395 in fees for its own attorney and $70,000 in fees to the attorneys for the plaintiffs.

Copyright Cases and Issues

The widespread practice of taping copyrighted material off-air without permission is under scrutiny in school districts as a result of the judgment reached in the first copyright infringement case ever brought against a school district. In 1977, the plaintiffs, Encyclopaedia Britannica Educational Corporation, Time-Life Films, Inc., and Learning Corporation of America, brought suit against the Board of Cooperative Services (BOCES) of the First Supervisory District, Erie County, New York, and won a decision barring unauthorized off-air taping of its materials; the defendants were enjoined from copying the plaintiffs' copyrighted works. In March 1983, Judge John T. Curtin awarded court costs and damages amounting to $78,515. Curtin ruled that 1981 guidelines regarding "fair use" of off-air taping did not apply in this case and did not have the force of law. BOCES, a publicly owned cooperative, had kept a library of films taped off-air, which it circulated to teachers for classroom use.

Because New York University agreed to enforce a policy with guidelines for authorized photocopying, the Association of American Publishers (AAP) dropped its suit against the university for "unauthorized and unlawful reproduction, anthologizing, distribution, and sale of the publishers' copyrighted work." Determined to stop the growth of large-scale photocopying centers, AAP filed a suit as a test case on behalf of nine publishers. The policy which NYU has agreed to follow until January 1986 authorizes photocopying in specific instances: by a teacher; for use in scholarly research or teaching, of single copies of a book chapter, a periodical or newspaper article, a short story, an essay, a poem, chart, graph, diagram, drawing, cartoon, or picture.

[For a report on copyright developments in 1983, see the News Reports section of Part 1—Ed.]

Associations

Association for Educational Communications and Technology (AECT)

When Lyn Gubser took over as executive director of the Association for Educational Communications and Technology this spring, he had several obstacles to overcome: One was to eradicate a budget deficit of approximately $250,000; another was to set new priorities and directions for this association, which, as President Paul Welliver put it, was "going through a transition." In Gubser's favor are a unified board of directors and a successful annual conference—COMMTEX International Exposition (jointly sponsored with the International Communications Industries Association), which was first held in New Orleans in January 1983, when it drew 3,750 exhibitors and 3,500 AECT registrants—AECT realized $140,000 (net) from exhibitors and $190,000 (gross) from registration.

It was during this convention that progress was made to end the standoff over whether the American Association of School Librarians and AECT could (and would) cooperate in compiling and writing new standards for school library media centers to replace the outdated standards jointly published by the two associations in 1975. Members of AECT's newest division, DSMS (Division of School Media Specialists), worked hard to effect this cooperation. They were relieved to hear, at the AECT spring leadership meeting in Washington, that procedures had been drawn up to enable a selected group of members from both associations to get down to work on the new standards.

Canadian Library Association

In hopes of forestalling a projected budget deficit of $37,047, delegates attending the June conference of the Canadian Library Association reluctantly approved a two-stage increase in membership fees over a two-year period. The budget crisis was the result of postal increases and a shortfall in incoming revenues—the cost of serving a member ($89.30) was higher than the average membership fee ($74.51). A personal member's dues will increase from the current $49.50 to $60 in 1983–1984 and to $65 the next year. Students' fees will almost double—from the current $16.50 to $32 in 1983–1984 and $5 more in 1984–1985.

American Library Association (ALA)

At both the midwinter meeting of the American Library Association in San Antonio, Texas, and at its annual conference in Los Angeles, the council's chief concern was ALA's financial health, not national issues. The budget at the close of the 1982–1983 fiscal year showed a plunging deficit of $205,000 and then bounced back to a year-end balance of $116,000. But ALA Treasurer Herb Biblo and its Committee on Program Evaluation and Support (COPES), council's watchdog on ALA expenditures, told the executive board at its fall meeting that action must be taken to ensure that the association's budget remains in the black.

Because the Office of Personnel Management (OPM), a Civil Service agency, is considering lower entry-level grades for librarians with less than a two-year MLS degree, ALA's Steering Committee on Standards is studying the whole matter of downgrading professionals with MLS degrees.

American Association of School Librarians (AASL)

The American Association of School Librarians doesn't have a budget crisis, but other problems have surfaced. Some members have voiced the opinion that the time has come to form a new national organization to represent school library media specialists, independent from the American Library Association. In the May issue of *School Library Journal,* Marilyn Miller raised the issue, which was then debated in its August issue: "It's time for school library media specialists to have a national organization of their own." Disenchanted members have voiced this opinion for at least ten years. "AASL's potential has outgrown ALA's ability and willingness to support and foster the unique identity and need of the school library media center," says Miller, who stresses that AASL has the leadership available to develop a membership structure that would best represent the needs of the profession. The article drew mixed reactions: Some wanted AASL to remain an ALA division; others applauded her proposal. The issue is to be studied by an ad hoc Special Committee on Future Structure.

After a one-year suspension of the jointly sponsored (with Encyclopaedia Britannica companies) National School Library Media Program of the Year Awards, new criteria were established, and winners will be named this spring. Also on AASL's agenda is the compilation of the new school library media standards to be written by a committee of AECT and AASL members from both library and media fields. The work has begun and a draft should be ready in 1985.

Association for Library Service to Children (ALSC)

Phyllis J. Van Orden, 1983–1984 president of the Association for Library Service to Children, says that ALSC is experiencing a transition: "The division is reexamining its priorities in terms of long-range planning. We are moving forward in improving our fiscal and program management." Most members were pleased that the festive Newbery/ Caldecott dinner was reinstated in 1983. The first ALSC calendar proved successful.

Van Orden says the association is concerned about members' participation, particularly by newer members who want to serve on committees and programs, but cannot get away from their jobs to attend conventions; attracting personal members and keeping them are also top priorities. She also sees increasing interest in international relations.

Young Adult Services Division (YASD)

A background paper issued by the Young Adult Services Division at the annual conference of the American Library Association in June claimed that three major school book club publishers were expurgating books offered for sale through classrooms. The division has notified Scholastic, Xerox Education Publications, and Troll that they should not use YASD's designation of a "best book for young adults" on a book or its promotional material if the title or text has been changed from the original version. The problem arises when troublesome, four-letter words are excised or paragraphs rewritten for book-club editions and no indication is given that the new version differs from the original. At last report Scholastic is planning to include information on the copyright page of any book that has been altered in a paperback edition. "We feel that expurgation is censorship and . . . violates our *Library Bill of Rights,*" YASD Executive Secretary Evelyn Shaevel told the press. "No one except the parents should restrict what a child can read." YASD will continue to monitor book clubs to see whether publishers comply with its request.

1983—Programs and Events

A review of the year would not be complete without a summary of some outstanding events and programs:

Each year, children's librarians and publishers of children's books eagerly await the announcement of the winners of the prestigious Newbery/Caldecott Medals, *Dicey's Song* by Cynthia Voigt won the Newbery; Marcia Brown's *Shadow,* the Caldecott.

Perhaps more than in other years, libraries and reading came in for a great deal of television coverage. The Library of Congress Center for the Book created Cap'n O.G. Readmore, an animated character who made his debut on April 21; the Cap'n appeared to the nation's TV viewers in 30- to 60-second spots on ABC Television aimed at family viewers. He was made possible through a joint venture of the Library of Congress and ABC Entertainment.

On public television stations, the highly popular "Reading Rainbow," a 15-part, daily, magazine-style series was telecast over the summer months to keep children reading. Featuring film star LeVar Burton, guest personalities, and children who reviewed books, the series was supported by many educational associations and cost well over $1 million to produce. Lists of the featured books and a colorful magazine added to the summer reading fun for young viewers. This is a perfect example of what can be accomplished when TV producers and sponsors join forces with libraries to spread the word.

Late in August, New York City was host to "Everychild: The American Conference," organized by the Children's Book Council, Inc. More than 2,500 came to enjoy meeting authors, listening to storytellers, and to attend more than 132 sessions on a wide range of topics related to children and the media at this largely successful conference. It was the first such event held in an attempt to reach parents as well as early childhood educators. Judging from comments overheard from librarians, the opportunity to browse through a series of programs free of regular business meetings was reason enough to come and enjoy.

Radio is not dead yet. In Harrisburg, Pennsylvania, station WITF-FM carried a "Teen Issues Phone-In" program in which teen concerns, including sexuality, friendship, and death, were freely discussed. Librarians in the seven-county area who were involved in planning the programs displayed books related to the topics and reported a good response to the series.

The benefits of cooperation with community agencies paid off in Milwaukee, Wisconsin, where children of all ages were treated to an exciting poetry concert. Milwaukee Public Library enlisted guest poets, theater groups, the Milwaukee Art Museum, and the Wisconsin Conservatory of Music for a follow-up series of programs for the public. Organized by Children's Services Coordinator Jane Botham, the event was backed by a $9,000 grant from the Wisconsin Arts Board.

1984—A Look Ahead

In an overview of an entire year, it is impossible to review all the noteworthy events. Most libraries went about serving the public in their usual quiet way, with programs that were perhaps as innovative as those mentioned.

We've reached 1984; it may not be George Orwell's version yet, although the executive branch recently attempted—without success—to restrict free speech by forcing government employees to sign pledges not to disclose classified information and to clear speeches, articles, and books before they are made public—for the rest of their lives. One thing is certain in the year ahead: We will witness even more rapid advances in technology and information exchange.

PW News Report, 1983

John F. Baker
Editor in Chief, *Publishers Weekly*

After a couple years of deepening recession for the book industry, in 1983 the light began to show at the end of the tunnel. Christmas 1982 was a comparatively lackluster one for book sales, and the malaise lingered into the following spring. But by early summer 1983, the renewed confidence affecting much of the economy spread to book purchasers, too. Sales began to climb—slowly at first, but with increasing rapidity toward the end of the year. Final 1983 figures showed sales growth as much as 25 percent higher than 1982 in some categories, notably in hardcover books and children's paperbacks. Only direct mail sales figures were consistently down.

Perhaps as a result of the beginning recovery, the number of takeovers, bankruptcies, and mergers in the industry was not as high as in the previous year—or as high as

Note: Adapted from *Publishers Weekly,* March 16, 1984, where the article was entitled "1983: The Year in Review."

some had predicted. By far, the biggest takeover was the purchase by a group of Wall Street investors of New American Library for more than $50 million, from the Times Mirror Company. Gulf & Western bought Esquire Inc., an educational publishing company. Otherwise, much of the activity involved publishers buying into the potentially lucrative field of consumer software, either by acquiring existing software producers or forming their own special divisions to create product. Examples of publishers becoming increasingly involved in software, by one approach or the other, included Simon & Schuster, Random House, Warner, Bantam, Hayden, Dutton, SFN, McGraw-Hill, Prentice-Hall, and Addison-Wesley. Although comparatively little software appeared from these houses during 1983, it was clear that 1984 would see a great deal entering the marketplace.

Highlights

- After a couple years of deepening recession for the book industry, in 1983 the light began to show at the end of the tunnel.
- Much of the year's merger activity involved publishers buying into the potentially lucrative field of consumer software.
- The boom in the production of computer books begun in 1982 continued unabated.
- It was another litigious year for the book business.
- A number of issues sharpened the conflict between writers and publishers in 1983.

The Push for Software

Book wholesalers and retailers, too, started preparing for software sales. Ingrams, the big Nashville wholesaler, launched a major software distribution program, and the major bookstore chains began stocking software items on a highly selective test basis. A few independents also joined in, but for most booksellers various problems of knowing what software to stock, the lack of expertise among salespeople, the follow-up necessary on customer difficulties, and the need for adequate display and security for software items all contributed to a wait-and-see attitude. Meanwhile, the boom in the production of computer books begun in 1982 continued unabated, with approximately 2,000 in print at year's end.

The growing interest in computers and software was strikingly evident at the American Booksellers Association convention in Dallas in June. An otherwise slow convention in terms of sales and bookseller attendance was striking for the number of stands involving computer-related products and for the heavy attendance at various seminars examining the profit possibilities for booksellers in software. In an effort to improve the ease with which authors could communicate with their publishers electronically, using their word processors (and perhaps open the way to considerable cost savings in typesetting), the AAP launched a major pilot study to develop a series of standard communication codes.

The Changing Scene

There were some casualties of the economy. The Brentano's bookstore chain, which had been struggling and had filed for Chapter 11 bankruptcy protection in 1982, finally went out of business in 1983. A & W and Hastings House also filed for bankruptcy in 1983. As an economy move, the Dial Press, a subsidiary of Doubleday, was folded into the main company, with the loss of a number of jobs. Time-Life Books, which had suffered heavy losses in the Mexican devaluation and an abortive Japanese expansion, closed a number of offices and cut its staff, but was reported at year's end to be ready for a return to the black. At Viking Penguin, president Irv Goodman resigned in mid-year among complaints from the English parent company of "inadequate profitability," and a major reorganization was undertaken, also with the loss of a number of jobs.

An ambitious scheme to improve book distribution, based on the consolidation of shipments and making extensive use of address codes, ZIPSAN, was launched in mid-summer but foundered within six months. It was apparently undercapitalized, according to its founders, and not enough publishers took advantage of it, even though they claimed it did cut costs over its rivals, as promised. Two other attempts to streamline the book-ordering process were in preparation at year's end and ready for testing in early spring 1984: one, Booksellers Ordering Service, organized by the American Booksellers Association; the other, Bowker Acquisition System, prepared by the R. R. Bowker Company.

An attempt to solve the problem of ever-escalating midtown rents for a number of New York City-based publishers—a publishing center proposed by Martin Levin, retired chairman of the Times Mirror Company, that could be built with city aid, and in which a number of publishers could share services (and cheaper rents)—was gaining adherents and support during 1983. At last report, it was likely to become a reality by 1985. Meanwhile, a number of companies changed their locations during the year in search of lower rents: Viking Penguin, Abrams, R. R. Bowker, among others.

The American Book Awards, which have been through a number of format changes in the four years since they were restructured to replace the old National Book Awards, had a year of dizzying ups and downs. At first they were supposed to take place during the ABA meeting in Dallas; when this proved infeasible, they were switched, in a severely reduced format, to the New York Public Library. Debate continued as to how much could be spent on them, how commercial they could or should be, and in how many categories awards should be made. By the end of 1983, it had been resolved—perhaps only temporarily again—that the categories should be severely reduced and that the awards should be given in late fall 1984.

Suits and Countersuits

It was another litigious year for the book business, with new chapters written for a number of continuing cases and some brand new ones on the scene.

A long-running serial that has deeply interested publishers and civil libertarians, the Island Trees case, in which a school board's attempt to remove a number of books from a Long Island school library was opposed by a group of students, finally ended in February with a 4–3 decision by the board to let the books stay. The case had gone all the way to the Supreme Court, which had ruled in 1982 that board members could not remove books from a school library "simply because they dislike the ideas contained in those books" and sent it back to a local court.

Another continuing case now likely, after several reversals, to get to the Supreme Court is the one brought by Harper & Row and Reader's Digest against the *Nation* magazine for allegedly misappropriating part of former President Gerald Ford's memoirs. The *Nation* lost a court ruling in March, then won an appeal against the judge's decision in November. The money at issue—the $12,500 the plaintiffs claim they lost in first-serial sales as a result of the *Nation*'s alleged piracy—was minimal, but both sides view the case as a crucial one. The plaintiffs plead copyright violation; the defendants see it as a matter of their First Amendment right to publish news.

The publishers' continuing struggle against academic and organizational photocopying scored some successes during 1983. A test case brought against New York University and an adjacent copy shop on behalf of a number of publishers who complained that their works had been extensively duplicated for courses ended in a victory for the publishers. NYU and the shop agreed to abide by guidelines providing recompense for extensive copying. A case brought by paperback publishers against several dealers in stripped books survived a court challenge and is likely to be resolved in 1984, probably in the publishers' favor.

Writers' Problems

In these times of generally more strained relationships between writers and publishers, a number of issues sharpened their conflict in 1983.

California passed a law providing that writers employed by publishers on a "work for hire" basis should enjoy the same privileges, in terms of health and unemployment benefits, as full-time employees for the duration of their contracts; there was considerable anxiety in the publishing community lest this concept should spread. Meanwhile, publishers were looking carefully at their arrangements with California freelancers.

Writers continued their attempts to organize on a national basis into a more militant union than any of the existing writers' organizations. But despite a number of organizing meetings, and letters on controversial issues sent on National Writers Union letterhead from time to time, the hope of many writers that the union would become a serious bargaining force was still a long way from realization.

One issue on which the union and other writers' groups were particularly vocal was the case of Dodd, Mead and three of its authors. The house was recently taken over by Thomas Nelson, a Nashville-based religious publisher specializing in Bibles, whose management let it be known that it frowned on books containing words and expressions it found objectionable. Two novels already under contract were canceled as a result (the angry authors took them to other houses), but the third, Richard Coniff, compiler of the anthology *The Devil's Book of Verse,* was caught with his books already in print. Copies were simply left in the warehouse and not distributed. At year's end, he sued the company.

Another suit by a writer watched with great interest by publishers had been brought by Gerald Colby Zilg against Prentice-Hall. Zilg, who had written a book critical of the Du Pont family, alleged that his publisher had been pressured by Du Pont into suppressing his book by inadequately advertising it and cutting its initial print order. A judge had ruled in favor of Zilg in 1982, but in September 1983, this ruling was reversed on appeal. The appeals court ruled that providing a publisher makes a good-faith effort to make a book available, its judgment as to how extensively to print and promote is final.

A somewhat similar case involving author Deborah Davis had a different outcome. Soon after publication, her publisher, Harcourt Brace Jovanovich, in effect disavowed a book she had written on Katharine Graham, publisher of the *Washington Post,* when doubts were raised about some facts in the book. HBJ ordered copies already printed to be destroyed and reverted the rights to Davis. She sued for $6 million and settled out of court for $100,000 and her right to keep her advance.

Comings and Goings

As usual, there was a fair amount of movement among people in the book business. G. Roysce Smith, executive director of ABA, resigned (and so, coincidentally, did his deputy Robert Hale); the new head of the organization is to be Bernard Rath, former head of the Canadian Booksellers Association. Arbor House President Donald Fine was fired by the Hearst organization, and promptly formed his own line, including some of his former authors. Major moves included those of Marvin Brown from Atheneum to New American Library, John Macrae III from Dutton to Holt, Rinehart & Winston, Joseph Kanon from Coward McCann to Dutton, Erwin Glikes from Simon & Schuster to Macmillan's Free Press, and Seymour Turk from Harry Abrams to Book-of-the-Month Club. Norman Mailer's move from his longtime publisher Little, Brown to Random House, reportedly in a $4 million package deal, was the big author switch of the year; on a slightly lesser scale, John Irving moved from Dutton to Morrow. Two notable book figures died: Curtis Benjamin, former McGraw-Hill president, who had long been an industry guru, and Charles Haslam, much-loved proprietor of Haslam's Books in St. Petersburg, Florida.

Oddities

One of the year's odder stories was a suit brought by William Peter Blatty against the *New York Times Book Review.* He claimed that by reporting his book *Legion* on its bestseller lists later than it had appeared on lists elsewhere, the *NYTBR* had been guilty of negligence and "trade libel." The *Times* replied that the success of Blatty's suit would mean the end of its lists. The *Times* lists were in the news again at the end of the year when the *Book Review*'s new editor, Mitchel Levitas (replacing Harvey Shapiro, who went to the *Magazine*), redesigned them to eliminate the distinction between trade and mass market paperbacks and to add separate categories for "how-to," cartoon, and joke books. The jury was still out at the end of the year as to how the new lists would affect publishers and booksellers.

One of the most spectacular publishing recalls in memory took place when Random House was forced to order the return of all 58,000 shipped copies of *Poor Little Rich Girl,* a biography of heiress Barbara Hutton by C. David Heymann. Among other things, a doctor who had been described in the book as prescribing drugs for Hutton was no more than a teenager at the time the prescriptions were alleged to have been written, and he threatened to sue unless the book was withdrawn.

Fairs and Shows

An unusual addition to the international book fair scene during 1983 was the arrival in New York in March of a major contingent of German publishers, who set up their own book fair for a few days in the publishing capital. The idea was to ensure that American publishers, generally too busy at Frankfurt to spare much attention for the books of their host country, had a chance to examine current German production. Not much business was reported, but the fair received a good deal of attention, largely as a result of some controversial public appearances by author Günter Grass, who was outspoken about U.S. politics and the role of the writer.

Another Moscow Book Fair took place in September. As before, most U.S. trade publishers boycotted it, with only a small group of technical and scientific publishers—the ones who stand to do the most business with the Russians—attending. Some publishers stayed away for political reasons, some because they felt it was not worth making the trip in business terms. The former group received a mild rebuke at a lunch for dissident Soviet writers in exile, who said it was better to lend support to dissidents by presence at the fair than by staying away.

On the Home Front

It was a busy year for *Publishers Weekly* itself. The magazine added several regular features, including the Yellow Pages, embracing news highlights of the week at a glance, forecast highlights, interesting people in the news, a quote of the week, reminiscences of earlier publishing days, a gossip-style column, "Talk of the Trade," and an opinion column, "My Say," in which industry representatives and interested others are invited to express their views. The magazine also became available at bookstores and selected newsstands throughout the country on a limited basis, and at year's end was selling approximately 1,500 extra copies a week to consumers.

The explosion in the world of small press publishing, which according to the statisticians who put together Bowker's *Books in Print* involves nearly 200 new publishers a month, encouraged Bruce Gray, president of Bowker, to launch a new magazine, *Small Press: The Magazine of Independent Book Publishing,* to cater to their interests. The first issue of the new bimonthly appeared in September, and by the end of the year had a circulation approaching 7,000, ahead of target.

Copyright in 1983

Jerome K. Miller
Consultant in Copyright Law
Copyright Information Services, Box 2419, Station A, Champaign, IL 61820

The copyright system was under pressure in 1983 from changing technology and economic problems in the publishing and audiovisual industries. Publishers and producers are attempting to protect their positions; users fear proposed changes will reduce their rights. Important areas of change include redefinition of librarians' rights to duplicate articles and parts of books for patrons; teachers' rights to duplicate printed materials for classroom use; proprietors' rights to restrict data base downloading; and proprietors' efforts to regulate rental, performance, and duplication of films and videotapes.

Highlights

- The copyright system was under pressure in 1983 from changing technology and economic problems in the publishing and audiovisual industries.
- The Register of Copyrights' five-year report on library photocopying is critical of libraries and recommends that libraries participate in licensing agreements authorizing traditional photocopying practices.
- Teachers' rights to duplicate materials for classroom use have been restricted by the out-of-court settlement in the New York University case.
- If the district court decision in *Columbia Pictures* v. *Redd Horne* is upheld, public libraries may be forced to stop showing videocassettes in house or obtain licenses authorizing the practice.
- Hardcore downloading of copyrighted data bases is illegal, but downloading licenses now authorize this practice.

Duplicating Printed Materials in the Library

The first quinquennial report of the Register of Copyrights on library photocopying, issued in January 1983, is critical of the lack of balance between library photocopying practices and publishers' rights as defined in the law.[1] The report indicates that librarians misinterpret Section 108 of the Copyright Act to authorize copying in excess of fair use, and that the relationship between Sections 107 (on fair use) and 108 (on photocopying) must be reconsidered. The report also indicates that a substantial amount of photocopying in libraries is job-related rather than for private research or scholarship and that, in fact, the volume of copying in libraries is so great that libraries have become republishers of copyrighted works. The report suggests a surcharge on library photo-copying equipment or collective licensing agreements through a licensing agency. Finally, the report recommends further studies of the impact of new technologies on library photocopying.

The library community, spearheaded by the American Library Association (ALA), responded to the report by citing the *King Report* and other studies, which indicate that photocopying for interlibrary loan consistently falls within legislative guidelines.[2] Librarians reacted to the accusation that they confuse the relationship between Sections 107 and 108 by pointing to legislative reports indicating that library photocopying was intended to permit some copying in excess of fair use. The suggestion that libraries pay a surcharge for copying or participate in licensing agreements was rejected. Librarians argue that the amount of copying rarely exceeds authorized levels and that accepting the conditions of the report undermines librarians' rights provided in the Copyright Act.

The Register's report includes four recommendations for statutory revision. The first would permit reproduction of out-of-print music in its entirety for private study, scholarship, or research. The proposed revision, prepared by the Music Library Association and the Music Publishers Association,[3] is supported, with reservations, by ALA. The report also recommends adopting an "umbrella statute" limiting copyright proprietors' judicial remedies in copyright infringements if the infringed works are not registered with a licensing agency. ALA opposes the umbrella statute, as it requires libraries to register with the licensing agency. The third legislative recommendation is a clarification of the warning notice on photocopies mandated by Section 108(a)(3). Publishers and the Register recommend requiring the statutory copyright notice, which ALA opposes unless publishers agree to include the copyright notice on the first page of every article and on the verso of the title page of every book. The final legislative recommendation calls for the exclusion of unpublished works from the benefits of library photocopying in Section 108(d) and (e). Subsection (d) authorizes making single copies of a small part of a work or one article from a periodical, and subsection (e) authorizes reproduction of entire out-of-print works. ALA suggests further study of the issue. Although the concerned parties continue to discuss the issues, no bills or legislative hearings on this subject have been announced.

Classroom Use of Copyrighted Works

Teachers' rights to duplicate textual materials for classroom distribution are guaranteed in the fair use section (Section 107) of the Copyright Act and are described in detail in the accompanying congressional reports.[4] The congressional reports include an "Agreement on Guidelines for Classroom Copying in Not-for-Profit Educational Institutions"[5] (hereafter "Guidelines"), which identifies *minimum* levels of fair use copying. Many observers view the minimum level as a conservative application of fair use, perhaps suitable for the lower grades but impossible to apply to college teaching practices, which typically require reading lengthy selections from many sources. The conflict between the "Guidelines" and college teaching practices culminated in the New York University (NYU) case. The plaintiffs charged that NYU professors collaborated with a commercial copy shop to reproduce books of assigned readings for NYU classes. Several of these books were copyrighted, and reproduced without permission. NYU, the professors, and the copy shop settled out of court.[6] The settlement requires NYU to enforce the minimum level of copying identified in the "Guidelines." Colleges and universities throughout the country responded to the settlement by implementing copyright policies similar to those required at NYU.

The Special Libraries Association (SLA) responded to the NYU case with a position paper, "Reproduction of Copyrighted Materials for Classroom Use: A Briefing Paper for Teaching Faculty and Administrators," which includes classroom copying guidelines developed at the University of Wisconsin-Madison.[7] The Wisconsin guidelines identify works suitable for unrestricted copying and procedures for applying the congressionally approved "Guidelines." The SLA papers comment briefly on the application of the "Guidelines" to duplicating single and multiple copies of copyrighted materials for library reserve reading collections.[8]

Downloading Data Bases

As libraries and information centers develop sophisticated online searching techniques, they are beginning to encounter copyright problems. Many bibliographic, numeric, factual, and textual data bases are copyrighted works, and downloading (copying) them can be an infringement. There appear to be two types of downloading—softcore and hardcore. Softcore downloading is (1) copying information obtained from a search for the purpose of high-speed access with delayed (offline) printing on a slow-speed printer, or (2) offline editing of search results to remove duplicate or irrelevant information or to make search results more useful. In softcore downloading, the record is erased after the report is printed. Hardcore downloading is copying data to create a local data base, thereby eliminating or reducing the need for further searching of the copyrighted source. Although softcore downloading is a copyright infringement, copyright proprietors appear to accept it as a harmless service to users. On the other hand, hardcore downloading is a clear-cut copyright infringement, and proprietors are attempting to stop their losses by offering downloading licenses.[9] *Chemical Abstracts*, among others, recently introduced a downloading license that may be attractive to high-volume users.

Online Computer Library Center (OCLC) responded to potential misuse of its data base by retroactively claiming copyright protection for it.[10] OCLC's action was prompted by a concern that the data base would be reproduced by a commercial competitor. Most data bases are protected from misuse by subscriber contracts that prohibit sharing the data with nonparticipants, but OCLC's member agreements lack this protective language. Rather than renegotiate contracts with all member libraries, networks, etc., OCLC decided to claim copyright protection as an expedient solution to its problem. OCLC received considerable publicity (and excoriation) for its decision. Most data in OCLC and similar data bases are in the public domain, either because of their nature (e.g., proper names or titles) or because they were produced by the federal government. However, OCLC and other data base producers can claim copyright protection for (1) a compilation of public domain data, (2) copyrightable data (e.g., descriptions), and (3) the underlying program.[11] OCLC is attempting to resolve the dispute with its members by negotiating new member contracts, but the hostility engendered by the decision to claim copyright protection makes it difficult to arrive at mutually acceptable language.[12]

Film and Video Court Cases

The Motion Picture Association of America (MPAA) coordinated suits by several film companies to stop infringing performances of films on videocassettes. The most significant case was *Columbia Pictures* v. *Redd Horne*, in which seven film companies sued a video shop operator for infringing performances of videocassettes.[13] Viewers paid an admission fee to see the videocassettes shown in small viewing rooms at the back of the shops. The defendant claimed that these were private performances exempt under Sections 101 and 106 of the Copyright Act, but the court held that performances available on demand to the general public are not exempt from the proprietors' right to regulate public and semipublic performances. If this case is sustained by the higher courts, it may force public libraries to stop in-house video performances or to obtain licenses for this service.

In their effort to protect their public performance rights, some film companies distributed a sternly worded warning notice to schools, colleges, and public libraries. The warning notice, prepared by MPAA attorneys, indicates that showing a videocassette in a school is a "public performance," which is an exclusive right reserved to the copyright proprietor.[14] MPAA representatives now acknowledge educators' right to use films and videocassettes in face-to-face teaching situations under the terms of Section 110(1) of the Copyright Act,[15] but many educators and librarians have been misled by the confusing language of the warning notice and assume that they may not show videocassettes in classrooms without permission.

A related issue stems from the BOCES case, in which three educational film companies sued the Erie County, New York, Board of Cooperative Education (BOCES) for copyright infringements in videotaping films off-the-air and distributing copies to schools.[16] Many observers expected BOCES to lose the case, but were surprised when the court denied BOCES the right to videotape television programs off-the-air under the terms of the "Guidelines for Off-Air-Recording of Broadcast Programming for Educational Purposes" (hereafter "Off-Air Guidelines").[17] The "Off-Air Guidelines" are similar to the CONTU guidelines for library photocopying and the two fair-use guidelines for classroom copying. None of these guidelines has the force of law, but it was widely assumed that the courts would uphold them as evidence of legislative intent for applying Sections 107 and 108 of the Copyright Act. The "Off-Air Guidelines" appear to be weaker than the other guidelines because (1) they were rejected by several major educational film companies and the trade association that collaborated in writing them, and (2) their application can conflict with the fourth fair use criterion, "the effect of the use upon the potential market for or value of the copyrighted work."[18] In the BOCES case, the plaintiffs argued that their films were available in film and video formats through sales, rental, or lease and that permitting BOCES to copy them off-the-air violated the fourth fair use criterion by depriving them of legitimate income from their copyrighted works.[19] The court accepted the plaintiffs' argument. Some contend that the court order invalidates the "Off-Air Guidelines"; others suggest that the order only applies to BOCES and lacks universal application. A moderate interpretation suggests that the "Off-Air Guidelines" cannot (and never could) be applied to videotaping programs readily available for sale, rental, lease, or loan—but may not be applied to videotaping programs off-the-air if the programs are currently available in the educational market.

Rental and Duplication of Audiovisual Works

Congress is debating several amendments to the copyright law. S. 32 requires a surcharge on commercial rentals of sound recordings, with the income distributed to the copyright proprietors of the music and the performances.[20] H.R. 1029, the "Betamax Bill," authorizes home videotape recording but institutes a surcharge on the sale of blank tape and recorders, to be distributed to the copyright proprietors.[21] H.R. 1030 imposes a surcharge on commercial rentals of copyrighted videocassettes, to be distributed to the proprietors.[22] These bills are supported by the Copyright Office. H.R. 1029 passed the Senate and may become law in this session, but the other two are still in committee. Schools, colleges, and public libraries are not affected by these bills, as they are presently written.

Conclusion

Although the copyright law was not amended at the time of writing, it was effectively reinterpreted by the New York University, BOCES, and *Redd Horne* cases. Efforts to amend the law to restrict library photocopying and other uses are undoubtedly being prepared and will be debated in the next few years. If a trend is visible, it suggests greater control over copying, renting, and public performances of copyrighted works. If these changes are implemented, licenses or surcharges will undoubtedly be required for many uses that are now free or relatively unrestricted.

Notes

1. *Report of the Register of Copyrights: Library Reproduction of Copyrighted Works (17 U.S.C. 108)* (Washington, D.C.: Copyright Office, 1983).
2. *Comments of the American Library Association on the Report of the Register of Copyrights to Congress: Library Reproduction of Copyrighted Works (17 U.S.C. 108)* (Washington, D.C.: American Library Association, 1983); and Nancy H. Marshall, "Register of Copyrights' Five-Year Review Report: A View from the Field," *Library Trends* 32 (Fall 1983): 165–182.
3. The development of the legislative recommendation for reproduction of out-of-print music is described in Carolyn Owlett Hunter, "Library Reproduction of Musical Works: A Review of Revision," *Library Trends* 32 (Fall 1983): 241ff.
4. U.S. House of Representatives, *Report No. 94-1476*, Sect. 107; and U.S. House of Representatives, *Report No. 94-1733*, Sect. 107.
5. "Agreement on Guidelines for Classroom Copying in Not-for-Profit Educational Institutions," in U.S. House of Representatives, *Report No. 94-1476*, Sect. 107.
6. *Addison-Wesley Pub. Co., Inc.* v. *New York University*, (DC SD NY 1983) 82 CIV 83333 (ADS).
7. Special Libraries Association, "Reproduction of Copyrighted Materials for Classroom Use: A Briefing Paper for Teaching Faculty and Administrators." Position paper, 1983.
8. For further information on the application of the guidelines to reserve reading collections, see J. K. Miller, "Duplication of Journal Articles for Reserve Reading Collections," in *U.S. Copyright Documents: An Annotated Collection for Use by Educators and Librarians* (Littleton, Colo.: Libraries Unlimited, 1980), pp. 28–35.
9. Jerome K. Miller, "Copyright Protection for Bibliographic, Numeric, Factual, and Textual Databases," *Library Trends* 32 (Fall 1983): 199–210.
10. "Good Morning. © OCLC." *American Libraries* 14 (February 1983): 74.
11. Miller, "Copyright Protection for Bibliographic, Numeric, Factual, and Textual Databases."
12. Letters from Rowland C. W. Brown to member libraries and networks, October 18, 1983, and November 10, 1983.
13. *Columbia Pictures v. Redd Horne*, (DC WD Pa 1983) No. 83-0016 Erie.
14. Motion Picture Association of America, Inc., "Warning! 'For Home Use Only' Means Just That" (Hollywood, Calif., n.d.), broadside.
15. Burton H. Hanft to Jerome K. Miller, in Jerome K. Miller, *Using Copyrighted Videocassettes in Classrooms and Libraries* (Champaign, Ill.: Copyright Information Services, 1984).
16. *Encyclopaedia Britannica Educational Corp.* v. *Crooks*, (DC WD NY) 558 FSupp 1247; (DC WD NY 1982) 542 FSupp 1156, 214 USPQ 697; and (DC WD NY 1978) 447 FSupp 243, 197 USPQ 280.
17. "Guidelines for Off-Air Recording of Broadcast Programming for Educational Purposes," *Congressional Record*, October 14, 1981, p. E4751.
18. United States Code, Title 17, "Copyrights," Sect. 107(4).
19. *Encyclopaedia Brittannica Educational Corp.* v. *Crooks*, op. cit.
20. S. 32, 98th Cong., 1st Sess.
21. H. R. 1029, 98th Cong., 1st Sess.
22. H. R. 1030, 98th Cong., 1st Sess.

Library Networking in the United States, 1983

Glyn T. Evans

Assistant Vice Chancellor for Library Services
State University of New York
Director, SUNY/OCLC Network

The rapid growth of library networks in the past decade necessarily left many unanswered questions, some of which evaporated over time, some still lie dormant, and some, no longer latent, are beginning to dominate networking debate. Furthermore, the rapid technological and social changes of the last decade have changed the networking environment, and that environment in turn, is affecting networking. The resulting uncertainty has raised the temperature but has not increased the light. Indeed, the tensions have generated more autonomic knee jerks than calm deliberation. On the other hand, the issues are complex, and the long-range effects of poor decisions made now will be serious. Where, and how, the decisions will be made is a component of the uncertainty, particularly in two of the dominant issues.

Highlights
- The rapid growth of library networks in the past decade necessarily left many unanswered questions, some of which are beginning to dominate networking debate.
- The ecology of networking reveals both a changing, hostile ecosystem (telecommunications, copyright) and an unstable internal structure (contracts, ethics, consultation, governance).
- The copyright issue depends on the definition of OCLC. Is OCLC all of its members, rather than only its management, or is it 4,000 individual entities trying to protect themselves against each other?
- Networks are a new social structure in the library world that crosses geographic and political boundaries and the established patterns of discourse in the professional associations and among libraries.
- There is a clear consensus of expectations among network users and network managements, and the current discussions are more about means than ends.

In the report on library networking in the 1983 *Bowker Annual,* two "other developments" were noted that would affect networking, telecommunications tariffs and the OCLC claim to copyright of its data base. In 1983 they, along with the OCLC contract discussions with regional networks, became the three dominant issues. Events are never tidy at year's end, and these issues remain as unresolved problems.

Major Developments

The Ecology of Networking: Telecommunications

The major bibliographic networks were founded, planned, and implemented on the premise of large computer systems supplying a large data base of standard bibliographic records and auxiliary services (cataloging, interlibrary loan, and so on), all of which would be accessed online by libraries at remote locations. This strategy was expected to improve the cost efficiency of library operations, and indeed it has. The networks would not be successful if it had not. One substantial part of the cost equation is telecommunications costs, which when the systems were planned were expected to diminish. But one lurking unknown was the suit by the Justice Department against AT&T, which was resolved on August 24, 1982, when Federal District Court Judge Greene signed a negotiated settlement between the department and AT&T. The result was the divestiture of AT&T into its own long-distance service, with many local (some Bell, others not) services for local access and a bridging interface mechanism between them. The shoe dropped when AT&T filed its tariff proposal with the Federal Communications Commission early in October 1983, to take effect on January 1, 1984. The proposed rate increases shocked the network world, and education generally, into rapt attention. OCLC computed an average increase of 69 percent in telecommunications charges, with some networks, depending on configuration and density of use, expecting increases as high as 84 percent (CAPCON, Washington, D.C.), 83 percent (OHIONET), 78 percent (INCOLSA, Indiana) and four others (Illinois, Michigan, Pennsylvania, and New York) at 73 percent. OCLC computed a monthly networkwide increase of some $300,000. No improvement in service quality is expected; in fact, because multiple organizations are involved simply to add a terminal to a leased line, inefficiencies and delays are anticipated.

The structure of the charges is as much the culprit as the values assigned to the charge components. OCLC reports a shift in emphasis in long-distance charges from 75 percent (1983 tariffs) to 26 percent (proposed 1984), with the major increase in local access charges. ALA and ARL, concerned about the effects of divestiture early in 1983, invited local and regional networks and other associations to join a "coalition to monitor telecommunications developments affecting library and educational data transmission," with a positive response. Legislation passed in the House on November 10, 1983, the Universal Telephone Service Preservation Act (HR 4102), would, among other things, repeal local access charges to private citizens. Pending in the Senate is S.1660, scheduled for debate in January 1984, which proposes delay of access charges for two years. Both bills assume that others will pick up the costs; unfortunately, library networks are among the others. The Federal Communications Commission has delayed a decision on the AT&T tariff proposal until April 1984. As would be expected, lobbying and information filing with the FCC are intense. At the same time, the networks must review technical alternatives in telecommunications. One increasing activity, distributed systems development, is discussed later in this report.

The Ecology of Networking: Copyright

As noted earlier, OCLC filed a claim for copyright of its data base in December 1982. The Copyright Office has still not responded to that claim as of this writing (December 28,

1983)—a rather unusual delay. Again, it is necessary to look back at the early days of networking, before the Copyright Act of 1976 was passed and before the Commission on New Technological Uses of Copyrighted Works (CONTU) was established in 1975. The question of "ownership" of the OCLC data base, although asked, was never pursued. Libraries joined networks, networks signed contracts with OCLC, and OCLC worked with networks to establish a system of "shared cataloging," which obviously entails a "shared data base." That data base now exceeds 10 million records, and the environment has changed in the last decade.

Consider these factors. First, OCLC's governance has evolved to include a board of trustees and user council, the latter elected by library members. The regional networks, with which OCLC contracts for service, which are largely responsible for the growth of OCLC, and which are almost totally responsible for the field implementation of new libraries and systems, have no formal voice in the governance of OCLC (other than through the election of individual staff members to the governance bodies). This structure obscures the definition of OCLC. Second, OCLC is not claiming copyright of the records themselves but of the totality of the compilation. Such precedents as the Yellow Pages do exist, and ALA holds the copyright of the *National Union Catalog*. The degree to which this is widely understood and its effects are unsure. Third, CONTU's preoccupation was with photocopying and only to a lesser degree with data bases and software; apparently data and software from a single producer, rather than a compilation, were envisioned. Therefore, little guidance can be expected from the CONTU recommendations. Fourth, OCLC's concern is limited to machine-readable, not eye-readable, formats. With more libraries realizing the value of the tapes for COM catalogs, distributed systems, moving to other utilities and services, or developing one's own system, access to the tapes for legitimate uses is crucial. Further, downloading (the copying of machine-readable records in machine-readable form through a terminal printer port or micro attached to the online system) is more likely, even encouraged by such technical developments as OCLC's Model 300 terminal, which is basically an IBM Personal Computer. Fifth, there is a continuing investment of public money in the data base, through records input from MARC tapes and funded retrospective conversion projects such as HEA Title IIC programs, union lists of serials, and LSCA projects. Indeed, tracing the provenance of any record is almost impossible. And it is true that OCLC itself makes a contribution through error control and correction, indexing, and such related files as the Name-Address Directory (NAD).

However, also consider the following.

The data base is probably the most important asset in networking, and that asset is vulnerable. Reports such as the one in *Library Hotline,* October 3, 1983 (12, no. 3, p. 1), on the Autographics, Inc., Agile-2 data base of 6 million records, which represents several years of producing COM catalogs for libraries, are not comforting, particularly since Autographics claims to be able to "undersell OCLC by 20%." Clearly, OCLC management, regional networks, and the libraries are united in their assessment that the data base must be protected, that there are uses of the data base that are at least unethical. The discussion within the OCLC community is about means, not ends. Codes of responsible use, or codes of ethics, may not be strong enough.

The Research Libraries Group (RLG) declared in June that it did not intend to copyright its data base, although clause 1.3 of its standard contract states that "All data added to the RLIN database by member may be used by RLG for any purpose without restriction. . ."; and clause 1.5 states that "In no event shall user copy all or any portion of the RLIN database in machine-readable form except with the prior written consent of RLG." Apparently by December its view of copyright compilations had changed.

OCLC is a membership organization, not a public utility, although one would hardly believe so judging from the formal action of other organizations. Perhaps the most surprising was RLG's encouragement of its members in December to copyright their records in the OCLC system as compilation, thus, in one sense, acknowledging the validity of the OCLC claim. The action was even less comprehensible since OCLC had already stated that it would delete (and indeed had) holdings of records that carried a library copyright. When ARL "informed" its members in a carefully worded letter that a "senior official of the Copyright Office had stated that such claims would be considered along with the OCLC claim," other elements entered the picture, including the propriety of the behavior of the parties involved. The RLG action was all the more surprising since it had successfully loaded some 4.5 million records, basically from OCLC tapes (although that source was not acknowledged in the press release), into its data base earlier in the year. It also had been assured by OCLC that RLIN would have a royalty-free license to use data from the OCLC data base in the same manner libraries are now using OCLC, and that the copyright claim would have no effect on use of existing data by RLG libraries. If the purpose was not actually to copyright the records but to confuse the issue further and to embarrass OCLC, then it was at least temporarily successful. At a meeting between OCLC and the Copyright Office on December 22, 1983, the Office said it wished to delay a decision even further, perhaps expecting more individual claims.

The resolution of the issue depends on the definition of OCLC. If OCLC is all its members rather than only its management, and if it is necessary to protect the data base from external threat, then copyright may be the only viable mechanism. If OCLC is seen as almost 4,000 individual entities trying to protect themselves against each other, copyright is not appropriate. Further, it must be added that OCLC management is not entirely free of criticism, even if, in the long run, copyright is the correct procedure. It introduced the question abruptly, even worse, unilaterally, and did a poor job of explaining its position and purpose. It failed to understand that the word "copyright" would produce a visceral reaction among its community of members. OCLC did issue clarifying statements late in the year, but too late; the damage was done. Diplomatic efforts will be necessary among many groups before the problem is resolved. Whether such diplomacy will be used remains to be seen.

The Ecology of Networking: Contracts

The copyright issue spilled over into network contracts in 1983, contributing to further alarm and confusion. All of the regional networks that have contracts with OCLC have developed them over a period of time since they first joined OCLC, some contracts being almost unchanged since 1977. Everyone agrees that the contracts were obsolete and that a major revision was necessary; conditions have changed so much. Preparatory work was undertaken late in 1982 when regional networks and OCLC agreed on a Statement of Mutual Tenets, Commitments and Expectations. In April 1983, OCLC distributed a draft contract to networks with the expectation that it would be signed and created by July 1983. Once again, the ethical system broke down, and within days comments and advice, some of it self-serving, were being freely offered to all parties by outsiders, despite the expectation of confidentiality during contract negotiation. The contract was frankly unacceptable to the regional networks (it was permeated with the unanswered copyright question, it made unrealistic claims about ownership of tape records, and it used such language as marketing agent, which is just not appropriate for many of the networks affiliated with OCLC). The regional networks unanimously rejected the contract, formed a steering committee, and hired a law firm to draft the network view of a contract. The degree of solidarity among the networks was remarkable.

All of this takes time, particularly since the networks are dispersed throughout the country, meet infrequently, and each is responsible to its own board and members. OCLC, impatient, accused the networks of not negotiating, not realizing that they were negotiating intensively, with each other. A draft contract was delivered to OCLC in November. The passage of time was good for both parties. Copyright disappeared from subsequent OCLC drafts of its contract, as did the question of ownership of tapes. One central issue about which there is serious discussion is exactly what responsibilities a library undertakes when it joins in shared cataloging, both in the number and quality of the records and holdings it is expected to enter and the degree to which it will agree to a code of ethics. Libraries take this question seriously; they link the creation of the data base asset with its protection.

At this writing, discussions are continuing, and there is a real sense that the parties are moving closer. Ron Deiner, director of OHIONET, provided a valuable commentary on contract and copyright discussions in *Ohionetwork*[1] and in a guest editorial published in the December 1983 *American Libraries*. In the latter optimistic editorial, he remarks on "those whose greatest ecstasy would be achieved with a colossal failure, either on the part of OCLC or of regional networks."[2] But Deiner is correct; no one involved with the contract is talking of failure to reach agreement. There will be a contract that adequately expresses the needs of libraries, OCLC, and networks in terms of the current technical, fiscal, and operational realities.

The Ecology of Networking: Other Developments

Other changes in the ecology of networking need brief report. Fred Kilgour, in a discussion of public policy and networks, concluded that "public policy and law have not caught up with the potentials of machine-readable information flow." He continued: "Countries with modern governments characterized by centralized authority are likely to be more effective in shaping new policies and law related to transmission of computerized data, but if they are not, the struggle between the future and the past will intensify for a long time to come."[3]

The increased use of video display terminals (VDTs) in industry and business is prompting other expressions of social concern. Legislation that proposes work conditions for VDT operators has been proposed in Illinois and New York; and reports on the potential health hazards of VDTs are continuing to appear. The ergonomic aspects of working at terminals are also beginning to attract wider attention, although in fact both problems have been a significant component of online implementation by regional networks since the beginning.[4]

In a survey clearly stimulated by concern about computer security—or rather the lack of it—*American Libraries* questioned LC and the four major utilities, OCLC, RLIN, WLN, and UTLAS, about their security arrangements.[5]

Senate Concurrent Resolution 59 authorized the Librarian of Congress to study the changing role of the book in the future and report the findings to Congress. Taken in conjunction with the progress of LC's work on optical disc technology, and its appointment of a new advisory group drawn from all sectors, long-range developments that clearly are about to emerge will affect networking.

The problem of providing network sources to the small user at a fair economic rate is also a growing concern, as is the development of statewide data bases. OCLC has responded to the small library problem by allowing non-OCLC libraries into the local union list of serials; and in New York, Wisconsin and California, it is conducting a "group access experiment" in which a group of non-OCLC libraries (likely an existing OCLC regional union list) can dial OCLC via ILL within its region, with an "agent" referring questions outside the region. This solves the operational if not the fiscal problems; the libraries still need expensive training, and regional networks have to balance their budgets, too.[6]

Finally, the Ohio Board of Tax Appeals announced its decision that OCLC is liable for property taxes in the Franklin County, Ohio, area, giving a strict interpretation of the description of educational institutions in Ohio law, which expects that teaching (not training) be carried out on the premises. OCLC's back taxes, which could exceed $5 million, will obviously be reflected in OCLC's current income and members' costs. OCLC will appeal or seek legislative relief, or both. The implications of this action go far beyond OCLC, of course. As the public belt tightens, and local authorities seek revenue, other networks and utilities are likely to be in a similar position. AMIGOS, in Dallas, has already reported a tax ruling against it. The long-run implications for the not-for-profit status of networks and data base producers bear quiet contemplation.

Major Technical Developments

It is a relief to turn from the politics to the remarkable technical developments of the year.

Online Public Access Catalogs

The idea, and indeed the reality, of the online public access catalog (OPAC, an unfortunate acronym) gained ground in 1983, with considerable public discussion and report. The Council on Library Resources has played an important stimulative role in furthering and supporting fundamental research in OPACs. *CLR Recent Developments* lists reports that were stimulated by council effort.[7] Jaye Bausser edits columns on OPACs in *RTSD Newsletter*,[8] and other reports of current developments can be found in such publications as *College and Research Libraries, LITA Newsletter,* and *DLA Bulletin.*[9]

What is the current status of the OPAC? Some systems are operational, and basic studies have been performed. The year has uncovered some new questions and some perhaps surprising hypotheses and answers. The fundamental strategy clearly is to create a machine-readable data base using a bibliographic utility and reuse the data in an OPAC. Then the tactic becomes less clear: Does one choose to rely on the utility to provide an OPAC centrally; or go through a distributed system; or turn to another vendor for either a service or software; or develop one's own using a mainframe, mini-, or microcomputer? And how does one decide on need as well as opportunity (of which there is an abundance)?

It seems unlikely that the major utilities will supply a central OPAC. Crawford, reporting on long searches of RLIN, writes that "the RLIN II searching interface is not suitable, *as it stands* [author's italics] for a large public access catalog. Naive use of the system could lead to significant difficulties in overall responsiveness. To maintain good overall response, such a catalog would need methods of detecting long searches, preventing inadvertent long searches, and reducing the impact of deliberate long searches."[10]

A number of vendors offer OPACs, SUNY/OCLC and the New York Public Library are in the middle of a field test of the CARLYLE System, which is a revision of the MELVYL System built to serve the University of California. The Mankato State System, a homegrown system, is operational, as is ORION at UCLA, and New York University has announced an online catalog using the GEAC System. OCLC includes an OPAC within its LS/2000 (discussed later), as do many of the other circulation system vendors. Replication is a word with a checkered history in networking. In the early days, many networks signed contracts that would allow "replication" of the OCLC system. Grammarians had a fine time with the word; few thought it could be done. But here we are, a decade later, replicating madly without a second thought. The WLN System to the University of Illinois at Champaign-Urbana and SOLINET, and Biblio-Techniques Library and Information System (BLIS), a close relative of WLN, to Johns Hopkins University, University of California at San Diego, and, for a six-month trial, to Columbia University; and Georgetown University's LIS System to the University of Texas Health Science Library at San Antonio.[11] Replication of the Mankato State System in Westchester County, New York, is being discussed. Anderson and Miller, reporting a survey of user needs at the University of Cincinnati, state with some surprise that users there were more than ready for an OPAC; indeed they preferred it to a circulation system.[12] And so they should; a circulation system helps librarians control the patron; a catalog helps the patron control the collection.

An interesting account of the Summary Recommendations of the Subject Access Meeting, sponsored by the Council on Library Resources and held in Dublin, Ohio, was reported by C. Lee Jones of the council in the March 1983 *Information Technology and Libraries*.[13] Long-term projects and issues are defined, following a report of the discussions and the changing environment. All of the projects will have a profound effect on networking and libraries, and some of the issues will need patient resolution. There is plenty of constructive work here for everyone.

In short, the climate, the data bases, the stress on public service hours in academic libraries, the machines and software, the pressure of telecommunications tariffs, the growing familiarity of the user and the terminal or microcomputer, and user expectations—all point to a rapid expansion of OPACs. Cautions: There are still many unknowns, particularly about the discomfiting phrase "user-friendly system," and the quality of the data bases still leaves much to be desired. Subject access also continues to demand attention, with more research reports this year.[14] An appropriate end to this section is a statement attributed to C. Lee Jones of the Council on Library Resources: "CLR is debating the economics of authority control, and while they recognize the need for it, it is questioned *how much can be afforded* [italics added]. To fully examine this question, CLR may hire a consultant from outside the profession."[15]

Distributed Systems and Micros

Distributed systems, defined as "the dispatch, to local or regional components of an online network, of the functions that through reasons of volume of traffic and proximity of local data, or to facilitate other mechanisms to improve overall system efficiency, are best operated locally," continued to expand in 1983. The forces driving such development are obvious: Telecommunications, local control of local data, the large cost of maintaining central systems, the inherent security risks, and the availability of inexpensive, efficient hardware and software, all point to distribution as an appropriate mode. These forces only underscore the importance of early resolution of the copyright and data base maintenance issues and concerns regarding telecommunications tariffs, which through their shift in emphasis to local charges throw a curve at distributed system economics.

RLG received a grant of $250,000 from Carnegie Corporation to begin a study of distributed processing in January 1983. OCLC, after five years without progress, abandoned development of its own distributed system and acquired the Integrated Library System, originally developed at the National Library of Medicine Lister Hill Biomedical Communications Center, but since subject to further independent developments by both William Ford at On-line Systems, Inc., and Richard Dick at Avatar Systems. Both Ford and Dick were members of the original development teams at NLM, and OCLC acquired both versions, along with some personnel (Dick is now working in Columbus). The system offers circulation, OPAC, authority control, and administrative services. It will be linked to the OCLC online system and OCLC, renaming the system LS/2000, is putting in a major development and marketing effort, with the support of most of the networks, to promulgate the system. Expansions planned are for serials control and acquisitions. At year's end, the system is operating at Dublin, Ohio, for a number of other libraries (Hampshire College, University of Akron, and Ohio Wesleyan University). The first distributed (i.e., in the field) implementation was activated in December 1983 at the five colleges in Massachusetts (University of Massachusetts, Amherst, Mt. Holyoke, Smith, and Hampshire colleges), with implementation expected in January 1984. The development, training, and implementation of new staff is a major fiscal and social investment on the part of the networks; and the whole exercise will demand new skills and resources to meet the new service opportunities in libraries, networks, and OCLC.

The microcomputer continued its march into libraries in 1983, with numbers of vendors offering micro-based systems, sometimes freestanding, sometimes linked with networks.

After disappointing experiences with the Model 200 terminal in 1982 and 1983, OCLC announced the Model 300 terminal, which, as noted earlier, is basically an IBM PC with OCLC internal software and keyboard. OCLC functions as a value-added vendor of the PC, which will, of course, still be an OCLC sole-source item. Since the package will include two diskette drives and the capability of attaching hard disc drives, the unit is best described as a work station; it can be used both on- and offline. WLN has also adopted the PC as a terminal for its system. Many other micros can also be attached to online networks, causing some concern about system security, with networks needing to monitor system attachments. Given the proximity of the major disc storage, there is also the obvious temptation of system abuse through downloading. Again, technical opportunity precedes a commonly agreed social policy.

One attraction of the micro is that it can act as a remote work station to offload (distribute) some functions from the main system and store data and instructions for remote entry. OCLC has field-tested a "micro enhancer" system, which gives considerable support to the ILL system, and is making the software available for the PC and the

Apple; other subsystems (catalog, acquisitions, and serials check-in) offer further opportunities of improving the cost efficiency of library operations.

Other Developments

Some brief notes on other significant developments that affected networking in 1983: Both RLG and OCLC announced systems to input non-Roman alphabet data into their respective data bases, specifically Chinese, Japanese, and Korean, quickly dubbed CJK, although the techniques probably will be used for other alphabets as well. RLG was first in this race, and its terminals are in use at the Library of Congress. OCLC's system was to be fully operational early in 1984.

Two fundamentally different approaches were adopted. The RLIN terminal is specially designed, with 226 keys that reconstruct the character, and requires special software in the mainframe. OCLC adopted a system developed by Asiagraphics, Inc., which uses a standard (Western) keyboard, terminal screen, and dot matrix printer and a technique of phonetic encoding in Western characters so that the data are transmitted to the data base in a standard manner. On output to the terminal, the character strings are translated back into the required character. OCLC expects to develop the system as a package for its Model 300 terminal; the RLG special terminal costs about $38,000. It will be interesting to see which system will be preferred by users.

Another significant technical development is the introduction of the data base machine, a mainframe computer that does not have a revised system architecture, but also does not carry the overload of unnecessary computing functions (and as floating point arithmetic) found in general-purpose computing. The expectations, of course, are lower cost and improved efficiency.[16]

In the international arena, UTLAS announced an online link with its replicated system in Japan,[17] and OCLC Europe continued to add new libraries. The bibliographic utilities and circulation and OPAC system vendors were prominent in the exhibitions and discussions at the forty-ninth IFLA conference in Munich in August 1983. The obvious attractions of expansion to a true international bibliographic system must be tempered by the cautions expressed by Kilgour,[18] and, indeed, the attitudes to international organizations generally, given the December 1984 congressional resolution to withdraw from UNESCO.

The hard, serious work on standards continued through the year. Progress through drafts is noted in the areas of computerized ordering of books (two formats), nonserials holdings, a combined summary and detail serial holdings format, and computer-to-computer protocols. In the last area, one protocol to permit intersystem search and retrieval has already been developed in the Linked System Project (LC-LSP) of the Library of Congress, WLN, and RLG; and a second protocol for transfer of records is under consideration. The U.S. Office of Education awarded an HEA Title IIC grant of $400,000 to Yale and others to design a manuscript and archive project for RLIN. One wonders how different it will be from LC's MARC format and the National Archives Spindex II system, both developed by public agencies.[19]

R. R. Bowker Company announced the final test of its Bowker Acquisition System (BAS) with an agreement with Baker and Taylor for a regular exchange of bibliographic data to test the system. When operational, the system, which utilizes the *Books in Print* data base, will be accessible by terminals and will accommodate orders from any U.S. publisher, distributor, or wholesaler.

Each of the three major U.S. bibliographic utilities announced major accomplishments during the year. The significant RLG data base load, bringing its file to 12 million records, has already been noted. RLIN announced that its authorities file subsystem is ready for searching, with access to LC names and subjects and New York Public Libraries' 2.3 million name and subject authority records. WLN announced that it has augmented its acquisitions subsystem with an online service that automatically transmits orders to participating vendors, with the clear purpose of improving the efficiency and speed of the acquisitions process. Anticipated vendors are invited to apply to WLN.

OCLC installed its new CPV operating system in June and began the implementation of applications software written under CPV but not mountable until the operating system was in place. Release 1 included the long-awaited serials claiming module and brought with it some problems and surprises that needed quick handling. Duplicate record processing, improved serials searching, direct access to NAD from Serials Control, and acquisitions order file maintenance were also included in Release 1. Release 2 was added in December 1983. It includes Version 3 of ILL (including an improved statistical package), link from ILL and NAD, and corporate author search during prime time. OCLC also installed the Fibre Optics Link (FOX) between the data base processors and applications processors to improve internal system data flow. The NEH funded Newspaper Project for the conversion of newspaper records into OCLC expanded during 1983.[20]

Management Information Systems, based on data derived from networks, became more prominent in 1983. The papers of the 1982 Urbana clinic on that topic were published;[21] and Mary Jo Lynch, ALA director of research, was appointed distinguished research scholar at OCLC to work on the topic. Improved network/library statistics are becoming available in OCLC's Marketing Users Trend Reports (MUTRS) and ILL statistics, giving individual library managers improved performance statistics for their own libraries.[22] ARL announced the launching of a national inventory of collections based on the RLG Conspectus On-Line, and interesting management development.[23]

Finally, people and places. Richard McCoy took up his directorship of RLG in January 1983, and Henriette Avram, for so long the important influence in MARC development, was named assistant librarian for processing services at the Library of Congress on November 7, succeeding Joe Howard, who became director of the National Agricultural Library in July 1983. Jim Kennedy resigned his directorship of AMIGOS to become OCLC sales manager—western United States, in July 1983, with responsibilities for the regional development of LS/2000. He was succeeded by Louella Wetherbee, director of libraries at George Mason University, who served as assistant and then associate director for library services at AMIGOS between 1977 and 1980. All these people are accepting major responsibilities at a difficult time, and we wish them well.

In the network world, Five Associated University Libraries (FAUL), established in 1965 and one of the first consortia to contract with OCLC in 1971, closed its doors in July 1983; and OCLC Western, headquartered at Claremont, California, changed its name to OCLC Pacific Network, or PACNET, in November 1983. A new network, the Missouri Library Network Corporation, headquartered in St. Louis, affiliated with OCLC in 1983.

Summary

Of the two levels of discourse currently in networking, the one most apparent is the tedious, internecine sniping among the parties, which is more a reflection of uncertainty, ambition, and frustration than it is a contribution to problem resolution, particularly as networks try to survive in a hostile environment. The second, which is extremely serious and important, is the consideration that libraries actually participating in networks are giving to social and political questions raised by networking. These are the libraries that have committed themselves to the investment of money, staff, and intellectual and emotional effort in networking. The questions answered by these libraries in the next year or so will shape networking for the next decade, more than will any planning document.

Think about these questions. How much effort should a library make to input all its current cataloging and holdings into a shared network data base? How much effort must be expended to achieve a satisfactory level of quality control of input? What returns can a library expect from such effort? Will the data bases being built be both accessible *and* protected from internal and external violation? What standards of ethics and responsibility are necessary, and how should the governance of the networks establish and administer such standards? Are stronger legal (copyright or contract) structures necessary to ensure the continued viability of networks?

There are more questions, but they lead back to the environment in which the decisions are made. Networks have achieved remarkable levels of fiscal and technical stability, but socially they are still fragile organisms. The ecology of networking outlined in this paper reveals both a changing, hostile ecosystem (telecommunications, copyright) and an unstable internal structure (contracts, ethics, consultation, and governance). Yet libraries have considerable confidence in the ability of the utilities and networks to deliver, and satisfaction at the services being delivered. As Kermit the Frog once said, "It's better than great; it's acceptable."

Bob Wedgeworth, executive director of the American Library Association, wrote a thoughtful paper for the "Networks for Networkers" pre-White House conference in 1980. Discussing "Coordinating National Library Programs," Wedgeworth posed three concepts: governance (Who's in charge?); service (What do I get?); and finance (Who pays?).[24] For most libraries, questions 2 and 3 are answered; there is little public or private subsidy of most networks, and the technology is available but it must be used wisely to provide the best services. Although governance structures have evolved, they had not been stress tested until last year, and the testing continues. Networks, we should remember, are a new social structure in the library world that crosses geographic and political boundaries and the established patterns of discourse in the professional associations and among libraries of different types, disciplines, and sizes. The structures are, perhaps, without precedent, so one should not wonder at the mistakes, the stumbling. The environment is changing rapidly, and, as Wedgeworth observes, "the politics of change may be every bit as important as the substance of change."[25]

Those libraries committed to networking, fiscally and operationally, and the networks and utilities that serve them, will resolve the internal ecological problems insofar as that is possible. (The external problem of telecommunications is a different issue that will require the concerted effort of the network and library communities.) To quote Wedgeworth again, "shared expectations can lead to effective compromises on reality."[26] There is a clear consensus of expectations among network users and network managements, and the current discussions are more about means than ends.

Notes

1. *Ohionetwork* 5, nos. 7–11 (July 1983–November 1983).
2. *American Libraries* 14, no. 11 (December 1983): 690.

3. Frederick G. Kilgour, "Public Policy and National and International Networks," *Information Technology and Libraries* 2, no. 3 (September 1983): 239–245.
4. Louis Tijerina, "Optimizing the VDT Workstation: Controlling Glare and Postural Problems" (Dublin, Ohio: OCLC, 1983); R. Bruce Miller, "Radiation, Ergonomics, Ion Depletion and VDT's: Healthful Use of Visual Display Terminals," *Information Technology and Libraries* 2, no. 2 (June 1983): 151–158; Richard P. Koffler, "The Ergonomic Art." *Datamation* 29, no. 6 (June 1983): 235–238.
5. "Major Database Disasters: Could They Happen Here?" *American Libraries* 14, no. 12 (November 1983): 645–647.
6. *News from the Library of Congress,* PR 83-123, December 8, 1983; *Library of Congress Information Bulletin* 42, no. 51 (1983): 438; *American Libraries* 14, no. 6 (June 1983): 340–342.
7. *CLR Recent Developments* 11, no. 3 (June 1983): 3–4.
8. *RTSD Newsletter* 8, nos. 1–3 (January–June 1983).
9. Robert N. Broadus, "Online Catalogs and Their Users," *College and Research Libraries* 44, no. 6 (November 1983): 458–467; *LITA Newsletter,* no. 11 (Winter 1983), no. 12 (Spring 1983); *DLA Bulletin* (University of California Division of Library Automation) 3, no. 2 (5) (October 1983): 10–11, 20.
10. Walter Crawford, "Long Searches, Slow Response: Recent Experience on RLIN," *Information Technology and Libraries* 2, no. 2 (June 1983): 176–182.
11. *SOLINEWS: The Solinet Newsletter* 11, no. 3 (September 1983); "Biblio-Techniques," press release (Olympia, Wash.: Biblio-Techniques Library and Information System), December 14, 1983; "Georgetown Automation System Adopted by UP San Antonio Unit," *Library Journal* 108, no. 22 (December 15, 1983): 2285–2286.
12. Paul M. Anderson and Allen G. Miller, "Participative Planning for Library Automation: The Role of the User Opinion Survey," *College and Research Libraries* 44, no. 4 (July 1983): 245–254.
13. C. Lee Jones, "Summary Recommendations from Subject Access Meeting," *Information Technology and Libraries* 2, no. 1 (March 1983): 116–119.
14. See sources in Notes 7, 8, and 9.
15. *RTSD Newsletter* 8, no. 2 (March–April 1983): 12.
16. Robert Epstein, "Why Database Machines?" *Datamation* 29, no. 7 (July 1983): 139–144.
17. "UTLAS-Japan Communications Link," *Information, Technology and Libraries* 2, no. 1 (March 1983): 33–34.
18. Kilgour, "Public Policy and National and International Networks."
19. *LITA Newsletter,* no. 12 (Spring 1983): 7, no. 13 (Summer 1983): 6; *RTSD Newsletter* 8, no. 4 (July–August 1983): 46; Wayne E. Davison, "The WLN/RLG/LC Linked System Project," *Information Technology and Libraries* 2, no. 1 (March 1983): 35–46.
20. "NEH Puts Close to $1 Million into Newspaper Database," *Library Journal* 108, no. 2 (January 15, 1983): 82.
21. F. Wilfred Lancaster, ed., *Library Automation as a Source of Management Information.* Clinic on Library Applications of Data Processing, 1982 (Urbana-Champaign, Ill., 1983).
22. *OCLC Newsletter,* no. 149 (November 1983): 3.
23. *Association of Research Libraries,* press release (August 3, 1983).
24. Robert Wedgeworth, "Coordinating National Library Programs," in *Networks for Networkers: Critical Issues in Cooperative Library Network Development,* ed. Barbara Evans Markuson and Blanche Woolls (New York: Neal-Schuman, 1980), p. 101.
25. Ibid., pp. 103–104.
26. Ibid., p. 107.

Special Reports

Lean Years and Fat Years: Lessons to Be Learned

Public Libraries

Ann E. Prentice

Director, Graduate School of Library and Information Science,
University of Tennessee, Knoxville

As a local institution whose primary focus is on its users, the public library's major source of income is the local government unit it serves. Although state and federal dollars are an important component of public library funding, they constitute a relatively small percentage of overall funding and their main purpose is to further such broad objectives as networking and resource sharing that are best done at levels above the local level. Because the library survives or withers on the basis of its local support, it is within the context of local government funding that public library funding must be reviewed.

Highlights
- Except for the period 1957–1967, public library funding patterns show chronic underfunding between 1930 and 1983.
- In periods of retrenchment, public libraries fared worse than other public agencies.
- Today, public libraries view their communities as markets.
- With immediate prospects of stable funding, public libraries could benefit from private-sector measures of productivity.

The public library as an institution is built on the idea that education is a right. Education in its broadest sense is supported by the freely available access to information by everyone. When social attitudes become more conservative, as they tend to do in economically difficult times, institutions providing information have more difficulty obtaining funds than do agencies that maintain law and order. Because the library is built on the concept of self-improvement and free access to information, it is often accused of being an elitist institution designed by the classes for the masses and not necessarily needed by the masses. In part because of this, the public library is a chronically underfunded institution that has had occasional periods of good funding. The study of shifts in public library funding in relation to the social concerns of time and place is an aspect of the public library that merits further research.

A Historical Perspective

In the past 50 years, public library funding has moved from difficult times to good times and back to trying times. In the early 1930s, all local government agencies were in serious financial difficulty. Most cities cut salaries between 1930 and 1934, but jobs were so scarce that people stayed at their jobs anyway. During this period the public library had to struggle to keep its doors open. Despite aging book stock and reduced staff, it succeeded in providing service. Librarians were estimated to be doing 30–40 percent more work than they had done five years earlier. Still, at budget time library service was assigned the lowest priority—bread, not books, was the hard-to-refute attitude. The 1940s wartime economy left little for the refurbishment of the library. However, late in the 1940s attention was placed on planning with the design and implementation of the Public Library Inquiry. The American Library Association's National Plan for Public Library Service was prepared.

The 1950s saw a continuation of this trend with a plea for planning and for funding through some combination of federal and state support of local services. The passage of the Library Services Act in 1957 was a turning point for public libraries. Not only did it signal the acceptance by the federal government of a role in making information accessible through the public library, but the act also required that states receiving funds have a state library agency with a long-range plan for library service. At the time, the economy was healthy and more money was available for everything, including libraries. The library budget rose along with other budgets. However, the public library still remained close to the bottom in funding priorities, and the percentage of its budget increase was typically lower than that of the overall municipal budget. In some cities, although the dollar amount of the public library budget increased, its percentage of the total local budget actually decreased.

By 1967, resources of local governments began to diminish although the demands for services and salaries were increasing. With high inflation, reduced levels of local income, cuts in local budgets, and cuts in federal and state funding of mandated programs that had to be picked up locally, the past decade was a period of survival efforts by local government and the library as part of the local structure.

Reduction in budgets did not appear all at once. There were numerous signs that the Great Society was running low on money and that plans for social and educational programs had outrun the ability to pay. Further, the levels of service in these and related programs were in some cases moving beyond the interests of the taxpayer. Although librarians wished to provide comprehensive information service and numerous specialized programs, the communities served were not necessarily interested in the level of service the professionals wished to provide.

At the same time, the information world was being confronted with massive technological change in the way information was produced, transmitted, and stored. The cost of developing bibliographic data bases, of putting libraries and library resources on line, and of purchasing equipment, retraining staff, and adapting to the new information environment has been high. The increased demand for resources at a time when budgets were being cut back or not keeping pace with the rate of inflation demanded review of existing programs.

Survey of Public Libraries

A survey of 18 public libraries in the South was conducted for the years 1970, 1975, 1980, and 1983 to determine the trends in public library budgeting over this period. The libraries were selected from the annual statistical compilations done by the Memphis and Shelby County (Tennessee) Library, which annually collects financial data in several categories for approximately 100 libraries. The libraries selected are representative of medium- and large-size public libraries nationally. Because of the changing bases on which public library statistics are collected—e.g., reported population statistics may change annually or reflect the most recent census—the following analysis is of general trends only.

Between 1970 and 1983, budgets more than tripled in each of the libraries studied. During the same period in all but two libraries the percentage of the budget devoted to materials decreased (one increased and one remained the same). The materials budget median of 18 percent in 1970 with a range of 11–23 percent had dropped by 1983 to 14 percent with a range of 9–20 percent. Changes in the percent of the budget for personnel ranged from a 13 percent increase to a 20 percent decrease. How much of the personnel budget decrease resulted from attrition and how much from alternate ways of reporting is not known. One firm figure in the statistics available is the increase in beginning salaries for entry-level librarians, for department heads, and for library directors. Entry-level salaries doubled. Salaries for department heads doubled and in some cases nearly tripled during the period. Library directors' salaries followed a similar pattern of at least doubling in most of the libraries studied. (See Table 1.) The increases in budgets generally paralleled increases in overall municipal budgets in the cities studied, with 2 percent of the municipal budget allocated to library service throughout the period. (The actual figure is probably slightly lower, since libraries often include state and federal funding in their budget totals.)

Libraries appeared to fare no better or worse than other agencies in a steady or slightly growing budget period. In cities where reduced budgets and retrenchment were necessary, evidence suggests that library service suffered more than did other services. For example, in New York City in the mid-1970s, library service was cut 25 percent; other services with a stronger voice in city hall were cut 10 percent or less during the same period.

Table 1 / Salary Increases in Relation to Budget Increases and Inflation

Year	Budget Increase (%)	Consumer Price Index*	Average Salary		
			Beginning MLS	Dept. Head	Director
1970	5.9	116.3	$ 7,300	$12,421	$19,028
1975	9.1	161.2	10,610	16,591	26,990
1980	13.5	247.0	12,464	23,069	37,910
1983	6.7	287.1	16,180	29,502	49,577

*Base year 1967.

Coping with Reduced Revenues

During the past 10 years, local officials have tried to reduce demand on local revenue. One means of coping with restricted funds is to shift from city library to city/county combined library. As central cities lose population to suburban areas, this shift shows merit. The property tax base, which although declining still forms the backbone of support for local services, has shifted from central city to surrounding areas. The central city is expected to support its surrounding area but on reduced income. Among those moving to a county-wide base are Orlando, Florida, and Atlanta, Georgia.

Library administrators have had to make many difficult decisions regarding what to cut back and what to eliminate altogether. Those who developed long-range plans for service were in a much better position to preserve essential services than were those who lightened the budget load by tossing away a program here or a staff member there. Few local government agencies, libraries included, had such plans in the 1960s for growth or in the 1970s for cutting back. Since *A Planning Process for Public Libraries* became available in 1980,[1] numerous public libraries have begun planning their activities in relation to the community and its needs. This has placed the public library in a leading role in local government in terms of public agency planning.

Librarians have begun to look at their communities as markets to determine what the demand for specific programs and services may be, if demand is great enough to warrant the cost, and if not whether a given program should be subsidized and by whom. Some have reviewed their program objectives and set priorities in terms of program viability in relation to the community served. But public libraries are still not as far along in costing programs as are other types of libraries.

Unlike most other types of library and information centers, the public library does not have a mission clearly defined by the community in which it is located and which pays taxes for its support. The clientele is so potentially diverse that service to its various components encompasses a nearly unlimited range. Why one group is served and not another and why one program is stressed and not another may be determined by the interests of library staff and trustees or by the availability of external funding from federal or state government. When there is adequate funding to pursue a number of options, this unplanned method of providing service does not necessarily detract from the provision of service to the entire community. As budgets constrict and citizens begin to look carefully at the benefits they gain from their tax dollars, such haphazard means of providing service are not tenable.

The Next Few Years

Economic indicators point to an improved economic picture in the next year or so, which will be reflected in more local revenue. During the past year, state funding for public libraries has generally increased. At the fourth annual White House Conference on Library and Information Services Task Force meeting, it was reported that 21 states had increased or restored state aid to libraries. For the 1983–1984 period, state aid allocated to libraries increased by 2 percent, or $3,672,865, to a total of $200,406,433.[2] This provides $.79 per capita nationwide. The states with the highest per capita aid are West Virginia with $2.73, Alaska with $2.71, and New York with $2.52. Much of the state funding is earmarked for projects of value to the entire state, such as statewide automation programs, resource sharing, or special outreach programs. At the federal level, despite annual threats of zero funding, Library Services and Construction Act (LSCA) I (public library program aid) and III (cooperation) have been funded annually with an increase in 1983 to bring the titles to full funding. Given the inflationary spiral of the late 1970s and early 1980s, this is far from holding the line but it is considerably better than zero funding. Because of the year-to-year crisis atmosphere, planning for the use of federal funds is difficult and implementation of plans is often slow.

A result of recent difficult budget years has in some cases been leaner organizations ready to move ahead. In many cases it has been libraries starved for resources, depleted of key staff, and with major programs barely functioning. Now that times are looking better as the economic recovery continues, we can expect an easing of budget restrictions. It would be most unfortunate if libraries used new resources to continue to do business as usual or to revert to earlier models. Not all of our programs are worth reviving. Planning for tough times became for many libraries a way to cut without killing the patient. Planning for better times should aim to provide the best library service possible so that the patient is no longer a patient but healthy and forward looking.

In this age of information, the public library is an important part of the information system, but it cannot continue the service patterns of the past. Individuals in the private sector, seeing the economic potential of designing and implementing information delivery systems, are often now in competition with tax-supported services. Some provide services the public library needs in order to serve its clientele and for which it must pay a high price. A new set of patterns is emerging for public versus private information delivery.

New ways of defining the role of the public library and the way in which it uses its resources can be taken from the private sector. Citizen satisfaction with existing services is being reviewed throughout local government. Citizen participation in actual service delivery is both potentially cost-effective and an important public relations activity. It provides citizens with the opportunity to see how a library works and what its justifiable costs are.

Careful planning for library service is particularly important. This is the time to benefit from what has been learned from long-range planning, strategic planning efforts, and retrenchment decisions to provide a plan for library service that takes into consideration the technological revolution. There is no possibility of business as usual because the nature of the business has changed. Wise use of resources resulting from an improving economy can further the public library mission of information access and do so in innovative ways that meet the changing needs of our times.

Notes

1. Vernon E. Palmour, Marcia C. Bellassai, and Nancy V. DeWath, *A Planning Process for Public Libraries* (Chicago: American Library Association, 1980).
2. *Library Hotline* XII, no. 38 (November 21, 1983): 2.

Lean Years and Fat Years: Lessons to Be Learned

School Libraries and Media Centers

Eliza T. Dresang

Manager, Media Services, Madison Metropolitan
School District, Madison, WI 53703

During the 1950s and 1960s, funding for school library media centers (SLMCs) rose gradually to a crescendo. By the mid-1970s, however, this trend reversed itself and funding typically either ceased to grow or declined. Even where a modest increase in the dollar amount existed, a gain rarely matched or exceeded the rate of inflation. Paradoxically, the need for a strong school library media (SLM) program has grown as funding has diminished. SLMCs have been responsible for an even greater variety of materials, equipment, services, and functions, and control of and access to information have become increasingly complex.

Highlights

- An increase in the total school-age population by 1995 may present opportunities for media programs that will have been absent for two decades.
- Reports on the first two years of ECIA Chapter 2 funding indicate that a large portion of the funds went for microcomputer equipment and software.
- Foundations are still a largely untapped source of funding for SLM programs.
- Until 1974, book and AV expenditures were even with or ahead of the Consumer Price Index. But by 1983, both book and AV purchases were suffering.
- A renewed interest in "quality" education may signal new opportunities to come for funding for SLMCs.

Today, as sources and levels of funding fluctuate, school library media specialists face the challenge to be proactive rather than reactive: (1) to be aware of the context in which funding for SLMCs occurs; (2) to understand the sources for and trends in funding and expenditures for SLM programs; (3) to apply lessons from the past, working to modify or prevent reductions in funding and to anticipate and plan wisely for unavoidable fluctuations.

The Context of Funding

The SLMC not only joins with its parent institution, the school, in competing for public financial support, but within the parent institution a jockeying for resources inevitably occurs. In addition, the SLMC directly competes for funding from external sources for which other programs in the school are ineligible.

Societal factors, such as enrollment trends that impact on funding to schools, also affect the SLMC. A baby boom in the 1950s and 1960s, which produced rapidly expanding school-age populations, was followed by a steady decline in enrollment, largely at the elementary level. Demographics are showing signs of yet another shift with a slight increase in elementary population expected by 1985 and a substantial increase by 1995. However, according to statistics from the National Center for Education Statistics, during these same years the high-school population will decline as the elementary has in the past.[1] These numerical shifts have profound effects on school funding and programs. An increase in the total school-age population by 1995 may present opportunities for media programs that will have been absent for two decades.

As philosophies and practices in education change, so does the role of the SLMC. SLMCs moved into the audiovisual world far more rapidly than other types of libraries, as individualized and nontextbook-oriented instruction was slowly introduced in the schools. On the other hand, SLMCs sometimes lag behind other types of libraries, as they have in networking, because the educational institutions of which they are a part are not attuned to library trends.

Sources of Funding

Federal Support

Large-scale federal aid to libraries was unknown until the mid-1950s. Since that time both library and educational legislation have provided for assistance to SLMCs. A landmark year was 1960, when the Library Services Act (LSA), first passed in 1956, was extended with an authorization of $30 million for state agencies to develop library services in public elementary or secondary schools from 1962 to 1965. The Library Services and Construction Act, which replaced the LSA, has funded interlibrary cooperation since 1974. SLMCs may apply, but few have done so until recent years.

In 1964, when the National Defense Education Act (NDEA) of 1958 was extended for an additional three years, Title III granted $90 million for the purchase of school library materials and equipment. Such other legislation as the Vocational Education Act of 1963 also allowed for aid to school libraries. But the legislation with the most impact on SLMCs was the Elementary and Secondary Education Act (ESEA), first passed in 1965. Title II, funded at $100 million in the initial year, provided for school library resources, textbooks, and other instructional materials. Even though textbooks were included, 90 percent of the total funds were spent for school library materials in 1966. This act required support for private as well as public schools. (See *Bowker Annual, 1972*, pp. 220–225, for a summary of ESEA Title II benefits from 1966 to 1972.) ESEA Title I monies, designated for educationally disadvantaged children, also boosted SLMC programs.

The first erosion of federal funds for SLMCs began in 1974 with the renewal of the ESEA. The new act designated Title IV-B, effective in 1976, as a combination of ESEA guidance, counseling, and testing funds; ESEA library media funds; and NDEA media funds. In 1978, after much protest from the library world, guidance, counseling, and testing were separated from Title IV-B, leaving it entirely for library resources, effective 1980. (See *Bowker Annual, 1982*, p. 223, for a compilation of expenditures for 1976–1982.) Title IV-C competitive grants were also open to SLMCs.

By the time the ESEA ended its 17-year existence on June 30, 1982, funding for SLMCs had reached approximately $164 million. ESEA was replaced with the Education

Consolidation and Improvement Act (ECIA), known as the block-grant program. Chapter 2 of ECIA consolidates 33 programs, including former Title IV-B. A few years earlier, SLM specialists had fought to have guidance and counseling removed from the library media title. Now 32 other programs, including counseling and guidance, have joined it. Many of the federal programs from which SLMCs received funds in the past, e.g., Reading Is Fundamental, are now part of Chapter 2 of the block-grant program. As with the ESEA, under ECIA Chapter 2, local education agencies have no requirements to maintain local support.

Although funding was reduced for the 33 Chapter 2 programs in the first year of ECIA, SLMCs had a sum approximately three times as large as the last Title VI-B allocation for which they could apply. Reports on the first two years of Chapter 2 funding are relatively optimistic. (See the reports in Part 2 of the 1983 and 1984 editions of *The Bowker Annual*.) Phyllis Land Usher, director of the Division of Federal Resources and School Improvement, Indiana State Department of Public Instruction, reports that a large portion of the funding went for library materials and equipment. The results of a survey by the National Audio-Visual Association (NAVA) also show that an overwhelming number of school districts used Chapter 2 monies for library materials and equipment. Microcomputer equipment and software accounted for the largest part of the expenditures.[2]

State Support

The state plays a major role in the development of SLM programs through the administration of federal grant programs. Over the years a number of state library agencies used ESEA funds (available for use at their discretion) to provide consultation and support to local education agency programs. Twenty percent of ECIA funds may be used at the state level, some of which may be dedicated to SLMC development.

States also benefit SLM programs through general aid to local education agencies, usually based on a per-pupil allocation. On occasion, they provide emergency aid to local school districts. Enrollment has declined, however, and legislation (discussed later in this report) has put limits on collections and expenditures in several states, hampering their ability to provide aid.

Some states have special funds allocated to districts specifically for the purchase of library media materials. For example, in Wisconsin the "aggregate amount of all monies received as income in the common school fund" before December 1 each year is divided on a per-pupil basis among the school districts. This money must be used for "purchase of library books and other instructional materials for school libraries."[3]

A survey by Thomas Hart of state departments of education personnel requested information about legislative gains and losses affecting SLM programs during 1982. Of 44 respondents, 11 states had legislative platforms; 3 of the 6 with planks that had been accepted experienced increased funding for library media resources.[4]

No clear-cut comparison of spending by all states is available over the years. However, there is evidence that a greater burden has been placed on the states in recent years, along with the same limitations in resources felt at other levels.

Regional Support

Regional funding for SLMCs is a relatively new phenomenon. No parallel exists with the public library networks that provide funding for member libraries. In most states regional support is much more likely to come in the form of services, e.g., films, instructional television, in-service functions, and audiovisual repair, than as a grant-in-aid. The concept of networking for SLMCs received its first strong support on a national level in the 1975 standards *Media Programs: District and School.*[5] Since then, an increasing number of states have provided for SLMC participation in multitype library networks.[6]

Local Support

Most local monies for education come from property taxes. Substantial cuts in these taxes in the late 1970s resulted in reduced revenues for public schools in many states. In June 1978, Proposition 13 was passed by the voters of California. This amendment to the state constitution reduced California property taxes more than 57 percent and revenue for public schools about 27 percent. Even though the state of California participated in a massive aid program to local governments, school districts had to make reductions, and frequently these cuts affected SLM programs.[7] Within a few months, 12 other states had taxation limitation proposals on their ballots. Texas reduced property taxes by some $500 million; Idaho and Nevada set constitutional limits on property taxes. New Jersey, Colorado, Tennessee, Arizona, and Michigan passed legislation putting limits on government spending. Massachusetts voters passed Proposition 2 1/2, limiting property taxes to 2 1/2 percent of real value and causing a 26 percent cut in the state's budget. Other states came to the aid of local governments just as California did, for example, New York legislators approved a $3.7 million funding supplement for school and public libraries. But none of these aid programs compensated for losses at the local level.

Foundation Support

From 1963 to 1968, the Knapp Foundation invested $1,130,000 to establish eight demonstration SLMCs in various parts of the country, offering library service at the level recommended in *Standards for School Library Programs, 1960.*[8] Additional funding supported analysis of the tasks of SLM specialists and model educational programs.

As other sources of funding began to diminish, foundation support became increasingly more important to SLMCs. Although in 1975–1976, 220 academic libraries received grants, only 4 SLMC grants were reported in the *Foundation Grants Index.*[9] In the late 1970s school libraries began to appear under "Grants-in-Aid" in *Library Literature*. However, foundations are still largely an untapped source of funding for SLM programs. In 1982, an Illinois SLMC was the first to receive a grant from the National Foundation for the Humanities.

Expenditures

Over the past 30 years reports on expenditures by SLMCs have been sporadic (Table 1). Until recently, those that were available came from a stratified random sample of schools from the U.S. Office of Education list. The 1983 survey, sponsored by *School Library Journal* (October 1983) and conducted by Marilyn L. Miller and Barbara B. Moran, was undertaken to fill the gap left by the government's failure to maintain statistics. The survey, which will be conducted annually, is the only one to include private schools. The sample for the survey came from subscribers to *SLJ*. [The survey report is reprinted in its entirety in Part 4 of this volume—*Ed.*]

Table 1 / School Library Media Center Statistical Reports, 1954–1983

Date of Publication	Title	Source*
1954	Statistics of Public School Libraries, 1953–54	USOE
1959	Public School Library Statistics, 1958–59	USOE
1961	Statistics of Public School Libraries, 1960–61	USOE
1963	Public School Library Statistics, 1962–63	USOE
1974	Statistics of Public School Libraries Media Centers, Fall 1974	NCES
1978	Statistics of Public School Libraries Media Centers, Fall 1978	NCES
1983	Expenditures for Resources in School Library Media Centers, FY 1982–83	SLJ

*USOE (Library Services Branch, U.S. Office of Education); NCES (National Center for Education Statistics); SLJ (School Library Journal).

    One item that appears in every report on SLMC expenditures between 1954 and 1983 is the average expenditure for books. More sporadic is the average expenditure for AV materials. In Table 2, changes in book and AV expenditures from 1954–1983 are compared to the changes in the Consumer Price Index (CPI), an indicator of the rise in cost of living. The expected expenditures for books (EEB) and audiovisual materials (EEAV) were generated by increasing the average expenditure from the previous report by the same percentage that the Consumer Price Index (CPI) increased.

    All expenditure figures should be taken as indicators of trends rather than absolutes. As such, they substantiate that during the 1950s and 1960s, book and AV expenditures were even with or ahead of the CPI (except for a slight decrease in 1961, but the 1961 survey may be less accurate since it was less formal than the others). The EEB and EEAV were often lower than the actual expenditures. However, between 1974 and 1978, a drastic turnaround occurred for books: Average expenditures were consistently and increasingly less than the EEB and the EEAV. The 1978 figure for AV expenditures has no 1974 counterpart, so the start of hard times cannot be exactly pinpointed, but obviously by 1983 both book and AV purchases were suffering. Expenditures are no longer keeping up with the inflated dollar.

Lessons from Hard Times

The difficulties of the past decade caught many SLM specialists by surprise, as had the sumptuous times of a decade before. Being caught unprepared meant reacting to what

Table 2 / Average Book and AV Expenditures per Student, 1954–1983

Year	Book Expenditures					AV Expenditures				
	Av. Exp.	% Inc.	CPI	% Inc.	EEB	Av. Exp	% Inc.	CPI	% Inc.	EEAV
1954	0.79	—	80.5	—	—	0.15	—	80.5	—	—
1959	1.60	102.0	87.3	8.4	0.86	—	—	—	—	—
1961	1.47	−8.8	89.6	2.6	1.64	0.25	67.0	89.6	11.3	0.17
1963	2.28	55.0	91.7	2.3	1.50	—	—	—	—	—
1974	4.22	85.0	147.7	61.0	3.67	—	—	—	—	—
1978	4.25	0.7	195.4	32.0	5.57	1.69	576.0	195.4	118.0	0.54
1983	4.58	7.7	301.8	54.0	6.54	1.79	0.5	301.8	54.0	2.60

happened rather than actively shaping events. SLM specialists are learning to anticipate changes and plan accordingly.[10] *A Nation at Risk: The Imperative for Educational Reform* and *A Report on Secondary Education in America* are among the many educational reports that can help prepare SLM specialists for the changes to come.[11]

Planning

One important indicator of change for all educators is projected enrollment trends. High-school library media specialists are preparing for an enrollment decline. On the other hand, enrollments may climb again at the elementary level, and media specialists must plan for possible increases in funds available to the school district. Another indicator is developments in educational technology, including computers and telecommunications devices. NAVA's report that a large proportion of the first Chapter 2 monies went for computer hardware and software indicates that developments in this area are anticipated, with corresponding funding implications. SLM specialists also are closely watching the current move for "quality" education. Interest in education is aroused as it has not been since the late 1950s and early 1960s, possibly signaling new opportunities for funding for SLMCs.

Implementation

Careful implementation is important. When the large, unprecedented rush of federal funds came in the late 1960s, some publishers found a ready market in which to dump poor products. Librarians, seeking eagerly to use the funds and transform libraries into media centers, sometimes bought without proper evaluation of products. When federal funds started to decline, wastefulness, as well as inability to maintain and replace what was bought, became apparent. Media specialists are faced with a similar evaluation dilemma as computer software enters the scene. The lesson from the past should make apparent the need for careful evaluation.

Cooperation

As purchases of books and AV materials decline and as the information explosion fosters the need for more information, cooperation and networking become inevitable. SLMCs and the educational institutions of which they are a part must radically change their viewpoint on these issues. The Library Services and Construction Act should be remembered as a potential source of funding. NAVA's publication *AV Connection: The Guide to Federal Funds for AV Programs* describes a number of alternative sources as do other federal and state publications.[12]

Involvement

Active participation in the political and legislative processes and in professional associations is more vital than ever. One of the major political realities for SLM specialists is that federal funds designated for SLMCs no longer exist. Under block grants SLM programs have been thrust into competition with the very programs they support. On the local level, the SLM specialist must convince school administrators that Chapter 2 funds allocated to the centralized media program benefit all students and teachers. Moreover, SLM specialists must be involved with allocation of the vast sums designated for microcomputer-related items. Good public relations also is extremely important. Administrators who understand what a program does and are convinced of its worth are more likely to make cuts elsewhere. But of ultimate importance is involvement in the total curricular process—not only support but development of the curriculum. A SLM specialist's level of involvement may directly affect the level of funding for the SLM program. This issue is addressed in *Involving the School Library Media Specialist in Curriculum Development*, the latest book in the School Media Centers: Focus on Trends and Issues Series of the American Association of School Librarians.[13]

Conclusion

Block grants, enrollment shifts, computers, telecommunications, networking, curriculum development and a renewed search for quality education are among the many challenges of the 1980s. Lessons learned from the hard times of the past decade should prepare SLM specialists to be proactive and to plan for and seize funding opportunities for these and the other challenges to come.

Notes

1. Martin Frankel, "Projecting a School Enrollment Turnaround," *American Education* 17 (August–September 1981): 34–35.
2. Kenton Pattie and Mary Ernst, "Chapter II Grants: Libraries Gain," *School Library Journal* 29 (January 1983): 17–20.
3. Wisconsin State Statute 32.70.
4. Thomas Hart, "State Legislation for K–12 School Library Media Programs—1982," in *School Library Media Annual*, vol. 1 (Littleton, Colo.: Libraries Unlimited, 1983), pp. 72–94.
5. American Association of School Librarians and Association for Educational Communications and Technology, *Media Programs: District and School* (Chicago: American Library Association, 1975).
6. For a review of SLMCs and networking, see Barbara Immroth, "Networking and the School Library Media Program," in *School Library Media Annual*, vol. 1 (Littleton, Colo.: Libraries Unlimited, 1983), pp. 410–427.
7. See the reports on media and school library funding reductions due to Proposition 13 and other recent factors in *California Media and Library Educators Association Journal* 4 (February 1980): 3–18.
8. American Association of School Librarians, *Standards for School Library Programs* (Chicago: American Library Association, 1960).
9. *Foundation Grants Index*, 12th ed. (New York: Foundation Center/Columbia University Press), 1983.
10. For an excellent evaluation program, see James Liesener, *A Systematic Process for Planning Media Programs* (Chicago: American Library Association, 1976), and *Instruments for Planning and Evaluating Library Media Programs*, rev. ed. (College Park, Md.: University of Maryland. 1980).

11. David P. Gardner et al., *A Nation at Risk: The Imperative for Educational Reform* (Washington, D.C.: Government Printing Office, 1983); Ernest Boyer, *High School: A Report on Secondary Education in America* (Princeton, N.J.: Carnegie Foundation for the Advancement of Teaching, 1983).

12. *AV Connection: The Guide to Federal Funds for Audio-Visual Programs* (Fairfax, Va.: National Audio-Visual Association, 1981).

13. American Association of School Librarians, *Involving the School Library Media Specialist in Curriculum Development* (Chicago: American Library Association, 1983).

Lean Years and Fat Years: Lessons to Be Learned

College and University Libraries

Richard J. Talbot

Director of Libraries, University of Massachusetts, Amherst, Massachusetts

The patterns of academic library finance clearly indicate that on the average academic libraries receive a fixed percentage of their institution's budget and no more. This has been true for 30 years. (See Table 1.) Before 1960, the percentage of the parent institutional budget devoted to libraries was about 3.1%.[1] Then, in the late 1960s and early 1970s, in what some now fondly recall as the golden age of academic libraries, this percentage rose to above 4.0%.[2] But after 1976 it began to drift downward.

Highlights

- Academic libraries have fallen on hard times, in part because the percentage of the budget they receive has been effectively frozen or has declined.
- From 1967 to 1977, academic libraries were continually losing ground, with declines in library expenditures per student, number of staff per student, proportion of the library budget expended for materials, and the number of books added to collections. This downward trend has probably continued to the present.
- Despite the pressures of inflation, the pattern of library budgetary allocation for salaries, materials, and "other" remains unaffected. Most remarkable has been the shift in expenditures for books and serials.
- The "library cost disease," now in remission, will flare up anew as computer software costs become the dominant element in library automation costs.
- The success of librarians in the scholarly communication process will determine the degree to which they will receive funding.

**Table 1 / Comparison of Library Expenditures with General Higher
Education Expenditures, 1930–1980**
(in millions of dollars)

Year	General Expenditures	Library Expenditures	Percentage Share
1980	44,543	1,624	3.6
1979	39,833	1,427	3.6
1978	36,257	1,349	3.7
1977	33,152	1,250	3.8
1976	30,599	1,224	4.0
1975	27,548	1,002	3.6
1970	15,789	653	4.1
1969	13,835	572	4.1
1968	13,190	493	3.7
1966	9,951	346	3.5
1964	7,425	237	3.2
1962	5,768	177	3.1
1960	4,513	135	3.0
1958	3,604	110	3.1
1956	2,766	86	3.1
1954	2,271	73	3.2
1952	1,921	61	3.2
1950	1,706	56	3.3

Sources: Historical Statistics of the United States, Colonial Times to 1970, 2 vols. (Washington, D.C., Government Printing Office, 1975), p. 384; National Center for Education Statistics, *Digest of Education Statistics, 1982* (Washington, D.C., Government Printing Office, 1982), tables 133, 134; *Statistical Abstract of the United States, 1982–83* (Washington, D.C., Government Printing Office, 1982), p. 164, C. B. Osburn, *Academic Research and Library Resources: Changing Patterns in America* (Westport, Conn.: Greenwood Press, 1979), p. 102.

The Decline in Budgetary Allocations

Certainly this proposition is true for the average academic library between 1967 and 1977, a period for which we have national statistics.[3] We lack full data for the period after that, but an examination of the statistics of the libraries in the Association of Research Libraries for the period 1977–1982 reveals the same pattern.[4] Not only does the average percentage of university expenditure for all of these institutions remain nearly the same, but as a year-to-year comparison of the figures for each institution makes clear, the percentage remains stable for each institution. There is remarkably little variation from year to year. For those institutions where the percentage does vary, the variation is seldom more than two- or three-tenths of one percent. Only in very rare instances are there sharp year-to-year differences of a full percentage point or more.[5]

The true significance of this invariant pattern of library funding lies in what it reveals about library budgeting by academic institutions. Because almost all library funding is provided by the parent institution,[6] the determination of the fraction of the parent budget devoted to its library amounts to a determination of what the library should be or, perhaps less explicitly, what the library's appropriate share of the institution's budget should be.

What makes this share appropriate? Such a determination cannot be based on any analysis of academic need. If it were, the percentages of the total budget received by academic libraries would vary widely, simply because the budgets of their parent institutions differ widely. In other words, if library academic need were definable in precise terms, the amount of money per student needed to satisfy that need would be similar for similar students at similar institutions. If an institution then attempted to fully satisfy that need, the percentage of its budget that it allocated to its library would fluctuate from year to year far more widely than it does, as these needs and the fiscal fortunes of the institution fluctuate.

But this doesn't happen. Instead, libraries receive nearly the same percentage of the budget year after year. On reflection, this really shouldn't be surprising. Higher education finance in general is not determined by institutional needs.[7] There are so many different kinds and levels of need to which these institutions are called upon to respond that ". . . no precise need . . . can be objectively defined and defended. . . ."[8] If this is true for the parent, it must also be true for the library, which is not only a creature of the parent but explicitly charged with supporting some of the academic needs that can neither be "objectively defined" nor "defended."

The situation is further complicated by the way higher educational unit costs behave. They are governed by the revenue theory of cost: ". . . an institution's educational cost per student unit is determined by revenues available for educational purposes. . . ."[9] Each college and university raises all it can and spends all it raises in an ever-increasing spiral.[10] Thus higher education costs, even library costs, are not determined by need but by available revenue.

In this kind of environment there can be no absolute standards to be met, only relative or comparative ones. In fact, in some institutions it is well understood that there is a peer group of other institutions with which comparisons are regularly made. This reflects the fact that the mechanisms of institutional analysis for higher education as a whole are just as primitive as those for libraries, so presidents and chancellors in making many kinds of decisions must rely on comparisons. However, when comparisons become the basis for budgetary decision, true need analysis tends to be ignored in favor of a standard comparative norm, i.e., a fixed budgetary percentage.

Under this system, academic libraries dramatically improved their lot in the late 1960s and into the 1970s (Table 1), as the percentage of the parent budget that they received rose by a full percentage point over the practice of the preceding decade. But now, as every academic librarian can testify, these libraries have fallen on hard times, in part because the percentage of the budget has either been effectively frozen or has declined.

Of course, in writing about the percentage of expenditure, we are writing about operating budgets, not capital budgets. Obviously, the employment of funds from capital budgets to construct buildings and buy equipment can make enormous differences in library operations. Some libraries have been lucky enough to obtain such funds through grants, donations, legislative appropriations, or even campus budget reallocations. But the economic climate for higher education for most of the past decade and the beginning of this one has been such that few libraries have been able to fund changes and improvements from capital funds. Federal funds have markedly decreased and most local and private funds have gone to larger institutions.[11] Therefore, nearly all academic libraries principally rely on the operating budgets they receive from their parent institutions even to fund improvements that in other contexts would be funded from capital budgets.

From 1967 to 1977, as a number of indices compiled by the National Center for Education Statistics reveal, academic libraries were continually losing ground, giving up many of the gains they made in the early 1960s. Library expenditures per student fell in real terms and with them the number of staff per student. The proportion of the library budget expended for materials diminished and so did the number of books added to the collections.[12]

The basic reason for all this, of course, was inflation. Between 1967 and 1974 library expenditures in constant dollars per full-time-equivalent (FTE) student fluctuated between $92 and $94, then fell to $84 in 1976 before rising to $87 in 1977.[13] This hesitantly downward trend has probably continued to the present. Many academic institutional planners expect the demographic decline in the college student population that is occurring in the 1980s to have a negative impact on their institutions, with a particularly adverse effect on libraries.[14] An examination, through 1980, of the expenditures of the median library in the Association of Research Libraries supports this view. From a high expenditure of $3,030,179 in 1970, expenditures in constant dollars gradually trended downward, reaching a low of $2,673,678 in 1976 before rising to $3,046,006 in 1978 and then declining again to $2,813,004 in 1980.[15]

Patterns of Expenditure: Past, Present, and Future

Nevertheless, although the actual resources academic libraries have to deploy have contracted sharply, the patterns of library internal responses to this contraction do not seem to have changed. The three principal categories of expenditure—materials, staffing, and "other"—do show more variation than that in the percentage of institutional budget spent on academic libraries, but not much. At least since 1960, they have tended to follow the 60–30–10 rule: 60% for salaries, 30% for materials, and 10% for "other." In 1960, for example, on the average 61.3% of the academic library budget was spent on salaries, 29.7% on materials, and 9% on everything else.[16] The percentage spent on materials rose to 37% by 1968 and then fell to 28% by 1977. The percentage spent on salaries and wages declined as acquisitions rose from 61.3% in 1960 to 54% in 1968 and then rose as materials declined to 61% in 1977. The "other" portion of the budget remained at 9 or 10%.[17] The libraries in the Association of Research Libraries, as a subset of academic libraries, show only a slightly different pattern. Between 1970 and 1976 materials declined steadily from 32.8% of the library budget to 29.2%, and salaries rose from 56.2 to 60.3%. The "other" category fluctuated between 10.5 and 11%.[18] In 1981, the ARL pattern was 33.1% for materials, 56.25% for salaries, and 10.6% for "other."[19]

As far as these principal categories of expenditure are concerned, there have been no radical departures from past practices. Despite the pressures of inflation, which have actually reduced library buying power since 1974, the pattern of library budgetary allocation remains unaffected. Within these categories, however, there have been some changes. The most remarkable of these has been the shift in expenditures for acquisitions between books and serials. In 1970, 62% of the acquisitions budget was spent on books and 34% on serials, but by 1976, 44% was spent on books and 50% on serials.[20] Statistics compiled for ARL libraries, although perhaps not applicable to all academic libraries, indicate a continuation of this trend, with more and more spent on serials and less on books.[21] However, in 1982 the rate of expenditure increase for books went up slightly and that for serials down, which may indicate that even these libraries are seeking a balance of expenditure between books and serials. Nevertheless, the rate of increase for serial titles actually acquired, as distinguished from the rate of expenditure, had slowed to 1.7% and the rate of increase for numbers of books acquired was negative. As long as the fraction of the library budget devoted to acquisitions remains constant, it is likely that these trends will continue: Rates of expenditure in nominal dollars will continue to rise, but the rate of increase in items actually acquired will continue to fall, and each library will acquire a continually diminishing fraction of the world's publishing output.

Acquisitions and Holdings

The two principal causes of the decline in acquisitions are inflation in prices and increases in the numbers of items being published. Some believe that the growth of scholarly publication may moderate as the number of scholars working in research fields falls.[22] Monetary inflation is moderating. Indeed, many libraries are benefiting from a related effect—the strength of the dollar overseas has reduced the cost of foreign publications— but the publishing industry is highly labor intensive and its costs have tended to rise faster than the price levels in the general economy, so even if general inflation vanished, inflation in publishing would remain and, all other things being equal, the decline in library rate of growth would continue.

Whether or not this decline is truly damaging to instruction and research is debatable. Certainly it is by the uncritical standards of the past. Certainly one can identify on every campus individual professors or students whose work has been adversely affected by the lack of materials that the library formerly collected. Yet study after study of library circulation has shown that a small percentage of what any library acquires satisfies a very large percentage of use. Perhaps 20% of the material held satisfies 80% of the use. It is tempting to infer from findings like these that libraries collect far more than they need and to urge that they reduce collection activity. This would solve the problem of declining growth by redefining the question in order to concentrate acquisition efforts on "useful" material.

Unfortunately, these studies, although helpful in managing collections, do not really tell us what to collect in advance of the act of selection. They are after-the-fact results, which give us very little guidance in how we might adapt selection decisions in the future. Nor do they shed much light on how materials are used in libraries, especially research libraries.[23] The most we can conclude is that the numbers of books and journals acquired by any library could be reduced without damaging scholarly pursuits, if we could identify in advance what will not be used. But we can't do that with any certainty. We can only guess at what we can do without as the depreciating library dollar forces us continually to reduce library growth rates. Although it is tempting for the harassed library selector to solve the selection problem by buying 80% less than now, as a casual reading of these studies might suggest, it would be imprudent to do so.

Budgetary Options

The other alternative within the library budget is to shift funds from either salary and wages or "other." The "other" category of library expenditure has remained at 9–10% of the total library budget, at least since the early 1960s. It is a catchall category for everything else except books and personnel. On it depend such items as postage for interlibrary loan, automation, telecommunications, travel, and so on. Although some components of this portion of the budget can be reduced, most will need to rise if the library is to maintain cooperative relationships and to automate library functions. With the decline in the purchasing power of the library materials budget, these activities are more important than ever before. Cooperative activity in borrowing books, creating union lists of serials, and so on, is the one way libraries have of obtaining some of the materials they can no longer buy themselves. And most of these cooperative activities will increasingly depend upon automation and telecommunication to be effective. A choice to cut this portion of the library budget would be penny-wise and pound-foolish. It would not only reduce the quality of current service, since it would diminish access to alternative sources of supply, but it would also damage the possibility of future improvement, if it affects automation.

That leaves salaries and wages as the most tempting target in the library budget. Because this category constitutes 60% of the whole, and has remained at this level since at least 1960, it is natural to ask why it could not be cut in order to support the acquisitions budget. The first answer to this is that it wouldn't do much good. During most of the 1970s, to have maintained library acquisitions budgets at levels high enough to offset inflation entirely would have required annual increases of 18%.[24] At that rate of increase the acquisitions budget would have doubled every four years. If for eight years the other elements in the library budget had been held constant with no adjustment for inflation, the acquisitions budget at this rate of increase would have constituted two-thirds of the whole library budget by the end of the first four years and all of the budget before the second four years had ended. There would have been no one to buy and process the books purchased, let alone provide other library services.

Nor does the fact that this portion of the library budget has remained stable mean that nothing has happened to library staffing. Between 1967 and 1978 the number of library staff per 1,000 FTE of enrollment fell from 7.2 to 6.7 and for professionals alone from 3.2 to 2.7. In the same period, the number of student assistants per 1,000 FTE students fell from 2.9 to 2.4.[25] The total number of librarians and other permanent staff in academic libraries continued to rise even in 1979, but the total number of student hours of library work fell by 1%. In ARL libraries, since 1976, the rate of staff growth has fluctuated within a very narrow band of 1%. It was negative in 1977, positive in 1978, negative in 1979, and almost flat from 1980 to 1982.[26] Although the evidence is scanty, what we have indicates signs of stress. On the average, library staffing continued to grow in this period, despite the inflationary pressures of the 1970s, but the rate of growth slowed markedly in the late 1970s, turned negative for student hours in 1979, and may have turned negative for the permanent staff in the 1980s.

Still, fewer books were added to the collections of academic libraries from 1971 onward. In 1970–1971, 26.4 million books were added, but by 1978–1979 this had fallen to 21.6 million, a decline of more than 20%.[27] ARL statistics indicate that this trend has probably continued to the present.

Undoubtedly, this decline in receipts permitted academic libraries to shift staffing resources, but the extent of this shift was probably quite limited. Purchases of other types of materials increased as did transactions of every kind: circulation, interlibrary loan, reference inquiries.[28] Libraries continued to grow and that very growth demanded increased staff effort to manage the collections: to shelve, to reshelve, to inventory, and so on. In addition, the introduction of automation on an ever-widening scale doesn't seem to have saved any personnel costs.[29] In fact, it is questionable whether productivity in a library can be significantly raised even by the introduction of automated systems. As Baumol and Marcus point out, every service industry suffers from a "cost disease" to the extent that gains in productivity fail to offset increases in salaries. In the early 1970s, Baumol and Marcus expected the benefits of library automation to produce productivity gains in libraries.[30] By 1983, Baumol was much less sanguine. In a review of library cost trends, he and Blackman discovered that ". . . library costs have until recently been rising at a compounded rate significantly greater than the inflation in the rest of the economy."[31] This is the classic description of the cost disease. Apparently, to some extent the cost of materials is included in these increases, but the problem must also extend to labor.

Nevertheless, costs per volume held in constant dollars seem to have fallen by 40% between 1970 and 1980.[32] But Baumol and Blackman take no comfort from this, asserting that the cost disease in libraries has merely been suspended during this period of inflation, that libraries are not more efficient but that financial stringency and the magnitude of the decrease in computer hardware costs have produced this result.[33] Looking to the future, they believe that cost declines in computer operations will cease as software costs increase ". . . because of the reliance on people to do software. . . ."[34] The implication is that the library cost disease, now in remission, will flare up anew as the economy recovers and computer software costs become the dominant element in library automation costs.

This is a very bleak view of library productivity. It means that if an attempt is made to maintain library service at present levels without any changes in budgetary support, the library capacity to maintain these services will eventually fail.

Outlook for the Future

It is improbable that the following fundamental patterns will be reversed:

1 Academic libraries are unlikely to receive capital funds needed to make significant changes.[35]
2 Library operating funds as a percentage of the parent's budget have been fixed in constant dollars for three decades and are likely to remain so.
3 Similarly, the percentage of the library internal budget for acquisitions is fixed and declining in constant dollars. This means a continuing decline in the number of books and journals acquired.
4 The percentage of the library budget expended for personnel is also fixed but has not yet produced a sharp reduction in services, although this is likely to occur in the future as the library cost disease reasserts itself.
5 Automation will not raise library productivity to offset these costs.

Publications will continue to proliferate even if the rate of growth is slowed. The cost of publications will rise faster than costs in the general economy, because the labor-intensive nature of the publishing industry suffers from the cost disease also. The surcease some library acquisitions budgets are enjoying because of the strength of the dollar abroad is transitory, and the pressures on acquisitions budgets will resume. The information explosion with its emphasis on the electronic delivery of information will produce fundamental changes in the way information is used. If libraries fail to respond to these changes, much of their clientele will go elsewhere. Yet the patterns of library budgeting militate against the library obtaining the funding needed to finance improvements. Moreover, libraries will be in increasing competition for funding from computer centers and in many institutions they will lose the competition.

All of this is a prescription for lingering death, but Armageddon is not going to dawn tomorrow. Academic libraries and their institutions still have an opportunity to adapt. Information and knowledge will always remain the central concerns of colleges and universities. The true challenge for academic librarians is to participate in the electronic revolution, not to oppose it with Luddite hostility. But this participation must go beyond adding a terminal here and a terminal there. Academic librarians must truly become active participants in the scholarly information transfer process. To discharge that role, however, librarians need the support and understanding of their institutional communities. To obtain that support they must make greater efforts to explain how libraries are being affected by current trends and how libraries should be changed to accommodate them. Changes in the library to make realistic accommodations to new demands will be possible only to the extent that the library itself plays a central role in its parent's response. If libraries remain on the periphery of institutional response to the information age, they will become increasingly irrelevant. The success of librarians in explaining and asserting their present and potential future role in the scholarly communication process will determine the degree to which they will receive the funding they need to adapt realistically to change—whether they will continue to be relevant to the academic enterprise.

Notes

1. C. B. Osburn, *Academic Research and Library Resources: Changing Patterns in America* (Westport, Conn.: Greenwood Press, 1979), p. 102.
2. R. M. Beazley, *Library Statistics of Colleges and Universities: Trends, 1968–1977. Summary Data, 1977* (Washington, D.C.: National Center for Education Statistics, 1981), p. 11.
3. Ibid.
4. Association of Research Libraries, *ARL Statistics* (Washington, D.C., 1969–1982).
5. One may object that ARL libraries are not the same as other academic libraries. And it is true that larger academic libraries do try to collect books and journals more comprehensively than smaller ones. But the phenomenon being examined here is the remarkable stability of the percentage of the parent institutional budget received by its library. This pattern seems to be roughly the same for all academic libraries. An additional indication that appears to support this conclusion is the result of a statistical study by Paul Kantor in which he found that "unit costs do not vary in an obvious way with library size." In other words, differences of scale do not seem to affect library costs. Costs are not the same as expenditures, but an absence of differences in cost due to scale seems to remove a principal reason for variance in expenditure pattern between large and smaller libraries. See P. B. Kantor, "Cost and Productivity in Library Operations," photocopy of a paper that will appear in the *Proceedings of the 1983 Annual Meeting of the American Society for Information Science.* p. 7.
6. J. Cohen, and K. W. Leeson, "Sources and Uses of Funds of Academic Libraries," *Library Trends* 28, no. 1 (1979): 30.
7. H. R. Bowen, *The Costs of Higher Education: How Much Do Colleges and Universities Spend per Student and How Much Should They Spend?* (San Francisco: Jossey-Bass, 1980), p. 16.
8. Ibid., p. 16.
9. Ibid., p. 17.
10. Ibid.
11. Cohen and Leeson, "Sources and Uses of Funds of Academic Libraries," p. 32.
12. Beazley, *Library Statistics of Colleges and Universities*, p. 12.
13. Ibid., p. 12.
14. Daniel Sullivan, "Libraries and Liberal Arts Colleges: Tough Times in the Eighties," *College and Research Libraries* 43, no. 2 (1982): 119.
15. W. J. Baumol, and S. A. B. Blackman, "Electronics, the Cost Disease, and the Operation of Libraries," *Journal of the American Society for Information Science* 34, no. 3 (1983): 189.
16. Cohen and Leeson, "Sources and Uses of Funds of Academic Libraries," p. 36.
17. Beazley, *Library Statistics of Colleges and Universities*, p. 11.
18. Cohen and Leeson, "Sources and Uses of Funds of Academic Libraries," p. 38.
19. Association of Research Libraries, *ARL Statistics.*
20. Cohen and Leeson, "Sources and Uses of Funds of Academic Libraries," p. 41.
21. Association of Research Libraries, *ARL Statistics*, 1981–1982, p. 4.

22. Sullivan, "Libraries and Liberal Arts Colleges," p. 122.
23. R. M. Hayes, "The Distribution of Use of Library Materials: Analysis of Data from the University of Pittsburgh," *Library Research* 3 (1981): 22.
24. H. S. White, "Library Materials Prices and Academic Library Practices: Between Scylla and Charybdis," *Journal of Academic Librarianship* 5, no. 1 (1979): 20.
25. Beazley, *Library Statistics of Colleges and Universities*, p. 9.
26. Association of Research Libraries, *ARL Statistics*, 1981–1982, p. 4.
27. National Center for Education Statistics, *Library Statistics of Colleges and Universities: 1979. Institutional Data* (Washington, D.C., 1981), p. 1.
28. Ibid.
29. White, "Library Materials Prices and Academic Library Practices," p. 22.
30. W. J. Baumol, and M. Marcus, *Economics of Academic Libraries* (Washington, D.C.: American Council on Education, 1973), p. 52.
31. Baumol and Blackman, "Electronics, the Cost Disease, and the Operation of Libraries," p. 181.
32. Ibid., p. 185.
33. Ibid.
34. Ibid., p. 180.
35. Sullivan, "Libraries and Liberal Arts Colleges," p. 119.

Women Predominate, Men Dominate: Disequilibrium in the Library Profession

Katharine Phenix

Westminster Public Library, Westminster, CO 80030

The history of women in librarianship is rich with fervent declaration, heated debate, honest opinion, and, more recently, empirical data and governmental policy. The Australians have dubbed the struggle "bun fights," Americans study the "disadvantaged majority," and the British have written "2,000 to 1: A Sex Oddity." Melvil Dewey fought the same battle when he moved his library school from New York City to Albany; librarians in Fairfax County, Virginia, are involved in the same struggle for pay equity today. Only the names and the rules have changed, and it must be left to the scholars to name the dialectic.

Highlights

- The history of women in librarianship is rich with fervent declaration, heated debate, honest opinion, and, more recently, empirical data and governmental policy.
- Survey after survey has reported lower median salaries, fewer professional perquisites, and a clouded view of the career ladder for women.
- In the struggle for women's equality, two fronts were opened in the last decade.
- Women first surfaced to agitate for affirmative political action in the American Library Association in 1970.
- Comparable worth rises as the library issue of the 1980s.

Early reports of "disquiet in the stacks" raised a number of issues: whether women were capable of the same quality work as men; whether women should remain in the work force after marriage; and whether a woman should obtain the same salary as a man for the same work. For the most part, these questions were resolved in favor of women (and librarianship) by 1970, and a host of other topics arose.

In the late 1960s and early 1970s, literature on women in librarianship focused on the issue of salaries. Affirmative action, for women the precursor of equal pay for equal work, and later, equal pay for work of equal value, was the rallying point for activist librarians. Survey after survey reported lower median salaries for women, fewer professional perquisites, and a clouded view of the career ladder, which disclosed men at the top and a preponderance of women at the bottom of the library hierarchy.

A Decade of Political Action

A look at the activities of the proponents of women's equality in the library profession during the last ten years gives perspective to the position of women today. Two fronts were opened during this period, political action and scholarly research. The first was manifested in two ways: (1) the formation of professional association groups and (2) individual and group efforts in favor of the Equal Rights Amendment.

Activist Groups

Early ALA Activity

Women first surfaced to agitate for affirmative political action in the American Library Association in 1970 as a Task Force on Women under the auspices of the Social Responsibilities Round Table. A number of far-reaching projects were undertaken by this group: two preconferences on women (1974 and 1980); the compilation of a list of nonsexist subject headings, which led to the publication *On Equal Terms* by Joan K. Marshall; a bibliography of library women, which stimulated the publication of *The Role of Women in Librarianship, 1876–1976: The Entry, Advancement, and Struggle for Advancement in One Profession* by Kathleen Weibel and Kathleen Heim; and a successful attempt to create a standing committee of the American Library Association Council, the Committee on the Status of Women in Librarianship (COSWL), in 1976.

Women Library Workers

Another activist group, Women Library Workers, was established in 1975 to become advocates for both credentialed and noncredentialed library workers who otherwise may have had no access to support groups. In summer 1976, Carol Leita and Nancy Schimmel traveled across the United States gathering support for national chapters. Meanwhile, the American Library Association Committee on the Status of Women in Librarianship set about its charge to "officially represent the diversity of women's issues within ALA . . . to promote and initiate the collection, analysis, dissemination, and coordination of information on the status of women in librarianship. . . ."[1]

ALA since 1977

Since its first meeting in 1977, COSWL has worked on several major projects. Through its efforts, a profile of ALA membership has been developed with which researchers can study the differences in career patterns between women and men. Other committee publications include *Equality in Librarianship: A Guide to Sex Discrimination Laws; The Library: A Room of One's Own / Women's Resources and Services;* and two editions of the *Directory of Library and Information Profession Women's Groups.* Networking has been an important activity for both COSWL and the Task Force on Women (which changed its name to Feminist Task Force in 1980). Links have been made with such outside groups as the Federation of Organizations for Professional Women, National Women's Studies Association, National Committee on Pay Equity, and National Political Women's Caucus, among others.

The mid-1970s witnessed a great upsurge of women's library groups. The American Library Association Reference and Adult Services Division (RASD) sponsored a new discussion group on Women's Materials and Women Library Users in 1977. At the same time, the Library Administration and Management Association (LAMA) gave rise to the Women Administrators Discussion Group. A later arrival was the Association of College and Research Libraries Women's Studies Discussion group, formed in 1982.

Other Library Groups

Outside the American Library Association, the Society of American Archivists had already established an ad hoc committee on the status of women in 1972. It was replaced by the Status of Women Committee in 1975, with a Women's Caucus as its activist arm. A few years later, the Special Libraries Association was confronted with the Women's Caucus when it met in New York in December 1979. (The caucus is still looking for a permanent home within the association.) Another group, the Association of Library and Information Science Education (ALISE), formed a women's interest group at its 1977 annual meeting.

State Groups

The COSWL *Directory* (May 1983) lists ten state groups that concern themselves with the status of women in libraries. Among the state library association groups are the Women in Libraries Caucus in Florida, the Women's Concerns Task Force in Illinois, the New York Library Association Round Table on the Status of Women in Librarianship, and the Ohio Library Association's Women on the Rise in Library Management. Women Library Workers has active chapters in Rhode Island, Massachusetts, and Wisconsin.

Library of Congress

In a category by itself is the Library of Congress Women's Program Advisory Committee, established by the Women's Program Office in 1976, when the office had already been in operation five years and it became staffed full time. The committee's major accomplishment was the completion of a 255-page report on the position of women at the Library of Congress from 1968 to 1978.

Women in the Community

During the past decade, women librarians also have been active in the area of services to women. In 1981, the Arthur and Elizabeth Schlesinger Library of the History of Women in America, funded by a grant from the National Endowment for the Humanities, assisted seven communities with library projects aimed at women.

International Activity

Women outside the United States are equally aware of their status in libraries. In Canada, a major study funded by the Canada Council examined career paths of male and female librarians in Canada in the early 1970s.[2] Other articles on the status of women in libraries have been published in the Netherlands, Japan, the Soviet Union, France, Nigeria, and a number of other countries. Women's library support groups are known to exist in Canada, Great Britain, Australia, and New Zealand.

The Equal Rights Amendment

Some of the nascent political activity of women in U.S. libraries can be attributed to the galvanizing effect of national action in favor of the Equal Rights Amendment. In 1974, the American Library Association passed a resolution in favor of the Equal Rights Amendment. In 1977, ALA membership and Council forums favored boycotting states that had not passed the ERA by holding ALA conferences outside the unratified states, and at the 1979 midwinter meeting, then President Russell Shank broke the tie vote in the ALA Council in favor of boycotting Chicago for a meeting in 1980. But when a petition circulated by anti-ERA members forced reconsideration of the issue by ALA membership-at-large through a mail vote, the membership decided against boycotting Illinois.

At the 1979 midwinter meeting, ALA Council established an ERA Task Force headed by Kay Cassell and Alice Ihrig. Using funds approved by ALA members and raised by a dues checkoff and by Council members, the ERA Task Force funneled support for ERA into library association groups in unratified states. In 1982, a resolution sponsored by COSWL member Cynthia Johanson was passed to discontinue the boycott while affirming the association's support for equal rights for women.

Publications

All of the library women's groups formed during the past decade have continued to operate and act on a number of issues. Ten years have produced four editions of the national *SHARE* (Sisters Have Resources Everywhere) *Directory of Feminist Librarians* and state (California, Wisconsin, and Illinois) directories. The Indiana Library Association Division on Women in Libraries has also published a number of editions of its *Women in Indiana Libraries Network Directory*. Newsletters and journals that continue to thrive are the *WLW Journal: News/Views/Reviews for Women and Libraries*, published by the national Women Library Workers; *Women in Libraries*, compiled for the ALA Feminist Task Force; the *SAA Women's Caucus Newsletter;* and the newsletter of Wisconsin Women Library Workers.

A Decade of Research

Paralleling the decade's political activity has been a trend toward closer scrutiny of the empirical data reflecting women's positions in libraries. National associations such as the American Library Association, the Association for Library and Information Science Education, the Society of American Archivists, the American Association of Law Libraries, and the Music Library Association sponsored studies addressing this issue, and a number of institutions collected data on librarians working in academic, public, school, state, and medical libraries. Other surveys focused on library science educators, the Library of Congress, and online searching personnel,[3] and several state and local studies of librarians were published.

The Widening Wage Gap

In every study, women achieved lower salaries and fewer administrative positions than men. In fact, a longitudinal look at the placements and salaries of entry-level librarians published annually by the *Library Journal* identifies the trend of a widening wage gap. According to *Library Journal* data, women earned 95.5 percent of what men earned in 1972. Women's salaries were up to 98.3 percent of men's in 1979, but dropped to 95.7 percent in 1980. They dropped again, to 96.8 percent in 1981, and lower still, to 96.3 percent in 1982.[4]

Salary and position of library school faculty have also been monitored for a number of years. At the dean and director levels, women increased their representation from 19.7 percent in 1976 to 25.4 percent in 1983. However, their salaries did not match those of their male counterparts. Women deans earned 96.8 percent of what male deans earned in 1976, and 86.2 percent in 1982. The number dropped to 85.6 percent in 1983. Salary data at all faculty levels show men with a financial advantage.

Other 1983 salary data reported by the Special Libraries Association,[5] the Medical Libraries Association,[6] and the Society of American Archivists[7] indicate lower average salaries for women. Some state reports issued in 1983 also confirm this trend. A study of librarians in academic libraries in Oregon revealed a 22.4 percent wage gap between women and men.[8] In Illinois, women academic librarians earned less than their male counterparts according to analysis of NCES HEGIS/LIBGIS data.[9] In North Carolina public libraries, male directors earned an average of $23,887 in 1982 as compared to $19,947 for female directors.[10]

A New Body of Research

Recently, a new body of research has emerged that looks beyond simple salary statistics to determine variables that affect women's status in libraries. Several doctoral dissertations and other essays that look at particular aspects of women in librarianship were compiled by Kathleen M. Heim in her *Status of Women in Librarianship: Historical, Sociological and Economic Issues,* published in 1983. Recruitment, mobility, assertiveness, and career interruption are a few of the key variables studied. Taking up the challenge to fill the gaps in the study of women in libraries, several reports were published that looked at particular library groups with these variables in mind. First and foremost among the projects reflecting the new focus of study is the Committee on the Status of Women's *Career Profiles and Sex Discrimination in the Library Profession,* the first research project to study the relationship of sex, status, and salary to a number of personal, demographic, and career patterns.

Library deans and directors were a particular target of 1983 research on the sexual composition of library workers. All the studies reported similar data: Women attained top positions at an older age; marriage was a negative variable for women and a positive variable for men; and men appeared to have higher educational credentials than women. Most clearly revealed in each of the studies were the opposite career patterns of women and men. Women were far more likely to be hired for a top position within the same institution, and men were far more likely to be hired from the outside.[11]

CDACL

Addressing the issue of career path and pattern is the Career Development and Assessment Center for Librarians (CDACL) at the University of Washington Graduate School of Library Science in Seattle. Funded by the Kellogg Foundation and supported by the Washington State Library and the Pacific Northwest Library Association, as well as the library school, the CDACL manifests a new approach toward improving women's status in libraries. In its three-year history, it has provided 89 librarians with assessment of present and potential management skills and career development guidance.

CDACL's three-year report is a positive statement of success. Peter Hiatt, its principal investigator, wrote "We have been able to explore the impact of assessment center technology and career planning on a feminized profession in which women have been discriminated against as managers and administrators.[11, 12] The center also has developed the skills of 53 "assessors" in observation and categorization of specific competencies. Those involved look forward to obtaining funds from the W. K. Kellogg Foundation and support from the American Library Association and its Office for Library Personnel Resources for a five-year project to expand the Northwest program to five regional career development and assessment centers in the United States and Canada.

Comparable Worth

Comparable worth rises as the library issue of the 1980s. Pay equity struggles have been documented in libraries in Canada, Maryland, St. Paul, Philadelphia, San Diego, San Jose, and Fairfax County, Virginia.

For the last decade, librarians have been primary advocates of equal pay for work of equal value. The American Library Association is a founding member of the National Committee on Pay Equity. Margaret Myers, director of the ALA Office for Library Personnel Resources (OLPR), has testified before the Equal Employment Opportunity Commission, as did Elizabeth Stone, when she was the association's president. OLPR also published a Topics in Personnel packet called *Pay Equity: Comparable Worth Action Guide.*

Comparable worth is an issue from which all librarians stand to gain. It is a women's issue. The library profession, with its preponderance of women, has historically excused librarians' depressed salary scale relative to other job categories that require less education and fewer supervisory responsibilities.

The Gains for Women

What is the status of women in libraries and the information profession today? Still low. Women continue to predominate in numbers and men dominate in power. In the last decade, however, activists have counted a number of victories. Sexist language and discriminatory remarks have been removed from ALA publications, and policy dictates that they not be accepted in the future. Nominations for ALA Council, which are carefully monitored and reported, are still disproportionately male, as is the number of male speakers and moderators at ALA conferences, but female representation is increasing. American Library Association policy also requests that salary ranges be published with job announcements, so that hidden higher salaries are not offered to men, and women applicants are encouraged to negotiate starting salaries. A good deal of support and work has gone into a current research project to identify the problems of women whose careers have been interrupted by personal obligations, and at the ALA Annual Conference in June 1984, the first Equality Award will be presented for "an outstanding contribution towards promoting equality between women and men in the library profession." Kathleen Weibel and Kathleen M. Heim documented 100 years of women in the library profession in *The Role of Women in Librarianship, 1876–1976: The Entry, Advancement, and Struggle for Equalization in One Profession. On Account of Sex: An Annotated Bibliography on Women in Librarianship, 1977–1981* by Kathleen M. Heim and Katharine Phenix, the five-year supplement, contains the same number of citations as the hundred-year compilation, and the ALA Committee on the Status of Women in Librarianship continues to provide yearly updates to these bibliographies.

Conclusion

A decade of activism has fostered women's support and action groups, association commitment, professional mechanisms such as the Career Development and Assessment Center for Librarians, governmental policy and comparable worth litigation, and political know-how. The groundwork has been laid. Closer investigation of the historical, sociological, and economic conditions that affect women and men in the library environment will hopefully reveal new methods to enfranchise the majority. But the technological revolution may bring yet a new host of problems or inequities. Librarians must be vigilant and prepared to act against sex discrimination, both subtle and overt.

Notes

1. *ALA Handbook of Organization, 1983/1984* (Chicago: American Library Association, 1983), p. 22.
2. This study, *Career Paths of Male and Female Librarians in Canada: Report to Canada Council,* was not widely disseminated. Some of the findings are published in Sherrill Cheda, Linda Fischer, Mary Ann Wasylycia-Coe, and Phyllis Yaffee, "Salary Differentials of Male and Female Librarians in Canada," *Emergency Librarian* 5 (January–February 1978): 3–13; and Mary Ann Wasylycia-Coe, "Profile: Canadian Chief Librarians by Sex," *Canadian Library Journal* 38 (June 1981): 159–163. The study is also carefully analyzed in Elizabeth Futas, "An Analysis of the Study, 'Career Paths of Male and Female Librarians in Canada' " in *Status of Women in Librarianship: Historical, Sociological, and Economic Issues,* ed. Kathleen M. Heim (New York: Neal-Schuman, 1983), pp. 393–423.
3. All of these studies were gathered and analyzed in Kathleen M. Heim, "The Demographic and Economic Status of Librarians in the 1970s, with Special Reference to Women," In *Advances in Librarianship,* ed. Wesley Simonton (New York: Academic Press, 1982), Vol. 12, pp. 1–45.
4. "Placements and Salaries," *Library Journal* (September/October): 1972–1983.
5. *SLA Triennial Salary Survey* (New York: Special Libraries Association, 1983).
6. "Salary Survey Results," *MLA News* 155 (May 1983): 1, 7–11.
7. David Bearman, "82 Survey of the Archival Profession," *American Archivist* 46 (Spring 1983): 233–241.
8. "Library Faculty Survey" (Portland, Oreg.: State System of Higher Education, December 1982).
9. Katharine Phenix, "Analysis of the 1981/82 HEGIS/LIBGIS Responses of Illinois Academic Libraries" (Springfield: Illinois State Library, August 1983).

10. Rex Klett and Karen Seawell, "The Tar Heel Enclave: Public Library Salaries in North Carolina," *North Carolina Libraries* (Spring 1983): 15–22.
11. The studies referred to are Barbara B. Moran, "Career Patterns of Academic Library Administrators," *College & Research Libraries* 44 (September 1983): 334–344; Raymond Kipela, "A Profile of Library School Deans, 1960–81," *Journal of Education for Librarianship* 23 (Winter 1983): 173–192; William Skeh Wong and David S. Zubatsky, "The First-Time Appointed Academic Library Director, 1970–1980: A Profile," *Journal of Library Administration* 4 (Spring 1983): 41–49; and Dale Karr, "Becoming a Library Director," *Library Journal* 108 (February 15, 1983): 343–346.
12. Peter Hiatt, Letter in the preface to *Your Assessment Center in Action: Third Year* (Seattle, Wash.: Career Development and Assessment Center for Librarians, June 1982).

Access to Federal Information: Issues in 1983–1984

Patricia Wilson Berger

President, Federal Librarians Roundtable
American Library Association

A review of what has been said and written on federal information access issues during the last two years reveals few conclusions, several contradictions, and reason for concern. One thing is certain, however—there is no scarcity of information on the growing scarcity of federal information or the associated access problems.

Highlights

- The federal government's two assessments of the relative worth of unclassified federal information constitute an odd, dichotomous policy.
- Concerns about the unauthorized or inadvertent release of classified information have expanded future security restrictions on greater numbers of federal employees.
- The Office of Management and Budget announced its intention to review present "cost recovery" methods and to consider "several principles of information resources management."
- The "identifiable damage" and "balancing" tests for withholding information from Freedom of Information Act petitioners were dropped from a recent executive order.
- Proposed changes to the Printing and Binding Regulations would redefine printing to include all copying, duplicating, and printing, by whatever means.
- Information access discussions today center not only on how to obtain information from or about a federal agency but also on whether information is still obtainable.

> People who mean to be their own Governors must arm themselves with the power which knowledge gives. [James Madison[1]]

> Surrounded by trash bags stuffed with [government] documents at a White House briefing, [Presidential Counselor Edwin] Meese said the publications were judged either unnecessary or redundant. . . . Since President Reagan took office three years ago, the Administration has eliminated one of every four government publications then printed. [Pete Early in the *Washington Post*[2]]

> Our national allegiance to the idea that information has value is being challenged by current policies aimed at restricting what the American people learn about their government. [Bruce W. Sanford[3]]

Between July 1982 and January 1984, Anne Heanue, of the American Library Association's (ALA) Washington, D.C., office, twice updated her chronology "Less Access to Less Information by and about the U.S. Government," first issued in January 1982.[4] In June 1983, ALA established a Commission on Freedom and Equality of Access to Information to focus association concerns about these issues. Throughout 1983 and early 1984, senators and representatives of the U.S. Congress discussed proposals for Freedom of Information Act (FOIA) amendments and explored ways to counteract increased classification and censorship activity in executive agencies. On September 25, 1983, Attorney Floyd Abrams' article on information control appeared in the *New York Times Magazine*,[5] and the April and October 1983 issues of *Special Libraries* carried articles by Marc Levin[6] and Bruce W. Sanford[7] and an address by UCLA Dean Robert M. Hayes.[8] John Berry's editorial in the July 1983 issue of *Library Journal* called for national focus and debate on "the information access agenda." He proposed that ALA's new Access Commission

> develop and offer to both the Republicans and Democrats the information planks for their 1984 platforms, planks designed to place our national debate on these information issues exactly where it belongs, at the center of our democratic, electoral process. Ultimately the American people will have to decide the issues on the information access agenda.[9]

Information access discussions today center not only on how to obtain information from or about a federal agency but also on whether information is still obtainable from that federal source—indeed, whether it is obtainable from any source. Cutbacks in agency publishing budgets plus orders from the Office of Management and Budget (OMB) to reduce the numbers of periodic titles published have stopped the production of such standbys as the annual *Handbook of Labor Statistics* and have shifted the publication of such titles as the *Higher Education Directory* to the private sector. A review of ALA's three chronologies reveals that these changes in access and availability have often been made quickly and with little or no previous discussion, resulting in confusion, cynicism, and misunderstanding regarding the intent of the changes. How is it that an administration that prides itself on effective public discourse and that refers to its leader as the "great communicator" could have overlooked the merits of announcement and discussion of contemplated changes?

Federal Information Policy and National Security

In his June 1983 address to the Special Libraries Association (SLA), Dean Robert Hayes, of UCLA's Graduate School of Library and Information Sciences, speaking on the politics of access, especially open access, said that "from the earliest days of our history, open access to information has been a matter of national public policy," which is embodied in the First Amendment of the Constitution and was reaffirmed by the Supreme Court when it ruled: "It is not only the right, but the duty of Congress to see to it that intercourse among the states and the transmission of intelligence are not obstructed or unnecessarily encumbered by state legislation."[10] Hayes speculated that the "continued effort on the part of the current administration to impose restraints on the open availability of information" comes from its overriding concerns about national security. These concerns have reinforced

> a belief that the country is being besieged and that a release of any information is tantamount to "revealing it all." The result is that "national security" is broadened from "military security" to "industrial security" to "economic security" and becomes a catchall for dealing with any threat, real or imaginary, military or industrial.[11]

President Reagan acknowledged in a 1983 memorandum to federal employees the necessity to "protect military secrets" and to "gather intelligence information" about "nuclear dangers, terrorism and aggression" without fear of public disclosure; but he also stipulated that "only a fraction of information concerning national security policy" is denied the public. He added that the nation's history of "free speech, robust debate, and the right to disagree strongly over all national policies [is a proud tradition] no one would ever want to change."[12]

Unclassified Information

At least two disparate judgments of the value of unclassified federal information can be identified today. One is represented by Edwin Meese's January 4, 1983, garbage bag display of some 3,800 government publications on their way to the trash heap. The other is manifest in such proposals as the one announced by the Department of Energy (DOE) on April 1, 1983, which would place stringent controls on certain kinds of nuclear data and would restrict public use of documents (including documents already published and distributed) that contain "unclassified controlled nuclear information."[13] The two views seem contradictory. There may be merit in periodic reviews and general housecleanings of unclassified publications programs, but to couple such a budget-cutting approach with an elaborate, expensive control mechanism for collection of unclassified material—material that may or may not remain technologically relevant—is odd. Few systems in or out of government are as costly to operate as security systems, and none is more difficult to set aside, even after the need for it has passed.

In his article in the *New York Times Magazine*, September 25, 1983, Floyd Abrams observed:

> There can be no quarrel with its purpose—to frustrate the efforts of terrorist organizations to produce nuclear weapons or sabotage nuclear facilities . . . [but] the proposed rules are so vague [permitting DOE to withhold almost any information about nuclear facilities] and so unlikely to work [once information is public it is all but impossible to make it "secret" again] that an extraordinarily diverse array of groups—from state officials, universities and public-interest organizations to libraries, Indian tribes and unions—have questioned them.[14]

He added:

> We can hardly be sure that all unclassified information is harmless information. But if we are to restrict the spread of information because we cannot guarantee its harmless effects, we will have much restricting to do in the future.[15]

Taken together, the government's two assessments of the relative worth of un-classified federal information—it is garbage and should be dumped versus it is danger-ous and should be controlled—constitute an odd, dichotomous policy, which discounts the need for a substantial component of unclassified federal information on the one hand and prohibits public access to a substantial component of what unclassified federal information remains on the other.

Classified Information

Concerns about the unauthorized or inadvertent release of classified information have expanded future security restrictions on greater numbers of federal employees. On March 11, 1983, the Presidential National Security Decision Directive "Safeguarding National Security Information" was released. One of its requirements is:

> All persons with authorized access to Sensitive Compartmented Information (SCI) shall be required to sign a nondisclosure agreement. . . . All such agreements must include a pro-vision for prepublication review to assure deletion of SCI and other classified information.[16]

Estimates of persons with authorized access to SCI in the Department of Defense alone range as high as 100,000. Bruce Sanford describes the directive as "breathtaking in its clumsiness and awesome in its contempt for the public."[17] He says:

> [It] would prohibit high officials of one Administration from criticizing the . . . policies of a succeeding Administration without first submitting their criticisms to their successors for clearance. This . . . [could] deny the public the views of former officials and the lessons of their experience in government.[18]

Abrams shares the view that the directive could diminish the public's knowledge of how or why executive policies were formulated and why certain decisions or courses of ac-tion were taken, because "those people most knowledgeable about subjects of overrid-ing national concern will be least able to comment without the approval of those they wish to criticize."[19]

A Federal Information Management Policy

The 1984 information access agenda promises to be crowded with debates on censor-ship, freedom of information, privacy, public access, and classification issues, as well as discussions about user fees, public sector versus private sector publishing rights, and who controls what aspects of executive agency publishing programs. On September 12, 1983, the Office of Management and Budget published a solicitation for comment on "the development of a policy circular concerning federal information management.[20] OMB announced its intention to review present "cost recovery" methods and to consider "several principles of information resources management," such as "information is not a free good but a resource of substantial economic value and should be treated as such."[21] OMB also said:

> Policy guidance may be needed to ensure that Federal agencies do not compete unfairly with the private sector when they provide information products and services to the public. . . . Many agencies' practices in charging for information products and services have been questioned in recent years. What special policy guidance is needed as regards the application of user charges to government information products and services?[22]

ALA's Position

Both ALA's Federal Librarians Roundtable (FLRT) and the Government Documents Roundtable (GODORT) helped to draft the association's response to OMB's solicitation. The response indicates that the ALA Council had "adopted a revision of its policy relating to federal information issues," which stipulates: "a democratic society depends on the federal government ensuring the right of all its citizens of access to a comprehensive range of knowledge and a diversity of communication media."[23] ALA noted that "information has value to the American public beyond the economic value";[24] on the matter of "unfair" competition with the private sector, ALA said that "subsequent drafts will need to elaborate this point both in terms of defining 'unfair' and the many complex considerations which determine who acquires what under which conditions." Finally, ALA stated its opposition to "full-cost recovery which includes the costs of creating information."[25]

On January 11, 1984, ALA's Council passed two resolutions regarding public access to federal information. The first of these called on President Reagan and "other appropriate federal agencies to ensure that information management policies promulgated protect and provide for equal and ready access to federally produced information."[26] The second resolution was cosponsored by FLRT and GODORT and took note of OMB's emphasis on full-cost recovery and private sector publishing interests. It urged OMB to include in its "final policy circular concerning Federal information management" the principle "that there should be equal and ready access to data collected, compiled, produced and published in any format by the government of the United States."[27]

A draft of OMB's proposed policy circular should be published in spring 1984. Since the Information Industry Association (IIA) has supported in principle many sections of the OMB solicitation criticized by ALA, the debate promises to be lively and vigorous.

Congressional Debate

The administration's request for substantial revisions to the Freedom of Information Act, the prepublication review restrictions of the March 11, 1983, Presidential National Security Decision Directive, and the security procedures set out in Executive Order 12356 on "National Security Information"[28] continue to receive attention, comment, and action from Congress.

Freedom of Information Protection Act

On May 19, 1983, Senator David F. Durenberger (R–Minn.) introduced S.1335, the Freedom of Information Protection Act of 1983.[29] S.1335 was prompted by Executive Order 12356, which Durenberger claimed

> [was] drafted by security bureaucrats who think only of how to keep everything secret, and by legal bureaucrats who think only of how to get away with filing fewer affidavits. Nobody gave much thought to the public's right to know what their Government is doing. Nobody worried about maintaining public support for the governmental secrecy system. . . . A year has gone by and what has happened? The public is ever more cynical about government secrecy. Bureaucrats and policymakers are ever more cynical about the information they control. Instead of sensible declassification we have selective leaks, both official and unofficial. And to fight those leaks we now have a Presidential directive that calls for more lie detectors and more censorship. Is that the best we can do?[30]

Durenberger said that Executive Order 12356 "told bureaucrats to be rigid" and "allows them to ignore the public interest in disclosure." To counter this:

> [his bill] will make sure that information withheld from FOIA petitioners . . . meets two tests that used to apply to all classification decisions: First, that it be information the disclosure of which could reasonably be expected to cause identifiable damage to national security, and, second, that the agency withholding the information first consider the public interest in disclosure.[31]

Durenburger stated that such tests for releasability "send a signal that moderation and thoughtfulness are the keys to effective security," and that protecting the FOIA is protecting the most basic element of open Government."[32] The two tests Durenberger referred to, commonly called the "identifiable damage" and "balancing" tests, were both included in security regulations in force throughout the Nixon, Ford, and Carter administrations, but were dropped from President Reagan's Executive Order 12356.

Senator Patrick Moynihan (D–N.Y.) spoke in support of S.1335 and observed that the prepublication review requirements spelled out in the Presidential Directive of March 11, 1983

> [appear] to call for a mandatory, and most likely, ineffective censorship bureaucracy. This from a President who staunchly opposes intrusive big government and, indeed, advocates private voluntary action as an alternative to governmental programs to meet basic social needs.[33]

Senator Joseph Biden (D–Del.) described S.1335 as the first step in the process of clarifying "the proper relationship among the three branches of Government in information policy matters.[34] He noted with regret:

> It is ironic but established fact that this administration, with its scorn for the values of Government and the people who work in it, has tried on a wide range of fronts to limit the access of the American people to information about the workings of the Government. . . .
> Through all these acts, the administration has given vent to crude ideological impulses against people who would dare to question its conduct of Government, its management of Federal agencies.[35]

Senator Patrick Leahy (D–Vt.) said that he hesitated

> to urge . . . colleagues to codify common sense, as this bill admittedly does. But the President's Executive order has made this proposal necessary. Statutes like the Freedom of Information Act work best when they enjoy the good will of the administration and the agencies charged with their implementation. In the absence of evidence that the presumption of openness will be held high as a standard, the present bill becomes crucial.[36]

On May 19, 1983, Durenberger's bill was referred to the Committee on the Judiciary. As of this writing, it is under study by a subcommittee of that committee.

Prepublication Review

Concerns about overclassification and censorship by the executive branch are shared by many other members of Congress in both chambers. On November 22, 1983, President Reagan signed into law the Department of State's Authorization Act for Fiscal Years 1984 and 1985. Section 1010 of that law is an unrelated amendment added to the act in order to suspend until April 15, 1984, implementation of the prepublication review rights spelled out in the March 11, 1983, Presidential Directive:

SEC. 1010. The head of a department or agency of the Government may not, before April 15, 1984, enforce, issue, or implement any rule, regulation, directive policy, decision, or order which (1) would require any officer or employee to submit, after termination of employment with the Government, his or her writings for prepublication review by an officer or employee of the Government, and (2) is different from the rules, regulations, directives, policies, decisions, or orders (relating to prepublication review of such writings) in effect on March 1, 1983.[37]

The amendment was introduced by Senators Charles "Mac" Mathias (R–Md.) and Thomas Eagleton (D–Mo.) on October 20, 1983.

In his remarks, Senator Mathias noted that members of the Senate share "President Reagan's justified concerns about leaks of classified information" and are disturbed that "national secrets seem to have become the common currency of the daily press," but that the amendment "simply would delay . . . implementation of a new program of censorship of the writings of private citizens." At a hearing convened on September 13, 1983, by the Senate Committee on Governmental Affairs, Mathias said members "were struck by how little evidence there is that former officials have abused their trust."[38]

Senator Jeremiah Denton (R–Ala.) spoke against the amendment because he believes that "classified information must be protected from even an inadvertent disclosure from those within our Government who have lawful access."[39]

Senator Moynihan spoke in support of the amendment because he believes "the net the administration has cast with this directive is . . . far wider than is proper and necessary and is therefore unconstitutional."[40] Senators Durenberger, Walter D. Huddleston (D–Ky.), Carl Levin (D–Mich.), and Jeff Bingaman (D–N. Mex.) also spoke in support of the amendment. The amendment passed in the Senate by a vote of 56 to 34.

On January 30, 1984, Representative Jack Brooks (D–Texas) introduced H.R. 4681, the "Federal Polygraph Limitation and Anticensorship Act of 1984." H.R. 4681 would severely restrict the use of the polygraph for screening purposes by executive agencies and would limit prepublication review requirements to only employees of the Central Intelligence Agency and the National Security Agency. Employees of both these agencies were covered by prepublication agreements before the Presidential Directive was issued March 11, 1983. At this writing, H.R. 4681 is under study by the House Committee on Post Office and Civil Service.

A joint oversight hearing closed to the public was held on February 7, 1984, by a House Judiciary Committee subcommittee chaired by Representative Don Edwards (D–Calif.) and a House Post Office and Civil Service Committee subcommittee chaired by Representative Patricia Schroeder (D–Calif.). The purpose of the closed hearing was to "review policies for prepublication materials by government employees."

The Freedom of Information Reform Act

In addition to the changes to the FOIA outlined in Senator Durenberger's Freedom of Information Protection bill, a host of others are proposed in S.774, called the Freedom of Information Reform Act by its sponsor, Senator Orrin Hatch (R–Utah). The major changes to the FOIA proposed in S.774 are:

1 New user fees to provide for the payment of "all costs . . . attributable to . . . the request [including] . . . reasonable standard charges for . . . search[ing], duplicat[ing], and other processing of the request."[41]

2 New royalties to provide for a "fair value fee" for records containing "commercially valuable technological information."[42]

3 New classifications of requestors to permit agencies to "recoup costs from 'special beneficiaries'" (as opposed to public interests).

4 Protective measures for proprietary documents that will require agencies to "permit submitters of trade secrets . . . to present claims of confidentiality" before information is released to an FOIA requestor.[43]

5 New provisions for the withholding of "sensitive noninvestigative law enforcement materials . . . and the protection of confidential sources."[44]

6 New exemptions "from mandatory disclosure of technical data that may not be exported lawfully."[45]

7 New agency flexibility "in deciding whether the release of . . . information would be lawful. The agency may take account of other information which it knows or reasonably believes to be available to the requestor."[46]

8 Prohibition of "FOIA requests by foreign nationals; . . . prescribed limitations [to requests] . . . by incarcerated felons; and toll time requirements . . . to requests from parties to adjudicatory proceedings in which the Government is also a party."[47]

9 Exemption from FOIA requests of "documents . . . generated or acquired in the course of a lawful organized crime investigation within the [last] five years."[48]

10 A new requirement that "within 270 days of enactment, agencies that want to rely on specific statutory exemptions will have to publish a list of them in the *Federal Register*."[49]

In its September 1983 report on the bill, the Senate Committee on the Judiciary said:

> [S.774 has] received the unanimous approval of this Committee as an indication of (its) success . . . in amending FOIA's most glaring weaknesses without compromising its vital strengths. . . . This bill will . . . fine-tune the most important component of our nation's information policy, a policy which distinguishes the United States among other nations.[50]

On September 12, 1983, S.774 was reported out of committee. As of this writing, it is on the Senate's calendar for a vote.

The Intelligence Information Act

On November 17, 1983, the Senate passed S.1324, the Intelligence Information Act of 1983, which exempts from FOIA requests "sensitive" files about CIA operations. The bill was approved on a voice vote and without debate.[51]

Senator Barry Goldwater (R–Ariz.) spoke in support of the bill and said that "every single Senator" on the Senate Select Committee on Intelligence voted in favor of the bill. Senator Moynihan also spoke for S.1324 and described it as "legislation which strikes a proper balance between the security requirements of the Central Intelligence Agency and the public's right to know."[52] Senators Durenberger, Huddleston, Strom Thurmond (R–S.C.), and Leahy also spoke in support of S.1324.

On November 13, 1983, S.1324 was referred for action to three House of Representatives committees, the Committee on Government Operations, the Permanent Select Committee on Intelligence, and the Committee on Post Office and Civil Service.

FOIA Fee Waivers

On January 7, 1983, the Department of Justice issued a policy memorandum to all agency and department heads on the subject of FOIA fee waivers.[53] In it, Assistant Attorney General Jonathan Rose reversed a Carter administration policy that recommended that agency discretion on fee waivers "be exercised generously," especially if the requestor represented the news media or a public interest organization or was a historical researcher. Rose's guidelines require more than a requestor's assertion before the FOIA fee can be waived. The agency must make an independent assessment of the requestor's personal interest and expertise before waiving fees. Agencies are also obliged

> [to] examine the value to the public of the records themselves. A fee waiver is appropriate only if the disclosable contents of the records are in fact informative on the issue found to be of public interest. No matter how interesting or vital the subject matter of a request, the public is benefited only if the information released meaningfully contributes to the public development or understanding of the subject.[54]

The Association of American Publishers (AAP) took exception to this reversal and in a letter to Rose said that the new policy guidance

> raises serious questions concerning the administration's commitment to a fundamental precept underlying our system of government—if the need for a citizenry well informed as to the affairs of government through the workings, among other means, of a vigorous press.[55]

AAP observed that the new guidelines "show no sensitivity to the public interest." The association concluded "that adherence to the letter and harsh spirit of the new fee waiver guidance will have a directly negative impact on authors and their publishers."[56]

Others have voiced similar complaints about the thrusts of both the newly passed and the currently proposed changes to the FOIA. Robert Hayes refers to Senator Hatch's proposed fee changes and the Department of Justice's January 1983 fee guidelines as "repeated attempts to gut the Freedom of Information Act . . . by instituting pricing policies to make it economically unfeasible to get access to information."[57] Bruce Sanford recommended to Congress that if "legislative fine tuning" of the act was needed, "Congress should use a screwdriver, not a crowbar,"[58] and Floyd Abrams describes the Department of Justice's guidelines as licensing "the Government itself to decide what information about its conduct—or misconduct—[is] 'meaningful' "[59]

On the other hand, University of Chicago's professor of law Antonin Scalia believes that "persons or corporations requesting information under the [FOIA] should pay a larger proportion of the taxpayers' cost of supplying it."[60] Scalia referred to "one horrible example" of a single request that cost the government "over $400,000" and added: "To say that the government's files should not be kept secret from its citizens is not to say that the government should become the world's largest free library reference service."[61] He noted that although FOIA is intended to benefit "the public at large," in practice, it has been employed "as a means of revealing what private companies are doing for the benefit of their adversaries and competitors."[62]

The Procter & Gamble (P&G) Company would no doubt agree with Scalia's last point. In 1979, the Food and Drug Administration released to a competitor firm a P&G report that "included details of a highly confidential technology." Similarly, the Federal Trade Commission "let slip highly secret ball bearings data it had received from Ingersoll-Rand" and the Environmental Protection Agency "disclosed under FOI a prized formula for a top-selling herbicide."[63] Senator Hatch's FOIA proposals would give companies time to argue against disclosure and advance notice when data are disclosed. James T. Reilly, a University of Cincinnati professor of law, believes the provisions would prevent companies from being "blind sided. At least [they would] know that competitors have the information."[64]

On the other hand, small companies are not too thrilled with the Hatch proposals. For example, Radionics, Inc., which makes spare parts for communications equipment manufactured by other companies, often obtains the equipment design data it needs via an FOIA to the federal government. Very often, FOIA is the only way Radionics can get the data it needs to compete. Radionics President Alfred Ozminkowski believes that the proposed Hatch reforms will "put a lot of small companies at a big disadvantage," because "if the Reagan Administration and the lobbyists prevail with their proposed revision of the act, it won't yield that kind of design data to . . . any . . . potential competitor anymore."[65]

The Paperwork Reduction Act

During 1983, Congress examined the activities of OMB's Office of Information and Regulatory Affairs (OIRA), which was established to administer the Paperwork Reduction Act of 1980. On November 7, 1983, Representative Brooks moved to suspend the House rules and pass H.R. 2718, the Paperwork Reduction Act Amendments of 1983. Section 110 of that bill establishes an Information Technology Fund, which combines "the capital and assets of the Federal telecommunications fund" with "the capital and assets of the automatic data processing fund" under the management of the General Services Administration.[66] Brooks stated that the new fund "will be used to finance the acquisition of technology for use by Federal agencies." He further noted:

> While OIRA has reported that it has substantially reduced the paperwork burden, it has not been successful in carrying out the information technology requirements contained in the Paperwork Reduction Act. Its lack of success in these areas is apparently due to OMB's decision to divert the scarce resources of OIRA to non-Paperwork Act functions. H.R. 2718 corrects this problem and establishes important new goals to even further reduce the paperwork burden.[67]

Senator Frank Horton (R–N.Y.) spoke in support of H.R. 2718, calling it "a good, sensible bill which will enable OMB and the agencies to continue management reforms they have recently begun."[68] H.R. 2718 passed the House on November 7, 1983, and was referred to the Senate Committee on Government Affairs on November 8, 1983.

Public assessments vary regarding how well OIRA and the Paperwork Reduction Act of 1980 have worked:

> The law has worked well. . . . This view is held by . . . the National Association of Manufacturers, the National Association of Broadcasters and the Business Advisory Council on Federal Reports, the virtual father of the act.

> It hasn't worked at all. The flood of federal forms is getting worse. This view was expressed repeatedly by heads of small businesses at recent Small Business Administration hearings around the country.

> It's worked too well, eliminating information vital to industry. Spokesmen for the American Meat Institute and the American Trucking Associations regret the loss of information that they say was useful in understanding their markets and keeping track of competitors.

It's been subverted by the Office of Management and Budget, which took money intended to corral stray federal paperwork and spent it in the more visible arena of regulatory relief. This is the complaint of some Congressional staffers and the General Accounting Office. . . .[60]

Marc Levin's criticism of the law is that it consolidated

within . . . OMB both information management and policy oversight. . . . [The] attempt to improve information policies has been less than successful due to OMB's inadequate staffing and concentration on regulatory reform and budget cuts. It is clear that information management and policy are not considered high priority issues in the current [Reagan] administration.[70]

Printing and Binding Regulations: Proposed Changes

On November 11, 1983, an additional source of controversy for OIRA developed when Representative Augustus F. Hawkins (D–Col.), chairman of the Joint Committee on Printing (JCP), entered into the *Congressional Record* the committee's proposed changes to its Printing and Binding Regulations of April 1977.[71] JCP's proposals redefine printing to include all copying, duplicating, and printing by whatever means. All agencies would be required to submit annual printing and publication plans to JCP, "enumerating equipment, printing environments, planned purchases of equipment and titles and types of publications to be issued, and the means of their distribution."[72] The revisions would also require agencies "to provide projected plans for a second and third year." These plus other adjustments would appear to shift both policy and operating authority for agency publishing programs from the executive to the legislative branch.

OMB's response to the JCP proposals was prompt and predictable. On December 12, 1983, David Stockman, director of OMB, wrote Representative Hawkins to protest the stipulation that the Government Printing Office (GPO) would be responsible for distribution of all government publications. First, Stockman said that "dissemination and use of information are integral . . . functions [of each executive] agency."[73] Stockman noted that OMB (OIRA) had "taken a number of actions regarding government publications which make it unnecessary to expand the Joint Committee's activities in this area,"[74] and that OMB's actions "call into question the need for the (proposed) annual three-year plan."[75] Second, OMB disputed JCP's redefinition of printing because it would divorce printing and publication decisions from agency "management of [its] information resources."[76] Third, the proposals would make "GPO the sole gatekeeper for the flow of government information to the public. As a matter of policy, we are opposed to the establishment and perpetuation of government information monopolies."[77] Fourth and fifth, the "budgetary implications" of the proposals are of "major concern" to OMB because they would reduce executive agency revenues while forcing agencies to spend additional "millions of dollars" in order to comply with the new requirements. Sixth, the proposals "ignore" the roles of NTIS, the National Library of Medicine, "and many technical information clearinghouses." Finally, Stockman said:

If literally applied, the regulations would not permit the President to issue a press release or the Supreme Court to issue an opinion, except through GPO and with the approval of JCP. We doubt that the Committee intends this result.[78]

On January 16, 1974, the Federal Publishers Committee, representing "publishing professionals from 120 executive departments . . . agencies and commissions," submitted 10 pages of objections and comments. Two overriding concerns emerged:

> Executive agencies have had little or no part in the drafting of these regulations and inadequate time to study them.
>
> The plan the draft regulations call for will cause additional paperwork, delay, inefficiency and duplication of effort by making executive . . . agencies report to yet another regulator.[79]

A number of individual agencies also submitted lengthy comments and suggestions for change.

On the other hand, ALA supported the JCP proposals. In a letter to JCP dated December 15, 1983, Eileen Cooke said: "the expanded definition of printing is extremely important for the continued effective operation of the depository library program."[80] Cooke noted the increase in the numbers of government publications published by private agents and endorsed the JCP proposal, which would "guarantee [GPO] distribution to depository libraries" of all future publications. ALA also supported the proposal to provide GPO "advance knowledge of all printing procurement orders," as a way to ensure the continued flow of documents to the depositories, and the prohibition against agencies "offering [government] information . . . to private entities for exclusive initial publication."[81]

The debate—essentially a turf fight to determine who controls government information under what circumstances—will undoubtedly continue and may even intensify in 1984.

Other Information Access Activities

Two other information access activities of importance began in 1983. The first was the National Commission on Libraries and Information Science (NCLIS) Blue Ribbon Panel on Archiving Satellite Data, which resulted from President Reagan's decision to investigate the possibility of selling the government's weather- and land-sensing satellites to private industry. The second was the introduction of H.R. 2514 on April 12, 1983, by Representative Doug Walgren (D–Pa.) "to enhance the transfer of technical information to industry, business and the general public by . . . [establishing] a Technical Information Clearinghouse Fund."[82]

A similar bill, S.808, introduced by Senator Bob Packwood (R–Oreg.) on March 31, 1983, was passed by the Senate on April 7, 1983. Both bills would establish a revolving fund of $5 million for the use of NTIS in lean times. During prosperous times, NTIS would be obliged to replenish the fund. As of this writing, H.R. 2514 is pending in the House Energy and Commerce Committee.

Conclusions

What can be deduced from all this activity? First, that our system of governmental checks and balances works—the executive branch acts and Congress reacts, and vice versa. Second, that pressures will continue to mount for accommodation of private sector interests in future deliberations of information policy issues. Third, that neither Congress nor the administration is sure of its proper role and responsibilities with respect to information policy formulation; therefore, we can expect efforts to revise information legislation and regulations to continue in the months ahead. Finally, John Berry's suggestion that ALA's new Access Commission develop and offer to both political parties "information planks for their 1984 platforms" makes good sense. Maybe, just maybe, the commission could elevate the information access debate to the level "where it belongs, at the center of our democratic, electoral process."[83]

Notes

1. James Madison to W. T. Barry, August 4, 1822, cited in *Writings of James Madison*, ed. G. Hunt (New York: Putnam, 1900–1910).
2. Pete Early, "U.S. Tightens Tourniquet on Flow of Paper," *Washington Post*, January 7, 1984, p. A5.
3. Bruce W. Sanford, "The Information-less Age," *Special Libraries* 74 (October 1983): 317–321.
4. "Less Access to Less Information by and about the U.S. Government," No. I. "A 1981 Chronology" (January 1982); No. II. "A 1982 Chronology: January–June" (July 1982); No. III. "A 1982–1983 Chronology: September 1982–December 1983" (January 1984) (Washington, D.C.: American Library Association).
5. Floyd Abrams, "The New Effort to Control Information," *New York Times Magazine*, September 25, 1983, pp. 22–28, 72–73.
6. Marc A. Levin, "Access and Dissemination Issues Concerning Federal Government Information," *Special Libraries* 74 (April 1983): 127–137.
7. Sanford, "The Information-less Age."
8. Robert M. Hayes, "Politics and Publishing in Washington: Are Our Needs Being Met in the 80's?" *Special Libraries* 74 (October 1983): 322–331.
9. John Berry, "America's Access Agenda," *Library Journal* 108 (July 1983): 1290.
10. Hayes, "Politics and Publishing in Washington," pp. 324, 325.
11. Ibid, p. 325.
12. Ronald Reagan, "Memorandum for Federal Employees, Subject: Unauthorized Disclosure of Classified Information" (Washington, D.C.: The White House, August 30, 1983), 2 pp.
13. "Identification and Protection of Unclassified Controlled Nuclear Information," *Federal Register* 48 (April 1, 1983): 13988.
14. Abrams, "The New Effort to Control Information," p. 27.
15. Ibid, p. 73.
16. "Safeguarding National Security Information," Presidential National Security Decision Directive 84, The White House, March 11, 1983, 3 pp.
17. Sanford, "The Information-less Age," p. 319.
18. Ibid., pp. 319, 320.
19. Abrams, "The New Effort to Control Information," p. 26.
20. "Development of an OMB Policy Circular on Federal Information Management; Solicitation of Public Comment," *Federal Register* 48 (September 12, 1983): 40964.
21. Ibid., p. 40964.
22. Ibid., pp. 40964, 40965.
23. Letter from Eileen D. Cooke, director, ALA Washington Office to J. Timothy Sprehe, Office of Information and Regulatory Affairs, Office of Management and Budget, November 10, 1983, 4 pp.
24. Ibid., p. 2.
25. Ibid., p. 3, 4.
26. American Library Association Council, "Resolution on the Right to Know" (Chicago, 1984).
27. _____, "Resolution Regarding OMB's Proposed Circular on Federal Information Management" (Chicago, 1984).
28. "National Security Information," Executive Order 12356, The White House, April 2, 1982.
29. *Congressional Record*, May 19, 1983, pp. S7161–7165.
30. Ibid., pp. S7161, 7162.
31. Ibid., p. S7163.

32. Ibid.
33. Ibid.
34. Ibid., p. S7165.
35. Ibid., p. S7164.
36. Ibid., p. S7165.
37. "Department of State Authorization Act, Fiscal Years 1984 and 1985," 97 Stat. 1017, Public Law 98-164, November 22, 1983 (H.R. 2915).
38. *Congressional Record*, October 20, 1983, pp. S14282–14283.
39. Ibid., p. S14291.
40. Ibid., p. S14286.
41. U.S. Congress Senate, Committee on the Judiciary, *Freedom of Information Reform Act. Report of the Committee on the Judiciary, United States Senate on S.774* (Washington, D.C.: U.S. Government Printing Office, 1983), p. 7.
42. Ibid., p. 8.
43. Ibid., p. 14.
44. Ibid., p. 23.
45. Ibid., p. 26.
46. Ibid., p. 27.
47. Ibid., p. 28.
48. Ibid., p. 30.
49. Ibid., p. 33.
50. Ibid., p. 1.
51. *Congressional Record*, November 17, 1983, pp. S16742–16746.
52. Ibid., p. S16743.
53. Jonathan C. Rose, assistant attorney general, Office of Legal Policy, Department of Justice, Memorandum to the Heads of All Federal Departments and Agencies. Subject: "FOIA Fee Waivers," January 7, 1983, 3 pp.
54. Ibid., p. 2.
55. "AAP Protests Fees for Use of FOIA Documents," *Publishers Weekly*, March 11, 1983, p. 18.
56. Ibid.
57. Ibid. Hayes, "Politics and Publishing in Washington," p. 330.
58. Sanford, "The Information-less Age," p. 321.
59. Abrams, "The New Effort to Control Information," p. 23.
60. "Cut Access to Government Data?" Interview with Antonin Scalia. *U.S. News & World Report*, January 18, 1982, p. 69.
61. Ibid.
62. Ibid.
63. William H. Miller, "Will Someone Leash Corporate Snooping?" *Industry Week*, June 27, 1983, pp. 94, 96.
64. Ibid., p. 96.
65. Tom Richman, "How Much Freedom Is Too Much?" *INC*, June 1982, p. 26.
66. *Congressional Record*, November 7, 1983, p. H9272.
67. Ibid., p. H9273.
68. Ibid.
69. Felicity Barringer, "A Cacophony of Opinions; Congress Must Sift Paperwork Act's Evaluations," *Washington Post*, July 20, 1983, p. A21.
70. Levin, "Access and Dissemination Issues Concerning Federal Government Information," p. 133.
71. *Congressional Record*, November 11, 1983, pp. H9709–H9713.
72. Ibid., p. H9709.
73. Letter, David A. Stockman, director, Office of Management and Budget to the Honorable Augustus F. Hawkins, chairman, Joint Committee on Printing, December 12, 1983, p. 1.
74. Ibid.

75. Ibid., p. 2.
76. Ibid.
77. Ibid.
78. Ibid., p. 4.
79. Letter with enclosure, Robin A. Atkiss, chairman, Federal Publishers Committee, to the Honorable Augustus F. Hawkins, January 16, 1984.
80. Letter, Eileen D. Cooke, director, ALA Washington Office to the Honorable Augustus F. Hawkins, December 15, 1983, p. 1.
81. Ibid., p. 2.
82. H.R. 2514, p. 1.
83. Berry, "America's Access Agenda."

The New Technologies

The Convergence of Computer-Based Library and Learning Systems

Greg Kearsley

Courseware,® Inc.

10075 Carroll Canyon Rd.,
San Diego, CA 92131
619-578-1700

For almost two decades, computer-based library systems and computer-based instruction (CBI) systems have been developing independently of each other. We are only now beginning to see the convergence of these two kinds of automated services in the context of information centers and computer networks. Over the years hardware has become secondary to content, organization, compatibility, reliability, and user acceptance. Today it is increasingly common to find computer-based library and learning systems integrated under a single information resources umbrella. Once a local or remote terminal network of sufficient size is established, the provision of both information and instruction by computer becomes feasible. Furthermore, emerging technologies such as videodisc and videotex make the convergence even more likely.

Parallel Histories

Computer-based instruction systems originated in the early 1960s and were based on time-shared mainframes. (PLATO represents the epitome of a large-scale CBI system.[1]) During the early 1970s, systems began to use minicomputers both for small time-sharing configurations (with 4–32 terminals) and in stand-alone mode. In the late 1970s, CBI using microcomputers began to take hold, originally as stand-alone terminals but later as part of local and remote networks. Systems in use today range from mainframe to microcomputer systems.[2,3]

Highlights

• Although computer-based instruction systems and library technology come from separate lines of development, they have many similarities.

• The increasing availability of microcomputers and networks is driving the convergence of computer-based information and instruction systems.

• Current examples of integrated library/learning centers provide a variety of different models.

• Newly emerging technologies, such as videodisc and videotex, are likely to encourage the development of multifunction information centers.

Automated library systems passed through a similar evolution of hardware stages.[4] Originally implemented on large time-sharing mainframes, these systems eventually became available on mini- and microcomputers. Along with this evolution, the systems became more affordable and available. Stand-alone (i.e., microcomputer-based) CBI and automated library systems can now be bought for under $10,000 complete with all hardware and software.

Early CBI and library automation software consisted of relatively unsophisticated programs that performed one basic major function (e.g., tutorials, testing, cataloging, or checkout). Today's systems generally feature software packages with a wide range of integrated functions. Modern CBI systems support instructional presentations as well as perform such functions as student management, lesson and graphics creation, and serve as multimedia interfaces. Similarly, current automated library systems provide for a diverse range of functions, including cataloging, circulation, bibliographic search, and patron access files. In the case of microcomputer-based systems, complete software packages are offered by many vendors for most of the popular machines.

CBI and automated library systems share commonalities in other respects. Both primarily involve data base applications. In the case of CBI, the data base consists of lessons, tests, and student performance data; with library systems, catalog records, abstracts, and circulation or patron data. Input and output of information are generally more important than computation, although such activities as bibliographic search and simulation can require substantial computational power. Finally, both fields are highly programmatic in their development, with advances being based more on experiences (collective and individual) than theory.

Organizations are now faced with a variety of alternatives. There are systems designed for large mainframes (e.g., NOVIS, IIAS/IIPS), minicomputer systems (e.g., ILS, TICCIT), and microcomputer systems (e.g., LIBRA, PASS). Various kinds of services can be bought on a subscription basis (e.g., OCLC, PLATO, DIALOG).

Some systems have adapted to the changes in the computer world. For example, the PLATO system is still based on a large mainframe but uses microcomputer-based terminals. Furthermore, certain PLATO courseware is available on popular microcomputers (e.g., Apple, Atari, and IBM). Similarly, OCLC continues to be a mainframe system but can be accessed by personal computers. Thousands of personal computer owners use information services such as DIALOG and BRS in their offices or homes. The affordability of microcomputers and the relative ease of connecting them to networks have made all these developments possible.

Some Examples of Computer-Based Library/Learning Centers

Computer-based library/learning centers can take a number of different forms, depending on the type of organization and the needs of the users. The information center at the IBM Santa Teresa Laboratory provides a model of an integrated library/learning facility in an industrial setting.[5] The center meets a wide range of user needs, including access to technical documentation, training, statistical analysis, and data base retrieval. It also plays an important role in career development and offers more than 850 multimedia courses that include slide/tape, video, and CBI. All of the computer programs (library and CBI) run on IBM mainframes located at the facility. An online bibliographic system was developed using an IBM information retrieval system called STAIRS. Since most professionals at the Santa Teresa Lab have terminals in their offices, they are able to use information center services without leaving their desks.

An example of integrated learning and library centers in an academic setting is found at Mission College in Santa Clara, California. The library and learning centers share the same computer system; however, in contrast to the Santa Teresa facility, where the instructional and information services are totally integrated, at Mission College the two centers are physically separate. Also the learning center does not provide direct instruction (i.e., CBI); instead it provides management of instructional materials (computer-managed instruction). Instructional materials are entered into a courseware data base to track the use of materials. The library system is based on a software package (ULISYS) and is used for online searching and circulation records. The computer system is a DEC 11/70 with a combination of video display and hard copy terminals.

The learning resource centers located at most major army posts have two completely separate systems for learning and library functions. These centers provide hundreds of courses using videotape, audiocassettes, filmstrips, and text. Some of the centers have PLATO terminals to provide CBI. It would be quite possible to have another computer system to manage the offline learning materials or to tap the Army Pentagon Library system (which uses ILS) via telecommunications.

Many public and school libraries are making substantial use of microcomputers for both learning and library functions. The library at Cumberland College, in Williamsburg, Kentucky, provides a good example.[6] Microcomputers are used by students for programming assignments, tutorials developed by the chemistry, religion, and education departments, and game playing. The faculty uses microcomputers for test creation and research via DIALOG searches. The library staff uses them to connect with OCLC for cataloging, to locate books for interlibrary loan through SOLINET, and for bookkeeping purposes.

The variety of approaches currently emerging for library/learning information centers reflects the diversity in institutional requirements. Factors such as organization size, number of users, availability of computer equipment, and the presence of knowledgeable staff determine the approach taken. For individuals who have micro-computers equipped with suitable communications capability in their office or home, there are information services, such as DIALOG or BRS, and instructional networks, such as PLATO. And, as courseware in the form of diskettes becomes increasingly available, significant changes will take place in the way instructional services are delivered in terms of facilities, occupational roles, and document forms.

Common Problems

Computer-based library and learning centers have encountered similar problems with content selection, organization, compatibility, reliability, and user acceptance.

In CBI systems, it is generally not desirable or economically feasible to put entire courses online, so some rules are needed to make selections. Instructors usually choose basic concepts or introductory materials, but such rules are at best arbitrary. In the library domain, although new acquisitions or the most frequently used items are often chosen for automation, the selection rule is similarly arbitrary.

The implementation of a computer-based library or learning system invariably introduces organizational changes. First, staff needs to be trained to run these systems. There are also new roles for staff. For example, instructors in CBI systems provide individual tutoring assistance and manage student progress rather than teach as they would in a classroom. Librarians help patrons use the systems and manage information processing or retrieval activities rather than actually performing search or cataloging functions. Computer-based library or learning systems often necessitate close interaction with data processing departments, blurring organizational lines. Furthermore, when the two systems are integrated in information centers, the functions of training, library, and data processing departments may be merged.

Compatibility is a problem that has plagued all realms of computer use. In CBI, courseware developed on one system is not transportable to another unless the same programming language and equipment are involved. The use of such languages as BASIC or PILOT helps, since courseware written in these languages can be run on a wide variety of machines with minor modifications. Courseware that involves sophisticated capabilities such as dynamic graphics or touch input is not likely to be transportable. With automated library systems, circulation or retrieval records developed for one system generally are not transportable to another. However, the widespread use of the MARC format and OCLC helps establish compatibility standards in computer-based library systems that do not exist for CBI.

Reliability is another classic problem across all fields of computing. The early time-sharing systems were inherently unreliable due to saturation and communications problems. Mini- and microcomputers have led to systems that are almost as dependable as cars, telephones, or TV sets. However, problems with unreliable software still arise from poor design and inadequate testing. This type of unreliability is likely to be with us for some time, since it stems from human rather than hardware failures. The use of high-level programming languages and program generators that minimize "bugs" should help both CBI and library software.

Finally, there is the issue of user acceptance. One of the major obstacles to achieving widespread user acceptance of either CBI or library systems in the past was the "unfriendliness" of the software interfaces, i.e., programs that were difficult to learn and cumbersome to use. In the past few years a great deal of attention has been paid to the human factors in computer interaction,[7,8] and recently designed software is much easier to use than older software. This includes CBI and library programs.

These problems are just beginning to become tractable, after two decades of computer-based learning and library systems development. The emergence of inexpensive microcomputers has significantly speeded up the evolutionary cycle by making systems and software widely available. However, the five major categories of problems just discussed do not magically go away with microcomputers. In fact, the easy availability of microcomputers and the pressure to computerize exacerbate the frequency and magnitude of these problems.

The Future

Just as the easy availability of microcomputers can aggravate existing problems, it also can be a great boon to integrating computer-based library and learning centers. The same microcomputer can easily run CBI or library programs stored on diskettes or shared from a central data base. As microcomputers become available en masse, the critical number of terminals needed for an automated library/learning center will be easily achieved. Furthermore, since the terminals could just as well be in someone's office in a remote location, instruction and information services can be distributed economically.

The emerging technologies of videodisc and videotex will undoubtedly facilitate integration of instruction and information services. Videodisc has already been widely used for education and training and is currently being explored in a number of library applications, including the Library of Congress.[9,10] Because of the tremendous information storage capacity plus the interactive capabilities of videodisc, it is a natural technology for integrated library/learning applications.

Videotex offers similar potential benefits. Microcomputers and television sets with appropriate interfaces can be used to provide learning or information services. Videotex has been successfully implemented for library and learning applications in England and Europe. Although videotex systems have not yet become popular in North America, information retrieval services such as DIALOG and BRS, and information utilities such as the SOURCE and COMPUSERVE, could evolve into full-fledged videotex systems. Videotex systems are equally well suited to instructional or information-delivery functions.

As shown in Figure 1, in an integrated information network of the future, stand-alone microcomputers might connect directly to remote courseware data bases, videotex services, or information retrieval systems via telecommunications. Use of such remote services would likely be on a subscription basis with an hourly usage charge. The microcomputers could also connect to local networks within the organization that contain shared courseware or bibliographic data bases. An information services management system would monitor use of such resources for internal accounting. Finally, the microcomputers would use local courseware/data bases in the form of diskettes or videodiscs. Local materials could be purchased commercially or created within the organization. Note that exactly the same delivery equipment (i.e., microcomputers) would be used for both instructional and information functions; only the nature of the software and data bases would distinguish between traditionally different domains.

In summary, computer-based library and learning systems are on a converging path, driven by the increasing prevalence of microcomputers and networks and hastened by the presence of other technologies such as videodisc and videotex. One of the implications of this convergence is that practitioners and researchers in the CBI and library automation domains must become more familiar with one another's applications. There is a great deal of experience and expertise in the two fields that could be profitably shared.

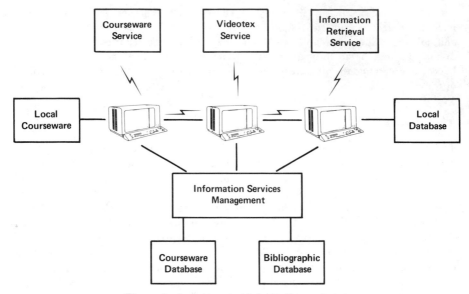

Figure 1. An integrated information network.

Notes

1. S. G. Smith and B. A. Sherwood, "Educational Uses of the PLATO Computer System," *Science* 162 (1982): 73–77.
2. G. Kearsley, *Computer-Based Training* (Reading, Mass.: Addison-Wesley, 1983).
3. J. Chambers and J. Sprecher, "Computer-Based Instruction: Current Trends and Critical Issues," *Communications of the ACM*, June 1980, pp. 332–342.
4. G. W. Lundeen and C. H. Davis, "Library Automation," in *Annual Review of Information Science and Technology*, ed. by M. E. Williams (White Plains, N.Y.: Knowledge Industry Publications, 1982).
5. K. T. Quinn, "The Information Center—Another Perspective," *Online*, July 1982, pp. 11–23.
6. J. Riley, "Computers in the Library," *T.H.E. Journal*, November 1983, pp. 123–124.
7. S. K. Card, T. P. Moran, and A. Newell, *The Psychology of Human-Computer Interaction* (Hillsdale, N.J.: Laurence Erlbaum, 1982).
8. G. Kearsley and M. J. Hillelsohn, "Human Factors Considerations for Computer-Based Training," *Journal of Computer-Based Instruction*, May 1982, pp. 74–84.
9. G. Kearsley, "Instructional Videodisc," *ASIS Perspectives*, November 1983.
10. C. Sneed, "The Videodisc Revolution: What's Ahead for Libraries?" *Wilson Library Bulletin*, November 1980, pp. 186–238; and M. Dennis, "The Videodisc as a Pilot Project of the Public Archives of Canada," *Videodisc/Videotex*, Summer 1981, pp. 154–161.

The New Technologies

The Impact of New Technology on Library Organization

Hugh C. Atkinson

Librarian

University of Illinois at Urbana-Champaign,
1408 W. Gregory Dr., Urbana, IL 61801

In most libraries, a separate organizational unit is required to work with the bibliographic utilities—Online Computer Library Center (OCLC), the Research Libraries Group/Research Libraries Information Network (RLG/RLIN), University of Toronto Library Automation System (UTLAS), and Washington Library Network (WLN). It can be a subsection of the cataloging department, a completely separate unit, or some variation of that pattern. The reasons most often given are outlined by Morita and Gapen in *Library Reviews and Technical Services*[1] and by Atkinson and Stenstrom in *Austerity Management in Academic Libraries*.[2] The main reasons, of course, are more efficient and higher output at lower cost than in the traditional library organization.

Highlights
- A 1977 survey indicates a trend among libraries toward the formation of a rapid cataloging unit.
- Decentralization of online data base searching will have to wait until more staff (not likely) or more sophisticated self-service microcomputer-based programs become available.
- Online reference services require a system or structure of formal appointments to replace the traditional "walk-in" approach to the reference interview.
- Patrons have always demonstrated a strong preference for either specialized or small local library units.
- The organizational structure of the future does seem to require an increasing number of smaller decentralized units, with a new kind of central administrator.

The Cataloging Department

In the past, the cataloging department did some original cataloging and some using Library of Congress copy as a basis. The primary difference between traditional and rapid cataloging units is not in the most obvious organizational patterns or work flow arrangements, although these certainly have had an impact. Rather, the perception of goals is different in a traditional cataloging department, which is primarily a professional organization, from that of a rapid cataloging unit, which is basically a clerical unit.

In the first case, the primary goal is to provide access to the library's collections in a format that meets national standards and local needs. This provision of access includes a commitment to a sufficiently high level of production to avoid a large backlog. But production is only one of its goals. The goal of the rapid cataloging unit, on the other hand, is simply to match as many items as possible to the records of the bibliographic utility. The unit also provides bibliographic access, but high-volume processing is the main goal; the intellectual activity of providing access is a lesser one. Thus, the primary areas of focus set the two departments apart. An attitudinal divergence rather than some other disparity in organization or approach is responsible for the great difference. Of course, an attitudinal difference does mean a different work flow and organizational pattern.

Rather than being an organization composed of professional librarians with some clerical support, as is the case in the cataloging department, the rapid cataloging unit is typically a clerical unit, often but not always directed by a professional cataloger. Within a relatively strict set of parameters, the unit matches book with record and makes minor modifications to adapt the record to the particular item at hand. It may also generate the local call number, but because that number is most often given as part of the proposed record, the main effort is to make modifications to meet the sequence on the library shelves.

The rapid cataloging unit almost never modifies the intellectual content of the record. That is, it almost never changes subject headings or added entries except as demanded by local practice. In such cases, changes are not made because of an intellectual commitment to a national standard but rather in a routine way, rearranging data already present on the record of the utility. In the end, the staff of the rapid cataloging unit reads little more than the title page of each item and may comprehend even less.

But in the original cataloging department, the staff must ascertain what the book is about, make an intellectual judgment as to the appropriate subject headings, ascertain the appropriate form of entry and the content of that form, and determine whether to use Library of Congress copy or that of another national library. In practice, the adaptation or editing of Library of Congress copy by an original cataloging department usually means many more changes than the adaptation of that same record by a rapid cataloging unit. In fact, the rapid cataloging unit does not do any cataloging and almost always passes on to a cataloger any item not found in the bibliographic utility.

Costs are decidedly less per item processed in a rapid cataloging unit than in almost all of the original and professional cataloging departments. The return for high production and lower cost is relatively small changes in format and a lack of absolute uniformity. And in some senses, local variations and the meeting of local needs are sacrificed in deference to standard national headings, especially in subject heading work.

A careful look at the work of the best cataloging departments in the United States reveals that it is not the national standard catalog variations and forms of heading and descriptive cataloging lost by the wholesale adaptation and use of edited records but rather the lack of subject access that is most noticeable in catalogs primarily derived by rapid cataloging units. Since the national libraries are at their weakest in providing adequate, up-to-date, and useful subject headings, the loss of good cataloging is most obvious there. However, over the last 20 years, so many catalog departments chose to concentrate on bibliographic control and descriptive cataloging rather than bibliographic access and analysis by subject that the loss is much less noticeable than might otherwise be the case or than would today be the case in England or on the European continent. Peter Spyers-Duran, in his survey of libraries in 1977, noted that a fair percentage of libraries had moved to the formation of a rapid cataloging unit, and that trend seems to be even more prevalent today.[3]

The Reference Department

The next most obvious impact by the newer technologies has been on the organization of library reference departments. The rise of online reference services, such as the American Chemical Society's C A Compendensates, the American Biological Association's Biosys, and the data bases of the U.S. Office of Education and National Technical Information Service, to name just a few of the many hundred services available, has provided a new and valuable reference tool.

Until recently (and often even now), the intervention of a trained librarian or other searcher with a high degree of skill was necessary before a patron could perform a satisfactory search. Online reference services require not only more staff but a system or structure of formal appointments to replace the traditional "walk-in" approach to the reference interview. Because new data bases require a knowledge of the subject or at least its language, not all members of a reference department can perform all searches. It may be better to decentralize online data base searching to various branch, departmental, and subject libraries, but that will have to wait until more staff is available (not likely) or more sophisticated "self-service" microcomputer-based programs become available for patrons to do their own searching.

No matter where it is found in libraries, automation demands closer analysis of work. In cataloging departments, that analysis suggested the separation of books that could be cataloged quickly, easily, and routinely by clerical staff from the items that had to be processed much more slowly and with more intellectual effort by a professional staff. The reference encounter also can be divided into three categories: first, activities that demand a significant block of time, such as an interview; second, professionally assisting patrons in the use of traditional reference sources; and third, the large volume of reference service that can be provided by upper-level clerical staff or perhaps even by those with somewhat less sophisticated training.

In addition to the formulation of a complex search, the provision of online service requires dialing the data bases and paying some fee for the service itself. Most directional and basic assistance questions can be handled by clerical staff. In more advanced departments, a patron may encounter at the reference desk a library technical assistant who answers the patron's question within a limited range of parameters or refers the patron to a data base searcher or a reference librarian. Such "information desk" or "ready reference" assistance will probably become more common in the near future.

The continued development of microcomputer-based assistance programs to enable a patron to search the large complex data bases without professional assistance may well change the organizational pattern again. However, as has been experienced with reference work using the traditional book and serial-based reference sources, the professional reference librarian must be able to intervene in cases where the preplanned program does not work, or where the patron's needs are so particular that the generalized program is inappropriate, or to carry the search beyond the limits of the microcomputer and its bibliographic assistance program.

Changes in Organizational Structure

Specialization

There has also been a series of administrative changes in libraries. One of the most common provides for an administrator of the outlying libraries or branches. Another provides for an administrator of the main library. Both report to the library director. In the traditional organizational pattern, technical services are organized under one head and public services or reader services under another. Both report to a chief librarian.

This reorganization was brought about by the realization that arbitrary divisions of labor within a library by reference, circulation, cataloging, or acquisitions do not meet patrons' needs for information or even for books or journals. The need for information is not related to the step in the library process at which the information is being handled. It is more likely to be met by those specializing by subject or by form (history or maps or government documents) than by those specializing in the acquisitions of everything, or the circulation of everything. Many large public libraries that have general neighborhood collections and large and specialized collections in the main library appear to have organization by geography. In fact, the geographic organization may be more accidental than substantial, with collections for browsing separated from specialized and research collections in the main library.

The Transfer to Online Systems

Most probably, the future will bring further reorganization, as libraries strive to provide more service with stable or shrinking budgets. The most obvious will occur because of the continued transfer to online systems of library record keeping and procedures. Online circulation is now commonplace in American libraries, and the online catalog is fast becoming so. Although not as universal as circulation or the use of the bibliographic utilities, online reference services are becoming far less rare. Thus, within the next decade most libraries' record keeping and access systems will be based on online computer systems.

A major effect on library organization will be to remove the patterns related to distance from the catalog, for example. One of the hallmarks of online systems is that they are distance independent; and they deliver copies of the record to a terminal at any location rather than relying on the single *locus*, as do manual and paper-based systems. One of the primary reasons for the traditional organizational patterns has been the necessary reliance on large, single-copy, paper files—the catalog, the order file, and the serials check-in file. The departments that use those files have to be within relatively short walking distance of them. With an online catalog, a cataloger does not have to be next to the catalog. The cataloger is as close to the catalog as he or she is to any terminal. Therefore, other factors that affect library organization will become more important than position relative to the catalog. The same is true for acquisitions and for serials check-in files.

Decentralization

Patrons have always demonstrated a strong preference for either specialized or small local library units.[4] The ideal library is one with one or two librarians, one or two library clerks, a handful of student assistants, a homogeneous identifiable clientele, and a collection large enough to satisfy that clientele. Whether the library is a neighborhood branch or a specialized unit on an academic campus, the organizational pattern of the future is likely to be a decentralized one.

Decentralization does not necessarily imply a "flat" organizational structure. It can mean a sharp pyramid with many administrative levels. The decentralizing trend of adding to the duties of those who service a collection the responsibilities of choosing and indexing the collection seems to be the natural outgrowth of the online system.

Over the last two decades, large public libraries have clearly moved from an almost standard policy of having all branch collections be full duplicates of the main library to a much more patron-centered system. In many cases, the main library selected items for the branches. The present pattern allows each branch to choose what it needs or considers appropriate for its clientele. The next step would clearly be to decentralize the cataloging necessary after the application of the bibliographic utility. The present structure of forming a unit devoted to using a bibliographic utility will remain only insofar as it continues to be cost-effective to keep terminals to the bibliographic utility fully occupied. When the terminal and the connect time (modem, lines, and the like) are no longer as costly as they are today, requiring an extensive and relatively large throughput to justify every additional terminal modem or line, then that too will be a decentralized unit.

The Central Administrator

The organizational structure of the future does seem to require an increasing number of smaller decentralized units. In academic libraries these are special libraries by subject or form and in public libraries by neighborhood or by ethnic culture. These changes will require a new kind of central administrator, a coordinator or evaluator rather than a supervisor, similar to the collection development officers beginning to appear in academic libraries and slowly moving into the public libraries. These are library administrators whose primary responsibility is not the purchase of individual items but the evaluation of the collection as a whole.

Decentralization of the efforts of acquisitions departments on one hand and the selectors in the departmental and branch libraries on the other set a pattern for similar activities in the fields of cataloging, reference, children's work, and other specialties within librarianship. Indeed, it has not been uncommon for public libraries to employ a central coordinator of children's services whose functions are similar to the academic collection development officer. That type of administrator is in charge of the activity, not the people. The new manager does not supervise personnel but rather provides the intellectual administration of the function.

The same kind of need arises in decentralized cataloging and reference as in decentralized selection of materials and children's work. A director of library catalogs will probably train librarians in the various branches who spend some portion of their time cataloging. The director will have official responsibility for quality control, to see that the library meets national standards for cataloging. He or she will probably administer the library's authority files and provide for the design of new systems. The coordinator of reference services will have similar responsibilities.

In a well-run, collegial, and participatory organization, central administrators will work closely with librarians in the branches for a continuously improving library service. This will clearly demand an extraordinarily talented administrative staff in order to avoid conflict between those who are actually performing the work in the various smaller units and those who coordinate the work in the central agencies, on the one hand, and between the line administrators who are in charge of the various branches and the central coordinating officers on the other.

Conclusion

There will no doubt be a long period of negotiation and experimentation with a good number of failures and retreats as the library community slowly sorts out what is to become traditional library activity, only to be changed again by the impact of some newer and different technology, sociology, or politics. One can already see the beginnings of new pressures and new organizational patterns with the advent of high-density optical digital discs, carbon fiber optics, and satellite communications, which provide even more distance independence and the potential for storage of large volumes of material in many remote locations so inexpensively that the very existence of a central store of data can be open to doubt. The rise of good, inexpensive, rapid, long-distance electronic document transmission may not only change the organizational patterns of individual libraries but may well change the patterns of librarianship as well. What is certain is that library organization will change, and that it will be different from what we expect.

Notes

1. Ichiko Morita and G. Kaye Gapen, "A Cost Analysis of the Ohio College Library Center On-Line Shared Cataloging System in the Ohio State University Libraries," *Library Reviews and Technical Services* 21 (1977): 286–301.
2. Hugh C. Atkinson and Patricia F. Stenstrom, "Automation in Austerity," in *Austerity Management in Academic Libraries* (New York: Scarecrow Press, 1984), pp. 277–285.
3. Peter Spyers-Duran, "The Effects of Automation on Organizational Change, Staffing, and Human Relations in Catalog Departments," in *Requiem for the Card Catalog Management Issues in Automated Cataloging*, ed. Daniel Dove, Joseph Kembrough, and Peter Spyers-Duran (Westport, Conn.: Greenwood Press, 1979), pp. 29–39.
4. Shoham Snuneth, "A Cost-Preference Study of the Decentralization of Academic Library Services," *Library Research* 4 (1982): 174–194.

Federal Agency and Federal Library Reports

National Commission on Libraries and Information Science

Seventh & D Sts. S.W., Suite 3122, Washington, DC 20024
202-382-0840

Toni Carbo Bearman
Executive Director

Dorothy Pollet Gray
Research Associate

The National Commission on Libraries and Information Science (NCLIS) was established by PL 91-345 in 1970 as a permanent, independent agency in the executive branch. Its mandate is to advise the president and Congress on national library and information policies and plans. The commission has four major roles: (1) *resident expert* for the executive and legislative branches; (2) *"honest broker,"* bringing together agencies in all branches and levels of government to focus on problems of common interest; (3) a *forum* for the entire library/information community, including both public and private sectors; and (4) a *catalyst* to assist in getting programs implemented. The commission's continuing overall goal is to help provide the people of the United States with equal opportunity of access to the library and information services they need.

For NCLIS, 1983 was an extremely productive year as well as a time of change. In late 1982, the commission's third chairperson and four other new members were confirmed by the Senate. They are Elinor Hashim, supervisor, Reference and Technical Services at Perkin-Elmer Corporation, Norwalk, Connecticut (chairperson); John E. Juergensmeyer, attorney, Juergensmeyer and Associates, Elgin, Illinois; Jerald C. Newman, president, chief administrative officer and trustee, The Bowery Savings Bank, New York, New York; Byron Leeds, vice president, Publishers Phototype, Inc., Carlstadt, New Jersey; and Julia Li Wu, head librarian, Virgil Junior High School, Los Angeles, California. Dr. Sarah G. Bishop was named deputy director of NCLIS in June.

Three meetings of the commission were held during 1983: in April, during National Library Week in Washington, D.C.; in June, in conjunction with the Special Libraries Association conference in New Orleans; and in October, in conjunction with the American Society for Information Science annual meeting in Arlington, Virginia. In February the commission moved from its original headquarters on K Street to a federal office building in southwest Washington, D.C. Office automation needs were studied thoroughly during the year, and a comprehensive office automation system was selected and installed.

1983 Program Highlights

In addition to its ongoing responsibilities in assisting the executive and legislative branches and the library/information community, the commission worked on three major program areas in FY 1983: (1) technology and productivity, (2) improving the dissemination of federal information, and (3) improving library and information services to meet changing needs.

The commission discussed the reports of three major NCLIS task forces during its 1983 meetings. The Task Force on Library Services to Cultural Minorities, the Task Force on Community Information and Referral Services (CI&R), and the Task Force on the Role of the Special Library in Nationwide Networks and Cooperative Programs completed their work and presented a total of 68 recommendations to the commission. NCLIS will now work with appropriate associations and agencies to implement the recommendations. The Cultural Minorities and CI&R task force reports were published during the year; next year NCLIS and the Special Libraries Association will publish *The Role of the Special Library in Networks and Cooperatives*. These task force reports represent a culmination of several years of study and analysis by a total of 39 experts from the library and information field.

Cooperative Activities

As part of its continuing responsibility to serve as resident expert to the Congress on policy issues in the library and information field, NCLIS has been instrumental in assisting the House Subcommittee on Postsecondary Education in evaluating the Library Services and Construction Act (LSCA). During 1983, NCLIS continued to assist in the development of specifications for the reauthorization of LSCA to strengthen the legislation administratively and substantively. The commission also helped identify witnesses for hearings the subcommittee held in April. NCLIS has been asked to assist with the Senate's review of this legislation in FY 1984.

The commission has also been asked to assist the Subcommittee on Postsecondary Education with reauthorization and amendments for the Higher Education Act (HEA) titles having an impact on libraries. Hearings are planned for 1984 and comments on HEA are being solicited.

Following President Reagan's recommendation to transfer the nation's weather and land-sensing satellites to private ownership, NCLIS was asked to advise the Department of Commerce on the archiving of data from these satellites. Under an interagency agreement, NCLIS assembled a distinguished blue ribbon panel composed of scientists, archivists, historians, and other experts from the public and private sectors who are knowledgeable about the issues surrounding the preservation and use of these types of data. The panel's objective is to provide guidance on the information policy issues related to archiving the satellite-produced data. The panel will consider the interests of the public, including the scientific, historical, and archival communities, and the needs of other users of satellite data in both the public and private sectors. At the panel's first meeting, on September 12, the group formulated tentative suggestions for Landsat and Metsat data. At its second and final meeting, on November 28, the panel agreed to a set of findings and recommendations. The commission will present its report to the Commerce Department early in 1984.

The commission assisted the Executive Office of the President with the White House Conference on Productivity held in Washington, D.C., September 22-23. NCLIS involved the library and information community in this effort in several ways. The commission prepared a briefing paper on the information component of productivity for distribution to all participants in the preconferences and main conference; it provided the names of experts and helped form panels for the preconferences; and it provided materials for distribution to make the participants aware of library and information concerns in relation to productivity. NCLIS commissioners and staff also participated in the national conference.

NCLIS continued to work with agencies in the executive branch to encourage and monitor the implementation of the 64 resolutions of the first White House Conference on Library and Information Services (WHCOLIS). As in the past, the NCLIS chairperson corresponded with the heads of agencies to learn of progress in the implementation of WHCOLIS resolutions pertaining to each agency.

There were numerous opportunities during 1983 for the commission to promote more effective communication among the members of the library and information community. For example, NCLIS continued to convene monthly meetings of the Public Affairs Roundtable and to compile semiannual statistical updates for staff of the National Center for Education Statistics and representatives from key library and information associations. The commission continued its membership on the Organizing Committee of the Coalition for Literacy, and it continued to assist Barbara (Mrs. George) Bush with her visits to libraries across the country, where she speaks on behalf of literacy and reading.

Technology and Productivity

Under a pioneering public sector/private sector partnership, NCLIS was assisted in a new project by outstanding young librarians from the IBM Corporation's Thomas J. Watson Research Center. The project's objectives are to examine the anticipated information environment of the coming years, assess the impact of technology on various segments of the population, and discover how the new information technologies can be used to promote a more productive society. The first report, available to the public early in 1984, discusses microcomputers, videodiscs, teletext, videotex, cable TV, satellite transmissions, and online data bases as the technologies expected to have the greatest impact on society in the future. The second report will examine the impact of the new technologies on knowledge workers, those whose work produces information rather than a specific product or service. Information is being gathered on ways in which the new technologies can make us more productive as a nation.

Improving Library Services

NCLIS continued to cooperate closely with the National Agricultural Library and other groups within the Department of Agriculture (USDA) in the National Rural Information Services Development Program. On August 4, Chairman Hashim presented a certificate of achievement and appreciation from the commission to Jason Hardman of Elsinore, Utah (pop. 680), for calling national attention to library service needs of people in rural areas. The ceremony was held in the Oval Office of the White House, where Hardman presented President Reagan with a sign bearing the national library symbol. Last year Hardman testified at the joint congressional hearing called "The Information Needs of Rural America—the Roles of Libraries and Information Technology," which was coordinated by the commission. NCLIS has prepared the record of this hearing for publication in 1984 in conjunction with the Department of Agriculture. At the 1983 annual meeting of the American Society for Information Science, NCLIS and USDA cosponsored a session entitled "Information, Innovation, and Productivity in Rural America." The commission has held preliminary discussions with USDA regarding the establishment of an advisory board on rural information needs.

As directed by its enabling legislation, NCLIS is investigating the current state of library and information services to an aging population. Literature searches and analyses have been conducted for reports of needs assessments pertaining to the elderly. NCLIS will work with the Administration on Aging to obtain information from older persons who are potential users of library and information services. A preliminary report on the library and information needs of senior citizens will be released in 1984.

International Activities

In January 1983, the NCLIS executive director served as the U.S. representative to the meeting of the Intergovernmental Council for the UNESCO General Information Program (UNESCO/PGI). In June, the commission assumed responsibility for the U.S. National Committee (USNC) for UNESCO/PGI. Official records were consolidated at NCLIS headquarters; new delegates and alternates to USNC were appointed by the member organizations; and an election of officers, bureau members, and at-large members was conducted. The first plenary meeting of USNC under the NCLIS secretariat took place on June 2. The USNC Bureau met September 22 to prepare the committee's response to the UNESCO draft program and budget for 1984–1985. The USNC has also been asked to advise the State Department in its new overall evaluation of U.S. participation in UNESCO.

During 1983 the commission played a leadership role in a new effort to coordinate participation of the U.S. library and information community in international organizations and programs. NCLIS is serving on the steering committee of an ad hoc international information group originally convened under the auspices of the Council on Library Resources. To further this effort, NCLIS staff put together a summary of U.S. focal points for the principal international library and information organizations. The commission continued to expand its coverage and understanding of international information issues that have implications for the library and information community. At its 1983 meetings the commission received briefings from several experts in the area of reciprocity and transborder data flow.

New Programs

At its October meeting, the commission appointed an ad hoc subcommittee, chaired by Commissioner Gordon Ambach, to study the report *A Nation at Risk*, which was prepared by the National Commission on Excellence in Education, and to present its findings and recommendations for NCLIS at the January 1984 meeting. In addition, NCLIS will continue to work closely with the Department of Education in examining how libraries contribute to excellence in education and lifelong learning and in emphasizing the importance of the "Fourth R"—the ability to find and use information through library and information services.

During the coming year the commission will build on and expand the major program areas for 1983. For example, in the program area of technology and productivity, NCLIS will examine barriers to use of the new information technologies and ways to expand access to information. In anticipation of launching a major new initiative in FY 1985, NCLIS will prepare an issue paper on the impact of fees on access to information. Other new program thrusts for the coming fiscal years will deal with national information policy and library and information science education.

Educational Resources Information Center (ERIC), 1983

Ted Brandhorst
ERIC Processing and Reference Facility

4833 Rugby Ave., Suite 301
Bethesda, MD 20814
301-656-9723

Despite continued reductions (down 15 percent for 1984) in the budget of its parent agency, the National Institute of Education (NIE), the Educational Resources Information Center (ERIC) has managed to retain its basic structure of 16 decentralized discipline-oriented clearinghouses, supported by contractors in the areas of computer services and micrographics. For a complete list of ERIC components, with addresses and telephone numbers, see the 1983 *Bowker Annual*, p. 100.

Products and Services: New Developments

Resources in Education Price Increase

Resources in Education (RIE), the ERIC system's flagship abstract journal, had its subscription price increased by the U.S. Government Printing Office (GPO) to $95/year in 1983.

Practitioner-Oriented Documents: Priority Status

The ERIC data base has always contained a significant amount of material relevant to educational practitioners. However, late in 1983, in connection with a special Practice File project, practitioner-oriented documents were assigned a high acquisitions and selection priority by ERIC. The results of this action will be seen in the content of *RIE* beginning with the December 1983 issue.

New Target Audience Data Element

Beginning with the January 1984 issue of *RIE*, documents processed for *RIE* will be assigned a "target audience" when such an audience is specified explicitly (or is evident) by the document. The permissible audiences are policymakers, researchers, practitioners, administrators, teachers, counselors, media staff, support staff, parents, and community. This new data element will be searchable online and should assist in limiting search output to material appropriate for the particular searcher.

New Publication Type Codes

Two new publication type codes have been approved for addition to the scheme: "Multilingual/Bilingual Materials (171)" and "Computer Software (101)." The former was implemented in mid-1983; the latter will be implemented in early 1984.

Online Data Entry

All ERIC clearinghouses are now performing data entry by transmitting data online to the ERIC facility. The new system supplants the old optical character recognition (OCR) system and bypasses dependence on the mails for receipt of these data.

New Publications

A new, tenth edition of the *Thesaurus of ERIC Descriptors* was published by Oryx Press early in 1984. This edition contains all ERIC terminological additions, changes, and deletions since the ninth edition was published in 1981. The price is $45 (including postage if prepaid).

A new edition of the *Directory of ERIC Microfiche Collections* was published by the GPO in early 1984. It lists 779 organizations with ERIC microfiche collections. The arrangement is geographic by country, state, and city.

In October 1983, the National Assessment of Educational Progress (NAEP) published a comprehensive 237-page bibliography, *National Assessment of Educational Progress, 1969–1983: A Bibliography of Documents in the ERIC Database*, announcing 575 documents and journal articles either directly produced by the NAEP or dealing with the NAEP and produced by others. The bibliography represents a record of the NAEP's accomplishments during the 14 years it was housed at the Education Commission on the States (ECS). Based on documentation collected by the ERIC data base during that period, the compilation serves as an archive of major domestic education documents. Basic arrangement is by specific assessment. Publications by the NAEP are listed separately from those by external organizations. Subject, institution, and personal author indexes are provided. Most of the documents listed in the compilation may be obtained through the regular ERIC channel, the ERIC Document Reproduction Service (EDRS).

Commissions/Task Forces/Study Groups

In 1983 an unusually large number of final reports were submitted by commissions, task forces, and study groups concerned with education, e.g., the National Commission on Excellence in Education, the Congressional Study on Merit Pay, the School

Finance Study, A Study of Schools (Goodlad Study), and the Carnegie Foundation Study of the Condition of Teaching. Extensive coverage of these documents in the popular press generated many requests for copies. In order to process requests expeditiously, ERIC developed small bibliographic information packets pertaining to several of these studies.

Online Computer Searching Survey

The results of a survey of online computer searching released by Infometrics, Inc., in 1983 revealed a strong showing by the ERIC data base. According to the survey:

1 ERIC is the second most used data base offered by DIALOG and BRS.
2 Among all data bases and all vendors, ERIC ranks fourth in total connect time and thirteenth in total revenues (the latter is partially attributable to ERIC's low hourly rate (no royalties need be paid to the government).
3 Among social science data bases, ERIC is the most used, with three times as much use as the second most used data base.
4 Within academia and government, ERIC is the second most used data base.
5 Within industry, ERIC is the fifteenth most used data base.
6 Within public libraries, ERIC is the fourth most used data base.
7 Within regions of the United States, ERIC ranks in usage as follows: (1) West, (2) Northeast, (3) North Central region, (4) South.

The Library of Congress

Washington, DC 20540
202-287-5000

James W. McClung
Public Affairs Specialist

Numerous important cultural events dominated the year 1983 at the Library of Congress, signaling increased public awareness of the library through its collections and resources, programs, and activities. These events included several major exhibitions and publications, busy seasons of literary and musical programs, many scholarly symposia, and the creation of new facilities and projects. The library also continued to be active in 1983 in the areas of preservation, technical processing, collections development and management, and copyright.

A major exhibition entitled "The American Cowboy" opened at the library in March. President and Mrs. Ronald Reagan led the list of distinguished guests at the reception marking the occasion. The exhibition moved to San Antonio, Texas, in December and, during 1984, will be seen in Denver, Colorado; Calgary, Alberta (Canada); and San Jose, California. Funded by United Technologies Corporation and organized by the library's American Folklife Center, the exhibition attracted both large numbers of visitors to the library and considerable attention in the press. The library published a lavishly illustrated paperbound catalog to accompany the exhibit (available for $18.95 plus $2 for postage and handling from the Library of Congress, Information Office, Box A, Washington, DC 20540), and a hardcover version was published by Harper & Row in the fall (available for $50).

In spring 1983, the Mary Pickford Foundation gave $500,000 to the library, to be funded over a ten-year period, to support screening and related programs, including seminars, lectures, publications, and other educational activities, to further the study and awareness of the history and development of the motion picture. A week-long celebration in May inaugurated the first of the funded programs. Events included the dedication of a film theater in the library in honor of Mary Pickford, an exhibition, a one-day symposium dealing with the life, times, and films of Mary Pickford, and a five-day film series of Mary Pickford and other silent film stars. The new 64-seat theater is located on the third floor of the Madison Building.

A major literary event of the year occurred in November, when 14 distinguished American poets, all of them either chancellors or fellows of the academy, gathered for two evenings of readings in honor of the fiftieth anniversary of the Academy of American Poets. The poets were Robert Fitzgerald, Daniel Hoffman, John Hollander, Stanley Kunitz, William Meredith, James Merrill, W. S. Merwin, Howard Nemerov, Mark Strand, May Swenson, Mona Van Duyn, David Wagoner, Robert Penn Warren, and Richard Wilbur.

Another major fiftieth anniversary observed in 1983 with an exhibition, opening reception, and a major new publication was the Historic American Buildings Survey (HABS). Launched in 1933 as a cooperative endeavor, with the U.S. Department of the Interior's National Park Service as the survey's administrator, the Library of Congress as the depository, and the American Institute of Architects as the adviser, HABS has documented more than 16,000 structures in 50 states, the District of Columbia, Puerto Rico, and the Virgin Islands, producing more than 40,000 measured drawings, 77,000 photographs, and 42,000 pages of written architectural data, all housed in the Library of Congress. The documentation program was expanded in 1969 with the creation of the Historic American Engineering Record, a parallel program with a similar structure, except that the American Society of Civil Engineers serves as adviser. *Historic America: Buildings, Structures and Sites*, published to coincide with the anniversary, includes a list of the more than 16,000 buildings and sites documented by HABS and a dozen interesting, fully illustrated essays. The 708-page publication is available for $29 from the Superintendent of Documents, U.S. Government Printing Office, Washington, DC 20402 (Stock No. 030-000-00149-4).

Two major musical events of 1983 included a week-long celebration marking the sesquicentenary of the birth of Johannes Brahms and the prestigious sixteenth Coolidge Festival of Chamber Music, continuing a series begun by the library's first patron of chamber music, Elizabeth Sprague Coolidge, in 1925. The Brahms International Festival and Conference included the presentation of papers by several world-renowned scholars, concerts by artists from several countries, and a display from the library's large collection of Brahms manuscripts and memorabilia. The sixteenth Coolidge Festival, held over four days in October, offered the world premieres of eight works by four composers from the United States, two from Israel, and one each from Hungary and Japan. All of the works were commissioned by three foundations in the library. The program also included a new production of a 1941 Coolidge commission, Paul Hindemith's *Hérodiade*, with a film prepared by the painter and filmmaker James Herbert.

Preservation

The emphasis in preservation in 1983 was on a three-year pilot program that will use optical disc technology to provide both secondary format preservation and timely access to frequently requested or rare and fragile materials. The program will also evaluate both the applicability of this technology and its costs. There are two portions of the program, one in which print materials will be stored on digital optical discs and one in which nonprint or image-based materials will be stored on analog optical discs, commonly known as videodiscs.

Print materials to be included in the project are selected high-use serials, legal collections, several collections of presidential papers, sheet music, and maps. Document preparation will be an assembly-line process in which materials will be scanned and digitized by a high-speed scanner and then transferred, by a laser writing process, onto the surface of an optical disc. Because of the high resolution of the digital process, the disc will contain substantially all of the information contained in the original. The digitized image will thus be capable of serving as a black-and-white secondary preservation format for the original.

The nonprint materials included in the project are approximately 50,000 images from several collections in the library's Prints and Photographs Division and from the Motion Picture, Broadcasting and Recorded Sound Division, some 90,000 to 100,000 motion picture publicity stills, films and film segments with special color preservation problems, selections from the paper print collection, and two newscasts. Two concerts will also be recorded on compact audio disc. All of the images except for the motion pictures will be copied on 35mm color motion picture film, which will then be used to prepare videodiscs.

Sensitive to the concerns of publishers and copyright owners, the library established an optical disc advisory group of publishers, librarians, and representatives from relevant associations to solicit their cooperation and advice to ensure the success of the program. The group held its first meeting in November.

Other preservation activities of 1983 included the filming by the library's Photoduplication Service of the collection of land ownership maps on 105mm microfiche and experimental microfilming of glass plate negatives. The library agreed to coordinate part of its preservation microfilming activity with the Research Libraries Group (RLG) Cooperative Microfilming Project. In cooperation with RLG members that have selected monographs—U.S. imprints and Americana—published between 1876 and 1900 as an initial target category, the library's Preservation Microfilming Office will film complementary materials in the target period, emphasizing serials and some heavily used historical and genealogical records.

National Library Service for the Blind and Physically Handicapped (NLS/BPH)

A highlight of 1983 for NLS/BPH was the completion of the voice-indexed version of *The Concise Heritage Dictionary*. The 55,000-entry dictionary was narrated in the NLS studio over a two-year period. The 56 four-sided cassettes are housed in five binders, each holding up to 12 cassettes, which occupy only seven inches of shelf space. The voice-indexing technique enables readers to locate dictionary entries more quickly. The American Printing House for the Blind, in Louisville, Kentucky, duplicated copies of the dictionary for NLS network libraries and will also sell the dictionary to blind readers at its production cost of $82.54. *The Concise Heritage Dictionary* is the first recorded dictionary available to blind readers.

In fall 1983, NLS announced publication of a collection of original essays, *That All May Read*. Designed primarily for use in library schools, the new publication will also be of interest to professional librarians. Topics include services in academic, public, and school libraries, international cooperation, education for leadership and research, and the history of NLS. A brief history of U.S. postal laws regarding the blind and physically handicapped and an extensive bibliography are appended. Copies of *That All May Read* are available upon request from the National Library Service for the Blind and Physically Handicapped, Library of Congress, Washington, DC 20542.

During 1983, NLS initiated and funded a contract with the American Library Association for a revision of the 1979 *Standards of Service for the Library of Congress Network of Libraries for the Blind and Physically Handicapped*, completed the first test of an automated magazine subscription merge process, and developed additional test procedures aimed at complete centralization of all mailing list activities. NLS also issued comprehensive procedures common to the functioning of NLS/BPH and the network of nearly 160 libraries that carry out the library's reading program for blind and physically handicapped individuals. These procedures, compiled and published as *Network Library Manual*, contain detailed instructions to ensure efficient delivery of reader services.

In 1983, NLS launched an analysis of its raised-line and raised-dot outline maps of foreign countries and states in the United States. This project was an outgrowth of the First International Symposium on Maps and Graphics. The head of the NLS Consumer Relations Section will chair a working group to compile a bibliography of available literature on the subject.

The Center for the Book

Early in 1983, Simon Michael Bessie of Harper & Row became the new chairperson of the Center for the Book's National Advisory Board and its executive committee. The board's February meeting preceded a luncheon celebrating the fortieth anniversary of the Armed Services Editions.

In May, the center held a symposium on "Radio and Reading," which attracted a diverse group of persons who share an interest in this area. The center's "Read More about It" project was subsequently expanded when the CBS Radio Network broadcast a "Read More about It" message during the All-Star baseball game in July. The televised versions of these messages began their fifth season on CBS Television in fall 1983.

In cooperation with ABC Children's Television, the center launched a new reading promotion campaign featuring Cap'n O. G. Readmore, an animated cat who knows a great deal because he reads so much. The Cap'n, who made his debut in September, will appear in 30-second messages to be broadcast during children's and family programming on ABC.

Other Center for the Book symposia during the year addressed the topics "The U.S. Book Abroad" and "Public Lending Right," the notion that authors are entitled to be compensated for the multiple uses of their books in libraries. Legislation was subsequently introduced in the U.S. Congress to name a commission to study this issue and to file a report after two years. Lecturers sponsored by the center in 1983 were Madeleine L'Engle, who spoke during National Children's Book Week; Harrison E.

Salisbury, who discussed "The Book Enchained"; James D. Hart, director of the Bancroft Library at the University of California at Berkeley, who delivered an illustrated Engelhard lecture on "Fine Printing: The San Francisco Tradition"; and noted book collector William Barlow, Jr., who delivered an Engelhard lecture on book collecting.

At the end of the year, a U.S. congressional concurrent resolution directed Librarian of Congress Daniel J. Boorstin to form a national advisory committee and hire consultants to study the role of the book in the future and the influence that computer and video technologies may have on books, reading, and the printed word. The study will be carried out under the auspices of the Center for the Book, and a report will be submitted to Congress by December 1, 1984.

American Folklife Center

In 1983, the American Folklife Center completed the preparations for and conducted the fieldwork portion of the Pinelands Folklife Project in New Jersey. Working with several New Jersey agencies and the U.S. National Park Service, the center's team of fieldworkers spent two months documenting the Pinelands' diverse human and cultural resources.

The center's Federal Cylinder Project continued developing the initial catalogs to accompany the cylinder collections that have been systematically duplicated and organized since the project began in 1979. A published recording of selected cylinder recordings made with the Omaha tribe in the early years of this century is also being developed. During the summer, the director of the project participated in the one hundred and fifty third pow wow of the Omaha Indians, at which he presented the Omaha Tribe Council copies of early Omaha cylinder recordings.

A major, invitational Washington Meeting on Folk Art was held at the Library of Congress in December under the joint sponsorship of the American Folklife Center and the Museum of American Folk Art in New York City. A recurring theme during the meeting was that to appreciate fully the artistic and cultural significance of an object, one must consider the circumstances under which it was made—when, where, by whom, and for what purpose. The need to define and understand folk art was demonstrated by the presence of approximately 400 folklorists, art historians, collectors, dealers, historians, and folk art enthusiasts who attended the meeting from all parts of the country.

During 1983, the center continued its outreach programs with an ongoing series of lectures, workshops, demonstrations, screenings, and concerts. Several new finding and reference aids were also prepared to help researchers use the collections of the center's Archive of Folk Culture.

Staff, Budget, and Services

As of October 1, 1983, there were 5,308 employees on the staff of the Library of Congress, only a slight increase over 1982. This continues a trend of virtually no growth in the size of the library's staff in the 1980s.

For the fiscal year beginning October 1, 1983, the library has an operating budget of $223,114,000. This is the first library budget under an appropriations act rather than a continuing resolution in four years. Other legislation affecting the library included bills that would restore a tax incentive for the donation of self-generated manuscripts and artwork materials to libraries and museums and that would make the library the repository of videotape recordings of the proceedings of the U.S. Senate.

With the relocation of the staff and collections of the Motion Picture, Broadcasting and Recorded Sound Division and several other administrative offices to the Madison Building, and the opening of a new sales and information counter in early 1983, the occupancy of the new library building was completed. The installation in early fall of the decorative bronze screen over the building's main entrance signaled the completion of all the original contract work on the building. Thus the library's third building project, originally discussed and planned in the mid-1950s, has been completed. Plans continued during the year, and hearings were held to seek funding for the restoration and renovation of the library's two older buildings on Capitol Hill.

During the fiscal year ending September 30, 1983, direct reference services—via telephone, correspondence, or in-person visit—answered 1,524,200 requests, the first significant increase in this figure in this decade. More than 3,013,800 volumes or items were circulated for use within the library, a slight increase, and 152,268 circulated outside the library, the first increase in that figure in recent years. The Congressional Research Service (CRS) responded during the fiscal year to 406,000 research and reference requests, reflecting the legislative, oversight, and representational needs of Congress. During 1983, CRS received permission from Congress to print and publish the *CRS Review* through the U.S. Government Printing Office. The authorization includes distribution to depository libraries and inclusion in the Superintendent of Documents sales program. *CRS Review* is a professional journal that carries primary articles on current issues before Congress, digests many of the latest CRS research studies, and routinely cites reports from the congressional community. Other CRS publications available through the GPO include *Major Legislation of Congress*, the *Digest of Public General Bills and Resolutions*, and *CRS Studies in the Public Domain*.

The library's third annual Cooperative Reference Exchange took place in September. A program designed to develop closer ties between state library and Library of Congress reference staff and to provide a better understanding of how to gain access to the services and resources of both state libraries and the national library, this offering of the exchange attracted 24 reference staff and managers from 20 states, primarily from the western United States.

Collections

Once again, the number of items in the library's collections grew by nearly 1 million in the fiscal year, bringing the new total near 81 million. The Collections Development Office continued to work with other library divisions to revise numerous acquisitions policy statements to clarify the library's responsibilities in these areas and to adjust to changing patterns in publishing. The office also gave high priority to the development of more specific guidelines for determining what categories of materials could be eliminated without compromising the research value of the library's collections.

The project to inventory the library's general collections, a task not undertaken in many years, was more than 35 percent complete by the end of 1983. The inventory continues to yield important dividends to the library. More than 4,500 linear feet of shelf space were emptied by the removal of some 50,000 duplicate or otherwise dispensable volumes, and more than 50,000 obsolete or invalid charge slips were removed from the Loan Division's files. The inventory project staff also identified volumes now known to be missing, about 2 percent of each of the classes surveyed to date. The not-on-shelf rate—the percentage of total books requested that is not available to readers—was cut in half for one of the classes inventoried.

Notable acquisitions in 1983 included a manuscript map of the Battle of Bunker Hill (June 17, 1775), drawn on the verso of two pages of music for colonial-era drinking songs; a survey plat of Frederick County, Virginia, drawn by George Washington when he was 18 years old; and the *Libro dei Globi* (1693), one of only seven known copies, representing the entire output of globe gores by Vincenzo Maria Coronelli. Books added to the collections during the year included Henri Matisse's *Jazz*, the greatest 20th-century illustrated book not heretofore represented in the Library's Rosenwald Collection; the first English translation of Andrea Palladio's *The First Book of Architecture* (London, 1663); and a collection of books of President John Quincy Adams, the first group of presidential association copies to be received in the library in many years. Manuscripts received on deposit included George Gershwin's holograph manuscript of his two-piano arrangement of *An American in Paris* and the personal papers of two figures closely associated with the New Deal, Thomas Corcoran and Robert Jackson.

Cataloging and Networking

The first issues of the new computer-generated microfiche publication of the *National Union Catalog (NUC)*, announced in 1982, were sent to subscribers in 1983. In addition to price and storage economies, the new register/index format offers multiple access points to the records. The *NUC* is available only in 48X computer-output microfiche. Requests for information on the *NUC* or orders should be directed to the Cataloging Distribution Service (CDS), Attn.: NUC Desk, Library of Congress, Washington, DC 20541.

Cataloging activities during 1983 also included the completion of the preliminary edition of the *National Level Authority Record* (available for $10 from CDS), the completion of the classification for the law of the Americas, Latin America, and the West Indies (a subclass of Class K), and the implementation of TOSCA (Total Online Searching for Cataloging Activities), a new procedure that has resulted in the shift from the card catalog to the online bibliographic and authority files for catalogers' routine searches. Because of TOSCA, cataloging productivity now exceeds former levels.

An important activity in 1983 that involved both technical processing staff and specialists from the library's research divisions was a project to reduce a cataloging backlog of at least 250,000 books in more than 100 languages acquired primarily over the past decade. Although most books had received some form of preliminary cataloging, reselection or additional cataloging was necessary to reduce the size of the collection and make the remaining books more accessible to readers. Nearly a quarter of the volumes will probably be transferred to other libraries or discarded, a limited number will be reselected for full cataloging, and the remainder will be given minimal-level cataloging. The project is expected to be completed early in 1984.

Cooperative cataloging endeavors continued to be important in 1983. The Name Authority Cooperative (NACO) Project, in which participating libraries have contributed more than 80,000 records to the library's automated name authority file, grew to 28 participants. Cooperation with two of the participants (the libraries of Harvard University and the University of Chicago) was expanded in spring 1983 to allow them direct access to the library's computer by terminal, with the capability of inputting and updating bibliographic and authority records online. Access to the library's data base was previously limited to a dial-up connection and in the search-only mode. Such cooperation has as one of its chief goals the enlargement of the Library's MARC data base, a project known as CODABASE (Cooperative Data Base Building System). Another major achievement in sharing occurred in fall 1983, when the Library of Congress input the first online vernacular Chinese bibliographic record into the RLIN (Research Libraries Information Network) data base, the automated information system of the Research Libraries Group (RLG). To accomplish this, it was necessary to install eight of RLG's Chinese-Japanese-Korean terminals, which will eventually allow the library to create machine-readable records for all its monographic holdings in these languages.

The Cataloging in Publication Division (CIP) gave several regional publishers' workshops in 1983. The series is designed to explain CIP goals and procedures and to give publishers an opportunity to ask questions about CIP. Officers of the division were also actively involved in directing a working group to develop an international standard format for CIP data printed in books.

The sixth in a series of meetings begun in 1977 between representatives of the Library of Congress and the National Library of Canada took place in spring 1983. Topics of discussion included "Standards," "Bibliographic Activities and Access to Records," and "Networking and Resource Sharing and New Technology Implications," and information was shared on such other subjects as preservation and reference and interlibrary loan services. Existing and potential cooperative endeavors in technical processing were also discussed.

Other areas of cooperation in 1983 included technical support by the library for the National Endowment for the Humanities' U.S. Newspaper Project, participation with RLG and the Washington Library Network in the Linked Systems Project (an endeavor supported by the Council on Library Resources, Inc.), and assistance to the British Library in the preparation of the *UNIMARC Interpretive Handbook*. At year's end, the Network Advisory Committee published its Planning Paper No. 8, *Public/Private Sector Interactions: The Implication for Networking*, in response to the NCLIS task force report on *Public Sector/Private Sector Interaction*. Planning Paper No. 8 is available for $5 from the library's Cataloging Distribution Service. In July 1983, the library signed a memorandum of understanding with the National Library of Medicine (NLM) to make the National Referral Center data base available to that library's user community through NLM's MEDLARS computer network.

Following the appointment of Joseph H. Howard as the new director of the National Agricultural Library in July 1983, Henriette D. Avram was named to succeed him as the assistant librarian for processing services. Avram had previously served the Library of Congress in several capacities, including chief of the MARC Development Office, director of the Network Development Office, and the library's first director for processing systems, networks, and automation planning.

[For a report on library networking in the United States in 1983, see Part 1—*Ed.*]

Other Educational and Cultural Activities

Other scholarly programs during 1983 included symposia devoted to Argentine writer Eduardo Mallea, Dutch/Indonesian writer Eduard Dowes Dekker (Multatuli), the tricentennial of German immigration, U.S.-Finnish cultural relations, and Arab-American literature, which also celebrated the centennial of the birth of Kahlil Gibran. These programs were organized by the library's various area studies divisions.

The Music Division held its second Summer Chamber Music Festival following a positive and enthusiastic response to the festival held in 1982. *Perspectives on John Philip Sousa*, a collection of essays on America's march king, was published in summer 1983, and the event was celebrated with an outdoor concert by the U.S. Marine Band. The publication is available from the Superintendent of Documents, U.S. Government Printing Office, Washington, DC 20402 (Stock No. 030-001-00103-2; $17).

Other new publications available from the Superintendent of Documents not mentioned elsewhere in this report are *American Doctoral Dissertations on the Arab World: Supplement, 1975-1981* (Stock No. 030-000-00145-1; $9), *Arab Oil: A Bibliography of Materials in the Library of Congress* (Stock No. 030-000-00143-5; $7.50), *Artists for Victory* (Stock No. 030-000-00146-0; $5.50), *Children's Books, 1982* (Stock No. 030-001-00102-4; $2.75), *Human Rights in Latin America, 1964-1980: A Selective Annotated Bibliography* (Stock No. 030-000-00144-3; $13), Volume 9 of *Letters of Delegates to Congress, 1774-1789* (Stock No. 030-000-00140-1; $19), *Literacy in Historical Perspective* (Stock No. 030-000-00142-7; $8), *Radio Broadcasts in the Library of Congress, 1924-1941: A Catalog of Recordings* (Stock No. 030-000-00139-7; $10), and *Wilbur & Orville Wright Pictorial Materials: A Documentary Guide* (Stock No. 030-001-00100-8; $6).

New publications available from the Library of Congress (Information Office, Box A, Washington, DC 20540, for the price stated plus $2 for postage and handling) are *The Early Illustrated Book: Essays in Honor of Lessing J. Rosenwald* ($50) and *Three Masters: The Stringed Instrument Collection in the Library of Congress* ($5).

Numerous other library publications, including technical processing materials and serials, as well as many free booklets and guides, are listed in *Library of Congress Publications in Print, 1983*, copies of which may be obtained free of charge from the Library of Congress, Central Services Division, Washington, DC 20540. Interested persons may also obtain copies of the library's annual gift and card or selected publications catalogs from the same address.

Other exhibitions mounted by the library during 1983 covered a wide range of subjects. A major new exhibition at year's end, "The Pennell Legacy: Two Centuries of Printmaking," displayed more than 200 fine prints of exceptional quality acquired by the library since the 1920s with income from the bequest of Joseph Pennell. The Pennell Fund has enabled the library to acquire several thousand prints as well as important additions to Pennell's own collection of the works of Whistler.

Smaller exhibitions were devoted to the photographs of Lewis Hine, the centennial of the Brooklyn Bridge, Currier & Ives, railroad maps of North America, and 150 years of U.S.-Thailand accord. Award-winning pictures taken by members of the White House News Photographers Association, a perennial favorite of visitors to the library, were on display during the summer months. The library also circulated several traveling exhibitions to a number of institutions around the United States during 1983.

National Agricultural Library

U.S. Dept. of Agriculture
Beltsville, MD 20705
301-344-3778

Eugene M. Farkas
Head, Educational Resources Staff

In 1983, Joseph H. Howard was appointed the new director of the National Agricultural Library (NAL), succeeding Richard A. Farley, who retired. Howard had been assistant librarian (processing services) at the Library of Congress (LC) before assuming his new position.

The new director initiated actions designed to coordinate and strengthen collection and dissemination of agricultural information through research and university libraries nationally, further improve and modernize NAL operations and services, and increase its role in international programs. The steps taken were consistent with recommendations made to the secretary of agriculture in August 1982 by a blue ribbon panel based on an assessment of the library's mission and operations.

During 1983, the NAL worked to (1) expand collection development and information access through coordination of holdings with and among land-grant universities, (2) initiate cooperative indexing/cataloging projects with public and private institutions, (3) strengthen agricultural library and information activities nationally through development and adoption of standardized formats and processing procedures essential for national networking, and (4) expand and strengthen ongoing regional document delivery and microfilming programs.

Collection Development

The NAL registered its interest with the Research Libraries Group of the Association of College and Research Libraries in conspectuses being developed on the holdings, collecting level, and collection responsibilities of major U.S. research libraries. In consultation with the Research Libraries Group, the NAL agreed to complete the conspectuses for agricultural subjects on which its own collections are based. The library also indicated its interest in being the prime coordinator among the land-grant institutions for collection development in agricultural fields.

The NAL began working with the Extension Service and the Food Safety and Inspection Service, U.S. Department of Agriculture (USDA), to create a Residue Avoidance Program (RAP) information project. It is joining forces with a network of veterinary toxicology centers located at the universities of Illinois, North Carolina, California, and Iowa State University to develop an automated data base of referred information on residues harmful to human health.

Analysis of resources and planning for a Grain Dust Safety Information Center at the NAL are in progress. Searches of relevant data bases were conducted to identify pertinent documents. Publications not already in the NAL collection will be acquired either in print copy, microfilm, or microfiche. Appropriate tags will identify the publications in the AGRICOLA data base.

Coordination and Standards

A request was forwarded to the Library of Congress to reactivate NAL participation in the CONSER Project and to assume national responsibility for the coordination and quality control of information on current agricultural journals, periodicals, and serials input into this project. The NAL has also asked the Library of Congress for national responsibility to maintain name authority records for current agricultural serial publications.

Initial discussions were held with the Commonwealth Agricultural Bureaux (CAB) on possible ways to strengthen and expand cooperation between the CAB and the NAL. The AGRICOLA data base of the NAL, the Commonwealth Agricultural Bureaux files, and the AGRIS data base of the Food and Agriculture Organization (FAO) constitute the major world bibliographical data bases on agriculture. Possibilities for strengthening relationships lie in coordination of training programs, sharing of bibliographic resources, and coordination of working relations with AGRIS. Opportunities to adapt for its own use either the AGROVOC thesaurus of FAO or the newly issued CAB controlled vocabulary are being explored by the library.

Cooperative Indexing/Cataloging

Arrangements were made by the National Agricultural Library, through a variety of cooperative agreements, for the indexing of specified agricultural journals and/or subject materials. Indexing will be done only once by the contracting institution, conforming to standard formats established by NAL. These records will be treated as NAL records (as if they were done within the National Agricultural Library) and will constitute the national record.

An agreement was negotiated with the University of Georgia to supply indexing data. Negotiations were begun with the University of Wisconsin Land Tenure Center, the University of Arizona Arid Lands Information Center, and the U.S. Forest Service to accept a common standard so that their indexing data can be incorporated into NAL's national bibliographic data base. Cost savings will be achieved by the one-time creation of an indexing record at the national level. Inclusion of these records in the NAL data base will make available unique collections of agricultural materials both nationally and internationally. The Online Computer Library Center, Inc. (OCLC), was asked to make the NAL coordinator of cataloging of agricultural publications for a group of land-grant institutions. This information would be distributed through AGRICOLA and MARC distribution service. NAL would provide training on standards and would establish sampling techniques for quality control.

Regional Document Delivery

During the last eight years an increasing number of land-grant university libraries have participated with the U.S. Department of Agriculture and the National Agricultural Library to provide documents and photocopies of articles to USDA personnel and libraries in their respective states and regions. A new region in the USDA Regional Document Delivery System began operation in July. The region covers Michigan, Ohio, Pennsylvania, and New York. The Albert R. Mann Library, Cornell University, is serving as regional coordinator. Seven regional centers serving 35 land-grant university libraries are now in operation: *Mid Continent*—Colorado, Kansas, Nebraska (Iowa State University, coordinator); *North Central*—Montana, North Dakota, South Dakota, Wisconsin (University of Minnesota, coordinator); *Northwest Intermountain*—Idaho, Utah (Washington State University, coordinator); *Southern Tier*—Alabama, Florida, Mississippi, North Carolina, South Carolina, Tennessee, Puerto Rico (University of Georgia, coordinator); *Southwestern*—Arkansas, Louisiana, New Mexico, Oklahoma (Texas A&M University, coordinator); *Western*—Arizona, Hawaii, Nevada (University of California, Davis, coordinator. A total of 67,500 requests, or 600 per month more than the same period during the previous year, were processed by these centers during 1983.

Microfilming

Purdue University, the University of Missouri, and Iowa State University libraries agreed to have their agricultural publications filmed in cooperation with the NAL. Agreements also were negotiated with a number of the states for microfilming materials issued by them from 1970 to 1980. Since NAL launched this cooperative program in 1974, the pre-1970 documents of 36 states, totaling over 2 million pages, have been microfilmed for archival, preservation, and storage purposes. Bulletins, circulars, reports, and other land-grant documents are filmed upon recommendation of a users and librarians advisory group.

Automated Systems

In response to the high priority placed by the NAL Blue Ribbon Panel on improving the library's automated data base, a comprehensive review and evaluation of the AGRICOLA system, the library's master bibliographic data base, was initiated by NAL through a contract with the Mitre Corporation. The study includes an objective review of current software and systems used by the library in various applications, along with consideration of future library applications that will interface with existing systems and programs. An initial report covering one phase of the review titled "Functional Requirements for a Bibliographic System" was issued in 1983.

In April 1982, the NAL began use of the OCLC Acquisitions Subsystem for all firm orders for monographs. Periodical renewals for 1984 have since been entered into the Acquisitions Subsystem, with plans made for input of preliminary records for books received on blanket arrangements, free, or otherwise received with no order. Use of the subsystem has eliminated typing and filing of temporary records, made order information available in several parts of the library and at several other locations, and eliminated keyboarding of many bibliographic entries (already in the system). Overall, it has saved time and allowed increased and easier access to records.

Electronic Mail

The library extended its use of electronic mail to three national and international systems: CLASS (California Library Authority for Systems and Services); COMET (COmputer

MEssage Transmission), a trademark of Computer Corporation of America; and DIALCOM Incorporated. It began accepting requests for documents on the OCLC interlibrary loan subsystem and developed procedures for receiving reference and general inquiries over the electronic communication network. An index to the NAL's Quick Bibliographies—AGRICOLA citations on topics of current interest—was introduced as a monthly feature on the USDA-sponsored Cooperative System Information Resource Network (DIALCOM).

Full-Text Transmission

A contract for development of a pilot data base for electronic transmission of the complete text of selected books, articles, pamphlets, flyers, and other documents was initiated in consultation with the Federal Extension Service, the Agricultural Research Service, and other federal and state units. The purpose is to enable NAL to produce and disseminate a full-text data base, utilizing state-of-the-art retrieval technology before the end of 1984. The result could be direct electronic access to agricultural information by technical information specialists, scientists, farmers, and the general public.

Videodisc

Another program involved testing the use of computer-aided instructional software linked to a laser videodisc to create and present library orientation and training programs. It could provide training for users of library data bases and systems as well as orientation for visitors. In addition, potential for full text storage and access to library documents using videodiscs may be explored.

The library again served as a satellite reception center for the American Library Association (ALA) annual teleconference broadcast live via satellite from Los Angeles with area libraries, government agencies, and others sending representatives to participate in the satellite program screened on television monitors in the NAL lobby.

User Services

Full reference, research, and document information services were made available from 8:00 A.M. to 4:30 P.M. at the main library in Beltsville, Maryland, as recommended by the blue ribbon panel report. As noted earlier, acceptance of interlibrary loan requests was expanded to include those sent via OCLC. In accordance with the National Interlibrary Code, requestors were asked to query first local and regional loan institutions listed in OCLC, New Serial Titles, and so on, before making a request of NAL. (See Table 1 for statistics on NAL activities and services in 1983.)

Current Awareness

The library initiated a request to lease a minicomputer system with an array processor—state-of-the-art equipment that will provide more efficient access to NAL's Current Awareness Literature Service (CALS). To augment its ongoing services, CALS

Table 1 / Statistics on NAL Operations, 1983

Library Operation	Productivity
Serials issues added	173,838
Titles cataloged	20,036
Articles indexed	127,732
Volumes bound	13,348
Document requests filled	253,626
Reference inquiries answered	29,480
Automated searches conducted	7,320
Current awareness (CALS) searches	290,242
Current awareness (CALS) profiles by all data bases	11,871

reinstated the full Chemical Abstracts CA Search file in lieu of Chemical Titles and added Telegen, a new data base on biotechnology/genetic engineering, and Water Resources Abstracts to the eight data bases already available to USDA personnel in the NAL computer-based literature searching system. These other data bases are AGRICOLA (NAL); Biological Abstracts/Reports, Reviews, Meetings; BioResearch Index; Commonwealth Agricultural Bureaux (CAB); Engineering Index; Food Science Technology Abstracts; Government Reports Announcement (NTIS) and World Textile Abstracts.

International Activities

Some 150,000 books and periodicals of foreign origin were added to the library's collection this year under agreements with 6,000 overseas exchange partners consisting of foreign governments and educational and research institutions. A newly streamlined exchange program will send an equal number of USDA publications overseas in return for foreign materials, which constitute about 60 percent of the total NAL collection of 1.8 million volumes. Bibliographically, the NAL contributed approximately 46,000 new citations to the AGRIS data base of the Food and Agriculture Organization in 1983. Under NAL auspices, AGRIS is expected to be available online in the United States through commercial vendors in 1984.

Online Training

The online training program, which includes introductory, basic, and advanced level workshops, continued to provide instruction on accessing the AGRICOLA and CRIS (Current Research Information System) data bases to librarians, technical information specialists, and scientists. Thirteen workshops were conducted in the Washington, D.C., area and at land-grant institutions. One hundred and eighty-eight persons from 26 states were instructed in the use of interrelated USDA bibliographic and computerized research information systems.

Chinese Study Team

More than 1,000 domestic and foreign visitors from public and private educational, scientific, and other institutions worldwide toured the library in 1983 and were briefed on its mission and operations. A five-member team from the National Agricultural Library and Information Center of the Chinese Academy of Agricultural Sciences spent ten weeks in the United States in an orientation and study program sponsored by the NAL. Visits were arranged to libraries on land-grant university campuses across the country as well as to other public and private technical information institutions. In a separate visit, the Chinese vice-minister of agriculture and president of the agriculture academy toured the library.

National Library of Medicine

8600 Rockville Pike, Bethesda, MD 20209
301-496-6308

Robert B. Mehnert
Public Information Officer

On September 30, 1983, Martin M. Cummings, M.D., retired as director of the National Library of Medicine (NLM). Harold M. Schoolman, M.D., was named acting director until a permanent successor is appointed. During the two decades under Dr. Cummings' leadership, NLM extended its mission as an international health information resource and emerged as a leader in computerized information handling. Among the most important accomplishments during his tenure is the extensive program of grant assistance that has benefited more than 1,000 U.S. health science libraries. Another is the Lister Hill National Center for Biomedical Communications, the research and development component of NLM that has played an important role in improving medical information transfer. The development of the online reference retrieval system, MEDLINE, was one of the center's first projects.

Online Services

The growth and widespread acceptance of MEDLINE and other computerized NLM systems have been remarkable. The number of U.S. institutions offering MEDLINE services stood at about 2,100 at the end of 1983, and more than 2.4 million searches were done on the various NLM data bases during the year. Three new data bases were added to the system in 1983. DIRLINE (Directory of Information Resources Online) lists 13,000 organizations that provide information on a variety of subjects. It is based on the National Referral Center data base of the Library of Congress. Two new cancer-related data bases were established on NLM's network in collaboration with the National Cancer Institute: CANCEREXPRESS, a selective, current file containing some 10,000 records describing cancer-related articles in several hundred high-quality journals; and a new PDQ (Protocol Data Query) file called PDQ/DIRECTORY, which contains the names of health care professionals and health care institutions that specialize in cancer treatment. Altogether there are now 20 current data bases and a number of backfiles of older references available for searching on NLM's domestic online network.

A new method of charging for online services became effective October 1, 1983.

Users are now billed on the basis of an algorithm that takes into account work performed by the NLM computers, the number of characters transmitted to the user's terminal, and the amount of time the user is connected to the system. Previously, charges were assessed only on the basis of time connected to the computers. Under the new method, most users will see little change in their bills; however, users who download and process large numbers of references will pay somewhat more.

The system under which NLM's data bases are made available is known as MEDLARS (Medical Literature Analysis and Retrieval System). MEDLARS became operational in 1964 and has gone through several evolutionary stages. A project known as MEDLARS III, after several years of planning, is now under actual development by a contractor. On August 31, 1983, NLM awarded a $3.9 million contract to Logicon, Inc., to develop, install, and test the first phase of MEDLARS III. Ultimately, the new system will fully automate NLM's processes for acquiring biomedical literature, for creating and distributing bibliographic records, for retrieving bibliographic information, and for providing document locator services.

Library Operations

NLM began charging $5 each for filled interlibrary loans to U.S. libraries on October 1, 1983. The existing fee of $4 for libraries abroad was raised to $7 at the same time. This change should encourage the self-sufficiency of local and regional resources, and it will bring NLM policy into conformance with other libraries in the Regional Medical Library Network. For the year ending September 30, 1983, NLM received 211,000 requests for interlibrary loans. The library filled 88.7 percent of these requests; 91 percent of the filled requests were sent out within four days. (See Table 1.)

The reconfiguration of the Regional Medical Library (RML) Network from 11 regions to 7, announced in 1982, was completed in January 1983. The network consists of local health science libraries (primarily at hospitals), resource libraries (at the medical schools), the seven regional medical libraries, and the National Library of Medicine as backstop to the network. The seven RMLs are the New York Academy of Medicine and the Universities of Maryland, Illinois (Chicago), Nebraska, Texas, Washington, and California (Los Angeles). The primary aim of the new configuration is to provide more cost-effective regional groupings and to preserve or improve the present level of reference, document delivery, and other information services to health professionals.

Table 1 / NLM Library Operations: Selected Statistics, 1983*

Library Operation	Volume
Collection (book and nonbook)	3,149,000
Serial titles received	23,500
Articles indexed for MEDLARS	310,400
Titles cataloged	18,400
Circulation requests filled	332,000
For interlibrary	174,600
For readers	157,400
Computerized searches (United States, all data bases)	2,412,300
Online	2.020,500
Offline	391,800

*For the year ending September 30, 1983.

Through this network approximately two million interlibrary loans are provided each year for the nation's health professionals.

NLM's online public access catalog became operational in January 1983. Six intelligent terminals in the main reading room provide rapid, convenient access to more than one-half million catalog records dating from 1500 to the present. Patrons may search the catalog by subject, personal or corporate author, title, series, conference name, or call number. The system, which has proven to be very popular with patrons, requires no previous training or special knowledge. Cards are no longer being added to the card catalog and it has become obsolete.

A new system of direct online input of bibliographic and name authority records by NLM catalogers was implemented this year. The new procedure eliminates some input and proofing steps, thereby reducing the overall time it takes to make a completed cataloging record available in the online and printed catalogs. In a parallel effort, improvements in the check-in and indexing processes have reduced the time between receipt of a journal and the appearance of cited references in MEDLINE and *Index Medicus*. More than 90 percent of the most heavily used journals are indexed and cited in 26 days or less.

Lister Hill National Center for Biomedical Communications

A major reorganization of the Lister Hill Center became effective in January 1983. The reorganization merged the functions of the library's National Medical Audiovisual Center with those of the Lister Hill Center. The realigned Lister Hill Center now consists of six branches: Communications Engineering, Computer Science, Health Professions Applications, Information Technology, Audiovisual Program Development, and Training and Consultation. Richard B. Friedman, M.D., was appointed director of the Lister Hill Center in March. Current programs are undergoing reappraisal by the new director and by the center's advisory group—the Board of Scientific Counselors —and a new research and development plan is being developed.

The Electronic Document Storage and Retrieval (EDSR) Program completed its first phase: the development of a prototype system capable of electronically scanning library documents, processing and storing the resulting electronic signals, and retrieving and displaying the stored images on paper or another medium. Work continues on research and evaluation activities using this prototype system as a laboratory test bed.

New in 1983 was the production by the Learning Resources Laboratory of several test videodiscs for use in health science education. Field-testing of a videodisc in basic medical pathology was begun in August in 25 schools. The videodisc, under microcomputer control, contains interactive tutorial sessions on *Cellular Alterations and Adaptations* and *Cell Injury and Death*. A second project, in radiology, will begin field-testing a videodisc, under microcomputer control, containing an instructional program using high-quality x-rays. Also compiled in 1983 was a technical evaluation of a new videodisc premastering facility that will be a critical component in developing future videodiscs. A report on the evaluation results is available.

Other NLM Programs

The library's Toxicology Information Program developed a number of support services for users of the MEDLARS chemical and toxicological files. A slide/tape presentation describing the Toxicology Information Program was produced and made available to introduce potential users to its services. Audiovisual instruction packages consisting of slides, a workbook, and a cassette were prepared for two of the toxicological files; two more will be prepared in 1984. Two new exhibits were constructed and, together with the audiovisual packages, were used with great success at a number of professional meetings in 1983.

The library's grant programs, carried out under the Medical Library Assistance Act, provide support for improving the resources and services of health science libraries, conducting research to improve biomedical communications, training for research careers in health computer sciences and health information, and publishing critical reviews and other works on important health topics. During FY 1983, awards totaling $7.5 million were made for 52 new projects, 46 projects begun in previous years, and contracts to support the regional medical libraries.

International Reports

The IFLA Conference, 1983, and Previews of the 1984 and 1985 Conferences

John G. Lorenz

Former Deputy Librarian of Congress
Consultant, Library and Information Services

Frank Kurt Cylke

Director

National Library Service for the Blind and Physically Handicapped,
The Library of Congress, 1291 Taylor St. N.W.,
Washington, DC 20542

The forty-ninth council and general conference of the International Federation of Library Associations and Institutions was held in Munich, Federal Republic of Germany, August 21–27, 1983. The theme of the conference, "Libraries in a Technological World," was based on the growing importance of technological developments for libraries and their services. Plenary sessions, more than 250 section and division meetings, and open forums dealt with such aspects as the new audiovisual and electromagnetic media; technology in the acquisition, cataloging, and preservation of materials; automated access to information and data; user fees based on higher costs; international cooperation to enhance standardization and data exchange; and transfer of appropriate technologies to developing countries. The conference was sponsored by the free state of Bavaria, the city of Munich, and the German Research Society. Most meetings were held at the University of Munich, with some events taking place at the Bavarian State Library. Approximately 1,200 representatives from more than 70 nations participated in the conference. Almost 200 of these participants were from the United States, the largest number from any country.

The Opening Session

The Growth and Importance of IFLA

At the official opening session of the conference, Franz Georg Kaltwasser, chairman of the local organizing committee and director of the Bavarian State Library, pointed out the significant growth in IFLA membership and program participation since IFLA last met in Munich in 1956, when total attendance was 68 libraries from 21 countries. Kaltwasser also stressed the basic importance of the book to present and future library and information services, despite the technological revolution in the dissemination of information. Kaltwasser's closing remarks honored the memory of Gustav Hofmann, former director-general of Bavarian state libraries and president of IFLA from 1958 to 1963. He quoted Hofmann from his opening address to the 1959 conference in Warsaw: "There is a vital necessity of a link between the various civilizations and a unity in the profession of librarian."

IFLA and UNESCO

The representative from UNESCO, Jacques Tocatlian, director of its General Information Program, outlined the objectives of the program to strengthen the capacity of each nation to collect, store, exchange, and use the information necessary for its development, in particular through the use of modern technology. He pointed out the marked convergence of IFLA and UNESCO programs, particularly in working toward the Universal Availability of Publications (UAP), one of the major program objectives of both organizations. Tocatlian also stressed the importance of greater involvement of the developing countries in IFLA sections, divisions, and programs. Problems that need to be overcome include currency restrictions, economic instability, and inconsistent support of delegate participation in meetings. Tocatlian emphasized the importance to developing countries of collecting, exchanging, and using scientific and technical information. Under one of its major programs, "Information Systems and Access to Knowledge," UNESCO plans to assist developing countries in the improvement of compatible information systems and services in their respective libraries.

The president of IFLA, Else Granheim of Norway, concluded the opening session by emphasizing the association's role as a catalyst in promoting the efficient use of new technologies in libraries, in close cooperation with UNESCO and other international organizations in the fields of documentation and archives. An important responsibility of the library profession is to convince the world's leaders and politicians that libraries are indispensable to the growth and development of both developing and industrialized nations. The president pledged her full support for an International Year of the Library, which has been proposed to UNESCO.

Plenary Session: The Future of Libraries

The opening plenary session of the conference featured speakers from the Federal Republic of Germany (Werner Knopp, president, Stifting Preussiche Kulturbesitz, Berlin); France (Denis Verloot, directeur des Bibliothèques, Ministère de l'Education Nationale, Paris); the United States (Thomas J. Galvin, dean, School of Library and Information Science, Pittsburgh); and the Union of Soviet Socialist Republics (N. S. Kartashov, director, Lenin State Library, Moscow). Each of the speakers spoke on the future of libraries and their use of the new technologies. Galvin stressed the importance of achieving a deeper understanding of the fundamental nature of information and the mutual responsibility of librarians and information scientists to develop an international research agenda to advance the future growth of knowledge in the information field. Verloot predicted a modified role for libraries in the future and recommended that libraries abandon present cataloging rules in an age of rapid transmission of information. He envisioned a paperless society with a declining use of libraries along with better methods of charging individuals for the information they need.

Open Forums

Universal Bibliographic Control

An open forum on one of the priority programs of IFLA, Universal Bibliographic Control (UBC), was opened by Barbara Jover, project officer of the program. She described the reduction in staff of the program, particularly the retirement of Dorothy Anderson, director of the office. She also reviewed the many accomplishments of the office under Anderson's direction. The British Library will provide guidance and administrative support through 1984, and Peter Lewis, director general of the Bibliographic Services Division, will provide overall direction and be responsible to the IFLA Program Management Committee. Beginning in 1985, funds are needed to support the projects relating to cataloging standards and the International Standard Bibliographic Description program.

Universal Availability of Publications

An open forum also was held on Universal Availability of Publications (UAP), another high priority IFLA program. The director of UAP's international office at Boston Spa, United Kingdom, Maurice Line, director general of the British Lending Library Division, led the program with the observation that "UBC without UAP is like a menu without a meal," since making available information and materials is a basic purpose of most libraries. The growing volume of publications on the subject includes the entire quarterly issue of the *Scandinavian Library Quarterly* and a new *UAP Newsletter.* Line supported a regional approach to the development of UAP, based on better understanding of needs, and advocated the development in each country of a community of publishers, booksellers, users, and librarians.

Council I Meeting

Changes in Rules of Procedure

At the Council I session of the conference, several changes in the association's rules of procedure were approved by council. The executive board may now, on the recommendation of the professional board, suspend the rule limiting standing committee members to two consecutive five-year terms in the case of very specialized sections; and standing committees may now select up to five corresponding members for the purpose of providing expert advice from countries or geographic areas that would not otherwise be regularly represented.

The rule concerning member association dues was modified in three ways: (1) The ceiling on the contribution to be paid by the library associations of any one country was changed from 12 to 10 percent of the total sum of all the contributions of national association members; (2) the dues classification was added for developing countries— nations with an annual per capita gross domestic product of U.S. $2,000 or less, as recorded in the *UN Statistical Yearbook;* and (3) in those cases where library association(s) and other bodies jointly contribute to the payment of national dues, the question of voting rights arising from the joint contribution shall be determined by consultation between the parties concerned. The rule concerning definition of and procedures for motions and resolutions was modified to codify current practice, and the specific obligations of outgoing officers of divisions and sections to inform and supply documentation to their successors were delineated.

New Executive Board

The council elected a slate of candidates to comprise the new executive board, all of whom were unopposed. Else Granheim (Oslo, Norway) will serve another two-year term as president. Elected to two-year terms on the executive board were Marie-Louise Bossuat (Paris, France), Gotthard Ruckl (Berlin, DDR), and Joseph S. Soosai (Kuala Lumpur, Malaysia). Elected to four-year terms were Henriette D. Avram (Washington, USA), Anthony J. Evans (Loughborough, UK), and Engelsina V. Pereslegina (Moscow, USSR). Hans Peter Geh (Stuttgart, FRG) continues to serve a four-year term.

Financial Report

Marie-Louise Bossuat, treasurer, presented a summary of the 1982–1983 accounts and the financial guidelines for 1983–1984. Although the 1982 accounts appeared to show a surplus, unless outstanding membership dues are paid, a deficit will remain for 1982–1983. The 1983–1984 estimated budget shows a slight surplus and reflects restriction of travel costs and the decision not to publish a separate directory of IFLA members, but to update membership through announcements in the *IFLA Journal*. Particular appreciation was extended to the Royal Library in The Hague, for providing new quarters, which greatly reduces headquarters costs. The four largest financial contributors to the association in 1982–1983 were the United States, West Germany, the Soviet Union, and Japan. IFLA gained 79 new members in 1982–1983, increasing the total membership to 1,101 members in 119 countries.

Program Management

Universal Bibliographic Control

The report of the Program Management Committee on the progress of the principal IFLA programs was given by Adam Wysocki (Poland). In the ten years since its founding, the Universal Bibliographic Control program has provided leadership in such areas as the development of the International Standards for Bibliographic Description, the development and dissemination of UBC publications, and support and follow-up on the international conference on Cataloging-in-Publication. Wysocki gratefully acknowledged the managerial support of the British Library, which made it possible for this important work to be continued.

Universal Availability of Publications

The International Office for the Universal Availability of Publications at Boston Spa, United Kingdom, has also made great strides in improving programs at all levels, identifying the problems in achieving the objectives of the programs and outlining the necessary research. UNESCO held an international conference on the subject in Paris in May 1982, which resulted in a number of recommendations for future activities. Wysocki closed by outlining the work of the International MARC program, centered at the Deutsche Bibliothek, Frankfurt (FRG), particularly in relation to UNIMARC, which will provide a universal standard for machine-readable cataloging.

The Professional Board

Activities of the Professional Board during the past year were described by its chairperson, Henriette Avram. These included the streamlining of conferences and meetings, the selection of plenary speakers and conference themes, closer cooperation with the International Standards Organization, and the development of guidelines for IFLA publications. The Professional Board is also charged with the responsibility of assigning priorities to the work of IFLA's professional groups.

Announcements

The publications officer of the association, Willem R. H. Koops (Groningen, Netherlands), announced that IFLA had again contracted with Verlag Dokumentation, K. G. Saur, to publish the major IFLA publications, continuing a ten-year working relationship, which has resulted in 30 publications. The winner of the annual Nijhoff Study Grant, Gloria Angela Gaspolini of Uruguay, was also announced.

Council II Meeting

Removal of an Officer

At the Council II meeting, several important actions were taken. IFLA Rules of Procedure were revised, giving the executive board the authority, on the recommendation of the professional board, to remove an officer if, in the opinion of a majority of the professional board, the person is considered not to be fulfilling the duties of the office, for example, by failing to make the required reports to the secretary general.

Program Evaluation and Structure

The following recommendations of the IFLA task force to evaluate programs and structure were accepted:

1 There is a need both to continue the activities of divisions, sections, and round tables and to establish programs in pursuance of IFLA's priorities. In addition to the three existing major programs—UBC, UAP, and International MARC— three added priorities were identified: (a) the advancement of librarianship in the Third World, (b) preservation and conservation, and, (c) transborder data flow and related problems of data exchange. Present divisions, sections, and round tables will have an important role in the implementation of these programs.

2 UBC and International MARC should be continued at the level of maintenance of the existing standards and manuals, including appropriate training for national usage.

3 The UAP should be considered a development program.

4 Programs involving the new technology, for example, videodiscs and optical discs, are to be treated as cross-sectional activities and assigned initially to Information Technology.

5 A new strategy is to be developed with regard to IFLA's financing, including (a) preparing and presenting programs to attract external funding; (b) establishing a more direct link to UNESCO at the highest level through the IFLA president; (c) supporting existing division, section, and round table programs from general IFLA income; (d) preparing an integrated budget showing all IFLA activities; (e) centralizing administration and management to achieve increased efficiency and savings; (f) exploring the improvement of revenues from conferences, seminars, publications, and personal and institutional affiliates.

Nairobi Protocol

An important resolution on the Nairobi Protocol to the Florence Agreement approved unanimously at the Council II session reads as follows:

> WHEREAS the Florence Agreement (Agreement on the Importation of Educational, Scientific and Cultural Materials) by eliminating import duties on books, periodicals, printed music and other educational, scientific and cultural material in over 70 adhering countries has provided great benefits to libraries and their users, as well as to educational institutions and the general public; and
> WHEREAS a 1976 Nairobi Protocol (supplement) to the Florence Agreement making further improvements in the original is now in force in 12 countries; and
> WHEREAS most of the countries thus far adhering to the protocol have adopted optional Annex C-2 which severely limits the duty free import of audio, visual, and micro-form materials rather than optional Annex C-1, which extends duty free status to these materials on the same basis as books and other publications; and
> WHEREAS the United States of America has eliminated import duties on audio, visual, and microform materials from all countries for a trial period of two years ending August 12, 1985 to encourage other countries to adhere to the Protocol and optional Annex C-1; and
> WHEREAS the International Federation of Library Associations and Institutions, the International Publishers Association, the International Federation of the Phonographic Industry, and other international associations have long supported the Protocol and optional Annex C-1,
> Now, therefore, BE IT RESOLVED that the International Federation of Library and Information Associations urge its component national associations to recommend strongly to their national governments prompt adherence to the Protocol and optional Annex C-1; and
> BE IT FURTHER RESOLVED that copies of this resolution be printed in the *IFLA Journal* and be sent to member associations of IFLA, to the Secretary General of UNESCO, to UNESCO national committees in all countries adhering to the Florence Agreement, and to the International Publishers Association, the International Federation of the Phonographic Industry and other international associations concerned.

Freedom of Opinion Resolution

A controversial resolution sponsored by the French delegation called on IFLA to intervene in specific cases where librarians are "persecuted for their opinions." Despite attempts by Soviet bloc delegates to forestall a vote, the resolution carried by a 254 to 99 margin with strong U.S. support.

Section and Division Meetings

Literally hundreds of section and division meetings were held during the conference on a wide variety of subjects ranging from "Electronic Publishing" to "Hospital Libraries in the Federal Republic of Germany." In many respects, the smaller meetings and discussion sessions are the heart of the conference, at which much of the planning and program development is accomplished. Because of the large number of programs, it is not possible to describe or summarize each one. However, complete sets of all papers in English or sets of papers presented in section, division, and round table meetings can be ordered from ERIC Document Reproduction Service, Box 190, Arlington, VA 22210.

Section of Libraries for the Blind

Forty-three librarians and technical experts representing 17 countries participated in meetings of the Section of Libraries for the Blind. Georgette Rappaport, chief librarian, Central Library for the Hospitals, Paris, France, briefly described the activities of the Antony Public Library, in Antony, France, serving blind and physically handicapped individuals.

Library Service in Poland

Clifford Law, chief librarian, Library Services for the Handicapped, National Library of Australia, read a paper titled "Reading Programs for the Blind and Physically Handicapped in Public Libraries of the Polish People's Republic," prepared by Franciszek Czajkowski, chairman, Section for the Propagation of Reading Programs for Invalids and Physically Handicapped Persons, Torun, Poland.

Czajkowski said an agreement concluded toward the end of 1975 between the Ministry of Culture and Art and the board of directors of the Polish Association of the Blind concerning the collection and availability of recorded books in public libraries provides for the acquisition and dissemination of talking books in Poland. Approximately 150 titles are recorded annually in the recording studio at the headquarters of the Polish Teachers Union in Warsaw for the use of public libraries, predominantly in the fields of general education and belles-lettres. Several are taken from classic Polish and foreign literature.

Czajkowski also described a survey of the regional branches of the Association of Polish Librarians and provincial libraries (a total of 49) which revealed that 35 provincial agencies have organized sections for talking books, frequently including recording studios in music departments or in libraries. In Torun and Lublin, special technical library branches are operating. In other areas, through cooperation between libraries and local administrations of the Polish Teachers Association, studios have been set up in community centers or in clubs. These libraries carry on library activity in the strict sense of the word, but some of them also organize rehabilitative educational and training programs.

The special library branch for the blind and physically handicapped at the Provincial Public Library and City Library in Torun, which evolved from the existing library studio in 1982, is situated on the ground floor (no stairs) of a historic apartment house in the center of town. In addition to standard library equipment, it has a collection of 390 talking book titles. Catalogs are being prepared in print and in braille, and a collection of rehabilitation and typhlological literature is being established. Two booths with equipment for reproducing cassettes and records will be installed in the near future, and funds to buy talking books, tape recorders, and other equipment are increasing.

Library Service in the Federal Republic of Germany

Rainer F. V. Witte, deputy director and head of Library Services and Braille Production, at the Deutsche Blindenstudienanstalt (BLISTA), the German Institute for the Blind, in Marburg/Lahn, Federal Republic of Germany offered a paper titled "Library Services for the Blind in the Federal Republic of Germany," in which he summarized the activities in the field. On August 17-19, 1983, 51 librarians and technical experts from 15 countries serving blind and physically handicapped individuals, held a preconference meeting at the German Institute for the Blind, under the auspices of the IFLA Section of Libraries for the Blind. The three-day agenda included nine technical sessions and three professional tours.

The German Institute for the Blind

Describing the work of the German Institute for the Blind, Director Jurgen Hertlein indicated that the 65-year-old institution provides "the visually handicapped with possibilities for higher education, resulting in mainstreaming, performance in scientific programs, and the development of technical devices." Its aim is "the professional integration of the visually handicapped into society."

In addition to its special schools, which presently offer education to 230 blind and low-vision students, the institute's Emil Kruckmann Library (with about 53,000 volumes in braille) offers books covering all scientific and literary fields as well as novels at no cost to readers in Germany and abroad; its documentation services (AIDOS) aid in finding information concerning the blind and low vision; the reference library of printed books helps in research; and the Braille Publishing House publishes and prints schoolbooks, scientific literature, novels, law compendiums, and magazines in braille—60 books in 50 copies and 6 braille magazines on a regular basis in quantities ranging from 100 to 750 copies each year. The institute also produces and distributes braillers, braille slates, braille printers and duplication machines for braille texts, standard typewriters with special devices for the blind, and many other materials for the visually handicapped, including drawing devices and materials, calculation aids, measuring devices, Audilux devices and accessories, clocks and watches, canes, arm bands and other traffic safety materials, television converters, tape recorders and cassettes, reading aids, games, and maps. These products are exported to more than 80 countries all over the world.

Tactile Maps

Hans Doove, the Netherlands Library for the Blind, coordinated a meeting addressed by Wilfred Laufenberg, BLISTA, and Paulli Thomsen, Danish State Institute for the Blind.

Laufenberg, Diplom-Psychologe, described various existing technologies for producing tactile maps. The simplest techniques involve hand construction of master pieces for thermocopying or gluing, such as used in the Nottingham Kit for making raised maps. Additional skill is required to produce relief pictures by embossing aluminum sheets or plates from which solid plaster masters can be made.

A second group of technologies produces large series of tactual reliefs without master pieces by photocopying or printing processes. The newly developed Minolta stereocopying process translates black-and-white drawings into tactually legible reliefs by use of a special paper, which expands, or "blows up," when exposed to heat. Techniques that require the use of photomechanical equipment to form masters for vacuum copying include one that uses Nyloprint newspaper printing plates. The technique involves photographing a black-and-white drawing of the relief. The Nyloprint plate hardens where the film negative allows ultraviolet light to pass through, and the parts of the plate not exposed to light are washed away. In the OTAC system, a combination of quartz powder and toner subjected to heat produce a photocopy of a black-and-white original on standard paper.

Both stereocopying and OTAC technology have advantages when used to produce simple dot-and-line drawings, but show disadvantages with complicated illustrations. Both are only capable of showing symbols of one standard height. To produce complex tactual information, silk screen printing is a better technique.

Paulli Thomsen gave a progress report on the International Register of Maps project being developed by the IFLA Section of Libraries for the Blind. The register, which will be based on input received from an international questionnaire, will be located in the Netherlands Library for the Blind. If plans hold, the register will be available for consultation in early 1984.

Paperless Braille

Manfred Harres, production coordinator, BLISTA, presented a paper titled "The Blind and the New Technologies: Paperless Braille and Reading Machines," in which he described new devices that have been developed to facilitate the three work steps involved in the brailling of a page: text editing, translation or code conversion, and storage. He concluded with a perspective on the future:

> A blind person would like to borrow a book which is not available in braille. He calls a central library, the book is available there in inkprint. There is no data carrier on which the same book is stored. The book can be read in the library by means of an automatic reading machine. The data edited in the library's computer are then entered into the blind person's personal computer via telephone. The blind person can get the text translated into Braille Grade 2 with his personal computer. He first reads the book on his tactile display. Then he can print the whole book or parts of it on his electric sheet brailler.

Talking Books

Karl Britz, graduate physical scientist and teacher for the blind, BLISTA, reviewed "Talking Book Libraries in the Federal Republic of Germany." He described the development of talking book technology beginning with the magnetic tape recording technique developed by the German AEG Company during World War II and experiments with recordings on magnetic wire at a Swiss braille library in 1949. The Tefifon mechanical technique (similar to the record disc), which used an endless plastic tape, was first discussed in 1952 at a conference organized by Carl Strehl, director of the Blindenstudienanstalt in Marburg, to examine the technological possibilities available at the time to produce a talking book. To listen to the tapes produced by the Tefifon technique, the reader of the talking book had to purchase an apparatus, which could be used to make recordings as well.

The first German talking book library was founded in Marburg in 1954 and several other libraries followed shortly afterward in various cities. They organized a federation of talking libraries in Germany that was soon joined by a number of foreign libraries (Austria, Switzerland, France, Holland, Luxembourg, and Sweden) also offering German literature to their listeners. At present 19 nonprofit institutions belong to the federation.

Third World

Wolfgang Stein, director, Christoffel Blindenmission, e.V., Federal Republic of Germany, described the state of blindness in the Third World. Of the more than 40 million blind and visually handicapped individuals in the world, 80 percent are in developing countries, and one of every 40 or 50 blind children in school has no access to braille materials.

Braille Production in Africa

Frank Kurt Cylke, director, National Library Service for the Blind and Physically Handicapped, Library of Congress, Washington, D.C., and Rainer Witte, deputy director, BLISTA, led a discussion of the current UNESCO-IFLA contract to study the status and feasibility of enhancing braille production in Africa. Witte made reference to UNESCO-sponsored activities that had established the aims and objectives of the current UNESCO/IFLA contract: *African Braille Production: A Statistical Review and Evaluation of Countries and Costs* by Marc Mayer and Frank Kurt Cylke (UNESCO Contract No. 594560) and the Seminar on Library Service to the Visually Handicapped in African Developing Countries (Arusha, Tanzania, November 3–11, 1980). The seminar, organized by Anna Ubostad, Norway, and Paulli Thomsen, Denmark, produced two publications, a final report on the seminar (UNESCO No. PGI-81/WS/21) and the supplement to the final report. *Establishing Braille Production Facilities in Developing Countries: A Handbook, 1980* by Barry Hampshire, Sweden, was noted as another useful publication.

Witte then gave a progress report on the current UNESCO/IFLA contract, outlining the purposes, problems, and activities to date. The scheduled paper "Thoughts about the Production and Spreading of Braille in Africa," prepared by Hans-Eugen Schulze, member of the Federal Supreme Court (Albert-Braun St. 10b, D-7500 Karlsruhe, Federal Republic of Germany), was not delivered. Copies are available on request.

Voice Indexing System

Franco Consadori, Vancouver, Canada, offered a demonstration of the Van Schyndel Voice Indexing System (VS/VIS), which offers a simple and effective solution to the problem of searching for a specific section (chapter, page, and so on) of a voice recording on audiocassettes. This problem is common to all audiorecordings, but poses special problems in the case of talking books for the blind. The VS/VIS was designed specifically with this application in mind.

The basic principle of operation of the VS/VIS is similar to the one widely utilized to index talking books, by which audiotones (beeps) are added to the normal recording. State-of-the-art technology now makes it possible to articulate the simple beeps into clearly spoken labels. The VS/VIS captures a message, encodes and manipulates it into a special format, and records it together with the regular text, so that it can only be heard in the fast forward mode.

The VS/VIS satisfies all the requirements of a successful indexing system. Its many features make it the only real solution to the indexing problem. Further information on the U.S. $2,000 machine may be obtained from: Q-VOX International, Inc., 2190 W. 12 Ave., Vancouver, B.C. V6K 2N2, Canada (Telex 04-352848 VCR).

Adapting to New Technology

Paul E. Thiele, librarian and head, Charles Crane Memorial Library, University of British Columbia, Vancouver, Canada, directed his paper to all those interested in serving the information needs of blind and physically handicapped individuals, concluding with the following comment:

> The on-going development of new technologies for the blind and sight-impaired has good and bad aspects. For the professional charged with programming reading services for the visually impaired either in a dedicated special setting or in public or education libraries and institutions, almost every new technology requires new methodology in administering, circulating, storing, packaging and dissemination. Every change requires large outlays of capital and continuing financial support. At the beginning of this paper, I complimented librarians, information science and education personnel on their positive attitudes and willingness to adapt. But I would be more than remiss not to point out and compliment the tremendous adaptability of the blind and partially-sighted themselves. Each new technology is accomplished by them at tremendous costs of learning new skills, adapting new methods, and devising new approaches. Many accomplished blind readers command several technologies, switching with ease from talking book to braille, tactile print and computer-generated speech. The perfect reading technology for the largest number of blind people has obviously not yet been developed, although the talking book comes close as being the most widely accepted. But the fact that the blind are coping with the many methods of accessing information and ready to embrace new technologies as they are developed, should demonstrate clearly their tremendous desire to read.

Standing Committee

On Friday, August 26, 1983, the Section of Libraries for the Blind held a meeting of its standing committee. Winnie Vitzansky assumed the position of chairperson and Judith Thiele the position of secretary. Frank Kurt Cylke will continue to serve as executive secretary.

Closing Session

At the closing session, tributes were given to several members for distinguished service to the association: Jean Lowrie (USA), outgoing executive board member; Henriette Avram (USA), Vladimir Popov (Bulgaria), Wolfgang Dietz (FRG), and Johannes Daugbjerg (Denmark), all outgoing professional board members; Dorothy Anderson (UK); Milisa

Coops (Netherlands); E. R. S. Fifoot (UK); Ludmila Gvishiana-Kosygina (USSR); Istovan Poppe (Hungary); and Franz Georg Kaltwasser (FRG).

1984 Nairobi Conference

The head of Kenya's delegation invited participants to the fiftieth IFLA conference in Nairobi, August 19–25, 1984. This will be the first IFLA meeting to be held in Africa. The 1984 theme, "The Basis of Library and Information Services for National Development," will be specifically covered in plenary sessions on "Promotion of the Reading Habit and Adult Education"; "Manpower for Library and Information Services"; and "Library and Information Systems and Services." A preconference seminar on "Education for Librarianship at the Grassroots Level" will be held August 13–18, 1984. A limited group of 20 to 30 experts will be invited to participate and discuss topics of current interest in this area.

The conference, including all professional meetings, will take place at the Kenyatta International Conference Center. The $150 registration fee for delegates and accompanying persons covers attendance at all sessions, exhibitions, and other official social events. Completed application forms should be returned to the Local Organizing Committee with full payment not later than May 31, 1984. Payments should be made by banker's transfer, not personal checks, to Kenya Library Association, Conference Account Number 1815774, Barclays Bank of Kenya Limited, Queensway House Branch, Box 30011, Nairobi, Kenya.

Visitors to Kenya must have vaccination certificates for yellow fever and cholera. Malaria protection and vaccination against typhoid and paratyphoid are also recommended. Hotel bookings must be made by April 30, 1984, with a one night deposit. Early bookings are advised. The United Touring Company, the conference official tour operator, will arrange all pre- and postconference tours.

1985 Chicago Conference

Henriette Avram (USA) issued a cordial invitation to the delegates to come to the fifty-first IFLA conference in Chicago, Illinois, August 18–24, 1985. The theme of the conference will be "Libraries and Universal Availability of Information." Conference activities will take place in a hotel in the Chicago Loop. The registration fee has been tentatively fixed at U.S. $175 for conference participants and $150 for accompanying persons. One day during the conference week will be devoted to study tours of notable libraries and historic sites in Illinois. Chicago's many libraries—public, private, and special—will be open for visitors during the conference for informal scheduled visits. For further information, address inquiries to IFLA 1985 Secretariat, 50 E. Huron St., Chicago, IL 60611.

Frankfurt, 1983: Quietly Bullish

Herbert R. Lottman
International Correspondent, *Publishers Weekly*

For the first time in years public confessions of contentment were heard at a Frankfurt Book Fair. There may have been smaller staffs on many stands, fewer free-floating bodies in the aisles, but there were more smiles than usual at the thirty-fifth Frankfurt (October 12–17). "It's one of the most active fairs in a long time," Seymour Lawrence, now copublisher at New York's Dutton, summed it up. "Good fair!" Alewyn Birch of London's Granada exclaimed as he rushed off for an airport taxi. "*Extremely* good fair!" "I've never liked a fair so much," agreed Allan Eady of Crown. "I had people coming to see what we do as much as what we have." Indeed, there was a broad consensus that the upturn in the American and British book trade had stirred hopes in most of the rest of the world. "When you do well, we all do well," explained Raúl Rispa of Spain's giant Salvat.

It seemed a quieter fair, but true professionals smiled indulgently at the notion that this was bad for business. "It's quieter," said Jaco Groot of Amsterdam's small, innovative and prosperous De Harmonie, "so we can really do things." And a five-star general of the rights trade, New York attorney-agent Morton L. Janklow, expressed his appreciation of the calmer atmosphere; the essential thing for him was that all the people he needed to see were around. "It's a good sign," he told *Publishers Weekly's* correspondent. "The more efficient publishers are, the better it is for authors."

The fair authorities had signed up 5,890 exhibitors this year, 4,274 of them from outside the two Germanys (the corresponding figures for 1982 had been 5,688 and 4,169). There were 4,195 individual exhibitors (up from 4,076); as one way to deal with the overflow, fair director Peter Weidhaas had set up an International Publishers' Meeting Point in a corner of International Hall 5 for publishers who couldn't get booths, and there were 28 of them, 20 from the United Kingdom alone. Weidhaas in his opening press conference pointed out that most of the fair's growth was in the German sector (with 1,558 imprints from the Federal Republic versus 1,462 last year), and most of the newcomers were medium-size or small. "Despite the often-denounced giantism, these firms, which use much sharper pencils in their calculations than do their large and established colleagues, see realistic chances for success."

A Fair for All Reasons

Frankfurt can be seen as several fairs in one. Certainly for most of its users it is Germany's equivalent of the American Booksellers Association's trade exhibit: publisher promotion aimed at the nation's booksellers and libraries, increasingly to its public at large; it's a fair of attractive, individually designed stands, round-the-clock author appearances, television, and other media coverage. For non-German participants it is also a bookselling fair, for they meet their customers from the world over. For both the Germans and the outlanders it is the world's leading rights market; indeed, the case could be made that it is first of all a rights fair for English-language publishers—call it "the autumn London Book

Note: Adapted from *Publishers Weekly,* November 18, 1983.

Fair," since the most important thing that goes on at the Frankfurt event is the contact between visiting U.S. and U.K. book people and their foreign counterparts. If a satellite photograph could be taken of the fair's international exhibition building, it would show the constant movement of people toward the northwest corner of Hall 5, where English-language trade publishers are concentrated; the photograph might also show forays out of that corner by agents armed with outlines (and this in a year when dollars were more expensive than ever).

Just before Frankfurt, Distripress held its annual meeting of magazine and mass market paperback distributors and their suppliers. There, Pocket Books president Ronald Busch heard his distributors describe their pricing problems: American paperbacks simply aren't able to compete with cheaper British editions anymore. Paul Feffer of the export house Feffer & Simons explained that most American hardcover books sold abroad go to institutional customers with fixed budgets in local currencies; the rise of dollar values simply decreases acquisition budgets. He was less concerned about British competition, because "it's always been there"; in any case, traditional British markets buy British editions of American titles published on license.

As for the sale of rights, Paul Gottlieb of Abrams found the fair a good one, considering the higher cost of films as well as rights to traditional European partners. "Almost every foreign publisher with depressed currency is making smaller offers apologetically," observed agent Morton Janklow, "telling us that it's as much money in their own currency as for the last book." In his contracts Janklow specifies payment in the currency he thinks will be strongest; it's dollars for the next two or three years.

Although few American agents bother to fly over for the fair, leaving the job of representing their authors to U.K., Continental, and Japanese subagents, some do, when the stakes are high enough. *PW* met Jonathan Silverman of Scott Meredith, who had come to sell Norman Mailer's next novel, *Tough Guys Don't Dance* (legal, sex, health, drug problems in a Cape Cod setting). A month before the fair it was decided to offer the book on the basis of five chapters (representing five-eighths of the complete manuscript), and it turned out to be a good decision; sales were quickly made to Sweden, Spain, Italy, the Netherlands, and Brazil. (In the case of Spain, acquiring publisher Planeta had never done Mailer before; in the Netherlands, Unieboek took on *Tough Guys* as part of a three-book deal, the other two not yet written.) For the U.K. market an auction was staged at the fair. Three contenders were in the running on day one; bids rose on the third day, and one contender dropped out; on Friday October 14 the bidding heated up between the two remaining publishers. At 1:00 P.M. that day Michael Joseph came up with the high bid: the rival had until 2:00 P.M. to top it and did not. The price was "even higher" than the amount paid for *Ancient Evenings* (which was reportedly $120,000). It happened to be Silverman's first fair, and he was struck by its optimism.

PW talked to London-based Ed Victor at the busy compound set aside for literary agents and scouts. He had come to Frankfurt with *Roman by Polanski* (sold before the fair to Laffont and to Sweden's Norstedt). In Victor's vision the Frankfurt fair is a race, where normal rules don't apply. "The first person who comes up to you and gives you a number, you say yes to." The week's surprise for him was a novel about a sheepdog, *Nop's Trials* by Donald McHaig, which he was handling for U.K. and non-English sales on behalf of New York agent Knox Burger, and which was sold to Crown for $150,000 before the Frankfurt week. Prior to Frankfurt, Victor had staged a London auction, won by Collins and Pan (£50,600); on the strength of that, fairgoers began seeking Victor out. "Publishers help other publishers. A British publisher, for example, will tell Ivan

Nabokov of Albin Michel in Paris: 'You have to get that book!'" Working for Victor, Andrew Nurnberg sold *Nop's Trials* to Rowohlt at the fair for $75,000. Nurnberg was also selling Polanski to the Germans in an auction, but again it was a Frankfurt auction, with fast-changing rules. Victor remembered the time that Roger W. Straus, Jr. walked by while he was showing a book to someone else and asked how much it was, and then said he'd take it. "There is a great concentration of powerful people here—heads of companies who can read a few pages and say yes or no."

For Ed Victor, Frankfurt is *two* fairs: a foreign rights fair, but also a New York–London fair, and he divides his time between the two. Because they were all in Frankfurt, for example, he worked out a joint venture deal between Richard Snyder and Ronald Busch (Simon & Schuster/Pocket Books) on one hand, Crown's Alan Mirken and Bruce Harris on the other, and in 48 hours, more quickly than he could have done it in New York.

The Janklow Operation

PW also got to talk to Morton Janklow, the attorney-agent who has often made news with big Frankfurt sales. Actually, he plays the fair in low key, leaving most of the negotiating to the U.S. publishers who have acquired world rights to his authors; he feels that his role is to help them. And at the Frankfurt fair Janklow sees people he never gets to see at any other time, the editors-in-chief and rights managers who don't come to New York. But Frankfurt is also the place, he says, where he can spend hours with Dick Snyder or with Bantam's Jack Romanos, something it's hard to do back home; he does a lot of his American work in Germany.

For his most successful international client, Danielle Steel (17 novels, 45 million copies in print worldwide), Janklow has an opportunity at Frankfurt to see how the books are being published. In all, he handles 65 authors (7 of them Pulitzer Prize winners), although he never has more than 6 to 9 projects to show at one time. This allows him to handle all deals directly; he never uses subagents, and all royalty statements come to New York for careful scrutiny. Some of his Frankfurt appointments are made months in advance; half are informal calls, or last-minute appointments made during a chance encounter in the aisles. Just before the fair Marc Jaffe had acquired *Moscow Rules* by Robert Moss for Random House, on the basis of an 80-page outline (it's the story of a military coup in the Soviet Union). Random House has world rights, but Janklow pitched in at Frankfurt to help sell it (he has approval of all foreign contracts); there were no formal auctions, but offers were coming in from just about everywhere. He also helped Simon & Schuster with Jackie Collins's *Hollywood Wives,* and was talking up Dominique Lapierre's nonfiction story of an American lay saint in Calcutta, *A Light in the Monsoon* (already sold to Doubleday and Laffont); he was doing things with recent books by Barbara Taylor Bradford. Sidney Sheldon, too. All this in an atmosphere he felt to be more buoyant than in recent years; the U.S. upturn was clearly contagious.

Curtis Brown (London) was showing an outline of Frederick Forsyth's *The Fourth Protocol,* the manuscript to be delivered on the last day of this year. Roaming the aisles, *PW*'s correspondent heard of impressive offers for Forsyth, for Mailer, for Doubleday's new Arthur Hailey (*Strong Medicine*). A publisher for the still weak Spanish market *lost* one of these authors with his $200,000 bid, which shows where things are. Indeed, one Frankfurt story was the epic combat of Spanish giants—Planeta with its Midas touch,

Plaza y Janés with Bertelsmann backing, for the big international bestsellers. Among the victims were leading Latin American publishers, whose diminished buying power keeps them out of the race these days.

Holt and its agents around the world were talking about Claire Sterling's version of the shooting of Pope John Paul II, but to read the manuscript one had to sit behind closed curtains in the Holt booth at the fair. With 63 pages to be shown, Mick Jagger's autobiography was the hottest item on the Weidenfeld stand. When *PW* talked with them, that house's Bud MacLennan was considering a high offer for Swedish rights. (In fact, Norstedt got the book as part of a three-book deal that included two other Weidenfeld offerings, a biography of Herbert van Karajan, and an autobiography by Plácido Domingo.) Warner's Howard Kaminsky was promoting William Goldman (who was under a three-book contract); you could find Frank Herbert's *Dune* movie tie-in on the Putnam stand, with a whole new world of Supergirl.

Keen interest was coming in for *War Day,* a novel by Whitley Strieber and James Kunetka that describes America after a limited nuclear war. Back home, Book-of-the-Month had won an auction conducted by Holt's Pat Breinin, and there was a $350,000 paperback floor and a movie in the works; Curtis Brown (New York) had sold rights to the United Kingdom's Hodder & Stoughton and Germany's Piper before the fair.

One way to learn where the money was going was to talk with the people at Bra Böcker, Sweden's package book club, which has been challenging traditional trade publishers in that country in the bestseller market. Bra Böcker had previously made news with a record offer for Mailer's *Ancient Evenings;* at Frankfurt it acquired *Tough Guys Don't Dance.* But despite a $150,000 offer, it lost the Arthur Hailey book to club rival Bonnier. In another field, Bra Böcker acquired a 20-volume Time-Life Library of Nations, to be offered to its club members a book at a time.

Barcelona agent Carmen Balcells was trying to promote to world class her Brazilian novelist Rubem Fonseca; she was being listened to because she had already brought in Mario Vargas Llosa, Gabriel García Márquez, Juan Carlos Onetti, José Donoso and folks like that; at least one major European house thought that a sufficient guarantee and bought Fonseca almost without reading him. Jonathan Cape's Tom Maschler was making a killing with the ultimate pop-up called *The Facts of Life*—conception and birth—which he expects to sell in one million copies in the United Kingdom alone; he had an impressive list of copublishers before the fair was over. Perhaps the fair's most precious manuscript was the new fairy tale by Wilhelm Grimm offered by Farrar, Straus & Giroux (actually on the basis of a rough English translation that potential buyers had to read under the watchful eyes of Farrar's Peggy Miller); the original manuscript, purchased by Straus for an undisclosed five-figure sum, was under lock and key in New York. Straus himself was excited about his own Frankfurt acquisition, Breyten Breytenbach's jail experiences in South Africa, acquired by Amsterdam's Robert van Gennep.

Economic Health Checkups

Walking around the international hall at Frankfurt was a good way to take the temperature of the major publishing nations. "We're moving into quite a strong period," Penguin's Peter Mayer said of the United Kingdom, where publishers were optimistic for the first time in five years. Mayer and Penguin's editorial director Peter Carson attribute improvement to a shaking down, a weeding of nonessential books. "We're publishing better," Mayer said, "paying more attention to the right quantity, the right price." Tom Rosenthal (chairman of Heinemann as well as of Secker & Warburg) agreed that you can now make money if you publish good books well, but you have to work twice as hard as ten years ago. From the giants *PW* went over to Marion Boyars, one of Britain's smaller houses. Like the biggest, American-born Boyars had seen hard times, but she is now showing a profit again; she feels the secret is highest possible quality, "not to compete with the entertainment industry." (Her list happens to include Elias Canetti, Heinrich Böll, Samuel Beckett, Eugenio Montale—all published before they received their respective Nobels.)

Caution among booksellers has caused many a German publisher to despair, says Paul Fritz of the Linder agency in Zurich, but across the board the book trade will survive. Those who make a living selling rights are satisfied, although advances have come down from their peak. Klaus Piper of Munich's Piper Verlag said that this year growth would exceed inflation—recently running at 3 percent per year; the business climate has improved, but one has to publish quality, avoiding the "mediocre." For Japan, giant Kodansha's Toshiyuki Hattori reports a 6 percent increase in copies produced, but less than 2 percent growth of sales; it's a matter of more sales of cheaper books. Inflation is at least as high as growth, resulting in stagnation. Growth continues in magazines, which is significant because Japan's largest book houses also do magazines; for the first time, Iwanami Shoten's Toru Midorikawa told *Publishers Weekly*, magazine sales exceeded book sales in the most recent business year.

In the Netherlands, the big four groups (Elsevier, Kluwer, VNU, and Wolters Samson) all announced higher profits in first 1983 returns—and if you don't look too closely at the results of trade publishers, you can be optimistic about that country (notes Johan Somerwil of Kluwer). French publishers generally appeared optimistic, although just prior to the fair their trade association had released statistics pointing to "the end of growth" in the 1979–1982 period, with sales up only 1.6 percent in constant francs last year; part of the problem was a price freeze, and higher business taxes; most of the problem was France's slump. In the book trade, Norway had Scandinavia's best track record, as Cappelen's Sigmund Stromme confirmed. Finnish houses, and clubs, continue to work miracles in their small market. But Sweden, agent Lennart Sane tells us, is still the best market in the region. Denmark? Copenhagen agent Ib Lauritzen holds up his fingers to form a zero.

The Italians came to Frankfurt bearing stories of general trade crisis, a result of undercapitalization and persistent inflation; reduced print runs require ever higher list prices. Nuova Italia's Mario Casalini points out that companies that used to be able to fall back on schoolbooks must cope with a sharp decline in school-age population; some larger companies such as Mondadori have protected themselves with diversification into television and other electronic media. Agent Elfriede Pexa describes the plight of publishers who must pay out nearly twice as many lire for their dollar acquisitions as they did a few short years ago. Many Italians at the fair wore pensive expressions—one could call it mourning—and few encountered in the aisles failed to evoke the crisis at one of their country's most prestigious houses, Turin's family-owned Einaudi; during Frankfurt fair week the Italian press was unraveling a story of indebtedness (30-billion lire, just about equivalent to total sales last year). No one thought that Einaudi would be allowed to die; although the firm has had to file for Italy's equivalent of Chapter 11, it is hoped that new capital and a reduction of about a third of its payroll of 350 will save it from liquidation.

At the end of the fair the word was spreading of Warner Communications' losses, and that froze smiles, although everyone knew that it was not the fault of the book publishing division.

Entertaining Traditions

Frankfurt has its traditions, such as the elegant Saturday night buffet in the palatial decor of the Hessischer Hof, hosted by Reader's Digest book divisions in Europe for non-American publishing partners. On the same evening, outside town at Kronberg Castle, Sweden's Bra Böcker offered another glamorous soirée to its friends. Amsterdam's Meulenhoff sponsored a sit-down dinner; the book trade's captains and generals wore their darkest suits for a reception held by the Mexican organizers of the International Publishers Congress, to be held in March 1984 in Mexico City.

A number of German houses hold regular Frankfurt parties, e.g., the Springer-Verlag Friday noon gathering at the Hessischer Hof; Piper, at the same hotel not far from the fairgrounds, threw a smaller party in the early evening; Thienemann, who gave the world Michael Ende, staged a Frankfurter Hof party to present its new program, showing that it didn't end with Ende. The lavish S. Fischer Verlag reception on the eve of the fair opening has also become a tradition; it is held in the fair's offices, but guests soon forget that; few Frankfurt restaurants could duplicate the display. French publishers invited foreign counterparts for cocktails at country's collective stand. Methuen used a downtown hotel to celebrate the launching of its adaptation of the pacesetting Gallimard children's book program, which they were calling Moonlight Books.

Once more Stuttgart's Ernest Klett Verlag offered fellow educational publishers an afternoon seminar on a subject of common concern. Last year it was "Microcomputers in Schools"; this time, "Text Processing in Publishing," with a case study by Hallstein Laupsa of Oslo's Aschehoug.

Surely the most moving event at this fair was the memorial hour organized for Ljubivoje Stefanović, who had been the international bookman par excellence, and who died early in the year. Publishers he worked with, Peter Jovanovich of Harcourt Brace Jovanovich and Academic Press, Sergio Giunti of Italy's Giunti, and Hans and Hilde Weitpert of Germany's Belser, were hosts at a reception at Ljubo's favorite Frankfurt hotel, the Frankfurter Hof. With its contingents of Japanese and Yugoslav and Swiss publishers, this was perhaps the most international gathering at Frankfurt, observed former McGraw-Hill book group chairman Edward E. Booher through tears. "I can't recall a ceremony like this for any other publisher," said Heinemann's Tom Rosenthal.

The Linder party was unique in two ways: agents usually don't hold parties; this one was held to introduce Michael Dennis Linder, son and heir of one of Europe's leading agents, the late Erich Linder; it brought together the elite of U.S. and European publishing—it would be easier to report who wasn't there.

Among American houses holding parties, the most elegant has always been Harper & Row's; it takes place on opening day and offers the opportunity to discover which European heads of houses have come to the fair. Holt, Rinehart and Winston presented its bestselling author Leo Buscaglia, preceding its party with the screening of a short film about him. Another author was in town—Umberto Eco—and his publisher Bompiani staged a party for fellow Eco publishers such as Harcourt Brace Jovanovich; Secker & Warburg, France's Grasset, the Netherlands' Bert Bakker, Finland's Tammi, Sweden's Bromberg, as well as for those who hadn't yet signed contracts. As for Eco, he was renewing acquaintanceship with a fair he had attended 13 times as a Bompiani editor; he even got married at a Frankfurt fair; he hadn't been back in a decade. Asked what he was doing to follow up *The Name of the Rose,* he provided the title of his forthcoming book: *Semiotics and the Philosophy of Language.*

For the first time in memory, the German book trade's Peace Prize went to a publisher (under his author's hat): Manès Sperber, formerly a Paris editor of foreign books, best known in Germany and around the world as author of works on his own and the Jewish experience.

No matter how early one gets to Frankfurt before the fair, one encounters publishers who arrived a day or more earlier. Those valuable pre-fair days allow longer, less hectic discussions. Companies with subsidiaries spread around the world, international organizations in the book world, hold their formal meetings before (or during) the fair. On the Tuesday preceding the Wednesday opening of the fair, STM—the International Group of Scientific, Technical and Medical Publishers—holds its general assembly; this was the fifteenth. The annual report of the STM Group Executive led off with an evocation of the way new technology permeates the publishing process within the STM constituency, and the stress was on the need to protect the products of publishers; indeed, much of the morning assembly was taken up with copyright and the problem of illicit copying. In the year since the fourteenth assembly, STM had staged a seminar in New York (under the chairmanship of Elsevier Science Publishing's Charles Ellis) on the U.S. market (and on new technologies in journal publishing); there had been a meeting in Amsterdam on electronic manuscript preparation and a seminar in Oslo on promotion; STM's omnipresent secretary Paul Nijhoff Asser had represented his group at public and private conferences around the world, notably with a lively defense of the publishing community when it seemed to be serving as a handy scapegoat at a WIPO Forum on Piracy at Geneva in March 1983. Among upcoming events: an STM marketing seminar to precede the opening of the New Delhi World Book Fair in February 1984.

Perhaps every major sci-tech publisher in the world was present at STM's ballroom meeting at Frankfurt's Intercontinental Hotel on October 11: heads of houses, directors, editors-in-chief; surely more capital investment, more turnover were represented in that room than in any equivalent gathering of trade houses that week. STM now serves 140 members in 21 nations; the group's committee on marketing, copyright, innovations, and scientific journals has now been augmented by an Ibero-American section under the chairmanship of Daniel Waingart of Mexico's Nueva Editorial Interamericana. At Frankfurt STM elected new officers: John J. Hanley (W. B. Saunders), chairman; Robert G. B. Duncan (Churchill Livingston, U.K.), vice-chairman. James J. L. Kels (Elsevier Science) stayed on as treasurer.

Copyright in Trouble

The assembly had opened with some disabused comments on the shortcomings of international governmental organizations with respect to copyright protection by outgoing chairman Robert H. Craven (F. A. Davis); he proposed that STM dispatch regular delegations to WIPO and UNESCO to make known its grievances. As chairman of STM's copyright committee, W. Bradford Wiley (John Wiley) reported some bad news from India: a new law allowing that country's publishers to reprint normally protected works without seeking permission. Alexander Hoffman (Doubleday), chairman of the U.S. Copyright Clearance Center, offered an update on that agency's achievements and announced the agreement of major American corporations to a system of one-time annual payments—the amounts to be based on sampling—for permissions to copy. He appealed to the world's publishers to back the project by entering their own titles into the system. "It would be foolish for any publisher not to join in," Andrew H. Neilly, Jr. of Wiley pitched in from the floor. Meanwhile, STM's model agreement—a set of permissions guidelines offering an international standard of fair use between publishers—had already received the endorsement of 93 publishing houses around the world.

Each year the publishing community's experiment in international copublishing cooperation, the Motovun Group, meets for Sunday morning breakfast. Representatives of some of the world's best-known imprints rub shoulders with coproduction packagers and printers from the United States, Europe, and Japan. Many of them will go on to the summer gathering in the Yugoslav village of Motovun, where publishers and creators meet in formal and informal sessions to dream over new projects. Under the chairmanship of Edward Booher, the Frankfurt meeting heard Motovun organizer Nebojša Tomašević (of Belgrade's Revija) announce the formal participation of the Motovun Group at the upcoming Belgrade book fair. There is now to be a Motovun Publishing House for appropriate copublishing ventures; in Tokyo veteran agent Hideo Aoki runs the world's first Motovun agency; this past summer at the medieval Yugoslav village there was a contingent of five mainland Chinese publishers. "What is unique about Motovun meetings," commented Booher, "is that everyone there can make an immediate decision, which wasn't even true of me when I ran McGraw-Hill."

One alumnus of McGraw-Hill, and of Motovun, introduced a new venture to Frankfurt visitors this year: Alfred van der Marck Editions had recently been founded in New York by van der Marck to do the sort of ambitious illustrated projects that "the giants don't do anymore." He had brought his first book to the fair, The Way of the Animal Powers, the first of a four-volume Historical Atlas of World Mythology; he had gambled by doing 20,000 copies for the American market, although he knew he couldn't make money with that. At Frankfurt he sold 8,000 more to the United Kingdom, was waiting for a 12,000-copy order to be confirmed from Germany when Publishers Weekly met him; he hoped for 40–50,000 foreign sales in all. And he had brought along dummies of other ambitious projects.

Promoting Other Fairs

Once again the organizers of the world's other book fairs used Frankfurt to promote them. Thus the Bologna Children's Book Fair people offered advance material on next spring's event (April 5–8, 1984), talking up the new features: a special exhibit on children and computers, with emphasis on the school market.

The London Book Fair passed out reminders (April 10–13, 1984), promising over 500 exhibitors. And there is a brand-new fair in the making: the Tokyo International Book Fair, to run from May 18–21, 1984, in order "to introduce to Japanese publishers and to Japanese readers the current state of publishing in as many countries as possible and to encourage the Japanese to take even more interest in a wider range of foreign publications," according to the prospectus of the Publishers Association for Cultural Exchange in Tokyo. Finally, there is to be a first International Feminist Book Fair, set for London from June 7-9, 1984, designed for the book trade, the public and "for all women"; the organizers, Feminist Book Fair at London House, Church Street, London N. W. 8, hope to see it used as a rights market.

As for Frankfurt, it convenes next year from October 3-8, 1984, when visitors will have to learn how to use a totally new layout; the fair will be transferred to four facing buildings at the eastern (town) side of the fairgrounds, connected by moving sidewalks; wonderful old *Halle Funf* is being retired. Every second year the fair comes with a theme, and the 1984 edition is inspired by George Orwell's novel, though it has been christened "Orwell 2000." There seemed no hope to changing the dates of the fair, despite the fact that Yom Kippur, the holiest of Jewish holy days, begins right in the middle of it (sundown on October 5); by the time the fair authorities discovered this, it was too late. The computers had apparently spewed out the dates of the various trade events organized by Frankfurt's fair authorities, and the book fair drew Yom Kippur. New technology had won out; 1984 was being commemorated appropriately.

National Associations

American Library Association

50 E. Huron St., Chicago, IL 60611
312-944-6780

Brooke E. Sheldon
President

Membership in the world's oldest and largest library association reached an all-time high of 39,124 in August 1983. As it has over the past 108 years, in 1983 the association involved itself in the key issues affecting its constituents and the library community at large. Major concerns of 1983 were the various federal government initiatives placing increased restraints on public access to government publications and information and continuing opposition to the U.S. Office of Personnel Management's proposed lowering of standards for the employment of federal librarians. As the Intellectual Freedom Committee noted in its annual report to the ALA Council, "This [Los Angeles] Conference is taking place in an atmosphere marked by increasing concern about the frightening growth of governmental restrictions on access to information and about increasing governmental secrecy." These concerns are reflected in a number of membership and Council resolutions and in other official statements of policy. [See the special report on access to federal information in Part 1—*Ed.*]

The association began the year with a substantial deficit, but several management initiatives, combined with the general rebound in the nation's economy, resulted in a balanced budget by the end of the fiscal year. It was a year of making new "connections," as President Carol Nemeyer carried out her theme through the development of funding for the first Business Council for Libraries, an ALA group dedicated to cooperation between libraries and industry. President Nemeyer also announced the creation of a Commission on Freedom and Equality of Access to Information. This commission, chaired by Dan Lacey, former senior vice president, McGraw-Hill, is studying the rapid growth of electronically based information systems, and will make recommendations on how these systems can be made available to library users.

The Annual Conference

Some 11,000 librarians, trustees, and friends of libraries attended more than 2,000 meetings and workshops at the ALA's annual conference held June 25–30, 1983, in Los Angeles. The President's Program featured talks by a number of "library champions," including such well-known personalities as Sir Richard Attenborough, producer-director of the film *Gandhi* (1982); Hollywood producer Samuel Goldwyn, Jr., a major library supporter; and Louis L'Amour, author of many best-selling novels about the Old West.

At the Los Angeles conference, the ALA took a major step forward in demonstrating new methods of communicating with members and in providing continuing education opportunities. A five-hour program that included highlights of the annual conference was transmitted to ALA members at more than 100 video-receiving locations throughout the United States. It was the association's third and most ambitious video teleconference, and the first from an annual meeting. The program included a review of new technology in libraries and a live interactive "bibliographic institute," sponsored by the ALA Resources and Technical Services Division.

International Meetings

It was a year in which the ALA president called for members to be "closer to each other within the profession and also to link us more securely to others in allied fields, in business and industry, in the political arena," and it was also a year in which our international connections were not neglected. Nearly 200 U.S. librarians attended the forty-ninth general conference of the International Federation of Library Associations and Institutions in Munich, August 21–27. The American delegation included 1983–1984 ALA President Brooke E. Sheldon, President-elect E. J. Josey, and Executive Director Robert Wedgeworth. Thomas J. Galvin, chairperson of ALA's International Relations Committee, along with representatives from the Federal Republic of Germany, France, and the Soviet Union, spoke at the opening plenary session on the conference theme "Libraries in a Technological World." More than 1,200 delegates from 74 countries attended the conference where Henriette Avram (Library of Congress) was elected to the IFLA executive board, and Irwin Pizer (Medical Library Association) was named treasurer of the IFLA professional board. [See the report on the IFLA conference in Part 1—*Ed.*] In December, ALA was represented by its president at the thirtieth anniversary celebration of the founding of the Library Association of China (R.O.C.), in Taipei.

Highlights of 1983

Most ALA members did not travel abroad, to Los Angeles, or to the high-spirited and balmy midwinter meeting in San Antonio, but a surprisingly high number of librarians, trustees, illustrators, members of the book trade, information scientists, and friends of the library in the United States, Canada, and 70 other countries who make up the ALA membership, participated actively in its 850 divisions, round tables, committees, task forces, and other voluntary units. The membership represents all types of libraries—state, public, school, academic, and special libraries—serving persons in government, commerce, the armed services, hospitals, prisons, and other institutions.

Although individual members have richly diverse interests, the overall goal of ALA, "the promotion of libraries and librarianship to assure the delivery of user-oriented library information service to all," forms an umbrella under which its many committees/units can accomplish their specific objectives. Current priorities, as adopted by the ALA Council, are access to information, legislation, funding, intellectual freedom, public awareness, and personnel resources. Major activities include research on library problems, development of standards and guidelines, accreditation of library education programs, clarification of legislative issues, vigorous support for intellectual freedom, publishing, awards, library cooperation, and continuing education.

Continuing Education Events

The following are examples of literally hundreds of continuing education events held both at the annual conference and throughout the year by the various units of ALA. More than 2,600 members, exhibitors, and friends attended the Public Library Association's (PLA) first national conference in Baltimore, which was also the site for the first conference of the Library and Information Technology Association (LITA), held in September. LITA reports that more than 1,500 attended, and 75 vendors held exhibits. Both of these conferences were exclusively devoted to continuing education events and featured such outstanding speakers and scholars as Isaac Asimov (PLA) and Ithiel de Sola Pool (LITA). LITA's pre–Los Angeles conference institute "Online Catalogs, Online Reference" drew 331 registrants.

The American Association of School Librarians (AASL) moved into high gear in planning its third national conference for Atlanta in fall 1984. Members of the American Library Trustee Association (ATLA) presented their Workshop in Library Leadership (WILL) in 13 states. The Association of Specialized and Cooperative Library Agencies (ASCLA) cosponsored a workshop on library service to disabled college students with the Florida State University's School of Library Science and spearheaded ALA's recognition of the Decade of Disabled Persons.

Six new continuing education courses were developed by the Association of College and Research Libraries (ACRL), bringing the total to 13. Continuing education courses were offered at the midwinter meeting, annual conference, and at ACRL chapter meetings. ACRL held its second series of library programming workshops funded by the National Endowment for the Humanities (NEH). These workshops brought together academic librarians and humanist scholars to consider humanities programming for the general public using the resources of academic libraries. ACRL's third national conference is scheduled for April 1984 in Seattle.

In addition to its live video telecast on rules and formats from Los Angeles, the Resources and Technical Services Division (RTSD) held the first in a series of institutes on preservation, "Library Preservation: The Administrative Challenge." This institute was funded by the Council on Library Resources and the Mellon Foundation.

The Intellectual Freedom Office has developed training modules for the "front-line" librarian on utilizing the media, the legislative process, the law, and interpersonal communication skills. The Office for Library Personnel Resources (OLPR) presented the 1983 annual conference program on administering staff cutbacks and began a pilot training program on specific personnel topics.

Legislation and Funding

The year 1983 was characterized by ups and downs in federal library funding. Welcome news was the authorization of $50 million for LSCA Title II public library construction as part of the emergency jobs bill and a 12 percent increase in LSCA Title I and III public library services and interlibrary cooperation. However, 1983 also brought the loss of all funding for HEA Title IIA college library resources. The ALA Washington Office monitored congressional hearings closely, presented testimony as appropriate, and coordinated all efforts of the association and its divisions in this regard.

Major areas of concern and accomplishment included the development of a response to the Register of Copyrights' first five-year report on library photocopying provisions; continuation of ALA's strong opposition to OPM-proposed standards for federal librarians through numerous developments throughout the year; efforts to publicize and oppose an increasing number of regulatory threats to citizen access to government information; and increasing involvement in telecommunications legislation, particularly that involving data communication by libraries, since proposed FCC policy and AT&T tariffs would cause major cost increases for libraries. Working closely with the District of Columbia Library Association, the ALA Washington Office held a highly successful ninth annual National Library Week Legislative Day, involving 350 library supporters from 37 states who spent the day visiting members of Congress.

In divisions and other units, the Association for Library Services to Children (ALSC) initiated a national legislative network of children's librarians; the Committee on the Status of Women in Librarianship developed legislative fact sheets on issues affecting women; and ASCLA published a "Checklist of Multitype Library Cooperation State Laws and Regulations," a detailed analysis of the components of legislation and regulation from 11 states, grouped by topic for study and comparison.

Recognizing the importance of seeking private sources of library funding, the Library Administration and Management Association (LAMA) board approved a new section for fund raising and financial development and a preconference on this topic was conducted at the annual meeting in Los Angeles. Other ALA units were successful in gaining funds from outside sources for special projects.

ACRL received a $210,000 grant to conduct workshops with the PLA for teams of academic and public librarians and humanist scholars; RTSD received the Bailey K. Howard-World Book Encyclopedia-ALA Goal Award for "Adult Services in the Eighties," a survey project designed to update the 1952–1953 landmark survey by Helen Lyman Smith; the ALA Office for Research was awarded a $105,000 grant by NCES to design a national data collection system; and the Public Information Office (PIO) won a $44,000 contract to encourage public library educational programs on the PBS series "Heritage: Civilization and the Jews." In October 1983, ASCLA began a two-year project funded by the National Endowment for the Humanities, "Let's Talk about It—Reading Discussion Programs in America's Libraries." The project, budgeted at $900,000, is designed to promote and support reading discussion programs for public libraries in at least 10 to 15 states. Several other units of ALA are actively involved in seeking grants and in sponsoring fund raising, proposal writing, and other workshops designed to increase public awareness and legislative support.

Publishing

ALA Publications

In 1982–1983, ALA published 30 books, including *Cartographic Materials* (Hugo Stibbe, general editor), *Bibliographic Record and Information Technology* (Ronald Hagler and Peter Simmons), *Cataloging Machine-Readable Data Files* (Sue Dodd), *Communicate!* (Anne J. Matthews), and *Sequels* (Janet Husband). Barbara Baskin and Karen Harris produced *The Mainstreamed Library: Issues, Ideas, Innovations.* Other previous authors for ALA and popular new editions include *The Intellectual Freedom Manual,* Music Library Association's *Basic Music Library,* and Ruth Gregory's *Anniversaries and Holidays.* Two important reference works, *ALA Glossary of Library and Information Science* and the *ALA Yearbook,* wrapped up the year. The new edition of the *ALA Glossary* (first since 1943) will shortly appear in Japanese translation.

Guide to the Literature of Art History* by Etta Arntzen and Robert Rainwater won the Art Libraries Association Award for best reference work. *Ways of the Illustrator* by Joseph Schwary was selected for *Choice*'s "Outstanding Academic Books List." Planning began for new editions of *Guide to Reference Books* and the *ALA World Encyclopedia of Library and Information Services.*

For ALA publishing, 1983 was an outstanding year, and substantial revenues were returned to the ALA general fund. Selected *Booklist* reviews are now available as part of Key Fax National Teletext magazine and in the Viewtron interactive home videotext system. These two projects mark ALA's first entry into the electronic publishing field.

Library Technology Reports, a unique bimonthly subscription service, provides critical evaluations of products and services used in libraries, media centers, and other educational institutions. Its purpose is to enable librarians to make wise purchasing decisions and also to alert manufacturers to the specific needs of libraries and to the standards of quality expected. In March 1983, *LTR* received a grant of $64,400 from the National Endowment for the Humanities for the development of a prototype face-up photocopier for copying from bound volumes without harming the book.

Selected Divisional and ALA Office Publications

In addition to its quarterly publication *Interface,* ASCLA published "Checklist of Multitype Library Cooperation State Laws and Regulations." A result of several years' work by the Multitype Library Cooperation Section's Legislative Committee, this is a detailed analysis of the components of legislation and regulations from 11 states. Another ASCLA publication was *Materials Packet: Library Service to Deaf Children, Young Adults and Their Parents,* and as 1983 ended ASCLA members were completing work on the revision of *Standards of Service for the Library of Congress Network of Libraries for the Blind and Physically Handicapped.* YASD, in addition to *Top of the News,* a joint publication with ALSC, published *Best Books, Selected Films, High-Interest/Low Reading Level Book List, Best of Best Books, Youth Participation in Library Decision Making Handbook,* and *Positive Aspects of the Contemporary American Family Media List.*

ALTA issued three new publications, *Securing a New Library Director, Library Trustees and Personnel,* and *Evaluating the Library Director.* ALSC published the 1984 Caldecott Wall Calendar and created a combined list of outstanding audiovisual materials for children. RTSD completed work on two guidelines: *Coordinated and Cooperative Collection Development* and *Guide to Collection Evaluation through Use and User Studies.* ACRL maintained an active program of more than 65 publications and added 8 new items in 1983. *Choice, College and Research Libraries,* and *College and Research Libraries News* each had a successful year. PLA reports a record year for publishing activity, and 64 projects with publishing potential have been identified within the division.

The Office of Research issued *Library Statistics, 1972–1982: A Guide to Sources.* A new chapter handbook was published by the Chapter Relations Committee to provide state associations, offices, and staff with comprehensive information about ALA and chapter relationships. The entries for the first annual Gale Research Financial Development Award were summarized in a new publication, *Success Stories,* edited by the Public Information Office and underwritten by the Gale Research Company. PIO also published the *Library Symbol Clip Art Book* and a special collection, *The ALA Library Clip Art Book*, with instructions on how to do basic design and paste-up.

The Office for Library Personnel Resources (OLPR) brought out two new kits in its *Topics in Personnel* series: #4, *Humanizing the Work Place: Quality of Work Life in Libraries,* and #5, *Administering Staff Cutbacks: Planning and Implementing a Reduction in Force.* As a result of committee projects, the Committee on the Status of Women in Librarianship published *Career Profiles and Sex Discrimination in the Library Profession, On Account of Sex,* and *Directory of Library and Information Profession Women's Groups.*

Accreditation

The ALA Committee on Accreditation (COA) reviewed self-study applications from ten library education programs and scheduled reaccreditation visits to ten schools. Accreditation actions in 1983, including action on programs visited in late 1982, resulted in the reaccreditation of 11 programs and withdrawal of accreditation from one. Two open meetings of the COA were held at ALA conferences to target attention on matters of particular interest to library educators. Interviews and orientation sessions were held for new site visitors who will join in the accreditation process in the future. In October 1983, there were 67 accredited library education programs, 7 in Canada and 60 in the United States.

ALANET—Electronic Mail Services

In fall 1983, ALA announced the availability of its electronic mail and information network (ALANET) to organization members. The system allows subscribers to communicate electronically with libraries, suppliers, library associations, and other subscribers across the United States and Canada. In addition, such data bases as the ALA *News Bulletin, Washington Newsline, Publication News, PR Power Tools,* conference schedules, online orders for publications and graphics, *Official Airline Guide, UMI Article Clearinghouse,* and United Press International, ALANET's computer-based services allow dial-up access through almost any type of terminal. Through ALANET, members can communicate directly with ALA headquarters in both Chicago and Washington, D.C., and follow legislation and intellectual freedom issues affecting libraries.

Newbery-Caldecott Awards

Cynthia Voigt, author of *Dicey's Song,* won the 1983 Newbery Medal for the most distinguished contribution to American literature for children published in 1982. Marcia Brown, illustrator and translator of *Shadow,* won her third Caldecott Medal for the most distinguished American picture book for children. Maurice Sendak, a trendsetter in juvenile books, was named winner of the 1983 Laura Ingalls Wilder Award, presented every three years to an author or illustrator whose books have made a lasting contribution to literature for children. These awards were presented at the revived Newbery-Caldecott banquet sponsored by the Association for Library Services to Children in Los Angeles. [For other ALA awards, see "Library Scholarship and Award Recipients, 1983" in Part 3—*Ed.*]

Coalition for Literacy

The ALA has been concerned for some time that there are more than 23 million adult functional illiterates in the United States. Since 1979, the Office for Library Outreach Services (OLOS) has been training resource personnel who in turn train others in the library field to conduct literacy programs.

ALA determined six years ago that its own training resources, and those of other literacy groups alone, were not sufficient. It has organized the Coalition for Literacy, a group of 11 national organizations, each with a distinctive role to play nationally and locally in the delivery of information and services. In addition to the ALA, the coalition includes the American Association of Advertising Agencies; American Association for Adult and Continuing Education; B. Dalton Bookseller; CONTACT, Inc.; International Reading Association; Laubach Literacy International; Literacy Volunteers of America, Inc.; National Advisory Council on Adult Education; National Commission on Libraries and Information Science; and National Council of State Directors of Adult Education.

A national Advertising Council campaign alerts both volunteers and persons needing information on local literacy programs and resources. By dialing a national toll-free hot line (1-800-228-8813), persons will be placed in touch with appropriate local agencies.

Planning

The year 1983 was characterized by planning and study of future directions for several ALA divisions. The AASL engaged in a year-long study of future options for that division. A major objective for the organization is the involvement of larger numbers of media professionals in its activities. The president of LITA appointed a committee to plan the implementation of the reorganization of LITA according to the recommendations of a previous Goals and Long-Range Planning Committee.

ASCLA celebrated its fifth anniversary on September 1, 1983, prompting the division's leadership to examine ASCLA's operation and structure to see if it is effective in meeting members' needs. Following discussions at ASCLA's meetings in Los Angeles, the division officers began streamlining the division in 1983-1984, with the goal of designing a structure that responds to members' needs and meets the division's overarching goal of access to libraries and information.

At the 1983 midwinter meeting LAMA began a self-study and planning effort relating to membership services and future role. As a result, the board approved seven goals in such important areas as activities, services, and membership participation.

National Library Week

With Jedi Yoda of the movie *Star Wars* as "spokescreature," PIO experienced another successful National Library Week campaign, providing materials to more than 15,000 participating libraries. Feature stories were placed, public service ads were run in national magazines, and radio announcements featuring Bill Cosby, John Jakes, Studs Terkel, and Jim Fixx were placed with networks and made available to local libraries. The National Library Week theme for April 1984 is "Knowledge Is Real Power." Posters, clip art, and bookmarks are available from the Public Information Office, ALA headquarters.

Chris Hoy Retires

Chris Hoy, conference arrangement officer for the association, retired in July 1983, after 24 years of service to ALA. He was honored at the Los Angeles conference by the ALA Council and several other groups for his "service with patience and distinction."

Council of National Library and Information Associations

John T. Corrigan, C.F.X.

CNLIA Secretariat, 461 W. Lancaster Ave., Haverford, PA 19041
215-649-5250

The first effort toward coordination of library associations was the creation by the council of the American Library Association of a Joint Committee on Relations between National Library Associations in 1939. The onset of World War II and the urgent need for cooperation in this national emergency spurred 14 associations to meet in 1942 to form a council of library associations, each with equal voting power, to take over the function of the joint committee. The Council of National Library and Information Associations, Inc. (CNLIA) has served since 1942 as a forum in which library and information associations have discussed their common library and information problems of each successive era.

The constitution states that the object of the Council of National Library/ Information Associations is "to promote a closer relationship among the national library and information associations of the United States and Canada by providing a central agency to foster cooperation in matters of mutual interest, by gathering and exchanging information among its member associations, and by cooperating with learned, professional and scientific societies in forwarding matters of common interest."

The council may be in its own right an operating body for carrying out its proper purposes, but no member association can be bound to any statement of policy, course of action, or financial commitment except by affirmative vote of its own governing body. Each member association reserves all rights of action either individually or jointly between two or more associations in any field of activity.

Each member association is represented on the council by two appointed delegates. Meetings are held twice a year, in May and November, usually in New York City. At the present time, 19 associations hold membership in CNLIA: American Association of Law Libraries, American Library Association, American Society of Indexers, American Theological Library Association, Art Libraries Society/North America, Association of

Christian Librarians, Association of Jewish Libraries, Catholic Library Association, Chinese American Librarians Association, Church and Synagogue Library Association, Council of Planning Librarians, Library Binding Institute, Library Public Relations Council, Lutheran Library Association, Medical Library Association, Music Library Association, Society of American Archivists, Special Libraries Association, and Theatre Library Association.

The primary purpose of the council is to provide a meeting place in which matters of library/information science interest and concern to more than one association can be discussed and appropriate action considered. A second purpose is to foster cooperative projects of value to North American librarianship information science as a whole; this has been done primarily through the activities of joint committees on which any interested associations may be represented. The committees sponsored by the council are usually initiated at council meetings, have a chairperson appointed by the council, and are authorized to proceed autonomously, making regular reports to the council. These independent groups have accomplished much serious and effective work.

CNLIA Projects

The Bowker Annual

One of the early interests of CNLIA was the revival of the *American Library Annual,* which had been dormant since 1918. In 1955, under the editorial sponsorship of CNLIA, R. R. Bowker Company resumed this publication under the new title *The Bowker Annual.* It featured a comprehensive listing of international, national, and regional library associations, their committees, and joint committees. Also included was an "activity index to the profession," which was an analytical cross-index of the subject interests of the committees. Other parts of the volume brought together statistical and factual information of practical concern to librarians: library statistics, salaries, building costs, postal regulations, literary prizes, library awards, news, and special reports. Now in its twenty-ninth edition, *The Bowker Annual, 1984* continues the format of the first edition.

ANSI Committee Z39

The American National Standards Committee Z39: Library and Information Sciences and Related Publishing Practices exemplifies the council's objective to cooperate with learned and scientific societies in forwarding library projects. The American National Standards Institute determines committee organization; the council sponsors the effort. Committee Z39 was reorganized in 1978 and was incorporated in 1983. It will soon receive independent agent status from ANSI, after which it will no longer need the sponsorship of the council. [See the annual report on Committee Z39, also in this section of Part I—*Ed.*]

Universal Serials and Book Exchange, Inc.

In 1945 the Joint Committee on Devastated Libraries (CNLIA's first joint committee) established the American Book Center for War Devastated Libraries. Then, in 1948, the United States Book Exchange, Inc. (USBE) was set up as a two-way exchange of American and foreign publications. In 1951, when foreign libraries were able to begin paying for the service, the Exchange became self-supporting. Renamed the Universal Serials and Book Exchange, Inc., USBE continues as one of the longest-lived cooperative agencies in the library profession today.

Other Projects

Other CNLIA-sponsored projects include the library manpower project, *Who's Who in Library and Information Services,* and CLENE (Continuing Library Education Network and Exchange), which grew out of a study group on library education established by CNLIA.

CNLIA's cooperative activities are reflected in its many past and present joint committees. Past joint committees include Library Services in Hospitals, Placement of Librarians, Library Work as a Career, Visiting Foreign Librarians, Library Problems Related to the Peace Corps, Prison Libraries, the Protection of Cultural and Scientific Resources, Exhibit Managers, and the Preservation of Materials. Current CNLIA joint committees include the Ad Hoc Committee on Copyright Practice and Interpretation, the Joint Committee on Specialized Cataloging, and the Joint Committee on Association Cooperation.

How to Join CNLIA

Application for membership in CNLIA is open to any national library/information or related area association of the United States or Canada, with admittance to membership based on a majority vote at any biannual meeting of the council. Inquiries may be addressed to the council chairperson at 461 W. Lancaster Ave., Haverford, PA 19041 (215-649-5250).

American National Standards Committee Z39: Library and Information Sciences and Related Publishing Practices
and
International Organization for Standardization Technical Committee (TC) 46—Documentation

U.S. Department of Commerce, National Bureau of Standards
Library E-106, Washington, DC 20234
301-921-3241

Sandra K. Paul
Chairperson

Patricia R. Harris
Executive Director

American National Standards Committee Z39: Library and Information Sciences and Related Publishing Practices has the principal responsibility in the United States for developing and promoting the voluntary technical standards used by libraries, information systems, data base services, and publishing. Committee Z39 was established in 1939 by the American National Standards Institute, on the request of the American Library Association, the Medical Library Association, the Special Libraries Association, and the American Association of Law Libraries. At the close of 1983, Committee Z39 had 40 published standards. Two of the best known standards are *Book Numbering* (Z39.21), which defines the International Standard Book Number (ISBN), and Z39.9, which establishes the International Standard Serial Number.

Committee Z39 Activities, 1983

Development and Approval of Standards

Formal procedures for the development and approval of American national standards are established by the American National Standards Institute. Once a draft standard is developed by a Z39 subcommittee, it is submitted to the Z39 voting membership for comment and vote. Negative votes can lead to a revised standard, which must be reballoted by the Z39 membership. Comment is also solicited from interested persons outside Z39 through a notice in the ANSI biweekly publication *Standards Action*. Z39 responds in writing to any negative comments that are received. Once this public review is completed and the Z39 voting members have achieved agreement on the draft standard, the standard is submitted to the ANSI Board of Standards Review, along with a certification that the ANSI procedural requirements have been met. Notice of approval by the Board of Standards Review is published in *Standards Action*, and the standard is published by ANSI.

Membership

Committee Z39 has two categories of members: voting members and information members. At the close of 1983, 45 voting members were participating in the work of Z39.

Z39's voting members include the major professional organizations in library and information sciences and publishing, federal libraries and agencies, library networks, and bibliographic services. Voting members participate actively in the work of Z39 by voting on and critiquing all draft standards developed by Z39 standards subcommittees and deciding on new standards to be developed. Membership is open to any organization that has a substantial interest in Z39's area of standards development. New voting members in 1983 included Colorado Alliance of Research Libraries, the Cooperative College Library Center in Atlanta, and the University of Alabama Press.

There were 81 information members at the close of 1983. Information members receive a subscription to Z39's newsletter, *Voice of Z39*, copies of draft standards under development, and other informational materials on standards published during the year.

Organizational Changes

In January 1983, Z39 filed articles of incorporation establishing itself as an independent educational association in the District of Columbia. Also in 1983, the officers of Z39 sponsored a national contest to solicit suggestions for a new name for the organization that would communicate the purpose and scope of the group's work. The new name, National Information Standards Organization (Z39), will be presented to the voting members for approval in early 1984 and will become effective shortly thereafter.

Officers and Committees

As of December 31, 1983, the officers of Z39 were the following: Sandra K. Paul, chairperson; Ted Brandhorst, vice-chairperson/chairperson elect; John Lorenz, treasurer; members of the Executive Council included: (representing libraries) Linda Bartley, Mary Ellen Jacob, and Larry X. Besant; (representing information services) James Rush, Lynne Neufeld, and Robert Tannehill; and (representing publishing) Karl Heumann, Seldon Terrant, and Jeffrey Heynen. Chairpersons of the Executive Council committees are Ted Brandhorst, Program Committee; Seldon Terrant, Finance Committee; Larry X. Besant, Membership Committee; Linda Bartley, Publicity Committee; and Henriette Avram, International Committee. A special Executive Council Committee on Future Planning was appointed in 1983 with Susan Vita as chairperson.

Publicity and Exhibits

In 1983, Z39 displayed its professional exhibit at the conferences of a number of library and information associations: American Library Association (annual meeting), National Federation of Abstracting and Information Services, Special Libraries Association (conference), American Society for Information Science, and the first national meetings of the Library and Information Technology Association and the Public Library Association.

Liaisons with Other Groups

Z39 works closely with standards committees in other related areas. The Z39 representative to American National Standards Committee X3 (Information Systems) is

Ray Dennenberg (Library of Congress). Ted Brandhorst, vice-chairperson/chairperson-elect of Z39, is representing Z39 on the review board of the Association of American Publishers' project to develop industrywide standards for preparing and processing electronic manuscripts. The goal of this project is to enable authors to create a transferable electronic file that can be processed on any machine and used as input for any publication. This project is cosponsored by the Council on Library Resources and is being carried out by Aspen Systems Corporation.

Standards in Development

The development and writing of Z39 standards are carried out by volunteer standards subcommittees composed of representatives of Z39's constituent groups, libraries, information services, and publishing communities. In 1983, two new standards subcommittees were appointed: Subcommittee CC, chaired by Wendy Reidel (Library of Congress), is defining a standard identifier for issues of serials and each item published in a serial; Subcommittee BB, chaired by David Cohen (Technique Learning Corporation), is charged to develop a standard identifier for computer software. Work continues on 14 other new standards, including "Romanization of Yiddish"; "Language Codes"; "Computer to Computer Protocols"; "Serials Holdings Statements"; "Bibliographic Data Source File Identification"; "Romanization"; "Coded Character Sets for Bibliographic Information Interchange"; "Environmental Conditions for Storage of Paper-based Materials"; "Permanent Paper for Library Materials"; "Standard Order Form for the Purchase of Multiple Titles"; "Standard Format for Computerized Book Ordering"; "Standard Identification Number for Libraries"; Non-serial Holdings Statement"; "Eye-Legible Information on Microfilm Leaders"; "Trailers and Containers of Processed Microfilm"; and "Interlibrary Loan Form."

In accordance with ANSI requirements, Z39 standards are reviewed and updated on a regular basis. Z39 published standards now being revised are Z39.1, *Periodicals: Format and Arrangement;* Z39.1, *Abbreviation of Titles and Periodicals;* Z39.10, *Directories of Libraries and Information Centers;* Z39.18, *Guidelines for Format and Production of Technical Reports;* and Z39.29, *Bibliographic References.*

New or Revised Z39 Standards Published in 1983

Five new or revised Z39 standards were published in 1983: Z39.45, *Claims of Missing Issues of Serials,* which identifies the data elements to be included in a serial claim and presents a model serial claim form; Z39.46, *Identification of Bibliographic Data on and Relating to Patent Documents,* which defines approximately 50 distinct pieces of bibliographic data widely used on the first page of patent documents; Z39.20, *Criteria for Price Indexes of Library Materials,* which describes the essential characteristics of a variety of library materials to enable the library market to track price changes in a reliable fashion; Z39.7, *Library Statistics;* Z39.23, *Standard Technical Report Number,* which outlines a numbering system to facilitate the bibliographic retrieval of technical reports.

An annotated list of Z39 published standards is available on request from the Z39 office. All Z39 standards are published and sold by the American National Standards Institute, 1430 Broadway, New York, NY 10018. They are available only from ANSI.

International Standardization Activities

Committee Z39 serves as the Technical Advisory Group (TAG) to the American National Standards Institute on the work of Technical Committee 46 (Documentation) of the International Standardization Organization. TC 46 is the counterpart of Z39 in the international arena. Z39 is responsible for representing the United States at TC 46 meetings and makes recommendations regarding the U.S. vote on draft international standards prepared by TC 46.

In May 1983, TC 46 held its biennial plenary assembly in Vienna. The United States was represented by Sandra K. Paul and Sally H. McCallum. At that meeting, the United States was elected to the TC 46 Advisory Group, which assists the secretariat in planning the program of work for the technical committee's many subcommittees and working groups (64 at the close of 1983). The United States is actively engaged in the work of Subcommittee 4, Automation in Documentation, and Subcommittee 6, Bibliographic Data Elements in Manual and Machine Processing. During 1983, three TC 46 working groups were established: Criteria for Price Indexes for Library Materials; International Library Statistics; and Back of the Book Indexes. ISO/TC 46 standards are available in the United States from the American National Standards Institute, 1430 Broadway, New York, NY 10018.

Association of American Publishers

One Park Ave., New York, NY 10016
212-689-8920

2005 Massachusetts Ave. N.W.
Washington, DC 20036
202-232-3335

Jane Lippe-Fine
Coordinator, Public Relations

The Association of American Publishers, the major voice of the book publishing industry in the United States, was founded in 1970 as the result of the merger of the American Book Publishers Council and the American Educational Publishers Institute. AAP members—some 350 companies representing all regions of the United States—publish the great majority of printed materials sold to American schools, colleges, libraries, and bookstores and by direct mail to homes. Member firms publish hardcover and paperback books—textbooks, general trade, reference, religious, technical, scientific, medical, professional, and scholarly—and journals. They also produce a range of other educational materials, including classroom periodicals, maps, globes, films and filmstrips, audio- and video-tapes, records, slides, transparencies, test materials, looseleaf and data base services, and computer software learning packages.

AAP operates under an organizational plan that ensures central direction of association affairs and gives important initiatives to the seven AAP divisions, each covering a major product line or distinct method of distribution of the industry. Marketing, promotion, research projects, and relations with other associations regarding mutual problems are central features of divisional programs. Each AAP division annually elects a chairperson and sponsors committees to plan and implement independent projects.

Association policies are established by an elected 29-member board of directors. AAP President Townsend Hoopes, chief operating officer, is responsible for managing AAP within the framework of policies set by the board. Approximately 40 professional and nonprofessional personnel staff AAP's two offices, in New York and Washington.

Highlights of 1983 Activities

In 1983, AAP submitted testimony to House and Senate committees on appropriations, copyright, education, library, and postal matters. It also reached successful settlements in lawsuits against American Cyanamid; E. R. Squibb and Sons; and New York University, its faculty, and an off-campus copy shop for their photocopying activities.

A major and continuing legislative objective during 1983 was the effort to maintain and improve public access to government information and to combat excessive government secrecy and censorship, which limit information available to writers and publishers and hence to the general public. In October, the chairperson of the Freedom to Read Committee testified before a House Government Operations subcommittee, along with other government officials and spokespersons for national media and scholarly organizations. The House subcommittee reviewed the March 1983 presidential directive "On Safeguarding National Security Information," which would severely curtail First Amendment rights, mandating prepublication review of writings by current or former government officials with access to classified information. Subsequently, the Congress imposed a moratorium on implementation of the directive until April 15, 1984. [See the special report on access to federal information in Part 1 of this volume—Ed.]

AAP filed friend-of-the-court briefs in two libel cases during 1983. In *Rogers* v. *Doubleday*, AAP's brief to the Texas Supreme Court challenged imposition of a $2 million punitive damage award against a book publisher that had unknowingly published a false fact about a private plaintiff. And in *Springer* v. *Viking*, in a brief to the New York State Court of Appeals (which subsequently dismissed the case), AAP addressed the critically important subject of applying the libel laws to works of fiction. (AAP had dealt with this subject in two previous cases.)

After a long battle, just before adjournment Congress passed a continuing resolution that will enable nonprofit mailings (including library rate and classroom periodicals) to continue at the present Step 14 of the phasing schedule. The $879 million appropriated for revenue foregone runs until the end of the current fiscal year on September 30, 1984. The Reagan administration had requested only $400 million for this purpose, which would have ended phasing and greatly increased costs.

After three years of consideration, Congress passed the Mail Order Consumer Protection Amendments. Of special concern to publishers, the new law incorporated the mirror image doctrine advocated by AAP, assuring that an advertisement cannot be subjected to mail fraud proceedings if it accurately reflects the contents of the book it promotes. This fundamental protection of the First Amendment rights of publishers in the new law was the keystone of AAP congressional testimony on the bill.

On April 28, 1983, the fourth annual American Book Awards were presented for 27 books at a ceremony in the New York Public Library.

Divisions

General Publishing Division

The General Publishing Division (GPD), chaired by Seymour Turk (Book-of-the-Month Club), represents 136 publishers of fiction, nonfiction, children's literature, religious, and reference books. It also frequently works cooperatively with publishers of professional and scholarly books and with mass market paperback publishers within AAP. The division's programs focus on three key objectives: broadening the audience for books, strengthening relationships with librarians and booksellers for the solution of common problems, and improving the management and marketing skills of publishers.

Among the activities the division supports are the American Book Awards program, a major recipient of divisional funds as well as contributed services and materials in its effort to call public attention to the best of American books. The program is also supported by authors, agents, booksellers, wholesalers, and librarians.

Under the sponsorship of the American Booksellers Association (ABA), members of the division serve as faculty members at schools for booksellers and promote the marketing of books through special activities for booksellers. Other educational initiatives include such programs as dissemination of bumper stickers and buttons bearing the message "I'd Rather Be Reading." Active liaison with librarians is maintained through joint committees with the American Library Association and the Special Libraries Association. A group of smaller publishers within the GPD plans programs and publications of particular interest to the growing number of smaller publishers within all AAP divisions.

Paperback Publishing Division

The Paperback Publishing Division, chaired by Bob Diforio (New American Library), primarily directs its efforts toward the promotion of the paperback book as an integral tool for both educational and recreational readers in America today. As it continues to explore new approaches to the marketing, production, and distribution of the paperback, the division takes on such serious problems as the illegal sale of stripped books and the question of release date rights in the open market.

This division remains in close contact with booksellers across the United States through its liaison with the American Booksellers Association, the Council of Periodical Distributors Association, and the National Association of College Stores (NACS). With support from the ABA, the division sponsors the Top Ten Bestseller program and the I'd Rather Be Reading promotional campaign. It also collaborates with NACS to produce the Monthly Campus Paperback Bestsellers list. The division serves as the official representative for the mass market paperback industry at the annual meetings of both ABA and NACS. It also works closely with the ABA and AAP's General Publishing Division in support of the American Book Awards program, now in its fifth year of operation under the auspices of the AAP.

In 1983, the division completed its fifth year of support for the Rack Clearance Center (RCC), which serves as a clearinghouse, processing reimbursement claims for the installation of racks in retail outlets where mass paperbacks are sold. The RCC receives claims from wholesalers and rack manufacturers, assesses them for accuracy, and ensures that appropriate backup papers are supplied. In 1982–1983, there was a 30 percent increase in the number of claims processed by the RCC over the previous year.

Higher Education Division

The Higher Education Division, chaired by James Levy (Scott, Foresman), is directly concerned with all aspects of the marketing, production, and distribution of textbooks to the postsecondary education field. It pays special attention to maintaining open communications between the publishing industry and college faculty, students, and bookstore managers. To develop and maintain strong relations with college students, the division has established the AAP Student Service, a public relations program featuring a series of publications directed to college students. They include *How to Get the Most out of Your Textbook, How to Prepare for Examinations, How to Improve Your Reading Skills, How to Build Your Writing Skills, How to Get the Most out of Your College Education, How to Read Technical Textbooks, How to Succeed in College: A Guide for the Non-Traditional Student,* and *How to Succeed in Your College Courses: A Guide for the ESL Student.* Several division publications directed to college faculty include *Links* and the newly revised *An Author's Guide to Academic Publishing. An Author's Primer to Word Processing* is an overview of manuscript preparation using a word processor.

The Higher Education Division maintains close contact with college bookstores through the NACS-College Division Liaison Committee and operates the AAP College Textbook Fiche Service. College bookstores subscribe to the service for a nominal fee; in return, they are provided with microfiches (updated monthly) of about 50,000 textbook titles available from more than three dozen leading textbook publishers. The Liaison Committee also publishes a booklet for college bookstore managers, *Textbook Questions and Answers,* and each spring it cosponsors an Advanced Financial Management Seminar for college store managers.

The Higher Education Division Marketing Committee sponsored a "Rely on Your Textbook" advertising campaign, with posters and news releases appearing in campus newspapers and college bookstores. The Marketing Committee is currently sponsoring a campaign addressed to first-year college students, entitled "Textbooks: An Investment in Your Future." Another important part of the division's public relations program is its sponsorship of a series of panels at various academic association annual meetings. Recently, the division sponsored a series of AAP panels at the NACS regional state bookstore association meetings. Past programs dealt with such subjects as "The Copyright Law and the Teacher," "Airing the Issues," and "How the New Technology Affects the Academic World."

The Higher Education Division has been alerted to the serious implications of illegal copy mill activities. Recently, an out-of-court settlement with New York University attracted national attention to the problem of such illegal activities.

Professional and Scholarly Publishing Division

The Professional and Scholarly Publishing Division (PSP), chaired by William Begell (Hemisphere), is primarily concerned with production, marketing, and distribution of technical, scientific, medical, and scholarly books, journals, and looseleaf services. Essentially, although not exclusively, many of these publications are for the practicing engineer, scientist, and businessperson. The division monitors relevant government activity and policies, levels of funding, and related matters. It provides for a continuous exchange of information and experience through seminars in journal publishing, marketing, sales, new technology, and copyright, and maintains relations with other professional associations, including the International Group of Scientific, Technical and Medical Publishers, government agencies, and industrial research groups. Professional societies and university presses play an integral role in divisional activities.

In 1982, a data base committee of publishers was added to the division and, accordingly, the annual PSP Awards program was expanded to include them. The Government Relations Committee continued to monitor the course of various pieces of legislation and participated in developing AAP's position on them. The PSP Marketing Committee developed a presentation on selling professional books for the American Booksellers Association Convention and other booksellers' meetings; it has also developed a booth for the ABA convention, as well as a marketing booklet. The PSP Journals and Marketing committees conducted an extensive program of seminars and workshops. Other standing committees are concerned with statistics and public relations.

School Division

The School Division, chaired by Richard T. Morgan (Scott, Foresman), is concerned with the production, marketing, and distribution of textbooks and other instructional materials for kindergarten through twelfth grade. It works to increase levels of funding and to simplify adoption procedures. It also sponsors seminars and conferences on topics of interest to educators and publishers.

The School Division works closely with state boards of education, legislatures, departments of education, and other state organizations in areas of mutual concern. Legislative advocates represent the School Division in key states.

Division committees work to acquaint parents, educators, and others with concerns of educational publishers through seminars and such publications as *Parents' Guide to More Effective Schools, Textbook Publishers and the Censorship Controversy, How a Textbook Is Made*, and *Standardized Testing*. Public service ads and radio spots are also part of the division's grass-roots public information campaign.

Now in its third year, the Education Research Awards Competition has provided grants to seven graduate students thus far. The division also works closely with professional organizations such as the International Reading Association and National Council of Teachers of English by participating in cosponsored sessions at annual meetings of these organizations.

Standing committees of the division include Executive, Communications, Critical Issues in Education, Research, Statistics, Test, Textbook Specifications, Order Flow Improvement, and selected state committees.

International Division

The International Division, chaired by Paul S. Feffer (Feffer & Simons), was formed in response to the rising importance of foreign markets for U.S. books. It focuses on issues that affect the marketing of books to other countries and the ever-growing complexities of the international marketplace. The division represents the entire spectrum of publishing in both size of publishing firm and product line.

Among the division's priorities are improving trade relations with the third world;

developing the professional skills of members through seminars and workshops; developing strong relationships with U.S. government agencies (U.S. Information Agency and the State and Commerce departments) interested in promoting the book abroad through national fairs and exhibits; promoting respect for international copyright; developing international sales statistics; and promoting attendance and active participation at international book fairs. Continuing its efforts to combat piracy around the world, the division collects and disseminates information in cooperation with the International Publishers Association and lends support to members in their individual efforts.

The division's annual meeting included reports on international trade barriers and incentives, market updates, professional and scholarly publishing in the international marketplace, mass market paperbacks, and Education in a Foreign Language (EFL) publishing. Its publications include an international fairs calendar and profiles of major international book fairs.

Direct Marketing Club / Book Division

The Direct Marketing/Book Club Division is actively concerned with the marketing and distribution of books through direct response and book clubs. The division works closely with the AAP Postal Committee to study the effects of new postal rates and regulations and to monitor new postal developments. The division's Marketing Committee sponsors seminars during the year. Issues of concern are privacy legislation, copyright, and improved statistical programs. Merrill Vopni (Prentice-Hall) is division chairperson; Arthur Heydendael (Meredith Corporation) is division vice chairperson.

Core Activities

Core activities include matters related to copyright, new technology, freedom to read, postal rates and regulations, statistical surveys, book distribution, public information, press relations, international freedom to publish, and education for publishing.

The Copyright Committee

The Copyright Committee, chaired by Charles Ellis (Elsevier-Science Publishing), safeguards and promotes the proprietary rights of authors and publishers domestically and internationally. Closely monitoring copyright activity in the United States and abroad, the committee prepares congressional testimony for appropriate AAP spokespersons, assigns representatives to attend national and international copyright meetings, and sponsors seminars on copyright matters.

The Copyright Committee plays an active role in disseminating information about the copyright law. It provides speakers to address publisher, librarian, and educator groups and prepares and distributes printed information.

The Copyright Committee maintains liaison with the U.S. Copyright Office and informs publishers of new and proposed regulations that relate to their activities. It participates in negotiations concerning copyright-related policy to be followed by users of copyright material and also maintains an active copyright enforcement campaign. In 1983, AAP coordinated lawsuits against American Cyanamid; E. R. Squibb & Sons; and

New York University, its faculty, and an off-campus copy shop for their photocopying activities. All suits resulted in settlements favorable to AAP. The Copyright Committee has two active subcommittees, the Computer Software Subcommittee, chaired by Mary Maher (SFN Companies), and the Rights and Permissions Advisory Committee, chaired by Camille Truchel (McGraw-Hill).

The New Technology Committee

The New Technology Committee was created in 1981 to meet the need expressed by member publishers to monitor the new technologies—the new means of distributing published information and the new products, that is, online data bases, computer programs, videodiscs, videotapes, teletexts, and videotexts. Functioning as an information clearinghouse, the committee publishes a monthly column on technologies that affect the publishing business and sponsors workshops and seminars to assist publishers in gaining the knowledge required to enter these fields. Robert Badger (John Wiley) chairs this committee.

In 1983, the New Technology Committee began a major effort to develop industry-wide standards for the processing of manuscripts in electronic format. The Council on Library Resources is cosponsoring this $300,000 project. The Project Management Team is chaired by Nicholas Alter (University Microfilms), and the contractor is Aspen Systems Corporation.

The Freedom to Read Committee

The Freedom to Read Committee, chaired by Heather Grant Florence (Bantam Books), is concerned with protecting freedoms guaranteed by the First Amendment. In addition to a major educational role, the committee analyzes individual cases of attempted censorship by Congress, state legislatures, federal, state, or municipal governments, local school boards, or any other institution. Its actions may take the form of a legal brief in support of a position against censorship, testimony before appropriate legislative committees, or public statements and communications protesting any attempt to limit freedom of communication. The committee works closely with other organizations that support its goals.

In addition to testimony provided regarding prepublication review of writings by government officials with access to classified information (see under "Highlights of 1983 Activities"), the committee mounted a continuing defense of the federal Freedom of Information Act (FoIA) against efforts to weaken it and thus make government information less accessible to the public. In September 1982, the committee filed with the Senate Judiciary Committee a statement identifying more than a dozen books as a partial list of many "responsible and important works which have benefited from information released by the CIA, FBI and other federal agencies pursuant to the FoIA." [For a special report on access to federal information, see Part 1—Ed.]

The one-hour videotaped program *Censorship or Selection: Choosing Books for Public Schools*, made in collaboration with the American Library Association's Intellectual Freedom Committee (see *The Bowker Annual, 1983*, pp. 148–149), was released by the Public Broadcasting Service to its 300-member public television stations and was broadcast by many of them. The videotaped program, accompanied by a useful discussion guide, is calculated to stimulate thoughtful community discussion of important educational issues.

The committee is embarking on a study of diversity in public library collections and the extent to which their content is influenced by outside pressures. This project is cosponsored by the ALA Intellectual Freedom Committee and the Fund for Free Expression.

For the first time in many years, the U.S. Supreme Court has three libel cases on its docket and AAP filed briefs in all. The briefs called the Court's attention to the specific aspects of each case that affect book publishing, even though none of the parties is a book publisher. Issues at stake range from "forum-shopping" (*Keeton* v. *Hustler, Calder* v. *Jones*) to the basic standards for appellate review (*Bose* v. *Consumers Union*).

The Postal Committee

The Postal Committee monitors the activities of the U.S. Postal Service, the Postal Rate Commission, and congressional committees responsible for postal matters. It presents the publisher's point of view to those in policymaking positions through direct testimony, by economic analyses of proposed postal programs, and through a variety of other means. Jon Mulford (Doubleday) chairs the committee.

The International Freedom to Publish Committee

The International Freedom to Publish Committee is the only body formed by a major group of publishers in any country for the specific purpose of protecting and expanding the freedom of written communication. The committee monitors the general status of freedom to publish and discusses problems of restriction with the U.S. government, other governments, and international organizations. When appropriate, it makes recommendations to these organizations and issues public statements.

During 1983, the committee investigated violations of free expression in Argentina, China, Cuba, Czechoslovakia, Haiti, Indonesia, Iran, Poland, South Africa, the Soviet Union, and Yugoslavia. Committee members testified at congressional hearings dealing with free expression and maintained contact with persecuted writers and publishers in repressive countries and with émigré writers from those countries. John Macrae III (Holt, Rinehart & Winston) is chairperson.

The Book Distribution Project

Reorganized in 1983 from the AAP Book Distribution Task Force, the Book Distribution Project has two objectives: (1) to keep publishers informed about current information in the distribution area through a series of information *Bulletins* and (2) to stimulate the development of more efficient book distribution systems through existing organizations within and outside the book publishing arena.

In 1983, individuals with operations responsibility within their company were convened as an ad hoc group to review the contents of *Book Distribution in the United States: Issues and Perceptions,* a report prepared for the Book Industry Study Group, Inc., by Arthur Andersen & Company. As a result of that effort, two separate projects are underway. One project is attempting to determine when it is cost-effective for electronic orders to be sent online rather than on computer tape. The second is an effort to analyze order cycle time—from transmittal of the order to receipt of books—to determine if time savings are possible.

At the request of AAP, the American Booksellers Association agreed to poll its members to determine if any of them maintained order-by-order records that would enable the AAP to break order cycle time into components relating to incoming mail, in-house processing, and freight. More than 25 booksellers have offered to supply such records, and analysis of the records should take place in 1984.

In addition to these specific efforts within the U.S. book trade, Book Distribution Project staff organized and conducted the fifth annual International Distribution Specialists meeting in Frankfurt on October 12, 1983. Project staff represented the AAP at meetings of the Network Advisory Committee to the Library of Congress, the Council on Library Resources, and the National Commission on Libraries & Information Science concerned with document delivery, decentralization of data bases, and telecommunications. They also analyzed all proposed and existing national standards sent for review by American National Standards Committee Z39.

The Education for Publishing Program

Established by AAP in 1978, the Education for Publishing Program develops and organizes conferences, seminars, and workshops that meet current industry needs. It also works to promote and advance the continuing education of employees in the industry. Among the activities sponsored by the program each year are orientation to book publishing courses in New York, Boston, and Chicago and two ongoing series, the Personnel Professionals Roundtable and Micro Users Group. Other programs are held on book manufacturing (at the Rochester Institute of Technology), microcomputer applications in book publishing, telemarketing, direct mail, mail-order space ads and premium sales, hiring, developing, and managing the field staff for educational publishers, and many other topics. Education for Publishing helps new talent to enter the industry by providing career and other information about book publishing. It also counsels educational institutions on useful book publishing courses. Andrew H. Neilly, Jr. (John Wiley) chairs the Education for Publishing Committee.

The Publishing Education Information Service

Established in 1979 and administered by the Education for Publishing Program, the Publishing Education Information Service acts as a research, referral, and communication resource for publishers, educators, and serious students seeking information about book publishing. The Stephen Greene Memorial Library contains a collection of more than 300 books, 40 periodicals, and archival material dealing with the industry. The library, staffed by a professional librarian, is open by appointment.

Other Areas of Interest

Reports of industry sales are published monthly by the AAP. The AAP annual report, which includes information on sales, operating costs, inventory turnover, and accounts receivable agings, is produced by the Statistical Service Center, an independent consulting firm, under procedures designed to protect the confidentiality of financial data reported by individual publishing houses. The form and content of AAP reports are regularly reviewed.

The AAP Compensation Survey is designed to enable members to make more informed decisions in matters of compensation and fringe benefits. Surveys (prepared in conjunction with Sibson & Company, compensation consultants) conducted approximately every two years, provide information on compensation levels (including salaries, bonuses, medical insurance, vacations, and pension plans) by size of company and geographic location.

A comprehensive, low-cost group insurance plan is available to members, covering medical and dental benefits, life insurance, accidental death, and short- and long-term disability. Because each member may choose a part or all of the coverage, every company can develop a custom-tailored plan to meet its particular needs and budget. More than $5 million in total annual premiums provide the buying power for the group to obtain premium rates not available to individual companies.

Awards

On April 28, 1983, the fourth annual American Book Awards were presented to 27 books at a ceremony in the halls of the New York Public Library. For the first time, the awards ceremony was divided into three parts—children's literature, graphics, and literary awards.

The eighth annual Curtis G. Benjamin Award for Creative Publishing was presented during the AAP annual meeting in March 1983. The association administers this award on behalf of its founders. This year's recipient was W. Bradford Wiley, chairman of John Wiley, who was cited as the "leader of a great family enterprise and ambassador-at-large for the industry."

The Professional and Scholarly Publishing Division completed the sixth year of its awards program, recognizing the best books and journals in its field; the program was expanded to include looseleaf publications and other media.

The School Division completed the second year of its Education Research Awards program. Four awards were granted to doctoral students for educational research.

The first Mary E. McNulty Award was presented to James R. Squire at the AAP Consolidated Divisional Meeting on November 15, 1983. This award will be given each year to a person whose work on behalf of School Division goals and educational publishing demonstrates the qualities of service, excellence, and commitment to education exemplified by Mary McNulty.

Liaison with Other Associations

The AAP has effective working relations with a large number of professional associations and agencies with allied interests. These include the American Booksellers Association, American Library Association, Association of American University Presses, Book Industry Study Group, Book Manufacturers Institute, Children's Book Council, Council of the Great Cities Schools, Information Industry Association, International Publishers Association, International Reading Association, National Association of College Stores, National Commission on Libraries and Information Science, National Council of

Teachers of English, National Education Association, PEN American Center, Publishers Publicity Association, Publishers Library Marketing Group, Special Libraries Association, and UNESCO.

Publications

Although some AAP publications are circulated to members only, many are available to nonmembers by subscription. The *AAP Newsletter* provides members with a periodic report on issues of concern to the publishing industry. The *Capital Letter,* issued monthly, offers news of federal government actions relating to the book community. Newsletters are prepared by the Higher Education, International, School, General Publishing, Paperback Publishing, and Professional and Scholarly Publishing divisions and the Copyright Committee. Periodic bulletins are published by the Book Distribution Project.

The AAP also publishes *The AAP Industry Statistics Report* on sales and operating expenses and the *AAP Survey of Compensation and Personnel Practices in the Publishing Industry.* The annual *AAP Exhibits Directory* lists about 300 book fairs and association meetings. The International Division publishes an annual *Profiles of International Book Fairs.* A publications list is available from AAP on request.

Information Industry Association

316 Pennsylvania Ave. S.E., Suite 400
Washington, DC 20003
202-544-1969

Fred S. Rosenau
Editorial Director

In a paper by President Paul Zurkowski entitled "Integrating America's Infostructure" released late in 1983, the Information Industry Association (IIA) set forth its "conceptual map" of the information business. The map (see Figure 1) is an attempt to depict the characteristics of the information industry as a new, self-created entity and of the information firms that comprise it.

Characteristics of IIA Member Companies

According to Zurkowski, these distinctive attributes include the following:

1. *Information companies create their own products,* in contrast to traditional book publishers, which maintain a stable of authors to write materials that the publishers then edit, package, publish, and market. Many information companies do rely on outside sources for their raw material, but in the process of adding value to these data they make them their own. Although copyright is generally considered an author's statute, it is used by traditional publishers to create a proprietary position on which the publishing and marketing investment can safely be made. In contrast, it is the information company itself

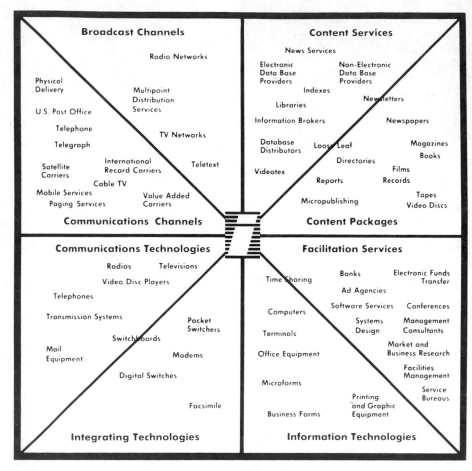

Figure 1. A conceptual map of the information business.

that has a legitimate claim to a copyright for the "author" functions it performs in adding value to information.

2. *Information companies maintain close end-user relations.* As contrasted to publishers' concerns about titles in print and the condition of a backlist, the information company works closely with the people who actually use an information product or service. This relationship creates a key role for the customer service people, who are expected to translate user needs into product enhancements and new product ideas. This characteristic of information companies results in the implementation of criteria 3 and 4.

3. *Information products are customized.* Close user relations lead directly to the process of customizing the information service provided. The product is often delivered in "custom" packaging, whether or not it has been customized in all aspects. In addition, customers seldom find information products on a discount table. Producers and users of information alike know that out-of-date information is "disinformation" and cannot be discount-priced.

4. *Information companies are media independent.* They must either be media

independent or use a multimedia approach. Once an information product is marketed, numerous applications for the content of the product quickly become apparent. Often these needs can be better satisfied in media other than the one in which the product was first offered. To fail to provide the information in these alternate media forms or to fail to take a media-independent posture is to concede to competitors shares of the market for the information.

5. *Information products are decision directed.* The object of an information company is to get its information product or service into the decision-making processes of the user. Information companies recognize that users need information, not for its intrinsic value, but because it assists them in making sound judgments. Information is like the proverbial quarter-inch drill bit: Millions are sold each year, not to people who want drill bits, but to people who want holes.

6. *Information companies price on the basis of benefits provided.* Pricing of information is based more closely on what it would cost the end user to reproduce the product than on a pro rata share of the cost of producing the information. This factor distinguishes the information company from the traditional publisher, which, when marketing its product, anticipates or forecasts sales volume, packages and promotes the product to appeal to as wide a market as is feasible, and calculates price on some multiple of each volume's first-copy cost.

7. *Information companies are repositories of what's known or knowable.* The seventh criterion was identified in a discussion with a public relations firm that claimed to meet all the above criteria (as it clearly may). But a public relations firm does not serve as a repository of what is known or knowable about a given area of business or human activity. Most information content companies, by definition, do.

8. *Information companies perceive their product to be information.* The essence of information company activity is one of perception. If the information company recognizes that its basic product is information content, that firm is in the information industry whether or not it meets any or all of the above criteria. If the perception exists, the pattern of behavior is sure to follow.

In 1982, the content services segment of the information industry (see top right-hand quadrant of Figure 1) represented an aggregate annual business volume of some $13.6 billion in revenues worldwide, an increase of 12.3 percent over the 1981 reported estimate. The U.S. market accounted for 81 percent of the worldwide totals. Moreover, some 28 percent of 1982 information revenue was delivered in machine-readable form—the most rapid rate of gain for any mode of delivery in the industry's latest financial survey, *The Business of Information, 1983* (ISBN 0-942774-12-4).

The producers of content services—the member companies of IIA—are the driving force that is expected to bring about the integration depicted in Figure 1. They are accomplishing this integration in these ways:

1 By producing their own products in multimedia formats, information companies are forcing various technologies to work together to deliver their products.

2 By offering decision-directed services, information companies integrate themselves and their products, and the technologies they use, into the mainstream of other enterprises.

3 By value pricing their products, information companies are able to fund the practical research necessary to establish "theories of use" essential to integrating content and technologies.

4 By focusing on information content, information businesses signal other participants shown in Figure 1 of the need for integration.

IIA 1983 Activities: A Brief Review

Between its fourteenth annual convention in Florida in 1982 (described in *Business Realities in the Information Industry* [1983]) and its fifteenth annual convention and exhibition in New York City's financial district in late 1983, IIA expanded to its present membership of nearly 300. Descriptions of the products and services of the various member firms and of the individual members may be found in the just-released *Information Sources, 1984* (ISBN 0-942744-13-2), the annual IIA directory. This all-new revised edition is the largest yet published with some 550 pages. IIA's sixteenth annual convention and exhibition ("New Actors, New Factors") is scheduled to be held in San Francisco, November 11-14, 1984.

The various IIA regional chapters across the nation launched a popular series of luncheon programs for local executives in New York City, the Washington, D.C., area, the West Coast, New England, the Midwest, the Rocky Mountain area, and the Philadelphia area. The first midyear management conference was held in Chicago in May 1983, organized around a theme now spelled out in considerable detail in a new IIA publication, *So You Want to Be a Profitable Database Publisher* (ISBN 0-942774-14-0).

IIA's industry newsletter for member-firm executives, known as *Friday Memo,* is now also available online via NewsNet.

Among the 1983 featured workshops and seminars conducted by the three IIA councils, which perform the work of the association, were

"Moving and Marketing Information for Profit" (Boca Raton, Florida, February), sponsored by the Future Technology & Innovation Council.

"Increasing Your Sales through Customer Service: A Critical Function in Transition" (Philadelphia, September), sponsored by the Business Operations Council and published by IIA under the same title early in 1984 (ISBN 0-942774-15-9).

"Integrating External Databases with the Corporate MIS" (San Francisco, December), sponsored by the Future Technology & Innovation Council.

"Information: Today's Key to Effective Lobbying" (Washington, D.C., February), sponsored by the Washington, D.C., chapter.

Marketing Directors' Roundtable (New York City, June), sponsored by the Business Operations Council.

"Making Effective Finance and Corporate Development Decisions" (New York City, April), sponsored by the Business Operations Council.

Association Leadership

IIA's resurgence in 1983 was led by Roy Campbell (Dun & Bradstreet) as chairperson of the board of directors. In November 1983, he was succeeded in that leadership role by Norman Wellen (Business International). Other new board officers for 1984 are Robert November (ITT Communications & Information Services), chairperson-elect; Peter Marx (Chase Econometrics/Interactive Data Corporation), treasurer; and Paul Massa

(Congressional Information Service), secretary. New board members include William Giglio (McGraw-Hill, Inc.), Marlene Hurst (University Microfilms International), John Jenkins (Bureau of National Affairs), and Carl Valenti (Dow Jones & Company).

Dan Sullivan (Frost & Sullivan) and Haines Gaffner (LINK Resources) continued to chair the Future Technology & Innovation Council and the Business Operations Council, respectively. Charles Tower (Dun & Bradstreet) became chairperson of the Public Policy & Government Relations Council late in 1983.

The IIA headquarters staff was enlarged during the year to cope with the heightened association activity level. Alison Caughman became director of finance and administration, Judy Russell directed membership development, and Linda Cunningham became meetings coordinator. Susan Dahlquist joined the government relations staff, Jennifer Googins assumed responsibility for special projects, and Virginia Nelson took over the receptionist position.

In November, IIA designated Forest Woody Horton, Jr., as a new distinguished professional member. It also announced that its 1983 Hall of Fame Award had been given to two recipients (for the first time since its inception in 1975): Philip Estridge, president, Entry Systems Division, International Business Machines Corporation, and Daniel Fylstra, chairman and chief executive officer, VisiCorp. The award honors individuals who have made landmark contributions to the growth and development of the information industry. Recent recipients include Roger Summit of DIALOG Information Services, Carlos Cuadra of Cuadra Associates, and the late William T. Knox, founder of IIA.

Special Libraries Association

235 Park Ave. S., New York, NY 10003
212-477-9250

David R. Bender
Executive Director

Richard Griffin
Associate Executive Director

The Special Libraries Association (SLA) was founded in 1909 by John Cotton Dana and other forward-looking library leaders concerned with the professional needs of librarians employed in the field of business. The association had 56 charter members, and Dana served as its first president.

As history was soon to show, the new organization was to witness the most spectacular scientific and industrial development the world has ever known. The following years saw the birth and development of aviation, motion pictures, radio and television, and an industrial and business environment that produced the material to win two world wars and split the atom. Keeping pace with all this activity was an ever-growing flood of knowledge, and access to knowledge became as vital to industrial and scientific success as good machinery. Special libraries and the Special Libraries Association were involved in early efforts to devise efficient methods and tools to store, retrieve, and disseminate the needed information.

SLA's board of directors has designated 1983–1984 the association's seventy-fifth anniversary year. Throughout the year, SLA's 54 chapters in the United States, Canada, and Europe and many of its 29 divisions are planning special activities and commemorative events. The official observance will be at the annual conference in New York City, June 9–14, 1984. Library associations and organizations are invited to join the SLA board of directors and staff at that time to mark this milestone in SLA's history.

Chapters and Divisions

SLA's strong organization of active chapters and divisions enables members to become active locally in the affairs of the association. Chapter meetings are held throughout the year. Divisions provide a channel of direct communication for members who share a common subject interest or information format in their libraries. It is the informal information network created by the chapters and divisions that is frequently cited by SLA members as the single most important reason for joining the association. No new chapters or divisions were established in 1983.

Statistics and Finances

A dues increase in January 1981 combined with a fluctuating economy caused a 3 percent decrease in membership in 1981. The effects of the dues increase were reversed in 1982 and 1983. Membership is currently at an all-time high of 11,600. The association has maintained its position as the world's third largest library association; only the American Library Association and the Library Association (U.K.) are larger.

SLA's financial position has been consistently positive over the last four years as a result of surplus income generated by the annual conferences, continuing education offerings, the investment program, and the publications program. This excess income subsidizes membership services, since dues income covers only about 70 percent of these costs.

Despite SLA's recent run of fiscal good health, the association cannot depend on annual conferences and other nondues income sources for producing a budgetary surplus year after year. An unprofitable conference, for example, could easily place SLA in a deficit position. Thus the SLA board and staff are dedicated to the development and implementation of creative programming and the following of sound fiscal policies in order to see the association through any potential lean years.

Government Relations

SLA's Government Relations Program, in cooperation with the Government Relations Committee, the Government Information Services Committee, and the Copyright Implementation Committee, continues to serve the needs of the special libraries community. Among SLA's legislative activities are the following:

Copyright. SLA monitored the Register of Copyright's five-year review of the

Copyright Law and legal actions filed by the Association of American Publishers and others against American Cyanamid, New York University, Squibb, Pfizer, and Texaco.

Paperwork Reduction Act of 1980. SLA monitored administrative implementation of the law to ensure fair and equitable collection and release of data needed by the information community.

Occupational Standards for Federal Librarians. SLA prepared testimony and news releases, collected data, and monitored various activities.

Circular A-76. SLA prepared testimony and news releases and continued monitoring activities concerning the contracting out for library and audiovisual services provided by various federal departments/agencies.

Medicare/Medicaid. SLA prepared testimony against the rule changes that would remove the words "medical libraries" from the current regulations.

Postal legislation. SLA monitored postal legislation, directives, and releases to determine the effect changes will have on special libraries and the association.

Numerous discussions were held, correspondence sent, and testimony prepared in keeping with the association's Government Relations Policy, 1983 Legislative Program, and its 501(c)(3) tax-exempt status.

Long-Range Plan

Definite steps toward the drafting and adoption of a five-year long-range plan were taken in 1983. Priorities for the plan were established by the SLA board of directors in late 1982 and further refined by the chapters and divisions in spring 1983. (See *Bowker Annual, 1983,* p. 161.) In June the board discussed and agreed on the assumptions on which the plan will be based. The following mission statement was adopted: "The mission of the Special Libraries Association is to advance the leadership role of its members in putting knowledge to work in the Information Society." The final draft of the plan was scheduled for the board's consideration and adoption in January 1984.

Staff Reorganization

In May 1983 the completion of the staff reorganization program, as approved by the board of directors in June 1982, was announced. Four new professional positions were created, three of which replaced existing jobs. The reorganization places the functions of information services, program services, and administrative services under the administration of directors and establishes a public relations program as a permanent association activity under the direction of the Information Services Department. The three department directors, the executive director and the associate executive director function as an administrative cabinet for planning, budgeting, and developing new programs and services and for overall staff review of association office operations.

The Program Services Department, the first to become operational under the staff reorganization, is responsible for membership records and services, conference and meeting arrangements, and professional development activities.

The Information Services Department, the second to become operational, is involved in a number of particularly interesting activities. With the addition of Martha Johnson, communications specialist, to the staff, the association can now move to implement a priority established at the beginning of the 1980s, the improvement of communications with and among the membership, their client groups, allied associations/organizations, and other appropriate groups. Other components of the Information Services Department are the serials and book publications programs and the SLA Information Center, which is being used with growing frequency by members, researchers, business and industry managers, and students as a primary source of information on special librarianship, information management, and technology.

The last SLA department to be established under the reorganization was the Administrative Services Department. Its responsibilities are fiscal and accounting operations and office support services (including data processing, order and fulfillment, and shipping and receiving).

Conclusion

Only associations that are responsive to the needs of their members survive for any length of time. One measure of SLA's success is its 75 years of service to special librarians. With its new staff organization, SLA is more capable than ever of providing quality service to its members. SLA continues to be highly proactive and, more and more frequently, its programs and activities reflect the various forces (technological and otherwise) that are continually shaping and reshaping the information profession. As always, the association's board and staff are prepared to meet the current needs of the special libraries community, and they continue to expend much effort in anticipating future needs and planning how best they can be met.

Part 2
Legislation, Funding, and Grants

Legislation and Regulations Affecting Librarianship in 1983

Eileen D. Cooke

Director, Washington Office, American Library Association

Carol C. Henderson

Deputy Director, Washington Office, American Library Association

It was a year of contrasts. The president again proposed to eliminate most federal library programs, but Congress funded the public library construction program for the first time in ten years, then followed by providing the highest appropriations ever for public library services and interlibrary cooperation. However, Congress declined to provide any funding for college library resource grants, the first time that HEA II-A has been without funds since Higher Education Act funding began in FY 1966.

Telecommunications became a major issue for libraries with the news that the FCC access charge plan and the AT&T private line tariff on phone lines leased for data communications (such as access to OCLC, RLIN, WLC) would cause rate increases averaging 73 percent. Both the FCC and Congress have the power to counteract such a drastic increase, but the outcome is uncertain. The American Library Association and the Association of Research Libraries, with assistance from other library associations, networks, and bibliographic utilities, have hired a consultant to help track these complex developments.

The Register of Copyrights issued the first five-year review of the library photocopying provisions of the 1976 copyright law. There were continuing developments on the proposed standards for federal librarians and on contracting out government activities to the private sector. Several regulatory developments affected access to government information, and, perhaps not surprisingly, there were congressional hearings near the end of the session titled "1984: Civil Liberties and the National Security State."

Funding, FY 1983

For the first time in ten years, Congress appropriated funds under the Library Services and Construction Act, Title II public library construction program. Given final approval in March, HR 1718 (PL 98-8), the FY 1983 emergency "jobs" supplemental appropriations bill contained $50 million, the highest amount ever appropriated for LSCA II, to remain available until expended for construction and renovation of public library facilities. The library funds originated in the Senate version of the bill at the instigation of Senate Appropriations Committee Chairman Mark Hatfield (R–Oregon).

Funding, FY 1984

Congressional Budget

For the first time since Ronald Reagan became president, House Democrats were able to pass their own budget. The 229–196 vote in March was due to a number of factors. The administration's budget, with its record high deficits, massive defense increases, and further domestic spending cuts, was an embarrassment even to Republicans. Unlike the previous two years, when alternative budgets developed by House Republicans with Office of Management and Budget assistance attracted enough conservative Democratic votes to pass, no substitute budget was offered this time. A final factor was the increased size of the Democratic majority due to congressional elections in fall 1982.

After Senate passage and resolution of details, the final congressional budget targets (later turned into binding budget ceilings) were much more generous for education ($16.1 billion) than either the previous year's actual funding ($15.2 billion in FY 1983) or FY 1984 appropriations ($15.3 billion). The budget resolution (H.Con.Res. 91) also assumed there would be enough postal revenue foregone subsidy to avoid nonprofit postal rate increases.

Administration Budget

President Reagan recommended a federal spending freeze in his FY 1984 budget, but dipped way below freezing to propose another zero budget for library grant programs. The president's budget message to Congress attempted to be conciliatory—admitting that the administration had made maximum possible cuts in many places and would work with Congress to accommodate special congressional concerns. But despite congressional rejection of the 1983 zero budget for libraries, the FY 1984 budget again recommended elimination of the Library Services and Construction Act and all Higher Education Act, Title II library programs.

According to Education Department justification papers, categorical library programs were proposed for termination because of possible support from other sources, as well as, in the case of LSCA, "the program's past success at establishing the highest practical levels of access across the country to library services, and at developing models of interlibrary cooperative arrangements to stimulate further expansion of the concept." The administration also proposed an 18 percent cut for the National Commission on Libraries and Information Science and a minuscule cut in the school block grant, which can be used for, among other things, school library resources.

Library Programs

For the first time in five years, Congress completed action on a regular Labor-HHS-Education Appropriations bill (HR 3913, PL 98-139) for FY 1984. For the previous four fiscal years, these programs were funded under continuing resolutions. The House made several attempts, on HR 3913 and on various supplementals and continuing resolutions, to raise education funding closer to the level approved in the congressional budget resolution. For the most part, these efforts were not successful. However, PL 98-139 contained both good news and bad news for library programs.

The Library Services and Construction Act, Titles I and III were raised to their authorized ceilings of $65 million and $15 million, respectively, the highest levels ever appropriated for public library services and interlibrary cooperation. The Senate version increased LSCA I and left LSCA III at 1983 levels, but House-Senate conferees agreed to the higher House figure. The House and Senate also differed on NCLIS, with the Senate maintaining level funding, but the House dipping to the president's budget request. Conferees kept the Senate's $674,000, avoiding a cutback in NCLIS staff and activities.

The bad news was that conferees went along with the Senate on the Higher Education Act, Title II-A College Library Resources program, which means no funds for college library grants in FY 1984. The Senate Appropriations Committee report (S. Rept. 98-247) explained its action: "The Committee shares the administration's concern over the lack of any needs-based standards for making such awards and recommends that the program be modified accordingly before consideration is given to any future appropriations." HEA II-B library training and research and II-C research library grants were funded at previous levels of $880,000 and $6,000,000, respectively.

Not all the usual funding bills were enacted into law. Congress finally provided the postal revenue foregone subsidy in a continuing resolution (H.J.Res. 413, 98-151) good for the entire 1984 fiscal year. It includes the full $879 million needed to prevent increases in nonprofit postal rates, including the fourth-class library rate. The president's budget had recommended only $400 million, less than half the amount needed.

The same funding resolution provided $90,805,000 for the National Archives and Records Service, of which $4 million was earmarked for the grants program of the National Historical Publications and Records Commission (NHPRC). For the commission, hard hit by funding cuts over the last few years, it was a return to the FY 1981 funding level.

The FY 1984 Interior and Related Agencies Appropriations bill (HR 3363, PL 98-146) provided $140 million for the National Endowment for the Humanities. House-Senate conferees agreed with the House in earmarking $3 million of the total for public libraries, but noted that NEH will include the public library program within "Program Development" under the Division of General Programs.

The Legislative Branch Appropriations bill (HR 3135, PL 98-51) for FY 1984 included $223,114,000 for the Library of Congress, a marginal increase over the previous year's $221,505,000 and less than the requested $231,257,000. This bill also included $25,700,000 for Superintendent of Documents activities (mainly the depository library program) in the Government Printing Office.

Other funding measures provided $9,873,000 (a 12 percent increase) for the National Agricultural Library and $42,113,000 (an 8 percent increase) for the National Library of Medicine, plus $7 million for the Medical Library Assistance Act. Table 1 shows funding details for these and other library and related programs.

Contracting Out Federal Activities

Over the course of the year, the Office of Management and Budget revised its Circular No. A-76, "Performance of Commercial Activities." The circular and its lengthy supplement establish federal policy regarding the operation of commercial activities and set forth procedures for determining whether such activities should be performed under contract with commercial sources or in-house using government facilities and personnel.

Library services and facility operation and cataloging are among the examples of commercial activities in both the proposed revision issued in January and the final revision published in the August 16 *Federal Register,* pp. 37110–37116. The final version has a new footnote, which says that "... some Federal libraries are primarily recreational in nature and would be deemed commercial activities. However, the National Archives or certain functions within research libraries might not be considered commercial activities. Agency management must use informed judgment on a case-by-case basis in making these decisions."

Table 1 / Appropriations for Library and Related Programs, FY 1984 (Appropriations in Thousands)

Library Programs	FY 1983 Appropriations	FY 1984 Budget	FY 1984 House	FY 1984 Senate	FY 1984 Appropriations
ECIA Act, Chapter 2 (includes school libraries)	$ 479,420	$ 478,879	$ 478,879	$ 479,420	$ 479,420
GPO Superintendent of Documents	27,291	25,738	25,700	25,700	25,700
Higher Education Act Title II	8,800	0	8,800	6,880	6,880
Title II-A, College Libraries	1,920	0	1,920	0	0
Title II-B, Training & Research	880	0	880	880	880
Title II-C, Research Libraries	6,000	0	6,000	6,000	6,000
Library of Congress	221,505	231,257	222,028	224,194	223,114
Library Services & Construction Act	71,520	0	80,000	76,520	80,000
Title I, Public Library Services	60,000	0	65,000	65,000	65,000
Title II, Public Library Construction	50,000	0	0	0	0
Title III, Interlibrary Cooperation	11,520	0	15,000	11,520	15,000
Medical Library Assistance Act	13,400*	7,653	defer	defer	7,500
National Agricultural Library	8,849	9,873	9,873	9,873	9,873
National Commission on Libraries & Information Science	674	553	553	674	674
National Library of Medicine	38,902	41,963	42,263	41,963	42,113
Library-Related Programs					
Adult Education Act	95,000	—†	100,000	100,000	100,000
Bilingual Education	138,057	94,534	142,057	139,000	139,365
Corporation for Public Broadcasting‡	130,000	75,000	130,000	130,000	130,000
ECIA Chapter 1 (ESEA I Disadvantaged Children)	3,200,394	3,013,969	3,480,000	3,480,000	3,480,000
Education for Handicapped Children (state grants)	1,017,900	998,180	1,017,900	1,071,850	1,068,875
HEA Title III, Developing Institutions	134,416	134,416	129,600	134,416	134,416
Title IV-C, College Work Study	590,000	800,000	550,000	550,000	555,000
Title VI, International Education	21,000	0	30,600	21,000	25,800
Indian Education Act	69,185	1,243	71,243	67,248	68,780
National Archives & Records Service	83,000	87,105	88,305	86,805	86,805
National Center for Education Statistics	8,589	8,747	8,747	8,747	8,747
National Endowment for the Arts	143,875	125,000	165,000	143,000	162,000
National Endowment for the Humanities	130,060	112,200	150,000	130,000	140,000
National Historical Publications & Records Commission	3,000	0	1,500	4,000	4,000
National Institute of Education	55,614	48,231	48,231	48,231	48,231
Postal Revenue Foregone Subsidy	789,000	400,000	879,000	802,000	879,000
Postsecondary Education Improvement Fund	11,710	6,000	11,710	11,710	11,710
Public Telecommunications Facilities	15,000	0	12,000	11,880	11,880
Women's Education Equity	5,760	0	5,760	5,760	5,760

*Includes one-time supplemental funding of $5.9 million for the Oregon Health Network.

†Included in block grant proposal for Vocational and Adult Education.

Former librarian Representative Major Owens (D–New York) testified at public hearings on the revision, calling for improvement of the circular to provide full and equitable partnership between public and private sectors, retention of the government's core information capabilities, and free and open access to government information.

Copyright

The first report of the Register of Copyrights as required by Section 108(i) of the 1976 copyright law was transmitted to Congress in January 1983. Section 108 on reproduction by libraries and archives required a report at five-year intervals on the "extent to which this section has achieved the intended balancing of the rights of creators, and the needs of users." The 363-page *Report of the Register of Copyrights—Library Reproduction of Copyrighted Works (17 U.S.C. 108),* with its seven volumes of appendices, was the culmination of a five-year process of meetings, hearings, data collection, analysis, and written comments.

The Register states that Section 108 "provides a workable structural framework for obtaining a balance between creators' rights and users' needs," but concludes that "the balance has not been achieved in practice." It is important to keep in mind, however, that although creators' rights are granted by acts of Congress, users also have rights, and these are guaranteed by the Constitution. As evidence of an imbalance in practice, the Register says that substantial quantities of library photocopies are made for job-related reasons, that many librarians are confused about how the law works and why enforcement is often their responsibility, and that some publishers strongly believe the present system is seriously unbalanced.

In the report, the Copyright Office makes seven nonstatutory and five statutory recommendations that represent its "best judgment about possible solutions to the copyright issues relating to library reproduction of copyrighted works." Very briefly summarized, they are as follows:

Copyright Office Nonstatutory Recommendations

1 All parties are encouraged to participate in collective licensing arrangements.
2 Interested parties are encouraged to develop voluntary guidelines with respect to present photocopying practices and the impact of new technological developments.
3 A copyright compensation scheme based on a surcharge on photocopying equipment should be studied.
4 Systems for copyright compensation should be studied based on samplings of photocopies made.
5 New technological developments should be studied as they affect library use of copyrighted works.
6 Interested parties should review new preservation techniques and their copyright implications to develop a common position for legislative action.
7 All levels of government should understand the need for adequate funding of libraries to enable them to pay their share of creation-dissemination costs.

Copyright Office Statutory Recommendations

1 An amendment should be enacted to permit library reproduction of an entire musical work (or substantial parts thereof) for private study, scholarship, or

research, following an unsuccessful, diligent search for the name and address of the copyright proprietor of the musical work, as recommended by the Music Library Association and the Music Publishers' Association.

2 A new Section 511 should be added limiting copyright owners to a single remedy—a reasonable copying fee—for copyright infringement of their scientific, technical, medical, or business periodicals or proceedings, if certain conditions are met by the user of the work, including membership in a collective licensing arrangement, unless the work was entered in a qualified licensing system or program. The purpose of the "umbrella statute," as recommended by the Association of American Publishers, is to encourage publisher and user participation in collective licensing arrangements.

3 A clarifying amendment should be enacted to make clear that the notice of copyright required on photocopies is *the* notice on the work itself, as publishers, but not librarians, have contended.

4 An amendment should be enacted to clarify that unpublished works are not covered by the copying privileges granted in Section 108(d) and (e).

5 An amendment should be enacted to permit the filing of the periodic five-year report on or about March 1 rather than in January.

The American Library Association's Washington office issued a response, "Comments of the American Library Association on the Report of the Register of Copyrights to Congress," which concludes:

Throughout the Register's Report the implication is made that librarians and the library community have engaged in copying that far exceeds the limits of the law. In his Executive Summary, the Register clearly points his finger at the library community as the cause of the imbalance he sees between the creator's rights and those of the user. At one point he strongly implies that librarians "have failed to comport with the behavior intended by Congress." Because of this, we feel the Report is heavily weighted on the side of proprietary groups and lacks balance and objectivity, despite massive amounts of statistical data in the King Research Report which is based on observation.

Oversight hearings were held in both the House and Senate Judiciary subcommittees, with jurisdiction over the Copyright Office, at which Register of Copyrights David Ladd urged hearings on the report and consideration of its recommendations. Neither panel took any action. The House subcommittee, however, held a series of hearings on copyright and technological change.

[See the copyright update for 1983 in the News Reports section of Part 1—*Ed.*]

Federal Information Policies

Federal Information Management

In September, the Office of Management and Budget solicited public comment in the development of a policy circular concerning federal information management, as part of its responsibility to implement the Paperwork Reduction Act of 1980 (PL 96-511). The 16 policy issues for which comment was requested included: (1) How should the principle that information is not a free good but a resource of substantial economic value be expressed as policy guidance to federal departments and agencies? (2) Since OMB Circular A-76 prescribes policy under which the government shall not compete unfairly with the private sector, policy guidance may be needed to ensure that federal agencies do not compete unfairly with the private sector when they provide information products and services to the public. And (3) What special policy guidance is needed as regards the application of user charges to government information products and services?

National Security Information Directive

Stating that additional safeguards are needed to protect classified information, the president issued a directive on safeguarding national security information on March 11. The directive mandates greater use of polygraph examinations in investigations of leaks of classified information and requires all individuals with access to certain types of classified information to sign a lifelong prepublication review agreement. The agreement requires the submission for governmental review of all writings and proposed speeches that touch on intelligence matters.

A November report of the House Government Operations Committee, "The Administration's Initiative to Expand Polygraph Use and Impose Lifelong Censorship on Thousands of Government Employees" (H.Rept. 98-578), recommended that Congress prohibit these changes in polygraph use and the infringement on free speech and political debate if the administration fails to withdraw the initiative. In an end of session amendment, Congress prohibited implementation of the directive until April 15, 1984, thus allowing time for further congressional action.

[See the special report on public access to federal information in Part 1 of this volume—*Ed.*]

UCNI Restrictions

In April 1983, the Department of Energy (DOE) proposed regulations concerning the identification and protection of unclassified controlled nuclear information (UCNI). The regulations would give the secretary of energy broad authority to define nuclear materials and the information that would be subject to control under the Atomic Energy Act of 1954. At a series of public hearings, librarians pointed out that although the proposal did not mention libraries, the potential scope of the documentation and information covered raised concern about access to information on nuclear research in libraries that are depositories of DOE nuclear materials. A revised DOE proposal is expected early in 1984.

Civil Liberties and the National Security State

Under this heading, Representative Robert Kastenmeier, chairperson of the Judiciary Subcommittee on Courts, Civil Liberties and the Administration of Justice, began a series of hearings on November 2 and 3. Although he felt that George Orwell's *1984* had not yet arrived, Kastenmeier was concerned that the pendulum had begun to swing back toward restrictions on civil liberties. He cited several examples, including some of the developments mentioned earlier, which have generally been viewed in isolation, but together, Kastenmeier concluded, produce a degree of secrecy incompatible with democracy.

Florence Agreement—Nairobi Protocol

The Educational, Scientific and Cultural Materials Importation Act (PL 97-446), signed by President Reagan in January 1983, implements the Nairobi Protocol to the Florence Agreement. The protocol provides for the removal of import duties among adhering countries on audiovisuals, microforms, and materials for the physically handicapped not included in the original Florence Agreement.

By Presidential Proclamation 5021, the United States dropped import duties on these materials in February for a 30-month trial period. Senate Finance Committee Chairman Robert Dole (R–Kansas) gave a progress report on these developments in the December 14 interim issue of the *Congressional Record* (pp. S17206–17207), and included the text of a resolution on the Nairobi Protocol adopted in November by the steering bodies of the International Federation of Library and Information Associations.

LSCA Reauthorization

In May, the House Education and Labor Committee approved HR 2878, a five-year reauthorization and revision of the Library Services and Construction Act, although the bill had not come up for a vote on the House floor as the year ended. HR 2878 was introduced May 3 by House Postsecondary Education Subcommittee Chairman Paul Simon (D–Illinois), based on a series of hearings in 1982 and early 1983 at which more than 200 witnesses testified and in reaction to an earlier draft bill prepared by Representative Simon and widely circulated in the library community in December 1982.

As introduced by Representative Simon and amended somewhat in committee, the bill reflects the expanded role libraries have assumed as community information centers. It places more emphasis on service and less on reaching all geographic locations in a revised Title I, makes minor changes to Title II public library construction, provides further encouragement for resource sharing in a revised Title III, authorizes funding directly to Native American tribes for library services in a new Title IV, and adds two new competitive library grant programs—Title V for acquisition of foreign-language materials and Title VI for library literacy programs.

Medical Libraries

On November 17, 1983 the House passed HR 2350, the Health Research Extension Act of 1983, including a three-year extension of the Medical Library Assistance Act (MLAA), with authorizations of $10 million for FY 1984, $11 million for 1985, and $12 million for 1986. Debate over the organization of National Institutes of Health research management kept MLAA from receiving a regular authorization for the last three years. It was reauthorized for one year (FY 1982) through the 1981 reconciliation process, and operated in FYs 1983 and 1984 through general authority provided in funding measures. A dispute over fetal research kept a pending Senate bill (S. 773) from enactment.

Standards for Federal Librarians

In December 1981, when the Office of Personnel Management issued the first of three drafts of its controversial proposed revision of classification and qualification standards for federal librarians, library technicians, and technical information specialists, it seemed unlikely that the issue would still be alive two years later. However, as 1983 ended the standards had been neither withdrawn nor published.

In January 1983, the General Accounting Office (GAO) began its review of the proposed librarian standards as the first part of a major pay equity study requested by several members of Congress. GAO issued its report in August, concluding that although OPM did not exceed its authority in developing the proposed standards, it failed to address librarians' criticisms concerning the reduced entry grade level and lowered minimum qualifications, and failed to demonstrate that the current minimum qualifications for federal librarians were inappropriate.

Several members of Congress called on OPM to withdraw the proposed standards in light of the GAO criticisms. OPM issued a detailed response in October to the GAO review. At year's end the American Library Association and OPM were in dispute over ALA's requests under the Freedom of Information Act for the data OPM used to respond to the GAO report.

Telecommunications

Pending telecommunications developments will have a major impact on library phone bills and data communications costs. As a result of the settlement of an antitrust suit brought by the Justice Department against AT&T, as of January 1, 1984, Bell Telephone will be divested of its local operating companies, which will become seven separate regional Bell operating companies. Divestiture removed the income from long-distance service, which AT&T claims subsidized local service.

Meanwhile, a Federal Communications Commission decision proposed access charges as a mechanism for compensating local companies for the capability to originate and terminate long-distance service. Access charges levied on the phone line of each end user and on certain carriers will raise library phone bills and increase dial-access telecommunications charges for users of Telenet, Tymnet, Uninet, and other value-added networks. The FCC's access charge plan required AT&T and other companies to file new tariffs for telecommunications charges, including the type of private, leased-line telecommunications that link many libraries to OCLC, RLIN, and WLN.

Analysis from OCLC and AT&T indicates an average increase of at least 73 percent in the cost of private/leased lines used by libraries for data communications as a result of the proposed tariff. Increases for individual libraries could be as high as 200 percent. The pricing structure of these data circuits is being totally reconfigured, with expenses moving much closer to the ends of the circuits. Some modest reductions in portions of the long-distance charges are more than offset by dramatically increased terminating channel costs.

In a partial response to the high increases that would result from the new tariffs, the FCC has delayed both the access charge plan and the proposed tariffs for 90 days, to April 3, 1984. Meanwhile, on November 10 the House passed legislation (HR 4102), which would repeal access charges for residential customers and single-line businesses, set up a universal service fund, and authorize lifeline phone service. A pending Senate bill (S. 1660) would delay access charges for home users and small businesses for two years.

Both bills assume that other users of telecommunications services will be able to absorb the vastly increased costs for existing facilities and services. For libraries, this is

Table 2 / Status of Legislation of Interest to Librarians (98th Congress, 1st Session, Convened January 3, 1983, Adjourned November 18, 1983)

Legislation	House					Senate					Final Action		
	Introduced	Hearings	Reported by Subcommittee	Committee Report Number	Floor Action	Introduced	Hearings	Reported by Subcommittee	Committee Report Number	Floor Action	Conference Report	Final Passage	Public Law
Bicentennial of Constitution	S 118				X	S 118			68	X	none	X	PL 98-101
Cable Telecommunications Act	HR 4103	X				S 66	X		67	X			
Copyright—Home Recording	HR 175, 1030		X			S 32	X		162	X			
Correctional Education Assistance	HR 3684					S 625							
ECIA Technical Amendments	HR 1035	X	X	51	X	S 1008		X	166	X	574	X	PL 98-211
Foreign Language Assistance	HR 2708	X	X	162	X	S 1795							
Freedom of Information Act Amendments						S 774	X		221				
Information Science & Technology Act	HR 480												
LC Study of Changing Role of Book	SConRes 59			451	X	SConRes 59			200	X	none	X	
LSCA Reauthorization	HR 2878	X	X	165	X								
Math and Science Education	HR 1310	X		6	X	S 1285	X	X	151				
Medical Library Assistance Act Extension	HR 2350		X	191	X	S 773	X		110				

	House Bill	H. Rpt.		Senate Bill		S. Rpt.		Conf. Rpt.			Public Law
National Archives, Independence	HR 3987			S 905	X		X	none	X		PL 98-189
NHPRC Reauthorization	HR 2196	129	X	S 1513	X	219	X				
Public Lending Right Study Commission											
Public Works	HR 1036	199	X	S 2192; S 724	X	94	X				
Revenue Sharing Extension	HR 2780	179	X	S 1426	X	189	X	550	X		PL 98-185
Taxation — Computer Contributions	HR 91, 701			S 1194							
Taxation — Libraries as Public Charities	HR 2183			S 1649							
Taxation — Manuscript Donations	HR 1285			S 427, 776							
Taxation — Thor Power Tool	HR 3004			S 1105, 2086							
Telephone Rate Legislation	HR 4102	479	X	S 1660	X	270	X				
Appropriations, FY 1984											
Further Continuing Resolution	HJRes 413	473	X	SJRes 194	X	304	X	540	X		PL 98-151
Supplemental Appropriations	HR 3959	375	X	HR 3959		275	X	551			PL 98-181
Agriculture	HR 3223	231	X	HR 3223	X	160	X	450			
Commerce, State Department	HR 3222	232	X	S 1721	X	206	X	478	X		PL 98-166
HUD, Independent Agencies	HR 3133	223	X	HR 3133	X	152	X	264	X	X	PL 98-45
Interior	HR 3363	253	X	HR 3363	X	184	X	399	X	X	PL 98-146
Labor-HHS-Education	HR 3913	357	X	HR 3913	X	247	X	422	X	X	PL 98-139
Legislative	HR 3135	227	X	HR 3135	X	161	X	271	X	X	PL 98-51
Treasury, Postal	HR 4139	417	X	S 1646	X	186	X				

For bills, reports, and laws, write to: House and Senate Documentation Rooms, U.S. Capitol, Washington, DC 20515 and 20510, respectively.

simply not the case. During debate on the Universal Telephone Service Preservation Act (HR 4102), Representative Bill Ford (D–Michigan) noted that libraries "provide universal access for all our citizens to information-age technology." He also noted that various federal aid programs and subsidized postal rates encourage libraries to share resources, yet disproportionate and unanticipated increases in telecommunications costs may make linkages between libraries unaffordable.

Other Legislative and Regulatory Activity

Education became a major political topic following the issuance in April of *A Nation at Risk,* the hard-hitting report of the National Commission on Excellence in Education. The president addressed the subject of excellence in education on several occasions, and it continued to generate discussion and activity, if not much additional financial support for education. The president also lent his support to the Education Department's Adult Literacy Initiative. Within the Education Department, the proposed elimination of the Office of Libraries and Learning Technologies in favor of a Center for Education Improvement was fortuitously changed to the Center for Libraries and Education Improvement.

The House passed a bill (HR 1310) to upgrade math and science education, but a similar Senate measure (S. 1285) is still pending. Tax measures to restore a deduction to authors and artists for donating their own manuscripts and artwork to libraries and museums, and to provide a deduction for donations of new scientific equipment and computers to schools and libraries, were introduced but not passed. The Senate passed cable television legislation (S. 66), but a House bill (HR 4104) is still in committee. The general revenue sharing program was extended for three years (HR 2780, PL 98-185).

In January 1983, the Office of Management and Budget proposed regulations limiting political advocacy by federal grantees and contractors that would have precluded most nonprofit organizations from lobbying if they received any federal funding. In November, a modified version was proposed, and the comment period was extended into 1984. Also in November, the Joint Committee on Printing proposed a major revision of the *Government Printing, Binding and Distribution Regulations* in an attempt to respond to technological change in information handling. On the last day of the session, a bill (S. 2192) was introduced to establish a commission to study the desirability of a U.S. public lending right system, whereby authors would be compensated for the public lending of their books by libraries.

Table 2 shows the status of legislation of interest to librarians as of the end of 1983.

Legislation Affecting Publishing in 1983

AAP Washington Staff*

For the first time in five years, a separate Labor-HHS-Education appropriations bill became law. The FY 1984 funding measure appropriated $9.2 billion more than the president's budget request.

Education and Library Affairs

Funding

Education and library programs suffered a mixed fate. On the plus side, the $4.669 billion for elementary and secondary education programs was an increase over last year's $4.352 billion. The $6.233 billion for college student assistance was down from last year's $6.718 billion, principally because of declining interest rates. Public Library Services (LSCA I) rose from $60 to $65 million, but funding for hard-pressed College Library Services (Title II-A, Higher Education Act) was terminated. The National Library of Medicine was reduced to $42.1 million from the previous year's $44.8 million.

Library Services and Construction Act

In March, in an appearance before a subcommittee of the House Committee on Education and Labor, the AAP testified in support of extension and expansion of the Library Services and Construction Act (LSCA). Among other things, the testimony urged assistance to libraries for literacy training activities for adults and school dropouts. The Library Services and Construction Act Amendments of 1983 (HR 2878), the bill reported by the committee on May 16, in addition to extending and revising LSCA, added three new titles for literacy training, purchase of foreign-language materials, and library services for Native Americans. The measure was pending on the House calendar at year's end.

On another front, libraries benefited by $50 million for public library construction as part of the $4.6 billion emergency jobs bill (Public Law 98-8) enacted in March.

Technology Education

In January 1983, Robert C. Bowen (McGraw-Hill), then chairman of AAP's School Division, testified before the House Committee on Education and Labor presenting the division's views on pending technology education legislation, known as the Mathematics and Science Education Act (HR 1310). He stressed the need for up-to-date instructional materials as an indispensable complement to new technology hardware and urged that

*The Association of American Publishers (AAP) general Washington staff includes Richard P. Kleeman, Roy H. Millenson, Diane Rennert, and Carol A. Risher, all of whom contributed to this article.

"prime emphasis be given to the development of high-quality courseware, embodying both the latest knowledge and techniques and involving . . . the combined efforts of the private sector and the academic community." He also urged that the legislation mandate research on instructional uses of the new technology to determine what kinds of instructional materials should be developed and to study how students learn through the use of new technology and how the new hardware and instructional materials can best be utilized in curricula. Similar testimony was submitted to the Senate.

The Mathematics and Science Education Act, which passed the House overwhelmingly on March 2, incorporated almost all AAP's recommendations. The Senate committee reported a comparable bill, S-1285, on June 13. It was awaiting floor action in January 1984.

Education Reports and Conferences

In April, the National Commission on Excellence in Education submitted its report, *A Nation at Risk*. Among the commission's findings were (1) that schools are not spending enough on texts and other instructional materials and (2) that many textbooks insufficiently challenge students.

Commission recommendations included: (1) textbooks should be upgraded and updated to assure more rigorous content; (2) in adopting textbooks, states and localities should evaluate them on the clarity of presentation of rigorous and challenging material, and should require publishers to furnish data on the materials' effectiveness; (3) funds should be made available to support text development in "thin-market" areas; (4) publishers should furnish evidence of the quality and appropriateness of textbooks; and (5) new instructional materials should reflect the most current applications of technology and the best scholarship and research. The commission also recommended that the federal government undertake support of curriculum improvement and research on teaching, learning, and school management.

Subsequently, in December in Indianapolis, Indiana, more than 2,000 education leaders from throughout the nation convened to discuss the report at a meeting sponsored by the Department of Education. Publishers attended and participated actively. Featured was a panel on textbook selection.

Other Issues

In testimony submitted to the Senate Subcommittee on Education, AAP urged inclusion of the Federal Correctional Education Assistance Act as an amendment to the Vocational Education Act extension measure pending before the subcommittee. The bill would authorize $25 million annually to state educational agencies for the education of inmates in state and local institutions.

AAP Education and Library Affairs Director Roy H. Millenson chaired a task force of the American Council on Education (ACE), the umbrella group for higher education, to devise proposals supported by the higher education community for legislation extending and revising Title II of the Higher Education Act, which deals with college and research library support programs and training of librarians. That report was to be presented to the House, the Senate, and the administration early in 1984.

Postal Affairs

Rate Increase Postponed

Late in 1983, the U.S. Postal Service (USPS) filed a package of requests for rate increases with the Postal Rate Commission. The special rate fourth class (book rate) would rise about 11 percent, considerably less than the 16 percent increase for first class, or the 22 percent proposed for third-class tariffs. Rates would not be increased until October 1984, at the earliest, in keeping with Postmaster General William Bolger's promises. More likely, because of the national elections and the Christmas mailing season, rates will probably go up in January 1985.

As in the past, AAP was to participate in the so-called rate case before the Postal Rate Commission. The commission, based on the comments of intervenors in the case, *can* alter the proposed rates, but *cannot* alter the total amount requested by the Postal Service. During early 1984, users of the other classes of mail were expected to try to get their rates reduced—but they could do so only be deriving additional dollars from another rate classification. This is one powerful reason for AAP intervention in this case. At least one organization—United Parcel Service—does not use the postal service and therefore favors raising the book rate as much as possible.

Revenue Foregone

After another long and tedious battle, Congress passed a continuing resolution in the closing days of the first session of the Ninety-eighth Congress that will permit eligible nonprofit mailings, including classroom periodicals and materials mailed at the library rate, to continue at the present Step 14 of the phasing schedule. The $879 million contained in the resolution runs until September 30, 1984. The administration had sought a funding level of $400 million, which would have terminated phasing and greatly escalated costs. AAP, along with a broad coalition of concerned groups, worked throughout 1983 to obtain full funding.

Mail Fraud Bill Enacted

After a three-year struggle, Congress passed the Mail Order Consumer Protection Amendments. The new law will strengthen the Postal Service's investigative and enforcement authority to combat misrepresentation through the mails. Of special interest to publishers is the provision strongly advocated by AAP that applies the mirror image doctrine to book advertising. This assures that as long as an advertisement accurately reflects the content of the book, it cannot be subject to false representation statutes.

Zip + 4 Goes Into Operation

After years of controversy, the nine-digit zip codes (zip + 4) became operative on October 1. Zip +4 is a voluntary system, designed for large-volume first-class business mailers. USPS believes it will improve efficiency and hold down costs by utilizing special equipment that automatically reads the zip code and sorts mail down to a city block. As an incentive for business mailers to use the expanded zip, eligible mailers receive a half-cent discount for each piece of presorted first-class mail, and a discount of 9/10 of a cent for nonpresorted first-class mail bearing the zip + 4.

Floppy Discs and 24-Page Rule

In December 1982 the Rates and Classification Department of the Postal Service ruled that computer tapes, floppy discs, and similar electronic-storage devices could not be mailed special rate fourth class. Representatives of AAP, through its Postal Committee, vigorously opposed this decision. The problem must now go to the Postal Rate Commission for resolution. Modification of the 24-page rule (specifying this as the minimum size for a book) will also be part of this proceeding.

Postal Rate-Making Decision Issued by Supreme Court

On June 22, more than a year after it agreed to hear the case regarding the proper interpretation of the postal rate-making statutes, the U.S. Supreme Court handed down its decision. On one side of the litigation were the National Association of Greeting Card Publishers and United Parcel Service, both of which believe that the statutes call for rigid cost-accounting-type rate setting. On the other side was the Postal Service's more discretionary approach. AAP supported the Postal Service interpretation. The overall effect of the decision will benefit mailers using second-class, special rate fourth-class and library rates. However, the decision leaves unresolved a number of questions on costing principles.

Mail Forwarding Period Extended

In October the forwarding period for first-class mail and express mail was extended from 12 to 18 months. This change will last for three years. The purpose of the three-year extension is to give mailers an opportunity to improve their mailing lists. AAP had filed comments asking for extension of this same forwarding privilege for the book rate. Unfortunately, it was not granted. However, the Postal Service will provide address correction service for 18 months for *all* classes of mail.

UPS and "Lost in the System"

The Postal Committee has dealt with the problem of books becoming lost in the United Parcel Service system. Publishers using UPS over a period of time seemed to be increasingly experiencing a problem with lost shipments. A representative from AAP's Operations Committee of the Mass Paperback Division traveled to Atlanta to see the UPS retail facility there for disposing of merchandise that becomes lost in its system and to meet with representatives of UPS. The subsequent report indicated that the magnitude of the problem is uncertain and may vary considerably from publisher to publisher. It was concluded that the appropriate course is for each company to negotiate its own return book procedures with UPS. From follow-up comments it appears that UPS is cooperating in such negotiations. The U.S. Postal Service, on the other hand, will return lost books to publishers, if specifically requested to do so.

Canadian Postal Increase for Publications

The Canadian government has announced plans to eliminate the existing postal subsidy for foreign publications. Under present Canadian policy, there is intragovernmental subsidy for publications printed in Canada or printed elsewhere and trucked into Canada for distribution through the Canadian postal system. The Department of Communications of Canada pays the Canadian Postal Corporation a subsidy to encourage this flow of information. However, the Department of Communications of Canada has announced its intention to stop "purchasing preferential rate reductions for foreign publications from the Canadian Postal Corporation." Canadian authorities are apparently contemplating a phase-in of the rate escalation, but no date has been set, nor has the phasing schedule been announced.

Copyright

The year 1983 was a busy one in the copyright field.

The Register's Report on Library Photocopying was issued by the Copyright Office on January 5, 1983. This was the first of the mandated five-year reviews to ascertain how well the copyright law is achieving the intended statutory balancing of the rights of copyright holders and the needs of copyright users. The Register found unauthorized photocopying but did not recommend extensive changes to the copyright law. No hearings were held on the report in 1983, but some might be scheduled during 1984. [See the copyright update for 1983 in the News Reports section of Part 1—*Ed.*]

The Copyright Office opened an inquiry concerning the deposit of computer software and received multiple comments causing the extension of time to respond to the inquiry.

The International Trade Commission conducted a study in response to the request made by the Ways and Means Trade Subcommittee and found that the repeal of the manufacturing clause would not cause a loss of jobs and great economic hardship on the printing industry. However, despite the findings, the manufacturing clause is scheduled to remain in the copyright law until July 1, 1986. The European Economic Community filed a complaint against the United States before the GATT because of the retention of the manufacturing clause, but the panel has not yet decided whether the United States owes reparations to the EEC.

The Caribbean Basin Initiative was passed August 5 with special language supported by AAP that the extent of protection provided for intellectual property be considered before granting beneficiary status to Caribbean Basin countries. This language serves to emphasize the U.S. government commitment to copyright protection.

Both Senate and House subcommittees with jurisdiction over copyright held hearings at which AAP testified on protection for microchip designs. In response to issues raised in the AAP testimony and comments, the House committee plans to introduce a new draft bill for consideration during the second session.

At the close of the second session, three copyright-related bills were introduced: (1) a revision of the "work for hire" provisions of the copyright law; (2) a commission to study the Public Lending Right; and (3) a bill to prohibit designation of "beneficiary developing countries" under the Trade Act unless adequate protection is provided for U.S. trademarks.

The Treasury Department has proposed new regulations for importing books, and new Federal Acquisitions Regulations were issued for comment. The Supreme Court held a second set of oral arguments on the Betamax case and everyone awaits its ruling, due during the Ninety-eighth session.

The Library of Congress project to convert print and audiovisual holdings to optical and video disc images has the publishing industry participation to assure adequate protections for all.

First Amendment

A large measure of AAP attention along with that of other print and electronic media groups in the First Amendment area was directed toward seeking withdrawal, or at least modification, of a presidential directive issued by the Reagan administration in March 1983. With the laudable aim of preventing leaks of crucial national security information, this excessively broad presidential order mandated lifelong prepublication review of all public writings or utterances of active or former government officials with access to highly classified materials, and greatly increased the use of lie detectors on government employees in an effort to ferret out those responsible for such leaks.

As the Ninety-eighth Congress rested between sessions, the directive was suspended, at least in theory, until April 15 by action of both houses. Although the extent to which the administration was complying with this moratorium was at least a matter of speculation, the *New York Times* did report in December that no top-ranking officer of the administration, and relatively few in lower ranks, had signed the lifelong secrecy agreements that the directive mandated.

The House Committee on Government Operations denounced the directive's proposals for widespread prepublication review and expanded use of lie detectors, recommended that neither provision be implemented, and stated that, if the administration failed to follow these recommendations, Congress should enact legislation to prohibit both.

Almost from the first announcement of the presidential directive, AAP was in the forefront of groups opposing and criticizing it. On October 19, Heather Grant Florence (Bantam), chairperson of the AAP Freedom to Read Committee, recited to the Government Operations Committee the extreme difficulties that implementation of the directive would impose on book authors and publishers. A statement by AAP President Townsend Hoopes, as a former high government official *and* spokesperson for publishers, plus a detailed analysis by Freedom to Read Counsel Bruce Rich, were also placed in the committee record. Earlier AAP had registered similar statements with two House committees and one from the U.S. Senate, protesting the curtailing of open public expression that would result from subjecting even former government officials to the directive's restrictions. Hoopes raised these points in an article on the Op Ed page of the *New York Times* on December 8, headlined "Block Reagan's Crude Attempt at Censorship," and he wrote a letter congratulating Chairman Jack Brooks (D-Texas) for the Government Operations Committee report cited earlier, which the AAP president termed "a valiant move to hold the bridge against an unprecedented assault on our constitutional rights of free speech and free expression."

Throughout the year, AAP was part of a print and electronic media coalition that successfully resisted administration-proposed weakening of the federal Freedom of

Information Act. Sweeping changes in this legislation—on the books to assure broad public access to information about federal government activities—was not expected during the second session of the Ninety-eighth Congress, which will be shortened by a recess for preelection campaigning.

During the year AAP also filed objections to a Reagan administration action making it more costly to obtain information under the Freedom of Information Act, and to another expanding officials' authority to classify government documents.

Also uncertain at midpoint between congressional sessions was the fate of another Reagan administration initiative to amend the Freedom of Information Act by allowing the government to charge a "fair value fee" or royalty, or both, when making available "commercially valuable technological information" gathered at government expense. In a letter to the Senate Judiciary Committee, AAP termed this proposal "vague, unworkable, unprincipled and imprudent" and said it appeared to give government the equivalent of an illicit copyright protection for such information. [See the special report on public access to federal information in Part 1 of this volume—*Ed.*]

For the first time in many years, the U.S. Supreme Court had three libel cases on its docket—and AAP filed briefs in all, calling the court's attention to the specific aspects of the cases that affect book publishing, even though none of the parties is a book publisher. Issues at stake range from "forum-shopping" (*Keeton* v. *Hustler, Calder* v. *Jones*) to the basic standards for appellate review (*Bose* v. *Consumers Union*).

Legislation Affecting the Information Industry in 1983

Robert S. Willard
Vice President, Government Relations
Information Industry Association

When the Ninety-eighth Congress convened its first session in January 1983, the comfortable majority that supporters of President Ronald Reagan had enjoyed in the Ninety-seventh Congress was no longer there. The party composition remained the same in the Senate (54 Republicans, 46 Democrats), but in the House of Representatives, where every member is up for election every two years, the Democrats outnumbered the Republicans (268–166). More important than the party orientation was the ideological alignment. Whereas in the Ninety-seventh Congress the conservative members of the Democratic party (referred to as the Boll Weevils) were able to add their numbers to the Republican minority in the House in sufficient numbers to pass significant parts of the president's program in 1981 and 1982, this strength was gone in 1983.

Instead, the legislative program of 1983 was characterized by a spirit of partisanship, with an eye ever on the 1984 elections; the presidential campaign was approaching full steam as the year ended, even though Reagan would wait another month before confirming that he would like to serve another four years. Both Houses would pass partisan legislation, and the Republican Senate would more than once be called on to prevent legislation dismantling the Reagan economic program passed the year before. It

Note. The opinions expressed in this article are those of the author and do not necessarily represent those of the Information Industry Association.

was successful in stalling a House-passed cap to the tax reduction legislation but was unable to forestall efforts to repeal the provision of the Reagan tax program that would require withholding for interest and dividends.

Congress's turnabout on this particular provision is instructive in understanding the mood of Congress. The withholding provision created no new taxes; it simply required financial institutions paying dividends and interest to withhold a certain percentage for federal taxes, just as an employer does from a paycheck. Any over- or underpayment would be adjusted when the individual filed a tax return. However, financial institutions, claiming inordinate processing burdens, urged customers to write Congress to seek a repeal. Many customers mistakenly thought the withholding was a new, additional tax and flooded the legislature with expressions of concern. Most members of Congress, rather than explaining the reason for the withholding provision they had passed in the previous Congress, decided to support the repeal. In fact, so many legislators were anxious to be identified with the repeal movement that hundreds of them introduced identical legislation under their name.

This sort of stampede mentality, where legislators can take the lead in an issue without really coming to grips with its complexity, was also evident later in 1983. Numerous legislators, reacting to simplistic analyses by consumer groups of the impact of the impending restructuring of AT&T, introduced legislation to postpone or even cancel some of the related provisions of the divestiture. Part of the cost of local service, which had long been subsidized by long-distance users, was clearly to be shifted to the local user, resulting in a small increase in the local component of telephone bills of all users; this charge was identified as an "access" charge. At the same time, the cost of long-distance service would decrease, and its users, principally business establishments, would be able to pass these savings along to consumers in the form of lower prices for goods and services. Admittedly, the issue was rife with economic and social policy complexities, but Congress, rather than dealing with the complexity, approached the issue simplistically: The House passed legislation prohibiting the access charges for most users. (Only a last minute postponement of the effective date of the access charges by the Federal Communications Commission prevented the Senate in early 1984 from passing similar legislation.)

In addition to dividend and interest withholding and telephone access charges, other issues attracted the interest of Congress during 1983. A number of liberal legislators introduced legislation calling for some form of "industrial policy," a popular buzzword in 1983 referring to a whole range of activities designed to involve the government in private economic decision making; the closest the Reagan administration would come to this concept was its bill promoting research and development. The combination of *Time* magazine's selection of the computer as the "machine of the year" and a host of study reports decrying the quality of education led to the introduction of numerous bills supporting science, math, and computer education. International issues, both localized (such as Central America and Lebanon) and global (such as the nuclear freeze movement), were the subjects of congressional attention in 1983. The bitter harshness of East-West conflict was brought home to members of Congress in chilling detail when one of their own colleagues was shot down by Russian fire; Representative Larry McDonald (D-Ga.) was among the 269 people aboard Korean Airlines Flight 007, which reportedly strayed into Soviet territory.

Especially noteworthy was the fact that Congress passed 10 of the 13 required funding bills, including—for the first time in five years—the labor, health, and education appropriations; the funding for the remaining three areas was approved by a continuing resolution, which leaves the money levels essentially unchanged from the previous year.

Like most first sessions of Congress, the first session of the Ninety-eighth Congress probably enacted only 25 to 35 percent of the legislation it will pass during its two-year term. Congress passed 215 public laws (more than a third of which dealt with such matters as designating certain commemorative days, weeks, or months, or naming federal buildings in honor of veteran politicians). Less than a half dozen of these laws have anything to do with information policy issues, yet during the year a large number of information policy bills were introduced and many of them were the subject of some action. Some of the more significant or interesting bills will be discussed in this article. Legislation will be classified in one of five categories. First are proposals that mandate or encourage the government to become involved in the information marketplace. Second are measures aimed at protecting the economic value of information resources. Comprising the third category are government rules affecting the transport of information, or communications. Fourth are legislative items that address civil liberty issues in the information arena, such as privacy and First Amendment rights. Finally, the fifth category contains proposals that may be an incentive or an impediment to the flow of information.

Government Information Activities

For the third year, the Senate majority leader, Howard Baker (R–Tenn.), failed to convince his colleagues to allow Senate floor proceedings to be televised (as is done in the House of Representatives). The Senate Rules and Administration Committee did approve a resolution (S. Res. 66) in favor of such broadcasts, but opponents have stalled further consideration.

Congress also stymied administration plans to transfer government meteorological and geodetic satellites to the private sector. Arguing that competitive marketplace forces would improve the efficiency and drive down prices charged for weather and other information collected by remote sensing satellites, the Department of Commerce initiated a comprehensive plan to sell these facilities. Congress, however, arguing that the principal purchaser of weather data was the government itself, passed legislation that effectively put an end to the proposal. The appropriation bill for the Commerce Department prohibited the department from spending any money on the sale idea, and the authorizing legislation for the National Aeronautics and Space Administration (PL 98-52) required that before any transfer of ownership or management a "comprehensive statement of recommended policies, procedures, conditions, and limitations" must be submitted to the Congress and Congress must enact a law authorizing such a transfer.

Congress handled a number of bills dealing with how the government should act when it procures goods and services from the private sector. Although this group of bills did not focus on information products and services, one bill enacted into law (PL 98-72) was designed to improve small business access to federal procurement information; it set parameters for publishing details about planned procurements. Other bills that advanced through the legislative process during 1983 focused on expanding the degree of competition in the federal procurement process and opening up the process to greater participation by small business. One bill that was introduced but received no action was identified as the Freedom from Government Competition Act (S. 1746). Its sponsor,

Senator Warren Rudman (R–N.H.), intended the bill to provide a statutory basis for the contracting policy contained in Office of Management and Budget Circular A-76, claiming "it is in the public interest that the government establish a consistent policy to rely on the private sector of the economy to provide goods and services necessary for or beneficial to the operation and management of government agencies and to avoid government competition with the private sector of the economy. . . ." Hearings on this bill are expected in early 1984.

The Government Printing Office (GPO), one of the major points of government information activities, was the subject of a trio of bills introduced by Representative Dan Glickman (D–Kans.) and cosponsored by more than 50 colleagues. The object of each of these bills (H.R. 4049, H.R. 4050, and H.R. 4051) was simply to reduce expenses of the GPO incurred in gratuitous distribution of the *Congressional Record* and other printing and binding performed for Congress. Another bill, H.R. 846, introduced by Representative McDonald seven months before his death in the Korean airline tragedy, would require that government publications distributed free to the public, as well as advertisements for such publications, must carry the message that "the printing and distribution of the publications are financed by United States taxpayers." None of these bills received further action during 1983.

However, a major congressional initiative concerning the GPO took place during 1983 that was not technically legislation but would, nevertheless, lead to a major change in its operation and government information activities. In November, just before the adjournment of the first session of Congress, the little-noticed Joint Committee on Printing, a body composed of five senators and five representatives, published a draft version of new regulations in the *Congressional Record* dealing with printing, binding, and distribution. One of the anomalies of Congress is that this committee can promulgate regulations that, without any further congressional action or involvement of the president, will control the activities of the entire government with regard to printing.

The regulations attempt to put into effect many of the provisions that were included in the unsuccessful 1979–1980 effort to amend Title 44 of the United States Code dealing with government printing. Especially troublesome in the proposed new version of the regulations is a definition of printing that goes far beyond the traditional ink-on-paper and more recent image-on-microfilm concepts. To some observers, this definition would embrace every form of information technology now known or to be developed. Because of existing law (passed in 1895), which requires that all printing be performed by the GPO, the new regulations would establish the GPO as the centralized, monopoly source of all government information.

The proposed regulations have been criticized by a whole spectrum of interests, including both the private sector and government entities. A segment of the library community, seeing the new regulations as a vehicle for providing depository libraries access to government information in electronic form, has endorsed the changes. It is certain that wholesale modifications to the draft will have to be made before these regulations can be put into effect.

Proprietary Rights

Perhaps no area of information policy legislation was more fecund in 1983 than that dealing with means to protect the economic value of information products, principally the means of copyright law. Little legislation was actually passed, but a large number of bills dealing with a broad range of issues were introduced and many took significant steps in the legislative process. Much of this activity took place in the shadow of two significant 1983 events: the report of the Register of Copyrights on library photocopying and the Supreme Court consideration of the videotape recording case, *Universal Studios* v. *Sony,* known popularly as the Betamax case.

The principle of government protection of intellectual efforts goes back to the drafting of the Constitution, and legislation was introduced in 1983 to celebrate the roots of this protection. Senator Charles McC. Mathias (R-Md.) introduced S.J. Res. 165 "to commemorate the bicentennial anniversary of the constitutional foundation for patent and copyright laws" in 1987.

Mathias, chairman of the Senate Judiciary Subcommittee on Patents, Copyright, and Trademarks (which was created in 1983 to deal with a wide range of intellectual property issues), also introduced a number of bills that called on Congress to determine what type of protection new forms of technology should be afforded. In light of controversy surrounding off-the-air recording, he introduced S. 31, which would allow home video recording but would also allow a royalty fee (characterized by opponents as a tax) to be assessed against recording hardware and blank tapes; these fees would subsequently be distributed to creators of movies and television productions. (Bills authorizing video copying without the payment of royalties were also introduced in both the House and Senate.) Mathias's S. 32 and S. 33 also addressed issues concerning tape recording; the bills would prohibit the purchasers of copyrighted audio and video material from renting, leasing, or lending that material for commercial purposes without approval of the copyright owner. The audio bill, S. 32, passed the Senate in June.

June also was the occasion of a surprise announcement from the Supreme Court concerning videotaping. The Betamax case had been argued before the Court, and as the Court session concluded there was a growing level of curiosity about whether the Court would agree with the district court ruling that off-the-air videotaping for personal use is allowable, or with the appeals court decision that such copying is an infringement. However, instead of a ruling, the Court issued a short statement that it had not reached a decision and would hear further oral arguments after its next term began in October. (Early in 1984, the Supreme Court did rule, siding with the lower court and affirming the right of individuals to tape television shows for later viewing. This ruling is certain to force Congress to address legislation such as Mathias's S. 31, but at this time one can only guess the final congressional outcome.)

The blurry boundary between patent and copyright protection is demonstrated most vividly in the problems of those who design and produce integrated circuits, or chips, for modern information processing devices. The chips, which can cost many hundreds of thousands of dollars to develop, can be examined and reproduced ("reverse engineered") for a small fraction of that cost. The program embodied in the chip can be protected by copyright and the overall device in which the chip is employed may be protected by patent, but the level of protection for the chip itself is unclear. Mathias introduced S. 1201, the Semiconductor Chip Protection Act, and held hearings on the bill to explore this issue. The bill would amend the Copyright Act in a number of significant ways that trouble some copyright experts: It would allow chips and certain intermediate products to be copyrighted but would limit the period of protection to ten years instead of the "life plus 50 years" available to other works created by individuals; it would introduce the concept of "innocent infringement"; and it would force owners of such copyrights to license the use of their property under certain circumstances of infringement. Alternatives to this copyright scheme are under consideration, such as a "design protection" for useful articles. There is broad support for some protection for computer chips and it is widely believed that Congress will resolve this issue in 1984.

There was equally wide appreciation of a whole host of problems under the rubric "computer crime," but it is less clear what action Congress may take to deal with this issue, which, like copyright, is concerned with the property value of information. During 1983 a few bills were introduced and at least two or three hearings were held. A flurry of activity took place during the summer when national media attention was directed toward young computer whizzes, termed "hackers," who had gained unauthorized access to a large number of computers, including one at the Los Alamos nuclear research facility. The only bill to be passed by either house was a rather innocuous bill, the so-called Small Business Computer Crime Prevention Act, H.R. 3075, which passed the House. This bill would establish a computer crime and security task force in the Small Business Administration to study the problem and make recommendations.

A bill with more power is H.R. 3075, the Counterfeit Access Device and Computer Fraud Act, introduced by William Hughes (D–N.J.). This legislation would amend the criminal code to provide fines up to $100,000 and prison terms up to 20 years for those who use a computer with intent to execute a scheme to defraud or who traffic in access devices (cards, codes, account numbers, and so on, used to access accounts to obtain something of value).

The preeminent legislative vehicle for addressing the computer crime issue is a bill introduced in various forms since the Ninety-fifth Congress. First sponsored in 1977 by then Senator Abraham Ribicoff, the bill was reintroduced in 1983 as H.R. 1092, the Federal Computer Systems Protection Act, by Representative Bill Nelson (D–Fla.). (Nelson, as a member of the state legislature, was instrumental in securing the passage of similar legislation at the state level in Florida.) This bill, which has continued to attract many cosponsors and has been the subject of a number of hearings, appeared no closer to passage in 1983 than it had in earlier Congresses. However, the public attention to problems of unauthorized access to computers may finally cause Congress to give the Ribicoff-Nelson legislation a much closer look and perhaps see it to enactment in 1984.

The question to ownership of information appeared in a rather unlikely place during 1983. Amendments to the Freedom of Information Act contained in S. 774 of Senator Orrin Hatch (R–Utah) and approved by the Senate Judiciary Committee, included a provision that would allow government agencies to charge a fee or royalty for "commercially valuable technological data." Some information industry representatives opposed this provision as a means of conferring copyright-like protection to the government, which is prohibited by Section 105 of the Copyright Act from claiming copyright for its works. Library interests also opposed the provision because of its potential restrictions on access. The Senate is likely to pass the bill with this provision intact, but any legislation passed by the House would probably not contain such a provision.

Although no copyright or computer crime legislation was enacted into law in 1983, one act signed by the president did contain a significant provision dealing with copyright; this was the Caribbean Basin Economic Recovery Act, which was included in P.L. 98-67. (Ironically, this provision was coupled with the repeal of the withholding on dividends and interest mentioned earlier. Congress, to forestall a threatened veto of the repeal provision, merged it with the president's own Caribbean Basin initiative. Reluctantly, the president signed the package into law in August.)

The copyright provisions of this legislation, although somewhat narrow, show a willingness on the part of Congress to speak for the interests of owners of intellectual property. The Caribbean plan allows special trade treatment for designated countries, but prohibits such favorable treatment "if a government-owned entity in such country engages in the broadcast of copyrighted material, including films or television material, belonging to United States copyright owners without their express consent." Moreover, the law directs the president, in evaluating a country for such favored treatment, to examine "the extent to which such country provides under its law adequate and effective means for foreign nationals to secure, exercise, and enforce exclusive rights in intellectual property," and "the extent to which such country prohibits its nationals from engaging in the broadcast of copyrighted material, including films or television material, belonging to United States copyright owners without their express consent." Such provisions may be extended to other trade preference legislation in 1984.

Finally, and again introduced by Senator Charles Mathias, S. 2192 calls on the Congress to put into place a mechanism for examining questions of equity in the area of copyright and libraries. The National Commission on the Public Lending of Books Act would establish a body within the Library of Congress to explore fully means of conferring on authors economic returns for the public lending of their works.

Communications

Congress handled comparatively little communications legislation of direct concern to the information industry. As indicated in the introduction to this article, a great deal of congressional attention was devoted to bills dealing with the AT&T divestiture and the proposed access charges. The House did pass Tim Wirth's H.R. 4102 (the Universal Telephone Service Preservation Act), but the Colorado Democrat is not likely to see his bill approved on the Senate side. The delaying action of the Federal Communications Commission with regard to the widespread imposition of access charges took the pressure off the Senate, which was not anxious to tackle telephone legislation in 1984, an election year. Although the House action may mark the first time in a half century that a major common carrier (i.e., telephone) bill was approved by the House, it appears improbable that any further action will occur.

Broadcast deregulation is another area that received attention in 1983, but no final resolution. Still undetermined is the degree to which the federal government can put day-to-day requirements on radio and television operations; the conflict comes between those who want to lift as many regulations as possible and see competition in the marketplace drive the decisions of broadcasters and those who feel broadcasters will only live up to their public interest responsibilities if the government forces them to do so.

A much narrower regulatory matter that nonetheless absorbed an inordinate amount of congressional attention was an arcane rule concerned with the right of networks to have certain financial interests in programs they broadcast. The FCC was moving to lift this rule, but the House, under pressure from Hollywood program owners, passed a bill prohibiting such action until the middle of 1984. The FCC agreed to suspend its action at least until May 1984, and the Senate deferred further action until it could evaluate the efforts of the networks and program producers to arrive at some compromise.

One congressional initiative that became law in 1983 had less to do with broadcasting and more with government propaganda, but nonetheless was a cause of concern to U.S. broadcasters. This was the administration proposal to beam Spanish-language news and other programs to Cuba. Originally identified as Radio Marti and patterned after Radio Free Europe, the service as finally enacted (PL 98-111, the Radio Broadcasting to Cuba Act) was folded into the Voice of America operations. The authorization of broadcasting on a frequency within the standard AM band raised the fear that retaliatory Cuban jamming would have a detrimental effect on some U.S. broadcasting operations.

Civil Liberties

For those concerned with governmental controls on information, perhaps no event drew as much attention as National Security Decision Directive-84 on Safeguarding National Security Information, issued by President Reagan on March 11, 1983. The directive required federal employees with access to certain categories of classified information to sign agreements to submit their writings to the government for prepublication review for the rest of their lives. It also allowed for use of polygraphs on federal employees in the investigation of security leaks. [See the special report on access to federal information in Part 1—Ed.]

Although not a legislative act, this directive immediately drew the attention of the Congress, and before the year was out the House Government Operations Committee had held hearings and issued a critical report on the directive. In addition, the State Department authorizing legislation, PL 98-164, contained a provision prohibiting any action that would implement the prepublication review requirements before April 15, 1984. Although not prohibiting the prepublication review outright, this temporary embargo gives Congress time to examine the issue more fully and, if necessary, to take remedial steps.

As in the past, a number of bills dealing with personal privacy were introduced, but the privacy provision that received the most congressional attention was contained in legislation passed by the Senate dealing with cable television. Section 611 of S. 66, the Cable Telecommunications Act, deals with the protection of subscriber privacy. The legislation addresses the fact that a whole host of information about an individual's viewing and (with the increase of transaction services) other personal habits can be collected and retained by a cable facility offering two-way service. The bill would prohibit the collection of personally identifiable information, except that needed for billing, unless the subscriber had given consent, either in writing or electronically. The bill delineates certain additional rights of the subscriber with regard to personal information maintained by the system, including the right to have access to one's own personal data and to be notified if the personal data are being sought through any court action. The bill also authorizes civil damages in the event of a violation of the rights authorized by this section.

Two bills dealing with the First Amendment freedoms of speech and the press were introduced in 1983, one attempting to extend the application of these rights, the other seeking to lift what some interpreted as a misapplication. The Freedom of Expression Act, S. 1917, was introduced by Senator Robert Packwood (R–Oreg.) to prohibit the

FCC from enforcing restrictions on information content imposed on broadcasters. On the other hand, H.R. 1157, which was introduced by Representative Joseph Addabbo (D–N.Y.) and has been called the Opinion Molder Legislation, would restrict the authority of the Small Business Administration to deny financial assistance to firms that are involved in the communication of ideas. Small business loan guarantees and other financial assistance have been withheld from such companies in the past because such assistance has been interpreted as a violation of the First Amendment prohibition on laws restricting freedom of speech or of the press. Hearings have been held on this subject in the past, and SBA officials have indicated a willingness to modify such restrictions administratively, yet no action has been taken.

Regulation of Information Flow

This final category includes a wide range of legislative efforts dealing with government activities that are either an incentive or an impediment to the use of information and information technology, including measures that seek to establish mechanisms to deal with information policy.

One such measure enacted into law is Section 124 of the State Department authorization (PL 98-164), which establishes a policy apparatus within the department for dealing with international communications and information policy. Another, which was passed by both the House and Senate but did not require presidential action, was S.Con.Res. 59. This resolution directs the Librarian of Congress to study the changing role of the book in the future, especially in light of changing technology.

Still subject to further action is the House-passed reauthorization of the Paperwork Reduction Act. H.R. 2718, introduced by Jack Brooks (D–Tex.) and Frank Horton (R–N.Y.), extends the authority of the Office of Information and Regulatory Affairs within the Office of Management and Budget (OMB) through 1986, consolidates two separate General Services Administration (GSA) funds into a single Information Technology Fund and further clarifies the relationship between OMB and GSA, and calls for separate ("line item") funding for the information resource management responsibilities assigned by the legislation. Senate action is expected on this bill in early 1984. (Another information policy aspect of the relationship between OMB and GSA was addressed in PL 98-169, which transferred the responsibility for producing the catalog of domestic assistance to GSA, while retaining within OMB the overall program management.)

Congressional action is not expected on H.R. 480, according to its sponsor, George Brown (D–Calif.), but he still argues for the Institute for Information Policy and Research that this bill (and its predecessors in the two preceding Congresses) would establish. Although it is claimed that the federal government, under the current administration, will not establish any new organization to examine policy implications of the information revolution, it is argued that H.R. 480 may act as a stimulus for other organizations to develop such institutions. At least two associations are advancing related ideas: The Association for Data Processing Service Organizations has developed a proposal for a Temporary National Information Commission, based on a predecessor organization established to deal with aspects of the Great Depression in the 1930s; and the Computer and Business Equipment Manufacturers Association is attempting to launch a research body known as the Information Age Institute.

Conclusion

Congress continues to be called on to address more and more complex issues of the information age. It remains to be seen whether, as an institution, it can give these issues the thoughtful, analytical attention they deserve, or whether, as was evident at times in the first session of the Ninety-eighth Congress, it will respond to insistent political pressure of constituents who have failed to give these issues anything but the simplest review.

Funding Programs and Grant-Making Agencies

Council on Library Resources, Inc.

1785 Massachusetts Ave. N.W., Washington. DC 20036
202-483-7474

Jane A. Rosenberg
Program Associate

Established in 1956, the Council on Library Resources (CLR) is a privately operated foundation that operates its own programs and provides funds for work to assist the solution of library problems, especially those of academic and research libraries. The council currently is funded by a number of foundations. It awards grants to individuals and institutions to carry out projects in several areas: bibliographic services; professional education, training, and research; library management and services; library resources and preservation; information delivery services; and international programs. CLR also relies on many expert individuals and groups to help plan and implement activities.

The council's board of directors consists of 22 individuals from academic institutions, research libraries, business, and the professions. During 1983, Whitney North Seymour (deceased, May 1983) served as chairman and Louis B. Wright was vice chairman; Warren J. Haas is president; and Mary Agnes Thompson is secretary and treasurer.

Bibliographic Service Development Program

As the council's largest program, the Bibliographic Service Development Program (BSDP) has a total program budget of $6.2 million. Eighteen new grants were made during FY 1983 and 24 grants were active at the end of the year.

Linked Systems Project

In the Linked Systems Project (LSP), the Research Libraries Group (RLG), the Washington Library Network (WLN), and the Library of Congress (LC) are developing and implementing sets of rules, or protocols, that govern the transfer of information from one computer to another. These protocols, collectively known as the Standard Network Interconnection (SNI), will eventually link the participants' computer systems, enabling them to exchange bibliographic records and other information. During 1983, James Aagaard, Northwestern University, completed work on the Application Level protocol and prepared to test SNI. A successful communication link between Library of Congress and Research Libraries Group computers early in the year utilized a portion of the protocols.

Final plans for the Name Authority File Service were in preparation in fiscal 1983, and in April, LSP participants began a bibliographic analysis project to plan new uses of the system links.

Standards and Guides

The council made a two-year grant to the American National Standards Institute in June 1982 to provide assistance for its Committee Z39 activities related to book paper quality, recording information about library holdings, and telecommunications protocols. Also, the Pittsburgh Regional Library Center has finished its project to develop a method of recording and communicating serials cancellation decisions via an online union list, and the council has provided funding to help the Committee on Research Materials on Southeast Asia, Association for Asian Studies, promote a universally acceptable romanization scheme for bibliographic descriptions. In November 1982, the University of Florida used CLR funds for a conference to review the design and plan the implementation of the proposed MARC format for locations and holdings to be recorded in a machine-readable union list of serials. The format is being developed by the Southeastern Association of Research Libraries Cooperative Serials Project, in conjunction with the Library of Congress.

The Association of American Publishers has received CLR assistance for a two-year project to develop standards for preparing and processing electronic manuscripts. Aspen Systems Corporation, the contractor for this work, will develop a proposed system of command codes, keyboarding conventions, and author guidelines for preparing manuscripts by machine. The University of Chicago Press has offered to incorporate the guidelines in a future edition of *The Chicago Manual of Style*.

The recently completed online public-access catalog evaluation was the first research project to obtain information from a large number of library users working with different online catalogs. Five groups conducted the two-year study: the Library of Congress; J. Matthews & Associates; the OnLine Computer Library Center, Inc. (OCLC); the Research Libraries Group; and the University of California's Division of Library Automation. Over 7,000 online catalog users and 3,000 nonusers at 29 research, college, community college, public, and government libraries were asked for information. A major synthesis of the data, *Using Online Catalogs: A Nationwide Study,* was published by Neal-Schuman in June 1983.

The council has contracted with J. Matthews & Associates, in cooperation with the University of California, to undertake a more detailed analysis of the online catalog study data, including differences in systems, data bases, support services, and characteristics of user and nonuser groups. Invitational meetings also were held on characteristics and costs of online catalogs and the design and improvement of user training programs. Publications from these meetings, titled *Costs and Features of Online Catalogs: The State of the Art* by J. Matthews & Associates and Charles Miller, Florida State University, and *Training Users of Online Public Access Catalogs,* were issued in 1983. Additional work on training is underway at Northwestern University.

To explore planning and managerial issues related to the introduction of online catalogs, BSDP sponsored a three-day conference for 27 library directors and systems designers in December 1982. The report of the conference, *Online Catalogs: Require-*

ments, Characteristics and Costs, was issued in March 1983. A meeting of online catalog system designers was held in the fall of 1983.

Other projects relating to bibliographic access include work by the Association of Research Libraries (ARL) to improve access to the contents of microform collections and two projects to provide information about machine-readable files. The Research Libraries Group is adding bibliographic records for machine-readable data files to its Research Libraries Information Network, and Rutgers University received CLR funding to develop record formats and create a sample data base for an international inventory of machine-readable texts in the humanities.

Conversion of Serials (CONSER)

The Association of Research Libraries and the National Federation of Abstracting and Indexing Services have undertaken a project to add information on the coverage of titles by abstracting and indexing services to the CONSER data base. Participants will also ensure that the data base includes a core group of widely used titles.

Bibliographic Products and Services

Pauline Cochrane, Syracuse University, has submitted a report on her work with the LC Subject Cataloging Division to strengthen the Library of Congress subject headings. As a result of this work, four libraries have begun submitting new cross-references for LC approval. Under another grant for work related to subject headings, Lois Chan, University of Kentucky, is revising her text, *Library of Congress Subject Headings: Principles and Application.*

C. Donald Cook, University of Toronto, continued work on a project to assess differences in applications of AACR 2 rules for headings for corporate bodies. Cook had analyzed 25 percent of the headings assigned by four national libraries by May 1983. Victor Rosenberg, University of Michigan, who received CLR funding to construct computer programs for extracting, formatting, and storing bibliographic citations from shared cataloging data bases, has completed software for several different micro-computers.

Professional Education, Training, and Research

The Professional Education and Training for Research Librarianship (PETREL) program, established in 1981, has funded three such programs, at the universities of Chicago, Michigan, and California at Los Angeles. During 1983, 10 students graduated from Michigan's basic professional education program and Chicago's postgraduate program in management. Twenty-nine selected senior library administrators have participated in the Senior Fellows program begun in 1982 at UCLA.

The PETREL program has also funded two frontiers conferences designed to bring librarians, library educators, university officials, and others together to discuss current issues and future library needs. The theme of the second conference, held in June 1983 at the University of British Columbia, was "Changing Technology: Its Impact on Scholarly Communication, Research Libraries, and Education for Librarianship and Information Science." Proceedings of both meetings will be published.

A new series of PETREL grants was made possible by funding from the Pew Memorial Trust. Part of the funding supports research projects conducted by teaching faculty and senior staff members of academic and research libraries. In 1983, 16 projects were funded.

Academic Library Management Intern Program

The Management Intern Program resumed in 1983. Five interns were chosen from a group of 90 applicants for the 1983–1984 program, bringing the total number of participants to 40. The new interns are: Jill B. Fatzer, University of Delaware, working with Millicent Abell, university librarian, University of California at San Diego; Susan F. Rhee, San Diego State University, at Columbia University, interning with Patricia Battin, vice-president and university librarian; Gordon S. Rowley, Northern Illinois University, working with Charles Churchwell, dean of library services, Washington University, St. Louis; Helen H. Spalding, University of Missouri, Kansas City, interning with John McGowan, university librarian, Northwestern University; and Sarah E. Thomas, Research Libraries Group, working with David Bishop, director of libraries, University of Georgia.

Library Management and Services

CLR support for the Academic Library Program of the Association of Research Libraries Office of Management Studies continued during FY 1983. The program now consists of six separate self-study procedures for academic and research libraries plus a consultant training program. Self-studies are available in general management, collection analysis, preservation planning, programs for medium-size and small academic libraries, and public services. Seventy-nine librarians have been selected to participate in the Consultant Training Program since its inception in 1979; the final group was trained in the fall of 1983.

Begun in 1969, the College Library Program is in its final year of operation. The program assisted 35 libraries in designing instruction-related activities. Many participants report that institutional resources have been provided to continue the programs.

Grants provided to Earlham College (Richmond, Indiana) for workshops designed to bring librarians and faculty at many institutions together to seek improved methods for integrating the library into academic life also will end after this year. The council provided Whittier College (Los Angeles, California) with support to bring Earlham faculty to the Whittier campus to replicate the program for West Coast participants, and also assisted Ohio State University with an April 1983 colloquium for faculty from other research universities. The colloquium emphasized faculty-librarian partnerships to improve research techniques among both graduate and undergraduate students.

Another project in the area of faculty-library communications, the ARL–American Association for the Advancement of the Humanities distribution of a national newsletter, *Library Issues,* to faculty at three institutions, ended in 1983. Most faculty indicated they prefer a locally produced publication tailored to their own campus community, and ARL will consider its role in continuing work in this area. The Society of American Archivists completed its project to design a self-assessment and peer-review process for archival agencies and published a guide titled *Evaluation of Archival Agencies.* At the University of Michigan, an investigation of faculty attitudes toward remote storage facilities is underway.

Library Resources and Their Preservation

The council's interest in preservation continues, although there is less activity than previously because more institutions are establishing programs. The final report of the Committee on Production Guidelines for Book Longevity, titled *Book Longevity,* appeared in December 1982. It is the basis for another CLR-supported activity, the American National Standards Institute's work on a standard for permanent paper for library materials.

The Resources and Technical Services Division, American Library Association, received a grant to help pay expenses for a series of four preservation conferences to be held over a two-year period. The conferences are cosponsored by LC's National Preservation Program. To help improve knowledge about practices elsewhere, the council has provided a grant to Nancy Bell, Johns Hopkins University, to complete preservation internships in England and document British practices.

Grants to assist the production of aids to research and professional literature include funding for a guide to microform collections. Ann Niles, Carleton College (Northfield, Minnesota), is preparing the guide to previously unindexed series. Ellis Mount, Columbia University (New York City), who published his *University Science and Engineering Libraries* (Westport, CT: Greenwood Press, 1975) as the result of a CLR fellowship, has received support to assist preparation of a new edition.

Several projects support development of methods for evaluating library holdings. Paul Metz, Virginia Polytechnic Institute and State University (Blacksburg), has completed a study of the use of library materials, focusing on the extent to which faculty and students rely on the literature of their own versus other disciplines. A manual resulting from a collection assessment project at four college libraries (Atlanta College of Art; Dillard University, New Orleans; Tougaloo College, Tougaloo, Mississippi; and Tuskegee University, Tuskegee, Alabama) will be published after revisions by the ARL Office of Management Studies. Collection overlap is the topic of research by Wiliam Gray Potter, University of Illinois. Potter is matching circulation records from 20 libraries using the Library Computer System, a shared circulation system.

Technology and Information Delivery Services

Late in 1982, the Alfred P. Sloan Foundation granted $400,000 to the council for use over five years to explore the potential value for library operations and services of recently developed technologies. Funds are used in part to support CLR technical staff, for technical studies, and for assistance from consultants in the field.

The council set up a new Ford Foundation–supported program to improve access to documents and information. A task force drawn from the library and information service communities has assisted with preliminary discussions and gathering information.

Information Systems Consultants, Inc. (ISCI) received a CLR contract to report on the potential of telefacsimile for helping improve interlibrary loan services. A report on current interlibrary loan activity and document delivery, titled *Document Delivery in the United States,* also was prepared by ISCI.

In July 1983, the Association of Research Libraries began a project to develop tools and procedures needed to describe collections across a wide spectrum of research libraries. CLR funding will be used by ARL's Office of Management Studies to develop manuals for bibliographers and training programs for library staff. At Syracuse University, Mona Farid and Eileen Snyder are investigating information-seeking behavior of students enrolled in Ph.D. programs.

International Programs and Special Projects

Council funding supported preparation of background papers and the final report of the August 1982 International Federation of Library Associations and Institutions (IFLA) international meeting to consider cataloging-in-publication programs, and also an ongoing two-year review of the International Standard Bibliographic Descriptions. To assist developing countries to establish national bibliographic services, the council has supported consultation services by the director of IFLA's International Office for Universal Bibliographic Control. The director has worked with the African Standing Conference on Bibliographic Control, and the UBC office has completed a survey of classification practices in African countries. The *Manual of Bibliographic Control* was prepared to assist countries in participating in international bibliographic programs.

During fiscal 1983, CLR funds were used to support a meeting of four international organizations interested in use of copyrighted materials by handicapped readers, and to send IFLA representatives to a UNESCO/World Intellectual Property Organization Working Group meeting in October 1982. The relation of document availability to planning for library and information services was the subject of a May 1983 IFLA Universal Access to Publications program report titled *Guidelines on National Planning for the Availability of Publications*.

CLR assistance has been provided for producing materials for professionals abroad. The *Manual on the Management of Archival Institutions* by Cesar A. Garcia Belsunce, Archivo de la Nacion, Argentina, will be published by the Archives of Spain. An edition of the Dewey decimal classification for Arab countries, begun with the aid of a 1980 council grant to Forest Press, publisher of the Dewey schedules, is also being published.

Travel grants were made during FY 1983 to Anthony J. Loveday, secretary of the Standing Conference of National and University Libraries and chairperson of the IFLA Section of University and Other General Research Libraries, to attend the joint spring meeting of ARL and the Canadian Association of Research Libraries; and to Rutherford D. Rogers, chairperson, IFLA Programme Management Committee, to attend committee meetings in Munich in November 1982.

Records of Government

The council is cooperating with the American Council of Learned Societies and the Social Science Research Council to sponsor the Committee on the Records of Government. Chaired by Ernest May, Harvard University, the committee began its 18-month inquiry in September 1983.

Wingspread Conference and Forum II

In December 1982, an invitational conference was held at Wingspread, Racine, Wisconsin, titled "Toward the 21st Century: A Conference on Research Libraries and

Their Users," culminating a project begun in 1981 by the Association of American Universities and the council. A result of the conference was an October 1983 meeting to consider national aspects of research library collections and preservation.

University of Chicago Conference

The council provided funding for the University of Chicago Graduate Library School's forty-second annual conference, "Publishing Today: Opportunities and Challenges in the Dissemination of New Knowledge and Literature," held in spring 1983.

New Grants and Contracts, FY 1983

American Library Association
Preservation conferences — $5,000

Association of Research Libraries
National Inventory of Research Collections — $23,427

Nancy J. Bell
Conservation internships — $2,500

Carleton College, Northfield, Minnesota
Guide to microform collections — $2,250

International Federation of Library Associations
and Institutions, The Hague, Netherlands
Guidelines for national UAP planning,
policy, and development — $3,500

IFLA representation at the UNESCO/WIPO Meeting — $2,000

Anthony J. Loveday
Travel grant for ARL/CARL conference — $1,500

Ellis Mount
Revision of *University Science and Engineering Libraries* — $2,250

Ohio State University
Colloquium on Library User Education — $4,500

University of Chicago
Forty-second annual conference — $14,300

University of Illinois
Collection overlap and diversity in the LCS network — $6,500

Whittier College (Los Angeles, California)
Bibliographic Instruction Workshop — $3,000

Bibliographic Service Development Program

Association of Research Libraries
CONSER A & I coverage project — $75,500

Giok Po Oey
Travel grant to explore romanization of Southeast Asian
language material — $2,200

Library of Congress
Joint Project: Bibliographic Analysis Linked Systems Project $4,620
LSP participation—SNI project (Session and Transport Layer design) $24,576
Preparation of intersite test plan for SNI $24,576
Protocol Layer Interface Design-SNI $25,000
Telenet connection for SNI development $8,500
J. Matthews & Associates
Detailed analysis of CLR online catalog data $27,000
Northwestern University
Educating the catalog user: A model for instructional
development and evaluation $57,000
Research Libraries Group, Inc.
Joint Project: Bibliographic analysis For Linked Systems Project $16,470
Planning the integration of machine-readable data files into RLIN $7,000
University of California, Berkeley
Features and costs of online catalogs: The state of the art $17,500
University of Florida Foundation Inc., Gainesville
Invitational conference on MARC format for holdings and locations $8,550
University of Georgia Research Foundation, Athens
Analysis of subsets of data gathered in the online public-access
catalog study $2,500
University of Kentucky Research Foundation
Second ed. of *Library of Congress Subject Headings:*
Principles and Applications $3,860
Washington Library Network
Joint project: Bibliographic analysis for Linked Systems Project $9,887

Information Delivery Services Program

Association of Research Libraries
National Inventory of Research Collections, Phase I $23,428
Information Systems Consultants Inc.
Document delivery survey, Phase I $12,800
Telefacsimile as a means of improving interlibrary document delivery $600
Syracuse University
Information-seeking behavior of Ph.D. students in selected disciplines $3,000

Professional Education and Training for Research Librarianship

Faculty/Librarian Cooperative Research Projects

Iowa State University $650
Indiana University $2,995
Michigan State University $2,800
Rutgers University $3,000

State University of New York	$3,000
Syracuse University	$2,000
University of California	$3,000
University of Illinois	$2,026
University of Iowa	$3,000
University of Minnesota	$3,000
University of Oklahoma	$2,930
University of Tennessee	$2,500
University of Western Ontario	$1,950
Vanderbilt University (Nashville, Tennessee) (2 awards)	$3,000
	$3,000
Wayne State University (Detroit, Michigan)	$3,000
University of British Columbia	
Frontiers Conference II	$33,000

Council on Library Resources Publications

Annual Report

CLR Recent Developments (newsletter; irregular)

U.S. Department of Education Library Programs, 1983

Ray M. Fry

Director, Division of Library Programs
Center for Libraries and Education Improvement
Office of Educational Research and Improvement
Department of Education
202-254-5680

During 1983, a major organizational shift transferred the Division of Library Programs from the Office of Libraries and Learning Technologies (OLLT) to the Center for Libraries and Education Improvement (CLEI), one of the three components of the Office of Educational Research and Improvement. (The other components are the National Institute of Education and the National Center for Education Statistics.)

HEA Programs

The four discretionary programs funded under the Higher Education Act (HEA) of 1965—training; research and demonstration; college library resources; and strengthening research libraries—are managed by the Library Education, Research, and Resources Branch of the Division of Library Programs. Three of the programs continue the same focus of previous years:

The Strengthening Research Library Resources program assists in the improvement and preservation of library collections and encourages the sharing of those collections.

The College Library Resources program assists in the improvement of library resources and encourages the sharing of resources through networking.

The Library Career training program still focuses on the recruitment of minorities and economically disadvantaged students and on the upward mobility of women.

However, over the past few years, the Research and Demonstration program fund has been reduced.

Despite limited funding, the Research and Demonstration program has continued to support a number of critical studies. The first major library personnel study funded since the department's effort in the early 1970s was completed in 1983. The survey report, *Human Resources: A Study of Supply and Demand*, was published by the American Library Association. [For a summary of the survey results, see the report by Nancy Roderer in Part 3—*Ed.*]

The major study of library education, "New Directions in Library and Information Science Education," continued throughout FY 1983 and will be completed in FY 1984. The purpose of the study is to identify, describe, and validate the competencies needed by library and information science professionals, with an emphasis on future competencies in the technology areas. Hopefully, the results of the study will provide a basis for revision and improvement of library and information science education.

A new study funded in 1983 will look at innovations developed and adopted for use in library and information science and will make recommendations for building a dissemination network for library and information science innovation. Another small, but vital, contract was awarded to study HEA II-B training fellows, with particular emphasis on their contributions to librarianship. In the area of technology, a contract was awarded to look at the role of libraries in creating and providing viewtext information services.

Potentially, one of the most significant library projects ever funded by the Department of Education was launched in 1983: "Libraries and the Learning Society" was an outgrowth of (and hopefully will be a complement to) *A Nation at Risk: The Imperative for Educational Reform* (National Commission on Excellence in Education, 1983). More than 100 librarians in four seminar deliberations will examine the role of libraries in the development of a learning society and in supporting the findings and recommendations of the National Commission on Excellence in Education.

LSCA Programs

The two state grant programs funded under the Library Services and Construction Act (LSCA), public library services (Title I) and interlibrary cooperation (Title III), are managed by the State and Public Library Services Branch of the Division of Library Programs. The Public Library Services Program continues to provide funding to extend library service to areas without service, to improve service in areas with inadequate service, to provide services to special clientele such as the disadvantaged and physically handicapped, and to strengthen state library administrative agencies. The Interlibrary Cooperation Program continues to promote cooperation among all types of libraries resulting in improved services, often at lower costs to millions of citizens.

The Instructional Materials and School Library Resources Program, a state grant program formerly administered by the Division of Library Programs, is now part of

Chapter 2 of the Education Consolidation and Improvement Act of 1981. Under this block grant program, public and private nonprofit schools at both the elementary and secondary school levels receive funds for the purchase of instructional equipment and materials, textbooks, and other school library resources.

Library Services and Construction Act

State and Public Library Services Branch Staff*

Division of Library Programs
Office of Libraries and Learning Technologies
Department of Education

In FY 1983–1984, funding for the Library Services and Construction Act reached the highest levels in more than 25 years of program activity. Funding for Public Library Services (Title I) was $60 million in FY 1983 and $65 million in FY 1984. Under the Emergency Jobs Act (PL 98-8), enacted March 24, 1983, $50 million was made available for Public Library Construction (Title II), an authorization that had not been funded in ten years. For the Interlibrary Cooperation Program (Title III), Congress appropriated $11,520,000 in FY 1983 and $15 million in FY 1984.

With the LSCA authorization expiring in FY 1984, Congressman Paul Simon held hearings before the House of Representatives Postsecondary Subcommittee, March 15–17, 1983, to consider the reauthorization of LSCA. Senate hearings were also anticipated for early 1984.

A Study of Historical Impact

The historical impact of LSCA on public library services and interlibrary cooperation over the years was carefully documented in a study of Titles I and III conducted by Applied Management Sciences of Silver Spring, Maryland. The results of the study were published by K. G. Saur, New York, in two volumes: *An Evaluation of Title I of the Library Services and Construction Act* (January 1981) and *A Study of Library Cooperatives, Networks and Demonstration Projects* (March 1978). Some of the findings follow.

LSCA Title I

Public Library Institutional Structure

1 LSCA I funds have contributed significantly to the establishment of regional systems of public libraries. This has led to an increase in library services through books-by-mail and bookmobiles and the improved capability of local libraries to respond to information requests through centralized purchasing and processing of

*Written by Nathan Cohen, Clarence Fogelstrom, Dorothy Kittel, Evaline Neff, Trish Skaptason, and Robert Klassen, branch chief.

library materials, interlibrary loan and delivery systems, and links with computerized bibliographic centers.

2 LSCA I helped establish the state library's role in coordinating, serving, and planning statewide public library service programs.

Public Library Services

1 Since 65 percent of LSCA I funds was used by state, regional, and local public libraries "to support and/or improve library services," the impact of LSCA on public library services could only be inferred. Also, among public libraries receiving an LSCA I grant, 25.3 percent indicated that such funds generated increased local funding. The study concluded that it would be "both misleading and incorrect to attempt to attribute any direct causal effect of LSCA Title I on the adequacy of public libraries."

2 But, in 90 percent of the states, LSCA I was responsible for the introduction of new public library services involving technology, community outreach, and audiovisual materials and for providing continuing education for practicing librarians.

3 Also, 94 percent of the nation's libraries were able to cite at least one change in service or the introduction of a new service as a result of LSCA I. The benefits most often cited were the promotion of resource sharing through regional and multitype library systems, more adequate staff and book/nonprint materials, and the initiation of programs for the blind and physically handicapped.

Extended or Improved Public Library Service

Between 1965 and 1978, 12.4 percent of all localities without public libraries in the United States established some type of public library service (e.g., bookmobile or books-by-mail) as a direct result of LSCA I.

Access to Public Libraries by Specific Groups

1 LSCA I has had a significant impact on the establishment and extension of library services to residents of state-supported institutions (prisons, mental homes, and so on).

2 LSCA I has had a significant impact on the development and the provision of a variety of library services to the blind. These library services were found to dovetail with Library of Congress support of the regional libraries operated under the National Library Services for the Blind and Physically Handicapped. On the other hand, there was little evidence that LSCA I funds were meeting the needs of other handicapping conditions.

3 There was little evidence that LSCA I funds had any measurable impact on the access to library services of persons identified as urban or rural disadvantaged or those with limited English-speaking ability—all priorities under LSCA I. (In fairness to the analysis for limited English-speaking persons, this priority was added to LSCA in FY 1974. The LSCA I study looked at FY 1978 reports, so the long-term trends could not be established.)

LSCA Title III

Institutional Patterns of Organization among Libraries

1 LSCA III funds were a major driving force behind the nationwide development of multilibrary cooperation and networking.

2 Along with LSCA Title I, Title III funds brought about a greater centralization of public library planning and coordination on the state and regional government levels.

3 Approximately 20 percent of present LSCA I appropriations were used by the states to support multilibrary and networking activities.

State Support

LSCA III funds were credited with having a major influence on state legislatures to modify and pass state legislation favoring interlibrary cooperation and networking.

Access to Library Resources

1 Access to computer-based information services was enhanced greatly through LSCA III funding of regional, state, and multistate cooperative networks.

2 Access to book and periodical library materials was enhanced through LSCA support of information processing systems linked to bibliographic data banks, such as OCLC, Inc., and RLIN (Research Libraries Information Network).

3 A major outcome of LSCA III support has been the substantial increase in access to all of the nation's library resources.

Innovation in Library Services

1 More than 85 percent of the LSCA III project activities involved basic library operational programs, rather than experimental research and development activities.

2 There was increased funding for technology-based programs.

3 Significant investments of LSCA III funds were made in continuing education programs for librarians involved in technology-based projects for enhancing interlibrary cooperation and networking.

LSCA Program Eligibility

To participate in any LSCA program, each state library administrative agency must submit a basic state plan, which has to be approved by the secretary of education, or a designated official (now the assistant secretary for the Office of Educational Research and Improvement), plus a long-range plan (three to five years) on state priorities for meeting the library and information needs of the citizens of the state. The latest basic state plan was a two-year agreement for FY 1983 and 1984.

An annual program plan for project activities must also be submitted for review. To be eligible, each state must match the LSCA I contribution in proportion to its per capita income and must maintain the same level of library expenditures for the second preceding year.

Grants are awarded after the approval of the basic state plan and the acceptance of the long-range plan update and the annual program. These awards are based on a combination of a minimum basic allotment and a formula based on the state's population.

The financial and annual reports are due 90 days after the conclusion of the fiscal year. These reports provide the data from which the following analyses and descriptions are taken. The detailed FY 1982 reports compiled by the State and Public Library Services Branch staff are available to readers on request.

Title I—Public Library Services

The legislative mandate of the Public Library Services Program is to:

1 Extend public library services to geographic areas and groups of persons without library services and to improve services in areas and for groups that may have adequate public library services.
2 Establish, expand, and operate programs and projects providing library services to the disadvantaged, the state institutionalized, the physically handicapped, and those who have limited English-speaking ability.
3 Improve and strengthen state library administrative agencies and strengthen metropolitan public libraries that serve as national or regional resource centers.
4 Support and expand services of Major Urban Resource Libraries (MURLs).

During the past 26 years (FY 1957–1983), nearly $1 billion ($965,173,500) of LSCA Title I funds provided increased access to public libraries and basic information services in areas where they were nonexistent or inadequate. Funds were also used to develop and improve public library services to special population groups. The breakdown of expenditures by major program emphasis is as follows: 74.4 percent went to areas without services or with inadequate services, to strengthen metropolitan and major urban libraries as resource centers, and to strengthen state administration; 25.6 percent was spent on the disadvantaged, physically handicapped, state institutionalized, limited English-speaking, and the aged. A selected review of some of these services is included here as reported in the annual reports from the states in FY 1982.

Major Urban Resource Libraries

MURL provisions are triggered when the Title I appropriation exceeds $60 million. In FY 1982 and 1983, the appropriation did not reach this level. But with the FY 1984 appropriation of $65 million, MURL program activity will be resumed. (See Table 1 for the expenditures for FY 1979–1981.) To receive these funds urban libraries must meet criteria pertaining to the value of their collections, the extent to which the needs of users are met, and the regional importance of their collections.

Services to Physically Handicapped Persons

LSCA defines services to the physically handicapped as "library services, through public or other nonprofit libraries, agencies, or organizations, to physically handicapped persons (including the blind and other visually handicapped) certified by competent authorities as unable to read or to use conventional printed materials as a result of

Table 1 / LSCA Title I, Public Library Services:
Final Expenditures for Major Urban Resource Libraries (MURL),*
FYs 1979–1981

FY	Federal	State	Local
1979	$1,666,225	$ 15,264	$ 187,197
1980	1,722,990	18,138	497,883
1981	1,775,566	678,724	502,593
Total	$5,164,781	$712,126	$1,187,673

*Figures updated from Table 3 in *The Bowker Annual, 1983*, p. 208.

physical limitations." In practice, library services to the disabled are of a broader nature and encompass the entire handicapped community, including parents, relatives, teachers, and others involved with the handicapped. One of the significant outcomes of the LSCA priority is a promoted public awareness in this broader community of the needs and problems of the disabled and the new approaches to such library service that have been developed.

According to the FY 1982 reports, $3.3 million in LSCA funds was coupled with state and local expenditures totaling $14.7 million to support library projects serving some 580,000 handicapped persons, of whom 439,000 were blind. The numbers served represented a 22 percent increase over FY 1981.

In all states, regional libraries for the blind and physically handicapped supported by the National Library Service (NLS) of the Library of Congress serve as distribution centers for audio-recorded materials and playback equipment. LSCA funds are often combined with state and local funds to provide the operating capital for these centers. The services of these regional centers include the purchase of books and magazines on disc, cassette, magnetic tape, braille, and large-type print books for the visually impaired. Custom recordings of textbooks and specialized publications are also made for blind students and researchers. In addition, 13 states used LSCA funds to support statewide radio reading service programs, which provide persons who cannot read printed materials access to the latest best-sellers, magazines, and newspapers over special FM radio bands.

Selected highlights of LSCA projects serving the physically handicapped follow:

Florida. The Miami-Dade Library in cooperation with the Greater Miami Opera Association makes operatic performances accessible to the disabled by taping commentary for each of the productions as well as describing the visual aspects of the stage settings.

Massachusetts. Workshops to train individuals who serve the disabled were conducted for staffs of the Amherst College library, interns from community and senior centers, and employees of the town clerk's office and a local foundation. An experiential day allowed staff members to use the library while simulating a variety of disabilities. These exercises resulted in building modifications, changes in staff attitudes toward the handicapped, and a substantial commitment of local funds by town administrators for library services to the disabled.

Pennsylvania. The Philadelphia Free Library conducted a program on "Computers and the Visually Handicapped" attended by 60 blind computer programmers who learned about computer equipment from five participating computer companies. The program demonstrated the need for a centralized clearinghouse of information on programs available for blind persons interested in computers.

Tennessee. The West Tennessee Talking Library·in the Memphis Public Library combined LSCA funds with the largest National Telecommunications Information Agency (U.S. Department of Commerce) grant of any radio reading service in the nation. It is the only such service that provides an emergency weather broadcast by means of a staff-built device that responds automatically to a unique code assigned by the National Weather Watch. No radio operator is needed.

Services to Persons of Limited English-Speaking Ability

Since the passage of the Education Amendments of 1974, one of the LSCA program priorities has been library service to areas with high concentrations of persons of limited English-speaking ability. The majority of these projects have been to provide library services to Spanish-speaking communities.

In FY 1982, $2.9 million in LSCA funds was coupled with state and local expenditures totaling $4.2 million to support these service projects in 26 states and territories, serving more than 2.6 million persons of limited English-speaking ability. Over half of the funds were in support of programs to service Hispanic persons. Selected highlights follow:

California. The Spanish Language Data Base is designed to meet the information needs of Spanish-speaking people in California and other states. The goals are to facilitate selection, acquisition, organization, and dissemination of materials, and bibliographic and statistical information for libraries. Activities include the publication of *LECTOR,* a selection tool for Spanish-language publications; an automated acquisitions and cataloging system for Spanish-language monographs; Spanish equivalents of Library of Congress subject headings; and an online retrieval system for periodical publications.

New Jersey. Newark Public Library has an information and referral service related to Hispanic concerns, which is available to any library with Spanish-speaking patrons. The library has received many kudos from organizations serving Hispanic populations.

New York. New York Public Library published a *Directory of Community Services* for the Bronx, Manhattan, and Staten Island in English and Spanish in 1982.

North Carolina. The Foreign Language Center is a statewide program operated by the Cumberland Public Library. The project has developed one of the best nonprint multilanguage collections in the Southeast. The center houses a vast range of materials covering more than 50 languages, from Afrikaans to Zulu.

Services to State Institutionalized Persons

One of the priorities of LSCA is to establish and maintain library services to those who are inmates, patients, or residents of state penal institutions, reformatories, residential training schools, orphanages, and hospitals. The funding at the state level for these purposes must remain constant; the act requires that once spending levels are established, they cannot be less than the second preceding year. (Similar maintenance-of-effort provisions exist for "Services to Physically Handicapped Persons" and overall LSCA Title I expenditures.)

In FY 1982, $2.3 million in LSCA funds was used in projects representing $14.1 million of state and local funds combined to reach nearly 650,000 persons living in state institutions with library services. This is an expenditure of nearly $25 per capita. Selected highlights follow:

Hawaii. The Hawaii State Office of Library Services added audiovisual materials and equipment, provided consultant visits and evaluations, and developed Minimum Standards for Libraries in Residential Institutions involving 27 institutions. Programs in these institutions included bibliotherapy projects and the building of unique collections of ethnic materials.

New Mexico. The state library provided consultant services and training for institutional librarians. A formal statement of policy services signed by the Department of Corrections and the coordinator of library services brought about improved services. Library programs focused on the innovative use of bibliotherapy, poetry, and writing. The remaining funds were used for reference books, AV materials and equipment, multicultural and living skills materials, high/low materials, adult literacy materials and filmstrips, and large-print books.

New York. New York State Library provided consultant services and initiated a survey resulting in the publication of statewide statistics for institutional libraries. Grants to institutional libraries went to Helen Hayes Hospital for salaries and materials to serve 600 institutionalized physically handicapped persons; the Department of Correctional Services to serve 500 correctional inmates through support for institutional salaries and equipment; and a special information and referral system (Pre-release Liaison Agency Network) for 500 inmates to make them aware of local agencies that will help them once they are out of the institutions. Additional state funds went for collection development.

South Carolina. The South Carolina State Library provided consultant services, which included library visits, program consultation, reference service, program monitoring, collection development, book selection, film previewing, hiring, training, and orientation of institutional librarians, and workshops on budgeting and bibliotherapy. Special programs for the incarcerated were supported in adult literacy and basic education, computer literacy, job skills and information, crafts, and how-to-do-it information.

Vermont. The Vermont State Library provided the following services: ordering of library materials; assistance to institutional librarians; and orientation and training programs on literacy, alcohol and drug abuse, and adult education. A special cooperative program between the correctional centers and the Department of Libraries was supported for the repair of talking book machines.

Washington. The Washington State Library provided consultant services including supervision of institutional librarians, evaluation of programs, establishment of new libraries, and the remodeling of others. Library programs included films; topical kits that included books, filmstrips, toys, and games for use with the developmentally disabled; and the preparation of an index of tasks performed by those working with the developmentally disabled.

Title II—Public Library Construction

During the seven-year period from FY 1976 to FY 1982 when there were no appropriations, 58 construction projects were administered under the Title II authority, through the transfer of $10.7 million from other federal programs. Federal funds represented 41 percent of the total cost of these construction efforts. Of the 58 projects, 49

Table 2 / Public Library Construction Projects Administered Under the
Library Services and Construction Act, Title II, with Appalachian Regional
Development Act (ARDA) Funds, FY 1982

Project	Funding (by Source)		
	Federal ARDA	Local/State	Total
Alabaster Public Library, Alabaster, Alabama	$300,000	$ 75,000	$375,000
Your Home Public Library, Johnson City, New York	39,900	32,000	71,900
Floyd County Library, Floyd, Virginia	210,753	101,937	312,690
Total	$550,653	$208,937	$759,590

were funded by the Appalachian Regional Development Act in the amount of $9.2 million. In FY 1982, three projects received over $550,000 under the LSCA Title II authority (see Table 2).

An appropriation of $50 million for public library construction was made by the Emergency Jobs Act (PL 98-8) in FY 1983 to be administered under the authority of the Title II program for public library construction. The program was intended to provide jobs for the long-term unemployed. Federal and local/state matching funds for the library construction segment of this program will create an estimated 13,000 new jobs. In FY 1983, a total of 27 states received federal funding of $28.5 million for 208 library construction projects. The final report on this special program will appear in *The Bowker Annual, 1985*.

Title III—Interlibrary Cooperation

During its 17 years of program operation (FY 1967–1983), LSCA Title III has provided nearly $80 million to support institutional library networks through projects involving telecommunications, bibliographic access, interlibrary loan, and other resource sharing activities. In FY 1982, Title III funds assisted the states in supporting more than 250 cooperative library projects, involving nearly 30,000 libraries.

The projects demonstrate cost-saving library service concepts, often supported by emerging technologies, but they are rarely discrete LSCA activities. Significant state expenditures are reported to supplement the federal funds, even though matching funds are not required as under Title I. The functional breakdown of federal expenditures follows:

Project	% of LSCA Funds
1. Projects linking libraries through telecommunications systems to data bases	50
2. Resource sharing projects not linked to automation	40
3. Training for these activities	10

A selected review of some of the projects as reported in the annual reports from the states in FY 1982 follows:

Some Selected Highlights, FY 1982

Arkansas. The Arkansas Reference and Interlibrary Loan Network (ARLIN) contracted with AMIGOS Bibliographic Council to coordinate all aspects of the publication of a computer-output-microfiche (COM) catalog, which combines all Arkansas holdings input into the OCLC data base. AMIGOS staff extracted the records, which were then consolidated into one bibliographic data base by Bro-Dart and used as a master copy for the production of the *Arkansas Union Catalog on Microfiche* (AUC).

Colorado. The state of Colorado set up a computerized communication system among the seven regional library systems, the state library, Denver Public Library, the University of Colorado-Boulder, and the Bibliographical Center for Research. This system has improved the reporting of such statistical information required by state and/ or federal law as the flow of interlibrary loans, annual statistical reports from public libraries, and county equalization grant fiscal reports. The system has provided a reliable, fast, assured means of communication between the systems and other libraries, reducing the need for telephone toll calls and meetings.

Another project is a statewide interlibrary loan study to (1) determine methods for improving the effectiveness and efficiency of interlibrary loan traffic; (2) to assess the feasibility of a specific courier route over the mountains; and (3) to look at document delivery problems and patterns of lending throughout the state.

Florida. The state continued the Florida Library Information Network, which provides access to information and materials to 464 libraries: 193 public libraries, 78 academic libraries, 40 special libraries, 40 institutional libraries, and 113 school libraries. Two medium-sized libraries received grants to participate in the SOLINET/OCLC system, thus adding their resources to the Florida Library Information Network.

Idaho. LSCA funds were provided for Idaho libraries to participate in the Washington Library Network (WLN). They also assisted the University of Idaho Law Library to purchase WLN terminals and Idaho Falls Public Library to convert its circulation tapes into the WLN data base.

Indiana. The Area Library Service Authorities (ALSA) membership has continued to increase, with 95 percent of the state's public libraries now participating. Interlibrary loan and reference referral services are well established in all areas. State workshops, staff visits to libraries, and individual consultations were continued. ALSA staff worked closely with state library staff in developing a Continuing Library Information Media Education (CLIME) Plan. A workshop was held for all continuing education program staff, with seven of the nine ALSAs represented. The Cooperative Bibliographic Center for Indiana Libraries continued development of INCOLSA data base services and cooperative information retrieval services begun with previous funding.

Kansas. Southeast Kansas Library System received a grant for installation of an OCLC terminal for member libraries to begin data input. Some objectives are to process materials for member libraries more efficiently, to record location information for use in the *Kansas Union Catalog*, and to include more school library and community college library materials in the statewide data base. An earlier LSCA project had incorporated school library holdings into the southeast Kansas holding catalog.

The contract with Bibliographical Center for Research continued to provide access for all Kansas users to its data base and interlibrary loan locations and bibliographic verification to Kansas libraries.

Maryland. A bibliographic control center was established at the state library resource center. With the magnitude and growth of statewide listing of library holdings, an office was needed to coordinate the data collection, the editing process, and the addition/deletion of records. This center should help to improve future editions of the state's holdings data base.

Michigan. Fifteen multitype library regions of cooperation used funds to convert their serials records to the OCLC holdings listing and to record interlibrary loan activities, including photocopying charges, telefacsimile transmission, and purchase of Michigan library consortia coupons. Some systems also used LSCA funds for computer searches of informational data bases for participating libraries.

Montana. The state of Montana replaced the TWX machines in six federation headquarters' libraries and the state library with seven microcomputers that were used to process interlibrary loan requests. Total communications costs for the microcomputers were $8,600, in contrast with the approximate cost of $30,000 per year for the entire TWX operation.

New Jersey. The East Brunswick Public Library received a grant to develop a prototype microcomputer-based online system for circulation control and inventory management, which would allow county, high school, and public libraries to share their circulation files.

South Carolina. To encourage cooperative planning of library automation, the state established a Task Force on Library Automation and Networking composed of 16 members from all types of libraries and the library education field. The task force received a final report, which suggested a five-phase approach to coordinate development of a statewide network. It also asked the South Carolina Library Association to revise the state interlibrary loan code. The new code was presented to the association membership for adoption in October 1982. A Serials Control Group was appointed to investigate the feasibility of establishing a holdings list of serials in South Carolina.

West Virginia. Via the Mini-MARC system, the West Virginia Library Commission produced 435,306 catalog cards for 56 public, school, and church libraries. The references were then added to the statewide holdings list. In addition, OCLC archival tapes covering the input from the nine member libraries of the Pittsburg Regional Library Council were purchased quarterly. These tapes were also added to the statewide holdings list and provided another source of records input.

Higher Education Act, Title II-A, College Library Resources

Beth Phillips Fine

Program Officer

Library Education, Research, and Resources Branch
Division of Library Programs
Center for Libraries and Education Improvement
Office of Educational Research and Improvement
Department of Education

The College Library Resources Program under Title II-A of the Higher Education Act of 1965, as amended, awards discretionary grants to improve the library resources of eligible institutions of higher education and certain other eligible library agencies. Since 1966, an average of 2,500 institutions of higher education have participated annually, and more than 45,000 awards for basic, supplemental, and special purpose grants exceeding $196 million have been made.

In FY 1981, Congress reauthorized the Title II-A program until FY 1985 by enacting the Education Amendments of 1980. This legislation established a Resource Development Grant, similar to the basic grant, which assists the institution in its acquisition of library materials, including books, periodicals, documents, magnetic tapes, phonograph records, audiovisual materials, and other related library materials. Institutions are also encouraged to use grant funds to pursue eligible networking activities for the purpose of resource sharing. Eligible networking activities include, but are not limited to, user fees, membership fees, and transaction expenses.

Funding is based on eligibility and fulfillment of the maintenance of effort requirement. Eligible applicants include public and nonprofit private institutions of higher education, as well as nonprofit library institutions whose primary function is to provide library and information services to students, faculty, and researchers of higher education on a formal cooperative basis. In addition, combinations of institutions of higher education may also apply. Members of eligible combinations of institutions of higher education may choose to allow the combination to apply on their behalf, relinquishing their option to apply for their own grants. If an eligible combination applies successfully on behalf of its members, as well as for its own grant, the grant award will equal the standard grant amount multiplied by the number of members plus the combination's award. The Associated Colleges of Kansas and the Consortium of Universities of the Washington Metropolitan Area are examples of combinations with six members that also applied on behalf of their members and each received an equivalent of seven awards.

The maintenance of effort requirement asks for consistency between the institution's proposed budget for library materials expenditures and its two-year average of spending prior to the year of application. It may be calculated through actual expenditures or average annual expenditures per full-time equivalent student. Waiver of the maintenance of effort requirement is limited to "very unusual circumstances."

The Title II-C Strengthening Research Library Resources Program assists major research libraries in the collection, preservation, and dissemination of research materials. Although institutions may apply for assistance under both programs, the legislation

**Table 1 / Higher Education Act, Title II-A,
College Library Resources, FY 1983**

State or Area	No. of Grants	1983 Obligations	State or Area	No. of Grants	1983 Obligations
Alabama	42	$ 37,380	Nevada	3	$ 2,670
Alaska	8	7,120	New Hampshire	21	18,690
Arizona	20	17,800	New Jersey	38	33,820
Arkansas	23	20,470	New Mexico	11	9,790
California	136	121,040	New York	177	157,530
Colorado	24	23,140	North Carolina	75	66,750
Connecticut	29	25,810	North Dakota	11	9,790
Delaware	10	8,900	Ohio	87	77,430
District of Columbia	6	10,680	Oklahoma	26	23,140
Florida	65	57,850	Oregon	28	24,920
Georgia	44	39,160	Pennsylvania	132	117,480
Hawaii	12	10,680	Rhode Island	14	12,460
Idaho	7	6,230	South Carolina	47	41,830
Illinois	95	84,550	South Dakota	28	24,920
Indiana	46	40,940	Tennessee	42	37,380
Iowa	45	40,050	Texas	90	80,100
Kansas	32	33,820	Utah	7	6,230
Kentucky	34	30,260	Vermont	15	1,350
Louisiana	19	16,910	Virginia	61	54,290
Maine	17	15,130	Washington	44	39,160
Maryland	30	27,590	West Virginia	19	16,910
Massachusetts	83	73,870	Wisconsin	64	56,960
Michigan	60	53,400	Wyoming	4	3,560
Minnesota	44	39,160	American Samoa	1	890
Mississippi	28	24,920	Puerto Rico	31	27,590
Missouri	43	38,270	Trust Territories	2	1,780
Montana	19	16,910	Virgin Islands	2	1,780
Nebraska	25	22,250	Total	2,126	$1,905,490

**Table 2 / Higher Education Act, Title II-A,
College Library Resources, FY 1983**

FY	Appropriation	Basic	Supplemental	Special Purpose	Obligations
1966	$10,000,000	1,830	—	—	$ 8,400,000
1967	25,000,000	1,983	1,266	132	24,500,000
1968	25,000,000	2,111	1,524	60	24,500,000
1969	25,000,000	2,224	1,747	77	24,900,000
1970	12,500,000	2,201	1,783	—	9,816,000
1971	9,900,000	548	531	115	9,900,000
1972	11,000,000	504	494	21	10,993,000
1973	12,500,000	2,061	—	65	12,500,000
1974	9,975,000	2,377	—	—	9,960,000
1975	9,975,000	2,569	—	—	9,957,416
1976	9,975,000	2,560	—	—	9,958,754
1977	9,975,000	2,600	—	—	9,946,484
1978	9,975,000	2,568	—	—	9,963,611
1979	9,975,000	2,520	—	—	9,903,201
1980	4,988,000	2,595	—	—	4,926,970
1981	2,988,000	2,471	—	—	2,977,400
1982	1,920,000	2,265	—	—	1,915,200
1983	1,920,000	2,126	—	—	1,905,490

prohibits an institution from receiving funding from both Title II-A and II-C in the same fiscal year.

In FY 1983 each successful applicant received an award of $890. Grantees are found in every state, the District of Columbia, American Samoa, Puerto Rico, the Virgin Islands, and the Trust Territories. Approximately $1.9 million was awarded to a total of 2,141 institutions of higher education, including 28 nonprofit library institutions and 24 combinations of institutions of higher education.

Notification of grant awards was made on May 20, 1983, with the monies to be used during the grant period of October 1, 1983 through September 30, 1984. (See Table I for the number of awards and funding by state. Table 2 traces the funding history of Title II-A from FY 1966 to date.)

The FY 1984 Appropriations Act for the Department of Education, PL 98-139, did not include funding for the College Library Resources Program. The Department of Education does not anticipate making awards under the College Library Resources Program in FY 1984.

Higher Education Act, Title II-B, Library Career Training

Frank A. Stevens
Chief, Library Education, Research, and Resources Branch
Division of Library Programs
Center for Libraries and Education Improvement
Office of Educational Research and Improvement, Department of Education

Janice Owens
Educational Technician, Library Education, Research, and Resources Branch

Title II-B (Library Career Training) of the Higher Education Act of 1965, as amended (20 U.S.C. 1021, 1032), authorizes a program of federal financial assistance to institutions of higher education and other library organizations and agencies to assist in training persons in librarianship and to establish, develop, and expand programs of library and information science, including new techniques of information transfer and communication technology. Grants are made for fellowships and traineeships at the associate, bachelor, master, postmaster, and doctoral levels for training in librarianship. Grants may also be used to assist in covering the costs of institutes or courses of training or study to upgrade the competencies of persons serving in all types of libraries, information centers, or instructional materials centers offering library and information services and those serving as educators.

The current program regulations were published on March 5, 1982, in the *Federal Register* (pp. 9786–9793). These regulations, which are part of the application package that is provided upon request to all interested parties at the time of the annual program announcement, define program objectives to include the statutorily mandated emphasis on information acquisition and transfer (and communication technology). The program criteria conform with the Education Division General Administrative Requirements

**Table 1 / HEA, Title II-B, Library Career Training,
Academic Year 1983–1984**

Institution	Project Director	No.	Level	Amount
Arizona				
University of Arizona	Ellen Altman	2	M	$16,000
California				
California State University	Marilyn Greenberg	2	M	$16,000
University of California, Los Angeles	Dorothy Anderson	2	M	$16,000
Colorado				
University of Denver	Camila Alire	5	M(3) PM(2)	$48,000
Connecticut				
Southern Connecticut State College	Emanuel T. Prostano	1	PM	$12,000
District of Columbia				
Catholic University	Elizabeth Stone	3	PM	$31,200
University of District of Columbia	Edith Griffin	6	M(2) B(4)	$30,000
Florida				
Florida State University	Harold Goldstein	2	M(1) D(1)	$20,000
Georgia				
Atlanta University	Lorene Brown	2	M	$16,000
Illinois				
University of Illinois	Lawrence Auld	2	M(1) PM(1)	$20,000
Indiana				
Indiana University	Herbert White	1	M	$8,000
Iowa				
University of Iowa	Carl Orgren	1	M	$8,000
Maryland				
University of Maryland	Anne Scott MacLeod	3	M	$24,000
Massachusetts				
Simmons College	Robert Stueart	2	M	$16,000
Michigan				
University of Michigan	Russell Bidlack	3	M(1) D(2)	$32,000
Mississippi				
University of Southern Mississippi	Onva K. Boshears	2	M	$16,000
Missouri				
University of Missouri	Mary Lenox	2	M	$16,000
New Jersey				
Rutgers University	Betty Turock	1	M	$ 8,000
New York				
Columbia University	Richard Darling	4	M(2) D(2)	$41,150
CUNY, Queens College	David Cohen	1	M	$ 8,000
St. John's University	Jovian Lang	1	M	$ 8,000
SUNY at Albany	Lucille Whalen	3	M	$24,000
SUNY at Buffalo	George Bobinski	1	M	$ 8,000
North Carolina				
North Carolina Central University	Benjamin F. Speller, Jr.	2	M	$16,000
Ohio				
Kent State University	Lubomyr Wynar	1	M	$ 8,000

**Table 1 / HEA, Title II-B, Library Career Training,
Academic Year 1983–1984 (cont.)**

Institution	Project Director	No.	Level	Amount
Pennsylvania				
Drexel University	Guy Garrison	3	M	$25,650
University of Pittsburgh	Patricia Pond	4	M(2) D(2)	$40,000
Texas				
North Texas State University	Kenneth Ferstl	4	M(3) D(1)	$36,000
Texas Woman's University	Lotsee Smith	1	M	$ 8,000
University of Texas	Ronald Wyllys	2	M	$16,000
Washington				
University of Washington	Margaret Chisholm	3	M	$24,000
Wisconsin				
University of Wisconsin, Milwaukee	Mohammed Aman	2	M	$16,000
University of Wisconsin, Oshkosh	Norma Jones	1	M	$ 8,000

(EDGAR) and specify special program criteria. The point system for all categories of training is standardized.

Fellowship Program

The entire FY 1983 appropriation of $640,000 was awarded for fellowships. Thirty-three library and information science education programs received 75 fellowship awards (8

Table 2 / Library Education Fellowship Traineeship Program, Academic Year 1966–1983

| Academic Year | Insti- tutions | Fellowships/Traineeships | | | | | | |
		Doctoral	Post- master	Master	Bachelor	Asso- ciate	Total	FY
1966/67	24	52	25	62	—	—	139	1966
1967/68	38	116	58	327	—	—	501	1967
1968/69	51	168	47	494	—	—	709	1968
1969/70	56	193	30	379	—	—	602	1969
1970/71	48	171	15	200	20[a]	—	406	1970
1971/72	20	116	6	—	20[a]	—	142	1971
1972/73	15	39	3	20[a]	—	—	62	1972
1973/74	34	21	4	145 + 14[a]	—	20	204	1973
1974/75	50	21	3	168 + 3[a]	—	5	200	1974
1975/76	22	27	6	94	—	—	127	1975
1976/77	12	5	3	43	—	—	51	1976
1977/78	37	18	3	134	—	5	160	1977
1978/79	33	25	9	139	10	5	188	1978
1979/80	36	19	4	134	2	3	162	1979
1980/81	32	17	5	72	—	7	101	1980
1981/82	34	13	2	59	—	5	79	1981
1982/83	33	13	2	56	—	3	74	1982
1983/84	33	8	7	56	4	—	75	1983
Total		1,042	232	2,562 + 37[a]	16 + 40[a]	53	3,982	

[a] Indicates traineeships.

doctoral, 7 postmaster, 56 master, and 4 bachelor). The order of priorities for fellowship training levels in FY 1983 was as follows: master, doctoral, postmaster, and baccalaureate. Stipend levels varied, depending on the level of study and length of program, within a range of $1,750 to $6,000 per fellow plus dependency allowance as permitted. Additionally, grantee institutions received an institutional allowance equal to the amount of stipend per fellow. Table 1 shows the institutions to which fellowship grants were awarded in academic year 1983. (A more detailed analysis of these awards is contained in a booklet available upon request from the Center for Libraries and Education Improvement.) Table 2 reviews the fellowship program since it began in 1966.

The selection of persons as fellowship recipients is, and has been throughout the history of the program, the responsibility of the grantee institution. However, such selection and program operation must be consistent with the grant application on which the award of funds is based.

Key factors given substantial consideration in the review process are the extent to which the fellowship program award will increase opportunities for members of underrepresented groups to enter the library profession and to advance professionally and the extent to which the fellowship program award can prepare librarians to work more responsively with the underserved and develop viable alternatives to traditional library service patterns.

In 1983, the recruitment efforts of 33 institutions were directed toward the following groups:

Recruitment Category	Number of Institutions
Asians	1
Blacks	7
Economically disadvantaged	7
Handicapped	2
Hispanics	3
Minorities	17
Native Americans	3
Women	3
Underrepresented	5

Nineteen of the 33 institutions indicated two or more recruitment categories, and 14 indicated one. Examples of program objectives for FY 1983 were to increase the number of blacks and other minorities in the profession; to provide training for women to advance to management positions; and to train librarians for service to the underserved, the economically disadvantaged, and the handicapped in the use of computer technology in libraries.

How to Apply

Announcement of the closing date for receipt of applications is published each year in the *Federal Register*. Application packages and further information on the Title II-B Library Career Training Program are available on request from: Frank A. Stevens, Chief, Library Education, Research, and Resources Branch, Center for Libraries and Education

Improvement, 400 Maryland Avenue S.W., Brown Building, Rm. 613, Washington, DC 20202.

Institute Program

The Institute Program provides long- and short-term training and retraining opportunities for librarians, media specialists, information scientists, and those persons desiring to enter these professions. Many institutes have given experienced practitioners the opportunity to update and advance their skills in a given subject. Institute Program applications have not been requested since 1979 due to the limited appropriation for this program.

Higher Education Act, Title II-B, Library Research and Demonstration Program

Yvonne B. Carter
Program Officer
Library Education, Research, and Resources Branch
Division of Library Programs
Center for Libraries and Education Improvement
Office of Educational Research and Improvement
Department of Education

The Library Research and Demonstration Program of the Center for Libraries and Education Improvement (CLEI) is authorized to award and administer grants and contracts for research and demonstration projects related to the improvement of libraries, for training in librarianship and information technology, and for the dissemination of information derived from these projects. On July 20, 1981, new grant regulations for this program were published in the *Federal Register* (p. 37484), with such significant changes as the expansion of the program to include the promotion of economic and efficient information delivery and cooperative effort related to librarianship, the support of developmental projects, and the improvement of information technology. The grant regulations also expand program eligibility to include profit-making organizations, agencies, and institutions.

Since late 1980, the Library Research and Demonstration Program has awarded only contracts. It will continue to do so during FY 1984. The projects described below include projects funded or completed in 1983, as well as updates on projects funded in an earlier year. All project reports are available through the Educational Research Information Center (ERIC). Announcement of availability appears in ERIC's *Resources in Education*, together with an abstract, the price of the report in hard copy or microfiche, and instructions for ordering. (Table 1 provides additional information on these projects.)

Table 1 / HEA, Title II-B, Library Research and Demonstration,
FY 1967–1983

FY	Obligation	No. of Projects
1967	$ 3,381,052	38
1968	2,020,942	21
1969	2,986,264	39
1970	2,160,622	30
1971	2,170,274	18
1972	2,748,953	31
1973	1,784,741	24
1974	1,418,433	20
1975	999,338	19
1976	999,918	19
1977	995,193	18
1978	998,904	17
1979	980,563	12
1980	319,877	4
1981	239,954	12
1982	243,438	1
1983	237,643	4
Total	$24,686,209	327

Projects Completed in FY 1983

The National Center for Education Statistics and the Division of Library Programs jointly funded in 1981 a study of the supply and demand for librarians which was completed by King Research Associates, Inc., during FY 1983. The study describes the current library labor market, estimates the current supply and demand and their rates of change, and forecasts the future market. Two surveys, one of library schools and one of libraries as employers of librarians, were conducted as part of the study. The report, *Library Human Resources: A Study of Supply and Demand*, was published by the American Library Association (ALA) and is available from ALA. [See the report on the results of this study in Part 3—*Ed.*]

Projects Funded in FY 1982 and Continuations

"New Directions in Library and Information Science Education," funded in FY 1982, has a projected completion date of March 1984. The identification of the present and future competencies needed by library and information science professionals is the major thrust of the project.

Projects Funded in FY 1983 with Completion Dates in 1984

Historical Review of HEA II-B Fellowships ($20,000)
Project Director: Dr. Mildred Lowe, Director, Division of Library and Information Science, St. John's University, Jamaica, N.Y. *Purpose:* To determine the contributions that have been made to the library and information science profession by recipients of Higher Education Act (HEA), Title II-B, fellowships since passage of the act.

Diffusion of Innovations in Library and Information Science ($78,643)
Project Director: Dr. Jose-Marie Griffiths, King Research, Inc., Bethesda, Md.

Purpose: To identify innovations developed and adopted for use in library and information science, to trace the development and distribution of innovation(s), to develop a model for planned diffusion, and to recommend options for building a diffusion network for library and information science innovation.

Role of Libraries in Creating and Providing Viewtext Information Services ($60,000)
Project Director: Dr. Mary De Weaver, Lawrence Johnson and Associates, Inc., Washington, D.C. *Purpose:* To determine the role of libraries in creating and providing viewtext information services and to determine the information resources now or soon to be available in a sample of libraries that can make a unique contribution to viewtext home or business information sources in their communities.

Libraries and Learning Society ($79,000)
Project Director: Dr. Regina Kyle, E. H. White Company, Washington, D.C. *Purpose:* To identify the role of the nation's libraries in responding to the findings and recommendations of the National Commission on Excellence in Education. To be conducted in two phases: Phase I (subject to this procurement) included the establishment of an advisory group, employment of a writer-consultant and commissioning of position papers on specialized aspects of the profession.

Historical Funding Data

Table 1 shows the number of projects funded and the totals for each year since 1967.

Requests for Contracts

During FY 1984, CLEI will conduct directed contract research in the area of library and information science research and demonstration. Requests for Contracts (RFC) that describe the work to be done will be prepared for public response. Announcements are published in the *Commerce Business Daily*, the publication in which all U.S. government solicitations are advertised. From 30 to 45 days are usually provided for response to an RFC. The *Commerce Business Daily* provides information on how to obtain the RFC, which in turn provides all the information needed to prepare a proposal for consideration by CLEI and the Department of Education.

Higher Education Act, Title II-C, Strengthening Research Library Resources

Louise V. Sutherland

Program Officer
Library Education, Research, and Resources Branch
Division of Library Programs
Center for Libraries and Education Improvement
Office of Educational Research and Improvement
Department of Education

Janice Owens

Education Technician
Library Education, Research, and Resources Branch

The Education Amendments of 1976 created a new Part C of the Higher Education Act of 1965, entitled Strengthening Research Library Resources, to promote research and education of higher quality throughout the United States by providing financial assistance to major research libraries. In authorizing the program, Congress recognized that the expansion of educational and research programs, together with the rapid increase in the production of recorded knowledge, was placing unprecedented demands upon these libraries by requiring programs and services beyond the financial capabilities of the individual and collective library budgets. Furthermore, the nation's major research libraries were acknowledged as essential elements to advanced and professional education and research. Major research libraries were defined as public or private nonprofit institutions having collections available to qualified users that make a significant contribution to higher education and research, are broadly based, are unique in nature and contain material not widely available, are in substantial demand by researchers and scholars not connected with the institution, and have national or international significance for research. The legislation directed the (then) commissioner of education to establish criteria designed to achieve regional balance in the allocation of funds. Also, it limited the number of institutions receiving grants to 150. The 1976 amendments authorized funds for the program for three years—FY 1977, 1978, and 1979—and were signed into law by President Gerald Ford on October 12, 1976. However, no funds were appropriated until FY 1978.

The program was reauthorized by the Higher Education Amendments of 1980 with some modifications: The requirement that limited the number of beneficiaries to 150 was dropped and the requirement that there must be regional balance in the allocation of funds was reworded to instruct the secretary, in making grants, to endeavor to achieve broad and equitable geographic distribution throughout the nation. These modifications are reflected in the revised program regulations, which appeared in final form in the *Federal Register* on August 13, 1982.

During the six years of operation of the II-C program, 511 applications have been received. Of these, 168 were funded, benefiting 218 institutions. A total of $34,752,264 has been awarded to further the purposes of the program. (See Table 1.)

FY 1983 Grants

In FY 1983, 82 applications were received, requesting a total of $16,899,849. (See Table 2.) The 35 top-ranking applications were funded, using the entire amount appropriated

Table 1 / HEA, Title II-C, Strengthening Research Library Resources, Summary of Program Funding, 1977–1983

Fiscal Year	Authorization	Budget Request	Appropriation	Awarded
1977	$10,000,000	0	0	0
1978	$15,000,000	$5,000,000	$5,000,000	$4,999,996
1979	$20,000,000	$5,000,000	$6,000,000	$6,000,000
1980	$20,000,000	$6,000,000	$6,000,000	$5,992,268
1981	$10,000,000	$7,000,000	$6,000,000	$6,000,000
1982	$ 6,000,000	$6,000,000	$5,760,000	$5,760,000
1983	$ 6,000,000	0	$6,000,000	$6,000,000
1984	$ 6,000,000	0	$6,000,000	

($6,000,000), with the average grant being $171,429. Four of these proposals were jointly sponsored, directly benefiting 14 additional institutions and making a total of 49 institutions overall benefiting in FY 1983. Twenty-seven of the recipients were institutions of higher education, four were independent research libraries, two were museums, one was a state library, and one was a public library. Eight applicants were funded for the first time, sending $862,499, or 14 percent of the FY 1983 monies, to new institutions.

Institution	Amount
Johns Hopkins University	$ 71,456
Metropolitan Museum of Art	101,850
Michigan State University	165,337
Pierpont Morgan Library	89,675
Washington University	205,168
University of California, San Diego	108,623
University of Connecticut	68,372
University of Tennessee	51,918

Bibliographic control and access, which emerged as the major activity in the first year of the program with 57 percent of the funds, continued to receive the major portion, with 70 percent of the funds earmarked for this activity. Preservation projects accounted for 21 percent, with only 9 percent going for collection development. All projects were funded for one year only. (See Tables 3 and 4.)

Table 2 / HEA, Title II-C, Strengthening Research Library Resources, Applications, FY 1983

Type of Library	Applications	
	No. Received	No. Funded*
Institutions of higher education	57	27
Independent research libraries	11	4
Public libraries	5	1
State libraries	3	1
Museums	5	2
Other	1	0
Total	82	35

*Four of these proposals are jointly sponsored, directly benefiting 14 additional institutions.

Table 3 / HEA, Title II-C, Strengthening Research Library Resources, Analysis of FY 1983 Grant Awards by Major Activity*

Institution	Program Activity		
	Bibliographic Control	Preservation	Collection Development
Boston Public Library	—	$157,577	—
Center for Research Libraries	$299,488	—	—
Columbia University	$178,432	$171,098	—
Cornell University	$241,204	—	—
Folger Shakespeare Library	$ 20,431	—	$ 38,430
Harvard University	$ 57,627	$192,207	—
Huntington Library	$ 35,750	—	—
Indiana University	$160,347	$ 55,653	$ 14,080
Johns Hopkins University	$ 48,102	$ 23,354	—
Massachusetts Institute of Technology	$127,065	$ 14,070	—
Metropolitan Museum of Art	$ 72,250	$ 29,600	—
Michigan State University	$150,277	$ 15,060	—
New York Botanical Garden	$273,359	—	—
New York State Education Department	$152,748	—	—
Ohio State University	$ 43,078	—	$ 70,015
Pierpont Morgan Library	$ 79,570	$ 10,105	—
Stanford University	$287,448	—	—
State University of New York at Buffalo	$168,489	—	—
University of Alaska	—	$187,269	—
University of Arizona	$ 98,978	—	—
University of California, San Diego	$ 46,958	$ 21,857	$ 39,808
University of Chicago	$ 81,119	$ 20,000	$ 35,000
University of Connecticut	$ 68,372	—	—
University of Florida	$378,459	—	—
University of Illinois	$ 84,903	—	$ 25,780
University of Kansas	$132,551	$ 11,762	—
University of Minnesota	$122,602	—	—
University of North Carolina, Chapel Hill	$305,951	—	—
University of Pennsylvania	$108,875	—	—
University of South Carolina	$ 96,612	—	—
University of Tennessee	$ 51,918	—	—
University of Texas	$180,998	—	—
University of Virginia	$ 85,146	—	—
Washington University	$ 76,468	—	$128,700
Yale University	$425,000	—	—
Total	$4,738,575	$909,612	$351,813

*The nature of the Title II-C program is such that the grants do not conveniently break down into detailed categories of program activity. Further, some grants include more than one activity. For the purposes of this table, each grant is analyzed by the amount of funding for three general program activities: bibliographic control, preservation, and collection development.

New Regulations Implemented

Final regulations for the II-C program were published in the *Federal Register* on August 13, 1982, and became effective September 27, 1982. These regulations established a new procedure for evaluating applications, using two sets of criteria set forth in the regulations. The first set was applied by a panel of experts in determining the applicant's significance as a major research library, using such measures as the resources and funds

Table 4 / Projects Funded Under HEA, Title II-C, Strengthening Research Library Resources Program, FY 1983

Institution and Project Director	Grant Award	Project Description
Boston Public Library Laura Monti	$157,577	To continue for a third year the preservation of fragile, deteriorating research materials in the special collections of the library, including rare books, notebooks, pamphlets, manuscripts, maps, and historic documents.
Center for Research Libraries Donald B. Simpson	$299,488	To continue for a second year the retrospective conversion of all serial titles except South and Southeast Asian non-English titles, enter records into two union lists on OCLC, and distribute to bibliographic systems other than OCLC.
Columbia University Rachael Goldstein	$349,530	To improve access to and preservation of art and architecture materials in the Avery Library.
Cornell University Shirley Harper	$241,204	To provide for retrospective conversion of a collection of industrial relations materials and preparation of machine-readable records, which will be entered into RLIN and OCLC data bases.
Folger Shakespeare Library Philip A. Knachel	$ 58,861	To develop and service a collection of Shakespeare films and adaptations on film and videotape and organize and catalog a collection of photographic slide negatives and microfilm master negatives.
Harvard University Oscar Handlin	$249,834	To microfilm several collections of ephemera, including European World War II publications, and prepare guides and issue regular reports to the *National Register of Microform Masters* and the *National Union Catalog*.
Henry E. Huntington Library and Art Gallery Mary Robertson	$ 35,750	To organize, index, and prepare simplified finding aids for the Otis Marston collection of materials pertaining to the Colorado River and the states through which it runs.
Indiana University Elaine Sloan	$230,080	To strengthen and make accessible folklore research materials through the retrospective conversion and preservation of serials and monographs and acquisition of selective items.
Johns Hopkins University Susan K. Martin	$ 71,456	To catalog and enter into RLIN 1,200 antislavery pamphlets, treat those in need of preservation, and prepare a short-title index to the collection.

Table 4 / Projects Funded Under HEA, Title II-C, Strengthening Research Library Resources Program, FY 1983 (cont.)

Institution and Project Director	Grant Award	Project Description
Massachusetts Institute of Technology Jay Lucker	$141,135	To continue for a second year entering into the OCLC data base research materials focused on technology and its impact on society, arranging, describing, and cataloging important manuscript collections and preserving deteriorating items.
Metropolitan Museum of Art William B. Walker	$101,850	To preserve materials on arms, armor, and heraldry; enter machine-readable data into RLIN; and publish cataloging data in supplements to the library catalog.
Michigan State University Richard Chapin	$165,337	To catalog and bind French Monarchy materials and enter bibliographic records into the OCLC data base.
New York Botanical Garden Charles R. Long	$273,359	To enable the libraries of the New York Botanical Garden and the Missouri Botanical Garden to enter into the OCLC data base full bibliographic records for over 19,000 titles of plant science literature.
New York State Library Barbara Rice	$152,748	To inventory an extensive newspaper collection, which emphasizes New York titles from 1725 to the present, catalog these holdings in CONSER format, and enter records into the OCLC data base.
Ohio State University William J. Crowe and Robert A. Tibbetts	$113,093	To continue for a second year a project to strengthen and improve bibliographic access to a collection of American fiction published between 1901 and 1925.
Pierpont Morgan Library Francis Mason	$ 89,675	To preserve, catalog, and enter into the RLIN data base a collection of historical autograph manuscripts and letters and other autograph materials from the Gilbert and Sullivan Collection.
State University of New York at Buffalo Saktidas Roy	$168,489	To support the retrospective conversion of monograph titles from a unique collection of twentieth-century English-language poetry and produce bibliographic tools to provide access to nonmonographic materials in the poetry collection.
Stanford University David Weber	$287,448	To provide full bibliographic records for titles included in the microprint set Early American Imprints: Second Series, 1811–1815, and enter these records into RLIN.

Table 4 / Projects Funded Under HEA, Title II-C, Strengthening Research Library Resources Program, FY 1983 (cont.)

Institution and Project Director	Grant Award	Project Description
University of Alaska Rober Geiman	$187,269	To preserve historic photographs and films from the Alaska and Polar Regions Collection by producing working masters and contact prints from master negatives obtained from nitrate originals.
University of Arizona James Enyeart	$ 98,978	To organize manuscript collections acquired since 1975 by the Center for Creative Photography, publish several finding aids, and report to the *National Union Catalog of Manuscripts*.
University of California, San Diego Millicent Abell	$108,623	To acquire, process, preserve, and make available materials in the area of Melanesian Studies.
University of Chicago Martin Runkle	$136,119	To acquire, catalog, or preserve materials in two area study programs: Far Eastern Studies and Middle Eastern Studies.
University of Connecticut Norman D. Stevens	$ 68,372	To catalog and place into the OCLC data base and the *National Union Catalog* a collection of Puerto Rican research materials.
University of Florida Sam Gowan	$378,459	To continue the Southeast Cooperative Serials Project by providing local programming and implementation of the new "MARC Format for Holdings and Locations," which was created by ten cooperating institutions.
University of Illinois, Urbana Timothy Kearley	$110,683	To develop a catalog of historical materials on Western European law and make the materials available through an online bibliographic system.
University of Kansas Lorraine Moore	$144,313	To continue the cataloging of the William J. Griffith Collection of Central American materials, making them accessible through the OCLC data base and preserving fragile items within the collection.
University of Minnesota Eldred Smith	$122,602	To catalog and enter into the RLIN data base monographic titles in the Polish American and Ukrainian American Collections.
University of North Carolina James Govan	$305,951	To continue the development of a local online access network linking the library collections of Duke University, North Carolina State University, and the University of North Carolina at Chapel Hill.
University of Pennsylvania Richard DeGennaro	$106,875	To continue cataloging of seventeenth- and eighteenth-century imprints in the Rare Book Collection, entering records into the RLIN data base.

Table 4 / Projects Funded Under HEA, Title II-C, Strengthening Research Library Resources Program, FY 1983 (cont.)

Institution and Project Director	Grant Award	Project Description
University of South Carolina Kenneth Toombs	$ 96,612	To continue the production of an online catalog of the Fox Movietonews newsfilm, covering the period 1919–1963.
University of Tennessee, Knoxville Pauline S. Bayne	$ 51,918	To convert to machine-readable form and enter into the OCLC data base unique music cataloging records.
University of Texas, Austin Harold Billings	$180,998	To catalog and enter into OCLC 10,000 Latin American titles of the Nettie Lee Benson Collection.
University of Virginia L. Gayle Cooper	$ 85,146	To convert the shelflist of the Tracy W. McGregor Library of American History into machine-readable records, enter the records into the SOLINET/OCLC data base, and produce a microfiche catalog.
Washington University Holly Hall	$205,168	To acquire the literary papers of eight writers central to the Modern Literature Collection and prepare a published guide to all contemporary literary manuscripts.
Yale University Jack Siggins	$425,000	To continue entering into the RLIN data base the 18,000 manuscript collections of Cornell, Stanford, and Yale universities.

made available to support research projects in the past year; evidence of recognition by the research community; the size and the comprehensiveness of the collection; the number and nature of special collections; the number of loans made outside the primary clientele; the demands for materials; formal, cooperative agreements for resource sharing with other information services; and active membership in a major computer-based bibliographic data base.

Fifty-nine applicants scored at least 65 of 100 possible points on institutional significance under the first set of criteria, making their proposals eligible for further review. These proposals were evaluated strictly on the quality of the projects by a second panel of experts using the second set of criteria. Points of consideration under this set include clarity of the project proposal; concise description of the project; evidence of adequate planning; the need for the project; the size of the intended audience; effectiveness of the management plan; the effective use of personnel to achieve each objective; the quality of key personnel; adequacy and cost-effectiveness of budget; the quality of the evaluation plan; and the institutional commitment to the project. The separation of the criteria to evaluate significance as a major research library from the criteria to evaluate the quality of the proposed project was intended to enable smaller institutions to compete successfully with the larger institutions that in the past years may have received funding chiefly on the basis of institutional strength. The change was made in an effort to be responsive to the needs and wishes of the library community.

The secretary, in accordance with the regulations, reviewed the findings and recommendations of the second panel and determined that the most highly rated applications were broadly and equitably distributed. The secretary could have selected other applications for funding if doing so would have improved the geographic distribution of the projects.

Additional Information

In order to respond to requests from libraries and other members of the public for information about the projects funded in FY 1983, the Department of Education, on request, will make available in abstract form descriptions of the goals and activities of each project, together with several tables that summarize the funding record of the Title II-C program from FY 1978 through FY 1983. Similar information is available on projects funded in previous years. Requests should be addressed to Frank A. Stevens, Chief, Library Education, Research, and Resources Branch, Division of Library Programs, 400 Maryland Avenue, S.W., Room 613, Brown Building, Washington, DC 20202.

Education Consolidation and Improvement Act of 1981, Chapter 2: A Follow-up Report

Phyllis Land Usher

Director, Division of Federal Resources and School Improvement
Indiana Department of Public Instruction

The Education Consolidation and Improvement Act (ECIA), Chapter 2, when passed in 1981, was considered an early achievement of the Reagan administration and an important step toward making federal programs easier to administer, less burdensome in paperwork and regulation, and more flexible in responding to local needs. State, federal, and local officials believe that the Education Block Grant has been successful in reducing the paperwork and allowing more local control.

1983 Spending Patterns

Now that one full year of the funding cycle has been completed it is possible to examine the consolidation's effect on each of the antecedent programs. The legislation that created Chapter 2 authorized the activities of previous programs under three subchapters: Basic Skills Development (Subchapter A); Educational Improvement and Support Services (Subchapter B); and Special Projects (Subchapter C). [For a description of the types of activities authorized under these subchapters, see *Bowker Annual, 1983*, pp. 232 and 235—*Ed.*] The U.S. Department of Education conducted an informal survey to find out how ECIA, Chapter 2, dollars were being spent. The results of the survey, to which 32 states and the District of Columbia responded, indicated the following spending patterns:

Category	Percent
Basic skills development	7.35
Educational improvement and support services	73.6
Special projects	6.13

At the local level, 47.42 percent of the funds—$85 million—went to the category that includes library resources, textbooks, instruction materials, and equipment. Of the amount, $50 million went for instructional equipment. Most of that money was used to buy computer hardware and software.

Another survey conducted by the American Association of School Administrators indicates that 88 percent of the school districts are spending most of their grant for materials. Nearly 50 percent of the districts surveyed by AASA report spending some funds for computer hardware and software.

Emergency School Aid Act

According to several sources, the program most adversely affected by the consolidation was the Emergency School Aid Act (ESAA), which funded desegregation-related activites. The Subcommittee on Intergovernmental Relations and Human Resources of the Committee on Government Operations, which prepared the first congressional evaluation of ECIA in fall 1983, cited that little Chapter 2 money is being spent for desegregation. The panel recommended in its report that ESAA be taken out of the block grant and be authorized as a separate program. The committee report was only endorsed by Democrats on the panel. The Republican minority said in a dissenting opinion, "Frankly, we believe the report reflects an unabashed bias in favor of federal influence over and tight control of our nation's education system."

Another study, *No Strings Attached*, published by the National Committee for Citizens in Education, said, "Education block grants have resulted in a massive redistribution of federal funds away from states serving large numbers of poor, nonwhite children, toward more sparsely settled states with few minority children." This report, a product of 18 months of monitoring parent and public involvement in the new program, said 5.7 percent of the monies were funding desegregation programs.

Administration of Chapter 2 Funds

The administration of ECIA, Chapter 2, in the U.S. Department of Education is the responsibility of the Division of Educational Support Services. The act provides that the state education agency shall be responsible for the administration and supervision of programs assisted under ECIA, Chapter 2. Twenty percent of a state's allotment may be reserved for state programs in any educational activity that was merged into Chapter 2 and block grant administration. A national survey by the National Committee for Citizens in Education reports that 12.1 percent of the funds retained by the states were being used for Chapter 2 administration. Table 1 shows the 1983–1984 allotments for the 50 states, the District of Columbia, and the outlying areas. The funding levels showed a slight increase over 1982–1983 levels.

Table 1 / ECIA, Chapter 2, State Block Grants, FY 1983 Appropriation (for Distribution in 1983–1984)

State or Outlying Area	FY 1983 Estimate	State or Outlying Area	FY 1983 Estimate
Alabama	7,782,302	New Mexico	2,747,780
Alaska	2,229,304	New York	31,599,467
Arizona	5,283,483	North Carolina	11,267,741
Arkansas	4,453,616	North Dakota	2,229,304
California	42,415,393	Ohio	20,506,920
Colorado	5,394,131	Oklahoma	5,716,857
Connecticut	5,652,312	Oregon	4,748,680
Delaware	2,229,304	Pennsylvania	21,087,827
Florida	16,495,899	Rhode Island	2,229,304
Georgia	11,147,872	South Carolina	6,325,426
Hawaii	2,229,304	South Dakota	2,229,304
Idaho	2,229,304	Tennessee	8,732,038
Illinois	21,364,449	Texas	29,026,882
Indiana	10,677,614	Utah	3,347,128
Iowa	5,384,911	Vermont	2,229,304
Kansas	4,213,877	Virginia	9,967,617
Kentucky	7,155,292	Washington	7,579,446
Louisiana	8,833,467	West Virginia	3,734,399
Maine	2,229,304	Wisconsin	8,999,440
Maryland	7,920,614	Wyoming	2,229,304
Massachusetts	10,198,136	District of Columbia	2,229,304
Michigan	18,220,177	Puerto Rico	8,117,449
Minnesota	7,680,874	American Samoa	436,089
Mississippi	5,394,131	Northern Marianas	219,073
Missouri	8,980,998	Guam	1,233,725
Montana	2,229,304	Trust Territory	1,652,196
Nebraska	2,904,532	Virgin Islands	1,253,117
Nevada	2,229,304	Total	$450,655,000
New Hampshire	2,229,304		
New Jersey	13,591,367		

Note: Up to 1 percent of the total appropriation for Chapter 2 is reserved for the outlying areas. An additional amount of up to 6 percent is reserved for the secretary's discretionary funds. The remainder is distributed to the 50 states, the District of Columbia, and Puerto Rico on the basis of the 5–17-year-old population. No state receives less than 0.5 percent of the remainder. Ages 5–17 population source—U.S. Department of Commerce, Bureau of the Census: 50 states and District of Columbia, 1981 revised estimates, unpublished data; Puerto Rico and outlying areas, 1980 census.

The Department of Education released "non-regulatory guidance" for ECIA, Chapter 2, in late July 1983. The document provides nonbinding guidelines for allocation and use of block-grant funds, evaluation and audit requirements, record keeping, private school student participation, and use of "carryover" funds. State and local agencies were encouraged by the secretary of education to develop alternative approaches for the administration of Chapter 2 as long as they are consistent with the statute, regulations, and legislative history.

A number of states asked the Department of Education for assistance in establishing national standards to evaluate the block grant. However, department policy is that evaluation be done at the state and regional levels. A national conference planned by the department for spring 1983 apparently was cancelled, because of this policy.

National Endowment for the Humanities
Support for Libraries, 1983

Washington, DC 20506
207-786-0438

The National Endowment for the Humanities (NEH), an independent federal grant-making agency created by Congress in 1965, supports research, education, and public understanding in the humanities through grants to organizations, institutions, and individuals. According to the legislation that established the Endowment, the term "humanities" includes, but is not limited to, the study of archeology, ethics, history, the history and criticism of the arts, the theory of the arts, jurisprudence, language (both modern and classical), linguistics, literature, philosophy, comparative religion, and those aspects of the social sciences that have humanities content and employ humanistic methods.

The Endowment's grant-making operations are conducted through five major divisions. (1) The Division of Research Programs provides support for group research projects in the humanities, for research resources, for the preparation of important research tools, for the editing of significant texts in the humanities, and for the publication of scholarship in the humanities. (2) The Division of Fellowships and Seminars, through several programs, provides stipends that enable individual scholars, teachers, and members of nonacademic professions to study areas of the humanities that may be directly and fruitfully related to the work they characteristically perform. (3) The Division of Education Programs supports projects and programs through which institutions endeavor to renew and strengthen the impact of teaching in the humanities at all levels. (4) The Division of General Programs endeavors to fulfill the Endowment's mandate "to increase public understanding of the humanities." The division includes programs that assist institutions and organizations in developing humanities projects for presentation to general audiences. The Division of General Programs was established in June 1982 through a merger of the Divisions of Special and Public Programs. The new division is composed of the Offices of Museums and Historical Organizations, Media, and Special Projects (which consists of Youth Programs and Program Development sections). In the reorganization, Humanities Projects in Libraries was integrated into Program Development. Libraries, in the future, are encouraged to submit proposals to the Program Development Section of the Office of Special Projects. Applications must meet published deadlines. (5) Finally, the Division of State Programs makes grants to citizens' committees in each state to provide support for local humanities projects, primarily directed toward general audiences.

Other projects are eligible for support through the Office of Program and Policy Studies and through the Office of Challenge Grants.

In FY 1983 the National Endowment for the Humanities made 39 grants to libraries for a total of $7,195,533.36. Table 1 shows examples of grants in effect as of December 1983.

Categories of Support

The NEH seeks to cooperate with libraries in strengthening the general public's knowledge and use of the humanities through its various programs. These programs are described below.

Table 1 / Examples of Current NEH Library Grants (December 1983)

Recipient	Project Description	Amount
Office of Challenge Grants		
Concord Free Public Library Concord, MA	To renovate and expand present library facilities.	$ 50,000
Reading Public Library Reading, MA	To convert an old school for library use and increase the acquisitions fund.	$ 30,000
Division of General Programs		
North Suburban Library Wheeling, IL	To explore the vast changes in Western civilization from the First World War to the cold war by reading and discussing the works of selected Nobel prize winners at 48 libraries over a period of two years.	$119,979
Mobile Public Library Mobile, AL	To discover what it was like to grow up in Mobile during the 1930s and 1940s.	$ 6,850
Division of Research Programs		
Folger Shakespeare Library Washington, DC	To microfilm some 5,000 manuscripts from a sixteenth- and seventeenth-century English theatrical history collection.	$ 18,100
Folger Shakespeare Library Washington, DC	To establish a center for the study of British political thought between 1550 and 1800.	$181,000
Research Libraries Group, Inc. Stanford, CA	To microfilm about 30,000 U.S. imprints and Americana, 1876–1900, that survive in brittle, critical condition in seven RLG libraries.	$675,000

Division of General Programs

The Program Development Section awards grants for projects that draw upon those library resources in the humanities that are designed to serve general audiences. The specific goals of Program Development are to strengthen programs that stimulate and respond to public interest in the humanities; to enhance the ability of library staff to plan and implement these programs; and to increase the public's use of a library's existing humanities resources. Librarians are encouraged to replicate, combine formats, or create entirely new and imaginative approaches to humanities programming. Following is a list of project ideas that are eligible for support.

1 Programs on humanities themes that draw on the library's book, magazine, audiovisual, and staff resources. The theme must be directly related to the humanities disciplines or provide a humanities perspective on a topic or theme.

2 Projects involving work with community groups and humanities scholars to plan and present programs for the public, using and publicizing the library's humanities resources. Such projects could include humanities workshops for community leaders or the preparation of special print materials or displays on library holdings.

3 Projects to increase the use of humanities resources by planning programs in conjunction with television programs or exhibitions developed by other community institutions.

4 Projects that strengthen professional staff expertise in the humanities as well as provide humanities programming for the public. These could include workshops

on the humanities disciplines, reference training, or programming ideas in preparation for a public humanities program.

5 Projects to produce "packaged" programs that would include specially prepared humanities materials, scholars and experts in the humanities as speakers, and special activities designed for use in local public libraries.

6 Projects to produce educational programs for the public on humanities topics or issues of interest to the community.

Any nonprofit library may apply. Libraries may submit proposals individually or in cooperation with other community organizations. Academic and school libraries are also eligible if the proposed project is open to the general public.

Division of Education Programs

Libraries may receive grants directly or be part of a college or university effort to strengthen teaching in the central disciplines of the humanities. Grants directly to libraries are usually in support of humanities institutes in which scholars use the library's resources as part of a program of study with experts on the theme of the institute and simultaneous development of new curricula for the participant's home institution. The Folger Shakespeare Library and the Newberry Library are recent grantees. The division is currently encouraging applications that focus entirely or in part on fostering cooperation between college libraries and humanities departments for the purpose of preparing students to locate and use resources for study of the humanities.

Division of Fellowships and Seminars

Through its program of Fellowships at Centers for Advanced Study, this division provides funds to independent research libraries for stipends to resident scholars. In 1982, the Newberry Library, the Huntington Library, and the American Antiquarian Society were among the centers that housed NEH fellows.

Division of Research Programs

The Resources Program focuses on making raw research materials more accessible to scholars. It meets this goal through projects that address national problems in the archival and library field, through projects that serve as models in systems development and library automation, and through processing grants that are used to catalog, inventory, or otherwise gain bibliographic control of significant research collections. The program also offers title subsidies to assist in publication costs for scholarly works in the humanities.

The Basic Research Program supports exploratory and interpretive research in all fields of the humanities, provides funds for research conferences, and makes grants in the joint field of humanities, science, and technology.

The Reference Works Program supports the production of scholarly editions, dictionaries, encyclopedias, atlases, and translations.

Office of Challenge Grants

Libraries are eligible for support within the Endowment's program of challenge grants, now in the seventh year of funding. By inviting libraries to appeal to a broader funding public, challenge grants assist institutions to increase long-term capital support and thereby sustain or attain a high quality of humanities activities, humanities collections, and the financial stability of the institutions. To receive each federal dollar, a challenge grant recipient must raise three dollars from nonfederal funding sources. Both federal and nonfederal funds may apply to a variety of expenditures supporting the humanities: acquisitions, conservation, renovation, development (both programmatic and financial), equipment, and other managerial or program expenses related to the humanities.

Office of Program and Policy Studies

Through the Planning and Assessment Studies Program, the Endowment awards, on a competitive basis, a small number of grants each year to compile supplemental information, to analyze important policy issues, or to develop analytical tools for monitoring trends and studying programs in the humanities.

The program's broad areas of concern include the humanities labor force, funding patterns in the humanities, the financial status of humanities institutions, and trends in the demand for and use of humanities resources. Grant-supported studies in these areas generally fall into the following categories: humanities data bases, policy studies, and analytical tools.

Division of State Programs

The Endowment annually makes grants to state humanities councils in all 50 states, the District of Columbia, Puerto Rico, and the U.S. Virgin Islands. The state councils, in turn, award "regrants" to institutions and organizations within each state according to guidelines and application deadlines determined by each council. Most grants are for projects that promote public understanding and appreciation of the humanities. Guidelines and application deadlines may be obtained by contacting the appropriate state council directly.

State Humanities Councils

Committee for the Humanities in Alabama
Box A-40, Birmingham-Southern College,
Birmingham, AL 35254

Alaska Humanities Forum
429 D St., Rm. 312, Loussac Sogn Bldg.,
Anchorage, AK 99501

Arizona Humanities Council
First Interstate Bank Plaza, 100 W. Washington, Suite 1290, Phoenix, AZ 85003

Arkansas Endowment for the Humanities
Remmel Bldg., Suite 102, 1010 W. Third
St., Little Rock, AR 72201

California Council for the Humanities
312 Sutter St., Suite 601, San Francisco,
CA 94108

Colorado Humanities Program
1836 Blake St., #100, Denver, CO 80202

Connecticut Humanities Council
195 Church St., Wesleyan Sta., Middletown, CT 06457

Delaware Humanities Forum
2600 Pennsylvania Ave., Wilmington, DE 19806

D.C. Community Humanities Council
1341 G St., N.W., Suite 620, Washington, DC 20005

Florida Endowment for the Humanities
LET 468, Univ. of South Florida, Tampa, FL 33620

Georgia Endowment for the Humanities
1589 Clifton Rd., N.E., Emory Univ., Atlanta, GA 30322

Hawaii Committee for the Humanities
2615 S. King St., Suite 211, Honolulu, HI 96826

Association for the Humanities in Idaho
1409 W. Washington St., Boise, ID 83702

Illinois Humanities Council
618 S. Michigan Ave., Chicago, IL 60605

Indiana Committee for the Humanities
3135 N. Meridian St., Indianapolis, IN 46208

Iowa Humanities Board
Oakdale Campus, Univ. of Iowa, Iowa City, IA 52242

Kansas Committee for the Humanities
112 W. Sixth St., Suite 509, Topeka, KS 66603

Kentucky Humanities Council, Inc.
Ligon House, Univ. of Kentucky, Lexington, KY 40508

Louisiana Committee for the Humanities
Ten-O-One Bldg., 1001 Howard Ave., Suite 4407, New Orleans, LA 70113

Maine Humanities Council
Box 7202, Portland, ME 04112

Maryland Committee for the Humanities
516 N. Charles St., #304-305, Baltimore, MD 21201

Massachusetts Foundation for the Humanities and Public Policy
155 Woodside Ave., Amherst, MA 01002

Michigan Council for the Humanities
Nisbet Bldg., Suite 30, 1407 S. Harrison Rd., East Lansing, MI 48824

Minnesota Humanities Commission
LL 85 Metro Sq., St. Paul, MN 55101

Mississippi Committee for Humanities, Inc.
3825 Ridgewood Rd., Rm. 111, Jackson, MS 39211

Missouri State Committee for the Humanities
Loberg Bldg., Suite 204, 11425 Dorsett Rd., Maryland Heights, MO 63043

Montana Committee for the Humanities
Box 8036, Hellgate Sta., Missoula, MT 59807

Nebraska Committee for the Humanities
Cooper Plaza, Suite 405, 211 N. 12 St., Lincoln, NE 68508

Nevada Humanities Committee
Box 8065, Reno, NV 89507

New Hampshire Council for the Humanities
112 S. State St., Concord, NH 03301

New Jersey Committee for the Humanities
73 Easton Ave., New Brunswick, NJ 08903

New Mexico Humanities Council
1712 Las Lomas N.E., Univ. of New Mexico, Albuquerque, NM 87131

New York Council for the Humanities
33 W. 42 St., New York, NY 10036

North Carolina Humanities Committee
112 Foust Bldg., Univ. of North Carolina-Greensboro, Greensboro, NC 27412

North Dakota Humanities Council
Box 2191, Bismarck, ND 58502

Ohio Humanities Council
760 Pleasant Ridge Ave., Columbus, OH 43209

Oklahoma Foundation for the Humanities
Executive Terrace Bldg., 2809 Northwest Expressway, Suite 500, Oklahoma City, OK 73112

Oregon Committee for the Humanities
418 S.W. Washington, Rm. 410, Portland, OR 97204

Pennsylvania Humanities Council
401 N. Broad St., Philadelphia, PA 19108

Fundacion Puertorriquena de las Humanidades
Box S-4307, Old San Juan, PR 00904

Rhode Island Committee for the Humanities
463 Broadway, Providence, RI 02909

South Carolina Committee for the Humanities
6-C Monckton Blvd., Suite 6, Columbia, SC 29206

South Dakota Committee on the Humanities
University Sta., Box 35, Brookings, SD 57007

Tennessee Committee for the Humanities
1001 18th Ave. S., Nashville, TN 37212

Texas Committee for the Humanities
1604 Nueces, Austin, TX 78701

Utah Endowment for the Humanities
10 W. Broadway, Broadway Bldg., Suite 900, Salt Lake City, UT 84101

Vermont Council on the Humanities and Public Issues
Grant House, Box 58, Hyde Park, VT 05655

Virgin Islands Humanities Council
College of the Virgin Islands, 215 Humanities Bldg., St. Thomas, VI 00802

Virginia Foundation for the Humanities and Public Policy
One-B West Range, Univ. of Virginia, Charlottesville, VA 22903

Washington Commission for the Humanities
Olympia, WA 98505

Humanities Foundation of West Virginia
Box 204, Institute, WV 25112

Wisconsin Humanities Committee
716 Langdon St., Madison, WI 53706

Wyoming Council for the Humanities
Box 3274, University Sta., Laramie, WY 82701

National Science Foundation Support for Research in Information Science and Technology

1800 G St. N.W., Washington, DC 20550
202-357-9572

Edward C. Weiss

Division of Information Science and Technology

The National Science Foundation (NSF), an independent agency of the federal government, was established by Congress in 1950 to promote the progress of science. The objective of the Division of Information Science and Technology is to discover and formulate in general terms the principles governing the generation, transmission, and use of information. This is accomplished through the support of research to increase understanding of the properties and structure of information and information transfer; to contribute to the store of scientific and technical knowledge that can be applied in the design of new information technologies; and to improve understanding of the impact of information and information technology on the economic and social fabric of society.

The Information Science and Technology subactivity supports research under three related program elements:

Information Science deals with the study of information as idealized organization or structure as well as with its many facets, i.e., measurement, storage, manipulation, coding, and interpretation. Emphasis is placed on investigations of human information processing, including those aspects of learning, memory, problem solving, and pattern recognition that are relevant to information processing principles.

Information Technology supports research that is fundamental to the design of information-intensive systems. It includes studies of the syntactical structure of documents and files of textual and graphic data, the basic transformations of such data, and the optimization of electronic information presentation formats. Emphasis is placed on the extraction of useful information from large, complex data files and on the human aspects of information retrieval.

Information Impact focuses on the roles of information in the economy as an input to production and as a commodity itself. Emphasis is placed on noneconomic impacts such as studies of the effects of information technology on the work force and other segments of society and the potential of advanced information technologies for education, training, and productivity improvement in information-intensive jobs.

The NSF Role

The foundation is the primary source of federal support of fundamental research in information science and technology. Research in this area draws on related research supported by NSF in computer science, electrical and computer engineering, cognitive science, linguistics, and economics. Close coordination among these areas is maintained to minimize redundancy.

Progress in computer and electrical sciences stimulates opportunities for research in information science and technology. In particular, new instrumentation and such new capabilities as increased capacities for information storage, manipulation, retrieval, and communication suggest new approaches to long-standing information science problems—new challenges for research in the field.

Research Priorities

The highest priority is assigned to research that will extend the theoretical foundations of the discipline. It includes the development of basic theories of information beyond the present entropy, probabilistic, fuzzy-set, and vector-space models. It also involves information processing in biological organisms (including humans) where the emphasis is on selective omission of information and its implications for more efficient classification, abstracting, and indexing by artificial systems.

Another important research priority focuses on providing the fundamental knowledge base to enable the augmentation of the human intellect by information-intensive machines. Research categories include how knowledge is represented in humans and machines, and the interface between them. They are concerned with the extent to which information-bearing forms of communication such as language can be processed and manipulated by artificial systems in a manner that will match the efficiency of and be compatible with human information-processing mechanisms.

The fact that we are entering an information age is being proclaimed by the media, yet surprisingly little is known about the economics of information as a commodity. Basic research is lacking, and the development of new scientific theory is an essential first step. Research categories include: (1) theoretical analysis of information in economic behavior of firms and individuals and (2) modeling the role of information-sector activity in the U.S. and world economies.

Research is also needed on social effects of new information technologies, to examine the special characteristics of interactivity made possible by new technology and the changing modes and structures of information distribution. Research categories include: (1) theoretical and empirical studies of the effects of information technologies on information acquisition and use; (2) the changing organization of communication and information services; and (3) the impact of new forms of information distribution.

The organization and structuring of information need general principles of information-system design. If design is to evolve from a base of scientific knowledge and technique, it must include: studies of the interface between information systems and users; the formal characterization of the interaction between an information resource and its user; and the inference of an interface design requirement from such formal characterizations.

Information science has been primarily a logical science but it has now progressed to the point where experimentation is both possible and necessary. As in all sciences, the ability to validate theory and test hypotheses is essential. The need for such experimentation is especially evident in the human aspects of information machines. Research categories include development of (1) methodologies, (2) measures, (3) representations, and (4) display requirements.

Library-related Research

Much of the research sponsored by the Division of Information Science and Technology will eventually have an impact on library affairs or operations. Research in FY 1983 with direct relevance to library activities was as follows:

J. N. Danziger, University of California at Irvine, "The Effects of Personal Computing on Professional Knowledge Workers," $6,500

G. Salton, Cornell University, "Mathematical Models in Automated Information Retrieval," 13,505

J. T. Tou, University of Florida, "Advanced Information Technology for Document Processing," $109,495

J. M. Hammer, Georgia Institute of Technology, "Models of Human Performance Using Text Editors," $74,506

D. Bell, Harvard University, "The Information Society: A Comprehensive Framework," $75,544

D. M. Liston, King Research, Inc., "Research into the Structure, Accessing, and Manipulation of Numeric Databases: Phase II," $203,510

N. K. Roderer, King Research, Inc., "Statistical Indicators of Scientific and Technical Communication in the U.S.," $83,044

J. J. O'Connor, Lehigh University, "Computer Selection of Search Words for Text Search Retrieval," $72,900

R. S. Marcus, Massachusetts Institute of Technology, "Investigation of Models for Enhanced Information Retrieval through Computer-Mediated Assistance," $103,735.

G. Nagy, University of Nebraska, "A Methodology for Characterizing Interactive Performance," $49,938

W. J. Baumol, New York University, "Knowledge: Its Creation, Distribution, and Economic Significance," $27,022

H. C. Lucas, New York University, "Test of a General Model of Information System Implementation," $186,073

M. H. Olson, New York University, "An Investigation of the Impacts of Remote Work Environments Supporting Technology," $142,678

L. Miller, University of Oklahoma, "Investigations into Parallel File Organizations," $44,476

S. M. Goldfeld, Princeton University, "The Disciplines of Information: Completion of Fritz Machulup's Research," $21,584

B. H. Weinberg, St. John's University, "Textual, Posting and Online Searching Frequencies of Index Terms," $47,160

R. R. Korfhage, Southern Methodist University, "Interaction of Queries with User Profiles," $56,183

D. E. Walker, SRI International, "Natural Language Access to Text," $92,764

J. Katzer, Syracuse University, "Research on Information Retrieval: Document Representation and Information Systems," $85,510

M. M. Sebrechts, Wesleyan University, "The Role of Schemata in the Acquisition and Use of Complex Systems: Computer Text-Editing and File Manipulation," $99,043

Foundation Grants

The Foundation Center as a Funding Resource

The Foundation Center
888 Seventh Ave., New York, NY 10106
212-975-1120

The Foundation Center is an independent, national service organization established by foundations to provide an authoritative source of information on philanthropic activity. The center's vast public service and publications programs are designed to assist grant seekers in identifying appropriate funding sources and to supply reliable descriptive and statistical data on philanthropic foundations and their programs in particular to grant makers, government officials, scholars, and journalists, but generally to anyone seeking information on private philanthropy.

The center maintains three computer data bases (all of which are currently available to the public through the Lockheed DIALOG system) and publishes a wide variety of directories, indexes, and technical assistance materials. All corporate, community, and private foundations actively engaged in grant making, regardless of size or geographic location, are included in one or more of the center's publications. Data are gathered from foundation reports and publications, mailing responses, and the public information returns filed by private foundations with the Internal Revenue Service.

The center also operates extensive public service and education programs through two national libraries, two regional field offices, and more than 130 cooperating collections in public, university, government, and foundation libraries in all 50 states, Canada, Mexico, Puerto Rico, the Virgin Islands, and Great Britain. The libraries provide free public access to all of the center's publications, plus a wide range of other books, services, periodicals, and research papers relating to foundations and philanthropy.

Fund raisers with a continuing need for information on foundations and grants may enroll in the center's Associates Program, which entitles them, for an annual fee of $275, to toll-free telephone reference service, access to custom searches of the center's computerized data bases, paper and microfilm duplicating service, and library research service. For more information about this program, the location of the library nearest you, or the center's publications, call toll free 800-424-9836.

Foundation Center Publications

Publications of The Foundation Center are the primary working tools of every serious grant seeker. Copies of the center's publications are available for free use in its libraries, as well as in cooperating collections. Publications may also be ordered prepaid from The Foundation Center, 888 Seventh Ave., New York, N.Y. 10106.

The Foundation Directory, 1983. 9th Ed., 775 pp. $60. The authoritative guide to the grant-making interests of major American foundations. The ninth edition covers 4,063 foundations that hold assets of at least $1 million or award grants of $100,000 or more annually. Indexes provide access to foundation officers and trustees, philanthropic interests, and geographic location. These foundations represent more than 90 percent of all U.S. foundation dollars.

Source Book Profiles is an annual subscription service offering in-depth analyses of the nation's 1,000 largest foundations. The service operates on a two-year publishing cycle, with 500 foundations analyzed in each annual subscription year. Each entry provides breakdowns of foundation grant making by subject, type of recipient, geographic focus, and type of support; background on grant-making patterns; and information on officers and trustees, publications, and application procedures. The 1982 and 1983 cumulative volumes are available for $200 each; 1984 subscriptions are $250.

National Data Book, 1984. 8th Ed., 2 vols. approx. 150 and 700 pp. $50. The only directory that includes all currently active grant-making foundations in the United States. Volume 1 includes three sections: independent and company-sponsored foundations, community foundations, and operating foundations. Each section is arranged by state to allow geographic access. Volume 2 is an alphabetical index to all sections by foundation name. Published annually in January.

Foundation Grants Index Annual, 1983. 12th Ed., 650 pp. $35. Lists 27,000 grants of $5,000 or more awarded by about 450 foundations, including the nation's top 100 grant makers. Grants are indexed by recipient name and location, subject focus, population served, and type of support awarded. Published annually in April.

COMSEARCH Printouts provide convenient access by subject or geographic focus to grant records listed in the *Foundation Grants Index Annual*. Grant listings are provided in 11 broad subject categories, 68 specific subject groupings, and 16 geographic areas to assist grant seekers in identifying grant makers active in specific fields of interest. Write to The Foundation Center for a complete title and price list. Published annually in May.

Foundation Grants Index Bimonthly. A current-awareness subscription service. Each bimonthly issue provides descriptions of more than 2,000 recently awarded grants, listings of recent foundation publications and other books and articles on fund raising and philanthropy received by The Foundation Center library, and updates on changes in grant makers' addresses, personnel, and funding priorities. Subscriptions are $20 for 6 issues.

Foundation Grants to Individuals, 1984. 4th Ed. approx. 250 pp. $18. The only publication devoted entirely to foundation grant opportunities for individual applicants. Not many of the 22,000 active U.S. foundations make grants directly to individuals, and most of the grants that are available have specific eligibility requirements. Entries include foundation telephone numbers, names of trustees and staff, sample grants, interview and deadline information, and financial data.

Foundation Fundamentals: A Guide for Grantseekers, 1981, Rev. ed. 148 pp. $6.50. This handy guidebook takes grant seekers step by step through the funding research process to identify appropriate funding sources for their organizations or projects. More than 50 illustrations, worksheets, and checklists help identify foundations by subject interest, geographic focus, types of support, and so on. Also gives advice on presenting ideas to a foundation. A second edition with current facts and figures on foundation funding is scheduled for publication in May 1984.

America's Voluntary Spirit: A Book of Readings, by Brian O'Connell. 1983. 450 pp. $19.95; $14.95 pap. A unique collection of 45 speeches, articles, book chapters, and papers that celebrate and examine the diversity and strength of America's voluntary sector. Contributors range from de Tocqueville to John D. Rockefeller, Thoreau to Max Lerner, Erma Bombeck to Vernon Jordan. This is an invaluable reference for all who speak, write, or are simply interested in learning more about the history and breadth of philanthropy and volunteering in the United States.

How to Get Foundation Funding

It is no secret that competition for foundation support is strong—and growing stronger as more and more nonprofit organizations face cutbacks in government funding and increases in operating costs. Foundations receive many thousands of worthy requests each year. Most of these requests must be declined because of insufficient funds or because the applications clearly fall outside the foundation's fields of interest. Like other grant seekers, librarians must be prepared to expend some time and energy to identify appropriate funding sources. Limiting the search for funding sources to those few national foundations that have historically been associated with library funding or choosing a scatter-shot or mass mailing approach to fund raising will not only severely restrict chances of getting grant support but can also damage credibility and options for future fund raising.

The Foundation Center provides a number of resources (listed earlier in this article) that can help identify foundations that might be interested in funding a library program. Librarians should consider foundations that have demonstrated an interest in informational programs nationally or in their specific geographic area, support for a broad variety of activities within a specific community, or an interest in the specific subject area in which the library conducts or is planning to conduct programs. For example, a library that needs funding to provide better access to its facilities for the handicapped should investigate foundations that have provided funding for community services to the handicapped, whether or not they have ever funded a program in a library.

In investigating foundation funding sources, librarians should bear in mind the following questions:

1 Does it seem likely that the foundation will make grants in your geographic location? Examine grant records carefully for explicit or implicit geographic restrictions. Company-sponsored foundations, for example, often restrict their giving to communities where the company has operations; community foundations are almost exclusively limited to giving within their own city or county.

2 Has the foundation indicated a real commitment to your subject field? Although preliminary research may have uncovered one or more grants awarded to a library, closer examination may reveal that these grants were made for other reasons, such as a geographic commitment, a commitment to a particular organization, or a short-term grant program.

3 Does the amount of money you are requesting fit within the foundation's grant range? It would be inappropriate to request $50,000 from a foundation that has never made a grant for more than $10,000.

4 Does the foundation have any policy prohibiting grants for the type of support you are seeking? Many foundations are restricted from giving grants for operating budgets, construction or equipment, or endowment funds; others only provide one type of support.

5 What types of organizations does the foundation tend to support? Some foundations limit their grants to large, national organizations; others focus only on community-based groups. Many foundations are unable to provide funding to organizations that receive a substantial amount of government support and would therefore be unable to award grants to public libraries supported primarily by tax dollars.

6 Does the foundation prefer to make grants to cover the full cost of a project, or does it favor projects where other foundations or funding sources share the cost?

7 Does the foundation have specific application deadlines and procedures?

Using the many state and local directories of grant makers, publications and guidelines statements issued by grant makers themselves, and Foundation Center indexes and directories—most of which can be found in a local cooperating collection near you—a library can conduct a thorough, yet inexpensive funding search. The key to successful fund raising for libraries is initiative and effort, but in today's competitive market, the effort is well worthwhile.

Analysis of Foundation Grants to Libraries, 1983

The Foundation Center
888 Seventh Ave., New York, NY 10016
212-975-1120

Each year The Foundation Center collects data from private and community foundations on recently awarded grants of $5,000 or more for inclusion in the Foundation Grants Index Database. Although this data base is designed primarily as a current-awareness tool for grant seekers, it also provides statistical data on the general funding patterns of the nation's largest foundations. The full listing of grants reported each year is published in *The Foundation Grants Index Annual,* and listings of grants in specific subject or geographic areas are published in the annual *COMSEARCH Printouts* series.

The center's most recent analysis of foundation funding patterns, reported in the twelfth edition of the *Grants Index Annual,* included 27,121 grants awarded by 444 foundations, reported to the center between October 1981 and September 1982. These grants have a total value of $1.49 billion, approximately 44 percent of the total dollars awarded by private foundations annually. The sample is heavily weighted toward large foundations, since it includes the 101 largest grant makers in the United States, whose grant dollars accounted for 72 percent of the total dollars in the sample.

Libraries and information services received 568 grants with a total value of $35.1 million, accounting for 2.4 percent of the total grant dollars in the sample. Of the 444 foundations reporting, 197 foundations, or 44 percent, reported grants for library-related projects, including grants for public, academic, and special libraries, library schools, and

Table 1 / Ten Largest Library Funders, October 1981–September 1982

Foundation Name	Total Dollars Awarded	No. of Grants
Pew Memorial Trust	$3,823,100	26
Andrew W. Mellon Foundation	2,543,000	11
Ford Foundation	2,159,048	22
Mabel Pew Myrin Trust	2,000,000	1
Council on Library Resources	1,572,014	30
George Foundation	1,562,000	2
Herbert H. and Grace A. Dow Foundation	1,150,000	1
Kresge Foundation	1,135,000	6
W. K. Kellogg Foundation	1,048,855	4
Ahmanson Foundation	941,500	18

Source: Foundation Grants Index Annual, 1983, 12th Ed.

Table 2 / Largest Grants to Libraries, 1980–1982

Foundation	Recipient	Amount/Purpose	Date Awarded
Mabel Pew Myrin Trust (Pennsylvania)	Drexel University	$2,000,000 for construction of a new library	1981
George Foundation (Texas)	County of Fort Bend, Texas	$1,512,000 for construction of central library	1980
Herbert H. and Grace A. Dow Foundation (Michigan)	University of Michigan, Ann Arbor	$1,150,000 for installments on pledges to Ford Library, Chemical Engineering Building, and Law School	1981
Pew Memorial Trust (Pennsylvania)	Johns Hopkins University	$930,000 for Eisenhower Library Information Retrieval System	1981
Herrick Foundation (Michigan)	Herrick Public Library	$702,500 for general purposes	1981
J. E. and L. E. Mabee Foundation (Oklahoma)	Texas Christian University	$500,000 for library expansion	1981
Andrew W. Mellon Foundation (New York)	Atlanta University Center	$500,000 for cataloging and training activities associated with consolidation of library collections of center's six constituent institutions into single central library	1981
Lilly Endowment (Indiana)	DePauw University	$484,150 for renovation of library, energy conservation, and computer equipment	1982
J. E. and L. E. Mabee Foundation (Oklahoma)	Saint Mary College	$400,000 for library	1981

Table 3 / Leading Library Grant Recipients, 1980–1982

Recipient	Foundation	Grant Amount	No. of Grants
Drexel University	Mabel Pew Myrin Trust	$2,000,000	1
County of Fort Bend (Public Library)	George Foundation	1,562,000	2
University of Michigan	Ahmanson Foundation	5,000	1
	Council on Library Resources	275,000	1
	Herbert H. and Grace A. Dow Foundation	1,150,000	1
	McGregor Fund	40,000	2
	Alfred P. Sloan Foundation	9,000	1
	Charles J. Strosacker Foundation	70,000	1
	Subtotal	1,549,000	7
Johns Hopkins University	Andrew W. Mellon Foundation	185,000	1
	Pew Memorial Trust	930,000	1
	Subtotal	1,115,000	2
Newberry Library	Amoco Foundation	30,000	1
	Chicago Community Trust	510,000	2
	Continental Bank Foundation	30,000	1
	Exxon Education Foundation	75,000	1
	Field Foundation of Illinois	50,000	1
	John D. and Catherine T. MacArthur Foundation	40,000	1
	Robert R. McCormick Charitable Trust	200,000	1
	Monticello College Foundation	7,500	1
	Subtotal	942,500	9
Herrick Public Library	Herrick Foundation	702,500	1
Scientists' Institute for Public Information	John D. and Catherine T. MacArthur Foundation	125,000	1
	Andrew W. Mellon Foundation	450,000	2
	Charles Stewart Mott Foundation	40,000	1
	Subtotal	615,000	4
Pierpont Morgan Library	Vincent Astor Foundation	65,000	3
	Booth Ferris Foundation	50,000	1
	Mary Flagler Cary Charitable Trust	297,165	4
	Morgan Guaranty Trust Company	10,000	1
	Pew Memorial Trust	27,600	1
	Surdna Foundation	141,000	1
	Subtotal	590,765	11
Atlanta University Center	Andrew W. Mellon Foundation	500,000	1
Texas Christian University	J. E. and L. E. Mabee Foundation	500,000	1

Source: Foundation Grants Index Annual, 1983, 12th Ed.

citizen and consumer information centers. Support was provided to these organizations for a wide variety of purposes, including endowment funds, building construction or renovation, acquisitions, equipment purchase, computerization projects, and special research or educational efforts. All grants for library and information programs are listed in The Foundation Center's COMSEARCH Printout number 23, which can be purchased from the center for $15 or consulted free of charge at any of the center's 130 cooperating library collections. The printout provides the name, address, and funding restrictions of the foundations reporting grants in the area, plus the name and location of each grant recipient, the amount awarded, and a brief description of the purpose of the grant.

Ten foundations accounted for 51 percent of the total grant dollars reported for library programs. (See Table 1.) As with all foundations, there is great diversity among these ten grant makers in terms of the number of grants awarded, the size of the grant awards, and their relationship to the overall grant program of the foundation. The Herbert H. and Grace A. Dow Foundation in Michigan, the Mabel Pew Myrin Trust in Pennsylvania, and George Foundation in Texas have programs that primarily focus on the local community or region; each awarded large grants to a specific library project in its area. The Ahmanson Foundation grants focus on the state of California: It awarded 18 grants largely for acquisitions to university libraries in California.

The other six foundations on the list are national foundations whose grants to libraries represent an interest in the field rather than in a specific geographic locale. The Andrew W. Mellon Foundation has had a tradition of support for efforts to strengthen the nation's research and academic libraries; its 11 grants provided funding for a variety of projects at these institutions. The Council on Library Resources, established in 1956 with funding from the Ford Foundation, only funds "programs that show promise of helping to provide solutions to problems that affect libraries in general, and academic and research libraries in particular." Although the council operated for many years as the Ford Foundation's "library program," Ford has continued to offer funding through its program for library-related projects. Its 22 grants included 7 grants to foreign libraries, as well as a variety of information services in nonlibrary settings, ranging from a $6,000 grant to the Potomac Institute for Economic Research for an information service on voting rights to a $250,000 gift to the National Association for Equal Opportunity in Higher Education to establish a clearinghouse for data on black colleges and blacks in higher education. The W. K. Kellogg Foundation has provided funding for information systems related to health care, reflecting the foundation's commitment to the health field. The Kresge Foundation generally limits its funding to challenge grants for construction, renovation, equipment, and real estate. Several of its grants have been for the renovation and expansion of university libraries. The Pew Memorial Trust has a broad funding program in the areas of health, education, human services, and cultural activities. Its 26 grants for library programs were primarily awarded to university and research libraries throughout the country for programs ranging from computerization of catalog records to new acquisitions projects.

The largest gift to a library was $2 million from the Mabel Pew Myrin Trust to Drexel University for the construction of a new library (Table 2). The George Foundation awarded two grants with a total value of $1.562 million for the construction of a central public library in Fort Bend County, Texas. For a list of other leading library grant recipients between 1980 and 1982, together with the total amount and the number of grants each received, see Table 3.

Part 3
Library Education, Placement, and Salaries

Trends in Information Science Education

Susan Bonzi

School of Information Studies
Syracuse University, Syracuse, New York 13210

Rapid advances in technology, changes in the organizational use of information, and expansion of the theories of information transfer are responsible for a continual state of growth and change in information science education. Traditionally, library schools have dealt with information in its printed form. More recently, however, information beyond the context of the printed word under the broad heading of information science has become a more central focus. Other disciplines, such as computer science, business, and communications, recognizing their roles in information transfer, have incorporated different aspects of information science into their curricula as well. But library schools appear to have integrated information science into their course offerings more thoroughly than other fields.

This discussion of trends in information science education is based largely on examination of course catalogs of 60 of the 68 schools of library and information science accredited by the American Library Association. Several course catalogs of other types of schools offering information science in their curricula were also reviewed. Readers are cautioned that courses advertised in a catalog may not be taught regularly, and courses dealing with information science may exist only under the headings "Special Topics" or "Seminar." Also, both titles and descriptions of courses may sometimes be misleading.

Definition

The American Society for Information Science defines information science as:

> the study of the characteristics of information and how it is transferred or handled. It is concerned with the way people create, collect, organize, label, store, find, analyze, send, receive, and use information in making decisions[1]

This definition, as well as the majority of other definitions of information science presented in the literature, allows inclusion of most if not all of the courses offered in library schools. For the purposes of this article, however, a more rigorous definition of information science has been used. Only courses that strongly imply the study of information outside the context of libraries were considered. In addition to course descriptions, catalog rhetoric also yielded clues on the extent to which library schools include the broader concept of information science.

Programs Incorporating Information Science

The trend toward information science education in library schools is often reflected in the descriptions of the schools' programs. Typical is the Simmons College catalog, which states that "The Graduate School of Library and Information Science's programs reflect a concern for the social, economic, and technological aspects of information organization and transfer."[2] For the most part, information science has become an integral part of library school curricula. But the degree to which information science is taught in library schools varies a great deal. A small number of schools still only offer traditional library science courses.

Most ALA-accredited library schools offer at least one or two courses in information science. These are generally such basic courses as "Introduction to Information Science" and "Information Storage and Retrieval." Schools that do not offer separate courses in information science generally incorporate the theories and skills of information science into their traditionally based courses: "Foundation" courses tend to cover both library science and information science, and "Information Sources in the Humanities/Social Sciences/Sciences" includes machine-readable data bases in its survey of sources.

A few schools offer a wide variety of information science courses. Schools that offer a degree in information science, such as the University of Pittsburgh, Syracuse University, and Long Island University, offer the greatest number of courses dealing with information science. Courses in bibliometrics, vocabulary control, data base management, scientific and technical communication, and information needs, uses, and users are included in the curricula of a number of library schools in the United States and Canada, for example Case Western Reserve University and the University of Maryland.

Several library schools either recommend or require one or more courses in information science as part of their core curricula. Again, these tend to be the introductory courses concerned with fundamental theories and basic courses exploring information systems. The Clarion University of Pennsylvania College of Library Science requires a course in information storage and retrieval, and the University of Iowa School of Library Science strongly recommends an introductory course in information science.

Many library schools either suggest or require that their students specialize in one area, with information science as one alternative. In a few schools information science specializations are quite specific and may incorporate both library and information science theory and skills. The Pratt Institute Graduate School of Library and Information Science, for example, offers specialties in information management, records management, information retrieval, and information analysis. The Drexel University School of Library and Information Science offers a doctorate in three areas of study: management of information resources, scholarly and professional communication, and information systems design and evaluation.

Some schools of library and information science do not emphasize information science at the master's level, but offer a postmaster's degree more oriented toward information science. The University of Hawaii Graduate School of Library Studies is one such school. Its Certificate in Advanced Library/Information Studies program has information science courses as part of its prerequisites as well as of its required core.

Outside the United States and Canada, information science education is taught in library schools in a variety of countries. Chen reports that information science specialties exist in library schools in China.[3] Saracevic, surveying information science education in Latin America, found that a few schools offer courses in information science.[4] Others have reported on information science education in library schools in India, Malaysia, Nigeria, Hong Kong, and Bolivia.[5]

Separate Degree Programs in Information Science

A number of schools have begun to offer degrees in information science. At Long Island University's C. W. Post Center, the Palmer School of Library and Information Science offers a master of science in information science in addition to its master of science in library science. The new information science program, first offered in fall 1982, includes a core of eight courses that cover "Theory and Fundamentals of Information." Students may specialize in one of three areas: information access, information resources management, or information technology.

The Syracuse University School of Information Studies offers a master of science in information resources management, a two-year program requiring ten courses in such areas as technology, structure, processing, policies, economics, and evaluation of information. The doctorate in information transfer, also oriented toward information science, emphasizes the same areas as the master's program but from the researcher's perspective. The school also offers an undergraduate dual major with the School of Arts and Sciences and an undergraduate minor in information studies.

The School of Library and Information Science at Western Michigan University offers a master of science with specialization in information science in addition to its master of science in librarianship and master of library administration. The 30-semester-hour interdisciplinary program is individually planned to meet each student's needs.

The University of Pittsburgh School of Library and Information Science is unique in that it has both a Department of Library Science and an Interdisciplinary Department of Information Science (IDIS). The IDIS offers a full complement of degrees in information science: bachelor's, master's, certificate of advanced study, and doctorate. The bachelor of science degree requires courses in behavioral science, computer programming, English composition, mathematics, and statistics, in addition to more general requirements in the humanities, social sciences, and natural sciences. Pittsburgh's master of science in information science is a 36-semester-hour program with prerequisite courses in behavioral science, statistics, computer language, and mathematics. There are three tracks in the master's program: information systems specialist, information systems designer, and information counselor. In addition, students may enroll in the Agricultural Information Specialist program or the Drug Information Specialist program, both of which may be incorporated into a master's degree in information science. Entrance to the Ph.D. program at IDIS requires successful completion of a preliminary examination, which covers theoretical structure, behavioral and philosophical foundations, and research methodology of information science, as well as information systems and technology. Clearly, Pittsburgh's Interdisciplinary Department of Information Science program is the most comprehensive of all information science curricula in library schools.

In fall 1984, the University of Denver Graduate School of Librarianship and Information Management will offer a master of arts in information resource management. The 64-quarter-hour curriculum, which includes prerequisite courses in technological and human aspects of information, also requires courses in information management, systems analysis, human resource management, and economics of information.

Information Science Education in Other Disciplines

Schools of library and information science are not the only means to a graduate education in information science. A number of other schools in the country offer degrees with a substantial information science orientation. Schools of computer science, business, and communication represent different approaches to information science education. The following represent a sample of the programs offered.

The Cornell University Department of Computer Science offers a concentration in information processing. Included in the program are courses in information organization and retrieval, data base systems, information processing, and file processing.

The Sloan School of Management at the Massachusetts Institute of Technology approaches information science from a management perspective. Its program in management information systems deals in part with technology, principles, and legal issues of computer-based information systems.

An interesting combination of computer science, management, and information science is offered by the Temple University Computer and Information Science Department. Located in the School of Business Administration, the department offers a master of business administration with a major in computer and information science. Included in the program are such courses as "Information Systems," "Online Systems and File Management," and "Problems in Information Sciences."

The Department of Information and Communication Studies, a part of the School of Communications at California State University, Chico, offers both bachelor's and master's degrees. One optional concentration is information studies, with emphasis in communication systems, instructional support systems, information storage and retrieval systems, or organizational information systems.

Sources in Information Science

Several sources identify educational programs in information science. The American Society for Information Science has compiled a representative list of educational programs in information science.[6] *Peterson's Annual Guide to Graduate Studies* contains a section on information science in its volume on engineering and applied sciences.[7] *The College Blue Book* also lists a variety of programs in information science.[8] For those interested in programs of study outside the United States and Canada, the *World Guide to Library Schools and Training Courses in Documentation* describes programs as well as courses taught in schools of library and information science.[9]

Conclusion

Information science has been and should continue to be an integral part of library school curricula. Nearly all schools accredited by the American Library Association include courses in information science, at least at a basic level, many offer specializations in the area, and a small number of library schools grant separate degrees in information science. Information science education programs in other disciplines appear to be increasing, with several schools of computer science, management, and communication offering specializations in the area. With the increased emphasis on the value of information in our society, education in the field of information science can be expected to continue to grow. There already appears to be a trend in library schools toward offering separate degrees in information science. This trend may soon become apparent in other disciplines as well.

Notes

1. American Society for Information Science, *Super Careers in Information Science*, brochure, n.d.
2. *Graduate School of Library and Information Science, 1982/84*: Simmons College, brochure, n.d., p. 7.

3. Ching-Chih Chen, "Education and Training in Information Science in the People's Republic of China," *Bulletin of the American Society for Information Science* 1 (April 1980): 16-18.
4. Tefko, Saracevic, "Training and Education of Information Scientists in Latin America," *Unesco Journal of Information Science, Librarianship and Archives Administration* 11 (July–September 1980): 170-179.
5. P. B. Mangla, "Library and Information Science Education in India: Trends and Issues," *Education and Training in Developed and Developing Countries: With Particular Attention to the Asian Region.* FID Publication 625 (The Hague: Federation Internaionale de Documentation, 1983), pp. 156-167; Lim, Huck-Tee, "Library Education in Malaysia," in *Education and Training,* pp. 169-177; B. Olabimpe Aboyade, "Education and Training of the Information Professionals in Nigeria—Establishing an Identity, in *Education and Training,* pp. 62-73; Kan Lai-Bin, "Hong Kong Library Education in Transition: 1977–1982," in *Education and Training,* pp. 119-126; Martha de Veizaga and Norah Camberos, "Education and Training in Information Sciences in Bolivia," in *Education and Training,* pp. 107-109.
6. Copies of the list may be obtained by sending a stamped, self-addressed envelope to SCHOOLS, American Society for Information Science, 1010 16 St. N.W., Washington, DC 20036.
7. *Peterson's Annual Guide to Graduate Studies* (Princeton, N.J.: Peterson's Guides, 1982).
8. *College Blue Book*, 19th ed. (New York: Macmillan, 1983).
9. *World Guide to Library Schools and Training Courses in Documentation*, 2nd ed. (London: Clive Bingley, 1981).

The Library Labor Market: A Study of Supply and Demand

Nancy K. Roderer

Project Director,
King Research, Inc.

A recently completed research project took a close look at the library labor force, estimating supply and demand at the current time and developing projections through 1990. The project was sponsored by the National Center for Education Statistics and the Office of Libraries and Learning Technologies of the Department of Education and was performed by King Research, Inc. The results are documented in a research report, *Library Human Resources: A Study of Supply and Demand,*[1] and an *American Libraries* article, "Librarians: A Study of Supply and Demand."[2] The study methodology and major findings are summarized here.

Study Methods

The Library Human Resources study required a description of the current library labor market, including its dynamics and the sources of supply and demand, estimation of the sizes of the current supply and demand and their rates of change, and forecasting of the market into the future. Methods used included an extensive literature review to identify existing data, the collection of new data by means of two surveys, and the development of regression models to project future supply and demand.

The surveys were addressed to library schools and to libraries as employers of librarians. The library school survey, which was sent to all of the approximately 275 library education programs identified, covered applicants, admissions, completions, and placement of graduates from 1977–1978 through 1980–1981. The employer survey was sent to a sample of 2,335 of the estimated 43,600 libraries in the United States. It covered number of employees by type, sex and educational status of librarians, and transfers into and out of the library. Numbers of employees were obtained for 1978–1982, and the remaining data were obtained for 1981 or 1982.

Forecasting models were developed using a variety of methods as appropriate to the data available. To project library employment, public, academic, school (public and private), and special libraries were examined separately. Regression models incorporating relevant variables for each library type were developed, fit to historical data, and then used to predict future demand. To project the new supply of librarians coming from library schools, models based on Freeman's theory of occupational choice were developed. The approach relies on multiple regression models in which supply is related to salaries, and salaries to market conditions. Other aspects of the supply and demand of librarians were projected based on current data and historical trends where available.

Study Findings

The Current Picture

A major outcome of the Library Human Resources study was a clear picture of the current employment situation in libraries. In 1982, there were approximately 136,000 full-time-equivalent librarians employed in libraries, with 48 percent employed in school libraries, 23 percent in public libraries, 15 percent in academic libraries, and 14 percent in special libraries. Librarians made up about 45 percent of total library staffs, with 5 percent being other professionals and 50 percent technical, clerical, and other support staff. About 80 percent of employed librarians had some type of library degree or certification, with the majority having an MLS degree. Individuals with BLS degrees made up about 12 percent of all employed librarians, and those with school library certification but no library degree accounted for about 7 percent of the total.

Some 23,000 librarians were hired and about 17,000 left libraries in 1981. About 34 percent of those hired came from academic programs; 44 percent came from other library employment. Twenty-two percent came from other kinds of employment or were previously unemployed. Of librarians leaving libraries, 37 percent went on to other library employment, 15 percent to other employment, and 48 percent retired, returned to school, became unemployed, and so on. About 4 percent of those hired came from nonlibrary information professional positions, and about 9 percent of those leaving went to this type of position.

In 1980–1981, there were about 4,200 graduates of accredited MLS programs, 800 graduates of nonaccredited MLS programs, 300 graduates of BLS programs, and 1,700 individuals who completed preparation for school library certification without receiving a library degree. Of the total of approximately 7,000 graduates, about 80 percent went on to library employment, about 4 percent to information professional employment, 6 percent to other employment, and 10 percent to student or unemployed status.

Future Supply and Demand

Study projections show the overall supply and demand situation through 1990. On the demand side, the number of positions for librarians will increase modestly into the early

1980s and then decline slightly to 1990. The decade of the 1980s is expected to show an even smaller increase in the employment level of librarians than the rather stable 1970s, with no anticipated return to the boom period of the 1960s. Most job openings created in the 1980s, especially later in the decade, will occur as a result of retirements and deaths rather than new positions.

As the number of jobs stays fairly constant in the 1980s, the number of individuals completing library education programs and seeking employment is also projected to remain fairly constant through the decade. MLS degrees from accredited programs are expected to reverse their decline of the 1970s and begin to increase again, but not rapidly; by 1990, the number of degrees will be the same as in 1969. MLS degrees from nonaccredited programs will follow the same pattern. School library certificates and BLSs, however, will decline steadily, offsetting the increases in the other areas. Our projections indicate that by 1990 the mix of library program completions will have changed from 59 percent to 73 percent for accredited MLS programs.

Although only small changes are projected in the number of graduates of library education programs and in the employment level of librarians, differences in the rates of change suggest that the job market will improve modestly between 1982 and 1986 and then tighten later in the decade. This statement reflects the job market for traditional librarians and could be countered by increasing movement of library program graduates to nonlibrary information professional positions.

How does the employment picture for librarians compare with that for other professionals? In contrast with the anticipated employment growth rate of 5 percent for librarians between 1980 and 1990, employment is projected to increase 19 percent for elementary school teachers, 23 percent for social workers, and 71 percent for systems analysts. Employment of college teachers, on the other hand, is expected to decline by 12 percent and employment of secondary school teachers by 14 percent. Employment of professional and technical workers generally is projected to increase by 22 percent.[3]

Employment projections for professionals, as well as for librarians, reflect only total demand. For a true picture of the future library labor market, it is also necessary to examine the relationship of supply to demand. Table 1 illustrates this relationship for librarians through 1990, reflecting total employment, job openings, and the additional

Table 1 / Supply and Demand for Librarians, 1978–1990

Years[1]	Total Employ- ment[2]	Job Openings			New Supply			Excess of Supply Over Demand[7]
		Growth[3]	Replace- ment[4]	Total	Grad- uates[5]	Other Additions[6]	Total	
1978–1982	130,600	2,400	12,800	15,200	7,400	9,000	16,400	1,200
1982–1986	137,500	1,300	13,100	14,400	5,700	9,200	14,900	500
1986–1990	136,900	−100	13,700	13,600	5,800	9,600	15,400	1,800

[1] Table data reflect annual averages for the periods indicated. Data for 1978–1982 are derived from NCES/OLLT Library Human Resources Survey, 1982. Projections for 1982–1986 and 1986–1990 were developed by King Research, Inc.
[2] Total annual employment in public, academic, school, and special libraries.
[3] Annual job openings due to increase (or decrease) in employment.
[4] Annual job openings due to death, retirement, occupational transfers, and others leaving the library labor force.
[5] Library program graduates seeking to enter the labor force each year (95 percent of all graduates). Includes graduates of accredited and nonaccredited MLS, BLS, and school library certificate programs.
[6] Other entrants into the library labor force each year. Includes reentrants, delayed entrants, and occupational transfers.
[7] Projected number of individuals available annually for other positions, including nonlibrary information professional positions.

supply of librarians. Data for 1978–1982 are based on results from the surveys of library schools and employers of librarians. Data for 1982–1986 and 1986–1990 are based on projections developed as a part of this study.

In the table, the number of job openings within the total employment is given in terms of additional positions created and positions available because of individuals leaving library employment. The new supply of librarians is expressed as the number of graduates of library education programs and of "other additions," which includes individuals obtaining library employment who had previously been unemployed and seeking work, otherwise not employed, or working at another occupation—that is, reentrants, delayed entrants, or occupational transfers. Strictly speaking, this category should include both individuals who obtain library employment and those who unsuccessfully seek library employment. But since estimates are not available for the latter category, the table only shows those who do obtain library employment. In contrast, the estimate given for graduates includes all those seeking to enter the labor force.

The final table column, labeled "excess of supply over demand," is the difference between the totals for openings and new supply, thereby estimating the number of persons expected to require other employment. Other employment could include work in a field outside librarianship, as a nonprofessional library worker, or as a nonlibrary information professional.

Between 1978 and 1982, the average number of employed librarians was 130,600. About 15 percent of job openings was due to increases in the number of positions and about 85 percent to replacement demand, including deaths, retirements, and other departures. The total number of openings in libraries included the approximately 15,000 positions indicated here plus an estimated 8,000 positions created and filled by transfers between libraries. Based on these data, the total number of job openings per year would be about 23,000, or 18 percent of all jobs.

The average number of new graduates of library education programs between 1978 and 1982 was 7,400. This includes graduates of programs leading to the MLS and BLS degrees and programs preparing people for school library certification. About 70 percent of these graduates received master's degrees from library education programs (60 percent from ALA-accredited programs versus 10 percent from nonaccredited master's programs). About 5 percent obtained bachelor's degrees from library education programs, and 25 percent did not obtain a library degree but completed a program leading to school library certification.

The other source of new supply, as described above, is other additions. This is estimated at 9,000 for 1978–1982. Thus the total new supply averaged 16,400. The excess of supply over demand in these terms, about 1,200 individuals, includes librarians who took nonprofessional library positions, nonlibrary information professional positions, or positions outside the information profession or were unemployed (voluntarily or otherwise).

As seen in Table 1, small decreases are projected for 1982–1986 in the average number of job openings and of graduates. The decrease in the number of graduates is relative to the 1978–1982 average and occurs despite the expectation of increases in the late 1980s; this is because the decreases of the late 1970s were greater than the corresponding increases in the late 1980s. Data for 1982–1986 suggest a somewhat smaller excess in the supply of librarians over the demand for them than in the previous period, about 500 individuals annually. This number is less than might be expected to go into nonlibrary information professional positions, based on a 1981 movement of about 800 with projected increases through the 1980s. Thus, in this period, an improved job market is expected. It seems likely that there will be some increase in transfers into librarianship between 1982 and 1986, with some of those having difficulty entering the field in the late 1970s now having a new opportunity, and other positions continuing to be filled.

As we have projected them, the number of library program graduates is related to salaries, which in turn are related to the library job market and other factors. Thus, the number of graduates responds to employment levels and the average number of library program graduates is expected to increase in the late 1980s. Table 1 shows an anticipated number of 5,800 graduates seeking to enter the labor force each year between 1986 and 1990. Combined with an estimated 9,600 other additions, this yields a new supply of 15,400. In the same period, library employment is expected to drop, and only 13,600 job openings are projected annually. The difference is 1,800 individuals available for other positions, again including nonlibrary information professional positions. Thus, an excess in the supply of librarians within the traditional library labor market is projected for the late 1980s.

Future Training of Nonlibrary Information Professionals

What cannot be predicted quantitatively is the effect of the movement by library schools toward the training of nonlibrary information professionals. This is potentially a large market, conservatively estimated at one-third again the size of librarianship in 1980 and felt to be growing rapidly. Although less than 4 percent of library graduates currently go into such positions, greater emphasis by individual schools has led to more placements. Opportunities appear to be available for the different types of library programs, all of which currently have about the same level of nonlibrary information professional placement.

It is possible that in the near future the higher salaries earned by information professionals will attract more people into library/information science education programs and more graduates into nonlibrary information professional positions. The supply model shows that potential library students are sensitive to salaries. It is generally believed that nonlibrary information positions pay more than those in libraries, at least in part because the nonlibrary positions are also competing for the well-paid graduates of business and computing programs. As more potential students learn more about nonlibrary work, more may enroll in library programs to train for nonlibrary work, and more of those intending to work in libraries may decide instead to seek nonlibrary positions. This could increase library program completions substantially beyond what has been projected. It could conceivably also present libraries with serious competition for new graduates, resulting in a shortage of new librarians available to libraries.

Currently, only a small percentage of new graduates is going into nonlibrary information work. The trend out of libraries is more noticeable among experienced librarians, who may be more willing to try a career change or may see more similarity between libraries and other settings than do new graduates. Library education programs may not be successfully marketing themselves to individuals interested in nonlibrary work. Almost exclusively people who enroll in these programs want to work in libraries, although some proportion either changes career goals while in school or is forced into nonlibrary employment upon graduation by the exigencies of the job market.

Another tentative area in the projections of this report is transfers and reentrants. Without data over time on the effect of changes in the market for librarians on reentrants and transfers, it is difficult to make projections. One would assume that individuals are more likely to reenter or transfer into a profession when job opportunities are plentiful. Given the relatively somber employment projections, it is possible that the reentry and transfer projections in Table 1 are high. On the other hand, it is impossible to estimate how many former librarians in the population would be willing and able to reenter the library labor force should the market improve. Some who have left the profession have done so permanently, never to return, but others have been forced out by the poor employment situation of the last few years and would return if conditions improved.

Trends by Library Type

According to the survey results, librarians tend not to change the type of library in which they are employed. In 1981, for example, only about 2 percent of all employed librarians transferred from one type of library to another. There is also segmentation by type of education—91 percent of all employed librarians with school library certification and no library degree are in school libraries, as are 73 percent of BLS recipients and 66 percent of graduates of nonaccredited MLS programs. MLS recipients make up 80 percent of all employed librarians from the three types of programs and 60 percent of the total of employed librarians, including 90 percent of academic librarians, 73 percent of special librarians, 63 percent of public librarians, and 47 percent of school librarians. We can thus talk about the market for different types of libraries and of the supply generated by the different types of programs.

According to our projections, the jobs for new librarians in the late 1980s will be in school, public, special, and academic libraries, in that order. Due to levels of supply, jobs will be more readily available in public and particularly special libraries. With the projected excess of supply over demand, jobs for librarians will also need to be found outside libraries, such as in nonlibrary information professional settings.

Geographic Trends

It is difficult to project the future employment situation by geographic area; the 1977–1981 surveys provided data on graduates and positions by region but none on mobility patterns. If it were assumed that graduates generally stay within the region in which they attend school, the Library Human Resources survey results for 1977–1981 would suggest small excesses of supply over demand in the North Atlantic, Great Lakes, and southeastern regions and an excess of demand over supply in the West and Southwest. There would also be local differences in the supply and demand picture, with more positions available in rural areas. As the mix of librarians changes in the 1980s, with proportionately fewer academic and school librarians, the geographic distribution of jobs should change as well, suggesting that the mobility of individuals may play a factor both now and in the future in finding professional library employment. Precisely in what way this will happen is unknown, but there could continue to be shortages in rural public libraries.

The study also did not look in depth at distinctions between areas within librarianship, such as administration, reference, cataloging, technical processing, and so on. Again, no comprehensive data are available on the current mix of positions in libraries. In the reference area, though, the market for the academic subject specialist is likely to decline, and more positions will become available in special libraries in business, industry, law, medicine, and so on. Generally, the average library size (in terms of number of librarians) will probably decrease in the late 1980s, requiring a reevaluation of the mix of tasks to be performed by professional staff. Although the need for technical processing activity is not likely to decline as the volume of available information increases, automation and networking activities may reduce the number of professional librarians needed in this area. As is true for the total U.S. job market for the 1980s, individuals with computer-related skills can be expected to be in demand.[4]

Conclusions

The implications of this study for currently employed and prospective librarians seem clear. Little change is expected in employment overall, with decreases in school and academic library positions. There will be strong competition for jobs in the late 1980s. Although the study does not address the specific functional areas in which opportunities will be best, subject expertise in business and industry and computer-related skills are likely to be helpful. With job shortages, geographic mobility will also be desirable. For individuals considering librarianship as a profession, opportunities to carry out similar functions in a nonlibrary environment should also be investigated.

The study also has implications for library educators: MLS program enrollments are projected to increase, but slowly, during the 1980s, and enrollments in BLS and school library certificate programs are expected to decrease throughout the 1980s. Responses are needed to new patterns of demand for librarians and to changes in the types of skills required of librarians. There appears to be potential for library training programs at all levels to also take on the training of information professionals for nonlibrary settings.

For employers of librarians, this study implies that, on the average, they will not be hiring many librarians. Job openings will result from retirements and from current employees changing jobs, not from expansion. Although supply will be below its past levels, it will still exceed demand, resulting in a buyer's market. The low level of turnover, however, suggests that libraries will have to place increasing emphasis on staff development. Unable to create new positions, and with fewer people leaving voluntarily (as the poor market discourages them from seeking greener pastures), libraries will have to rely more on retraining and less on hiring to bring in new skills in changing areas such as automation of library processes and of information storage and retrieval. Library educators may therefore want to switch some of their efforts from the training of new librarians to continuing education.

The surveys conducted as a part of this study established the feasibility of collecting much of the data relevant to research on employment of librarians, especially data on transfers. They also established baseline data on employment by all types of libraries and on graduates from all library education programs. The models developed provide a means of evaluating the supply and demand situation. This function should be performed periodically for the library profession overall and would also be of interest within specific geographic areas and other subdivisions of the field. Finally, the results obtained from this study challenge library researchers to explore aspects of the employment picture in greater depth, such as changes in functional requirements in libraries, mobility patterns of librarians and job transfers, and to monitor job openings.

Notes

1. Nancy K. Roderer, Nancy A. Van House, Michael Cooper, and Ellen Sweet, *Library Human Resources: A Study of Supply and Demand,* prepared for the National Center for Education Statistics, Office of Libraries and Learning Technology (Rockville, Md.: King Research, Inc., March 1983). Available from the ALA Order Department, 50 E. Huron St., Chicago, IL 60611, at a cost of $20 (0-8389-0394-0).
2. Nancy A. Van House, Nancy K. Roderer, and Michael D. Cooper, "Librarians: A Study of Supply and Demand," *American Libraries* (June 1983).
3. U.S. Bureau of Labor Statistics, *Occupational Projections and Training Data, 1982 Edition,* Bulletin 2202. A Statistical and Research Supplement to the 1982–1983 *Occupational Outlook Handbook* (Washington, D.C.: U.S. Government Printing Office, 1982).
4. U.S. Bureau of Labor Statistics, *Occupational Outlook Quarterly* 26, no. 1 (October 1982).

Guide to Library Placement Sources

Margaret Myers

Director, Office for Library Personnel Resources,
American Library Association

This year's guide updates the listing in the 1983 *Bowker Annual* with information on new services and changes in contacts and groups listed previously. The sources listed primarily give assistance in obtaining professional positions, although a few indicate assistance with paraprofessionals. The latter, however, tend to be recruited through local sources.

General Sources of Library Jobs

Library Literature. Classified ads of library vacancies and positions wanted are carried in many of the national, regional, and state library journals and newsletters. Members of associations can sometimes list position wanted ads free of charge in their membership publications. Listings of positions available are regularly found in *American Libraries, Catholic Library World, Chronicle of Higher Education, College & Research Libraries Newsletter, Journal of Academic Librarianship, Library Journal, LJ/SLJ Hotline,* and *Wilson Library Bulletin.* State and regional library association newsletters, state library journals, foreign library periodicals, and other types of periodicals carrying such ads are listed in later sections.

Newspapers. The Sunday *New York Times* Week in Review section carries a special section of job openings for librarians in addition to the regular classifieds. Local newspapers, particularly the larger city Sunday editions, often carry job vacancy listings in libraries, both professional and paraprofessional.

Note: The author wishes to acknowledge the assistance of Sandra Raeside, OLPR administrative assistant, in compiling the information for this article.

Library Joblines

New joblines were added in 1983 for Connecticut and Missouri. Library joblines or job hot lines give recorded telephone messages of job openings in a specific geographic area. Most tapes are changed once a week on Friday afternoon, but individual listings may sometimes be carried for several weeks. Although the information is fairly brief and the cost of calling is borne by the individual job seeker, a jobline provides a quicker and more up-to-date listing of vacancies than is usually possible with printed listings or journal ads.

Most joblines carry listings for their state or region only, although some will occasionally accept out-of-state positions if there is room on the tape. A few list technician and other paraprofessional positions, but the majority are for professional jobs only. When calling the joblines, one may occasionally get no answer; this usually means that the tape is being changed or that there are no new jobs for that period.

The classified section of *American Libraries* carries jobline numbers in each issue. The following are in operation: *American Society for Information Science*, 202-659-1737; *Arizona State Library/JAM*, 602-278-1327; *Association of College and Research Libraries*, 312-944-6795; *British Columbia Library Association*, 604-263-0014 (B.C. listings only); *California Library Association*, 916-443-1222, for northern California, and 213-629-5627, for southern California (identical lists); *California Media and Library Educators Association*, 415-697-8832; *Colorado State Library*, 303-866-2210 (Colorado listings only; includes paraprofessional); *Connecticut Jobline*, 203-727-9675 (cosponsored by Connecticut Library Association and Connecticut State Library); *Florida State Library*, 904-488-5232 (in-state listings only); *Illinois Library Job Hotline*, 312-828-0930 (cosponsored by Special Libraries Association, Illinois Chapter, and Illinois Library Association—all types of jobs listed); *Maryland Library Association*, 301-685-5760; *Metropolitan Washington Council of Governments* (D.C.), 202-223-2272; *Midwest Federation of Library Associations*, 517-487-5617 (also includes paraprofessional and out-of-state positions if room on tape; cosponsored by six state library associations—Illinois, Indiana, Michigan, Minnesota, Ohio, and Wisconsin); *Missouri Library Association*, 314-449-4627 (5:00 PM–8:00 AM weekdays and all weekend); *Mountain Plains Library Association*, 605-624-2511 (includes listings for Colorado, Kansas, Montana, Nebraska, Nevada, North and South Dakota, Utah and Wyoming; updated on Thursdays); *Nebraska*, 402-471-2045 (during regular business hours); *New England Library Board*, 617-738-3148; *New Jersey Library Association/State Library*, 609-695-2121; *New York Library Association*, 212-227-8483; *North Carolina State Library*, 919-733-6410 (professional jobs in North Carolina only); *Oklahoma Jobline*, 405-521-4202 (5:00 PM–8:00 AM, Monday through Friday and all weekend); *Oregon Library Association*, 503-585-2232 (cosponsored by Oregon Educational Media Association and Oregon State Library); *Pacific Northwest Library Association*, 206-543-2890 (Alaska, Alberta, British Columbia, Idaho, Montana, Oregon, and Washington; includes both professional and paraprofessional and other library-related jobs); *Pennsylvania Cooperative Jobline*, 717-234-4646 (cosponsored by Pennsylvania Library Association; Pennsylvania Learning Resources Association; Medical Library Association—Philadelphia and Pittsburgh groups; American Society for Information Science—Delaware Valley Chapter; Pennsylvania School Librarians Association; and West Virginia Library Association [also accepts paraprofessional out-of-state listings]); *Special Libraries Association*, 212-460-9716; *Special Libraries Association, New York Chapter*, 212-753-7247; *Special Libraries Association, San Francisco Bay Chapter*, 415-968-9748; *Special Libraries Association, Southern California Chapter*, 213-795-2145; *Texas Library Association Job Hotline*, 713-782-0570

(4:00 PM Friday–8:30 AM Monday); *Texas State Library Jobline*, 512-475-0408 (Texas listings only); *University of South Carolina College of Librarianship*, 803-777-8443; *Virginia Library Association Jobline*, 804-355-0384. Delaware jobs are listed on the New Jersey and Pennsylvania joblines.

For those employers who wish to place vacancy listings on the jobline recordings, the following numbers can be called: *ACRL*, 312-944-6780; *ASIS*, 202-659-3644; *Arizona*, 602-269-2535; *California*, 916-447-8541; *District of Columbia*, 202-223-6800, ext. 458; *Florida*, 904-487-2651; *Illinois*, 312-644-1896; *Missouri*, 314-449-4627; *New Jersey*, 609-292-6237; *New York*, 212-227-8032; *New York/SLA*, 212-790-0639; *North Carolina*, 919-733-2570; *Oklahoma*, 405-521-2502; *Oregon*, 503-378-4243; *Pennsylvania*, 717-233-3113; *San Francisco/SLA*, 408-277-3784; *Southern California/SLA*, 213-356-6329; *Special Libraries Association*, 212-477-9250; *Texas*, 512-475-4110; *Virginia*, 804-257-1101.

Write: *British Columbia Library Association*, Box 46378, Sta. G, Vancouver, B.C., Canada V6R 4G6; *California Media and Library Educators Association*, 1575 Old Bayshore Hwy., Suite 204, Burlingame, CA 94010; *Colorado State Library Jobline*, 1362 Lincoln, Denver, CO 80203; *Connecticut Library Association/State Library Jobline*, 231 Capitol Ave., Hartford, CT 06106; *Illinois Library Job Hotline*, Illinois Library Association, 425 N. Michigan Ave., Suite 1304, Chicago, IL 60611 ($20 fee/2 weeks); *Maryland Library Association*, 115 W. Franklin St., Baltimore, MD 21201; *Mountain Plains Library Association*, c/o I.D. Weeks Library, Univ. of South Dakota, Vermillion, SD 57069; *Nebraska Job Hotline*, Library Commission, 1420 P St., Lincoln, NE 68508; *New England Library Jobline*, c/o James Matarazzo, GSLIS, Simmons College, 300 The Fenway, Boston, MA 02115; *New York Library Association*, 15 Park Row, New York, NY 10025; *Oregon Library Association JOBLINE*, Oregon State Lib., Salem, OR 97310; *PNLA Jobline*, c/o School of Librarianship, Univ. of Washington FM-30, Seattle, WA 98195; *Texas Library Association Job Hotline*, 8989 Westheimer, Suite 108, Houston, TX 77063; *University of South Carolina, College of Librarianship*, Placement, Columbia, SC 29208 (no geographic restrictions). For the *Midwest Federation Jobline*, employers should send listings to their state association executive secretary, who will refer them to the Michigan Library Association where the recording equipment is housed. The employer is charged a $5 fee for each listing. Paraprofessional positions are also accepted.

Specialized Library Associations and Groups

The National Registry for Librarians, formerly housed in the Illinois State Job Service at 40 W. Adams St., Chicago, IL 60603, is no longer in operation. Referral service will still be carried out through state and local Job Service offices but no independent registry will be maintained for librarians.

American Association of Law Libraries, 53 W. Jackson Blvd., Chicago, IL 60604, 312-939-4764. Placement service is available without charge. Lists of openings and personnel available are published ten times per year in a newsletter distributed to membership. Applicants are referred to placement officers for employment counseling.

American Libraries, c/o Beverly Goldberg, 50 E. Huron St., Chicago, IL 60611. Career LEADS EXPRESS provides advance galleys (3–4 weeks) of job listings to be published in next issue of *American Libraries*, giving early notice of some 60–80 positions open. Galleys that are sent about the seventeenth of each month do not include editorial corrections and late changes as they appear in the regular *AL* LEADS section, but they do include some late job notices. For each month, send $1 check made out to AL EXPRESS, self-addressed, standard business-size envelope (4 × 9), and 20¢ postage on envelope.

American Libraries, Consultants Keyword Clearinghouse (CKC), an *AL* service that helps match professionals offering library/information expertise with institutions seeking it. Published quarterly, CKC appears in the Career LEADS section of the January, April, June, and October issues of *AL*. Rates: $4/line—classified; $40/inch—display. Inquiries should be made to Beverly Goldberg, LEADS Ed., *American Libraries*, 50 E. Huron St., Chicago, IL 60611, 312-944-6780, ext. 326.

American Library Association, Office for Library Personnel Resources, 50 E. Huron St., Chicago, IL 60611, 312-944-6780. A placement service is provided at each annual conference (June or July) and midwinter meeting (January). Request applicant or employer registration forms prior to each conference. Persons not able to attend conference can register with the service and can also purchase job and applicant listings, which will be sent directly from the conference site. Information included with registration forms upon request. Handouts on interviewing, preparing a résumé, and other job-seeking information are available from the ALA Office for Library Personnel Resources.

American Library Association, Association of College and Research Libraries, Fast Job Listing Service, 50 E. Huron St., Chicago, IL 60611, 312-944-6780. Monthly circular listing job openings received in ACRL office during previous four weeks (supplements listings in *C&RL News*). $10 to ACRL members requesting service (indicate ALA/ACRL membership number); $15 to nonmembers. Renewable each six months. Jobline recorded telephone message updated each Friday lists current job openings. Phone 312-944-6795 for listings. Employers who wish to have a listing for two weeks should send a check for $30 (ACRL members) or $35 (non-ACRL members).

ALA Social Responsibilities Round Table, Rhode Island Affiliate, c/o Mary Frances Cooper, Providence Public Lib., 150 Empire St., Providence, RI 02903. SRRT Jobline appears monthly in *RILA Bulletin*, listing positions in southeast New England, including paraprofessional and part-time jobs. Job seekers desiring copy of most recent monthly Jobline, send self-addressed, stamped envelope. Groups of envelopes may also be sent. To post a notice, contact Lucinda Manning, 150 Empire St., Providence, RI 02903.

American Society for Information Science, 1010 16 St. N.W., 2nd fl., Washington, DC 20036, 202-659-3644. An active placement service operates at ASIS annual meetings (usually October) and mid-year meetings (usually May) (locales change). All conference attendees (both ASIS members and nonmembers), as well as ASIS members who cannot attend the conference, are eligible to use the service to list or find jobs. Job listings are also accepted from employers who cannot attend the conference. Interviews are arranged and special seminars are given. During the rest of the year, current job openings are listed on the ASIS JOBLINE, 202-659-1737. Seventeen of the ASIS chapters have placement officers who further assist members in finding jobs.

The ASIS JOBLINE operates 24 hours a day, 7 days a week. Brief descriptions—including contact information—of current job openings around the country are recorded biweekly. New jobs are listed first, starting with overseas or West Coast jobs and ending with jobs in the Washington, D.C., area. Thereafter, jobs still available from the preceding recording are listed. The number to call is 202-659-1737.

Art Libraries Society/North America (ARLIS/NA), c/o Exec. Dir., 3775 Bear Creek Circle, Tucson, AZ 85749. Art librarian and slide curator jobs are listed in the *Art Documentation* (5/year).

Associated Information Managers, c/o Sheila Brayman, Exec. Dir., 1776 E. Jefferson St., Suite 470S, Rockville, MD 20852, 301-231-7447. AIM Career Exchange Clearinghouse lists positions open and wanted on a biweekly basis in conjunction with the *AIM Network*. Position applicants send résumé and cover letter to AIM for forwarding to employers. Employers listing positions open may list their organization name and contact person and telephone number, or they may request that AIM serve as the clearinghouse. Reference numbers for all listings are assigned by AIM. Minimum salary level for all positions is $25,000. The Career Exchange Clearinghouse is open to AIM members *only*.

Association for Educational Communication & Technology, Placement Service, 1126 16 St. N.W., Washington, DC 20036, 202-466-4780. Positions available are listed in the association publication *Instructional Innovator* by code number and state. Responses to ads are forwarded by the association to the appropriate employer. A referral service is also available at no charge to AECT members only. A placement center operates at the annual conference, free to all conference registrants.

Catholic Library Association, 461 W. Lancaster Ave., Haverford, PA 19041, 215-649-5250. Personal and institutional members of CLA are given free space (35 words) to advertise for jobs or to list job openings in *Catholic Library World* (10/year). Others may advertise at $1 per printed line.

Council of Library/Media Technicians, c/o Shirley Daniels, Newsletter Ed., 5049 Eighth St. N.E., Washington, DC 20017. *COLT Newsletter* appears 11 times a year and will accept listings for library/media technician positions. However, correspondence relating to jobs cannot be handled.

Gossage Regan Associates, 15 W. 44 St., New York, NY 10036, 212-869-3348. Gossage Regan Associates works with library trustees, faculty search committees, or with library directors, systems heads, library search committees, chief executive officers of corporations, higher education institutions, or other organizations to locate, screen, assess, and recommend candidates for library management positions such as directors, division heads, or information specialists.

Information Exchange System for Minority Personnel (IESMP, Inc.), Box 668, Fort Valley, GA 31030, 912-825-7645: Nonprofit organization designed to recruit minority librarians for EEO/AA employers. *Informer*, quarterly newsletter. Write for membership categories, services, and fees.

Medical Library Association, 919 N. Michigan Ave., Suite 3208, Chicago, IL 60611, 312-266-2456: Monthly *MLA News* lists positions wanted and positions available in its Employment Opportunities column (up to 20 free lines for MLA members and $5 per line over this; $6 per line for nonmembers). MLA members may request advance mailings of employment opportunities at no charge for six months; this service is available to nonmembers for a prepaid fee of $25. Also offers placement service at annual conference each summer.

Online, Inc., c/o Jean-Paul Emard, 11 Tannery Lane, Weston, CT 06883, 203-227-8466: The JOBLINE column is no longer carried in the *Online* or *Database* magazines. Position openings in the online field are now available through DIALOG in an online file as part of the *ONLINE Chronicle*.

Reforma, National Association of Spanish-Speaking Librarians in the United States, Anita Peterson, Ed., Inglewood Public Lib., 101 W. Manchester Blvd., Inglewood, CA 90301. Quarterly newsletter lists and invites listings, especially those for bilingual and minority librarians. In addition, job descriptions are matched and sent to those who submit résumé and job qualifications to REFORMA JOBLINE at above address (members free; nonmembers $10/year for job-matching service). For a listing of Spanish-speaking/Spanish-surnamed professionals, *Quien Es Quien: A Who's Who of Spanish-Heritage Librarians in the U.S.* (rev. ed., 1981), send $5.50 to Mexican American Studies, College of Arts & Sciences, Univ. of Arizona, Tucson, AZ 85721. The *Amoxcalli* quarterly newsletter of the Reforma El Paso Chapter also lists job openings. Contact chapter at Box 2064, El Paso, TX 79951.

Society of American Archivists, 330 S. Wells, Suite 810, Chicago, IL 60606, 312-922-0140. The *SAA Newsletter* (bimonthly) is sent to members only and lists jobs and applicants, as well as details of professional meetings and courses in archival administration. The *Employment Bulletin* is sent to members who pay a $10 subscription fee. Issues of the *Bulletin* alternate with the *Newsletter*.

Special Libraries Association, 235 Park Ave. S., New York, NY 10003, 212-477-9250. In addition to the Conference Employment Clearing House, a jobline, the SpeciaLine, is in operation 24 hours a day, 7 days a week: 212-460-9716. Most SLA chapters also have employment chairpersons who act as referral persons for employers and job seekers. The official newsletter of the association, *SpeciaList* (monthly), carries classified advertising each month.

Theresa M. Burke Employment Agency, 25 W. 39 Street, New York, NY 10018, 212-398-9250. A licensed professional employment agency that has specialized for over 30 years in the recruitment of library and information personnel for academic, public, and special libraries. Staffed by employment counselors who have training and experience in both library service and personnel recruitment. Presently the majority of openings are in special libraries in the Northeast and require subject backgrounds and/or specific kinds of experience. Fees are paid by the employer.

State Library Agencies

In addition to the joblines mentioned previously, some of the state library agencies issue lists of job openings within their areas. These include: Indiana (monthly on request); Iowa (*Joblist*, monthly); Kentucky (monthly on request); Minnesota (*Position Openings in Minnesota and Adjoining States*, semimonthly, sent to public and academic libraries); Mississippi (job vacancy list, monthly); and Ohio (*Library Opportunities in Ohio*, monthly, sent to accredited library education programs and interested individuals upon request).

On occasion, state library newsletters or journals list vacancies: Alabama (*Cottonboll*, bimonthly); Indiana (*Focus on Indiana Libraries*); Kansas (*Kansas Libraries*, monthly); Louisiana (*Library Communique*, monthly); Massachusetts (*Massachusetts Position Vacancies*, monthly, sent to all public libraries in-state and to interested individuals on a one-time basis); Missouri (*Show-Me Libraries*, monthly); Nebraska (*Overtones*, 13/year); New Hampshire (*Granite State Libraries*, bimonthly); New Mexico (*Hitchhiker*, weekly newsletter); Utah (*Horsefeathers*, monthly); Virginia (*News*, irregular); and Wyoming (*Outrider*, monthly).

Many state library agencies refer applicants informally when vacancies are known to exist, but do not have formal placement services. The following states primarily make referrals to public libraries only: Alabama, Georgia, Idaho, Louisiana, South Carolina (institutional also), Tennessee, Vermont, and Virginia. Those who refer applicants to all types of libraries are Alaksa, Delaware, Florida, Kansas, Maine, Maryland, Massachusetts, Mississippi, Montana, Nebraska, Nevada (largely public and academic), New Hampshire, New Mexico, North Dakota, Ohio, Rhode Island, South Dakota, Utah, West Virginia (public, academic, special), and Wyoming.

Bulletin boards in the Connecticut State Library, Library of Michigan, and State

Library of Ohio post library vacancies for all types of libraries. Addresses of the state agencies are found in Part 6 of this volume of *The Bowker Annual.*

State and Regional Library Associations

State and regional library associations often make referrals, run ads in association newsletters, or operate a placement service at annual conferences, in addition to the joblines sponsored by some groups. The following associations refer applicants when job openings are known: Arkansas, Delaware (also for Delaware listings, call the New Jersey or Pennsylvania joblines), Hawaii, Louisiana, Michigan, Nevada, Pennsylvania, South Dakota, Tennessee, Texas, and Wisconsin. Although listings are infrequent, job vacancies are placed in the following association newsletters or journals when available: Alabama (*Alabama Librarian*, 10/year); Alaska (*Sourdough*, 4/year); Arkansas (*Arkansas LA Newsletter*, 8/year); District of Columbia (*Intercom*, 11/year); Indiana (*Focus on Indiana Libraries*, 10/year); Iowa (*Catalyst*, 6/year); Kansas (*KLA Newsletter*, 3/year); Massachusetts (*Bay State Letter*, 8/year); Minnesota (*MLA Newsletter*, 10/year); Missouri (bimonthly); Mountain Plains (*MPLA Newsletter*, bimonthly, lists vacancies and position wanted ads for individual and institutional members or area library school students); Nevada (*Highroller*, 4/year); New England (*NELA Newsletter*, 6/year); New Hampshire (*NHLA Newsletter*, 6/year; *Granite State Libraries*); New Jersey (*New Jersey Libraries*, 4/year); New Mexico (shares notices via State Library's *Hitchhiker*, weekly); New York (*NYLA Bulletin*, 10/year); Rhode Island (*RILA Bulletin*, monthly); South Dakota (*Bookmarks*, bimonthly); Vermont (*VLA News*, Box 803, Burlington, VT 05402, 10/year); Virginia (*Virginia Librarian*, bimonthly); and Wyoming (*Roundup*, 3/year). The *Southeastern Librarian* lists jobs in that geographic area.

At their annual conference the following associations have indicated some type of placement service, although it may only consist of bulletin board postings: Alabama, Connecticut, Illinois, Indiana, Kansas, Louisiana, Maryland, Missouri, Mountain Plains, New Jersey, New York, Pennsylvania, South Dakota, Texas, Vermont, and Wyoming.

The following associations have indicated they have no placement service at this time: Minnesota, Mississippi, Montana, Nebraska, New Mexico, North Dakota, Pacific Northwest, and Tennessee.

State and regional association addresses are found in Part 6 of this volume of *The Bowker Annual.*

Library Education Programs

Library education programs offer some type of service for their current students as well as alumni. Of the ALA-accredited programs, the following handle placement activities through the library school: Alberta, Atlanta, British Columbia, Clarion, Columbia, Dalhousie, Denver, Drexel, Emory, Hawaii, Illinois, Long Island, Louisiana, McGill, Michigan, Missouri, Pittsburgh, Pratt, Queens, Rosary, Rutgers, Tennessee, Texas-Austin, Toronto, Western Ontario, and Wisconsin-Madison.

The central university placement center handles activities for the following schools: California-Berkeley, Case Western, North Carolina, Peabody/Vanderbilt, and Southern California. However, in most cases, faculty in the library school still do informal job counseling.

In some schools, the placement services are handled in a cooperative manner; in such cases the university placement center usually sends out credentials and the library school posts or compiles the job listings. Schools utilizing both sources include Alabama, Albany, Arizona, Ball State, Brigham Young, Buffalo, Catholic, Chicago, Clarion, Denver, Florida State, Indiana, Iowa, Kent, Kentucky, Maryland, Montreal, North Carolina-Greensboro, North Carolina Central, North Texas, Northern Illinois, Oklahoma, Peabody/Vanderbilt, Pratt, Queens, Rhode Island, St. John's, San Jose, Simmons, South Carolina, South Florida, Southern Connecticut, Southern Mississippi, Syracuse, Tennessee, Texas Woman's, UCLA, Washington, Wayne State, and Wisconsin-Milwaukee. Schools vary as to whether they distribute placement credentials free, charge a general registration fee, or request a fee for each file or credential sent out.

Those schools that post job vacancy notices for review but do not issue printed lists are Alabama, Albany, Alberta, Arizona, Atlanta, Ball State, British Columbia, Buffalo, Case Western, Catholic, Chicago, Columbia, Emory, Florida State, Hawaii, Kent, Louisiana, Maryland, McGill, Montreal, North Carolina-Greensboro, North Carolina Central, Northern Illinois, Oklahoma, Peabody/Vanderbilt, Queens, St. John's, San Jose, Simmons, South Carolina, South Florida, Southern California, Southern Mississippi, Syracuse, Tennessee, Texas Women's, Toronto, Washington, Wayne State, Western Ontario, and Wisconsin-Milwaukee.

In addition to job vacancy postings, some schools issue a printed listing of positions open, which is distributed primarily to students and alumni and only occasionally is available to others. The following schools issue listings free to students and alumni *only* unless indicated otherwise: Albany (weekly to SLIS graduates registered with placement office); Brigham Young; California-Berkeley (alumni receive 10/year out-of-state listings if registered—$45 fee for service; also a jobline, call 415-642-1716 to list positions); Case Western (alumni $10 for 6 lists); Clarion (free to students and alumni); Dalhousie ($5/year for students, alumni, and others); Denver (alumni $8/year, biweekly); Drexel (free in office; by mail to students and alumni who supply self-addressed stamped envelopes—12 for 6 months); Illinois (free in office; 8 issues by mail for $2 and 8 self-addressed, stamped no. 10 envelopes to alumni, $4 and 8 SASEs to nonalumni); Indiana (free for one year following graduation; alumni and others may send self-addressed stamped envelopes); Iowa (weekly, $5/4 months for registered students and alumni); Long Island (issues printed job list biweekly, free for 6 months following graduation; all others $5 for 6 months); Michigan (free for one year following graduation; all other graduates, $10/year, 24 issues); Missouri (Library Vacancy Roster, triweekly printout, 50¢/issue, with minimum of 5 issues, to anyone); North Carolina (available by mail to alumni and students who pay $15 referral fee); North Texas State ($5/6 months, students and alumni); Peabody/Vanderbilt (students and alumni if registered for fee); Pittsburgh (free for 6 months following graduation; other graduates $2/6 months; others $3/6 months); Pratt (alumni—weekly during spring, fall, and summer sessions; others—renew every 3 months); Rhode Island (monthly, $3/year); Rosary (every 2 weeks, $15/year for alumni); Rutgers (subscription $4/6 months, $8/year—twice a month to anyone); Southern Connecticut (printed listing twice a month, free in office, mailed to students/alumni free); Texas-Austin (bimonthly placement bulletin free to alumni and students one year following graduation, $6/6 months or $11/year thereafter); UCLA (alumni—every 2 weeks by request—renew every 3 months); Wisconsin-Madison (subscription $8/year for 12 issues, to anyone); Western Ontario sends notices of positions open as they are received to graduates on the school's placement mailing list.

A number of schools provide job-hunting seminars and short courses or are more actively trying to help graduates obtain positions. Most schools offer at least an annual or semiannual discussion on placement, often with outside speakers representing different types of libraries or recent graduates relating experiences. Some additional programs offered by schools include Albany (alumni/student career day, career possibilities colloquium series; sessions on résumé writing, interviewing, job counseling; computer-based placement file); Arizona (job hunting, résumé writing workshops); Atlanta (seminar on résumé writing); Ball State (job hunting, résumé writing, videotaped job interview role-playing sessions); Brigham Young (students write résumé, which is critiqued in basic administration class); British Columbia (seminars, personal assistance with résumés, jobline liaison); Buffalo (assists laid-off local employees; sends list of graduates to major libraries in the United States; operates selective dissemination of information [SDI] service; résumé seminar and follow-up critique, strategy sessions for conference job seeking; "Put a Buffalo in Your Library" buttons); California-Berkeley (career awareness workshops on résumés, interview and job search; also provides a career planning and information workbook for entering students); Case Western (résumé writing, interviewing skills, including videotape critique, job counseling; alumni as well as current graduates); Chicago (workshop on career opportunities, résumé writing and interviewing skills); Clarion (colloquium series—résumé writing, position interviewing and searching, individual counseling); Columbia (alumni/student career day; sessions on résumé writing, interviewing, individual and group job counseling during the spring); Dalhousie (sessions on job searching, etc., with critiquing of résumés); Denver (résumé writing in administration course, interview workshop, profile of students so job listings can be sent matching interests, Career Day for students/alumni, career awareness workshop with university placement personnel, individual counseling, postings); Drexel (job search workshops: résumé, cover letters, interviewing; individual job counseling by appointment available to students and alumni); Emory (job strategy meeting each term, résumé assistance and job counseling); Florida State (individual consultation with faculty critiques of résumés, etc.); Hawaii (sessions on job searching, résumé writing, cover letters, interviewing; individual job counseling by appointment available to students and alumni); Illinois (résumé writing, interview role playing in library administration class, counseling/critiquing for individuals in library school placement office, computer-based placement profiles for students and alumni, job search workshops by university-wide placement service); Indiana (convocation on job search, seminar on résumé writing, critique of individual résumés and letters); Iowa (job strategy and résumé writing session each term, individual counseling); Kent (annual placement workshops, résumé writing, interviewing strategies); Kentucky (interviewing, résumé preparation, career opportunities, career counseling, summaries of past placement for prospective employers); Long Island (job hunting workshops); Louisiana (cover letters, résumés, job search strategy, interview techniques); Maryland (placement colloquia; job search workshops, and videotapes available); McGill (résumé writing, interview techniques, counseling for job hunting, reception for employers); Michigan (seminar sessions on job hunting, résumé writing, interviewing and search strategies); Mississippi (résumé writing, letters, and interviewing); Missouri (student seminars, individual conseling); and Montreal (discussion on placement with speakers representing a certain type of library; résumé writing and interview techniques in administration course).

The following schools also offer additional programs: North Carolina (workshop on résumé preparation, job-seeking strategy, interview techniques; students may do mock interview on videotape with critique); North Carolina-Greensboro (job hunting, résumé workshops); North Carolina Central (seminars, counseling); Oklahoma (orientation session on placement services offered by university, job search workshops offered by university placement office); Peabody/Vanderbilt (regular seminars on library market-place, résumé preparation, interviews, and so on); Pittsburgh (individual counseling, preconference strategy sessions, placement colloquium sessions, two day-long workshops covering search strategy, résumés, and other means of access, interview techniques, interaction with recent graduates and other alumni, employers' open house); Pratt (job clinics throughout the year, book of résumés sent to employers); Rhode Island (résumés critiqued in library administration course, jobs seminar annually); Rutgers (seminars on job search and résumé writing, individual counseling, interview role playing by video in Contemporary Issues class, paper bag lunchtime panel discussions, postings); San Jose (two-day workshops on alternative careers, twice a year; one-day session on résumé writing, interviews and strategies); Simmons (series of four programs each semester); South Carolina (seminars on job search and résumé writing offered as part of curriculum); South Florida (résumé writing and interview sessions); Southern California (workshops on résumé writing, interviewing, cover letters, and role play in the interview process); Southern Mississippi (placement seminar); Syracuse (job search strategy workshops, career possibilities colloquium series, résumé critiques, career counseling); Tennessee (placement colloquium; assistance in résumé writing); Texas-Austin (job postings, active job opening solicitations, on-campus interviews for students and alumni; one-hour to one-day seminars each semester on job-hunting strategies, résumé and cover letter writing, and interviewing; extensive handouts; small library); Toronto (résumé writing, job search workshops, individual job counseling by appointment); UCLA (career planning, colloquia series; seminar sessions on résumé writing, cover letters, and interviewing, mock interviews on videotapes with critique, individual placement counseling); Washington (job search strategy, résumé writing, interviewing programs); Western Ontario (job search strategy workshops); Wisconsin-Madison (job-finding programs, résumé writing, interview role playing and career day); and Wisconsin-Milwaukee (Job Fair with interview role playing and résumé writing).

Employers often only list jobs with schools in their particular geographic area; some library schools give information to nonalumni regarding their specific locales, but advice is usually given in person since they are *not* staffed to handle mail requests. Schools that allow librarians in their areas to view listings are Alabama, Albany, Alberta, Arizona, Ball State, Brigham Young, British Columbia, Buffalo, Case Western, Catholic, Chicago, Clarion, Columbia, Dalhousie, Denver, Drexel, Emory, Florida State, Illinois, Indiana, Iowa, Kent, Kentucky, Louisiana, Maryland, McGill, Michigan, Missouri, Montreal, North Carolina, North Carolina-Greensboro, North Texas, Northern Illinois, Oklahoma, Peabody/Vanderbilt, Pittsburgh, Pratt, Queens, Rhode Island, Rutgers, St. John's, San Jose, South Carolina, Southern California, Southern Connecticut, Southern Mississippi, Syracuse, Tennessee, Texas-Austin, Texas Woman's, Toronto, UCLA, Washington, Wayne State, Western Ontario, Wisconsin-Madison, and Wisconsin-Milwaukee.

A list of addresses of accredited programs is included in Part 3 of this *Bowker Annual*. Individuals interested in placement services of other library education programs should contact the schools directly.

Federal Library Jobs

The first step in obtaining employment in a federal library is to be listed on the Librarian's Register, a subset of files maintained by the U.S. Office of Personnel Management (OPM) to match federal job applicants with federal job vacancies (Washington Area Office [SSS], Box 52, Washington, DC 20044). Applicants should obtain a Qualifications Information Statement for Professional Librarian Positions (QI-1410), a Federal Employment Application Instructions and Forms Pamphlet (OPM Form 1282), and an Occupational Supplement for Professional Librarian Positions (OPM Form 1203-B) from any federal job information center. (Federal job centers are located in many cities across the country and are listed under "U.S. Government" in major metropolitan area telephone directories. A *Federal Job Information Centers Directory* is available from OPM.)

Job applicants are considered for all grades for which they are qualified that they are willing to accept. As vacancies occur, applications are evaluated in relation to an agency's specific requirements, and the best qualified candidates are referred for consideration. Eligibility remains in effect for one year, after which an applicant must submit updated information to remain eligible.

Although federal job examiners do not select those to be hired, they do play a crucial role in weighing the relative experience of those on the register. When selecting the most qualified candidates whose forms are to be forwarded to the hiring agency, the examiner must consider many factors simultaneously, such as work experience, education (formal and informal), and geographic preference. It is important that all pertinent information regarding education and experience be on these forms. An applicant who fails to provide complete information may never reach the interview stage.

Applications are accepted only when the register is "open." The frequency with which and the length of time the register is open depend on the size of the inventory. The inventory is judged to be too low when a significant proportion of applicants who are qualified for positions decline them. This so-called declination rate is reversed by opening the register, thereby expanding the applicant pool.

In recent years the register has been opened once each year, generally only for several weeks at a time. However, the general register for librarians has not been open since January 1982, and OPM is uncertain if it will be open for any period during 1984. Advance notice goes to all local federal job information centers, so it is important to check frequently in order to be alerted to the registration period. However, the Librarian's Register is open on a continuing basis for persons with training and experience in the fields of medical and law librarianship, engineering, the physical and biological sciences, and for Veterans Administration positions.

In addition to filing the appropriate forms, applicants can attempt to make personal contact directly with federal agencies in which they are interested. Over half the vacancies occur in the Washington area. Most librarian positions are in three agencies—Army, Navy, and Veterans Administration. The Veterans Administration Library Network (VALNET) employs over 350 professional librarians at 175 health care facilities located throughout the United States and Puerto Rico. Although most VALNET positions require training in medical librarianship, many entry-level GS-9 positions require no previous experience; GS-11/13 positions require experience specific to the duties of each vacancy. For a copy of the current vacancy list, telephone 202-389-2820 Monday through Friday, 8:00 AM–4:30 PM EST, or contact your closest VA medical center library service.

Some "expected" agencies are not required to hire through the usual OPM channels. Although these agencies may require the standard forms, they maintain their own employee selection policies and procedures. Government establishments with positions outside the competitive civil service include Energy Research and Development Administration; Board of Governors of the Federal Reserve System; Central Intelligence

Agency; Department of Medicine and Surgery; Federal Bureau of Investigation; Foreign Service of the United States; National Science Foundation; National Security Agency; Central Examining Office; Tennessee Valley Authority; U.S. Nuclear Regulatory Commission; U.S. Postal Service; Judicial Branch of the Government; Legislative Branch of the Government; U.S. Mission to the United Nations; World Bank and IFC; International Monetary Fund; Organization of American States; Pan American Health Organization; and United Nations Secretariat.

The Library of Congress, the world's largest and most comprehensive library, is an excepted service agency in the legislative branch and administers its own independent merit selection system. Job classifications, pay, and benefits are the same as in other federal agencies, and qualifications requirements generally correspond to those used by the U.S. Office of Personnel Management. The library does not use registers, but announces vacancies as they become available. A separate application must be submitted for each vacancy announcement. For most professional positions, announcements are widely distributed and open for a minimum period of 30 days. Qualifications requirements and ranking criteria are stated on the vacancy announcement. The Library of Congress Recruitment and Placement Office is located in Room LM-107 of the James Madison Memorial Building, 101 Independence Ave., S.E., Washington, DC 10540, 202-287-5627.

The Federal Employment Handbook by William C. Robison (New York: Julian Messner, 1981) is a useful book on general procedures for finding a job with the federal government. The *Federal Times* and the Sunday *Washington Post* sometimes list federal library openings.

Additional General and Specialized Job Sources

Affirmative Action Register, 8356 Olive Blvd., St. Louis, MO 63132. The goal of this organization is to "provide female, minority and handicapped candidates with an opportunity to learn of professional and managerial positions throughout the nation and to assist employers in implementing their Affirmative Action Programs." Free distribution of monthly bulletin is made to leading businesses, industrial and academic institutions, and over 4,000 agencies that recruit qualified minorities and women, as well as to all known female, minority, and handicapped professional organizations, placement offices, newspapers, magazines, rehabilitation facilities, and over 8,000 federal, state, and local governmental employment units with a total readership in excess of 3.5 million (audited). Individual mail subscriptions are available for $15 per year. Library job listings are in most every issue. Sent free to libraries on request.

The Chronicle of Higher Education (published 48 times a year—2-week breaks in August and December; 1333 New Hampshire Ave. N.W., Washington, DC 20036) is receiving more classified ads for library openings than previously, although many are at the administrative level; *Academe* (bulletin of the American Association of University Professors, One DuPont Circle, Washington, DC 20036) also lists jobs for librarians at times.

Education Information Service, Box 662, Newton Lower Falls, MA 02162. Instant Alert service for $29 sends 12 notices of domestic or overseas openings on same day EIS learns of opening. Also publishes periodic list of educational openings including library job openings worldwide. Library jobs are small portion of this publication. Cost $6.

School Libraries. School librarians often find that the channels for locating positions in education are of more value than the usual library ones, e.g., contacting county or city school superintendent offices. The *School Library Media Quarterly* 11 (Fall 1982):63–65, contains a discussion under the "Readers' Queries" column on recommended strategies for seeking a position in a school library media center. Primary sources include university placement offices, which carry listings for a variety of school system jobs, and *local* information networks among teachers and library media specialists. A list of commercial teacher agencies may be obtained from the National Association of Teachers' Agencies, c/o Spears Teacher Placement Service, 207 Jackson Keller, San Antonio, TX 78216.

Overseas

Opportunities for employment in foreign countries are limited and immigration policies of individual countries should be investigated. Employment for Americans is virtually limited to U.S. Government libraries, libraries of U.S. firms doing worldwide business, and American schools abroad. Library journals from other countries sometimes list vacancy notices. Some persons have obtained jobs by contacting foreign publishers or vendors directly. Non-U.S. government jobs usually call for foreign-language fluency.

Action, P305, Washington, DC 20525. An umbrella agency that includes the Peace Corps and Vista sometimes needs librarians in developing nations and host communities in the United States. For further information, call toll-free 800-424-8580 and ask for Recruitment. Recruiting offices are in many large cities.

Council for International Exchange of Scholars, Suite 300, 11 DuPont Cicle, Washington, DC 20036, 202-833-4950. Administers U.S. government Fulbright awards for university lecturing and advanced research abroad; usually six to eight awards per year are made to specialists in library science. In addition, many countries offer awards in any specialization of research or lecturing for which specialists in library and information science may apply. Open to U.S. citizens with university or college teaching experience. Request registration forms to receive spring announcement for academic year to start 12–18 months later. Applications and information may be obtained, beginning in April each year, from the office of the graduate dean, chief academic officer, or international programs on U.S. college and university campuses, or directly from CIES.

Department of Defense, c/o Dir., Dept. of Defense Dependent Schools, 2461 Eisenhower Ave., Alexandria, VA 22331. Overall management and operational responsibilities for the education of dependent children of active duty U.S. military personnel and DOD civilians who are stationed in foreign areas. Also responsible for teacher recruitment. For complete application brochure, write to above address.

Education Information Service, Box 662, Newton, MA 02162. Provides a monthly update on overseas education openings, including positions for librarians, media center directors, and audiovisual personnel.

Home Country Employment Registry, National Association for Foreign Student Affairs, 1860 19 St. N.W., Washington, DC 20009. Services are offered to U.S.-educated foreign students to assist them in locating employment in their home countries following completion of their studies. The registry has been temporarily suspended, however, for an evaluation of the service.

International Association of School Librarianship, c/o School of Librarianship, Western Michigan Univ., Kalamazoo, MI 49008. Informal contacts might be established through this group.

International School Services, Box 5910, Princeton, NJ 08540. Private, nonprofit organization established to provide educational services for American schools overseas, other than Department of Defense schools. These are American elementary and secondary schools enrolling children of business and diplomatic families living away from their homeland. ISS seeks to register men and women interested in working abroad in education who meet basic professional standards of training and experience. Specialists, guidance counselors, department heads, librarians, supervisors, and administrators normally need one or more advanced degrees in the appropriate field as well as professional experience commensurate with position sought. ISS also publishes a comprehensive directory of overseas schools. Information regarding this publication and other services may be obtained by writing to the above address.

U.S. Information Agency (U.S. Information Service overseas) will occasionally seek librarians with MLS and four years of experience for regional library counsultant positions. Candidates must have proven administrative ability, and skills to coordinate the overseas USIS library program with other information functions of USIS in various cities worldwide. Relevant experience might include cooperative library program development, community outreach, public affairs, project management, and personnel training. (Five years U.S. citizenship also is required.) USIA maintains more than 132 libraries in over 80 countries, with one million books and 400 local library staff worldwide. Libraries provide reference service and material about the United States for foreign audiences. Overseas allowances and differentials where applicable. Vacation leave, term life insurance, medical and retirement programs. Send standard U.S. Government Form 171 to Employment Branch, USIA, Washington, DC 20547. All types of jobs within USIA are announced through a recording, 202-485-2539. However, chances of librarian positions being announced are slim.

Overseas—Exchange Programs

International Exchanges. Most exchanges are handled by direct negotiation between interested parties. A few libraries, such as the Chicago Public Library, have established exchange programs for their own staff. In order to facilitate exchange arrangements, the *IFLA Journal* (issued February, May, August, and November) provides a listing of persons wishing to exchange positions *outside* their own country. All listings must include the following information: full name, address, present position, qualifications (with year obtained), language, abilities, preferred country/city/library, and type of position. Send to International Federation of Library Associations and Institutions (IFLA) Secretariat, Box 95312, CH-2509 The Hague, Netherlands.

A Librarian's Directory of Exchange Programs/Study Tours/Funding Sources and Job Opportunities Outside of the U.S. by Diane Stine lists additional information on groups that sponsor exchanges and contacts for possible positions abroad. Order from OLPR/ALA, 50 E. Huron St., Chicago, IL 60611 for $1.50 *prepaid.*

Additional clearinghouses for information on exchanges are:

Bureau for International Staff Exchange, c/o A. Hillier, College of Librarianship Wales, Llanbadarn Fawr, Aberystwyth, Dyfed SY23 3AS, Wales, Great Britain. Assists in two-way exchanges for British librarians wishing to work abroad and for librarians from the United States, Canada, France, and the Federal Republic of Germany who wish to work in Britain.

American Library Association, Association of College and Research Libraries, ACRL Exchange Librarian Program, 50 E. Huron St., Chicago, IL 60611, 312-944-6780. Maintains file of American and foreign academic libraries that might be interested in providing opportunity for librarians to work on their staff in an exchange arrangement, as a temporary replacement, or as a nonsalaried visitor.

American Libraries. Professional Exchange, 50 E. Huron St., Chicago, IL 60611, 312-944-6780, ext. 326. Classified section for persons who are interested in trading jobs and/or housing on a temporary basis.

Using Information Skills in Nonlibrary Settings

A great deal of interest has been shown in alternative careers and in using information skills in nonlibrary settings. These jobs are not usually found through the regular library placement sources, although many library schools are trying to generate such listings for their students and alumni. Job listings that do exist may not specifically call for "librarians" by that title, so that ingenuity may be needed to identify jobs where information management skills are needed.

Some librarians are working on a free-lance basis by offering services to businesses, alternative schools, community agencies, and legislators; these opportunities are usually not found in advertisements but through contacts and publicity over a period of time. A number of information brokering business firms have developed from individual free-lance experiences. Small companies or other organizations often need one-time service for organizing files or collections, bibliographic research for special projects, indexing or abstracting, compilation of directories, and consulting services.

Bibliographic networks and online data base companies are using librarians in such positions as information managers, trainers, researchers, systems and database analysts, online services managers. Jobs in this area are sometimes found in library network newsletters or data processing journals. Classifieds in *Publishers Weekly* may lead to information-related positions. One might also consider reading the Sunday classified sections in metropolitan newspapers in their entirety to locate advertisements calling for information skills under a variety of job titles. Librarians can be found working in law firms as litigation case supervisors (organizing and analyzing records needed for specific legal cases); with publishers as sales representatives, marketing directors, editors, and computer services experts; and with community agencies as adult education coordinators, volunteer administrators, and grants writers.

Information on existing information services or methods for using information skills in nonlibrary settings can be found in: *Wilson Library Bulletin* 49 (February 1975):440–445; *Special Libraries* 67 (May/June 1976):243–250; *ASIS Bulletin* 2 (February 1976): 10–20; *RQ* 18 (Winter 1978):177–179; *New York Times* (December 12, 1979). Careers section; *Show-Me Libraries* 31 (May 1980):5–8; *Bay State Librarian* 69 (Winter 1980):9–11; and *Savvy* (January 1981):20–23. The *Canadian Library Journal* (34, no. 2, April 1977) has a whole issue on alternative librarianship. Syracuse University, School of Information Studies, 113 Euclid Ave., Syracuse, NY 13210, has available *Proceedings of the Information Broker/Free-Lance Librarian Workshop* (April 1976) for $5 and *Alternative Careers in Information/Library Services: Summary of Proceedings of a Workshop* (July 1977) for $5.50.

The Directory of Fee-Based Information Services lists information brokers, free-lance librarians, independent information specialists, and institutions that provide services for a fee. Individuals do not need to pay for listings; 1984 directory is available for $18.95 (prepaid), plus $2 postage and handling, from Burwell Enterprises, 5106 F.M. 1960 W., Suite 349, Houston, TX 77069 (713-537-9051). It is supplemented by *The Journal of Fee-Based Information Services* (price to be determined). Issues include new listings, changes of address, announcements, feature articles, and exchange column. Another publication is *So You Want to Be an Information Broker?* (proceedings of a May 1–2, 1981, workshop at SUNY-Albany School of Library and Information Sciences; $29.50 plus $1.50 postage), available from Information Alternative, Box 5571, Chicago, IL 60680 (312-461-0890).

Other publications include *What Else You Can Do with a Library Degree*, edited by Betty-Carol Sellen, published by Neal-Schuman Publishers and Gaylord Brothers (Box 4901, Syracuse, NY 13221), for $14.95 plus 25¢ postage; *Fee-Based Information Services: A Study of a Growing Industry* by Lorig Marajian and Richard W. Boss (New York: R. R. Bowker, 1980, $24.95); *The Information Brokers: How to Start and Operate Your Own Fee-Based Service* by Kelly Warnken (New York: R. R. Bowker, 1981, $24.95); and *Information Brokering: A State-of-the-Art Report* by Gary M. Kaplan (Emerald Valley Publishing Co., 2715 Terrace View Dr., Eugene, OR 97405. Write for current list of other titles in the Business of Information series). Directories such as *Information Sources: The Membership Directory of the Information Industry Association*, *Library Resources Market Place*, and *Information Industry Market Place* might provide leads of possible organizations in which information skills can be applied. "Information Resource(s) Mangement—IRM" in the *Annual Review of Information Science and Technology* 17 (1982):228–266, provides a listing of associations and journals involved with IRM, as well as an extensive bibliography on the topic.

"A National Profile of Information Professionals" by Donald W. King et al. (*Bulletin of the American Society for Information Science* 6 [August 1980]:18–22) gives the results of a 1980 study funded by the National Science Foundation and carried out by the University of Pittsburgh School of Library and Information Science and King Research, Inc. *The Information Professional: Survey of an Emerging Field* published in 1981 by Marcel Dekker is based on the study.

"Careers in Online" is a new series in *Online*, starting with Vol. 7, November 1983. *Careers for Information Professionals* is a fact sheet from the ERIC Clearinghouse on Information Resources, Syracuse University School of Education, Syracuse, NY 13210. *Careers in Information*, edited by Jane F. Spivack (White Plains, N.Y.: Knowledge Industries, 1982), includes chapters on the work of information specialists, entrepreneurship in the information industry, and information professionals in the federal government, as well as guidance on finding a job and information on placements and salaries for the broader information field as well as librarianship. A new publication in 1983 by Neal-Schuman is *New Options for Librarians: Finding a Job in Related Fields*, edited by Betty-Carol Sellen and Dimi Berkner.

Job Hunting in General

Wherever information needs to be organized and presented to patrons in an effective, efficient, and service-oriented fashion, the skills of professional librarians can be applied, whether or not they are in traditional library settings. However, it will take considerable investment of time, energy, imagination, and money on the part of an individual before a satisfying position is created or obtained, in a conventional library or another type of information service. Usually, no one method or source of job hunting can be used alone. *Finding a Position: Strategies for Library School Graduates* by Robert F. Delzell gives useful information on job-searching procedures, what to expect from the employer, and what the employer expects from you. This is available as Occasional Paper No. 153 (April 1982) for $3 from Publications Office, Univ. of Illinois at Urbana-Champaign, 249 Armory Bldg., 505 E. Armory St., Champaign, IL 61820 (ISSN 0276 1769).

Public and school library certification requirements often vary from state to state; contact the state library agency for such information in a particular state. Certification requirements are summarized in *Certification of Public Libraries in the U.S.* (3rd ed., 1979) available from the ALA Library Administration and Management Association ($3). A summary of school library/media certification requirements by state is found in *Requirements for Certification*, edited by Elizabeth H. Woellner and published annually by the University of Chicago Press. State supervisors of school library media services may also be contacted for information on specific states; *see* Part 6 of this volume of *The Bowker Annual* for a list of these contact persons.

Civil service requirements either on a local, county, or state level often add another layer of procedures to the job search. Some civil service jurisdictions require written and/or oral examinations; others assign a ranking based on a review of credentials. Jobs are usually filled from the top candidates on a qualified list of applicants. Since the exams are held only at certain time periods and a variety of jobs can be filled from a single list of applicants (e.g., all Librarian I positions regardless of type of function), it is important to check whether a library in which one is interested falls under civil service procedures.

If one wishes a position in a specific subject area or in a particular geographic location, remember those reference skills to ferret information from directories and other tools regarding local industries, schools, subject collections, and so on. Directories such as the *American Library Directory*, *Subject Collections*, *Directory of Special Libraries and Information Centers*, *Directory of Health Sciences Libraries*, as well as state directories or other special subject areas, can provide a wealth of information for job seekers. Some students have pooled resources to hire a clipping service for a specific time period in order to get classified listings of library job openings for a particular geographic area.

Working as a substitute librarian or in temporary positions while looking for a regular job can provide valuable contacts and experience. A description of a corps of temporary library workers who tackle all types of jobs through a business called Pro Libra Associates, Inc. (Box 707, Maplewood, NJ 07040, 201-762-0070), can be found in *American Libraries* 12 (October 1981):540–541. Similar agencies that hire library workers for part-time or temporary jobs might be found in other geographic areas, such as C. Berger and Co., 0-North 469 Purnell St., Wheaton, IL 60187 (312-653-1115), in the Chicago area, and Gossage Regan Associates, 15 W. 44 St., New York, NY 10036 (212-869-3348), in the New York area. Part-time jobs are not always advertised; they are often found by canvassing local libraries and leaving applications.

For information on other job-hunting and personnel matters, please request a checklist of personnel materials available from the ALA Office for Library Personnel Resources, 50 E. Huron St., Chicago, IL 60611.

Placements and Salaries, 1982: Slowing Down

Carol L. Learmont

Associate Dean, School of Library Service, Columbia University, New York

Stephen Van Houten

Cataloger, Gustave L. and Janet W. Levy Library,
Mount Sinai Medical Center, New York

For this thirty-second annual report on placement and salaries of graduates of ALA-accredited library school programs, 64 of the 69 eligible schools responded to all or part of the questionnaire. One Canadian school and four U.S. schools (one in the Northeast, two in the Southeast, and one in the Midwest) did not participate.

In 1982 the average beginning level salary of both men and women was $16,583, based on 1,554 known full-time professional salaries reported by 4,050 graduates of 64 library school programs.

'Salaries for 1982 improved over those for 1981, but again fell below the increase in the cost of living. The 1982 salaries increased at the rate of 6 percent compared with 9.9 percent in 1981 and 8.4 percent in 1980. In 1982 the average (mean) beginning salary for women was $16,335, a 6 percent increase over 1981; and for men $17,641, a 7 percent increase. Median salaries were $16,000 for all graduates, $15,885 for women, and $16,500 for men (see Table 7). Table 12 shows that, for new graduates with relevant prior experience, the average beginning salary was $17,687, up from $17,014 in 1981; without experience, $15,248, up from $14,385 in 1981.

Among placement officers in the schools, 48 reported no major difficulty placing graduates in 1982; 6 reported major difficulty; 1 reported some difficulty. This was about the same as in 1981. The usual shortages of people with science, math, and engineering backgrounds are still with us. There continues to be a need for technical services people and, increasingly, for children's specialists. There are at least 228 temporary professional placements reported in 1982 compared with 255 in 1981 and 201 in 1980. On a percentage basis, the figures for 1981 and 1982 are almost the same. Once again, Canadian salaries are given in U.S. dollars. Nontraditional positions are found in the category "Other Information Specialties."

Placements

First professional degrees were awarded to 4,050 graduates by the 64 schools reporting in 1982 (see Table 1). In 1981 the 65 reporting schools awarded 4,512 first professional degrees; in 1980, 63 reporting schools awarded 4,396 degrees. In 1978 the average number of graduates of schools reporting was 88; in 1979, 84; in 1980, 70; in 1981, 69; in 1982, 63. The number of graduates continues to decline.

Table 1 shows permanent and temporary professional placements, as well as nonprofessional library placements and totals for the three. These are library or information-related positions. Table 1 also shows the number of graduates reported who were not in library positions or whose employment status was unknown at the beginning

Note: Adapted from *Library Journal,* September 15, 1983.

Table 1 / Status of 1982 Graduates, Spring 1983*

	No. of Graduates			Not in Library Positions			Empl. Not Known			Permanent Prof. Placements			Temp. Prof. Placements			Nonprof. Library Placements			Total in Library Positions		
	Women	Men	Total	Women	Men	Total	Women	Men	Total	Women	Men	Total	Women	Men	Total	Women	Men	Total	Women	Men	Total
United States	2767	602	3602	397	109	510	528	108	859	1588	327	1919	137	25	163	117	33	151	1842	385	2233
Northeast	896	212	1261	91	30	122	200	37	387	526	130	658	50	8	58	29	7	36	605	145	752
Southeast	472	83	600	61	19	80	90	14	147	300	48	349	12	0	12	9	2	12	321	50	373
Midwest	760	187	960	137	36	174	121	32	165	431	96	527	24	9	33	47	14	61	502	119	621
Southwest	256	40	296	35	7	42	42	4	46	163	21	184	8	3	11	8	5	13	179	29	208
West	383	80	485	73	17	92	75	21	114	168	32	201	43	5	49	24	5	29	235	42	279
Canada	336	102	448	47	20	69	38	5	44	188	56	247	49	13	65	14	8	23	251	77	335
All Schools	3103	704	4050	444	129	579	566	113	903	1776	383	2166	186	38	228	131	41	174	2093	462	2568

*Totals include graduates undifferentiated by sex.

of April 1983. Of these, 14 percent were known not to be in library positions compared with 13 percent in 1981 and 15 percent in 1980. In April 1983 the whereabouts of 22 percent were unknown compared with 23 percent in April 1982 and 19 percent in April 1981. Of the 1982 graduates, 63 percent were known to be employed either in professional or nonprofessional positions in libraries or information-related work, as were 64 percent of the 1981 graduates and 66 percent of the 1980 graduates. Of the 1982 graduates, 53 percent were known to be employed in permanent professional positions compared with 54 percent of the 1981 graduates and 57 percent of the 1980 graduates. Employment distribution for 2,063 of the 4,050 graduates is shown in Table 2, Table 3, and Table 11. In all, there were reportedly 2,166 full-time professional placements. Of the people finding professional jobs who reported how long they actively sought professional employment after getting their degrees, 562 (26 percent) reported searching for less than 90 days. There were 146 people (7 percent) who looked for 3–4 months, 93 (4 percent) who looked for 4–6 months, and 57 (3 percent) who looked for more than 6 months. A total of 501 people (23 percent) went back to their previous positions, and 561 (26 percent) found jobs before graduation. Nothing is known about 246 others (11 percent).

In 1982, 4 percent of the graduates were in nonprofessional library and related positions (Table I). In 1981 and 1980 these placements also represented 4 percent of the total. About 4 percent of the women and 4 percent of the men were in nonprofessional jobs. In 1981 it was the same. In 1980 it was 4 percent of the women and 6 percent of the men. The percentage of graduates in this category has hardly changed in recent years.

The percentage of placements by type of library or other information specialties in 1982 was similar to that of 1981 and 1980. College and university library placements dropped by 54 individuals, school libraries by 93, public libraries by 51, and other library agencies by 92. However, there were 103 professional placements that were not differentiated by type of library or related work. If we knew the type of work or library in which those 103 were placed, the picture might be significantly different. In the 1981 statistics there were 89 such undifferentiated positions.

Comparison of U.S. and Canadian placements appears in Table 5. Table 6, showing special placements, is self-explanatory and gives a rough picture of new-hire activity in various specialties in 1982.

Demand and Supply

A total of 54,378 positions was listed with 56 schools. The lowest number reported was 55; the highest was 5,100. The listings were for positions at all levels, and many were duplicated in several places. In 1981, 56 schools reported 55,677 vacancies. The average number reported for each school in 1982 was 971 compared with 994 in 1981 and 1,032 in 1980.

Increases in position listings in 1982 over 1981 ranging from 5 to 100 percent were reported by 13 schools. The median was 12 percent, with 18 schools reporting no significant change from 1981. A decline, ranging from 2 1/2 to 35 percent, was reported by 23 schools; the median was 15 percent. As indicated above, 6 placement officers reported major difficulty in placing 1982 graduates; 1 reported some difficulty; 48 reported no major difficulty. Thirteen placement officers thought that they had more difficulty placing graduates in 1982 than in 1981; 11 thought they had less difficulty; and 35 thought they had about the same level of difficulty both years.

Table 2 / Placements by Type of Library*

Schools	Public			Elementary & Secondary			College & Univ.			Special			Other Specialties			Total		
	Women	Men	Total	Women	Men	Total	Women	Men	Total	Women	Men	Total	Women	Men	Total	Women	Men	Total
Alabama	11	3	14	8	0	8	7	1	8	6	1	7	0	0	0	32	5	37
Albany	11	0	11	9	2	11	2	4	6	0	1	1	1	0	1	26	8	34
Arizona	5	0	5	2	1	3	5	0	5	2	1	3	2	0	2	16	2	18
Atlanta	3	0	3	1	0	1	5	3	8	3	0	3	0	0	0	12	4	16
Brigham Young	4	3	7	1	1	2	3	1	4	3	1	4	0	0	0	12	5	17
British Columbia	8	3	11	1	1	2	2	0	2	10	1	11	2	0	2	23	5	28
Buffalo	4	0	4	4	2	6	9	1	10	3	0	3	1	0	1	21	4	25
California (Berk.)	7	1	8	0	0	0	8	2	10	8	0	8	5	0	5	31	4	34
California (LA)	4	1	5	3	0	3	4	0	4	7	1	8	3	1	4	21	3	24
Case Western	8	1	9	5	1	6	7	3	10	6	1	7	5	2	7	41	11	52
Catholic	9	2	11	3	0	3	3	6	9	10	8	18	2	0	2	27	16	43
Chicago	3	1	4	0	0	0	7	2	9	5	1	6	1	0	1	16	4	20
Clarion	10	1	11	4	1	5	1	0	1	4	3	7	3	1	4	23	6	29
Columbia	6	1	7	2	0	2	6	0	6	12	2	14	1	0	1	27	3	30
Dalhousie	5	0	5	1	0	1	5	1	6	6	0	6	0	0	0	17	1	18
Denver	9	0	9	8	1	9	3	2	5	9	4	13	3	0	3	32	7	39
Drexel	2	3	5	6	1	7	11	1	12	20	3	23	9	5	14	50	13	63
Emory	7	4	11	6	0	6	9	1	10	3	1	4	0	0	0	25	5	30
Florida State	12	1	13	14	0	14	7	2	9	2	2	4	0	0	0	36	5	41
Hawaii	3	2	5	7	0	7	3	0	3	4	3	7	3	0	3	20	5	25
Illinois	12	2	14	1	0	1	11	3	14	5	1	6	0	0	0	29	6	35
Indiana	17	1	18	7	2	9	17	5	22	4	2	6	1	4	5	46	14	60
Iowa	6	2	8	3	0	3	7	4	11	1	1	2	2	1	3	19	8	27
Kent State	18	3	21	7	2	9	10	2	12	9	3	12	0	0	0	44	10	54
Kentucky	12	3	15	6	0	6	14	2	16	9	0	9	3	0	3	44	5	49
Long Island	5	2	7	5	1	6	2	0	2	5	0	5	1	0	1	18	3	21
Louisiana State	5	0	5	7	1	8	6	2	8	6	0	6	3	0	3	27	3	30
Maryland	4	2	6	5	0	5	6	2	8	1	1	2	0	0	0	16	5	21
McGill	0	1	1	1	0	1	8	2	10	8	4	12	3	1	4	20	8	28
Michigan	16	1	17	9	2	11	22	4	26	18	1	19	2	0	2	67	8	75
Minnesota	2	2	4	5	1	6	2	4	6	14	0	14	0	0	0	23	7	30

Missouri	8	1	5	4	2	6	3	2	5	8	0	8	2	0	2	26	6	32
Montreal	4	1	5	0	0	0	7	5	12	10	3	13	3	2	5	25	11	36
North Carolina	8	2	10	5	0	5	3	2	5	7	1	8	3	0	3	26	5	31
North Carolina Central	2	0	2	4	0	4	7	2	5	0	0	0	0	0	0	13	2	15
Northern Illinois	3	1	4	3	1	3	0	0	0	2	0	2	0	0	0	9	2	11
Northern Texas State	7	0	7	9	0	10	8	6	14	6	1	6	0	0	0	30	7	37
Oklahoma	5	1	5	6	1	6	4	0	4	6	0	4	0	0	0	21	1	22
Peabody	7	2	8	6	0	6	12	1	13	6	1	7	1	0	2	30	2	32
Pittsburgh	10	4	12	5	0	5	8	3	10	8	4	12	4	1	4	40	9	49
Pratt	4	4	8	12	0	12	1	1	4	14	0	16	0	0	0	27	8	36
Queens	5	0	5	4	0	4	0	1	1	3	1	3	1	0	1	9	1	10
Rhode Island	7	3	10	1	1	1	3	1	4	4	0	5	0	0	0	19	6	25
Rosary	18	3	20	3	1	2	2	1	3	9	1	9	0	0	0	38	4	42
Rutgers	26	3	29	5	2	15	15	9	24	21	2	23	2	0	2	72	16	88
St. Johns	2	1	3	5	0	3	3	0	3	2	1	4	0	0	0	11	5	16
San Jose	6	2	8	5	0	5	3	0	3	3	1	3	2	0	2	20	3	23
Simmons	24	1	25	6	1	28	28	11	39	33	5	38	2	1	3	91	18	109
South California	0	0	0	0	0	3	3	1	3	5	1	6	0	0	0	11	2	14
South Carolina	4	0	4	14	0	1	1	0	2	4	0	5	2	1	3	24	2	26
Southern Connecticut	16	1	17	5	1	1	1	1	1	5	0	5	0	0	0	29	2	31
South Florida	4	1	5	9	1	3	3	0	4	2	0	3	2	0	0	19	3	23
Southern Mississippi	5	0	5	10	0	2	2	3	5	2	2	4	0	2	2	21	5	26
Syracuse	3	2	5	7	0	2	2	2	4	1	0	1	1	0	1	21	7	28
Tennessee	5	1	6	2	0	8	8	2	12	3	0	3	7	2	9	18	5	23
Texas	6	4	10	8	0	4	4	2	4	11	1	12	5	0	5	34	8	42
Texas Woman's	13	0	13	13	0	9	4	0	13	5	0	5	0	0	0	35	0	35
Toronto	18	3	21	0	1	3	9	4	5	27	3	30	3	0	3	62	11	73
Washington	3	2	5	4	0	3	3	2	5	4	3	4	0	0	0	21	4	25
Wayne	2	0	2	6	1	5	1	0	1	2	1	3	1	0	1	12	2	14
Western Michigan	12	2	12	6	1	4	5	0	2	2	1	3	0	1	0	28	2	30
Western Ontario	20	4	25	2	5	3	4	8	12	12	5	17	2	0	2	43	22	64
Wisconsin (Madison)	10	3	13	8	1	3	3	3	6	4	2	6	2	0	2	26	9	35
Wisconsin (Milwaukee)	1	0	1	1	0	1	0	3	3	3	0	2	0	0	0	7	3	10
Total	**496**	**90**	**588**	**319**	**39**	**358**	**367**	**138**	**505**	**418**	**80**	**501**	**87**	**23**	**111**	**1,776**	**383**	**2,166**

*From 1951 through 1966 these tabulations were for "special and other placements" in all kinds of libraries. From 1967 to 1979 these figures include only placements in library agencies that do not clearly belong to one of the other three groups. In the 1980 through 1982 report these figures include the sum of responses to placements in special libraries and in other information specialties.

Table 3 / Placements by Type of Library, 1951-1982

Year	Public	School	College & Universities	Other Library Agencies	* Total
1951-1955†	2,076 (33%)	1,424 (23%)	1,774 (28%)	1,000 (16%)	6,264
1956-1960†	2,057 (33)	1,287 (20)	1,878 (30)	1,105 (17)	6,327
1961-1965	2,876 (30)	1,979 (20)	3,167 (33)	1,600 (17)	9,622
1966-1970	4,773 (28)	3,969 (23)	5,834 (34)	2,456 (15)	17,032
1971	999 (29)	924 (26)	1,067 (30)	513 (15)	3,503
1972	1,117 (30)	987 (26)	1,073 (29)	574 (15)	3,751
1973	1,180 (31)	969 (25)	1,017 (26)	712 (18)	3,878
1974	1,132 (31)	893 (24)	952 (26)	691 (19)	3,668
1975	994 (30)	813 (24)	847 (25)	714 (21)	3,368
1976	764 (27.1)	655 (23.2)	741 (26.3)	657 (23.2)	2,817
1977	846 (28.4)	673 (22.6)	771 (25.9)	687 (23.1)	2,977
1978	779 (26.1)	590 (19.8)	819 (27.4)	798 (26.7)	2,986
1979	778 (27.4)	508 (17.9)	716 (25.3)	835 (29.4)	2,837
1980	659 (27.1)	473 (19.5)	610 (25.1)	687 (28.3)	2,429
1981	642 (27.3)	451 (19.2)	556 (23.6)	704 (29.9)	2,353
1982	588 (28.5)	358 (17.4)	505 (24 5)	612 (29.7)	2,063

*See footnote to Table 2.
†Figures for individual years are reported in preceding articles in this series.

Several placement officers thought that lack of geographic mobility (or a reluctance to move) accounted for the difficulty many had finding professional jobs. The economic squeeze at local, county, and state levels was blamed for lack of jobs, especially in regions outside major metropolitan areas.

Salaries

The salary statistics reported include only full-time annual salaries and exclude such variables as vacations and other fringe benefits, which may be part of total compensation. They do not reflect differences in hours worked per week. Such information might provide more precise comparability, but such data are probably beyond the needs of most library schools and of the profession. In any case, the validity of this analysis rests on comparable statistics collected since 1951.

All of the 64 schools reporting supplied some salary data. Not all schools could provide all the information requested, nor could they supply it for all employed graduates. Schools were asked to exclude data for graduates in irregular placements such as those for graduates from abroad returning to posts in their homelands, appointments in religious orders or elsewhere where remuneration is in the form of some combination of salary plus living, and all salaries for part-time employment. These exclusions were added to the number of salaries not known or not reported. As a result, there is known salary information for 1,554 of the 1982 graduates (1,259 women, 292 men, and 3 undifferentiated by sex). This represents 72 percent of the known placements and 38 percent of all graduates reported. In 1981 there was salary information on 71 percent of known placements, representing 38 percent of the number of graduates reported. Salary data as reported by the 64 schools are contained in Table 4 and summarized in Table 7 in U.S. dollars.

Average (Mean) Salaries

The 1982 average salary for all graduates was $16,583, an increase of $950 (6 percent) over the 1981 average of $15,633. For women the average was $16,335, and for men the

Table 4a / Placements and Salaries of 1982 Graduates—Summary by Region*

	Place-ments	Salaries Known			Low Salary ($)			High Salary ($)			Average Salary ($)			Median Salary ($)		
		Women	Men	Total	Women	Men	Total	Women	Men	Total	Women	Men	Total	Women	Men	Total
United States	1,919	1,138	256	1,397	4,940	8,000	4,940	40,815	45,000	45,000	16,317	17,540	16,545	15,600	16,434	15,800
Northeast	658	393	106	500	8,190	11,000	8,190	27,600	45,000	45,000	16,140	18,284	16,595	15,600	16,895	16,000
Southeast	349	207	40	248	4,940	8,000	4,940	25,400	22,000	25,400	15,365	15,329	15,361	15,000	15,000	15,000
Midwest	527	288	65	353	8,800	8,591	8,591	33,336	34,020	34,020	15,969	16,918	16,143	15,000	15,500	15,000
Southwest	184	117	18	135	10,000	12,279	10,000	29,000	26,753	29,000	17,071	17,166	17,084	16,500	15,500	16,500
West	201	133	27	161	9,600	12,000	9,600	40,815	33,700	40,815	18,416	19,640	18,640	18,000	18,000	18,000
Canada	247	121	36	157	10,044	11,340	10,044	22,680	29,160	29,160	16,495	18,360	16,923	16,200	18,144	17,010
All Schools	**2,166**	**1,259**	**292**	**1,554**	**4,940**	**8,000**	**4,940**	**40,815**	**45,000**	**45,000**	**16,335**	**17,641**	**16,583**	**15,885**	**16,500**	**16,000**

*Totals include salaries undifferentiated by sex.

Table 4b / Placements and Salaries of 1982 Graduates*

Schools	Place-ments	Salaries Known			Low Salary ($)			High Salary ($)			Average Salary ($)			Median Salary ($)		
		Women	Men	Total	Women	Men	Total	Women	Men	Total	Women	Men	Total	Women	Men	Total
Alabama	37	29	5	34	12000	11186	11186	20238	16600	20238	16212	15157	16057	16681	16500	16500
Albany	34	16	7	23	10000	12000	10000	20000	17000	20000	14624	15082	14763	14340	15200	14980
Arizona	18	15	2	17	13500	15200	13500	21500	26753	26753	16894	20977	17374	16000	15200	16000
Atlanta	16	10	4	14	11000	12000	11000	25400	16500	25400	15419	13375	14835	14688	14011	14000
Brigham Young	17	10	3	13	13800	14000	13800	21900	25029	25400	16304	17680	16621	15084	19900	15084
British Columbia	28	5	0	5	16524	0	16524	18630	0	18630	17593	0	17593	17172		17172
Buffalo	25	18	4	22	10500	19900	10500	22032	32000	32000	15378	23014	16767	14690	20400	15000
California (Berk.)	34	27	3	30	12000	15384	12000	25500	26400	26400	17573	20728	17889	18000	18600	18000
California (L.A.)	24	13	3	16	14500	17000	14500	25012	32000	32000	18924	22533	19601	18192	19750	18192
Case Western	52	13	6	19	12096	13500	12096	33336	24000	33336	16588	14417	15902	14800	16500	14800
Catholic	43	25	16	41	12100	13000	12100	27000	45000	45000	18717	22277	20106	18000	16250	18500
Chicago	20	12	3	15	13000	13000	13000	20160	21700	21700	15330	17067	15677	14400	18200	15000
Clarion	29	16	1	17	8700	16250	8700	25000	16250	25000	15418	16250	15467	15314	16250	15600
Columbia	30	23	3	26	13500	17400	13500	23885	19500	23885	16203	18367	16453	16500	18200	16700
Dalhousie	18	9	0	9	14985	0	14985	22275	0	22275	16617	0	16617	16200		16200
Denver	39	30	7	37	12000	14500	12000	40815	33700	40815	18912	23615	19802	18500	24000	18500
Drexel	63	43	13	56	12684	13000	12684	26500	34500	34500	17158	19158	17622	16000	16500	16000
Emory	30	22	4	26	12810	14124	12810	19800	14580	19800	15116	14341	14997	14592	16160	14500
Florida State	41	14	5	19	11796	13000	11796	18500	18000	18500	14804	15598	15013	14536	15506	15000
Hawaii	25	16	3	19	12000	12000	12000	25000	18000	25000	17681	15473	17332	16764	16418	16764
Illinois	35	24	4	28	11780	12500	11780	30700	18000	30700	15502	14500	15359	14100	12500	14100
Indiana	60	30	8	38	8865	13500	8865	20280	34020	34020	14379	17635	15065	14000	14500	14500

Table 4b / Placements and Salaries of 1982 Graduates* (cont.)

Schools	Place-ments	Salaries Known			Low Salary ($)			High Salary ($)			Average Salary ($)			Median Salary ($)		
		Women	Men	Total	Women	Men	Total	Women	Men	Total	Women	Men	Total	Women	Men	Total
iowa	27	14	5	19	12000	12000	12000	18000	32000	32000	14823	19002	15923	14800	16000	14800
Kent State	54	32	7	39	11000	12260	11000	23700	28000	28000	15809	18713	16330	15000	19977	15408
Kentucky	49	16	2	18	8000	8000	8000	20000	15000	20000	13677	11500	13435	13452	8000	13452
Long Island	21	11	3	14	10000	15500	10000	23000	30000	30000	16723	21067	17654	18000	17700	17700
Louisiana State	30	14	2	16	10000	15000	10000	19000	15000	19000	14403	15000	14477	14000	15000	14000
Maryland	21	11	4	15	12500	16200	12500	24786	29000	29000	18075	19359	18417	18000	16200	17436
McGill	28	9	3	12	15390	16200	15390	20250	17010	20250	16740	16470	16673	17010	16200	16200
Michigan	75	46	4	50	11500	14000	11500	32000	22000	32000	16674	16500	16660	16000	15000	16000
Minnesota	30	14	7	21	12700	14400	12700	25600	23500	25600	16258	17871	16129	16000	16770	16836
Missouri	32	24	5	29	10058	8591	8591	24000	22242	24000	15234	13067	14860	14500	11502	14300
Montreal	36	13	7	20	15957	17820	15957	21060	21240	21240	18118	19728	18682	17820	20544	17820
North Carolina	31	25	5	30	12000	13000	12000	24000	18825	24000	16039	15805	16000	14917	15400	14917
North Carolina Central	15	8	1	9	12700	16889	12700	17752	16889	17752	15357	16889	15527	14256	16889	16000
Northern Illinois	11	8	2	10	8800	11000	8800	22000	11000	22000	15463	11000	14570	16000	11000	16000
North Texas State	37	24	6	30	12504	14000	12504	20927	17450	20927	16468	16267	16428	16500	*	16500
Oklahoma	22	0	1	1		15000	15000		15000	15000	0	15000	15000	0	15000	15000
Peabody	32	18	2	20	7300	12000	7300	21000	20000	21000	14054	16000	14249	13400	12000	13400
Pittsburgh	49	17	3	20	11900	11500	11500	18000	15500	18000	14176	13220	14033	14500	12660	14500
Pratt	36	13	4	18	15600	15000	15000	27600	20000	27600	19263	17209	18653	18750	16434	18000
Queens	10	8	1	9	14000	11000	14000	24000	14000	24000	17687	14000	17277	16746	14000	16746
Rhode Island	25	18	6	24	8190	11000	8190	20800	30000	30000	14840	17200	15430	14000	14000	14000
Rosary	42	26	2	28	10500	19000	10500	22022	29500	29500	15417	24250	16048	15072	19000	15500
Rutgers	88	66	16	82	9100	12500	9100	26000	24000	26000	16366	16759	16443	15500	17000	15500
St. Johns	16	11	5	16	14000	13164	13164	22000	23000	23000	17265	17893	17461	16000	16500	16000
San Jose	23	16	2	18	17500	15000	15000	29000	18000	29000	21844	16500	21250	20000	15000	20000
Simmons	109	61	13	74	15618	13000	15000	24500	23100	24500	15246	16369	15443	15000	16000	15000
South California	14	8	2	11	12000	19000	12000	23920	24000	24000	19655	21500	20140	15000	19000	19000
South Carolina	26	23	2	25	9000	13000	9000	20000	17050	20000	16254	15025	16156	15927	13000	15927
Southern Connecticut	31	28	1	29	4940	13750	4940	22950	17500	22950	14553	17500	14655	14700	17500	14750
South Florida	23	19	3	23	12000	14000	12000	23000	22000	23000	15909	18083	16197	15000	18500	16000
Southern Mississippi	26	20	5	25	10000	13880	10000	23000	22000	23000	14755	16220	15048	13500	15000	14200
Syracuse	28	8	6	14	12000	14000	12000	23000	24000	24000	14613	18230	16163	15299	15000	15500
Tennessee	23	3	2	5	12576	12279	12279	21600	17500	21600	16492	16100	16335	16000	14700	15299
Texas	42	32	7	39	11064	14700	11064	25000	23500	25000	17231	17777	17329	15000	18000	16900
Texas Woman's	35	32	0	32	10044		10044	29000		29000	18615		18615	17700		17700
Toronto	73	61	11	72	9600	11340	9600	22400	29160	29160	16027	18042	16335	16200	15795	16200
Washington	25	13	4	17	9750	13500	9750	19920	17000	19920	16065	14936	15799	16000	14244	15600
Wayne	14	10	2	12	12150	19926	12150	33000	32000	33000	21846	25963	22532	21000	19926	21000
Western Michigan	30	9	1	10	10000	17500	10000	19400	17500	19400	15157	17500	15391	14500	17500	15600
Western Ontario	64	24	15	39	12960	13650	12960	22680	23085	23085	16440	18332	17168	16200	18630	17010
Wisconsin (Madison)	35	23	6	29	12150	13650	12000	25500	19477	25500	15494	16507	15704	14616	15500	15000
Wisconsin (Milwaukee)	10	3	3	6	13500	13500	13500	25500	14500	25500	19500	13833	16667	19500	13500	13500

*Includes placements and salaries undifferentiated by type of library or by sex.

Table 5 / U.S. and Canadian Placements Compared
(Percents may not add to 100 because of rounding)

	Placements	Public Libraries	School Libraries	College & University Libraries	Special Libraries	Other Info. Specialties
All Schools*	2063	588 (28.5%)	358 (17.4%)	505 (24.5%)	501 (24.3%)	111(5.4%)
Women	1687	496 (29.4)	319 (18.9)	367 (21.8)	418 (24.8)	87 (5.2)
Men	370	90 (24.3)	39 (10.5)	138 (37.3)	80 (21.6)	23 (6.2)
U.S. Schools*	1827	520 (28.5)	346 (18.9)	450 (24.6)	412 (22.6)	99 (5.4)
Women	1451	428 (29.5)	307 (21.2)	312 (21.5)	329 (22.7)	75 (5.2)
Men	315	79 (25.1)	32 (10.2)	118 (37.5)	65 (20.6)	21 (6.7)
Canadian Schools*	236	68 (28.8)	12 (5.1)	55 (23.3)	89 (37.7)	12 (5.1)
Women	178	55 (30.9)	5 (2.8)	35 (19.7)	73 (41.)	10 (5.6)
Men	55	11 (20.)	7 (12.7)	20 (36.4)	15 (27.3)	2 (3.6)

*Includes individuals undifferentiated by sex.

Table 6 / Special Placements*

	Women	Men	Total
Government jurisdiction (U.S. and Canada)			
State and provincial libraries	53	7	60
Other government agencies (except USVA hospitals)	36	14	50
National libraries	33	8	41
Armed Services libraries (domestic)	5	1	6
Overseas agencies (incl. Armed Services)	2	2	4
Total government jurisdiction	129	32	161
Library science			
Advanced study	25	7	32
Teaching	13	7	20
Children's services—school libraries	138	19	157
Children's services—public libraries	114	7	121
Business, finance, industrial, corporate	71	13	84
Medical	67	5	72
Law	57	14	71
Youth Services—school libraries	58	5	63
Science and technology	46	15	61
Audio-visual and media centers	42	16	58
Youth services (public libraries)	36	9	45
Rare books, manuscripts, archives	32	9	41
Systems analysis; automation	26	8	34
Information Services (non-library)	28	5	33
Commuications industry (publishing, TV, etc.)	22	6	28
Religion (seminars, theological school)	17	10	27
Databases (publishing, servicing)	22	3	25
Records management	19	6	25
Hospitals (inc. USVA hospitals)	21	3	24
Indexing	17	7	24
Art and Museum	21	2	23
Historical agencies	13	7	20
Research and development	14	6	20
Outreach activities and services	15	2	17
Theater, motion pictures, dance, music	10	5	15
Youth services—other	13	1	14
Bookstore	9	3	12
Services to the handicapped	8	4	12
Social sciences	6	4	10
Pharmaceutical	8	1	9
Freelance	6	1	7
Networks and consortia	6	1	7
Children's services—other	6		6
International agencies	6		6
Maps	3	2	5
Correctional institutions	1	3	4
Genealogical	1	3	4
Documentation	2		2
Environmental	1	1	2
Professional associations	1	1	2
Spanish Speaking Centers	2		2
Architecture		1	1
Editor		1	1
Women's organization	1		1
Total Special Placements	**1,153**	**255**	**1,408**

*Includes special placements in all types of libraries.

Table 7 / Salary Data Summarized

	Women	Men	Total
Average (Mean) Salary	$16335	$17641	$16583
Median Salary	15885	16500	16000
Individual Salary Range	4940-40815	8000-45000	4940-45000

Table 8 / Average Salary Index for Starting Library Positions, 1967–1982

Year	Library Schools	Fifth-Year Graduates	Average Beginning Salary	Increase in Average	Beginning Index
1967	40	4,030	$7,305	—	—
1968	42	4,625	7,650	$355	105
1969	45	4,970	8,161	501	112
1970	48	5,569	8,611	450	118
1971	47	5,670	8,846	235	121
1972	48	6,079	9,248	402	127
1973	53	6,336	9,423	175	129
1974	52	6,370	10,000	617	137
1975	51	6,010	10,594	554	145
1976	53	5,415	11,149	555	153
1977	53	5,467	11,894	745	163
1978	62	5,442	12,527	633	171
1979	61	5,139	13,127	600	180
1980	63	4,396	14,223	1,096	195
1981	65	4,512	15,633	1,410	214
1982	64	4,050	16,583	950	227

Table 9 / High Salaries by Type of Library

	Public			School			College & Univ.			Special			Other		
	Women	Men	Total	Women	Men	Total	Women	Men	Total	Women	Men	Total	Women	Men	Total
$10,000									1	1	1	1	1		
11,000				1	1	1	1	1				2		2	
12,000		3	3	1		1				2	2	1		1	
13,000	1	3	4	1	1	2	2	4	6	1	1	2			
14,000	3	3	6	2	1	3	7	4	11	2	1	3	3	1	4
15,000	14	6	20	1	3	4	7	6	13	3	4	7	2	1	3
16,000	10	3	13	5	2	7	8	3	11	2	2	4	3	1	4
17,000	8	7	15	2	1	3	8	6	14	6	5	11			
18,000	7	6	13	7	1	8	5	3	8	9	2	11		1	1
19,000	3	1	4	7	3	10	3	1	4	4	3	7	3	1	4
20,000	6	2	8	6		6	5	3	8	5	1	6	4		4
21,000	2		2	2		2	9	2	11	3	4	7	2	1	3
22,000	2	2	4	6	3	9	1		1	4	2	6			
23,000				2	1	3	1	2	3	3	2	5	2		2
24,000	1	1	2	2		2				4	1	5	2	3	5
25,000	2		2	4	1	5	1		1	6		6	3		3
26,000		1	1	1	1	2	1		1	2		2	1	1	
27,000										1			1		1
28,000											1	1			
29,000		1	1	1		1		2	2	2	2	4			
30,000		1	1				1	1	2						
31,000															
32,000				1	1	1	2		2						
33,000				2	1	2									
34,000					1	1	1	1		1		1			
40,000				1		1									
45,000											1	1			

Table 10 / Low Salaries by Type of Library

	Public			School			College & Univ.			Special			Other		
	Women	Men	Total	Women	Men	Total	Women	Men	Total	Women	Men	Total	Women	Men	Total
$ 4,000							1		1						
5,000															
6,000															
7,000							1		1						
8,000	2	1	3	1	1	2	1		1	1		1			
9,000	1		1	3		3				1		1			
10,000	7		7	1		1	1		1	3		3	2		2
11,000	7	3	10	4	1	5	4	1	5	3		3	1		1
12,000	16	7	23	9		9	9	2	11	5	2	7	2		2
13,000	6	5	11	5	1	6	10	11	21	8	1	9	2		2
14,000	7	5	12	6	1	7	13	13	26	10	3	13	3	2	5
15,000	8	5	13	8	3	11	9	4	13	11	7	18	5	2	7
16,000	2	4	6	3	2	5	5	6	11	5	5	10	3	2	5
17,000	2	6	8	3	1	4	4		4	2	6	8	1		1
18,000	1	2	3	5	1	6				7	3	10	2	1	3
19,000				1	4	5				1	1	2	2	1	3
20,000				4	1	5	1	3	4		2	2	5		5
21,000											2	2		1	1
22,000		1	1	2		2									
23,000											2	2	1		1
24,000										1	1	2			
25,000				1	1	2							1		1
26,000				1		1									
27,000															
28,000															
29,000		1	1												
30,000								1	1						
31,000															
32,000				1		1	1		1					1	1
33,000				1		1									

average was $17,641, a difference of $1,306. Annual changes in average salaries since 1967 are shown in Table 8, which also includes a beginning salary index figure that may be compared with the Annual Cost of Living Index (COL) reports issued by the government.

The COL index for 1982 was 289.1, an increase of 16.7 points over the 1981 figure of 272.4, a gain of 6.1 percent. The comparable increase in the beginning salary index is 13 points, 3.7 points below the increase in the cost of living.

In 1982 the range in the category of average salaries for women was from a low of $13,677 to a high of $21,846, a difference of $8,169; for men the range was $11,000 to $25,963, a $14,963 difference. In the 60 schools that reported average salaries for both men and women, the women's average was highest in 22 schools, and the men's average was highest in 38 schools.

Table 11 summarizes the salaries of men and women in the different types of libraries and other information specialties. The average salary is higher for men (the difference ranging from $1,075 to $2,590) in every category.

Median Salaries

In 1982 the median for all graduates was $16,000, an increase of $1,000 over the 1981 median of $15,000. The median for women was $15,885; for men, $16,500. Of the 59 schools reporting on both men and women, the median salary for women was higher in 26 schools; for men, in 31; and it was the same in 2.

Table 11 / Comparison of Salaries by Type of Library

	Placements	Salaries Known			Low Salary ($)			High Salary ($)			Average Salary ($)			Median Salary ($)		
		Women	Men	Total	Women	Men	Total	Women	Men	Total	Women	Men	Total	Women	Men	Total
Public Libraries																
United States	520	334	66	400	8190	8000	8000	25025	30000	30000	14816	15967	15006	14500	15384	14748
Northeast	176	113	23	136	8190	11000	8190	24786	30000	30000	14704	16530	15013	14500	15506	14700
Southeast	96	58	13	71	10000	8000	8000	21195	18825	21195	14252	14463	14291	14000	14580	14124
Midwest	156	106	16	122	9750	12000	9750	19400	29500	29500	14363	16412	14632	14060	14000	14060
Southwest	45	29	4	33	11064	12279	11064	22572	18700	22572	15642	16485	15744	15700	16960	15885
West	47	28	10	38	12000	14000	12000	25025	18000	25025	17292	15706	16422	16075	15000	16032
Canada	68	39	8	47	12150	12960	12150	22680	20250	22680	16355	16751	16875	17010	15390	17010
All Schools	588	373	74	447	8190	8000	8000	25025	30000	30000	14977	16052	15155	14800	15390	15000
School Libraries																
United States	346	234	25	259	8800	8591	8591	40815	34020	40815	17691	19217	17838	17000	19000	17200
Northeast	98	60	9	69	9000	13000	9000	26500	19900	26500	16007	16467	16067	15600	15500	15600
Southeast	85	65	1	66	11000	22000	11000	23000	22000	23000	16365	22000	16451	16168	22000	16168
Midwest	84	46	10	56	8800	8591	8591	33336	34020	34020	19507	19360	19481	19000	19000	19000
Southwest	48	36	3	39	12000	15000	12000	25500	26753	26753	18594	19301	18648	17500	16150	17500
West	31	27	2	29	9600	25029	9600	40815	33700	40815	20329	29365	20953	19920	25029	20250
Canada	12	1	4	5	19440	11340	11340	19440	23085	23085	19440	18934	19035	19440	20250	20250
All Schools	358	235	29	264	8800	8591	8591	40815	34020	40815	17699	19178	17861	17000	19000	17200
College/Univ. Libraries																
United States	450	235	93	328	4940	11502	4940	30700	34700	34700	15696	16808	16012	15300	15400	15300
Northeast	138	76	36	112	11300	12750	11300	23885	34700	34700	16190	17877	16732	16000	16895	16000
Southeast	101	45	18	63	4940	12000	4940	21600	20000	21600	14560	14778	14622	14500	14160	14500
Midwest	133	65	25	90	8865	11502	8865	30700	32000	32000	15233	16053	15461	15000	15000	15000
Southwest	41	22	8	30	10000	14000	10000	25000	21000	25000	16027	16431	16134	15500	16500	15500
West	37	27	6	33	12672	13500	12672	21900	29000	29000	17047	20133	17608	17000	17000	17000
Canada	55	18	13	31	13527	14985	13527	21060	29160	29160	16696	19221	17755	15390	18630	17010
All Schools	505	253	106	359	4940	11502	4940	30700	34700	34700	15768	17104	16162	15390	16000	15500
Special Libraries																
United States	412	272	53	327	8000	12000	8000	29280	45000	45000	17255	19925	17681	16800	18200	17000
Northeast	180	118	26	145	9500	12000	9500	27000	45000	45000	17400	20841	18011	17000	18200	17100
Southeast	54	32	8	41	8000	14484	8000	25400	22000	25400	16134	17142	16327	15000	16500	16000
Midwest	85	59	9	68	10058	15000	10058	25300	28000	28000	16961	20068	17372	16500	19926	16650
Southwest	41	25	3	28	12600	12000	12600	29000	23500	29000	16711	17900	16839	16000	15200	15400
West	52	38	7	45	12000	12000	12000	29280	29000	29280	18561	20387	18845	18000	20106	18500
Canada	89	51	10	61	10044	15795	10044	22275	22822	22822	16146	18319	16502	16200	17010	16200
All	501	323	63	388	8000	12000	8000	29280	45000	45000	17080	19670	17496	16524	18000	17000
Other libraries																
United States	99	51	16	68	10000	14000	10000	27600	32000	32000	18204	19578	18573	18000	19000	18000
Northeast	46	23	12	35	10500	14800	10500	27600	24000	27600	17687	18688	18030	16800	16750	16800
Southeast	8	6	0	6	11500		11500	19500		19500	16103		16103	15895		15895
Midwest	21	6	2	8	10000	14000	10000	24000	24000	24000	16549	19000	17162	14496	14000	14496
Southwest	7	5	0	5	18000	0	18000	25012	0	25000	20800	0	20800	20000		20000
West	17	11	2	14	13992	19000	13992	25012	32000	32000	20155	25500	21000	20000	19000	20000
Canada	12	7	1	8	15795	18144	15795	21250	18144	21250	18680	18144	18613	20250	18144	18144
All Schools	111	58	17	76	10000	14000	10000	27600	32000	32000	18262	19494	18577	18000	19000	18144

Salary Ranges

The 1982 range of individual salaries again shows a wide range between the high and low salaries. Table 12 shows the effects of experience and no experience on salary levels. For the purposes of the survey, prior experience, if known, consisted of work of a professional and/or subject nature of a year or more. The range in 1982 (see Table 7) was from a low of $4,940 to a high of $45,000, a difference of $40,060. The low salaries were in a college library and a public library; the high salaries, in a school library and a special library. In 1982 the range of high salaries was from $15,000 tp $45,000, a difference of $30,000. Thirteen schools showed highs of $30,000 or more (5 women, 10 men). The median high salary for all graduates was $22,250; for women, $22,975; for men, $22,000. For the ninth year, women show the highest median. The median high salary in 1981 was $24,200, with a range of salary from $11,000 to $37,000. Thirteen salaries were $30,000 or more (8 women, 5 men) in 1981. Distribution of high salaries by type of library is shown in Table 9 and in different context in Table 11.

In 1982 the category "Specialist Libraries" accounted for 27 percent of the 63 highest salaries reported, and the category "Other Information Specialties" accounted for 10 percent. In 1981 "Special Libraries" accounted for 30 percent of the 63 highest salaries, and "Other" for 8 percent. School libraries accounted for 37 percent, down from 44 percent in 1981; academic libraries accounted for 16 percent, up from 13 percent in 1981; and public libraries had an 11 percent share, up from 5 percent. The positions were scattered geographically and included 27 states, the District of Columbia, and 5 provinces. New York provided 6 of the high-salaried positions; California, 5; Illinois, 4; Louisiana, Michigan, Texas, and Alberta, 3 each.

The lowest beginning-level salaries offered to 1982 graduates ranged from $4,940 to $16,524, with the median low salary of $12,000 for all graduates. Of the 60 schools reporting low salaries for men and women, 7 reported higher low salaries for women, 47 reported higher low salaries for men, and 6 schools reported the same.

Based on reports from 63 schools, public libraries once again accounted for the majority of the lowest salaries, 42 percent, down from 50 percent in 1981. Academic libraries accounted for 25 percent, up from 17 percent in 1981. School libraries accounted for 15 percent, up from 14 percent in 1981. Special libraries accounted for 13 percent and other information specialties for 4 percent, down from 14 percent and 5 percent respectively in 1981.

There was no significant pattern in the geographic location of the placements in 29 states, Puerto Rico, and 3 provinces. New York led with the 7 lowest salary placements; Illinois had 6; Texas and California, 4 each; North Carolina, Ohio, Michigan, Pennsylvania, and Ontario had 3 each. Distribution of low salaries is shown in Tables 10 and 11.

Next Year?

Placement officers in 26 schools see no change in the number of job vacancies reported so far in 1983 compared with 1982. An increase is predicted by 16, and 13 think there will be a decrease. Placement officers in 14 schools think that 1983 graduates will have the same difficulty finding professional positions as did the 1982 graduates; 31 expect less difficulty; 15 expect more difficulty.

Table 12 / Effects of Experience on Salaries

	Salaries without Previous Experience (53 Schools)			Salaries with Previous Experience (53 Schools)		
	Women	Men	Total	Women	Men	Total
Number of Positions	404	99	504	588	120	710
Range of Low Salaries	$7300-23633	$8000-21060	$7300-23633	$4940-25400	$8591-32000	$4940-30000
Mean (Average)	12918	14280	12821	14180	17598	14372
Median	10058	16200	10000	14000	8591	14000
Range of High Salaries	$12500-25012	$8000-24000	$8000-25012	$15876-33000	$15000-45000	$15876-45000
Mean (Average)	18330	16439	18467	22684	24151	25094
Median	17000	16200	17000	32000	22242	32000
Range of Average Salaries	$12167-13500	$8000-13833	$8000-13750	$13677-22500	$13834-15500	$13755-22500
Mean (Average)	15127	15683	15248	17205	20073	17687
Median	13006	16200	12255	18426	13834	18198

Salaries for 1983 will probably be stronger by about $1,000 on the average according to 20 schools; another 19 schools foresee no significant change.

The responses to a question about types of libraries that are noticeably increasing or decreasing the number of positions to be filled are summarized as follows by number of schools reporting:

Schools Reporting	Increasing	Decreasing
Public libraries	11	7
School libraries	6	15
Academic libraries	10	10
Special libraries	15	13

Several schools reported that filling positions that required such undergraduate majors as math and sciences was less of a problem in 1982 than it has been. This is a heartening change, even though there probably will continue to be a shortage for the next few years. The same backgrounds that have been in short supply for years are still in short supply: business, math, science, engineering, languages, and law. Two schools found it difficult to fill jobs that required a second master's degree. Cataloging is still highest on the list of specializations for which an increasing demand is seen, followed by information science and systems, health science, law, and children's work.

Schools continue to pay more and more attention to seeking out nontraditional placements. Some mention was made of the return of recruiters from public libraries, a bright note on an otherwise rather dull employment scene shaped by budget cuts and the depressed economy.

A trend worth noting and watching, although peripheral to this salary survey, is the increasing number of foreign students being trained in the United States and Canada and returning to their homelands. Foreign students from at least 33 countries are represented in the figures for graduates although they could not be included in the salary statistics.

The authors thank all of the reporting schools for their continuing cooperation in making this report possible.

Accredited Library Schools

This list of graduate schools accredited by the American Library Association was issued in October 1983. A list of more than 400 institutions offering both accredited and nonaccredited programs in librarianship appears in the thirty-sixth edition of the *American Library Directory* (Bowker, 1983).

Northeast: Conn., D.C., Mass., Md., N.J., N.Y., Pa., R.I.

Catholic University of America, School of Lib. and Info. Science, Washington, DC 20064. Raymond F. Vondran, Acting Dean. 202-635-5085.

Clarion University, College of Lib. Science, Clarion, PA 16214. Elizabeth A. Rupert, Dean. 814-226-2271.

Columbia University, School of Lib. Service, New York, NY 10027. Richard L. Darling, Dean. 212-280-2291.

Drexel University, School of Lib. and Info. Science, Philadelphia, PA 19104. Guy Garrison, Dean. 215-895-2474.

Long Island University, C. W. Post Center, Palmer School of Lib. and Info. Science, Greenvale, NY 11548. Ralph J. Folcarelli, Dean. 516-299-2855, 2856.

Pratt Institute, Grad. School of Lib. and Info. Science, Brooklyn, NY 11205. Nasser Sharify, Dean. 212-636-3702.

Queens College, City University of New York, Grad. School of Lib. and Info. Studies, Flushing, NY 11367. Richard J. Hyman, Dir. 212-520-7194.

Rutgers University, School of Communication, Info., and Lib. Studies, New Brunswick, NJ 08903. James D. Anderson, Chpn. 201-932-7917.

St. John's University, Div. of Lib. and Info. Science, Jamaica, NY 11439. Mildred Lowe, Dir. 212-990-6161, ext. 6200.

Simmons College, Grad. School of Lib. and Info. Science, Boston, MA 20115. Robert D. Stueart, Dean. 617-738-2225.

Southern Connecticut State University, School of Lib. Science and Instructional Technology, New Haven, CT 06515. Edward J. Jennerich, Dean. 203-397-4532.

State University of New York at Albany, School of Lib. and Info. Science, Albany, NY 12222. Richard S. Halsey, Dean. 518-455-6288.

State University of New York at Buffalo, School of Info. and Lib. Studies, Buffalo, NY 14260. George S. Bobinski, Dean. 716-636-2411.

Syracuse University, School of Info. Studies, Syracuse, NY 13210. Evelyn H. Daniel, Dean. 315-423-2911.

University of Maryland, College of Lib. and Info. Services, College Park, MD 20742. Anne S. MacLeod, Acting Dean. 301-454-5441.

University of Pittsburgh, School of Lib. and Info. Science, Pittsburgh, PA 15260. Thomas J. Galvin, Dean. 412-624-5230.

University of Rhode Island, Grad. Lib. School, Kingston, RI 02881. Lucy V. Salvatore, Acting Dean. 401-792-2947.

Southeast: Ala., Fla., Ga., Ky., Miss., N.C., S.C., Tenn.

Atlanta University, School of Lib. and Info. Studies, Atlanta, GA 30314. Lorene B. Brown, Dean. 404-681-0251, ext. 230.

Emory University, Div. of Lib. and Info. Management, Atlanta, GA 30322. A. Venable Lawson, Dir. 404-329-6840.

Florida State University, School of Lib. and Info. Studies, Tallahassee, FL 32306. Harold Goldstein, Dean. 904-644-5775.

North Carolina Central University, School of Lib. Science, Durham, NC 27707. Benjamin F. Speller, Acting Dean. 919-683-6485.

University of Alabama, Grad. School of Lib. Service, University, AL 35486. James D. Ramer, Dean. 205-348-4610.

University of Kentucky, College of Lib. and Info. Science, Lexington, KY 40506-0027. Timothy W. Sineath, Dean. 606-258-8876.

University of Mississippi, Grad. School of Lib. and Info. Science, University, MS 38677. Steven B. Schoenly, Acting Dir. 601-232-7440.

University of North Carolina, School of Lib. Science, Chapel Hill, NC 27514. Edward G. Holley, Dean. 919-962-8366.

University of North Carolina at Greensboro, Dept. of Lib. Science/Educational Technology, Greensboro, NC 27412. Keith C. Wright, Chpn. 919-379-5100.

University of South Carolina, College of Lib. and Info. Science, Columbia, SC 29208. F. William Summers, Dean. 803-777-3858.

University of South Florida, Grad. Dept. of Lib., Media and Info. Studies, Tampa, FL 33620. John A. McCrossan, Chpn. 813-974-3520.

University of Southern Mississippi, School of Lib. Service, Hattiesburg, MS 39406. Onva K. Boshears, Jr., Dean. 601-266-4228.

University of Tennessee, Knoxville, Grad. School of Lib. and Info. Science, Knoxville, TN 37996-4330. Ann E. Prentice, Dir. 615-974-2148.

Vanderbilt University, George Peabody College for Teachers, Dept. of Lib. and Info. Science, Nashville, TN 37203. Edwin S. Gleaves, Chpn. 615-322-8050.

Midwest: Iowa, Ill., Ind., Kans., Mich., Minn., Mo., Ohio, Wis.

Ball State University, Dept. of Lib. and Info. Science, Muncie, IN 47306. Ray R. Suput, Chpn. 317-285-7180, 7189.

Case Western Reserve University, Matthew A. Baxter School of Info. and Lib. Science, Cleveland, OH 44106. Phyllis A. Richmond, Dean. 216-368-3500.

Indiana University, School of Lib. and Info. Science, Bloomington, IN 47405. Herbert S. White, Dean. 812-335-2848.

Kent State University, School of Lib. Science, Kent, OH 44242. A. Robert Rogers, Dean. 216-672-2782.

Northern Illinois University, Dept. of Lib. Science, DeKalb, IL 60115. Cosette N. Kies, Chpn. 815-753-1733.

Rosary College, Grad. School of Lib. and Info. Science, River Forest, IL 60305. Richard Tze-chung Li, Dean. 312-366-2490.

University of Chicago, Grad. Lib. School, Chicago, IL 60637. W. Boyd Rayward, Dean. 312-962-8272.

University of Illinois, Grad. School of Lib. and Info. Science, 1407 W. Gregory, 410 DKH, Urbana, IL 61801. Charles H. Davis, Dean. 217-333-3280.

University of Iowa, School of Lib. Science, Iowa City, IA 52242. Carl F. Orgren, Dir. 319-353-3644.

University of Michigan, School of Lib. Science, Ann Arbor, MI 48109. Russell E. Bidlack, Dean. 313-764-9376.

University of Minnesota, Lib. School, 117 Pleasant St. S.E., Minneapolis, MN 55455. George D'Elia, Dir. 612-373-3100.

University of Missouri, Columbia, School of Lib. and Info. Science, Columbia, MO 65211. Edward P. Miller, Dean. 314-882-4546.

University of Wisconsin-Madison, Lib. School, Madison, WI 53706. Jane B. Robbins-Carter, Dir. 608-263-2900.

University of Wisconsin-Milwaukee, School of Lib. and Info. Science, Milwaukee, WI 53201. Mohammed M. Aman, Dean. 414-963-4707.

Wayne State University, Div. of Lib. Science, Detroit, MI 48202. Edith B. Phillips, Coord. 313-577-1825.

Southwest: Ariz., La., Okla., Tex.

Louisiana State University, School of Lib. and Info. Science, Baton Rouge, LA 70803. Kathleen M. Heim, Dean. 504-388-3158.

North Texas State University, School of Lib. and Info. Sciences, Denton, TX 76203. Dewey E. Carroll, Dean. 817-565-2445.

Texas Woman's University, School of Lib. Science, Denton, TX 76204. Brooke E. Sheldon, Dean. 817-387-2418.

University of Arizona, Grad. Lib. School, Tucson, AZ 85721. Ellen Altman, Dir. 602-626-3565.

University of Oklahoma, School of Lib. Science, Norman, OK 73019. Sylvia G. Faibisoff, Dir. 405-325-3921.

University of Texas at Austin, Grad. School of Lib. and Info. Science, Austin, TX 78712-7576. Ronald E. Wyllys, Acting Dean. 512-471-3821.

West: Calif., Colo., Hawaii, Utah, Wash.

Brigham Young University, School of Lib. and Info. Sciences, Provo, UT 84602. Nathan M. Smith, Dir. 801-378-2977.
San Jose State University, Div. of Lib. Science, San Jose, CA 95192. Robert E. Wagers, Interim Dir. 408-277-2292.
University of California-Berkeley, School of Lib. and Info. Studies, Berkeley, CA 94720. Michael K. Buckland, Dean. 415-642-1464.
University of California-Los Angeles. Grad. School of Lib. and Info. Science, Los Angeles, CA 90024. Robert M. Hayes, Dean. 213-825-4351.
University of Denver, Grad. School of Libnshp. and Info. Management, Denver, CO 80208. Bernard M. Franckowiak, Dean. 303-753-2557.
University of Hawaii, Grad. School of Lib. Studies, Honolulu, HI 96822. Miles M Jackson, Dean. 808-948-7321.
University of Southern California, School of Lib. and Info. Management, Los Angeles, CA 90089-0031. Roger C. Greer, Dean. 213-743-2548.

University of Washington, Grad. School of Lib. and Info. Science, Seattle, WA 98195. Margaret Chisholm, Acting Dir. 206-543-1794.

Canada

Dalhousie University, School of Lib. Service, Halifax, N.S. B3H 4H8. Norman Horrocks, Dir. 902-424-3656.
McGill University, Grad. School of Lib. Science, Montreal, P.Q. H3A 1Y1. Hans Möller, Dir. 514-392-5930.
Université de Montréal, Ecole de bibliothéconomie, Montréal, P.Q. H3C 3J7. Richard K. Gardner, Dir. 514-343-6044.
University of Alberta, Faculty of Lib. Science, Edmonton, Alta. T6G 2J4. William Kurmey, Dean. 403-432-4578.
University of British Columbia, School of Libnshp., Vancouver, B.C. V6T 1W5. Basil Stuart-Stubbs, Dir. 604-228-2404.
University of Toronto, Faculty of Lib. and Info. Science, Toronto, Ont. M5S 1A1. Katherine H. Packer, Dean. 416-978-3234.
University of Western Ontario, School of Lib. and Info. Science, London, Ont. N6G 1H1. William J. Cameron, Dean. 519-679-3542.

Library Scholarship Sources

For a more complete list of the scholarships, fellowships, and assistantships offered for library study, see *Financial Assistance for Library Education* published annually by the American Library Association.

American Library Association. (1) The David H. Clift Scholarship of $3,000 is given to a varying number of U.S. or Canadian citizens who have been admitted to accredited library schools. For information, write to: Staff Liaison, David H. Clift Scholarship Jury, ALA, 50 E. Huron St., Chicago, IL 60611; (2)

the Louise Giles Minority Scholarship of $3,000 is given to a varying number of minority students who are U.S. or Canadian citizens and have been admitted to accredited library schools. For information, write to: Staff Liaison, Louise Giles Minority Scholarship Jury, ALA, 50 E. Huron St., Chicago, IL

60611; (3) the F. W. Faxon Scholarship of $3,000 is given to a U.S., Canadian, or foreign student who has been admitted to an accredited library school. Scholarship includes ten-week expenses-paid internship at F. W. Faxon in Westwood, Massachusetts. For information, write to: Staff Liaison, F. W. Faxon Scholarship, ALA, 50 E. Huron St., Chicago, IL 60611; (4) the ACRL Doctoral Dissertation Fellowship of $1,000 for a student who has completed all coursework in the area of academic librarianship; and (5) the Samuel Lazerow Fellowship of $1,000 for a librarian currently working in acquisitions or technical services in an academic or research library. For information, write to: Sandy Whiteley, Program Officer, ACRL/ALA, 50 E. Huron St., Chicago, IL 60611; (6) the Sarah C. N. Bogle Travel Fund of varying amounts for a varying number of librarians attending an international conference for the first time. For information, write to: Exec. Dir., International Relations Committee, American Library Association, 50 E. Huron St., Chicago, IL 60611.

American-Scandinavian Foundation. Fellowships and grants for 25 to 30 students, in amounts from $1,500 to $7,500, for advanced study in Denmark, Finland, Iceland, Norway, or Sweden. For information, write to: Exchange Div., American-Scandinavian Foundation, 127 E. 73 St., New York, NY 10021.

American Society for Information Science. A scholarship of $1,000 for active doctoral study in information science. For information, write to: Research Committee Chpn., ASIS, 1010 16 St. NW, Washington, DC 20036.

Association for Library and Information Science Education. A varying number of research grants of $2,500 (maximum) for members of ALISE. For information, write to: Janet Phillips, Exec. Secy., ALISE, 471 Park Lane, State College, PA 16801.

Association of Jewish Libraries. A grant of $250 for graduate study. For information, write to: A. Metz, Braude Lib., Temple Beth El, 70 Orchard Ave., Providence, RI 02906.

Beta Phi Mu. (1) The Sarah Rebecca Reed Scholarship of $1,500 each for a varying number of persons accepted in an ALA-accredited library program; (2) the Frank B. Sessa Scholarship of $750 each for a varying number of Beta Phi Mu members for continuing education; (3) the Harold Lancour Scholarship of $1,000 each for a varying number of students for graduate study in a foreign country related to the applicant's work or schooling. For information, write to: Exec. Secy., Beta Phi Mu, Grad. School of Lib. and Info. Science, Univ. of Pittsburgh, Pittsburgh, PA 15260.

Canadian Library Association. (1) The Howard V. Phalin-World Book Graduate Scholarship in Library Science of $2,500; (2) the H. W. Wilson Scholarship of $2,000; and (3) the Elizabeth Dafoe Scholarship of $1,750 are given to a Canadian citizen or landed immigrant to attend an accredited Canadian library school. For information, write to: Scholarships and Awards Committee, Canadian Lib. Assn., 151 Sparks St., Ottawa, Ont. K1P 5E3, Canada.

Catholic Library Association. (1) Rev. Andrew L. Bouwhuis Scholarship of $1,500 for a person with a B.A. degree who has been accepted in an accredited library school. (Award based on financial need and proficiency.) (2) World Book-Childcraft Awards: one scholarship of a total of $1,000 to be distributed among no more than four recipients for a program of continuing education. Open to CLA members only. For information, write to: Scholarship Committee, Catholic Lib. Assn., 461 W. Lancaster Ave., Haverford, PA 19401.

Information Exchange System for Minority Personnel. Scholarship of $500, intended for minority students, for graduate study. For information, write to: Dorothy M. Haith, Chpn., Clara Stanton Jones School, Box 668, Fort Valley, GA 31030.

Medical Library Association. (1) Varying number of scholarships of $2,000 each for minority students, for graduate study in medical librarianship. (2) Grants of varying amounts for continuing education for medical librarians with an MLS and two years' professional experience. Open to MLA members only. For information, write to: Scholarship Committee, Medical Lib. Assn., Suite 3208 919 N. Michigan Ave., Chicago, IL 60611.

The Frederic G. Melcher Scholarship (administered by Association of Library Service to Children, ALA). Two scholarships of $4,000 each for a U.S. or Canadian citizen admitted to an accredited library school who plans to work with children in school or public libraries. For information, write to: Exec. Secy., Assn. of Lib. Service to Children, ALA, 50 E. Huron St., Chicago, IL 60611.

Mountain Plains Library Association. Ten grants of $500 (maximum) each for residents of the association area. Open only to MPLA members with at least two years of membership. For information, write to: Joseph R. Edelen, Jr., MPLA Exec. Secy., Univ. of South Dakota Lib., Vermillion, SD 57069.

Natural Sciences and Engineering Research Council. (1) A varying number of scholarships of $10,500 each and (2) a varying number of scholarships of varying amounts for postgraduate study in science librarianship and documenta-

tion for a Canadian citizen or landed immigrant with a bachelor's degree in science or engineering. For information, write to: J. H. Danis, Scholarships Officer, Programs Branch, Natural Sciences and Engineering Research Council, Ottawa, Ont. K1A OR6, Canada.

New England Library Association. A scholarship of $500 for graduate study. For information, write to: Ronald B. Hunte, Exec. Secy., NELA, 292 Great Neck Rd., Acton, MA 01720.

REFORMA, the National Association of Spanish-Speaking Librarians in the U.S. A scholarship of $1,000 to attend an ALA-accredited program. For information, write to: Ali Mattei, Box 25605, TWU Station, Denton, TX 76204.

Special Libraries Association. (1) Two $5,000 scholarships for U.S. or Canadian citizens, accepted by an ALA-accredited library education program, who show an aptitude for and interest in special libraries. (2) One $1,000 scholarship for a U.S. or Canadian citizen with an MLS and an interest in special libraries who has been accepted in an ALA-accredited Ph.D. program. (3) One $1,000 scholarship for a U.S. or foreign student with an MLS and an interest in special libraries who has been accepted in an ALA-accredited Ph.D. program. For information, write to: Scholarship Committee, SLA, 235 Park Ave. S., New York, NY 10003. (4) Two scholarships of $2,500 each for minority students with an interest in special libraries. Open to U.S. or Canadian citizens only. For information, write to: Positive Action Program for Minority Groups, c/o SLA.

Library Scholarship and Award Recipients, 1983

AASL Distinguished Library Service Award for School Administrators. For exemplary leadership in the development and support of library media programs at the building and district levels. *Offered by:* ALA American Association of School Librarians. *Winner:* James Thompson, Supt. of Schools, Blue Valley U.S.D., Stanley, Kans.

AASL/Baker & Taylor President's Award—$2,000. For demonstrating excellence and providing an outstanding national or international contribution to school librarianship and school library development. *Offered by:* ALA American Association of School Librarians. *Donor:* Baker & Taylor. *Winner:* Rachel Wingfield DeAngelo, professor emeritus, Univ. of Hawaii, Honolulu.

AASL/SIRS Intellectual Freedom Award—$1,000. For a school library media specialist who has upheld principles of intellectual freedom. *Offered by:* ALA American Association of School Librarians and Social Issues Resources Series, Inc. *Winner:* Patsy R. Scales, librarian, Middle School, Greenville, S.C.

ACRL Academic/Research Librarian of the Year Award—$2,000. For an outstanding national or international contribution to academic and research librarianship and library development. *Offered by:* ALA Association of College and Research Libraries. *Donor:* Baker & Taylor. *Winner:* Richard M. Dougherty, director, University Library, Univ. of Michigan, Ann Arbor.

ACRL Doctoral Dissertation Fellowship. For research in academic librarianship. *Offered by:* ALA Association of College and Research Libraries. *Winner:* Stanton F. Biddle, assoc. dir. for planning and development, University Library, State Univ. of New York, Buffalo.

ALA Honorary Life Membership Award. *Offered by:* American Library Association. *Winners:* Johnny Carson, Jack Dalton, Clara Stanton Jones, The Honorable Claiborne Pell.

ALISE Doctoral Student Forum Award. For an outstanding doctoral dissertation. *Offered by:* Association for Library and Information Science Education. *Winners:* Elfreda Chatman, Univ. of California, Berkeley, for "Information Diffusion among the Working Poor"; Edna F. Reid, Univ. of Southern California, for "An Analysis of Terrorism Literature: A Bibliometric and Content Analysis Study"; and Adeline W. Wilkes, Florida State Univ., for "A Study of Managerial Functions Performed by Beginning Academic Librarians and Their Perception of Their Preparation for These Responsibilities."

ALISE Research Grant Award—$1,500—$2,500. For a project that reflects ALISE goals and objectives. *Offered by:* Association for Library and Information Science Education. *Winners:* John V. Richardson, Jr., Univ. of California, Los Angeles, for "Primary Source Materials for a Critical Biography of Pierce Butler"; and Alvin M. Schrader, Univ. of Alberta, Canada, for "A Bibliometric Study of the *Journal of Education for Librarianship.*"

ALISE Research Paper Competition—$500. For a research paper concerning any aspect of librarianship or information studies by a member of ALISE. *Offered by:* Association for Library and Information Science Education. *Winners:* Nancy Van House, Univ. of California, Berkeley, for "The Return on the Investment in Library Education"; and Wayne A. Wiegand, Univ. of Kentucky, for "Establishing ALA Headquarters in Chicago: An Analysis of the Forces Which Brought the Association to the Midwest in 1909."

ALTA Literacy Award. For an outstanding contribution to the extirpation of illiteracy. *Offered by:* ALA American Library Trustee Association. *Winner:* George McLean.

ALTA Major Benefactors Honor Awards. *Offered by:* ALA American Library Trustee Association. *Winners:* The Fremont Area Foundation, Fremont, Mich.; Gerber Baby Food Fund, Gerber Products Co., Fremont, Mich.; Raymond Bryan, Sr. (posthumous); and Donald Graham.

ASCLA Exceptional Achievement Award. For recognition of leadership and achievement in the areas of library cooperation and state library development. *Offered by:* ALA Association of Specialized & Cooperative Library Agencies. *Winner:* Forrest H. Carhart, Jr.

ASCLA Exceptional Service Award. For exceptional service to ASCLA or any of its component areas of service, namely, services to patients, the homebound, medical, nursing, and other professional staff in hospitals, and inmates; demonstrating professional leadership, effective interpretation of program, pioneering activity, or significant research or experimental projects. *Offered by:* ALA Association of Specialized & Cooperative Library Agencies. *Winner:* Brenda Vogel.

Joseph L. Andrews Bibliographic Award. For a significant contribution to legal bibliographical literature. *Offered by:* American Association of Law Libraries (AALL). *Winner:* Ted L. McDorman for *Maritime Boundary Delimitation: An Annotated Bibliography.*

Armed Forces Librarians Achievement Citation. For significant contributions to the development of armed forces library service and to organizations encouraging an interest in libraries and reading. *Offered by:* Armed Forces Librarians Section, ALA Public Library Association. *Winner:* Mary L. Shaffer, former director, Army Library, The Pentagon.

Beta Phi Mu Award—$500. For distinguished service to education for librarianship. *Offered by:* ALA Awards Committee. *Donor:* Beta Phi Mu Library Science Honorary Association. *Winner:* J. Periam Danton.

Blackwell North America Resources Section Scholarship Award (formerly National Library Service Resources Section Publication Award). Presented to the author/authors of an outstanding monograph, published article, or original paper on acquisitions pertaining to college or university libraries. *Offered by:* ALA Resources and Technical Services Division, Resources Section. *Donor:* Blackwell North America. *Winner:* Phyllis J. Van Orden.

Rev. Andrew L. Bouwhuis Scholarship—$1,500. For a person with a B.A. degree who has been accepted in an accredited library school. (Award is based on financial need and proficiency.) *Offered by:* Catholic Library Association. *Winner:* Mary Frances Rufe, Ephrata, Pa.

CASLIS Award for Special Librarianship in Canada. *Offered by:* Canadian Assn. of Special Libraries and Information Services. *Winner:* Nita Cooke, Edmonton, Alta.

CIS/GODORT/ALA Documents to the People Award—$1,000. For effectively encouraging the use of federal documents in support of library services. *Offered by:* ALA Government Documents Round Table. *Donor:* Congressional Information Service, Inc. *Winner:* Nancy Cline.

CLA Dafoe Scholarship—$1,750. For a Canadian citizen or landed immigrant to attend an accredited Canadian library school. *Offered by:* Canadian Library Association. *Winner:* Joann Hamilton, Winnipeg, Man.

CLA Outstanding Service to Librarianship Award. *Offered by:* Canadian Library Association. *Winner:* Sheila Egoff, School of Librarianship, Univ. of British Columbia.

CLA Research & Development Award—$1,000. For theoretical and applied research that advances library and information science. *Offered by:* Canadian Library Association. *Winner:* John Leide, Graduate School of Library Science, McGill Univ.

CLR Fellowships. For a list of the recipients for the 1982–1983 academic year, see the report from the Council on Library Resources, Inc., in Part 2 of this *Bowker Annual.*

CLR Management Interim Program. *Offered by:* Council on Library Resources, Inc. *Winners:* Jill B. Fatzer, Susan F. Rhee, Gordon S. Rowley, Helen H. Spalding, and Sarah E. Thomas.

CSLA Award for Outstanding Congregational Librarian. For distinguished service to the congregation and/or community through devotion to the congregational library. *Offered by:* Church and Synagogue Library Association. *Winner:* Carolyn Zimmerman, librarian, Hatboro Baptist Church, Hatboro, Pa.

CSLA Award for Outstanding Congregational Library. For responding in creative and innovative ways to the library's mission of reaching and serving the congregation and/or the wider community. *Offered by:* Church and Synagogue Library Association. *Winner:* Pearce Memorial Library/Media Center of Monte Vista Christian Church, Albuquerque, N.M.

CSLA Award for Outstanding Contribution to Librarianship. For providing inspiration, guidance, leadership, or resources to enrich the field of church or synagogue librarianship. *Offered by:* Church and Synagogue Library Association. *Winner:* Not awarded in 1983.

CLSA Distinguished Service Award for School Administrators. *Offered by:* Canadian School Library Association. *Winner:* Virginia Andrew, Winnipeg, Manitoba.

Francis Joseph Campbell Citation. For an outstanding contribution to the advancement of library service to the blind. *Offered by:* Section on Library Service to the Blind and Physically Handicapped of the Association of Specialized and Cooperative Library Agencies. *Winner:* Raymond Kurzweil.

Canadian Library Trustees Merit Award. For exceptional service as a trustee in the library field. *Offered by:* Canadian Library Trustees Association. *Winner:* Frances Corbett, Saint John, New Brunswick.

James Bennett Childs Award. For a distinguished contribution to documents librarianship. *Offered by:* ALA Government Documents Round Table. *Winner:* Bernard M. Fry.

David H. Clift Scholarship—$3,000. For a worthy student to begin a program of library education at the graduate level. *Offered by:* ALA Awards Committee, Standing Committee on Library Education. *Winners:* Aron D. Roberts and Hope Mayo.

Cunningham Fellowship. A six-month grant and travel expenses in the United States and Canada for a foreign librarian. *Offered by:* Medical Library Association. *Winner:* Palled Fangappa Mahefh (India).

John Cotton Dana Award. For exceptional support and encouragement of special librarianship. *Offered by:* Special Libraries Association. *Winner:* Arleen N. Somerville.

John Cotton Dana Library Public Relations Awards. *Offered by:* American Library Association. *Winners:* Council for Florida Libraries, Tallahassee, Fla.; Gustavus Adolphus Library, Saint Peter, Minn.; Pennsylvania State Library, Harrisburg, Pa.; Salt Lake City Public Library, Salt Lake City, Utah; Travis Air Force Base, Calif.; Tulsa City-County Library, Tulsa, Okla.; Union Public School District, Tulsa, Okla.

Dartmouth Medal. For achievement in creating reference works of outstanding quality and significance. *Offered by:* ALA Reference and Adult Services Division. *Winner:* Congressional Information Service, Inc., Washington, D.C.

Melvil Dewey Medal. For recent creative professional achievement of a high order, particularly in library management, library training, cataloging and classification, and the tools and techniques of librarianship. *Offered by:* ALA Awards Committee. *Donor:* Forest Press. *Winner:* Edward G. Holley.

Janet Doe Lectureship. *Offered by:* Medical Library Association. *Winner:* Susan Crawford, Ph.D., dir., School of Medicine Library, and professor, Biomedical Communications, Washington Univ., St. Louis, Mo.

Ida and George Eliot Prize—$100. For an essay published in any journal in the preceding calendar year that has been judged most effective in furthering medical librarianship. *Offered by:* Medical Library Association. *Winner:* Louise Darling for vol. 1 of *The Handbook of Medical Library Practice,* 4th ed. (Medical Library Assn.).

Facts on File Award—$1,000. For a librarian who has made current affairs more meaningful to adults. *Offered by:* ALA Reference and Adult Services Division.

Winner: Barbara Harris, Brown County Lib., Wisconsin.

Frederick Winthrop Faxon Scholarship—$3,000. *Offered by:* American Library Association. *Winner:* Margaret A. Warner Curl.

Gale Research Company Financial Development Award. *Offered by:* American Library Association. *Donor:* Gale Research Co. *Winner:* Altoona Area Public Library, Altoona, Pa.

Louise Giles Minority Scholarship—$3,000. For a worthy student who is a U.S. or Canadian citizen and is also a member of a principal minority group. *Offered by:* ALA Awards Committee, Office for Library Personnel Resources Advisory Committee. *Winners:* Curtis L. Kendrick and Patricia Mei Yung Wong.

Murray Gottlieb Prize—$100. For the best unpublished essay submitted by a medical librarian on the history of some aspect of health sciences or a detailed description of a library exhibit. *Offered by:* Medical Library Association. *Winner:* Charles Gordon Forrest, Univ. of Illinois, Chicago.

Grolier Award for Research in School Librarianship in Canada—$1,000. For theoretical or applied research that advances the field of school librarianship. *Offered by:* Canadian Library Trustees Association. *Winner:* Ken Haycock, Vancouver, B.C.

Grolier Foundation Award—$1,000. For an unusual contribution to the stimulation and guidance of reading by children and young people through high school age, for continuing service, or one particular contribution of lasting value. *Offered by:* ALA Awards Committee. *Donor:* Grolier Foundation. *Winner:* Zena Sutherland.

Grolier National Library Week Award—$1,000. For the best plan for a public relations program. *Awarded by:* National Library Week Committee of the

American Library Association. *Donor:* Grolier Educational Corp. *Winner:* Virginia Library Association.

Bailey K. Howard–World Book Encyclopedia–ALA Goal Award—$5,000. To support programs that recognize, advance, and implement the goals and objectives of the American Library Association. *Donor:* World Book-Childcraft International, Inc. *Winner:* ALA Reference and Adult Services Division for "Adult Services in the Eighties."

John Phillip Imroth Memorial Award for Intellectual Freedom—$500. For a notable contribution to intellectual freedom and remarkable personal courage. *Offered by:* ALA Intellectual Freedom Round Table. *Donor:* Intellectual Freedom Round Table. *Winner:* Nat Hentoff.

ISI Scholarship—1,000. For graduate study leading to a doctorate in library or information science. *Offered by:* Institute for Scientific Information/Special Libraries Association. *Winner:* Stephen Foster Cummings.

Information Industry Association Hall of Fame Award. For leadership and innovation in furthering the progress of the information industry. *Offered by:* Information Industry Association. *Winners:* Philip Estridge, president, Entry Systems Division, International Business Machines Corp., and Daniel Fylstra, chairman and chief executive officer, Visicorp.

Information Industry Association Honorary Professional Member Award. For long-term services to the information industry. *Offered by:* Information Industry Association. *Winner:* Forest Woody Horton, Jr.

JMRT Professional Development Grant. *See* 3M Company Professional Development Grant.

J. Morris Jones–World Book Encyclopedia–ALA Goal Award—$5,000. To support programs that recognize,

advance, and implement the goals and objectives of the American Library Association. *Donor:* World Book-Childcraft International, Inc. *Winner:* Nine ALA divisions for ALA Divisional Leadership Enhancement Program.

William T. Knox Outstanding Information Manager Award. For excellence in managing information resources or for a distinctive contribution to the information management field. *Offered by:* Associated Information Managers. *Winner:* Dr. Craig M. Cook, former principal, Arthur Young & Co., Washington, D.C.

LITA/Gaylord Award for Achievement in Library and Information Technology. For distinguished leadership, notable development or application of technology, superior accomplishments in research or education or original contributions to the literature of the field. *Offered by:* Library and Information Technology Association. *Winner:* Lawrence F. Buckland, Inforonics, Inc.

LRRT Research Award—$500. To encourage excellence in library research. *Offered by:* ALA Library Research Round Table. *Winner:* Not awarded in 1983.

Samuel Lazerow Fellowship—$1,000. For outstanding contributions to acquisitions or technical services in an academic or research library. *Offered by:* ALA Association of College and Research Libraries and the Institute for Scientific Information. *Winner:* Denise D. Bedford, asst. to the director for technical services, Stanford Univ. Libraries.

Joseph W. Lippincott Award—$1,000. For distinguished service to the profession of librarianship, such service to include outstanding participation in the activities of professional library associations, notable published professional writing, or other significant activity on behalf of the profession and its aims. *Offered by:* ALA Awards Committee.

Donor: Joseph W. Lippincott. *Winner:* Russell Bidlack.

MLA Continuing Education Award—$350. For continuing education courses in medical librarianship. *Offered by:* Medical Library Association. *Winners:* Janet Ann Kubinec, Columbia Univ., and Dana M. Neeley, West Texas State Univ., Canyon, Tex.

MLA Minority Scholarship—$2,000. For a minority student entering an ALA-accredited library school. *Offered by:* Medical Library Association. *Winner:* Katherine Love, Drexel Univ., Philadelphia. Pa.

MLA President's Award. For an outstanding contribution to medical librarianship. *Offered by:* Medical Library Association. *Winner:* Nina Matheson for her work on the *AAMC Report* (Assn. of American Medical Colleges).

John P. McGovern Award Lectureship. *Offered by:* Medical Library Association. *Winner:* Lois DeBakey, Ph.D., professor of scientific communication, Baylor College of Medicine, Baylor, Tex.

Margaret Mann Citation. For outstanding professional achievement in the area of cataloging and classification. *Offered by:* ALA Resources and Technical Services Division/Cataloging and Classification Section. *Winner:* Frances Hinton.

Allie Beth Martin Award—$2,000. For an outstanding librarian. *Offered by:* ALA Public Library Association. *Donor:* Baker & Taylor. *Winner:* Hardy Franklin, Washington, D.C., Public Library.

Frederic G. Melcher Scholarship—$4,000. For young people who wish to enter the field of library service to children. *Offered by:* ALA Association for Library Service to Children. *Winners:* Eileen F. King and Judith Ann Mann.

Isadore Gilbert Mudge Citation. For a distinguished contribution to reference librarianship. *Offered by:* ALA Reference and Adult Services Division. *Winner:* Charles A. Bunge.

Gerd Muehsam Award—$100 + $250 travel expenses. For the best paper by a graduate student in library or information science on a topic dealing with art librarianship or visual resource curatorship. *Offered by:* Art Libraries Society of North America. *Winner:* Nancy M. Pike, Univ. of Wisconsin.

Noyes Award—$250 and travel expenses to MLA annual meeting. For an outstanding contribution to medical librarianship. *Offered by:* Medical Library Association. *Winner:* Harold Bloomquist, former director, Countway Library of Medicine, Harvard Univ.

Eunice Rockwell Oberly Award. For the best bibliography in agriculture or related sciences. *Offered by:* ALA Association of College and Research Libraries. *Winners:* J. Richard Blanchard, university librarian emeritus, Univ. of California, Davis, and Lois Farrell, librarian, Natural Resources Library, Univ. of California, Berkeley, for *Guide to Sources for Agricultural and Biological Research* (Univ. of California).

Shirley Olofson Memorial Award. For individuals to attend their second annual conference of ALA. *Offered by:* ALA Junior Members Round Table. *Winners:* Linda Cochran, Barbara Schanzer, and Lorretta Turnage.

Helen Keating Ott Award. Presented to an individual or institution for a significant contribution to children's literature. *Offered by:* Church and Synagogue Library Association. *Winner:* Isabelle Holland, New York.

Howard V. Phalin-World Book Graduate Scholarship in Library Science—$2,500 (maximum). For a Canadian citizen or landed immigrant to attend an accredited library school in Canada or the United States. *Offered by:* Canadian

Library Association. *Winner:* Martha Wolfe, Windsor, Ont.

Esther J. Piercy Award. For contribution to librarianship in the field of technical services by younger members of the profession. *Offered by:* ALA Resources and Technical Services Division. *Winner:* Sue A. Dodd.

Plenum Scholarship Award—$1,000. For graduate study leading to a doctorate in library or information science. *Offered by:* Special Libraries Association. *Winner:* Not awarded in 1983.

Rittenhouse Award—$200. For the best unpublished paper on medical librarianship submitted by a student enrolled in, or having been enrolled in, a course for credit in an ALA-accredited library school, or a trainee in an internship program in medical librarianship. *Offered by:* Medical Library Association. *Winner:* Dorothy Manderschied, School of Library Science, Univ. of Michigan.

Frank Bradway Rogers Information Advancement Award—$500. For an outstanding contribution to knowledge of health science information delivery. *Offered by:* Medical Library Association. *Winner:* Frank Bradway Rogers.

SLA Hall of Fame. For an extended and sustained period of distinguished service to the Special Libraries Association in all spheres of its activities. *Offered by:* Special Libraries Association. *Winner:* Lorraine Ann Ciboch.

SLA Honorary Member. For a non-member's contribution to SLA or to special librarianship. *Offered by:* Special Libraries Association. *Winner:* Andrew A. Aines.

SLA Minority Stipends—$2,000. For students with financial need who show potential for special librarianship. *Offered by:* Special Libraries Association. *Winner:* Patrick C. Ravines.

SLA Professional Award. For a member's contribution to the work of SLA or to special librarianship. *Offered by:* Special Libraries Association. *Winners:* Ron Coplen and James M. Matarazzo.

SLA Special Programs Fund Grant—$5,000 (total). For a project that promotes SLA's objectives. *Offered by:* Special Libraries Association. *Winners:* SLA Boston Chapter, James M. Matarazzo, and Marcy Murphy.

SLA Scholarships—$5,000. For students with financial need who show potential for special librarianship. *Offered by:* Special Libraries Association. *Winners:* Karen K. Kreisel and Donna Wells Dzierlenga.

Margaret B. Scott Award of Merit. For an outstanding school librarian. *Offered by:* Canadian School Library Association. *Winner:* Kathleen Snow, Calgary, Alta.

Margaret B. Scott Memorial Award—$400. For the development of school libraries in Canada. *Offered by:* Canadian School Library Association and Ontario Library Association. *Winners:* Reginald Crossman, Keith Medley, and Ronald Crawford.

Charles Scribner's Sons Award—$325. To attend ALA's annual conference. *Offered by:* ALA Association for Library Service to Children. *Donor:* Charles Scribner's Sons. *Winners:* Debbie Abilock, Judith A. Logan, Paula Morrow, and Barbara Tupper.

John Sessions Memorial Award. For significant efforts to work with the labor community. *Offered by:* ALA Reference and Adult Services Division. *Winner:* Wisconsin State Historical Society, Madison, Wis.

3M/JMRT Company Professional Development Grant. To encourage professional development and participation of new librarians in ALA and JMRT activities. To cover expenses for recipients to attend ALA conference. *Offered by:*

ALA Junior Members Round Table. *Winners:* Cynthia Comer, Germaine McCarthy, and Lynn McCauley.

Trustee Citations. For distinguished service to library development whether on the local, state, or national level. *Offered by:* ALA American Library Trustee Association. *Donor:* ALA. *Winners:* Diana Hunter and C. Vernon Cooper, Jr.

H. W. Wilson Co. Award—$500. For the best paper published in *Special Libraries* in 1981. *Offered by:* Special Libraries Association. *Winner:* Miriam A. Drake for "Information Management and Special Librarianship" (October 1982).

H. W. Wilson Foundation Award—$2,000. Available to Canadian citizen or landed immigrant for pursuit of studies at an accredited Canadian library school. *Offered by:* Canadian Library Association. *Winner:* Gary Deane, Regina, Sask.

H. W. Wilson Library Periodical Award—$500. To a periodical published by a local, state, or regional library, library group, or library association in the United States or Canada that has made an outstanding contribution to librarianship. *Offered by:* ALA Awards Committee. *Donor:* H. W. Wilson Co. *Winner:* *The Idaho Librarian* (Idaho Library Association), ed. by Jeanne Otten Lipscomb.

H. W. Wilson Library Staff Development Grant—$250. *Offered by:* ALA Awards Committee. *Winner:* Jackson-George Regional Library System, Pascagoula, Miss.

Justin Windsor Essay Prize—$500. For excellence in research in library history. *Offered by:* ALA Library History Round Table. *Winner:* Robert S. Martin for his essay, "Maurice F. Tauber's *Louis Round Wilson.*"

George Wittenborn Memorial Award. For excellence of content and physical design of an art book, exhibition catalog, and/or periodical published in North America. *Offered by:* Art Libraries Society of North America. *Winners:* Cooper Hewitt Museum/Harry N. Abrams, Inc.; Macmillan Publishing Co.; Canadian Centre for Architecture; Univ. Press of New England.

World Book–Childcraft Awards—$1,000. For continuing education in school or children's librarianship; distributed among no more than four recipients (candidates must be members of Catholic Library Association). *Offered by:* Catholic Library Association. *Winners:* Sister M. Clare Boehmer, ASC, Waterloo, Ill., and Sister Rose Anthony Moos, CSJ, Salina, Kans.

Part 4
Research and Statistics

Library Research and Statistics

Research on Libraries and Librarianship, 1983

Mary Jo Lynch

Director, ALA Office for Research

Aspects of personnel for library and information service headed the list of topics for research activity in 1983.

Personnel

A Study of Supply and Demand

The long-awaited report on *Library Human Resources: A Study of Supply and Demand* was published in July by the American Library Association. This report was prepared for the National Center for Education Statistics and the Office of Libraries and Learning Technologies by King Research, Inc. It contains 55 tables and substantial accompanying text describing the library labor market as of 1981–1982 and projecting supply and demand to 1990. This report will be of use to anyone who wants to know how many librarians are currently employed in a particular type of library and is a useful indicator of what the future might hold for personnel in this field. [For a report on the results of the study, see Part 3—*Ed.*]

New Directions in Professional Education

A second project related to information professionals was also funded by the Department of Education and conducted by King Research, Inc. Work on "New Directions in Library and Information Science Education" began late in 1982 and continued throughout 1983. The project seeks to determine the present and future competencies needed by library and information science professionals and to examine educational requirements for achieving those competencies. The project team will document the study process so that education for the library and information science profession can be kept up-to-date with future studies.

The study team established a four-part framework for the project: (1) trends affecting information professionals through 1990; (2) work settings within which information professionals perform; (3) functions performed across work settings; and (4) levels of professional work (i.e., entry level, mid-level, senior level). Within this framework the team has identified competencies needed now and in the future by information professionals. The term "competencies" is broadly defined to include knowledge, skills, and abilities required to perform a function well.

Two methodologies have been used to identify competencies: a thorough review of the literature and an extensive series of interviews with information professionals and the managers to whom they report in a variety of work settings. The progress of the project team has been reported through a newsletter and a series of speeches by the project director, Jose-Marie Griffiths. The final report, expected by the end of March 1984, will be in three parts. Volume I will be a background report describing the information professions, the environment within which information professionals operate, key trends influencing the profession, and a perspective on future developments. Volume II, which will constitute the formal project report, will include competencies identified and reviewed during the project and a discussion of the implications of project findings on future education and training of information professionals. Volume III will be a manual describing how the profession can continue the process of competency identification and validation so that changes in the work place can be communicated to educators.

Public Libraries

Research on public libraries faced turbulent times in 1983. In April, the Department of Education issued a Request for Proposal (RFP) entitled "Alternative Funding Possibilities for Publicly Supported Library and Information Services," based on a suggestion made in *A Library and Information Science Research Agenda for the 1980s* (see the 1981 *Bowker Annual*, p. 267). The "Statement of Work" attached to the RFP explains that this contract would explore the assigned topic through "a survey of a random sample of libraries from each subtype of library and case studies of libraries successful in procuring alternative sources of funds in addition to or in place of federal, state, or local funding sources. The RFP was criticized in the library press and elsewhere. After responses were received, the RFP was withdrawn for reasons which were never fully explained.

Two monographs published in 1983 report results of research on topics related to the question of how public libraries should be financed. Lawrence J. White, currently professor of economics at New York University, has been working for several years on a project financed by the Twentieth Century Fund. His investigation covered a broad area, "public libraries in the United States—their goals, their orientation, their functions, their roles, their problems, their policies," but of most interest to the library world is his conclusion that given the present pattern of use and the potential number of services that could be offered, public libraries should start to charge fees. White believes that most of the dilemmas he identifies in *The Public Library in the 1980s* (Lexington, Mass.: D. C. Heath, 1983) could be eliminated if public libraries would charge fees for many services.

Another perspective on the question of how public library service should be financed is offered by Nancy Van House in *Public Library User Fees* (Westport, Conn.: Greenwood Press, 1983). Van House tries to answer the question "What is the proper role of user fees in public libraries?" by consideration of two different kinds of choices: (1) the community's decision to support a public library and (2) the individual's decision to use it. Analysis of the first choice applies public finance theory to explain why libraries are publicly supported in the first place. Analysis of the second choice applies time allocation theory to various kinds of fees a public library could possibly charge in order to predict use as a function of cost to the user in both time and money. Like White, Van House concludes that public libraries can and should be at least partially supported by fees. Both books provide research results in a form useful to practitioners faced with hard financial choices.

Public Library Research Funding

Two attempts to promote research related to public libraries were begun in 1983. One was a proposal made to the board of directors of the Public Library Association (PLA) by its Research Committee, chaired by Kenneth Dowlin. As Dowlin explained in the fall 1983 issue of *Public Libraries,* when the PLA Research Committee examined *A Library and Information Science Research Agenda for the 1980s* the committee was struck by the absence of a mechanism to ensure that research recommended by the *Agenda* would actually be done. The committee proposed creation of a center for public library research that would "help practitioners and administrators of public library service to apply new research methods and to acquire funds for the improvement of library operations." Dowlin's proposal for the center was discussed at the PLA national conference in Baltimore (March 1983) and was brought to the PLA board in Los Angeles. Although the proposal was not accepted as such by the PLA board, it has generated considerable discussion in the public library community regarding the need for and the possibility of research.

Another attempt to promote research on public libraries was initiated by Herbert Goldhor, director of the Library Research Center of the Graduate School of Library and Information Science at the University of Illinois. Goldhor has asked large public libraries and state library agencies to pay dues of $1,000 (public libraries) or $2,000 (state libraries) to support a Coalition for Public Library Research. In return they will be entitled to a vote on the topic to be explored, a vote on the advisory committee to the project, and a copy of the report. As of this writing (mid-December 1983) it is not certain whether the coalition will actually be launched, but dues have already been received from several libraries.

Academic Libraries

Research on topics of special interest to academic librarians flourished in 1983 thanks largely to the Council on Library Resources (CLR). The January 1983 issue of *CLR Recent Developments* announced that ten faculty-librarian teams had received the first grants under the Professional Education and Training for Research Librarianship (PETREL) Program's Cooperative Research Project. This project was established in April 1982 by the CLR board to encourage faculty members and librarians to join forces in solving problems facing academic and research libraries. The program provides small grants to help defray research costs such as charges for computer time, data organization and input, and part-time assistance. Five more faculty-librarian teams were announced in June. Teams commonly consist of one or more librarians and one or more faculty members from either the campus library school or another academic department. Three of the 15 studies funded in 1983 deal with some aspect of the online catalog; two deal with government document collections; the others cover a wide range of topics.

Library Use Studies

The Council on Library Resources also supported research by Paul Metz at the Virginia Polytechnic Institute and State University, which was published by ALA in 1983 as *The Landscape of Literatures: Use of Subject Collections in a University Library* (ACRL Publications in Librarianship no. 43). Metz answered the questions "Who uses research libraries?" and "What materials are most in demand?" by analyzing circulation data from VPI&SU and other institutions. The study tried to identify subject literature of interest to faculty and students in various disciplines and examined those reading patterns "as data that reveal the orientations of disciplines in fundamental ways." In addition it sought to "discover to what extent reading patterns may be an outcome of basic library policies." Based on his analysis Metz suggests the need for several changes in the way book collections are built and managed. He also concludes that many more such studies should be done and probably will be done now that automated circulation systems have made data more manageable. Help for librarians conducting such studies has been provided by ALA's Resources and Technical Services Division in a "Guide to Collection Evaluation through Use and User Studies" (*Library Resources and Technical Services* 27 [October/ December 1983]: 432–440).

Grants and Awards

The Association for Library and Information Science Education (ALISE), formerly the Association of American Library Schools (AALS), expanded its program of support for research by sponsoring both research grant awards and a research paper competition in 1982. Winners were announced at the group's annual conference in January 1983. Research grants were awarded to Mike Marchant and Nathan Smith for a study of competencies public library directors seek when hiring staff and to Robert Swisher and Rosemary DuMont for a study of career patterns of female academic librarians. In the research paper competition, awards of $500 each went to "In Search of a Name: Information Science and Its Antecedents," by Alvin M. Schrader, and "Assessing the Quality of Reference Service for Government Publications," by Charles McClure and Peter Hernon.

ALA's Association of College and Research Libraries (ACRL) granted two fellowship awards funded by the Institute for Scientific Information. The Samuel Lazerow Fellowship for Research in Acquisitions or Technical Services in an Academic or Research Library, consisting of a citation and $1,000, was given to Denise Bedford, assistant to the director for technical services at the Stanford University Libraries. Her study will investigate "Technical Processing Costs in Large Academic Research Libraries." ACRL's doctoral dissertation fellowship was awarded to Stanton F. Biddle, associate director for planning and development at the State University of New York at Buffalo Library. Biddle, who is a doctoral candidate at the School of Library and Information Studies, University of California at Berkeley, received a citation and $1,000 for his proposal entitled "The Planning Function in the Management of University Libraries: Survey, Analysis, Conclusions and Recommendations." ALA's Library Research Round Table (LRRT) chose not to make an award in its Research Paper Competition for 1983.

Periodical Publications

Two leading journals covering research on libraries and librarianship changed in a major or minor way during 1983. The minor change was in the journal formerly known as *Library Research*, which became *Library and Information Science Research* with the publication of Volume 5, Number 1, in spring 1983. As editor Jane Robbins-Carter explained in that issue "the rationale for the name change is to reflect more accurately the nature of the articles which are published in the journal." A major change was made in the periodical formerly known as *RADIALS Bulletin*, which became *Current Research* in 1983. The title change in this publication of the Library Association (Great Britain) marks two important developments: expanded international coverage and more frequent publication, from semiannual to quarterly issues. *Current Research* provides (in English) abstracts of library and information science research from all over the world.

Research in ALA

Research played a quiet but pervasive role at the one hundred and second annual conference of the American Library Association in Los Angeles (June 1983). In addition to the traditional research forums sponsored by the Library Research Round Table (LRRT), there were research forums sponsored by the American Association of School Librarians (the tenth annual), the Young Adult Services Division, and the Library History Round Table. Poster sessions, designed to present research findings or describe innovative programs or solutions to problems, included a substantial number of research presentations, approximately 25 percent of the total.

In addition to programs there was discussion at the policy level regarding research functions that should be carried out by ALA. In a document presented to the ALA executive board, the Committee on Research proposed that the ALA Office for Research (OFR) sharpen its focus on three research-related functions essential to the financial and professional strength of the association: (1) to collect, analyze, and interpret data about the membership of ALA and users of ALA products and services on an ongoing basis for organizational decision making; (2) to conduct and/or promote the collection of statistics about libraries and librarians; and (3) to monitor ongoing research related to libraries and disseminate information about such studies to the profession. The Committee on Research believes that these functions are best carried out by the Office for Research. The move to sharpen OFR's focus comes at a time when ALA's difficult fiscal situation threatens the very existence of the office.

Statistics

An opportunity to make real progress on the second research function was presented in September when the National Center for Education Statistics (NCES) awarded OFR a $105,000 contract to analyze current NCES data collection activities in libraries and develop plans for a more efficient and effective system. The project staff began by studying current forms used by NCES and by state agencies to collect data from libraries. After this material has been studied and project staff has determined how it is used by federal, state, and local officials, a planning committee will be convened to help develop plans for the future.

Researchers and practitioners looking for national-level statistics on libraries will be aided by an ALA publication produced by the Office for Research and published late in 1983. *Sources of Library Statistics, 1972–1982* describes the data that have been published during this period on academic, public, school, and special libraries, as well as on several other topics related to library service.

Innovation

Two years ago *A Library and Information Science Research Agenda for the 1980s* recommended that a study be done on how innovation is disseminated in the library and information science field. In March 1983 the Department of Education responded to that suggestion by issuing a Request for Proposal (RFP) with the title "Diffusion of Innovations in Library and Information Science." According to the RFP's "Statement of Work," the contractor will be expected to study: "1) when and why innovation occurs in the library and information field; 2) what linkages (communication channels) exist that result in a flow (dissemination) of information; 3) what model(s) and methods were effectively used in the diffusion process; and 4) what options and recommendations are needed to develop a plan for the diffusion networks for library innovation(s)." King Research, Inc., was awarded the contract for this study.

One innovation that will probably affect libraries greatly in the future is electronic publishing. In fall 1983, the Association of American Publishers launched a two-year, $250,000 Electronic Publishing Project, which will develop publishing industry standards for preparation, coding, and processing of author-generated electronic manuscripts. Aspen Systems Corporation was named contractor for the project. Its first task will be to conduct a comprehensive survey of existing publishing practices to gather information about electronic manuscript publication that has never before been available in one place for the industry as a whole.

A unique source of intelligence about another aspect of the electronic information industry became available to subscribers for the first time in 1983. Information Market Indicators (IMI) produced by InfoMetrics, Inc., whose president is Martha Williams, presents an audit of how the online data base industry serves the information center/ library market in the United States. IMI staff collected and analyzed all of the bills for publicly available online data base services purchased by a carefully selected sample of 550 user organizations, many of them libraries. The resulting statistical tables show revenues and use patterns for some 247 data bases, their 151 producers, and the 15 vendors who offer the services. IMI reports are issued quarterly for an annual subscription fee. Williams plans to expand the service to include the home computer use market and to cover numeric data bases.

Developments in Library Statistical Activities, 1983

Louise Berry

Chairperson, Statistics Section, ALA Library
Administration and Management Division

and Director, Darien Library, 35 Leroy Ave., Darien, CT 06820
203-655-2568

The major development in statistics for libraries in 1983 was the acceptance and publishing of the new *American National Standard for Library and Information Sciences and Related Publishing Practices—Library Statistics* (generally referred to as ANSI Z39.7—1983) by the American National Standards Institute (ANSI), a nongovernmental organization.

The New ANSI Standard

The ANSI standard applies to all types and sizes of libraries in the United States and was developed by a voluntary committee made up of representatives from approximately 40 organizations affiliated with ANSI.

The revision of the 1968 standard for collecting library statistics provides categories and definitions of terms for national and local reporting on libraries. The purpose of the standard is to provide a pool of defined statistical data items about libraries from which various surveys and studies may be designed and to promote the exchange of information about libraries. The use of standardized definitions and categories will reduce the burden on libraries responding to surveys and, more importantly, will produce compatible sets of data for the library manager, researcher, government official, or other user. It will also aid individual library managers in developing measures of library use, for example, ANSI Z39.7—1983 contains standardized definitions for reference and directional questions, bibliographic instruction, data base reference transactions, and cultural presentations to groups.

ALA Activities

Statistical Sources

Another new library statistics publication, Mary Jo Lynch's *Sources of Library Statistics, 1972-82*, published in 1983 by the American Library Association (ALA), provides background information on the nationwide collection of statistics about libraries. The pamphlet lists all publications with national library statistics that have been issued regularly since 1972. It also describes sources of statistics on such areas as library buildings, costs, salaries, and library education.

From Input to Output: A Shift in Focus

The ever-increasing demand for more accountability and the need for better statistical data to help libraries evaluate their effectiveness culminated in 1982 with the publication of *Output Measures for Public Libraries* by Douglas Zweizig and Eleanor Jo Rodger.

This ALA publication marked the shift in focus in the library field away from the collection of input statistics (materials, personnel, money) to output statistics (services provided to the library user). Output measures include reference fill rate, library visits per capita, and materials availability. This new focus is reflected in the current activities of several divisions of the American Library Association. The Association of College and Research Libraries (ACRL) has a task force on statistics that is exploring output measures for college and university libraries, and the Reference and Adult Services Division's committee on Evaluation of Reference and Adult Services is looking at output measures for reference.

LAMA Statistics Section

The Statistics Section of ALA's Library Administration and Management Association (LAMA) division advises other associations, organizations, and agencies regarding needs for and uses of statistical measurement of library resources, services, and facilities. The section played an active role in the development of the ANSI Z39.7—1983 standard. Current projects of the Statistics Section include the following:

The Statistics for School Library Media Centers Committee, chaired by Herb Achleitner of Emporia State University, is planning a project to measure the benefit of library services to users.

The Statistics for State Library Agencies Committee, chaired by Ed Klee, Kentucky Department for Libraries, is investigating the use of microcomputers for the collection and analysis of library statistics and is planning a program on the topic at the American Library Association annual conference in June 1986.

The Statistics for Nonprint Media Committee, chaired by Evelyn King, Texas A&M University, is sponsoring a program at the ALA annual conference in June 1984 on one of the most complex areas of library statistics—the collection and analysis of statistics for graphic arts, media, cartographic, and microfilm collections and for machine-readable data base services and other nonprint materials.

The Statistics for College and University Libraries Committee, chaired by Roger Harris, University of North Carolina, has identified the agencies that collect descriptive statistics on college and university libraries at the state and regional level and is preparing the data for possible future publication.

The Statistics for Circulation Services Committee, chaired by Ruth Fraley, SUNY Albany, and the Statistics for Technical Services Committee, chaired by Suzanne Striedieck, Pennsylvania State University, developed a checklist to aid library managers in the evaluation of the data collection components of automated circulation control systems. The checklist is available from the LAMA office of the American Library Association.

NCES

The federal government, through the National Center for Education Statistics (NCES), has been the major compiler of descriptive statistics about libraries. In 1983, NCES initiated an exciting new project by awarding a one-year contract to the American Library Association to study NCES procedures for collecting and publishing data about libraries. According to a press release from ALA, the project "seeks to plan a national library data collection system serving federal, state and local government and the greater library community." The study will be coordinated by ALA's Office for Research Director Mary Jo Lynch.

Although severely hampered by cutbacks by the federal government, NCES is working on several library surveys. A questionnaire on public library use will be mailed to 65,000 households as part of the October 1984 supplement to the Current Population Survey. The statistics of the latest public library survey are to be released by the end of 1984. NCES is also planning two new statistical surveys—one on public school library media centers and the other on library networks.

Selected Characteristics of the U.S. Population

W. Vance Grant
Head, Statistical Information Office, National Center for Education Statistics

	Number	Percent
Total U.S. population (July 1, 1983)[1]	234,249,000	100.0
Resident population of 50 states and D.C.	233,722,000	99.8
Armed forces overseas	527,000	0.2
Resident population of U.S. outlying areas (July 1, 1982)[2]	3,645,000	—
U.S. population, five years and over, including armed forces abroad (July 1, 1982)[3]	214,685,000	100.0
5–9 years	15,956,000	7.4
10–14 years	18,024,000	8.4
15–19 years	19,845,000	9.2
20–24 years	21,935,000	10.2
25–64 years	112,099,000	52.2
Age 65 and over	26,824,000	12.5
Public and private school enrollment (fall 1983)*	56,775,000	100.0
Kindergarten through grade 8	30,780,000	54.2
Grades 9–12	13,595,000	23.9
Higher education, total enrollment	12,400,000	21.8
Private school enrollment[4]	7,670,000	13.5
Kindergarten through grade 8*	3,625,000	11.8
Grades 9–12*	1,335,000	9.8
Higher education, total enrollment*	2,710,000	21.9

	Number	Percent
Educational status of population aged 25 and over		
Total aged 25 and over (March 1981)[5]	132,899,000	100.0
With four or more years of college	22,726,000[†]	17.1
With one to three years of college	20,068,000[†]	15.1
With four years of high school or more	92,631,000[†]	69.7
With less than four years of high school	40,268,000[†]	30.3
Residence in and outside metropolitan areas[5]		
Total noninstitutional population (April 1, 1980)	226,500,000	100.0
Nonmetropolitan areas	57,100,000	25.2
Metropolitan areas	169,400,000	74.8
In central cities	68,000,000	30.0
Outside central cities	101,500,000	44.8
Employment status[6]		
Total noninstitutional population 16 years old and over (October 1983)	176,474,000	—
Civilian labor force, total[7]	111,815,000	100.0
Employed[7]	101,928,000	91.2
Unemployed[7]	9,886,000	8.8
Total faculty and students in colleges and universities (fall 1983)[8]	13,270,000	100.0
Faculty*	870,000	6.6
Students*	12,400,000	93.4

*Unpublished estimates of the National Center for Education Statistics.

[†]This number, derived from a percentage, is an approximation only.

[1]Estimates of the Bureau of the Census, *Current Population Reports*, Series P-25, no. 940.

[2]Unpublished estimates of the Bureau of the Census.

[3]Estimates of the Bureau of the Census, *Current Population Reports*, Series P-25, no. 929.

[4]A segment of public and private school enrollment reported above. Percentages for private school enrollment are based on the total figures for public and private school enrollment at each level.

[5]Data from the Bureau of the Census, *Statistical Abstract of the United States, 1982–83*.

[6]Data from the Bureau of Labor Statistics, published in *Economic Indicators*, November 1983.

[7]Seasonally adjusted.

[8]Includes full-time and part-time instructional staff and students.

Note: Because of rounding, numbers may not add to totals.

Number of Libraries in the United States and Canada

Statistics are from the thirty-sixth edition of the *American Library Directory* (*ALD*) edited by Jaques Cattell Press (R. R. Bowker, 1983). In addition to listing and describing almost 32,300 individual libraries, the thirty-sixth edition of *ALD* lists over 300 library networks consortia, and other cooperative library organizations, including processing and purchasing centers and other specialized organizations. Data are exclusive of elementary and secondary school libraries. The directory does not list small public libraries. Law libraries with fewer than 10,000 volumes are included only if they specialize in a specific field.

Libraries in the United States

A. Public libraries 8,822
   Public libraries with
   branches 1,344
   Public library branches ... 6,146
   Total public libraries
   (including branches) ... 14,968*
B. Junior college libraries ... 1,279
   Departmental 18
   Medical 5
   Religious 3
   University and college 1,901
   Departmental 1,702
   Law 188
   Medical 233
   Religious 98
   Total academic
   libraries 4,900*
C. Armed forces
   Air Force 132
   Medical 16
   Army 188
   Law 1
   Medical 32
   Navy 163
   Medical 21
   Total armed forces
   libraries 483*
D. Government libraries 1,591
   Law 437
   Medical 245
   Total government
   libraries 1,591*
E. Special libraries 4,281*
F. Law libraries 430*

G. Medical libraries 1,552*
H. Religious libraries 839*

Total law (including
   academic, armed forces,
   and government) 1,056
Total medical (including
   academic, armed forces,
   and government) 2,104
Total religious (including
   academic) 940
Total special (including
   all law, medical,
   and religious) 8,381
Total libraries
   counted (*) 29,044

Libraries in Regions Administered by the United States

A. Public libraries 13
   Public libraries with
   branches 4
   Public library branches ... 24
   Total public libraries
   (including branches) ... 37*
B. Junior college libraries ... 9
   University and college
   libraries 29
   Departmental 17
   Law 3
   Total academic
   libraries 55*

C. Armed forces
    Air Force 1
    Army 1
    Navy 4
    Total armed forces 6*
D. Government libraries 11
    Law 7
    Medical 1
    Total government
    libraries 11*
E. Special libraries 9*
F. Medical libraries 3*
    Total libraries counted (*) 121

Libraries in Canada

A. Public libraries 746
    Public libraries with
    branches 135
    Public library branches ... 927
    Total public libraries
    (including branches) ... 1,673*
B. Junior college libraries ... 90
    Departmental 18
    Medical 3
    Religious 1

    University and college 159
    Departmental 221
    Law 17
    Medical 28
    Religious 16
    Total academic
    libraries 488*
C. Government libraries 292*
    Law 24
    Medical 4
D. Special libraries 476*
E. Law libraries 30*
F. Medical libraries 127*
G. Religious libraries 46*
    Total libraries
    counted (*) 3,132

Summary

Total U.S. libraries 29,044
Total libraries administered
  by the United States 121
Total Canadian libraries 3,132
Grand total of libraries
  listed 32,297

*Note: Numbers followed by an asterisk are added to find "Total libraries counted" for each of the three geographic areas (United States, U.S.-administered regions, and Canada). The sum of the three totals is the "Grand total of libraries listed" in the ALD (shown in the Summary). For details on the count of libraries, see the preface to the thirty-sixth edition of the ALD—Ed.

An Inventory of Statistical Surveys by State Library Agencies

Theodore Samore

Professor, School of Library and Information
Science, University of Wisconsin-Milwaukee

Box 413, Milwaukee, WI 53201
414-963-4707

Some ten years ago, S. Herner and Company issued the *National Inventory of Library Statistics Practices,* which was published in two volumes. Volume 1, *Data Collection on National, State and Local Levels* (U.S. Office of Education, Washington, D.C., 1974), was a listing of surveys conducted and distributed on national, state, and local levels.

Volume 2, *Agency Profiles and Individual Site Descriptions,* was published by the National Center for Education Statistics, Washington, D.C., in 1972. At the time of the survey, 40 states were collecting and publishing library statistical data.

In an attempt to update a portion of Herner's work, in December 1983, a letter was sent to the 50 state library agencies requesting a listing of statistical surveys recently conducted, planned, or financed within the state. Twenty-eight states responded with information on published reports of surveys conducted or planned for the most part since 1982. Some earlier surveys also were included. One state, Alaska, indicated that it no longer issues library statistical reports. For information on any of the 21 nonresponding states, readers should write to the state library agency. [Agency addresses are listed in Part 6 of this volume—*Ed.*]

In the listing that follows, publications are arranged by state and, when appropriate, by type of library within the state. For each publication, states were requested to provide author, title, date of survey, place of publication, price, number of pages, and ordering information. In some cases, however, such information as the price of the publication was not provided. Readers should contact the state library (or other source) to determine whether there is a charge for the publication. A number of states also indicate the previous survey and/or the next survey planned in the series.

Alabama

Alabama Public Library Service. *Annual Report.* Montgomery: The Service. Survey reports public library statistics. Distributed annually to all Alabama public libraries and state library agencies. Copies may be borrowed on interlibrary loan from the Alabama Public Library Service or purchased from ERIC.

Colorado

Maffeo, Steven E. "Jobs Nationally Advertised by Colorado Libraries during 1982: A Statistical Analysis," *Colorado Libraries* 9, no. 2 (June 1983), 5 pp. Nominal cost.

Available from: Steven E. Maffeo, Municipal Reference Library, 1470 S. Havana, #626, Aurora, CO 80012.

Connecticut

Connecticut State Library, Department of Planning and Research. *Salary Survey: Connecticut Public Libraries, 1982.* Unpaged. Free. Compiled from information received by the Connecticut State Library between July 1, 1981 and June 30, 1982. Next survey to be published in spring 1984.

Connecticut State Library. *Public Library Statistical Report, 1982.*
Hartford: Connecticut State Library, 1982. Free.

Publications available from Connecticut State Library, Dept. of Planning and Research, 231 Capitol Ave., Hartford, CT 06106.

Delaware

1983 Reports of the Delaware Public Libraries. FY 1983 survey covers July 1, 1982 through June 30, 1983. Dover: Delaware Division of Libraries, 1983. 40 pp. Free.

Annual survey. Available from Delaware Div. of Libraries, Box 639, Dover, DE 19903-0639.

Florida

Moeller, Helen Morgan, and E. Walter Terrie. *1983 Florida Library Directory with Statistics for 1982.* Tallahassee: Florida Department of State, Division of Library Services, 1983. 186 pp. $12.50.

Available from State Library of Florida, R. A. Gray Bldg., Tallahassee, FL 32301. Survey conducted 1983.

Georgia

Georgia Department of Education, Division of Public Library Services. *1982 Georgia Public Library Statistics.* Atlanta: Department of Education, Division of Public Library Services, 1983. 65 pp.

Annual survey. Available from Div. of Public Library Services, Georgia Dept. of Education, 156 Trinity Ave. S.W., Atlanta, GA 30303.

Curry, Betsy, Vicki Williams, and Edward Moeller. *Microcomputers in Public Libraries in Georgia Survey, 1983.* Decatur: DeKalb Library System, 1983. 15 pp.

Available from DeKalb Library System, 3560 Kensington Rd., Decatur, GA 30032.

Illinois

Copies of all Illinois publications (except those that are out of print) are available without cost from: Publications Unit, Illinois State Library, Centennial Bldg., Rm. 065, Springfield, IL 62756.

Academic

Daugherty, Robert, and Lois M. Pausch. *Bibliographic Instruction in Illinois Academic Libraries: A Survey Report.* Springfield: State Library, 1983. 86 pp. Illinois Statistical Report, no. 11.

Goldhor, Herbert. *Results of a Survey of Illinois Academic Libraries Affiliated with ILLINET.* Springfield: State Library, 1982. 20 pp. Illinois Library Statistical Report, no. 5.

Jackson, Bryant H. *"Higher Education General Information Survey, 1980–1981."* In *Illinois Libraries* 64, no. 7 (September 1982): 889–910. Eleventh annual summary of HEGIS/LIBGIS statistical data for state university libraries.

Phenix, Katharine. *Analysis of the 1981/82 HEGIS/LIBGIS Responses of Illinois Academic Libraries.* Springfield: State Library, 1983. 65 pp. Illinois Library Statistical Report, no. 9.

Public

Analyses of the 1981-82 Illinois Public Library Statistics. Springfield: 1982. 82 pp.

Baker, Sharon L. *Two Studies of Illinois Public Libraries: An Adult User Survey; and Fines, Fees and Charges Levied.* Springfield: State Library, 1983. 73 pp. Illinois Library Statistical Report, no. 7.

Goldhor, Herbert. *Analysis of Responses to the Public Library Supplemental Annual Report for 1980/81.* Springfield: State Library, 1982. 39 pp. Illinois Library Statistical Report, no. 4.

"Public Library Statistics, 1982–1983." In *Illinois Libraries* 65, no. 9 (November 1983): 533–557. Prepared annually at the Library Research Center from public library reports submitted to the state library.

Studies of Illinois Public Libraries Using Data from 1978-79 and 1979-80. Springfield: State Library, 1981. 92 pp. Illinois Library Statistical Report, no. 1. Prepared by staff members of the Library Research Center, Graduate School of Library and Information Science, University of Illinois at Urbana-Champaign.

Studies of Illinois Public Libraries Using Data from 1980-81. Springfield: State Library, 1982. 57 pp. Illinois Library Statistical Report, no. 3. Prepared by staff members of the Library Research Center, Graduate School of Library and Information Science, University of Illinois at Urbana-Champaign.

Wallace, Danny P., and Herbert Goldhor. *An Index of Quality of Illinois Public Library Service,* and *The Comparative Performance of Illinois Public Libraries.* Springfield: State Library, 1983. 54 pp. Illinois Library Statistical Report, no. 10.

School

Goldhor, Herbert, and Cora E. Thomassen. *The 1981 Survey of Illinois Public School Library Media Centers.* Springfield: State Library, 1983. 73 pp. Illinois Library Statistical Report, no. 6.

Special

Wallace, Danny P. *1981 Survey of Illinois Special Libraries.* Springfield: State Library, 1982. 125 pp. Illinois Library Statistical Report, no. 2.

Wallace, Danny P. *Performance Measures in Illinois Special Libraries.* Springfield: State Library, 1983. 49 pp. Illinois Library Statistical Report, no. 8 (o.p.).

Indiana

Indiana State Library. *Statistics of Indiana Libraries, 1982.* Indianapolis: Indiana State Library, 1983. 134 pp. $6.

Annual survey. Available from Extension Div., Indiana State Library, 140 N. Senate Ave., Indianapolis, IN 46204-2296.

Iowa

State Library of Iowa. *Iowa Public Library Statistics,* 1981–82. Des Moines. 198 pp. Free.

Data for 1982–1983 available spring 1984 from State Library of Iowa, Office of Library Development, E. 12th and Grand, Des Moines, IA 50319.

Kansas

Gardiner, Allen. *Kansas Public Library Statistics.* Topeka: State Library. $6.50.

Annual survey. Available from the Kansas State Library, State Capitol, Topeka, KS 66612.

Kentucky

Frank R. Levstik. *Historical Records Needs Assessment.* Frankfort: Historical Records Advisory Board, 1983. 92 pp. Free.

Survey conducted 1982. Available from Public Records Div., Dept. for Libraries and Archives, Box 537, Frankfort, KY 40602.

Louisiana

Louisiana State Library. *Public Libraries in Louisiana: Statistical Report, 1983.* Baton Rouge: State Library, 1984. 36 pp.

Annual survey. Limited distribution. Available from Library Development Section, Louisiana State Library, Box 131, Baton Rouge, LA 70821.

Massachusetts

Massachusetts Board of Library Commissioners. *Data for Massachusetts, FY83: Comparative Public Library Report.* Boston: Board of Library Commissioners, December 1983. 63 pp.

Massachusetts Board of Library Commissioners. *Data for Massachusetts, 1983: Public Library Personnel Report.* Boston: Board of Library Commissioners, January 1984. 97 pp.

Both surveys are conducted annually in the summer/fall and published in the winter.

The publications are available at no cost (while supply lasts) from the Massachusetts Board of Library Commissioners, 648 Beacon St., Boston, MA 02215, or for a fee from ERIC Document Reproduction Service, Box 190, Arlington, VA 22210.

Michigan

Library of Michigan. *1983 Michigan Library Statistics*. Lansing: Library of Michigan, 1983. 98 pp. Free.

Data for 1984 available summer 1984 from Library of Michigan, Box 30007, Lansing, MI 48909. Statistical information gathered from public libraries and library cooperative forms, filed on or before February 1, 1983.

Michigan Library Consortium. *Michigan Library Automation Directory*. Lansing, 1983. 180 pp. Members $22.95; nonmembers $27.95. First survey in 1983. Next planned for spring 1984.

Available from Michigan Library Consortium, 6810 S. Cedar, Suite 8, Lansing, MI 48910.

Michigan Library Association (MLA). *Salary and Fringe Benefit Survey*. Lansing, October 1983. 57 pp. $6.50 (20% discount to MLA members).

Available from Michigan Library Association, 415 W. Kalamazoo, Lansing, MI 48933. Next survey tentatively planned for October 1984.

Montana

Montana Library Directory, 1983, with Statistics of Montana Public Libraries, July 1, 1981–June 30, 1982. Helena: Montana State Library, 1983. 92 pp. Free.

Annual survey. Available from Montana State Library, 1515 E. Sixth Ave., Helena, MT 59620.

Nevada

Nevada State Library. Nevada Library Directory and Statistics, 1984. Carson City: Nevada State Library, 1984. 70 pp. $3.

Survey conducted 1983. Annual publication. Available from the Library Development Div., Nevada State Library, Capitol Complex, Carson City, NV 89710.

New Hampshire

New Hampshire State Library. *New Hampshire Library Statistics, January–December, 1982*. Concord: The Library, 1983. ca. 30 pp.

Available from New Hampshire State Library, 20 Park St., Concord, NH 03301.

New Mexico

New Mexico State Library. *Annual Report: Library Statistics, 1983*. 28 pp. Free. Fiscal Year 1982–1983 survey. Available from New Mexico State Library, 325 Don Gaspar, Santa Fe, NM 87503.

New York

New York State Education Department. Division of Library Development. *A Directory of College and University Libraries in New York State, 1982.* Albany: State Education Department, 1983. 198 pp. Free.

Data collected October 1981. Available from Gifts and Exchange Section, New York State Library, Cultural Education Center, Albany, NY 12230.

New York State Education Department. Bureau of Specialist Library Services. *Selected Statistics on Postsecondary Libraries in New York State; Fall 1982 and Fiscal Year 1981–82 Data.* Albany: State Education Department, 1983. unpaged. Free.

Data (5 tables) collected October 1982. Available from Bureau of Specialist Library Services, New York State Library, Cultural Education Center, Albany, NY 12230.

New York State Education Department. Division of Library Development. *A Directory of College and University Libraries in New York State, 1983.* Albany: State Education Department, 1984.

Data collected October 1982. Available in mid-1984 from Gifts and Exchange Section, New York State Library, Cultural Education Center, Albany, NY 12230.

New York State Education Department, *Institution Libraries Statistics/1981–82.* Albany: State Education Department, 1983. 36 pp. Free.

Data collected 1982. Available from Gifts and Exchange Section, New York State Library, Cultural Education Center, Albany, NY 12230.

North Carolina

North Carolina. Department of Cultural Resources. Division of State Library. *Statistics & Directory of North Carolina Public Libraries, July 1, 1982–June 30, 1983.* Raleigh, 1984. 34 pp. Free.

Survey conducted 1983. Next survey 1983–1984.

North Carolina Department of Cultural Resources. Division of State Library. *Statistics of North Carolina Special Libraries, July 1, 1981—June 30, 1982.* Raleigh, 1983. 7 pp. Free.

Survey conducted 1983. Next survey report will cover 1982–1983.

North Carolina Department of Cultural Resources. Division of State Library. *Statistics of North Carolina University and College Libraries, July 1, 1981–June 30, 1982.* Raleigh, 1982. 7 pp. Free.

Survey conducted 1982. Next report survey will cover 1982–1983. Publications available from Div. of State Library, 109 E. Jones St., Raleigh, NC 27611.

Ohio

Scott, Sandra. "Survey of Public Library Homebound Programs." Currently in progress. Will be available from State Library of Ohio, State Office Bldg., 65 S. Front St., Columbus, OH 43215.

Oklahoma

Oklahoma Department of Libraries. *Annual Report & Directory of Oklahoma Libraries, July 1, 1981–June 30, 1982.* Oklahoma City, 1983. 114 pp. Free. Survey conducted annually in the summer.

Oklahoma Department of Libraries. *Long-Range Program, 1984–1988 Update & Extension and Annual Program FY1984.* Oklahoma City, 1983. Includes 76 pp. of statistics. Free. Updated annually.

Oklahoma Department of Libraries. *Continuing Education State Plan, 1983.* Oklahoma City, 1983. 11 pp. Free. Updated annually.

Publications available from Oklahoma Dept. of Libraries, 200 N.E. 18th St., Oklahoma City, OK 73105.

Rhode Island

Rhode Island Department of State Library Services. *Table Showing Comparable Statistics for Services of Public Libraries of Rhode Island.* Providence: Department of State Library Services, January 1984. 18 pp. Free.

Annual publication based on public library annual reports to the department. Available from Reference Dept., Rhode Island. Dept. of State Library Services, 95 Davis St., Providence, RI 02908.

Rhode Island Library Association. Personnel Committee. *Annual Salary Survey.*

To be published in February issue of the *RILA Bulletin* beginning in 1984. (1982 survey was published in the January 1983 issue of the *RILA Bulletin.*) Available from Editor, *RILA Bulletin,* 95 Davis St., Providence, RI 02908.

South Carolina

South Carolina Public Library Annual Statistical Summary, FY 83. Columbia: South Carolina State Library, 1983. 30 pp.

Survey conducted during fiscal year ending June 30, 1983. Available through interlibrary loan from the South Carolina State Library, 1500 Senate St., Columbia, SC 29201.

Texas

Texas State Library and Texas Council of State University Librarians. *Texas Academic Library Statistics.* Austin: Texas State Library, 1982. 160 pp. Free. Annual survey.

Texas State Library. *Public Library Statistics for 1982.* Austin: Texas State Library, 1982. 227 pp. Free. Annual survey.

Texas State Library. *Texas Public Library Statistics for 1982: An Analysis.* Austin: Texas State Library, 1982. 227 pp. Free. Publication available May 1984. Annual survey.

Texas State Library and Texas Chapter. Special Libraries Association. *Directory of Special Libraries and Information Centers in Texas: 1983.* Austin: Texas State Library, 1983. 142 pp. Free. Report for 1983 available June 1984. Survey conducted biennially.

Publications available from Texas State Library, Library Development Div., Box 12927/Capitol Sta., Austin, TX 78711.

Virginia

Virginia State Library. *Statistics of Virginia Public Libraries and Institutional Libraries, 1981–1982.* Richmond, 1983. 40 pp. Annual.

Available from Library Development Branch, 12th and Capitol St., Richmond, VA 23219.

West Virginia

West Virginia Library Commission. *Annual Statistical Report.* The Commission. 20 pp. Annual. Free. Data available in February.

(Supplements to this report available on FRIENDS groups, bookmobile service, Mail-a-Book programs, service to schools, registered borrowers, and professional librarians.) Available from WVLC, Cultural Center, Charleston, WV 25305.

Wyoming

Wyoming State Library. *Wyoming Public Library Statistics, 1982.* Cheyenne: Wyoming State Library, 1983. 5 pp. Free. Annual survey, 1982– .

Available from Public Information Office, Wyoming State Library, Supreme Court and State Library Bldg., Cheyenne, WY 82002.

U.S. College and University Library Statistics in Series

Frank L. Schick

Consulting Editor, *Bowker Annual*

Library statistics of national scope have been compiled through public and private initiative since the second half of the nineteenth century.[1] But a continuing series of academic library statistics have been collected only during the past 50 years by the U.S. Department of Education (formerly Office of Education), the American Library Association (ALA), the Association of College and Research Libraries (ACRL), and other private sponsors.

Department of Education

Between 1938 and 1958, the Statistics Division of the Office of Education (now the National Center for Education Statistics, NCES) collected and published college and university library statistics on an irregular basis, roughly every four to six years. In 1958, the series was moved to an annual cycle. In the foreword to the first annual survey (1959–1960), John G. Lorenz, then director of the Library Services Branch, explained the change:

> With this volume, the Office of Education initiates a series of annual surveys of libraries in institutions of higher education. In doing so, the Office takes a major step toward its goal of furnishing current data on all types of libraries. Public library statistics have been issued annually since 1945 and the first annual survey of school libraries (using sample techniques) was undertaken in 1960. Thus the compilation of academic library statistics completes the series of annual reports on the status of three basic types of libraries, thereby filling the gaps between the comprehensive surveys published approximately every 5 years.
>
> Plans for the survey of college and university libraries were developed by the Library Services Branch, in close cooperation with officers and committee members of ACRL and . . . ALA. Coordination was essential since this survey replaced the annual statistics formerly published in the January issues of *College and Research Libraries*. . . Thus, the Office of Education aims to maintain the familiar format of the discontinued ALA statistical series while giving for the first time a detailed analysis of the data.[2]

The content of the series was enlarged and changed over the years, but the format—an institutional report followed one or two years later by an analytical report—was maintained through the 1960s. Since 1965, when all Office of Education statistical functions were transferred to NCES, greater emphasis has been given to the analytical reports.

Table 1 shows the trend toward reduction in the number of surveys and publications between 1960 and 1984.[3] This trend is even more noticeable if nonsurvey years are considered: During the 1960s, the only nonsurvey year was 1965; in the 1970s, there were surveys in all even years except 1976; thus far in the 1980s, one survey was conducted in 1982—no surveys are scheduled for 1984. The reduced frequency is due not only to reduction of funds and staff but also to increases in survey costs, absence of new library support programs (which sparked the increase of surveys in 1959), and the Paper Reduction Act of 1980 (PL 96-511).

Association of Research Libraries

The collection of annual statistics of the largest university libraries has its origin in Princeton University surveys conducted annually from 1919 to 1962. In 1963, ARL assumed this function for its members in the United States and Canada. The data cover more than 100 of the largest academic libraries. The series is extensive in content and

Table 1 / Academic Library Surveys, 1960–1984

Survey Years	No. of Surveys	No. of Publications
1960–1969	9	15
1970–1979	6	11
1980–1984	1	1

provides a detailed ranking of member institutions in the United States and Canada by various criteria. The terminology of the surveys is compatible with that of NCES.

ALA/ACRL Statistics

Like most large professional associations today, ALA concerns itself with statistics through its committee structure. The results of the first series of ALA salary surveys, conducted between 1923 and 1934, were published in volumes 17–28 of the *ALA Bulletin*. In 1935, data on holdings and related items were added. Then in 1942, when statistical surveys were transferred to the various divisions, ACRL began to collect academic data and continued to do so until 1960. Results of its surveys were published in *College and Research Libraries*. ACRL discontinued direct participation in data collection with the 1958–1959 survey, when NCES started its annual series of college and university surveys.[4] Some 20 years later, as the federal government was slowing down its data collection, ACRL resumed direct surveys with the publication of ACRL university library statistics for 1978–1979 and 1981–1982. ACRL surveys are not truly national in scope; they represent only non-ARL university libraries. Even ACRL and ARL statistics combined provide data for no more than 200 of the major academic libraries in the United States; in contrast, NCES surveyed nearly 3,200 postsecondary institutions in 1983.

R. R. Bowker Company

For about 25 years, the R. R. Bowker Company has published a limited amount of statistical data on all types of libraries in its *American Library Directory*. The regularity of this publication qualifies the statistics as a series, but the limited scope of the data and the use of nonstandard terminology reduce their usefulness as a national survey system.

Other Statistical Sources

The Medical Library Association and the American Association of Law Libraries serially collect statistics for medical and law school libraries. Regional and state library associations and some state libraries also conduct surveys of academic institutions. Detailed information about some of these surveys is given in a recent article by Sandy Whiteley.[5]

Outlook

The drastic reduction by NCES in its collection of nationwide college and university library statistics and the incompleteness in scope or geographic coverage of the other series give reason for concern. Hopefully, the new ACRL Task Force on Library Statistics will find solutions for these problems. Also, an NCES contract was recently awarded to the American Library Association to study data acquisitions problems. Sharing of public and private funding and of the responsibility for various segments of the large statistical universe may be possible, if care is taken to standardize data input and processing. Definitive steps in this direction are important, because a profession without access to frequent and reliable data by which to evaluate its performance will be limited in its ability to plan for the future.

Notes

1. Frank L. Schick. "Developments in Library Statistical Activities," *Bowker Annual 1982.* 27th ed. (New York: R. R. Bowker Co., 1982), pp. 309–312.
2. U. S. Department of Health, Education and Welfare, *Library Statistics of Colleges and Universities* (Washington, D.C.: Government Printing Office, 1961), p. iii.
3. U. S. Department of Education, *Learning Resources Statistics Publications, 1960–1980.* Typescript. (Washington, D.C., 1981).
4. *Library Statistics of Colleges and Universities,* p. iii.
5. Sandy Whiteley, "Sources of Statistics of Academic Libraries," *College and Research Library News* 44, no. 7, pp. 221–222, 224–225.

Survey of Federal Libraries, FY 1978

Anne Heanue

Assistant Director, ALA Washington Office

The results of the long-awaited survey of federal libraries, FY 1978, conducted by Marcia C. Bellassai with funds provided by the Federal Library Committee and the National Center for Education Statistics (NCES), were published by NCES in March 1983.[1] The survey provides a wealth of data about the activities, expenditures, resources, functions, and staff of federal libraries not available anywhere else. These data are much needed by the broad range of people grappling with two of the major issues currently facing federal librarians—the revision of classification and qualification standards for librarians, library technicians, and information specialists in the federal government by the Office of Personnel Management (OPM) and the implementation of the Office of Management and Budget's Circular A-76, which sets federal policy on private-sector contracts for "commercial" activities, including library operations.[2] As Patricia Berger pointed out in her article in the 1983 *Bowker Annual,* "The New Federalism: How It Is Changing the Library Profession in the United States": "Because of the size and pervasiveness of this work force, government decisions about the status of federal librarians and the programs they operate tend to have ripple effects on the library community at large."[3]

The 1978 survey is the fifth comprehensive survey of federal libraries. Other surveys, in 1876, 1963, 1969, and 1972, contributed toward the development of a broad base from which to view the surprising variety of libraries that serve the federal establishment and its agencies throughout the world.

Survey Results

More than 2,100 federal libraries were surveyed in 1978. Nearly 1,400 libraries submitted individual data, and data were obtained from other sources for another 491 libraries. Thus, significant data are included for 1,880 federal libraries, representing 88 percent of the survey universe. During FY 1978, federal libraries spent more than $565 million. Of this amount, 57 percent was for salaries and wages, 19 percent for library materials and supplies, and 5 percent for automation. A total of 20,526 full-time equivalent (FTE) employees was reported. Of these employees, 65 percent were female, and the percentage of females decreased as salary increased. Less than one-third of the total work force was classified in the library series and about half of these were library professionals in the GS-1410 librarian series. The median number of staff in a federal library was three.

The results of the survey indicate a wide variety in the mission of federal libraries and the composition and size of their collections. At the end of FY 1978, federal libraries reported collection holdings of approximately 200 million items and an estimated total of 60 million individual service contacts. Circulation of materials comprised three-fourths of total estimated service contacts. Collection size ranged from the large holdings of the three national libraries (almost 80 million items, or two-fifths of the total) to the small holdings of the penal libraries, half of which reported collections of fewer than 3,000 items. The median collection consisted of about 12,500 items. In his foreword to the 1978 survey, Frank L. Schick observes that "Possibly the most revealing information about the size of Federal Libraries is that nearly three-quarters of them have collections of less than 30,000 items, and almost half have collections of less than 12,000 items. The number of titles reported held by Federal libraries in 1978 was nearly 71,000,000, a figure that seems low."[4] The survey shows that nearly 50,000 new periodical titles were added during the year for a total of more than 597,000 current periodical titles. (See Table 1.)

Distribution of Libraries

The mission of the library/system was the principal criterion used to determine the 16 types or subtypes in the federal library universe:

> *National libraries* have government-wide responsibilities and missions, including concern for both national and international matters.
>
> *Presidential libraries* specialize in the official records, memorabilia, literature, and other materials of a specific former president of the United States.
>
> *Systems headquarters* provide administrative and/or technical services to autonomous or semiautonomous libraries. The headquarters may or may not operate service outlets of its own.
>
> *Audiovisual libraries* support a variety of missions but are distinguished by collections consisting primarily of nonprint materials.
>
> *Engineering and science libraries* have collections devoted primarily to engineering and/or the sciences, except health sciences.
>
> *Medical libraries* are those with collections devoted primarily to medicine and the health sciences.
>
> *Law libraries* have collections devoted primarily to legal materials and support the efforts of courts and lawyers located throughout the federal government.
>
> *Special libraries* support specific special or technical mission plans, but their collections do not fall into any of the types thus far noted.
>
> *General (quasi-public) libraries* serve the general library needs of personnel assigned to a location or facility. These include base, post, and station libraries serving military members and their dependents throughout the world.
>
> *Patient libraries* meet the general library needs of persons in federal hospitals.
>
> *Penal libraries* provide general materials and services to inmates of federal correctional institutions.

Table 1 / Survey of Federal Libraries, FY 1978: Summary of Key Data Items

Item	National Libraries (n = 3)		Libraries Reporting Individual Data (n = 1,414)		Libraries Reporting Aggregate Data (n = 463)		Total (n = 1,880)	
	%*	No./Amount	%*	No./Amount	%*	No./Amount	%*	No./Amount
Collections								
Total collection items	100	79,875,902	99[a]	107,018,490	100	3,249,406	99	190,143,798
Total current periodical titles	100	198,711	93	397,998	17	474	74	597,183
Services								
Circulation	100	2,787,391	82	33,065,381	83	6,292,119	82	42,144,891
All interlibrary loan transactions	100	327,901	74	961,046	14	5,388	56	1,294,335
Information transactions	100	1,430,260	89	11,200,858	83	173,576	88	12,804,694
Photocopies for patrons†	100	198,276	46	3,377,548	—	—	47	3,575,824
Total service contacts	100	4,743,828	96	48,604,833	100	6,471,083	97	59,819,744
Automation								
Number of libraries reporting automation	67[b]	2	31	445	14[c]	63	27	510
Of technical services	67	2	24	338	—	—	18	340
Current	67	2	22	308	—	—	16	310
Under development	33	1	5	72	—	—	4	73
Online data bases	67	2	21	299	14	63	19	364
Expenditures								
Total	100	$210,016,912	98	$174,918,514	83	$180,604,932	95	$565,540,358
Salaries and wages	100	101,593,000	94	94,914,087	83	125,881,730	91	322,388,817
Materials‡	100	37,188,612	93	56,547,033	83	11,677,573	90	105,413,218
Automation	100	24,035,000	18	6,136,467	—	—	14	30,171,467
Employees								
Total	100	5,511	95	6,566	83	8,446	92	20,526
Female %	100	54	95	74	—	—	71	65
Total in 1410 series	100	1,162	57	2,043	—	—	43	3,205
Female %	100	53	57	73	—	—	43	66
Total GS 14 and above	100	447	4	84	—	—	3	531
Female %	100	24	4	44	—	—	3	28

*Percent of libraries in category responding to item.
†Estimated data.
‡Includes binding and materials for other libraries.
[a] Thirteen systems headquarters had no collections; another nine libraries did not report these data.
[b] Only cost data reported for the Library of Congress.
[c] No information is available concerning automation in the 383 AV libraries.

**Table 2 / Survey of Federal Libraries, FY 1978:
Distribution of Libraries**

Category	Number of Libraries	
	Identified	Responding
All Libraries	2,142	1,880
Governmental Organization		
Judicial branch	42	29
Legislative branch	8	5
Executive branch		
Civilian departments	517	432
Military departments	1,157	1,025
Independent agencies	418	389
Type of Library		
National	3	3
Special or technical	983	791
General	433	379
Educational	136	121
Multitype	162	162
Presidential	6	5
Systems headquarters	36	36
Audiovisual	383	383
Location		
Washington metropolitan area	220	167
Rest of United States	1,131	962
Outside United States	314	288
Multiple locations*	477	463

*Aggregate data.

Academic libraries serve the educational mission of federal colleges, universities, graduate and postgraduate schools, and nondegree-granting programs that enable students to derive college credit for course offerings.

Elementary, intermediate, and/or secondary school libraries provide curriculum support to students and faculty at military dependents schools and schools on Native American reservations.

Technical school libraries support vocational and/or technical nondegree-granting courses or training schools.

Multitype medical-patient libraries serve hospitals and medicenters.

Other multitype libraries include administrative combinations of two or more types of libraries other than medical-patient.

Table 2 shows the distribution of federal libraries identified for and responding to the 1978 survey, by governmental organization, type of library, and location in the United States.

Expenditures

A primary purpose of the FY 1978 federal survey was to update the data collected in FY 1972.[5] The 1,744 federal libraries reporting in FY 1972 had a total operating expenditure of $191,825,882. By FY 1978, 1,880 federal libraries reported expenditures of $565,540,358, with 57 percent spent on salaries and wages, 19 percent on library materials and supplies, and 5 percent on automation. Substantial variations in both amounts and distribution of expenditures reflected significant differences in the size and mission of the federal libraries. Apart from the national libraries, median reported library expenditures were highest in presidential libraries, followed by academic libraries and systems headquarters. Law libraries had the lowest median expenditures reported, followed by penal and school libraries. Expenditures for the Library of Congress totaled $165,686,912, or 29 percent of all expenditures reported. Some 11 tables in the survey report data on expenditures.

Staffing in Federal Libraries

In FY 1978, 20,526 full-time equivalent (FTE) staff worked in the 1,728 libraries reporting that data; in FY 1972, 11,080 FTE employees staffed 1,744 federal libraries.[6] Fourteen tables in the 1978 survey provide a comprehensive picture of the number of staff, distribution of employees in various types of libraries, numbers of employees in the various library classification series, salary grades in federal libraries, sex of library employees, and the educational level of library directors. Since OPM released the first draft of its controversial proposed classification and qualification standards in December 1981, allegations of discrimination against a female-dominated occupation have flourished. Table 3 indicates the percentage of women in the various library series.

Of the total 20,526 library employees, 3,205 (16 percent) were professional librarians in the GS-1410 librarian series. More than 36 percent of these were employed in national libraries. Veterans Administration libraries, and 63 percent of their employees in the GS-1410 series, had the highest proportion of professional librarians. Sixty-six percent of federal librarians in 1978 were female; however, 72 percent of librarians in grades GS-13 and above were male. These figures are almost unchanged since 1972, when 64 percent of

Table 3 / Percentage of Female Employees in Federal Libraries, by Library Classification and GS Salary Grade, FY, 1978

	Percent
Classification	
Appropriated fund	
1410 series	66
1411 series	72
1412 series	54
All others	60
Nonappropriated fund	66
Assigned military	32*
GS Salary Grade	
1–6	76
7–8	64
9	68
10–11	64
12	55
13	40
14	32
15	22
16 and over	17

*Does not include military employees of AV libraries.

Table 4 / Number of Titles in Federal Library Collections, FY 1978

Item	Number of Titles				% of All Titles	% of Microform Titles
	Print	Microform	Other	Total		
Bookstock	31,028,978	2,882,918	—	33,911,896	48	9
Periodicals	968,747	507,606	—	1,476,353	2	34
Loose-leaf services	48,222	—	—	48,222	*	—
Documents/reports	9,262,034	21,871,307	—	31,133,341	44	70
AV materials	—	—	3,052,112	3,052,112	4	—
Not specified	—	1,250,000†	—	1,250,000	2	100
Total	41,307,981	26,511,831	3,052,112	70,871,924	100	37

*Less than 1 percent.
†Includes periodicals and documents/reports.

all federal librarians were female, but 71 percent of those employed in grades GS-13 and above were male, despite the increase in the number of libraries reporting in 1978. [For a retrospective report on the status of female librarians, see "Women Predominate, Men Dominate: Disequilibrium in the Library Profession" in the Special Reports section of Part 1—*Ed.*]

Library Collections

At the end of FY 1978, almost 71 million titles were held by federal libraries, 58 percent of which were print materials, and 37 percent were microforms (Table 4). Although more than two-fifths of total items held were in national libraries, less than 20 percent of total titles held were there. More than one-quarter of all titles (25.5 percent) were held in science libraries, which included 43 percent of all microform titles. Current periodical subscriptions (exclusive of title duplication) totaled more than 597,000 at the end of FY 1978. By comparison, in FY 1972, approximately 59 million volumes were held in reporting libraries and 32 percent of those were held in the three national libraries.

Service to Users

Both the average number of service contacts and the percentage distribution of these contacts varied according to governmental organization and by type of library. Service contacts in the national libraries were highest for all service categories. Table 5 identifies the number of individual service contacts reported, by category of service.

Automation

Some form of automation was reported by 27 percent of all responding libraries (510), with online data bases the most used automated service. More than 71 percent of the libraries with automated services were special and technical libraries. Ninety-six percent of all data files used were commercial; only the national libraries reported more than half of online data files prepared in-house. In 1978, federal libraries spent almost $11 million on automation, representing 5 percent of total federal library expenditures that year. Comparable data are not available for the 1972 survey.

Table 5 / Service Contacts Reported by Federal Libraries, by Category of Service, FY 1978

Type of Service	% of Respondents	Total No.	Median No.	% of Total
Direct circulation	83	42,144,891	10,709	71
Interlibrary loan	56	1,294,335	—	2
Items loaned	—	703,795	78	—
Items borrowed	—	590,540	198	—
Information transactions	88	12,804,694	—	21
Reference	—	7,070,996	1,716	—
Directional	—	5,266,874	2,080	—
Online reference	—	466,824	520	—
Photocopies made for				
patrons (estimated)	35	3,575,824	—	6
Total service contacts	—	59,819,744	—	100

Cooperative Arrangements

One-quarter of the responding federal libraries reported participation in a network or other cooperative arrangement. According to the survey, most of these arrangements were designed to improve the flow of materials between libraries through interlibrary loan, although cataloging, technical processing services, centralized procurement, and bibliographic tools were also reported.

Overall, 471 libraries reported membership in an average of 2.2 cooperative groups; however, this would appear to be only a part of total federal library involvement in cooperative activities. A number of federal libraries have access to OCLC (Online Computer Library Center) through FEDLINK, the Federal Library and Information Network of the Federal Library Committee, and thus have access to the largest bibliographic network in the United States for cataloging data and location of interlibrary loan materials. Formal and informal interagency regional or topical networks also provide for resource sharing. These include the Regional Medical Library Network through the National Library of Medicine and such agency networks as those of the Department of Agriculture, the Environmental Protection Agency, the National Oceanic and Atmospheric Administration, and the Veterans Administration. [For an update on library networking in 1983, see the News Reports section of Part I—*Ed.*]

Cooperative arrangements are important not only to the federal establishment but to other libraries and their users because of the unique resources of federal libraries. In 1982, Alphonse F. Trezza submitted a report of the Intergovernmental Library Cooperation Project, titled *Toward a Federal Library and Information Services Network: A Proposal.* The report, a joint undertaking of the National Commission on Libraries and Information Science and the Library of Congress, extensively used the data of the 1978 survey to recommend a federal library and information services network to provide more and improved services to the government and the nation. Trezza noted that federal librarians are willing to participate more fully at the local, state, and national levels and that "the sharing of resources between federal and non-federal libraries hold the promise of more efficient and effective services to the primary users of all libraries."[7]

Conclusion

The *Survey of Federal Libraries, Fiscal Year 1978* is a milestone report—a benchmark against which changes in federal sector libraries should be measured, weighed, and compared. But this comprehensive profile of federal libraries in 1978 should be updated soon. Current data are needed not only to provide a base of general information about federal libraries but to measure the impact of changes now underway in federal government policies toward the operation of its libraries. Budget cuts, personnel changes, and the continued participation of federal libraries in established automation and other networks (as more of these libraries are contracted out to the private sector) are just a few of the significant shifts likely to happen in the near future. However, it is extremely difficult to make projections in 1984 on the basis of 1978 data. For data to be current, statistics should be updated every three to four years. Although a survey of federal libraries was projected for 1983 (every five years after 1972),[8] plans for the 1983 survey, as well as for a number of other statistical studies, were unfortunately eliminated because of budget cuts. Whether the project will be included in the 1985 budget is yet undetermined.

Only a few hundred copies for the 1978 survey were printed by the National Center for Education Statistics; however, the publication is available through ERIC, although it is costly in the paper edition (pap. $44.15; microfiche $1.37). Order the 619-page document, ED 231391, from CMIC-ERIC, Box 190, Arlington, VA 22210.

Notes

1. National Center for Education Statistics, *Survey of Federal Libraries, Fiscal Year 1978*, Marcia Bellassai, contractor (Washington, D.C.: National Center for Education Statistics, 1983).
2. U.S. Office of Management and Budget, OMB Circular No. A-76 (rev.), "Performance of Commercial Activities," *Federal Register*, August 16, 1983, pp. 37110–37116.
3. Patricia W. Berger, "The New Federalism: How It Is Changing the Library Profession in the United States," *Bowker Annual* (New York: R. R. Bowker, 1983), p. 36.
4. *Survey of Federal Libraries, Fiscal Year 1978*, p. v.
5. National Center for Education Statistics, *Survey of Federal Libraries, Fiscal Year, 1972* (Washington, D.C.: U.S. Government Printing Office, 1975).
6. Ibid., p. 11.
7. Alphonse F. Trezza, *Toward a Federal Library and Information Services Network: A Proposal*, Report of the Intergovernmental Library Cooperation Project, a joint undertaking of the National Commission on Libraries and Information Science and the Library of Congress (Washington, D.C.: U.S. Government Printing Office, 1982), p. vi.
8. Loretta Wright, *The Condition of Education, Part 2*, 1982 ed., NCES Programs and Plans, National Center for Education Statistics (Washington, D.C.: U.S. Government Printing Office, 1982), p. 30.

Expenditures for Resources in School Library Media Centers, FY 1982–1983

Marilyn L. Miller

Associate Professor, School of Library Science,
University of North Carolina, Chapel Hill

Barbara B. Moran

Assistant Professor, School of Library Science,
University of North Carolina, Chapel Hill

The ability to assess the development of school library service in the United States has been a persistent problem that is hampered by the irregularity of the availability of dependable statistics. For instance, during the last 20 years, only three national surveys of public school library media centers (LMCs) have been published. In 1963, a landmark survey, *Public School Library Statistics 1962–63,* was published by the U.S. Office of Education.[1] Fourteen years later, the department published *Statistics of Public School Library Media Centers, 1974* (LIBGIS I).[2] This was followed by *Statistics of Public School Libraries/Media Centers, 1978* (LIBGIS II), published in 1981.[3] The time lag between these reports, the failure of any other government department or professional

Note: Adapted from *School Library Journal,* October 1983.

organization to systematically gather statistics on LMCs, and the decision of the current federal administration to diminish the government's role in providing statistical data have prevented school librarians from monitoring levels of expenditures for resources and programs in LMCs.

It must be conceded that it is nearly impossible to account for all funding for LMCs. From building to building, district to district, county to county, and state to state, there is no uniformity to the way in which funds are obtained for and allocated to LMCs. Some library media specialists receive and all-inclusive budget from local school boards to cover the purchase or rental of all resources. Others, depending on location, may have access to supplementary funds from their counties and states in addition to federal funds. Still others rely heavily for additional money on gifts and fund-raising activities.

Methodology

In early April 1983, a questionnaire was mailed to the 2,000 LMCs included in the sample; the envelopes were stamped "Attention Librarian." Two follow-up mailings were subsequently sent to nonrespondents. By mid-June, 1,297 librarians had returned their questionnaires—a response rate of nearly 65 percent. Of these responses, 1,251 were usable, producing a final, usable rate of approximately 62 percent.

Responses were considered unusable for a variety of reasons, the most common being omission of most budget figures or reporting budget figures for more than one school. In addition, all responses from new schools were excluded from the data analysis because it was thought that the large start-up expenses of these schools would not represent the material-buying patterns of the typical school. Although the total number of respondents was 1,251, not all data reported are based on this total since, in some cases, respondents failed to report one or more items. For example, some respondents did not supply the information requested about salaries.

Every response was checked for accuracy, then coded and keypunched. Data analysis was done using the Statistical Analysis System (SAS), a packaged computer program. Measures of central tendency (means and medians) were produced for all of the budget items on the survey. It was decided to report both of these measures of central tendency to give a more accurate description of the data. Although the mean (or average) is the descriptive statistic most commonly used in studies of this type (for instance, in the LIBGIS studies), analysis showed that much of the data collected was positively skewed because a few respondents reported spending extremely large amounts for various types of library materials.

With a data distribution of this type, the few large scores make the mean a less desirable measure of central tendency because those large scores cause the mean itself to be unrealistically large. In instances where the data was skewed, simply reporting the mean would be misleading. For example, ten respondents reported spending more than $7,500 for audiovisual (AV) materials. When these ten responses were averaged with the other responses, the computed mean for AV expenditures was $978. If only the mean were reported, the reader might be led to think that a majority of LMCs spend about $1,000 a year on AV material. However, most spend considerably less than that amount. In this case, the median ($559) is a much more accurate assessment of spending (the median is simply the middle score reported by respondents). Here the median shows that one-half of the LMCs spend less than $559 a year on AV materials and one-half spend more. This provides a more realistic measure of expenditure.

Table 1 / Distribution of Respondents by School Level and Census Region

School Level	No. of Responses	Census Region	No. of Responses
Elementary	587	South	462
Jr. High/Middle	308	North Central	305
High School	304	Northeast	291
Other	49	West	190

The systematic sample of 2,000 was drawn from the approximately 33,000 school library subscribers to *School Library Journal* (*SLJ*). The *SLJ* subscription list is the most easily identifiable national list of LMCs. It is impossible to say how representative these are of all LMCs in the United States. LIBGIS II estimated that there were more than 70,000 schools with LMCs in 1978; an unknown number of schools have closed since then. We assume that many or most of the media specialists who serve more than one LMC enter only one subscription to *SLJ*; therefore it is our estimate that subscribers to *SLJ* constitute nearly one-half of all LMCs. Since LMCs subscribing to *SLJ* are probably more affluent than those that do not, it is likely that the data on expenditures in this survey are higher than if the sample had been drawn from all LMCs in the United States.

The Survey Instrument

Recipients of the survey, library media specialists, were asked to provide various demographic information such as geographic location, population served, and the size and level of the school. (Tables 1–3 present these distributions.) They were asked to describe themselves in terms of certification, employment status, years of experience, salary, and sex; and to describe the size of the school's library media collection, the type of clerical and unpaid volunteer assistance, whether the school system employed a district media coordinator, and their budgeting procedures.

The survey also asked respondents to report in detail specific amounts expended for a variety of materials, including microcomputer software and online services. A concluding section sought to identify: (1) the numbers of microcomputers in the LMC or the number located outside the center but managed by the library media center staff; (2) how the micros are used by students, media staff, and faculty.

Findings

Represented in this survey are 1,179 public and 72 private schools. The LMCs in these schools are administered by 1,192 certified library media specialists, 1,016 of whom work full-time in one school. In 141 (11 percent) of the schools, there are two certified media

Table 2 / Distribution of Respondents by School District Size and School Enrollment

School District Size	No. of Responses	Enrollment	No. of Responses
Under 50,000	751	Under 300	151
50,000–199,999	266	300–499	356
200,000–749,999	77	500–699	278
Over 750,000	32	700–999	227
		1,000–1,999	156
		Over 2,000	18

Table 3 / Distribution of Responses by Geographic Location and School District Population

	Under 50,000		50,000–199,000		200,000–749,000		750,000 & over		Total	
	No. of Responses	%	No. of Responses	%	No. of Responses	%	No. of Responses	%	No. of Responses	%
Northeast	212	18.79	42	3.72	7	0.62	1	0.09	262	23.23
South	231	20.48	113	10.02	40	3.55	21	1.86	405	35.90
North Central	211	18.71	58	5.14	10	0.89	6	0.53	285	25.27
West	98	8.69	54	4.79	20	1.77	4	0.35	176	15.60
Total	752	66.67	267	23.67	77	6.83	32	2.84	1,128	100.00

Table 4 / Expenditures and Collection Size in School Library Media Centers by Level of School

	Elementary N=587		Junior High/Middle N=308		Senior High N=304		Other N=49	
	Median	Mean	Median	Mean	Median	Mean	Median	Mean
Enrollment	450	476	696	718	900	976.33	520	507
Total materials expenditure (TME)[1]	$3,280	$3,984	$4,899	$5,779.24	$7,743.5	$9,155.87	$4,140	$5,008
TME per pupil	$7.29	$9.06	$7.33	$8.99	$9.04	$11.54	$10.07	$12.50
Size of book collection	8,000	8,593.3	10,000	10,567.4	12,000	13,633.7	10,000	11,681
Average books per pupil	17.51	20.42	14.50	16.29	14.51	17.06	22.31	28.62
Volumes added, 82–83	250	295.8	320	393.01	367	465.96	280	364.97
Size of AV collection	1,200	1,656	1,287.5	2,069.56	1,000	2,326.66	675	1,448.24
Average AV per pupil	2.62	3.71	2.00	2.97	1.25	2.70	1.42	3.06
AV added, 82–83	27.50	61.13	25	68.56	29.5	112.97	26	87.53
Media specialist Years experience	9	10.04	11	11.79	11	12.02	7.5	9.84
Salary	$19,000	$19,596	$21,013	$21,613	$19,987	$20,069.30	$15,500	$15,954.40

[1]Includes funds budgeted directly to the LMC through the LEA, federal funds, and gift funds.

Table 5 / Expenditures and Collection Size in School Library Media Centers by Region

	Northeast N=291		South N=464		North Central N=306		West N=190		All N=1251	
	Median	Mean	Median	Mean	Median	Mean	Median	Mean	Median	Mean
Enrollment	509	628	590	675	500	625	590	712	546	651
Total materials expenditures (TME)[1]	$4,383	$5,833	$4,120	$5,169	$4,800	$6,347	$4,762	$5,961	$4,400	$5,733
TME per pupil	$8.45	10.13	$6.85	8.29	$9.14	11.44	$7.69	10.20	$7.66	9.79
Size of book collection	10,000	11,160	9,080	9,922	9,000	10,352	9,512	10,653	9,442	10,431
Average books per pupil	18.20	22.3	14.7	16.6	16.9	19.8	15.6	17.9	16.01	18.9
Volumes added, 82–83	285	343	294	357	300	369.6	300	403	300	363
Size of AV collection	1,075	2,008.55	1,400	2,108	914	1,804	1,000	1,455	1,106	1,910
Average AV per pupil	2.16	3.47	2.5	3.4	1.6	3.3	1.44	2.47	2.05	3.26
AV added, 82–83	25	63.5	36	103	25	66	20	47	27	76
Media specialist Years experience	11	11.8	10	10.9	10	10.5	9	10.4	10	10.98
Salary	$20,000	$20,719	$18,366	$18,565	$19,810	$20,081	$24,000	$22,910	$19,870	$20,079

[1]Includes funds budgeted directly to the LMC through the LEA, federal funds, and gift funds.

Table 6 / Expenditures and Collection Size in School Library Media Centers by Size of Population Served by School District

	Below 50,000 N=752		50,000 to 199,999 N=267		200,000 to 749,000 N=77		Over 750,000 N=32	
	Median	Mean	Median	Mean	Median	Mean	Median	Mean
Enrollment	501	602	640	790	652	716	600	822
Total materials expenditures (TME)[1]	$4,521	$5,812	$4,410	$5,978	$3,662	$4,564	$5,090	$6,346
TME per pupil	$8.67	$11.01	$6.61	$7.76	$6.15	$6.33	$6.88	$8.04
Size of book collection	9,200	10,024	10,000	11,363	9,060	10,092	10,000	11,032
Average books per pupil	16.6	19.5	14.4	17.4	14.2	15.8	14.6	15.6
Books added, 82–83	300	359	300	368	225	306	349	577
Size of AV collection	1,000	1,739	1,259	2,332	1,319	1,929	1,900	2,255
Average AV per pupil	1.95	3.2	2.2	3.3	2.3	2.8	2.6	3.1
AV added, 82–83	25	66	31	100	20	71	30	88
Media specialist								
Years experience	10	10.8	10	11.7	11	11.6	10	11.2
Salary	$19,000	$19,590	$21,000	$21,281	$22,714	$22,325	$21,000	$21,861

[1]Includes funds budgeted through the LEA, federal funds, and gifts funds.

specialists, and 19 (0.15 percent) of the schools have three certified media specialists. The head media specialist in 91 percent of the schools is female. The reported years of experience range from five who were in their first year of service as media specialists to one who reported 47 years of service. Reported salaries for full-time staff range from $5,900 to $39,393. The typical or average LMC is administered by an experienced media specialist who earns barely $20,000 (see Table 4). (The "other" category, which represents only 49 combined K–12 schools and special schools of various kinds, must be excluded from comparison.)

Full-time clerical assistance is available in 63 percent of the LMCs, and 34 percent of the centers use adult volunteers, ranging from 113 schools, each of which has one, to a center that uses 51. Students volunteer in 71 percent of the schools, ranging from the 22 schools that reported only one student to the 3 in each of which 99 students work. Slightly more than half of the library media specialists work directly with district-level media coordinators.

School library media specialists reported spending, from all building-assigned funds, a total of $6,948,265, or $9.79 per pupil, on print, audiovisual, and computer materials, and materials for producing resources. The majority of school library media specialists do not administer funds received as a result of budget preparation and presentation to meet identified needs. Rather, they administer funds generally allocated on a per-pupil basis by their administrations. If a library media specialist does develop a budget, it is a line-item expenditure budget.

Only elementary schools meet the lower level for the basic book collection recommended by *Media Programs: District and School,* the American Association of School Librarians/Association of Educational Communications and Technology national standards published in 1965, which we will call *The Standards.* It should be remembered, however, that *The Standards*, which recommend 8,000–12,000 volumes for an enrollment of 500 (or 16–24 books per user), assume that the collection has been

Table 7 / Comparison of Private and Public School Library
Media Centers

	Private N=72		Public N=1179	
	Median	*Mean*	*Median*	*Mean*
Enrollment	440	460	550	669
Total material expenditures (TME)[1]	$4,299	$5,131	$4,405	$5,767.68
TME, per pupil	$10.88	$12.55	$7.60	$9.62
Size of book collection	8,500	9,783	9,500	10,470.2
Average books per pupil	20	27.08	15.86	18.44
Volumes added, 82–83	336	387.14	300	362
Size of AV collection	600	1,190.25	1,200	1,952.53
Average AV per pupil	1.42	3.20	2.08	3.26
AV added, 82–83	25	99.38	27	74.77
Media specialist Years experience	8	8.92	10	11.08
Salary	$13,600	$13,880	$20,000	$20,389

[1]Includes funds budgeted directly to the LMC through the LEA on school governance board, federal funds and gift funds.

Table 8 / School Library Media Center Collections, Expenditures, and Volunteer Assistance by School Enrollment

	Under 300 Students N=151		300–499 Students N=356		500–699 Students N=278	
	Median	Mean	Median	Mean	Median	Mean
Collections						
Size of book collection	6,125	6,740	8,000	8,378	9,000	9,806
Volumes added '82–'83	200	233	230	280	300	362
Number of books per pupil	28	32	20	21	16	17
Size of AV collection	500	1,049	1,009	1,528	1,200	1,725
Number of AV added '82–'83	15	37	25	55	34	89
Number of AV items per pupil	2.3	4.6	2.70	3.82	2	3
Expenditures						
Salary of head school library media specialist	$17,071	$17,000	$19,500	$20,043	$19,000	$19,416
Amount spent for books	1,425	1,543	1,429	1,863	2,200	2,514
Amount spent per pupil for books	6.00	7.00	3.80	4.70	3.73	4.33
Amount spent for periodicals	354	470	400	545	500	667
Amount spent per pupil for periodicals	1.53	2.30	.98	1.36	.89	1.14
Amount spent for AV materials	365	614	400	708	663	966
Amount spent per pupil for AV materials	1.60	2.70	1.00	1.77	1.11	1.64
Volunteer assistance						
Adult volunteers	—	2	—	3	—	2
Student volunteers	—	8	—	8	—	10

	700–999 Students N=227		1000–1999 Students N=156		2000 and above N=18	
	Median	Mean	Median	Mean	Median	Mean
Collections						
Size of book collection	10,971	11,843	15,000	16,197	25,000	26,265
Volumes added '82–'83	325	417	500	588	656	784
Number of books per pupil	14	14	12	12	12	11
Size of AV collection	1,380	1,994	2,000	3,557	1,705	4,270
Number of AV added '82–'83	30	62	35	151	20	132
Number of AV items per pupil	1.6	2.4	1.6	2.6	.81	1.58
Expenditures						
Salary of head school library media specialist	$20,000	$20,721	$22,000	$22,437	$25,600	$23,778
Amount spent for books	2,536	3,189	4,262	4,578	8,203	11,398
Amount spent per pupil for books	3.06	3.9	3.34	3.47	4.09	4.68
Amount spent for periodicals	700	852	1,200	1,400	2,700	2,754
Amount spent per pupil for periodicals	.83	1.02	.90	1.05	1.14	1.12
Amount spent for AV materials	750	1,231	950	1,542	1,409	2,375
Amount spent per pupil for AV materials	.94	1.46	.68	1.16	.63	1.02
Volunteer assistance						
Adult volunteers	—	2	—	3	—	3
Student volunteers	—	11	—	17	—	17

weeded and that it represents appropriate and usable volumes. This survey requested neither the number of books discarded in 1982–1983 nor an assessment of the quality of the book collection, which would include, among other things, an assessment of relevance of titles to the curriculum, the currency of titles, and the adequacy of the number of copies.

As students progress through the schools, they have access to smaller collections of both print and AV materials. We realize, of course, that no media specialist has enough funds to buy one hardcover book per pupil per year in addition to other resources, and no average school meets the minimum recommended numbers of AV materials. It should also be noted that respondents were not asked to describe the existing AV collection in their schools by type of material. However, the size of the average AV collection is so small that, at this stage, the lack of this information is not necessarily a problem. Playing the numbers game is risky, and the writers acknowledge that there is no research that substantiates quantitative recommendations, but experience and common sense lead to the inevitable conclusion that the average LMC in the United States, as described in this study, has not yet been developed into an adequately stocked, multimedia center.

Interesting differences begin to appear when the average LMC is described regionally (see Table 5) and by size of school district served (see Table 6). Although the schools are smaller in the north central region, media specialists there spent more money per pupil, added more books in 1982–1983, and, with their colleagues in the Northeast, provided their students with slightly more books per pupil than did media specialists in the other two regions. Although media specialists in the West have slightly less experience than their colleagues in other parts of the country, their salaries are the highest.

Students in the South have access to the smallest total collections of resources, although southern schools have the largest collections of AV resources. Schools in the South make the lowest per-pupil expenditures for resources. Media specialists serving southern schools earn the lowest salaries in the country—the median salary is $1,500 below the national median.

Table 9 / Comparison of Schools with and without District-
Level Library Media Coordinators

	Districts with Media Coordinator N=666		Districts without Media Coordinator N=597	
	Median	Mean	Median	Mean
Enrollment	595	695	505	617
Total materials expenditures (TME)	$4,210	$5,699	$4,636	$5,789
TME per pupil	$6.98	$8.80	$8.80	$10.92
Book collection	10,000	10,702	9,000	10,129
Ave. books per pupil	15.8	18	16	20
Books added, 83–83	300	368	300	360
AV collection	1,364	2,248	934	1,493
Ave. AV per pupil	2.38	3.45	1.67	3.03
AV added, 82–83	31	95	25	54.5
Media specialist salary	$20,000	$20,699	$18,657	$19,354
Clerical assistance	——	.83	——	.77
Adult volunteers	——	2.46	——	1.85

Presently, small school districts are spending the most per pupil on resources for their LMCs, which house the largest per-pupil collections, and they are paying the lowest salaries to media specialists (see Table 6). Data organized this way are possibly the least meaningful to readers, but they do indicate that collection development in the largest schools in areas serving a population of 200,000 to 749,000 is difficult to maintain with a materials expenditure of $6.15 per pupil.

No attempt was made to determine the affiliations (or any other special characteristic) of the private schools represented in the survey. Since only 72 private schools responded, the only comparison that can be made with public schools is at the national level. As shown in Table 7, media specialists in private schools serve fewer students, have more money to spend on resources, administer smaller collections, and earn more modest salaries.

Table 8 summarizes the major data by size of school enrollment. Although larger schools have larger total collections, their 1982–1983 per-pupil expenditures were much less than those in the smaller schools. Only the smaller schools now exceed the standards for book collections; with an expenditure of $7.00 per pupil for books, only the smaller schools can hope to add one hardcover trade book per student. Such expenditures, maintained at this level, will quickly lead to collection erosion. AV materials collections in all schools remain markedly small by national standards.

District Media Coordinators

The advantages to a school media program of a district media coordinator are not clearly demonstrated in this study, since respondents were not asked to describe district-level resources and services. As reported in Tables 9–11, schools without district coordinators

Table 10 / Budget Preparation with and without District-Level Library Media Coordinators

Budget Preparation	Districts with Media Coordinator %	(No.)	Districts w/o Media Coordinator %	(No.)	Total %	(No.)
Prepare budget on perceived needs and/or objectives	10.85	(134)	12.79	(158)	23.64	(292)
Prepare budget based on per pupil allocation and stated objectives	11.09	(137)	5.59	(69)	16.68	(206)
Receive stated amount allocated by administration with no budget input	29.80	(368)	25.67	(317)	55.47	(685)
Spend until "No More Funds Available"— no budget	0.73	(9)	1.13	(14)	1.86	(23)
Do not use budget—no funds allocated to LMC	0.32	(4)	0.40	(5)	0.73	(9)
Other	0.81	(10)	0.81	(10)	1.62	(20)

Table 11 / Use of Library Media Advisory Committee with and without District-Level Library Media Coordinator

	Districts with Media Coordinator		Districts w/o Media Coordinator		Total	
	%	(No.)	%	(No.)	%	(No.)
Use of Library Media Advisory Committee	13.2	(164)	6.36	(79)	19.57	(243)
Prediction of budget for 83–84						
About same as 82–83	30.26	(367)	25.97	(315)	56.22	(682)
Less than 82–83	15.09	(183)	12.86	(156)	27.95	(339)
More than 82–83	8.16	(99)	7.67	(93)	15.83	(192)
	53.51	(649)	46.50	(564)	100	(1,213)

have more money per pupil to spend on resources and have more books per pupil than those schools with district coordinators. However, in those same schools, the media specialist is paid less, has slightly less clerical assistance, and uses fewer adult volunteers. Audiovisual expenditures and collection size are still low for schools in both categories, although the supervised school has a larger AV collection and, in 1982–1983, acquired slightly more AV items.

In looking at the data relating to budgets and use of faculty media selection committees, factors that might imply the value of district-level leadership, the differences are still not clearly apparent. Of the 498 media specialists who prepare a budget (either to present as rationale for funding or to handle per-pupil allocated funds), only 54 percent work with district coordinators. In addition, although the 30 percent of the total that work with district media coordinators prepare no budget and deal with per-pupil allocations, only 25.6 percent of those without coordinators operate the same way (see Table 10).

A second leadership indicator might be in the number of schools in which media specialists select materials with the assistance of a library media advisory committee. In this instance, twice as many media specialists with coordinators, 13.2 percent, as those lacking district-level leadership, 6.36 percent, use this selection help.

Budget forecasting is barely more supportive of the presence of coordinators if maintaining the same level of financing in this bleak school economy is viewed as positive. If this view is held, only 15 percent that have media coordinators expect to have less money in the 1983–1984 school year, as compared with 12.86 percent of those who do not have coordinators and expect to have less money. Slightly more (8.16 percent) district-led centers predict more available funds in 1983–1984, as compared with the 7.67 percent who do not have central leadership, but who look forward to increased funding.

Expenditures for Types of Resources

How school library media center administrators allocate 1982–1983 funds among a variety of instructional resources is reported in Table 12. Many states request detailed annual reporting of collection development, so it was a surprise in this era of accountability to find that many media specialists do not keep acquisitions records in a

Table 12 / Average Expenditures by School Library Media Centers by Region*

	Northeast N=291		South N=461		North Central N=306		West N=190	
	No. of Responses	Amt.	No. of Responses	Amt.	No. of Responses	Amt.	No. of Responses	Amt.
Books	200	$2,301.40	349	$1,972.95	209	$2,113.71	127	$2,271.77
Paperbacks	200	152.03	347	80.37	207	133.97	127	248.56
Permabounds	200	120.76	348	104.99	207	153.04	127	187.88
Professional Books	200	79.32	349	52.86	208	62.55	127	66.00
General Periodicals	215	676.16	369	449.80	214	695.08	144	722.15
Professional Periodicals	215	135.88	369	110.18	214	121.13	144	108.35
Microforms	279	103.36	435	33.72	290	35.96	175	56.93
Filmstrips (incl. sound)	180	565.78	280	560.00	168	455.32	103	390.85
Audiotapes, cassettes, and disc recordings	179	56.54	282	53.66	168	48.50	103	50.81
Transparencies (commercial)	179	8.50	280	5.18	168	5.73	103	12.60
Multi Media Kits	180	138.43	280	147.19	169	108.30	103	137.94
Picture/Poster(s) Sets	179	14.79	280	15.52	168	11.80	103	27.42
Recorded Videotapes/ Cassettes	179	21.56	280	27.79	168	49.69	103	64.56
Realia	179	4.18	280	3.01	168	7.64	103	9.22
Loop Films	179	4.16	280	3.96	168	8.92	103	2.99
16mm Films	178	77.07	280	14.71	168	194.92	103	23.39
8mm Films	178	—	280	0.12	169	—	103	5.82
AV Supplies-transparency film, blank tapes, photo. film, etc.	274	235.32	438	168.41	289	283.92	178	164.33

*This table presents expenditures from only the schools that could report subdivided expenditures for specific resources, and only mean expenditures are reported. Because expenditures for computer software and services are made by so few LMCs at this stage, these data have been reported in Table 13.

way that allows them to report easily and quickly the actual or estimated expenditures for specific resources.

Reports from those who could detail specific expenditures revealed, to no one's surprise, that books and periodicals for students take the major share. With funds currently limited, it is noteworthy that so little is spent for paperbacks and microforms. More original publishing in paperback, the development of so-called quality paperback publishing, demonstrated student affinity for paperbacks, and the inexorable climb of hardcover book prices make these low expenditures of particular interest.

Amounts expended for AV materials ranged from $0–$14,850, and approximately 21 percent of the respondents reported spending no funds at all on AV resources. Most AV expenditures are concentrated on filmstrips, multimedia kits, production supplies, and audio recordings.

We believe the status of AV materials in LMCs and schools needs more investigation. For instance, the amount being expended for print and AV materials that go directly into the classroom, bypassing the acquisition and management procedures of the media center, is unknown, as is the amount of district-level centralization of AV materials. Whether the centralized administration and distribution of AV materials, popular in the sixties and during the early days of the media center concept, will be resumed or continued in the face of critically low budgets is also a matter of speculation. Also unknown is just how much and what kind of use is made, generally, of AV materials. Since the characteristics of AV use are not known, we have to ask whether the levels recommended by *The Standards* for any materials reflect the need for and the use of resources in quality instructional programs.

Microcomputers and LMCs

The following quotations from two survey respondents typify the hopes and the despairs of media specialists as they confront the impact of the microcomputer.

> "Electronic learning" (computers) is considered a logical extension of the role the library has traditionally played. The librarian is the logical person to coordinate the use of the library computer center, *and* to have primary responsibility for the acquisition of software.
>
> *—Junior High School Respondent*

> The push for computers means that the money... formerly used for library materials is all being used to put computers in the school. This is a definite setback for library funds.
>
> *—Secondary School Respondent*

Nearly 30 percent of the responding media specialists manages microcomputers located in or near the LMC. The majority of the media specialist-managed micros are located in the LMC (see Table 13), where 54 percent of them are permanently housed for use by students and school staff (see Table 14). Table 13 also reports the mean expenditures of LMC allocations from local funds for microcomputer software by the schools reporting such expenditures. Elementary schools report the highest expenditures ($595) for microcomputer software. Table 15 reports how micros located permanently in the LMC are used. It is noteworthy that the major microcomputer use is by students, with only 108 media specialists (fewer than one-third of the respondents) reporting that they were using micros for LMC management functions.

Table 13 / Microcomputer Location, Management, and Software Expenditures in School Library Media Centers ($n = 362$)

	Elementary		Junior/High Middle School		Senior High		Combination	
	No. of responses	Mean	No. of responses	Mean	No. of responses	Mean	No. of responses	Mean
Micros located in LMC	186	2.46	70	2.0	96	2.52	9	2.0
Micros located outside LMCs and managed by media specialist	84	3.69	22	4.09	32	5.75	6	7.33
Local expenditures for software	81	$595	37	$322	46	$381	5	$523

Table 14 / Management of Micros Located in School Library Media Centers

	Elementary		Junior/Middle School		Senior High		Combination	
	No. of Responses	%	No. of Responses	%	No. of Responses	%	No. of Responses	%
Circulated to classrooms	87	25	32	9	25	7	2	.56
Located permanently and available to students and school staff	100	28	57	16.06	35	10	4	1
Located permanently in LMC but available only to LMC staff	1	.28	5	1	5	1	1	.28
Total*	188	53	94	26	66	19	7	2

*Most figures have been rounded.

Table 15 / Uses of Microcomputers in School Library Media Centers

Use	No. of Respondents
Computer-assisted instruction	265
Computer awareness	255
Programming	180
Games	135
LMC management	110
Computer-managed instruction	68
Word processing	65
Other	10

Summary of Total Expenditures

Tables 16 and 17 summarize the total expenditures for resources from local and federal funds. Funds from gifts, fund raising, and so on, were relatively minor, with 455 schools (36 percent) reporting media gifts of $300, or $0.53 per pupil. Although a full picture of the results of the first year of the new federal block grants program has not been drawn, it is obvious from Table 16 that federal funds were not a major force in acquisitions for LMCs in 1982–1983. Only 40 percent of the schools reported receiving funds for a total per-pupil allocation of $3.32, the majority of which was spent for books.

LIBGIS I (1974) reported an average per-pupil expenditure of $4.22 for books and LIBGIS II (1978) an average expenditure of $4.25 per pupil for books. That LMCs are seriously continuing to lose ground in the purchasing of resources can be verified by comparing those amounts with the 1982–1983 mean expenditures of $4.58 (median, $3.71)—a modest average increase of $0.33 over a five-year period during which juvenile book prices rose 30 percent. Media specialists purchasing adult nonfiction and reference books face even greater increases.[4]

Conclusion

School library media specialists have obviously made progress over the last 20 years in their efforts to provide a library resource center in every school. There are, however, disquieting signs in this data. We are obviously a long way from seeing adequately stocked and adequately maintained multimedia collections in all schools, since more than

Table 16 / Use of Federal Funds for Resources
(*n* = 504)*

	Mean Amount
Books	$1,152
Audiovisual resources	502
Periodicals	52
Microforms	19
AV supplies	30
Computer software and services	156
Total federal funds	1,912
Total federal funds per pupil	3.32

*Only schools reporting use of federal funds

Table 17 / Mean and Median Expenditures on Books, AV, and Periodicals:
Total and Per-Pupil

Type of Expenditures	Total Expenditures		Per-Pupil Expenditures	
	Mean	Median	Mean	Median
Audiovisual	$978	$559	$1.70	$1.00
Books	2,725	2,023	4.58	$3.71
Periodicals	775	550	1.33	.96

one-quarter of the respondents fear they will have lower budgets in 1983–1984. At the reported level of present funding, collection erosion is a serious threat; the lack of available money for AV resources comes at a time when we purport to know a great deal about the value of multimedia resources and their use in the teaching-learning process.

Survey research often raises more questions than it answers—this study is no exception. In next year's survey we intend to continue determining and describing the use of microcomputers in the schools. After we reviewed the responses to the microcomputer section of the questionnaire, it became evident that we should have tried to describe the use of micros throughout the school rather than just in the LMC. We also expect to trace whether declining LMC budgets are due in any part to a diversion of funds to micro software purchases. We will try to study expenditures for resources that go into classroom media collections, the resources provided by district resource centers, and how resources are selected. We will also attempt to learn more about media specialists themselves.

Notes

1. U.S. Office of Education, *Public School Library Statistics, 1962–63* (Washington, D.C.: U.S. Office of Education, 1963).

2. Nicholas Osso, *Statistics of Public School Library Media Centers, 1974* (Washington, D.C.: U.S. Dept. of Health, Education, and Welfare, 1977).

3. National Center for Education Statistics, *Statistics of Public School Libraries/Media Centers, 1978* (Washington, D.C.: Dept. of Education, 1981).

4. Consult Chandler B. Grannis, "Title Output and Average Prices. 1982 Preliminary Figures." *Publishers Weekly,* March 11, 1983, p. 44.

Public and Academic Library
Acquisition Expenditures, 1982–1983

Every two years until 1983 and annually since then, the R. R. Bowker Company has compiled statistics on library acquisition expenditures from information reported in the *American Library Directory* (*ALD*). The statistics given here are based on information from the thirty-sixth edition of the directory (1983). In most cases, the statistics reflect expenditures for the 1982–1983 period. The total number of public libraries listed in the thirty-sixth edition of *ALD* is 8,822; the total number of academic libraries is 4,900.

Understanding the Tables

Number of libraries includes only those libraries in *ALD* that reported annual acquisition expenditures (7,615 public libraries; 2,847 academic libraries). For the second consecutive year, libraries that reported annual income but not expenditures are not included in the count. Academic libraries include university, college, and junior college libraries. Special academic libraries, such as law and medical libraries, that reported acquisition expenditures separately from the institution's main library are counted as independent libraries.

Total acquisition expenditures for a given state is almost always greater than (in a few cases equal to) the sum of the categories of expenditure. This is because the total acquisition expenditures amount also includes the expenditures of libraries that did not itemize by category.

Figures in *categories of expenditure* columns represent only those libraries that itemized expenditures. Libraries that reported a total acquisition expenditure amount but did not itemize are only represented in the total acquisition expenditures column.

Unspecified includes monies reported as not specifically for books, periodicals, audiovisual, microform, or binding (e.g., library materials). This column also includes monies reported for categories in combination, for example, audiovisual *and* microform. When libraries report only total acquisition expenditures without itemizing by category, the total amount is not reflected as unspecified.

Estimated percent of acquisitions is based on a comparison of the total expenditures for each of the categories and the total of all of the categories, that is, the total amount spent on books in the United States was compared with the sum of all of the categories of expenditure. The reader should note, therefore, that the percentages are not based on the figures in the total acquisition expenditures column.

Special Note for 1982–1983: Through refinement of the computer program in 1983, the proportion of the 1982–1983 expenditures identified as unspecified has been considerably reduced, with corresponding increases in the percentages of the other categories of expenditure. Readers should bear this in mind when comparing the 1982–1983 percentages with those for 1981–1982.

Table 1 / Public Library Acquisition Expenditures, 1982–1983

State	Number of Libraries	Total Acquisition Expenditures	Categories of Expenditure					
			Books	Periodicals	Audiovisual	Microform	Binding	Unspecified
Alabama	129	$3,613,104	$1,873,780	$409,816	$302,911	$238,032	$28,950	$22,444
Alaska	24	1,605,025	557,697	59,516	204,363	212,800	26,175	—
Arizona	66	3,657,416	2,623,203	319,701	124,785	22,820	73,960	300
Arkansas	46	1,527,312	839,924	110,258	19,478	43,548	11,927	—
California	173	36,702,411	21,997,744	3,689,224	1,337,682	444,241	272,459	17,118
Colorado	107	3,325,107	3,546,446	434,090	96,047	25,407	66,906	—
Connecticut	149	6,524,305	3,061,571	349,252	260,656	26,649	65,256	—
Delaware	23	986,771	604,266	138,705	89,539	4,361	—	3,500
District of Columbia	1	726,700	600,205	94,103	32,392	—	—	—
Florida	130	12,255,164	6,179,507	883,581	513,539	255,715	118,575	3,437
Georgia	52	5,279,634	1,646,596	192,302	162,982	107,245	39,601	2,302
Hawaii	2	2,020,155	—	—	—	—	—	—
Idaho	92	1,151,998	649,495	42,011	42,041	10,178	3,570	—
Illinois	526	22,198,901	10,850,798	1,527,259	1,642,245	373,175	247,901	43,909
Indiana	212	9,476,904	4,322,544	393,614	396,702	57,590	151,011	8,800
Iowa	474	4,713,563	2,470,274	369,836	191,517	72,831	23,789	—
Kansas	288	3,819,533	2,584,493	372,163	75,799	36,732	35,393	—
Kentucky	109	8,790,382	4,065,326	192,223	186,893	43,568	32,922	—
Louisiana	62	4,569,257	2,691,969	339,134	222,080	1,225	60,222	500
Maine*	169	1,687,186	854,617	101,335	18,313	14,810	16,427	—
Maryland	28	9,466,330	6,141,492	386,461	612,862	28,695	45,402	—
Massachusetts	311	11,570,082	6,137,281	581,658	267,593	151,758	95,887	7,334
Michigan	344	13,213,286	7,343,073	1,136,439	659,298	71,587	140,876	13,713
Minnesota	114	7,226,740	5,087,157	484,344	538,371	44,063	87,110	987
Mississippi	47	2,471,672	1,111,169	150,665	71,665	34,533	23,798	4,773
Missouri	117	5,515,311	3,864,210	654,168	366,986	157,569	78,910	—
Montana	73	992,264	603,558	90,765	5,075	4,671	4,678	2,626
Nebraska	190	2,413,621	1,053,658	64,084	67,604	30,002	29,871	—
Nevada	20	1,144,222	838,110	37,299	22,158	—	3,425	—
New Hampshire	214	1,834,072	1,457,141	49,601	21,967	8,855	6,262	350

Table 1 / Public Library Acquisition Expenditures, 1982–1983 (cont.)

State	Number of Libraries	Total Acquisition Expenditures	Categories of Expenditure					
			Books	Periodicals	Audiovisual	Microform	Binding	Unspecified
New Jersey	278	$14,321,194	$8,315,504	$1,192,282	$432,878	$177,342	$89,538	$65,978
New Mexico	46	1,413,197	677,524	102,657	36,205	3,200	6,300	—
New York	677	46,213,738	32,112,980	2,964,098	975,421	296,534	296,959	17,100
North Carolina	118	7,632,097	4,464,610	698,136	432,833	140,148	75,778	—
North Dakota	42	974,686	541,170	51,213	65,824	11,500	1,400	—
Ohio	236	23,075,435	14,964,273	2,042,891	1,660,105	279,191	344,644	—
Oklahoma	83	3,626,813	2,155,766	359,024	196,835	104,518	51,237	—
Oregon	94	3,010,007	1,630,994	191,045	55,682	5,446	6,777	—
Pennsylvania	419	11,878,607	8,843,406	1,075,539	248,870	307,848	65,394	600
Rhode Island	45	1,665,713	674,953	85,594	119,249	13,500	17,231	—
South Carolina	39	3,207,975	1,826,494	140,476	132,849	6,035	22,234	—
South Dakota	62	884,143	463,577	88,402	84,288	27,537	8,631	—
Tennessee	108	3,617,275	2,229,812	372,170	261,517	37,678	39,827	—
Texas	367	18,265,055	11,511,613	1,806,007	858,168	90,362	360,624	1,370,015
Utah	41	2,141,282	519,467	35,916	24,318	1,133	26,331	—
Vermont	145	1,079,548	484,431	50,195	22,278	5,018	3,842	—
Virginia	79	8,927,533	5,124,350	606,442	289,605	109,232	101,497	549,432
Washington	62	8,407,217	4,770,147	712,977	520,851	39,433	29,442	15,565
West Virginia	68	2,300,348	1,271,519	153,208	292,568	4,789	13,188	88,092
Wisconsin	287	7,782,971	2,990,919	389,666	391,242	52,119	52,438	2,058
Wyoming	24	1,283,502	484,477	44,580	56,775	2,500	11,850	—
Pacific Islands	1	252,718	71,347	24,717	29,795	—	500	—
Puerto Rico	1	165,694	—	—	—	—	—	—
Virgin Islands	1	30,000	—	—	—	—	—	—
Total U.S.	7,615	$362,635,176	$211,786,637	$26,840,842	$15,741,699	$4,237,723	$3,416,925	$2,238,863
Estimated % of acquisitions			80.1	10.2	6.0	1.6	1.3	0.8

*The 1981–1982 total acquisition expenditures figure for Maine in *The Bowker Annual*, 1983, p. 340, should be corrected to $1,603,973. The "Total U.S." figure also should be adjusted accordingly.

Table 2 / Academic Library Acquisition Expenditures, 1982–1983

State	Number of Libraries	Total Acquisition Expenditures	Categories of Expenditure					
			Books	Periodicals	Audiovisual	Microform	Binding	Unspecified
Alabama	49	$7,456,771	$3,914,544	$1,787,368	$97,770	$96,877	$189,133	$6,744
Alaska	11	1,889,466	739,714	268,448	60,841	31,675	45,045	—
Arizona	28	9,215,304	1,947,990	1,427,108	102,216	47,931	170,429	—
Arkansas	31	4,746,208	1,495,195	917,570	24,121	148,647	84,863	154,522
California	225	65,507,580	24,041,302	18,255,103	1,096,576	1,130,178	3,347,905	54,203
Colorado	38	6,878,095	2,600,613	2,508,124	222,639	63,012	196,893	19,518
Connecticut	47	10,539,740	2,401,639	2,389,998	123,623	103,795	383,811	—
Delaware	8	2,136,780	1,773,563	17,408	3,738	2,092	141,383	6,000
District of Columbia	25	11,530,702	4,676,187	3,012,481	92,936	141,500	259,335	—
Florida	86	20,513,507	8,426,933	6,562,941	572,286	392,796	900,536	538,674
Georgia	67	11,997,589	4,442,353	4,634,838	171,182	256,891	526,517	266,120
Hawaii	14	2,893,168	1,251,556	1,390,896	69,049	63,517	217,200	—
Idaho	10	2,175,952	556,226	660,456	53,213	28,605	35,793	—
Illinois	126	31,287,852	9,981,847	2,126,194	825,012	304,088	1,224,231	3,800
Indiana	47	12,356,915	4,657,669	3,040,677	129,809	107,684	482,787	112,000
Iowa	52	9,249,404	1,950,257	3,981,496	87,693	146,191	396,344	—
Kansas	50	6,907,173	3,112,489	2,664,238	103,869	72,506	295,522	—
Kentucky	40	8,743,671	4,254,065	2,708,998	89,929	74,927	306,333	18,000
Louisiana	34	8,629,649	3,782,346	2,225,644	91,122	254,366	399,883	—
Maine	26	2,711,391	888,991	1,019,352	58,332	30,826	52,770	500
Maryland	39	5,076,703	1,665,045	1,284,317	121,763	199,052	97,499	500
Massachusetts	135	30,652,543	19,577,911	5,437,467	267,778	284,002	1,713,326	69,800
Michigan	85	21,117,517	8,343,908	3,996,298	245,315	203,433	713,991	—
Minnesota	55	8,248,952	3,410,507	3,130,103	130,433	60,749	385,140	—
Mississippi	46	5,913,631	1,703,586	1,378,650	119,091	205,364	139,891	—
Missouri	72	10,108,439	3,385,776	4,084,161	214,021	331,562	468,249	15,000
Montana	12	1,425,266	505,600	738,276	16,500	3,800	20,040	—
Nebraska	31	5,088,517	1,868,093	2,145,749	75,568	31,789	248,840	113,794
Nevada	7	1,287,655	480,841	513,302	41,600	—	75,583	—

Table 2 / Academic Library Acquisition Expenditures, 1982–1983 (cont.)

State	Number of Libraries	Total Acquisition Expenditures	Categories of Expenditure					
			Books	Periodicals	Audiovisual	Microform	Binding	Unspecified
New Hampshire	26	$3,862,921	$1,271,879	$1,608,755	$36,272	$199,058	$118,376	$23,650
New Jersey	56	13,153,953	6,166,630	2,866,222	380,520	194,322	576,864	23,600
New Mexico	24	4,218,892	1,245,696	1,200,731	44,439	26,399	202,066	—
New York	206	50,291,217	21,042,815	13,830,725	639,968	1,113,714	1,742,566	163,285
North Carolina	110	20,943,590	9,744,647	6,000,856	398,462	257,759	917,791	2,000
North Dakota	13	1,155,346	447,095	559,118	31,763	37,500	21,150	—
Ohio	119	19,662,882	8,192,397	7,776,199	391,197	416,490	863,328	16,600
Oklahoma	46	8,772,318	1,798,448	2,057,512	55,472	126,909	189,405	1,205,694
Oregon	43	7,826,297	1,815,227	3,196,686	146,073	104,088	238,119	492,951
Pennsylvania	153	26,378,222	9,991,689	8,758,735	401,615	620,852	1,518,163	34,448
Rhode Island	12	2,188,555	561,776	397,366	16,489	32,465	45,866	—
South Carolina	50	5,076,008	2,306,114	2,779,098	77,527	110,164	311,583	270,922
South Dakota	18	1,901,423	565,587	588,392	40,143	15,581	44,320	—
Tennessee	60	9,772,565	3,597,255	4,000,389	153,785	61,808	472,693	31,500
Texas	143	30,663,798	14,048,728	8,021,183	672,406	1,031,717	1,135,625	392,046
Utah	12	1,476,105	506,486	671,885	78,380	12,000	52,300	2,000
Vermont	19	2,585,647	1,036,239	1,166,724	22,186	44,933	112,329	—
Virginia	71	14,843,315	4,634,261	4,880,209	231,177	229,967	405,111	450
Washington	47	10,759,952	3,316,767	4,845,907	202,185	87,417	475,803	59,084
West Virginia	28	3,605,344	682,892	597,320	97,512	60,600	35,825	—
Wisconsin	62	11,597,544	4,865,299	4,736,814	324,954	199,733	395,110	—
Wyoming	8	2,744,067	1,372,224	1,092,900	38,300	6,000	78,043	—
Pacific Islands	2	94,000	6,000	3,000	—		—	—
Puerto Rico	21	2,877,797	1,616,320	804,553	105,700	14,000	61,724	—
Virgin Islands	2	166,000	91,000	30,000			5,000	—
Total U.S.	2,847	$582,903,898	$228,760,217	$166,769,940	$9,894,550	$9,821,331	$23,535,432	$4,097,405
Estimated % of acquisitions			51.7	37.7	2.2	2.2	5.3	0.9

Price Indexes for School and Academic Library Acquisitions

Kent Halstead

National Institute of Education

Inflation is a persistent debilitating factor in the U.S. economy. Every organization, institution, and business operates with rising input costs that require offsetting revenue increases if an operating balance or profit is to be maintained. The erosion of purchasing power is of special concern to public-service enterprises, such as educational institutions, where additional funding support must be legislated. Schools, colleges, and universities must make a strong, well-documented case to ensure responsible public support.

Highlights

- Books, periodicals, and other library materials have traditionally exhibited rapid price inflation. Libraries must correspondingly increase their budgets if real investment in new acquisitions is to be maintained.
- College and university library acquisitions were underfunded in 1982 by 15 percent compared to 1975, resulting in a single year loss in real investment of $80 million.
- The Library Acquisition Price Indexes (LAPI) for schools and colleges measure price change in library materials and may be projected to estimate future funding requirements necessary to offset anticipated price increases.

To provide this documentation, institutions use the School Price Index (SPI) and the Higher Education Price Index (HEPI), which report changes in the prices of goods and services purchased by elementary and secondary schools (SPI) and colleges and universities (HEPI) for their current operations.[1] Of relevance to the library community are the components of the indexes that report price changes in new acquisitions. These data can be used to project estimated future funding required to offset anticipated price increases. Also, past expenditures can be compared with price movements to ascertain whether spending has kept pace with price level changes. A decline in constant dollars means that the library's acquisitions budget has lost real purchasing power.

We cannot overemphasize the importance of incorporating measures of inflation in library acquisitions budget analysis and projection. New acquisitions are a key element in the scholarly development of every educational institution. And although it is desirable to expand the acquisitions rate, a more realistic and critical requirement is assurance that real investment will be maintained. Less than constant dollar input means erosion of the collection's relative standing, and this may not always be recognized when actual dollar funding is increasing.

The historical magnitude of inflation affecting acquisitions budgets is another

Table 1 / Average Prices and Indexes for Elementary and Secondary School Library Acquisitions, FY 1975–1983

Year		Hardcover Books					Mass Market Paperback Books					
		Elementary[1]		Secondary[2]		Total Index[3]	Elementary[1]		Secondary[2]		Total Index[3]	
Calendar	Fiscal	Av. Price	Index	Av. Price	Index		Av. Price	Index	Av. Price	Index		
1974	1975	$5.01	100.0	$14.09	100.0	100.0	$ .98	100.0	$1.28	100.0	100.0	
1975	1976	5.82	116.2	16.19	114.9	115.6	1.07	109.2	1.46	114.1	111.5	
1976	1977	5.87	117.2	17.20	122.1	119.5	1.22	124.5	1.60	125.0	124.7	
1977	1978	6.64	132.5	18.03	128.0	130.4	1.41	143.9	1.71	133.6	139.1	
1978	1979	6.59	131.5	20.10	142.7	136.8	1.47	150.0	1.91	149.2	149.6	
1979	1980	7.13	142.3	22.80	161.8	151.5	1.48	151.0	2.06	160.9	155.7	
1980	1981	8.21	163.9	23.57	167.3	165.5	1.65*	168.4	2.50	195.3	181.0	
1981	1982	8.29	165.5	26.88	190.8	177.4	1.79	182.7	2.65	207.0	194.1	
1982	1983	8.87	177.1	30.59	217.1	195.9	2.02	206.2	2.95	230.4	217.6	

Year		U.S. Periodicals					Audiovisual Materials								
		Elementary[4]		Secondary[5]		Total Index[6]	Microfilm[7]		16mm Film[8]		Videocassettes		Filmstrip[9]		
Calendar	Fiscal	Av. Price	Index	Av. Price	Index		Av. Price	Index	Av. Price	Index	Av. Price	Index	Av. Price	Index	
1974	1975	$3.72	100.0	$11.43	100.0	100.0	$.1060*	100.0	$11.55	100.0	—	—	$63.76	100.0	
1975	1976	4.69	126.1	14.36	125.6	125.8	.1190	106.0	12.85	111.3	—	—	73.91	115.9	
1976	1977	5.32	143.0	15.24	133.3	137.4	.1335*	125.9	12.93	111.9	—	—	58.41	91.6	
1977	1978	5.82	156.5	16.19	141.6	147.9	.1475*	139.2	13.95	120.8	—	—	76.26	119.6	
1978	1979	6.34	170.4	17.26	151.0	159.1	.1612	152.1	13.56	108.7	—	—	62.31	97.7	
1979	1980	6.70	180.1	18.28	159.9	168.4	.1750*	165.1	13.62	117.9	—	—	65.97	103.5	
1980	1981	7.85	211.0	19.87	173.8	189.4	.1890*	178.3	12.03	104.2	$ 7.58	100.0	67.39	105.7	
1981	1982	8.56	230.1	21.83	191.0	207.4	.2021	190.7	16.09	139.3	14.87	196.2	71.12	111.5	
1982	1983	9.90	266.1	23.93	209.4	233.2	.2627	247.9	15.01	129.9	10.47	138.1	81.62	128.0	

Audiovisual Materials (cont.)

Year		Prerecorded Cassette Tape		Multimedia Kits		Total Index[10]	Library Acquisitions Price Index[11]	Free Textbooks to Students				
								Hardbound		Paperbound		Total Index[12]
Calendar	Fiscal	Av. Price	Index	Av. Price	Index			Av. Price	Index	Av. Price	Index	
1974	1975	$10.76	100.0	$100.00	100.0	100.0	100.0	$4.01	100.0	$1.61	100.0	100.0
1975	1976	10.32	95.9	140.25	140.3	118.9	117.2	4.25	106.0	1.97	122.4	109.1
1976	1977	12.08	112.3	93.63	93.6	110.5	115.7	4.50	112.2	2.21	137.3	117.0
1977	1978	10.63	98.8	93.65	93.7	111.2	123.9	4.76	118.7	2.32	144.1	123.5
1978	1979	12.57	116.8	117.38	117.4	108.2	130.9	5.14	128.2	2.39	148.4	132.0
1979	1980	12.58	116.9	85.70	85.7	104.7	139.4	5.32	132.7	2.47	153.4	136.6
1980	1981	9.34	86.8	92.71	92.7	100.0	148.7	5.54	138.2	2.69	167.1	143.7
1981	1982	12.48	116.0	46.99	47.0	104.5	159.0	5.59	139.4	2.87	178.3	146.8
1982	1983	10.47	99.8	57.52	57.5	107.7	174.5	6.09	151.9	3.13	194.5	160.0

*Estimates.

1 Juvenile book category (age 8 or younger, fiction).

2 All book categories.

3 Weighted average: elementary (K–6) books, 53 percent; secondary (7–12) books, 47 percent. Weights based on data reported in the National Center for Education Statistics' *Statistics of Public School Library Media Centers, 1973–1974.*

4 Children's periodicals (76 titles in 1982).

5 General interest periodicals (176 titles in 1982).

6 Weighted average: elementary (K–6) periodicals, 42 percent; secondary (7–12) periodicals, 58 percent. Weights based on data reported in the National Center for Education Statistics' *Statistics of Public School Library Media Centers, 1973–1974.*

7 Average price per foot, 35mm positive microfilm.

8 Average cost per minute, color purchase.

9 Average cost of filmstrip set (cassette).

10 Weighted average: 16mm film, 31.4 percent; videocassettes, 0.6 percent; film-strips, 32.5 percent; prerecorded tapes, 9.6 percent; multimedia kits, 25.9 percent. Based on industry sales data from *Survey of 1975 Educational Media Sales,* Association of Media Producers, Washington, D.C.

11 Weighted average: hardcover books, 56 percent; paperback books, 3 percent; periodicals, 9 percent; microfilm, 2 percent; audiovisual materials, 30 percent.

Weights based on data reported in the National Center for Education Statistics' *Statistics of Public School Library Media Centers, 1973–1974.*

12 Weighted average: hardbound textbooks, 81 percent; softbound textbooks, 19 percent. Weights based on data for 1974 reported in *Trends in Textbook Markets—Status Report.* Paine Webber Mitchell & Hutchins, Inc. New York.

Sources: Prices of hardcover books and of mass market paperback books before 1980 are based on books listed in the Weekly Record of *Publishers Weekly* for the calendar year with an imprint for the *same* year (usually cited as *preliminary* data). After 1980 data on mass market paperbacks are taken from *Paperbound Books in Print.* Not included in the hardcover category are government documents and certain multivolume encyclopedias. The average prices are published in *The Bowker Annual of Library & Book Trade Information,* R. R. Bowker, New York.

Prices of microfilm are compiled by Imre T. Jarmy from the *Directory of Library Reprographic Services: A World Guide* and supplemental data and are published in *The Bowker Annual of Library & Book Trade Information,* R. R. Bowker, New York.

Prices of audiovisual materials are compiled by David B. Walch based on information derived from selected issues of *Previews* and *Booklists* and are published in *The Bowker Annual of Library & Book Trade Information,* R. R. Bowker, New York.

Prices of hardbound and softbound textbooks from J. Kendrick Noble, Jr., *Trends in Textbook Markets—Status Report,* prepared for the Book Industry Study Group, Inc., published by Paine Webber Mitchell & Hutchins, Inc., New York.

Table 2 / Average Prices and Indexes for College and University Library Acquisitions, FY 1975–1983

| Year | | U.S. Hardcover Books | | U.S. Periodicals | | Foreign Monographs[1] | | Library Acquisitions Price Index[2] |
Calendar	Fiscal	Av. Price	Index[3]	Av. Price	Index[3]	Av. Price	Index[3]	
1974	1975	$14.09	100.0	$34.55	100.0	$ 6.42	100.0	100.0
1975	1976	16.19	114.9	38.94	112.7	7.59	118.3	114.7
1976	1977	17.20[4]	122.1	41.85	121.1	7.91	123.2	122.0
1977	1978	18.03	128.0	45.14	130.6	8.89	138.5	130.4
1978	1979	20.10	142.7	50.11	145.0	9.41	146.6	144.0
1979	1980	22.80	161.8	57.23	165.6	11.52	179.5	165.6
1980	1981	23.57	167.3	67.81	196.3	13.05	203.3	181.4
1981	1982	26.88	190.8	73.89	213.9	13.84	215.6	201.5
1982	1983	30.59	217.1	78.04	225.9	11.91	185.5	215.0

[1] All hardcover books, paperbacks, and pamphlets purchased during the fiscal year by the Library of Congress from approximately 100 foreign countries.

[2] Weighted average based on the estimated proportion of the total acquisitions budget expended for each category. Weights used—U.S. hardcover books, 55 percent; U.S. periodicals, 30 percent; and foreign monographs, 15 percent.

[3] Indexes are not fixed-weight indexes; they reflect changes in the type and mix of books and periodicals from year to year. The fiscal year index refers to average price in the previous calendar year due to the normal time delay between published date and purchase.

[4] In 1976, Publishers Weekly reported a book price of $17.39 for an 18-month period (1976–1977). An adjusted value of $17.20 for calendar year 1976 was determined from the trend line.

Source: Prices of hardcover books are published in The Bowker Annual of Library & Book Trade Information, R. R. Bowker, New York, based on books listed in the Weekly Record section of Publishers Weekly for the calendar year with an imprint for the same year. Not included are mass market paperbacks, government documents, and certain multivolume encyclopedias. U.S. periodicals are priced by the F. W. Faxon Co. and reported by F. F. Clasquin in the October issues of Library Journal. Foreign monographs are priced according to an unpublished price series prepared by the Library of Congress.

factor. Books, periodicals, and other library materials, being labor-intensive products, traditionally have exhibited rapid price increases. In higher education, the library acquisitions component of the Higher Education Price Index increased 6.8 times from 1961 to 1983, whereas the HEPI itself increased only four times. This means that college and university libraries had to increase their acquisitions budget nearly seven times over the last 22 years to purchase essentially the same amount of new materials. The average increase of 9 percent yearly for library acquisitions exceeds all other components of the HEPI, including utilities, with the exception of fringe benefits. During this same 22-year period the Consumer Price Index, by comparison, increased 3.3 times.

Price increases for library acquisitions at elementary and secondary schools have been more moderate, 7.2 percent yearly from 1975 to 1983 compared to 10 percent during the same period in the higher education sector.

Have acquisitions budgets increased sufficiently to offset these inflation rates? Recent expenditure data are not available for elementary and secondary schools, but college and university libraries have fallen short of the requirement. Their 1982 book and periodical budget of $513,823,000 is 1.7 times the 1975 budget of $295,873,000,[2] less than the twofold increase in the prices of these materials. The 1982 budget is deficient by $77.9 million and earlier years are similarly short, resulting in a considerable loss of real investment in new acquisitions since 1975.

Description of Indexes and Data Base

Tables 1 and 2 show prices and indexes of new acquisitions for school libraries and academic libraries. In both tables, the Library Acquisitions Price Index (LAPI) is a weighted aggregative index number with "fixed," or "constant," weights, often referred to as a "market basket" index. The LAPI measures price change by repricing each year and comparing the aggregate costs of the library materials bought by institutions in the base year. For college and university libraries the base year is 1971–1972; for elementary and secondary schools the 1973–1974 buying pattern has been used. Because the academic index was first published nearly a decade earlier, its composition is not as sophisticated as the index for schools. Work is currently under way to add other library materials to the academic index.

Both the amount and quality of the various items that comprise the acquisitions market basket must remain constant so that only the effects of price changes are reflected. Weights are changed infrequently—only when there is clear evidence of a shift in the relative *amounts* of various items purchased, or when new items are introduced. Institutions with substantially different buying patterns may wish to construct a tailored composite index using weights based on their own budget proportions. However, once established for a selected base year, the weights must be held constant.

The indexes for each acquisitions category (books, periodicals, and so on) are calculated with FY 1975 as the base. This means that current prices are expressed as a percentage of prices for 1975. An index of 110 means that prices have increased 10 percent since the base year. The index may be converted to any desired base period by dividing each index number to be converted by the index for the desired base period.

Sources of the price series are listed in the tables. Prices for library materials are generally quoted for the calendar year. The corresponding fiscal years are also listed for budget year identification.

Notes

1. See Kent Halstead, *Inflation Measures for Schools and Colleges*, National Institute of Education, U.S. Department of Education, 1983, 183 pp. Available from the Superintendent of Documents, U.S. Government Printing Office, Washington, DC 20402, Document #065-000-00186-1, $6 includes shipping. Available in microfiche from the ERIC Document Reproduction Service, Box 190, Arlington, VA 22210, ED #230083, $.98 plus $.20 postage. The HEPI and SPI are updated annually by Research Associates of Washington, 2605 Klingle Road N.W., Washington, DC 20008.
2. Unpublished data provided by Richard M. Beazley, National Center for Education Statistics.

College and University Libraries, 1978-1979 and 1981-1982: Three Years of Change

Robert A. Heintze

Project Officer
Division of Multilevel Education Statistics
National Center for Education Statistics

400 Maryland Ave. N.W., Rm. 606, Washington, DC 20202
202-254-7351

This report summarizes some of the findings of a National Center for Education Statistics (NCES) survey of college and university libraries for the academic year ending in 1982 and compares them with the previous NCES survey of college and university libraries for the academic year ending in 1979. All library data are reported with reference to academic years 1978-1979 and 1981-1982, except for library staff and student enrollment data, which are reported as of fall 1979 and 1982, and library reference transactions, which are reported as of spring 1979 and 1982. The 1982 survey had a 91 percent response rate from a universe of 3,326 college and university libraries in 50 states and the District of Columbia. Data were estimated for all nonrespondents, with the exception of 89 institutions that were not in the 1979 survey.

Holdings and Acquisitions

Although total book volumes increased from 517.2 million in 1978-1979 to 567.8 million in 1981-1982 (Table 1), acquisitions of book volumes and titles decreased by 9.1 percent and 11.6 percent, respectively (Table 2). This decline in book acquisitions continues the downward trend that began in 1972-1973. Periodical subscriptions, however, increased 3.0 percent. The popularity of periodicals carried over into microforms, where the number of periodical titles available on microforms increased a substantial 58.3 percent and the acquisitions of periodicals on microforms was up 52.5 percent from 1978-1979 to 1981-1982. Audiovisual materials were being added at a slower rate, down 22.4 percent from 1978-1979.

Expenditures and Receipts

Operating expenditures in academic libraries increased by $452.9 million, or 30.4 percent, from 1978-1979 to 1981-1982 (Table 3). During the same three-year period, the inflation

Table 1 / Holdings of Library Materials by Type in College and
University Libraries, 1979 and 1982

| | (in thousands) | | % |
Type of Library Materials	1978–1979	1981–1982	Change
Book volumes	517,152	567,826	+9.8
Book titles	338,426	369,916	+9.3
Government documents (in separate collections)	89,974	106,285	+18.1
Microforms—book titles	39,094	46,631	+19.3
Microforms—periodical titles	2,493	3,947	+58.3
Microforms—other	223,502	307,443	+37.6
Audiovisual materials	20,738	24,762	+19.4
All other library materials (titles)	118,952	160,182	+34.7

rate, based on the Consumer Price Index (derived from monthly figures published by the Bureau of Labor Statistics), was 37.3 percent. Expenditures for library staff salaries increased 30.0 percent, but expenditures for fringe benefits increased considerably more—up 47.8 percent. In 1981–1982, total expenditures for staff compensation (salaries, fringe benefits, and wages for student assistants) of $1.2 billion were approximately double the amount spent on library materials (books, periodicals, microforms, audiovisuals, and other library materials).

In comparing the two survey years, the 47.8 percent increase in fringe benefits represents the largest percentage increase of any expenditures item, followed closely by the 44.7 percent increase of expenditures for periodicals. By comparison, expenditures for books increased only 14.6 percent. Total 1982 expenditures for periodicals exceeded total expenditures for books, $258.1 million and $255.8 million, respectively. Only one expenditure item—audiovisual materials—showed a decrease (down 7.6 percent). Total receipts from federal government grants showed a 23.2 percent decrease.

Staff

A total of 58,476 full-time equivalent (FTE) persons served on college and university library staffs in fall 1982 (Table 4), a 1 percent increase over fall 1979. This total represents approximately 155 FTE students per FTE library staff member in 1982, as compared with 147 FTE students per FTE library staff member in 1979. (Source of enrollment data: U.S. Department of Education, National Center for Education Statistics, *Fall Enroll-*

Table 2 / Acquisitions of Library Materials by Type in College and
University Libraries, 1979 and 1982

| | (in thousands) | | % |
Type of Library Materials	1978–1979	1981–1982	Change
Periodical subscriptions	4,749	4,890	+3.0
Book volumes	21,460	19,507	−9.1
Book titles	14,405	12,735	−11.6
Government documents (in separate collections)	7,270	6,303	−13.3
Microforms—book titles	3,275	3,054	−6.3
Microforms—periodical titles	282	430	+52.5
Microforms—other	21,609	26,375	+22.0
Audiovisual materials	2,089	1,621	−22.4
All other library materials (titles)	5,328	4,690	−11.9

Table 3 / Operating Expenditures and Receipts of College and University Libraries by Type, 1979 and 1982

Types of Expenditures/Receipts	(in thousands)		% Change
	1978–1979	1981–1982	
Total library operating expenditures	1,490,862	1,943,770	+30.4
Salaries and wages*	703,280	914,379	+30.0
Fringe benefits	113,310	167,515	+47.8
Wages of students†	79,086	100,847	+27.5
Books	223,207	255,767	+14.6
Periodicals	178,385	258,066	+44.7
Microforms	20,029	22,384	+11.8
Audiovisual material	16,960	15,661	−7.6
All other library materials	9,174	9,321	+1.6
Binding and rebinding	25,176	30,351	+20.6
All other library operating expenditures	122.256	169,478	+38.6
Total receipts from federal government grants	25,186	19,343	−23.2

*Includes estimated value of contributed services.
†Serving on hourly basis.

Table 4 / Full-Time-Equivalent (FTE) Staff by Sex and Hours of Student Assistance in College and University Libraries, 1979 and 1982

Staff Level/Sex/Hours	Fall 1979	Fall 1982	% Change
Total staff	57,918	58,476	+1.0
Total men	14,397	14,512	+0.8
Total women	43,221	43,964	+1.7
Administrators*	5,412	5,515	+1.9
Men	2,716	2,634	−3.0
Women	2,696	2,881	+6.9
Librarians	15,285	15,589	+1.9
Men	4,826	4,795	−0.4
Women	10,459	10,794	+3.2
Other professionals†	2,569	2,712	+5.6
Men	1,067	1,092	+2.4
Women	1,502	1,620	+7.9
Technical and clerical	34,352	34,660	+0.8
Men	5,788	5,991	+3.5
Women	28,564	28,669	+0.4
Hours of student assistance‡	38,994,204	40,068,400	+2.8

*Includes chief, deputy, associate, assistant chief librarian.
†Includes other professional staff charged to library budget.
‡Includes hours of student assistance charged to both the library budget and other budgets.

Table 5 / Transactions in College and University Libraries by Type, 1979 and 1982

Type of Transactions	1978–1979	1981–1982	% Change
Circulation	199,328,299	200,070,483	+0.4
Interlibrary loans			
To other libraries	3,086,007	4,138,367	+34.1
From other libraries	1,886,568	2,226,345	+18.0
Reference transactions*	999,755	1,647,107	+64.8

*Typical week in the spring of the academic year.

ment in Higher Education 1979, and unpublished fall 1982 data.) Females represented approximately 75 percent of college and university library staff in both years, but only 52 percent of college library administrators in 1982. Between 1979 and 1982 the number of female administrators increased by 6.9 percent, and the number of male administrators decreased by 3.0 percent.

Library Usage

Although circulation of library materials was virtually unchanged—up 0.4 percent (Table 5)—reference transactions increased substantially, up 64.8 percent, since 1979. In spring 1982, reference transactions exceeded 1.6 million in a typical week. Interlibrary loans rose substantially; total loans to other libraries increased by 34.1 percent and loans from other libraries by 18.0 percent over 1979.

For More Information

Inquiries about the data used in this analysis should be directed to the Statistical Information Office, National Center for Education Statistics, 400 Maryland Ave. N.W. (Brown Building, Rm. 606), Washington, DC 20202; 202-254-6057. For additional information about this report, contact Robert A. Heintze.

Library Buildings in 1983

Bette-Lee Fox
Associate Editor, *Library Journal*

Ann Burns
Associate Editor, *Library Journal*

Deborah Waithe
Assistant Editor, *Library Journal*

This report includes statistics on 45 new public library buildings and 33 public addition/renovation projects completed between July 1, 1982 and June 30, 1983 (Tables 1–4). For those who swear by *Library Journal* statistics, a caveat: The information questionnaire was mailed slightly later this year than in past years. It is possible that some libraries could not meet the deadline and did not respond to the request for data. Therefore more than 78 building projects may have been completed during FY 1983.

What can be discerned from these figures is the following: The number of additions to and renovations of existing structures is catching up to completely new construction. Staff members are contributing to individual project concepts and design. Energy efficiency is still a priority in most projects, and contributions of labor from volunteer work forces stresses the need for economic efficiency.

Note: Adapted from *Library Journal*, December 1, 1983.

Table 1 / New Public Library Buildings

Community	Pop. in M	Code	Project Cost	Gross Sq. Ft.	Const. Cost	Sq. Ft. Cost	Equip. Cost	Site Cost	Other Costs	Vols.	Reader Seats	Fed. Funds	State Funds	Local Funds	Gift Funds	Architect
ALABAMA																
Alabaster	7	M	391,866	5,400	301,000	55.74	29,210	15,000	46,656	15,000	30	300,000	0	75,000	15,000	Moss & Associates
CALIFORNIA																
Crescent City	19	M	397,179	6,250	296,947	47.51	24,960	34,539	40,733	36,500	45	225,963	0	154,721	16,495	Kappeler
Stockton	27	B	869,404	9,600	680,975	70.93	67,333	35,000	86,096	44,000	80	0	0	869,404	0	Morris & Wenell
COLORADO																
Vail	5	M	1,832,000	14,000	1,372,000	98.00	250,000	owned	210,000	60,000	105	0	0	2,000,000	30,000	Snowdon & Hopkins
FLORIDA																
Davie	40	B	1,378,161	10,000	856,328	85.53	96,483	303,423	121,927	55,000	60	0	0	1,378,161	0	McDonald & Assoc.
Plantation	250	B	3,576,383	27,680	3,026,194	109.32	382,984	owned	167,205	130,000	170	0	0	3,576,383	0	Haack/Craford . . .
GEORGIA																
Evans	30	B	600,000	10,690	472,317	44.18	76,020	owned	51,663	35,000	66	0	400,000	200,000	0	Holroyd & Johnson
Soperton	6	B	295,452	5,000	224,995	44.99	32,500	12,000	25,957	20,000	48	0	187,660	70,000	31,409	Buckley & Assoc.
ILLINOIS																
Glendale Hgts.	21	M	2,428,945	25,910	1,916,446	74.00	121,414	175,000	216,085	100,000	102	0	0	2,428,945	0	Wight & Co.
Roselle	18	M	2,484,900	24,000	1,795,909	74.83	203,780	240,000	245,211	100,000	109	0	0	2,474,900	10,000	O'Donnell . . .
INDIANA																
Indianapolis	40	B	1,237,471	13,500	996,397	73.81	94,074	60,000	87,000	70,000	108	0	0	1,237,471	0	Brandt . . .
Indianapolis	73	B	1,079,640	13,500	932,116	69.04	94,074	12,450	41,000	70,000	108	0	0	1,079,640	0	Brandt . . .
MARYLAND																
Cumberland	25	B	868,462	9,000	671,345	75.00	77,770	68,667	50,680	26,000	68	100,000	131,421	637,041	0	Gaudreau, T. L.
MICHIGAN																
Marine City	8	B	277,259	4,000	206,919	50.00	20,340	50,000	n/a	15,000	36	0	0	0	277,259	Nofs, R.C.
MINNESOTA																
Minnetonka	150	BS	4,290,127	94,000	2,818,792	29.99	272,286	270,575	928,474	100,000	148	0	0	4,290,127	0	Griswold & Rauma
MISSISSIPPI																
Brandon	10	B	256,900	3,900	151,335	38.80	72,261	3,156	30,148	15,000	27	0	128,450	128,450	0	Lewis-Eaton . . .
Jackson	5	B	274,000	6,607	231,240	35.00	28,000	owned	14,760	8,325	11	0	0	274,000	0	Larry Bishop
Poplarville	3	B	332,163	5,257	230,345	43.82	45,694	40,000	16,124	26,000	28	0	163,500	163,663	5,000	Wagner, Fred
Tchula	2	B	109,508	3,110	87,426	28.11	6,716	10,000	5,366	12,000	20	1,816	53,878	15,246	38,568	Bowman & Bowman
MISSOURI																
St. Charles	50	B	588,029	15,000	515,341	34.36	35,656	owned	37,032	90,000	84	0	0	581,691	6,338	M. Thomas Hall
MONTANA																
Helena	12	M	6,283,246	101,500	4,597,513	45.30	993,851	106,256	585,626	70,000	52	0	6,283,246	0	0	Page & Werner . . .

Location		Code												Architect
NORTH CAROLINA														
Clinton[1]	50	MS	626,673	9,600	424,760	89,013	80,000	32,900	48,000	78	0	60,300	320,563	245,810	J.J. Rose
Kinston	68	MS	1,499,500	20,850	897,000	83,000	455,000	64,500	72,000	124	0	160,000	710,000	629,500	Hargett, Warren E.
Selma	5	M	166,430	3,230	125,145	26,485	5,895	8,905	16,878	28	0	60,300	65,000	41,130	Coble, Wesley M.
Spindale	54	M	275,050	5,035	217,562	35,959	owned	21,529	30,000	32	104,150	70,900	100,000	0	Holland, L. Pegram
OKLAHOMA														
Altus[2]	35	MS	1,777,018	24,564	1,228,490	352,750	52,400	143,378	90,000	99	0	0	1,777,018	0	Appleby & Assoc.
Pauls Valley	6	M	426,782	5,800	347,696	58,806	0	20,280	20,000	48	0	0	75,000	400,000	MNT Inc. Porter
Stroud	4	n/a	206,363	3,000	180,000	14,029	owned	12,334	4,500	20	0	0	206,363	0	Everett...
Tulsa	45	B	1,282,857	18,900	1,123,229	90,215	owned	69,413	50,000	133	0	60,675	1,222,182	0	Coleman-Ervin
OREGON														
McMinnville	15	M	1,399,325	16,500	1,177,325	122,000	owned	100,000	100,000	50	0	0	1,399,325	0	Herbert & Keller
SOUTH CAROLINA														
Hardeeville	5	BS	49,741	1,352	29,864	11,277	8,600	0	6,000	15	25,000	10,000	7,000	7,741	none
TEXAS														
Houston	43	B	2,572,260	25,800	2,175,000	246,000	owned	151,260	65,000	130	1,145,000	0	1,427,260	0	Ray B. Bailey
Houston	25	B	1,287,300	8,500	969,800	89,000	171,000	57,500	40,000	73	969,800	0	317,500	0	Molina & Assocs.
Port Neches	14	M	600,000	10,450	485,135	81,319	owned	33,546	75,000	56	0	0	350,000	250,000	S. M. Vaught
Sweeny	4	B	154,614	4,000	129,977	16,046	owned	8,592	20,000	24	0	0	0	154,614	not reported
UTAH														
North Ogden	26	B	1,200,000	21,200	725,000	100,000	225,000	150,000	35,000	60	0	0	800,000	400,000	Richardson Assocs.
VIRGINIA														
Chase City	7	B	287,294	5,393	199,436	44,876	20,000	22,982	16,000	22	0	0	9,500	277,794	Edgerton Assocs.
Mechanicsville[3]	25	B	360,356	6,000	282,731	35,125	25,000	17,500	25,000	40	0	0	327,837	32,519	DGR...
Scottsville	3	B	255,349	3,940	230,349	0	25,000	25,000	12,000	50	0	0	255,349	0	John B. Farmer
WASHINGTON														
Edmonds	60	B	2,981,005	20,000	2,596,871	60,000	50,000	274,134	90,000	159	0	0	2,874,000	0	ARAI...
Sequim[4]	12	B	550,000	6,000	385,000	60,000	0	105,000	40,000	35	0	0	350,000	200,000	BJSS Architects
Spokane	40	B	537,297	5,750	441,114	31,097	30,470	34,616	30,000	68	516,627	0	20,670	0	Donald Erickson
WISCONSIN														
Ashland	137	S	105,000	3,800	96,300	0	8,700	0	25,000	0	0	105,000	0	0	not reported
WYOMING														
Gillette	33	M	3,530,000	44,145	2,411,274	588,174	owned	530,552	150,000	175	0	0	3,530,000	0	Christopher Hard
Kemmerer[5]	5	M	904,000	11,000	845,000	50,000	owned	9,000	60,000	n/a	514,469	0	360,531	29,000	Alfred Lauber
BRITISH COLUMBIA														
Delta	42	B	1,347,240	11,400	1,000,000	80,000	owned	267,240	40,000	43	0	0	1,347,240	0	Terry Teupah
QUEBEC														
Quebec City	166	M	10,773,186	100,000	8,128,016	1,000,000	owned	1,645,170	250,000	650	0	2,779,560	860,440	4,133,186	Gauthier...
Stean-Richelieu	36	M	2,540,059	23,500	1,791,400	160,000	75,000	513,659	120,000	163	656,425	561,405	1,322,229	0	DeMontigny....

Symbol Code: B—Branch Library; HS—Branch & System Headquarters; M—Main Library; MS—Main & System Headquarters; S—System Headquarters; SC—School District; NA—Not Available.

Table 2 / Public Libraries: Additions and Renovations

Community	Pop in M	Code	Project Cost	Gross Sq. Ft.	Const. Cost	Sq. Ft. Cost	Equipt. Cost	Site Cost	Other Costs	Vols.	Reader Seats	Fed. Funds	State Funds	Local Funds	Gift Funds	Architect
ALABAMA																
Birmingham[6]	25	B	550,525	8,400	468,866	55.81	39,129	owned	42,530	55,000	82	4,000	0	546,525	0	Giattina . . .
Birmingham	14	B	59,475	3,800	31,810	13.47	19,411	leased	8,254	15,000	36	4,254	0	55,221	0	Garrett & Assocs
Montevallo	4	M	209,498	3,682	71,500	57.00	6,553	125,000	6,445	8,200	35	0	0	0	209,498	Arnold & Barrow
CALIFORNIA																
South Pasadena	23	M	2,135,542	25,502	1,666,400	65.34	103,089	owned	366,053	100,000	142	0	0	2,039,576	95,966	Morgridge . . . .
Stockton	312	MS	293,001	69,900	220,657	3.16	28,003	owned	44,341	350,000	340	0	0	293,001	0	Public Works Dept.
ILLINOIS																
Glencoe	9	M	40,267	1,370	36,000	26.27	0	owned	4,267	n/a	80	0	0	30,267	10,000	n/a
INDIANA																
Nashville[7]	13	M	316,509	5,600	89,545	15.99	14,012	198,106	14,846	30,000	28	0	0	316,509	0	Wright . . . .
KANSAS																
Kiowa	2	M	82,130	1,300	70,278	54.06	6,230	owned	5,622	12,000	29	0	0	0	82,130	Miller . . .
MICHIGAN																
Bay City[8]	120	B	291,194	5,888	233,730	49.45	32,707	owned	24,757	112,000	35	29,250	0	260,930	1,014	John Meyer
Tecumseh	14	M	192,146	3,200	178,000	55.63	10,146	owned	4,000	12,250	21	0	0	0	192,146	Dave Siler
MISSISSIPPI																
Louin	1	M	7,156	460	1,225	15.56	896	owned	5,035	2,500	12	0	0	7,156	0	n/a
Walnut Grove	1	B	30,805	960	27,879	29.04	2,926	owned	0	10,000	32	0	0	27,879	2,926	n/a
Waveland	4	B	156,000	1,786	126,015	70.56	20,464	owned	9,521	10,000	20	0	78,000	58,231	19,769	Lewis-Eaton
NEW JERSEY																
Stirling[9]	7	M	200,766	1,750	148,973	85.10	26,350	owned	25,443	30,000	37	0	0	24,000	176,766	Hoagland Assocs.
Teaneck	39	B	1,115,243	25,000	865,307	34.61	150,000	owned	99,936	154,000	200	837,000	0	278,243	0	Beyer Blinder
NEW YORK																
Locust Valley	9	M	575,047	12,240	463,351	37.86	54,303	owned	57,393	45,000	46	109,800	0	325,247	140,000	Bentel & Bentel

NORTH CAROLINA																
Eden[10]	83	S	209,226	4,420	178,303	40.00	13,060	owned	17,863	12,180	0	0	60,300	148,926	0	Grier-Fripp
Landis[11]	25	B	194,394	4,100	118,227	28.84	36,334	30,000	9,833	20,000	38	40,000	50,000	14,000	90,394	James F. Kluttz
Yanceyville[12]	21	S	100,867	1,500	85,231	56.00	4,895	owned	10,741	40,000	56	0	46,500	49,367	5,000	John Anderson
OREGON																
Medford[13]	60	M	456,000	1,400	430,000	30.71	5,000	owned	21,000	155,000	55	0	0	456,000	0	Daniels . . .
PENNSYLVANIA																
Wilkes-Barre	357	M	605,295	3,288	429,108	102.76	67,600	owned	109,587	39,000	57	0	0	0	605,295	Everman . . .
RHODE ISLAND																
Pawtucket[14]	71	M	2,550,000	42,351	2,241,264	53.00	108,557	owned	200,179	200,000	400	0	1,250,000	1,250,000	50,000	Robinson . . .
SOUTH CAROLINA																
Belton	9	B	74,938	2,000	62,500	31.25	6,438	owned	6,000	12,500	25	10,000	10,000	10,938	44,000	Neal Archs.
TEXAS																
Coleman[15]	9	M	197,794	6,264	157,394	31.58	0	36,000	4,400	25,000	92	0	0	104,694	93,100	Wukasch . . .
Comfort	3	M	145,000	4,600	30,000	6.66	15,000	100,000	0	5,000	24	9,000	4,041	0	131,959	William Nelson
Jacksonville	13	M	802,255	14,200	545,255	38.40	45,319	157,500	54,181	60,000	74	0	157,500	157,500	644,755	George A. Rogers
Littlefield[16]	19	M	100,436	3,820	39,909	10.00	340	59,987	200	19,000	10	0	0	0	100,436	n/a
Matador	2	B	2,723	460	397	.86	2,326	owned	0	5,439	13	2,186	0	66	471	n/a
UTAH																
Park City[17]	4	M	759,000	5,000	425,000	85.00	70,000	owned	269,000	15,000	60	0	0	0	9,000	Cooper . . .
VIRGINIA																
Boydton[18]	42	M	24,335	660	23,000	35.00	0	owned	1,335	4,477	15	0	0	14,335	10,000	Edgerton . . .
WASHINGTON																
Spokane	33	B	17,500	5,283	17,500	3.31	0	leased	0	52,000	44	0	0	17,500	0	J. Steve Hindley
Spokane	171	M	21,416	4,600	21,416	4.66	0	owned	0	0	0	0	0	18,303	3,113	n/a
WYOMING																
Pinedale	5	M	70,264	1,350	64,040	47.44	6,224	owned	0	3,800	12	1,000	0	7,905	61,359	Dolence & Frullo
BRITISH COLUMBIA																
Clearbrook	74	B	160,000	11,000	135,000	12.27	0	owned	25,000	27,000	46	0	0	160,000	0	n/a

Table 3 / New Buildings Not Previously Reported

Community	Pop in M	Code	Project Cost	Gross Sq.Ft.	Const. Cost	Sq.Ft. Cost	Equip. Cost	Site Cost	Others Costs	Volumes	Reader Seats	Fed. Funds	State Funds	Local Funds	Gift Funds	Architect
Harlan, IA (1981)	15	M	$610,007	15,270	$486,500	$31.86	$83,270	owned	$40,237	29,310	70	$206,515	0	$68,485	$335,007	Frevert...
Dumont, NJ (1982)	18	M	652,765	9,424	554,128	58.80	45,000	27,037	26,600	40,000	82	0	0	636,765	16,000	LoMonte, F.
Riverhead, NY (1982)	25	M	754,172	11,512	609,661	52.96	58,742	owned	85,769	50,000	48	0	0	710,206	19,000	Denis, D.
Fort Worth, TX (1982)	26	B	n/a	3,000	n/a	62.22	32,296	152,590	77,898	17,000	35	n/a	0	n/a	0	Martinez, R.
Round Rock, TX (1980)	15	M	550,000	20,000	501,550	25.00	48,450	owned	0	23,000	44	0	0	550,000	0	Gill, Ray

1. Includes passive solar features.
2. Transformed from 1,900 square foot WPA building (1936) to modern 24,500 square foot building with audio, video, and microcomputer services.
3. Circulation desk designed by librarian and built by volunteers from local men's club.
4. Includes an "earth bermed" exterior which was designed for energy efficiency and noise control.
5. Utilizes passive solar heating.
6. Situated in park with glass wall for light and view.
7. Locally made crafts and artwork displayed to reflect heritage of county.
8. Restoration and renovation of 99-year-old building, oldest in state in continuous use.
9. All funds raised through volunteer effort.
10. Computer room built to house future installation of Automated Integrated Library System.
11. Large-scale model train in children's area.
12. Gravelled entranceway enclosed to provide new children's area; former children's area converted into public meeting room.
13. Remodeled and renovated 1912 Carnegie building and its 1952 addition.
14. Two buildings of different architectural styles joined to make a single library complex.
15. Four light wells utilizing passive solar energy; preservation of original 1925 tin ceiling.
16. Project organized and funded by corporation made up of business and community people; corporation owns building and county maintains it.
17. Gift funds restored national historic building.
18. One of ten buildings in Virginia donated by the late David Bruce, former U.S. ambassador.

Table 4 / Public Library Buildings: Six-Year Cost Summary

	Fiscal 1978	Fiscal 1979	Fiscal 1980	Fiscal 1981	Fiscal 1982	Fiscal 1983
Number of new bldgs.	135	168	100	82	91	45
Number of ARRs[1]	85	112	66	76	75	33
Sq. ft. new bldgs.	1,355,130	2,898,585	1,662,699	1,134,748	2,052,813	692,713
Sq. ft. ARRs	663,915	912,567	508,528	954,106	736,707	276,134
New bldgs.						
Construction cost	$54,508,361	$96,010,260	$79,984,894	$64,658,453	$107,707,038	$40,105,938
Equipment cost	7,433,541	13,336,842	9,712,822	9,059,027	14,571,251	5,310,577
Site cost	5,508,018	3,233,751	3,234,525	3,265,157	3,556,109	2,568,131
Other costs	6,712,240	8,523,617	9,602,584	7,167,009	13,203,141	4,900,664
Total—Project cost	74,162,160	121,109,470	102,538,025	86,019,599	141,684,901	52,885,310
ARRs—Project cost	18,891,111	29,930,142	20,948,544	55,388,161	37,921,545	12,586,747
New & ARR Project cost	$93,053,271	$151,039,612	$123,486,569	$141,407,760	$179,606,446	$65,472,057
Fund sources						
Federal, new bldgs.	$13,304,652	$63,354,045	$29,005,800	$18,269,728	$11,922,851	3,902,825
Federal, ARRs	4,046,901	18,414,336	4,253,080	4,105,877	5,497,522	1,046,490
Federal, total	$17,351,553	$81,768,381	$33,258,880	$22,375,605	$17,420,373	4,949,315
State, new bldgs.	$5,803,920	$13,897,410	$1,394,677	$3,537,248	$23,513,456	7,875,330
State, ARRs	2,658,733	1,404,067	3,367,304	1,343,174	1,049,493	1,498,841
State, total	$8,462,653	$15,301,477	$4,761,981	$4,880,422	$24,562,949	9,374,171
Local, new bldgs.	$47,193,528	$73,994,629	$63,348,408	$57,099,210	$87,730,798	38,139,941
Local, ARRs	10,371,229	9,854,905	9,740,767	43,598,892	24,401,171	6,512,319
Local, total	$57,564,757	$83,849,534	$73,089,175	$100,698,102	$112,131,969	44,652,260
Gift, new bldgs.	$7,860,060	$11,398,318	$5,506,812	$5,699,152	$20,143,884	3,098,177
Gift, ARRs	1,658,467	1,352,053	3,560,915	6,366,551	2,736,493	2,779,097
Gift, total	$9,518,527	$12,750,371	$9,067,727	$12,065,703	$22,880,377	5,877,274
Total funds used	$92,897,490	$193,669,763	$120,177,763	$140,109,832	$175,995,668	64,853,020

1. Additions, remodeling, renovations.

Table 5 / Academic Libraries, 1973–1983

	1973	1974	1975	1976	1977	1978–79	1980	1981	1982	1983
New libraries	17	21	18	15	6	38	14	19	20	8
Additions	1	9	2	5	5	8	2	0	9	1
Additions plus Renovation	3	10	5	8	7	22	11	11	6	11
TOTALS	21	40	25	28	18	66	27	30	35	20
Combined Additions and Addition plus renovation	4	19	7	13	12	30	13	11	15	12
Percentage of Combined A and A & R	19.04	47.50	28.00	46.42	66.66	45.45	48.15	36.66	42.85	60.00

Table 6 / New Academic Libraries, 1983

Name of Institution	Project Cost	Gross Area	Assignable	Non-Assignable	Sq.Ft. Cost	Building Cost	Equipment Cost	Book Capacity	Seating Capacity	Architect
Univ. of Texas Health Science Ctr., San Antonio	9,500,000	93,000	74,400	18,600	77.77	7,300,000	2,200,000	250,000	950	Chumney . . . & Phelps
Univ. of North Carolina Art Lib., Chapel Hill[1]	6,800,000	11,000	n/a	n/a	72.50	5,500,000	n/a	71,000	97	Clark . . .
Western New England College, Springfield, Mass.	4,400,000	47,103	37,621	9,482	76.49	3,603,000	308,000	176,000	650	The Hillier Group
Biscayne College, Miami, Fla.	2,772,500	51,205	39,205	12,000	50.00	2,560,000	212,500	250,000	410	Spillis Candela
Swarthmore Coll. Lib. of Sci. & Engineering, Pa.	2,089,455	18,000	15,200	2,800	100.00	1,809,947	97,002	120,000	178	H2L2 Design Co.
Western Michigan Univ., Music/Dance Lib., Kalamazoo	884,000	9,360	9,360	0	80.00	748,000	136,000	60,000	115	Harley . . .
Ball State Univ., Coll. Arch. & Planning, Muncie, Ind.	n/a	4,149	4,149	0	87.00	360,963	0	40,000	55	Crumlish/Sporleder
City College, CUNY[2]	n/a	n/a	167,900	0	n/a	871,000	1,994,000	1,300,000	1,800	Warnecke & Assocs.

1. Project cost and figures refer to total Art Classroom Studio Building which houses the library.
2. Part of 810,000 square foot building costing $125 million.

Name of Institution		Project Cost	Gross Area	Assignable	Non-Assignable	Sq.Ft. Cost	Building Cost	Equipment Cost	Book Capacity	Seating Capacity	Architect
Drew University, Madison, N.J.	Total	9,350,000	136,000	106,750	29,460	68.64	8,649,100	700,900	750,000	472	The Hillier Group
	New	7,350,000	84,110	66,500	17,610	87.39	6,820,600	529,400	450,000	200	
	Renovated	2,000,000	52,100	40,250	11,850	38.39	1,828,500	171,500	300,000	272	
Texas Christian Univ., Fort Worth, Tex.	Total	7,957,869	158,605	121,712	36,893	n/a	6,175,487	900,000	1,500,000	1,100	Skidmore . . .
	New	6,485,787	74,260	61,712	12,548	87.34	5,175,487	750,000	838,500	498	
	Renovated	1,472,082	84,345	60,000	24,345	17.45	1,000,000	150,000	661,500	602	
Colby College, Waterville, Me.	Total	7,500,000	100,000	75,000	25,000	75.00	5,314,800	250,000	470,000	599	Shepley Bulfinch . . .
	New	n/a	40,000	n/a	n/a	75.00	3,152,400	n/a	183,000	352	
	Renovated	n/a	60,000	n/a	n/a	50.00	2,162,400	n/a	287,000	247	
Brandeis Univ., Waltham, Mass.	Total	7,000,000	166,412	116,500	49,912	n/a	6,600,000	400,000	985,000	876	Abramovitz . . .
	New	6,275,000	60,407	42,300	18,107	103.88	6,000,000	275,000	95,000	350	
	Renovated	725,000	106,005	74,200	31,805	6.84	600,000	125,000	890,000	526	
Virginia Polytech. Inst/State Univ., Blacksburg	Total	6,440,000	226,630	183,099	43,531	n/a	5,350,000	500,000	1,200,000	1,800	VVKR Partnerhip
	New	5,440,000	115,035	85,358	29,677	47.20	4,538,000	500,000	600,000	1,000	
	Renovated	1,000,000	111,595	97,741	13,854	8.96	812,000	0	600,000	800	
U.S. Air Force Acad., Colorado Springs	Total	5,401,319	141,990	117,083	24,907	76.63	4,507,897	893,422	549,000	1,359	Henningson . . .
	New	5,050,364	54,242	46,098	8,144	n/a	4,156,942	893,422	154,000	586	
	Renovated	350,955	87,748	70,985	16,763	n/a	350,955	0	395,000	773	
Western Carolina Univ., Cullowhee, N.C.	Total	5,245,000	135,355	111,640	n/a	n/a	4,056,079	555,740	600,000	1,000	Six Associates Inc.
	New	n/a	20,000	n/a	n/a	n/a	n/a	n/a	n/a	n/a	
	Renovated	n/a	15,000	n/a	n/a	n/a	n/a	n/a	n/a	n/a	
Univ. of North Dakota, Grand Forks	Total	4,500,000	153,758	111,222	42,536	29.27	3,600,000	650,000	103,000	1,312	Myron Denbrook
	New	n/a	80,583	56,468	24,115	n/a	n/a	n/a	n/a	n/a	
	Renovated	n/a	73,175	54,754	18,421	n/a	n/a	n/a	n/a	n/a	
Franklin & Marshall Coll., Lancaster, Pa.	Total	4,000,000	82,000	62,000	20,000	36.59	3,000,000	280,000	300,000	535	Shepley Bulfinch . . .
	New	n/a	32,000	n/a	n/a	n/a	n/a	n/a	150,000	251	
	Renovated	n/a	50,000	n/a	n/a	n/a	n/a	n/a	150,000	284	
Grinnell Coll., Ia.	Total	3,418,654	54,250	n/a	n/a	54.50	2,956,654	592,428	540,000	402	Weese Hickey Weese
	New	n/a	11,000	n/a	n/a	n/a	n/a	337,428	n/a	80	
	Renovated	n/a	43,250	n/a	n/a	n/a	n/a	255,000	n/a	322	
College of Saint Rose, Albany, N.Y.	Total	1,920,063	46,490	37,547	8,943	39.50	1,545,063	220,000	200,000	350	The Hillier Group
	New	1,528,723	17,700	16,621	1,079	65.00	1,153,723	220,000	75,000	188	
	Renovated	391,340	28,790	20,926	7,864	14.00	391,340	0	125,000	162	

Renovation Only

Name of Institution	Project Cost	Gross Area	Assignable	Non-Assignable	Sq.Ft. Cost	Building Cost	Equipment Cost	Book Capacity	Seating Capacity	Architect
Catholic Univ. of America, Washington, D.C.	2,000,000	100,000	82,000	18,000	n/a	1,500,000	500,000	n/a	500	Leo A. Daly Co.

As in the past, most of the funds for the projects come from local governments, with a small percentage from federal funding. Gift funds this year are only slightly higher than federal contributions. One original community incorporated several business and local people solely for the undertaking of the library reconstruction.

The academic buildings include the University of Texas Health Science Center at San Antonio and 11 projects with new and renovated space headed by Drew University and including the United States Air Force Cadet Library in Colorado Springs. (See Tables 5–7.)

Two-Year College Library Resource Center Buildings

D. Joleen Bock

Appalachian State University, Boone, North Carolina

Over the past 20 years, overall enrollments in two-year institutions have increased 500 percent, from 818,869 in 1962 to 4,964,379 in 1982. Part-time enrollments account for approximately 60 percent of that figure. During that time, the number of public institutions has nearly doubled, from 678 to 1,177. Although the number of independent colleges has decreased to 142 from a high of 329, enrollments in these institutions have increased 50 percent. In those 20 years, student, faculty, and learning resource personnel have often decried the fact that there was never enough space, equipment, materials, or people. However, a review of new facilities reported shows that community colleges built 433 new learning resource centers (LRCs) during that time. This represents a very large capital investment in instructional support services facilities, in addition to equipment, materials, and personnel to staff them. It indicates phenomenal support by college administrators, boards of trustees, and state and federal legislators. Without these key individuals, funding would not have been made available for these new facilities.

Major Trends

What are the major trends, as seen through reports of new facilities? Since 1965, average square foot costs increased 156 percent from $23 to $59 (Table 1). Even this is not extravagant, considering inflation.

One of the biggest changes was in the formats of public catalogs. In 1979, the first year this information was collected, only one of the 13 new LRC buildings used other-than-card formats. In the past four years, 23 out of 52 new LRCs reported other-than-card public catalogs in a wide variety of formats; nine of these are in LRCs built in 1983:

Book Catalog
Pennsylvania Institute of Technology
Aiken Technical (South Carolina)

Note: Adapted from *Library Journal*, December 1, 1983.

Table 1 / LRC Building Square Foot Costs, 1965–1983

School Year(s)	No. New Bldgs. Reporting Cost	$ Range	Avg.
1965–71	114	9.76–34.63	$23.07
1971–72	29	17.12–61.11	32.76
1972–73	45	5.30–88.92	31.25
1973–75	89	18.00–206.97	42.50
1975–76	31	23.00–89.49	38.61
1976–77	30	16.56–89.49	39.90
1978–79	8	7.00–45.00	33.29
1979–81	17	35.62–100.00	54.49
1981–83	15	35.00–88.61	59.03

Computer Terminal plus Card Catalog
Olive-Harvey (Illinois)
Trident Technical (South Carolina)

Fiche Catalog
Dallas Richland Campus
Cuyahoga East Campus (Ohio)
Mohave Havasu Campus (Arizona)

Fiche plus Card Catalog
Clark County (Nevada)

Film Catalog
Evergreen Valley (California)

One of a number of growing new services, as reported in building plans, was the area of learning assistance. In the 1971–1981 period, 122 learning assistance centers were included in 225 new buildings. The current report (Table 2) again indicates that 50 percent of the buildings include these services. This is a tribute to the integration of learning resources with instructional programs, one of the prime objectives in LRC programs. Seventy-three institutions also reported career information centers in the past ten years.

Another area of service growth was in audio-video production, where 183 out of 225 buildings included audio-video production facilities, and 161 included graphic/

Table 2 / Services in 24 LRCs
Built July 1, 1981–June 30, 1983

Services	No. of LRCs
Library	23
AV distribution	22
Graphic/photographic production	14
Audio-video production	18
Reprographic production	10
Audio-video learning lab	15
Learning assistance center	12
Career information center	7
CAI terminals	7

Table 3 / New LRC Buildings, July 1, 1981–June 30, 1983

COLLEGE	FTE 1982	GROSS AREA	TOTAL ASF	SQ.FT. COST	FURN/EQUIPT COST	SEATS	KEY TO FACILITIES
ARIZONA							
Mohave Havasu Campus	1,092	NA	1,945	54.00	NA	28	ABD
CALIFORNIA							
Evergreen Valley	NA	71,353	45,024	72.12	623,989	1,133	ABCDEFGHI
Long Beach City	NA	45,898	37,124	85.26	542,917	650	ABCDEFGHI
Palomar College	1,085	55,892	43,628	76.00	319,000	451	ABCDEFI
ILLINOIS							
Olive-Harvey	NA	64,000	NA	NA	NA	450	ABCDFI
IOWA							
Iowa Western	680	5,403	3,843	60.00	5,984	70	ABCDE
KANSAS							
Donnelly	392	26,790	26,790	35.00	NA	75	ABDFG
MARYLAND							
Prince George's	8,300	75,000	53,000	50.82	383,000	700	ABCDEF
MICHIGAN							
Oakland	NA	2,864	2,356	65.00	21,500	NA	DG
MISSOURI							
State Community of East St. Louis	1,160	31,520	NA	NA	9,000	82	ABCDEFGH
NEVADA							
Clark County	3,526	21,450	19,950	53.73	360,000	295	ABD
NEW HAMPSHIRE							
N.H. Voc-Tech	240	5,300	4,150	60.21	53,000	84	A
NEW MEXICO							
N.M. State Alamogordo	NA	15,000	NA	NA	NA	NA	ABCDEG
NORTH CAROLINA							
Anson Technical	392	5,116	NA	NA	NA	32	ABDFGH
Beaufort County	1,000	NA	NA	NA	NA	100	ABF
Carteret Technical	985	15,000	10,295	56.82	30,000	95	ABCDFG
Surry	1,649	23,650	NA	41.00	72,000	150	ABCD
OHIO							
Cuyahoga East Campus	1,902	NA	30,511	88.61	212,088	198	ABCDEFGHI
OREGON							
Umpqua	NA	NA	NA	NA	NA	NA	ABDFGH
PENNSYLVANIA							
Pennsylvania Inst. of Technology	NA	8,000	7,500	NA	NA	50	ABG
SOUTH CAROLINA							
Trident Technical	NA	100,000	65,000	NA	NA	107	ABF
TEXAS							
Dallas County Richland Campus	6,092	32,460	NA	NA	NA	233	ABCDF
Texas State Technical Institute	NA	21,000	16,000	50.00	147,251	211	ABEFH
WYOMING							
Sheridan College	1,049	39,344	NA	37.00	152,162	175	ABCDEGI

Table 4 / Remodeled LRC Buildings, July 1, 1981–June 30, 1983

COLLEGE	FTE 1982	GROSS AREA	TOTAL ASF	SQ.FT. COST	FURN/EQUIPT COST	SEATS	KEY TO FACILITIES
ALASKA							
Northwest	1-¾	NA	22,500	NA	NA	12	ABF
ARIZONA							
Eastern Arizona	NA	9,020	NA	$26.50	$ 22,221	175	ABDF
Pima West Campus	4,695	13,500	NA	11.11	NA	NA	BGHI
CALIFORNIA							
El Camino	30,612	NA	NA	NA	NA	NA	AFGI
Golden West	8,937	58,991	48,660	NA	NA	NA	ADFI
Mira Costa	3,027	20,332	19,833	22.37	225,000	205	ABDFI
San Diego Miramar	NA	3,000	NA	NA	NA	50	ABCDGH
FLORIDA							
Bauder	NA	2,022	1,752	NA	NA	75	AB
GEORGIA							
Gainesville Jr. Coll.	NA	30,415	21,379	65.00	114,921	450	ABCDFGI
GUAM							
Guam Community Coll.	516	5,400	5,725	2.06	18,010	94	AB
HAWAII							
Leeward Community	NA	3,450	NA	NA	NA	90	FGI
ILLINOIS							
Danville Area	NA	15,280	13,133	77.80	44,650	140	ABCDFG
MASSACHUSETTS							
Central New England	2,600	NA	400	NA	NA	16	ABCDEFGHI
Greenfield	NA	544	544	3.35	4,404	7	AI
NEW HAMPSHIRE							
N.H. Voc-Tech	829	380	5,380	NA	NA	77	ABCDEHI
OREGON							
Bassist	NA	1,000	800	NA	NA	32	ABCDH
SOUTH CAROLINA							
Tri-County Technical	NA	9,000	8,500	4.66	NA	28	ABCDEFG
Univ. of SC at Union	NA	10,000	5,700	87.71	27,610	72	ABEFG
TEXAS							
Austin Community	8,342	18,000	NA	NA	50,000	320	ABCDF
VIRGINIA							
Northern Virginia	NA	24,568	20,824	52.38	42,618	244	ABCDEFGHI
Piedmont Virginia	1,454	13,670	10,882	61.05	69,809	136	ABCDEFG
WASHINGTON							
Shoreline Community	4,852	2,042	2,042	2.93	91,348	92	ABCDEF

Key to Facilities: A = Library; B = AV Distribution; C = Graphic/Photographic Distribution; D = Audio-Video Production; E = Reprographic Production; F = Audio-Video Learning Lab; G = Learning Assistance Center; H = Career Information Center; I = CAI Terminals.

photographic production facilities. In 1978–1979, CAI terminals were reported for the first time. Since then, 27 percent of the LRCs have included this capability.

Tables 3 and 4 indicate data for 24 new and 22 remodeled LRC buildings.

Flat Roof Disaster

Although the thrust of this report is related to construction of facilities, it is necessary to note that *destruction* of buildings was also taking place. Two days before Thanksgiving 1982, Hurricane Iva hit Kauai, Hawaii. It destroyed LRC Director Kathy Peters' home in Po'ipu. The 100-mile-per-hour winds blew waterproofing and insulation materials off the flat roof of the LRC at Kauai Community College. The next morning, large sheets of plastic were placed over the stacks to protect the collection from newly sprung leaks. The roof, built like a swimming pool, with inadequate drains, became a catch basin for thousands of gallons of water. The roofing ruptured, acoustic tile ceilings buckled, and the building became flooded. Ankle-deep water covered the floors; carpeting soaked up hundreds of gallons. Plastic shrouds that had saved the books from the heavy rain created optimum conditions for mold growing thickly on walls, books, furniture, and equipment.

The decision was made to evacuate the books. The Matson Navigation Company agreed to donate three large refrigerator cars until the LRC could be dried out. Every salvable volume was removed, wiped free of mold with Lysol-saturated cloths, and then packed. Without electricity to run the elevator, the resourceful salvage crews devised a ramp out of the stairwell banisters and a human chain moved the loaded boxes from the second floor to the refrigerator cars. Approximately 35,000 volumes were removed in less than two days, thereby saving the collection from irreversible damage.

When electricity was restored to the campus, work crews began the arduous task of cleaning and drying the LRC. Vacuum cleaners with water suction devices were used to extract hundreds of gallons of water. Lysol and Clorox solutions were used to scrub the thick mold off walls, furniture, and equipment. By January 4, six weeks after Iva, the building was dried out sufficiently to start bringing back the books that had been dried in the college's autobody paint drier at 80° to 85° F.

By January 31, when they reopened the LRC, most of the 35,000 volumes were back in shelflist order, except for portions of the Reference and Hawaii/Pacific collections. Some 3,200 volumes had been repaired and approximately 350 nonsalvable volumes had been withdrawn. Only 1 percent of the collection was lost, a tribute to the heroic efforts of community helpers, the LRC staff, the faculty, and administration of Kauai Community College. In retrospect, Ms. Peters said, "It was grossly wrong to design a flat roof for a location like this where the average annual rainfall is over 60 inches." Architects, please take note.

Book Trade Research and Statistics

Book Title Output and Average Prices:
1983 Preliminary Figures

Chandler B. Grannis
Contributing Editor, *Publishers Weekly*

American book title output continued its moderate annual rise in 1983, but average per-volume prices were holding steady or even beginning to drop slightly in a number of subject categories for the first time in several years, according to R.R. Bowker Company computations.

Of U.S. book title output in 1983, nearly 42,000 titles had been accounted for by the end of the year. Many more will be added as computations continue, and the final total, to be completed by late summer, will probably exceed the final 1982 total of about 47,000 titles. Figures are compiled and computed under the direction of Peter Simon and Beverly Lamar of Bowker's Data Services Division, using the *American Book Publishing Record* (*Weekly Record*) data base for hardcover and trade paperback books and the *Paperbound Books in Print* data base for mass market paperbacks.

So far, as can be seen in Table 1, the 1983 output comes to 41,888 titles, of which 3,825 are mass market paperbound volumes (Table 2) and 10,962 are paperbacks other than mass market (Table 3). The principal addenda in the final report will probably occur in the hardcover and trade paperback groups.

Table 4, showing imported books (hardbound and trade paperbound volumes only), is a report that had been missing from these surveys for several years because only incomplete data could be extracted from the *Weekly Record* entries. The situation is now rectified, and import totals similar to those of the late 1970s (in the 4,500–5,000 range) can be expected in the final report for 1983.

The reader will correctly conclude from Table 2 that a breakdown between new books and new editions could not be given for mass market books; that information is not consistently available in the *Paperbound Books in Print* data base, from which mass market figures are derived. Similarly, the *PBIP* data base does not now provide information on imported titles, so mass market titles are not included in Table 4. Even if they were, however, the number probably would not be great.

Table 5 deals with average prices of hardcover volumes and indicates, at least for this preliminary report, an overall price increase of 50 cents above the 1982 final figure of $30.34. Table 6, with average hardcover prices of all volumes priced below $81, shows—again, on a preliminary basis—an increase of only 12 cents over the final 1982 average, $23.26.

Note: Adapted from *Publishers Weekly,* March 16, 1984.

Table 1 / American Book Title Production, 1981–1983

(Hardbound and paperbound books, domestic and imported from listings in Bowker's *Weekly Record* and *Paperbound Books in Print*)

Categories with Dewey Decimal Numbers	1981 titles (final) Hardbound & trade paperbound only			1981 All hardbound & paperbound	1982 titles (final) Hardbound & trade paperbound only			1982 All hardbound & paperbound	1983 titles (preliminary) Hardbound & trade paperbound only			1983 All hardbound & paperbound
	New Books	New Editions	Totals	Totals	New Books	New Editions	Totals	Totals	New Books	New Editions	Totals	Totals
Agriculture (630–639; 712–719)	393	76	469	474	338	97	435	439	347	86	433	440
Art (700–711; 720–779)	1,450	235	1,685	1,693	1,453	260	1,713	1,722	1,294	172	1,466	1,472
Biography (920; 929; B)	1,407	379	1,786	1,860	1,447	240	1,687	1,752	1,356	203	1,559	2,059
Business (650–659)	1,031	302	1,233	1,342	979	335	1,314	1,327	990	268	1,258	1,266
Education (370–379)	1,006	152	1,158	1,172	887	148	1,035	1,046	739	111	850	856
Fiction	1,906	653	2,558	5,655	2,042	406	2,448	5,419	1,814	273	2,087	4,946
General Works (000–099)	1,428	229	1,657	1,743	2,055	283	2,338	2,398	1,945	222	2,167	2,216
History (900–909; 930–999)	1,813	465	2,278	2,321	1,696	443	2,139	2,177	1,350	368	1,736	1,761
Home Economics (640–649)	848	151	999	1,108	886	133	1,019	1,099	815	113	928	1,006
Juveniles	2,761	201	2,962	3,102	2,677	150	2,827	3,049	2,313	108	2,421	2,651
Language (400–499)	629	112	741	761	447	122	569	576	415	96	511	531
Law (340–349)	1,128	316	1,444	1,448	1,065	385	1,450	1,451	974	269	1,243	1,245
Literature (800–810; 813–820; 823–899)	1,477	256	1,733	1,777	1,454	250	1,704	1,742	1,337	216	1,553	1,597
Medicine (610–619)	3,128	625	3,753	3,788	2,691	510	3,201	3,229	2,352	486	2,838	2,869
Music (780–789)	298	101	397	398	265	77	342	346	265	56	321	323
Philosophy, Psychology (100–199)	1,141	244	1,385	1,465	1,151	242	1,393	1,465	980	207	1,187	1,277
Poetry, Drama (811; 812; 821; 822)	1,047	120	1,167	1,183	925	96	1,021	1,049	867	82	949	967
Religion (200–299)	1,905	347	2,252	2,278	1,762	291	2,053	2,075	1,533	226	1,759	1,781
Science (500–599)	2,781	577	3,358	3,375	2,604	506	3,110	3,124	2,164	424	2,588	2,605
Sociology, Economics (300–339; 350–369; 380–399)	6,627	1,122	7,749	7,807	6,319	1,081	7,400	7,449	5,660	1,056	6,716	6,759
Sports, Recreation (790–799)	921	165	1,086	1,264	832	150	982	1,191	749	135	884	1,056
Technology (600–609; 620–629; 660–699)	1,866	436	2,302	2,313	1,911	400	2,311	2,328	1,772	403	2,175	2,223
Travel (910–919)	372	96	468	472	352	107	459	482	330	94	424	442
Total	37,259	7,359	44,618	48,793	36,238	6,712	42,950	46,935	32,361	5,692	38,053	41,888

Note: In Tables 1–9, figures for mass market paperbound book production are based on entries in *Paperbound Books in Print*. All other figures are from the *Weekly Record* (American Book Publishing Record) data base.

Table 7, giving per-volume averages in the mass market field, presents a highly erratic picture, with an overall average 21 cents above the 1982 final average of $2.93. Table 8, per-volume averages of trade paperbacks, indicates, in the preliminary compilation for 1983, a decline of 68 cents, or 5.5%, from the 1982 final average of $12.32. *This overall decline, however, is attributable almost entirely to declines in two categories, Biography and Sociology/Economics,* where, for reasons not traced, the 1982 averages turned out to be abnormally high. The only other category where the average per-volume price of trade paperbacks fell off was in Technology, with a 51-cent drop from 1982's $14.78.

Table 2 / Mass Market Paperback Titles, 1981–1983

	1981 final	1982 final	1983 prelim.
Agriculture	5	4	7
Art	8	9	6
Biography	74	65	50
Business	9	13	8
Education	14	11	6
Fiction	3,097	2,971	2,859
General works	86	60	49
History	43	38	25
Home Economics	109	80	78
Juveniles	240	222	230
Language	20	7	20
Law	4	1	2
Literature	44	38	34
Medicine	35	28	31
Music	1	4	2
Philosophy, Psychology	80	72	90
Poetry, Drama	16	28	18
Religion	26	22	22
Science	17	14	17
Sociology, Economics	52	49	43
Sports, Recreation	178	209	172
Technology	11	17	48
Travel	4	23	18
Total	**4,175**	**3,985**	**3,835**

SOURCE: Paperbound Books in Print (R. R. Bowker Co.)

Table 3 / Paperbacks Other Than Mass Market, 1981–1983

Categories	1981 titles (final) Totals	1982 titles (final)			1982 titles (prelim.)		
		New Bks.	New Eds.	Totals	New Bks.	New Eds.	Totals
Fiction	399	238	73	311	281	48	329
Nonfiction	12,011	10,299	2,048	12,347	8,866	1,767	10,633
Total	**12,410**	**10,537**	**2,121**	**12,658**	**9,147**	**1,815**	**10,962**

Table 4 / Imported Titles, Hardbound and Trade Paperbound Only, 1983
(From listings in *Weekly Record*)

	New Books	New Editions	Totals
Agriculture	46	14	60
Art	96	9	105
Biography	100	9	109
Business	76	14	90
Education	109	11	120
Fiction	98	18	116
General Works	143	29	172
History	188	29	217
Home Economics	26	8	34
Juveniles	61	4	65
Language	113	16	129
Law	78	16	94
Literature	158	9	167
Medicine	273	18	291
Music	43	4	47
Philosophy, Psychology	115	12	127
Poetry, Drama	124	12	136
Religion	84	2	86
Science	607	72	679
Sociology, Economics	924	81	1,005
Sports, Recreation	69	6	75
Technology	269	47	316
Travel	33	5	38
Total	**3,833**	**445**	**4,278**

Table 5 / Average Per-Volume Prices of Hardcover Books, 1977–1983
(From Weekly Record listings of domestic and imported books)

Categories with Dewey Decimal Numbers	1977 vols. (final) Average prices	1980 vols. (final) Total volumes	1980 vols. (final) Average prices	1981 vols. (final) Total volumes	1981 vols. (final) Average prices	1982 vols. (final) Total volumes	1982 vols. (final) Average prices	1983 vols. (preliminary) Total volumes	1983 vols. (preliminary) Total prices	1983 vols. (preliminary) Average prices
Agriculture (630–639; 712–719)	$16.24	360	$27.55	390	$31.88	299	$33.54	301	$ 9,478.61	$31.49
Art (700–711; 720–779)	21.24	1,132	27.70	1,094	31.87	1,009	31.68	898	31,468.16	35.04
Biography (920; 929; B)	15.34	1,508	19.77	1,348	21.85	1,230	22.27	1,136	25,536.72	22.47
Business (650–659)	18.00	898	22.45	1,045	23.09	976	25.58	890	24,905.80	27.98
Education (370–379)	12.95	626	17.01	697	18.77	621	20.74	507	10,794.11	21.29
Fiction	10.09	5,100	12.46	1,855	15.49	1,972	13.91	1,663	23,618.12	14.20
General Works (000–099)	30.99	1,190	29.84	1,295	35.02	1,165	37.29	1,230	43,781.72	35.59
History (900–909; 930–999)	17.12	1,743	22.78	1,761	23.15	1,558	26.25	1,202	29,923.88	24.89
Home Economics (640–649)	11.16	517	13.31	584	16.07	569	16.42	519	9,139.07	17.60
Juveniles	6.65	2,742	8.16	2,660	8.31	2,290	8.77	2,062	19,997.82	9.69
Language (400–499)	14.96	318	22.16	328	22.95	346	22.85	295	7,109.62	24.10
Law (340–349)	25.04	759	33.25	1,175	36.30	1,047	35.61	826	31,786.30	38.48
Literature (800–810; 813–820; 823–899)	15.78	1,266	18.70	1,190	19.79	1,162	21.40	1,023	23,914.31	23.37
Medicine (610–619)	24.00	2,596	34.28	3,065	36.47	2,559	38.88	2,276	86,612.52	38.05
Music (780–789)	20.13	273	21.79	284	25.82	219	26.42	202	5,256.67	26.02
Philosophy, Psychology (100–199)	14.43	1,045	21.70	982	22.41	964	23.28	802	19,777.20	24.65
Poetry, Drama (811; 812; 821; 822)	13.63	753	17.85	699	19.34	568	19.96	523	12,133.76	23.20
Religion (200–299)	12.26	1,109	17.61	1,147	18.54	991	17.89	950	16,360.50	17.22
Science (500–599)	24.88	2,481	37.45	2,778	40.63	2,437	44.44	1,992	87,704.82	44.02
Sociology, Economics (300–339; 350–369; 380–399)	29.88	5,138	31.76	5,616	29.28	5,089	45.12	4,531	212,844.12	46.97
Sports, Recreation (790–799)	12.28	644	15.92	738	18.82	603	20.20	518	10,397.12	20.07
Technology (600–609; 620–629; 660–699)	23.61	1,742	33.64	1,864	36.76	1,558	40.65	1,458	55,070.49	37.77
Travel (910–919)	18.44	253	16.80	234	19.55	225	22.20	220	5,115.07	23.25
Total	**$19.22**	**31,234**	**$24.64**	**32,829**	**$26.63**	**29,457**	**$30.34**	**26,024**	**$802,726.51**	**$30.84**

Table 6 / Average Per-Volume Prices of Hardcover Books, Eliminating All Volumes Priced at $81 or More, 1977–1983
(From *Weekly Record* listings of domestic and imported books)

Dewey Classifications	1977 (final)	1980 (final)	1981 (prelim. only)	1982 (final) Total volumes	1982 (final) Average prices	1983 volumes (preliminary) Total volumes	1983 volumes (preliminary) Total prices	1983 volumes (preliminary) Average prices
Agriculture (630–639; 712–719)				281	$29.08	284	$ 7,434.36	$26.17
Art (700–711; 720–779)				971	26.88	846	22,288.66	26.34
Biography				1,204	19.68	1,156	22,468.72	20.15
Business (650–659)				964	23.48	874	20,541.05	23.50
Education (370–379)				618	20.41	506	10,689.11	21.12
Fiction				1,966	13.57	1,661	23,283.12	14.01
General Works (000–099)	$22.45	$23.34	$25.15	1,095	26.93	1,178	30,710.08	26.06
History (900–909; 930–999)				1,538	23.70	1,189	28,504.38	23.97
Home Economics (640–649)				566	15.80	516	7,602.57	14.73
Juveniles				2,289	8.74	2,058	18,497.32	8.98
Language (400–499)	$14.55	$20.14	$20.65	343	22.09	291	6,620.97	22.75
Law (340–349)				997	29.30	785	23,253.52	29.62
Literature (800–810; 813–820; 823–899)				1,153	20.39	1,012	21,320.81	21.06
Medicine (610–619)				2,353	33.01	2,109	66,803.07	31.67
Music (780–789)				216	25.28	198	4,699.22	23.73
Philosophy, Psychology (100–199)	$14.17	$20.18	$21.61	960	22.75	799	19,152.25	23.92
Poetry, Drama (811; 812; 821; 822)				559	18.12	509	10,025.76	19.69
Religion (200–299)	11.98	15.55	16.58	984	16.61	945	15,260.50	16.14
Science (500–599)	23.78	32.67	33.97	2,200	35.20	1,839	63,935.95	34.76
Sociology, Economics (300–399; 350–369; 380–399)				4,957	23.81	4,405	108,151.68	24.55
Sports, Recreation (790–799)				595	18.61	511	9,694.62	18.97
Technology, (600–609; 620–629; 660–699)				1,433	31.27	1,371	44,586.89	32.52
Travel (910–999)				220	19.29	215	4,082.57	18.98
Total	**$17.32**	**$22.48**	**$24.33**	**28,462**	**$23.26**	**25,216**	**$589,607.18**	**$23.38**

Table 7 / Average Per-Volume Prices of Mass Market Paperbacks, 1981-1983
(From *Paperbound Books in Print*)

	1981 volumes (final)	1982 volumes (final)		1983 (preliminary)		
	Average prices	Total volumes	Average prices	Total volumes	Total prices	Average prices
Agriculture	$2.54	3	$3.61	7	$ 35.65	$5.09
Art	5.49	9	8.45	6	27.80	4.63
Biography	3.82	65	4.29	49	227.05	4.63
Business	4.63	13	3.89	8	40.15	5.02
Education	3.96	11	4.25	6	33.25	5.54
Fiction	2.47	2,900	2.72	2,838	8,135.40	2.88
General Works	3.62	49	3.90	48	255.40	5.32
History	3.53	38	4.25	25	110.45	4.42
Home Economics	4.34	78	4.68	77	360.95	4.69
Juveniles	1.79	221	2.04	223	500.30	2.24
Language	3.41	7	3.61	20	68.45	3.42
Law	3.08	1	3.50	2	5.90	2.95
Literature	3.41	37	3.65	32	127.05	3.98
Medicine	3.66	27	5.08	31	160.50	5.18
Music	—	4	5.67	2	10.90	5.45
Philosophy, Psychology	2.83	70	3.57	90	390.55	4.33
Poetry, Drama	3.21	19	3.41	18	88.30	4.90
Religion	2.70	22	3.55	22	84.95	3.86
Science	4.45	14	4.70	17	72.35	4.26
Sociology, Economics	3.43	49	4.05	43	182.70	4.24
Sports, Recreation	3.04	207	2.90	171	592.50	3.47
Technology	4.20	15	4.33	47	188.80	4.02
Travel	3.22	23	7.55	18	178.65	9.92
Total	**$2.65**	**3,882**	**$2.93**	**3,790**	**$11,878.00**	**$3.13**

Table 8 / Average Per-Volume Prices of Trade Paperbacks, 1977–1983

(From Weekly Record listings of domestic and imported books)

Categories	1977 volumes (final)	1980 volumes (final)		1981 volumes (final)		1982 volumes (final)		1983 volumes (preliminary)		
	Average prices	Total volumes	Average prices	Total volumes	Average prices	Total volumes	Average prices	Total volumes	Total prices	Average prices
Agriculture	$ 5.01	104	$ 8.54	96	$ 9.74	116	$11.91	118	$1,729.64	$14.65
Art	6.27	563	9.09	651	10.07	625	12.75	434	6,383.97	13.19
Biography	4.91	363	6.57	444	7.33	414	26.50	368	3,733.13	10.14
Business	7.09	285	9.90	309	10.10	302	12.82	316	4,959.22	15.69
Education	5.72	382	8.42	484	9.54	383	10.22	310	3,538.60	11.41
Fiction	4.20	432	5.71	479	5.81	449	6.70	398	2,855.14	7.17
General Works	6.18	544	8.00	578	10.90	1,120	9.10	855	9,960.95	11.65
History	5.81	478	7.57	634	9.10	525	10.64	467	5,883.44	12.59
Home Economics	4.77	360	6.33	465	7.01	422	7.94	380	3,380.25	8.89
Juveniles	2.68	460	3.50	504	3.35	475	4.04	315	1,508.16	4.78
Language	7.79	215	8.59	252	8.56	208	10.51	198	2,214.40	11.18
Law	10.66	317	11.33	307	12.34	335	12.25	274	3,619.90	13.21
Literature	5.18	424	7.26	477	8.14	504	9.07	476	4,871.23	10.23
Medicine	7.63	682	11.46	814	12.35	573	13.13	503	6,885.06	13.68
Music	6.36	83	9.36	126	10.12	113	10.69	103	1,175.60	11.41
Philosophy, Psychology	5.57	382	7.57	415	9.66	395	10.93	348	4,039.06	11.69
Poetry, Drama	4.71	442	5.09	525	6.00	424	6.87	390	3,002.75	7.69
Religion	3.68	937	6.15	1,142	6.81	1,000	7.63	758	6,038.96	7.96
Science	8.81	630	13.46	648	14.75	605	15.29	510	8,977.18	17.60
Sociology, Economics	6.03	2,016	9.75	2,275	11.56	2,128	18.85	1,923	24,196.26	12.58
Sports, Recreation	4.87	326	7.11	414	7.86	355	9.28	338	3,185.51	9.48
Technology	7.97	601	13.52	918	14.60	673	16.78	593	9,653.51	16.27
Travel	5.21	247	6.73	263	8.20	221	8.17	190	1,769.55	9.31
Total	**$ 5.93**	**11,279**	**$ 8.60**	**13,220**	**$ 9.76**	**12,365**	**$12.32**	**10,613**	**$123,561.47**	**$11.64**

Book Sales Statistics:
Highlights from AAP Annual Survey, 1982

Chandler B. Grannis

Contributing Editor, *Publishers Weekly*

Net receipts of more than $7.971 billion were recorded by American book publishers from sales in 1982, according to the Association of American Publishers (AAP) in its annual statistical report, compiled by Touche, Ross & Company. This was an increase of only 4% over 1981 net sales and almost certainly meant a decline or, at best, a negligible rise in the number of copies sold, as suggested clearly in the surveys of another industry organization, the Book Industry Study Group (BISG). (For purposes of comparison, dollar sales increases for each recent year over the previous year have been estimated for AAP as follows: 1982, 4%; 1981, 8.9%; 1980, 11.2%; 1979, 9.3%; 1978, 12.7%.)

For 1983, however, a considerably brighter picture is foreseen. Trade book sales generally improved through the year, and retail sales in the fall and Christmas seasons were especially strong, according to the AAP monthly reports. Year-end sample surveys by AAP also suggested healthy increases in most categories. Final AAP estimates, with projections of industry totals, are usually released in the late spring for the preceding year.

In 1982, as Table 1 indicates, trade book net receipts showed virtually no increase overall, in spite of a good showing in trade paperbacks and juvenile paperbacks. Among the other major categories, only mass market and sci-tech sales registered increases more than 10% above 1981.

Publishers' sales estimates by BISG, prepared by John P. Dessauer, differ somewhat from those of AAP, though both sources reflect the same trends substantially. Differences derive from the fact that truly complete reports from every book publishing entity in the United States can never be obtained. As the AAP explains in its annual survey reports, the basic data used by industry statisticians are those reported in the U.S. Census of Manufactures, most recently released in 1980 for the year 1977. To these figures, industry analysts add their estimates reflecting *actual* changes shown in the industry's own annual surveys. For final, supposedly complete figures, analysts have to apply their own well-informed judgment.

One difficulty, as noted in the AAP annual reports, is that "the Census does not obtain data on most university presses or on other institutionally sponsored and not-for-profit publishing activities." Also, AAP includes figures on audiovisual and other materials not covered by the census, nor by BISG; and the census includes Sunday school materials and certain pamphlets not covered by AAP.

Consumer expenditures on books (not the same as publishers' receipts), along with data on channels of sale, are reported by John Dessauer later in this section of the *Bowker Annual.*

Table 1 / Estimated Book Publishing Industry Sales 1972, 1977, 1981, and 1982
(Millions of Dollars)

	1972	1977		1981			1982		
	$	$	% Change from 1972	$	% Change from 1977	% Change from 1972	$	% Change from 1981	% Change from 1972
Trade (total)	444.8	887.2	99.5	1,353.7	52.5	204.3	1,355.5	0.1	204.7
Adult hardbound	251.5	501.3	99.3	735.6	46.7	192.5	671.6	−8.7	167.0
Adult paperbound*	82.4	223.7	171.5	384.7	72.0	366.9	452.0	17.5	448.6
Juvenile hardbound	106.5	136.1	27.8	190.2	40.8	78.6	180.3	−5.2	69.3
Juvenile paperbound	4.4	26.1	493.2	43.2	65.5	881.8	51.5	19.3	1,071.3
Religious (total)	117.5	250.6	113.3	360.1	43.7	206.5	390.0	8.3	231.9
Bibles, testaments, hymnals, and prayer books	61.6	116.3	88.8	171.1	47.1	177.8	163.7	−4.3	165.8
Other religious	55.9	134.3	140.2	189.0	40.7	238.1	226.2	19.7	304.7
Professional (total)	381.0	698.2	83.2	1,140.7	63.4	199.4	1,230.5	7.9	223.0
Technical and scientific	131.8	249.3	89.2	391.1	56.9	196.7	431.4	10.3	227.3
Business and other professional	192.2	286.3	49.0	492.7	72.1	156.4	530.6	7.7	176.1
Medical	57.0	162.6	185.3	256.9	58.0	350.7	268.5	4.5	371.0
Book clubs	240.5	406.7	69.1	571.1	40.4	137.5	590.0	3.3	145.3
Mail-order publications	198.9	396.4	99.3	653.6	64.9	228.6	604.6	−7.5	204.0

Mass market paperback Rack-sized	250.0	487.7	95.1	735.6	50.8	194.2	823.1	11.9	229.2
University presses	41.4	56.1	35.5	86.0	53.3	107.7	92.4	7.5	123.3
Elementary and secondary text	497.6	755.9	51.9	998.6	32.1	100.7	1,051.5	5.3	111.3
College text†	375.3	649.7	73.1	1,074.7	65.4	186.4	1,142.4	6.3	204.4
Standardized tests	26.5	44.6	68.3	62.6	40.4	136.2	69.7	11.4	163.2
Subscription reference	278.9	294.4	5.6	386.2	31.2	38.5	396.6	2.7	42.2
AV and other media (total)	116.2	151.3	30.2	166.8	10.2	43.6	148.0	−11.2	27.4
El-Hi	101.2	131.4	29.8	148.9	13.3	47.1	130.1	−12.6	28.6
College	9.2	11.6	26.1	6.7	−42.2	−27.2	7.9	17.9	−14.1
Other	5.8	8.3	43.1	11.2	34.9	93.1	10.0	−10.8	72.2
Other sales‡	49.2	63.4	28.9	75.4	18.9	53.2	77.1	2.3	56.8
Total	3,017.8	5,142.2	70.4	7,665.1	49.1	154.0	7,971.5	4.0	164.1

Source: AAP Industry Statistics, 1982 (New York: Association of American Publishers, 1983).

*Includes nonrack size sales by mass market publishers of $92.9 million in 1981 and $113.5 million in 1982.
†An independent survey conducted by the Statistical Service Center for the AAP College Division indicated that 43 publishers, which represent the majority of college publishing, had 1982 net sales of $863.9 million. The AAP statistical agent and the Department of Commerce have been unable to reconcile the differences between U.S. Census figures and the College Division survey.
‡Other sales does not include any regular book sales. It covers only sheet, domestic and export (except sales to prebinders), and miscellaneous merchandise sales.

U.S. Consumer Expenditures on Books, 1982

John P. Dessauer
Book Industry Statistician

American consumers spent an estimated $9.7 billion on books in 1982, an increase of 6.2 percent over 1981. Consumers acquired 1.7 billion units in 1982, a decline of 0.4 percent from the previous year. These data emerge from an updated version of the annual estimate of industry sales in *Book Industry Trends*, published by the Book Industry Study Group.

The year 1982, a deep recession year, was one of the worst the industry experienced in recent memory. As Table 1 indicates, hardbound consumer books, which had performed strongly in recent years, fell on hard times. Adult trade and book club books and mail-order publications all posted significant unit losses. Among market channels (Table 2), general retailers fell off their double-digit pace of growth for the first time in a decade, and direct-to-consumer sales showed unprecedented dollar and unit declines.

Educational and institutional sales continued on the weak path they have been following in recent years, with unit losses posted by most textbook categories and by libraries and schools. The only reassuring record was established by the professional, religious, and university press categories.

Data for 1983 thus far indicates that the book industry is recovering, though with less vigor than some other sectors of the economy. One reason may be that price inflation in books has persisted at a time when general inflation has been abating. During 1982, some categories, notably adult trade paperbound, hardbound, and book clubs, posted substantial increases in average dollar rates per unit (see last two columns of Table 1). Book price behavior may have to resemble that of other commodities more closely before the industry can hope to benefit fully from the new wave of consumer spending.

Note: Reprinted from *Publishers Weekly*, November 4, 1983, where the article was entitled "1982 Book Purchases: A Hard Year."

Table 1 / Estimated U.S. Consumer Expenditures on Books, 1982 and 1981
(Millions of Dollars and Units)

	1982		1981		% Change		Dollars Per Unit		
	Dollars	Units	Dollars	Units	Dollars	Units	1982	1981	% Change
Trade	2,278.1	408.64	2,218.5	396.15	3.1	2.7	5.57	5.60	— .5
Adult Hardbound	1,225.6	139.27	1,333.2	166.74	— 8.1	— 16.5	8.80	7.99	10.1
Adult Paperbound	648.3	106.95	531.8	104.11	21.9	2.7	6.06	5.10	18.8
Children's Hardbound	286.9	76.98	263.3	70.18	9.0	9.7	3.72	3.75	— .8
Children's Paperbound	117.3	85.44	101.1	55.12	16.0	55.0	1.37	1.83	— 25.1
Religious	632.6	98.40	574.6	96.29	10.1	2.2	6.42	5.96	7.7
Hardbound	442.5	39.66	403.6	39.23	9.6	1.1	11.15	10.28	8.5
Paperbound	190.1	58.74	171.0	57.06	11.2	2.9	3.23	2.99	8.0
Professional	1,223.7	55.13	1,099.4	51.94	11.3	6.1	22.19	21.16	4.9
Hardbound	958.1	29.21	869.9	28.95	10.1	.9	32.80	30.04	9.2
Paperbound	265.6	25.92	229.5	22.99	15.7	12.7	10.24	9.98	2.6
Book Club	564.5	180.40	555.1	210.49	1.7	— 14.3	3.12	2.63	18.6
Hardbound	438.3	56.94	431.4	65.07	1.6	— 12.5	7.69	6.62	16.2
Paperbound	126.2	123.46	123.7	145.42	2.0	— 15.1	1.02	.85	20.0
Mail Order Publications	617.4	54.53	675.2	59.85	— 8.6	— 8.9	11.32	11.28	.4
Mass Market Publications	1,549.5	582.57	1,397.8	563.68	10.9	3.4	2.65	2.47	7.3
University Presses	94.0	9.80	86.6	9.64	8.5	1.7	9.59	8.98	6.8
Hardbound	65.8	4.12	60.5	3.94	8.8	4.6	15.97	15.35	4.0
Paperbound	28.2	5.86	26.1	5.70	8.0	.4	4.96	4.57	8.5
Elhi Text	1,075.0	247.25	996.0	252.75	7.9	— 2.2	4.34	3.94	10.2
Hardbound	595.5	101.71	558.5	102.13	6.6	— .4	5.85	5.46	7.1
Paperbound	479.5	145.54	437.5	150.62	9.6	— 3.4	3.29	2.90	13.4
College Text	1,338.5	97.88	1,209.7	98.04	10.6	— .1	13.67	12.33	10.9
Hardbound	997.6	62.66	908.9	63.50	9.8	— 1.3	15.92	14.31	11.3
Paperbound	340.9	35.32	300.8	34.54	13.3	2.3	9.65	8.79	9.8
Subscription Reference	333.4	1.00	328.5	1.00	1.5	.0	333.40	328.50	1.5
TOTAL	9,706.7	1,735.70	9,141.2	1,741.85	6.2	— .4	5.59	5.24	6.7

Table 2 / Channels of U.S. Book Distribution—Estimated Consumer Expenditures
(Millions of Dollars and Units)

	1982		1981		% Change	
	Dollars	Units	Dollars	Units	Dollars	Units
General Retailers	3,754.1	814.48	3,497.8	785.41	7.3	3.7
College Stores	1,791.9	204.32	1,624.5	201.47	10.3	1.4
Libraries & Institutions	751.2	62.42	683.2	66.16	10.0	— 5.7
Schools	1,329.6	282.61	1,267.9	293.45	4.9	— 3.7
Direct to Consumer	1,938.5	293.15	1,949.8	325.80	— .6	— 10.0
Other	141.4	78.79	118.0	69.54	19.8	13.3
TOTAL	**9,706.7**	**1,735.70**	**9,141.2**	**1,741.83**	**6.2**	**— .4**

Prices of U.S. and Foreign Published Materials

Dennis E. Smith

Coordinator, Library Financial Analysis and External Relations
University of California, Office of the President,
Berkeley, California 94720
415-642-2370

Single-digit inflation rates for the Consumer Price Index and the Producer Price Index appeared to have had a stabilizing effect on prices of hardcover books during the 1983 period. But once again, prices for U.S.-published periodicals climbed in the double-digit range. Norman Brown's and Jane Phillips's preliminary survey of 1984 subscription prices of U.S. periodicals indicates an increase of 13.2 percent over 1983. This increase should be viewed conditionally, because experience has shown that the preliminary January estimates of the percentages of increase of American periodical subscription prices are usually higher than the final percentages. Also, it is clear that the upward trend in prices for periodicals is affected by the continuing trend for professional associations to charge institutional rates for publications. Norman Brown points out that the American Psychological Association's decision to inaugurate institutional rates in 1984 for many of its journals caused a 90.5 percent increase in their prices.

U.S. Published Materials

The changes in the indexes for the principal categories of U.S. materials published in 1983 are as follows:

Materials	Index Change	Percent Change
Periodicals	22.1	12.1
Serial services	21.2	12.4
Hardcover books	2.6	1.7
Mass Market paperbacks	7.4	6.8
(Higher priced) paperbacks	−11.6	−5.6

Caution should be used when using the data in Table 4, which provides the actual price index broken out by subject class for mass market paperbacks. Several of the subject classes that make up the survey continue to be quite limited in size. For example, "Agriculture," with one of the highest rates of increase (40.6 percent), consists of 7 books, and "Law" and "Music," which recorded declines of 15.7 percent and 4.0 percent, respectively, consisted of only 2 titles each.

Libraries using the various U.S. price indexes, or any other index, should be careful, once again, not to be misled by overall or general rates of increase or decrease. The rates for specific subject classes within each index must be analyzed in relation to an individual library's purchasing pattern. For example, the overall preliminary price increase for 1983 over 1982 for hardcover books is only 1.7 percent, but art books increased 10.6 percent and business books 9.4 percent. Note, also, that poetry and drama books increased 16.2 percent.

Table 6 contains data on U.S. nonprint media. It is interesting to note that the

Table 1 / U.S. Periodicals: Average Prices and Price Indexes, 1980–1983*
(Index Base: 1977 = 100)

Subject Area	1977 Average Price	1980 Average Price	1980 Index	1981 Average Price	1981 Index	1982 Average Price	1982 Index	1983 Average Price	1983 Index
U.S. Periodicals†	$24.59	$34.54	140.5	$39.13	159.1	$44.80	182.2	$50.23	204.3
Agriculture	11.58	15.24	131.6	17.24	148.9	19.76	170.6	21.27	183.7
Business and economics	18.62	25.42	136.5	28.88	155.1	32.67	175.5	35.67	191.6
Chemistry and physics	93.76	137.45	146.6	156.30	166.7	177.94	189.8	207.94	221.8
Children's periodicals	5.82	7.85	134.9	8.56	147.1	9.90	170.1	11.49	197.4
Education	17.54	23.45	133.7	25.18	143.6	28.18	160.7	31.36	178.8
Engineering	35.77	49.15	137.4	54.55	152.5	61.54	172.0	73.18	204.6
Fine and applied arts	13.72	18.67	136.1	20.51	149.5	23.35	170.2	25.17	183.5
General interest periodicals	16.19	19.87	122.7	21.83	134.8	23.93	147.8	26.43	163.2
History	12.64	15.77	124.8	17.96	142.1	20.37	161.2	22.43	177.5
Home economics	18.73	24.63	131.5	27.34	146.0	34.27	183.0	35.68	190.5
Industrial arts	14.37	20.70	144.1	22.62	157.4	27.13	188.8	28.83	200.6
Journalism and communications	16.97	27.34	161.1	29.80	175.6	33.91	199.8	37.39	220.3
Labor and industrial relations	11.24	18.84	167.6	21.68	192.9	24.72	219.9	29.22	260.0
Law	17.36	23.00	132.5	24.80	142.9	27.53	158.6	29.66	170.9
Library and information sciences	16.97	23.25	137.0	28.47	167.8	33.52	197.5	36.72	216.4
Literature and language	11.82	15.30	129.4	17.30	146.4	19.39	164.0	21.19	179.3
Math, botany, geology, and general science	47.13	67.54	143.3	75.62	160.4	87.99	186.7	97.26	206.4
Medicine	51.31	73.37	143.0	86.38	168.3	102.87	200.5	112.72	219.7
Philosophy and religion	10.89	14.73	135.3	15.40	141.4	17.92	164.6	20.21	185.6
Physical education and recreation	10.00	13.83	138.3	15.42	154.2	16.91	169.1	19.07	190.7
Political science	14.83	19.30	130.1	22.69	153.0	25.89	174.6	28.97	195.3
Psychology	31.74	41.95	132.2	47.27	148.9	54.21	170.8	59.31	186.9
Sociology and anthropology	19.68	27.56	140.0	31.37	159.4	36.38	184.9	40.54	206.0
Zoology	33.69	44.58	132.3	48.32	143.4	61.07	181.3	70.74	210.0
Total number of periodicals	3,218	3,358		3,425		3,544		3,671	

*Compiled by Norman B. Brown and Jane Phillips. For further comments see Library Journal, September 1983. "Price Indexes for 1983: U.S. Periodicals and Serial Services," by Norman B. Brown and Jane Phillips. Note that this table uses a one-year (1977), rather than a three-year (1977–1979), base, conforming to the practice of the Bureau of Labor Statistics and making these price indexes comparable to the consumer price indexes. For average prices for years prior to 1980, see previous editions of the Bowker Annual.
†Based on the total group of titles included in the indexes in this table.

Table 2 / U.S Serial Services: Average Prices and Price Indexes, 1980–1983*†
(Index Base: 1977 = 100)

	1977 Average Price	1980 Average Price	1980 Index	1981 Average Price	1981 Index	1982 Average Price	1982 Index	1983 Average Price	1983 Index
Business	$216.28	$294.00	135.9	$343.29	158.7	$371.03	171.6	$417.83	193.2
General and humanities	90.44	124.28	137.4	142.04	157.1	160.03	176.9	186.67	206.4
Law	126.74	184.38	145.5	212.85	167.9	232.61	183.5	249.64	197.0
Science and technology	141.16	191.35	135.6	214.01	151.6	229.98	162.9	270.94	191.9
Social sciences (excluding business and law)	145.50	190.07	130.6	215.12	147.8	249.03	171.2	266.43	183.1
Soviet translations	175.41	229.68	130.9	253.79	144.7	298.22	170.0	341.04	194.4
U.S. documents	62.88	78.87	125.4	84.48	134.4	99.05	157.5	101.24	161.0
"Wilson Index"	438.00	541.92	123.7	600.58	137.1	583.83	133.3	606.58	138.5
U.S. serial services‡	$142.27	$194.21	136.5	$219.75	154.5	$244.52	171.9	$274.72	193.1
Total number of services	1,432	1,470		1,477		1,494		1,524	

*Compiled by Norman B. Brown and Jane Phillips. For further comments see *Library Journal*, September 1983. "Price Indexes for 1983: U.S. Periodicals and Serial Services," by Norman B. Brown and Jane Phillips. Note that this table uses a one-year (1977), rather than a three-year (1977–1979), base, conforming to the practice of the Bureau of Labor Statistics and making these price indexes comparable to the consumer price indexes. For average prices for years prior to 1980, see previous editions of the *Bowker Annual*.
†The definition of a serial service has been taken from the *American National Standard Criteria for Price Indexes for Library Materials* (ANSI Z39.20-1974).
‡Excludes "Wilson Index."

Table 3 / U.S. Hardcover Books: Average Prices and Price Indexes, 1980–1983*

(Index Base: 1977 = 100)

Categories with Dewey Decimal Numbers	1977 Average Price	1980 (Final) Vols.	1980 (Final) Average Price	1980 (Final) Index	1981 (Final) Vols.	1981 (Final) Average Price	1981 (Final) Index	1982 (Final) Vols.	1982 (Final) Average Price	1982 (Final) Index	1983 (Preliminary) Vols.	1983 (Preliminary) Average Price	1983 (Preliminary) Index
Agriculture (630–639; 712–719)	$16.24	360	$27.55	169.6	390	$31.88	196.3	299	$33.55	206.6	301	$31.49	193.9
Art (700–711; 720–779)	21.24	1,132	27.70	130.4	1,094	31.87	150.0	1,009	31.69	149.2	898	35.04	165.0
Biography	15.34	1,508	19.77	128.9	1,348	21.85	142.4	1,230	22.28	145.2	1,136	22.48	146.5
Business (650–659)	18.00	898	22.45	124.7	1,045	23.09	128.3	976	25.58	142.1	890	27.98	155.4
Education (370–379)	12.95	626	17.01	131.4	697	18.77	144.9	621	20.75	160.2	507	21.29	164.4
Fiction	10.09	2,100	12.46	123.5	1,855	15.49	153.5	1,972	13.92	138.0	1,663	14.20	140.7
General Works (000–099)	30.99	1,190	29.84	96.3	1,295	35.02	113.0	1,165	37.29	120.3	1,230	35.59	114.8
History (900–909; 930–999)	17.12	1,743	22.78	133.1	1,761	23.15	135.2	1,558	26.26	153.4	1,202	24.90	145.4
Home Economics (640–649)	11.16	517	13.31	119.3	584	16.07	144.0	569	16.43	147.2	519	17.61	157.8
Juvenile	6.65	2,742	8.16	122.7	2,660	8.31	125.0	2,290	8.78	132.0	2,062	9.70	145.9
Language (400–499)	14.96	318	22.16	148.1	328	22.95	153.4	346	22.86	152.8	295	24.10	161.1
Law (340–349)	25.04	759	33.25	132.8	1,175	36.30	145.0	1,047	35.62	142.3	826	38.48	153.7
Literature (800–810; 813–820; 823–889)	15.78	1,266	18.70	118.5	1,190	19.79	125.4	1,162	21.40	135.6	1,023	23.38	148.2
Medicine (610–619)	24.00	2,596	34.28	142.8	3,065	36.47	152.0	2,559	38.89	162.0	2,276	38.05	158.5
Music (780–789)	20.13	273	21.79	108.2	284	25.82	128.3	219	26.42	131.2	202	26.02	129.3
Philosophy, Psychology (100–199)	14.43	1,045	21.70	150.4	982	22.41	155.3	964	23.29	161.4	802	24.66	170.9
Poetry, Drama (811; 812; 821; 822)	13.63	753	17.85	131.0	699	19.34	141.9	568	19.97	146.5	523	23.20	170.2
Religion (200–299)	12.26	1,109	17.61	143.6	1,147	18.54	151.2	991	17.89	145.9	950	17.22	140.5
Science (500–599)	24.88	2,481	37.45	150.5	2,778	40.63	163.3	2,437	44.45	178.7	1,992	44.03	177.0
Sociology, Economics (300–339; 350–369; 380–399)	29.88	5,138	31.76	106.3	5,616	29.28	98.0	5,089	45.12	151.0	4,531	46.98	157.2
Sports, Recreation (790–799)	12.28	644	15.92	129.6	738	18.82	153.3	603	20.21	164.6	518	20.07	163.4
Technology (600–609; 620–629; 660–699)	23.61	1,742	33.64	142.5	1,864	36.76	155.7	1,558	40.66	172.2	1,458	37.77	160.0
Travel (910–919)	18.44	253	16.80	91.1	234	19.55	106.0	225	22.20	120.4	220	23.25	126.1
Total	$19.22	31,193	$24.63	128.1	32,829	$26.63	138.6	29,457	$30.34	157.9	26,024	$30.85	160.5

*Compiled by Dennis E. Smith from data supplied by the R. R. Bowker Company. Price indexes on Tables 3 and 5 are based on books recorded in the R. R. Bowker Company's *Weekly Record* (cumulated in the *American Book Publishing Record*). The 1983 preliminary figures include items listed during 1983 with an imprint date of 1983. Final data for previous years include items listed between January of that year and June of the following year with an imprint date of the specified year. (See the report "Book Title Output and

Table 4 / U.S. Mass Market Paperbacks: Average Prices and Indexes, 1982–1983*
(Index Base: 1981 = 100)

	1981 Average Prices	1982			1983 (Preliminary)		
		Total Volumes	Average Prices	Index	Total Volumes	Average Prices	Index
Agriculture	$2.54	3	$3.62	142.5	7	$5.09	200.4
Art	5.49	9	8.46	154.1	6	4.63	84.3
Biography	3.82	65	4.30	112.6	49	4.63	121.2
Business	4.63	13	3.90	84.2	8	5.02	108.4
Education	3.96	11	4.25	107.3	6	5.54	139.9
Fiction	2.47	2,900	2.73	110.5	2,838	2.87	116.2
General works	3.63	49	3.91	107.7	48	5.32	146.6
History	3.53	38	4.25	120.4	25	4.42	125.2
Home economics	4.35	78	4.69	107.8	77	4.69	107.8
Juvenile	1.79	221	2.05	114.5	223	2.24	125.1
Language	3.42	7	3.61	105.6	20	3.42	100.0
Law	3.09	1	3.50	113.3	2	2.95	95.5
Literature	3.42	37	3.65	106.7	32	3.97	116.1
Medicine	3.66	27	5.09	139.1	31	5.18	141.5
Music	—	4	5.68	—	2	5.45	—
Philosophy, psychology	2.84	70	3.57	125.7	90	4.34	152.8
Poetry, drama	3.22	19	3.42	106.2	18	4.91	152.5
Religion	2.70	22	3.56	131.9	22	3.86	143.0
Science	4.45	14	4.70	105.6	17	4.26	95.7
Sociology, economics	3.43	49	4.06	118.4	43	4.25	123.9
Sports, recreation	3.05	207	2.91	95.4	171	3.46	113.4
Technology	4.20	15	4.34	103.3	47	4.02	95.7
Travel	3.23	23	7.55	233.7	18	9.93	307.4
Total	$2.65	3,882	$2.93	110.6	3,800	$3.13	118.0

*Compiled by Dennis E. Smith from data supplied by the R. R. Bowker Company. Average prices of mass market paperbacks are based on listings of mass market titles in *Paperback Books in Print.*

average purchase cost per minute of 16mm film rose 3.1 percent in 1983, while the average cost of an entire 16mm film decreased by 2.0 percent. This is caused by a decrease of 4.5 percent in the average length of a film.

The price indexes for U.S. library microfilm (Table 7) and selected U.S. daily newspapers (Table 8) record moderate increases once again. The cost of negative microfilm increased 3.1 percent per exposure, and the cost of positive microfilm increased 4.1 percent per foot. The average subscription rate for U.S. daily newspapers increased 3.7 percent.

Foreign Published Materials

As indicated last year, the availability of price data for British books is limited to prices for British academic books, as reported in Table 9. The data reported here is based on price information published under the auspices of the Centre for Library and Information Management of Loughborough University of Technology for copyright books deposited in the Cambridge University Library.

The data reported in Table 9 should be used with extreme caution. CLAIM's report no. 27 indicates that the preliminary data for 1983, covering the period from January to June, cannot be taken at face value. It is reported that while prices have increased overall by 15 percent over the last five years to an average of £12.46, the figure has in fact dropped

Table 5 / U.S. Trade (Higher Priced) Paperback Books: Average Prices and Price Indexes, 1980–1983
(Index Base: 1977 = 100)*

	1977 Average Price	1980 (Final)			1981 (Final)			1982 (Final)			1983 (Preliminary)		
		No. of Books	Average Price	Index	No. of Books	Average Price	Index	No. of Books	Average Price	Index	No. of Books	Average Price	Index
Agriculture	$5.01	104	$8.54	170.5	96	$9.74	194.4	116	$11.92	237.9	118	$14.66	292.6
Art	6.27	563	9.09	145.0	651	10.07	160.6	625	12.76	203.5	484	13.19	210.4
Biography	4.91	363	6.57	133.8	444	7.33	149.3	414	26.51	539.9	368	10.14	206.5
Business	7.09	285	9.90	139.6	309	10.10	142.5	302	12.83	181.0	316	15.69	221.3
Education	5.72	382	8.42	147.2	484	9.54	166.8	383	10.23	178.8	310	11.41	199.5
Fiction	4.20	432	5.71	136.0	479	5.81	138.3	449	6.70	159.5	398	7.17	170.7
General works	6.18	544	8.00	129.4	578	10.90	176.4	1,120	9.10	147.2	855	11.65	188.5
History	5.81	478	7.57	130.3	634	9.10	156.6	525	10.64	183.1	467	12.60	216.9
Home economics	4.77	360	6.33	132.7	465	7.01	147.0	422	7.95	166.7	380	8.90	186.6
Juvenile	2.68	460	3.50	130.6	504	3.35	125.0	475	4.04	150.7	315	4.79	178.7
Language	7.79	215	8.59	110.3	252	8.50	109.1	208	10.52	135.0	198	11.18	143.5
Law	10.66	317	11.33	106.3	307	12.34	115.8	335	12.25	114.9	274	13.21	123.9
Literature	5.18	424	7.26	140.2	477	8.14	157.1	504	9.08	175.3	476	10.23	197.5
Medicine	7.63	682	11.46	150.2	814	12.35	161.9	573	13.13	172.1	503	13.69	179.4
Music	6.36	83	9.36	147.2	126	10.12	159.1	113	10.70	168.2	103	11.41	179.4
Philosophy, psychology	5.57	382	7.57	135.9	415	9.66	173.4	395	10.93	196.2	348	11.61	208.4
Poetry, drama	4.71	442	5.09	108.1	525	6.00	127.4	424	6.87	145.9	390	7.70	163.5
Religion	3.68	937	6.15	167.1	1,142	6.81	185.1	1,000	7.63	207.3	758	7.97	216.6
Science	8.81	630	13.46	152.8	648	14.75	167.4	605	15.29	173.6	510	17.60	199.8
Sociology, economics	6.03	2,016	9.75	161.7	2,275	11.56	191.7	2,128	18.86	312.8	1,923	12.58	208.6
Sports, recreation	4.87	326	7.11	146.0	414	7.86	161.4	355	9.29	190.8	336	9.48	194.7
Technology	7.97	601	13.52	169.6	918	14.60	183.2	673	16.79	210.7	593	16.28	204.3
Travel	5.21	247	6.73	129.2	263	8.20	157.4	221	8.18	157.0	190	9.31	178.7
Total	$5.93	11,273	$8.60	145.0	13,220	$9.76	164.6	12,365	$12.33	207.9	10,613	$11.64	196.3

*See footnote to Table 3.

Table 6 / U.S. Nonprint Media: Average Prices and Price Indexes, 1979–1983
(Index Base: 1977 = 100)

Category	1977 Average Price	1979 Average Price	1979 Index	1980 Average Price	1980 Index	1981 Average Price	1981 Index	1982 Average Price	1982 Index	1983 Average Price	1983 Index
16mm Films											
Rental cost per minute	$1.23	$1.35	109.8	$1.41	114.6	$1.65	134.1	$1.61	130.9	$1.82	148.0
Purchase cost per minute	13.95	13.62	97.6	12.03	86.2	16.09	115.3	15.01	107.6	15.47	110.9
Cost of film	308.85	328.24	106.3	279.09	90.4	343.79	111.3	432.35	140.0	423.87	137.2
Length per film (min.)	22.1	24.1	—	23.2	—	21.4	—	28.7	—	27.4	—
Videocassettes											
Purchase cost per minute	—	—	—	7.58	100.0	14.87	196.2	10.47	138.1	11.04	145.6
Purchase cost	—	—	—	271.93	100.0	322.54	118.6	337.40	124.1	320.16	117.7
Length per video (min.)	—	—	—	—	—	—	—	—	—	29.0	
Filmstrips											
Cost of filmstrip	18.60	21.42	115.2	21.74	116.9	25.40	136.6	29.14	156.7	28.60	153.8
Cost of filmstrip set	72.26	65.97	91.3	67.39	93.3	71.12	98.4	81.62	113.0	79.57	110.1
Number of filmstrips per set	4.1	3.08	—	3.1	—	2.8	—	2.8	—	2.8	—
Number of frames per filmstrip	64.2	71.8	—	67.9	—	71.4	—	67.8	—	70.7	—
Sound Recordings											
Average cost per cassette	10.63	12.58	118.3	9.34	87.9	12.48	117.4	10.74	101.0	11.23	105.6

*Compiled by David B. Walch from selected issues of Choice, School Library Journal, and Booklist.

Table 7 / U.S. Library Microfilm: Average Rates and Index Values, 1981–1983*
(Index Base: 1978 = 100)

Year	Negative Microfilm (35mm)			Positive Microfilm (35mm)		
	Average Rate/ Exposure	Index Value	Change in Index	Average Rate/ Foot	Index Value	Change in Index
1978	$0.0836	100.0	0	$0.1612	100.0	0
1981	$0.0998	132.8	+32.8	$0.2021	142.5	+42.5
1982	$0.1067	142.0	+ 9.3	$0.2184	154.0	+11.5
1983	$0.1100	147.0	+ 3.5	$0.2274	160.3	+ 4.1

in the last six months from an average £14.29. Similarly, the proportion of books costing less than £8.00 has fallen from 51 percent to 49 percent over five years, but has risen in the last six months from 37 percent. There was a seemingly high incidence of items appearing in the *British National Bibliography,* January through June 1983, with pre-1983 imprints. The British Library Bibliographic Services Division has described this as a temporary phenomenon. This anomaly obviously affects the accuracy of the figures, in that average prices are lower than if the pre-1982 imprints were not present. One assumes that once the backlog at British National Bibliography has been cleared, the data reported by CLAIM will more accurately reflect the prices of British books.

One of the three German book price indexes recorded a moderate increase in 1982. The combined index for both hardcover and all paperback books (Table 10) stabilized at a decrease of only 0.5 percent. The German paperback book index (Table 11) registered a moderate increase of 5.4 percent. The hardcover and scholarly paperback book index (Table 12) decreased by a moderate 4.7 percent.

As indicated for other indexes that have a subject breakdown, users of the German indexes should pay careful attention to their library's acquisition profile. The rate of change in each subject area can be a significant factor in estimating the impact of price changes on a library's book budget; for example, the combined index in Table 10 reports a decrease of 19.6 percent in law and administration and an increase of 16.7 percent in the social sciences. The same can be said for paperback books (Table 11), where there is a 26.2 percent increase for school textbooks versus a decrease of 17.7 percent in the general subject category.

The data reported for Latin American books (Table 13) reflects the widely divergent collection profiles of eight large research libraries, some of which aim for comprehensive coverage in all countries while others acquire very selectively in only a few. The total number of books acquired by all reporting libraries ranges from 35 for Surinam to 7,047 for Brazil, and the average cost runs from $3.63 (Guyana, based on 107 pieces) to $16.97

Table 8 / Selected U.S. Daily Newspapers: Average Subscription Rates and Index Values, 1981–1983*
(Index Base: 1978 = 100)

Year	Average Rate	Index Value	Change in Index
1978	$76.4391	100.0	0
1981	98.5521	128.9	+28.9
1982	103.6382	139.9	+8.5
1983	107.4728	145.0	+3.7

Table 9 / British Academic Books: Average Prices and Cost Indexes, 1980–1983*
(Index Base: 1979 = 100)

Dewey Classes‡	1979 Average Price £ p	1981 No. of Books	1981 Average Price £ p	1981 Index	1982 No. of Books	1982 Average Price £ p	1982 Index	1983 (Preliminary)† No. of Books	1983 (Preliminary)† Average Price £ p	1983 (Preliminary)† Index
000	14.17	507	12.10	85.4	587	14.31	101.0	309	12.33	87.0
100	8.89	409	10.29	115.7	384	13.47	151.5	155	12.27	138.0
200	5.47	481	5.97	109.1	541	6.51	119.0	350	8.37	153.0
300	9.15	3,687	10.69	116.8	3,305	12.21	133.4	1,605	9.80	107.1
400	7.62	147	11.09	145.5	194	10.05	131.9	76	9.07	119.0
500	16.67	1,225	18.51	111.0	1,339	21.76	130.5	429	21.73	130.4
600	14.32	2,460	16.78	117.2	2,298	20.33	142.0	805	19.55	136.5
700	9.57	949	11.83	123.6	907	12.92	135.0	510	12.31	128.6
800	7.19	1,163	7.37	102.5	1,060	8.85	123.1	572	9.16	127.4
900	7.78	1,256	9.04	116.2	1,094	10.02	128.8	584	9.59	123.3
Total	10.81	12,284	12.16	112.5	11,709	14.29	132.2	5,395	12.46	115.3

*Data compiled by Richard Hume Werking from Alan Cooper and Marilyn Hart, "CLAIM: Average Prices of British Academic Books, 1982," Report No. 25, and from Marilyn Hart and Lawraine Wood, "CLAIM: Average Prices of British Academic Books, January–June 1983," Report No. 27, published under the auspices of the Centre for Library and Information Management, Loughborough University of Technology.

†The preliminary data for 1983 covers the period from January through June. See narrative for caveats for use of this data.

‡000 General Works; Bibliographies; Librarianship
100 Philosophy; Psychology; Occultism, etc.
200 Not Subdivided
300 Sociology; Politics; Economics; Law; Public Administration; Social Problems and Services; Education; Social Customs, etc.
400 Language; School Readers
500 General Science; Mathematics; Astronomy; Physics; Chemistry; Geology; Meteorology; Pre-history; Anthropology
600 Medicine; Public Safety; Engineering/Technology; Agriculture; Domestic Economy; Business Management; Printing and Book Trade; Manufacturers; Chemical Technology; Building
700 Architecture; Fine Arts; Photography; Music; Entertainment; Sports; Amusements
800 General and Foreign Literature: English Literature
900 Geography; Travel; Biography; History

Table 10 / German Books: Average Prices and Price Indexes, 1980–1982*
(Index Base: 1977 = 100)

	1977 Average Price	1980 Average Price	1980 Index	1981 Average Price	1981 Index	1982 Average Price	1982 Index	1982 % Change
General, library science, college level textbooks	DM68.47	DM75.23	109.9	DM66.45	97.0	DM71.95	105.1	8.3
Religion, theology	23.21	24.06	103.7	23.00	99.1	22.90	98.7	-0.4
Philosophy, psychology	26.67	27.81	104.3	30.15	113.0	29.05	108.9	-3.6
Law, administration	33.92	47.04	138.7	62.65	184.7	50.36	148.5	-19.6
Social sciences, economics, statistics	25.97	32.98	127.0	32.30	124.4	37.71	145.2	16.7
Political and military science	22.91	25.50	111.3	24.90	108.7	27.83	121.5	11.8
Literature and linguistics	27.79	27.71	99.7	30.63	110.2	24.70	88.9	-19.4
Belles lettres	6.57	7.20	109.6	8.15	124.0	9.04	137.6	10.9
Juvenile	9.07	10.29	113.5	9.47	104.4	8.52	93.9	-10.0
Education	16.50	18.20	110.3	20.69	125.4	19.16	116.1	-7.4
School textbooks	10.88	11.58	106.4	13.61	125.1	13.69	125.8	0.6
Fine arts	49.70	51.76	104.1	54.30	109.3	48.82	98.2	-10.1
Music, dance, theater, film, radio	28.04	26.38	94.1	29.20	104.1	29.45	105.0	0.9
History, folklore	38.79	39.78	102.6	39.63	102.2	33.99	87.6	-14.2
Geography, anthropology, travel	32.20	31.14	96.7	29.83	92.6	29.09	90.3	-2.5
Medicine	50.29	59.91	119.1	65.57	130.4	66.35	131.9	1.2
Natural sciences	93.45	99.60	106.6	122.81	131.4	129.03	138.1	5.1
Mathematics	28.98	36.48	125.9	42.06	145.1	42.72	147.4	1.6
Technology	42.45	62.40	147.0	57.11	134.5	64.24	151.3	12.5
Touring guides and directories	21.78	31.02	142.4	29.03	133.3	28.24	129.7	-2.7
Home economics and agriculture	25.10	24.09	96.0	25.70	102.4	27.46	109.4	6.8
Sports and recreation	18.99	20.26	106.7	21.45	113.0	20.48	107.8	-4.5
Miscellaneous	11.30	13.60	120.4	11.69	103.5	15.69	138.8	34.2
Total	DM21.87	DM25.23	115.4	DM26.60	121.6	DM26.48	121.1	-0.5

*This is a combined index for numbered paperback books (Taschenbucher) and for bound volumes and scholarly paperbacks (andere Titel). See also Tables 11 and 12. The indexes are tentative and based on average prices unadjusted for title production. Figures for 1981–1982 were compiled by Peter Graham and Paul Peters from *Buch und Buchhandel in Zahlen* (Frankfurt, 1982 and 1983). The index year 1977 has been adopted to conform to the year used in the U.S. government's Consumer Price Index. *Information note.* At the end of the year 1982, the market exchange rate was 2.4266 Deutsche Marks per U.S. dollar as reported by the Bureau of Statistics, International Monetary Fund in its periodical *International Financial Statistics*.

Table 11 / German Paperback Books: Average Prices and Price Indexes, 1980–1982*

(Index Base: 1977 = 100)

	1977 Average Price	1980 Average Price	1980 Index	1981 Average Price	1981 Index	1982 Average Price	1982 Index
General, library science, college level textbooks	DM6.47	DM8.71	134.6	DM13.04	201.5	DM10.73	165.8
Religion, theology	7.03	7.29	103.7	8.92	126.9	8.79	125.0
Philosophy, psychology	8.06	9.44	117.1	9.18	113.9	9.75	121.0
Law, administration	8.95	13.41	149.8	10.42	116.4	12.04	134.5
Social sciences, economics, statistics	10.02	10.75	107.3	11.06	110.4	12.14	121.2
Political and military science	8.24	9.34	113.3	10.08	122.3	9.88	119.9
Literature and linguistics	8.36	10.21	122.1	10.02	119.9	10.59	126.7
Belles lettres	4.89	5.70	116.6	6.21	127.0	6.85	140.1
Juvenile	4.77	5.51	115.5	5.59	117.2	6.17	129.4
Education	10.88	11.63	106.9	10.70	98.3	11.86	109.0
School textbooks	2.52	3.12	123.8	3.05	121.0	3.85	152.8
Fine arts	10.28	11.77	114.5	11.11	108.1	11.45	111.4
Music, dance, theater, film, radio	8.11	8.60	106.0	9.64	118.9	10.78	132.9
History, folklore	8.35	9.22	110.4	10.75	128.7	11.57	138.6
Geography, anthropology, travel	6.82	9.09	133.3	9.90	145.2	10.29	150.9
Medicine	10.42	12.15	116.6	10.58	101.5	11.97	114.9
Natural sciences	10.85	12.31	113.5	12.86	118.5	12.92	119.1
Mathematics	15.00	16.21	108.1	17.53	116.9	16.74	111.6
Technology	20.63	28.22	136.8	36.72	178.0	33.17	160.8
Touring guides and directories	7.11	10.46	147.1	9.93	139.7	10.00	140.6
Home economics and agriculture	6.77	7.38	109.0	8.25	121.9	8.53	126.0
Sports and recreation	6.81	7.69	112.9	8.24	121.0	9.28	136.3
Miscellaneous	5.00	8.87	177.4	8.73	174.6	8.51	170.2
Total	DM6.69	DM7.76	116.0	DM8.13	121.5	DM8.57	128.1

*Indexes are tentative and based on average prices unadjusted for title production for numbered paperback books (Taschenbucher). Figures for 1981 –1982 were compiled by Peter Graham and Paul Peters from *Buch und Buchhandel in Zahlen* (Frankfurt, 1982 and 1983). The index year 1977 has been adopted to conform to the year used in the U.S. government's Consumer Price Index.

Information note: At the end of the year 1982, the market exchange rate was 2.4266 Deutsche Marks per U.S. dollar as reported by the Bureau of Statistics, International Monetary Fund in its periodical *International Financial Statistics*.

Table 12 / German Hardcover and Scholarly Paperback Books: Average Prices and Price Indexes, 1980–1982*

(Index Base: 1977 = 100)

	1977 Average Price	1980 Average Price	1980 Index	1981 Average Price	1981 Index	1982 Average Price	1982 Index
General, library science, college level textbooks	DM82.28	DM86.93	105.7	DM73.66	89.5	DM87.18	106.0
Religion, theology	27.67	28.63	103.5	26.24	94.8	25.47	92.0
Philosophy, psychology	40.38	38.14	94.5	44.68	110.6	42.13	104.3
Law, administration	37.50	50.79	135.4	70.32	187.5	55.88	149.0
Social sciences, economics, statistics	32.20	39.71	123.3	39.90	123.9	45.81	142.3
Political and military science	27.85	32.52	116.8	33.07	118.7	33.95	121.9
Literature and linguistics	40.90	36.06	88.2	42.57	104.1	31.18	76.2
Belles lettres	7.48	8.20	109.6	9.82	131.3	11.05	147.7
Juvenile	12.86	12.69	98.7	11.54	89.7	9.54	74.2
Education	18.19	19.40	106.7	23.07	126.8	20.66	113.6
School textbooks	10.98	11.79	107.4	13.80	125.7	13.64	124.2
Fine arts	58.51	63.70	108.9	65.08	111.2	56.45	96.5
Music, dance, theater, film, radio	37.89	38.73	102.2	46.13	121.7	41.26	108.9
History, folklore	49.82	53.43	107.2	54.73	109.9	44.62	89.6
Geography, anthropology, travel	34.76	34.05	98.0	35.19	101.2	32.59	93.8
Medicine	61.55	68.47	111.2	76.41	124.1	75.31	122.4
Natural sciences	131.28	118.89	90.6	143.29	109.1	149.80	114.1
Mathematics	32.83	41.55	126.6	46.60	141.9	44.69	136.1
Technology	45.39	67.79	149.4	60.87	134.1	68.00	149.8
Touring guides and directories	22.94	34.08	148.6	33.80	147.3	30.26	131.9
Home economics and agriculture	31.49	31.38	99.7	33.90	107.7	35.21	111.8
Sports and recreation	24.55	28.51	116.1	29.97	122.1	27.70	112.8
Miscellaneous	11.71	14.32	122.3	12.63	107.9	19.08	162.9
Total	DM27.68	DM32.18	116.3	DM35.39	127.9	DM33.74	121.9

*Indexes are tentative and based on average prices unadjusted for title production for numbered paperback books (Taschenbucher). Figures for 1981–1982 were compiled by Peter Graham and Paul Peters from *Buch und Buchhandel in Zahlen* (Frankfurt, 1982 and 1983). The index year 1977 has been adopted to conform to the year used in the U.S. government's Consumer Price Index.

Information note: At the end of the year 1982, the market exchange rate was 2.4266 Deutsche Marks per U.S. dollar as reported by the Bureau of Statistics, International Monetary Fund in its periodical *International Financial Statistics*.

Table 13 / Number of Copies and Average Cost of Latin American Books Purchased by Eight Selected U.S. Libraries in Fiscal Year 1983*

	Number of Books		Average Cost		%(+ or −) over 1982
	FY 1982	FY 1983	FY 1982	FY 1983	
Argentina	4,839	5,265	$10.52†	$7.61	−27.7
Bolivia	1,603	1,291	10.89†	7.86†	−27.8
Brazil	9,094	7,047	7.68	9.09	18.4
Chile	1,165	1,530	19.07†	16.97†	−11.0
Colombia	1,786	3,087	13.18†	12.22	−7.3
Costa Rica	592	958	7.70	8.18†	6.2
Cuba	119	380	9.83	9.73	−1.0
Dominican Republic	575	901	10.02	11.31	12.9
Ecuador	586	917	8.95†	9.48†	5.9
El Salvador	172	433	17.55	13.44	−23.4
Guatemala	280	184	9.14	11.65	27.5
Guyana	46	107	16.54	3.63	−78.1
Haiti	176	283	9.44	8.09	−14.3
Honduras	342	460	4.70	6.69	42.3
Jamaica	150	546	7.62	6.96†	−8.7
Mexico	3,673	3,615	9.02	8.65	−4.1
Nicaragua	227	295	8.82	11.10	25.9
Panama	66	102	8.64	8.55	−1.0
Paraguay	195	575	12.30	9.60†	−22.0
Peru	2,515	2,498	9.34†	9.50†	1.7
Puerto Rico	366	265	8.04	9.34	16.2
Surinam	26	35	‡	13.20	‡
Trinidad	32	49	6.94	11.39	64.1
Uruguay	1,606	1,199	14.93†	13.78†	−7.7
Venezuela	710	2,130	10.96	15.39†	40.4
Other Caribbean	1,654	2,756	8.95	7.70†	−14.0

*Compiled by Peter J. de la Garza, Seminars on the Acquisition of Latin American Library Materials (SALALM), Acquisition Committee, from reports on the number and cost of current monographs purchased by the libraries of Cornell University, University of Florida, University of Illinois, Library of Congress, University of Minnesota, New York Public Library, University of Texas, and University of Wisconsin.
†Includes some binding costs.
‡Data insufficient for meaningful comparison.

(Chile, 1,530 pieces). The one-year change in cost shows a low of −78.1 percent for Guyana to an increase of 64.1 percent for Trinidad.

Aside from collecting profiles, there are other variables that account for the striking divergences in Table 13. These variables are (a) levels of development of the book trade in the more than 25 countries, (b) the lack of meaningful "list" prices in most countries, (c) a high rate of inflation, (d) currency revaluation, (e) shipping, handling, service, and binding charges not consistently reflected in the reported costs, (f) changes in the scope of dealer coverage (e.g., entrepreneurial initiatives in Venezuela and some countries of Central America and the Caribbean), and (g) inconsistencies in reporting practices.

Peter de la Garza reports that a reassessment of the present statistics-gathering and tabulation program is being undertaken in 1984 by working groups of the Seminars on the Acquisition of Latin American Library Materials (SALALM) in the hope of improving the accuracy and predictive value of price data for Latin American materials. Expansion of the reporting base and the enforcement of stricter standards will be important goals of the revision.

U.S. libraries that spend a significant portion of their book budget for materials published in foreign countries will benefit from the continued rise in 1983 of the value of the U.S. dollar against the value of foreign currencies. A comparison of the value of the currencies of a representative group of countries with the U.S. dollar at the beginning and close of 1983 ("Nominal New York Closing Quotations for Interbank Payments of Listed Currencies as of Close of Business, January 31, 1983 and December 30, 1983," the Chase Manhattan Bank) illustrates the dramatic gain of U.S. purchasing power abroad during 1983.

Country	Jan. 31, 1983	Dec. 30, 1983	% Change
Canada	.8097	.8038	−0.7
France	.1441	.1200	−16.7
United Kingdom	1.5320	1.4495	−5.4
Germany	.4075	.3670	−9.9
Japan	.004144	.004319	4.2
Netherlands	.3715	.3265	−12.1
Spain	.0078	.006397	−18.0

Using the Price Indexes

In planning future budgets, libraries should bear in mind that the favorable trend in U.S. purchasing power noted above can be reversed. It is for this reason that the ALA/RTSD Library Materials Price Index Committee has sponsored the preparation and publication of the tables that accompany this article.

The price indexes that were designed to measure the rate of price change of newly published materials against those of earlier years on the national level are useful for comparing with local purchasing patterns. They reflect retail prices, not the cost to a particular library, and were never intended to be a substitute for information that a library might collect about its own purchases. The prices on which the indexes are based do not include discounts, vendor service charges, or other service charges. These variables naturally affect the average price for library materials paid by a particular library. However, as studies have shown, this does not necessarily mean that the rate of increase in prices paid by a particular library is significantly different from the rate of increase shown by the price indexes. The Library Materials Price Index Committee is interested in pursuing correlation of individual library's prices with national prices and would like to be informed of any studies undertaken.

Users are cautioned to use the indexes with care, noting the particulars of each index. For example, the use of preliminary data in comparison with final data can be risky, as previously noted for U.S. published periodicals and for British academic book prices.

For the users' information, the data reported on these tables were compiled for the first time on a personal computer which retains 15 decimal places for use in all computations. Thus, there will be some discrepancies if the user compares this data with the data reported in previous years.

In addition to the indexes presented here, there are at least two other published price indexes: "Price Indexes, Foreign and Domestic Music," which appears in the *Law Library Journal*. Also, timely updates of several of the indexes sponsored by the Library Materials Price Index Committee are published in the *RTSD Newsletter*.

The current members of the Library Materials Price Index Committee are Dennis E. Smith, chairperson; Mary Elizabeth Clack, Anne E. Foley, Peter Graham, and Richard Hume Werking. Consultants to the committee are Norman B. Brown, Imre Jármy, Jane Phillips, Nelson A. Piper, David B. Walch and Sally F. Williams.

U.S. Book Exports and Imports and International Title Output

Chandler B. Grannis

Contributing Editor, *Publishers Weekly*

United States book exports increased about 6.3% in 1982 over 1981, reaching a total of over $641.3 million (Table 1), and book imports increased at a similar rate, about 6.8%, for a recorded total of almost $315 million (Table 2), according to the U.S. Department of Commerce. The figures have been extracted and organized by *Publishers Weekly* from printouts supplied by William F. Lofquist, printing and publishing industry specialist at the department's Bureau of Industrial Economics, Washington, DC 20230.

The Commerce Department data omit export shipments valued under $500 and import shipments valued under $250; the actual amount of those shipments is not known.

In 1981 and 1982, imports were a little under half the value of exports; in 1980 and earlier, annual imports were reported at somewhat *over* half the export total.

Total figures are not available for units   numbers of copies of books exported and imported—since data on children's books are not given.

Broad Fluctuations

In all the Department of Commerce book categories, year-to-year fluctuations are typically very broad and seldom easy to explain. The key categories, of course, are "Books Not Elsewhere Classified" under exports and "Other Books" among imports; most trade books, presumably, are accounted for in these groups, but in fact the Department of Commerce categories can only remotely be correlated with the book industry's own customary classifications.

The relative positions of the principal countries (Table 3) receiving and sending books to the United States fluctuate considerably from year to year, but the top three countries in each column remain the same: Canada, the United Kingdom and Australia for exports, and the United Kingdom, and Canada and Japan for imports. Canada accounted for about 37% of U.S. book exports in 1982; the United Kingdom was the source of some 27% of book imports by the United States. Small shipments in each case, however, must have accounted for large additional quantities in unknown proportions.

Table 4 covers total book title output of principal leading book-producing countries. Table 5 reports numbers of translations, by original language, for the top 25 languages as of 1978.

Note: Adapted from *Publishers Weekly*, September 16, 1983, where the article was entitled "U.S. Exports, Imports, UNESCO Reports."

Table 1 / U.S. Book Exports, 1980–1982
Shipments Valued at $500 or More Only

	TO ALL COUNTRIES, Dollar Values				TO ALL COUNTRIES, Units				TO CANADA ONLY, Dollar Values		
	1980	1981	1982	% chg. 1981–82	1980	1981	1982	% chg. 1981–82	1980	1981	1982
Bibles, Testaments & Other Religious Books (2703020)	$31,867,260	$33,894,757	$31,873,724	− 6.0	43,501,521	35,871,584	34,872,569	− 2.8	$6,848,742	$7,710,272	$7,716,728
Dictionaries & Thesauruses (2703040)	6,018,536	7,098,264	5,750,959	−19.0	1,726,792	2,689,611	1,087,077	− 59.6	1,312,839	1,557,846	1,063,469
Encyclopedias (2703060)	27,944,503	25,819,529	25,344,932	− 1.8	6,462,048	4,619,219	4,195,293	− 9.2	9,340,069	7,011,290	6,127,968
Textbooks, Workbooks & Standardized Tests (2703070)	99,657,783	118,716,052	130,785,740	+ 10.2	———	———	28,297,679		37,395,796	41,283,009	51,537,407
Technical, Scientific & Professional Books (2703080)	53,927,278	79,637,779	118,491,757	+48.8	15,807,469	21,678,179	30,606,547	+ 41.2	11,816,779	15,745,842	19,982,424
Books Not Elsewhere Classified & Pamphlets (2704000)	284,159,654	327,185,497	319,643,723	− 2.3	199,852,375	215,360,345	195,882,465	− 9.1	121,136,963	143,059,209	147,171,845
Children's Picture & Coloring Books (7375200)	8,049,807	10,848,562	9,445,771	−12.9	———	———	———	———	3,451,007	4,718,255	4,191,463
Total Domestic Merchandise Omitting Shipments Under $500	$511,622,823	$603,200,440	$641,336,606	+ 6.3	———	———	———	———	$191,302,195	$221,085,723	$237,701,304

Source: U.S. Dept. of Commerce, Printing and Publishing issue of Spring-Summer 1980 and P&P editors; 1981 and 1982 figures compiled from data supplied to PW by U.S. Dept. of Commerce, Bureau of Industrial Economics (William S. Lofquist, Printing and Publishing Industry Specialist).

Table 2 / U.S. Book Imports, 1980–1982
Shipments Valued at $250 or More Only

	Dollar Values				TO ALL COUNTRIES, Units			
	1980	1981	1982	% Change 1981–1982	1980	1981	1982	% Change 1981–1982
Bibles & Prayerbooks (2702520)	$ 5,912,277	$ 5,363,579	$ 7,618,372	+ 42.0	1,513,528	2,234,254	8,560,438	+ 283.1
Books, Foreign Language (2702450)	30,100,817	27,021,249	27,081,560	+ 0.2	17,953,146	18,297,425	19,460,202	+ 6.4
Books Not Specially Provided for, wholly or in part the work of an author who is a U.S. national or domiciliary (2702560)	4,152,073	7,178,346	10,306,088	+ 43.6	1,148,235	15,202,787	38,699,397	+ 154.5
Other Books (2702580)	257,041,783	246,895,088	260,928,176	+ 5.7	196,199,815	202,306,063	217,021,948	+ 7.2
Toy Books & Coloring Books (7375200)	9,303,476	8,406,121	9,057,181	+ 7.7	—	—	—	
Total Imports, Omitting Shipments Under $250	**$308,510,938**	**$294,862,383**	**$314,991,377**	**+ 6.8**	—	—	—	

Source: See footnote to Table 1.

Table 3 / U.S. Book Exports and Imports: Principal Countries, 1981–1982

U.S. Exports (over $500 shipments only)

	Dollars 1981	Dollars 1982	% Change 1981–82
Canada	$221,085,723	$237,701,304	+ 7.5
United Kingdom	90,109,326	82,570,276	− 8.4
Australia	53,348,172	57,026,542	+ 6.9
Japan	21,343,698	24,909,000	+ 16.7
Nigeria	22,177,822	21,305,568	− 3.9
Netherlands	14,654,782	17,324,325	+ 18.2
Mexico	21,695,165	15,508,370	− 28.5
Rep. S. Africa	10,621,634	12,248,738	+ 15.3
Germany, W.	9,638,096	11,870,388	+ 23.2
Philippines	6,863,202	11,045,829	+ 60.9
Portugal	7,332,287	10,105,811	+ 37.8
Ireland	3,387,508	10,043,952	+ 196.5
Saudi Arabia	8,442,042	9,131,554	+ 8.2
Brazil	9,795,851	9,058,563	− 7.5
Singapore	8,255,662	8,994,100	+ 8.9
New Zealand	7.757,549	8,200,195	+ 5.7
All others	86,691,921	94,292,091	+ 8.9
Total, all countries	**$603,200,440**	**$641,336,606**	**+ 6.3**

U.S. Imports (over $250 shipments only)

	Dollars 1981	Dollars 1982	% Change 1981–82
United Kingdom	$90,840,357	$85,036,854	− 6.4
Canada	39,252,863	47,500,975	+ 21.0
Japan	44,585,307	46,889,045	+ 5.1
Hong Kong	15,520,380	19,306,161	+ 24.4
Spain	15,157,382	16,575,489	+ 9.4
Germany, W.	16,442,051	16,350,227	− .6
Italy	14,108,956	15,573,855	+ 10.4
Netherlands	8,795,091	9,501,430	+ 8.0
Switzerland	7,861,061	7,026,595	− 10.6
Mexico	5,578,452	6,902,932	+ 23.7
France	5,946,085	6,454,008	+ 8.5
Belgium	2,158,506	5,751,581	+ 58.4
Singapore	5,115,987	5,330,870	+ 4.2
All others	23,499,478	26,990,275	+ 14.8
Total, all countries	**$294,862,383**	**$314,991,377**	**+ 6.8**

Source: See footnote to Table 1.

Table 4 / Title Output: Principal Book-Producing Countries, 1978–1980

	1978	1979	1980		1978	1979	1980
AFRICA				**EUROPE**			
Egypt	1,680	——	——	Austria	6,439	6,783	7,098
Nigeria	1,175	——	2,316	Belgium	9,012	10,040	9,009
NORTH AMERICA				Bulgaria	4,234	4,600	4,681
Canada	22,168	21,793	19,063	Czechoslovakia	9,588	10,089	11,647
United States*	87,569	88,721	86,377	Denmark	8,642	9,415	9,256
SOUTH AMERICA				Finland	3,367	4,834	6,511
Argentina	4,627	4,451	4,698	France	21,225	25,019	32,318
Brazil	18,102	——	——	Germany, E.	5,680	5,816	——
Chile	——	——	1,109	Germany, W.	50,950	59,666	64,761
Colombia	——	——	5,492	Greece	——	4,664	4,048
Peru	968	857	766	Hungary	9,579	9,120	9,254
Uruguay	——	1,012	857	Italy	10,679	11,162	12,029
ASIA				Netherlands	13,393	13,429	14,591
Bangladesh	1,229	——	——	Norway	4,407	5,405	5,578
China	12,493	14,738	19,109	Poland	11,849	11,191	11,919
Cyprus	1,054	1,335	1,137	Portugal	6,274	5,726	——
Hong Kong	——	3,386	——	Romania	7,562	7,288	7,350
India	12,932	11,087	13,148	Spain	23,231	24,569	——
Indonesia	2,628	2,402	2,322	Sweden	5,256	5,396	7,598
Iran	2,657	——	——	Switzerland	10,077	10,765	10,362
Iraq	1,618	1,204	——	United Kingdom	38,641	41,864	48,069
Israel	2,397	——	——	Yugoslavia	10,509	12,061	11,301
Japan	43,973	44,392	45,596				
Korea, Rep.	16,424	16,081	20,978	**OCEANIA**			
Malaysia	1,328	2,037	——	Australia	7,658	8,392	——
Pakistan	1,317	1,184	1,279	New Zealand	2,079	2,496	2,850
Philippines	——	——	1,254				
Singapore	1,306	1,087	1,406	**USSR**	**84,727**	**80,560**	**80,676**
Sri Lanka	1,405	1,582	1,875	Byeloruss SSR	2,618	2,806	3,009
Thailand	——	3,779	4,091	Ukraine SSR	8,259	9,032	9,081
Turkey	——	5,071	3,396				
Vietnam	1,721	——	——				

Sources: UNESCO Statistical Yearbook 1982, Table 8.2 (New York, Unipub, 1983), except U.S.A. figures, which are supplied by R. R. Bowker Co. Data Services and University Microfilms. UNESCO figures are published late. *Includes books and pamphlets issued through U.S. Government Printing Office (in 1978, 14,814; in 1979, 13,506; in 1980, 13,000 est.); also university theses (in 1978, 31,529; in 1979, 30,035; in 1980, 31,000 est.). *Not* included in the U.S. figures are publications of state and local governments, publications of numerous institutions, and many reports, proceedings, lab manuals, and workbooks.

Table 5 / Translations by Original Language: Top 25 Languages in 1978

	1976	1977	1978
English	19,264	19,577	23,715
Russian	6,994	6,771	6,745
French	6,105	6,054	6,220
German	4,665	4,656	5,663
Italian	1,323	1,260	1,731
Swedish	1,166	1,158	1,177
Spanish	751	649	879
Danish	589	577	625
Czech	653	715	584
Polish	570	539	578
Hungarian	682	685	565
Dutch	367	448	528
Latin	479	432	508
Serbo-Croatian	463	437	477
Romanian	376	383	454
Classical Greek	496	387	437
Chinese	288	165	352
Arabic	260	227	318
Japanese	157	129	308
Norwegian	235	279	264
Bulgarian	284	289	256
Hebrew	232	215	246
Sanskrit	192	152	221
Portuguese	151	140	215
Ukrainian	216	203	156
Total, all languages	**50,381**	**50,047**	**57,147**

Source: UNESCO Statistical Yearbook 1982; Table 8.12.

British Book Production, 1983

British publishers set yet another output record in 1983, easily breaking the 50,000 barrier with the issue of 38,980 new titles, and 12,091 reprints and new editions (including paperbacks), making an overall total of 51,071 titles. (Tables 1–3). Contrasted with the 1982 figures (all of which represented record levels), the 1983 total is up by 5.7 percent; new books up by 2.7 percent; and reprints and new editions up by 16.7 percent. The general view is that these increases are not to be welcomed—although readers of *The Bookseller* will recall that dissenting opinions have been expressed—not least because of the implication that the trade is involved in more but shorter production runs. Fewer and longer are thought to be healthier.

There are two probable causes for the 1983 increase. Imported English-language books handled through British distributors (essentially U.S. imports) showed some growth. For several years these have represented just under 30 percent of the entire output; in 1983 they represented just over 30 percent. This advance was mostly in the sector of reprints and new editions, sharply up by 16.7 percent. New titles were little changed, up 2.7 percent. U.S. imports, particularly in the literature category, contributed perceptibly to this. So, too, did paperbacks. The manifest growth of trade in large-format paperbacks has especially increased output figures.

Although it is dangerous to read too much into statistics, it is interesting to note, if without comment, that in 1983 book categories broadly associated with reading for pleasure and relaxation—fiction, children's books, literature, and biography—showed considerable growth; the more vocational categories—chemistry and physics, commerce, and medical, political and natural sciences—all declined. And the small but devoted group that believes sociology to be the greatest disaster to strike Britain since the Black Death will be encouraged by a small decline in that category, too.

Note: Adapted from *The Bookseller* (12 Dyott Street, London WC1A 1DR, England), January 14, 1984, where the article was entitled "Another Annual Output Record."

Table 1 / Book Title Output, 1983

Classification	December, 1983				January–December, 1983			
	Total	Reprints & New Editions	Trans.	Ltd. Editions	Total	Reprints & New Editions	Trans.	Ltd. Editions
Aeronautics	16	2	—	—	206	36	1	—
Agriculture and forestry	35	2	1	—	427	68	18	2
Architecture	52	11	1	—	426	62	9	9
Art	170	16	1	2	1,312	186	30	—
Astronomy	25	5	3	—	171	40	5	—
Bibliography and library economy	73	14	—	—	675	136	3	—
Biography	132	30	1	3	1,969	734	78	5
Chemistry and physics	82	11	2	—	697	115	30	—
Children's books	189	47	24	1	3,449	790	194	11
Commerce	131	43	—	—	1,377	345	3	1
Customs, costumes, folklore	12	1	1	—	172	37	6	—
Domestic science	67	34	1	—	781	209	29	—
Education	127	13	—	—	1,421	245	5	—
Engineering	220	49	—	—	1,714	315	22	1
Entertainment	69	8	—	—	598	102	16	1
Fiction	272	114	9	—	5,265	2,156	204	6
General	144	12	—	—	856	97	2	—
Geography and archeology	29	12	3	—	437	118	5	—
Geology and meteorology	40	3	8	—	348	40	27	—
History	185	37	—	1	1,740	361	46	1
Humor	8	1	—	—	242	43	2	—
Industry	68	10	—	—	612	109	9	—
Language	67	15	—	—	708	129	7	1
Law and public administration	190	46	1	—	1,787	403	8	4
Literature	150	18	5	—	2,187	1,013	79	3

Table 1 / Book Title Output, 1983 (cont.)

Classification	December, 1983				January–December, 1983			
	Total	Reprints & New Editions	Trans.	Ltd. Editions	Total	Reprints & New Editions	Trans.	Ltd. Editions
Mathematics	133	15	3	—	1,011	142	22	—
Medical science	381	47	6	—	3,165	520	27	—
Military science	13	4	—	—	167	44	2	—
Music	38	7	1	—	489	113	22	—
Natural sciences	76	19	1	—	1,177	169	44	3
Occultism	11	3	—	—	188	35	17	—
Philosophy	66	20	11	—	695	167	59	—
Photography	16	1	—	—	294	40	2	6
Plays	26	6	—	2	381	201	35	2
Poetry	69	5	7	9	925	222	72	31
Political science and economy	438	96	4	—	4,177	823	92	—
Psychology	67	18	1	—	705	127	13	3
Religion and theology	290	66	23	—	2,257	394	189	—
School textbooks	165	47	1	—	1,964	288	9	—
Science, general	14	1	—	—	76	16	4	1
Sociology	110	16	1	—	1,162	172	16	1
Sports and outdoor games	52	13	—	—	610	123	2	3
Stockbreeding	23	5	—	—	265	53	7	—
Trade	47	9	—	—	563	127	2	—
Travel and guidebooks	93	50	1	4	956	379	24	2
Wireless and television	34	7	—	—	267	47	1	5
Totals	4,715	1,009	121	22	51,071	12,091	1,499	101

Note: This table shows the books recorded in December 1983 and the total for January—December 1983, with the numbers of new editions, translations, and limited editions.

Table 2 / Title Output, 1947–1983

Year	Total	Reprints and New Editions
1947	13,046	2,441
1948	14,686	3,924
1949	17,034	5,110
1950	17,072	5,334
1951	18,066	4,938
1952	18,741	5,428
1953	18,257	5,523
1954	18,188	4,846
1955	19,962	5,770
1956	19,107	5,302
1957	20,719	5,921
1958	22,143	5,971
1959	20,690	5,522
1960	23,783	4,989
1961	24,893	6,406
1962	25,079	6,104
1963	26,023	5,656
1964	26,154	5,260
1965	26,358	5,313
1966	28,883	5,919
1967	29,619	7,060
1968	31,470	8,778
1969	32,393	9,106
1970	33,489	9,977
1971	32,538	8,975
1972	33,140	8,486
1973	35,254	9,556
1974	32,194	7,852
1975	35,608	8,361
1976	34,434	8,227
1977	36,322	8,638
1978	38,766	9,236
1979	41,940	9,086
1980	48,158	10,776
1981	43,083	9,387
1982	48,307	10,360
1983	51,071	12,091

Table 3 / Comparison of Book Production by Subject, 1982 and 1983

	1982	1983	+ or −
New Books	37,947	38,980	+1,033
New Editions	10,360	12,091	+1,731
Totals	48,307	51,071	+2,764
Art	1,279	1,312	+33
Biography	1,491	1,969	+478
Chemistry and physics	754	697	−57
Children's books	2,917	3,449	+532
Commerce	1,493	1,377	−116
Education	1,175	1,421	+246
Engineering	1,662	1,714	+52
Fiction	4,879	5,265	+386
History	1,503	1,740	+237
Industry	569	612	+43
Law and public administration	1,464	1,787	+323
Literature	1,612	2,187	+575
Medical science	3,274	3,165	−109
Natural sciences	1,507	1,177	−330
Political science	4,263	4,177	−86
Religion	1,856	2,257	+401
School textbooks	1,807	1,964	+157
Sociology	1,174	1,162	−12
Travel and guidebooks	869	956	+87

Number of Book Outlets in the United States and Canada

The *American Book Trade Directory* has been published by the R. R. Bowker Company since 1915. Revised annually, it features lists of booksellers, publishers, wholesalers, periodicals, reference tools, and other information about the U.S. book market as well as markets in Great Britain and Canada. The data provided in Tables 1 and 2 for the

Table 1 / Bookstores in the United States (and Canada)*

Antiquarian	1,086 (86)	Museum store and art gallery**	
Mail order (antiquarian)	631 (22)	Newsdealer	131 (6)
College	2,857 (144)	Office supply	62 (2)
Department store	948 (109)	Paperback***	767 (35)
Drugstore	21 (4)	Religious	3,664 (205)
Educational	112 (20)	Remainders	21 (4)
Exporter-importer	30 (1)	Rental	4 (0)
Foreign language	17 (38)	Science-technology	71 (8)
General	5,757 (984)	Special****	1,723 (180)
Gift shop	110 (9)	Stationer	143 (24)
Juvenile	154 (29)	Used	724 (48)
Law	67 (3)		
Mail order (general)	361 (14)	Total listed in the United States	19,580
Medical	119 (3)	Total listed in Canada	1,978

*In Tables 1 and 2, the Canadian figure for each category is in parentheses following the U.S. figure.
**No figure available.
***This figure does not include paperback departments of general bookstores, department stores, stationers, drugstores, or wholesalers handling paperbacks.
****"Special" includes stores specializing in subjects other than those specifically given in the list.

Table 2 / Wholesalers in the United States (and Canada)

General wholesalers	951 (129)	Total listed in the United States	1,267
Paperback wholesalers	316 (21)	Total listed in Canada	150

United States and Canada, the most current available, are from the 1983 edition of the directory.

The 21,558 stores of various types shown in Table 1 are located in approximately 6,300 cities in the United States, Canada, and regions administered by the United States. All "general" bookstores are assumed to carry hardbound (trade) books, paperbacks, and children's books; special effort has been made to apply this category only to bookstores for which this term can properly be applied. All "college" stores are assumed to carry college-level textbooks. The term "educational" is used for outlets handling school textbooks up to and including the high school level. The category "mail order" has been confined to those outlets that sell general trade books by mail and are not book clubs; all others operating by mail have been classified according to the kinds of books carried. The term "antiquarian" covers dealers in old and rare books. Stores handling only secondhand books are classified by the category "used." The category "paperbacks" represents stores with stock consisting of more than an 80 percent holding of paperbound books. Other stores with paperback departments are listed under the major classification ("general," "department store," "stationers," etc.), with the fact that paperbacks are carried given in the entry. A bookstore that specializes in a subject to the extent of 50 percent of its stock has that subject designated as its major category.

Book Review Media Statistics

**Number of Books Reviewed by Major
Book-Reviewing Publications, 1982 and 1983**

	Adult		Juvenile		Young Adult		Total	
	1982	1983	1982	1983	1982	1983	1982	1983
Booklist[1]	3,387	3,427	1,540	1,546	1,225	1,118	6,584	6,386
Bulletin of the Center for Children's Books	—	—	490	439	418	375	908	814
Chicago Sun-Times	800	800	200	200			1,000	1,000
Chicago Tribune	750	600	150	150	—	—	900	750
Choice[2]	6,929	6,212	—	—	—	—	6,929	6,611
Horn Book	59	46	318	284	111	137	488	477
Kirkus Services	3,536	2,588	869	599	—	—	4,405	3,187
Library Journal	5,100	4,806	—	—	—	—	5,100	4,806
Los Angeles Times	2,858	2,900	125	125	—	—	2,983	3,025
New York Review of Books	400	400	—	—	—	—	400	400
New York Times Sunday Book Review[3]	2,266	2,200	234	250	—	—	2,500	2,450
Publishers Weekly[4]	4,515	4,610	585	600	—	—	5,100	5,210
School Library Journal	30	31	2,295	2,357	250	225	2,575	2,613
Washington Post Book World	1,870	1,811	121	219	—	—	1,991	2,030

[1]All figures are for a 12-month period from September 1 to August 31; 1983 figures are for September 1, 1982–August 31, 1983. Totals include reference and subscription books. In addition, Booklist publishes reviews of nonprint materials—1,297 in 1982 and 914 in 1983 (including 216 and 190 special nonprint lists, respectively)—and of special bibliographies—4,000 in 1982 and 3,362 in 1983.

[2]All figures are for a 12-month period beginning Septermber and ending July/August, 1983 figures are for September 1982–July/August 1983. Total for 1982 includes 399 nonprint materials.

[3]Adult figure includes paperbacks reviewed in "New and Noteworthy" column.

[4]Includes reviews of paperback originals and reprints.

Part 5
Reference Information

Bibliographies

The Librarian's Bookshelf

Olha della Cava

Librarian, School of Library Service,
Columbia University Libraries, New York

This bibliography is intended as a buying and reading guide for individual librarians and library collections. A few of the titles listed are core titles that any staff development collection might contain, but most are titles published since 1981 with an emphasis on continuing education. Bibliographic tools that most libraries are likely to have for day-to-day operations have been excluded from this list.

Books

General Works

The ALA Glossary of Library and Information Science, ed. by Heartsill Young. Chicago: American Library Association, 1983. $50.

ALA World Encyclopedia of Library and Information Services, ed. by Robert Wedgeworth. Chicago: American Library Association, 1980. $95.

The ALA Yearbook 1983: A Review of Library Events 1982, ed. by Robert Wedgeworth. Chicago: American Library Association, 1983. $65.

Advances in Librarianship, ed. by Michael Harris. New York: Academic Press, 1970– . Vol. 12, 1982. $32.

American Library Directory, 1983. 36th ed. New York: R. R. Bowker, 1983. $95.

Bowker Annual of Library & Book Trade Information 1984. 29th ed. New York: R. R. Bowker, 1984. $60.

Buckland, Michael K. *Library Services in Theory and Context.* New York: Pergamon Press, 1983. $23.25.

Encyclopedia of Library and Information Science. New York: Marcel Dekker, 1968–1983. Vols. 1–36. $55 per vol.

Fang, Josephine Riss, and Songe, Alice H. *International Guide to Library, Archival, and Information Science Associations.* 2nd ed. New York: R. R. Bowker, 1980. $32.50.

Ladenson, Alex. *Library Law and Legislation in the United States.* Metuchen, NJ: Scarecrow, 1982. $14.50.

Lilley, Dorothy, and Badough, Rose Marie. *Library and Information Science: A Guide to Information Sources.* Detroit: Gale, 1982. $44.

Schlachter, Gail A. *Library Science Dissertations, 1973–1981: An Annotated Bibliography.* Littleton, CO: Libraries Unlimited, 1982. $45.

The Status of Women in Librarianship, ed. by Kathleen Heim. New York: Neal-Schuman, 1983. $29.95.

Who's Who in Library and Information Services, ed. by Joel Lee. Chicago: American Library Association, 1982. $150.

Wilson, Pauline. *Stereotype and Status: Librarians in the United States.* Westport, CT: Greenwood Press, 1982. $27.50.

Advances in Library Administration and Organization, Vol. 2, ed. by Gerald B. McCabe, B. Kriessman, and W. Carl

Jackson. Greenwich, CT: JAI Press, 1983. $45.

Alley, Brian, and Cargill, Jennifer. *Keeping Track of What You Spend: The Librarian's Guide to Simple Bookkeeping.* Phoenix, AZ: Oryx Press, 1982. $25.

Bailey, Martha. *Supervisory and Middle Managers in Libraries.* Metuchen, NJ: Scarecrow, 1981. $12.

Bommer, Michael R. W., and Chorba, Ronald W. *Decision Making for Library Management.* White Plains, NY: Knowledge Industry, 1982. $34.50.

Chen, Ching-Chih. *Library Management without Bias.* Greenwich, CT: JAI Press, 1981. $37.50.

Corry, Emmett. *Grants for Libraries: A Guide to Public and Private Funding Programs and Proposal Writing Techniques.* Littleton, CO: Libraries Unlimited, 1982. $22.50.

Cowley, John. *Personnel Management in Libraries.* London: C. Bingley, 1982. $13.

Dougherty, Richard M. *Scientific Management of Library Operations,* 2nd ed. Metuchen, NJ: Scarecrow, 1982. $15.

Kohn, Rita, and Teppler, K. *You Can Do It: A PR Skills Manual for Librarians.* Metuchen, NJ: Scarecrow, 1981. $12.50.

Librarians' Affirmative Action Handbook, ed. by John F. Harvey and Elizabeth M. Dickinson. Metuchen, NJ: Scarecrow, 1983. $18.50.

Library Leadership: Visualizing the Future, ed. by Donald E. Riggs. Phoenix, AZ: Oryx Press, 1982. $27.50.

Line, Maurice B. *Library Surveys: An Introduction to the Use, Planning, Procedure and Presentation of Surveys,* 2nd ed. London: C. Bingley, 1982 (U.S. dist. by Shoe String, Hamden, CT). $17.50.

The Management Process: A Selection of Readings for Librarians, ed. by Ruth J. Person. Chicago: American Library Association, 1983. $20.

Martin, Murray S. *Issues in Personnel Management.* Greenwich, CT: JAI Press, 1981. $40.

Mathews, Anne J. *Communicate! A Librarian's Guide to Interpersonal Relations.* Chicago: American Library Association, 1983. $8.

Mitchell, Betty Jo. *ALMS, A Budget Based Library Management System.* Greenwich, CT: JAI Press, 1983. $42.50.

O'Reilly, Robert C., and O'Reilly, Marjorie I. *Librarians and Labor Relations: Employment under Union Contracts.* Westport, CT: Greenwood Press, 1981. $25.

Personnel Administration in Libraries, ed. by Sheila Creth and Frederick Duda. New York: Neal-Schuman, 1981. $24.95.

Planning for Library Services: A Guide to Utilizing Planning Methods for Library Management, ed. by Charles R. McClure. New York: Haworth Press, 1982. $29.95.

Prentice, Ann E. *Financial Planning for Libraries.* Metuchen, NJ: Scarecrow, 1983. $14.50.

Quirk, Dantia. *The Shrinking Library Dollar.* White Plains, NY: Knowledge Industry, 1982. $24.95.

Rowley, Jennifer E., and Rowley, P. J. *Operations Research: A Tool for Library Management.* Chicago: American Library Association, 1981. $10.

Sager, Donald J. *Participatory Management in Libraries.* Metuchen, NJ: Scarecrow, 1982. $14.50.

Simpson, I. S. *Basic Statistics for Librarians,* 2nd ed. London: C. Bingley, 1983. $19.50.

Smith, David. *Systems Thinking in Library and Information Management.* Hamden, CT: Shoe String, 1981. $16.

Smith, G. Stevenson. *Accounting for Librarians and Other Not-for-Profit Managers.* Chicago: American Library Association, 1983. $50.

Stevens, Norman D. *Communication throughout Libraries.* Metuchen, NJ: Scarecrow, 1982. $14.50.

Strategies for Library Administration: Concepts and Approaches, ed. by Charles R. McClure and A. R. Samuels. Littleton, CO: Libraries Unlimited. 1982. $28.50.

Stueart, Robert. Library Management. 2nd ed. Littleton, CO: Libraries Unlimited, 1981. $30.

Women and Library Management: Theories, Skills, and Values. Ann Arbor, MI: Pierian, 1982. $16.95.

Archives, Conservation, and Special Collections

Banks, Paul Noble. A Selective Bibliography on the Conservation of Research Libraries Materials. Chicago: Newberry Library, 1981. $10.

Clinton, Alan. Printed Ephemera: Collection, Organization and Access. Hamden, CT: Shoe String, 1981. $15.

Conservation in the Library: A Handbook of Use and Care of Traditional Materials, ed. by Susan Garretson Swartzburg. Westport, CT: Greenwood Press, 1983. $35.

Conserving and Preserving Library Materials, ed. by Kathryn Luther Henderson. Urbana-Champaign, IL: University of Illinois, Graduate School of Library and Information Science, 1983. $15.

Cunha, George D. Library and Archives Conservation: 1980's and Beyond, 2 vols. Metuchen, NJ: Scarecrow, 1983. Vol. 1 $16; Vol. 2 (Bibliography) $28.50.

Gracy, David B. An Introduction to Archives and Manuscripts. New York: Special Libraries Association, 1981. $7.25.

Harrison, Alice W. The Conservation of Archival and Library Materials: A Resource Guide to Audiovisual Aids. Metuchen, NJ: Scarecrow, 1982. $13.50.

Kyle, Hedi. Library Materials Preservation Manual: Practical Methods for Preserving Books, Pamphlets and Other Printed Materials. Bronxville, NY: N. T. Smith, 1983. $22.50.

Morrow, Carolyn Clark. Conservation Treatment Procedures: A Manual of Step-by-Step Procedures for the Maintenance and Repair of Library Materials. Littleton, CO: Libraries Unlimited, 1982. $18.50.

Morrow, Carolyn Clark. The Preservation Challenge: A Guide to Library Materials. White Plains, NY: Knowledge Industry, 1983. $34.50.

Roberts, Matt. Bookbinding and the Conservation of Books: A Dictionary of Descriptive Terminology. Washington, DC: Library of Congress, GPO, 1982. $27.

Society of American Archivists. Basic Manual Series, unnumbered series. $5 for members, $7 for nonmembers. (Most recent title is Sung, Carolyn Hoover. Archives and Manuscripts: Reprography. Chicago: SAA, 1982.

Young, Laura S. Bookbinding and Conservation by Hand. New York: R. R. Bowker, 1981. $35.

Audiovisual

Audio-Visual Equipment Directory 1983-84. 29th ed. Fairfax, VA: National Audio-Visual Association, 1983. $25.

Audiovisual Market Place, 1984: A Multimedia Guide, 14th ed. New York: R. R. Bowker, 1984. $45.

Cable for Information Delivery: A Guide for Librarians, Educators and Cable Professionals, ed. by Brigitte L. Kenney. White Plains, NY: Knowledge Industry, 1983. $34.50.

Educational Media Yearbook 1983, ed. by James W. Brown. Littleton, CO: Libraries Unlimited, 1983. $47.50.

Gothberg, Helen M. Television and Video in Libraries and Schools. Hamden, CT: Shoe String, 1983. $22.50.

Video Involvement for Libraries, ed. by Susan Spaeth Cherry. Chicago: American Library Association, 1981. $6.

Buildings, Furniture, Equipment

Building Renovation in ARL Libraries. Washington, DC: Association of Research Libraries, Office of Management Studies, 1983 (Spec kit 97). $15.

Cohen, Elaine. *Automation, Space Management, and Productivity: A Guide for Libraries.* New York: R. R. Bowker, 1982. $35.

Library Interior Layout and Design: Proceedings of the Seminar Held in Frederiksdal, Denmark, June 16-20, 1980, IFLA, ed. by Rolf Fuhltrott. Munich-New York: G. K. Saur, 1982 (U.S. dist. by Shoe String, Hamden, CT. $36.

Mallery, Mary S., and DeVore, Ralph E. *A Sign System for Libraries.* Chicago: American Library Association, 1982. $15.

Reynolds, Linda, and Barrett, S. *Library Signs and Guiding: A Practical Guide to Design and Production.* Hamden, CT: Shoe String, 1981. $32.50.

Children's and Young Adults' Services and Materials

Bauer, Caroline Feller. *This Way to Books.* New York: H. W. Wilson, 1983. $30.

Bernstein, Joanne E. *Books to Help Children Cope with Separation and Loss.* 2nd ed. New York: R. R. Bowker, 1983. $24.95.

Beyond Fact: Nonfiction for Children and Young People, comp. by Jo Carr. Chicago: American Library Association, 1982. $12.50.

Celebrating Children's Books: Essays on Children's Literature in Honor of Zena Sutherland, ed. by Betsy Hearne and Marilyn Kaye. New York: Lothrop, Lee & Shepard Books, 1981. $14.25.

Children and Books. 6th ed. Glenview, IL: Scott, Foresman, 1981. $24.50.

Children's Media Market Place, 1982. 2nd ed. New York: Neal-Schuman, 1982. $24.95.

Cianciolo, Patricia A. *Picture Books for Children.* 2nd ed. Chicago: American Library Association, 1981. $15.

Dreyer, Sharon. *The Bookfinder: A Guide to Children's Literature about the Needs and Problems of Youth.* Circle Pines, MN: American Guidance Service, 1977-1981. 2 vols. $73.50.

Egoff, Sheila. *Thursday's Child: Trends and Patterns in Contemporary Children's Literature.* Chicago: American Library Association, 1981. $15.

Ettlinger, John R. T. *Choosing Books for Young People: A Guide to Criticism and Bibliography, 1945-1975.* Chicago: American Library Association, 1982. $25.

Jones, Dolores Blythe. *Children's Literature Awards and Winners: A Directory of Prizes, Authors, and Illustrators.* New York: Neal-Schuman in Association with Gale, 1983 (Dist. by Gale, Detroit). $65.

Lima, Carolyn W. *A to Zoo: Subject Access to Children's Picture Books.* New York: R. R. Bowker, 1982. $29.95.

Lukens, Rebecca J. *A Critical Handbook of Children's Literature.* 2nd ed. Glenview, IL: Scott, Foresman, 1982. $9.95.

New Directions for Young Adult Services, ed. by Ellen V. LiBretto. New York: R. R. Bowker, 1983. $24.95.

Paulin, Mary Ann. *Creative Uses of Children's Literature.* Hamden, CT: Shoe String, 1982. $49.50.

Polette, Nancy. *E Is for Everybody: A Manual for Bringing Fine Picture Books into the Hands and Hearts of Children,* 2nd ed. Metuchen, NJ: Scarecrow, 1982. $12.50.

Reaching Young People through Media, ed. by Nancy Bach Pillon. Littleton, CO: Libraries Unlimited, 1983. $23.50.

Rohrlick, Paula. *Exploring the Arts: Films and Video Programs for Young Viewers.* New York: R. R. Bowker, 1982. $24.95 (pap.).

Special Collections in Children's Literature, ed. by Carolyn W. Field. Chicago: American Library Association, 1982. $18.

Vandergrift, Kay E. *Child and Story: The Literary Connection.* New York: Neal-Schuman, 1981. $17.95.

Collection Development

Acquisition of Foreign Materials for U.S. Libraries, 2nd ed., comp. and ed. by Theodore Samore. Metuchen, NJ: Scarecrow, 1982. $16.

Alternative Materials in Libraries, ed. by James P. Danky and E. Shore. Metuchen, NJ: Scarecrow, 1982. $16.

Collection Development and Acquisitions, 1970–1980: An Annotated, Critical Bibliography, comp. by Irene P. Godden, K. W. Fachan, and P. A. Smith, Metuchen, NJ: Scarecrow, 1982. $11.

Ethnic Collections in Libraries, ed. by E. J. Josey. New York: Neal-Schuman, 1983. $24.95.

Gardner, Richard K. *Library Collections: Their Origin, Selection and Development.* New York: McGraw-Hill, 1981. $24.

Hernon, Peter. *Developing Collections of U.S. Government Publications.* Greenwich, CT: JAI Press, 1982. $45.

Library Government Documents and Information Conference (First, 1981, Boston). *Collection Development and Public Access of Government Documents: Proceedings of the First Annual Library Government Documents and Information Conference,* ed. by Peter Hernon. Westport, CT: Meckler, 1982. $35.

New York Academy of Medicine. Library. *The New York Academy of Medicine Library Collection Development Policy,* prep. by Anne M. Pascarelli. New York: The Academy, 1982. $10.

Shaping Library Collections for the 1980's, ed. by Peter Spyers-Duran and Thomas

Mann, Jr. Phoenix, AZ: Oryx Press, 1981. $24.50.

Van Orden, Phyllis. *The Collection Program in Elementary and Middle Schools: Concepts, Practices, and Information Sources.* Littleton, CO: Libraries Unlimited, 1982. $18.50.

Weeding Library Collections—II, ed. by Stanley J. Slote. 2nd, rev. ed. Littleton, CO: Libraries Unlimited, 1982. $21.50.

College and University Libraries

ACRL University Library Statistics 1981–1982, comp. by Sandy Whiteley. Chicago: American Library Association, 1983. $15.

Academic Librarianship: Yesterday, Today and Tomorrow, ed. by Robert Stueart. New York: Neal-Schuman, 1982. $26.95.

Association of College and Research Libraries. National Conference (Second, 1981, Minneapolis). *Options for the 80s: Proceedings of the Second National Conference of the Association of College and Research Libraries,* 2 vols., ed. by Michael D. Kathman. Greenwich, CT: JAI Press, 1982. $125.

Association of Research Libraries. *Minutes,* Washington, DC: ARL, 1932– . 98th meeting entitled Resources for Research Libraries, 1981. $12.50.

Clark, Alice S. *Managing Curriculum Materials in the Academic Library.* Metuchen, NJ: Scarecrow, 1982. $14.

Cline, Hugh, and Sinnott, L. T. *Building Library Collections: Policies and Practices in Academic Libraries.* Toronto: Lexington Books, 1981. $18.95.

College Librarianship, ed. by William Miller and D. S. Rockwood. Metuchen, NJ: Scarecrow, 1981. $15.

Martell, Charles R. *The Client-Centered Academic Library: An Organizational Model.* Westport, CT: Greenwood Press, 1983. $29.95.

Priorities for Academic Libraries, ed. by Thomas J. Galvin and Beverly P. Lynch. San Francisco: Jossey-Bass, 1982. $7.95.

SPEC Kits. Washington, DC: Association of Research Libraries. 1973– . Nos. 1– . $7.50 for members, $15 for nonmembers. (Recent kits have been on such topics as Approval Plans, Public Service Goals and Objectives, and Personnel Classification Systems.)

Shiflett, Orvin Lee. *Origins of American Academic Librarianship.* Norwood, NJ: Ablex, 1981. $27.50.

Comparative and International Librarianship

Amadi, Adolphe A. *African Libraries: Western Tradition and Colonial Brainwashing.* Metuchen, NJ: Scarecrow, 1981. $14.

Andersen, Axel, Friis-Hansen, J. B., and Kajberg, L. *Library and Information Services in the Soviet Union.* Copenhagen: Royal School of Librarianship, 1981. n.p.

Biskup, Peter. *Australian Libraries,* 3rd ed. London: C. Bingley, 1982 (U.S. dist. by Shoe String, Hamden, CT). $23.

British Librarianship and Information Work 1976–1980. Vol. 1: *General Libraries and the Profession,* ed. by L. J. Taylor. London: The Library Association, 1983 (U.S. dist. by Oryx, Phoenix, AZ). $59.

Bunch, Allan. *Community Information Services: Their Origin, Scope and Development.* London: C. Bingley, 1982 (U.S. dist. by Shoe String, Hamden, CT). $17.50.

Burkett, Jack. *Library and Information Networks in Western Europe.* London: Aslib, 1982. £13.

Chandler, George. *International and National Library and Information Services: A Review of Recent Developments, 1970–1980.* New York: Pergamon Press, 1982. $20.

Indian Librarianship, ed. by Ravindra N. Sharma. New Delhi: Kalyani Publishers, 1982. $20.

International Book and Library Activities: The History of an Attempted U.S. Foreign Policy, ed. by Paxton P. Price. Metuchen, NJ: Scarecrow, 1982. $15.

International Handbook of Contemporary Developments in Librarianship, ed. by Miles M. Jackson. Westport, CT: Greenwood Press, 1981. $65.

Kunoff, Hugo. *The Foundations of the German Academic Library.* Chicago: American Library Association, 1982. $18.

Maack, Mary Niles. *Libraries in Senegal: Continuity and Change in an Emerging Nation.* Chicago: American Library Association, 1981. $20.

Simsova, Sylva. *A Primer of Comparative Librarianship.* Hamden, CT: Shoe String, 1982. $14.50.

Soviet-American Library Seminar (First, 1979, Washington, DC). *Proceedings of the First Soviet-American Library Seminar: May 4–6, 1979, Washington, D.C.,* ed. by Jean E. Lowrie. Chicago: American Library Association, 1983. $27.50.

Copyright

Johnston, Donald. *Copyright Handbook.* 2nd ed. New York: R. R. Bowker, 1982. $27.50.

Miller, Jerome K. *U.S. Copyright Documents: An Annotated Collection for Use by Educators and Librarians.* Littleton, CO: Libraries Unlimited, 1981. $27.50.

United States. Copyright Office. *Library Reproduction of Copyrighted Works (17 U.S.C. 108): Report of the Register of Copyrights.* Washington, DC: Library of Congress, Copyright Office, 1983. n.p.

Education for Librarianship

Coburn, Louis. *Classroom and Field: The Internship in American Library Educa-*

tion. Flushing, NY: Queens College Press, 1981. $7.50.

Cronin, Blaise. *The Education of Library-Information Professionals: A Conflict of Objectives?* London: Aslib, 1982. n.p.

Debons, Anthony et al. *The Information Professional: Survey of an Emerging Field.* New York: Marcel Dekker, 1981. $35.

Education for Information Management: Directions for the Future, cosponsored by the Information Institute, International Academy at Santa Barbara, and the Association of American Library Schools, May 6–8, 1982, ed. by Eric H. Boehm and Michael K. Buckland. Santa Barbara, CA: International Academy at Santa Barbara, 1983. $24.50.

Financial Assistance for Library Education: Academic Year 1983–84. Chicago: American Library Association, 1982. $1.

Roberts, Anne F. *Library Instruction for Librarians.* Littleton, CO: Libraries Unlimited, 1982. $26.

World Guide to Library Schools and Training Courses in Documentation. 2nd ed. Paris: Unesco, 1981 (U.S. dist. by Shoe String, Hamden, CT). $50.

Information and Society

Chen, Ching-Chih. *Information Seeking: Assessing and Anticipating User Needs.* New York: Neal-Schuman, 1982. $22.95.

An Information Agenda for the 1980s: Proceedings of a Colloquium June 17–18, 1980, ed. by Carlton Rochell. Chicago: American Library Association, 1981. $8.

Information and the Transformation of Society: Papers from the First Joint International Conference of the Institute of Information Scientists and the American Society for Information Science, held at St. Patrick's College, Dublin, Ireland, 28–30 June, 1982, ed.

by G. P. Sweeney. Amsterdam, NY: North-Holland, 1982. $51.

Information Industry Association. *Membership Directory, 1982–83.* Bethesda, MD: Information Industry Association, 1982. $21.

Information Industry Market Place, 1983. An International Directory of Information Products and Services. New York: R. R. Bowker, 1982. $42.50.

McGarry, K. J. *The Changing Context of Information: An Introductory Analysis.* Hamden, CT: Shoe String, 1982. $19.50.

Strategies for Meeting the Information Needs of Society in the Year 2000, ed. by Martha Boaz. Littleton, CO: Libraries Unlimited, 1981. $23.50.

Warnken, Kelly. *The Information Brokers: How to Start and Operate Your Own Fee-Based Service.* New York: R. R. Bowker, 1981. $24.95.

Intellectual Freedom

Censorship, Libraries and the Law, ed. by Haig A. Bosmajian. New York: Neal-Schuman, 1982. $24.95.

Censorship Litigation and the Schools: Proceedings of a Colloquium Held January 1981. Chicago: Office of Intellectual Freedom, American Library Association, 1983. $17.50.

de Grazia, Edward, and Newman, Roger K. *Banned Films: Movies, Censors and the First Amendment.* New York: R. R. Bowker, 1982. $24.95. pap. $14.95.

Freedom of Information Trends in the Information Age, ed. by Tom Riley and Harold Relyea. London: Frank Cass, 1983. £15.

Jones, Frances M. *Defusing Censorship: The Librarian's Guide to Censorship Conflict.* Phoenix, AZ: Oryx Press, 1983. $24.95.

Robotham, John S. *Freedom of Access to Library Materials.* New York: Neal-Schuman, 1983. $22.95.

Library History

Breed, Clara E. *Turning the Pages: San Diego Public Library History 1882–1982.* San Diego: Friends of the San Diego Public Library, 1983. $15.

Goodrum, Charles A., and Dalrumple, H. W. *The Library of Congress.* Boulder, CO: Westview, 1982. $30.

Hamlin, Arthur T. *The University Library in the United States: Its Origins and Development.* Philadelphia: University of Pennsylvania Press, 1981. $25.

Hyman, Richard Joseph. *Shelf Access in Libraries.* Chicago: American Library Association. 1982. $15.

Libraries in American Periodicals before 1876: A Bibliography with Abstracts and an Index, comp. and ed. by Haynes McMullen. Jefferson, NC: McFarland, 1983. $65.

McCrimmon, Barbara. *Power, Politics and Print: The Publication of the British Museum Catalogue, 1881–1900.* Hamden, CT: Shoe String, 1981. $17.50.

Miles, Wyndham D. *A History of the National Library of Medicine: The Nation's Treasury of Medical Knowledge.* Bethesda, MD: U.S. Department of Health and Human Services, National Library of Medicine, 1982 (for sale by the Supt. of Docs.), n.p.

Mount, Ellis. *Ahead of Its Time: The Engineering Societies Library 1913–1980.* Hamden, CT: Linnet Books, 1982. $22.50.

Richardson, John V. *The Spirit of Inquiry: The Graduate Library School at Chicago, 1921–1951.* Chicago: American Library Association, 1982. $35.

Library and Archival Security

Fennelly, Lawrence J. *Museum, Archive, and Library Security.* Boston: Butterworths, 1983. $55.

Gandert, Slade Richard. *Protecting Your Collection: A Handbook, Survey and Guide for the Security of Rare Books,* *Manuscripts, Archives, and Works of Art.* New York: Haworth Press, 1982. $19.95. (*Library and Archival Security,* vol. 4, nos. 1 & 2)

Jenkins, John Holmes. *Rare Books and Manuscript Thefts: A Security System for Librarians, Booksellers, and Collectors.* New York: Antiquarian Booksellers Associations of America, 1982. n.p.

Microforms and Computer Output Microforms

Folcarelli, Ralph J., Tannenbaum, A. C., and Ferragamo, R. C. *The Microform Connection: A Basic Guide for Libraries.* New York: R. R. Bowker, 1982. $35.

Meckler, Alan M. *Micropublishing: A History of Scholarly Micropublishing in America, 1938–1980.* Westport, CT: Greenwood Press, 1982. $23.95.

Microform Market Place 1982–1983, ed. by Deborah O'Hara. Westport, CT: Meckler, 1982. $29.95.

Microform Research Collections: A Guide, ed. by Suzanne Cates Dodson. Westport, CT: Meckler, 1983. $125.

Networks, Interlibrary Cooperation, and Resource Sharing

Cooperative Services: A Guide to Policies and Procedures in Library Systems, ed. by Helen A. Knievel. New York: Neal-Schuman, 1982. $24.95.

Interlibrary Loan in ARL Libraries. Washington, DC: Association of Research Libraries, Office of Management Studies, 1983 (Spec kit 92). $15.

Jones, C. Lee, *Linking Bibliographic Data Bases: A Discussion of the Battelle Technical Report.* Arlington, VA: ERIC Document Reproduction Service, 1981. ED 195 274. $3.65 + postage. MF $.91.

Morris, Leslie R. *Interlibrary Loan Policies Directory,* 2nd ed. Chicago: American Library Association, 1983. $27.50.

The Report on Library Cooperation, 1982, 4th ed., comp. and ed. by Nancy L. Wareham. Chicago: American Library Association-Association of Specialized and Cooperative Library Agencies, 1982. $25.

Periodicals and Serials

The Management of Serials Automation: Current Technology and Strategies for Future Planning, ed. by Peter Gellatly. New York: Haworth Press, 1982. $45.

Serials Automation for Acquisitions and Inventory Control, ed. by William G. Potter and A. F. Sirkin. Chicago: American Library Association. 1981. $15.

The Serials Collection: Organization and Administration, ed. by Nancy Jean Melin. Ann Arbor, MI: Pierian, 1982, $18.95.

Serials Collection Development: Choices and Strategies, ed. by Sul H. Lee. Ann Arbor, MI: Pierian, 1981. $18.95.

Serials Management in an Automated Age. Annual Serial Conference. Vol. 1. Westport, CT: Meckler, 1982. $35.

Taylor, David Carson. Managing the Serials Explosion: The Issues for Publishers and Libraries. White Plains, NY: Knowledge Industry, 1982. $34.50.

Tuttle, Marcia. Introduction to Serials Management. Greenwich, CT: JAI Press, 1982. $42.50.

Public Libraries

Fact Book of the American Public Library, comp. by Herbert Goldhor. Urbana, IL: University of Illinois, GSLIS, 1981. $3. (Occasional Papers, no. 150.)

Leerburger, Benedict A. Marketing the Library. White Plains, NY: Knowledge Industry, 1981. $24.50.

Public Librarianship: A Reader, ed. by Jane Robbins-Carter. Littleton, CO: Libraries Unlimited, 1982. $35.

Public Library Association. Output Measures for Public Libraries: A Manual of Standardized Procedures, by Douglas Zweizig and Eleanor Jo Rodger. Chicago: American Library Association. 1982. $8.

Sager, Donald J. Public Library Administrators' Planning Guide to Automation. Dublin, OH: OCLC, 1983. $12.50.

Stevens, Rolland Elwell. Reference Work in the Public Library. Littleton, CO: Libraries Unlimited, 1983. $34.

Sullivan, Peggy. Public Libraries, Smart Practices in Personnel. Littleton, CO: Libraries Unlimited, 1982. $13.50.

Van House, Nancy A. Public Library User Fees: The Use and Finance of Public Libraries. Westport, CT: Greenwood Press, 1983. $27.50.

Wheeler and Goldhor's Practical Administration of Public Libraries, completely revised by Carlton Rochell. New York: Harper & Row, 1981. $28.80.

White, Lawrence J. The Public Library in the 1980's: The Problems of Choice. Lexington, MA: Lexington Books, 1983. $22.95.

Reference Services, Online Searching, and Bibliographic Instruction

Back to Books: Bibliographic Instruction and the Theory of Information Sources, ed. by Ross Atkinson. Chicago: American Library Association-Association of College and Research Libraries, 1983. $15.

Beaubien, Ann K. et al. Learning the Library: Concepts and Methods for Effective Bibliographic Instruction. New York: R. R. Bowker, 1982. $35.

Breivik, Patricia Senn. Planning the Library Instruction Program. Chicago: American Library Association, 1982. $10.

Chen, Ching-Chih. Online Bibliographic Searching: A Learning Manual. New York: Neal-Schuman, 1981. $19.95.

Drake, Miriam A. *User Fees: A Practical Perspective.* Littleton, CO: Libraries Unlimited, 1981. $17.50.

Ethics and Reference Services, ed. by Bill Katz and Ruth A. Fraley. New York: Haworth Press, 1982. $24. (*The Reference Librarian,* no. 4.)

Freedman, Janet L. *Information Searching: A Handbook for Designing and Creating Instructional Programs,* rev. ed. Metuchen, NJ: Scarecrow, 1982. $16.

Katz, William A. *Introduction to Reference Work,* 4th ed., 2 vols. New York: McGraw-Hill, 1982. $23.50 per vol.

McClure, Charles R. *Improving the Quality of Reference Service for Government Publications.* Chicago: American Library Association, 1983. $35.

Meadow, Charles T., and Cockrane, P. A. *Basics of Online Searching.* New York: Wiley, 1981. $21.95.

Myers, Marcia J. *The Accuracy of Telephone Reference/Information Services in Academic Libraries.* Metuchen, NJ: Scarecrow, 1983. $17.50.

Online Search Strategies, ed. by Ryan E. Hoover. White Plains, NY: Knowledge Industry, 1982. $37.50.

Palmer, Roger C. *Online Reference and Information Retrieval.* Littleton, CO: Libraries Unlimited, 1983. $18.50.

Reference and Online Services Handbook: Guidelines, Policies and Procedures for Libraries, ed. by Bill Katz. New York: Neal-Schuman, 1982. $29.95.

Reference Service: A Perspective, ed. by Sul H. Lee. Ann Arbor, MI: Pierian, 1983. $18.95.

Reference Services Administration and Management, ed. by Bill Katz and Ruth A. Fraley. New York: Haworth Press, 1982. $24. (*The Reference Librarian,* no. 3.)

Reference Services and Library Education: Essays in Honor of Frances Neel Cheney, ed. by Edwin S. Gleaves. Lexington, MA: Lexington Books, 1982. $29.95.

Reference Services for Children and Young Adults, ed. by Bill Katz and Ruth A. Fraley. New York: Haworth Press, 1983. $14.95. (*The Reference Librarian,* no. 7/8.)

Rice, James, Jr. *Teaching Library Use: A Guide for Library Instruction.* Westport, CT: Greenwood Press, 1981. $25.

Sheehy, Eugene P. *Guide to Reference Books,* 9th ed. Chicago: American Library Association, 1976. $40. 1st supplement, 1980. $15.

Teaching Library Use Competence: Bridging the Gap from High School to College, ed. by Carolyn A. Kirkendall. Ann Arbor, MI: Pierian, 1982. $16.95.

Theories of Bibliographic Education: Designs for Teaching, ed. by Cerise Oberman and K. Strauch. New York: R. R. Bowker, 1982. $35.

Research

A Library and Information Science Research Agenda for the 1980's: Final Report Prepared by Cuadra Associates. Santa Monica, CA: Cuadra Associates, 1982. n.p.

Library Science Research Reader and Bibliographic Guide, ed. by Charles H. Busha. Littleton, CO: Libraries Unlimited, 1981. $23.50.

Magnotti, Shirley. *Library Science Research, 1974–1979.* Troy, NY: Whitston, 1983. $15.

Martyn, John, and Lancaster, F. Wilfrid. *Investigative Methods in Library and Information Science: An Introduction.* Arlington, VA: Information Resources, 1981. $30.50.

School Libraries/Media Centers

Baker, D. Philip, and Bender, D. R. *Library Media Programs and the Special Learner.* Hamden, CT: Shoe String, 1981. $19.50.

Carroll, Frances. *Recent Advances in School Librarianship.* New York: Pergamon, 1981. $30.

Children in Libraries: Patterns of Access to Materials and Services in School and Public Libraries. Proceedings of the Forty-First Conference of the Graduate Library School, May 16–17, 1980. Chicago: University of Chicago Press, 1981. $10.

Cleaver, Betty P. *Involving the School Library Media Specialist in Curriculum Development.* Chicago: American Library Association-American Association of School Librarians, 1983. $7.

Gillespie, John T., and Spirt, Diana L. *Administering the School Library Media Center.* New York: R. R. Bowker, 1983. $29.95.

Hicks, Warren. *Managing the Building-level School Media Program.* Chicago: American Library Association, 1981. $6. (School Media Centers: Focus on Trends and Issues. no. 7.)

The Library Media Specialist in Curriculum Development, ed. by Nevada Wallis Thomason. Metuchen, NJ: Scarecrow, 1981. $15.

Mancall, Jacqueline C. *Measuring Student Information Use: A Guide for School Library Media Specialists.* Littleton, CO: Libraries Unlimited, 1983. $19.50.

Microcomputers in the Schools, ed. by James L. Thomas. Phoenix, AZ: Oryx Press, 1981. $27.50.

Miller, Inabeth. *Microcomputers and the Media Specialist: An Annotated Bibliography.* Syracuse, NY: ERIC Clearinghouse on Information Resources, Syracuse University, 1981. $4.25.

Nonprint in the Secondary Curriculum: Readings for Reference, ed. by James L. Thomas, Littleton, CO: Libraries Unlimited, 1982. $19.50.

Petrie, Joyce. *Mainstreaming the Media Center.* Phoenix, AZ: Oryx Press, 1982. $22.50.

Silverman, Eleanor. *Trash into Treasure: Recycling Ideas for Library / Media Centers.* Metuchen, NJ: Scarecrow, 1982. $12.50.

Taylor, Mary M. *School Library and Media Center Acquisitions: Policies and Procedures.* Phoenix, AZ: Oryx Press, 1981. $29.50.

Van Orden, Phyllis J. *The Collection Program in Elementary and Middle Schools: Concepts, Practices, and Information Sources.* Littleton, CO: Libraries Unlimited, 1982. $18.50.

Walker, H. Thomas. *Teaching Library Media Skills: An Instructional Program for Elementary and Middle School Students,* 2nd ed. Littleton, CO: Libraries Unlimited, 1983. $19.50.

Services for Special Groups

Baechtold, Marguerite. *Library Service for Families.* Hamden, CT: Shoe String, 1982. $18.

Clendening, Corinne P. and Davies, Ruth Ann. *Challenging the Gifted: Curriculum Enrichment and Acceleration Models.* New York: R. R. Bowker, 1983. $32.50.

Dequin, Henry C. *Librarians Serving Disabled Children and Young People.* Littleton, CO: Libraries Unlimited, 1983. $22.50.

High/Low Handbook: Books, Materials and Services for the Teenage Problem Reader, ed. by Ellen V. LiBretto. New York: R. R. Bowker, 1981. $19.95.

Jail Library Service: A Guide for Librarians and Jail Administrators, ed. by Linda Bayley and others. Chicago: American Library Association, 1981. $17.50.

Jones, Edward V., III. *Reading Instruction for the Adult Illiterate.* Chicago: American Library Association, 1981. $15.

Library Services for the Handicapped Adult, ed. by James L. Thomas and

Carol H. Thomas. Phoenix, AZ: Oryx Press, 1982. $25.

Lucas, Linda. *The Disabled Child in the Library: Moving into the Mainstream.* Littleton, CO: Libraries Unlimited, 1983. $22.50.

The Mainstreamed Library: Issues, Ideas, Innovations, ed. by Barbara H. Baskin and Karen H. Harris. Chicago: American Library Association, 1982. $35.

Marshall, Margaret Richardson. *Libraries and the Handicapped Child.* Lexington, MA: Lexington Books, 1981. $26.50.

Needham, William L. *Improving Library Service to Physically Disabled Persons: A Self-Evaluation Checklist.* Littleton, CO: Libraries Unlimited, 1983. $18.50.

Pearlman, Della. *No Choice: Library Services for the Mentally Handicapped.* Phoenix, AZ: Oryx Press, 1981. $17.25.

Speaking Out: Personal and Professional Views on Library Service for Blind and Physically Handicapped Individuals, comp. and ed. by Leslie Eldridge. Washington, DC: National Library Service for the Blind and Physically Handicapped, Library of Congress, 1982. n.p.

Turock, Betty J. *Serving the Older Adult: A Guide to Library Programs and Information Sources.* New York: R. R. Bowker, 1983. $32.50.

Wright, Keith. *Library and Information Services for Handicapped Individuals,* 2nd ed. Littleton, CO: Libraries Unlimited, 1983. $20.

Special Libraries

Ahrensfeld, Janet L., Christianson, E. B., and King, D. E. *Special Libraries: A Guide for Management.* 2nd ed. New York: Special Libraries Association, 1981. $17.

The Basic Business Library: Core Resources, ed. by Bernard S. Schlessinger. Phoenix, AZ: Oryx Press, 1983. $32.50.

A Basic Music Library: Essential Scores and Books, 2nd ed., comp. by the Music Library Association, Committee on Basic Music Collection, ed. by Robert Michael Fling. Chicago: American Library Association. 1983. $12.

Cave, Roderick. *Rare Book Librarianship,* 2nd ed. London: C. Bingley, 1982 (U.S. dist. by Shoe String, Hamden, CT). $20.

Directory of Special Libraries and Information Centers in U.S.A. and Canada, 8th ed., Vol. 1, ed. by Brigitte Darnay. Detroit: Gale, 1983. $260.

Handbook of Medical Library Practice, ed. by Louise Darling, 4th ed. Vol. 1: *Public Services in Health Science Libraries.* Chicago: Medical Library Association, 1982. $22.50.

Handbook of Special Librarianship and Information Work, 5th ed. London: Aslib, 1982. £22.

Marke, Julius J. *Legal Research and Law Library Management.* New York: Law Journal Seminars-Press, 1982. $32.

Mount, Ellis. *Special Libraries and Information Centers: An Introductory Text.* New York: Special Libraries Association, 1983. $25.

Nichols, Harold. *Map Librarianship,* 2nd ed. London: C. Bingley, 1982. £15.

Picture Librarianship, ed. by Helen P. Harrison. Phoenix, AZ: Oryx Press, 1981. $39.50.

Report on Library Cooperation, 1982, ed. by Nancy L. Wareham, 4th ed. Chicago: Association of Specialized and Cooperative Library Agencies, 1982. $10.

State Libraries

The State Library Agencies: A Survey Project Report, 6th ed., comp. and ed. by ASCLA headquarters staff. Chicago: Association of Specialized and Cooperative Library Agencies, 1983. $25.

Technical Services

Carter, Ruth C. *Data Conversion.* White Plains, NY: Knowledge Industry, 1983. $34.50.

Technical Services: Acquisitions

Boss, Richard W. *Automating Library Acquisitions: Issues and Outlook.* White Plains, NY: Knowledge Industry, 1982. $27.50.

Kim, Ung Chon. *Policies of Publishers: A Handbook for Order Librarians,* Metuchen, NJ: Scarecrow, 1982. $15.

Technical Services: Cataloging and Classification

AACR2 Decisions and Rule Interpretations: A Consolidation of the Decisions and Rule Interpretations . . . 2nd ed., made by the Library of Congress, the National Library of Canada, the British Library and the National Library of Australia. Ottawa: Canadian Library Association, 1982 (U.S. dist. by ALA, Chicago). $50.

Anglo-American Cataloguing Rules. Second Edition: Revision of Rules. Chicago: American Library Association—Joint Steering Committee for Revisions of AACR, 1982. $2.50.

Authority Control: The Key to Tomorrow's Catalog. Proceedings of the 1979 Library and Information Technology Association Institutes, ed. by Mary W. Ghikas. Phoenix, AZ: Oryx Press, 1982. $29.95.

Berman, Sanford. *Joy of Cataloging. Essays, Letters, Reviews and Other Explosions.* Phoenix, AZ: Oryx Press, 1981. $32.50.

The Card Catalog—Current Issues, Readings and Selected Bibliography, ed. by Cynthia C. Ryans. Metuchen, NJ: Scarecrow, 1981. $16.

Cleveland, Donald B. *Introduction to Indexing and Abstracting.* Littleton, CO: Libraries Unlimited, 1983. $19.50.

Dodd, Sue A. *Cataloging Machine-Readable Data Files: An Interpretive Manual.* Chicago: American Library Association, 1982. $35.

Dowell, Arlene Taylor. *AACR 2 Headings: A Five-year Projection of Their Impact on Catalogs.* Littleton, CO: Libraries Unlimited, 1982. $22.50.

Foster, Donald L. *Managing the Catalog Department.* 2nd ed. Metuchen, NJ: Scarecrow, 1982. $15.

Gorman, Michael. *Concise AACR 2.* Chicago: American Library Association, 1981. $8.

Olson, Nancy B. *Cataloging of Audiovisual Materials: A Manual Based on AACR 2.* Mankato, MN: Minnesota Scholarly Press, 1981. $17.50.

Osborn, Jeanne. *Dewey Decimal Classification, 19th Edition: A Study Manual.* Littleton, CO: Libraries Unlimited, 1982. $27.50.

Rogers, JoAnn V. *Nonprint Cataloging for Multimedia Collections: A Guide Based on AACR 2.* Littleton, CO: Libraries Unlimited, 1982. $17.50.

Subject Access: Report of a Meeting Sponsored by the Council on Library Resources, Dublin, Ohio, June 7–9, 1982, comp. and ed. by Keith W. Russell. Washington, DC: Council on Library Resources, 1982. $10.

Tseng, Sally C. *LC Rule Interpretations of AACR 2, 1978–1982, Cumulated Edition.* Metuchen, NJ: Scarecrow, 1982. $10.

Periodicals

The journals in the list that follows might normally be purchased as part of a continuing education program in a library or as subscriptions for individual librarians. Titles used primarily for selection have been excluded.

ALA Washington Newsletter
The American Archivist
American Libraries
ASCATOPICS
Audiovisual Librarian
Behavioral and Social Sciences Librarian
CABLIS (Current Awareness Bulletin for Librarians and Information Scientists)
Cataloging and Classification Quarterly
Collection Building

Collection Management
College and Research Libraries
Community and Junior College Libraries
Conservation Administration News
Current Research in Library and Information Science
Database
Data Base Alert
Drexel Library Quarterly
IFLA Journal
The Indexer
Information and Referral
Information Processing and Management
Information Technology and Libraries
International Library Review
Journal of Academic Librarianship
Journal of Education for Librarianship
Journal of Library Administration
Journal of Library History, Philosophy, and Comparative Librarianship
LJ/SLJ Hotline
Library Acquisitions: Practice and Theory
Library and Archival Security
Library and Information Science Research Journal
Library Hi Tech

Library Journal
Library Management
Library of Congress Information Bulletin
Library Quarterly
Library Resources and Technical Services
Library Technology Reports
Library Trends
Microform Review
Newsletter on Intellectual Freedom
Online
Online Review
Public Library Quarterly
RQ
RSR (Reference Services Review)
The Reference Librarian
School Library Journal
School Media Quarterly
Science and Technology Libraries
Serials Librarian
Serials Review
Special Libraries
Top of the News
UNESCO Journal of Information Science, Librarianship and Archives Administration
Wilson Library Bulletin

High Technology Bibliography

Katharine Phenix
Westminster Public Library
Westminster, CO 80030

Claudia Perry-Holmes
University Library, University of Rhode Island
Kingston, RI 02881

Regular reading of the periodical literature is an absolute necessity for the librarian attempting to stay current in a field changing as rapidly as library automation. However, the phrase "library automation" is becoming so nearly inseparable from the concept of librarianship that it becomes impossible for one individual to remain continually well read in all areas of professional interest. At the same time, one about to embark on a new automation project, the library school student, or the computer novice seeking introduction to recent developments in information technologies needs the background, detailed examples, and summaries more often found in books than in periodical articles.

As the original data base managers, librarians are expected to embrace the new technologies, not only for themselves, but also to develop expertise to guide their clientele. The library professional's responsibility in this area is twofold. First, to investigate information technologies that expand the capabilities of libraries and information centers to control, coordinate, and make available their resources. This includes communication with other professionals to exchange knowledge gained from using new methods of library administration and service (automated serials check-in, online catalogs, software collection, and so on). Second, information professionals who have developed personal expertise in the computer sciences are expected to use their expertise to evaluate, acquire, catalog, and disseminate high technology materials for library users. Hence, the dual focus of this bibliography.

This selected annotated bibliography covers aspects of automation and technology of practical value to librarians and library students. Citations represent the best of what is available to date. Representative titles were selected for review in an attempt to establish some structure over the countless computer books published in the last few years.

"High Technology for Libraries," prepared by Claudia Perry-Holmes, covers new techniques for automating library processes and for providing better information services. Included are case studies, bibliographies, how-to's, and user guides for almost every aspect of information processing, as well as a number of new periodicals devoted to this area.

"High Technology for Library Users," prepared by Katharine Phenix, is representative of the myriad materials librarians have been reviewing and selecting for their collections to satisfy users' needs. Most of the publications are microcomputer-, as opposed to mainframe- or minicomputer-, oriented. (The large computers are still the province of computer scientists.) None of the titles is machine-specific, that is, appropriate only for a particular type of microcomputer.

As the first such compilation in the *Bowker Annual*, this bibliography includes books and periodicals published since 1980, and of necessity excludes many useful titles due to space considerations. However, subsequent annual updates will provide a more comprehensive view of the previous year's publications. Books from both traditional library publishers and related fields are included, the former grouped by general subject area. Periodicals are listed separately. Annotations are descriptive rather than annotative.

High Technology for Libraries

Overview or General

Boss, Richard. *Automating Library Acquisitions.* White Plains, N.Y.: Knowledge Industry Publications, 1982. 135 pp. bibliog. index. appendix. (Professional Librarian Series). $27.50 pap. LC 82-8941. ISBN 0-86729-006-4. A broad survey of the issues in acquisitions automation, geared to those considering such a step. Reviews the acquisitions process, describes the "ideal" system, and presents different types of acquisitions systems available. Includes evaluations of specific packages, a discussion of planning and implementation, and a look at future concerns.

Carter, Ruth C., and Scott Bruntjen. *Data Conversion.* White Plains, N.Y.: Knowledge Industry Publications, 1983. 169 pp. bibliog. index. appendix. (Professional Librarian Series). $34.50; pap. $27.50. LC 83-84. ISBN 0-86729-047-1; pap. 0-86729-046-3. A practical guide to planning and conducting a data conversion project. Compares various conversion methods and discusses the purposes of conversion, pitfalls, and project analysis and design. Special consideration is given to the conversion of serial records, reclassification in conjunction with conversion, and treatment of pre-AACR2 records.

Fosdick, Howard. *Computer Basics for Librarians and Information Specialists.* Arlington, Va.: Information Resources Press, 1981. 203 pp. bibliog. index. $19.95. LC 81-80539. ISBN 0-87815-034-X. An introduction to such essentials as storage considerations and media, operating systems, programming languages, documentation, data base systems, systems support software, memory management, and, somewhat briefly, mini- and microcomputer systems. The emphasis is on mainframe computers and software rather than commonly used library systems.

Hagler, Ronald, and Peter Simmons. *The Bibliographic Record and Information Technology.* Chicago: American Library Association, 1982. 346 pp. index. appendix. $25. LC 82-14706. ISBN 0-8389-0370-3. A well-organized text aimed at all librarians. Provides an overview of the purposes and methods of bibliography as a foundation for the understanding of the automated handling of bibliographic records. Discusses the content and format of the bibliographic record, access points, and the creation and sharing of bibliographic data.

Information Technology: Critical Choices for Library Decision-Makers. Edited by Allen Kent and Thomas J. Galvin. New York: Dekker, 1982. 477 pp. index. appendix. (Books in Library and Information Science, No. 40). $57.50. LC 82-14886. ISBN 0-8247-1737-6. A volume of conference proceedings from the University of Pittsburgh treating the impact of technology on libraries, local choice and local commitment, network-level decisions, human factors and human consequences, and competition and the private sector. A lengthy appendix presents a state-of-the-art summary of information technology of interest to librarians.

Online Terminal/Microcomputer Guide and Directory, 82–83. 3rd ed. Weston, Conn.: Online, 1982. 286 pp. $40 spiral. Annual supplements $15 each. ISSN 0198-697X. A substantial guide to online terminals, which has been expanded to include microcomputers in this edition. Features articles on computer selection, an annotated bibliography and glossary, as well as an extensive listing of specifications for print and video terminals, modems, and microcomputers, and a directory of brokers and manufacturers. Updated by two annual supplements, published in November 1982 and 1983.

Saffady, William. *Introduction to Automation for Librarians.* Chicago: American Library Association, 1983. 304 pp. bibliog. illus. index. $35. LC 83-7164. ISBN 0-8389-0386-X. Designed as a tutorial survey of technology and its applications to libraries. Discusses computer fundamentals—hardware, software, data processing concepts, and automated office systems—as well as automated library operations in circulation, cataloging, reference, acquisitions, and serials control.

Serials Automation for Acquisition and Inventory Control. Edited by William Gray Potter and Arlene Farber Sirkin. Chicago: American Library Association, 1981. 181 pp. bibliog. index. appendix. $12.50 pap. LC 81-10798. ISBN 0-8389-3267-3. Proceedings of the ALA Library and Information Technology Association (LITA) conference held September 4–5, 1980, in Milwaukee. Six essays treat the evolution of automated serials control, serials check-in at the University of California, Los Angeles, inventory and holdings features, serials control by agents, serials and the online catalog, and the future of serials control. Discussions and an appendix describe additional serials control systems.

Government Publications

New Technology and Documents Librarianship. Proceedings of the Third Annual Library Government Documents Information Conference. Edited by Peter Hernon. Westport, Conn.: Meckler, 1983. 107 pp. bibliog. $35. LC 83-896. ISBN 0-930466-64-0. A good summary of automation as it relates to the management of government publications, which challenges documents librarians to greater involvement in new technologies. Topics include improved access through better bibliographic control, strategies to follow in utilization, applications, and technologies available.

Library Systems and Planning for Automation

Corbin, John. *Developing Computer-Based Library Systems.* Phoenix, Ariz.: Oryx, 1981, 226 pp. bibliog. index. appendix. (A Neal-Schuman Professional Book). $30. LC 81-1232. ISBN 0-912700-10-6. A detailed look at the step-by-step procedures involved in planning and implementing an automated library system. Provides an overview of the systems approach and discusses project planning and management, new system requirements, system evaluation and comparison, design specifications, requests for proposals, and implementation.

Matthews, Joseph R. *Choosing an Automated Library System: A Planning Guide.* Chicago: American Library Association, 1980. 119 pp. bibliog. index. $12.50 pap. LC 80-17882. ISBN 0-8389-0310-X. A general guide to the selection and implementation of automated systems, geared to small and medium-sized libraries. Discusses initial considerations, needs assessment, systems alternatives (manual, batch processing, and online automation), selection, contracts, installation, and implementation.

Sager, Donald J. *Public Library Administrator's Planning Guide to Automation.* Dublin, Ohio: OCLC, 1983. 144 pp. bibliog. index. (OCLC Library, Information and Computer Science Series No. 2). $12.50 pap. ISBN 0-933418-43-4. A useful introduction to automation planning, which summarizes factors to be considered in the decision-making process. Includes good discussion of cost determinations for manual vs. automated operations.

Microcomputers

Microcomputers for Libraries: How Useful Are They? Edited by Jane Beaumont and Donald Krueger. Ottawa: Canadian Library Association, 1983. 124 pp. bibliog. appendix. $12 pap. spiral. ISBN 0-088802-170-4. A practical, detailed guide to microcomputer applications in libraries, based on a 1982 CLA conference workshop. Articles include discussions of communications software, management uses of microcomputers, applications software and its selection, electronic messaging systems, data base management systems, and the use of micros in research.

Microcomputers in Libraries. Edited by Ching-Chih Chen and Stacey E. B. Bressler. New York: Neal-Schuman, 1982. 259 pp. bibliog. illus. index. (Applications in Information

Management and Technology Series). $22.95 pap. LC 82-6493. ISBN 0-918212-61-8. A useful introduction geared to the computer novice, based on presentations made at the Institute on Microcomputers sponsored by Simmons College in November 1981 and March 1982. Discusses microcomputer hardware and software, applications in various types of libraries, staff development, and planning.

Woods, Lawrence A., and Nolan F. Pope. *Librarian's Guide to Microcomputer Technology and Applications.* White Plains, N.Y.: Published for American Society for Information Science by Knowledge Industry Publications, 1983. 209 pp. bibliog. index. appendix. $36.50; pap. $27.50. LC 83-13548. ISBN 0-87629-045-5; pap. 0-87629-044-7. A comprehensive look at microcomputer applications in public services, technical services, and library management. Discusses software and hardware technology, and design and selection issues and describes library microcomputer applications in actual use. Numerous helpful appendices. Valuable for present and potential microcomputer users at all levels.

Online Public Access Catalogs

Hildreth, Charles R. *Online Public Access Catalogs: The User Interface.* Dublin, Ohio: OCLC, 1982, 263 pp. bibliog. index. appendix. (OCLC Library, Information and Computer Science Series). $18 pap. LC 82-8224. ISBN 0-933418-34-5. A detailed study of ten quite different online catalog systems, including OCLC, RLIN, three large university libraries, four small academic libraries, and one public library system. The systems are compared for command languages, searching capabilities, online access, output, and user assistance. Other chapters review the literature on the user-system interface and human communication with computers. A technical report geared to the systems analyst rather than the general reader.

Matthews, Joseph R. *Public Access to Online Catalogs: A Planning Guide for Managers.* Weston, Conn.: Online, 1982. 345 pp. bibliog. illus. index. appendix. $28.50 pap. LC 82-18777. ISBN 0-910965-00-5. A basic handbook in two parts, presenting a discussion of the planning and implementation of an online catalog, as well as profiles of various systems currently available. Examines types of catalogs, design choices, components, searching the catalog, effects on staff, users, and services, and the future of the online catalog.

Public Access to Library Automation. Edited by J. L. Divilbliss. Urbana: Graduate School of Library and Information Science, University of Illinois, 1981. 128 pp. illus. index. (Clinic on Library Applications of Data Processing: 1980). $10. LC 81-11685. ISBN 87845-065-3. A collection of papers treating both the practical and philosophical aspects of public access. Articles deal with design considerations and principles, online catalog use determined through queuing analysis, access by the handicapped, and user resistance to technology. Several operational systems are described.

Using Online Catalogs: A Nationwide Survey. Edited by Joseph R. Matthews, Gary S. Lawrence, and Douglas K. Ferguson. New York: Neal-Schuman, 1983. 255 pp. $24.95 pap. LC 83-8061. ISBN 0-918212-76-6. Presents the findings of a survey of users and nonusers of online catalogs in 31 U.S. libraries. Describes the study, the participating libraries and their systems, then analyzes the survey results, with particular emphasis on human-computer interactions. Patrons were found to exhibit a definite preference for an online catalog over a traditional catalog. Implications of the study for library managers, reference staffs, systems designers, and the library profession are discussed.

Online Searching

Chen, Ching-Chih, and Susanna Schweizer. *Online Bibliographic Searching: A Learning Manual.* New York: Neal-Schuman, 1981. 227 pp. bibliog. illus. index. appendix. (Applications in Information Management and Technology Series). $22.95 pap. LC 81-83497. ISBN 0-918212-59-6. A good introduction to the concepts and fundamentals of retrieving online bibliographic information, "designed to serve as a self-instruction manual." Specific search examples are provided for DIALOG, but the three major U.S. systems—BRS, DIALOG, and SDC—are also compared for various features. Management issues are examined briefly, and answers are provided in the *Dialog Lab Workbook*, third edition.

Hartner, Elizabeth P. *An Introduction to Automated Literature Searching.* New York: Dekker, 1981. 145 pp. bibliog. index. appendix. (Books in Library and Information Science, Vol. 36). $23.50 pap. LC 81-7831. ISBN 0-8247-1293-5. A precisely defined guide to automated retrieval of information in the sciences and technology. Without discussing specific systems, Hartner clearly examines the process of finding information, files available for mechanized retrieval, search strategies, the presentation and evaluation of search results, as well as briefly introducing how computerized retrieval works.

Meadow, Charles T., and Pauline Atherton Cochrane. *Basics of Online Searching.* New York: Wiley, 1981. 245 pp. illus. index. appendix. (Information Science Series; A Wiley Interscience Publication). $21.95. LC 80-23050. ISBN 0-471-05283-3. A basic text geared for use in conjunction with search service user manuals. Presents the principles rather than the mechanics of online searching, with examples from DIALOG, BRS, and ORBIT (SDC). Introduces vocabulary, elements of interactive searching and search languages, and discusses the presearch interview, data bases, basic commands, text searching, beginning and ending a search, storing searches, and strategy.

Online Search Strategies. Edited by Ryan E. Hoover. White Plains, N.Y.: Knowledge Industry Publications, 1982. 345 pp. bibliog. index. appendix. (Professional Librarian Series). $37.50; pap. $29.50. LC 82-17179. ISBN 0-86729-005-6; pap. 0-86729-004-8. A practical guide to improving search skills, geared to the searcher with some online experience in one of the four major U.S. services: BRS, SDC, DIALOG, and NLM. Subject areas range from U.S. government information and the social and behavioral sciences to chemical and health science information. Illustrative searches are included.

Periodicals

ACCESS: Microcomputers in Libraries. Quarterly. Edited by Deborah Christian, Box 764, Oakridge, Oreg. 97463. DAC Publications. July 1981– . $11/yr. ISSN 0277-0784. A useful journal devoted to microcomputers and their applications in libraries. Features articles on such topics as justifying the purchase of a microcomputer, printers, word processing roles in information management, present and future applications of micros, memory needs, and minicomputer systems adaptable for micros. Also publishes reviews, news items, a calendar of events, and actual computer programs.

Library Hi Tech. Quarterly. Edited by Nancy Jean Melin. Pierian Press, Box 1808, Ann Arbor, Mich. 48106. Summer 1983– . Institutions, $39.50; Individuals $19.50. ISSN 0737-8831. A journal featuring articles, interviews, and annotated bibliographies treating "all available and forthcoming technologies applicable to libraries and information centers." Articles range from discussions of electronic mail and automated circulation systems to cordless telephones at the reference desk and robotics. Includes book reviews, conference reports, a calendar of events, and indexes to reviews of software and data bases.

Small Computers in Libraries. Monthly. Edited by Allen Pratt. Published by the Graduate Library School, University of Arizona, Tucson, Ariz. 85721. April 1981– . $20/yr. ISSN 0275-6722. A newsletter presenting brief practical articles, software and book reviews, announcements, and letters. Especially helpful as an information clearinghouse on library projects and applications for microcomputers.

High Technology for Library Users

Personal Computing

Most of the currently popular publications fall into this category. A number of them are buying guides, some contain hardware specifications, and a few focus on how to live with a personal computer, or basic maintenance and care, or the social implications of home computers. All are written in a simple, conversational style that attempts to dispel general misconceptions and commonly held fears about computer technology. Most of them feature pictures and cartoons.

McWilliams, Peter A. *The Personal Computer Book,* Los Angeles: Prelude Press, 1982. 335 pp. pap. $9.95. ISBN 0-345-31106-X.

Although soon to be out-of-date, as prices, availability, and software for the personal computer change daily, McWilliams' book stands as the original demystifier of microcomputers, their use, abuse, and place in the home. It is a guide, "sincere but not serious," that the uninitiated can depend on to answer most of their questions.

Business Applications

Numerous books that target special business applications have begun to appear on the market. Law is a particular favorite. Word processing titles fall into this category, as do buying guides for small and medium-sized businesses. Publications on microcomputer data base management systems are also aimed at the business community.

McWilliams, Peter A. *The Personal Computer in Business Book.* Los Angeles: Prelude Press, 1983. 287 pp. pap. $9.95. ISBN 0-345-31294-5. McWilliams' strength is his ability to simplify potentially confusing concepts. He deals with computer networking, online data bases, software, and potential business applications with a deceptively easy reading style.

Programming

Career opportunities in computer technology have generated more than a passing interest in programming skills. Publications on higher level languages such as PL/I and PASCAL, or big business languages like COBOL and FORTRAN, are still generally at the textbook level. Microcomputers, on the other hand, usually accept some dialect of BASIC, and mass market publishers are aiming at the personal computer user with a number of E-Z BASIC books.

Zaks, Rodney. *Your First BASIC Program.* Berkeley, Calif.: Sybex Computer Books, 1983. 187 pp. $9.95 pap. LC 83-60488. ISBN 0-89588-092-X. This title does it best, combining pink dragons with flowcharts and algorithms that guarantee BASIC programming ability to those who persevere. Zaks is well known in computer education and writes with the confident style of one who knows the material well enough to describe it in simple terms.

Software Catalogs

As book publishers move into software production, users, computer dealers, and librarians need centralized control over software availability. Software catalogs offer the same service as *Books in Print* does for the publishing world.

The Software Catalog: Microcomputers and *The Software Catalog: Minicomputers.* 2 vols. New York: Elsevier, 1983– . $69 and $95. ISBN 0-686-45987-3; 0-686-45988-1. The printed counterpart of the International Software Database (Imprint Software, Fort Collins, Colo.), *The Software Catalog* bridges the information gap for mini- and microcomputer software. It is published four times a year as two catalogs and two updates.

History

The introduction of computing technology into personal and social consciousness gives rise to a new genre of social, historical, and economic commentary. For those who are more interested in the form of computers in society, several publications offer this approach.

Ledgard, Henry F., E. Patrick McQuaid, and Andrew Sinter. *From Baker Street to Binary: An Introduction to Computers and Computer Programming with Sherlock Holmes.* New York: McGraw-Hill, 1983. $10.95 pap. ISBN 0-07-036983-6. Authors use whimsical settings to describe some early computer principles and concepts. A most popular introduction to computer literacy.

Rochester, Jack B., and John Gantz. *The Naked Computer: A Layperson's Almanac of Computer Lore, Wizardry, Personalities, Memorabilia, World Records, Mindblowers and Tomfoolery.* New York: Morrow, 1983. 335 pp. $15.95. LC 83-61793. ISBN 0-688-02450-5. Provides more than just cocktail conversation. In this book, one can pick up the inside story of the development of Intel's 4004 microprocessor chip and later the 8080, which represents the birth of the microcomputer industry. The author also credits the public library in Nashua, New Hampshire, with the first public access coin-operated Apple computer.

Children and Computers

Children and young adults in school today, the first real inheritors of high technology, make up a large portion of the microcomputer user population. At long last, school and children's librarians are welcoming computer books aimed at this population. Parents' guides, teachers' handbooks, and educational software descriptions are all included in this category.

Burke, Anna Mae Walsh. *Microcomputers Can Be Kidstuff.* New York: Hayden, 1983. 192 pp. $8.95 pap. ISBN 0-8104-5202-2. Designed for children aged 11 to 16, this book covers the same concepts as adult introductory books: Programming, hardware and software descriptions, approaches to problem analysis, and a glossary are all presented in an easily understandable style.

Goldberg, Kenneth P., and Robert D. Sherwood. *Microcomputers: A Parent's Guide.* New York: Wiley, 1983. 196 pp. $8.95 pap. LC 83-1129. ISBN 0-471-87278-4. Most important here are the central chapters on the microcomputer at home and in the schools. Both educational and recreational uses are described. Also supplies questions and answers for parents who want to understand and encourage the use of microcomputers in primary and secondary schools.

Basic Publications for the Publisher and the Book Trade

Nancy Tremmel Dvorin

Librarian, R. R. Bowker Company

Bibliographies of Books about Books and the Book Trade

These six books contain extensive bibliographies.

Gottlieb, Robin. *Publishing Children's Books in America, 1919–1976: An Annotated Bibliography.* New York: Children's Book Council, 1978. $15.

Lee, Marshall. *Bookmaking: The Illustrated Guide to Design/Production/Editing.* New York: R. R. Bowker, 1980. $32.50. Bibliography is divided into four parts: Part 1 covers books and includes a general bibliography as well as extensive coverage of books on all technical aspects of bookmaking; Part 2 lists periodicals; Part 3 lists films, filmstrips, etc.; Part 4 lists other sources.

Lehmann-Haupt, Hellmut, Wroth, Lawrence C., and Silver, Rollo. *The Book in America.* 2nd ed. New York: R. R.

Bowker, 1951, o.p. Bibliography covers cultural history, bibliography, printing and bookmaking, book illustration, bookselling, and publishing.

Melcher, Daniel, and Larrick, Nancy. *Printing and Promotion Handbook.* 3rd ed. New York: McGraw-Hill, 1966. $38.50. Bibliography covers general reference, advertising, artwork, book publishing, color, copyright, copywriting, direct mail, displays, editing and proofreading, layout and design, lettering, magazine publishing, newspaper publishing, packaging, paper, photography, printing, publicity, radio and TV, shipping, typography, and visual aids.

The Reader's Adviser: A Layman's Guide to Literature. 12th ed. 3 vols. New York: R. R. Bowker, 1974–1977. $120. (3-vol. set); $45. (ea. vol.). Vol. 1. *The Best in American and British Fiction, Poetry, Essays, Literary Biography, Bibliogra-*

phy, and Reference, edited by Sarah L. Prakken. 1974. Chapters "Books about Books" and "Bibliography" cover history of publishing and bookselling, practice of publishing, bookmaking, rare book collecting, trade and specialized bibliographies, book selection tools, best books, etc. Vol. 2. *The Best in American and British Drama and World Literature in English Translation,* edited by F. J. Sypher. 1977. Vol. 3. *The Best in the Reference Literature of the World,* edited by Jack A. Clarke. 1977.

Tanselle, G. Thomas. *Guide to the Study of United States Imprints.* 2 vols. Cambridge, Mass.: Belknap Press of Harvard University Press, 1971. $70. Includes sections on general studies of American printing and publishing as well as studies of individual printers and publishers.

Trade Bibliographies

American Book Publishing Record Cumulative, 1876–1949: An American National Bibliography. 15 vols. New York: R. R. Bowker, 1980. $1,975.

American Book Publishing Record Cumulative, 1950–1977: An American National Bibliography. 15 vols. New York: R. R. Bowker, 1979. $1,975.

American Book Publishing Record Five-Year Cumulatives. New York: R. R. Bowker, 1960–1964 Cumulative. 5 vols. $150. 1965–1969 Cumulative. 5 vols. $150. 1970–1974 Cumulative. 4 vols. $150. 1975–1979 Cumulative. 5 vols. $175. Annual vols.: 1978, $59; 1979, $59; 1980, $59; 1981, $68; 1982, $76.50; 1983, $81.

Books in Print. 6 vols. New York: R. R. Bowker, ann. $169.

Books in Print Supplement. New York: R. R. Bowker, ann. $75.50.

Books in Series 1876–1949. 3 vols. New York: R. R. Bowker, 1982. $150.

Books in Series in the United States. 3rd ed. New York: R. R. Bowker, 1980. $175.

British Books in Print: The Reference Catalog of Current Literature. New York: R. R. Bowker, 1983. $160 (plus duty where applicable).

Canadian Books in Print, edited by Marian Butler. Toronto: University of Toronto Press, ann. $50.

Canadian Books in Print: Subject Index, edited by Marian Butler. Toronto: University of Toronto Press, ann. $50.

Cumulative Book Index. New York: H. W. Wilson. Monthly with bound semiannual and larger cumulations. Service basis.

El-Hi Textbooks in Print. New York: R. R. Bowker, ann. $49.50.

Forthcoming Books. New York: R. R. Bowker, $67.50 a year. $18 single copy. Bimonthly supplement to *Books in Print.*

International Books in Print. 3rd ed. 2 vols. Munich: K. G. Saur, 1983. Dist. by R. R. Bowker. $175.

Large Type Books in Print. New York: R. R. Bowker, 1982. $49.50.

Paperbound Books in Print. New York: R. R. Bowker. 3 vols. $69.50.

Publishers' Trade List Annual. New York: R. R. Bowker, ann. 5 vols. $95.

Robert, Reginald, and Burgess, M. R. *Cumulative Paperback Index, 1939–59.* Detroit: Gale, 1973. $48.

Small Press Record of Books in Print, edited by Len Fulton. Paradise, Calif.: Dustbooks, 1983. $25.95.

Subject Guide to Books in Print. 4 vols. New York: R. R. Bowker, ann. $110.

Subject Guide to Forthcoming Books. New York: R. R. Bowker. $45 a year. $95 in combination with *Forthcoming Books.*

Subject Guide to International Books in Print. 1st ed. 2 vols. Munich: K. G. Saur, 1983. Dist. by R. R. Bowker. $175.

Book Publishing

Education and Practice

Association of American University Presses. *One Book—Five Ways: The Publishing Procedures of Five University Presses.* Los Altos, Calif.: William Kaufmann, 1978. $19.95. pap. $11.95.

Bailey, Herbert S., Jr. *The Art and Science of Book Publishing.* Austin: University of Texas Press, 1980. pap. $7.95.

Bodian, Nat G. *Book Marketing Handbook: Tips and Techniques for the Sale and Promotion of Scientific, Technical, Professional, and Scholarly Books and Journals.* New York: R. R. Bowker, 1980. $45.

———. *Book Marketing Handbook, Volume Two: 1,000 More Tips and Techniques for the Sale and Promotion of Scientific, Technical, Professional, and Scholarly Books and Journals.* New York: R. R. Bowker, 1983. $60.

Brownstone, David M. *The Dictionary of Publishing.* New York: Van Nostrand Reinhold, 1982. $18.95.

Carter, Robert A. *Trade Book Marketing: A Practical Guide.* New York: R. R. Bowker, 1983. $29.95. pap. $19.95.

Crutchley, Brooke. *To Be a Printer.* New York: Cambridge University Press, 1980. $22.50.

Dessauer, John P. *Book Publishing: What It Is, What It Does.* New York: R. R. Bowker, 1981. $23.95. pap. $13.95.

Glaister, Geoffrey. *Glaister's Glossary of the Book: Terms Used in Paper-Making, Printing, Bookbinding, and Publishing.* 2nd ed., completely rev. Berkeley: University of California Press, 1979. $75.

Grannis, Chandler B. *Getting into Book Publishing.* New York: R. R. Bowker, 1983. Pamphlet, one free; in bulk 75¢ each.

——— ed. *What Happens in Book Publishing.* 2nd ed. New York: Columbia University Press, 1967. $30.

Greenfeld, Howard, *Books: From Writer to Reader.* New York: Crown, 1976. $8.95. pap. $4.95.

Hackett, Alice Payne, and Burke, James Henry. *Eighty Years of Best Sellers, 1895–1975.* New York: R. R. Bowker, 1977. $18.95.

Peters, Jean, ed. *Bookman's Glossary.* 6th ed. New York: R. R. Bowker, 1983. $21.95.

Analysis, Statistics, Surveys

ANSI Standards Committee Z-39. *American National Standard for Compiling Book Publishing Statistics, Z-39.8.* New York: American National Standards Institute, 1978. $4.

Altbach, Philip G., and Rathgeber, Eva-Marie. *Publishing in the Third World: Trend Report and Bibliography.* New York: Praeger, 1980. $27.95.

Arthur Andersen & Co. *Book Distribution in the U.S.: Issues and Perceptions.* New York: Book Industry Study Group, 1982. $60.

Association of American Publishers 1982 Industry Statistics. New York: Association of American Publishers, 1983. Nonmemb. $250.

Association of American Publishers. *1982 Survey of Compensation and Personnel Practices in the Publishing Industry.* Prepared and Conducted by Sibson & Company, Inc. New York: Association of American Publishers, 1982. Participant $45. Non-part. $90.

Benjamin, Curtis G. *A Candid Critique of Book Publishing.* New York: R. R. Bowker, 1977. o.p.

Book Industry Study Group, Inc. *Special Reports.* New York: Book Industry Study Group. Vol. 1, No. 1. Lambert, Douglas M. *Physical Distribution: A Profit Opportunity for Printers, Publishers, and Their Customers.* August, 1982. $25. Vol. 1, No. 2. Noble, J. Kendrick. *Trends in Textbook Markets.* 1983. $50. Dist. to nonmembers by R. R. Bowker.

Bowker Annual of Library and Book Trade Information. New York: R. R. Bowker, ann. $55.

Bowker Lectures on Book Publishing. New York: R. R. Bowker, 1957, o.p.

Bowker Lectures on Book Publishing, New Series. New York: R. R. Bowker. 10 vols. 1973–1982. $3 each. No. 1. Pilpel, Harriet F. *Obscenity and the Constitution.* 1973. No. 2. Ringer, Barbara A. *The Demonology of Copyright.* 1974. No. 3. Henne, Frances E. *The Library World and the Publishing of Children's Books.* 1975. No. 4. Vaughan, Samuel S. *Medium Rare: A Look at the Book and Its People.* 1976. No. 5. Bailey, Herbert S. *The Traditional Book in the Electronic Age.* 1977. No. 6. Mayer, Peter. *The Spirit of the Enterprise.* 1978. No. 7. De Gennaro, Richard. *Research Libraries Enter the Information Age.* 1979. No. 8. Dystel, Oscar. *Mass Market Publishing: More Observations, Speculations and Provocations.* 1980. No. 9. Giroux, Robert. *The Education of an Editor.* 1981. No. 10. Martin, Lowell. *The Public Library: Middle Age Crisis or Old Age?* 1982.

The Business of Publishing: A PW Anthology. New York: R. R. Bowker, 1976. $18.50.

Cheney, O. H. *Economic Survey of the Book Industry, 1930–31.* The Cheney Report. Reprinted. New York: R. R. Bowker, 1960. o.p.

Compaine, Benjamin. *The Book Industry in Transition: An Economic Analysis of Book Distribution and Marketing.* White Plains, N.Y.: Knowledge Industry Publications, 1978. $29.95.

———. ed. *Who Owns the Media?* 2nd ed. White Plains, N.Y.: Knowledge Industry Publications, 1982. $45.

Coser, Lewis A., Kadushin, Charles, and Powell, Walter W. *Books: The Culture and Commerce of Publishing.* New York: Basic Books, 1982. $19.

Dessauer, John P. *Book Industry Trends 1983.* New York: Book Industry Study Group, 1983. Dist. by R. R. Bowker. $150. *Book Industry Trends 1982* also available from R. R. Bowker.

———. *Trends Update* (monthly). Expands upon statistics in the annual compilation and explains forecasting techniques. $240 a year. $25 single copy. Both publications distributed to nonmembers by R. R. Bowker.

Gedin, Per. *Literature in the Marketplace.* Trans. by George Bisset. Woodstock, N.Y.: Overlook, 1977. $12.95.

Graubard, Steven R., ed. *Reading in the 1980's.* New York: R. R. Bowker, 1983. $14.95.

Machlup, Fritz, and Leeson, Kenneth W. *Information through the Printed Word: The Dissemination of Scholarly, Scientific, and Intellectual Knowledge.* 4 vols. Vol. 1. *Book Publishing.* Vol. 2. *Journals.* Vol. 3. *Libraries.* Vol. 4. *Books, Journals, and Bibliographic Services.* New York: Praeger, 1978. Vol. 1, $31.95; Vol. 2, $33.95; Vol. 3, $29.95; Vol. 4, $32.95.

Shatzkin, Leonard. *In Cold Type: Overcoming the Book Crisis.* Boston: Houghton Mifflin, 1982. $17.95.

Smith, Roger H., ed. *The American Reading Public: A Symposium.* New York: R. R. Bowker, 1964. o.p.

Whiteside, Thomas. *The Blockbuster Complex.* Middletown, Conn.: Wesleyan University Press. Dist. by Columbia University Press, 1981. $16.95.

Yankelovich, Skelly, and White, Inc. *The 1978 Consumer Research Study on Reading and Book Purchasing.* New York: Book Industry Study Group, 1978. Apply for price scale.

History

Bonn, Thomas L. *Under Cover: An Illustrated History of American Mass-Market Paperbacks.* New York: Penguin Books, 1982. $12.95.

Briggs, Asa, ed. *Essays in the History of Publishing: In Celebration of the 250th*

Anniversary of the House of Longman, 1724-1974. New York: Longman, 1974. $15.

Carpenter, Kenneth E., ed. *Books and Society in History: Papers of the ACRL Rare Books and Manuscripts Preconference June 1980, Boston, Mass.* New York: R. R. Bowker, 1983. $29.95.

Cave, Roderick. *The Private Press.* New York: R. R. Bowker, 1983. $59.95.

Cerf, Bennett. *At Random: The Reminiscences of Bennett Cerf.* New York: Random House, 1977. $12.95.

Crider, Allen Billy. *Mass Market Publishing in America.* Boston: G. K. Hall, 1982. $35.

Haydn, Hiram. *Words & Faces.* New York: Harcourt Brace Jovanovich, 1974. $8.95.

Hodges, Sheila. *Gollancz: The Story of a Publishing House.* London: Gollancz, 1978. £7.50.

Kurian, George. *Directory of American Book Publishing: From Founding Fathers to Today's Conglomerates.* New York: Monarch, 1975. $25.

Lehmann-Haupt, Hellmut. *The Book in America.* 2nd ed. New York: R. R. Bowker, 1951. o.p.

Madison, Charles. *Jewish Publishing in America.* New York: Hebrew Publishing Co., 1976. $11.95.

Moore, John Hammond. *Wiley: One Hundred and Seventy-five Years of Publishing.* New York: Wiley, 1982. $25.

Morpurgo, J. E. *Allen Lane: King Penguin.* New York: Methuen, 1979. $25.

Mott, Frank Luther. *Golden Multitudes: The Story of Best Sellers in the United States (1662-1945).* Reprint ed. New York: R. R. Bowker, 1960. o.p.

Norrie, Ian. *Mumby's Publishing and Bookselling in the Twentieth Century.* 6th ed. London: Bell & Hyman, 1982. Dist. by R. R. Bowker. $35.

O'Brien, Geoffrey. *Hardboiled America: The Lurid Years of Paperbacks.* New York: Van Nostrand Reinhold, 1981. $16.95.

Regnery, Henry. *Memoirs of a Dissident Publisher.* New York: Harcourt Brace Jovanovich, 1979. $12.95.

Schick, Frank L. *The Paperbound Book in America: The History of Paperbacks and Their European Background.* New York: R. R. Bowker, 1958. o.p.

Schreuders, Piet. *Paperbacks U.S.A.: A Graphic History, 1939-1959.* Trans. from the Dutch by Josh Pachter. San Diego: Blue Dolphin Enterprises, 1981. $10.95.

Stern, Madeleine B. *Books and Book People in 19th-Century America.* New York: R. R. Bowker, 1978. $28.50.

———. *Publishers for Mass Entertainment in Nineteenth Century America.* Boston: G. K. Hall, 1980. $28.

Tebbel, John. *A History of Book Publishing in the United States.* 4 vols. Vol. 1. *The Creation of an Industry, 1630-1865.* Vol. 2. *The Expansion of an Industry, 1865-1919.* Vol. 3. *The Golden Age between Two Wars, 1920-1940.* Vol. 4. *The Great Change, 1940-1980.* New York: R. R. Bowker, 1972, 1975, 1978, 1981. $37.50 each.

Electronic Publishing

Knowledge Industry Publications Staff and Bailey, Janet, eds. *Data Base-Electronic Publishing Review and Forecast 1983.* White Plains, N.Y.: Knowledge Industry Publications, 1983. $175.

Martin, James. *Viewdata and the Information Society.* Englewood Cliffs, N.J.: Prentice-Hall, 1982. $29.95.

Neustadt, Richard M. *The Birth of Electronic Publishing: Legal and Economic Issues in Telephone, Cable and Over-the-Air Teletext and Videotext.* White Plains, N.Y.: Knowledge Industry Publications, 1982. $32.95.

Spigai, Frances, and Sommer, Peter. *Guide to Electronic Publishing: Opportunities in Online and Viewdata Services.* White

Plains, N.Y.: Knowledge Industry Publications, 1982. $95.

Tydeman, John, and Lipinski, Hubert. *Teletext and Videotext in the United States: Market Potential, Technology and Public Policy Issues.* New York: McGraw-Hill, 1982. $34.95.

Editors, Agents, Authors

Applebaum, Judith, and Evans, Nancy. *How to Get Happily Published.* New York: Harper & Row, 1978. $11.95.

Berg, A. Scott. *Max Perkins: Editor of Genius.* New York: Pocket Books. pap. $2.95.

Commins, Dorothy Berliner. *What Is an Editor? Saxe Commins at Work.* Chicago: University of Chicago Press, 1978. $5.95.

Curtis, Richard. *How to Be Your Own Literary Agent.* Boston: Houghton Mifflin, 1983. $12.95.

Henderson, Bill, ed. *The Art of Literary Publishing: Editors on Their Craft.* Yonkers, N.Y.: Pushcart, 1980. $15.

Madison, Charles. *Irving to Irving: Author-Publisher Relations: 1800-1974.* New York: R. R. Bowker, 1974. $15.95.

Meyer, Carol. *Writer's Survival Manual: The Complete Guide to Getting Your Book Published.* New York: Crown, 1982. $13.95.

Reynolds, Paul R. *The Middle Man: The Adventures of a Literary Agent.* New York: Morrow, 1972. $6.95.

Unseld, Siegfried. *The Author and His Publisher.* Chicago: University of Chicago Press, 1980. $12.50.

Watson, Graham. *Book Society: Reminiscences of a Literary Agent.* New York: Atheneum, 1980. $10.95.

Book Design and Production

Grannis, Chandler B. *The Heritage of the Graphic Arts.* New York: R. R. Bowker, 1972. $24.95.

Lee, Marshall. *Bookmaking: The Illustrated Guide to Design and Production.* 2nd ed. New York: R. R. Bowker, 1980. $32.50.

Mintz, Patricia Barnes. *Dictionary of Graphic Arts Terms: A Communication Tool for People Who Buy Type & Printing.* New York: Van Nostrand Reinhold, 1981. $17.95.

Rice, Stanley. *Book Design: Systematic Aspects.* New York: R. R. Bowker, 1978. $18.95.

———. *Book Design: Text Format Models.* New York: R. R. Bowker, 1978. $18.95.

Roberts, Matt T., and Etherington, Don. *Bookbinding and the Conservation of Books: A Dictionary of Descriptive Terminology.* Washington, D.C.: Library of Congress. For sale by the Supt. of Docs., U.S. G.P.O., 1982. $27.

Strauss, Victor. *The Printing Industry: An Introduction to Its Many Branches, Processes and Products.* New York: R. R. Bowker, 1967. $34.95.

White, Jan. *Editing by Design.* 2nd ed. New York: R. R. Bowker, 1982, pap. $24.95.

Williamson, Hugh. *Methods of Book Design: The Practice of an Industrial Craft.* 3rd ed. New Haven, Conn.: Yale University Press, 1983. $40. pap. $12.95.

Wilson, Adrian. *The Design of Books.* Layton, Utah: Peregrine Smith, 1974. pap. $10.95.

Bookselling

Anderson, Charles B., ed. *Bookselling in America and the World: A Souvenir Book Celebrating the 75th Anniversary of the American Booksellers Association.* New York: Times Books, 1975. o.p.

Bliven, Bruce. *Book Traveller.* New York: Dodd, Mead, 1975. $4.95. o.p.

Manual on Bookselling: How to Open and Run Your Own Bookstore. 3rd ed. New York: American Booksellers Association, 1980. Distr. by Harmony Books. $15.95. pap. $8.95.

White, Ken. *Bookstore Planning and Design.* New York: McGraw-Hill, 1982. $44.50.

Censorship

de Grazia, Edward, comp. *Censorship Landmarks.* New York: R. R. Bowker, 1969. $29.50.

Ernst, Morris L., and Schwartz, Alan U. *Censorship.* New York: Macmillan, 1964. $6.95.

Haight, Anne Lyon. *Banned Books.* 4th ed., updated and enlarged by Chandler B. Grannis. New York: R. R. Bowker, 1978. $14.95.

Hentoff, Nat. *The First Freedom: The Tumultuous History of Free Speech in America.* New York: Delacorte, 1980. $11.95. pap. $2.50.

Jenkinson, Edward B. *Censors in the Classroom: The Mind Benders.* Carbondale, Ill.: Southern Illinois University Press, 1979. $17.95.

Copyright

Copyright Revision Act of 1976: Law, Explanation, Committee Reports. Chicago: Commerce Clearing House, 1976. $12.50.

Current Developments in Copyright Law, 1982. Patents, Copyrights, Trademarks and Literary Property Course Handbook Series. New York: Practising Law Institute, 1982. $30.

Johnston, Donald F. *Copyright Handbook.* 2nd ed. New York: R. R. Bowker, 1982. $27.50.

McDonald, Dennis D., and Bush, Colleen G. *Libraries, Publishers and Photocopying: Final Report of Surveys Conducted for the United States Copyright Office.*

Rockville, Md.: King Research, Inc., 1982. $25.

Wittenberg, Philip. *Protection of Literary Property.* Boston: The Writer, Inc., 1978. $12.95.

Book Trade Directories and Yearbooks

American and Canadian

American Book Trade Directory, 1983. 29th ed. New York: R. R. Bowker, ann. $95.

Book Publishers Directory: An Information Service Covering New and Established, Private and Special Interest, Avant-Garde and Alternative, Organization and Association, Government and Institution Presses, edited by Linda S. Hubbard. Detroit: Gale, 1983. $195. Supplement, 1983. $110.

Chernofsky, Jacob L., ed. *AB Bookman's Yearbook.* 2 vols. Clifton, N.J.: AB Bookman's Weekly, ann. $10; free to subscribers to *AB Bookman's Weekly.*

Congrat-Butlar, Stefan, ed. *Translation & Translators: An International Directory and Guide.* New York: R. R. Bowker, 1979. $35.

Kim, Ung Chon. *Policies of Publishers.* Metuchen, N.J.: Scarecrow, 1982. pap. $15.

Literary Market Place, 1984, with Names & Numbers. New York: R. R. Bowker, ann. $45. The business directory of American book publishing.

Publishers, Distributors, & Wholesalers of the United States: A Directory. New York: R. R. Bowker, 1983. pap. $35.

Publishers Weekly Yearbook 1982; News, Analyses and Trends in the Book Industry. New York: R. R. Bowker, 1983. pap. $29.95.

U.S. Book Publishing Yearbook and Directory, 1981/82. White Plains, N.Y.: Knowledge Industry Publications, 1982. $65.

Foreign and International

International Directory of Little Magazines and Small Presses. Paradise, Calif.: Dustbooks. ann. $25.95.

International ISBN Publisher's Directory 1983. Berlin: International ISBN Agency, 1983. Distr. by R. R. Bowker. $99.50.

International Literary Market Place 1983–84. New York: R. R. Bowker, 1983. $55.

Publishers' International Directory. 2 vols. New York: K. G. Saur. Distr. by Gale Research, 1982. $175.

Taubert, Sigfred, ed. *The Book Trade of the World.* Vol. I. *Europe and International Sections.* Vol. II. *U.S.A., Canada, Central and South America, Australia and New Zealand.* Vol. III. *Africa, Asia.* New York: R. R. Bowker. Vol. I, 1972, $70; Vol. II, 1976, $70; Vol. III, 1980, $70.

UNESCO Statistical Yearbook, 1982. New York: Unipub, 1983. $109.75.

Who Distributes What and Where: An International Directory of Publishers, Imprints, Agents, and Distributors. New York: R. R. Bowker, 1983. $55.

Newspapers and Periodicals

Editor and Publisher International Year Book. New York: Editor and Publisher. ann. $50.

IMS '83 Ayer Directory of Publications. Fort Washington, Pa.: IMS Press, 1983. $95.

Irregular Serials and Annuals: An International Directory. New York: R. R. Bowker, 1984. $95.

Magazine Industry Market Place: The Directory of American Periodical Publishing. New York: R. R. Bowker, 1984. $45.

New Serial Titles 1950–1970. New York: R. R. Bowker, 1973. 4 vols. o.p. Available on microfilm, $100; or xerographic reprint, $250.

New Serial Titles 1950–1970, Subject Guide. New York: R. R. Bowker, 1975. 2 vols. $138.50.

Sources of Serials: An International Publisher and Corporate Author Directory to Ulrich's and Irregular Serials. New York: R. R. Bowker, 1981. $65.

Standard Periodical Directory: 1983–1984. 8th rev. Edited by Patricia Hagood. New York: Oxbridge Communications, 1982. $160. Distr. by Gale Research.

Ulrich's International Periodicals Directory. 22nd ed. 2 vols. New York: R. R. Bowker, 1983. $110.

Working Press of the Nation: Newspapers, Magazines, Radio and TV, and Internal Publications. Chicago: National Research Bureau, ann. 5 vols. $241.

Editing

Barzun, Jacques. *Simple and Direct: A Rhetoric for Writers.* New York: Harper & Row, 1976. $12.50.

Bernstein, Theodore. *The Careful Writer.* New York: Atheneum, 1965. pap. $9.95.

The Chicago Manual of Style, 13th rev. ed. Chicago: University of Chicago Press, 1982. $30.

Fowler, H. W. *Dictionary of Modern English Usage.* 2nd rev. ed. New York: Oxford University Press, 1965. $15.

Jordan, Lewis. *The New York Times Manual of Style and Usage.* New York: Times Books, 1982. pap. $5.95.

Skillin, Marjorie E., and Gay, Robert M. *Words into Type.* Rev. ed. Englewood Cliffs, N.J.: Prentice-Hall, 1974. $22.95.

Strunk, William, Jr., and White, E. B. *Elements of Style.* 3rd ed. New York: Macmillan, 1978. $7.95. pap. $2.95.

Zinsser, William. *On Writing Well: An Informal Guide to Writing Nonfiction.* 2nd ed. New York: Harper & Row, 1980. $12.45.

Periodicals

AB Bookman's Weekly (weekly including yearbook). Clifton, N.J.: AB Bookman's Weekly. $35.

American Book Publishing Record (monthly). New York: R. R. Bowker. $44.50.

The American Bookseller (monthly). New York: American Booksellers Association. $18.

BP Report: On the Business of Book Publishing (weekly). White Plains, N.Y.: Knowledge Industry Publications. $215.

EPB: Electronic Publishing and Bookselling (bimonthly). Phoenix, Ariz.: Oryx Press. $60.

Electronic Publishing Review (quarterly). Medford, N.J.: Learned Information, Inc. $66.

Publishers Weekly. New York: R. R. Bowker. $68.

Scholarly Publishing: A Journal for Authors & Publishers (quarterly). Toronto: University of Toronto Press. $25.

Small Press (bimonthly). New York: R. R. Bowker. $18.

Weekly Record. New York: R. R. Bowker. $47.50. A weekly listing of current American book publications, providing complete cataloging information.

For a list of periodicals reviewing books, see *Literary Market Place*.

Distinguished Books

Literary Prizes, 1983

ASCAP-Deems Taylor Awards. *Offered by:* American Society of Composers, Authors, and Publishers. *Winners:* Samuel Adler for *The Study of Orchestration* (Norton); David Beach and Jurgen Thum, trans., for *The Art of Strict Musical Composition* by Johann Phillip Kirnberger (Yale Univ.); Samuel Charters for *The Roots of the Blues* (Perigee); B. Lee Cooper for *Images of American Society in Popular Music* (Nelson-Hall); Joseph Horowitz for *Conversations with Arrau* (Knopf); Carol J. Oja for *Stravinsky in Modern Music* (Da Capo); Sally Placksin for *American Women in Jazz* (Wideview Books); Mark Slobin for *Tenement Songs* (Univ. of Illinois); Emanuel Winternitz for *Leonardo da Vinci as a Musician* (Yale Univ.).

Academy of American Poets Fellowship Award. For distinguished poetic achievement. *Winners:* James Schuyler and Philip Booth.

Jane Addams Children's Book Award. For a book promoting the cause of peace, social justice, and world community. *Offered by:* Women's International League for Peace and Freedom and the Jane Addams Peace Association. *Winner:* Toshi Maruki for *Hiroshima No Pika* (Lothrop).

Alan Award. For a significant contribution to adolescent literature. *Offered by:* National Council of Teachers of English. *Winner:* Kenneth Donelson for research and writing on the use, effect, and history of adolescent literature in a special issue of the *Arizona English Bulletin*.

American Academy and Institute of Arts and Letters Awards in Literature. *Winners:* Alfred Corn; Stephen Dixon; Robert Mezey; Mary Oliver; David Plante; George Starbuck; Leo Steinberg; Edmund White.

American Academy and Institute of Arts and Letters Short Story Award. *Winner:* Elizabeth Spencer.

American Academy in Rome Fellowship in Creative Writing. *Offered by:* American Academy and Institute of Arts and Letters. *Winner:* Gjertrud Schnackenberg.

American Book Awards. *Winners:* (autobiography/biography) Judith Thurman for *Isak Dinesen: The Life of a Storyteller* (St. Martin's) and James R. Mellow for *Nathaniel Hawthorne in His Times* (Houghton); (fiction) Alice Walker for *The Color Purple* (Harcourt); Eudora Welty for *The Collected Stories of Eudora Welty* (Harvest/Harcourt); (first novel) Gloria Naylor for *The Women of Brewster Place* (Viking); (general nonfiction) Fox Butterfield for *China: Alive in the Bitter Sea* (Times Books) and James Fallows for *National Defense* (Vintage); (history) Alan Brinkley for *Voices of Protest: Huey Long, Father Coughlin and the Great Depression* (Knopf) and Frank E. Manuel and Fritzie P. Manuel for *Utopian Thought in the Western World* (Belknap); (original paperback) Lisa Goldstein for *The Red Magician* (Timescape/Pocket Books); (poetry) Galway Kinnell for *Selected Poems* (Houghton) and Charles Wright for *Country Music* (Wesleyan Univ.); (science) Abraham Pais for *Sub-*

tle *Is the Lord: The Science and Life of Albert Einstein* (Oxford Univ.) and Philip J. Davis and Reuben Hersh for *The Mathematical Experience* (Houghton); (translation) Richard Howard for *Les Fleurs du Mal* by Charles Baudelaire (Godine).

American Book Awards for graphics. *Winners:* (book design—pictorial) Barry Moser and Steve Renick for *Alice's Adventures in Wonderland* by Lewis Carroll (Univ. of California); book design—typographical) David Lance Goines and William F. Luckey for *A Constructed Roman Alphabet* (Godine); (book illustration—collected art) Howard Morris, Nancy Grubb, and Dana Cole for *John Singer Sargent* by Carter Ratcliff (Abbeville); (book illustration—original art) Erick Ingraham and Cynthia Basil for *Porcupine Stew* by Beverly Major (Morrow); (book illustration—photographs) Eleanor Morris Caponigro for *Alfred Stieglitz: Photographs and Writings* by Sarah Greenough and Juan Hamilton (National Gallery of Art/Callaway Editions); (cover design) Martha Sedgwick and Matt Tepper for *Key Exchange* by Kevin Wade (Avon) and Doris Ettlinger and Neil Stuart for *Bogmail* by Patrick McGinley (Penguin); (jacket design) Fred Marcellino and Frank Metz for *Souls on Fire* by Elie Wiesel (Summit Books/Simon and Schuster).

American Book Awards—Children's Books. *Winners:* (fiction—hardcover) Jean Fritz for *Homesick: My Own Story* (Putnam); (fiction—paperback) Paula Fox for *A Place Apart* (Signet/New American Library); (nonfiction) James Cross Giblin for *Chimney Sweeps,* illus. by Margot Tomes (Crowell); (picture books—hardcover) Barbara Cooney for *Miss Rumphius* (Viking) and William Steig for *Doctor De Soto* (Farrar, Straus); (picture books—

paperback) Mary Ann Hoberman for *A House Is a House for Me,* illus. by Betty Fraser (Puffin Books/Viking).

American Printing History Association Award. For a distinguished contribution to the study of the history of publishing and printing. *Winners:* Leona Rostenberg and Madeleine B. Stern of Leona Rostenberg Rare Books.

American-Scandinavian Foundation/PEN Translation Prizes. For previously unpublished translations of poetry and fiction by Scandinavian writers born in the last century. Not awarded in 1983.

Hans Christian Andersen Medals. For the entire body of work of one author and one illustrator. *Offered by:* International Board on Books for Young People. Not awarded in 1983.

Joseph L. Andrews Bibliographical Award. For a significant contribution to legal bibliographical literature. *Offered by:* American Association of Law Libraries. *Winner:* Ted L. McDorman for *Maritime Boundary Delimitation: An Annotated Bibliography.*

Anisfield-Wolf Awards. For contributions to the improvement of racial or ethnic understanding. *Offered by:* Cleveland Foundation. Not awarded in 1983.

Associated Writing Programs Awards. For book-length manuscripts to be published by university presses. *Winners:* (novel) Douglas Finn for *Heart of a Family* (State Univ. of New York); (poetry) Lisa Ress for *Flight Patterns* (Univ. Press of Virginia); (short fiction) Charles Baxter for *Harmony of the World* (Univ. of Missouri).

Association of Jewish Libraries Book Awards. For outstanding contributions in the field of Jewish literature for children. *Winners:* (children's book) Linda Heller for *Castle on Hester Street* (Jewish Publication Society); (older children's book) Marilyn Sachs for *Call Me Ruth* (Doubleday).

Association of Logos Bookstores Book Awards. For excellence in religious publishing. Not awarded in 1983.

Australian Children's Book Awards. For literary merit, but with attention to the quality and design of the book as a whole. *Winners:* (book of the year) Victor Kelleher for *Master of the Grove* (Penguin); (medal for junior readers) Robin Klein for *Thing,* illus. by Alison Lester (Oxford Univ.); (picture book of the year) Pamela Allen for *Who Sank the Boat?* (Nelson—Australia).

Bancroft Prizes—$4,000 each. For books of exceptional merit and distinction in American history, American diplomacy, and the international relations of the United States. *Offered by:* Columbia University. *Winners:* John P. Demos for *Entertaining Satan: Witchcraft and the Culture of Early New England* (Oxford Univ.) and Nick Salvatore for *Eugene V. Debs: Citizen and Socialist* (Univ. of Illinois).

Banta Award. For literary achievement by a Wisconsin author. *Offered by:* Wisconsin Library Association. *Winner:* Susan Engberg for *Pastorale* (Univ. of Illinois).

Alice Hunt Bartlett Award (Great Britain). *Offered by:* Poetry Society. *Winner:* Medbh McGuckian for *The Flower Master* (Oxford Univ.).

Mildred L. Batchelder Award. For an American publisher of a children's book originally published in a foreign language in a foreign country and subsequently published in English in the United States. *Winner:* Toshi Maruki for *Hiroshima No Pika* (Lothrop).

Beefeater Club Prize for Literature. For works of true literary merit, having significance for both England and the United States. Not awarded in 1983.

Before Columbus Foundation American Book Awards. For literary achievement by people of various ethnic backgrounds. *Winners:* Nash Candelaria for *Not by the Sword* (Bilingual Press); Barbara Christian for *Black Women Novelists* (Greenwood); Judy Grahn for *Queen of Wands* (Crossing Press); Peter Guralnick for *Lost Highway: Journeys and Arrivals of American Musicians* (Godine); Jessica Hagedorn for *Pet Food and Tropical Apparitions* (Momo's Press); James D. Houston for *Californians* (Knopf); Joy Kogawa for *Obasan* (Godine); Cecilia Liang, trans., for *Chinese Folk Poetry* (Beyond Baroque); Sean O'Tuma and Thomas Kinsella, ed., for *An Duainne: Poems of the Dispossessed* (Univ. of Pennsylvania); Harriet Rohmer for *The Legend of Food Mountain* (Children's Book Press); John Williams for *Click Song* (Houghton); Evangelina Vigil for *Thirty an' Seen a Lot* (Arte Publico). *Special Lifetime Achievement Award:* Kay Boyle.

Curtis G. Benjamin Award for Creative Publishing. *Winner:* W. Bradford Wiley.

Bennett Award. For a writer who has not received full recognition, or a writer at a critical stage of creative development. *Offered by:* Hudson Review. Not awarded in 1983.

Gerard and Ella Berman Award. For a book of Jewish history. *Offered by:* Jewish Book Council of the National Jewish Welfare Board. *Winner:* Yosef Hayim Yerushalmi for *Zakhor: Jewish History and Jewish Memory* (Univ. of Washington).

Irma Simonton Black Award. For unified excellence of story line, language, and illustration in a published work for young children. *Offered by:* Bank Street College of Education. *Winner:* Charlotte Graeber for *Mustard,* illus. by Donna Diamond (Doubleday).

James Tait Black Memorial Prizes (Great Britain). For the best biography and the best novel of the year. *Offered by:* University of Edinburgh. *Winners:* (biography) Richard Ellman for *James Joyce* (Oxford Univ.); (novel) Bruce Chatwin for *On the Black Hill* (Cape).

Elmer Holmes Bobst Award for Arts and Letters. *Offered by:* New York University. *Funded by:* Elmer and Mamdouha Bobst Foundation. *Winners:* Russell Baker; Kenneth Burke; Alfred Knopf; Denise Levertov; Bernard Malamud; Arthur Miller.

Bollingen Prize for Poetry. *Offered by:* Yale University Library. *Winners:* Anthony Hecht and John Hollander.

Bologna Children's Book Fair Prizes (Italy). *Offered by:* Bologna Trade Fair Promotion Agency. *Winners:* (younger children) Roy Gerrard for *The Fayershams* (Gollancz—Great Britain/Farrar—U.S.); *Il était une fois les mots* (La Farandole—France); (junior critics) Ingrid Selberg for *Our Changing World,* illus. by Andrew Miller (Collins—Great Britain).

Books in Canada Award (Canada). For literary achievement by a first novelist. *Winner:* W. P. Kinsella for *Shoeless Joe* (Houghton).

Boston Globe—Horn Book Awards. For excellence in text and illustration. *Winners:* (fiction) Virginia Hamilton for *Sweet Whispers, Brother Rush* (Philomel); (nonfiction) Daniel S. Davis for *Behind Barbed Wire: The Imprisonment of Japanese Americans during World War II* (Dutton); (illustration) Vera B. Williams for *A Chair for My Mother* (Greenwillow).

Brandeis University Creative Arts Award in Fiction. *Winner:* Robert Penn Warren.

John Nicholas Brown Prize. *Offered by:* Mediaeval Academy of America. *Winner:* David Berger for *The Jewish-Christian Debate in the High Middle Ages: A Critical Edition of the Nizzahon Vetus with an Introduction, Translation*

and Commentary (Jewish Publication Society).

John Burroughs Medal. *Winner:* Alexander S. Skutch for *A Naturalist on a Tropical Farm* (Univ. of California).

Witter Bynner Foundation Prize for Poetry. *Offered by:* American Academy and Institute of Arts and Letters. *Winner:* Douglas Crase.

Caldecott Medal. For the artist of the most distinguished picture book. *Offered by:* R. R. Bowker Company. *Winner:* Marcia Brown for *Shadow* (Scribner's).

John W. Campbell Award. For an author whose first professional story was published in the preceding two years. *Offered by:* World Science Fiction Convention. *Winner:* Paul O. Williams.

John W. Campbell Memorial Award. For an outstanding science fiction novel. *Offered by:* Science Fiction Research Association. *Winner:* Brian Aldiss for *Helliconia Spring* (Atheneum).

Canada-Australia Literary Prize. For an outstanding body of work. *Offered by:* Canada Department of External Affairs, the Canada Council, and the Australia Council. *Winner:* Barry Oaklay.

Canada Council Children's Literature Prizes. For an outstanding author and illustrator. *Winners:* (English-language book) Monica Hughes for *Hunter in the Dark* (Clarke Irwin) and Vlasta van Kampen, illus., for *ABC, 123: The Canadian Alphabet and Counting Book* (Hurtig); (French-language book) Ginette Anfousse for *Fabien 1* and *Fabien 2* (Leméac) and Darcia Labrosse, illus., for *Agnès et le singulier bestiaire* (Pierre Tisseyre).

Canada Council Translation Prizes. For the best translation in English and in French. *Winners:* (French into English) Raymond Y. Chambelain, Jr. for *Jos Connaissant* by Victor-Lévy Beaulieu (Cercle du Livre de France); (English into French) Claude Aubry for *Je t'at-*

tends à Peggy's Cove by Brian Doyle (Exile Editions).

Canadian Association of Children's Librarians Book of the Year. *Winner:* Brian Doyle for *Up to Low* (Douglas and McIntyre).

Canadian Authors Association Literary Awards. For literary excellence without sacrificing popular appeal. *Winners:* (drama) W. O. Mitchell for *Back to Beulah* (Macmillan); (nonfiction) Christina McCall-Newman for *Grits* (Macmillan); (novel) W. P. Kinsella for *Shoeless Joe* (Houghton); (poetry) George Amabile for *The Presence of Fire* (McClelland & Stewart).

Canadian Library Association Children's Book of the Year Award. *Winner:* Brian Doyle for *Up to Low* (Douglas and McIntyre).

Melville Cane Award. For an outstanding book of poems and a book on poetry or a poet. *Offered by:* Poetry Society of America. *Winner:* Ian Hamilton for *Robert Lowell: A Biography* (Random).

Carey-Thomas Awards. For a distinguished project of book publishing. *Offered by:* R. R. Bowker Company. *Winner:* Penguin Books: Penguin Contemporary American Fiction Series and Penguin Original Series. *Honor Citation:* Literary Classics of the United States for *Literary America. Special Citations:* Callaway Editions/National Gallery of Art for *Alfred Stieglitz: Photographs and Writings;* Sierra Club Books for books on environmental issues; Philomel Books for books for blind children.

Carnegie Medal (Great Britain). For an outstanding book for children. *Offered by:* British Library Association. *Winner:* Margaret Mahy for *The Haunting* (Dent).

Children's Book Guild Award. *See Washington Post/* Children's Book Guild Nonfiction Award.

Gilbert Chinard Prize. For a distinguished scholarly book or manuscript in the history of Franco-American relations. *Offered by:* Institut Francais de Washington and the Society for French Historical Studies. *Winner:* Orville T. Murphy for *Charles Gravier, Comte de Vergennes: French Diplomacy in the Age of Revolution, 1719-1787* (State Univ. of New York).

Cholmondeley Award (Great Britain). For contributions to poetry. *Offered by:* Society of Authors. *Winners:* John Fuller; Craig Raine; Anthony Thwaite.

Christopher Book Awards. For books that affirm the highest values of the human spirit. *Winners:* (adult books) James MacGregor Burns for *The Vineyard of Liberty* (Knopf); James Tunstead Burtchaell for *Rachel Weeping* (Andrews and McMeel); Yaffa Eliach for *Hasidic Tales of the Holocaust* (Oxford Univ.); Stephen B. Oates for *Let The Trumpet Sound: The Life of Martin Luther King, Jr.* (Harper); Richard Reeves for *American Journey* (Simon and Schuster); Barbara Rosen and Barry Rosen, with George Fiefer, for *The Destined Hour* (Doubleday); Jonathan Schell for *The Fate of the Earth* (Knopf); (children's books) Jim Arnosky for *Drawing from Nature* (Lothrop); Jean Fritz for *Homesick: My Own Story,* illus. by Margot Tomes (Putnam); Zibby O'Neal for *A Formal Feeling* (Viking); James Stevenson for *We Can't Sleep* (Greenwillow).

Frank and Ethel Cohen Award. For a book of Jewish thought. *Offered by:* Jewish Book Council. *Winner:* Bernard Septimus for *Hispano-Jewish Culture in Transition: The Career and Controversies of Ramah* (Harvard Univ.).

Carr P. Collins Award. For an outstanding book of nonfiction. *Offered by:* Texas Institute of Letters. *Winner:* Robert A. Caro for *The Path to Power: The Years of Lyndon Johnson, Vol. 1* (Knopf).

Collectors' Institute Award. For best book design. *Winners:* Barbara Whitehead and Fred Whitehead, designers, for *Journey to Pleasant Hill: The Civil War Letters of Captain Elijah P. Petty, Walker's Texas Division, C.S.A.* (Univ. of Texas Institute of Texan Cultures).

Columbia University Translation Awards. For excellence in translation. *Winners:* Roger Greenwald for *The Silence Afterwards: Selected Poems* by Rolf Jacobson (from the Norwegian); Carol Rubenstein for traditional works of the Sarawak Dayaks; Lawrence Venuti for *The Colomber* by Dino Buzzati (from the Italian); Craig Williamson for *A Feast of Creatures: Anglo-Saxon Riddle Songs* (from the Old English); Jeno Brogyanyi for *The Line* by Geza Paskandi (from the Hungarian); Stanley F. Lombardo for *Hesiod's Works and Days* (from the Greek); Moss Roberts for *The Three Kingdoms* by Lo Guanzhong (from the Chinese); and Lisa Sapinkopf for *For the Lure of the Threshold* by Yves Bonnefoy (from the French).

Common Wealth Award. For distinguished service in literature. *Winner:* Christopher Isherwood.

Commonwealth Club of California. To honor the finest works of literature by California authors. *Offered by:* Commonwealth Club of California. *Winners:* (gold medals) Gina Berriault for *The Infinite Passion of Expectation: Twenty-five Stories* (North Point) and Robert Middlekauff for *The Glorious Cause: The American Revolution, 1763–1789* (Oxford Univ.) (silver medals) Margot Zemach for *Jake and Honeybunch Go to Heaven* (Farrar); Thomas Perry for *The Butcher's Boy* (Scribner's); Clayton Bess for *Story for a Black Night* (Parnassus); Barry Spacks for *Spacks Street: New & Selected Poems* (Johns Hopkins); and Ruth Teiser and Catherine Harroun for *Winemaking in California* (McGraw).

Commonwealth Poetry Prize (Great Britain). For a first published book of poetry in English by an author from a Commonwealth country other than Great Britain. *Offered by:* Commonwealth Institute and the National Book League. *Winner:* Grace Nichols for *I Is a Long-Memoried Woman* (Carribbean Cultural International).

Thomas Cook Travel Book Awards (Great Britain). For the best travel book and the best guide book. *Offered by:* National Book League. *Winners:* Vikram Seth for *From Heaven Lake* (Chatto & Windus) and Michael Leapman for *The Companion Guide to New York* (Collins).

Duff Cooper Memorial Prize (Great Britain). For a distinguished book on history, biography, politics, or poetry. *Winner:* Richard Ellman for *James Joyce* (Oxford Univ.).

Daedalian Poetry Award. For an outstanding volume of poetry. *Sponsored by:* Paul Voertman. *Winners:* Naomi Shihab Nye for *Hugging the Jukebox* (Dutton) and Thomas Whitbread for *Whomp and Moonshiver* (Boa Editions).

Delacorte Press First Young Adult Novel Prize. To encourage the writing of contemporary young adult fiction. *Offered by:* Delacorte Press. *Winner:* Joyce Sweeney for *The Center Line.*

Alice Fay Di Castagnola Award. *Offered by:* Poetry Society of America. *Winner:* Thomas Lux for *Fireplace Full of Crutches.*

Elliott Prize. For a first article in the field of medieval studies. *Offered by:* Medieval Academy of America. *Winner:* Lance W. Brunner for "A Perspective on the Southern Italian Sequence: The Second Tonary of the Manuscript Monte Cassino 318" from *Early Music History* 1 (1981): 117–164.

Ralph Waldo Emerson Award. *Offered by:* Phi Beta Kappa. *Winner:* Daniel Joseph Singal for *The War Within* (Univ. of North Carolina).

Kurt Maschler Emil Award. For a work of the imagination in which text and illustration are of excellence. *Winner:* Anthony Browne for *Gorilla* (Julia MacRae).

English-Speaking Union Awards: For books of outstanding merit sent to English-speaking countries abroad to serve as interpreters of American life and culture. *Winners:* (adult books) Thomas Boylston Adams for *A New Nation* (Globe Pequot); Susan Mary Alsop for *Yankees at the Court: The First Americans in Paris* (Doubleday); Jervis Anderson for *This Was Harlem* (Farrar); Jackson R. Bryer for *The Letters of Eugene O'Neill to Kenneth MacGowan* (Yale Univ.); Justin Kaplan for *Whitman: Poetry and Prose* (Library of America); Henry Kissinger for *Years of Upheaval* (Little, Brown); Olga Maynard for *Judith Jamison: Aspects of a Dancer* (Doubleday); Robert Middlekauff for *The Glorious Cause: The American Revolution* (Oxford Univ.); Hal Morgan and Andreas Brown for *Prairie Fires and Paper Moons: The American Photographic Post Card* (Godine); Roy Harvey Pearce for *Hawthorne: Tales and Sketches* (Library of America); Kate Simon for *Bronx Primitive* (Viking); Kathryn Kish Sklar for *Harriet Beecher Stowe: Three Novels* (Library of America); Jane S. Smith for *Elsie De Wolfe: A Life in the High Style* (Atheneum); Thomas G. Tanselle for *Herman Melville: Typee, Omoo, Mardi* (Library of America); Edward Weeks for *Writers and Friends* (Atlantic-Little); Theodore White for *America in Search of Itself* (Harper); Roy Wilkins with Tom Mathews for *Standing Fast: The Autobiography of Roy Wilkins* (Viking); (children's books) Diana H. Cross and Jan Brett for *Some Birds Have Funny Names* (Crown); Jean Lipman with Margaret Aspinwall for *Alexander Calder and His Magical Mobiles* (Hudson Hills Press); John F. Loeper for *The House on Spruce Street* (Hudson Hills Press); Lorus J. Milne and Margery Milne for *Dreams of a Perfect Earth* (Atheneum); Helen Plotz for *Gladly Learn and Gladly Teach: Poems of the School Experience* (Greenwillow); Cynthia Rylant and Diane Goode for *When I Was Young in the Mountains* (Dutton).

William and Janice Epstein Award. For a book of Jewish fiction. *Winner:* Robert Greenfield for *Temple* (Summit).

Geoffrey Faber Memorial Prize (Great Britain). *Offered by:* Faber & Faber Ltd. *Winner:* Graham Swift for *Shuttlecock* (Faber).

Eleanor Farjeon Award (Great Britain). For distinguished services to children's books. *Offered by:* Children's Book Circle. *Winner:* Jean Russell.

Dorothy Canfield Fisher Children's Book Award. For a children's book by a distinguished Vermont author selected by Vermont schoolchildren. *Offered by:* Vermont Department of Libraries and Vermont Congress of Parents and Teachers. *Winner:* Judy Blume for *Tiger Eyes* (Bradbury).

William Frank Memorial Award. To promote an appreciation of Jewish children's literature. *Offered by:* Jewish Book Council. *Winner:* Barbara Cohen for *King of the Seventh Grade* (Lothrop).

George Freedley Memorial Award. *Offered by:* Theatre Library Association. *Winner:* J. C. Furnas for *Fanny Kemble: Leading Lady of the Nineteenth Century Stage* (Dial); (honorable mention) Laurence Senelick for *Gordon Craig's Moscow Hamlet: A Reconstruction* (Greenwood).

R. T. French Tastemaker Awards. For the outstanding cookbooks of the year. *Offered by:* R. T. French Company. *Winners:* (American) Melinda M. Vance, ed., for *Connecticut à la Carte* (Connecticut à la Carte of West Hartford); (basic/general) Anne Willan for *The Varenne Cooking Course* (Morrow); (best cookbook) Evan Jones and Judith Jones for *The Book of Bread* (Harper); (international) Giuliano Bugialli for *Giuliano Bugialli's Classic Techniques of Italian Cooking* (Simon and Schuster); (natural foods/special diet) Joyce Trollope, ed., for *Better Homes and Gardens Dieter's Cookbook* (Meredith Corp.); (original softcover—basic/general) Janeth Nix, Elaine Woodard, and other editors of Sunset Books and *Sunset Magazine* for *Easy Basics for Good Cooking* (Lane); (original softcover—international/American regional) Rose Dosti for *Middle Eastern Cooking* (HP Books); (original softcover—meat/fish/eggs) Yvonne Young Farr for *The Great East Coast Seafood Book* (Random); (original softcover—specialty) Lou Seibert Pappas for *Vegetable Cookery* (HP Books); (specialty) John Clancy for *John Clancy's Christmas Cookbook* (Hearst).

Friends of American Writers. *Winners:* Will D. Campbell for *The Glad River* (Holt); John Madson for *Where the Sky Began* (Houghton); Kathy Callaway for *Bloodroot Flower* (Knopf).

Friends of the Dallas Public Library Award. For a book that makes an important contribution to knowledge. *Winner:* David J. Weber for *The Mexican Frontier, 1821–1846: The American Southwest under Mexico* (Univ. of Mexico).

Garden State Children's Book Awards. For children's books with literary merit that are popular with readers. *Offered by:* New Jersey Library Association. *Winners:* (easy to read) James Stevenson for *Clams Can't Sing* (Greenwillow); Jane Yolen for *Commander Toad in Space* (Coward, McCann); (younger fiction) Judy Blume for *Superfudge* (Dutton); (younger nonfiction) Mary Beth Sullivan and Linda Bourke for *A Show of Hands: Say It in Sign Language*, illus. by Linda Bourke (Addison-Wesley).

Christian Gauss Award. For an outstanding book in the field of literary scholarship or criticism. *Offered by:* Phi Beta Kappa. *Winner:* W. R. Johnson for *The Idea of Lyric* (Univ. of California).

Georgia Children's Book Awards. *Offered by:* University of Georgia College of Education. *Winners:* (children's book) Judy Blume for *Superfudge* (Dutton); (children's picture book) Kelly Oechsli for *Herbie's Troubles* by Carol Chapman (Dutton).

Leon L. Gildesgame Award. For excellence in visual arts. *Winners:* Andrew S. Ackerman and Susan L. Braunstein for *Israel in Antiquity* (Jewish Museum).

Tony Godwin Award. For an American or British editor (in alternate years) to spend six weeks working at a publishing house in the other's country. *Offered by:* Harcourt Brace Jovanovich. *Winner:* Patricia Mulcahy, Penguin Books.

Golden Kite Awards. *See* Society of Children's Book Writers.

Governor General's Literary Awards. To honor literary excellence. *Offered by:* Canada Council. *Winners—English-language works:* (fiction) Guy Vanderhaeghe for *Man Descending* (Macmillan); (poetry) Phyllis Webb for *The Vision Tree: Selected Poems* (Talonbooks); (drama) John Gray for *Billy Bishop Goes to War* (Talonbooks); (nonfiction) Christopher Moore for *Louisbourg Portraits: Life in an Eighteenth-Century Garrison Town* (Macmillan). *Winners—French-language works:* (fiction) Roger Fournier for *Le cercle des arènes* (Albin Michel); (poetry) Michel

Savard for *Forages* (Noroît); (theater) Réjean Ducharme for HA ha! . . . (Lacombe); (nonfiction) Maurice Lagueux for *Le marxisme des années soixante: une saison dans l'histoire de la pensée critique* (Hurtubise). *Translation:* (English into French) Claude Aubry for *Je t'attends à Peggy's Cove* by Brian Doyle (Exile Editions); (French into English) Raymond Y. Chamberlain, Jr., for *Jos Connaissant* by Victor-Lévy Beaulieu (Cercle du Livre).

Grand Prix du Roman (France). For a work of "higher inspiration" by a young novelist. *Offered by:* Académie Francaise. *Winner:* Liliane Guignabodet for *Natalia* (Albin Michel).

Great Lakes Colleges Association Awards. For literary merit in a first book of fiction and a first book of poetry. *Winners:* (fiction) Michael Joyce for *The War outside Ireland* (Tinkers Dam Press); (poetry) Maria Flook for *Reckless Wedding* (Houghton).

Kate Greenaway Medal (Great Britain). For distinguished illustration of a book for children. *Offered by:* British Library Association. *Winners:* Michael Foreman for *Long Neck and Thunder Foot* by Helen Piers (Kestrel/Penguin) and *Sleeping Beauty and Other Favourite Fairy Tales*, trans. by Angela Carter (Gollancz).

Eric Gregory Trust Awards (Great Britain). For poets under the age of 30. *Offered by:* Society of Authors. *Winners:* Martin Stokes; Hilary Davis; Michael O'Neill; Lisa St. Aubin de Teran; Deirdre Shanahan.

Guardian Fiction Prize (Great Britain). For a novel of originality and promise by a British or Commonwealth writer. *Offered by:* Manchester *Guardian. Winner:* Graham Swift for *Waterland* (Heinemann).

Sarah Josepha Hale Award. For a writer of distinction who reflects the literary tradition of New England. *Offered by:*

Friends of the Richards Library, Newport, N.H. *Winner:* Donald Hall.

Alice and Edith Hamilton Prize. For the best original, scholarly book-length manuscript on women. *Offered by:* University of Michigan Rackham School of Graduate Studies. *Winner:* Leslie W. Rabine for *Reading the Romantic Heroine: Text, History, Ideology* (Univ. of Michigan).

Haskins Medal. For a distinguished book in the field of medieval studies by a scholar in the United States or Canada. *Winner:* Jean Bony for *The English Decorated Style: Gothic Architecture Transformed, 1250–1350* (Oxford Univ.).

R. R. Hawkins Award. For the most outstanding book of the year from the fields of science, medicine, technology, and business. *Offered by:* Association of American Publishers Professional and Scholarly Publishing Division. *Winner:* Sybil P. Parker, ed., *Synopsis and Classification of Living Organisms, Vols. 1 and 2* (McGraw-Hill).

Hawthornden Prize (Great Britain). For a work of imaginative literature by an English writer under the age of 41. *Offered by:* Society of Authors. *Winner:* Timothy Mo for *Sour Sweet* (André Deutsch).

Florence Roberts Head Memorial Award. For an outstanding book about the Ohio scene. *Offered by:* Ohioana Library Association. *Winner:* Jack Bickham for *I Still Dream about Columbus* (St. Martin's).

Hugh Hefner First Amendment Award. For a work that contributes to protect the First Amendment. *Offered by:* Playboy Foundation. Not awarded in 1983.

Heinemann Award (Great Britain). For a genuine contribution to literature. *Offered by:* Royal Society of Literature. *Winner:* Derek Walcott for *The Fortunate Traveller* (Faber).

Drue Heinz Literature Prize. For an outstanding collection of unpublished short fiction. *Offered by:* University of Pittsburgh Press and the Howard Heinz Endowment. *Winner:* Jonathan Penner for *Private Parties* (Univ. of Pittsburgh).

Ernest Hemingway Foundation Award. For a work of first fiction by an American. *Winner:* Bobbie Ann Mason for *Shiloh and Other Stories* (Harper).

Sidney Hillman Foundation Prize. For an outstanding work on civil liberties, race relations, social and economic welfare, or world understanding. *Offered by:* Sidney Hillman Foundation of the Amalgamated Clothing and Textile Workers Union. *Winner:* Jonathan Schell for *The Fate of the Earth* (Knopf).

Winifred Holtby Prize (Great Britain). For the best regional novel. *Winner:* Kazuo Ishiguro for *Pale View of the Hills* (Faber).

Clarence L. Holte Prize. For a contribution by a living writer to the public understanding of the cultural heritage of Africa and the African diaspora. *Winner:* Vincent Harding for *There Is a River: The Black Struggle for Freedom in America* (Harcourt).

Amelia Frances Howard-Gibbon Award (Canada). For the illustrator of an outstanding book. *Offered by:* Canadian Library Association, Canadian Association of Children's Librarians. *Winner:* Lindee Climo for *Chester's Barn* (Tundra Books).

Hugo Awards. *See* World Science Fiction Convention.

International Reading Association Children's Book Award. For a first or second book of fiction or nonfiction by an author of promise. *Winner:* Meredith Ann Pierce for *The Darkangel* (Atlantic/Little).

Iowa School of Letters Award. For short fiction. *Offered by:* Iowa Arts Council Writers Workshop and the University of Iowa Press. *Winner:* Ivy Goodman for *Heart Failure* (Univ. of Iowa).

Joseph Henry Jackson Award. For an unpublished work of fiction, nonfictional prose, or poetry. *Offered by:* San Francisco Foundation. *Winner:* Michael Covino for *Full Particulars.*

Jerusalem Prize (Israel). For an author who has contributed to the understanding of the freedom of the individual in society. *Offered by:* Jerusalem Municipality. *Winner:* V. S. Naipaul.

Jewish Chronicle Awards. *See* H. W. Wingate Awards.

Leon Jolson Award. For a book on the holocaust. *Winners:* Irving Abella and Harold Troper for *None Is Too Many: Canada and the Jews of Europe, 1933-1948* (Denys/Random).

Jesse Jones Award. For an outstanding book of fiction. *Winner:* Allen Hannay for *Love & Other Natural Disasters* (Atlantic/Little).

Juniper Prize. For an outstanding manuscript of original English poetry. *Offered by:* University of Massachusetts Press. *Winner:* Marc Hudson for *Afterlight* (Univ. of Massachusetts).

Jane Heidinger Kafka Prize. For an outstanding work of fiction by an American woman. *Offered by:* University of Rochester English Department and Writers' Workshop. *Winner:* Mary Lee Settle for *The Killing Ground* (conclusion to the Beulah Quintet) (Farrar).

Morris J. Kaplun Memorial Award. For a book on Israel. *Winner:* J. Robert Moskin for *Among Lions* (Arbor).

Sue Kaufman Prize. For a first work of fiction. *Offered by:* American Academy and Institute of Arts and Letters. *Winner:* Susanna Moore for *My Old Sweetheart* (Houghton).

Robert F. Kennedy Book Awards. For works that reflect Robert Kennedy's purposes. *Winners:* Stephen B. Oates for *Let the Trumpet Sound: The Life of*

Martin Luther King, Jr. (Harper) and Jonathan Schell for *The Fate of the Earth* (Knopf).

Irvin Kerlan Award. For singular attainments in the creation of children's literature. *Offered by:* University of Minnesota Kerlan Collection Committee. *Winner:* Katherine Paterson.

Coretta Scott King Award. For a work that promotes the cause of peace and brotherhood. *Offered by:* American Library Association Social Responsibilities Round Table. *Winners:* Virginia Hamilton for *Sweet Whispers, Brother Rush* (Philomel) and Peter Magubane, illus., for *Black Child* (Knopf).

Robert Kirsch Award. For an outstanding body of work by an author from the West or featuring the West. *Offered by:* Los Angeles Times. *Winner:* M. F. K. Fisher.

Roger Klein Award. For an outstanding editor. *Offered by:* PEN American Center. Not awarded in 1983.

Janusz Korczak Award. For a book about the welfare and nurturing of children. *Offered by:* Anti-Defamation League of B'nai B'rith. Not awarded in 1983.

Sarah H. Kushner Memorial Award for Scholarship. *Winner:* Jeremy Cohen for *Friars and Jews* (Cornell Univ.).

Lamont Poetry Selection. *Offered by:* American Academy and Institute of Arts and Letters. *Winner:* Sharon Olds for *The Dead and the Living* (Knopf).

Evelyn Sibley Lampman Award. For a significant contribution to children's literature in the Pacific Northwest area. *Offered by:* Oregon Library Association. *Winner:* Patricia Feehan.

Jules F. Landry Award. For the best manuscript in southern history, biography, or literature. *Offered by:* Louisiana State University Press. *Winner:* Fred Hobson for *Tell about the Southern Rage to Explain.*

Allen Lane Award. For a book that furthers public understanding of mental illness and/or handicap. *Winner:* Dorothy Rowe for *Depression: The Way Out of Your Prison* (Routledge & Kegan Paul).

Peter I. B. Lavan Younger Poets Awards. *Offered by:* American Academy and Institute of Arts and Letters. *Winners:* Edward Hirsch; Brad Leithauser; Gjertrud Schnackenberg.

Abraham Lincoln Literary Award. For an outstanding contribution to American literature. *Offered by:* Union League Club. *Winner:* William Manchester for *The Last Lion, Winston Spencer Churchill: Visions of Glory, 1874–1932* (Little, Brown).

Mildred and Harold Strauss Livings Award. *Offered by:* American Academy and Institute of Arts and Letters. *Winners:* Raymond Carver and Cynthia Ozick.

Loins Award for Poetry. *Offered by:* American Academy and Institute of Arts and Letters. *Winner:* Geoffrey Hill.

Locus Awards. *Offered by:* Locus Publications. *Winners:* (anthology) Terry Carr, ed., for *The Best Science Fiction of the Year #11* (Timescape); (artist) Michael Whelan; (fantasy novel) Gene Wolfe for *The Sword of the Lictor* (Timescape); (magazine) *Locus;* (nonfiction/reference) Barry Malzberg for *The Engines of the Night* (Doubleday); (novelette) Harlan Ellison for *Djinn, No Chaser* (TZ 4/82) (novella) Joanna Russ for "Souls" (*Fantasy and Science Fiction*, January 1982); (publisher) Pocket/Timescape; (science fiction novel) Isaac Asimov for *Foundation's Edge* (Doubleday); (short story) Ursula K. Le Guin for "Sur" from *The Compass Rose* (Harper); (single-author collection) Ursula K. Le Guin for *The Compass Rose* (Harper).

Los Angeles Times Book Awards. Honor literary excellence. *Winners:* (biography) Seymour M. Hersh for *The Price of Power: Kissinger in the Nixon White House* (Summit); (current interest) Walker Percy for *Lost in the Cosmos: The Last Self-Help Book* (Farrar); (fiction) Thomas Keneally for *Schindler's List* (Simon and Schuster); (history) Fernand Braudel for *The Wheels of Commerce: Civilization and Capitalism, 15th–18th Century* (Harper); (poetry) James Merrill for *The Changing Light at Sandover* (Atheneum).

James Russell Lowell Prize. For an outstanding literary or linguistic study, a critical edition, or a critical biography. *Offered by:* Modern Language Association of America. *Winner:* Thomas M. Greene for *The Light in Troy: Imitation and Discovery in Renaissance Poetry* (Yale Univ.).

Booker McConnell Prize (Great Britain). For a full-length novel in English by a citizen of Britain or the British Commonwealth, Republic of Ireland, or South Africa. *Offered by:* National Book League. *Winner:* J. M. Coetzee for *The Life and Times of Michael K.* (Secker and Warburg).

Dorothy McKenzie Award. For service on behalf of children. *Offered by:* Southern California Council on Literature. *Winner:* Michael Cart.

Howard R. Marraro Prize. For a distinguished scholarly study on any phase of Italian literature or comparative literature involving Italy. Not awarded in 1983.

Lenore Marshall/Nation Prize. For an outstanding book of poems published in the United States. *Offered by: The Nation* and the New Hope Foundation. *Winner:* George Starbuck for *The Argot Merchant Disaster: Poems New and Selected* (Atlantic/Little).

Somerset Maugham Awards (Great Britain). For young British authors to gain experience in foreign countries. *Offered by:* Society of Authors. *Winner:* Lisa St. Aubin de Teran for *Keepers of the House* (Cape).

Frederic G. Melcher Award. For a work that makes a significant contribution to religious liberalism. *Offered by:* Unitarian Universalist Association. *Winner:* Jonathan Schell for *The Fate of the Earth* (Knopf).

Kenneth W. Mildenberger Medal. For an outstanding research publication in the field of teaching foreign languages and literature. Not awarded in 1983.

Mitchell Prizes. For an outstanding book on the history of art. *Winners:* Hugh Honour and John Fleming for *A World History of Art* (Macmillan—Great Britain), published in the United States as *The Visual Arts: A History* (Prentice-Hall); Keith Christiansen for *Gentile da Fabriano* (Chatto—Great Britain; Cornell Univ.—U.S.).

Mother Goose Award (Great Britain). For children's book illustration. *Offered by:* Books for Your Children Booksellers. *Winner:* Satoshi Kitamura for *Angry Arthur* (Andersen).

Frank Luther Mott-Kappa Tau Alpha Award. For the best researched book dealing with the media. *Offered by:* National Journalism Scholarship Society. *Winner:* John Naisbitt for *Megatrends* (Warner).

National Arts Club Gold Medal of Honor for Literature. *Winner:* James Laughlin.

National Book Critics Circle Awards. *Winners:* (biography/autobiography) Joyce Johnson for *Minor Characters* (Houghton); (criticism) John Updike for *Hugging the Shore* (Knopf); (fiction) William Kennedy for *Ironweed* (Viking); (general nonfiction) Seymour Hersh for *The Price of Power: Kissinger in the Nixon White House* (Simon and Schuster); (poetry) James Merrill for *The Changing Light at Sandover* (Atheneum).

National Catholic Book Awards. For an outstanding religious book. *Offered by:*

Catholic Press Association and Associated Church Press. *Winner:* (children's) David R. Collins for *Thomas Merton: Monk with a Mission*, illus. by Mary Beth Froehlich (St. Anthony Messenger Press); (general) John Welch for *Spiritual Pilgrims: Carl Jung and Teresa of Avila* (Paulist Press); (professional/educational) Adam J. Maida, ed., *Issues in the Labor-Management Dialogue: Church Perspectives* (Catholic Health Assn.); (design and production) Regis J. Armstrong and Ignatius Brady, trans., for *Francis and Clare: The Complete Works* (Paulist Press); Simon Tugwell, ed., for *Early Dominicans: Selected Writings* (Paulist Press).

National Council of Teachers of English Award for Excellence in Scientific and Technical Writing. *Winner:* Carolyn J. Mullins for *The Complete Manuscript Preparation Style Guide* (Prentice-Hall).

Nebula Awards. For outstanding works of science fiction. *Offered by:* Science Fiction Writers of America. *Winners:* (novel) Michael Bishop for *No Enemy but Time* (Timescape); (novella) John Kessel for "Another Orphan" (*Fantasy and Science Fiction*, 9/82); (novelette) Connie Willis for "Fire Watch" (*Isaac Asimov's Science Fiction Magazine*, 2/15/82); (short story) Connie Willis for "A Letter from the Clearys" (*Isaac Asimov's Science Fiction Magazine*, 7/82).

Nene Award. For an outstanding children's book selected by Hawaii's schoolchildren. *Offered by:* Hawaii Association of School Librarians and the Hawaii Library Association Children's and Youth Section. *Winners:* Deborah and James Howe for *Bunnicula: A Rabbit Tale of Mystery* (Atheneum).

Frederic W. Ness Book Award. For a significant contribution to the study of liberal education. *Winner:* Howard R. Bowen for *The State of the Nation and the Agenda for Higher Education* (Jossey-Bass).

Neustadt International Prize for Literature. For distinguished and continuing artistic achievement in poetry, drama, or fiction. *Offered by:* University of Oklahoma. Not awarded in 1983.

New York Academy of Sciences Awards. For quality books about science for children. *Winners:* (younger category) Joanne Rider for *The Snail's Spell*, illus. by Lynne Cherry (Warne); (older category) Judith St. George for *The Brooklyn Bridge* (Putnam); (younger children's reference book) Lerner Natural Science Books.

New York Times Best Illustrated Children's Book Awards. *Winners:* Leonard Baskin for *Leonard Baskin's Miniature Natural History: First Series* (Pantheon); Henrik Drescher for *Simon's Book* (Lothrop); Roy Gerrard for *The Favershams* (Farrar); Ann Jonas for *Round Trip* (Greenwillow); Martin Leman for *Twelve Cats for Christmas* (Pelham/Merrimack); Ken Robbins for *Tools* (Four Winds); Chris Van Allsburg for *The Wreck of the Zephyr* (Houghton); Ed Young for *Up a Tree* (Harper); Lisbeth Zwerger for *Little Red Cap* by the Brothers Grimm (Morrow).

John Newbery Medal. For the most distinguished contribution to literature for children. *Donor:* ALA Association for Library Service to Children. *Medal contributed by:* Daniel Melcher. *Winner:* Cynthia Voigt for *Dicey's Song* (Atheneum).

Nobel Prize for Literature. For the total literary output of a distinguished writer. *Offered by:* Swedish Academy. *Winner:* William Golding (English novelist).

Noma Award for Publishing in Africa (Japan). To encourage publication in Africa of books by African writers. *Winner:* A. N. E. Amissah for *Criminal Procedure in Ghana* (Sedco—Ghana).

Flannery O'Connor Short Fiction Awards. *Offered by:* University of Georgia Press. *Winner:* Sandra Thompson for *Close-Ups* (Univ. of Georgia).

Ohioana Book Awards. To honor Ohio authors. *Offered by:* Ohioana Library Association. *Winners:* (fiction) Helen Hooven Santmyer for "And Ladies of the Club" (Ohio Univ. and Putnam); (history) Lawrence J. Friedman for *Gregarious Saints* (Cambridge Univ.); (Ohio subjects) James Westwater for *Ohio* (Graphic Arts Center); (science) Milton B. Trautman for six books on biological subjects including *The Fishes of Ohio* (Ohio State Univ.).

George Orwell Award. *Offered by:* National Council of Teachers of English. *Winner:* Haig A. Bosmajian for *The Language of Oppression* (Univ. Press of America).

Pegasus Prize for Literature. For an important foreign work from a country whose literature is rarely translated into English. *Offered by:* Mobil Corporation. Not offered in 1983.

PEN American Center and PEN South PEN/Faulkner Award. For outstanding fiction by an American author. *Winner:* Toby Olson for *Seaview* (New Directions).

PEN American Center Awards. Not awarded in 1983.

PEN Los Angeles Center Awards. For writing that exemplifies the principles of freedom of expression. *Winners:* (distinguished body of work) Christopher Isherwood; (first work of fiction) Henry Bean for *False Match* (Poseidon); (first work of poetry) Thomas Dunn for *Passages of Joy* (Farrar); (children's book) Clare Bell for *Ratha's Creature* (Atheneum) and Zilpha Keatley Snider for *The Birds of Summer* (Atheneum).

PEN Translation Prize. For an outstanding book-length translation into English. *Winner:* Richard Wilbur for *Four Comedies* (Molière) (Harcourt).

PEN Writing Awards for Prisoners. To promote literacy and literature in America's prisons. *Winners:* (Malcolm Braly Fiction Prize) Steven Pannell for *A Simple Game of Chance;* (nonfiction) Nicholas Wolf for *Tour San Quentin;* (Muriel Rukeyser Poetry Prize) W. M. Aberg for *Reductions.*

Maxwell Perkins Editors Award. *Offered by:* PEN Los Angeles Center. *Winner:* Barry Gifford.

Maxwell Perkins Prize. For a first work of fiction about the American experience. *Offered by:* Charles Scribner's Sons. *Winner:* Stephen Wright for *Meditations in Green* (Scribner's).

Pfizer Award. For the best book on the history of science. *Offered by:* History of Science Society. *Winner:* Richard S. Westfall for *Never at Rest: A Biography of Isaac Newton* (Cambridge Univ.).

James D. Phelan Award. For an unpublished work of fiction, nonfictional prose, poetry, or drama. *Offered by:* San Francisco Foundation. *Winner:* Gary Young for *A Dream of a Moral Life* (poetry).

Phi Beta Kappa Science Award. *Winner:* Stephen Jay Gould for *Hen's Teeth and Horses' Toes* (Norton).

Pilgrim Award. For a work of outstanding scholarship in science fiction. *Offered by:* Science Fiction Research Association. *Winner:* H. Bruce Franklin.

Edgar Allan Poe Awards. For outstanding mystery, crime, and suspense writing. *Offered by:* Mystery Writers of America. *Winners:* (critical/biographical study) Roy Hoopes for *Cain* (Holt); (fact crime) Richard Hammer for *The Vatican Connection* (Holt); (first novel) Thomas Perry for *The Butcher's Boy* (Scribner's); (novel) Rick Boyer for *Billingsgate Shoal* (Houghton); (paperback) Teri White for *Triangle* (Ace/Charter); (short story) Frederick Forsyth for "There Are No Snakes in Ireland" from *No Comebacks* (Viking); (Grand Master Award) Margaret Millar; (children's mystery) Robbie Branscum for *The Murder of Hound Dog Bates* (Viking).

Renato Poggiolo Translation Awards. For an unpublished translation of a work of Italian literature. *Offered by:* PEN Translation Committee. *Sponsored by:* Arnaldo Mondadori Editore (Milan) and the Ingram Merrill Foundation. *Winners:* Sarah Henry for *Uomini e No (Men and No Others)* by Elio Vittorini and Janice Thresher for *Early Novellas of Giovanni Verga.*

George Polk Memorial Awards. For outstanding achievement in journalism. *Offered by:* Long Island University Department of Journalism. Not awarded in 1983.

Marcia and Louis Posner Award. For children's picture books, to promote an appreciation of Jewish children's literature. *Offered by:* Jewish Book Council. *Winner:* Barbara Cohen for *Yussel's Prayer: A Yom Kippur Story,* illus. by Michael Deraney (Lothrop).

Prix Fémina (France). For an outstanding novel. *Winner:* Florence Delay for *Riche et légère* (Gallimard).

Prix Goncourt (France). For a work of imagination in prose, preferably a novel, exemplifying youth, originality, *esprit,* and form. *Winner:* Frederick Tristan for *Les Egarés* (Balland).

Prix Interallié (France). For a distinguished novel. *Winner:* Jacques Duquesne for *Maria Vandamme* (Grasset).

Prix Médicis (France). To honor experimental fiction written in French. *Winner:* Jean Echenoz for *Cherokee* (Editions de Minuit).

Prix Médicis Étranger (France). For the best foreign novel translated into French. *Winner:* Kenneth White for *La Route Bleue* (Grasset).

Prix Renaudot (France). For a distinguished novel. *Winner:* Jean-Marie Rouart for *Avant-guerre* (Grasset).

PSP Awards. For the most outstanding books in the fields of science, medicine, technology, and business. *Offered by:* Professional and Scholarly Publishing Division, Association of American Publishers. *Winners:* (architecture and ur-

ban planning) Adolf K. Placzek for *Macmillan Encyclopedia of Architects* (Macmillan); (book design and production) Edward C. Papenfuse and Joseph M. Coale III for *The Hammond-Harwood House Atlas of Historical Maps of Maryland, 1608–1908* (Johns Hopkins Univ.); (business, management, and economics) William O. Cleverley, ed., for *Handbook of Health Care Accounting and Finance* (Aspen Systems); (engineering) Gabriel Salvendy, ed., for *Handbook of Industrial Engineering* (Wiley); (health sciences) Marvin Wagner and Thomas L. Lawson for *Segmental Anatomy: Applications to Clinical Medicine* (Macmillan); (humanities) Charlotte Streifer Rubinstein for *American Women Artists: From Early Indian Times to the Present* (Hall); (law) Richard A. Givens, ed., for *Legal Strategies for Industrial Innovation* (Shepard's/McGraw-Hill); (life sciences) Ernst Mayr for *The Growth of Biological Thought: Diversity, Evolution, and Inheritances* (Harvard Univ.); (physical and earth sciences) Gerard R. Case for *A Pictorial Guide to Fossils* (Van Nostrand); (social and behavioral sciences) Stanley H. Cath, Alan R. Gurwitt, and John Munder Ross for *Father and Child: Developmental and Clinical Perspectives* (Little, Brown); (technology) Carl H. Meyer and Stephen M. Matyas for *Cryptography: A New Dimension in Computer Data Security* (Wiley); (new project) Linda Schele for *Maya Slyphs: The Verbs* (Univ. of Texas).

Pulitzer Prizes in Letters. To honor distinguished works by American writers, dealing preferably with American themes. *Winners:* (biography) Russell Baker for *Growing Up* (Congdon & Weed); (fiction) Alice Walker for *The Color Purple* (Harcourt); (general nonfiction) Susan Sheehan for *Is There No Place on Earth for Me?* (Houghton); (history) Rhys L. Isaac for *The Transformation of Virginia, 1740–1790* Univ. of North Carolina); (poetry) Galway Kinnell for *Selected Poems* (Houghton).

Pushcart Press Editors' Book Award. For an unpublished book of exceptional quality. *Winner:* Frank Stiffel for *The Tale of the Ring: A Kaddish* (Pushcart).

Gregory Rabassa Prize. *Offered by:* American Literary Translators Association and the University of Missouri. *Winner:* Margaret Kidder Ewing for *A Night in the Forest* by Blaise Cendrars (Univ. of Missouri).

Trevor Reese Memorial Prize (Great Britain). For the best scholarly book published in Great Britain in the field of British Imperial and Commonwealth history. *Offered by:* University of London Institute of Commonwealth Studies. Not awarded in 1983.

Regina Medal. For excellence in the writing of literature for children. *Offered by:* Catholic Library Association. *Winner:* Tomie De Paola.

Howard U. Ribalow Prize. To honor the best work of fiction on a Jewish theme. *Offered by:* Hadassah Magazine. *Winner:* Chaim Grade for *Rabbis and Wives* (Knopf).

Richard and Hilda Rosenthal Foundation Award. For a work of fiction that is a considerable literary achievement though not necessarily a commercial success. *Offered by:* American Academy and Institute of Arts and Letters. *Winner:* A. G. Mojtabai for *Autumn* (Houghton).

David H. Russell Award. *Offered by:* National Council of Teachers of English. *Winner:* Margaret Donaldson for *Children's Minds* (Norton).

Ralph Coats Roe Award. For a work that contributes toward better public understanding and appreciation of the engineer's worth in contemporary society. *Offered by:* American Society of Mechanical Engineers. *Winner:* Tracy Kidder for *The Soul of a New Machine* (Little, Brown).

Carl Sandburg Awards. For exceptional achievement in literature by Chicago area writers. *Offered by:* Friends of the Chicago Public Library. *Winners:* (fiction) Harry Mark Petrakis for *Days of Vengeance* (Doubleday); (nonfiction) Louise B. Young for *The Blue Planet* (Little, Brown); (poetry) Sterling Plumpp for *The Mojo Hands Call, I Must Go* (Thunder Mouth Press); (children's books) Mildred Johnson for *Wait, Skates!* (Children's Press).

Delmore Schwartz Memorial Poetry Award. *Offered by:* New York University College of Arts and Science. Not awarded in 1983.

Scribner's Crime Novel Award. *Winner:* Ted Wood for *Dead in the Water* (Scribner's).

Seal Books Award (Canada). For an outstanding first novel. *Winners:* David Kendall for *Lázaro* (McClelland and Stewart/Seal Books) and Jonathan Webb for *Pluck* (McClelland and Stewart/Seal Books).

Mina P. Shaughnessy Medal. For an outstanding research publication in the field of teaching English language and literature. *Winners:* Marie Ponsot and Rosemary Deen for *Beat Not the Poor Desk: Writing—What to Teach, How to Teach It and Why* (Boynton/Cook).

Shelley Memorial Award for Poetry. *Offered by:* Poetry Society of America. *Winners:* Jon Anderson and Leo Connellan.

Kenneth B. Smilen/Present Tense Literary Awards. To honor authors and translators of works that have intrinsic value and lasting quality and reflect humane Jewish values. *Offered by:* American Jewish Committee. *Winners:* (biography/autobiography) Elisabeth Young-Bruehl for *Hannah Arendt: For Love of the World* (Yale Univ.); (fiction) Aharon Meggedd for *Asahel* (Taplinger); (general nonfiction) Thérèse Metzger and Mendel Metzger for *Jewish Life in the Middle Ages* (Alpine); (history) David

Vital for *Zionism: The Formative Years* (Oxford Univ.); (contribution to Jewish Literature) Gabriel Preil; (social and political analysis) Stephen Sharot for *Messianism, Mysticism and Magic* (Univ. of North Carolina); (translation) Stephen Mitchell for *Points of Departure* (Yale Univ.); (special citation) Chaim Potok, representing the committee, on completion of the new translation of the Hebrew Bible; (children's book) Barbara Cohen for *King of the Seventh Grade* (Lothrop).

John Ben Snow Prize. For an outstanding nonfiction manuscript dealing with some aspect of New York State. *Offered by:* Syracuse University Press. *Winner:* Mary Ann Smith for *Gustav Stickley, the Craftsman* (Syracuse Univ.)

Society of Children's Book Writers Golden Kite Awards. *Winners:* (fiction) Beverly Cleary for *Ralph S. Mouse* (Morrow); (nonfiction) James Giblin for *Chimney Sweeps* (Clarion); (illustration) Tomie De Paola for *Marianna May and Nursey* (Holiday House).

Society of Midland Authors Awards. For outstanding books about the Midwest or by Midwest authors. *Winners:* (biography) Richard Dunlop for *Donovan: America's Master Spy* (Rand McNally); (fiction) Susan Engberg for *Pastorale* (Univ. of Illinois); (nonfiction) Robert Pisor for *The End of the Line—The Siege of Khe Sanh* (Norton); (poetry) Carolyn Forché for *The Country between Us* (Harper); (career of literary excellence) Studs Terkel; (children's book) Patricia DeMuth for *Joel Growing Up a Farm Man* (Dodd).

Southern California Council on Literature for Children and Young People Award. *Winners:* (fiction) Patricia Beatty for *Jonathan Down Under* (Morrow); (nonfiction) Ann Elwood and Linda Wood for *Windows in Space* (Walker); (series) Tom Bethancourt for *Doris Fein Mysteries* (Holiday House); (cultural signifi-

cance) Clayton Bess for *Story for a Black Night* (Houghton).

Agnes Lynch Starrett Poetry Prize. *Offered by:* University of Pittsburgh Press. *Winner:* Kate Daniels for *The White Wave* (Univ. of Pittsburgh).

Texas Bluebonnet Award. *Offered by:* Texas Association of School Librarians and Children's Round Table of the Texas Library Association. *Winner:* Bill Wallace for *A Dog Called Kitty* (Holiday House).

Texas Institute of Letters Special Award. For continuing excellence in Texas letters. *Winners:* John Graves and Glen Rose.

Theatre Library Association Award. For the outstanding book in the field of motion pictures and broadcasting. *Winners:* Jay Leyda and Zina Voynow for *Eisenstein at Work* (Pantheon/MOMA); (honorable mention) Thomas Nelson for *Kubrick: Inside a Film Artist's Maze* (Indiana Univ.).

Thomas Thompson Nonfiction Book Award. *Winner:* Tom Reiterman for *Raven: The Untold Story of the Reverend Jim Jones and His People* (Dutton).

Travelling Scholarships (Great Britain). To enable British writers to travel. *Winners:* Rosemary Dinnage and Richard Holmes.

University of Southern Mississippi School of Library Service Silver Medallion. *Winner:* Katherine Paterson.

Voertman's Poetry Award. *See* Daedalean Poetry Award.

Harold D. Vursell Memorial Award. *Offered by:* American Academy and Institute of Arts and Letters. *Winner:* Jonathan D. Spence for *The Gate of Heavenly Peace* (Viking/Penguin).

Washington Post/Children's Book Guild Nonfiction Award. *Winner:* Patricia Lauber.

Wattie Book of the Year (New Zealand). *Offered by:* Book Publishers Association of New Zealand. *Winner:* Janet Frame for *To the Is-land* (Hutchinson).

Western Heritage Awards. For writing of artistic quality that accurately depicts the West. *Offered by:* National Cowboy Hall of Fame and the Western Heritage Center. *Winners:* (art book) William Albert Allard Award for *Vanishing Breed: Photographs of the Cowboy and the West* (New York Graphic Society/ Little, Brown); (magazine article) Patricia Nell Warren for "Saga of an American Ranch" (*Reader's Digest*); (non-fiction book) Margaret F. Maxwell for *A Passion for Freedom: The Life of Sharlot Hall* (Univ. of Arizona).

Whitbread Literary Awards (Great Britain). For literature of merit that is readable on a wide scale. *Offered by:* Booksellers Association of Great Britain. *Winners:* (novel) William Trevor for *Fools of Fortune* (Bodley Head); (first novel) John Fuller for *Flying to Nowhere* (Salamander); (biography) Victoria Glendinning for *Vita: The Life of V. Sackville-West* (Weidenfeld) and Kenneth Rose for *King George V* (Weidenfeld); (children's novel) Roald Dahl for *The Witches* (Cape).

William Allen White Children's Book Award. *Winner:* Barbara Brooks Wallace for *Peppermints in the Parlor* (Atheneum).

Walt Whitman Award. For an American poet who has not yet published a book of poems. *Winner:* Christopher Gilbert for *Across the Mutual Landscape* (Graywolf).

Richard Wilbur Prize for Poetry. *Offered by:* American Literary Translators Association and University of Missouri. *Winner:* Sandra Reyes for *Sermons and Homilies of the Christ of Elqui* by Nicanor Parra (Univ. of Missouri).

Laura Ingalls Wilder Medal. *Offered by:* American Library Association. *Winner:* Maurice Sendak.

Thornton Wilder Prize. For a distinguished translation of contemporary American literature into foreign languages. *Offered by:* Columbia University Translation Center. *Winner:* Rita Rait.

William Carlos Williams Award. For a book of poetry published by a small press, nonprofit press, or university press. *Offered by:* Poetry Society of America. *Winner:* David Wojahn for *Icehouse Lights* (Yale Univ.).

H. W. Wilson Indexing Award. *Offered by:* American Society of Indexers. Not awarded in 1983.

H. W. Wingate Awards (Great Britain). For fiction or nonfiction that stimulates an awareness of Jewish interest. *Winners:* Chaim Herzog for *The Arab-Israeli Wars* (Arms & Armour Press) and Chaim Raphael for *The Springs of Jewish Life* (Chatto and Windus).

Laurence L. Winship Book Award. For a book having some relation to New England. *Offered by:* Boston Globe. *Winner:* Cynthia Zaitzevsky for *Frederick Law Olmstead and the Boston Park System* (Harvard Univ.).

Nero Wolfe Award for Mystery Fiction. *Offered by:* The Wolfe Pack. *Winner:* Martha Grimes for *The Anodyne Necklace* (Little, Brown).

Workmen's Circle Award for Yiddish Literature. *Winners:* Chaim Spilberg and Yaacov Zipper for *Canadian Jewish Anthology* (National Committee on Yiddish of the Canadian Jewish Congress).

World Fantasy Convention Awards. *Winners:* (anthology) Charles L. Grant, ed., for *Nightmare Seasons* (Doubleday); (life achievement) Roald Dahl; (novel) Michael Shea for *Nifft the Lean* (Daw); (novella) Karl Edward Wagner for "Beyond All Measure" (*Whispers* 15/16); (short story) Tanith Lee for "The Gorgon" (*Shadows* 5).

World Science Fiction Convention Hugo Awards. For outstanding science fiction writing. *Winners:* (novel) Isaac Asimov for *Foundation's Edge* (Doubleday); (novella) Joanna Russ for "Souls" (*Fantasy and Science Fiction*, 1/82); (novelette) Connie Willis for "Fire Watch" (*Isaac Asimov's SF Magazine*, 2/15/82); (nonfiction) James Gunn for *Isaac Asimov: The Foundations of Science Fiction* (Oxford Univ.); (short story) Spider Robinson for "Melancholy Elephants" (*Analog*, 6/82).

Yale Series of Younger Poets Award. *Winner:* Richard Kenney for *The Evolution of the Flightless Bird* (Yale Univ.).

Morton Dauwen Zabel Award. *Offered by:* American Academy and Institute of Arts and Letters. *Winner:* Judy Blume for *Superfudge* (Dutton).

Notable Books of 1983

This is the thirty-seventh year in which this list of distinguished books has been issued by the Notable Books Council of the Reference and Adult Services Division of the American Library Association.

Bradford, Sarah. *Disraeli.* Stein & Day.

Bricktop, with James Haskins. *Bricktop.* Atheneum.

Carver, Raymond. *Cathedral: Stories.* Knopf.

Chase, Joan. *During the Reign of the Queen of Persia: A Novel.* Harper.

Chatwin, Bruce. *On the Black Hill.* Viking.

Clampitt, Amy. *The Kingfisher: Poems.* Knopf.

Didion, Joan. *Salvador.* Simon & Schuster.

Drew, Elizabeth. *Politics and Money: The New Road to Corruption.* Macmillan.

Dubus, Andre. *The Times Are Never So Bad: A Novella & Eight Short Stories.* Godine.

Egerton, John. *Generations: An American Family.* University Press of Kentucky.

Fossey, Dian. *Gorillas in the Mist.* Houghton.

Gage, Nicholas. *Eleni.* Random.

García Márquez, Gabriel. *Chronicle of a Death Foretold.* Translated from the Spanish by Gregory Rabassa. Knopf.

Heat Moon, William Least. *Blue Highways: A Journey into America.* Little/Atlantic.

Helprin, Mark. *Winter's Tale.* Harcourt.

Hersh, Seymour M. *The Price of Power: Kissinger in the Nixon White House.* Summit.

Hilts, Philip J. *Scientific Temperaments: Three Lives in Contemporary Science.* Simon & Schuster.

Isaacs, Arnold R. *Without Honor: Defeat in Vietnam and Cambodia.* Johns Hopkins University Press.

Jensen, Robert, and Patricia Conway. *Ornamentalism: The New Decorativeness in Architecture & Design.* Potter.

Kennedy, William. *Ironweed: A Novel.* Viking.

Lamb, David. *The Africans.* Random.

LeVot, André. *F. Scott Fitzgerald: A Biography.* Translated from the French by William Byron. Doubleday.

Liang, Heng, and Judith Shapiro. *Son of the Revolution.* Knopf.

Loewinsohn, Ron. *Magnetic Field(s): A Novel.* Knopf.

McElvaine, Robert S., ed. *Down & Out in the Great Depression: Letters from the "Forgotten Man."* University of North Carolina Press.

MacLaverty, Bernard. *Cal.* Braziller.

Malamud, Bernard. *The Stories of Bernard Malamud.* Farrar.

Murdoch, Iris. *The Philosopher's Pupil.* Viking.

Page, Joseph A. *Perón: A Biography.* Random.

Pancake, Breece D'J. *The Stories of Breece D'J Pancake.* Little/Atlantic.

Parry, Linda. *William Morris Textiles.* Viking.

Petrosky, Anthony. *Jurgis Petraskas: Poems.* Louisiana State University Pr.

Porter, Eliot. *All under Heaven: The Chinese World.* Text by Jonathan Porter. Pantheon.

Radosh, Ronald, and Joyce Milton. *The Rosenberg File: A Search for the Truth.* Holt.

Rockwell, John. *All American Music: Composition in the Late Twentieth Century.* Knopf.

Rushdie, Salman. *Shame.* Knopf.

Silverman, Jonathan. *For the World to See: The Life of Margaret Bourke-White.* Viking.

Song, Cathy. *Picture Bride.* Yale University Press.

Theroux, Paul. *The London Embassy.* Houghton.

Updike, John. *Hugging the Shore: Essays and Criticism.* Knopf.

Warner, William W. *Distant Water: The Fate of the North Atlantic Fisherman.* Little/Atlantic.

Wideman, John Edgar. *Sent for You Yesterday.* Avon.

Wilcox, Fred A. *Waiting for an Army to Die: The Tragedy of Agent Orange.* Random.

Wright, Stephen. *Meditations in Green.* Scribner.

Best Young Adult Books of 1983

Each year a committee of the Young Adult Services Division of the American Library Association compiles a list of best books for young adults selected on the basis of young adult appeal. These titles must meet acceptable standards of library merit and provide a variety of subjects for different tastes and a broad range of reading levels. *School Library Journal (SLJ)* also provides a list of best books for young adults. This year the list was compiled by *SLJ*'s young adult review committee, which is chaired by Ron Brown, young adult specialist at Boston Public Library, and made up of public and school librarians in the greater Boston Area. The *SLJ* list was published in the December 1983 issue of the journal. The following list combines the titles selected for both lists. The notation ALA or *SLJ* following the price indicates the source of titles chosen.

Adler, C. S. *The Shell Lady's Daughter.* Coward-McCann. pap. $10.95. ALA.

Arrick, Fran. *God's Radar.* Bradbury. $10.95. ALA.

Asimov, Isaac, ed. *Creations.* Crown. $16.95. ALA.

Bell, Clare. *Ratha's Creature.* Atheneum. $11.95. ALA.

Binchey, Maeve. *Light a Penny Candle.* Viking. $17.75. *SLJ.*

Boulle, Pierre. *The Whale of the Victoria Cross.* Vanguard. $12.95. ALA.

Briggs, Raymond. *When the Wind Blows.* Schocken. $10.95. ALA.

Brown, Dee. *Killdeer Mountain.* Holt. $14.45. *SLJ.*

Chambers, Aidan. *Dance on My Grave.* Harper. $12.89. ALA.

Chernin, Kim. *In My Mother's House: A Daughter's Story.* Clarion. $14.95. *SLJ.*

Coney, Michael. *The Celestial Steam Locomotive.* Houghton. $13.95. *SLJ.*

Cormier, Robert. *The Bumblebee Flies Anyway.* Pantheon. $10.95. ALA.

Costello, Elaine. *Signing: How to Speak with Your Hands.* Illustrated by Lois A. Lehman. Bantam. pap. $8.95. *SLJ.*

Crutcher, Chris. *Running Loose.* Greenwillow/Morrow. $9. ALA.

Eriksenn, Eric, and Els Sincebaugh. *Adventures in Closeup Photography: Rediscovering Familiar Environments through Details.* Amphoto/Watson-Guptill. $24.50. *SLJ.*

Faber, Doris. *Love & Rivalry.* Viking. $13.95. ALA.

Ferry, Charles. *Raspberry One.* Houghton. $10.95. ALA.

Fretz, Sada. *Going Vegetarian: A Guide for Teenagers.* Morrow. $11. ALA.

Gaan, Margaret. *Little Sister.* Dodd, Mead. $13.95. ALA.

Gaines, Ernest J. *A Gathering of Old Men.* Knopf. $13.95. ALA.

Geras, Adele. *Voyage.* Atheneum. $10.95. ALA.

Gold, Gerald. *Gandhi: A Pictorial Biography.* Newmarket. $16.95. pap. $9.95. *SLJ.*

Golden, Frederic. *The Trembling Earth: Probing and Predicting Quakes.* Scribner. $13.95. ALA.

Goldman, Peter, and Tony Fuller. *Charlie Company: What Vietnam Did to Us.* Morrow. $15.95. ALA.

Gordon, Suzanne. *Off Balance: The Real World of Ballet.* Pantheon. $15.95. ALA.

Greenberg, Joanne. *The Far Side of Victory.* Holt. $14.45. ALA.

Hamilton, Virginia. *The Magical Adventures of Pretty Pearl.* Harper. $11.89. ALA.

Harrington, John W. *Dance of the Continents: Adventures with Rocks and Time.* Tarcher, distributed by Houghton. $15. pap. $9.50. *SLJ.*

Hayden, Torey L. *Murphy's Boy.* Putnam. $13.95. ALA, *SLJ.*

Heidish, Marcy. *The Secret Annie Oakley.* Daw. $14.95. ALA.

Holman, Felice. *The Wild Children.* Scribner. $11.95. ALA.

Hughes, Monica. *Hunter in the Dark.* Atheneum. $9.95. ALA.

Janeczko, Paul, ed. *Poetspeak: In Their Work, About Their Work.* Bradbury. $12.95. ALA.

Jordan, Ruth. *Daughter of the Waves: Memories of Growing Up in Pre-War Palestine.* Taplinger. $12.95. *SLJ.*

Kerr, M. E. *Me Me Me Me Me: Not a Novel.* Harper. $9.89. ALA.

Korschunow, Irina. *A Night in Distant Motion.* Translated from the German by Leigh Hafrey. Godine $10.95. ALA.

Krementz, Jill. *How It Feels to Be Adopted.* Knopf. $11.95. ALA.

Lasky, Kathryn. *Beyond the Divide.* Macmillan. $11.95. ALA.

Lee, Tanith. *Red as Blood.* Daw. pap. $2.50. ALA.

Liang, Heng, and Judith Shapiro. *Son of the Revolution.* Knopf. $15. ALA.

McGuire, Paula. *It Won't Happen to Me: Teenagers Talk about Pregnancy.* Delacorte. $6.95. ALA.

Madaras, Lynda. *What's Happening to My Body? A Growing Up Guide for Mothers and Daughters.* Newmarket. $14.95. pap. $7.95. ALA.

Martin, David. *The Road to Ballyshannon.* St. Martin's. $10.95. *SLJ.*

Mason, Robert C. *Chickenhawk.* Viking. $17.75. ALA.

Mazer, Norma Fox. *Someone to Love.* Delacorte. $13.95. ALA.

Newton, Suzanne. *I Will Call It Georgie's Blues.* Viking. $11.95. ALA.

Nicholls, Peter, and David Langford, eds. *The Science in Science Fiction.* Knopf. $14.95. ALA, *SLJ.*

Oberski, Jona. *Childhood.* Translated from Dutch by Ralph Manheim. Doubleday. $11.95. *SLJ.*

Page, Tim. *Tim Page's Nam.* Knopf. $25. pap. $14.95. ALA, *SLJ.*

Paulsen, Gary. *Dancing Carl.* Bradbury. $9.95. ALA.

Peck, Richard. *This Family of Women.* Delacorte. $15.95. *SLJ.*

Pollock, Dale. *Skywalking: The Life and*

Times of George Lucas. Harmony/ Crown. $14.95. ALA.

Pray, Lawrence M. *Journey of a Diabetic.* Illustrated by Richard Evans. Simon & Schuster. $14.95. *SLJ.*

Reese, Lyn, ed. *I'm on My Way Running: Woman Speak on Coming of Age.* Avon. $4.95. ALA.

Richards, Arlene Kramer, and Irene Willis. *What to Do if You or Someone You Know Is Under 18 and Pregnant.* Lothrop. $9.55. pap. $7. ALA.

Rushing, Jane Gilmore. *Winds of Blame.* Doubleday. $14.95. *SLJ.*

Santiago, Danny. *Famous All over Town.* Simon & Schuster. $14.95. ALA, *SLJ.*

Sargent, Pamela. *Earthseed.* Harper & Row. $10.95. pap. $6.95. ALA.

Severin, Tim. *The Sindbad Voyage.* Putnam. $17.95. ALA.

Singer, Marilyn. *The Course of True Love Never Did Run Smooth.* Harper. $10.95. ALA.

Skurzynski, Gloria. *The Tempering.* Clarion. $11.50. ALA.

Slepian, Jan. *The Night of the Bozos.* Dutton. $10.95. ALA.

Smith, Robert Kimmel. *Jane's House.* Morrow. $13.95. ALA.

Smith, Rukshana. *Sumitra's Story.* Coward-McCann. $9.95. ALA.

Speare, Elizabeth. *The Sign of the Beaver.* Houghton. $8.95. ALA.

Steinem, Gloria. *Outrageous Acts and Everyday Rebellions.* Holt. $14.95. ALA.

Sutcliff, Rosemary. *The Road to Camlann: The Death of King Arthur.* Dutton. $11.50. ALA.

Tevis, Walter. *The Queen's Gambit.* Random. $13.95. ALA.

Thomas, Lewis. *The Youngest Science.* Viking. $15.95. ALA.

Trull, Patti. *On with My Life.* Putnam. pap. $9.95. ALA.

Ure, Jean. *See You Thursday.* Delacorte. $12.95. ALA.

Van Devanter, Lynda. *Home before Morning: The Story of an Army Nurse in Vietnam.* Beaufort. $16.95. ALA.

Voigt, Cynthia. *Solitary Blue.* Atheneum. $10.95. ALA.

Von Canon, Claudia. *The Inheritance.* Houghton. $10.95. ALA.

Wilcox, Fred A. *Waiting for an Army to Die: The Tragedy of Agent Orange.* Random. pap. $6.95. ALA.

Willey, Margaret. *The Bigger Book of Lydia.* Harper. $11.95. ALA.

Best Children's Books of 1983

A list of notable children's books is selected each year by the Notable Children's Books Committee of the Association for Library Service to Children of the American Library Association (ALA). The committee is aided by suggestions from school and public children's librarians throughout the United States. The book review editors of *School Library Journal* (*SLJ*) also compile a list each year, with full annotations, of best books for children. The following list is a combination of ALA's Notable Children's Books of 1983 and *SLJ*'s selection of "Best Books 1983," published in the December 1983 issue of *SLJ*. The source of each selection is indicated by the notation ALA or *SLJ* following each entry. [See the article "Literary Prizes" for Newbery, Caldecott, and other award winners—*Ed.*]

Adkins, Jan. *A Storm without Rain: A Novel in Time.* Little, Brown. $12.95. ALA.

Ahlberg, Janet, and Allan Ahlberg. *The Baby's Catalogue.* Atlantic Monthly Press. $10.50. ALA, *SLJ.*

Aliki. *A Medieval Feast.* Crowell. $9.95. *SLJ.*

Anno, Masaiciro, and Matsumasa Anno. *Anno's Mysterious Multiplying Jar.* Illus. by Mitsumasa Anno. Philomel. $10.95. ALA.

Arnosky, Jim. *Secrets of a Wildlife Watcher.* Lothrop. $10. ALA.

Ashabranner, Brent. *The New Americans: Changing Patterns in U.S. Immigration.* Photos by Paul Conklin. Dodd, Mead. $13.95. ALA.

Bang, Molly. *Ten, Nine, Eight.* Greenwillow. $10.50. ALA, *SLJ.*

Bellairs, John. *The Mummy, the Will, and the Crypt.* Maps by Edward Gorey. Dial. $11.95. *SLJ.*

Bierhorst, John, ed. *The Sacred Path: Spells, Prayers and Power Songs of the American Indians.* Morrow. $9.50. ALA.

Branley, Franklyn N. *Saturn: The Spectacular Planet.* Illus. by Leonard Kessler. Crowell. $11.95. *SLJ.*

Brittain, Bill. *The Wish Giver: Three Tales of Coven Tree.* Illus. by Andrew Glass. Harper. $9.95. ALA, *SLJ.*

Brooks, Polly Schoyer. *Queen Eleanor: Independent Spirit of the Medieval World—A Biography of Eleanor of Aquitaine.* Lippincott. $9.95. ALA, *SLJ.*

Cassedy, Sylvia. *Behind the Attic Wall.* Crowell. $11.95. ALA, *SLJ.*

Ceserani, Gian Paolo. *Grand Constructions.* Illus. by Piero Ventura. Putnam. $12.95. *SLJ.*

Cleary, Beverly. *Dear Mr. Henshaw.* Illus. by Paul O. Zelinsky. Morrow. $8.50. ALA, *SLJ.*

Cleaver, Vera, and Bill Cleaver. *Hazel Rye.* Lippincott. $11.89. ALA.

Cole, Joanna. *Bony-Legs.* Illus. by Dirk Zimmer. Four Winds. $8.95. ALA, *SLJ.*

———. *Cars and How They Go.* Illus. by Gail Gibbons. Crowell. $9.89. ALA, *SLJ.*

Conford, Ellen. *Lenny Kandell, Smart Aleck.* Illus. by Walter Gaffney-Kessell. Little, Brown. $9.50. *SLJ.*

Cooper, Susan, *The Silver Cow: A Welsh Tale.* Illus. by Warwick Hutton. Atheneum. $11.95. ALA, *SLJ.*

Corbett, W. J. *The Song of Pentecost.* Illus. by Martin Ursell. Dutton. $10.63. *SLJ.*

Cormier, Robert. *The Bumblebee Flies Anyway.* Pantheon. $10.95. ALA, *SLJ.*

Dahl, Roald. *The Witches.* Illus. by Quentin Blake. Farrar, Straus. $10.95. ALA.

dePaola, Tomie. *Sing, Pierrot, Sing: A Picture Book in Mime.* Harcourt. $11.95. *SLJ.*

Dubanevich, Arlene. *Pigs in Hiding.* Four Winds. $10.95. *SLJ.*

Ferry, Charles. *Raspberry One.* Houghton. $8.95. *SLJ.*

Fischer-Nagel, Heiderose, and Andreas Fischer-Nagel. *A Kitten Is Born.* Trans. from German by Andrea Mernan. Putnam. $9.95. *SLJ.*

Fritz, Jean. *The Double Life of Pocahontas.* Illus. by Ed Young. Putnam. $9.95. ALA, *SLJ.*

Froehlick, Margaret Walden. *Hide Crawford Quick.* Houghton. $9.95. ALA.

Garfield, Leon. *Fair's Fair.* Illus. by S. D. Schindler. Doubleday. $10.95. *SLJ.*

Greer, Gery, and Bob Ruddick. *Max and Me and the Time Machine.* Harcourt. $11.95. *SLJ.*

Griffith, Helen V. *More Alex and the Cat.* Illus. by Donald Carrick. Greenwillow. $8.95. *SLJ.*

Grimm Brothers. *The Devil with the Three Golden Hairs.* Retold and illus. by Nonny Hogrogian. Knopf. $10.95. *SLJ.*

———. *Little Red Riding Hood.* Retold and illus. by Trina Schart Hyman. Holiday House. $13.95. ALA.

Hahn, Mary Downing. *Daphne's Book.* Clarion. $10.95. *SLJ.*

Hamilton, Virginia. *The Magical Adventures of Pretty Pearl.* Harper. $11.50. ALA.

———. *Willie Bea and the Time the Mar-*

tians Landed. Greenwillow. $11.50. ALA.

Hancock, Sibyl. *Esteban and the Ghost.* Illus. by Dirk Zimmer. Dial. $10.95. ALA.

Herbst, Judith. *Sky Above and Worlds Beyond.* Photos by George Lovi. Atheneum. $13.95. *SLJ.*

Hoban, Tana. *Round and Round and Round.* Greenwillow. $9.50. ALA.

Hoguet, Susan Ramsay. *I Unpacked My Grandmother's Trunk: A Picture Book Game.* Dutton. $9.95. *SLJ.*

Hopkins, Lee Bennett. *The Sky Is Full of Song.* Illus. by Dirk Zimmer. Harper. $9.95. *SLJ.*

Hopkins, Lee Bennett, selector. *A Song in Stone: City Poems.* Photos by Anna Held Audette. Crowell. $9.95. ALA.

Hughes, Shirley. *Alfie's Feet.* Lothrop. $8.50. ALA.

Hurwitz, Johanna. *Rip-Roaring Russell.* Illus. by Lillian Hoban. Morrow. $8.50. ALA.

Janeczko, Paul B., selector. *Poetspeak: In Their Work, about Their Work.* Bradbury. $12.95. *SLJ.*

Jaspersohn, William. *Magazine: Behind the Scenes at Sports Illustrated.* Little, Brown. $12.95. *SLJ.*

Jonas, Ann. *Round Trip.* Greenwillow. $8.50. ALA.

Jukes, Mavis. *No One Is Going to Nashville.* Illus. by Lloyd Bloom. Knopf. $8.95. *SLJ.*

Kidd, Ronald. *Sizzle and Splat.* Lodestar. $10.95. *SLJ.*

Kipling, Rudyard. *The Elephant's Child.* Illus. by Lorinda Bryan Cauley. Harcourt. $12.95. *SLJ.*

Korschunow, Irina. *A Night in Distant Motion.* Trans. from German by Leigh Hafrey. Godine. $10.95. *SLJ.*

Larrick, Nancy. *When the Dark Comes Dancing—A Bedtime Poetry Book.* Illus. by John Wallner. Philomel. $15.95. ALA.

Lasky, Kathryn. *Sugaring Time.* Photos by Christopher G. Knight. Macmillan. $10.95. ALA.

Lerner, Carol. *Pitcher Plants—The Elegant Insect Traps.* Morrow. $11. ALA.

Lindgren, Astrid. *Ronia, the Robber's Daughter.* Trans. by Patricia Compton. Viking. $12.50. ALA.

Lindgren, Barbro. *Sam's Bath.* Illus. by Eva Eriksson. Morrow. $5.50. ALA.

———. *The Wild Baby Goes to Sea.* Adapt. from Swedish by Jack Prelutsky. Illus. by Eva Eriksson. Greenwillow. $9. *SLJ.*

Lobel, Arnold. *The Book of Pigericks—Pig Limericks.* Harper. $9.95. ALA.

Longfellow, Henry Wadsworth. *Hiawatha.* Illus. by Susan Jeffers. Dial. $11.95. *SLJ.*

Lowry, Lois. *The One Hundredth Thing about Caroline.* Houghton. $8.95. ALA.

Lunn, Janet. *The Root Cellar.* Scribner's. $12.95. ALA, *SLJ.*

Mabey, Richard. *Oak & Company.* Illus. by Clare Roberts. Greenwillow. $9. *SLJ.*

Macaulay, David. *Mill.* Houghton. $14.95. ALA, *SLJ.*

Marshak, Samuel. *The Month-Brothers: A Slavic Tale.* Trans. from Russian by Thomas P. Whitney. Illus. by Diane Stanley. Morrow. $10.95. *SLJ.*

Oxenbury, Helen. *The Dancing Class.* Dial. $5.95. ALA.

Porte, Barbara Ann. *Harry's Visit.* Illus. by Yossi Abolafia. Greenwillow. $7. ALA.

Prelutsky, Jack, selector. *The Random House Book of Poetry for Children.* Illus. by Arnold Lobel. Random. $13.95. ALA, *SLJ.*

Provensen, Alice, and Martin Provensen. *The Glorious Flight across the Channel with Louis Blériot.* Viking. $12.95. ALA, *SLJ.*

Ritter, Lawrence S. *The Story of Baseball.* Morrow. $12, pap. $8. ALA, *SLJ.*

Rosenberg, Maxine B. *My Friend Leslie: The Story of a Handicapped Child.*

Illus. by George Ancona. Lothrop. $9.50. ALA.

Sancha, Sheila. *The Luttrell Village: Country Life in the Middle Ages.* Crowell. $12.95. ALA, *SLJ.*

Schwartz, Alvin. *Unriddling.* Illus. by Sue Truesdell. Lippincott. $9.95. ALA.

Skurzynski, Gloria. *The Tempering.* Clarion. $10.95. *SLJ.*

Sleator, William. *Fingers.* Atheneum. $10.95. *SLJ.*

Slepian, Jan. *The Night of the Bozos.* Dutton. $10.95. ALA.

Smith, Doris Buchanan. *The First Hard Times.* Viking. $10.95. ALA.

Speare, Elizabeth George. *The Sign of the Beaver.* Houghton. $8.95. ALA, *SLJ.*

Stevenson, James. *What's under My Bed?* Greenwillow. $10.50. ALA, *SLJ.*

Tafuri, Nancy. *Early Morning in the Barn.* Greenwillow. $10.95. *SLJ.*

Uchida, Yoshiko. *The Best Bad Thing.* Atheneum. $9.95. ALA, *SLJ.*

Van Allsburg, Chris. *The Wreck of the Zephyr.* Houghton. $14.95. ALA.

Van Leeuwen, Jean. *Tales of Amanda Pig.* Illus. by Ann Schwinger. Dial. $8.89. ALA.

Voigt, Cynthia. *A Solitary Blue.* Atheneum. $10.95. ALA.

Wangerin, Walter, Jr. *Thistle.* Harper. $8.95. *SLJ.*

Williams, Vera B. *Something Special for Me.* Greenwillow. $10. *SLJ.*

Wolkstein, Diane. *The Magic Wings: A Tale from China.* Illus. by Robert Andrew Parker. $10.95. *SLJ.*

Wrightson, Patricia. *A Little Fear.* Atheneum. $9.95. ALA.

Bestsellers of 1983: Hardcover Fiction and Nonfiction

Daisy Maryles

Senior Staff Editor, *Publishers Weekly*

Hardcover book sales in 1983, at least for bestsellers, continued to rack up impressive numbers, always matching last year's record-breaking figures and in some cases establishing new sales records.

Once again all of the top 25 novels boasted sales of over 100,000 and a few fiction titles with sales just into the six-figure mark didn't even make the list of top sellers.

In nonfiction, each of the top 10 titles sold over 300,000 copies, a first-time-ever feat. A new record of sorts was also set by the #1 bestseller of the year, *In Search of Excellence,* with its sales of over 1 million copies in 1983; the only other bestseller to achieve that distinction on these end-of-the-year lists was *The Living Bible* in 1972 and 1973. Also, at least ten nonfiction books that sold well over 100,000 this past year did not achieve one of the 25 nonfiction spots.

In fiction, name authors with track records continued to dominate the list. Once again, as in 1982, 17 of the top 25 fiction titles were by authors who have previously appeared on these end-of-the-year bestseller charts (the same was true for 1982). While two of the three first novels were written by well-known figures in the book or entertainment fields, the third, *The Name of the Rose,* could be dubbed one of the most

Note: Adapted from *Publishers Weekly,* March 16, 1984, where the article was titled "The Year's Bestselling Books: Hardcover Top Sellers."

unlikely bestselling novels ever—it was written by an Italian professor of semiotics, set in a fourteenth-century monastery, and filled with numerous untranslated Latin passages.

The bestselling nonfiction fare in 1983 was more predictable. But here, too, there were some surprises. While business, self-improvement, humor, and religious titles dominated, a book about America's backroads made the list of top 15. By far, the strongest category in 1983 was business books, and the top three books in this group—*In Search of Excellence, Megatrends,* and *The One Minute Manager*—were also the longest-running bestsellers on *PW*'s 1983 lists.

The books on *PW*'s annual bestseller lists, including runners-up, are based on sales figures supplied by publishers. These figures, according to the respective firms, reflect only 1983 U.S. trade sales—that is, sales to bookstores, wholesalers, and libraries only. Not included, claim publishers, are book club, overseas, and direct mail transactions. Some books appear in the listings without accompanying sales figures. These were submitted to *PW* in confidence, for use only in placing the titles in their correct positions on a specific list.

"Sales," as used on these lists, refers to books shipped and billed in calendar year 1983. Publishers were asked to reflect returns made through January 15, 1984. Still, in many cases, the 1983 sales figures include books on bookstore and wholesaler shelves and/or books on the way back to the publishers' warehouses, as well as books already stacking up on returns piles.

The Fiction Bestsellers

At $6.95 with about 60 illustrated pages, the novelization *Return of the Jedi Storybook* could very easily be considered a children's title. Yet it enjoyed a 22-week run on *PW*'s and the *New York Times* hardcover adult bestseller charts, several times in the #1 spot. A title similar in appeal and scope to last year's leading fiction bestseller, *E.T. The Extra-Terrestrial Storybook,* it shares an even more significant feature with its outer space cousin. Both books managed to knock a new James Michener book off a much-deserved spot on top of the year's annual fiction bestselling chart.

Michener's *Poland* sold 786,235 copies to *Jedi*'s 882,124. But at $17.95 and 560-pages—covering that Eastern European country's history from the thirteenth century to the present day—Michener's book clearly ranks as #1 in terms of dollar sales for a 1983 novel. And although *Space* was the #2 fiction bestseller in 1982, many of the author's previous works were leading novels when they were published, including *The Source* (1965), *Centennial* (1974), and *Chesapeake* (1978).

A distinction that occurs rarely on these annual lists is for an author to have two novels among the top 10 of the year. Stephen King captured the #3 and #5 spots with two new books, *Pet Sematary* and *Christine,* with 657,741 (his highest ever year-end sales figure) and 303,589 copies respectively. Three other novelists who have achieved similar laurels were Frederick Forsyth in 1972, John O'Hara in 1960, and James Hilton in 1935. Two books on the same list by a nonfiction writer is a bit more common; in 1982, Leo Buscaglia and Andrew A. Rooney both had two titles on the end-of-the-year hardcover list. This year William Manchester has two major biographies in the top 25.

The #4 position on these annual lists seems to be a favorite spot for John le Carré. His latest thriller, *The Little Drummer Girl,* sold over 400,000 copies in 1983 and was the year's longest-running fiction hardcover bestseller on *PW*'s weekly list; it was on the list for 35 weeks, 18 weeks in the #1 spot. Four previous le Carré titles also made the year-end #4 spot—*The Honourable Schoolboy* (1977), *Tinker, Tailor, Soldier, Spy* (1974), *A Small Town in Germany* (1968), and *The Looking Glass War* (1965).

Three science fiction/fantasy novels, in addition to *Return of the Jedi Storybook,* were among the top 15 fiction bestsellers for the year—the same figure as last year. Again, this points to the continued strong showing of this category on hardcover bestseller lists; just a few years ago the appearance of just one book in this genre was a noteworthy event.

Isaac Asimov takes the #12 spot with sales of more than 171,300 for *The Robots of Dawn.* Last year, the prolific author made it to the end-of-the-year hardcover list for the first time with the fourth novel in his famous Foundation series, *Foundation's Edge.* Another 1982 bestselling author in the genre returning in 1983 is Stephen R. Donaldson, with sales of about 267,000 in 1983 for *White Gold Wielder: Book Three of The Second Chronicles of Thomas Covenant,* enough to give it the #8 spot on the fiction list. Rounding off the science fiction/fantasy category and the top 15 fiction list is a newcomer to these annual bestseller charts, Anne McCaffrey with the continuing saga of Pern in *Moreta: Dragonlady of Pern;* sales of about 151,000 gives it the #15 spot on the 1983 fiction list.

Another category, usually reserved for paperback bestsellerdom, is westerns. But Louis L'Amour crosses into the hardcover topseller frontier with *The Lonesome Gods,* #10 with 1983 sales of 205,000. This is the first time Bantam has published an original L'Amour in hardcover. It has been about 60 years since western hardcovers have made these annual charts; at that time one could count on a Zane Grey title showing up on an annual list. L'Amour is hardly a stranger to the bestseller world; according to his publisher, he is one of the world's four bestselling living novelists with over 130 million copies of his fiction works in print. In 1982, he became the first novelist in American history to be voted a special National Gold Medal by the United States Congress for "his distinguished career as an author and his contribution to the nation through his historically based works."

There was an extra incentive for consumers to pay $9.95 for this year's #11 fiction bestseller, *Who Killed the Robins Family.* In what Morrow called "an unprecedented publishing event," the publisher was offering a $10,000 cash reward to the reader who came up with the best solution to the mystery posed by the novel. Created by agent/packager Bill Adler and written by veteran mystery writer Thomas Chastain, *PW* called it "a most ingenious puzzle that would have had even Sherlock Holmes guessing." As of this writing, that continues to hold true for readers of this plot.

Ten years in the writing, Norman Mailer's opus on Egypt was published to mixed reviews; still, enough fans (over 151,000) bought the book to place it #14 on the 1983 fiction list. Mailer is no stranger to these lists, making his first appearance in 1948 with a first novel, *The Naked and the Dead;* it was #2 that year with over 137,000 copies sold. In 1979, his true-life novel of the life and death of Gary Gilmore was among the top 25 fiction bestsellers.

As noted earlier, a most unusual first novel made it to the list of top 15. With sales of 275,000, Umberto Eco's *The Name of the Rose* placed #7 on this year's list of fiction top sellers. The book was a bestseller in Italy, France, and Germany and had won some prestigious literary prizes, including two major Italian honors and France's Prix Medicis for best foreign novel in France. Still, it was a surprise to almost all, including the hardcover publisher who reportedly bought the manuscript for somewhere between $4,000 and $5,000. Warner Books paid $550,000 for paperback reprint rights. The book was on *PW*'s bestseller list for 26 weeks, five weeks in the #1 spot (it got bumped by Michener's *Poland*).

Judith Rossner returned to a New York setting for *August,* #13 on the end-of-the-year list with sales of over 157,500. The city was also the setting for her previous title that made it onto these annual lists—*Looking for Mr. Goodbar,* #4 in 1975 with sales of over 163,000.

Another veteran of these lists, Danielle Steel, outdid her previous hardcover record attained only last year with *Crossings* (it garnered the #13 position with sales close to 199,000). Her 1983 bestseller, *Changes,* attained the #6 position with sales reaching 295,000.

A newcomer to these lists is Jackie Collins (she is Joan's younger sister). Her book *Hollywood Wives* racked up sales of 226,505 in 1983, enough to give it the #9 fiction spot for the year. She has written eight other novels, currently published in more than 30 languages; according to her publisher, each of her books has sold more than 1 million copies worldwide.

The Fiction Runners-Up

The second tier of bestsellers is also dominated by authors whose previous books have been major bestsellers. Len Deighton has written 15 thrillers, many of which have made it onto these end-of-the-year lists. In fact, the only newcomers to annual fiction bestseller lists are Bette Midler and Nora Ephron. Midler, who toured extensively on behalf of this work, certainly is no new name. While this is Ephron's first novel, her nonfiction books have enjoyed excellent sales. Also, the fact that many reviewers and journalists drew parallels between Ephron's marriage to Carl Bernstein and what happens to *Heartburn*'s heroine didn't hurt the book's sales.

New hardcover novels selling over 100,000 copies in 1983 that did not make the top-25 fiction list include *Banker* by Dick Francis, *Delta Star* by Joseph Wambaugh, and *Monimbo* by Robert Moss and Arnaud de Borchgrave.

In ranked order, the 10 fiction runners-up are: *The Seduction of Peter S.* by Lawrence Sanders (Putnam, 8/83; 145,117); *Voice of the Heart* by Barbara Taylor Bradford (Doubleday, 3/83; 144,356); *The Saga of Baby Divine* by Bette Midler (Crown, 11/83;140,798); *Ascent into Hell* by Andrew M. Greeley (Warner, 6/83; 139,681); *Berlin Game* by Len Deighton (Knopf, 1/84, books were shipped in 12/83; 138,909); *The Wicked Day* by Mary Stewart (Morrow, 10/83); *Summer of Katya* by Trevanian (Crown, 6/83; 130,597); *Heartburn* by Nora Ephron (Knopf, 4/83; 123,751); *The Auerbach Will* by Stephen Birmingham (Little, Brown, 8/83); and *Godplayer* by Robin Cook (Putnam, 7/83; 117,530).

The Nonfiction Leaders

Without contest, business was the hottest bestselling subject in 1983; there were a couple of months during 1983 when the top four spots on *PW*'s weekly list were commanded by the four leaders in this category—*In Search of Excellence, Megatrends, The One Minute Manager,* and *Creating Wealth.* They ranked #1, #2, #4, and #9, respectively, on the 1983 nonfiction list. Except for *Creating Wealth,* the other three titles also made the top 25 1982 bestseller list, but in much lower spots.

Perhaps the most remarkable performance by any bestseller in many years was achieved by *In Search of Excellence*. The book reached 1 million copies in sales within 10 months of publication, making it one of the fastest-selling books of all time. The sales figure is even more astounding when compared with the publisher's sales advance of 8,100 copies prior to its November 1982 publication date. It was one of the most sought-after books of Christmas 1982 and dominated the top of the 1983 bestseller charts for almost three-quarters of the year. With sales of 1,160,491 in 1983, added to about 122,000 copies in 1982, this title was the best-selling book in Harper & Row's 166-year history.

The #2 nonfiction bestseller, *Megatrends*, sold 788,260 copies in 1983. Its 1982 sales of 210,708 made it #15 on last year's annual list. Both *Megatrends* and *In Search of Excellence* did not miss a week on *PW*'s weekly charts.

Offering advice on the quickest way to increase productivity, *The One Minute Manager,* the #3 nonfiction seller, scored high on the weekly charts until the trade paperback edition was published in late fall (that quickly became the #1 trade paperback seller). Sales of more than 200,000 in 1982 earned it the #16 spot that year.

In *Creating Wealth,* the author shares some of the steps in the wealth-building program that made him a multimillionaire before the age of 35. (Writing bestsellers was certainly a contributing factor to his new financial status.) The popularity of *Creating Wealth,* with sales of over 315,000 books in 1983, also propelled his first book, *Nothing Down,* back on the national bestseller charts. That title captured the #9 spot in 1980 with sales of 197,000 copies; in mid-February 1984, it was the #1 hardcover bestseller at Waldenbooks and the #2 hardcover bestseller at B. Dalton.

Body and face tone-up were also the themes of several major bestsellers. Last year's nonfiction leader, *Jane Fonda's Workout Book,* sold an additional 420,617 in 1983, enough to capture the #5 spot. For the lead position in 1982, the Fonda book sold over 692,000 books. Fonda's very attractive colleague in the acting field, Victoria Principal, also scored with her first book on an exercise program based on isometric exercises designed to take about 30 minutes a day. Close to 308,000 consumers picked up the book, enough to make it the #10 nonfiction bestseller in 1983.

Once the figure is attended to, the face comes next (or maybe the order is reversed). A well-coordinated marketing campaign by the publishers and the Mary Kay Cosmetic Company quickly launched this bestselling title, #6 for 1983 with sales totals for the year of more than 334,500; one week after shipping, it captured the #1 spot on B. Dalton's bestseller list.

Three veterans of these hardcover lists made it again to the top 15 with their latest works. In the #3 spot, Erma Bombeck, one of the most popular funny ladies, managed to sell 725,372 copies of *Motherhood: The Second Oldest Profession.* Obviously, many customers took the publisher's advice seriously when it stated that "this book was not for everyone—only for those who are mothers or who had one." Bombeck has been on the year-end lists a number of times, most recently in the #1 spot in 1979 for *Aunt Erma's Cope Book* with sales of 692,000 for that year.

Well-known British veterinarian James Herriot has been a bestselling author ever since his first book appeared in 1972, *All Creatures Great and Small.* The author's latest work, an illustrated anthology, is a collection chosen by Herriot of the best of all his previous writings. Sales of over 388,905 made it the #6 bestselling nonfiction hardcover of the year.

A regular on these end-of-the-year charts on the fiction list is Ken Follett. His nonfiction debut in *On Wings of Eagles* earns him one of his most impressive sales records of his career—sales of more than 315,000 gives him the #8 nonfiction spot in 1983. His last appearance on an annual list was in 1982 when *A Man from St. Petersburg* placed #10 on the fiction list with sales of over 225,000.

Three religious titles made it on the top 15 list, an impressive number for the annual list. All were by well-known religious personalities with widespread television exposure. Billy Graham's *Approaching Hoofbeats,* with sales of 259,000, gave it the #11 spot for the year-end nonfiction list. Graham's first appearance on a *PW* annual list was in 1955 with *The Secret of Happiness;* sales of 115,697 made it #7 that year. Exactly 20 years later, his book *Angels: God's Secret Agents* took the #1 spot for the year with sales of 810,000.

Two titles from Thomas Nelson are in the #12 and #14 spots. Robert H. Schuller's *Tough Times Never Last, But Tough People Do* sold 257,641 books in 1983, and Pat Robertson's *The Secret Kingdom* sold 214,899 books. Both authors are also well known on television—Schuller is one of the best-known TV preachers and Robertson is host of the "700 Club," a major religious talk show with weekly viewers estimated at about 15 million.

William Least Heat Moon scored with his first published book, *Blue Highways,* #13 on *PW*'s annual 1983 hardcover list. According to Little, Brown, it is one of the most successful books ever published by Atlantic Monthly Press.

Another newcomer to these annual lists, but certainly not to weekly national charts, is Art Buchwald. His satirical look at the President enjoyed sales of over 185,417 books, enough to get it the #15 spot in 1983. Buchwald's syndicated column appears in 550 newspapers worldwide.

The Nonfiction Runners-Up

This year's 10 runners-up in nonfiction were all books that enjoyed long runs on weekly national bestseller charts. William Manchester scored with two impressive biographical works. A 13-part PBS-TV special based on Stanley Karnow's *Vietnam* helped that book's bestseller run. Other books making up this second tier of nonfiction bestsellers are a first collection of essays by *Ms. Magazine* editor Gloria Steinem; books from two well-known people from the entertainment field, as well as more books on diet and fitness.

1983 nonfiction bestsellers that did not make a top-25 list include such titles as *No More Hot Flashes and Other Good News* by Penny Budoff, *The Love You Make: An Insider's Story of the Beatles* by Peter Brown and Steven Gaines, *A Hero for Our Time: An Intimate Story of the Kennedy Years* by Ralph G. Martin, *Richard Simmons' Better Body Book* by Richard Simmons, and *The Price of Power: Kissinger in the Nixon White House* by Seymour M. Hersh. All sold 119,000 copies or more in 1983.

In ranked order, the 10 nonfiction runners-up are: *Vietnam: A History* by Stanley Karnow (Viking, 10/83; 176,635 books); *Out On a Limb* by Shirley MacLaine (Bantam, 6/83; 175,000); *Fatal Vision* by Joe McGinniss (Putnam, 9/83; 168,342); *Working Out* by Charles Hix (Simon & Schuster, 2/83; 165,285); *Outrageous Acts and Everyday Rebellions* by Gloria Steinem (Holt, Rinehart and Winston, 9/83; 158,107); *The Peter Pan Syndrome* by Dr. Dan Kiley (Dodd, Mead, 9/83; 141,000); *One Brief Shining Moment: Remembering Kennedy* by William Manchester (Little, Brown, 11/83); *The Diet Center Program* by Sybil Ferguson (Little, Brown, 4/83); *How to Live to Be 100 . . . or More* by George Burns (Putnam, 5/83; 135,806); and *The Last Lion: Winston Spencer Churchill* by William Manchester (Little, Brown, 5/83).

Publishers Weekly 1983 Hardcover Bestsellers

Fiction

1 *Return of the Jedi Storybook* adapted by Joan D. Vinge (published May 1983) Random House; 882,124 copies sold in 1983

2 *Poland* by James A. Michener (August 1983) Random House; 786,235

3 *Pet Sematary* by Stephen King (November 14, 1983) Doubleday; 657,741

4 *The Little Drummer Girl* by John le Carré (March 21, 1983) Knopf; 400,444

5 *Christine* by Stephen King (April 29, 1983) Viking; 303,589

6 *Changes* by Danielle Steel (September 2, 1983) Delacorte; 295,000

7 *The Name of the Rose* by Umberto Eco (June 9, 1983) A Helen and Kurt Wolff Book/Harcourt Brace Jovanovich; 275,000

8 *White Gold Wielder: Book Three of The Second Chronicles of Thomas Covenant* by Stephen R. Donaldson (April 1983) A Del Rey Book/Ballantine; 267,000

9 *Hollywood Wives* by Jackie Collins (July 29, 1983) Simon & Schuster; 226,505

10 *The Lonesome Gods* by Louis L'Amour (April 1983) Bantam; 205,000

*11 *Who Killed the Robins Family* by Bill Adler and Thomas Chastain (August 1983) Morrow

12 *The Robots of Dawn* by Isaac Asimov (October 21, 1983) Doubleday; 171,322

13 *August* by Judith Rossner (August 15, 1983) Houghton Mifflin; 157,535

*14 *Ancient Evenings* by Norman Mailer (April 1983) Little, Brown

15 *Moreta: Dragonlady of Pern* by Anne McCaffrey (November 1983) A Del Rey Book/Ballantine; 151,000

Nonfiction

1 *In Search of Excellence: Lessons from America's Best-Run Companies* by Thomas J. Peters and Robert H. Waterman, Jr. (October 21, 1982) Harper & Row; 1,160,491

2 *Megatrends: Ten New Directions Transforming Our Lives* by John Naisbitt (October 18, 1982) Warner; 788,260

3 *Motherhood: The Second Oldest Profession* by Erma Bombeck (October 3, 1983) McGraw-Hill; 725,372

*4 *The One Minute Manager* by Kenneth Blanchard and Spencer Johnson (September 1, 1982) Morrow

5 *Jane Fonda's Workout Book* by Jane Fonda (November 16, 1981) Simon & Schuster; 420,617

6 *The Best of James Herriot* by James Herriot (September 1983) St. Martin's Press; 388,905

Note: Rankings on this list are determined by sales figures provided by publishers; the numbers reflect reports of copies "shipped and billed" only and should not be regarded as net sales figures since publishers do not yet know what their final returns will be.
*Sales figures were submitted to *PW* in confidence, for use only in placing the titles in their correct positions on a specific list.

  7 *The Mary Kay Guide to Beauty: Discovering Your Special Look* by the Beauty Experts at Mary Kay Cosmetics (September 26, 1983) Addison-Wesley; 334,580

 *8 *On Wings of Eagles* by Ken Follett (September 1983) Morrow

  9 *Creating Wealth* by Robert G. Allen (April 28, 1983) Simon & Schuster; 315,193

 10 *The Body Principal: The Exercise Program for Life* by Victoria Principal (September 19, 1983) Simon & Schuster; 307,976

 11 *Approaching Hoofbeats: The Four Horsemen of the Apocalypse* by Billy Graham (November 1983) Word; 259,000

 12 *Tough Times Never Last, But Tough People Do* by Robert H. Schuller (May 1, 1983) Thomas Nelson; 257,641

*13 *Blue Highways: A Journey into America* by William Least Heat Moon (January 1983) Atlantic Monthly Press/Little, Brown

 14 *The Secret Kingdom by Pat Robertson with Bob Slosser* (October 1, 1982) Thomas Nelson; 214,899

 15 *While Reagan Slept* by Art Buchwald (October 14, 1983) Putnam; 185,417

Part 6
Directory of Organizations

Directory of Library and Related Organizations

National Library and Information-Industry Associations, United States and Canada

American Association of Law Libraries

53 W. Jackson Blvd., Chicago, IL 60604
312-939-4764

Object

"To promote librarianship, to develop and increase the usefulness of law libraries, to cultivate the science of law librarianship and to foster a spirit of cooperation among members of the profession." Established 1906. Memb. 3,610. Dues (Active) $65; (Inst.) $65; (Assoc.) $65 & $125; (Student) $10. Year. June 1 to May 31.

Membership

Persons officially connected with a law library or with a law section of a state or general library, separately maintained; and institutions. Associate membership available for others.

Officers (June 1983–1984)

Pres. M. Kathleen Price, Univ. of Minnesota, Law Lib., 229 19 Ave. S., Minneapolis, MN 55455; *V.P./Pres.-Elect.* Jacquelyn J. Jurkins, Multnomah Law Lib., County Courthouse, 4th fl., 1021 S.W. Fourth Ave., Portland, OR 97204; *Secy.* Mary L. Fisher, General Electric Co., Corporate Legal Operation, 3135 Easton Turnpike, Fairfield, CT 06431; *Treas.* Richard L. Beer, Adams-Pratt Oakland County Law Lib., 1200 N. Telegraph Rd.,

Pontiac, MI 48053; *Immediate Past Pres.* Leah F. Chanin, Mercer Univ. Law Lib., Macon, GA 31207.

Executive Board (1983–1984)

Officers: Margaret A. Leary; Harry S. Martin III; Maureen M. Moore; Betty W. Taylor; O. James Werner; Sarah K. Wiant.

Committee Chairpersons (1983–1984)

Awards. Nancy Johnson, Georgia State Univ., College of Law Lib., University Plaza, Altanta, GA 30303.
Certification Board. Edgar J. Bellefontaine, Social Law Lib., 1200 Court House, Boston, MA 02108.
CONELL. Catherine H. Gillette, Cleveland-Marshall Law Lib., Cleveland State Univ., E. 18 & Euclid Ave., Cleveland, OH 44115.
CONELL Co-Chair. Mickie A. Voges, Univ. of Texas, Tarlton Law Lib., 727 E. 26 St., Austin, TX 78705.
Constitution and Bylaws. Vivian L. Campbell, Georgetown Univ., Fred O. Dennis Law Lib., 600 New Jersey Ave., N.W., Washington, DC 20001.
Copyright. Laura Gasaway, Univ. of Okla-

homa, 300 Timberdell Rd., Norman, OK 73019.

Directory—Biographical. Gail Daly, Univ. of Minnesota, 229 19 Ave. S., Minneapolis, MN 55455.

Directory—1984 Edition AALL. Kamla J. King, Bureau of National Affairs, 1231 25 St. N.W., Washington, DC 20037.

Co-Chair Directory—1984 Edition AALL. Anne H. Butler, Alston & Bird, 35 Broad St., 1200 C&S National Bank Bldg., Atlanta, GA 30335.

Education. Alan Holoch, Villanova Univ. Law Lib., Gary Hall, Villanova, PA 19085.

Elections. Francis Doyle, Loyola Univ. Law Lib., One E. Pearson St., Chicago, IL 60611.

Exchange of Duplicates. Margaret A. Lundahl, Lundahl Enterprises, 10128 Ave. J, Chicago, IL 60617.

Financial Planning. Lorraine A. Kulpa, General Motors Corp., Information Systems, 15–235 General Motors Bldg., Detroit, MI 48202.

Foreign, Comparative, and International Law. Margaret A. Aycock, Univ. of Virginia Law Lib., Charlottesville, VA 22901.

Index to Foreign Legal Periodicals. James Hoover, Columbia Univ. Law Lib., 435 W. 116 St., New York, NY 10027.

Indexing of Periodical Literature. George Grossman, Northwestern Univ., School of Law Lib., 367 E. Chicago Ave., Chicago, IL 60611.

Law Library Journal. Robert L. Summers, St. Mary's Univ., School of Law Lib., One Camino Santa Maria, San Antonio, TX 78284.

Lawnet. Betty W. Taylor, Univ. of Florida College of Law, Legal Information Center, Gainesville, FL 32611.

Legislation & Legal Developments. Kathleen T. Larson, United States Dept. of Justice, Civil Rights Lib., Rm. 7618, Tenth & Constitution Aves., N.W., Washington, DC 20530.

Membership/Recruitment. Dan J. Freehling, Univ. of Maine, School of Law, 246 Deering Ave., Portland, ME 04102.

Memorials. George Skinner, Univ. of Arkansas, School of Law Lib., Fayetteville, AR 72701.

National Law Library. Roy Mersky, New York Law School, 57 Worth St., New York, NY 10013.

Newsletter. Gayle S. Edleman, Univ. of Chicago Law Lib., 1121 E. 60 St., Chicago, IL 60637.

Nominations. Peter Schanck, Univ. of Kansas School of Law, Law Lib., Lawrence, KS 66045.

Placement. Barbara Gontrum, Univ. of Maryland, Thurgood Marshall Law Lib., 20 North Paca St., Baltimore, MD 21201.

Public Relations. Joyce Saltalmachia, New York Law School Lib., 57 Worth St., New York, NY 10013.

Publications. Marian F. Parker, Univ. of Tulsa, 3120 E. Fourth Place, Tulsa, OK 74104.

Relations with Publishers & Dealers. Margaret Maes Axtmann, Cornell Law Lib., Myron Taylor Hall, Ithaca, NY 14853.

Scholarships & Grants. Kathleen M. Carrick, Case Western Reserve Univ., Law Lib., 11075 East Blvd., Cleveland, OH 44106.

Service to the Public. Anita K. Shew, Butler County Law Lib., Court House Annex, Hamilton, OH 45011.

SIS Steering. Margaret A. Leary, Univ. of Michigan Law Lib., 801 Monroe St., Ann Arbor, MI 48109.

Standards. Anita L. Morse, Univ. of Wisconsin Law Lib., Madison, WI 53706.

Statistics. David Thomas, Brigham Young Univ., Law Lib., Provo, UT 84602.

Special-Interest Section Chairpersons

Academic Law Libraries. Kathleen Carrick, Case Western Reserve Univ., Law

Lib., 11075 East Blvd., Cleveland, OH 44106.

Automation & Scientific Development. Duncan Webb, Michigan State Law Lib., Box 30012, Lansing MI 48909.

Contemporary Social Problems. Susan M. Wood, Supreme Court Lib. at Syracuse, 500 Court House, Syracuse, NY 13202.

Government Documents. Marian F. Parker, Univ. of Tulsa, College of Law Lib., 3120 E. Fourth Place, Tulsa, OK 74104.

Micrographics & Audio-Visual. Nina Cascio, State Univ. of New York at Buffalo, Amherst Campus, Buffalo, NY 14260.

On-Line Bibliographic Services. Suzanne Thorpe, Hennepin Co. Law Lib., C-2451 Government Center, Minneapolis, MN 55487.

Private Law Libraries. Austin Doherty, Hogan & Hartson, 815 Connecticut Ave. N.W., Washington, DC 20006.

Readers' Services. Bobbie Snow, Univ. of Michigan Law Lib., Legal Research Bldg., Ann Arbor, MI 48109.

State, Court & County Law Libraries. Carol Meyer, Cincinnati Law Lib. Assn., 601 Court House, Cincinnati, OH 45202.

Technical Services. Melody Lembke, Los Angeles County Law Lib., 301 W. First St., Los Angeles, CA 90012.

Representatives

ABA (American Bar Association). M. Kathleen Price.

American Bar Association. Committee on Economics of Law Practice. Donna M. Tuke.

American Correctional Association. E. Ann Puckett.

American Library Association. Committee on Cataloging. Phyllis C. Marion.

American National Standards Institute. Committee PH-5. Larry Wenger.

American National Standards Institute. Committee Z-39. Anita L. Morse.

American Society for Information Science. Jill Mubarak.

Association of American Law Schools. M. Kathleen Price.

Association of Legal Administrators. Francis Gates.

British-Irish Association of Law Libraries. David A. Thomas.

CLENE. Dennis J. Stone.

Copyright Committee. Lynn Wishart.

CNLA—Joint Committee on Cataloging. Margaret Maes Axtmann.

Council of National Library and Information Associations. Ad Hoc Committee on Copyright. Jack S. Ellenberger, William H. Jepson.

International Association of Law Libraries. Claire Germain.

Library of Congress. Patrick E. Kehoe.

National Association of Secretaries of State. Carol Boast.

Special Libraries Association. Laura N. Gasaway.

American Library Association

Executive Director, Robert Wedgeworth
50 E. Huron St., Chicago, IL 60611
312-944-6780

Object

The American Library Association is an organization for librarians and libraries with the overarching objective of promoting and improving library service and librarianship. Memb. (Indiv.) 34,992; (Inst.) 2,952. Dues (Indiv.) 1st year, $25; 2nd and 3rd years, $35; 4th year and beyond, $50; (Nonsalaried Libns.) $15; (Trustee & Assoc. Membs.) $20; (Student) $10; (Foreign Indiv.) $30; (Inst.) $50 & up (depending upon operating expenses of institution).

Membership

Any person, library, or other organization interested in library service and librarians.

Officers

Pres. Brooke E. Sheldon, Dir., School of Lib. Science, Texas Woman's Univ., Denton, TX 76204; *V.P./Pres.-Elect.* E.J. Josey, Chief, Bur. of Special Lib. Service, The State Lib., Cultural Education Center, Empire State Plaza, Albany, NY 12230; *Treas.* Herbert Biblo, Dir., Long Island Lib. Resources Council, Inc., Box 31, Bellport, NY 11713; *Exec. Dir. (Ex officio)* Robert Wedgeworth, ALA Headquarters, 50 E. Huron St., Chicago, IL 60611.

Address general correspondence to the executive director.

Executive Board

Immediate Past Pres. Carol A. Nemeyer (1984). Other members; Jane Anne Hannigan (1984); Margaret E. Chisholm (1984); Judith R. Farley (1985); Regina Minudri (1985); David Snider (1986); F. William Summers (1986); Arthur Curley (1987); Beverly Lynch (1987).

Endowment Trustees

William V. Jackson (1986); John Juergensmeyer (1984); Albert W. Daub (1985).

Divisions

See the separate entries that follow: American Assn. of School Libns.; American Lib. Trustee Assn.; Assn. for Lib. Service to Children; Assn. of College and Re-
search Libs.; Assn. of Specialized and Cooperative Lib. Agencies; Lib. Admin. and Management Assn.; Lib. and Info. Technology Assn.; Public Lib. Assn.; Reference and Adult Services Div.; Resources and Technical Services Div.; Young Adult Services Div.

Publications

American Libraries (11 per year; memb.).
ALA Handbook of Organizations and Membership Directory 1983-1984 (ann.).
ALA Yearbook (ann.; $65).
Booklist (22 issues; $45).
Choice (11 issues; $85).

Round Table Chairpersons

(ALA staff liaison is given in parentheses.)
Ethnic Materials. David Cohen, Proj. Dir., Queens College, School of Lib. & Info. Studies, Flushing, NY 11367 (Jean E. Coleman).
Exhibits. Jon Malinowski, 17 Observatory Dr., Croton, NY 10520 (Walter Brueggen).
Federal Librarians. Patricia W. Berger, Natl. Bur. of Standards, Washington, DC 20234 (Anne A. Heanue).
Government Documents. Sandra K. Peterson, Docs., Swem Lib., College of William & Mary, Williamsburg, VA 23185 (Bill Drewett).
Intellectual Freedom. James B. Nelson, Cabell County Public Lib., 455 Ninth St. Plaza, Huntington, WV 27501 (Judith F. Krug).
International Relations. Warren M. Tsuneishi, Dir. for Area Studies, Lib. of Congress, Washington, DC 20540 (to be appointed).
Junior Members. J. Linda Williams, Rte. 4, Box 4146, LaPlata, MD 20646 (Patricia Scarry).
Library History. Lee Shiflett, School of Lib. & Info. Science, Louisiana State

Univ., Baton Rouge, LA 70803 (Joel M. Lee).

Library Instruction. Linda Anne Dougherty, Chicago Public Lib., Brighton Park Branch, 4314 S. Archer Ave., Chicago, IL 60632 (Jeneice Guy).

Library Research. Daniel O'Connor, School of Communications Info. and Lib. Studies, Rutgers Univ., New Brunswick, NJ 08903 (Mary Jo Lynch).

Map and Geography. James A. Coombs, Maps, Meyer Lib., Southwest Missouri State Univ., Springfield, MO 65804 (to be appointed).

Social Responsibilities. Linda Pierce, 3634 Edwards Rd., No. 27, Cincinnati, OH 45208 (Jean E. Coleman).

Staff Organizations. Barbara Waserman, George Mason Regional Lib., 7001 Little River Turnpike, Annandale, VA 22003 (to be appointed).

Committee Chairpersons

Accreditation (Standing). Robert M. Hayes, Univ. of California, Los Angeles, CA 90024 (Elinor Yungmeyer).

"American Libraries"—Editorial Advisory Committee for (Standing). Jean Pelletiere, Shaffer Lib., Union College, Schenectady, NY 12308 (Arthur Plotnik).

Awards (Standing). Patricia Senn Breivik, Auraria Lib. & Media Center, Lawrence at 11th St., Denver, CO 80204 (to be appointed).

Chapter Relations (Standing). Bonnie B. Mitchell, OHIONET, 1500 W. Lane Ave., Columbus, OH 43221 (Patricia Scarry).

Conference Program (Standing). William A. Gosling, Mary Lankford, John A. Humprhey (to be appointed).

Constitution and Bylaws (Standing). Frances V. Sedney, Harford County Lib., 100 Pennsylvania Ave., Bel Air, MD 21014 (Miriam L. Hornback).

Council Orientation (Special). Caroline

Arden, School of Lib. & Info. Science, Catholic Univ. of America, Washington, DC 20064 (Miriam L. Hornback).

Instruction in the Use of Libraries (Standing). Judith Pryor, Lib./Learning Center, Univ. of Wisconsin-Parkside, Box 2000, Kenosha, WI 53411 (Andrew M. Hansen).

Intellectual Freedom (Standing, Council). J. Dennis Day, Dir., Public Lib., 209 E. Fifth St. S., Salt Lake City, UT 84111 (Judith F. Krug).

International Relations (Standing, Council). Thomas J. Galvin, School of Lib. & Info. Science, Univ. of Pittsburgh, 135 N. Bellefield, Pittsburgh, PA 15260 (to be appointed).

Legislation (Standing, Council). Gary E. Strong, State Libn., California State Lib., Box 2037, Scaramento, CA 95809 (Eileen D. Cooke).

Library Education (Standing, Council). Peggy O'Donnell, 1135 W. Webster, Chicago, IL 60614 (Margaret Myers).

Library Outreach Services, Office for (Standing, Advisory). Thomas Alford, Los Angeles Public Lib., 630 W. Fifth St., Los Angeles, CA 90071 (Jean E. Coleman).

Library Personnel Resources, Office for (Standing, Advisory). Lora Landers, Hennepin County Lib., 12601 Ridgedale Dr., Minnetonka, MN 55343 (Margaret Myers).

Mediation, Arbitration, and Inquiry, Staff Committee on (Standing). Roger H. Parent, ALA Headquarters, 50 E. Huron St., Chicago, IL 60611.

Membership (Standing). Alphonse F. Trezza, School of Lib. & Info. Studies, Florida State Univ., Tallahassee, FL 32306 (Patricia Scarry).

Minority Concerns (Standing, Council). Doreitha R. Madden, State Lib., CN520, 185 W. State St., Trenton, NJ 08625 (Jean E. Coleman).

National Library Week (Standing). Elizabeth W. Stone, 4000 Cathedral Ave., Washington, DC 20016 (Peggy Barber).

Organization (Standing, Council). Robert Rohlf, Hennepin County Lib., 12601 Ridgedale Dr., Minnetonka, MN 55343 (to be appointed).

Planning (Standing, Council). Gerald R. Shields, School of Info. & Lib. Studies, State Univ. of New York at Buffalo, Amherst, NY 14260 (to be appointed).

Professional Ethics (Standing, Council). Ann E. Prentice, Grad. School of Lib. Info. Science, Univ. of Tennessee, 804 Volunteer Blvd., Knoxville, TN 37916 (Judith F. Krug).

Program Evaluation and Support (Standing, Council). Janis C. Keene, Tulsa City-County Lib., 400 Civic Center, Tulsa, OK 74103 (Sheldon I. Landman).

Publishing (Standing, Council). Robert D. Stueart, Grad. School of Lib. & Info. Science, Simmons College, Boston, MA 02115 (Gary Facente).

Research (Standing). Miriam Drake, Purdue Univ. Lib., Stewart Center, West Lafayette, IN 47907 (Mary Jo Lynch).

Resolutions (Standing, Council). Sharon A. Hammer, Odegaard Undergraduate Lib., DF-10 Univ. of Washington, Seattle, WA 98115 (Miriam L. Hornback).

Standards (Standing). E. Blanche Woolls, School of Lib. & Info. Science, Univ. of Pittsburgh, Pittsburgh, PA 15260 (to be appointed).

Women in Librarianship, Status of (Standing, Council). Neel Parikh, 3027 Richmond Blvd., Oakland, CA 94611 (Margaret Myers).

Joint Committee Chairpersons

American Correctional Association — ASCLA Committee on Institution Libraries. Co-Chpn. Priscilla K. Linsley, 2 Cleveland Rd., W. Princeton, NJ 08540 (ALA). (ACA to be appointed.)

American Federation of Labor/Congress of Industrial Organizations — ALA, Library Service to Labor Groups, RASD. ALA Chpn. Arthur S. Meyers, 2105 Concord, Muncie, IN 47304; AFL/CIO Co-Chpn. Jim Auerback, AFL/CIO, Dept. of Educ., 815 16 St. N.W., Rm. 407, Washington, DC 20006.

Anglo-American Cataloguing Rules Common Revision Fund. ALA Rep. Gary Facente, Assoc. Exec. Dir. for Publishing; CLA Rep. Laurie Bowes, Canadian Lib. Assn., 151 Sparks St., Ottawa, Ont. K1P 5E3 Canada; (British) Lib. Assn. Rep. Joel C. Dowling, c/o Lib. Assn., 7 Ridgmount St., London, WC 1E 7AE, England.

Anglo-American Cataloguing Rules, Joint Steering Committee for Revision of. ALA Chpn. Helen F. Schmierer, 5550 S. Dorchester, Apt. 408, Chicago, IL 60637.

Association for Educational Communications and Technology — AASL. Thomas L. Hart, School of Lib. Science, Florida State Univ., Tallahassee, FL 32306 (AASL).

Association of American Publishers — ALA. ALA Brooke E. Sheldon, School of Lib. Science, Texas Woman's Univ., Denton, TX 76204; AAP chpn. to be appointed.

Association of American Publishers — RTSD. ALA Chpn. Susan H. Vita, 3711 Taylor St., Chevy Chase, MD; AAP Chpn., Dedria Bryfonski, Gale Research Book Tower, Detroit, MI 48226.

Children's Book Council — ALA. ALA Co-Chpn. Amy Kellman, 211 Castlegate Rd., Pittsburgh, PA 15221; CBC Co-Chpn. Judith R. Whipple, Macmillan, 899 Third Ave., New York, NY 10022.

Society of American Archivists — ALA Joint Committee on Library-Archives Relationships. SAA Chpn. Peter Parker, Historical Society of Pennsylvania, 1300 Locust St., Philadelphia, PA 19107.

U.S. National Park Service — ALSC Joint Committee. ALSC Co-Chpn. Joanne Fields, 2179 E. 28 St., Brooklyn, NY 11229; U.S. National Park Service Co-Chpn. Patricia M. Stanek, Cowpens National Battlefield, Box 335, Chesnee, SC 29323.

American Library Association
American Association of School Librarians

Executive Director, Alice E. Fite
Administrative Assistant, Gail Piernas-Davenport
50 E. Huron St., Chicago, IL 60611
312-944-6780

Object

The American Association of School Librarians is interested in the general improvement and extension of library media services for children and young people. AASL has specific responsibility for planning programs of study and service for the improvement and extension of library media services in elementary and secondary schools as a means of strengthening the educational program; evaluation, selection, interpretation, and utilization of media as they are used in the context of the school program; stimulation of continuous study and research in the library field and to establish criteria of evaluation; synthesis of the activities of all units of the American Library Association in areas of mutual concern; representation and interpretation of the need for the function of school libraries to other educational and lay groups; stimulation of professional growth, improvement of the status of school librarians, and encouragement of participation by members in appropriate type-of-activity divisions; and conduct activities and projects beyond the scope of type-of-activity divisions, after specific approval by the ALA Council. Established in 1951 as a separate division of ALA. Memb. 7,000.

Membership

Open to all libraries, school library media specialists, interested individuals and business firms with requisite membership in the ALA.

Officers

Pres. Judith M. King, 3333 University Blvd. W., #201, Kensington, MD 20895;

1st V.P./Pres.-Elect. Bettie Day, Santa Barbara County Schools Lib., 4400 Cathedral Oaks Rd., Box 6307, Santa Barbara, CA 93111; *2nd V.P.* Lucille C. Thomas; *Rec. Secy.* Joanne Troutner; *Past Pres.* Dorothy W. Blake; *Exec. Dir.* Alice E. Fite.

Board of Directors

Officers; *Regional Dirs.* Edna M. Bayliss, Region I (1985); E. Blanche Woolls, Region II (1984); Richard J. Sorensen, Region III (1984); Edna Louise Dial, Region IV (1985); Thomas L. Hart, Region V (1984); Charlie Lou Rouse, Region VI (1986); M. Maggie Rogers, Region VII (1985); *Regional Dirs. from Affiliate Assembly.* Hugh A. Durbin (1985); Bernice Yesner (1984); *Affiliate Assembly Chpn.* Albert H. Saley; *NPSS Chpn.* Stephen L. Matthews; *SS Chpn.* Constance J. Champlin; *Ex officio Ed. School Library Media Quarterly.* Jack R. Luskay.

Publication

School Library Media Quarterly (q.; memb.; nonmemb. $20). *Ed.* Jack R. Luskay, John Jay Senior H.S., Katonah, NY 10536.

Section Committees — Chairpersons

Nonpublic Schools Section (NPSS)

Executive. Stephen L. Matthews, Box 1233, Middleburg, VA 22117.
Bylaws. Walter E. DeMelle, Jr. Edsel Ford Memorial Lib., Hotchkiss School, Lakeville, CT 06039.

Exchanges and Study Visits. Jeanette M. Smith, Dir. of Media Services, Forsyth Country Day School, 5501 Shallowford Rd., Lewisville, NC 27023.

Nominating—1984 Election. Ellen M. Mintz, Harvard School Lib., 3700 Coldwater Canyon, North Hollywood, CA 91604.

Program—Dallas, 1984. Diane Dayton, Head Libn., Carlyle Fraser Lib., Westminster Schools, 1424 W. Paces Ferry Rd. N.W., Atlanta, GA 30327.

Role of the Nonpublic School in Networks and Community Cable (task force). Nancy P. Minnich, Tower Hill School Lib., 13 W. 17 St., Wilmington, DE 19806.

Supervisors Section (SS)

Executive. Constance J. Champlin, W. Maple IMC, 8800 Maple St., Omaha, NE 68134.

Bylaws. Judith K. Meyers, Coord. of Media Services, City Schools, 1470 Warren Rd., Lakewood, OH 44107.

Critical Issues Facing School Library Media Supervisors (Discussion Group). Christina Carr Young, 1253 Girard St. N.E., Washington, DC 20017.

Nominating—1984 Election. Richard J. Sorensen, 215 N. Jefferson St., Verona, WI 53593.

Publications (Ad Hoc). Mary Oppman, 7740 Oak Ave., Gary, IN 46403.

Program—Dallas, 1984. Theresa M. Fredericka, 337 E. Beck St., Columbus, OH 43206.

Committee Chairpersons

Program Coordinating. Dorothy W. Blake, Coord. of Planning Media Resources & Utilization, 2930 Forrest Hill Dr. S.W., Atlanta, GA 30315.

Unit Group I—Organizational Maintenance

Unit Head. Winifred Duncan, 800 Oak St., 2F, Winnetka, IL 60093.

Bylaws. O. Mell Busbin, Box 411, Boone, NC 28607.

Conference Program Planning—Los Angeles, 1984. Paula Montgomery, No. 32, 5842 Stevens Forest Rd., Columbia, MD 21045.

Local Arrangements—Dallas, 1984. Lu Ouida Phillips, Independent School Dist., 3700 Ross Ave., Dallas, TX 75204.

Nominating—1984 Election. Helen Lloyd Snoke, School of Lib. Science, Univ. of Michigan, 580 Union Dr., Ann Arbor, MI 48109.

Resolutions. Lucille C. Thomas, 1184 Union St., Brooklyn, NY 11225.

Unit Group II—Organizational Relationships

Unit Head. Diane A. Ball, 2410 Fairmont Ave., Dayton, OH 45419.

American Association of School Administrators (Liaison). Marie Harris, 1801 30 St. S.E., Washington, DC 20020.

American University Press Services, Inc. (Advisory). Raymond W. Barber, 4616 Larchwood Ave., Philadelphia, PA 19143.

Association for Educational Communications and Technology (Joint). Thomas L. Hart, Professor, School of Lib. Science, Florida State Univ., Tallahassee, FL 32306.

Association for Supervision and Curriculum Development (Liaison). Karen A. Dowling, Professional Lib., Rm. 50, Montgomery County Public Schools, 850 Hungerford Rd., Rockville, MD 20850.

International Reading Association (Liaison). Virginia Mathews, 17 Overshore Dr. W., Hamden, CT 06514.

National Association of Secondary School Principals (Liaison). Edward W. Barth, 13802 Loree Lane, Rockville, MD 20853.

National Congress of Parents and Teachers (Liaison). Doris Masek, 6815 N. Algonquin Ave., Chicago, IL 60646.

National Council for the Social Studies (Liaison). Margaret B. Lefever, 7106 Beechwood Dr., Chevy Chase, MD 20815.

National Council of Teachers of English (Liaison). W. Duane Johnson, Lib. Science Dept., Univ. of Northern Iowa, Cedar Falls, IA 50613.

National Council of Teachers of Mathematics (Liaison). Edward W. Barth, 13802 Loree Lane, Rockville, MD 20853.

Unit Group III—Media Personal Development

Unit Head. Jill M. Sienola, 253 College St. S.W., Apt. 3-A, Valley City, ND 58072.

Library Education. Leah Hiland, Dept. of Lib. Science, Univ. of Northern Iowa, Cedar Falls, IA 50613.

Networking—Interconnection of Learning Resources. Donald C. Adcock, School Dist. No. 41, 793 N. Main St., Glen Ellyn, IL 60137.

Professional Development. Geraldine W. Bell, Public Schools, 2015 Park Place, Birmingham, AL 35202.

Research. Milbrey L. Jones, 201 I St. S.W., Apt. 819, Washington, DC 20024.

Video Communications. To be appointed.

Unit Group IV—Media Program Development

Unit Head. Wanna M. Ernst, 16 Brisbane Dr., Charleston, SC 29407.

Early Childhood Education. Charlie Lou Rouse, 2623 Black Oak Dr., Stillwater, OK 74074.

Elementary School Materials Selection

(Ad Hoc). Anne Ida King, 3-25 Dorothy St., Fair Lawn, NJ 07410.

Evaluation of School Media Programs. Judith K. Meyers, Bd. of Educ., 1470 Warren Rd., Lakewood, OH 44107.

Facilities, Media Center. Rebecca T. Bingham, Dir. of Lib. Media Services, Burrett Center, 4409 Preston Hwy., Louisville, KY 40213.

Library Media Skills Instruction (Ad Hoc). Patricia L. Meier, 2230 1/2 Ripley, Davenport, IA 52083.

School Faculty Materials Selection (Ad Hoc). Joan Myers, Dir. of Libs., School Dist. of Philadelphia, Rm. 301, 21 St., S. of the Pkwy., Philadelphia, PA 19103.

School Library Media Services to Children with Special Needs. Jeannine L. Laughlin, School of Lib. Science, Univ. of Southern Mississippi, Box 5146, Southern Sta., Hattiesburg, MS 39401.

Secondary School Materials Selection (Ad Hoc). Margaret Lefever, 7106 Beechwood Dr., Chevy Chase, MD 20815.

Standardization of Access to Library Media Resources. Thomas L. Hart, School of Lib. Science, Florida State Univ., Tallahassee, FL 32306.

Standards for School Library Media Programs: Writing. James Liesener, 14108 Ansted Rd., Silver Spring, MD 20904.

Standards Program and Implementation. Elizabeth Martin, 330 Oregon, Cedar Falls, IA 50613.

Student Involvement in the Media Center Program. Norma Jane Humble, 1197 Harper, Mason, MI 48854.

Vocational/Technical Materials Selection (Ad Hoc). Barbara Hull, 35-20 Cpl. Stone St., Bayside, NY 11361.

Unit Group V—Public Information

Unit Head. Paula M. Short, 302 Colony Woods Dr., Chapel Hill, NC 27514.

AASL Distinguished Library Service Award for School Administrators.

Mildred Lee, 18756 Park Lee Lane, Sonoma, CA 95476.

Intellectual Freedom Award/AASL SIRS. Susan Schlein, 3039 Pecan Pt., Sugarland, TX 77478.

Intellectual Freedom Representation and Information. Ethel C. Kutteroff, Rte. 3, M56, Chester, NJ 07930.

International Relations. Caroline F. Bauer, 6892 Seaway Circle, Huntington Beach, CA 92648.

Legislation. Estelle B. Williamson, Ruxton Towers, Apt. 312, 8415 Bellona Lane, Baltimore, MD 21204.

National School Library Media Program of the Year Award Selection, AASL/ Encyclopaedia Britannica. Donald A. Colberg, SEMBCS, 3301 Monaco, Denver, CO 30222.

President's Award Selection. AASL/Baker & Taylor. Yvonne B. Carter, 301 G St. S.W., Apt. 213, Washington, DC 20024.

Public Relations. Ann T. White, Dir., Spartanburg School Dist. 3, Box 267 Glendale, SC 29346.

School Library Media Week. Lucille C. Thomas, 1184 Union St., Brooklyn, NY 11225.

Committees (Special)

AASL General Conference — Atlanta, 1984. Theresa M. Fredericka, 337 E. Beck St., Columbus, OH 43206.

Future Structure for AASL. Carolyn L. Cain; Glenn E. Estes; Karen Whitney (members — no chair).

Nation at Risk. Betty Day, Coord. of Lib. Services, Santa Barbara County Schools, 4400 Cathedral Oaks Rd., Box 6307, Santa Barbara, CA 93110.

Publications Advisory. Helen Lloyd Snoke, School of Lib. Science, Univ. of Michigan, 580 Union Dr., Ann Arbor, MI 48109.

Discussion Groups

Microcomputer Utilization for School Library Media Centers. Joanne Troutner, 3002 Roanoke Circle, Lafayette, IN 47905.

Online School Libraries Users Group. Hugh A. Durbin, 4240 Fairoaks Dr., Columbus, OH 43214.

Representatives

ALA Appointments. Judith M. King.

ALA Chicago Conference (1985). Betty Day.

ALA Dallas Conference. Judith M. King.

ALA Legislation Assembly. Estelle B. Williamson.

ALA Membership Promotion Task Force. Gail Piernas-Davenport.

ALA Planning and Budget Assembly. Judith M. King.

Associated Organizations for Professionals in Education. Leah Hiland.

Catalog Form, Function, and Use. Winifred E. Duncan.

Education U.S.A. Advisory Board. Alice E. Fite.

International Assn. of School Librarianship. Alice E. Fite.

Freedom to Read Foundation. Ethel C. Kutteroff.

Library Education Assembly. Leah Hiland.

National Assn. of State Educational Media Professionals. Alice E. Fite.

RTSD/CCS/AASL Cataloging of Children's Materials. Winifred E. Duncan.

Affiliate Assembly

The Affiliate Assembly is composed of the representatives and delegates of the organizations affiliated with the American Association of School Librarians. The specific purpose of this assembly is to provide a channel for communication for reporting concerns of the affiliate organizations and their membership and for reporting the actions of the American Association of School Librarians to the affiliates.

Executive Committee

Albert H. Saley, Rte. 1, Box 111, Blairstown, NJ 07028.

Bylaws

Carol Stanke, 3543 W. Shady Lane, Neenah, WI 54956.

Nominating Committee — 1984 Election

Judith F. Davie, Dept. of Lib. Science, Univ. of North Carolina, Greensboro, NC 27402.

Affiliate Assembly Organizational Review

Jerry Wicks, Instructional Materials, Glenbrook North H.S., 2300 Shermer Rd., Northbrook, IL 60062.

Affiliates

Region I. Connecticut Educational Media Assn.; Massachusetts Assn. for Educational Media; New England Educational Media Assn.; Vermont Educational Media Assn.

Region II. District of Columbia Assn. of School Libns.; Maryland Educational Media Organization; Educational Media Assn. of New Jersey; Pennsylvania School Libns. Assn.; School Lib. Media Sec., New York Lib. Assn.

Region III. Assn. for Indiana Media Educators; Illinois Assn. for Media in Education; Iowa Educational Media Assn.; Michigan Assn. for Media in Education; Minnesota Educational Media Organization; Missouri Assn. of School Libns.; Ohio Educational Lib. Media Assn.; Wisconsin School Lib. Media Assn.; School Div., Michigan Lib. Assn.

Region IV. Colorado Educational Media Assn.; Kansas Assn. of School Libns.; Nebraska Educational Media Assn.; Nebraska Lib. Assn. School, Children's & Young People's Sec.; North Dakota Assn. of School Libns.; Wyoming School Lib. Media Assn.

Region V. Alabama Instructional Media Assn.; Children & School Libns. Div., Alabama Lib. Assn.; Florida Assn. for Media in Education, Inc.; Georgia Lib. Media Dept.; School & Children's Sec., Georgia Lib. Assn.; Kentucky School Media Dept.; North Carolina Assn. of School Libns.; School & Children's Sec., Southeastern Lib. Assn.; South Carolina Assn. of School Libns.; School Lib. Sec., Tennessee Education Assn.; Virginia Educational Media Assn.

Region VI. Louisiana Assn. of School Libns.; Oklahoma Assn. of School Lib. Media Specialists; School Libs. Div., Arizona State Lib. Assn.; School Libs. Div., Arkansas Lib. Assn.; Texas Assn. of School Libs.

Region VII. AASL-Alaska; California Media & Lib. Educators Assn.; Hawaii Assn. of School Libs.; Oregon Educational Media Assn.; School Lib./Media Div., Montana Lib. Assn.; Washington State Assn. of School Libns.

American Library Association
American Library Trustee Association

ALTA Program Officer, Sharon L. Jordan
50 E. Huron St., Chicago, IL 60611
312-944-6780

Object

The development of effective library service for all people in all types of communities and in all types of libraries; it follows that its members are concerned as policymakers with organizational patterns of service, with the development of competent personnel, the provision of adequate financing, the passage of suitable legislation, and the encouragement of citizen support for libraries. Open to all interested persons and organizations. Organized 1890. Became an ALA division 1961. Memb. 1,710. (For dues and membership year, see ALA entry.)

Officers (1983–1984)

Pres. Barbara D. Cooper, 936 Intracoastal Dr., #6-D, Ft. Lauderdale, FL 33304; *1st V.P./Pres.-Elect.* Joanne Wisener, 860 19 Place, Yuma, AZ 85364; *2nd V.P.* Herbert Davis; *Secy.* Norma Buzan; *Council Rep./ Parliamentarian.* Jean M. Coleman.

Board of Directors

Officers; *Council Administrators*, Jeanne Davies (1984); Gloria Glaser (1984); Jo Anne Thorbeck (1984); Esther Lopato (1983); Carol Neuhauser (1984); *Reg. V.Ps.* Kay Vowvalidis (1984); Schuyler Mott (1984); Pat Nixon (1985); Mary Womack (1985); Mildred King (1984); Irving Portman (1985); Eugene Harple (1983); Aileen Schrader (1984); Dorothe Peterson (1985); James Voyles (1984); *Past Pres.* M. Don Surratt; *PLA Past Pres. Ex officio.* Don Sager (1984); Ed. *The ALTA Newsletter.* Nancy Stiegemeyer.

Publication

The ALTA Newsletter. Ed. Nancy Stiegemeyer, 215 Camellia Dr., Cape Girardeau, MO 63701.

Committee Chairpersons

Action Development. Charles Reid, 620 West Dr., Paramus, NJ 07652.
ALTA Foundation Committee. James Voyles, 1088 Starks Bldg., Louisville, KY 40202.
ALTA Future Committee. Barbara Cooper, 936 Intracoastal Dr., #6-D, Ft. Lauderdale, FL 33304.
Awards. Lila Milford, 1225 Northwood Ct., Marion, IN 46952.
Budget. Joanne Wisener, 860 19 Place, Yuma, ZA 85364.
Specialized Outreach Services Committee. Marguerite W. Yates, 190 Windemere Rd., Lockport NY 14094; Arthur Kirschenbaum, Washington, DC.
Conference Program and Evaluation. Carol Nuehauser, 436 N. Stark Dr., Palatine, IL 60067.
Education of Trustees. Kay Vowvalidis, 100 Deer Path Rd., Ozark, AL 36360.
Intellectual Freedom. Patricia Turner, 3419 Redman Rd., Baltimore MD 21207; Madeleine Grant, 3300 Rance Terr., Lincoln, IL 60646.
Jury on Trustee Citations. Virginia Young, 10 E. Parkway Dr., Columbia, MO 65201; Minnie-Lou Lynch, 404 E. Sixth St., Oakdale, LA 71463.
Legislation. Sylvia Shorstein, 6908 La-Loma Dr., Jacksonville FL 32217; Norma Mihalevich, Box 287, Crocker, MO 65452.

Nominating. James Hess, 91 Farms Rd. Circle, East Brunswick, NJ 08816.
Publications. Ira Harkavy, 1784 E. 29 St., Brooklyn, NY 11229.
Publicity. Ella Nothern, Rte. 1, Box 88, Glasco, KS 67445; Gloria Dinerman, 82 Fordham, Colonia, NJ 07067.
Resolutions Committee. John Parsons, Skyline Plaza, 2013-N, 3701 S. George Mason Dr., Falls Church, VA 22041.
Speakers Bureau. Allan Kahn, 2265

Glenkirk Dr., San Jose, CA 95124.
State Associations. Herbert Davis, Box 108, Brooklandville, MD 21022.
Task Force on Liaison with Leagues of Municipalities. Theodore Wenzl, 83 Jordan Blvd., Delmar, NY 12054.
Task Force on Membership. Joanne Wisener, 860 19 Place, Yuma, AZ 85364; Deborah Miller, 840 Rosedale Lane, Hoffman Estates, IL 60195.

American Library Association
Association for Library Service to Children

Executive Director, Ann Carlson Weeks
50 E. Huron St., Chicago, IL 60611
312 944-6780

Object

Interested in the improvement and extension of library services to children in all types of libraries. Responsible for the evaluation and selection of book and nonbook materials for, and the improvement of techniques of, library services to children from preschool through the eighth grade or junior high school age, when such materials or techniques are intended for use in more than one type of library. Founded 1900. Memb. 3,108. (For information on dues see ALA entry.)

Membership

Open to anyone interested in library services to children.

Officers (July 1983–June 1984)

Pres. Phyllis Van Orden, 2281 Trescott Dr., Tallahassee, FL 32312; *V.P.* Margaret Bush, 319 Tenth St. S.E., Apt. 2, Washington, DC 20003; *Past Pres.* Margaret M. Kimmel, School of Lib. and Info. Science, Univ. of Pittsburgh, 135 N. Bellefield,

Pittsburgh, PA 15260; *Exec. Dir.* Ann Carlson Weeks, ALSC/ALA, 50 E. Huron St., Chicago, IL 60611.

Directors

Marianne Carus; Eliza T. Dresang; Adele Fasick; Ruth Gordon; Elizabeth Huntoon; Barbara Immroth; Virginia McKee; Susan Roman; Mary Somerville; Caroline Ward.

Committee Chairpersons

Priority Group I: Child Advocacy

Consultant. Marilyn Berg Iarusso, Office of Children's Services, New York Public Lib., 455 Fifth Ave., New York, NY 10016.
Boy Scouts of America (Advisory). Linda Ward Callaghan, West Belmont Branch, Chicago Public Lib., 3104 N. Narragansett, Chicago, IL 60634.
Legislation. Mary K. Conwell, 400 Central Park W., #2Y, New York, NY 10025.
Liaison with Mass Media. Judith Rovenger, Westchester Lib. System, Cross Westchester Executive Branch, 8 Westchester Plaza, Elmsford, NY 10523.

Liaison with National Organizations Serving the Child. Elizabeth W. Simmons, 4801 S. 23 Rd., Arlington, VA 22206.

U.S. National Park Service/ALSC (Joint Committee). Joanne E. Fields, 2179 E. 28 St., Brooklyn, NJ 11229.

Priority Group II: Evaluation of Media

Consultant. Ellen M. Stepanian, Shaker Heights City School Dist., 3468 Lee Rd., Shaker Heights, OH 44120.

Film Evaluation. Hilda W. Parfrey, Sandberg Elementary School, 217 Karen Ct., Madison, WI 53705.

Filmstrip Evaluation. Maria B. Salvadore, Children's Services, D.C. Public Lib. System, 901 G St. N.W., Washington, DC 20001.

"Multimedia Approach to Children's Literature Revision" (ad hoc). Lynne R. Pickens, 1481 Hampton Glen Ct., Decatur, GA 30033.

Notable Children's Books. Beverly J. Bruan, 3966 N. Sherman Ave., Fresno, CA 93726.

Notable Children's Books 1976-1980 Reevaluation Committee (ad hoc). Amy Kellman, 211 Castlegate Rd., Pittsburgh, PA 15221.

Recording Evaluation. Kathy J. Woodrell, 625 Wiley Ave., Salisbury, NC 28144.

Selection of Children's Books from Various Cultures. Frances F. Povsic, 604 Knollwood Dr., Bowling Green, OH 43402.

Toys, Games and Realia Evaluation. Rosemary Nuclo, 3701 Lochearn Dr., Baltimore, MD 21207.

Priority Group III: Professional Development

Consultant. Barbara Barstow, 13412 Sprecher, Cleveland, OH 44135.

Arbuthnot Honor Lecture. Sybille Jagusch, 3 Chesham Ct., Cockeysville, MD 21030.

Continuing Education. Linda Gayle Cole, Stockton-San Joaquin County Public Lib., 605 N. El Dorado St., Stockton, CA 95202.

Managing Children's Services (Discussion Group). Mary B. Bauer, 1026 Edgewood Ave., Silver Springs, MD 20901; Nancy Schifrin, Fairfax County Public Lib., 5502 Port Royal Rd., Springfield, VA 21151.

Frederic G. Melcher Scholarship. Mary Alice Hunt, 1603 Kolopakin Nene, Tallahassee, FL 32301.

Putnam Publishing Group Award. Patricia E. Latch, Cobb County Public Lib. System, 30 Atlanta St., Marietta, GA 30060.

State and Regional Leadership (Discussion Group). Margo Daniels, 7400 Old Dominion Dr., McLean, VA 22101.

Teachers of Children's Literature (Discussion Group). Judith Weedman, Univ. of Michigan, SLIS, 580 Union Dr., Ann Arbor, MI 48109.

Priority Group IV: Social Responsibilities

Consultant. Jane McGregor, 1419 Valparaiso Dr., Apt. U-11, Florence, SC 29501.

Intellectual Freedom. Mae M. Benne, 331 W. 53, Seattle, WA 98107.

International Relations. Mary Lou White, 2530 Brookdale Dr., Springfield, OH 45502.

Library Service to Children with Special Needs. Judith F. Davie, 251A Patriot Way, Greensboro, NC 27408.

Preschool Services and Parent Education. Frances A. Smardo, 3539 Vancouver Dr., Dallas, TX 75229.

Program Support Publications (Special). Mary Beth Babikow, Baltimore County Public Lib., 320 York Rd., Towson, MD 21204.

Social Issues in Relation to Materials and Services for Children (Discussion Group). Anitra T. Steele, Mid-Continent Public Lib., 15616 E. 24 Hwy., Independence, MO 64050.

Priority Group V: Planning and Research

Consultant. Mary C. Paulus, 120 Harry Lane, Owings Mills, MD 21117.

Caldecott Medal Calendar Committee. Marilyn Berg Iarusso, Office of Children's Services, New York Public Lib., 455 Fifth Ave., New York, NY 10016.

Collections of Children's Books for Adult Research (Discussion Group). Winifred Ragsdale, 2990 Maiden Lane, Altadena, CA 91001.

Local Arrangements—Dallas 1984. Jo Ann Bell, 801 Carney Dr., Garland, TX 75041.

Membership. Jill L. Locke, Farmington Community Lib., 32737 W. 12 Mile Rd., Farmington Hills, MI 48018.

National Planning of Special Collections. Margaret N. Coughlan, 510 N St. S.W., Washington, DC 20024.

Nominating—1984. Amy Kellman, 211 Castlegate Rd., Pittsburgh, PA 15521.

Organization and Bylaws. Ethel B. Manheimer, 2373 Woolsey St., Berkeley, CA 94705.

Program Evaluation and Support. Adele M. Fasick, 4351 Bloor St. W., Unit 40, Etobicoke, ON M9C 2A4, Canada.

Publications Committee. Marjorie Jones, The Junior Literary Guild, 245 Park Ave., New York, NY 10167.

Research and Development. Ellin Greene, Univ. of Chicago, Graduate Lib. School, 1100 E. 57 St., Chicago, IL 60637.

"Top of the News" Editorial, Joint ALSC/ YASD. Marilyn Kaye, SLIS, St. John's Univ., Grand Central & Utopia Pkwys., Jamaica, NY 11439.

Priority Group VI: Award Committees

Consultant. Bette J. Peltola, 4109 N. Ardmore, Milwaukee, WI 53211.

Mildred L. Batchelder Award Selection— 1984. M. Jean Greenlaw, 2600 Sheraton Rd., Denton, TX 76201.

Mildred L. Batchelder Award Selection— 1985. Mary Kingsbury, School of Lib. Science, Manning Hall, 026-A, Univ. of North Carolina, Chapel Hill, NC 27514.

Caldecott Award—1984. Ellin Greene, Univ. of Chicago, Graduate Lib. School, 1100 E. 57 St., Chicago, IL 60637.

Caldecott Award—1985. Karen Nelson Hoyle, 1554 Fulham St., St. Paul, MN 55108.

Newbery Award—1984. Elizabeth M. Greggs, King County Lib. System, 300 Eighth Ave. N., Seattle, WA 98109.

Newbery Award—1985. Julie Cummins, Children's Services Consultant, Monroe County Lib. System, 115 South Ave., Rochester, NY 14604.

Representatives

ALA Budget Assembly. Margaret Bush.

ALA Legislation Assembly. Mary K. Conwell.

ALA Library Education Assembly. Linda Gayle Cole.

ALA Dallas Conference (1984) Conference Program. Phyllis Van Orden.

ALA Membership Promotion Task Force. Jill L. Locke.

International Board on Books for Young People, U.S. Section, Executive Board. Ann Carlson Weeks, Mary Lou White, Phyllis Van Orden.

RTSD/CCS Cataloging of Children's Materials. Marilyn Karrenbrock; Divna Todorovich.

Liaison with Other National Organizations

American Association for Gifted Children. Naomi Noyes.

American National Red Cross. Red Cross Youth. To be appointed.

Association for Children and Adults with Learning Disabilities. To be appointed.

Big Brothers and Big Sisters of America. Helen Mullen.

Boys Clubs of America. Jane Kunstsler.

Camp Fire Inc. Anitra T. Steele.

Child Welfare League of America. Ethel Ambrose.

Children's Defense Fund. Effie Lee Morris.

Children's Theatre Association. Amy E. Spaulding.

Day Care and Child Development Council of America. James W. Hoogstra.

Four-H Programs, Extension Service. Elizabeth Simmons.

Girls Club of America. Karen Breen.

Girl Scouts of America. Margo M. Daniels.

National Association for the Education of Young Children. Jeanette Studley.

National Association for the Perpetuation and Preservation of Storytelling. Elizabeth Simmons.

National Story League. Linda Hansford.

Parents Without Partners. Marian B. Peck.

Puppeteers of America. Darrell Hildebrandt.

Salvation Army. Margaret Malm.

Young Men's Christian Association. Jill L. Locke.

Young Women's Christian Association. Elizabeth Simmons.

American Library Association
Association of College and Research Libraries

Executive Director, Julie A. Carroll Virgo
50 E. Huron St., Chicago, IL 60611
312-944-6780

Object

Represents research and special libraries and libraries in institutions of postsecondary education, including those of community and junior colleges, colleges, and universities. Founded 1938. Membership 9,000. (For information on dues, see ALA entry.)

Publications

ACRL Nonprint Media Publications (occasional). *Ed.* Jean W. Farrington, 221 Martroy Lane, Wallingford, PA 19086.

ACRL Publications in Librarianship (formerly *ACRL Monograph Series*) (occasional). *Ed.* Arthur P. Young, Univ. of Rhode Island, Kingston, RI 02881.

Choice (11 per year; $75); *Choice Reviews on Cards* ($150). *Ed.* Rebecca D. Dixon, 100 Riverside Center, Middletown, CT 06457.

College & Research Libraries (6 per year, memb.; nonmemb. $35). *Ed.* C. James Schmidt, Research Lib. Group, Jordan Quad, Stanford, CA 94305.

College & Research Libraries (11 per year; memb.; nonmemb.; $10). *Ed.* George M. Eberhart, ACRL Headquarters.

Officers (July 1983–July 1984)

Pres. Joyce Ball, California State Univ., Sacramento, CA 95819; *V.P./Pres.-Elect.* Sharon J. Rogers, Bowling Green State Univ. Libs., Bowling Green, OH; *Past Pres.* Carla J. Stoffle, Univ. of Wisconsin-Parkside, Kenosha, WI 53141.

Board of Directors

Officers; section chairs and vice-chairs; *Dirs.-at-Large.* Imogene I. Book (1984); Sara Lou Whildin (1984); Barbara Collinsworth (1985); Betty L. Hacker (1985); Willis M. Hubbard (1985); Jean A. Major (1986); Bob D. Carmack (1987); Alexandra Mason (1987).

Section Chairpersons

Anthropology and Sociology. Patricia W. Silvernail, Univ. of Oregon Library, Eugene, OR.

Art. Roland Hasen, School of the Art Institute of Chicago Lib., Chicago, IL 60603.

Asian and African. Tze-chung Li, Rosary College Grad. School of Lib. Science, River Forest, IL 60305.

Bibliographic Instruction. Maureen D. Pastine, Clark Lib., San Jose State Univ., San Jose, CA.

College Libraries. Patricia G. Oyler, Simmons College Grad. School of Lib. and Info. Science, Boston, MA.

Community and Junior College Libraries. Mary Sue Ferrell, Western Nevada Community College, Carson City, NV.

Education and Behavioral Sciences. Virginia Parr, Central Lib., Univ. of Cincinnati, Cincinnati, OH.

Law and Political Science. Abner J. Gaines, Univ. of Rhode Island Lib., Kingston, RI 02881.

Rare Books and Manuscripts. Stephen Ferguson, Firestone Lib., Princeton Univ., Princeton, NJ 08540.

Slavic and East European Section. Jan Kennedy-Olsen, Mann Lib., Cornell Univ., Ithaca, NY 14853.

Science and Technology Section. Jan Kennedy-Olsen, Mann Lib., Cornell Univ., Ithaca, NY 14853.

University Libraries. Jane Ross Moore, Grad. School and Univ. Center, City Univ. of New York, New York, NY 10036.

Western European Specialists. Joan F. Higbee, Lib. of Congress, Washington, D.C.

Discussion Groups

Black Studies Librarianship. Jeff Jackson, Reference Dept., Univ. of Wisconsin-Parkside, Wood Rd., Kenosha, WI 53141.

Cinema Librarians. Nancy H. Allen, Communications Lib., Univ. of Illinois, 122 Gregory HL, Urbana, IL 61501.

English and American Literature. Valmai R. Fenster, Univ. of Wisconsin Lib. School, 600 N. Park St., Madison, WI 53706.

Extended Campus Library Services. Robert M. Cookingham, Meriam Lib., California State Univ., Chico, CA 95929.

Fee Based Information Service Centers in Academic Libraries. Elizabeth A. Lunden, Rice Univ., Houston, TX 77001.

Heads of Public/Readers Services. Peter D. Haikalis, San Francisco State Univ., San Francisco, CA 94132.

Librarians of Library Science Collections. Olha T. Della Cava, Columbia Univ. Lib., New York, NY 10027.

Committee Chairpersons

ACRL Academic or Research Librarian of the Year Award. Kenneth G. Peterson, Morris Lib., Southern Illinois Univ. at Carbondale, Carbondale, IL 62901.

ACRL Academic and Research Library Personnel Study Group. Page Ackerman, Santa Monica, CA 90402.

ACRL Academic Status Committee. Barbara J. Ford, Univ. of Illinois at Chicago, Chicago, IL.

ACRL Appointments (1983) and Nominations (1984). Mary Sue Ferrell, Western Nevada Community College, Carson City, NV.

ACRL Appointments (1984) and Nominations (1985). Mary Reichel, Pullen Lib., Georgia State Univ., 100 Decatur St., Atlanta, GA 30303.

Audiovisual. Linda Piele, Public Services Div., Lib./Learning Center, Univ. of

Wisconsin-Parkside, Kenosha, WI 53141.

"Books for College Libraries—Third Edition." Richard D. Johnson, James M. Milne Lib., State Univ. College, Oneonta, NY 13820.

Budget and Finance Committee. Robert Almony, Ellis Lib., Univ. of Missouri, Columbia, MO 65201.

College and Research Libraries Editor Search Committee (Ad Hoc). Lawrence J. Wilt, Univ. Lib., Univ. of Maryland-Baltimore County, Catonsville, MD 21228.

College Library Standards Committee (Ad Hoc). Jacquelyn M. Morris, Univ. of the Pacific, Stockton, CA 95211.

Conference Executive Committee—ACRL National Conference, Seattle, 1984. Gary L. Menges, Public Services, Suzzallo Lib., Univ. of Washington, Seattle, WA 98195.

Conference Program Planning Committee—Dallas, 1984. Joyce Ball, Univ. Lib., California State Univ., Sacramento, CA 95819.

Conference Program Planning Committee—Chicago, 1985. Sharon J. Rogers, Bowling Green State Univ. Libs., Bowling Green, OH.

Continuing Education Committee. Keith M. Cottman, William Robertson Coe Lib., Univ. of Wyoming, Laramie, WY 82071.

Copyright Committee. Barbara B. Rystrom, Univ. of Georgia Libs., Athens, Georgia.

Doctoral Dissertation Fellowship. Sara Fine, School of Lib. and Info. Science, Univ. of Pittsburgh, Pittsburgh, PA 15260.

J. Morris Jones—ALA Divisional Leadership Enhancement Program Planning. Kathleen Weibel, Univ. of Wisconsin-Parkside, Kenosha, WI 53141.

Legislation. Elaine Sloan, Indiana Univ., Bloomington, IN 47401.

Membership. Elizabeth M. Salzer, J.

Henry Meyer Memorial Lib., Stanford Univ., Stanford, CA 94305.

Planning. Carla Stoffle, Univ. of Wisconsin-Parkside, Kenosha, WI 53141.

Publications. Joanne R. Euster, J. Paul Leonard Lib., San Francisco State Univ., San Francisco, CA 94132.

Samuel Lazerow Fellowship Committee for Research in Acquisitions or Technical Services. Jay Martin Poole, Texas A & M, College Sta., Galveston, TX.

Standards and Accreditation. Patricia Ann Sacks, Muhlenberg and Cedar Crest College, Allentown, PA.

Supplemental Funds. Carlton C. Rochell, New York Univ. Lib., New York, NY 10012.

Representatives

American Association for the Advancement of Science. Jacquelyn Morris.

American Association for the Advancement of Science, Consortium of Affiliates for International Programs. Jacquelyn Morris.

American Council on Education. Joseph A. Boisse.

ALA Committee on Appointments. Sharon J. Rogers.

ALA Committee on Professional Ethics. Ann Bristow Beltran.

ALA Conference Program Planning Committee (Dallas, 1984). Joyce Ball.

ALA Conference Program Planning Committee (Chicago, 1985). Sharon Rogers.

ALA Legislation Assembly. Elaine Sloan.

ALA Membership Promotion Task Force. Elizabeth M. Salzer.

ALA Planning and Budget Assembly. Joyce Ball.

ALA Resources and Technical Services Division, Committee on Cataloging: Description and Access. Jennifer A. Younger.

ALA RTSD Interdivisional Committee on Catalog Form, Function, and Use. Brian Nielsen.

ALA RTSD Preservation of Library Materials Section. Carolyn Harris.
ALA Standing Committee on Library Education (SCOLE). Barbara J. Ford, Keith M. Cottam, Olha T. Della Cava.
Association for Asian Studies, Committee

on East Asian Libraries. Warren Tsuneishi.
Freedom to Read Foundation. James N. Myers.
LC Cataloging in Publication Advisory Group. Susan U. Golden.

American Library Association
Association of Specialized and Cooperative Library Agencies

Executive Director, Sandra M. Cooper
50 E. Huron St., Chicago, IL 60611
312-944-6780

Object

To represent state library agencies, specialized library agencies, and multitype library cooperatives. Within the interest of these types of library organizations, the Association of Specialized and Cooperative Library Agencies has specific responsibility for:

1. Development and evaluation of goals and plans for state library agencies, specialized library agencies, and multitype library cooperatives to facilitate the implementation, improvement, and extension of library activities designed to foster improved user services, coordinating such activities with other appropriate ALA units.

2. Representation and interpretation of the role, functions, and services of state library agencies, specialized library agencies, and multitype library cooperatives within and outside the profession, including contact with national organizations and government agencies.

3. Development of policies, studies, and activities in matters affecting state library agencies, specialized library agencies, and multitype library cooperatives relating to (a) state and local library legislation, (b) state grants-in-aid and appropriations, and (c) relationships among state, federal, regional, and local governments, coordi-

nating such activities with other appropriate ALA units.

4. Establishment, evaluation, and promotion of standards and service guidelines relating to the concerns of this association.

5. Identifying the interests and needs of all persons, encouraging the creation of services to meet these needs within the areas of concern of the association, and promoting the use of these services provided by state library agencies, specialized library agencies, and multitype library cooperatives.

6. Stimulating the professional growth and promoting the specialized training and continuing education of library personnel at all levels in the areas of concern of this association and encouraging membership participation in appropriate type-of-activity divisions within ALA.

7. Assisting in the coordination of activities of other units within ALA that have a bearing on the concerns of this association.

8. Granting recognition for outstanding library service within the areas of concern of this association.

9. Acting as a clearinghouse for the exchange of information and encouraging the development of materials, publications, and research within the areas of concern of this association.

Board of Directors

Pres. Christine L. Kirby, Cons. for Service to the Disadvantaged, Massachusetts Bd. of Lib. Commissioners, 648 Beacon St., Boston, MA 02215; *V.P./Pres.-Elect.* James A. Nelson, State Libn., Dept. of Libs. and Archives, Box 537, Frankfort, KY 40602; *Past Pres.* Nancy L. Wareham, Exec. Dir., Cleveland Area Metropolitan Lib. System, 11000 Euclid Ave., Rm. 309, Cleveland, OH 44106; *Div. Councillor.* Barratt Wilkins (1985); *Dirs.-at-Large.* John D. Christenson (1984); Jane Gray (1985); Rhea J. Rubin (1984); Patricia H. Smith (1985); *Sec. Reps.* Kathleen O. Mays, HCLS chpn. (1984); Barbara L. Perkis, LSBPH chpn. (1984); Mary E. Flournoy, LSDS chpn. (1984); Linda S. Lucas, LSIES chpn. (1984); Catharine D. Cook, LSPS chpn. (1984); Sheila J. Merrell, MLCS chpn. (1984); Peter Paulson, SLAS chpn. (1984); *Ex Officio* (Nonvoting). Sue O. Medina, *Interface* ed. (1985); Marcia King, Planning, Organization, and Bylaws Committee chpn. (1985); *Exec. Dir.* Sandra M. Cooper.

Publications

Bibliotherapy Discussion Group Newsletter. (q.; $5 memb.; $7 nonmemb.). *Newsletter Coord.* Lethene Parks, 8532 State Rd. N. 302, Gig Harbor, WA 98335.
Interface (q.; memb.; nonmemb. $10). *Ed.* Sue O. Medina, 663 Hillsboro Rd., Montgomery, AL 36109.

Committees

American Correctional Association — ASCLA Committee on Institutional Libraries (Joint). Priscilla K. Linsley, 2 Cleveland Rd. W., Princeton, NJ 08540.
Awards. S. Stephen Prine, Jr., 223 Sixth St. S.E., #2, Washington, DC 20003.

Exceptional Achievement Award Jury. Stefan B. Moses, Exec. Dir., California Lib. Assn., 717 K St., Suite 300, Sacramento, CA 95814-3477.
Bibliotherapy. Frank L. Turner, Jr., Box 1024, Lake Dallas, TX 75065.
Budget and Finance. James A. Nelson, State Libn., Dept. of Libs. and Archives, Box 537, Frankfort, KY 40602.
Catalog Form, Function and Use. Dorothy McGarry, Physical Science & Technical Libs., 8251 Boelter Hall, Univ. of California, Los Angeles, CA 90024.
Conference Program Coordination. Susan E. Stroyan, 2013 E. Taylor St., Bloomington, IL 61701.
Continuing Education. Peggy O'Donnell, 1135 W. Webster, Chicago, IL 60614.
Exceptional Service Award Jury. Jan L. Ames, Dir., Washington Regional Lib. for the Blind and Physically Handicapped, 811 Hamson St., Seattle, WA 98129.
"Interface" Advisory. William M. Duncan, Metropolitan Lib. Service Agency, Griggs Midway Bldg., S-322, St. Paul, MN 55104.
Legislation. Barbara F. Weaver, State Libn., New Jersey State Lib., CN 520, Trenton, NJ 08625.
Membership Promotion. Beverly A. Jones, Chief Planning Officer, Oklahoma Dept. of Libnshp., 200 N.E. 18 St., Oklahoma City, OK 73105.
Nominating. Carmela M. Ruby, 121 45 St., Sacramento, CA 95819.
Planning, Organization, and Bylaws. Marcia King, Dir., Public Lib., Box 27470, Tucson, AZ 85726.
Publications. Donna O. Dziedzic, 2124 N. Sedgwick, Chicago, IL 60614.
Research. Katherine M. Jackson, Head, Reference Div., Sterling C. Evans Lib., Texas A & M Univ., College Station, TX 77843.
Standards for Library Functions at the State Level (Ad Hoc Subcommittee). Denny R. Stephens, Asst. Dir., Okla-

homa Dept. of Libnshp., 200 N.E. 18 St., Oklahoma City, OK 73105.

Standards Review. Richard T. Miller, Jr., Projects Coord., State Lib., Box 387, 308 E. High St., Jefferson City, MO 65102.

Standards Review for Library Service to the Blind and Physically Handicapped (Ad Hoc Subcommittee). Alphonse F. Trezza, 2205 Napoleon Bonaparte Dr., Tallahassee, FL 32308.

Representatives

ALA Government Documents Round Table (GODORT). Patricia K. Sloan (1985).

ALA International Relations Assembly. Blane K. Dessy (1985).

ALA Legislation Assembly. Elliot Shelkrot (1984); Barbara F. Weaver (1984).

ALA Library Education Assembly. Peggy O'Donnell (1984).

ALA Membership Promotion Task Force. Beverly A. Jones (1984).

ALA/LAMA/BES Committees for Facilities for Specialized Library Services. Richard E. Bopp (1984).

ALA/RASD Interlibrary Loan Committee. Theresa A. Trucksis (1984).

ALA/RTSD/CCS Cataloging: Description and Access Committee. To be announced.

American Correctional Association (ACA). To be announced.

Association for Radio Reading Services, Inc. Barbara L. Wilson (1985).

Chief Officers of State Library Agencies (COSLA). Exec. Dir., Sandra M. Cooper.

Freedom to Read Foundation. Susan B. Madden (1985).

Interagency Council on Library Resources for Nursing. Barbara Van Nortwick (1985).

Section Chairpersons

Health Care Libraries Section (HCLS). Kathleen O. Mayo, Rte. 1, Box 3425, Havana, FL 32333.

Library Service to the Blind and Physically Handicapped (LSBPH). Barbara L. Perkis, Asst. Dir., Regional Lib. for the Blind and Physically Handicapped, 1055 W. Roosevelt Rd., Chicago, IL 60608.

Library Service to the Deaf Section (LSDS). Mary E. Flournoy, 419 S. Quince St., Philadelphia, PA 19147.

Library Service to the Impaired Elderly Section. (LSIES). Linda S. Lucas, Assoc. Professor, College of Lib. & Info. Science, Univ. of South Carolina, Columbia, SC 29208.

Library Service to Prisoners Section (LSPS). Catharine D. Cook, Public Lib. Consultant, Dept. of Libnshp., 200 NE 18 St., Oklahoma City, OK 73105.

Multitype Library Cooperation Section (MLCS). Sheila J. Merrell, 37 Magnolia Dr., St. Louis, MO 63124.

State Library Agency Section (SLAS). Peter Paulson, 24 Tilinghast Ave., Albany, NY 12204.

American Library Association
Library Administration and Management Association

Executive Director, Roger H. Parent
50 E. Huron St., Chicago, IL 60611
312-944-6780

Object

"The Library Administration and Management Association provides an organizational framework for encouraging the study of administrative theory, for improving the practice of administration in libraries, and for identifying and fostering administrative skill. Toward these ends, the division is responsible for all elements of general administration which are common to more than one type of library. These may include organizational structure, financial administration, personnel management and training, buildings and equipment, and public relations. LAMA meets this responsibility in the following ways:

1. Study and review of activities assigned to the division with due regard for changing developments in these activities.

2. Initiating and overseeing activities and projects appropriate to the division, including activities involving bibliography compilation, publication, study, and review of professional literature within the scope of the division.

3. Synthesis of those activities of other ALA units which have a bearing upon the responsibilities or work of the division.

4. Representation and interpretation of library administrative activities in contacts outside the library profession.

5. Aiding the professional development of librarians engaged in administration and encouragement of their participation in appropriate type-of-library divisions.

6. Planning and development of those programs of study and research in library administrative problems which are most needed by the profession."

Established 1957.

Officers

Pres. Nancy R. McAdams, Univ. of Texas, Austin, TX 78712; *V.P./Pres.-Elect.* Gary Strong; *Past Pres.* David R. Smith; *Exec. Dir.* Roger H. Parent.

(Address correspondence to the executive director.)

Board of Directors

Dirs. B. Franklin Hemphill; Daniel J. Bradbury; Dale Montanelli; Mary Jordon Coe; Sally Brickman; Laurence Miller; Louise P. Berry; *Dirs.-at-Large.* Sue Fontaine; Thomas E. Alford; *Councillor.* Dale Canelas; *Ex Officio.* Peter Spyers-Duran; Carol L. Anderson; William W. Sannwald; Maureen Sullivan; Nancy C. Woodall; David F. Kohl; Eleanor Jo Rodger; *Committee Organizer.* William G. Jones.

Publications

LAMA Newsletter (q.; memb.) *Ed.* Edward D. Garten, Tennessee Technical Univ., Box 5066, Cookeville, TN 38501.

Committee Chairpersons

Budget and Finance. Gary M. Shirk, 3741 20 Ave., Minneapolis, MN 55407.
Membership. Eugene T. Neely, Rutgers Univ. Lib., 185 University Ave., Newark, NJ 07102.
Nominating. Patricia Paine, 3915 Benton St. N.W., Washington, DC 20007.
Organization. William G. Jones, 329 Ridge Rd., Kenilworth, IL 60043.
Orientation. Betty Bender, Spokane Pub-

lic Lib., W906 Main, Spokane, WA 99201.

Program. David R. Smith, Hennepin County Lib., 12601 Ridgedale Dr., Minnetonka, MN 55343.

Publications. Gary Kraske, McKeldin Lib., Univ. of Maryland, College Park, MD 20742.

Small Libraries Publications. Kay Cassell, Huntington Public Lib., 338 Main St., Huntington, NY 11743.

Special Conferences and Programs Committee. Donald Kelsey, 499 Wilson Lib., 309 19 Ave. S., Minneapolis, MN 55455.

Discussion Group Chairpersons

Asst.-to-the-Dir. John Kupersmith, General Libs., Box P, Univ. of Texas, Austin, TX 78712.

Middle Management. Barton M. Lessin, Central Michigan Univ. Lib., Mt. Pleasant, MI 48859.

Racism Sexism Awareness. Honore Francois, Prince George's County Memorial Lib., 6532 Adelphi Rd., Hyattsville, MD 20782.

Women Administrators. Sarah P. Hunt, Loudoun County Public Lib., 21 E. Cornwall, Leesburg, VA 22075; Noreen S. Alldredge, Montana State Univ. Lib., Bozeman, MT 59719.

Section Chairpersons

Advisory Committee on LAMA Newsletter (ad hoc). Mary A. Seng, General Lib., Box P, Univ. of Texas, Austin, TX 78712.

Buildings and Equipment Section. B. Franklin Hemphill, 1809 Landrake Rd., Towson, MD 21204.

Catalog Form, Function, and Use Committee. Susan Phillips, 4606 Creek Ridge, Austin, TX 78735.

Fund Raising and Financial Development Section. Daniel J. Bradbury, Public Lib., 311 E. 12 St., Kansas City, MO 64106.

Library Education Assembly. Janet Steiner.

Library Organization and Management Section. Dale Montanelli, 230 Lib., Univ. of Illinois, 1408 W. Gregory Dr., Urbana, IL 61801.

Personnel Administration Section. Mary Jordan Coe, Santa Fe Regional Lib., 222 E. University Ave., Gainesville, FL 32601.

Public Relations Section. Sally Brickman, Freiberger Lib., Case Western Reserve Univ., 11161 East Blvd., Cleveland, OH 44106.

Statistics Section. Louise P. Berry, Darien Lib., 35 Leroy Ave., Darien, CT 06820.

Systems and Services Section. Laurence Miller, Florida International Univ., Tamiami Trail, Miami, FL 33199.

Task Force on Evaluation Methods. Gary Strong, California State Lib., Box 2037, Sacramento, CA 95809.

Task Force on Governmental Affairs. Ann Heidbreder Eastman, College of Arts and Sciences, VA Polytechnic Univ., Blacksburg, VA 24061.

Task Force on Institutional Membership. Sherman Hayes, Chester Fritz Lib., Univ. of North Dakota, Grand Forks, ND 58202.

Task Force on Membership Involvement. Gloria J. Stockton, Northern Regional Lib. Facility, Univ. of California, Richmond Field Station, Richmond, CA 94804.

Task Force on Non-Library Management Association. Kenneth E. Toombs, Thomas Cooper Lib., Univ. of South Carolina, Columbia, SC 29208.

Task Force on Recognition of Achievement. Nolan Lushington, Box 1624, Greenwich, CT 06836.

American Library Association
Library and Information Technology Association

Executive Director, Donald P. Hammer
50 E. Huron St., Chicago, IL 60611
312-944-6780

Object

"The Library and Information Technology Association provides its members and, to a lesser extent, the information dissemination field as a whole, with a forum for discussion, an environment for learning, and a program for action on all phases of the development and application of automated and technological systems in the library and information sciences. Since its activities and interests are derived as responses to the needs and demands of its members, its program is flexible, varied, and encompasses many aspects of the field. Its primary concern is the design, development, and implementation of technological systems in the library and information science fields. Within that general precept, the interests of the division include such varied activities as systems development, electronic data processing, mechanized information retrieval, operations research, standards development, telecommunications, networks and collaborative efforts, management techniques, information technology and other aspects of audiovisual and video cable communications activities, and hardware applications related to all of these areas. Although it has no facilities to carry out research, it attempts to encourage its members in that activity.

Information about all of these activities is disseminated through the division's publishing program, seminars and institutes, exhibits, conference programs, and committee work. The division provides an advisory and consultative function when called upon to do so.

It regards continuing education as one of its major responsibilities and through the above channels it attempts to inform its members of current activities and trends, and it also provides retrospective information for those new to the field."

Officers

Pres. Kenneth E. Downlin, Dir., Pikes Peak Regional Lib. Dist., 20 N. Cascade Ave., Colorado Springs, CO 80901; *V.P./Pres.-Elect.* Nancy L. Eaton, Bailey-Howe Lib., Univ. of Vermont, Burlington, VT 05405; *Past Pres.* Carolyn M. Gray, Asst. Dir. for Technical Services & Automation, Goldfarb Lib., Brandeis Univ., 415 South St., Waltham, MA 02254.

Directors

Officers: Hugh Atkinson (1984); Patricia Barkalow (1986); Joyce Capell (1984); Lois M. Kershner (1985); Jerome Yavarkovsky (1984); *Councillor.* Bonnie K. Juergens (1985); *Ex officio. Bylaws and Organization Committee Chpn.* Heike Kordish (1984); *Exec Dir.* Donald P. Hammer.

Publications

Information Technology and Libraries (ITAL, formerly *JOLA)* (q.; memb.; nonmemb. $25; single copies $7.50.). *Ed.* William G. Potter, 246A Lib., Univ. of Illinois, 1408 W. Gregory Dr., Urbana, IL 61801. For information or to send manuscripts, contact the editor.
LITA Newsletter (3/yr.; memb.) *Ed.* Carol A. Parkhurst, Systems Libn., Univ. of Nevada Lib., Reno, NV 89557.

Committee Chairpersons

Awards. Mary Fisher Ghikas, Asst. Commissioner, Public Lib., 425 N. Michigan Ave., Chicago, IL 60611.

Budget Review. Carolyn M. Gray, Asst. Dir., Technical Services & Automation, Goldfarb Lib., Brandeis Univ., 415 South St., Waltham, MA 02554.

Bylaws and Organization. Heike Kordish, Columbia Univ. Libs., 322 Butler Lib., New York, NY 10027.

Catalog Form, Function, and Use. Dorothy McGarry, Physical Science & Technical Libs., 8251 Boelter Hall, UCLA, Los Angeles, CA 90024.

Education. Janet J. Bausser, Perkins Lib., Rm. 120, Duke Univ., Durham, NC 27706.

Emerging Technologies. Brigitte L. Kenney, Infocon, Inc., 400 Plateau Pkwy., Golden, CO 80401.

ITAL Editorial Board. William G. Potter, Univ. of Illinois Lib., Rm., 246A, 1408 W. Gregory Dr., Urbana, IL 61801.

Legislation and Regulation. David H. Brunell, FLC/FEDLINK, Lib. of Congress, Washington, DC 20540.

LITA/Gaylord Award. Patricia Earnest, Public Lib., 500 W. Broadway, Anaheim, CA 92895.

Membership. Frances Carducci, Univ. of Rochester, Rush Rhees Lib., Rochester, NY 14627.

Long-Range Plan Implementation. Nancy L. Eaton, Bailey-Howe Lib., Univ. of Vermont, Burlington, VT 05405.

Nominating. Sherrie Schmidt, Univ. of Texas, 2601 N. Floyd, Box 643, Richardson, TX 75080.

Program Planning. Richard G. Akeroyd, Jr., Public Lib., 1357 Broadway, Denver, CO 80203.

Publications. Michael J. Gorman, 246A Lib., Univ. of Illinois, 1408 W. Gregory Dr., Urbana, IL 61801.

Representation in Machine-Readable Form of Bibliographic Information, RTSD/LITA/RASD (MARBI). Richard O. Green, OCLC, 6565 Frantz Rd., Dublin, OH 43017.

Technical Standards for Library Automation (TESLA). Ruth C. Carter, Head, Cataloging Dept., G49 Hillman Lib., Univ. of Pittsburgh, Pittsburgh, PA 15260.

Telecommunications. Janet L. Bruman, CLASS, 1415 Koll Circle, Suite 101, San Jose, CA 95112.

Discussion Group Chairpersons

Consultant/User Discussion Group. Ernest A. Muro, V.P., Technical Services, Baker & Taylor Co., 6 Kirby Ave., Somerville, NJ 08876.

Vendor/User Discussion Group. James K. Long, OCLC, 6565 Frantz Rd., Columbus, OH 43017.

Section Chairpersons

Information Science & Automation Section (ISAS). Jerome Yavarkovsky, Dean, Lib. School, Adelphi Univ., Garden City, NY 11530.

Video and Cable Communications Section (VCCS). Joyce Capell, Mission College LRS, 3000 Mission College Blvd., Santa Clara, CA 95054.

American Library Association
Public Library Association

Executive Director, Shirley Mills-Fischer
50 E. Huron St., Chicago, IL 60611
312-944-6780

Object

To advance the development, effectiveness, and financial support of public library service to the American people; to speak for the library profession at the national level on matters pertaining to public libraries; and to enrich the professional competence and opportunities of public librarians. In order to accomplish this mission, the Public Library Association has adopted the following goals:

1. Conducting and sponsoring research about how the public library can respond to changing social needs and technological developments.

2. Developing and disseminating materials useful to public libraries in interpreting public library services and needs.

3. Conducting continuing education for public librarians by programming at national and regional conferences, by publications such as the journal, and by other delivery methods.

4. Establishing, evaluting, and promoting goals, guidelines, and standards for public libraries.

5. Maintaining liaison with relevant national agencies and organizations engaged in public administration and human services such as National Association of Counties, Municipal League, Commission on Post-Secondary Education.

6. Maintaining liaison with other divisions and units of ALA and other library organizations such as the Association of American Library Schools and the Urban Libraries Council.

7. Defining the role of the public library in service to a wide range of user and potential user groups.

8. Promoting and interpreting the public library to a changing society through legislative programs and other appropriate means.

9. Identifying legislation to improve and to equalize support of public libraries.

Organized 1951. Memb. 5,600.

Membership

Open to all ALA members interested in the improvement and expansion of public library services to all ages in various types of communities.

Officers (1983–1984)

Pres. Nancy M. Bolt, 1088 Fox Run Rd., Milford, OH 45150; *V.P.* Charles W. Robinson, Baltimore County Public Lib., 320 York Rd., Towson, MD 21204; *Past Pres.* Donald J. Sager, Milwaukee Public Lib., 814 West Wisconsin Ave., Milwaukee, WI 53233.

Board of Directors (1983–1984)

Officers; Melissa Forinash Buckingham; Anna A. Curry; Nina S. Ladof; Jerome G. Pennington; Jacquelyn E. Thresher; Albert V. Tweedy; *Sec. Reps. AEPS Pres.* Carol Ann Desch; *AFLS Pres.* Egon Weiss; *CIS Pres.* Lillie J. Weward; *MLS Pres.* Patricia Olsen Wilson; *PLSS Pres.* Rosemary S. Martin; *SMLS Pres.* Matthew C. Kubiak; *Ex officio. PLA-ALA Membership Rep.* Catherine O'Connell; *Past Pres. ALTA.* M. Don Surratt; *Councillor.* Kathleen Mehaffey Balcom; *Ex officio. Public Libraries ed.* Kenneth D. Shearer; *Exec. Dir.* Shirley Mills-Fischer.

Publications

Public Libraries (q.; memb.; nonmemb. $18). *Ed.* Kenneth D. Shearer, Jr., 1205 LeClair St., Chapel Hill, NC 27514.
Public Library Reporter (occas.). Ed. varies. Standing orders or single order available from Order Dept., ALA, 50 E. Huron St., Chicago, IL 60611.

Section Heads

Alternative Education Programs (AEPS). Carol Ann Desch.
Armed Forces Librarians (AFLS). Egon Weiss.
Community Information (CIS). Lillie J. Seward.
Metropolitan Libraries (MLS). Patricia Olsen Wilson.
Public Library Systems (PLSS). Rosemary S. Martin.
Small & Medium Sized Libraries Section (SMLS). Matthew C. Kubiak.

Committee and Task Force Chairpersons

Accreditation (Task Force). To be announced.
Allie Beth Martin Award. Arthur Curley, New York Public Lib., Fifth Ave. & 42 St., New York, NY 10018.
Audiovisual. Victor Frank Kralisz, Dallas Public Lib., 1515 Young St., Dallas, TX 75201.
Bylaws. Pat Woodrum, Tulsa City-County Lib., 400 Civic Center, Tulsa, OK 74103.
Cataloging Needs of Public Libraries. Maurice Freedman, Westchester Lib. System, 8 Winchester Plaza, Elmsford, NY 10523.
Children, Service to. Laureen F. Riedesel, Public Lib., 218 N. Fifth, Beatrice, NE 68301.
Conference Program Coordinating. Jon Scheer, Audelia Rd., Branch Lib., 10045 Audelia Rd., Dallas, TX 75238.

Division Program—Dallas, 1984. Sandra Stephan, Maryland State Dept. of Educ., 200 W. Baltimore St., Baltimore, MD 21201.
Division Program—Chicago, 1985. Evelyn C. Minick, 176 Merion Rd., York, PA 17403.
Education of Public Librarians. Vee Friesner, Kansas State Lib., Topeka, KS 66612.
Goals, Guidelines, and Standards for Public Libraries. Ronald A. Dubberly, Seattle Public Lib., 1000 Fourth St., Seattle, WA 98104.
Output Measures Data Collection (Subcommittee). Carolyn Additon Anthony, Baltimore County Public Lib., 320 York Rd., Towson, MD 21204.
Intellectual Freedom. Joan Collett, St. Louis Public Lib., 1301 Olive St., St. Louis, MO 63103.
International Relations (Task Force). Jane Hale Morgan, Detroit Public Lib., 5201 Woodward Ave., Detroit, MI 48202.
Legislation. Nettie Barcroft Taylor, State Dept. of Educ., Lib. Development Div., Baltimore, MD 21201.
Library Investment. Donald J. Sager, Milwaukee Public Lib., 814 W. Wisconsin Ave., Milwaukee, WI 53233.
Marketing of Public Library Services. Joyce A. McMullin, 7609 95 Ave. S.W., Tacoma, WA 98498.
Membership. Catherine O'Connell, Washington County Free Lib., 100 S. Potomac St., Hagerstown, MD 21740.
Multilingual Library Service. Patrick Valentine, North Carolina Foreign Language Lib., 328 Gillespie St., Fayetteville, NC 28301.
National Conference Evaluation. Jane Robbins-Carter, Lib. School, Helen C. White Hall, Univ. of Wisconsin, Madison, WI 53706.
Network Relations (Task Force). Betty Turock, Rutgers Univ. Grad. School of Lib. & Info. Studies, 185 College Ave., New Brunswick, NJ 08903.

New Standards (Task Force). Karen Krueger, South Central Lib. System, 201 W. Mifflin St., Madison, WI 53701.

Nominating—1984. Robert H. Rohlf, Hennepin County Lib., Ridgedale Dr. at Plymouth Rd., Minnetonka, MN 55343.

Nominating—1985. Agnes M. Griffen, Montgomery Dept. of Public Lib., 99 Maryland Ave., Rockville, MD 20850.

Organization. Claudya B. Muller, State Lib. of Iowa, Historical Bldg., 12th and Grand, Des Moines, IA 50319.

Orientation. Dorothy S. Puryear, Nassau Lib. System, 900 Jerusalem Ave., Uniondale, NY 11553.

Planning. Thomas C. Phelps, National Endowment for the Humanities, 806 15 St. N.W., MS 406, Washington, DC 20506.

Planning Process Discussion Group. Estelle M. Black, Rockford Public Lib., 215 North Wyman St., Rockford, IL 61101.

Planning Process Financial Development (Task Force). Patrick M. O'Brien, Cuyahoga County Public Lib., 4510 Memphis, Cleveland, OH 44144.

"Public Libraries" Editorial Board. Barbara Webb, Fairfax County Public Lib., 5502 Port Royal Rd., Springfield, VA 22151.

Public Library Heritage. Donald D. Foos, Lib. & Info. Science Programs, Univ. of Arkansas, Little Rock, AR 72204.

"Public Library Reporter" (Subcommittee). W. Bernard Lukenbill, Univ. of Texas, GSLS, Box 7576, Austin, TX 78712.

Publications. Peter Hiatt, Grad. School of Lib. Science, Univ. of Washington, 133 Suzzallo Lib., FM-30, Seattle, WA 98195.

Research. Eleanor Jo Rodger, Fairfax County Public Lib., 5502 Port Royal Rd., Springfield, VA 22151. *Public Library Data Base (Subcommittee).* To be announced.

State and Regional Affiliates (Task Force). Sarah Ann Long, Dauphin County Lib. System, 101 Walnut St., Harrisburg, PA 17101.

Use of Microcomputers in Public Libraries. Russell E. Walker, Upper Arlington Public Lib., 2800 Tremont Rd., Columbus, OH 43221.

Videotex. Kevin Hegarty, Tacoma Public Lib., 1102 Tacoma Ave. S., Tacoma, WA 98402.

American Library Association
Reference and Adult Services Division

Executive Director, Andrew M. Hansen
50 E. Huron St., Chicago, IL 60611
312-944-6780

Object

The Reference and Adult Services Division is responsible for stimulating and supporting in every type of library the delivery of reference/information services to all groups, regardless of age, and of general library services and materials to adults. This involves facilitating the development and conduct of direct service to library users, the development of programs and guidelines for service to meet the needs of these users, and assisting libraries in reaching potential users.

The specific responsibilities of RASD are:

1. Conduct of activities and projects within the division's areas of responsibility.

2. Encouragement of the development

of librarians engaged in these activities, and stimulation of participation by members of appropriate type-of-library divisions.

3. Synthesis of the activities of all units within the American Library Association that have a bearing on the type of activities represented by the division.

4. Representation and interpretation of the division's activities in contacts outside the profession.

5. Planning and development of programs of study and research in these areas for the total profession.

6. Continuous study and review of the division's activities.

Formed by merger of Adult Services Division and Reference Services Division, 1972. Memb. 5,469. (For information on dues, see ALA entry.)

Officers (1983-1984)

Pres. Kay A. Cassell, Huntington Public Lib., 338 Main St., Huntington, NY 11743; *V.P./Pres.-Elect.* Gary R. Purcell, Grad. School of Lib. & Info Science, Univ. of Tennessee, 804 Volunteer Blvd., Knoxville, TN 37916; *Secy.* Jean A. Coberly, History Dept., Seattle Public Lib., 100 Fourth Ave., Seattle, WA 98104.

Directors

Officers; Jeanne Gelinas; James Rettig; Susan DiMattia; Elaine Z. Jennerich; Tina Roose; Clyde C. Walton; *Councillor.* Ruth M. Katz; *Past Pres.* Danuta A. Nitecki; *Ex officio, History Sec. Chpn.* Judith P. Reid; *Machine-Assisted Reference Sec.* Rebecca J. Whitaker; *Ed. RASD Update.* Steven D. Atkinson; *Ed. RQ.* Kathleen M. Heim; *Council of State and Regional Groups Chpn.* Carl Stone, Anderson County Lib., Box 4047, 202 E. Greenville St., Anderson, SC 29622; *Exec. Dir.* Andrew M. Hansen.

(Address general correspondence to the executive director.)

Publications

RQ (q.; memb.; nonmemb. $20). *Ed.* Kathleen M. Heim, Louisiana State Univ., School of Lib. & Info. Science, Coates Hall, Rm. 267, Baton Rouge, LA 70803.

RASD Update (periodic; memb.; nonmemb. $6). *Ed.* Steven D. Atkinson, State Univ. of New York Lib., Box 22728, 1400 Washington Ave., Albany, NY 12222.

Section Chairpersons

History. Judith P. Reid, Local History and Genealogy Sec., Lib. of Congress, Washington, DC 20540.

Machine-Assisted Reference (MARS). Rebecca J. Whitaker, Information Retrieval, Indiana Cooperative Lib., Services Authority, 1100 W. 42 St., Indianapolis, IN 46208.

Committee Chairpersons

Adult Library Materials. Margaret J. Thomas, 15506 Oak Dr., Livonia, MI 48154. *Multilingual Subcommittee.* William E. McElwain, Foreign Language Sec., Chicago Public Lib., 78 E. Washington, Chicago, IL 60602.

"Adult Services in Action" Advisory. Leandra Fox, 6316 Jackson St., Pittsburgh, PA 15206.

Adults, Library Service to. Thomas T. Jones, Veteran's Memorial Public Lib., 520 Ave. A East, Bismarck, ND 58501.

Aging Population, Library Service to an. Lethene Parks, 8532 State Rd. 302 N.W., Gig Harbor, WA 98335.

AFL/CIO-ALA (RASD) Joint Committee on Library Service to Labor Groups.

Arthur S. Meyers, 2105 Concord, Muncie, IN 47304.

Bibliography. Judith B. Quinlan, Perkins Lib., Reference Dept., Duke Univ., Durham, NC 27706.

Business Reference. Sarah G. W. Kalin, E105 Pattee Lib., Pennsylvania State Univ., University Park, PA 16802.

Catalog Use. Douglas Ferguson, 1801 Rose St., Berkeley, CA 94703.

Conference Program. Jane Cumming Selvar, 15 Beech Tree Lane, Bronxville, NY 10708.

Contracted Reference Services (Ad Hoc). Susan S. DiMattia, 44 Chatham Rd., Stamford, CT 06903.

Cooperative Reference Service. Ellen Zabel Hahn, General Reading Rms. Div., LJ 144, Lib. of Congress, Washington, DC 20540.

Dartmouth Medal. Richard W. Grefrath, Instructional Services Lib., Univ. of Nevada Lib., Reno, NV 89557.

Evaluation of Reference and Adult Services. Charles A. Bunge, Lib. School, Univ. of Wisconsin, 600 N. Park St., Madison, WI 53706.

Executive. Kay A. Cassell, Huntington Public Lib., 338 Main St., Huntington, NY 11743.

Facts On File. Jane K. Hirsch Montgomery County Dept. of Public Libs., 99 Maryland Ave., Rockville, MD 20850.

Interlibrary Loan. Mary U. Hardin, 1501 Locust St., Norman, OK 73069.

Isadore Gilbert Mudge Citation. Peter G. Watson, Box 1543, Paradise, CA 95969.

John Sessions Memorial Award. Ginny Cooper, Alameda County Lib., 3121 Diablo Ave., Hayward, CA 94545.

Legislation. Marvin W. Mounce, 3104 Huntington Woods Blvd., Tallahassee, FL 32303.

Membership. Priscilla Ciccariello, Port Washington Public Lib., 245 Main St., Port Washington, NY 11050.

Nominating. Linda Beaupre, 2509 Friar Tuck Lane, Austin, TX 78704.

Notable Books Council. Kenneth L. Ferstl, Box 13256, North Texas State Univ., Denton, TX 76203.

Organization. Susan S. Di Mattia, 44 Chatham Rd., Stamford, CT 06903.

Planning. Danuta A. Nitecki, 11328 Cherry Hill Rd., Beltsville, MD 20705.

Professional Development. George M. Bailey, 2129 Villa Maria Rd., Claremont, CA 91711.

Publications. Helen B. Josephine, Box 246, Berkeley, CA 94701.

Reference Intern/Exchange Project (Ad Hoc). David F. Kohl, Jr. Undergrad. Lib., Univ. of Illinois, 1408 W. Gregory Dr., Urbana, IL 61801.

Reference Services to Children and Young Adults. Neel Parikh, Alameda County Lib. System, Costro Valley, CA 94546.

Reference Sources. Kevin M. Rosswurm, Akron-Summit County Public Lib., 55 South Main St., Akron, OH 44326.

Reference Sources for Small and Medium-sized Libs. (4th ed.) (Ad Hoc). Deborah C. Masters, B16 Univ. Lib., State Univ. of New York, 1400 Washington Ave., Albany, NY 12222.

Reference Tools Advisory. Elaine Z. Jennerich, 1264 Highview Terrace, Cheshire, CT 06410.

Regional Workshops (Ad Hoc). Glenda S. Neely, Ekstrom Lib., Univ. of Louisville, Louisville, KY 40292.

RQ Editorial Advisory Board. Kathleen M. Heim, Louisiana State Univ., School of Lib. & Info. Science, Coates Hall, Rm. 267, Baton Rouge, LA 70803.

Spanish-Speaking, Library Service to the. Nathan A. Josel, Jr., El Paso Public Lib., 501 N. Oregon St., El Paso, TX 79901.

Spanish-Speaking, Basic Buying List for the (Subcommittee). Fabio Restrepo, Box 1321, Denton, TX 76202.

Speakers/Consultants (Ad Hoc). Jean A. Coberly, History Dept., Seattle Public Lib., 1000 Fourth Ave., Seattle, WA 98104.

Standards & Guidelines. Winston Tabb, 11303 Handlebar Rd., Reston, VA 22091.

Wilson Indexes. Larry Earl Bone, Mercy College Libs., 555 Broadway, Dobbs Ferry, NY 10522.

ence Dept., Univ. of California Lib., Riverside, CA 92517.

Women's Materials and Women Library Users. Gurley Turner, Catalyst, 14 E. 60 St., New York, NY 10022; Co. Ch., Susan E. Searing.

Discussion Group Chairpersons

Adult Materials and Services. Nancy Fisher, Cuyahoga Public Lib., 25501 Shaker Blvd., Beachwood, OH 44122.

Interlibrary Loan. Jane G. Rollins, 18 Vatrand Ave., Loudonville, NY 12211.

Library Service to an Aging Population. Allan Kleiman, Service to the Aging/ SAGE Program, Brooklyn Public Lib., 2115 Ocean Ave., Brooklyn, NY 11229.

Multilingual Services and Materials. William E. McElwain, Foreign Language Sec., Chicago Public Lib. 78 E. Washington, Chicago, IL 60602.

Performance Standards for Reference/Information Librarians. Rebecca Kellogg, Central Reference Dept., Univ. of Arizona Lib., Tucson, AZ 85721.

Reference Services in Large Research Libraries. Paula Watson, 715 W. Delaware Ave., Urbana, IL 61801.

Reference Services in Medium-sized Research Libraries. Nancy Huling, Refer-

Representatives

ALA Legislation Assembly. Marvin Mounce, 3104 Huntington Woods Blvd., Tallahassee, FL 32303.

ALA Legislation Committee (Ad Hoc Copyright Subcommittee). Mary U. Hardin, 1501 Locust St., Norman, OK 73069.

ALA Library Instruction Round Table. Sheila M. Laidlaw, Univ. Lib., Box 7500, Univ. of New Brunswick, Fredericton, New Brunswick E3B 5H5, Canada.

ALA Membership Promotion Task Force. Priscilla Ciccariello, Port Washington Public Lib., 245 Main St., Port Washington, NY 11050.

Coalition of Adult Education Organizations. Andrew M. Hansen, ALA, 50 E. Huron St., Chicago, IL 60611.

Freedom to Read Foundation. Deborah Ellis Dennis, 923 Deland Ave., Cherry Hill, NJ 08034.

American Library Association
Resources and Technical Services Division

Executive Director, William I. Bunnell
50 E. Huron St., Chicago, IL 60611
312-944-6780

Object

The division is responsible for the following activities: "acquisition, identification, cataloging, classification, reproduction, and preservation of library materials; the development and coordination of the country's library resources; and those areas of selection and evaluation involved in the acquisition of library materials and pertinent to the development of library resources. Any member of the American Library Association may elect membership in this division according to the provisions of the bylaws." Established 1957. Memb. 6,351. (For information on dues, see ALA entry.)

Officers (June 1983–June 1984)

Pres. Susan Brynteson, Dir. of Libraries, Univ. of Delaware Lib., Newark, DE 19711; *V.P./Pres.-Elect.* William J. Myrick, Jr., Dir. for Library Planning & Development, Office of Academic Affairs, City Univ. of New York, 535 E. 80 St., New York, NY 10021; *Chpn. Council of Regional Groups.* Doris H. Clack, 1115 Frazier Ave., Tallahassee, FL 32304; *Past Pres.* Norman J. Shaffer, 11505 Soward Dr., Silver Spring, MD 20902.

(Address correspondence to the executive director.)

Directors

Officers. *Section chairpersons:* Lizbeth Bishoff (CCS); Sally A. Buchanan (PLMS); Margaret M. Byrnes (RLMS); Noreen G. Alldredge (RS); Rex Bross (SS). *Dirs.-at-Large.* Joe A. Hewitt (1985); Marcia Pankake (1986); *Council of Regional Groups vice-chpn./chpn.-elect.* Elizabeth J. Dickinson, *LRTS ed.* Elizabeth Tate (1985); *Parliamentarian.* Edward Swanson (1985). *RTSD Newsletter ed.* Arnold Hirshon (1985); *RTSD Planning and Research Committee chpn.* Judith N. Kharbas (1984).

Publications

Library Resources & Technical Services (q.; memb. or $20). *Ed.* Elizabeth Tate, 11415 Farmland Dr., Rockville, MD 20852.

RTSD Newsletter (bi-mo.; memb. or *LRTS* subscription, or $8 yearly). *Ed.* Arnold Hirshon, Asst. Dir. for Technical Services, Cabell Lib., Virginia Commonwealth Univ., 901 Park Ave., Richmond, VA 23284.

Section Chairpersons

Cataloging and Classification. Lizbeth Bishoff, Ela Area Public Lib. Dist., 135 S. Buesching Rd., Lake Zurich, IL 60047.

Preservation of Library Materials. Sally A. Buchanan, Conservation Officer, Green Lib., Rm. 401, Stanford Univ., Stanford, CA 94305.

Reproduction of Library Materials. Margaret M. Byrnes, Univ. of Michigan, 20 Harlan Hatcher Grad. Lib., Ann Arbor, MI 48109.

Resources. Noreen G. Alldredge, Univ. Lib., Montana State Univ., Bozeman, MT 59717.

Serials. Rex Bross, Serials Dept., Perkins Lib., Duke Univ., Durham, NC 27706.

Committee Chairpersons

Association of American Publishers/ RTSD Joint Committee. Susan H. Vita, 3711 Taylor St., Chevy Chase, MD 20815.

Audiovisual. Sheila Intner, Asst. Professor, School of Lib. Service, Columbia Univ., New York, NY 10027.

Catalog Form, Function and Use. Dorothy McGarry, Physical Science & Technical Libs., 8251 Boelter Hall, Univ. of California, Los Angeles, CA 90024.

Commercial Technical Services Committee. Eunice P. Drum, 3001 Sherry Dr., Raleigh, NC 27604.

Conference Program — Dallas, 1984. Susan Brynteson, Dir. of Libs., Univ. of Delaware Lib., Newark, DE 19711.

Conference Program — Chicago, 1985. William J. Myrick, Jr., Dir. for Lib. Planning & Development, Office of Academic Affairs, City Univ. of New York, 535 E. 80 St., New York, NY 10021.

Duplicates Exchange Union. Priscilla C. Yu, Univ. of Illinois Lib., 1408 W. Gregory Dr., Urbana, IL 61801.

Education. Carolyn Frost, School of Lib. Science, Univ. of Michigan, 580 Union Dr., Ann Arbor, MI 48109.

International Relations. E. Dale Cluff,

Dir. of Libs., Texas Technical Univ., Lubbock, TX 79409.

Legislative. David F. Bishop, Dir., Univ. of Georgia Libs., Athens, GA 30605.

Membership. Sally Voth Rausch, 3880 Laurel Ct., Blommington, IN 47401.

Nominating. Paul H. Mosher, Green Lib., Stanford Univ., Stanford, CA 94305.

Organization and Bylaws. Norman J. Shaffer, 11505 Soward Dr., Silver Spring, MD 20902.

Piercy Award Jury. Donald L. Lanier, 613 Ball Ave., Dekalb, IL 60115.

Planning and Research. Judith N. Kharbas, Asst. Dir. for Technical Services, Univ. of Rochester Lib., Rochester, NY 14627.

Preservation Microfilming. Jeffrey Heynen, Information Interchange, 503 11 St. S.E., Washington, DC 20003.

Program Evaluation and Support. William J. Myrick, Jr., Dir. for Lib. Planning & Development, Office of Academic Affairs, City Univ. of New York, 535 E 80 St., New York, NY 10021.

Representation in Machine-Readable Form of Bibliographic Information, RTSD/LITA/RASD (MARBI). Richard O. Green, OCLC, 6565 Frantz Rd., Dublin, OH 43017.

Representation in Machine-Readable Form of Bibliographic Information (MARBI), Character Set Task Force (Ad Hoc). Charles Payne, 5807 Blackstone, Chicago, IL 60637.

Technical Services Costs. Charlene Renner, Technical Services, Rm. 168, Iowa State Univ. Lib., Ames, IA 50011.

Representatives

ALA Freedom to Read Foundation. Karin A. Trainer.

ALA Government Documents Round Table. Gail M. Nichols.

ALA Legislation Assembly. David F. Bishop.

ALA Library and Information Technology Association. Nolan F. Pope (Bylaws & Organization); Pamela Bluh (Implementation).

ALA Membership Promotion Task Force. Sally Voth Rausch.

American National Standards Institute, Inc. (ANSI), Standards Committee Z39 on Library Work, Documentation and Related Publishing Practices. Sally H. McCallum; Janice E. Anderson, alternate.

CONSER Advisory Group. Jean Cook.

Joint Advisory Committee on Nonbook Materials. Sheila Inter & Nancy B. Olson.

Joint Steering Committee for Revision of AACR. Helen F. Schmierer.

National Institute for Conservation. John P. Baker.

Universal Serials and Book Exchange Inc. Pamela M. Bluh.

Discussion Groups

Acquisition of Library Materials. Helen I. Reed, Acquisitions Libn., Perkins Lib., Duke Univ., Durham, NC 27705.

Automated Acquisitions/In-Process Control Systems. Steven P. Lane, Box 3045, Shawnee, KS 66203.

Booksellers. Jay Askuvich, Midwest Lib. Service, 141 Nevada Ave., Chatesworth, CA 91311.

Cataloging Management. Deborah Rae, Assoc. Libn., Cataloging Dept., Univ. of Delaware Lib., Newark, DE 19711.

Cataloging Norms. Nancy Romero, Univ. of Illinois Lib., Original Cataloging Libn., 200 N. Lib., 1408 W. Gregory Dr., Urbana, IL 61801.

Chief Collection Development Officers of Large Research Libraries. John R. Kaiser, 1136 S. Atherton St., State College, PA 16801.

Commercial Automation, Support of Technical Services in Medium-Sized Research Libraries. Marcia A. King-

Blandford, Head of Copy Cataloging, Univ. of Notre Dame Libs., Notre Dame, IN 46556.

Copy Cataloging. Virginia Drake, Cataloging Coord., Eisenhower Lib., Johns Hopkins Univ., Baltimore, MD 21218.

Heads of Cataloging Departments. Colleen Bednar, Head of Monographs, Cataloging Dept., Michigan State Univ., East Lansing, MI 48824.

Pre-order & Pre-catalog Searching. Robert Eckert, Head, Acquisitions Dept., Univ. Research Lib., UCLA, Los Angeles, CA 90024.

Preservation of Library Materials. Ann G. Swartzell, Preservation Libn., Harvard Univ. Libs., Cambridge, MA 02138.

Reproduction of Library Materials. Helga Borck, Public Lib., Fifth Ave. at 42 St., New York, NY 10018.

Research Libraries. Frank Orser, Serials Dept., Univ. of Florida, Gainesville, FL 32611; Ludmilla Sak, Cataloger, Rutgers Univ. Lib., New Brunswick, NJ 08901.

Retrospective Conversion. Susan A. Matson, 112A N. Rod Lane, Carbondale, IL 62901; Virginia H. Drake, Johns Hopkins Univ. Lib., Baltimore, MD 21218.

Role of the Professional in Academic Research Technical Services Departments. Lawrence R. Keating, M.D. Anderson Lib., Univ. of Houston Central Campus, 4800 Calhoun Blvd., Houston, TX 77004.

Technical Services Administrators of Large Public Libraries. Annie M. Gilbert, Chief, Materials Processing Service, Public Lib., 1515 Young St., Dallas, TX 75201.

Technical Services Administrators of Medium-sized Research Libraries. Charlene Renner, Asst. Dir. of Technical Services, Iowa State Univ. Lib., Ames, IA 50011.

Technical Services Directors of Large Research Libraries. Jean Hamrick, Asst. Dir. for Automation & Information Systems Planning, PCL 3.200, Univ. of Texas, Austin, TX 78712.

Technical Services Directors of Processing Centers. Dallas Shawkey, Public Lib., 109 Montgomery St., Brooklyn, NY 11225.

American Library Association
Young Adult Services Division

Executive Director, Evelyn Shaevel
50 E. Huron St., Chicago, IL 60611
312-944-6780

Object

"Interested in the improvement and extension of services to young people in all types of libraries; has specific responsibility for the evaluation, selection, interrelation and use of books and nonbook materials for young adults except when such materials are intended for only one type of library."

Established 1957. Memb. 3,000. (For information on dues, see ALA entry.)

Membership

Open to anyone interested in library services to young adults.

Officers (July 1983–July 1984)

Pres. Penelope S. Jeffrey, 4733 Morningside Dr., Cleveland, OH 44109; *V.P.* Lydia Lafleur, New York Public Lib., Manhattan Borough Office, 20 W. 53 St., New York, NY 10019; *Past. Pres.* Barbara Newmark, 11 Lake St., #3G, White Plains, NY 10603; *Division Councillor.* Gerald Hodges, Dept. of Lib. Science & Educ. Technology, Univ. of North Carolina at Greensboro, Greensboro, NC 27412.

Directors

Jack Forman; Ellen LiBretto; Larry Rakow; Suzanne Sullivan; Christy Tyson; Jacqueline Brown Woody.

Committee Chairpersons

Best Books for Young Adults. Nancy Rolnick, Croton Free Lib., Croton-on-Hudson, NY 10520.

Computer Applications. Jack Forman, 7072 Hillsboro St., San Diego, CA 92120.

Education. Mary K. Biagini, 740 W. Main St., Kent, OH 44240.

High-Interest, Low-Literacy Level Materials Evaluation. Elizabeth Acerra, 1097 E. 95 St., Brooklyn, NY 11236.

Ideas and Activities. Rhonna A. Goodman, New York Public Lib., Staten Island Borough Office, 10 Hyatt St., Staten Island, NY 10301.

Intellectual Freedom. Gayle Keresey, 2148 Harrison St., Wilmington, NC 28401.

Leadership Training. Penelope S. Jeffrey, 4733 Morningside Dr., Cleveland, OH 44109.

Legislation Committee. Eleanor Pourron, Arlington County Public Lib., 1015 N. Quincy, Arlington, VA 22201.

Library of Congress, YASD Advisory Committee to the Collection and Development Section and the National Library Service for the Blind and Physically Handicapped of the Library of Congress. Linda Lapides, Enoch Pratt Free Lib., 400 Cathedral St., Baltimore, MD 21201.

Media Selection and Usae. Scott Bunn,

c/o General Delivery, Cobb Island, MD 20625.

Membership Promotion. Bruce Daniels, Rhode Island State Lib., 95 Davis St., Providence, RI 02908.

National Organization Serving the Young Adult Liaison. Ricki Fairtile, 82-24 135 St., #3A, Kew Gardens, NY 11435.

Nominating 1982. Eleanor Pourron, Arlington County Public Lib., 1015 Quincy St., Arlington, VA 22201.

Organization and Bylaws. Mary Ann Schwehr, Chicago Public Lib., Legler Branch, 115 S. Pulaski, Chicago, IL 60624.

Program Planning Clearinghouse. Evie Wilson, 8602 Champlain Ct., Apt. 85, Tampa, FL 33614.

Public Relations. Elizabeth Talbot, 4008 Loma Vista Ave., Oakland, CA 94619.

Publications. Patsy Perritt, 226 Middleton Lib., Louisiana State Univ., Baton Rouge, LA 70803.

Publishers Liaison. Neal Porter, Scribner Book Companies, 597 Fifth Ave., New York, NY 10017.

Research. Henry C. Dequin, Northern Illinois Univ., DeKalb, IL 60115.

Selected Films for Young Adults. Vivian Wynn, Mayfield Regional Lib., 6080 Wilson Mills Rd., Mayfield Village, OH 44404.

Spanish Speaking Youth Committee, Library Service to. John W. Cunningham, 979 N. Fifth St., Philadelphia, PA 19123.

Television. Roslyn Rubinstein, Queens Borough Public Lib., 89–11 Merrick Blvd., Jamaica, NY 11432.

Top of the News Editorial. Marilyn Kaye, Div. of Lib. & Info. Services, St. John's Univ., Grand Central & Utopia Pkwys., Jamaica, NY 11439.

Young Adults with Special Needs. Jo-Anne Weinberg, 272 Old Kensico Rd., White Plains, NY 10607.

Youth Participation. Connie Lawson, 20667 Ellacott Pkwy., #601, Warrensville Heights, OH 44128.

American Merchant Marine Library Association

(Affiliated with United Seamen's Service)
Executive Director, Mace Mavroleon
One World Trade Center, Suite 2601, New York, NY 10048
212-775-1033

Object

Provides ship and shore library service for American-flag merchant vessels, the Military Sealift Command, the Coast Guard, and other waterborne operations of the U.S. government.

Officers

Chpn. of the Bd. RADM Bruce Keener, III; *Pres.* Thomas J. Smith; *Treas.* Hubert Carr; *Secy.* Capt. Franklin K. Riley.

Trustees

W.J. Amoss; Ralph R. Bagley; Vice Adm. W.E. Caldwell; Hubert Carr; Nicholas Cretan; Rebekah T. Dallas; Maj. Gen. H.R. DelMar; John I. Dugan; Arthur W. Friedberg; Capt. Robert E. Hart; James J. Hayes; RADM Bruce Keener, III: RADM Thomas A. King; George F. Lowman; Frank X. McNerney; Thomas Martinez; Mace G. Mavroleon; Capt. Howard E. Miniter, USN; Andrew Rich; George J. Ryan; Thomas J. Smith; Richard T. Soper; Anthony J. Tozzoli; Rev. James R. Whittemore.

American Society for Information Science

Executive Director, Samuel B. Beatty
1010 16 St. N.W., Washington, DC 20036
202-659-3644

Object

The American Society for Information Science provides a forum for the discussion, publication, and critical analysis of work dealing with the design, management, and use of information systems and technology. Memb. (Indiv.) 4,700; (Student) 480; (Inst.) 100. Dues (Indiv.) $75; (Student) $15; (Inst.) $350; (Sustaining Sponsor) $800.

Officers

Pres. Donald W. King, King Research, Inc., Rockville, MD 20852; *Pres.-Elect.* Bonnie Carroll, Box 62, Oak Ridge, TN 37830; *Treas.* Frank Spaulding, Bell Telephone Labs, Rm. 3C202, Holmdel, NJ 07733; *Past Pres.* Charles Davis, Univ. of Illinois Champaign/Urbana, Champaign, IL 61820.

(Address correspondence to the executive director.)

Board of Directors

Officers; *Chapter Assembly Dir.* Joe Ann Clifton; *SIG Cabinet Dir.* George Abbott; *Dirs.-at-Large.* Ching Chih Chen; Ward Shaw; David Penniman; Stephanie Normann, Robert Tannehill, Daniel Robbins.

Publications

Note: Unless otherwise indicated, publications are available from Knowledge Industry Publications, 701 Westchester Ave., White Plains, NY 10604.

Annual Review of Information Science and Technology (vol. 3, 1968–vol. 10, 1975, $35 each, memb. $28; vol. 11, 1976–vol. 14, 1979, $37.50 each, memb. $30; vol. 15, 1980–vol. 18, 1983, $45 each, memb. $36).

Bulletin of the American Society for Information Science ($45 domestic, $52.50 foreign). Available directly from ASIS.

Collective Index to the Journal of the American Society for Information Science (vol. 1, 1950–vol. 25, 1974, $67.95). Available from John Wiley & Sons, 605 Third Ave., New York, NY 10016.

Computer-Readable Data Bases: A Directory and Data Sourcebook 1982 $120, memb. $96.

Cumulative Index to the Annual Review of Information Science and Technology (vol. 1, 1966–vol. 10, 1975, $35 each, memb. $28).

Journal of the American Society for Information Science; formerly *American Documentation* (bi-mo.; memb. or $85 domestic and $106 foreign). Available from John Wiley & Sons, 605 Third Ave., New York, NY 10016.

Key Papers in the Design and Evaluation of Information Systems. Ed. Donald W. King ($25, memb. $20).

Library and Reference Facilities in the Area of the District of Columbia (11th ed., 1983, $39.50, memb. $31.60).

Proceedings of the ASIS Annual Meetings (vol. 5, 1968–vol. 9, 1972, $15 each, memb. $12; vol. 10, 1973–vol. 19, 1982, $19.50 each, memb. $15.60; vol. 20, $19.50 each, memb. $15.60).

Committee Chairpersons

Awards and Honors. Mauro Pittaro, Engi-

neering Information, Inc., 345 E. 47 St., New York, NY 10017.

Budget and Finance. Frank Spaulding, Bell Telephone Labs, Rm. 3C202, Holmdel, NJ 07733.

Conferences and Meetings. Frank Slater, Mgr., Lib. Systems Development, Univ. of Pittsburgh, G-33 Hillman Lib., Pittsburgh, PA 19482.

Constitution and Bylaws. Barbara Sanduleak, Imperial Clevite, Inc., 540 E. 105 St., Cleveland, OH 44108.

Education. Carol Tenopir, Univ. of Illinois, Urbana, IL 61801.

Executive. Donald W. King, Pres., King Research, Inc., 6000 Executive Blvd., Suite 200, Rockville, MD 20852.

International Relations. M. Lynne Neufeld, 425 W. Mermaid Lane, Philadelphia, PA 19118.

Marketing. N. Bernard Basch, Pres., The Turner Subscription Agency, 235 Park Ave. S., New York, NY 10003.

Membership. Frances Roberts, 9435 Goshen Lane, Burke, VA 22015.

Nominations. Charles H. Davis, Dean, Univ. of Illinois, GSLIS, 410 David Kinley Hall, 1407 W. Gregory Dr., Urbana, IL 61801.

Professionalism. Pamela Cibbarelli, Cibbarelli Assocs., 18652 Florida, Huntington Beach, CA 92648.

Public Affairs. Jeffrey Davidson, 2708 Fenimore Rd., Wheaton, MD 20902.

Publications. Elizabeth Fake, 15516 Straughn Dr., Laurel, MD 20810.

Research. Manfred Kochen, Mental Health Research Institute, Univ. of Michigan, Ann Arbor, MI 48104.

Standards. David Liston, King Research, 6000 Executive Blvd., Rockville, MD 20852.

American Theological Library Association

Executive Secretary, Albert E. Hurd
5600 S. Woodlawn Ave., Chicago, IL 60637

Object

"To bring its members into closer working relationships with each other, to support theological and religious librarianship, to improve theological libraries, and to interpret the role of such libraries in theological education, developing and implementing standards of library service, promoting research and experimental projects, encouraging cooperative programs that make resources more available, publishing and disseminating literature and research tools and aids, cooperating with organizations having similar aims and otherwise supporting and aiding theological education." Founded 1947. Memb. (Inst.) 160; (Indiv.) 460. Dues (Inst.) $50–$300, based on total library expenditure; (Indiv.) $10–$55, based on salary scale. Year. May 1–April 30.

ATLA is a member of the Council of National Library and Information Associations.

Membership

Persons engaged in professional library or bibliographical work in theological or religious fields and others who are interested in the work of theological librarianship.

Officers (June 1983–June 1984)

Pres. Martha Aycock, Union Theological Seminary, 3401 Brook Rd., Richmond, VA 23227; *V.P./Pres.-Elect.* Ronald F. Deering, Southern Baptist Theological Seminary, 2825 Lexington Rd., Louisville, KY 40280; *Past Pres.* Robert Dvorak, Gordon-Conwell Theological Seminary, South Hamilton, MA 01982; *Treas.* Robert A. Olsen, Jr., Libn., Brite Divinity School, Texas Christian Univ., Fort Worth, TX 76129.

Board of Directors

Dorothy Ruth Parks; Richard D. Spoor; Betty O'Brien; Lawrence H. Hill; Roslyn Lewis; Peter Deklerk.

Publications

Newsletter (q.; memb. or $10).
Proceedings (ann.; memb. or $20).
Religion Index One (formerly *Index to Religious Periodical Literature, 1949–date*).
Religion Index Two: Multi-Author Works.
Research in Ministry: An Index to Doctor of Ministry Project Reports.

Committee Chairpersons

ATLA Newsletter. Donn Michael Farris, Ed., Divinity School Lib., Duke Univ., Durham, NC 27706.
ATLA Representative to ANSI Z39. Warren Kissinger, 6309 Queen's Chapel Rd., Hyattsville, MD 20782.
ATLA Representative to the Council of National Library and Information Associations. James Irvine, Princeton Theological Seminary, Box 111, Princeton, NJ 08540.
ATS Representative. Sara B. Little, Union Theological Seminary, 3401 Brook Rd., Richmond, VA 23227.
Archivist. Gerald W. Gillette, Presbyterian Historical Society, 425 Lombard St., Philadelphia, PA 19147.
Bibliographic Systems. Elizabeth Flynn, Grad. Theological Union, 2400 Ridge Rd., Berkeley, CA 94709.

Collection Evaluation and Development. W. Terry Martin, Southeastern Baptist Theological Seminary, Box 752, Wake Forest, NC 27587.

Microtext Reproduction Board. Maria Grossmann, Andover-Harvard Lib., 45 Francis Ave., Cambridge, MA 02138; Charles Willard, Exec. Secy., Speer Library, Princeton Theological Seminary, Princeton, NJ 08540.

Nominating. H. Eugene McLeod, Southeastern Baptist Theological Seminary, Box 752, Wake Forest, NC 27587.

Oral History. Alice Kendrick, Dir., Center for Documental Resources, Lutheran Council on the U.S.A., 360 Park Ave. S., New York, NY 10010.

Periodical Indexing Board. Norman Kansfield, Libn., Colgate Rochester/Bexley Hall/Crozer Divinity School, 1100 S. Goodman St., Rochester, NY 14620.

Preservation of Religious Monographs. Jerry Campbell, Bridwell Lib., Perkins School of Theology, Southern Methodist School of Theology, Dallas, TX 75275.

Program. Erich Schultz, Univ. Libn., Wilfrid Laurier Univ., Waterloo, Ont. N2L 3C5, Canada.

Publication. Betty O'Brien, 7818 Lockport Blvd., Dayton, OH 45449.

Reader Services. John Dickason, Reference Libn., Princeton Theological Seminary, Box 111, Princeton, NJ 08540.

Relationships with Learned Societies. Andrew Scrimgeour, Iliff School of Theology Lib., 2233 S. University Blvd., Denver, CO 80210.

Statistician and Liaison with ALA Statistics Coordinating Committee. David Green, General Theological Seminary, 175 Ninth Ave., New York, NY 10011.

Systems and Standards. Doralyn Hickey, Reporter, School of Lib. & Info. Sciences, North Texas State Univ., Denton, TX 76203.

Art Libraries Society of North America (ARLIS/NA)

Executive Director, Pamela J. Parry
3775 Bear Creek Circle, Tucson, AZ 85749
602-749-9112

Object

"To promote art librarianship and visual resources curatorship, particularly by acting as a forum for the interchange of information and materials on the visual arts." Established 1972. Memb. 1,100. Dues (Inst.) $60; (Indiv.) $35; (Business Affiliate) $60; (Student) $20; (Retired/unemployed) $25; (Sustaining) $150; (Sponsor) $500. Year. Jan.–Dec. 31.

Membership

Open and encouraged for all those interested in visual librarianship, whethery they be professional librarians, students, library assistants, art book publishers, art book dealers, art historians, archivists, architects, slide and photograph curators, or retired associates in these fields.

Officers (Feb. 1984–Feb. 1985)

Chpn. Mary Ashe, San Francisco Public Lib., Civic Center, San Francisco, CA 94102; *Past Chpn.* Nancy Allen, Museum of Fine Arts Lib., Boston, MA 02115.

(Address correspondence to the executive director.)

Committees

(Direct correspondence to headquarters.)
Cataloging Advisory.

Conference.
Education.
Fund Raising.
International Relations.
Membership.
Gerd Muehsam Award.
Nominating.
Publications.
Standards.
Wittenborn Award.

Executive Board

The chairperson, past chairperson, chairperson-elect, secretary, treasurer, and four regional representatives (East, Midwest, West, and Canada).

Publications

Art Documentation (bi-mo.; memb.)
Handbook and List of Members (ann.; memb.)
Occasional Papers (price varies).
Miscellaneous others (request current list from headquarters).

Chapters

Allegheny; Arizona; DC-Maryland-Virginia; Delaware Valley; Kansas-Missouri; Kentucky-Tennessee; Michigan; Mid-States; New England; New Jersey; New York; Northern California; Northwest; Ohio; Southeast; Southern California; Texas; Twin Cities; Western New York.

Asian/Pacific American Librarians Association

President, Lourdes Y. Collantes
SUNY College at Old Westbury Library
Box 229, Old Westbury, NY 11568
516-876-3154

Object

"To provide a forum for discussing problems and concerns of Asian/Pacific American librarians; to provide a forum for the exchange of ideas by Asian/Pacific American librarians and other librarians; to support and encourage library services to the Asian/Pacific American communities; to recruit and support Asian/Pacific American librarians in the library/information science professions; to seek funding for scholarships in library/information science schools for Asian/Pacific Americans; and to provide a vehicle whereby Asian/Pacific American librarians can cooperate with other associations and organizations having similar or allied interests." Founded 1980; incorporated 1981; affiliated with ALA 1982. Dues (Inst.) $25; (Indiv.) $10; (Students and Unemployed Librarians) $5.

Membership

Open to all librarians/information specialists of Asian/Pacific descent working in U.S. libraries/information centers and other such related organizations and to others who support the goals and purposes of APALA. Asian/Pacific Americans are defined as those who consider themselves Asian/Pacific Americans. They may be Americans of Asian/Pacific descent, or Asian/Pacific people with the status of permanent residency, or Asian/Pacific people living in the United States.

Officers (July 1983–June 1984)

Pres. Lourdes Y. Collantes, SUNY College at Old Westbury Lib., Box 229, Old Westbury, NY 11568; *V.P.* Victor Okim, Japanese American Cultural and Community Center, 244 South San Pedro, Los Angeles, CA 90012; *Treas.* Ravindra Nath Sharma, Beaver Campus Lib., Pennsylvania State Univ., Monaca, PA 15061; *Secy.* Pei-ling Wu, Macomb County Community College Lib., 14500 12 Mile Rd., Warren, MI 48098.

Advisory Committee

The president, immediate past president, vice-president/president-elect, secretary, treasurer, chairpersons of the regional chapters and an elected representative of the Standing committees.

Publications

APALA Newsletter (q.; memb.) *Ed.* Sharad Karkhanis, Kingsborough Com-

munity College Lib., Oriental Blvd., Brooklyn, NY 11235. Membership Directory.

Committee Chairpersons

Constitution and By-Laws. Henry C. Chang, Bureau of Libs., Museums & Archaeological Services, Box 390, St. Thomas, VI 00801.

Membership. Conchita J. Pineda, Citibank, N.A. – Financial Lib., 153 E. 53 St., New York, NY 10043.

Publicity and Program. Suzine Har-Nicolescu, CUNY Medgar Evers College, 402 Eastern Pkwy., Brooklyn, NY 11225.

Recruitment and Scholarship. Michael M. Lee, Ward Edwards Lib., Central Missouri State Univ., Warrensburg, MO 64093.

Associated Information Managers

Executive Director, Sheila Brayman
1776 E. Jefferson St., Suite 470S, Rockville, MD 20852
301-231-7447

Object

To advance information management as a profession and to promote information management as an executive function by improving recognition of its applicability as a strategic and tactical tool in achieving organizational and executive effectiveness. AIM provides the meeting ground for the professionals responsible for meeting the present and future information needs of their organizations within the information management context. Established January 1981. Membership, 1,000 (Indiv.); 15 (Corporate members).

Membership

Corporate planners, vice presidents of communication and marketing, administration managers, on-line users, data processing, telecommunications, librarianship, records management, office automation, and management information systems (MIS) personnel. Its primary focus is on the management of these information activities and on making the total information base supportive of management and the decision-making process. Board of Directors made up of leading information professionals in industry, academia, and government. Dues (corporate) sustaining $3,000, supporting $1,000, contributing $500; (regular) $85; (foreign) $120; (student) $35.

Board of Directors

Herbert R. Bringberg, Pres. & CEO, Aspen Systems Corp.; Ramona C. T. Crosby, Supv., Info. Services, Stauffer Chemical Co.; J. William Doolittle, Sr. Partner, Prather, Seeger, Doolittle & Farmer; Elizabeth Bole Eddison, Pres., Warner/Eddison Assocs., Inc. Robert J. Judge, Assoc. Dir., Div. Support Services, General Foods; James G. Kollegger, Pres., EIC/Intelligence, Inc.; Rhoda R. Mancher, Deputy Asst. Attorney General, Office of Info. Technology, Dept. of Justice; Donald A. Marchand, Inst. of Info. Management, Technology & Policy, Univ. of South Carolina; Herbert N. McCauley, V.P., Management Info. Systems, Harris Corp.; Morton F. Meltzer, Info. Mgr., Martin Marietta Corp.; Peter C. Robinson, Corporate V.P., Blount, Inc.; Molly A. Wolfe, V.P./Gen. Mgr., Info. Programs Div., Informatics General Corp.

Publications

AIM Network (bi-weekly; free to membs.). Newsletter.

Marketing Yourself in Your Organization, by Morton Meltzer. (memb. $9.95; nonmemb. $14.95).

Partners in Fact: Information Managers/ Information Company Executives Talk. (memb. $14.95; nonmemb. $19.95).

Who's Who in Information Management. (ann.; nonmemb. $35).

Association for Information and Image Management

(Formerly National Micrographics Association)
Executive Director, O. Gordon Banks
8719 Colesville Rd., Silver Spring, MD 20910
301-587-8202

Object

To serve the professional and trade members of the Association in promoting education on and applications for information and imaging technologies which facilitate the effective storage, transfer, retrieval, and processing of images and information. Founded 1943. Memb. 8,000. Dues. (Indiv.) $60. Year. July 1, 1983–1984.

Officers (1983–1984)

Pres. John P. Luke, Eastman Kodak Co, 343 State St., Rochester, NY 14650; *V.P.* Roger E. Blue, Total Information Management Corp., 1545 Park Ave., Emeryville, CA 94608; *Treas.* Edward W. Mackin, MICOR, 3494 Progress Dr., Cornwells Heights, PA 19020.

Publication

Journal of Information and Image Management (mo.; memb. subscriptions). *Ed.* Ellen T. Meyer. Book reviews included; product review included. Ads accepted.

Association for Library and Information Science Education

(Formerly Association of American Library Schools)
Executive Secretary, Janet Phillips
471 Park Lane, State College, PA 16801
814-238-0254

Object

"To advance education for librarianship." Founded 1915. Memb. 790. Dues (Inst.) $125; (Assoc. Inst.) $75; (Indiv.) $25; (Assoc. Indiv.) $20. Year. Sept. 1983–1984.

Membership

Any library school with a program accredited by the ALA Committee on Accreditation may become an institutional member; any educator who is employed full time for a full academic year in a library school with an accredited program may become a personal member.

Any school that offers a graduate degree in librarianship or a cognate field but whose program is not accredited by the ALA Committee on Accreditation may become an associate institutional member; any part-time faculty member or doctoral student of a library school with an accredited program of any full-time faculty member employed for a full academic year at other schools that offer graduate degrees in librarianship or cognate fields may become an associate personal member. [Any other individual interested in the goals and objectives of the association may become an associate personal member.]

Officers (Feb. 1984–Jan. 1985)

Pres. Jane Robbins-Carter, Lib. School, Univ. of Wisconsin at Madison, Madison, WI 53706; *Past Pres.* Robert D. Stueart, Grad. School of Lib. & Info. Science, Simmons College, Boston, MA 02115; (Address correspondence to the executive secretary.)

Directors

F. William Summers (South Carolina); Charles R. McClure (Oklahoma); Joan C. Durrance (Michigan).

Publication

Journal of Education for Librarianship (5 per year; $20).

Committee Chairpersons

Conference. Ching-chih Chen, Grad. School of Lib. & Info. Science, Simmons College, Boston, MA 02115.
Continuing Education. Joan C. Durrance, School of Lib. Science, Univ. of Michigan, Ann Arbor, MI 48109.
Editorial Board. Charles D. Patterson, School of Lib. & Info. Science, Louisiana State Univ., Baton Rouge, LA 70803.
Governmental Relations. Herbert White, Dean, School of Lib. & Info. Science, Indiana Univ., Bloomington, IN 47405.
Nominating. Adele M. Fasick, Faculty of Lib. Science, Univ. of Toronto, Toronto, Ont. M5S 1A1, Canada.
Research. Douglas Zweizig, Lib. School, Univ. of Wisconsin-Madison, Madison, WI 53706.

Representatives

ALA SCOLE. Shirley Fitzgibbons (Indiana).
Council of Communication Societies. Guy Garrison (Drexel).
IFLA. Jane Robbins-Carter (Wisconsin-Madison); Josephine Fang (Simmons).
Organization of American States. Travis White (Denver).

Association of Academic Health Sciences Library Directors

Secretary-Treasurer, Joan Zenan
Savitt Medical Lib., Univ. of Nevada, Reno, NV 89557
702-784-4625

Object

"To promote, in cooperation with educational institutions, other educational associations, government agencies, and other non-profit organizations, the common interests of academic health sciences libraries located in the United States and elsewhere, through publications, research, and discussion of problems of mutual interest and concern, and to advance the efficient and effective operation of academic health sciences libraries for the benefit of faculty, students, administrators, and practitioners."

Membership

Regular membership is available to nonprofit educational institutions operating a school of health sciences that has full or provisional accreditation by the Association of American Medical Colleges. Annual dues $50. Regular members shall be represented by the chief administrative officer of the member institution's health sciences library.

Associate membership (and nonvoting representation) is available to organizations having an interest in the purposes and activities of the association.

Officers (June 1983–June 1984)

Pres. Elizabeth J. Sawyers, Health Sciences Lib., Ohio State Univ., 376 W. Tenth Ave., Columbus, OH 43210; *Pres.-Elect.* Ralph Arcari, Lyman Maynard Stowe Lib., Univ. of Connecticut Health Center, Farmington, CT 06032; *Past Pres.* Richard Lyders, Texas Medical Center Lib., Houston Academy of Medicine, Jesse H. Jones Lib. Bldg., Houston, TX 77030; *Secy.-Treas.* Joan Zenan, Savitt Medical Lib., Univ. of Nevada, Reno, NV 89557.

Board of Directors (June 1983–June 1984)

Officers; Rachael Goldstein, Health Sciences Lib., Columbia Univ., 701 W. 168 St., New York, NY 10032; Virginia H. Holtz, Middleton Health Sciences Lib., 1305 Linden Dr., Madison, WI 53706; L. Yvonne Wulff, Alfred Taubman Medical Lib., Univ. of Michigan, 1135 E. Catherine, Ann Arbor, MI 48109.

Committee Chairpersons

Audit. David Curry.
Bylaws. Dana McDonald.
Development of Standards and Guidelines. Erika Love.
Information Control and Technology. Cyril Feng.
Medical Education. David Kronick.
Newsletter Advisory. Thomas Higdon.
Program. Robert Chesier.
Statistics: Annual Statistics of Medical Libraries in the U.S. and Canada. Editorial Board. Richard Lyders.

Meetings

An annual business meeting is held in conjunction with the annual meeting of the Medical Library Association in June. Annual membership meeting and program is held in conjunction with the annual meeting of the Association of American Medical Colleges in October.

Association of Jewish Libraries

c/o National Foundation for Jewish Culture
122 E. 42 St., Rm. 408, New York, NY 10017

Object

"To promote and improve library services and professional standards in all Jewish libraries and collections of Judaica; to serve as a center of dissemination of Jewish library information and guidance; to encourage the establishment of Jewish libraries and collections of Judaica; to promote publication of literature which will be of assistance to Jewish librarianship; to encourage people to enter the field of librarianship." Organized 1966 from the merger of the Jewish Librarians Association and the Jewish Library Association. Memb. 600. Dues (Inst.) $25; (Student/retired) $18. Year. July 1–June 30.

Officers (June 1982–June 1984)

Pres. Philip E. Miller, Klau Lib., Hebrew Union College-Jewish Institute of Religion, New York, NY 10012; *Treas.* Debra Reed, Klau Lib., Hebrew Union College-Jewish Institute of Religion, New York, NY 10012; *Corres. Secy.* Edith Lubetski,

Hedi Steinberg Lib., Yeshiva Univ., 245 Lexington Ave., New York, NY 10016; *Rec. Secy.* Ralph R. Simon, Temple Emanu El, 2200 S. Green Rd., University Heights, OH 44121.

(Address correspondence to the president.)

Publications

AJL Newsletter (bienn.) *Ed.* Irene S. Levin, 48 Georgia St., Valley Stream, NY 11580.
AJL Bulletin (2 per year).
Proceedings.

Divisions

Research and Special Libraries. Charles Cutter, Brandeis Univ. Lib., Waltham, MA 02154.
Synagogue School and Center Libraries. Hazel B. Karp, Hebrew Academy of Atlanta Lib., 1892 N. Druid Hills Rd. N.E., Atlanta, GA 30319.

Association of Research Libraries

Executive Director, Shirley Echelman
1527 New Hampshire Ave. N.W., Washington, DC 20036
202-232-2466

Object

To initiate and develop plans for strengthening research library resources and services in support of higher education and research. Established 1932 by the chief librarians of 43 research libraries. Memb. (Inst.) 117. Dues (ann.) $5,010. Year. Jan.-Dec.

Membership

Membership is institutional.

Officers (Oct. 1983–Oct. 1984)

Pres. Eldred Smith, Univ. of Minnesota Libs., Minneapolis, MN 55455; *V.P.* Richard J. Talbot, Univ. of Massachusetts Libs., Amherst, MA 01002; *Past Pres.* James F. Govan, Univ. of North Carolina Libs., Chapel Hill, NC 27515.

Board of Directors

Hugh C. Atkinson, Univ. of Illinois Libs.; Patricia Battin, Columbia Univ. Libs.; Graham H. Hill, McMaster Univ. Libs.; Herbert F. Johnson, Emory Univ. Libs.; W. David Laird, Univ. of Arizona Libs.; William J. Studer, Ohio State Univ. Libs.; Paul Vassallo, Univ. of New Mexico Libs.; Anne Woodsworth, Univ. of Pittsburgh Libs.

Publications

ARL Annual Salary Survey (ann.; memb. or $10).

The ARL Index and Quantitative Relationship in the ARL. Kendon Stubbs ($5).

ARL Minutes (s. ann.; memb. or $12.50 each).

ARL Newsletter (approx. 5 per year; memb. or $15).

ARL Statistics (ann.; memb. or $10).

Cataloging Titles in Microform Sets. Report based on a study conducted for ARL in 1980 by Information Systems Consultants, Inc., Richard W. Boss, Principal Investigator ($12).

Cumulated ARL University Library Statistics, 1962–63 through 1978–79. Compiled by Kendon Stubbs and David Buxton ($15).

Our Cultural Heritage: Whence Salvation? Louis B. Wright; *The Uses of the Past,* Gordon N. Ray; remarks to the 89th membership meeting of the association ($3).

76 United Statesiana. Seventy-six works of American Scholarship relating to America as published during two centuries from the Revolutionary era of the United States through the nation's bicentennial year. Ed. by Edward C. Lathem ($7.50; $5.75 paper). Dist. by the Univ. of Virginia Press.

13 Colonial Americana. Ed. by Edward C. Lathem ($7.50). Dist. by the Univ. of Virginia Press.

Committee Chairpersons

ARL/CRL Joint Committee on Expanded Access to Journal Collections. Elaine F. Sloan, Indiana Univ. Libs., Bloomington, IN 47401.

ARL Statistics. Herbert F. Johnson, Emory Univ. Lib. Atlanta, GA 30322.

Bibliographic Control. Joseph Rosenthal, Univ. of California, Berkeley Lib., Berkeley, CA 94720.

Center for Chinese Research Materials. To be announced.

Library Education. Margot B. McBurney, Queen's Univ. Lib., Kingston, Ont. K7L 5C4, Canada.

Membership Committee on Nonuniversity Libraries. Roy L. Kidman, Univ. of Southern California Libs., Los Angeles, CA 90007.

Nominations. ARL vice-president.

Office of Management Studies. Jay K. Lucker, Massachusetts Institute of Technology, Cambridge, MA 02139.

Preservation of Research Library Materials. Margaret A. Otto, Dartmouth College Libs., Hanover, NH 03755.

Task Force Chairpersons

Collection Development. Robert C. Miller, Notre Dame Univ. Libs., Notre Dame, IN 46556.

Research Library Staffing. Eldred Smith, Univ. of Minnesota Libs., Minneapolis, MN 55455.

Scholarly Communication. Charles B. Osburn, Univ. of Cincinnati Libs., Cincinnati, OH 45221.

ARL Membership in 1983

Nonuniversity Libraries

Boston Public Lib.; Canada Inst. for Scientific and Technical Information; Center for Research Libs.; John Crerar Lib.; Lib. of Congress; Linda Hall Lib.; National Agricultural Lib.; National Lib. of Canada; National Lib. of Medicine; New York Public Lib.; New York State Lib.; Newberry Lib.; Smithsonian Institution Libs.

University Libraries

Albama; Alberta; Arizona; Arizona State; Boston; Brigham Young; British Columbia; Brown; California (Berkeley); California (Davis); California (Irvine); California (Los Angeles); California (Riverside); California (San Diego); California (Santa Barbara); Case Western Reserve; Chicago; Cincinnati; Colorado; Colorado State; Columbia; Connecticut; Cornell; Dartmouth; Delaware; Duke; Emory; Florida; Florida State; Georgetown; Georgia; Georgia Institute of Technology; Guelph; Harvard; Hawaii; Houston; Howard; Illinois; Indiana; Iowa; Iowa State; Johns Hopkins; Kansas; Kent State; Kentucky; Louisiana State; McGill; McMaster; Manitoba; Maryland; Massachusetts; Massachusetts Institute of Technology; Miami; Michigan; Michigan State; Minnesota; Missouri; Nebraska; New Mexico; New York; North Carolina; North Carolina State; Northwestern; Notre Dame; Ohio State; Oklahoma; Oklahoma State; Oregon; Pennsylvania; Pennsylvania State; Pittsburgh; Princeton; Purdue; Queen's (Kingston, Canada); Rice; Rochester; Rutgers; Saskatchewan; South Carolina; Southern California; Southern Illinois; Stanford; SUNY (Albany); SUNY (Buffalo); SUNY (Stony Brook); Syracuse; Temple; Tennessee; Texas; Texas A & M; Toronto; Tulane; Utah; Vanderbilt; Virginia; Virginia Polytechnic; Washington; Washington State; Wayne State; Western Ontario; Wisconsin; Yale; York.

Association of Visual Science Librarians

c/o Pat Carlson, Librarian
Southern California College of Optometry
2001 Associate Rd., Fullerton, CA 92631

Object

"To foster collective and individual acquisition and dissemination of visual science information, to improve services for all persons seeking such information, and to develop standards for libraries to which members are attached." Founded 1968. Memb. (U.S.) 51; (foreign) 13. Annual meeting held in December in connection with the American Academy of Optometry; Houston, Texas (1983); St. Louis, Missouri (1984); and mid-year mini meeting with the Medical Library Association; Denver, Colo. (1984); New York City (1985).

Officers

Chpn. Pat Carlson, Libn., Southern California College of Optometry, 2001 Associated Rd., Fullerton, CA 92631; *Chpn.-Elect.* Suzanne Ferimer, Libn., Univ. of Houston, College of Optometry, Cullen Blvd., Houston, TX 77004.

Publications

Opening Day Book Collection — Visual Science.
PhD Theses in Physiological Optics (irreg.).
Standards for Vision Science Libraries.
Union List of Vision-Related Serials (irreg.).

Beta Phi Mu

(International Library Science Honor Society)
Executive Secretary, Blanche Woolls
School of Library and Information Science
University of Pittsburgh, Pittsburgh, PA 15260

Object

"To recognize high scholarship in the study of librarianship, and to sponsor appropriate professional and scholarly projects." Founded at the University of Illinois in 1948. Memb. 18,500.

Membership

Open to graduates of library school programs accredited by the American Library Association who fulfill the following requirements: complete the course requirements leading to a fifth-year or other advanced degree in librarianship with a scholastic average of 3.75 where A equals 4 points. This provision shall also apply to planned programs of advanced study beyond the fifth year that do not culminate in a degree but that require full-time study for one or more academic years; receive a letter of recommendation from their respective library schools attesting to their demonstrated fitness of successful professional careers. Former graduates of accredited library schools are also eligible on the same basis.

Officers

Pres. H. Joanne Harrar, Dir. of Libs., Univ. of Maryland, College Park, MD 20742; *V.P./Pres.-Elect.* Edward G. Holley, School of Lib. Science, Univ. of North Carolina, Chapel Hill, NC 27514; *Past Pres.* Robert D. Stueart, Grad. School of Lib. & Info. Science, Simmons College, Boston, MA 02115; *Treas.* Marilyn P. Whitmore, Univ. Archivist, Hillman Lib., Univ. of Pittsburgh, Pittsburgh, PA 15260; *Exec. Sec.* Blanche Woolls, School of Lib. & Info. Science, Univ. of Pittsburgh, Pittsburgh, PA 15260; *Admin. Sec.* Mary Y. Tomaino, School of Lib. & Info. Science, Univ. of Pittsburgh, Pittsburgh, PA 15260.

Directors

David L. Searcy, 703 Durant Place N.E., Apt. #1, Atlanta, GA 30308 (Zeta Chapter—Atlanta Univ./1984); Dorothy M. Shields, School of Lib. & Info. Sciences Brigham Young Univ., Provo, UT 84602 (Beta Theta Chapter—Brigham Young Univ./1984); Trudi Bellardo, College of Lib. & Info. Science, Univ. of Kentucky, Lexington, KY 40506 (Upsilon Chapter—Univ. of Kentucky/1985); Gordon Eriksen, 220 S. Kendall, #13, Kalamazoo, MI 49007 (Kappa Chapter—Western Michigan Univ./1985); Joseph J. Mika, School of Lib. Service, Univ. of Southern Mississippi, Southern Station, Box 5146, Hattiesburg, MS 39401 (Beta Psi Chapter—Univ. of Southern Mississippi/1986); Edward P. Miller, School of Lib. & Info. Science, Univ. of Missouri, Columbia, Columbia, MO 65211 (Psi Chapter—Univ. of Missouri, Columbia/1986); *Directors-at-Large.* Charles D. Patterson, School of Lib. & Info. Science, Louisiana State Univ., Baton Rouge, LA 70803 (1985); Robert John Grover, School of Lib. Science, Emporia State Univ., Emporia, KS 66801 (1986).

Publications

Newsletter (bienn.). Beta Phi Mu sponsors a modern Chapbook series. There small volumes, issued in limited editions, are intended to create a beautiful combination of text and format in the interest of the graphic arts and are available to members only.

Chapters

Alpha. Univ. of Illinois, Grad. School of Lib. & Info. Science, Urbana, IL 61801; *Beta.* Univ. of Southern California, School of Lib. Science, University Park, Los Angeles, CA 90007; *Gamma.* Florida State Univ., School of Lib. Science, Tallahassee, FL 32306; *Delta* (Inactive). Loughborough College of Further Education, School of Libnshp., Loughborough, England; *Epsilon.* Univ. of North Carolina, School of Lib. Science, Chapel Hill, NC 27514; *Zeta.* Atlanta Univ., School of Lib. & Info. Studies, Atlanta, GA 30314; *Theta.* Pratt Institute, Grad. School of Lib. & Info. Science, Brooklyn, NY 11205; *Iota.* Catholic Univ. of America, School of Lib. & Info. Science, Washington, DC 20064, and Univ. of Maryland, College of Lib. & Info. Services, College Park, MD 20742; *Kappa.* Western Michigan Univ., School of Libnshp., Kalamazoo, MI 49008; *Lambda.* Univ. of Oklahoma, School of Lib. Science, Norman, OK 73019; *Mu.* Univ. of Michigan, School of Lib. Science, Ann Arbor, MI 48109; *Nu.* Columbia Univ., School of Lib. Service, New York, NY 10027; *Xi.* Univ. of Hawaii, Grad. School of Lib. Studies, Honolulu, HI 96822; *Omicron.* Rutgers Univ., Grad. School of Lib. & Info. Studies, New Brunswick, NJ 08903; *Pi.* Univ. of Pittsburgh, School of Lib. & Info. Science, Pittsburgh, PA 15260; *Rho.* Kent State Univ., School of Lib. Science, Kent, OH 44242; *Sigma.* Drexel Univ., School of Lib. & Info. Science, Philadelphia, PA 19104; *Tau.* State Univ. of New York at Geneseo, School of Lib. & Info. Science, College of Arts and Science,

Geneseo, NY 14454; *Upsilon.* Univ. of Kentucky, College of Lib. Science, Lexington, KY 40506; *Phi.* Univ. of Denver, Grad. School of Libnshp. and Info. Mgmt., Denver, CO 80208; *Pi Lambda Sigma.* Syracuse Univ., School of Info. Studies, Syracuse, NY 13210; *Chi.* Indiana Univ. School of Lib. & Info. Science, Bloomington, IN 47401; *Psi.* Univ. of Missouri, Columbia, School of Lib. & Info. Science, Columbia, MO 65211; *Omega.* San Jose State Univ., Div. of Lib. Science, San Jose, CA 95192; *Beta Alpha.* Queens College, City College of New York, Grad. School of Lib. & Info. Studies, Flushing, NY 11367; *Beta Beta.* Simmons College, Grad. School of Lib. & Info. Science, Boston, MA 02115; *Beta Delta.* State Univ. of New York–Buffalo, School of Info. & Lib. Studies, Buffalo, NY 14260; *Beta Epsilon.* Emporia State Univ., School of Lib. Science, Emporia, KS 66801; *Beta Zeta.* Louisiana State Univ., Grad. School of Lib. Science, Baton Rouge, LA 70803; *Beta Eta.* Univ. of Texas at Austin, Grad. School of Lib. & Info. Science, Austin, TX 78712; *Beta Theta.* Brigham Young Univ., School of Lib. & Info. Science, Provo, UT 84602; *Beta Iota.* Univ. of Rhode Island, Grad. Lib. School, Kingston, RI 02881; *Beta Kappa.* Univ. of Alabama, Grad. School of Lib. Service, University, AL 35486; *Beta Lambda.* North Texas State Univ., School of Lib. & Info. Science, Denton, TX 76203, and Texas Woman's Univ., School of Lib. Science, Denton, TX 76204; *Beta Mu.* Long Island Univ., Palmer Grad. Lib. School, C.W. Post Center, Greenvale, NY 11548; *Beta Nu.* St. John's Univ., Div. of Lib. & Info. Science, Jamaica, NY 11439; *Beta Xi.* North Carolina Centeral Univ., School of Lib. Science, Durham, NC 27707; *Beta Omicron.* Univ. of Tennessee, Knoxville, Grad. School of Lib. & Info. Science, Knoxville, TN 37916; *Beta Pi.* Univ. of Arizona, Grad. Lib. School, Tucson, AZ 85721; *Beta Rho.* Univ. of Wisconsin–Milwaukee, School of Lib. Science, Milwaukee, WI 53201; *Beta Sigma.* Clarion State College, School of Lib. Science, Clarion, PA 16214; *Beta Tau.* Wayne State Univ., Div. of Lib. Science, Detroit, MI 48202; *Beta Upsilon.* Alabama A & M Univ., School of Lib. Media, Normal, AL 35762; *Beta Phi.* Univ. of South Florida, Grad. Dept. of Lib., Media & Info. Studies, Tampa, FL 33620; *Beta Chi.* Southern

Connecticut State College, School of Lib. Science & Instructional Technology, New Haven, CT 06515; *Beta Psi.* Univ. of Southern Mississippi, School of Lib. Service, Hattiesburg, MS 39406; *Beta Omega.* Univ. of South Carolina, College of Libnsp., Columbia, SC 29208; *Beta Beta Gamma.* Rosary College, Grad. School of Lib. & Info. Science, River Forest, IL 60305.

Bibliographical Society of America

Executive Director, Deirdre C. Stam
Box 397, Grand Central Sta., New York, NY 10163

Object

"To promote bilbliographical research and to issue bibliographical publications." Organized 1904. Memb. 1,400. Dues. $20. Year. Calendar.

Taylor; (1985) John Bidwell; William Matheson; Roger Stoddard; Roderick Stinehour; (1986) Joan M. Friedman; Richard G. Landon; Bernard M. Rosenthal; Elizabeth A. Swain.

Officers (Jan. 1984–Jan. 1986)

Pres. G. Thomas Tanselle, Guggenheim Memorial Foundation, 90 Park Ave., New York, NY 10016; Marjorie Wynne; *Treas.* R. Duke Benjamin, Lazard Freres and Co., 1 Rockerfeller Plaza, New York, NY 10020; *Secy.* Peter VanWingen, Rare Book Rm., Lib. of Congress, Washington, DC 20540.

Publication

Papers (q.; memb.). *Eds.* John Lancaster and Ruth Martimer, Box 467, Williamsburg, MA 01096.

Committee Chairpersons

Fellowship Program. William L. Joyce, New York Public Lib., 42 St. and Fifth Ave., New York, NY 10018.

Publications. G. Thomas Tanselle, Guggenheim Memorial Foundation, 90 Park Ave., New York, NY 10016.

Council

Officers; (1984) Roland Folter; Paul Needham; Katharine Pantzer; W. Thomas

Canadian Association for Information Science
(Association Canadienne Des Sciences De L'Information)

Secretariat/Secretariat, c/o Robert Leitch
44 Bayswater Ave., Suite 100, Ottawa, Ont. K1Y 4K3, Canada
613-725-0332

Object

Brings together individuals and organizations concerned with the production, ma-

nipulation, storage, retrieval, and dissemination of information with emphasis on the application of modern technologies in these areas. CAIS is dedicated to enhancing the activity of the information transfer process, utilizing the vehicles of research, development, application, and education, and serves as a forum for dialogue and exchange of ideas concerned with the theory and practice of all factors involved in the communication of information. Dues (Inst.) $75; (Regular) $25; (Student) $10.

Membership

Institutions and all individuals interested in information science and who are involved in the gathering, the organization, and the dissemination of information (computer scientists, documentalists, information scientist, librarians, journalists, sociologists, psychologists, linguists, administrators, etc.) can become members of the Canadian Association for Information Science.

Officers

Pres. Mary F. Laughton, 265 Poulin Ave., Apt. 1602, Ottawa, Ont. K2B 7Y8; *V.P./ Pres.-Elect.* Gils des Chatelets, 1119 Des Chasseurs, Cap-Rouge, Quebec G0A 1K0; *Treas.* Felicity Pickup, 145 Saint George St., Apt. 901, Toronto, Ont. M5R 2M1; *Secy.* Yves Marie LaCroix, Information Services, CIS TI, NRC, Montreal Rd., Ottawa, Ont. K1A 0S2.

Publications

CAIS Bulletin. (irreg.; free with membership).
The Canadian Conference of Information Science; Proceedings (ann.; ninth ann., 1981, $16.50).
The Canadian Journal of Information Science (ann.; nonmemb. $12).

Canadian Library Association

Executive Director, Paul Kitchen
151 Sparks St., Ottawa, Ont. K1P 5E3, Canada
613-232-9625

Object

To develop high standards of librarianship and of library and information service. CLA develops standards for public, university, school, and college libraries and library technician programs; offers library school scholarships and book awards; carries on international liaison with other library associations; and makes representation to government and official commissions. Founded in Hamilton in 1946, CLA is a nonprofit voluntary organization governed by an elected council and board of directors. Memb. (Indiv.) 4,100; (Inst.) 1,000. Dues (Indiv.) $60 & $90, depending on salary; (Inst.) $60 & $100, depending on budget. Year. July 1–June 30.

Membership

Open to individuals, institutions, and groups interested in librarianship and in library and information services.

Officers (1983–1984)

Pres. Lois M. Bewley, School of Libnshp., Univ. of British Columbia, Vancouver, B.C. V6T 1W5; 1st V.P./Pres.-Elect. Judith McAnanama, Chief Lib., Hamilton Public Lib., 55 York Blvd., Hamilton, Ont. L8P 3K1; *2nd V.P.* Hazel Fry, Area Head, Environment-Science-Technology Lib., Univ. of Calgary, Calgary, Alta. T2N 1N4; *Treas.* Ken Jensen, Asst. Chief Libn., Regina Public Lib., 2311 12 Ave., Regina,

Sask. S4P 0N4; *Past Pres.* Pearce Penney, Chief Provincial Libn., Nfld. Public Lib. Services, St. John's, Nfld. A1B 3A3.

(Address general correspondence to the executive director.)

Board of Directors

Officers, division presidents.

Council

Officers; division presidents; councillors, including representatives of ASTED and provincial/regional library associations.

Councillors-at-Large

To June 30, 1984: Madge Mac Gown, Donald Mills; to June 30, 1985: Claire Cote, Donald Harvey; to June 30, 1986: Gerry Meek and Carole Brégaint-Joling.

Publications

Canadian Library Journal (6 issues; memb. or nonmemb. subscribers, Canada $20, U.S. $25 (Can.), International $30 (Can.).

CM: Canadian Materials for Schools and Libraries (6 per year, $30).

Division Chairpersons

Canadian Association of College and University Libraries. Donna Duncan, Asst. Area Libn., Humanities & Social Sciences Area Lib., McLennan Lib., 3459 McTavish St., Montreal, Quebec, H3A 1Y1.

Canadian Association of Public Libraries. Madge Aalto, Chief Libn., 2 Thorncliffe Park Dr., Unit 34, Toronto, Ont. M4H 1H2.

Canadian Association of Special Libraries and Information Services. Carrol Lu-

nau. Sr. Advisor, (Systems Planning) National Lib. of Canada, 395 Wellington St., Ottawa, Ont. K1A 0N4.

Canadian Library Trustees Association. Harold Brief, Sheppard Centre, Suite 605, 2 Sheppard Ave. E., Willowdale, Ont. M2H 5Y7.

Canadian School Library Association. Warren Grabinsky, Supv. of Instruction (Teaching & Learning Resources) S.D. No. 22 (Vernon), Box 1030, Vernon, B.C. V1T 6N2.

Association Representatives

Association pour l'Avancement des Sciences et des Techniques de la Documentation (ASTED). Lise Brousseau, Dir.-Gen. ASTED, 7243 rue Saint-Denis, Montreal, P.Q. H2R 2E3.

Altantic Provinces Library Association. André Guay, Technical Service, Acadian Univ. Lib., Wolfville, Nova Scotia B0T 1X0.

British Columbia Library Association. Margaret Friesen, Interlibrary Loan, Univ. of British Columbia Lib., 1956 Main Mall, Vancouver, B.C. V6T 1Y3.

Library Association of Alberta. Nora Robinson, Alberta Vocational Centre, 332 Sixth Ave. S.E., Calgary, Alta. T2G 4S6.

Manitoba Library Association. W. R. Converse, Chief Libn., Univ. of Winnipeg Lib., 515 Portage, Winnipeg, Man. R3B 2E9.

Ontario Library Association. Beth Miller, Special Collections Libn., D. B. Weldon Lib., Univ. of Western Ontario, London, Ont. N6A 3K7.

Quebec Library Association. Diane Mittermeyer, Asst. prof. McGill Univ. Grad. School of Lib. Science, 3459 McTavish St., Montreal, Quebec H3A 1Y1.

Saskatchewan Library Association. John Murray, Gabriel Dumont Institute, 121 Broadway Ave. E., Regina, Sask. S4N 0Z6.

Catholic Library Association

Executive Director, Matthew R. Wilt
461 W. Lancaster Ave., Haverford, PA 19041
215-649-5250

Object

The promotion and encouragement of Catholic literature and library work through cooperation, publications, education, and information. Founded 1921. Memb. 3,250. Dues. $25-$500. Year. July 1983-June 1984.

Officers (April 1983-April 1985)

Pres. Sister Mary Dennis Lynch, SHCJ, Rosemont College, Rosemont, PA 19010; *V.P.* Mary A. Grant, St. John's Univ., Jamaica, NY 11439; *Past Pres.* Kelly Fitzpatrick, Mt. St. Mary's College, Emmitsburg, MD 21727. (Address general correspondence to the executive director.)

Executive Board

Officers; Sally Anne Thompson, Orangedale School, Phoenix, AZ 85008; Irma C. Godfrey, 6247 Westway Place, St. Louis, MO 63109; Sister Chrysantha Rudnik, CSSF, Felician College, Chicago, IL 60659; Gayle E. Salvatore, Brother Martin H.S., New Orleans, LA 70122; Sister Barbara Anne Kilpatrick, RSM, St. Vincent de Paul School, Nashville, TN 37208; Reverend Kenneth O'Malley, CP, Catholic Theological Union, Chicago, IL 60615.

Publications

Catholic Library World (10 issues; memb. or $30).
The Catholic Periodical and Literature Index (subscription).

Committee Chairpersons

Advisory Council. Mary A. Grant, St. John's Univ., Jamaica, NY 11439.
Catholic Library World Editorial. James P. Clarke, Marywood College, Scranton, PA 18509.
The Catholic Periodical and Literature Index. Arnold Rzepecki, Sacred Heart Seminary College Lib., Detroit, MI 48206.
Constitution and Bylaws. Eileen Searls, St. Louis Univ. Law School, St. Louis, MO 63108.
Continuing Education. Richard Fitzsimmons, Worthington Campus Lib., Pennsylvania State Univ., Dummore, PA 18512.
Elections. Susie Gremillion, Brother Martin H.S., New Orleans, LA 70122.
Finance. Mary A. Grant, St. John's Univ., Jamaica, NY 11439.
Membership. John T. Corrigan, CFX, CLA Headquarters, 461 W. Lancaster Ave., Haverford, PA 19041.
Nominations. Sister Franz Lang, OP, Barry Univ. Lib., Miami, FL 33161.
Program Coordinator. John T. Corrigan, CFX, CLA Headquarters, 461 W. Lancaster Ave., Haverford, PA 19041.
Public Relations. Owen T. McGowan, Bridgewater State College, Bridgewater, MA 02324.
Publications. Sister M. Catherine Blooming, HM, Central Catholic H.S., Canton, OH 44708.
Regina Medal. Marland L. Schrauth, St. Alphonsus School, Brooklyn Center, MN 55429.
Scholarship. Brother Emmett Corry, OSF, St. John's Univ., Jamaica, NY 11439.

Organizations to Which CLA Has Representation

American Theological Library Association. Reverend Simeon Daly, OSB, St. Meinrad Archabbey, St. Meinrad, IN 47577.

Catholic Health Association. Mary A. Grant, St. John's Univ., Jamaica, NY 11439.

Catholic Press Association. John T. Corrigan, CFX, CLA Headquarters, 461 W. Lancaster Ave., Haverford, PA 19041.

Council of National Library and Information Association (CNLIA). John T. Corrigan, CFX, CLA Headquarters, 461 W. Lancaster Ave., Haverford, PA 19041.

Independent Schools Association. Gloria A. Kelley, John Street School, Hempstead, NY 11550.

Special Libraries Association. Mary-Jo DiMuccio, Sunnyvale Public Lib., Sunnyvale, CA 94087.

College, University, Seminary Libraries. Sister Marie Joseph Morhan, OP, St. Thomas Aquinas College, Sparkill, NY 10976.

High School Libraries. Thomas O'Connor, Josephinum H.S., Chicago, IL 60622.

Library Education. Peggy Sullivan, Northern Illinois Univ., De Kalb, IL 60115.

Parish/Community Libraries. Sister Justain Heintzman, OSU, Ursuline Motherhouse of the Immaculate Conception, Louisville, KY 40206.

Section Chairpersons

Archives. John J. Prentzel, Diocese of Wilmington Archives, Wilmington, DE 19807.

Children's Libraries. Sister Rita Ann Bert, OSF, Oak Lawn Public Lib., Oak Lawn, IL 60453.

Round Table Chairpersons

Cataloging and Classification Round Table. Tina-Karen Weiner, La Salle College, Philadelphia, PA 19141.

Public Libraries Round Table. Miriam Crespi, The Free Lib. of Philadelphia, Philadelphia, PA 19103.

Chief Officers of State Library Agencies

Robert L. Clark, State Librarian,
Oklahoma Department of Libraries
200 N.E. 18 St., Oklahoma City, OK 73105

Object

The Object of COSLA is to provide "a means for cooperative action among its state and territorial members to strengthen the work of the respective state and territorial agencies. Its purpose is to provide a continuing mechanism for dealing with the problems faced by the heads of these agencies which are responsible for state and territorial library development."

Membership

The Chief Officers of State Library Agencies is an independent organization of the men and women who head the state and territorial agencies responsible for library development. Its membership consists solely of the top library officers of the 50 states and one territory, variously designated as state librarian, director, commissioner, or executive secretary.

Officers (Nov. 1982–Nov. 1984)

Chpn. Robert L. Clark, State Libn., Oklahoma Dept. of Libs., c/o 200 N.E. 18 St., Oklahoma City, OK 73105; *V. Chpn.* Gary Strong, State Libn., California State Lib., Box 2037, Sacramento, CA 95809; *Secy.*

John L. Kopischke, Dir., Nebraska Lib. Commission, 1420 P, Lincoln, NE 68508; *Treas.* Barbara Weaver, Asst. Commissioner & State Libn., State Dept. of Educ., Div. of State Libs., Archives & History, 185 W. State St., CN520, Trenton, NJ 08625; *ALA Affiliation.* Sandra Cooper, ALA, Exec. Secy. ASCLA.

Directors

Officers; immediate past chpn.: Patricia Klinck, State Libn., Vermont Dept. of Libs., c/o State Office Bldg., Montpelier, VT 05602; two elected members: Elliot L. Shelkrot, State Libn., State Lib. of Pennsylvania, Harrisburg, PA 17120; David M. Woodburn, Dir., Mississippi Lib. Commission, Box 3260, Jackson, MS 39207.

Committee Chairpersons

Committee on Network Development. Anthony Miele, Dir., Alabama State Lib.

Continuing Education Committee. Anne Marie Falsone, Dir., Colorado State Lib.

Legislation. Richard Cheski, Dir., Ohio State Lib.

Liaison with ALA and Other National Library-Related Organizations. Gary Nichols, Dir., Maine State Lib.

Liaison with Library of Congress. Betty Callaham, Dir., South Carolina State Lib.

Liaison with Library of Congress, Division for Blind and Physically Handicapped. Russell Davis, Utah State Lib. Commission.

Liaison with National Commission on Libraries and Information Science. Elliot Shelkrot, Pennsylvania State Lib.

Liaison with U.S. Department of Education. Barratt Wilkins, State Libn., Florida State Lib.

Chinese-American Librarians Association

Executive Director, John Yung-hsiang Lai
Harvard-Yenching Library, Harvard University
2 Divinity Ave., Cambridge, MA 02138

Object

"(1) To enhance communication among Chinese-American librarians as well as between Chinese-American librarians and other librarians; (2) to serve as a forum for discussion of mutual problems and professional concerns among Chinese-American librarians; (3) to promote Sino-American librarianship and library services; and (4) to provide a vehicle whereby Chinese-American librarians may cooperate with other associations and organizations having similar or allied interest."

Membership

Membership is open to everyone who is interested in the association's goals and activities. Memb. 400. Dues (Regular) $15; (Student and Nonsalaried) $7.50; (Inst.) $45; (Permanent) $150.

Officers (July 1983–June 1984)

Pres. Norma Yueh, Dir., Ramapo College Lib., Mahwah, NJ 07430; *V.P./Pres.-Elect.* Sally Tseng, Univ. Lib., Univ. of

California, Irvine, CA 92713; *Exec. Dir.* Amy Seetoo Wilson, University Microfilms, Ann Arbor, MI 48106; *Treas.* Cecilia Chen, Educational Resources Center, California State Univ. Dominguez Hills, Carson, CA 90747.

Publications

Journal of Library and Information Science (2 per year; memb. or $15).
Membership Directory, 1983 (memb.).
Newsletter (3 per year; memb.).

Committee Chairpersons

Annual Program. Sally Tseng, Univ. of Calif., Irvine, CA 92713.
Awards. Lillian Chan, San Diego State Univ., San Diego, CA 92182.
Books to China, Susana Liu, San Jose State Univ., San Jose, CA 95192.
Constitution and By-laws. Henry Chang, Bureau of Lib., St. Thomas, VI 00801.
Foundation. Hwa-wei Lee, Ohio Univ. Lib., Athens, OH 45701.
Membership. Lena Yang, Institute for Advanced Studies of World Religions, SUNY, Stony Brook, NY 11794.
Nominating. Bessie Hahn, Brandeis Univ. Lib., Waltham, MA 02254.
Public Relations. Barbara Liaw, Huntsville Madison Public Lib., AL 35803.

Publications. John Yung-hsiang Lai, Harvard-Yenching Lib., Harvard Univ., Cambridge, MA 02138.

Chapter Chairpersons

California. George W. Huang, Calif. State Univ., Chico, CA 95929.
Mid-Atlantic. Peter C. Ku, Learning Resources Center, Howard Community College, Columbia, MD 21044.
Mid-West. William S. Wong, Univ. of Illinois Lib., Urbana, IL 61801.
Northeast. Nelson Chou, East Asia Lib., Rutgers Univ., New Brunswick, NJ 08903.
Southwest. Cecilia Tung, Libn., Texas Instruments, Garland, TX 75042.

Journal Officers

John Yung-hsiang Lai, executive ed., 40 Twin Circle Dr., Arlington, MA 02174.
Newsletter Ed. Marjorie Li, Rutgers Univ. Lib., New Brunswick, NJ 08903.

Distinguished Service Awards

The 1983 distinguished service award was presented to Dr. Hwa-wei Lee, Ohio Univ. Lib., on June 28, 1983.

Church and Synagogue Library Association

Executive Secretary, Dorothy J. Rodda
Box 1130, Bryn Mawr, PA 19010

Object

"To act as a unifying core for the many existing church and synagogue libraries; to provide the opportunity for a mutual sharing of practices and problems; to inspire and encourage a sense of purpose and mission among church and synagogue librarians; to study and guide the development of church and synagogue librarianship toward recognition as a formal branch of the library profession." Founded 1967. Memb. 1,600. Dues (Contributing) $100; (Inst.) $75; (Affiliated) $35; (Church or Synagogue) $20; (Indiv.) $10. Year. July 1983–June 1984.

Officers (July 1983–June 1984)

Pres. Ruth Sawyer, 2826 San Gabriel, Austin, TX 78705; *1st V.P./Pres.-Elect.* Marilyn P. Demeter, 3145 Corydon Rd., Cleveland Heights, OH 44118; *2nd V.P.* Elizabeth M. Burton, R.R. 1, Box 287, Cicero, IN 46034; *Treas.* Patricia W. Tabler, Box 116, Keedysville, MD 21756; *Past. Pres.* Anita Dalton, 41 Aberdeen Rd. N., Cambridge, Ont. N1S 2X1, Canada; *Publns. Dir. and Bulletin Ed.* William H. Gentz, 300 E. 34 St., Apt. 9C, New York, NY 10016.

Executive Board

Officers; committee chairpersons.

Publications

A Basic Book List for Church Libraries: Annotated Bibliography ($3.00).

Church and Synagogue Libraries (bi-mo.; memb. or $15, Can. $18). *Ed.* William H. Gentz. Book reviews, ads, $145 for full-page, camera-ready ad, one-time rate.

CSLA Guide No. 1, Setting Up a Library: How to Begin or Begin Again ($2.50).

CSLA Guide No. 2, rev. 2nd ed. *Promotion Planning All Year 'Round* ($4.50).

CSLA Guide No. 3, rev. ed. *Workshop Planning* ($6.50).

CSLA Guide No. 4, rev. ed. *Selecting Library Materials* ($2.50).

CSLA Guide No. 5. Cataloging Books Step by Step ($2.50).

CSLA Guide No. 6. Standards for Church and Synagogue Libraries ($3.75).

CSLA Guide No. 7. Classifying Church or Synagogue Library Materials ($2.50).

CSLA Guide No. 8. Subject Headings for

Church or Synagogue Libraries ($3.50).

CSLA Guide No. 9. A Policy and Procedure Manual for Church and Synagogue Libraries ($3.75).

CSLA Guide No. 10. Archives in the Church or Synagogue Library ($4.50).

Church and Synagogue Library Resources: Annotated Bibliography ($2.50).

The Family Uses the Library. Leaflet (5¢; $3.75/100).

Helping Children Through Books: Annotated Bibliography ($3.75).

Know Your Neighbor's Faith: An Annotated Interfaith Bibliography ($3.00).

Promotion Planning Year 'Round. Slide set with reading script. ($100; rental fee $15).

Religious Books for Children: An Annotated Bibliography ($5.00).

Setting Up a Library: How to Begin or Begin Again. Slide set with reading script ($75; rental fee $10).

The Teacher and the Library—Partners in Religious Education. Leaflet (10¢; $7/100).

Committee Chairpersons

Awards. Jean S. Good.

Chapters. Fay W. Grosse.

Constitution and Bylaws. Lois S. Seyfrit.

Continuing Education. Joyce L. White.

Finance and Fund Raising. Robert Dvorak.

Library Services. Judith Stromdahl.

Library World Liaison. Carolyn Albert.

Membership. Lois Seyfrit.

Nominations and Elections. Smith Gooch.

Public Relations. Maryanne J. Dotts.

Publishers' Liaison. Doris G. Metzler.

Sites. Ruth Roth.

Continuing Library Education Network and Exchange (CLENE), Inc.

Executive Director, Patsy Haley Stann
620 Michigan Ave. N.E., Washington, DC 20064
202-635-5825

Object

The basic missions of CLENE, Inc., are (1) to provide equal access to continuing education opportunities, available in sufficient quantity and quality over a substantial period of time to ensure library and information science personnel and organizations the competency to deliver quality library and information services to all; (2) to create an awareness and a sense of need for continuing education of library personnel on the part of employers and individuals as a means of responding to societal and technological change. Founded 1975. Memb. 260. Dues (Indiv.) $25; (Inst. assoc.) $50–$150; (State agency) $750–$3,000 according to population. Year. Twelve months from date of entry.

Membership

CLENE, Inc., welcomes as members institutions—libraries, information centers, data banks, schools and departments of library, media, and information science—any organization concerned with continuing education; professional associations in library, media, information science, and allied disciplines; local, state, regional, and national associations; individuals; state library and educational agencies; consortia.

Officers (June 1983–June 1984)

Pres. John Hinkle, Continuing Education Coord., Oklahoma Dept. of Libs., 200 N.E. 18 St., Oklahoma City, OK 25202; *Pres.-Elect.* Vee Friesner, Dir. of Lib. De-velopment, Kansas State Lib., Box 7, Rte. 1, St. George, KS 66535; *Exec. Dir.* Patsy Haley Stann, 620 Michigan Ave. N.E., Washington, DC 20064; *Treas.* Sydelle Popinsky, Continuing Education Consultant, Texas State Lib., 1004 Eason, Austin, TX 78703; *Past Pres.* Alphonse F. Trezza, Assoc. Professor, School of Lib. & Info. Studies, Florida State Univ., Tallahassee, FL 32306. (Address correspondence to the executive director.)

Board of Directors

Officers; Ann Armbrister, Assoc. Dir. for Lib. Services, AMIGOS Bibliographic Council, Inc., 11300 N. Central Expressway, Suite 321, Dallas, TX 75243; Evalyn Clough, Asst. to the Dean, School of Lib. & Info. Science, Univ. of Pittsburgh, Pittsburgh, PA 15260; Joan C. Durrance, Coord. of Continuing Education, School of Lib. Science, Univ. of Michigan, Ann Arbor, MI 48109; Dottie Hiebing, Lib. Continuing Education Consultant, Wisconsin Dept. of Public Instruction, 126 Langdon, Madison, WI 53705; Elizabeth Stone, Dean Emeritus, The Catholic Univ. of America, Washington, DC 20064; Sandra S. Stephan, Specialist in Staff Development & Continuing Education, Div. of Lib. Development & Services, Maryland State Dept. of Educ., 200 W. Baltimore St., Baltimore, MD 21201; Sharon A. Sullivan, Personnel Libn., Ohio State Univ. Libs., 1858 Neil Ave. Mall, Columbus, OH.

Publications

CLENExchange. (4/year). Newsletter $10.

Concept Papers

#2. *Guide to Planning and Teaching CE Courses.* Washtien (1975). $4.25 (memb.); $5 (nonmemb.).

#4. *Helping Adults to Learn.* Knox (1976) (out of print).

#5. *Continuing Library Education: Needs Assessment & Model Programs.* Virgo, Dunkel, Angione (1977). $10.20 (memb.); $12 (nonmemb.).

#6. *Recognition for Your Continuing Education Accomplishments.* James Nelson (June 1979).

#7. *Planning Coordinated Systems of Continuing Library Education, A Workbook and Discussion Guide.* Kathleen Weibel (1982). $6 (memb.); $6.90 (nonmemb.).

Bibliography on Nontraditional Learning. Elizabeth Stone and Mary Baxter (1978). $3.50.

Bibliography on Recognition Systems (1978). $3.50.

Continuing Education Resource Book (1977). $2.55 (memb.); $3 (nonmemb.).

Final Report to the NCIIS. Elizabeth Stone (1974). $5.

Model Continuing Education Recognition System in Library and Information Science (1977). $1.50 (memb.); $2 (nonmemb.).

Planning for Statewide Continuing Education for Library/Information/Media Personnel. Eleanor Biscoe, ed. (1980). $4.25 (memb.); $5 (nonmemb.).

For more information or to order publications, write to CLENE, Inc., 620 Michigan Ave. N.E., Washington, DC 20064. (202-635-5825).

Committees

Finance.
Long Range Planning.
Membership Promotion.
Membership Services.
Publications Advisory.
Research & Development.
Voluntary Recognition.

Council of National Library and Information Associations, Inc.

461 W. Lancaster Ave., Haverford, PA 19041
215-649-5251

Object

To provide a central agency for cooperation among library/information associations and other professional organizations of the United States and Canada in promoting matters of common interest.

Membership

Open to national library/information associations and organizations with related interests of the United States and Canada. American Assn. of Law Libs.; American Lib. Assn.; American Society of Indexers; American Theological Lib. Assn.; Art Libs. Society/North America; Assn. of Christian Libs., Inc.; Assn. of Jewish Libs.; Catholic Lib. Assn.; Chinese-American Libns. Assn.; Church and Synagogue Lib. Assn.; Council of Planning Libns.; Lib. Binding Institute; Lib. Public Relations Council; Lutheran Lib. Assn.; Medical Lib. Assn.; Music Lib. Assn.; Society of American Archivists; Special Libs. Assn.; Theatre Lib. Assn.

Officers (July 1983–June 1984)

Chpn. David Bender, Exec. Dir., Special Libs. Assn., 235 Park Ave. S., New York,

NY 10003; *V. Chpn.* Robert DeCandido, The New York Public Lib., Research Libs., Fifth Ave. & 42 St., New York, NY 10018; *Secy.-Treas.* Jack S. Ellenberger, Shearman & Sterling, 53 Wall St., New York, NY 10005.

(Address correspondence to chairperson at 461 W. Lancaster Ave., Haverford, PA 19041.)

Directors

James Irvine, Princeton Theological Seminary, Box 111, Princeton, NJ 08540 (July 1981–June 1984); D. Sherman Clarke, Olin Lib., Rm. 110, Cornell Univ., Ithaca, NY 14853 (July 1982–June 1985); Wilma W. Jensen, Exec. Dir., Lutheran Church Lib. Assn., 122 W. Franklin Ave., Minneapolis, MN 55404.

Council of Planning Librarians, Publications Office

1313 E. 60 St., Chicago, IL 60637

Object

To provide a special interest group in the field of city and regional planning for libraries and librarians, faculty, professional planners, university, government, and private planning organizations; to provide an opportunity for exchange among those interested in problems of library organization and research and in the dissemination of information about city and regional planning; to sponsor programs of service to the planning profession and librarianship; to advise on library organization for new planning programs; to aid and support administrators, faculty, and librarians in their efforts to educate the public and their appointed or elected representatives to the necessity for strong library programs in support of planning. Founded 1960. Memb. 150. Dues. $35 (Inst.); $15 (Indiv.). Year. July 1–June 30.

Membership

Open to any individual or institution that supports the purpose of the council, upon written application and payment of dues to the treasurer.

Officers (1983–1984)

Pres. Marilyn Myers, Wichita State University Lib., Campus Box 68, Wichita, KS 67208; *V.P./Pres.-Elect.* Jon Greene, Architecture & Planning Lib., Univ. of California, Los Angeles, CA 90024; *Secy.* Olya Tymciurak, Tucson Planning Dept. Lib., Box 27210, Tucson, AZ 85726-7210; *Treas.* Coreen Douglas, Lib., City of Edmonton Planning Dept., Phipps McKinnon Bldg., 10020-101A Ave., 11th Fl. Edmonton, Alta. T5J 3G2, Canada; *Member-at-Large.* Lynne DeMerritt, Municipal Research & Services Center, 4719 Brooklyn Ave. N.E., Seattle, WA 98105; *Editor, Publications Program.* James Hecimovich, 1313 E. 60 St., Chicago, IL 60637.

Publications

CPL Bibliographies (approx. 30 bibliographies published per year). May be purchased on standing order subscription or by individual issue. Free catalog on request.

#84. *A Bibliography on Natural Resources and Environmental Conflict: Management Strategies and Processes.* John R. Ehrmann & Patricia A. Bidol ($10).

#85. *Health Care Cost Containment Strategies: A Bibliography.* Robert J. Juster & Joyce A. Lanning ($10).

#86. *Industrial Development of Urban Space: A Selected and Annotated Bibliography.* Rosalind G. Bauchum ($4).

#87. *The Sociology of Range Manage-*

ment: A Bibliography. Jere Lee Gilles ($8).

#88. *Women in Suburbia: A Bibliography.* Hugh Wilson & Sally Ridgeway ($6).

#89. *Shopping Centers: A Bibliography.* John A. Dawson ($10).

#90. *National Parks in Urban Areas: An Annotated Bibliography.* Kathleen Fahey ($10).

#91. *Hazardous Substances in Canada: A Selected Bibliography.* John J. Miletich ($5).

#92. *Revenue and Expenditure Forecasting in State and Local Government: A Selective, Annotated Bibliography.* Margaret B. Guss & David R. Brink ($6).

#93. *Studies Relating Automobile Design and Vehicle Safety: An Annotated Bibliography.* Margaret E. Shepard ($15).

#99. *Valuation and Property Taxation of Nonrenewable Resources: An Annotated Bibliography.* Robert M. Clatanoff ($8).

#102. *Urban Enterprise Zones: A Selected Review of the Literature with Annotations.* Andrew Garoogian ($8).

#103. *National Criminal Justice Reference Service Bibliographies: A Bibliography of Bibliographies.* John Ross ($5).

#104. *Skills in Community Practice: A Bibliography.* Barry Checkoway & Mary Blackstone ($8).

#106. *The Private Sector Role in Rural Outdoor Recreation in the U.S.: An Annotated Bibliography.* H. Ken Cordell & Barbara Stanley-Saunders ($15).

#107. *History of Urban Planning in the U.S.: An Annotated Bibliography.* Martin Gellen ($6).

#110. *Heavy Industry, Deepwater Ports, and Coastal Environments: A Bibliographic Case Study of Cherry Point, Washington.* Megan Barton ($6).

#119. *Cityshape: Research and References in Community Design.* Sherwin Greene & Rita Calvan ($12).

Council on Library Resources, Inc.

1785 Massachusetts Ave. N.W., Washington, DC 20036
202-483-7474

Object

A private operating foundation, the council seeks to assist in finding solutions to the problems of libraries, particularly academic and research libraries. In pursuit of this aim, the council makes grants to and contracts with other organizations and individuals, and calls upon many others for advice and assistance with its work. The council was established in 1956 by the Ford Foundation, and it now receives support from a number of private foundations and other sources. Current program emphases include establishment of a computerized system of national bibliographic control, professional education, library resources and their preservation, information delivery services, library costs and funding, and technology assessment.

Membership

The council's membership and board of directors is limited to 25.

Officers

Chpn. Maximilian Kempner; *V. Chpn.* Charles Churchwell; *Pres.* Warren J. Haas; *Secy.-Treas.* Mary Agnes Thompson. (Address correspondence to headquarters.)

Publications

Annual Report.
CLR Recent Developments.

Educational Film Library Association

Executive Director, Nadine Covert
45 John St., Suite 301, New York, NY 10038
212-227-5599

Object

"To promote the production, distribution and utilization of educational films and other audio-visual materials." Incorporated 1943. Memb. 1,800. Dues (Inst.) $140-$190; (Commercial organizations) $265; (Indiv.) $45. Year. July–June.

Officers

Pres. Catherine Egan (1981–1984), Asst. Dir., AV Services, Pennsylvania State Univ., Special Services Bldg., University Park, PA 16802; *Pres.-Elect.* Michael Miller (1982–1985), Head, AV Services, Mid-Hudson Lib. System, 103 Market St., Poughkeepsie, NY 12601; *V.P./Past Pres.* Clifford Ehlinger (1980–1984), Dir., Div. of Media, Grant Wood Area Education Agency, 4401 Sixth St. S.W., Cedar Rapids, IA 52404; *Secy.* Carol Doolittle (1982–1985), Dir., AV Resource Center, Cornell Univ., 8 Research Pk., Ithaca, NY 14850; *Treas.* Nadine Covert (Ex Officio), Exec. Dir., EFLA, 43 W. 61 St., New York, NY 10023.

Board of Directors

Officers; Peter Finney (1983–1986), Dir., Instructional Materials Center, Washtenaw Intermediate School Dist., 1819 S. Wagner Rd., Ann Arbor, MI 48106; Diane Henry (1983–1986), Asst. Chief, Technology & AV Div., Martin Luther King Memorial Lib., 901 G St. N.W., Washington, DC 20001; Lillian Katz (1981–1984), Head, Media Services, Port Washington Public Lib., 245 Main St., Port Washington, NY 11050; Angie Leclercq (1980–1986), Head, Undergrad. Lib., Univ. of Tennessee, 1015 Volunteer Blvd., Knoxville, TN 37916; George Zook (1983–1986), Dir., Instructional Materials Service, Lancaster-Lebanon Int. Unit #13, 1110 Enterprise Rd., East Petersburg, PA 17520.

Publications

American Film Festival Program Guide (ann.).
EFLA Bulletin (q.).
EFLA Evaluations. (5 per year). *Ed.* Judith Trojan.
Sightlines (q.). *Ed.* Nadine Covert.

Write for list of other books and pamphlets.

Federal Library Committee

Executive Director, James P. Riley
Library of Congress, Washington, DC 20540
202-287-6055

Object

"For the purpose of concentrating the intellectual resources present in the federal library and library related information community: To achieve better utilization of library resources and facilities; to provide more effective planning, development, and operation of federal libraries; to promote an optimum exchange of experience, skill, and resources; to promote more effective service to the nation at large. Secretariat efforts and the work groups are organized to: consider policies and problems relating to federal libraries; evaluate existing federal library programs and resources; determine priorities among library issues requiring attention; examine the organization and policies for acquiring, preserving, and making information available; study the need for a potential of technological innovation in library practices; and study library budgeting and staffing problems, including the recruiting, education, training, and remuneration of librarians." Founded 1965. Memb. (Federal libs.) 2,200; (Federal libns.) 3,300. Year. Oct. 1–Sept. 30.

Membership

Libn. of Congress, Dir. of the National Agricultural Lib., Dir. of the National Lib. of Medicine, representatives from each of the other executive departments, and delegates from the National Aeronautics and Space Admin., the National Science Foundation, the Smithsonian Institution, the U.S. Supreme Court, U.S. Information Agency, the Veterans Admin., and the National Archives. Six members will be selected on a rotation basis by the permanent members of the committee from independent agencies, boards, committees, and commissions. These rotating members will serve two-year terms. Ten regional members shall be selected on a rotating basis by the permanent members of the committee to represent federal libraries following the geographic pattern developed by the Federal Regional Councils.

These rotating regional members will serve two-year terms. The ten regional members, one from each of the ten federal regions, shall be voting members. In addition to the permanent representative of DOD, one nonvoting member shall be selected from each of the three services (U.S. Army, U.S. Navy, U.S. Air Force). These service members, who will serve for two years, will be selected by the permanent Department of Defense member from a slate provided by the Federal Library Committee. The membership in each service shall be rotated equitably among the special service, technical, and academic and school libraries in that service. DOD shall continue to have one voting member in the committee. The DOD representative may poll the three service members for their opinions before reaching a decision concerning the vote. A representative of the Office of Management and Budget, designated by the budget director and others appointed by the chairperson, will meet with the committee as observers.

Officers

Chpn. Carol Nemeyer, Assoc. Libn. for National Programs, Lib. of Congress, Washington, DC 20540; *Exec. Dir.* James P. Riley, Federal Lib. Committee, Lib. of Congress, Washington, DC 20540. (Address correspondence to the executive director.)

Publications

Annual Report (Oct.).
FLC Newsletter (irreg.).
Technical Notes (mo.).

Fedlink Network Office

Federal Library Committee, Library of Congress,
Washington, DC 20540
202-287-6454

Object

The Federal Library and Information Network (FEDLINK) is an FLC operating cooperative program, established to minimize costs and enhance services through the use of on-line data base services for shared cataloging, interlibrary loan, acquisitions, and information retrieval. FEDLINK was established to:

1. Expedite and facilitate on-line data base services among federal libraries and information centers.

2. Develop plans for the expansion of such services to federal libraries and information centers.

3. Promote cooperation and utilization of the full potential of networks and technologies to institutions and provide for formal relationships between library and information networks and the FEDLINK membership.

4. To serve as the major federal library and information cooperative system in the emerging national library and information service network.

5. Promote education, research, and training in network services and new library and information technology for the benefit of federal libraries and information centers.

Membership

FEDLINK membership is nationwide and is made up of over 550 libraries, information centers, and systems that participate in automated systems and services sponsored and coordinated by FLC.

Officers

Dir. James P. Riley.

Information Industry Association

President, Paul G. Zurkowski
316 Pennsylvania Ave. S.E., Suite 400, Washington, DC 20003
202-544-1969

Membership

For details on membership and dues, write to the association headquarters. Memb. Over 200.

Staff

Pres. Paul G. Zurkowski; *V.P., Government Relations.* Robert S. Willard; *Dir., Finance & Admin.* Alison Caughman; *Dir., Marketing & Publications.* Fred S. Rosenau; *Dir., Membership Development.* Judith Russell; *Meetings Coord.* Linda Cunningham.

Board of Directors

Chair: Norman M. Wellen, Business International Corp.; *Chair-Elect:* Robert S. November, ITT Communications and Information Services; *Treas.* Peter A. Marx, Chase Econometrics/Interactive Data Corp.; *Secy.* Paul P. Massa, Congressional Information Service; *Past Chair.* Roy K. Campbell, Dun & Bradstreet Credit Services; Robert F. Asleson, International Thomson Information; John H. Buhsmer, NewsNet; Peter A. Genereaux, Information Delivery Systems; William Giglio, McGraw-Hill; Lois Granick, PsycINFO; James H. Holly, Times Mirror Videotex Services; Marlene Hurst, University Microfilms International; John Jenkins, BNA Video Group; James G. Kollegger, EIC/Intelligence; Carl Valenti, Dow Jones & Co.

Publications

The Business of Information Report (1983).
Information Sources (6th ed., 1984).
Planning Product Innovation (1981).
So You Want to Be a Profitable Database Publisher (1983).
Understanding U.S. Information Policy (1982).

Lutheran Church Library Association

122 W. Franklin Ave., Minneapolis, MN 55404
612-870-3623
Executive Secretary, Wilma Jensen
(Home address: 3620 Fairlawn Dr., Minnetonka, MN 55404
612-473-5965)

Object

"To promote the growth of church libraries by publishing a quarterly journal, *Lutheran Libraries;* furnishing booklists; assisting member libraries with technical problems; providing meetings for mutual encouragement, assistance, and exchange of ideas among members." Founded 1958. Memb. 1,800. Dues. $15, $25, $100, $500, $1,000. Year. Jan.–Jan.

Officers (Jan. 1983–Jan. 1985)

Pres. Marlys Johnson, Libn., Fluidyne Engineering Corp. & Elim Lutheran Lib., 4709 Oregon Ave. N., Minneapolis, MN 55428; *V.P.* Mary Egdahl, Libn., Our Saviors Lutheran Lib., 3165 Maryola Ct., Lafayette, CA 94549; *Secy.* Vivian Thoreson, American Lutheran Church Women, 422 S. Fifth St., Minneapolis, MN 55415; *Treas.* Mrs. G. Frank (Jane) Johnson, 2930 S. Hwy. 101, Wayzata, MN 55391. (Address correspondence to the executive secretary.)

Executive Board

Ruby Forlan; Elaine Hanson; Mary Jordan; Charles Mann; Solveig Bartz; Astrid Wang.

Advisory Board

Chpn. Gary Klammer; Rev. Rolf Aaseng; Mrs. H. O. Egertson; Mrs. Donald Gauerke; Mrs. Harold Groff; Rev. James Gunther; Rev. A. B. Hanson; Malvin Lundeen; Mary Egdahl; Rev. A. C. Paul; Don Rosenberg; Stanley Sandberg; Les Schmidt; Aron Valleskey; Daniel Brumm.

Publication

Lutheran Libraries (q.; memb., nonmemb. $8). *Ed.* Erwin E. John, 6450 Warren St., Minneapolis, MN 55435.

Committee Chairpersons

Budget. Rev. Carl Manfred, 5227 Oaklawn Ave., Minneapolis, MN 55436.

Council of National Library & Info. Assn.
Wilma W. Jensen, Exec. Secy; Mary A.
Huebner, Libn., Concordia College, 171
White Plains Rd., Bronxville, NY
10708.
Library Services Board. Mrs. Forrest
(Juanita) Carpenter, Libn., Rte. 1, Prior
Lake, MN 55372.

Membership. Mrs. Lloyd (Betty) LeDell,
Libn., Grace Lutheran of Deephaven,
15800 Sunset D., Minnetonka, MN
55343.
Publications Board. Rev. Carl Weller,
Augsburg Publishing House, 426 S.
Fifth St., Minneapolis, MN 55415.

Medical Library Association

Executive Director, Raymond A. Palmer
919 N. Michigan Ave., Suite 3208, Chicago, IL 60611
312-266-2456

Object

The Medical Library Association (MLA)
was founded in 1898 and incorporated in
1934. MLA's major purposes are: (1) to
foster medical and allied scientific libraries; (2) to promote the educational and
professional growth of health science librarians, and (3) to exchange medical literature among the members. Through its
programs and publications, MLA encourages professional development of its membership, whose foremost concern is the
dissemination of health sciences information for those in research, education, and
patient care.

Membership

MLA has 1,360 institutional members and
3,731 individual members. Institutional
members are medical and allied scientific
libraries. Institutional member dues are
based on the number of subscriptions
(subscriptions up to 199—$100; 200–
299—$135; 300–599—$165; 600–999—
$200; 1,000 + —$235). Individual MLA
members are people who are (or were at
the time membership was established) engaged in professional library or bibliographic work in medical and allied
scientific libraries, or people who are interested in medical or allied scientific li-

braries. Annual dues for individual
members are $60, with special membership
categories for emeritus, associate, student, life, and sustaining members.

Officers

Pres. Nina W. Matheson, Planning Office,
National Lib. of Medicine, Bethesda, MD
20209; *Pres.-Elect.* Phyllis S. Mirsky, Cen-
tral Univ. Lib., Univ. of California at San
Diego, LaJolla, CA 92093; *Past Pres.*
Nancy W. Lorenzi, Medical Center Lib.,
Univ. of Cincinnati, Cincinnati, OH
45267.

Directors

Jana Bradley; Holly Shipp Buchanan; Alison Bunting; Rachael K. Goldstein;
Eleanor Goodchild; Mary Horres; Nancy
M. Lorenzi; Nina W. Matheson; Judith
Messerle; Phyllis S. Mirsky; Minnie Or-
fanos; Madeline V. Taylor; Ruth W. Wen-
der.

Publications

*Bulletin of the Medical Library Associa-
tion* (q.; $65).
Current Catalog Proof Sheets (w.; $65).

Handbook of Medical Library Practice,
4th ed, vol. 1. ($22.50).
Handbook of Medical Library Practice,
4th ed, vol. 2 ($27.50).
Hospital Library Management ($67.50).
Introduction to Reference Sources in the
Health Sciences ($18).
MLA Directory ($30).
MLA News (10 times per year; $25).

Standing Committee
Chairpersons

Audiovisual Standards and Practices.
Committee. Donna P. Johnson, Abbott
Northwestern Hospital Resource Cen-
ter, 800 E. 28 St., Minneapolis, MN
55407.
Bulletin Consulting Editors Panel. Susan
Crawford, School of Medicine Lib.,
Washington Univ., 4580 Scott Ave., St.
Louis, MO 63110.
Bylaws Committee. Jean K. Miller, Health
Science Center Lib., Univ. of Texas,
5323 Harry Hines Blvd., Dallas, TX
75235.
Certification Eligibility Committee. Susan
E. Swanson, 117 Oakview Dr., Morgan-
town, WV 26505.
Certification Examination Review Com-
mittee. Fred W. Roper, School of Lib.
Science, Univ. of North Carolina, Man-
ning Hall 026-A, Chapel Hill, NC
27514.
Committee on Committees. Phyllis S.
Mirsky, Central Univ. Lib., C-075-G,
Univ. of California at San Diego, La
Jolla, CA 92093.
Continuing Education Committee. Gary
D. Byrd, Health Sciences Lib., Univ. of
North Carolina, Chapel Hill, NC 27514.
Copyright Committee. Wayne J. Peay,
Eccles Health Sciences Lib., Univ. of
Utah, Salt Lake City, UT 84112.
Editorial Committee for the Bulletin. Byrd
S. Helguera, Medical Center Lib., Van-
derbilt Univ., Nashville, TN 37232.

Editorial Committee for the MLA News.
Sabina W. Sinclair, Acquisitions Dept.,
Main Lib., Indiana Univ., Blooming-
ton, IN 47405.
Elections Committee. Phyllis S. Mirsky,
Central Univ. Lib., C-075-G, Univ. of
California at San Diego, La Jolla, CA
92093.
Exchange Committee. Elizabeth A. Rob-
inson, Shank Memorial Lib., Good Sa-
maritan Hospital, 2222 Philadelphia
Dr., Dayton, OH 45406.
Executive Committee. Nina W. Matheson,
National Lib. of Medicine, 8600 Rock-
ville Pike, Bethesda, MD 20209.
Finance Committee. Alison Bunting, Cen-
ter for the Health Sciences, Univ. of Cal-
ifornia at Los Angeles Biomedical Lib.,
Los Angeles, CA 90024.
Health Sciences Library Technicians Com-
mittee. Rosemarie K. Taylor, 40 S.
Cleveland St., Wilkes-Barre, PA 18705.
Honors and Awards Committee. David A.
Kronick, Health Science Center, Univ.
of Texas, 7703 Floyd Curl Dr., San An-
tonio, TX 78284. *Janet Doe Lectureship*
Subcommittee. David A. Kronick,
Health Science Center, Univ. of Texas,
7703 Floyd Curl Dr., San Antonio, TX
78284. *Ida and George Eliot Prize Sub-*
committee. Catherine Siron, Leon
Gardner Health Science Lib., St. Joseph
Hospital, 333 N. Madison St., Joliet, IL
60435. *Frank Bradway Rogers Informa-*
tion Advancement Award Subcommit-
tee. Erich Meyerhoff, S.J. Wood Lib.,
Cornell Univ. Medical College, 1300
York Avenue, New York, NY 10021.
Murray Gottlieb Prize Subcommittee.
William E. Maina, Health Sciences
Center Library, University of Texas,
5323 Harry Hines Boulevard, Dallas,
TX 75236. *Rittenhouse Award Subcom-*
mittee. Paul E. Groth, Micromedex
Inc., 2750 S. Shoshone St., Englewood,
CO 80110.
Hospital Library Standards and Practices
Committee. Marilyn Cook, Washington

Hospital Center, 110 Irving St. N.W., Washington, DC 20010.

Interlibrary Loan & Resource Sharing Standards & Practices Committee. Suzanne Ferimer, College of Optometry Lib., Univ. of Houston, Houston, TX 77004.

International Cooperation Committee. Audrey Kidder, Health Sciences Lib., Wright State Univ., Dayton, OH 45435.

Legislation Committee. Gerald J. Oppenheimer, Health Sciences Lib., Univ. of Washington SB-55, Seattle, WA 98195.

Library Standards and Practices Committee. Donald Potts, Medical Lib. Center of New York, 5 E. 102 St., New York, NY 10029.

MLA/NLM Committee. Judith Messerle, Information Services, St. Joseph's Hospital, 915 E. Fifth, Alton, IL 62002.

Membership Committee. Nidia T. Scharlock, Health Sciences Lib., 223H, Univ. of North Carolina, Chapel Hill, NC 27514.

1984 National Program Committee. Charles R. Bandy, Medical Center Lib., Univ. of Colorado, 4200 E. Ninth Ave., Denver, CO 80206.

1985 National Program Committee. Rachael K. Goldstein, Health Sciences Lib., Columbia Univ., 701 W. 168 St., New York, NY 10032.

1986 Nominating Committee. Phyllis S. Mirsky, Central Univ. Lib., C-075-G, Univ. of California at San Diego, La Jolla, CA 92093.

Oral History Committee. James J. Kopp, National Lib. of Medicine, 86000 Rockville Pike, Bethesda, MD 20209.

Program and Convention Committee. Mary Ann Hoffman, Health Sciences Lib., Wright State Univ., 3640 Colonel Glenn Hwy., Dayton, OH 45435.

Publication Panel. Frances Groen, Medical Lib., McGill Univ., 3655 Drummond St., Montreal, PQ H3G 1Y6, Canada.

Publishing and Information Industries Relations Committee. Jacque-Lynne Schulman, 5964 Ranleigh Manor Dr., McLean, VA 22101.

Recertification Committee. Lynn M. Fortney, Hill Lib. of the Health Science, Univ. of Alabama in Birmingham, Univ. Sta., Birmingham, AL 35294.

Research Committee. Phyllis C. Self, Univ. of Illinois, Lib. of the Health Sciences, 102 Medical Sciences Bldg., Urbana, IL 60801.

Scholarship and Grants Committee. Cynthia Goldstein, Rudolph Mata Medical Lib., Tulane School of Medicine, 1430 Tulane Ave., New Orleans, LA 70112.

Status and Economic Interests of Health Sciences Library Personnel. Anthony R. Aguirre, College of Physicians of Philadelphia, 19 S. 22 St., Philadelphia, PA 19103.

Ad Hoc Committees

Ad Hoc Committee for a Membership Campaign. Joan Ash, Oregon Health Science Univ. Lib., Box 573, Portland, OR 97207.

Ad Hoc Committee on Automating the Exchange. Raymond A. Palmer, Medical Lib. Assn., Suite 3208, 919 N. Michigan Ave., Chicago, IL 60611.

Ad Hoc Committee on Professional Development. Fred Roper, School of Lib. Science, Univ. of North Carolina, Manning Hall 026-A, Chapel Hill, NC 27514.

Music Library Association

Box 487, Canton, MA 02021
617-828-8450

Object

"To promote the establishment, growth, and use of music libraries; to encourage the collection of music and musical literature in libraries; to further studies in musical bibliography; to increase efficiency in music library service and administration." Founded 1931. Memb. about 1,700. Dues (Inst.) $46; (Indiv.) $32; (Student) $16. Year. Sept. 1–Aug. 31.

Officers

Pres. Mary W. Davidson, Music Lib., Wellesley College, Wellesley, MA 02181; *Past Pres.* Donald W. Krummel, Grad. Lib. School, Univ. of Illinois, Urbana, IL 61801; *Secy.* George R. Hill, Music Dept., Baruch College/CUNY, 17 Lexington Ave., New York, NY 10010; *Treas.* Harold J. Diamond, Music Lib., Lehman College/CUNY, Bedford Park Blvd. W., Bronx, NY 10468; *Ed. of "Notes."* Susan T. Sommer, Special Collections-Music, New York Public Lib., 111 Amsterdam Ave., New York, NY 10023; *Exec. Secy.* Suzanne E. Thorin, 812 Arlington Mill Dr., #201, Arlington, VA 22204.

Directors

Officers; Judith Kaufman; Gordon Rowley; Jean Geil; Gillian Anderson; Neil M. Ratliff; Annie Thompson.

Publications

MLA Index Series (irreg.; price varies according to size).
MLA Newsletter (q.; free to memb.).
MLA Technical Reports (irreg.; price varies according to size).
Music Cataloging Bulletin (mo.; $12).
Notes (q.; inst. subscription $42; nonmemb. subscription $28).

Committee Chairpersons

Administration. Lenore Coral. Cornell Univ., Music Lib., Ithaca, NY 14850.
Audio-Visual. Philip Youngholm, Connecticut College Lib., New London, CT 06320.
Awards. Dena J. Epstein, Univ. of Chicago Lib., 5835 S. University Ave., Chicago, IL 60637.
Bibliographic Control. Richard Smiraglia, Univ. of Illinois, Music Lib., Univ. of Illinois, Urbana, IL 61801.
Constitution Revision. Walter Gerboth, Brooklyn College, CUNY, Brooklyn, NY 11210.
Education. Ruth Tucker, Univ. of California, Music Lib., Berkeley, CA 94720.
Legislation. Carolyn O. Hunter, Cornell Univ. Lib., Ithaca, NY 14850.
Microforms. Stuart Milligan, Sibley Music Lib., Eastman School of Music, Rochester, NY 14606.
Preservation. Barbara Strauss, Univ. of Wisconsin, Music Lib., Madison, WI 53706.
Public Libraries. Norma Jean Lamb, Buffalo and Erie County Public Lib., Lafayette Sq., Buffalo, NY 14203.
Publications. Michael Ochs, Harvard Univ., Music Lib., Cambridge, MA 02138.
Reference and Public Service. Richard E. Jones, Univ. of Wisconsin, Music Lib., Milwaukee, WI 53201.
Resources and Collection Development. David Fenske, Indiana Univ., Music Lib., Bloomington, IN 47401.

National Librarians Association

Secretary-Treasurer, Donna Hanson
Drawer B, College Station, Pullman, WA 99163
509-334-3167

Object

"To promote librarianship, to develop and increase the usefulness of libraries, to cultivate the science of librarianship, to protect the interest of professionally qualified librarians, and to perform other functions necessary for the betterment of the profession of librarianship. It functions as an association of librarians, rather than as an association of libraries." Established 1975. Memb. 450. Dues. $20 per year; $35 for 2 years; (Students and Retired and Unemployed Librarians) $10. Year. July 1–June 30.

Membership

Any person interested in librarianship and libraries who holds a graduate degree in library science may become a member upon election by the executive board and payment of the annual dues. The executive board may authorize exceptions to the degree requirements to applicants who present evidence of outstanding contributions to the profession. Student membership is available to those graduate students enrolled full time at any accredited library school.

Publication

NLA Newsletter: The National Librarian (q.; 1 year $15, 2 years $28, 3 years $39). *Ed.* George Gardner.

Society of American Archivists

Executive Director, Ann Morgan Campbell
600 S. Federal St., Suite 504, Chicago, IL 60605
312-922-0140

Object

"To promote sound principles of archival economy and to facilitate cooperation among archivists and archival agencies." Founded 1936. Memb. 4,000. Dues (Indiv.) $45–$75, graduated according to salary; (Associate) $40, domestic; (Student) $30 with a two-year maximum on student membership; (Inst.) $50; (Sustaining) $100.

Officers (1983–1984)

Pres. David B. Gracy II, Texas State Archives, Capitol Sta. Box 12927, Austin, TX 78711; *V.P.* Andrea Hinding, 107 Walter Lib., Univ. of Minnesota, Minneapolis, MN 55455; *Treas.* Paul H. McCarthy, Jr., Box 80687, College Sta., Fairbanks, AK 99708.

Council

Kenneth W. Duckett; John A. Fleckner; Robert S. Gordon; Larry J. Hackman; Edie Hedlin; Linda Henry; Sue E. Holbert; William L. Joyce; Virginia C. Purdy.

Staff

Exec. Dir. Ann Morgan Campbell; *Membership Asst.* Bernice E. Brack; *Program*

Asst. Sylvia Burck; *Publications Asst.* Suzanne Fulton; *Administrative Aide.* Antonia Pedroza; *Program Officer.* Mary Lynn Ritzenthaler; *Program Asst.* Linda Ziemer.

Publications

The American Archivist (q.; $30). *Ed.* Charles Schultz; *Managing Ed.* Deborah Risteen, 600 S. Federal, Suite 504, Chicago, IL 60605. Book for review and related correspondence should be addressed to the editor. Rates for B/W ads: full-page, $250; half-page, $175; outside back cover, $350; half-page minimum insertion; 10% discount for four consecutive insertions; 15% agency commission.

SAA Newsletter. (6 per year; memb.) *Ed.* Deborah Risteen. Rates for B/W ads: full-page, $300; half-page, $175; quarter-page, $90; eighth-page, $50. 10% discount for six consecutive insertions; 15% agency commission.

Special Libraries Association

Executive Director, David R. Bender
235 Park Ave. S., New York, NY 10003
212-477-9250

Object

"To provide an association of individuals and organizations having a professional, scientific or technical interest in library and information science, especially as these are applied in the recording, retrieval, and dissemination of knowledge and information in areas such as the physical, biological, technical and social sciences and the humanities; and to promote and improve the communication dissemination, and use of such information and knowledge for the benefit of libraries or other educational organizations." Organized 1909. Memb. 11,500. Dues. (Sustaining) $250; (Indiv.) $55; (Student) $12; Year. Jan.–Dec. and July–June.

Officers (June 1983–June 1984)

Pres. Pat Molholt, Rensselaer Polytechnic Inst., Folsom Lib., Troy, NY 12181; *Pres.-Elect.* Vivian J. Arterbery, Rand Corp., Lib., 1700 Main St., Santa Monica, CA 90406; *Chapter Cabinet Chpn.* Didi Pancake, Univ. of Virginia, Sci./Tech. Info. Center, Clark Hall, Charlottesville, VA 22901; *Chapter Cabinet Chpn.-Elect.* James Matarazzo, Simmons College, Grad. School of Lib. & Info. Science, 300 The Fenway, Boston, MA 02115; *Division Cabinet Chpn.* Jean K. Martin, Molycorp, Inc., Lib., Box 54945, Los Angeles, CA 90054; *Division Cabinet Chpn.-Elect.* James B. Tchobanoff, Pillsbury Co., Research Div., Technology Info. Center, 311 Second St., S.E., Minneapolis, MN 55414; *Treas.* Muriel Regan, Gossage-Regan Assoc., 15 W. 44 St., New York, NY 10036; *Immed. Past Pres.* Janet Rigney, Council on Foreign Relations, Lib., 58 E. 68 St., New York, NY 10021.

Directors

Jack Leister (1981–1984); M. Elizabeth Moore (1981–1984); Frank Spaulding (1982–1985); Mary Lou Stursa (1982–1985); Elizabeth S. Knauff (1983–1986); Jo An Segal (1983–1986).

Publications

Special Libraries (q.) and *SpeciaList* (mo.). Cannot be ordered separately ($36 for both; add $5 postage outside the U.S., including Canada). *Ed.* Doris Youdelman.

Committee Chairpersons

Awards. George H. Ginader, International Creative Management, Inc., 401 W. 57 St., New York, NY 10019.

Conference Program. Fred Roper, Univ. of North Carolina, School of Lib. Science, Manning Hall 026-A, Chapel Hill, NC 27514.

Consultation Service. Marilyn Stark, Colorado School of Mines, Arthur Lakes Lib., Golden, CO 80401.

Copyright Law Implementation. Laura N. Gasaway, Univ. of Oklahoma, Law Lib., 300 Timberdell, Norman, OK 73019.

Education. Mirian H. Tees, McGill Univ., Grad. School of Lib. Science, 3459 McTavish St., Montreal, P.Q. H3A 1Y1, Canada.

Government Information Services. John F. Kane, Aluminum Co. of America, Alcoa Tech. Center, Info. Dept., Alcoa Center, PA 15069.

Government Relations. Catherine A. Jones, Lib. of Congress, Congressional Research Service, Washington, DC 20540.

Networking. Beth A. Hamilton, Triodyne, Inc., 7855 Grosse Pointe Rd., Skokie, IL 60077.

Nominating. Betty A. Bassett, Xerox Research Center of Canada, Technical Info. Center, 2660 Speakman Dr., Mississauga, Ont., L5K 2L1, Canada.

Positive Action Program for Minority Groups. Thomasina Capel, Institute for Defense Analyses, Technical Info. Services, 1801 N. Beauregard St., Alexandria, VA 22311.

Publications. Mary Margaret Regan, New York Public Lib., Economics & Public Affairs Div., Fifth Ave. & 42nd St., New York, NY 10018.

Publisher Relations. Howard F. McGinn, Jr., Microfilming Corp. of America, 1620 Hawkins Ave., Sanford, NC 27330.

Scholarship. Marie A. Gadula, McLeod Young & Weir, Commerce Union Tower, Box 433-Toronto Dominion Center, Toronto, Ont. M5K 1M2, Canada.

Standards. Audrey N. Grosch, Univ. of Minnesota, Lib. Systems Dept. S-34, Wilson Lib., Minneapolis, MN 55455.

Statistics. David A. Self, Univ. of Illinois, Veterinary Medicine Lib., Urbana, IL 61801.

Student Relations Officer. Julie H. Bichteler, Univ. of Texas at Austin, Grad. School of Lib. Science, Box 7576, Univ. Sta., Austin, TX 78712.

H. W. Wilson Co. Award. Ronald R. Sommer, Univ. of Tennessee, Center for Health Sciences, Lib., 800 Madison Ave., Memphis, TN 38163.

Theatre Library Association

Secretary-Treasurer, Richard M. Buck
111 Amsterdam Ave., New York, NY 10023

Object

"To further the interests of collecting, preserving, and using theatre, cinema, and performing arts materials in libraries, museums, and private collections." Founded 1937. Memb. 500. Dues. (Indiv.) $20; (Inst.) $25. Year. Jan. 1–Dec. 31, 1984.

Officers (1983–1984)

Pres. Dorothy L. Swerdlove, Curator, Billy Rose Theatre Collection, The New York Public Lib. at Lincoln Center, 111 Amsterdam Avenue, New York, NY 10023; *V.P.* Mary Ann Jensen, Curator, William Seymour Theatre Collection, Princeton Univ.

Libs.; Princeton, NJ 08540; *Secy.-Treas.* Richard M. Buck, Asst. to the Chief, Performing Arts Research Center, New York Public Lib. at Lincoln Center, 111 Amsterdam Ave., New York, NY 10023; *Rec. Secy.* Birgitte Kueppers, Archivist, Shubert Archive, Lyceum Theatre, 149 W. 45 St., New York, NY 10036. (Address correspondence, except *Broadside & PAR* to the secretary-treasurer. Address *Broadside* correspondence to Alan J. Pally, General Lib. & Museum of the Performing Arts, New York Public Lib. at Lincoln Center, 111 Amsterdam Ave., New York, NY 10023. Address *PAR* correspondence to Barbara N.C. Stratyner, 300 Riverside Dr., 11B, New York, NY 10025.

Executive Board

Officers; William Appleton; Elizabeth Burdick; Geraldine Duclow; Mary Ann Jensen; Gerald M. Kahan; Lois Erickson McDonald; Margaret Mahard; Julian Mates; Robert L. Parkinson; Louis A. Rachow; Anne G. Schlosser; Alan L. Woods. *Ex officio.* Barbara Naomi Cohen Stratyner; Alan J. Pally. *Honorary.* Rosamond Gilder; Marguerite McAneny; Paul Myers.

Publications

Broadside (q.; memb.)
Performing Arts Resources (ann.; memb.).

Committee Chairpersons

Awards. Don B. Wilmeth.
Nominations. Mary Ann Jensen.
Program and Special Events. Richard M. Buck.
Publications. Julian Mates.

Universal Serials and Book Exchange, Inc.

Executive Director, Mary W. Ghikas
3335 V St. N.E., Washington, DC 20018
202-529-2555

Object

"To promote the distribution and interchange of books, periodicals, and other scholarly materials among libraries and other educational and scientific institutions of the United States, and between them and libraries and institutions of other countries." Organized 1948. Year. Jan. 1–Dec. 31.

Membership

Membership in USBE is open to any library that serves a constituency and is an institution or part of an institution or organization. The USBE corporation includes a representative from each member library and from each of a group of sponsoring organizations listed below.

Board of Directors

Pres. Susan K. Martin, Dir., Milton S. Eisenhower Lib., Johns Hopkins Univ., Baltimore, MD 21218; *V.P./Pres.-Elect.* Joseph M. Dagnese, Dir. of Libs., Purdue Univ., West Lafayette, IN 47907; *Secy.* Joyce D. Gartrell, Head, Serials Cataloging, Columbia Univ. Libs., New York, NY 10027; *Treas.* Murray S. Martin, Libn., Wessell Lib., Tufts Univ., Medford, MA 02155; *Past Pres.* Juanita S. Doares, Assoc. Dir., Collection Management and Development, New York Public Lib., New York, NY 10017.

Members of the Board

Mary W. Ghikas, Exec. Dir.; Patricia W. Berger, Chief, Lib. & Info. Services, National Bureau of Standards, Washington, DC 20234; H. Joanne Harrar, Dir. of Libs., Univ. of Maryland, College Park, MD 20742; Jospeh H. Howard, Dir., National Agricultural Lib., U.S. Dept. of Agriculture, Beltsville, MD 20705; Nancy H. Marshall, Assoc. Dir. of Libs. for Public Services, Univ. of Wisconsin-Madison, 728 State St., Madison, WI 53706; Frank H. Spaulding, Head, Lib. Operations, Bell Laboratories, Holmdell, NJ 07733; Benita M. Weber, Head, Serials Dept., Univ. of New Mexico General Lib., Albuquerque, NM 87131.

Sponsoring Members

Alabama Lib. Assn.; Alaska Lib. Assn.; American Assn. of Law Libs.; American Council of Learned Socieities; American Society for Info. Science; American Lib. Assn.; American Theological Lib. Assn.; Arizona State Lib. Assn.; Assn. of American Lib. Schools; Assn. of Jewish Libs.; Assn. of Research Libs; Assn. of Special Libs. of the Philippines; Associazione Italiano Biblioteche; British Columbia Lib. Assn.; California Lib. Assn.; Catholic Lib. Assn.; Colorado Lib. Assn.; District of Columbia Lib. Assn; Ethiopian Lib. Assn.; Federal Lib. Committee; Federation of Indian Lib. Assns.; Florida Lib. Assn.; Idaho Lib. Assn.; Interamerican Assn. of Agricultural Libns. and Documentalists; Jordan Lib. Assn.; Kenya Lib. Assn.; Lib. of Congress; Maryland Lib. Assn.; Medical Lib. Assn.; Michigan Lib. Assn.; Music Lib. Assn.; National Academy of Sciences; National Agricultural Lib.; National Lib. of Medicine; New Jersey Lib. Assn.; North Carolina Lib. Assn.; Pennsylvania Lib. Assn.; Philippine Lib. Assn.; Smithsonian Institution; Social Science Research Council; South African Lib. Assn.; Southeastern Lib. Assn.; Special Libs. Assn.; Special Libs. Assn. of Japan; Theatre Lib. Assn.; Uganda Lib. Assn.; Vereinigung Osterreichischer Bibliothekare.

State, Provincial, and Regional Library Associations

The associations in this section are organized under three headings: United States, Canada, and Regional Associations. Both the United States and Canada are represented under Regional Associations. Unless otherwise specified, correspondence is to be addressed to the secretary or executive secretary name in the entry.

United States

Alabama

Memb. 1,400. Founded 1904. Term of Office. Apr. 1982–Apr. 1983. Publication. *The Alabama Librarian* (10 per year). *Ed.* Bob Schremser, Huntsville Public Lib., Box 443, Huntsville 35804.

Pres. Pat Moore, 613 Winwood Dr., Birmingham 35226; *1st V.P./Pres.-Elect.* Niel Snider, Box 1, Livingston 35470; *2nd V.P.* Frances F. Davis, 1912 Washington St., Tuskegee 36088; *Secy.* Hope I. Cooper, 1103-C Thornwood Dr., Birmingham 35209; *Treas.* Frank Walker, 1006 Circleview Dr., Dothan 36301; *ALA Chapter Councillor.* James Ramer, Dean, Grad. School of Lib. Service, Univ. of Alabama, Box 6242, University 35486; *Past Pres.* Jane McRae, 4608 Scenic View Dr., Bessemer 35020.

Address correspondence to the executive secretary, Alabama Lib. Assn., Box BY, University 35486.

Alaska

Memb. (Indiv.) 276; (Inst.) 27. Term of Office. Mar. 1983–Mar. 1984. Publications. *Sourdough* (q.); *Newspoke* (bi-mo.).

Pres. Pat Wilson, 9215 Gee St., Juneau 99801; *V.P./Pres.-Elect.* To be announced; *Secy.* To be announced; *Treas.* Judy Monroe, 5240 E. 42, Anchorage 99504.

Arizona

Memb. 1,050. Term of Office. October 8, 1983–December 17, 1984. Publication. *ASLA Newsletter* (mo.). *Ed.* Arlene Bansal, Arizona State Lib., 3rd fl. Capitol, 1700 W. Washington, Phoenix 85007.

Pres. Donald E. Riggs, Arizona State Univ., Tempe 85287; *Pres.-Elect.* June Garcia, Phoenix Public Lib., 12 E. McDowell, Phoenix 85004; *Secy.* Susan Garvin, 4444 N. Seventh Ave., Apt. 407, Phoenix 85013; *Treas.* Jeanette Daane, 2123 S. Paseo Loma, Mesa 85202.

Arkansas

Memb. 1,150. Term of Office. Sept. 1983–Sept. 1984. Publications. *Arkansas Libraries* (q.); *ALA Newsletter* (monthly).

Pres. Janet Mitcham, Univ. of Arkansas for Medical Sciences Lib., UAMS Lib., Slot 586, 4301 W. Markham, Little Rock 72205; *Exec. Dir.* Alice Shands, Box 2275, Little Rock 72203.

Address correspondence to the executive director.

California

Memb. (Indiv.) 3,050; (Inst.) 178; (Business) 70. Term of Office. Jan. 1–Dec. 31, 1984. Publication. *The CLA Newsletter* (mo.).

Pres. Bernard Kreissman, Univ. of California, Davis 95616; *V.P./Pres.-Elect.* Linda M. Wood, Riverside City-County Lib., Box 468, Riverside 92502; *Treas.* Margaret C. Wong, Los Angeles County Public Lib., 320 W. Temple St., Los Angeles 90012; *ALA Chapter Councillor.* Gilbert W. McNamee, San Francisco Public Lib., Business Branch, 530 Kearny St., San Francisco 94108.

Address correspondence to Stefan B. Moses, Exec. Dir., California Lib. Assn., 717 K St., Suite 300, Sacramento 95814.

Colorado

Term of Office. Nov. 1983–Oct. 1984. Publication. *Colorado Libraries* (q.). *Ed.* Johannah Sherrer, Michener Lib., Univ. of Northern Colorado, Greeley 80639.

Pres. John Campbell, Pathfinder Lib. Service System, S. First and Uncompahgre, Montrose 81401; *1st V.P./Pres.-Elect.* Beverly Moore, U.S.C. Lib., 2200 Bonforte Blvd., Pueblo 81001; *2nd V.P.* Gail M. Dow, Denver Public Lib., 4048 S. Wisteria Way, Denver 80237; *Exec. Secy.* Susan Englese, Colorado Lib. Assn., Box 32113, Aurora 80041; *Past Pres.* Irene Godden, Univ. Libs., Colorado State Univ., Fort Collins 80523.

Connecticut

Memb. 750. Term of Office. July 1, 1983–June 30, 1984. Publication. *Connecticut Libraries* (11 per year). *Ed.* Gretchen Swackhammer, Bridgeport Public Lib., 925 Broad St., Bridgeport 06604.

Pres. Mary Dymek, Prosser Public Lib., One Tunxis Ave., Bloomfield 06002; *V.P./Pres.-Elect.* Michael Simonds, Norwalk Public Lib., Belden Ave., Norwalk 06850; *Treas.* Barbara Harris, Waterford Public Lib., 49 Rope Ferry Rd., Waterford 06385; *Secy.* Jeanne Simpson, Connecticut Lib. Assn., State Lib., 231 Capitol Ave., Hartford 06106.

Delaware

Memb. (Indiv.) 224; (Inst.) 22. Term of Office. May 1983–May 1984. Publication. *DLA Bulletin* (3 per year).

Pres. David Burdash, Wilmington Inst., Tenth & Market St., Wilmington 19801; *V.P./Pres.-Elect.* Atlanta T. Brown, Newark H.S., Newark 19711; *Secy.* Barbara K. Foster, Wilmington Inst., Tenth and Market St., Wilmington 19801; *Treas.* Margaret Wang, Univ. of Delaware Lib., Newark 19711; *Past Pres.* Judith Roberts, Cape Henlopen H.S., Cape Henlopen 19958.

Address correspondence to the Delaware Lib. Assn., Box 1843, Wilmington 19899.

District of Columbia

Memb. 1050. Term of Office. May 1983–May 1984. Publication. *Intercom* (mo.). *Ed.* Jacque-Lynne Schulman, Reference Section, National Lib. of Medicine, Bethesda, MD 20209.

Pres. Darrell H. Lemke, Consortium of Universities, 1346 Connecticut Ave. N.W., Washington, DC 20036; *Pres.-Elect.* Lawrence Molumby, District of Columbia Public Lib., 901 G St. N.W., Washington, DC 20001; *Treas.* Melinda Renner, Atomic Industrial Forum, 7101 Wisconsin Ave. N.W., 12 fl., Bethesda, MD 20814; *Secy.* Jacque-Lynne Schulman, National Lib. of Medicine, Bethesda, MD 20209.

Florida

Memb. (Indiv.) 1,000; (In-state Inst.) 80; (Out-of-state Inst.) 90. Term of Office. July 1, 1983–June 30, 1984.

Pres. Jean F. Rhein, Seminole County Public Lib., 101 E. First St., 3rd fl., Sanford 32771; *V.P./Pres.-Elect.* John McCrossan, Univ. of South Florida, Dept. of Lib. Studies, 13507 Palmwood Lane, Tampa 33624; *Secy.* Sue Crum Harrell, Wakulla County Public Lib., Rte. 1, Box 61C, Crawfordville 32327; *Treas.* Thomas L. Reitz, 1333 Gunnison Ave., Orlando 32804.

Georgia

Memb. 967. Term of Office. Oct. 1983–Oct. 1985. Publication. *Georgia Librarian.* *Ed.* James Dorsey, Emanuel Junior College, Swainsboro 30401.

Pres. Jane R. Morgan, Materials Specialist, Fulton County Public Schools, 3121 Norman Berry Dr., East Point 30344; *1st V.P.* Wanda J. Calhoun, Augusta Regional Lib., 902 Greene St., Augusta 30902; *2nd V.P.* Jan Rogers, Griffin/ Spaulding City Schools, Drawer N, Griffin 30224; *Treas.* Michael Dugan, Albany Dougherty City Regional Lib., 2215 Barnsdale Way, Albany 31707; *Secy.* Virginia Boyd, Brunswick Junior College, Altamaha at Fourth, Brunswick 31520; *Exec. Secy.* Ann W. Morton, Box 833, Tucker 30084.

Hawaii

Memb. 425. Term of Office. Mar. 1983–Mar. 1984. Publications. *Hawaii Library Association Journal* (ann.); *Hawaii Library Association Newsletter* (6 per year); *HLA Membership Directory* (ann.); *Directory of Libraries & Information Sources in Hawaii & the Pacific Islands* (irreg.).

Pres. Cynthia Timberlake, Libn., Bishop Museum, Box 19000A, Honolulu 96819; *V.P./Pres.-Elect.* Caroline Spencer, Branch Libn., Kalihi-Palama Lib., Honolulu 96819; *Secy.* Rose Crozier, 94-207 Loaa St., Waipahu 96797; *Treas.* Vernon Tam, 1649-F Kewalo St., Honolulu 96822.

Address correspondence to the president.

Idaho

Memb. 365. Term of Office. Oct. 31, 1983–Oct. 31, 1984. Publication. *The Idaho Librarian* (q.). *Ed.* Donna Hanson.

Pres. Anna Green, Portneuf District Lib., Chubbuck 83202; *Pres.-Elect.* Vera Kenyon, Wilder School District, Wilder 83676; *Secy.* Samuel Sayre, Idaho State Univ. Lib., Pocatello 83209.

Illinois

Memb. 3,500. Term of Office. Jan. 1984–Dec. 1984. Publication. *ILA Reporter* (6 per year).

Pres. Valerie Wilford; *V.P./Pres.-Elect.* Harold Hungerford; *Treas.* Doris Brown; *Exec. Dir.* Willine C. Mahony.

Address correspondence to the executive director, ILA, 425 N. Michigan Ave., Suite 1304, Chicago 60611.

Indiana

Memb. (Indiv.) 1,130; (Inst.) 231. Term of Office. May 1983–Mar. 1984. Publications. *Focus on Indiana Libraries* (10 per year). *Ed.* Beth Steele, ILA/ILTA Exec. Office, 1100 W. 42 St., Indianapolis 46208; *Indiana Libraries* (q.). *Ed.* Ray Trevis, Dept. of Lib. Science, Ball State Univ., Muncie 47306.

Pres. Linda Robertson, Wabash Public Lib., 188 W. Hill, Wabash 46992; *V.P./Pres.-Elect.* Harold W. Boyce, Marion College Lib., 4201 S. Washington St., Marion 46952; *Secy.* David Cooper, Noblesville Public Lib., 16 S. Tenth St., Noblesville 46060; *Treas.* Leslie R. Galbraith, Christian Theological Seminary, 1000 W. 42 St., Indianapolis 46208.

Iowa

Memb. 1,642. Term of Office. Jan. 1984–Jan. 1985. Publication. *The Catalyst* (bi-mo.). *Ed.* Naomi Stovall, 921 Insurance Exchange Bldg., Des Moines 50309.

Pres. Richard Doyle, Stewart Memorial Lib., Coe College, Cedar Rapids 52402.

Kansas

Memb. 1,000. Term of Office. July 1983–June 1984. Publications. *KLA Newsletter* (q.); *KLA Membership Directory* (ann.).

Pres. Arnita Graber, 200 W. Broadway, Newton 67114; *V.P./Pres.-Elect.* Louise Snyder, Kelsey Lib., Sterling College, Sterling 67579; *Secy.* Karyl Buffington, Coffeyville Public Lib., 311 W. Tenth, Coffeyville 67337; *Treas.* Rowena Olsen, McPherson College Lib., McPherson 67460.

Kentucky

Memb. 1,050. Term of Office. Oct. 1983–Oct. 1984. Publication. *Kentucky Libraries* (q.).

Pres. James A. Norsworthy, Jr., Audiovisual Center, Jefferson County Public Schools, 4409 Preston Hwy., Louisville 40213; *V.P.* Rebekah Heath, Jefferson Community College, 109 E. Broadway, Louisville 40202; *Secy.* Mildred Franks, Exstrom Lib., Univ. of Louisville, Louisville 40292.

Louisiana

Memb. (Indiv.) 1,435; (Inst.) 80. Term of Office. July 1983–June 1984. Publication. *LLA Bulletin* (q.).

Pres. Joy Lowe, Box 3061, Tech Stat., Ruston 71270; *1st V.P./Pres.-Elect.* Anthony Benoit, 4265 Hyacinth Ave., Baton Rouge 70808; *2nd V.P.* Jean Calhoun, 415 Georgia St., Vidalia 71373; *Secy.* Gloria Donatto, 4824 Odin St., New Orleans 70126; *Parliamentarian.* Marianne Puckett, 109 E. Southfield, #181, Shreveport 71105; *Exec. Dir.* Chris Thomas, Box 131, Baton Rouge 70821.

Address correspondence to the executive director.

Maine

Memb. 722. Term of Office. (*Pres. & V.P.*) Spring 1982–Spring 1984. Publications. *Downeast Libraries* (4 per year); *Monthly Memo* (mo.).

Pres. Schuyler Mott, Paris Hill, Paris 04271; *V.P.* Glenna Nowell, Gardiner Public Lib., Gardiner 04345; *Secy.* Catherine H. Cocks, Miller Lib., Colby College, Waterville 04901; *Treas.* J. Michael Francescki, Merrill Memorial Lib., Yarmouth 04096.

Address correspondence to Maine Lib. Assn., c/o Maine Municipal Assn., Local Government Center, Community Dr., Augusta 04330.

Maryland

Memb. 900. Term of Office. June 1, 1983–June 1, 1984.

Pres. Anne Shaw Burgan, Network Services Div., Enoch Pratt Free Lib., 400 Cathedral St., Baltimore 21201; *1st V.P.* Kenna Forsyth, Baltimore County Public Lib., 320 York Rd., Towson 21204; *Secy.* Jan Baird-Adams, INFER Office, Enoch Pratt Free Lib., 400 Cathedral St., Baltimore 21201; *Treas.* Alvin Miller, Lib. for the Blind and Physically Handicapped, 1715 N. Charles St., Baltimore 21201.

Address correspondence to the president.

Massachusetts

Memb. (Indiv.) 750; (Inst.) 150. Term of Office. July 1983–June 1984. Publication. *Bay State Librarian* (2 per year).

Pres. Constance Clancy, South Hadley Public Lib., South Hadley 01075; *V.P.* Susan Flannery, Lucius Beebe Memorial Lib., Wakefield 01880; *Rec. Secy.* Bertha Chandler, Sharon Public Lib., Sharon 02067; *Treas.* Ann Haddad, Falmouth Public Lib., Falmouth 02540; *Exec. Secy.* Ronald Hunte, 436 Great Rd., Acton 01720.

Address correspondence to the executive secretary.

Michigan

Memb. (Indiv.) 2,200; (Inst.) 150. Term of Office. Nov. 1, 1983–Oct. 31, 1984. Publication. *Michigan Librarian Newsletter* (10 per year).

Pres. Eleanor Pinkham, Kalamazoo College, Kalamazoo 49001; *Treas.* William Miller, Head, Reference Lib., Michigan State Univ., East Lansing 48823; *Exec. Dir.* Marianne Gessner, Michigan Lib. Assn., 226 W. Washtenaw Ave., Lansing 48933.

Address correspondence to the executive director.

Minnesota

Memb. 900. Term of Office. (*Pres.* & *V.P.*) Nov. 1, 1983–Oct. 31, 1984; (*Secy.*) Nov. 1, 1982–Oct. 31, 1984; (*Treas.*) Nov. 1, 1983–Oct. 31, 1985. Publication. *MLA Newsletter* (10 per year).

Pres. Michael Kathman, 414 Eighth Ave. N., Cold Spring 56320; *V.P./Pres.-Elect.* Joseph Kimbrough, Dir., Minneapolis Public Lib. & Info. Center, 300 Nicollet Mall, Minneapolis 55401; *ALA Chapter Councillor.* Laura Landers, Deputy Dir., Hennepin County Lib., 12601 Ridgedale Dr., Minnetonka 55343; *Secy.* Darlene Arnold, Office of Lib. Development & Services, 400 Capitol Sq., 550 Cedar St., St. Paul 55101; *Treas.* Edward Swanson, 1065 Portland Ave., St. Paul 55104; *Exec. Dir.* Adele Panzer Morris, Minnesota Lib. Assn., 4700 W. 28 St., Minneapolis 55416.

Address correspondence to the executive director.

Mississippi

Memb. 1,000. Term of Office. Jan. 1984–Dec. 1984. Publication. *Mississippi Libraries* (q.).

Pres. Anice C. Powell, Sunflower County Lib., 201 Cypress Dr., Indianola 38751; *V.P./Pres.-Elect.* Barbara Carroon, 5818 North Dale, Jackson 39211; *Secy.* Kendall Chapman, 807 S. Jackson St., Brookhaven 39601; *Treas.* Missy Lee, Rte. 1, Pinola 39149; *Exec. Secy.* DeLois Minton, MLA Office, Box 470, Clinton 39056.

Address correspondence to the executive secretary.

Missouri

Memb. 1,303. Term of Office. Oct. 21, 1983–Oct. 5, 1984. Publication. *Missouri Library Association Newsletter* (6 per year).
Pres. Martha Maxwell, Dir., Cape Girardeau Public Lib., 711 N. Clark, Cape Girardeau 63701; *V.P./Pres.-Elect.* Helen Wigersma, Missouri Western State College, 2627 Frederick, St. Joseph 64506; *Treas.* Nancy Bray, Cape Girardeau 63701; *Secy.* Dorothy Elliott, Dir., St. Joseph Public Lib., Tenth and Felix St., St. Joseph 64501.
Address correspondence to Exec. Coord., Missouri Lib. Assn., Parkade Plaza, Suite 9, Columbia 65201.

Montana

Memb. 560. Term of Office. June 1, 1983–May 31, 1984. Publication. *MLA President's Newsletter* (4–6 per year).
Pres. Rita Schmidt, 3721 Seventh Ave. N., Great Falls 59401; *V.P./Pres.-Elect.* Barbara Rudio, Extension Libn., City-County Lib. of Missoula, Missoula 59801; *Secy.* Suzy Holt, Libn., Shodair Children's Hospital, Box 5539, Helena 59601.

Nebraska

Memb. 776. Term of Office. Oct. 1983–Oct. 1984. Publication. *NLA Quarterly.*
Pres. Robert Trautwein, 2512 26 St., Columbus 68601; *V.P./Pres.-Elect.* Elaine Norton, Box 150, David City 68632; *Secy.* Margaret S. Mills, 660 N. State St., Box 427, Osceola 68651; *Treas.* Betty Werner, 512 W. 11, Cozad 69130; *Exec. Secy.* Ray Means, Dir., Alumni Memorial Lib., Creighton Univ., 2500 California St., Omaha 68178.

Address correspondence to the executive secretary.

Nevada

Memb. 300. Term of Office. Jan. 1, 1984–Dec. 31, 1984. Publication. *Highroller* (4 per year).
Pres. Gretchen Billow, Western Nevada Community College, 2201 W. Nye Lane, Carson City 89701; *V.P./Pres.-Elect.* Billie Mae Polson, Dickinson Lib., Univ. of Nevada-Las Vegas, 4505 Maryland Pkwy., Las Vegas 89154; *Exec. Secy.* Jean Spiller, Eldorado H.S., 1139 N. Linn Lane, Las Vegas 89110; *Treas.* Anne Hawkins, Washoe County Lib., Box 2151, Reno 89505; *Past Pres.* Mary Sue Ferrell, Western Nevada Community College, 2201 W. Nye Lane, Carson City 89701.

New Hampshire

Memb. 420. Term of Office. May 1983–May 1984. Publication. *NHLA Newsletter* (bi-mo.).
Pres. Andrew Carnegie, 5 Robin Lane, Exeter 03833; *V.P./Pres.-Elect.* Kathryn Wendelowski, Littleton Public Lib., 109 Main St., Littleton 03561; *2nd V.P.* John Courtney, Concord Public Lib., 35 Green St., Concord 03301; *Secy.* Carol West, Shapiro Lib., 2500 N. River Rd., Manchester 03104; *Treas.* Barry Hennessey, Dimond Lib., Univ. of New Hampshire, Durham 03824.

New Jersey

Memb. 1,550. Term of Office. May 1983–Apr. 1984. Publication. *New Jersey Libraries* (q.).
Pres. Elaine McConnell, Dir., Piscataway Township Libs., 500 Hoes Lane, Piscataway 08854; *V.P./Pres.-Elect.* Eleanor Brome, Dir., Cranford Public Lib., 224 Walnut Ave., Cranford 07016; *Past Pres.* Dorothy Johnson, Asst. Dir., Bloomfield

Public Lib., 90 Broad St., Bloomfield 07003; *Treas.* Rowland Bennett, Dir., Maplewood Memorial Lib., 51 Baker St., Maplewood 07040; *Exec. Dir.* Abigail Studdiford, New Jersey Lib. Assn., 116 W. State St., Trenton 08608.

Address correspondence to the executive director, NJLA Office, Trenton 08608.

New Mexico

Memb. 641. Term of Office. Apr. 1983–Apr. 1984. Publication. *New Mexico Library Association Newsletter. Ed.* Kin-Tree Van, Box 25084, Albuquerque 87125.

Pres. Linda J. Erickson, Sandia National Laboratories, R.R. 5, 104 Penasco Rd. N.E., Albuquerque 87123; *1st. V.P./Pres.-Elect.* Cheryl Wilson, New Mexico State Univ., 1109 Skyway, Las Cruces 88001; *2nd V.P.* Marcy Litzenberg, Santa Fe Public Lib., 438 Luisa Lane, Santa Fe 87501; *Secy.* Cherrill M. Whitlow, Rio Grande H.S., 2702 Morrow Rd. N.E., Albuquerque 87106; *Treas.* Lowell Duhrsen, New Mexico State Univ., Box 3813, Univ. Park Branch, Las Cruces 88003.

New York

Memb. 3,500. Term of Office. Oct. 1983–Oct. 1984. Publication. *NYLA Bulletin* (10 per year). *Ed.* Diana J. Dean.

Pres. Carol A. Kearney, Dir. of Libs., Buffalo City Schools, City Hall, Rm. 418, Buffalo 14202; *1st V.P.* Roy A. Miller, Jr., Coord. of Adult Servs., Brooklyn Public Lib., Grand Army Plaza, Brooklyn 11238; *2nd V.P.* Samuel L. Simon, Dir., Finkelstein Memorial Lib., 19 S. Madison Ave., Spring Valley 10977; *Exec. Dir.* Nancy W. Lian, CAE, New York Lib. Assn., 15 Park Row, Suite 434, New York City 10038.

Address correspondence to the executive director.

North Carolina

Memb. 2,000. Term of Office. Oct. 1983–Oct. 1985. Publication. *North Caro-lina Libraries* (q.). *Ed.* Robert Burgin, Forsyth Co. Public Lib., 660 W. Fifth St., Winston-Salem 27101.

Pres. Leland M. Park, Dir., Lib. of Davidson College, Davidson 28036; *1st V.P./Pres.-Elect.* Pauline F. Myrick, Dir. of Instruction & Educational Media, Moore County Schools, Box 307, Carthage 28327; *2nd V.P.* M. Jane Williams, Asst. State Libn., Div. of State Lib., 109 E. Jones St., Raleigh 27611; *Secy.* Roberta S. Williams, Dir., Transylvania County Lib., 105 S. Broad St., Brevard 28712; *Treas.* Eunice P. Drum, Chief, Technical Services, Div. of State Lib., 109 E. Jones St., Raleigh 27611; *Dir.* Shirley B. McLaughlin, Dir., Learning Resources, Asheville-Buncome Technical College, 340 Victoria Rd., Asheville 28801; *Dir.* Jerry A. Thrasher, Dir., Cumberland County Public Lib., Box 1720, Fayetteville 28302.

North Dakota

Memb. (Indiv.) 350; (Inst.) 30. Term of Office. (*Pres., V.P.,* and *Pres.-Elect*) Oct. 1983–Oct. 1985. Publication. *The Good Stuff* (q.).

Pres. Jerry Kaup, Dir., Minot Public Lib., Minot 58701; *V.P./Pres.-Elect.* Cheryl Bailey, Mary College Lib., Bismarck 58501; *Secy.* Connie Strand, Harley French Medical Lib., Univ. of North Dakota Lib., Grand Forks 58202; *Treas.* Mary Jane Chaussee, Veteran's Memorial Public Lib., Bismarck 58501.

Ohio

Memb. (Indiv.) 1,904; (Inst.) 226. Term of Office. Oct. 1983–Oct. 1984. Publications. *Ohio Library Association Bulletin* (3 per year); *Ohio Libraries: Newsletter of the Ohio Library Association* (9 per year).

Pres. Rachel Nelson, Cleveland Heights-Univ. Heights Public Lib., Cleveland Heights 44118; *V.P./Pres.-Elect.* Greg Byerly, Kent State Univ. Lib., Kent

44242; *Secy.* Rebecca Callender, Logan County District Lib., Bellefontaine 43311; *Exec. Dir.* A. Chapman Parsons, 40 S. Third St., Suite 409, Columbus 43215.

Address correspondence to the executive director.

Oklahoma

Memb. (Indiv.) 950; (Inst.) 100. Term of Office. July 1, 1983–June 30, 1984. Publication. *Oklahoma Librarian* (bi-mo.).

Pres. Frances Alsworth, Central State Univ. Lib., 100 N. University Dr., Edmond 73034; *V.P./Pres.-Elect.* Norman Nelson, Oklahoma State Univ. Lib., Stillwater 74078; *Secy.* Donna Skvarla, Pioneer Multi-County Lib., 225 N. Webster, Norman 73069; *Treas.* Marilyn Vesely, Oklahoma Dept. of Libs., 200 N.E. 18, Oklahoma City 73105; *Exec. Secy.* Kay Boies, 300 Hardy Dr., Edmond 73034.

Address correspondence to the executive secretary.

Oregon

Memb. (Indiv.) 589; (Inst.) 39. Term of Office. Apr. 1983–Apr. 1984. Publication. *Oregon Library News* (mo.). *Ed.* Patricia Feehan, Corvallis-Benton County Public Lib., 645 N.W. Monroe St., Corvallis 97330.

Pres. Stanley N. Ruckman, Linn-Benton Community College, 6500 S.W. Pacific Blvd., Albany 97321; *V.P./Pres.-Elect.* Mary Devlin-Willis, Library TB-5, Portland General Electric Corp., 121 S.W. Salmon, Portland 97204; *Secy.* Mary Baker, Eugene Public Lib., 100 W. 13 Ave., Eugene 97401; *Treas.* Maureen Seaman, Lib. Oregon Graduate Center, 19600 N.W. Walker Rd., Beaverton 97006.

Pennsylvania

Memb. 1,600. Term of Office. Oct. 1983–Oct. 1984. Publication. *PLA Bulletin* (mo.).

Pres. Priscilla Greco McFerren, Hano-

ver Public Lib., Library Place, Hanover 17331; *Exec. Dir.* Diane D. Ward, Pennsylvania Lib. Assn., 126 Locust St., Harrisburg 17101.

Puerto Rico

Memb. 300. Term of Office. Apr. 1982–Mar. 1984. Publications. *Boletin* (s. ann.); *Cuadernos Bibliotecologicos* (irreg.); *Informa* (mo.); *Cuadernos Bibliograficos* (irreg.).

Pres. Luisa Vigo.

Address correspondence to the Sociedad de Bibliotecarios de Puerto Rico, Apdo. 22898, U.P.R. Sta., Rio Piedras 00931.

Rhode Island

Memb. 625. Term of Office. Nov. 1983–Jan. 1985. Publication. *Rhode Island Library Association Bulletin.* *Ed.* Christine Chapman.

Pres. Frances Farrell-Bergeron, Providence Public Lib., Providence 02903; *V.P.* Connie Lachowicz, South Kingstown Public Lib., Peace Dale 02883; *Secy.* Christian A. King, East Providence Public Lib., East Providence 02914; *Treas.* Charles Moore, Woonsocket-Harris Public Lib., Woonsocket 02895; *Member-at-Large.* Jean Sheridan, Phillips Lib., Providence College, Providence 02818; *NELA Councillor.* Jacquelyn Toy, Providence Public Lib., Rochambeau Branch, Providence 02906; *ALA Councillor.* Margaret A. Bush, Providence Public Lib., Providence 02903.

Address correspondence to the secretary.

St. Croix

Memb. 48. Term of Office. Apr. 1982–May 1983. Publications. *SCLA Newsletter* (q.); *Studies in Virgin Islands Librarianship* (irreg.).

Pres. Wallace Williams; Florence A.

Williams Public Lib., 49-50 King St., Christianstead, St. Croix 08820; *V.P.* Helen Tompkins; *Secy.* Liane Forbes; *Treas.* Nancy Fisk; *Bd. Membs.* Marty Ammerman, Avi Whitney.

South Carolina

Memb. 820. Term of Office. Oct. 1983–Sept. 1984. Publication. *The South Carolina Librarian* (s. ann.). *Ed.* Laurance Mitlin, Dacus Lib., Winthrop College, Rock Hill 29733; *News and Views of South Carolina Library Association* (bi-mo.). *Ed.* William C. Cooper, Laurens County Lib., 321 S. Harper St., Laurens 29360.

Pres. Drucilla G. Reeves, Brookland-Cayce H.S., 1300 State St., Cayce 29033; *V.P./Pres.-Elect.* Carl Stone, Anderson County Lib., Box 4047, Anderson 29622; *2nd V.P.* Lea Walsh, South Carolina State Lib., Box 11469, Columbia 29211; *Treas.* David J. Cohen, College of Charleston, Charleston 29424; *Secy.* Mary R. Bull, USC-Coastal Carolina College, Conway 29526; *Exec. Secy.* Louise Whitmore, Box 25, Edisto Island 29438.

South Dakota

Memb. (Indiv.) 415; (Inst.) 52. Term of Office. Oct. 1983–Oct. 1984. Publications. *Bookmarks* (bi-mo.); *Newsletter. Co. eds.* Phil Brown, Hilton M. Briggs Lib., South Dakota State Univ., Box 2115, Brookings 57007; Tina Cunningham, Brookings Public Lib., 515 Third St., Brookings 57006.

Pres. Susan Stow Sandness, Minnehaha County Lib., Box 218, Hartford 57033; *V.P./Pres.-Elect.* Joe Edelen, I.D. Weeks Lib., Univ. of South Dakota, Vermillion 57069; *Secy.* Nancy Sabbe, Madison Public Lib., 209 E. Center, Madison 57042; *Treas.* Kitty Brewer, Madison H.S. Lib., Madison 57042; *ALA Councillor.* Leon Raney, Hilton M. Briggs Lib., South Dakota State Univ., Brookings 57007.

Tennessee

Memb. 1,175. Term of Office. May 1983–May 1984. Publication. *Tennessee Librarian* (q.).

Pres. Janet S. Fisher, Asst. Dean/Learning Resources, Medical Lib., East Tennessee State Univ., Johnson City 37614; *Pres.-Elect.* Evelyn P. Fancher, Dir., Tennessee State Univ. Lib., Nashville 37203; *Treas.* Julia G. Boyd, Dir., Upper Cumberland Regional Lib., Cookeville 38501; *Exec. Secy.* Betty Nance, Box 120085, Nashville 37212.

Texas

Term of Office. Apr. 1983–Apr. 1984.

Pres. James O. Wallace, Dir., San Antonio College Lib., 1001 Howard, San Antonio 78284; *Pres.-Elect.* Margaret Nichols, Asst. Professor, SLIS, North Texas State Univ., 2514 Royal Lane, Denton 76201; *Exec. Dir. (Continuing).* Ada M. Howard, TLA Office, 8989 Westheimer, Suite 108, Houston 77063.

Address correspondence to the executive director.

Utah

Memb. 550. Term of Office. (*Pres. & V.P.*) Mar. 1983–Mar. 1984. Publication. *HATU Newsletter* (q.).

Pres. Craige Hall, Weber State College, 3750 Harrison Blvd., Ogden 84408; *1st V.P.* Brad Mauer, Davis County Lib., 725 S. Main, Bountiful 84010; *2nd V.P.* Sherie Snyder, Utah State Lib., 2150 S. 300 W., Suite 9, Salt Lake City 84115; *Exec. Secy.* Gerald A. Buttars, Utah State Lib. Commission, 2150 S. 300 W., Salt Lake City 84115.

Vermont

Memb. 450. Term of Office. Jan. 1984–Dec. 1984. Publication. *VLA News* (10 per year).

Pres. Jean Marcy, St. Johnsbury Atheneum, 30 Main St., St. Johnsbury 05819; *V.P./Pres.-Elect.* Vivian Bryan, Dept. of Libs., Montpelier 05602; *Secy.* Anita Danigelis, 470 S. Willard, Burlington 05401; *Treas.* Janet Nielsen, Libn., Kellogg Hubbard Lib., Montpelier 05602; *Past Pres.* Dewey Patterson, Libn., Vermont Technical College, Randolph Center 05061.

Virginia

Memb. 1,200. Term of Office. Oct. 1983–Nov. 1984. Publication. *Virginia Librarian Newsletter* (6 per year).

Pres. Tim Byrne, Cabell Lib., Virginia Commonwealth Univ., 901 Park Ave., Richmond 23284; *V.P./Pres.-Elect.* Christie Vernon, Thomas Nelson Community College Lib., Box 9407, Hampton 23670; *Secy.* John Stewart, Asst. Dir., Virginia Beach Dept. of Public Libs., Administrative Offices, Municipal Center, Virginia Beach 23456; *Treas.* Lynne Dodge, Lynchburg Public Lib., 914 Main St., Lynchburg 24504; *Exec. Dir.* Deborah M. Trocchi, Publishers' Services, 80 S. Early St., Alexandria 22304.

Address correspondence to the executive director.

Washington

Memb. (Indiv.) 1,000; (Inst.) 50. Term of Office. Aug. 1, 1983–July 31, 1985. Publication. *Highlights* (bi-mo.).

Pres. Anne Haley, Walla Walla Public Lib., 238 E. Alder, Walla Walla 99362; *1st V.P.* Irene Heninger, Kitsap Regional Lib., 1301 Sylvan Way, Bremerton 98310; *2nd V.P.* Charlotte Jones, Spokane Public Lib., W. 906 Main, Spokane 99201; *Secy.* Makiko Doi, Central Washington Univ. Lib., Ellensburg 98926; *Treas.* Janice Hammock, Washington State Lib., AJ-11, Olympia 98504; *Corres. Secy.* Marjorie Burns, 1232 143 Ave. S.E., Bellevue 98007; *Past Pres.* Anthony M. Wilson,

Highline Community College Lib., 25-ID, Midway 98031.

West Virginia

Memb. (Indiv.) 642; (Inst.) 23. Term of Office. Dec. 1983–Nov. 1984. Publication. *West Virginia Libraries.*

Pres. Jeanne Moellendick, Parkersburg H.S., 2101 Dudley Ave., Parkersburg 26101; *1st V.P./Pres.-Elect.* Charles McMorran, Boone-Madison Public Lib., 375 Main St., Madison 25130; *2nd V.P.* Jo Ellen Flagg, Kanawha County Public Lib., 123 Capitol St., Charleston 25301; *Secy.* Catherine Apel, Huntington H.S., Eighth St. & Ninth Ave., Huntington 25701; *Treas.* Dave Childers, West Virginia Library Commission, Cultural Center, Charleston 25305; *ALA Councillor.* Judy K. Rule, Cabell County Public Lib., 455 N. St. Plaza, Huntington 25701.

Wisconsin

Memb. 1,780. Term of Office. Jan. 1984–Dec. 1984. Publication. *WLA Newsletter* (bi-mo.).

Pres. Dennis Ribbens, Lawrence Univ. Lib., Appleton 54912; *V.P.* Milton Mitchell, 400 Eau Claire St., Eau Claire 54701.

Address correspondence to the president.

Wyoming

Memb. (Indiv.) 440; (Inst.) 12; (Subscribers) 24. Term of Office. Apr. 1983–Apr. 1984. Publication. *Wyoming Library Roundup* (tri-mo.). *Ed.* Linn Rounds, Wyoming State Lib., Cheyenne 82002.

Pres. Barbara Fraley, Johnson County Lib., 90 N. Main St., Buffalo 82834; *V.P.* Henry Yaple, Univ. of Wyoming, Box 3334, Univ. Sta., Laramie 82071; *Exec. Secy.* Lucie P. Osborn, Laramie County Lib. System, 2800 Central Ave., Cheyenne 82001.

Canada

Alberta

Memb. (Indiv.) 309; (Inst.) 79; (Trustee) 36. Term of Office. May 1983–May 1984. Publication. *Letter of the L.A.A.* (mo.).

Pres. Nora Robinson, Alberta Vocational Centre Lib., 332 Sixth Ave. S.E., Calgary T2G 4S6; *1st V.P./Pres.-Elect.* Vince Richards, Dir. of Libs., Edmonton Public Lib., 7 Sir Winston Churchill Sq., Edmonton T5J 2V4; *2nd V.P.* Sylvia Dubrule, Extension Lib., Univ. of Alberta, 9403 63 Ave., Edmonton T6E 0G2; *Treas.* Pat Garneau, Lib., Edmonton Journal, Box 2421, Edmonton T5J 2S6.

Address correspondence to the president, Box 1357, Edmonton T5J 2N2.

British Columbia

Memb. 670. Term of Office. Apr. 1, 1983–Mar. 31, 1984. Publication. *The Reporter* (6 per year). *Ed.* Joan Aufiero.

Pres. Margaret Friesen; *V.P.* Garth Homer; *Secy.* Colleen Smith; *Treas.* Joan Wenman.

Address correspondence to BCLA, Box 35187 Sta. E., Vancouver V6M 4G4.

Manitoba

Memb. 300. Term of Office. Sept. 1983–Sept. 1984. Publication. *Manitoba Library Association Bulletin* (q.).

Pres. Don Mills, Winnipeg Public Lib., 251 Donald St., Winnipeg R3C 3P5; *Past Pres.* Eileen McFadden, John E. Robbins Lib., Brandon Univ., Brandon R7A 6A9.

Address correspondence to E. MacMillan, 6 Fermor Ave., Winnipeg R2M 0Y2.

Ontario

Memb. 2,200. Term of Office. Nov. 1, 1983–Oct. 31, 1984. Publications. *Focus* (bi-mo.); *The Reviewing Librarian* (q.).

Pres. Elizabeth Cummings; *1st V.P.* Alan Pepper; *2nd V.P.* Gerda Molson; *Past Pres.* Beth Miller; *Treas.* George Court; *Exec. Dir.* Diane Wheatley.

Address correspondence to Ontario Lib. Assn., Suite 402, 73 Richmond St. W., Toronto M5H 1Z4.

Quebec

Memb. (Indiv.) 160; (Inst.) 67; (Commercial) 6. Term of Office. May 1983–May 1984. Publication. *ABQ/QLA Bulletin.*

Pres. Diane Mittermeyer, McGill Univ., Grad. School of Lib. Science, 3459 McTavish, Montreal H3A 1Y1; *V.P./Pres.-Elect.* Sylvia Piggott, Bank of Montreal, Technical Information Centre, One Brome Place, Bonaventure, Montreal H5A 1A3; *Secy.-Treas.* George McCubbin, McGill Univ., 3459 McTavish, Montreal H3A 1Y1; *Exec. Secy.* Shirley Bernier, Quebec Lib. Assn., Box 2216, Dorval H9S 5J4.

Saskatchewan

Term of Office. (*Pres., 1st V.P./Pres.-Elect., Past Pres.*) July 1, 1983–June 30, 1984; (*2nd V.P., Secy.*) July 1, 1983–June 30, 1985; (*Treas.*) July 1, 1983–June 30, 1985. Publication. *Saskatchewan Library Forum* (5 per year).

Pres. Anne Smart, Programme Coord., Saskatoon Public Lib., 311 23 St. E., Saskatoon S7K 0J6; *1st V.P./Pres.-Elect.* Linda Fritz, Native Law Centre Lib., Univ. of Saskatchewan, Diefenbaker Centre, Saskatoon S7M 0W0; *2nd V.P.* John Murray, 1550 14 Ave., Apt. J, Regina S4P 0W6; *Secy.* Robert Kreig, Southeast Regional Lib., Box 550, Weyburn S4H 2K7; *Treas.* Michael Brydges, Wheatland Regional Lib., 806 Duchess St., Saskatoon S7K 0R5; *Past Pres.* Alan Ball, BCD Lib. and Automation Consultants, 2268 Osler St., Regina S4P 1W8.

Address correspondence to the secretary.

Regional

Atlantic Provinces: N.B., Nfld., N.S., P.E.I.

Memb. (Indiv.) 310; (Inst.) 185. Term of Office. May 1983–Apr. 1984. Publication. *APLA Bulletin* (bi-mo.).

Pres. André Guay; *Pres.-Elect.* William Birdsall; *V.P. Nova Scotia.* Margot Schenk; *V.P. Prince Edward Island.* Frances Dindial; *V.P. Newfoundland.* Suzanne Sexty; *V.P. New Brunswick.* Eric Swanick; *Secy.* Betty Jeffery; *Treas.* Jane Archibald.

Address correspondence to Atlantic Provinces Lib. Assn., c/o School of Lib. Service, Dalhousie Univ., Halifax B3H 4H8, N.S.

Middle Atlantic: Del., Md., N.J., W.Va., D.C.

Term of Office. July 1982–Mar. 1984.

Pres. Jane E. Hukill, Delaware Campus Lib., Widener Univ., Box 7139, Concord Pike, Wilmington, DE 19803; *V.P.* Nicholas Winowich, Kanawha County Public Lib., 123 Capitol St., Charleston, WV 25301; *Secy.-Treas.* Richard Parsons, Baltimore County Public Lib., 320 York Rd., Towson, MD 21204.

Address correspondence to the secretary-treasurer.

Midwest: Ill., Ind., Mich., Minn., Ohio, Wis.

Term of Office. Oct. 1983–Oct. 1987.

Pres. Walter D. Morrill, Dir., Duggan Lib., Hanover College, Box 287, Hanover, IN 47243; *V.P.* James L. Wells, Dir., Washington County Lib., 3825 Lake Elmo Ave. N., Lake Elmo, MN 55042; *Secy.* G. Gordon Lewis, Jr., Dir., Farmington Community Lib., 32737 W. 12 Mile Rd., Farmington, MI 48018; *Treas.* A. Chapman Parson, Exec. Dir., Ohio Lib. Assn./ Ohio Lib. Trustees Assn., 40 S. Third St., Columbus, OH 43215.

Address correspondence to the president, Midwest Federation of Lib. Assns.

Mountain Plains: Colo., Kans., Mont., Nebr., Nev., N. Dak., S. Dak., Utah, Wyo.

Publication. *MPLA Newsletter* (bi-mo.). *Ed. & Adv. Mgr.* Jim Dertien, Sioux Falls Public Lib., 201 N. Main Ave., Sioux Falls, SD 57101.

Pres. Donna R. Jones, Pioneer Memorial Lib., 375 W. Fourth, Colby, KS 67701; *V.P./Pres.-Elect.* Dorothy Liegl, South Dakota State Lib., State Lib. Bldg., Pierre, SD 57501; *Secy.* Jane Hatch, Dodge City Public Lib., 1001 Second Ave., Dodge City, KS 67801; *Exec. Secy.* Joe Edelen, Technical Services, I.D. Weeks Lib., Univ. of South Dakota, Vermillion, SD 57069.

New England: Conn., Mass., Maine, N.H., R.I., Vt.

Term of Office. Oct. 1983–Oct. 1984. Publications. *NELA Newsletter* (6 per year). *Ed.* Frank Ferro, 35 Tuttle Place, East Haven, CT 06512; *A Guide to Newspaper Indexes in New England; The Genealogists' Handbook for New England Research.*

Pres. Janice F. Sieburth, Univ. of Rhode Island Lib., Kingston, RI 02881; *V.P./ Pres.-Elect.* Sherman Pridham, Portsmouth Public Lib., Portsmouth, NH 03801; *Treas.* Ruth Rothman, Portland Public Lib., Portland, ME 04103; *Secy.* Connie Lachowicz, South Kingston Public Lib., Peace Dale, RI 02883; *Dirs.* Margo Brown-Crist, Central Massachusetts Regional Lib. System, Worcester, MA 01608; Margaret Allen, Bennington Free Lib., Bennington, VT 05201; *Past Pres.* Peggy Wargo, Fairfield Public Lib., Fairfield, CT 06430; *Exec. Secy. Ex officio.* Ronald B. Hunte, CAE, New England Lib. Assn., 436 Great Rd., Acton, MA 01720.

Address correspondence to the executive secretary.

Pacific Northwest: Alaska, Idaho, Oreg., Wash., Alta., B.C.

Memb. 950 (Active); 320 (Subscribers). Term of Office. (*Pres./1st V.P.*) Oct. 1983–Oct. 1984. Publication. *PNLA Quarterly.*

Pres. Vicki R. Kreimeyer, Asst. Dir., Lewis & Clark College Lib., Portland, OR 97219; *1st V.P.* Barbara Tolliver, School of Libnshp., 133 Suzzallo Lib., FM-30, Univ. of Washington, Seattle, WA 98195; *2nd V.P.* Carol Hildebrand, Eugene Public Lib., 100 13 Ave., Eugene, OR 97401; *Secy.* George Smith, Oregon State Lib., State Lib. Bldg., Salem, OR 97310; *Treas.* Audrey Kolb, Alaska State Lib., 1215 Cowles St., Fairbanks, AK 99701.

Southeastern: Ala., Fla., Ga., Ky., La., Miss., N.C., S.C., Tenn., Va., W.Va.

Memb. 2,500. Term of Office. Nov. 1982–Nov. 1984. Publication. *The Southeastern Librarian* (q.).

Pres. Barratt Wilkins, Pres., State Lib. of Florida, R.A. Gray Bldg., Tallahassee, FL 32301; *V.P./Pres.-Elect.* Rebecca T. Bingham, Dir. of Lib. Media Services, Jefferson County Public Schools, Durrett Education Center, 4409 Preston Hwy., Louisville, KY 40213; *Secy.* David L. Ince, The Library, Valdosta State College, Valdosta, GA 31698; *Treas.* Arial A. Stephens, Dir., Richard H. Thornton Public Lib., Box 339, Oxford, NC 27565; *Exec. Secy.* Ann W. Morton, Box 987, Tucker, GA 30084.

Address correspondence to the executive secretary.

State Library Agencies

The state library administrative agencies listed in this section have the latest information on state plans for the use of federal funds under the Library Services and Construction Act. The name of the director, address, and telephone number are given for each state agency.

Alabama

Anthony W. Miele, Dir., Alabama Public Lib. Service, 6030 Monticello Dr., Montgomery 36130. Tel: 205-277-7330.

Alaska

Richard B. Engen, Dir., Div. of State Libs. and Museums, Alaska Dept. of Educ., Pouch G, State Office Bldg., Juneau 99811. Tel: 907-465-2910.

Arizona

Sharon G. Womack, Dir., Dept. of Lib., Archives, and Public Records, 1700 W. Washington, State Capitol, Phoenix 85007. Tel: 602-255-4035.

Arkansas

John A. (Pat) Murphey, Jr., State Libn., Arkansas State Lib., One Capitol Mall, Little Rock 72201. Tel: 501-371-1526.

California

Gary E. Strong, State Libn., California State Lib., Box 2037, Sacramento 95809. Tel: 916-445-2585 or 4027.

Colorado

Anne Marie Falsone, Asst. Commissioner, Colorado State Lib., 1362 Lincoln St., Denver 80203. Tel: 303-866-3695.

Connecticut

Clarence R. Walters, State Libn., Connecticut State Lib., 231 Capitol Ave., Hartford 06115. Tel: 203-566-4192.

Delaware

Sylvia Short, Dir., Delaware Div. of Libs., Dept. of Community Affairs, Box 639, Dover 19901. Tel: 302-736-4748.

District of Columbia

Hardy R. Franklin, Dir., D.C. Public Lib., 901 G St. N.W., Washington 20001. Tel: 202-727-1101.

Florida

Barratt Wilkins, State Libn., State Lib. of Florida, R.A. Gray Bldg., Tallahassee 32201. Tel: 904-487-2651.

Georgia

Joe B. Forsee, Dir., Div. of Public Lib. Services, 156 Trinity Ave. S.W., Atlanta 30303. Tel: 404-656-2461.

Hawaii

Bartholomew A. Kane, Asst. Superintendent/State Libn., Office of Lib. Services, Dept. of Educ., Box 2360, Honolulu 96804. Tel: 808-735-5510.

Idaho

Charles M. Bolles, State Libn., Idaho State Lib., 325 W. State St., Boise 83702. Tel: 208-334-2150.

Illinois

Bridget L. Lamont, Dir., Illinois State Lib., Centennial Memorial Bldg., Springfield 62756. Tel: 217-782-2994.

Indiana

C. Ray Ewick, Dir., Indiana State Lib., 140 N. Senate Ave., Indianapolis 46204. Tel: 317-232-3692.

Iowa

Claudya Muller, Dir., State Lib. of Iowa, Capitol Complex, Des Moines 50319. Tel: 515-281-4113.

Kansas

Duane F. Johnson, State Libn., Kansas State Lib., 3rd fl., State Capitol, Topeka 66612. Tel: 913-296-3296.

Kentucky

James A. Nelson, State Libn. and Commissioner, Kentucky Dept. for Libs. and Archives, Box 537, Frankfort 40602. Tel: 502-875-7000.

Louisiana

Thomas F. Jaques, State Libn., Louisiana State Lib., Box 131, Baton Rouge 70821. Tel: 504-342-4923.

Maine

J. Gary Nichols, State Libn., Maine State Lib., State House Sta. 64, Augusta 04333. Tel: 207-289-3561.

Maryland

Nettie B. Taylor, Asst. State Superintendent for Libs., Div. of Lib. Development and Services, Maryland State Dept. of

Educ., 200 W. Baltimore St., Baltimore 21201. Tel: 301-659-2000.

Massachusetts

Roland R. Piggford, Dir., Massachusetts Bd. of Lib. Commissioners, 648 Beacon St., Boston 02215. Tel: 617-267-9400.

Michigan

Susan M. Haskin, Interim State Libn., Lib. of Michigan, Box 30007, Lansing 48909. Tel: 517-373-1580.

Minnesota

William G. Asp, Dir., Office of Public Libs. and Interlib. Cooperation, Minnesota Dept. of Educ., 301 Hanover Bldg., 480 Cedar St., St. Paul 55101. Tel: 612-296-2821.

Mississippi

David M. Woodburn, Dir., Mississippi Lib. Commission, 1100 State Office Bldg., Box 3260, Jackson 39207. Tel: 601-359-1036.

Missouri

Charles O'Halloran, State Libn., Missouri State Lib., Box 387, Jefferson City 65102. Tel: 314-751-2751.

Montana

Sarah Parker, State Libn., Montana State Lib., 1515 E. Sixth Ave., Helena 59620. Tel: 406-449-3004.

Nebraska

John L. Kopischke, Dir., Nebraska Lib. Commission, Lincoln 68508. Tel: 402-471-2045.

Nevada

Joseph J. Anderson, State Libn., Nevada State Lib., Capitol Complex, Carson City 89710. Tel: 702-885-5130.

New Hampshire

Shirley Adamovich, State Libn., New Hampshire State Lib., 20 Park St., Concord 03301. Tel: 603-271-2392.

New Jersey

Barbara F. Weaver, Asst. Commissioner for Education/State Libn., Div. of State Lib., Archives and History, 185 W. State St., Trenton 08625. Tel: 609-292-6200.

New Mexico

Virginia Downing, State Libn., New Mexico State Lib., 325 Don Gaspar St., Santa Fe 87503. Tel: 505-827-3804.

New York

Joseph F. Shubert, State Libn./Asst. Commissioner for Libs., Rm. 10C34, C.E.C., Empire State Plaza, Albany 12230. Tel: 518-474-5930.

North Carolina

David Neil McKay, Dir./State Libn., Dept. of Cultural Resources, Div. of State Lib., 109 E. Jones St., Raleigh 27611. Tel: 919-733-2570.

North Dakota

Ruth Mahan, State Libn., North Dakota State Lib., Liberty Memorial Bldg., Capitol Grounds, Bismarck 58505. Tel: 701-224-2492.

Ohio

Richard M. Cheski, Dir., State Lib. of Ohio, 65 S. Front St., Columbus 43215. Tel: 614-462-7061.

Oklahoma

Robert L. Clark, Jr., Dir., Oklahoma Dept. of Libs., 200 N.E. 18 St., Oklahoma City 73105. Tel: 405-521-2502.

Oregon

Wesley A. Doak, State Libn., Oregon State Lib., Salem 97310. Tel: 503-378-4367.

Pennsylvania

Elliot L. Shelkrot, State Libn., State Lib. of Pennsylvania, Box 1601, Harrisburg 17105. Tel: 717-787-2646.

Rhode Island

Fay Zipkowitz, Dir., Rhode Island Dept. of State Lib. Services, 95 Davis St., Providence 02908. Tel: 401-277-2726.

South Carolina

Betty E. Callaham, State Libn., South Carolina State Lib., 1500 Senate St., Box 11469, Columbia 29211. Tel: 803-758-3181.

South Dakota

Clarence Coffindaffer, State Libn., South Dakota State Lib., State Library Bldg., Pierre 57501. Tel: 605-773-3131.

Tennessee

Olivia K. Young, State Libn. and Archivist, Tennessee State Lib. and Archives, 403 Seventh Ave. N., Nashville 37219. Tel: 615-741-2451.

Texas

Dorman H. Winfrey, Dir. and Libn., Texas State Lib., Box 12927, Capitol Sta., Austin 78711. Tel: 512-475-2166.

Utah

Russell L. Davis, Dir., Utah State Lib., 2150 S. 300 W., Suite 16, Salt Lake City 84115. Tel: 801-533-5875.

Vermont

Patricia E. Klinck, State Libn., State of Vermont, Dept. of Libs., c/o State Office Bldg., Post Office, Montpelier 05602. Tel: 802-828-3261 ext. 3265.

Virginia

Donald R. Haynes, State Libn., Virginia State Lib., Richmond 23219. Tel: 804-786-2332.

Washington

Roderick G. Swartz, State Libn., Washington State Lib., Olympia 98504. Tel: 206-753-2915.

West Virginia

Frederic J. Glazer, Dir., West Virginia Lib. Commission, Science and Cultural Center, Charleston 25305. Tel: 304-348-2041.

Wisconsin

Leslyn M. Shires, Asst. Superintendent, Div. for Lib. Services, Wisconsin Dept. of Public Instruction, 125 S. Webster St., Madison 53707. Tel: 608-266-2205.

Wyoming

Wayne H. Johnson, State Libn., Wyoming State Lib., Barnett Bldg., Cheyenne 82002. Tel: 307-777-7283.

American Samoa

Sailautusi Avegalio, Federal Grants Mgr., Dept. of Educ., Box 1329, Pago Pago 96799. Tel: 633-5237.

Guam

Magdalena S. Taitano, Libn., Nieves M. Flores Memorial Lib., Box 652, Agana 96910. Tel: 472-6417.

Northern Mariana Islands

Ruth Tighe, Dir. of Lib. Services, Commonwealth of the Northern Mariana Islands, Saipan 96950. Tel: 6534.

Pacific Islands (Trust Territory of)

Harold Crouch, Chief of Federal Programs, Dept. of Educ., Trust Territory of the Pacific Islands, Saipan, Mariana Islands 96950. Tel: 9448.

Puerto Rico

Ana Martinez, Acting Dir., Dept. of Educ., Apartado 859, Hato Rey 00919. Tel: 809-753-9191 or 754-0750.

Virgin Islands

Henry C. Chang, Dir., Libs. and Museums, Bur. of Libs., Museums, and Archaelogical Services, Dept. of Conservation and Cultural Affairs, Government of the Virgin Islands, Box 390, Charlotte Amalie, St. Thomas 00801. Tel: 809-774-3407.

State School Library Media Associations

Unless otherwise specified, correspondence to an association listed in this section is to be addressed to the secretary or executive secretary named in the entry.

Alabama

Alabama Lib. Assn., Div. of Children's and School Libns. Memb. 405. Term of Office. Apr. 1983–Apr. 1984. Publication. *Alabama Librarian.*

Chpn. Vicky Dennis, 589 S. Forest Dr., Birmingham 35209; *Chpn.-Elect.* Mary Maude McCain, 548 Collette St., Birmingham 35204; *Secy.* Joan Lewis, Enterprise H.S., Enterprise 36330.

Alaska

[See entry under State, Provincial, and Regional Library Associations — *Ed.*]

Arizona

School Lib. Div., Arizona State Lib. Assn. Memb. 400. Term of Office. Oct. 1983–Oct. 1984. Publication. *ASLA Newsletter.*

Pres. Caryl Major, 3213 W. Sunnyside Ave., Phoenix 85029; *Pres.-Elect.* Hazel Robinson, 16819 N. 20 St., Phoenix 85022; *Secy.* Diane Cole, 7919 N. Zarragoza, Tucson 85704; *Treas.* Jerry Wilson, 4148 N. 23 Dr., Phoenix 85015.

Arkansas

School Lib. Div., Arkansas Lib. Assn. Memb. 294. Term of Office. Jan. 1984–Dec. 1984.

Chpn. Wanda Williams Jones, 19 Cardinal Valley Cove, North Little Rock 72116; *V. Chpn.* Joyce Schneider, 401 Devon Ave., Sherwood 72116; *Secy.* Ann Ayres, 1503 Ridgecrest, Springdale 72764.

California

California Media and Lib. Educators Assn. (CMLEA), Suite 204, 1575 Old Bayshore Hwy., Burlingame 94010. Tel. 415-692-2350. Job Hotline. 415-697-8832. Memb. 1,100. Term of Office. June 1983–May 1984. Publication. *CMLEA Journal* (bi-ann.).

Pres. Jack Stolz, Dir., Instructional Media Services, Santa Barbara County Schools, 4400 Cathedral Oaks Rd., Santa Barbara 93160; *Pres.-Elect.* David L. Rose, District Libn. and Media Specialist, Claremont Unified School District, 2080 N. Mountain Ave., Claremont 91711; *Secy.* Dorothy Baird, Coord. of Instructional Materials, Los Alamitos Unified School District, 10650 Reagan St., Los Alamitos 90720; *Treas.* Mel Nickerson, Coord., Instructional Media Center, California State College, Stanislaus, 801 W. Monte Vista Ave., Turlock 95380; *Business Office Secy.* Nancy Kohn, CMLEA, 1575 Old Bayshore Hwy., Burlingame 94010.

Colorado

Colorado Educational Media Assn. Memb. 680. Term of Office. Feb. 1983–Feb. 1984. Publication. *The Medium* (mo.).

Pres. Carol Newman, Boulder Valley Schools, 6500 E. Arapahoe, Boulder 80301; *Exec. Secy.* Terry Walljasper, Colorado Educational Media Assn., Box 22814, Wellshire Sta., Denver 80222.

Address correspondence to the executive secretary.

Connecticut

Connecticut Educational Media Assn. Term of Office. May 1983–May 1984.

Pres. Betsy Kenneson, 32 Corey St., Windsor 06095. Tel. 203-727-0131; *V.P.* Maureen Reilly, 48 W. District Rd., Unionville 06085. Tel. 203-673-1413. *Secy.* Rosemary Morante, 28 Welch St., Plainville 06062; *Treas.* Charles White, 12 Maple Row, Bethel 06801.

Address correspondence to Anne Weimann, Administrative Secy., 25 Elmwood Ave., Trumbull 06611. Tel. 203-372-2260.

Delaware

Delaware School Lib. Media Assn., Div. of Delaware Lib. Assn. Memb. 125. Term of Office. June 1983–June 1984. Publication. *DSLMA Newsletter.*

Pres. Patricia Robertson, Conrad Jr. H.S., Jackson Ave. & Boxwood Rd., Wilmington 19804; *Pres.-Elect.* Sue Gooden, Howard Career Center, 401 12 St., Wilmington 19801; *Secy.* Elsie Stephens, Mt. Pleasant H.S., Washington St. extended and Marsh Rd., Wilmington 19810; *Treas.* Sue Munsen, Sanford School, Hochessin 19707.

District of Columbia

D.C. Assn. of School Libns. Memb. 150. Term of Office. Aug. 1983–Aug. 1984. Publication. *Newsletter* (3 per year).

Pres. Patricia Copelin, Brookland School, Michigan Ave. and Randolph St. N.E., Washington 20017; *V.P./Pres.-Elect.* Kistler Farmer, Garnet-Patterson Jr. H.S., Tenth and U Sts. N.W., Washington 20001; *2nd V.P.* Nathalia Ramsundar, Marie Reed Learning Center, 2200 Champlain St. N.W., Washington 20009; *Rec. Secy.* Edna Mills, M. M. Washington Career Center, O St. between First and N.

Capitol N.W., Washington 20001; *Corres. Secy.* Patricia Bonds, Eliot Jr. High, 18 and Constitution Ave. N.E., Washington 20002; *Treas.* Ellevia Smith, Burroughs Elementary School, 18 and Monroe Sts. N.E., Washington 20018; *Immediate Past Pres.* Etrula Williams, Shadd Elementary School, 5601 E. Capitol St. S.E., Washington 20019.

Florida

Florida Assn. for Media in Education, Inc. Memb. 1,400. Term of Office. Oct. 1983–Oct. 1984. Publication. *Florida Media Quarterly* (q.).

Pres. Ruth Flintom, 444 N.E. 36 St., Boca Raton 33431; *V.P.* Winona Jones, 911 Manning Rd., Palm Harbor 33563; *Pres.-Elect.* Mary Newman, 140 N.E. 95 St., Miami Shores 33138; *Secy.* Nelson Towle, 4407 North Lake Dr., Sarasota 33582; *Treas.* Ron Johnson, 295 Hickory Dr., Mulberry 33830.

Georgia

School and Children's Lib., Div. of the Georgia Lib. Assn. Term of Office. Nov. 1983–Nov. 1985.

Chpn. Edna F. Adkins, Bartlett Middle School, 207 Montgomery Crossroad, Savannah 31406.

Hawaii

Hawaii Assn. of School Libns. Memb. 225. Term of Office. June 1, 1983–May 31, 1984. Publications. *The Golden Key* (ann.); *HASL Newsletter* (q.), c/o HASL, Box 23019, Honolulu 96822.

Pres. Myrna Nishihara, 45-685 Kuahulu Place, Kaneohe 96744; *1st V.P.* Kay Nagaishi, 6508 Hawaii Kai Dr. #503, Honolulu 96825; *2nd V.P.* Sharon deLeon, 315 Kuulei Rd., Kailua 96734; *Rec. Secy.* Sylvia Mitchell, 1669-A Makuakane Place, Honolulu 96817; *Corres. Secy.* Winifred

Kitaoka, 1742 Hooheno Place, Pearl City 96782; *Treas.* Ginger Enomoto, 94-361 Hokuili St., Mililani Town 96789; *Dir.* Beverly Fujita, 2870 Booth Rd., Honolulu 96813; *Dir.* Jane Kurahara; 3421 Pawaina St., Honolulu 96822.

Idaho

School Libs., Div. of the Idaho Lib. Assn. Term of Office. May 1983–May 1984. Publication. Column in *The Idaho Librarian* (q.).

Chpn. Barbara Gessner, Libn., Lapwai Public School, Lapwai 83540.

Illinois

Illinois Assn. for Media in Education (IAME). (Formerly Illinois Assn. of School Libns.) Memb. 670. Term of Office. Jan. 1983–Dec. 1984. Publication. *IAME News for You* (q.). *Ed.* Charles Rusiewski, 207 E. Chester, Nashville 62263.

Pres. Bernadette Winter, 2308 Silverthorn Dr., Rockford 61107.

Indiana

Assn. for Indiana Media Educators. Memb. 950. Term of Office. (*Pres.*) Apr. 30, 1983–Apr. 30, 1984. Publication. *Indiana Media Journal*.

Pres. Karen Niemeyer, Supv. of Media Services, Carmel-Clay Schools, Box 2099, Carmel 46032; *Exec. Secy.* Lawrence Reck, School of Education, Indiana State Univ., Terre Haute 47809.

Address correspondence to the executive secretary.

Iowa

Iowa Educational Media Assn. Memb. 650. Term of Office. Apr. 1983–Apr. 1984. Publication. *Iowa Media Message* (q.). *Ed.* Donald Rieck, 121 Pearson Hall, Iowa State Univ., Ames 50011.

Pres. Pat Severson, 2406 North Shore Dr., Clear Lake 50428; *V.P./Pres.-Elect.* Pat Meier, 2230½ Ripley, Davenport 52803; *Past Pres.* Chuck Ruebling, 9505 Clubhouse Rd., Eden Prairie; *Secy.* Paula Behrendt, 2306 Sixth, Harlan 51537; *Treas.* Don Powell, 212 Alpha N.W., Bondurant 50035; *Dirs.* (1984) Tim Graham, Elizabeth Morgan, Barbara Steen; (1985) Quentin Coffman, Margaret White, June Wishman; (1986) Lynn Myers, Ilene Rewerts, Betty Yunek.

Kansas

Kansas Assn. of School Libns. Memb. 800. Term of Office. July 1983–June 1984. Publication. *KASL Newsletter* (s. ann.).

Pres. Phyllis Monyakula, 5807 W. 99, Overland Park 66207; *V.P./Pres.-Elect.* Barbara Herrin, 126 W. 15, #6, Emporia 66801; *Treas.* Janice Ostrom, 519 Garden, Salina 67401; *Secy.* Joyce Funk, 916 S.E. Croco Rd., Topeka 66605.

Kentucky

Kentucky School Media Assn. Memb. 650. Term of Office. Oct. 1983–Oct. 1984. Publication. *KSMA Newsletter.*

Pres. Jacqueline VanWilligen, 657 Montclair Dr., Lexington 40502. Tel. 606-269-8301; *Pres.-Elect.* Linda Perkins, 9707 Holiday Dr., Louisville 40272. Tel. 502-935-3640; *Secy.* Mary Janet Cartmell, 325 Malabu Circle, Lexington 40502; *Treas.* Maude Teegarden, Box 201, Brooksville 41004.

Louisiana

Louisiana Assn. of School Libns., c/o Louisiana Lib. Assn., Box 131, Baton Rouge 70821. Memb. 415. Term of Office. July 1, 1983–June 30, 1984.

Pres. Sue Hill, 6780 Nellie Ave., Baton Rouge 70805; *1st V.P./Pres.-Elect.* Earl Hart, 2121 Charters St., New Orleans 70118; *Secy.* Florence Brumfield, 2041 Betty Blvd., Morrero 70072; *Treas.* Marvene Dearman, 1471 Chevelle Dr., Baton Rouge 70806.

Maine

Maine Educational Media Assn. Memb. 200. Term of Office. Oct. 1983–Sept. 1984. Publication. *Mediacy* (q.).

Pres. Jean LaBrecque, Bonny Eagle H.S., West Buxton 04093; *Pres.-Elect.* Marcia McGee, Sumner H.S., East Sullivan 04607; *V.P.* Barbara Warren, Oak Hill H.S., Wales 04280; *Secy.* Thomas Peterson, Windham H.S., R.F.D. 1, South Windham 04082; *Treas.* Alice Douglas, Morse H.S., Bath 04530.

Maryland

Maryland Educational Media Organization. Memb. 600. Term of Office. Oct. 1983–Oct. 1984. Publication: *MEMO-Random* (newsletter, q.).

Pres. K. Gary Ambridge, 1603 Deborah Ct., Forest Hill 21040; *Pres.-Elect.* Mary Ellen Kennedy, 219 Bright Oaks Dr., Bel Air 21014; *Secy.* Peter Shambarger, 1286 Graff Ct., Apt. 2D, Annapolis 21403; *Treas.* Sheila Grap, 800 Thimbleberry Rd., Baltimore 21220; *Past Pres.* Margaret Denman-West, Box 056, Westminster 21157.

Massachusetts

Massachusetts Assn. for Educational Media. Memb. 470. Term of Office. June 1, 1983–May 31, 1984. Publication. *Media Forum* (q.).

Pres. Garrett Mitchell, Jr., 40 Longfellow Rd., Worcester 01602. Tel. 617-755-4480; *Pres.-Elect.* Bruce H. Webb, Somerville H.S. Annex Lib., 15 Summer St., Somerville 02143. Tel. 617-666-5700; *Secy.* Nancy Lane, 42 Braeland St., Newton 02159; *Treas.* Vivian Robb, 15 Beach St., Marion 02738.

Address correspondence to the president.

Michigan

Michigan Association for Media in Education (MAME). Term of Office. One year.

Pres. Jeannine Cronkhite, 19182 Lancashire, Detroit 48223; *Pres.-Elect.* Beverly Rentschler, 6095 Pontiac Trail, Orchard Lake 48033; *Secy.* Maureen Corser, 1159 N. Chevrolet Ave., Flint 48504; *Treas.* Deborah Anthony, 1415 John R Rd., Rochester 48063; *Past Pres.* Mary Ann Paulin, 1205 Joliet, Marquette 49855; *Coord. of Special Interest Div.* Kristina Powers-Aubrey, 1819 E. Milham Rd., Kalamazoo 49002; *Coord. of Regions.* Gerald Lang, 6962 Surrey Lane, Jackson 49201.

Minnesota

Minnesota Educational Media Organization. Memb. 1,200. Term of Office. May 1983–May 1984. Publication. *Minnesota Media.*

Pres. Ray Birr, Rte. 1, Box 159, Sauk Centre 56378; *Secy.* Shari Pretzer, 1264 Whitney Dr., St. Cloud 56301; *Past Pres.* Larry Gifford, 1415 Tenth St. N.E., Rochester 55901.

Mississippi

Mississippi Assn. of Media Educators. Memb. 84. Term of Office. Mar. 1983–Mar. 1984. Publication. *MAME* (newsletter, bi-ann.).

Pres. Edward Garcia, Box 8338, Southern Sta., Univ. of Southern Mississippi, Hattiesburg 39401; *V.P./Pres.-Elect.* Burl Hunt, School of Education, Univ. of Mississippi, Oxford 38677; *V.P. Membership.* Ann Denison, Dir. of Media Services, Biloxi Public Schools, Biloxi 39533; *Secy.* Serita McGee, 511 Railway Ave.,

Belzonia 39038; *Treas.* Lynn Conerly, Drawer 1101, Mississippi ETV, Jackson 39205; *Past Pres.* Joseph L. Ellison, Media Center, Jackson State Univ., Jackson 39217.

Missouri

Missouri Assn. of School Libns. Memb. 600. Term of Office. Sept. 1, 1983–Aug. 31, 1984. Publication. *MASL Newsletter* (4 per year). *Ed.* Mary Reinert, Rte. 3, Nevada 64772.

Pres. Aileen Helmick, 318 Johnson, Warrensburg 64093; *V.P.* Curt Fuchs, 7301 Sunrise Ct., Columbia 65301; *Secy.* Jane Pounds, 2129 Apple Hill Lane, St. Louis 63122; *Treas.* Shirley Ross, 23 Ussery, Lexington 64067.

Montana

Montana School Lib. Media, Div. of Montana Lib. Assn. Memb. 170. Term of Office. May 1983–May 1984.

Chpn. Megan Fite, Box 127, Colstrip School, Colstrip 59323.

Address general correspondence to MSL/MA, c/o Montana Lib. Assn., Montana State Lib., 1515 E. Sixth Ave., Helena 59620.

Nebraska

Nebraksa Educational Media Assn. Memb. 400. Term of Office. July 1, 1983–June 30, 1984. Publication. *NEMA News* (4 per year). *Eds.* Cliff Lowell, Box 485, E.S.U. 11, Holdrege 68949; Kevin Traylor, Center for Instructional Technology, Creighton Univ., 2500 California St., Omaha 68718.

Pres. Sonya Collison, Roseland Public Schools, Box 8, Roseland 68973; *Pres.-Elect.* Rick Urwiler, Instructional Resources Center, Wayne State College, Wayne 68787; *Secy.* Jean Lienemann, Sutton Public Schools, Box 590, Sutton 68979.

Nevada

Nevada Assn. of School Libns. Memb. 67. Term of Office. Jan. 1, 1984–Dec. 31, 1984.

Chpn. Cynthia Smith, Elko Grammar School #2, Elko 89801.

New Hampshire

New Hampshire Educational Media Assn. Memb. 185. Term of Office. June 1983–June 1984. Publication. *Online* (irreg.).

Pres. Shelley Lochhead, Hopkinton H.S., Contoocook 03229; *Pres.-Elect.* Janet Zeller, Maple St. School, Contoocook 03229; *Treas.* Jane McKersie, Pelham H.S., Marsh Rd., Pelham 03076; *Rec. Secy.* Anne Bryant, Gilford Elementary School, Gilford 03246; *Corres. Secy.* Joyce Kendall, Fall Mt. Regional H.S., R.R. 1, Alstead 03602.

Address correspondence to the president.

New Jersey

Educational Media Assn. of New Jersey (EMAnj). (Organized Apr. 1977 through merger of New Jersey School Media Assn. and New Jersey Assn. of Educational Communication and Technology.) Memb. 1,000. Term of Office. June 1983–June 1984. Publications. *Signal Tab* (newsletter, mo.); *Emanations* (journal, q.).

Pres. Elsie Brainard, 100B Cedar Lane, Highland Park 08904; *Pres.-Elect.* Ruth Toor, 61 Greenbriar Dr., Berkeley Heights 07922; *V.P.* Sally Young, 8 Townsend Rd., Mendham 07945; *Rec. Secy.* Marjorie Horowitz, 10 Prospect Ave., Montclair 07042; *Corres. Secy.* Lily Chang, 16 Tuttle Ave., East Hanover 07936; *Treas.* Eleanor Gulick, 1006 Mount Pleasant Way, Cherry Hill 08034.

New Mexico

New Mexico Lib. Assn., School Libs. Children and Young Adult Services Div. Memb. 237. Term of Office. Apr. 1983–Apr. 1984.

Chpn. Alison Almquist, 10320 San Luis Rey N.E., Albuquerque 87111.

New York

School Lib. Media Sec., New York Lib. Assn., 15 Park Row, Suite 434, New York 10038. Tel. 212-227-8032. Memb. 720. Term of Office. Nov. 1983–Nov. 1984. Publications. Participates in *NYLA Bulletin* (mo. except July and Aug.); *SLMS Gram* (s. ann.).

Pres. Helen Flowers, Lib. Media Specialist, Bay Shore H.S., 155 Third Ave., Bay Shore 11706; *V.P.* Frances Roscello, 30 Kimberly Dr., Dryden 13053; *Secy.-Treas.* Ethel A. Keefer, 779 Pennsylvania Ave., Elmira 14904.

North Carolina

North Carolina Assn. of School Libns. Memb. 900. Term of Office. Oct. 1983–Oct. 1985.

Chpn. Judith F. Davie, Dept. of Lib. Science and Educational Technology, Univ. of North Carolina at Greensboro, Greensboro 27412; *Chpn.-Elect.* Helen Tugwell, Media Specialist, Hunt H.S., Wilson 27893; *Secy.-Treas.* Carolyne Burgman, Media Specialist, Bluford School, 1901 Tuscaloosa St., Greensboro 27401.

North Dakota

North Dakota Lib. Assn., School Lib. Media Sec. Memb. 85. Term of Office. One year. Publication. *The Good Stuff* (q.).

Pres. Neil V. Price, Box 8174, UND Sta., Grand Forks 58202.

Address correspondence to the president.

Ohio

Ohio Educational Lib. Media Assn. Memb. 1,700. Term of Office. Jan. 1983–Jan. 1984. Publication. *Ohio Media Spectrum* (q.).

Pres. Anne Hyland, Northeastern Local Schools, 1414 Bowman, Springfield 45502.

Address correspondence to the president.

Oklahoma

Oklahoma Assn. of School Lib. Media Specialists. Memb. 250. Term of Office. July 1, 1983–June 30, 1984. Publications. *School Library News* column in *Oklahoma Librarian* (q.); "Library Resources" section in *Oklahoma Educator* (mo.).

Chpn. Sybil Connelly, Windsor Hills Elementary School, 2909 Ann Arbour, Oklahoma City 73127; *Chpn.-Elect.* Mary Lou Divelbiss, 1815 Live Oak, Enid 73701; *Secy.* La Vonne Sanborn, Westwood Elementary School, 502 S. Kings Hwy., Stillwater 74074; *Treas.* Bettie Estes, 2124 Everglade Ct., Yukon 73099; *Past. Chpn.* Donnice Cochinour, 911 W. Main, Norman H.S., Norman 73069.

Oregon

Oregon Educational Media Assn. Memb. 800. Term of Office. Oct. 1, 1983–Sept. 30, 1984. Publication. *Interchange.*

Pres. Allan Quick, Supv. Lib. Services, West Linn School Dist., West Linn 97068; *Pres.-Elect.* Don Erickson, Lebanon Public Schools, c/o 375 Wendell, Lebanon 97355; *Exec. Secy.* Sherry Hevland, 16695 S.W. Rosa Rd., Beaverton 97007; *Past Pres.* Jim Heath, I.M.C. Dir., Douglas County ESD, 1871 N.E. Stephens, Roseburg 97470.

Pennsylvania

Pennsylvania School Libns. Assn. Memb. 1,300. Term of Office. July 1, 1982–June 30, 1984. Publications. *Learning and Media* (4 per year); *027.8* (4 per year).

Pres. Anna Harkins, 5630 Glen Hill Dr., Bethel Park 15102; *V.P./Pres.-Elect.* Sharon Nardelli, Baldwin School, Morris & Montgomery, Bryn Mawr 19010; *Secy.* Judith B. Palmer, 1218 Monterey St., Pittsburgh 15212; *Treas.* Hope Sebring, Box 74, Delmont 15626; *Past Pres.* Sue A. Walker, 6065 Parkridge Dr., East Petersburg 17520.

Rhode Island

Rhode Island Educational Media Assn. Memb. 225. Term of Office. June 1983–June 1984. Publications. *RIEMA* (newsletter, 9 per year).

Pres. Raymond Argamache, Regional Mgr., United Camera, 155 Slade St., Tiverton 02878; *Pres.-Elect.* Michael W. Mello, Dir. of Instruction, Portsmouth School Dept., Middle Rd., Portsmouth 02871; *V.P.* John J. McAniff, Jr., Media Coord., Tiverton Middle School, 23 Spruce Rd., Swansea 02777; *Secy.* Arlene Luber, Media Specialist, E. Providence School Dept., 2 Jackson Walkway, Apt. 1012, Providence 02903; *Treas.* Alice Reinhardt, School Libn., Slater Jr. H.S., 55 E. Knowlton, East Providence 02915.

South Carolina

South Carolina Assn. of School Libns. Memb. 600. Term of Office. Apr. 1983–Apr. 1984. Publication. *Media Center Messenger* (5 per year).

Pres. A'La Perle Hickman, Box 2602, Aiken 29801; *V.P./Pres.-Elect.* Peggy J. Hanna, 3 Chisolm St., Charleston 29401.

South Dakota

South Dakota School Lib. Media Assn., Sec. of the South Dakota Lib. Assn. and South Dakota Education Assn. Term of Office. Oct. 1983–Oct. 1984.

Pres. Donna Fisher, Libn., Douglas

H.S., Ellsworth AFB, Rapid City 57701; *Pres.-Elect*. Mary Schwartz, Media Dir., Redfield Public Schools, Redfield 57469; *Secy.-Treas*. Sonia Jordre, Selby H.S., Selby 57472.

Tennessee

Tennessee Education Assn., School Lib. Sec., 598 James Robertson Pkwy., Nashville 37219. Term of Office. May 1983–May 1984.

Chpn. Jane Sparks, 5513 Lakeshore Dr., Knoxville 37920.

Texas

Texas Assn. of School Libns. Memb. 1,800. Term of Office. Apr. 1983–Apr. 1984. Publication. *Media Matters* (2 per year).

Chpn. Kathryn Meharg, 2631 Pittsburg, Houston 77005; *Chpn.-Elect*. Elizabeth Haynes, 10165 Bermuda, El Paso 79925; *Secy.-Treas*. Marybeth Green, 7912 Merchant, Amarillo 79121; *Councillor*. Diantha Dawkins, 501 W. Louisiana #203, Midland 79701.

Utah

Utah Educational Lib. Media Assn. Memb. 225. Term of Office. Mar. 1983–Mar. 1984. Publication. *UELMA Journal* (q.).

Pres. Marilyn Taylor, Dee Elementary School, 500 22 St., Ogden 84401; *Pres.-Elect*. R. Kent Wood, Dept. of Instructional Technology, Utah State Univ., Logan 84321; *Secy.-Treas*. Rosette Summers-Accord, Huntsville School, Huntsville 84317.

Utah Lib. Assn., Children's and Young Adult's Section. Memb. 60. Publications. *Horsefeathers* (mo.); *HATU* (q.). Term of Office. Mar. 1983–Mar. 1984.

Pres. Vivien M. Milius, Salt Lake County Lib. System, Salt Lake City.

Vermont

Vermont Educational Media Assn. Memb. 114. Term of Office. May 1983–May 1984. Publication. *VEMA News* (q.).

Pres. Nancy Hunt, Orchard School, South Burlington 05401; *Pres.-Elect*. Georgeanne Bonifanti, Manchester Elementary School, Manchester Center 05255; *Secy*. Carol Kress, Monkton Central School, Monkton 05469; *Treas*. Tom Karlen, Randolph Union H.S., Randolph 05060.

Virginia

Virginia Educational Media Assn. (VEMA). Term of Office. Nov. 1983–Nov. 1984.

Pres. Mary B. Mather, 1005 Fleming Dr. #1, Virginia Beach 23451; *V.P./Pres.-Elect*. Gloria Davidson, T.C. Williams H.S., 307 Yoakum Pkwy., Alexandria 22304; *Secy*. Carolyn Nilsson, Randolph-Henry H.S., Rte. 1, Box 123A, Red Oak 23964; *Treas*. Vykuntapathi Thota, Box 5002N, Virginia State Univ., Petersburg 23808.

Washington

Washington Lib. Media Assn. Memb. 700. Term of Office. Jan. 1, 1984–Dec. 31, 1984. Publication. *The Medium* (q.); *The Newsletter* (irreg.).

Pres. Shirley Painter, 118 W. 23 Place, Kennewick 99336; *Pres.-Elect*. Mary Lou Gregory, 711 Spruce, Hoquium 98550; *V.P.* Marilyn Matulich, N. 7231 Fotheringham, Spokane 99208; *Secy*. Roy Bueler, 908 15 Ave. S.W., Puyallup 98371; *Treas*. Barbara Baker, 18645 101 Ave. N.E., Bothell 98011.

Address correspondence to the president.

West Virginia

West Virginia Educational Assn. Memb. 350. Term of Office. Oct. 1983–Oct. 1984. Publication. *WVEMA Newsletter* (q.).

Pres. Tom Blevins, Coord. of Audiovisual Services, Box 38, Bluefield State College, Bluefield 24701; *V.P./Pres.-Elect.* Linda Wilson-Mirarchi, Instructor/Dir. Learning Resources Center, Box 6122, College of Human Resources and Education, West Virginia Univ., Morgantown 26506; *Treas.* Earl Nicodemus, Associate Professor of Education, Box 239, West Liberty State College, West Liberty 26074; *Memb. Secy.* Trudy Berkey, Libn., West Virginia Northern Community College, New Martinsville 26155; *Rec. Secy.* Barbara Aguirre, Libn., Southern West Virginia Community College, Logan 25601; *Past Pres.* Robert Moore, Dept. of Communication Arts, 472 Wenger Center, Elizabethtown College, Elizabethtown 17022.

Wisconsin

Wisconsin School Lib. Media Assn., Div. of Wisconsin Lib. Assn. Term of Office. Jan. 1983–Dec. 1983. Publication. *WLA Newsletter* (6 per year). *Ed.* Don Johnson.

Pres. Roger Krentz, Platteville Public Schools, 1205 Camp St., Platteville 53818; *V.P./Pres.-Elect.* Helen R. Adams, Media Dir., Rosholt Public Schools, Rosholt 54473; *Secy.* Leora McGee, Milwaukee Public Schools, Milwaukee 53201; *Financial Adviser.* Vera Ludwigsen, Media Coord., Oconomowoc School Dist., Hartland 53029.

Wyoming

Wyoming School Lib. Media Assn. Memb. 25. Term of Office. May 1983–Apr. 1984.

Chpn. Sharlye Good, Box 392, Midwest 82643.

State Supervisors of
School Library Media Services

Alabama

Hallie A. Jordan, Educational Specialist, Lib. Media Services, 111 Coliseum Blvd., Montgomery 36193. Tel: 205-832-5810.

Alaska

Jo Morse, Alaska State Lib., School Lib. Media Coord., 650 International Airport Rd., Anchorage 99502. Tel: 907-561-1132.

Arizona

Mary Choncoff, Education Program Specialist, State Dept. of Educ., 1535 W. Jefferson, Phoenix 85007. Tel: 602-255-5961.

Arkansas

Betty J. Morgan, Specialist, Lib. Services, Arkansas Dept. of Educ., State Educ. Bldg., Rm. 301B, Little Rock 72201. Tel: 501-371-1861.

California

John Church, Dir., Resources Center, State Dept. of Educ., 721 Capitol Mall, Sacramento 95814. Tel: 916-322-0494.

Colorado

Boyd E. Dressler, Ed. D., Consultant, Special Projects Unit, Colorado Dept. of

Educ., 303 W. Colfax Ave., Denver 80204. Tel: 303-534-8871 ext. 244.

Connecticut

Robert G. Hale, Sr. Coord., Learning Resources & Technology Unit, and Instructional Television Consultant; Betty B. Billman, Lib. Media Consultant; Elizabeth M. Glass, Computer Technology Consultant; Dorothy M. Headspeth, Info. Specialist; and Brenda H. White, Lib. Media Consultant, Learning Resources and Technology Unit, State Dept. of Educ., Box 2219, Hartford 06154. Tel: 203-566-2250.

Delaware

Richard L. Krueger, Lib. Specialist, State Dept. of Public Instruction, John G. Townsend Bldg., Box 1402, Dover 19903. Tel: 302-736-4692.

District of Columbia

Marie Haris, Asst. Dir., Dept. of Lib. Science, Public Schools of the District of Columbia, 801 Seventh St. S.W., Washington 20024. Tel: 202-724-4952.

Florida

Sandra W. Ulm, Administrator, School Lib. Media Services, State Dept. of Educ., 506 Knott Bldg., Tallahassee 32301. Tel: 904-488-0095.

Georgia

Nancy V. Paysinger, Dir., Media Services Unit, Div. of Instructional Media, Georgia Dept. of Educ., Suite 2054 Twin Towers E., Atlanta 30334. Tel: 404-656-2418.

Hawaii

Patsy Izumo, Dir., Multimedia Services Branch, State Dept. of Educ., 641 18 Ave., Honolulu 96816. Tel: 808-732-5535.

Idaho

Rudy H. Leverett, Coord., Educational Media Services, State Dept. of Educ., Len B. Jordan Bldg., 650 State St., Boise 83720. Tel: 208-334-2281.

Illinois

Marie Rose Sivak, Program Consultant, Lib. Media Services & Gifted Education, State Bd. of Educ., 100 N. First St., Springfield 62777. Tel: 217-782-3810.

Indiana

Phyllis Land Usher, Dir., Div. of Federal Resources & School Improvement, State Dept. of Public Instruction, Indianapolis 46204. Tel: 317-927-0296.

Iowa

Betty Jo Buckingham, Consultant, Education Media, State Dept. of Public Instruction, Grimes State Office Bldg., Des Moines 50319. Tel: 515-281-3707.

Kansas

June Saine Level, Lib. Media Consultant, Educational Assistance Sec., Kansas State Dept. of Educ., 110 E. Tenth St., Topeka 66612. Tel: 913-296-3434.

Kentucky

Judy L. Cooper, Program Mgr. for School Media Services, State Dept. of Educ., 1830 Capital Plaza Tower, Frankfort 40601. Tel: 502-564-2672.

Louisiana

James S. Cookston, State Supv. of School Lib., State Dept. of Educ., Box 44064, Education Bldg., Rm. 408, Baton Rouge 70804. Tel: 504-342-3399.

Maine

John W. Boynton, Coord., Media Services, Maine State Lib., LMA Bldg., State House Sta. 64, Augusta 04333. Tel: 207-289-2956.

Maryland

Paula Montgomery, Chief, School Media Services Branch, Div. of Lib. Development & Services, State Dept. of Educ., 200 W. Baltimore St., Baltimore 21201. Tel: 301-659-2125.

Massachusetts

Position vacant. Write to: Dept. of Educ., 1385 Hancock St., Quincy 02169. Tel: 617-770-7500.

Michigan

Susan M. Haskin, Interim State Libn., Lib. of Michigan, Box 30007, Lansing 48909. Tel: 517-373-1580.

Minnesota

Robert H. Miller, Supv., Educational Media Unit, State Dept. of Educ., Capitol Square Bldg., St. Paul 55101. Tel: 612-296-6114.

Mississippi

John Barlow, State Dept. of Educ., Educational Media Services, Box 771, Jackson 39205. Tel: 601-359-3553.

Missouri

Carl Sitze, Asst. Dir. of School Supervisor, Dept. of Elementary & Secondary Educ., Box 480, Jefferson City 65102. Tel: 314-751-2603.

Montana

Sheila Cates, Lib. Media Specialist, Office of Public Instruction, Rm. 106 State Capitol, Helena 59620. Tel: 406-449-3126.

Nebraska

Jack Baillie, Administrative Asst., State Dept. of Educ., Box 94987, 301 Centennial Mall S., Lincoln 68509. Tel: 402-471-2486.

Nevada

William F. Arensdorf, Chpn., Instructional Materials and Equipment, State Dept. of Educ., Capitol Complex, Carson City 89710. Tel: 702-885-3136.

New Hampshire

Frank W. Brown, Chief, Div. of Instruction, State Dept. of Educ., 64 N. Main St., Concord 03301. Tel: 603-271-3235.

New Jersey

Anne Voss, Coord., School and College Media Services, State Dept. of Educ., State Lib., CN 520, Trenton 08625. Tel: 609-292-6256.

New Mexico

Mary Jane Annand, Lib./Media Specialist, State Dept. of Educ., 300 Don Gaspar, Santa Fe 87501. Tel: 505-827-6556.

New York

Beatrice Griggs, Chief, Bur. of School Lib. Media Programs, State Educ. Dept., Albany 12234. Tel: 518-474-2468.

North Carolina

Elsie L. Brumback, Deputy Asst., State Superintendent, Dept. of Public Instruction, Raleigh 27611. Tel: 919-733-3170.

North Dakota

Patricia Herbel, Coord. of Curriculum and NDN, Dept. of Public Instruction, State Capitol, Bismarck 58505. Tel: 701-224-2281.

Ohio

Theresa M. Fredericka, Lib. Media Consultant, State Dept. of Educ., 65 S. Front St., Rm. 1005, Columbus 43215. Tel: 614-466-2761.

Oklahoma

Barbara Spriestersbach, Asst. Administrator; Pam Allen, Betty Riley, and Clarice Roads, Coords.; Lib. & Learning Resources Div., State Dept. of Educ., 2500 N. Lincoln Blvd., Oklahoma City 73105. Tel: 405-521-2956.

Oregon

George Katagiri, Coord., Instructional Technology, Oregon Dept. of Educ., 700 Pringle Pkwy. S.E., Salem 97310. Tel: 503-373-7900.

Pennsylvania

Doris M. Epler, Div. of School Lib. Media, State Dept. of Educ., Box 911, 333 Market St., Harrisburg 17108. Tel: 717-787-6704.

Rhode Island

Richard Harrington, Coord. Consolidated Grant Programs, State Dept. of Educ., 22 Hayes St., Providence 02908. Tel: 401-277-2617.

South Carolina

Margaret W. Ehrhardt, Lib./Media Consultant, State Dept. of Educ., Rutledge Bldg., Rm. 810, Columbia 29201. Tel: 803-758-2652.

South Dakota

James O. Hansen, State Superintendent, Div. of Elementary & Secondary Education, Richard F. Kneip Bldg., Pierre 57501. Tel: 605-773-3243.

Tennessee

R. Jerry Rice, Dir., Instructional Resources, 130 Cordell Hull Bldg., Nashville 37219. Tel: 615-741-3379.

Texas

Mary R. Boyvey, Learning Resources Program Dir., Instructional Technology and Media Div., Texas Education Agency, 201 E. 11 St., Austin 78701. Tel: 512-834-4081.

Utah

Bruce Griffin, Assoc. Superintendent, Curriculum and Instruction Div., State Office of Educ., 250 E. Fifth S., Salt Lake City 84111. Tel: 801-533-5431.

Kenneth Neal, Media Services Coord., Curriculum and Instruction Div., State Office of Educ., 250 E. Fifth S., Salt Lake City 84111. Tel: 801-533-5573.

Vermont

Jean D. Battey, School Lib./Media Consultant, Vermont Dept. of Educ., Montpelier 05602. Tel: 802-828-3111.

Virginia

Mary Stuart Mason, Supv., School Libs. and Textbooks, State Dept. of Educ., Box 6Q, Richmond 23216. Tel: 804-225-2855.

Washington

Nancy Motomatsu, Supv., Learning Resources Services, Office of State Superintendent of Public Instruction, Old Capitol Bldg., Olympia 98504. Tel: 206-753-6723.

West Virginia

Carolyn R. Skidmore, Dir., ECIA Chapter 2, and Lib. Media & Learning Resources, 1900 Washington St. E., B-346, Charleston 25305. Tel: 304-348-3925.

Wisconsin

Dianne McAfee Hopkins, Dir., Bur. for Instructional Media and Technology, State Dept. of Public Instruction, Box 7841, Madison 53707. Tel: 608-266-1965.

Wyoming

Jack Prince, Coord., Instructional Resources, Wyoming Dept. of Educ., Hathaway Bldg., Cheyenne 82002. Tel: 302-777-6252.

American Samoa

Emma S. Fung Chen Pen, Program Dir., Office of Lib. Services, Dept. of Educ., Box 1329, Pago Pago 96799. Tel: 633-1181/1182.

Northern Mariana Islands (Commonwealth of the) (CNMI)

Emiliana S. Ada, Acting Head, Office of Lib. Services, CNMI Dept. of Educ., Saipan, CM 96950.

Ruth L. Tighe, Libn., Northern Marianas College, Box 1250, Saipan, CM 96950.

Pacific Islands (Trust Territory of)

Tamar Jordan, Supv., Lib. Services, Dept. of Educ., Majuor, Marshall Islands 96960.

Tomokichy Aisek, Supv., Lib. Services, Dept. of Educ., Truk, Caroline Islands 96942.

Puerto Rico

Ana Martinez Mora, Dir., Public Lib. Div., Dept. of Educ., Box 759, Hato Rey 00919. Tel: 809-753-9191; 754-0750.

Virgin Islands

Fiolina B. Mills, State Dir., Bur. of Lib. Services and Instructional Materials, Virgin Islands Dept. of Educ., Box 6640, St. Thomas 00801. Tel: 809-774-3725.

International Library Associations

Inter-American Association of Agricultural Librarians and Documentalists

IICA-CIDIA, 7170 Turrialba, Costa Rica

Object

"To serve as liaison among the agricultural librarians and documentalists of the Americas and other parts of the world; to promote the exchange of information and experiences through technical publications and meetings; to promote the improvement of library services in the field of agriculture and related sciences; to encourage the improvement of the professional level of the librarians and documentalists in the field of agriculture in Latin America."

Officers

Pres. Orlando Arboleda, Info. Specialists, IICA-CIDIA, San José, Costa Rica; *V.P.* Ubaldino Dantas Machado, EMBRAPA/DID, Brasilia, Brazil; *Exec. Secy.* Ana Maria Paz de Erickson, IICA-CIDIA, 7170 Turrialba, Costa Rica. (Address correspondence to the executive secretary.)

Publications

AIBDA Actualidades (irreg., 5 per year).
Boletín Informativo (q.).
Boletín Especial (irreg.).

Revista AIBDA (2 per year).
Páginas de Contenido: Ciencias de la Información (3 per year).
Proceedings. Tercera Reunión Interamericana de Bibliotecarios y Documentalistas Agrícolas, Buenos Aires, Argentina, April 10–14, 1972 (U.S. price: $10 including postage). Out of print. Available in Microfiche. (Price U.S. $10).
Proceedings. Cuarta Reunión Interamericana de Bibliotecarios y Documentalistas Agrícolas, Mexico, D.F., April 8–11, 1975 (U.S. price: Memb. $5 including postage; nonmemb. $10 including postage).
Proceedings. Quinta Reunión Interamericana de Bibliotecarios y Documentalistas Agrícolas, San José, Costa Rica, April 10–14, 1978 (U.S. price: Memb. $10 plus postage; nonmemb. $15 plus postage).

International Association of Agricultural Librarians and Documentalists

c/o P. J. Wortley, Secretary-Treasurer
Tropical Development and Research Institute
College House, Wrights Lane, London, England W8 5SJ

Object

"The Association shall, internationally and nationally, promote agricultural library science and documentation as well as the professional interest of agricultural librarians and documentalists." Founded 1955. Memb. 620. Dues (Inst.) $40; (Indiv.) $10.

Officers (1980–1985)

Pres. E. J. Mann, England; *V.Ps.* H. Haendler, Germany; G. Paez, Costa Rica; *Secy.-Treas.* P. J. Wortley, England; *Ed.* V. Howe, England.

Executive Committee

M. Bonnichon, France; A. d'Ambroso, Italy; L. Gregorio, Philippines; I. Berg Hansen, Denmark; W. Laux, Germany; A. Lebowitz, Italy; A. Rutgers, Netherlands; A. T. Yaikova, USSR; representatives of national associations of agricultural librarians and documentalists.

Publication

Quarterly Bulletin of the IAALD (memb.).

International Association of Law Libraries

Vanderbilt Law Library, Nashville, TN 37240, USA

Object

"To promote on a cooperative, non-profit, and fraternal basis the work of individuals, libraries, and other institutions and agencies concerned with the acquisition and bibliographic processing of legal materials collected on a multinational basis, and to facilitate the reseach and other uses of such materials on a worldwide basis." Founded 1959. Memb. over 600 in 64 countries.

Officers (1983–1986)

Pres. Igor I. Kavass, Vanderbilt Univ., Law School Lib., Nashville, TN 37240, USA; *1st V.P.* Klaus Menzinger, Bibliothek für Rechtswissenschaft der Universität Freiburg, D-7800 Freiburg, Fed. Rep. of Germany; *2nd V.P.* Ivan Sipkov, Lib. of Congress, Washington, DC 20540, USA; *Secy.* Adolf Sprudzs, Law School Lib., Univ. of Chicago, 1121 E. 60 St., Chicago, IL 60637, USA; *Treas.* Arno Liivak, Rutgers Univ., Law Lib., Camden, NJ 08102, USA.

Board Members (1983–1986)

Officers: Robert F. Brian, Australia; Myrna Feliciano, Philippines; Eric Gaskell, Belgium; Lajos Nagy, Hungary; Fernando de Trazegnies, Peru; Yoshiro Tsuno, Japan; Christian Wiktor, Canada; Shaikha Zakaria, Malaysia.

Services

1. The dissemination of professional information through the *International Journal of Legal Information* through continuous contacts with the affiliated national groups of law librarians and through work within other international organizations, such as IFLA and FID.

2. Continuing education through the one-week IALL Seminars in International Law Librarianship annually.

3. The preparation of special literature for law librarians, such as the *European Law Libraries Guide*, and of introductions to basic foreign legal literature.

4. Direct personal contacts and exchanges between IALL members.

IALL Representatives

A liaison between the law librarians of their regions and the IALL administration is being appointed for every country or major area.

Publication

International Journal of Legal Information (6 per year). *Ed.-in-Chief.* Arno Liivak, Rutgers Univ. Law Lib., Camden, NJ 08120, USA; *Assoc. Ed.* Igor I. Kavass, Vanderbilt Law Lib., Nashville, TN 37240, USA; Klaus Menzinger, Bibl. für Rechtswissenschaft der Universität Freiburg, Werthmannplatz 1, 7800 Freiburg i. Br., Fed. Rep. of Germany; Ivan Sipkov, Law Lib., Lib. of Congress, Washington, DC 20540, USA; Adolf Sprudzs, Univ. of Chicago Law School, 1121 E. 60 St., Chicago, IL 60637, USA.

International Association of Metropolitan City Libraries

c/o P. J. Th. Schoots, Director, Gemeentebibliothek Rotterdam,
Nieŭwe Markt 1, NL-3001 Rotterdam, Netherlands

Object

"The Association was founded to assist the worldwide flow of information and knowledge by promoting practical collaboration in the exchange of books, exhibitions, staff, and information." Memb. 97.

Officers

Pres. Pieter J. van Swigchem, Openbare Bibliothek, Bilderdiijkstraat 1-7, The Hague, Netherlands; *Secy.-Treas.* Piet J. Th. Schoots, Gemeentebibliothek, Nieŭwe Markt 1, NL-3001 Rotterdam, Netherlands; *Past Pres.* Juergen Eyssen, Stadtbibliothek Hildesheimer Str. 12, D-3000 Hannover 1, Fed. Rep. of Germany. (Address correspondence to the secretary-treasurer.)

Program

A research team and correspondents are engaged in drawing up a practical code of recommended practice in international city library cooperation and in formulating objectives, standards, and performance measures for metropolitan city libraries.

Publications

Annual International Statistics of City Libraries (INTAMEL).
Review of the Three Year Research and Exchange Programme 1968–1971.

International Association of Music Libraries, Archives and Documentation Centres (IAML)

Music Library/Hornbake Library,
University of Maryland, College Park, MD 20742, USA

Object

To promote the activities of music libraries, archives, and documentation centers and to strengthen the cooperation among them, to promote the availability of all publications and documents relating to music and further their bibliographical control, to encourage the development of standards in all areas that concern the association, and to support the protection and preservation of musical documents of the past and the present. Memb. 1,800.

Officers

Pres. Anders Lönn, Musikaliska akademiens bibliotek, Box 16 326, S-103 26, Stockholm, Sweden; *Past Pres.* Brian Redfern, 15 Tudor St., Birmingham B18 4DG, England; *V.Ps.* Maria Calderisi, National Lib., Music Div., Ottawa K1A ON4, Canada; Janos Kárpátri, Lib. of the Liszt Ferenc Adademy of Music, Box 206, H-1391 Budapest, Hungary; Nanna Schiødt, Svanevaenget 20, DK-2100 Kobenhavn O, Denmark; Heinz Werner, Berliner Stadtbibliothek, Breite Strasse 32-34, DDR-102 Berlin, German Democratic Rep.; *Secy.-Gen.* Neil Ratliff, Music Lib./Hornbake Lib., Univ. of Maryland, College Park, MD 20742, USA; *Treas.* Wolfgang Rehm, Schiffmanngasse 18, A-5020 Salzburg, Austria.

Publication

Fontes Artis Musicae (4 per year, memb.).

Commission Chairpersons

Bibliography. Maria Calderisi, National Lib., Music Div., Ottawa K1A ON4, Canada.
Broadcasting Music Libraries. Lucas van Dijck, Nederlandse Omroep Stichting, P.O.B. 10, NL-1200 JB Hilversum, Netherlands.
Cataloging. Lenore Coral, Music Lib., Lincoln Hall, Cornell Univ., Ithaca, NY 14853, USA.
International Inventory of Musical Sources. Kurt von Fischer, Laubholzstr. 46, CH-8703 Erlebach ZH, Switzerland.
International Repertory of Music Literature. Barry S. Brook, RILM Center City Univ. of New York, 33 W. 42 St., New York, NY 10036, USA.
International Repertory of Musical Iconography. Barry S. Brook, Research Center for Musical Iconography, City Univ. of New York, 33 W. 42 St., New York, NY 10036, USA.
Libraries in Music Teaching Institutions. Anthony Hodges, Royal Northern College of Music, 124 Oxford Rd., Manchester M13 9RD, England.

Music Information Centers. William Elias, Israel Music Institute, P.O.B. 11253, Tel-Aviv 61112, Israel.
Public Music Libraries. Eric Cooper, London Borough of Enfield, Music Dept., Town Hall, Green Lanes, Palmers Green, London N13 4XD, England.
Research Music Libraries. Richard Andrewes, Pendlebury Lib., Univ. Music School, West Road, Cambridge CB3 9DP, England.
Service and Training. Don L. Roberts, Music Lib., Northwestern Univ., Evanston, IL 60201, USA.

US Branch

Pres. Geraldine Ostrove, New England Conservatory of Music, Spaulding Lib., 33 Gainsborough St., Boston, MA 02115; *Secy.-Treas.* Don L. Roberts, Music Lib., Northwestern Univ., Evanston, IL 60201.

UK Branch

Pres. Roger Crudge, Avon County Libs., College Green, Bristol BS1 5 TL; *Gen. Secy.* Anna Smart, Royal Northern College of Music, 124 Oxford Rd., Manchester M13 9RD; *Hon. Treas.* Pam Thompson, Royal College of Music Lib., Prince Consort Rd., London SW7 2BS.

Publication

BRIO. Ed. Clifford Bartlett, 36 Tudor Rd., Godmanchester, Huntingdon, Cambs., PE18 8DP (2 per year; memb.).

International Association
of Orientalist Librarians (IALO)

c/o Secretary-Treasurer, William S. Wong
Assistant Director of General Services and
Professor of Library Administration
University Library, University of Illinois at Urbana-Champaign,
1408 W. Gregory Dr., Urbana, IL 61801

Object

"To promote better communication among Orientalist librarians and libraries, and others in related fields, throughout the world; to provide a forum for the discussion of problems of common interest; to improve international cooperation among institutions holding research resources for Oriental Studies." The term Orient here specifies the Middle East, East Asia, and the South and Southeast Asia regions.

Founded in 1967 at the 27th International Congress of Orientalists in Ann Arbor, Michigan. Affiliated with the International Federation of Library Associations and Institutions (IFLA) and International Congress of Human Sciences in Asia and North Africa.

Officers

Pres. Warren D. Tsuneishi; *Secy.-Treas.* William S. Wong; *Ed.* Helen D. Jarvis.

Publication

International Association of Orientalist Librarians Bulletin (s. ann., memb.).

International Association of School Librarianship

School of Library and Information Science,
Western Michigan University, Kalamazoo, MI 49008

Object

"To encourage the development of school libraries and library programs throughout all countries; to promote the professional preparation of school librarians; to bring about close collaboration among school libraries in all countries, including the loan and exchange of literature; to initiate and coordinate activities, conferences and other projects in the field of school librarianship." Founded 1971. Memb. (Indiv.) 700; 19 (Assn.).

Officers & Executive Board

Pres. Michael Cooke, Aberystwyth, Wales; *V.P.* John G. Wright, Edmonton, Alta., Canada; *Treas.* Anne Shafer, Evanston, IL, U.S.A.; *Exec. Secy.* Jean Lowrie, Kalamazoo, MI, U.S.A.; *Dirs.* David Elaturoti, Nigeria, Africa; Valerie Packer, Artarmon, Australia; Shirley Coulter, Nova Scotia, Canada; Axel Wisbom, Hellerup, Denmark; Mieko Nagajura, Kanagawa, Japan; Nelson R. Trujillo, Caracas; Venezuela.

Publications

Directory of National School Library Associations.
Getting Started: A Bibliography of Ideas and Procedures.
IASL Conference Proceedings (ann.).

IASL Monograph Series.
IASL Newsletter (q.).
Persons to Contact for Visiting School Libraries/Media Centers.

American Memberships

American Assn. of School Libs.; Hawaii School Lib. Assn.; Maryland Educational Media Organization; Oregon Educational Media Assn.

International Association of Sound Archives

c/o Helen Harrison, Media Librarian, Open University
Library, Walton Hall, Milton Keynes, MK7 6AA, England

Object

IASA is a UNESCO-affiliated organization established in 1969 to function as a medium for international cooperation between archives and other institutions that preserve recorded sound documents. This association is involved with the preservation, organization, and use of sound recordings; techniques of recordings and methods of reproducing sound; the international exchange of literature and information; and in all subjects relating to the professional work of sound archives.

Membership

Open to all categories of archives, institutions, and individuals who preserve sound recordings or have a serious interest in the purposes or welfare of IASA.

Officers (1981–1984)

Pres. David G. Lance, Curator of Audiovisual Records, Australian War Memorial, Box 345, Canberra City ACT 2601, Australia; *V.Ps.* Peter Burgis, National Lib. of Australia, Sound Recordings Lib., Canberra City, A.C.T. 2600, Australia; Dietrich Schüller, Phonogrammarchiv der Osterreichischen Akademie der Wissenshaften, Liebiggasse 5, A-1010 Vienna, Austria; Rolf Schuursma, Erasmus Universiteit, Universiteitsbibliotheek, Burg. Oudlaan 50, NL-3062 PA Rotterdam, Netherlands; *Ed.* Ann Briegleb, Music Dept. Univ. of California, Los Angeles, CA 90024, USA; *Secy.* Helen P. Harrison, Media Libn., Open Univ. Lib., Walton Hall, Milton Keynes MK7 6AA, England; *Treas.* Ulf Scharlau, Süddeutscher Rundfunk, Schallarchiv/Bandaustausch, Neckarstr. 230, D-7000 Stuttgart 1, Fed. Rep. of Germany.

Publications

An Archive Approach to Oral History.
Directory of IASA Member Archives, 2nd ed., 1982.
Phonographic Bulletin (3 per year, memb. or subscription).
Sound Archives: A Guide to Their Establishment and Development, 1983.

International Council on Archives

Secretariat, 60 rue des Francs-Bourgeois
F-75003 Paris, France

Object

"To establish, maintain, and strengthen relations among archivists of all lands, and among all professional and other agencies or institutions concerned with the custody, organization, or administration of archives, public or private, wherever located." Established 1948. Memb. 750 (representing 121 countries). Dues (Indiv.) $30; (Inst.) $50; (Archives Assns.) $50 or $100 (Central Archives Directorates) $250 minimum, computed on the basis of GNP and GNO per capita.

Officers

Pres. Carlos Wyffels; *V.Ps.* Hans Booms, Ms. Soemartini; *Exec. Secy.* C. Kesckeméti; *Treas.* Alfred Wagner. (Address all correspondence to the executive secretary.)

Publications

ADPA—Archives and Automation (ann. 250 FB or U.S. $9 memb.; subscriptions to M. Jean Pieyns, Archives de l'Etat, rue Pouplin, 8, B-4000 Liege, Belgium).

Archivium (ann.; memb. or subscription to KG Saur Verlag, Possenbacker Str. 2, Postfach 71 1009, D-8 Munich 71, Fed. Rep. of Germany).

Guides to the Sources of the History of Nations (Latin American Series, 10 vols. pub.; African Series, 10 vols. pub.; Asian Series, 3 vols. pub.).

ICA Bulletin (s. ann.; memb., or U.S. $5).

Microfilm Bulletin (subscriptions to Centro Nacional de Microfilm, serrano 15, Madrid 6, Spain).

List of other publications available upon request to ICA secretariat, Paris, France.

International Federation for Documentation

Box 90402, 2509 LK The Hague, Netherlands

Object

To group internationally organizations and individuals interested in the problems of documentation and to coordinate their efforts; to promote the study, organization, and practice of documentation in all its forms, and to contribute to the creation of an international network of information systems.

Program

The program of the federation includes activities for which the following committees have been established: Central Classification Committee (for UDC); Research on the Theoretical Basis of Information; Linguistics in Documentation; Information for Industry; Education and Training; Classification Research; Terminology of Information and Documentation; Patent Information and Documentation; Social Sciences Documentation; Informetrics. It also includes the BSO Panel (Broad System of Ordering).

Officers

Pres. Ricardo A. Gietz, CAICYT, Moreno 431/33, 1091 Buenos Aires, Argentina; *V.Ps.* S. Fujiwara, Dept. of Chemistry,

Chiba Univ., Yoyoi-cho 1-3, Chiba, Japan; M. W. Hill, Science Reference Libn., British Lib., 25 Southhampton Bldgs., Chancery Lane, London, England; A. I. Mikhailov, VINITI, Baltijskaja ul. 14, Moscow A219, USSR; *Treas.* Margarita Almada de Ascencio, Mexico City, Mexico; *Councillors.* Yone Sepulveda Chastinet, Brasilia, Brazil; Emilia Currás, Madrid, Spain; I. Essaid, Baghdad, Iraq; A. van der Laan, The Hague, Netherlands; P. Lázár, Budapest, Hungary; E.-J. von Ledebur, Bonn, Fed. Rep. of Germany; S. S. Ljungberg, Södertälje, Sweden; Elmer V. Smith, Ottawa, Canada; Marcel Thomas, Paris, France; Neva Tudor-Silović, Zagreb, Yugoslavia; Mu'azu H. Wali, Lagos, Nigeria; *Belgian Member.* Monique Jucquois-Delpierre, La Hulpe, Belgium; *Secy.-Gen.* Stella Keenan, The Hague, Netherlands; *Pres., FID/CLA* A. L. Carvalho de Miranda, Brasilia, Brazil; *Pres., FID/CAO.* B. L. Burton, Hong Kong. (Address all correspondence to the secretary-general.)

Publications

FID Annual Report (ann.).
FID Directory (bienn.).

FID News Bulletin (mo.) with supplements on document reproduction (q.).
FID Publications (ann.).
International Forum on Information and Documentation (q.).
Newsletter on Education and Training Programmes for Information Personnel (q.).
R & D Projects in Documentation and Librarianship (bi-mo.).
Proceedings of congresses; Universal Decimal Classification editions; manuals; directories; bibliographies on information science, documentation, reproduction, mechanization, linguistics, training, and classification.

Membership

Approved by the FID Council; ratification by the FID General Assembly.

American Membership

U.S. Interim National Committee for FID.

International Federation of Film Archives

Secretariat, Coudenberg 70, B-1000 Brussels, Belgium

Object

"To facilitate communication and cooperation between its members, and to promote the exchange of films and information; to maintain a code of archive practice calculated to satisfy all national film industries, and to encourage industries to assist in the work of the Federation's members; to advise its members on all matters of interest to them, especially the preservation and study of films; to give every possible assistance and encouragement to new film archives and to those interested in creating them." Founded in Paris, 1938. Memb. 72 (in 50 countries).

Executive Committee (June 1983–June 1985)

Pres. Wolfgang Klaue, DDR; *V.Ps.* Eileen Bowser, USA: David Francis, UK; Raymond Borde, France; *Secy.-Gen.* Robert

Daudelin, Canada; *Treas.* Jan de Vaal, Netherlands. (Address correspondence to B. Van der Elst, executive secretary, at headquarters address.)

Committee Members

Cosme Alves Netto, Brazil; Hector Garcia Mesa, Cuba; Guido Cincotti, Italy; Eva Orbanz, Fed. Rep. of Germany; Anna-Lena Wibom, Sweden.

Publications

Annual Bibliography of FIAF Members' Publications.
Film Cataloging.
Film Preservation (available in English or French).

Guidelines for Describing Unpublished Script Materials.
Handbook for Film Archives (available in English or French).
International Directory to Film & TV Documentation Sources.
International Index to Film and Television Periodicals (microfiche service).
International Index to Film Periodicals (cumulative volumes).
International Index to Television Periodicals (cumulative volumes).
The Preservation and Restoration of Colour and Sound in Films.
Proceedings of the FIAF Symposiums: 1977: L'Influence du Cinema Sovietique Muet Sur le Cinema Mondial/The Influence of Silent Soviet Cinema on World Cinema; 1978: Cinema 1900–1906; 1980: Problems of Selection in Film Archives.

International Federation of Library Associations and Institutions (IFLA)

c/o The Royal Library, Box 95312,
2509 CH The Hague, Netherlands

Object

"To promote international understanding, cooperation, discussion, research, and development in all fields of library activity, including bibliography, information services, and the education of library personnel, and to provide a body through which librarianship can be represented in matters of international interest." Founded 1927. Memb. (Lib. Assns.) 166, (Inst.) 819, (Aff.) 148; 117 countries.

Officers and Executive Board

Pres. Else Granheim, Dir., Norwegian Directorate for Public and School Libs., Oslo, Norway; *1st V.P.* Hans-Peter Geh, Dir., Württembergische Landsbibliothek, Stuttgart, Fed. Rep. of Germany; *2nd V.P.* Joseph Soosai, Libn., Rubber Research Institute, Kuala Lumpur, Malaysia; *Treas.* Marie-Louise Bossuat, Dir., Bibliographical Center of the National Lib., Paris, France; *Exec. Bd.* G. Rückl, Dir., Central Lib. Institute, Berlin, DDR; Henriette Avram, Dir. for Processing Systems, Networks, and Automation Planning, Lib. of Congress, Washington, DC, USA; A. J. Evans, Dir., Univ. Lib., Loughborough Univ. of Technology, Loughborough, UK; Engelsina V. Pereslegina, Deputy Dir., All-Union State Lib. of Foreign Literature, Moscow, USSR; *Ex officio Members.* Paul Kaegbein, Chpn., Professional Bd., Chair of Lib. Science, Cologne Univ., Cologne,

Fed. Rep. of Germany; Adam Wysocki, Chpn., Programme Management Committee, Consultant, Bureau for Labour Problems Analysis, International Labour Organization, Geneva, Switzerland; *Secy.-Gen.* Margareet Wijnstroom, IFLA Headquarters; *Programme Officer, IFLA International Office for Universal Bibliographic Control.* Barbara Jover, c/o Ref. Div., British Library, London, UK; *Dir., IFLA Office for International Lending.* M. B. Line, c/o British Lib. Lending Div., Boston Spa, Wetherby, West Yorkshire, UK; *Publications Officer.* W. R. H. Koops, Univ. Libn., Groningen, Netherlands; *Professional Coord.* A. L. van Wesemael, IFLA headquarters.

Publications

IFLA Annual.
IFLA Directory (biennial).

IFLA Journal (q.).
IFLA Publications Series.
International Cataloguing (q.).

American Membership

American Lib. Assn.; Art Libs. Society of North America; Assn. of American Lib. Schools; Assn. of Research Libs.; International Assn. of Law Libs.; International Assn. of Orientalist Libns.; International Assn. of School Libns.; Medical Lib Assn.; Special Libs. Assn. *Institutional Members:* There are 134 libraries and related institutions that are institutional members or affiliates of IFLA in the United States (out of a total of 903), and 37 Personal Affiliates (out of a total of 87).

International Institute for Children's Literature and Reading Research

Mayerhofg. 6, A-1040 Vienna, Austria

Object

"To create an international center of work and coordination; to take over the tasks of a documentations center of juvenile literature and reading education; to mediate between the individual countries and circles dealing with children's books and reading." Established Apr. 7, 1965. Dues. Austrian schillings 250 (with a subscription to *Bookbird*); Austrian schillings 270 (with a subscription of *Bookbird* and *Jugend und Buch*).

Program

Promotion of international research in field and collection and evaluation of results of such research; international bibliography of technical literature on juvenile reading; meetings and exhibitions; compilation and publication of recommendation lists; advisory service; concrete studies on juvenile literature; collaboration with publishers; reading research.

Officers

Pres. Hermann Lein; *Hon. Pres.* Adolf März; Richard Bamberger; Wilhelmine Lussnigg; *V.P. Dir.* Otwald Kropatsch; *Pres.* Hans Matzenauer; *Dir.* Lucia Binder; *V.-Dir.* Viktor Böhm. (Address all inquiries to director at headquarters address.)

Publications

Bookbird (q.; memb. or Austrian shillings 250 [appox. $14]).
Jugend und Buch (memb. or Austrian shillings 120 [approx. $7]).

Schriften zur Jugendlekture (series of books and brochures dealing with questions on juvenile literature and literary education in German).

International Organization for Standardization

ISO Central Secretariat
1 r. de Varembé, Case postale 56, CH-1211 Geneva 20, Switzerland

Object

To promote the development of standards in the world in order to facilitate the international exchange of goods and services and to develop mutual cooperation in the spheres of intellectual, scientific, technological, and economic activity.

Officers

Pres. D. C. Kothari, India; *V.P.* Jan Ollner, Sweden; *Secy.-Gen.* Olle Sturen, Sweden.

Technical Work

The technical work of ISO is carried out by over 160 technical committees. These include:

TC 46—Documentation (Secretariat, DIN Deutsches Institut fur Normung, 4-10, Burggrafenstr., Postfach 1107, D-1000 Berlin 30). Scope: Standardization of practices relating to libraries, documentation and information centers, indexing and abstracting services, archives, information science, and publishing.

TC 37—Terminology (Principles & Coordination) (Secretariat, Osterreisches Normungsinstitut, Leopoldgasse 4, A-1020 Vienna, Austria). Scope: Standardization of methods for creating, compiling, and coordinating terminologies.

TC 97—Information Processing Systems (Secretariat, American National Standards Institute ANSI, 1430 Broadway, New York, NY 10018, USA). Scope: Standardization, including terminology, in the area of information processing systems including computers and office equipment.

Publications

Bulletin (mo.).
Catalogue (ann.).
Liaisons.
Member Bodies.
Memento (ann.).

Foreign Library Associations

The following list of regional and national foreign library associations is a selective one. For a more complete list with detailed information, see *International Guide to Library, Archival, and Information Science Associations* by Josephine Riss Fang and Alice H. Songe (R. R. Bowker, 1980). The *Guide* also provides information on international associations, some of which are described in detail under "International Library Associations" (immediately preceding this section). A more complete list of foreign and international library associations also can be found in *International Literary Market Place* (R. R. Bowker), an annual publication.

Regional

Africa

International Assn. for the Development of Documentation, Libs. & Archives in Africa, *Secy.* Zacheus Sunday Ali, Box 375, Dakar, Senegal.

Standing Conference of African Lib. Schools, c/o School of Libns., Archivists & Documentalists, Univ. of Dakar, B. P. 3252, Dakar, Senegal.

Standing Conference of African Univ. Libs., Eastern Area (SCAULEA), c/o Univ. Libn., Univ. of Nairobi, Kenya.

Standing Conference of African Univ. Libs., Western Area (SCAULWA), c/o M. Jean Aboghe-Obyan, Bibliotheque Universitaire, Univ. Omar Bongo, Libreville, Gabon.

Standing Conference of East African Libns., c/o Tanzania Lib. Assn., Box 2645, Dar-es-Salaam, Tanzania.

The Americas

Asociación de Bibliotecas Universitarias, de Investigación e Institucionales del Caribe (Assn. of Caribbean Univ., Research & Institutional Libs.), *Exec. Secy.* Oneida R. Ortiz, Apdo. Postal S. Estación de la Universidad, San Juan, PR 00931.

Asociación Latinoamericana de Escuelas de Bibliotecologia y Ciencias de la Información (Latin American Assn. of Schools of Lib. and Info. Science), Colegio de Bibliotecologia, Universidad Nacional Autónoma de México, México 20, D. F., Mexico.

Seminar on the Acquisition of Latin American Lib. Materials, SALALM Secretariat, *Exec. Secy.* Suzanne Hodgman. Memorial Lib., Univ. of Wisconsin-Madison, Madison, WI 53706.

Asia

Congress of Southeast Asian Libns. (CONSAL), *Chpn.* Dr. Serafin Quiason, c/o National Lib. of the Philippines, T. M. Kalaw St., Manila, Philippines.

British Commonwealth of Nations

Commonwealth Lib. Assn., c/o Church Teachers College, Box 41, Mandeville, Manchester, Jamaica, West Indies.

Standing Conference on Lib. Materials on Africa (SCOLMA), c/o *Secy.* P. M. Larby, Institute of Commonwealth Studies, 27-28 Russell Sq., London WC1B 5DS, England.

Europe

LIBER (Ligue des Bibliothèques Européenes de Recherche), Assn. of European Research Lib., c/o H.-A. Koch, Universitatsbibliothek, Postfach 33 01 60, D-2800 Bremen 33, Federal Republic of Germany.

Nordiska Vetenskapliga Bibliotekarieförbundet (Scandinavian Assn. of Research Libns.), c/o Chefbibliotekarie Tor Holm, Svenska Handelshögskolans bibliotek, Arkadiagatan 22, SF-00100 Helsinki 10, Finland.

National

Argentina

Asociación Argentina de Bibliotecas y Centros de Información Científicos y Técnicos (Argentine Assn. of Scientific & Technical Libs. & Info. Centers), Santa Fe 1145, Buenos Aires. Exec. *Secy.* Olga E. Veronelli.

Australia

Australian School Lib. Assn., c/o *Secy.* Box 80, Balmain N.S.W. 2041.

Lib. Assn. of Australia, *Exec. Dir.* Susan Acutt, 376 Jones St., Ultimo, NSW 2007.

Lib. Automated Systems Info. Exchange (LASIE), *Pres.* Dorothy Peake, Box 602, Lane Cove, N.S.W. 2066.

The School Lib. Assn. of New South Wales, c/o *Secy.,* Box 80, Balmain N.S.W. 2041.

State Libns.' Council of Australia, *Chpn.* W. L. Brown, State Lib. of Tasmania, 91 Murray St., Hobart, Tasmania 7000.

Austria

Österreichische Gesellschaft für Dokumentation und Information—ÖGDI (Austrian Society for Documentation and Info.), *Exec. Secy.* Bruno Hofer, c/o ON, Österreichisches Normungsinstitut, Heinestrasse 38, POB 130, A-1021 Vienna.

Verband Österreichischer Volksbüchereien und Volksbibliothekare (Assn. of Austrian Public Libs. & Libns.), *Chpn.* Franz Pascher; *Secy.* Heinz Buchmüller, Langegasse 37, A-1080 Vienna.

Vereinigung Österreichischer Bibliothekare—VÖB (Assn. of Austrian Libns.), *Pres.* Ferdinand Baumgartner, c/o Österreichische Nationalbibliothek, Josefsplatz 1, A-1015 Vienna.

Belgium

Association Belge de Documentation-ABD/Belgische Vereniging voor Documentatie-BVD (Belgian Assn. for Documentation), Box 110, 1040 Brussels 26. *Pres.* De Backer Roger.

Association des Archivistes et Bibliothécaires de Belgique/Vereniging van Archivarissen en Bibliothecarissen van België (Belgian Assn. of Archivists & Libns.), *Exec. Secy.* T. Verschaffel, Bibliothèque Royale Albert I, 4 bd. de l'Empereur, B-1000 Brussels.

Association des Bibliothécaries-Documentalistes de l'Institute d'Etudes Sociales de l'Etat (Assn. of Libns. & Documentalists of the State Institute of Social Studies), *Secy.* Claire Gerard, 24 rue de l'Abbaye, B-1050 Brussels.

Vereniging van Religieus-Wetenschappelijke Bibliothécarissen (Assn. of Theological Libns.) Minderbroederstr. 5, B-3800 St. Truiden. *Exec. Secy.* K. Van de Casteele, Spoorweglaan 237, B-2610 Wilrijk.

Vlaamse Vereniging voor Bibliotheek, Archief, en Documentatiewezen—VVBAD (Flemish Assn. of Libns., Archivists, & Documentalists), *Pres.* F. Heymans; *Secy.* F. Franssens; Goudbloemstraat 10, 2008 Antwerpen.

Bolivia

Asocciación Boliviana de Bibliotecarios (Bolivian Lib. Assn.), *Pres.* Efraín Virreira Sánchez, Casilla 992, Cochabamba.

Brazil

Associação dos Arquivistas Brasileiros (Assn. of Brazilian Archivists), Praia de Botafogo 186, Sala B-217, CEP 22253 Rio do Janeiro, RJ. *Pres.* Lia Temporal Malcher.

Federaçáo Brasiliera de Associações de Bibliotecários (Brazilian Federation of Lib. Assns.), c/o *Pres.* Elizabeth Maria Ramos de Carvalho, rua Humberto de Campos 366, ap. 1302, 22430 Rio de Janeiro, R.J.

Bulgaria

Bulgarian Union of Public Libraries, ul. Alabin, Sofia.

Sekciylna na Bibliotechnite Rabotnitsi pri Zentrainija Komitet na Profesionalniya Suyuz na Rabotnicite ot Poligrafičeskata Promišlenost i Kulturnite Instituti (Lib. Sec. at the Trade Union of the Workers in the Polygraphic Industry & Cultural Institutions), c/o Cyril and Methodius National Lib. Blvd., Tolbuhin. *Pres.* Stefan Kancev.

Canada

Association Canadienne de Science de l'Information (Canadian Assn. for Info. Science), c/o Robert Leitch, 47 Gore St. E., Perth, Ont. K7H 1H6.

Association Canadienne des Écoles des Bibliothécaires (The Canadian Association of Library Schools); *Pres.* Samuel Rothstein, School of Libnshp., Univ. of British Columbia, Vancouver, B.C. V6T 1W5.

Association pour l'avancement des sciences et des techniques de la documentation (ASTED, Inc.), *Dir.-Gen.* Lise Brousseau, 7243 rue Saint-Denis, Montréal, P.Q. H2R 2E3.

Canadian Lib. Assn., *Exec. Dir.* Paul Kitchen, 151 Sparks St., Ottawa, Ont. K1P 5E3. (For detailed information on the Canadian Lib. Assn. and its divisions, see "National Library and Information Industry Associations, U.S. and Canada"; for information on the library associations of the provinces of Canada, see "State, Provincial, and Regional Library Associations.")

Conseil Canadien des Écoles Bibliothéconomie (CCLS/CCEB) (Canadian Council of Lib. Schools), *Pres.* William J. Cameron, Dean, School of Lib. & Info. Science, Univ. of Western Ontario, London, Ont. N6G 1H1, Canada.

La Société bibliographique du Canada (The Bibliographical Society of Canada), *Secy.-Treas.* Eleanor E. Magee, Box 1110, Sta. B., London, Ont. N6A 5K2.

Chile

Colegio de Bibliotecarios de Chile, A. G. (Chilean Lib. Assn.), *Pres.* Ursula Schadich Schonhals; *Secy. Gen.* Eliana Bazán del Campo, Casilla 3741, Santiago.

China (People's Republic of)

Library Assn. of China, c/o National Central Lib., 43 Nan Hai Rd., Taipei. *Exec. Dir.* Karl M. Ku.

Zhongguo Tushuguan Xuehui (China Society of Lib. Science [CSLS]), *Secy.-Gen.* Tan Xiangjin; 7 Wenjinjie, Beijing (Peking).

Colombia

Asociación Colombiana de Bibliotecarios — ASCOLBI (Colombian Assn. of Libns.), Apdo. Aéreo 30883, Bogotá, D.E.

Colegio Colombiana de Bibliotecarios — CCB (Colombian Academy of Libns.), Apdo. Aéreo 1307, Medellin.

Costa Rica

Asociación Costarricense de Bibliotecarios (Assn. of Costa Rican Libns.), Apdo. Postal 3308, San José.

Cyprus

Kypriakos Synthesmos Vivliothicarion (Lib. Assn. of Cyprus), c/o Pedagogical Academy, Box 1039, Nikosia. *Secy.* Paris G. Rossos.

Czechoslovakia

Ústřední knihovnická rada CSR (Central Lib. Council of the Czechoslovak Socialist Republic), *Chief, Dept. of Libs.* Marie Sedláčková, c/o Ministry of Culture of CSR, Valdštejnská 10, Prague 1-Malá Strana.

Zväz slovenských knihovníkov a informatikov (Assn. of Slovak Libns. & Documentalists), *Pres.* Vít Rak; *Exec. Secy.* Štefan Kimlička, Michalská 1, 814 17 Bratislava.

Denmark

Arkivforeningen (The Archives Society), *Exec. Secy.* Erik Gobel, Rigsarkivet, Rigsdagsgarden 9, DK-1218 Copenhagen K.

Danmarks Biblioteksforening (Danish Lib. Assn.), *Pres.* K. J. Mortensen, Trekronergade 15, DK-2500 Valby-Copenhagen.

Danmarks Forskningsbiblioteksforening (Danish Research Lib. Assn.), *Pres.* M. Laursen Vig, c/o Roskilde Universitetsbibliotek, Box 258, DK-4000, Roskilde.

Danmarks Skolebiblioteksforening (Assn. of Danish School Libs.), *Exec. Secy.* Niels Jacobsen, Frankrigsgade 4, 2300 Kobenham S.

Dansk Musikbiblioteksforening, Dansk sektion of AIBM (Danish Assn. of Music Libs., Danish Sec. of AIBM), c/o *Secy.*, Irlandsvej 90, DK-2300 Copenhagen K.

Dominican Republic

Asociación Dominicana de Bibliotecarios—ASODOBI (Dominican Lib. Assn.), c/o Biblioteca Nacional, Plaza de la Cultura, Santo Domingo. *Pres.* Prospero J. Mella Chavier; *Secy. Gen.* Hipólito González C.

Ecuador

Asociación Ecuatoriana de Bibliotecarios—AEB (Ecuadorian Lib. Assn.), *Exec. Secy.* Elizabeth Carrion, Casa de la Cultura Ecuatoriana, Casilla 87, Quito.

Egypt

See United Arab Republic.

El Salvador

Asociación de Bibliotecarios de El Salvador (El Salvador Lib. Assn.), c/o *Secy.-Gen.* Edgar Antonio Pérez Borja, Urbanización Gerardo Barrios Polígono, "B" No. 5, San Salvador, C.A.

Ethiopia

Ye Ethiopia Betemetshaft Serategnot Mahber (Ethiopian Lib. Assn. [ELA]), *Exec. Secy.* Asrat Tilahun, Box 30530, Addis Ababa.

Finland

Kirjastonhoitajaliitto-Bibliotekarieförbundet r.y. (Finnish Libns. Assn.), *Exec. Secy.* Anna-Maija Hintikka, Temppelikatu 1 A 12, SF-00100 Helsinki 10.

Suomen Kirjastoseura-Finlands Biblioteksförening (Finnish Lib. Assn.), *Exec. Secy.* Hilkka M. Kauppi, Museokatu 18, SF-00100 Helsinki 10.

Tieteellisten Kirjastojen Virkailijat-Vetenskapliga Bibliotekens Tjänstemannaförening r.y. (Assn. of Research & Univ.

Libns.), *Exec. Secy.* Kirsti Janhunen, Temppelikatu 1 A 12, 00100 Helsinki 10.
Tietopalveluseura-Samfundet för Informationstjänst i Finland (Finnish Society for Information Services), c/o *Pres.* Ritva Launo, The State Alcohol Monopoly of Finland (ALKO), Helsinki.

France

Association des archivistes français (Assn. of French Archivists), *Pres.* M. Charnier; *Exec. Secys.* Mme. Rey-Courtel and Mlle. Etienne, 60 r. des Francs-Bourgeois, F-75141 Paris, CEDEX 03.
Association des Bibliothécaires Français (Assn. of French Libns.), *Exec. Secy.* Jean-Marc Léri, 65 rue de Richelieu, F-75002 Paris.
Association des Bibliothèques ecclésiastiques de France (Assn. of French Theological Libs.), *Exec. Secy.* Paul-Marie Guillaume, 6 rue du Regard, F-75006 Paris.
Association Française des Documentalistes et des Bibliotécaires Spécialisés — ADBS (Assn. of France Info. Scientists & Special Libns.), *Exec. Secy.* J. C. Le Moal, 5, av. Franco russe, 75007 Paris.

German Democratic Republic

Bibliotheksverband der Deutschen Demokratischen Republik (Lib. Assn. of the German Democratic Republic), c/o *Exec. Secy.* Hermann-Matern-Str. 57, DDR-1040 Berlin.

Germany (Federal Republic of)

Arbeitsgemeinschaft der Kunstbibliotheken (Working Group of Art Libs.), *Exec. Secy.* Jürgen Zimmer, Bibliothek des Zentralinstituts für Kunstgeschichte in München, Meiserstr. 10, D-8000 München 2.
Arbeitsgemeinschaft der Spezialbibliotheken (Assn. of Special Libs.), *Chpn.* Wal-

ter Manz, Zentralbibliothek der Kernforschungsanlage Jülich GmbH, Postfach 1913, D-5170 Jülich 1.
Deutsche Gesellschaft für Dokumentation e.V. — DGD (German Society for Documentation), *Scientific Secy.* Hilde Strohl-Goebel, Westendstr. 19, D6000 Frankfurt am Main 1.
Deutscher Bibliotheksverband (German Lib. Assn.), *Secy.* Victoria Scherzberg. Bundesallee 184/185, 1000 Berlin 31.
Verband der Bibliotheken des Landes Nordrhein-Westfalen (Assn. of Libs. in the Federal State of North Rhine-Westphalia), *Chpn.* Johannes Schultheis, Direktor, Stadtbücherei Bochum, Vorsitzender, Rathausplatz 2-6, 4630 Bochum.
Verein der Bibliothekare an Öffentlichen Bibliotheken (Assn. of Libns. at Public Libs.), *Secy.* Roonstr. 57, 2800 Bremen 1.
Verein der Diplom-Bibliothekare an wissenschaftlichen Bibliotheken (Assn. of Graduated Libns. at Academic Libs.), *Chpn.* Ulla Usemann-Keller, c/o Deutsches Bibliotheksinstitut, Bundesallee 184/185, D-1000 Berlin 31.
Verein Deutscher Archivare — VDA (Assn. of German Archivists), *Chpn.* Eckhart G. Franz, Hessisches Staatsarchiv, Schloss, D-6100 Darmstadt.
Verein Deutscher Bibliothekare e.V. — VDB (Assn. of German Libns.), *Pres.* Ltd. Bibliotheksdirektor Dr. Rudolf Frankenberger; *Secy.* Bibliotheksoberrat Dr. Hans-Burkard Meyer, Universitätsbibliothek, Alter Postweg 120, D-8900 Augsburg.

Ghana

Ghana Lib. Assn., *Exec. Secy.* P. Amonoo, Box 4105, Accra.

Greece

Enosis Ellenon Bibliothakarion (Greek Lib. Assn.), Box 2118, Athens-124.

Guatemala

Asociación Bibliotecológica Guatemalteca ´ (Lib. Assn. of Guatemala), c/o *Dir..*, 18 Avenida "A," 4-04 Zona 15 V.H.I., Guatemala, C.A.

Guyana

Guyana Lib. Assn. (GLA), *Secy.* Wenda Stephenson, c/o National Lib., Box 10240, 76/77 Main St., Georgetown.

Honduras

Asociación de Bibliotecarios y Archivistas de Honduras (Assn. of Libns. & Archivists of Honduras), *Secy.-Gen.* Juan Angel Ayes R., 3 Av. 4y5C., no. 416, Comayagüela, DC, Tegucigalpa.

Hong Kong

Hong Kong Lib. Assn., *Chpn.* Malcolm Quinn, c/o Box 10095, G.P.O. Hong Kong.

Hungary

Magyar Könyvtárosok Egyesülete (Assn. of Hungarian Libns.), *Secy.* D. Kovács, Box 244, H-1368 Budapest.
Tájékoztatási Tudományos Társaság— MTESZ/TTT (Info. Science Society), c/o Pál Gágyor, Kossuth ter 6-8, Budapest 1055.

Iceland

Bókavarŏafélag Islands (Icelandic Lib. Assn.), *Pres.* Eiríkur Th. Einarsson, Box 7050, 127 Reykjavík.

India

Indian Assn. of Special Libs. & Info. Centres (IASLIC), *Gen. Secy.* S. K. Kapoor, P-291. CIT Scheme 6M, Kankurgachi, Calcutta 700 054.
Indian Lib. Assn. (ILA), *Pres.* P. B. Mangla; *Secy.* O. P. Trikha, A/40-41,

No. 201, Ansal Bldgs., Dr. Mukerjee Nagar, Delhi 110009.

Indonesia

Ikatan Pustakawan Indonesia—IPI (Indonesian Lib. Assn.), *Pres.* Mastini Hardjo Prakoso; *Secy.* Soemarno HS, Jalan Merdeka Selatan 11, Jakarta-Pusat.

Iran

Iranian Lib. Assn., *Exec. Secy.* M. Niknam Vazifeh, Box 11-1391, Tehran.

Iraq

Iraqi Lib. Assn., *Exec. Secy.* N. Kamal-al-Deen, Box 4081, Baghdad-Adhamya.

Ireland

Cumann Leabharlann Na h-Éireann (Lib. Assn. of Ireland), *Pres.* W. P. Smith; *Hon. Secy. (Acting).* P. M. Grant, 22 Crofton Rd., Dun Laoghaire, Dublin.
Cumann Leabharlannaith Scoile—CLS (Irish Assn. of School Libns.), Headquarters: The Lib., Univ. College, Dublin 4. *Exec. Secy.* Sister Mary Columban, Loreto Convent, Foxrock Co., Dublin.

Italy

Associazione Italiana Biblioteche—AIB (Italian Libs. Assn.), *Secy.* A. M. Caproni, c/o Istituto di Patologia del Libro, Via Milano 76, 00184 Rome.
Associazione Nazionale Archivistica Italiana—ANAI (National Assn. of Italian Archivists), *Secy.* Antonio Dentoni-Litta, Via di Ponziano 15, 00152 Rome.
Ente Nazionale per le Biblioteche Popolari e Scholastiche (National Assn. for Public & Academic Libs.), Via Michele Mercati 4, 1-00197 Rome.
Federazione Italiana delle Biblioteche Popolari—FIBP (Federation of Italian Public Libs.), c/o La Società Umanita-

ria, Via Davario 7, Cap. N., 1-20122 Milan.

Ivory Coast

Association pour le Développement de la Documentation des Bibliothèques et Archives de las Côte d'Ivoire (Assn. for the Development of Documentation, Libs. & Archives of the Ivory Coast), c/o Bibliothèque Nationale, B.P. 20915 Abidjan.

Jamaica

Jamaica Lib. Assn. (JLA), *Secy.* Hermine C. Salmon, Box 58, Kingston 5.

Japan

Nihon Toshokan Kyôkai (Japan Lib. Assn. [JLA]), *Secy.-Gen.* Hitoshi Kurihara, 1-10, Taishido 1-chome, Setagaya-ku, Tokyo 154.

Nippon Dokumentêsyon Kyôkai—NIPDOK (Japan Documentation Society), *Exec. Secy.* Tsunetaka Ueda, Sasaki Bldg., 5-7 Koisikawa 2-chome, Bunkyô-ku, Tokyo 112.

Senmon Toshokan Kyôgikai—SENTO-KYO (Japan Special Libs. Assn.), *Exec. Dir.* Yoshitaro Tanabe, c/o National Diet Lib., 1-10-1 Nagata-cho, Chiyoda-ku, Tokyo 100.

Jordan

Jordan Lib. Assn. (JLA), *Pres.* Anwar Akroush; *Secy.* Medhat Mar'ei; *Treas.* Butros Hashweh, Box 6289, Amman.

Korea (Democratic People's Republic of)

Lib. Assn. of the Democratic People's Republic of Korea, *Secy.* Li Geug, Central Lib., Box 109, Pyongyang.

Korea (Republic of)

Hanguk Tosogwan Hyophoe (Korean Lib. Assn.), *Exec. Secy.* Dae Kwon Park, 100-177, 1-Ka, Hoehyun-Dong, Choong-Ku, CPO Box 2041, Seoul.

Laos

Association des Bibliothécaires Laotiens (Laos Lib. Assn.), Direction de la Bibliothèque Nationale, Ministry of Education, Box 704, Vientiane.

Lebanon

Lebanese Lib. Assn. (LLA), *Pres.* L. Hanhan, Saab Medical Lib., AUB, Beirut.

Malaysia

Persatuan Perpustakaan Malaysia—PPM (Lib. Assn. of Malaysia), *Secy.* Aizan Mohd. Ali, Box 2545, Kuala Lumpur.

Mauritania

Association Mauritanienne des Bibliothécaires, des Archivistes et des Documentalistes—AMBAD (Mauritanian Assn. of Libns., Archivists & Documentalists), c/o *Pres.* Oumar Diouwara, Dir., National Lib., Nouakchott.

Mexico

Asociación de Bibliotecarios de Instituciónes de Enseñanza Superior e Investigación—ABIESI (Assn. of Libns. of Higher Education & Research Institutions), *Pres.* Elsa Barberena, Apdo. Postal 5-611, México 5, D.F.

Asociación Mexicana de Bibliotecarios, A.C. (Mexican Assn. of Libns.), *Pres.* Adolfo Rodriquez, Apdo. 27-102, Mexico 7, D.F.

Colegio Nacional de Bibliotecarios—CNB

(Mexico National College of Librariana), *Pres.* Estela Morales, Apdo. Postal 20-697, 01000 Mexico, D.F.

Netherlands

Nederlandse Vereniging van Bedrijfsarchivarissen — NVBA (Netherlands Assn. of Business Archivists), *Secy.* C. L. Groenland, Aalsburg 25 26-6602 WD Wijchen.

Nederlandse Vereniging van Bibliothecarissen, Documentalisten en Literatuuronderzoekers — NVB (Dutch Lib. Assn.), p/a Mw. H. J. Krikke-Scholten, Nolweg 13 d, 4209 AW Schelluinen.

UKB-Samenwerkingsverband van de Universiteits- en Hogeschoolbibliotheken en de Koninklijke Bibliotheek (Assn. of Univ. Libs. & the Royal Lib.), *Exec. Secy.* J. L. M. van Dijk, c/o Bibliotheek Rijksuniversiteit Limburg, Postbus 616, 6200 MD Maastricht.

Vereniging va Archivarissen in Nederland — VAN (Assn. of Archivists in the Netherlands), *Exec. Secy.* A. W. M. Koolen, Postbus 897, 8901 BR Leeuwarden.

Vereniging voor het Theologisch Bibliothecariaat (Assn. of Theological Libns.), *Exec. Secy.* R. T. M. Van Dijk, Postbus 289, 6500 AG Nijmegen.

New Zealand

New Zealand Lib. Assn. (NZLA), *Pres.* J. G. Brock, 20 Brandon St., Box 12-212, Wellington 1.

Nicaragua

Asociación de Bibliotecas Universitarias 6 Especializadas de Nicaragua — ABUEN (Assn. of Univ. & Special Libs. of Nicaragua), *Secy.* Cecilie Aguilar Briceño, Biblioteca Central, Universidad Nacional Autónoma de Nicaragua, Apdo. No. 68, León.

Nigeria

Nigerian Lib. Assn. (NLA), c/o *Hon. Secy.* E. O. Ejiko, P.M.B. 12655, Lagos.

Norway

Arkivarforeningen (Assn. of Archivists), *Secy.-Treas.* Atle Steinar Nilsen, Postboks 10, Kringsja, Oslo 8. Norsk Bibliothekforening — NBF (Norwegian Lib. Assn.), *Secy.-Treas.* G. Langland, Malerhaugveien 20, Oslo 6.

Norske Forskningebibliotekarers Forening — NFF (Assn. of Norwegian Research Libns.), *Secy.* G. Langland, Malerhaugveien 20, Oslo 6.

Pakistan

Pakistan Lib. Assn. (PLA), *Exec. Secy.* A. H. Siddiqui, c/o Pakistan Institute of Development Economics, Univ. Campus, Box 1091, Islamabad.

Society for the Promotion & Improvement of Libs. (SPIL), *Pres.* Hakim Mohammed Said, Al-Majeed, Hamdard Centre, Nazimabad, Karachi-18.

Panama

Asociación Panameña de Bibliotecarios (Panamanian Assn. of Libns.), c/o Departamento de Bibliotecología, Universidad de Panama, Estafeta Universitaria, Republic of Panama.

Papua New Guinea

Papua New Guinea Lib. Assn. (PNGLA), *Pres.* Margaret Obi; *V.P.* Ursula Pawe; *Secy.* Haro Raka; *Treas.* Lewis Kusso-Aless; *Pubns. Mgr.* Maria Teka, Box 5368, Boroko, PNG.

Paraguay

Asociación de Bibliotecarios Universitarios del Paraguay — ABUP (Paraguayan

Assn. of Univ. Libns.), c/o Zayda Caballero, Head, Escuela de Bibliotecología, Universidad Nacional de Asunción, Casilla de Correo, 1408 Asunción, Paraguay.

Peru

Agrupación de Bibliotecas para la Integración de la Información Socio-Económica — ABIISE (Lib. Group for the Integration of Socio-Economic Info.), *Dir.* Betty Chiriboga de Cussato, Apdo. 2874, Lima 100.

Asociación Peruana de Archiveros (Assn. of Peruvian Archivists), Archivo General de la Nación, C. Manuel Cuadros s/n., Palacio de Justicia, Apdo. 3124, Lima 100.

Asociación Peruana de Bibliotecarios (Assn. of Peruvian Libns.), *Exec. Secy.* Amparo Geraldino de Orban, Apdo. 3760, Lima.

Philippines

Assn. of Special Libs. of the Philippines (ASLP), *Pres.* Susima Lazo Gonzales, Box 4118, Manila.

Philippine Lib. Assn. Inc. (PLAI), *Pres.* Angelica A. Cabanero, Box 2926, Manila.

Poland

Stowarzyszenie Bibliotekarzy Polskich — SBP (Polish Libns. Assn.), *Pres.* Stefan Kubów; *Gen. Secy.* Wladyslawa Wasilewska, ul. Konopczyńskiego 5/7, 00-953 Warsaw.

Portugal

Associação Portuguesa de Bibliotecários, Arquivistas e Documentalistas — BAD (Portuguese Assn. of Libns., Archivists & Documentalists), *Exec. Secy.* José

Garcia Sottomayor, Rua Ocidental ao Campo Grande 83, 1751 Lisbon.

Rhodesia

See Zimbabwe.

Romania (Socialist Republic of)

Asociatia Bibliotecarilor din Republica Socialista Romania/Association des Bibliothecaires de la République Socialiste de Roumanie), *Pres.* G. Botez, Biblioteca Centrala de Stat, Strada Ion Ghica 4, 7001 8 Bucharest.

Scotland

See United Kingdom.

Senegal

Commission des Bibliothèques de l'ASD-BAM, Association Sénégalaise pour le Développement de la Documentation, des Bibliothèques, des Archives et des Musées (Senegal Assn. for the Development of Documentation, Libs., Archives & Museums), *Gen. Secy.* Miss Aïssatou Wade, B.P. 375, Dakar.

Sierra Leone

Sierra Leone Lib Assn. (SLLA), c/o *Secy.* F. Thorpe, Sierra Leone Lib. Bd., Rokell St., Freetown.

Singapore

Congress of Southeast Asian Libns. (CONSAL), *Chpn.* Mrs. Hedwig Anuar, c/o National Lib., Stamford Rd., Singapore 0617.

Lib. Assn. of Singapore (LAS), *Hon. Secy.,* c/o National Lib., Stamford Rd., Singapore 0617.

South Africa

South African Lib. Assn., c/o Lib., Univ. of the North, Private Bag X5090, Pietersburg 0700.

Spain

Asociación Nacional de Bibliotecarios, Archiveros, Arqueólogos y Documentalists (National Assn. of Libns., Archivists & Archeologists), *Exec. Secy.* C. Iniguez, Paseo de Calvo Sotelo 22, Apdo. 14281, Madrid 1.

Sri Lanka (Ceylon)

Sri Lanka Lib. Assn. (SLLA), *Exec. Secy.* N. A. T. de Silva, c/o Univ. of Colombo, Race Course, Reid Ave., Colombo 7.

Sudan

Sudan Lib.Assn. (SLA), *Exec. Secy.* Mohamed Omar, Box 1361, Khartoum.

Sweden

Svenska Arkivsamfundet (The Swedish Archival Assn.), c/o Riksarkivet, Box 12541, S-102 29 Stockholm.
Svenska Bibliotekariesamfundet — SBS (Swedish Assn. of Univ. & Research Libs.), c/o *Secy.* Birgit Antonsson, Uppsala universitets-bibliotek, Box 510, S-75120 Uppsala.
Sveriges Allmänna Biblioteksförening — SAB (Swedish Lib. Assn.), *Pres.* B. Martinsson, Box 1706, S-221 01 Lund.
Sveriges Vetenskapliga Specialbiblioteks Förening — SVSF (Assn. of Special Research Libs.), *Pres.* Anders Ryberg; *Secy.* Yvonne Olrog Hedvall, c/o Kungl. Skogs- och Lantbruksakademien. Biblioteket, Box 6806, 113 86 Stockholm.
Tekniska Litteratursällskapet — TLS (Swedish Society for Technical Documentation), *Secy.* Birgitta Levin, Box 5073, S-10242 Stockholm 5.
Vetenskapliga Bibliotekens Tjänstemannaförening — VBT (Assn. of Research Lib. Employees), *Pres.* Lillemor Lundström, The Royal Lib., Box 5039, S-102 41 Stockholm.

Switzerland

Schweizerische Vereingung für Dokumentation/Association Suisse de Documentation — SVD/ASD (Swiss Assn. of Documentation), *Secy.-Treas.* W. Bruderer, BID GD PTT 3030 Berne.
Vereinigung Schweizerischer Archivare — VSA (Assn. of Swiss Archivists), c/o *Pres.* Walter Lendi, Staatsarchivar, Staatsarchiv St. Gallen, Regierungsgebäude, CH 9901, St. Gallen.
Vereinigung Schweizerischer Bibliothkare/ Association des Bibliothécaires Suisses/ Associazione dei Bibliotecari Svizzeri — VSB/ABS (Assn. of Swiss Libns.), *Exec. Secy.* W. Treichler, Hallwylstrasse 15, CH-3003 Bern.

Tanzania

Tanzania Lib. Assn., *Exec. Secy.* T. E. Mlaki, Box 2645, Dar-es-Salaam.

Tunisia

Association Tunisienne des Documentalistes, Bibliothécaires et Archivistes (Tunisian Assn. of Documentalists, Libns. & Archivists), *Exec. Secy.* Rudha Tlili, 43 rue de la Liberté, Le Bardo.

Turkey

Türk Kütüphaneciler Derneği — TKD (Turkish Libns. Assn.), *Exec. Secy.* Nejat Sefercioglu, Necatibey Caddesi 19/ 22, P.K. 175, Yenisehir, Ankara.

Uganda

Uganda Lib. Assn. (ULA), *Chpn.* P. Birungi; *Secy.* L. M. Ssengero, Box 5894, Kampala.

Uganda Schools Lib. Assn. (USLA), *Exec. Secy.* J. W. Nabembezi, Box 7014, Kampala.

Union of Soviet Socialist Republics

USSR Lib. Council, *Pres.* N. S. Kartashov, Lenin State Lib., 3 Prospect Kalinina, 101 000 Moscow.

United Arab Republic

Egyptian School Lib. Assn. (ESLA), *Exec. Secy.* M. Alabasiri, 35 Algalaa St., Cairo.

United Kingdom

ASLIB (Association of Special Libraries & Information Bureaux), *Dir.* Dr. D. A. Lewis, 3 Belgrave Sq., London SW1X 8PL.

Assn. of British Theological and Philosophical Libs. (ABTAPL), *Hon. Secy.* Mary Elliott, King's College Lib., Strand, London WC2R 2LS.

Bibliographical Society, *Hon. Secy.* M. M. Foot, British Lib., Reference Div., Great Russell St., London WC1B 3DG.

British & Irish Assn. Of Law Libns. (BIALL), *Hon. Secy.* D. M. Blake, Libn., Harding Law Lib., Univ. of Birmingham, Box 363, Birmingham B15 2TT.

The Lib. Assn., *Exec. Secy.* Keith Lawrey, 7 Ridgmount St., London WCIE 7AE.

Private Libs. Assn. (PLA), *Exec. Secy.* Frank Broomhead, Ravelston, South View Rd., Pinner, Middlesex.

School Lib. Assn. (SLA), *Chpn.* Peter Matthews; *Exec. Secy.* Miriam Curtis, Victoria House, 29-31 George St., Oxford OXI 2AY.

Scottish Lib. Assn. (SLA), *Hon. Secy.* Robert Craig, Dept. of Libnshp., Univ. of Strathclyde, Livingstone Tower, Glasgow G1 1XH.

Society of Archivists (SA), *Exec. Secy.* C. M. Short, South Yorkshire County Record Office, Cultural Activities Centre, 56 Ellin St., Sheffield S1 4PL.

The Standing Conference of National & Univ. Libs. (SCONUL), *Exec. Secy.* A. J. Loveday, Secretariat & Registered Office, 102 Euston St., London NW1 2HA.

Welsh Lib. Assn., *Exec. Secy.*, c/o County Lib. Headquarters, County Civic Centre, Mold, Clwyd CH7 6NW.

Uruguay

Agrupación Bibliotecológica del Uruguay—ABU (Lib. & Archive Science Assn. of Uruguay), *Pres.* Luis Alberto Musso, Cerro Largo 1666, Montevideo.

Venezuela

Colegio de Bibliotecólogos y Archivólogos de Venezuela—COL-BAV (Assn. of Venezuelan Libns. & Archivists), *Exec. Secy.* M. Hermoso, Apdo. 6283, Caracas 101.

Wales

See United Kingdom.

Yugoslavia

Društvo Bibliotekara Bosne i Hercegovine—DB BiH (Lib. Assn. of Bosnia and Herzegovina), *Exec. Secy.* Nada Milićević, Obala 42, YU-71000 Sarajevo.

Društvo Bibliotekarjev Slovenije—DBS (Society of Libns. in Slovenia), *Exec. Secy.* Ana Martelanc, Turjaška 1, YU-61000 Ljubljana.

Hrvatsko bibliotekarsko društvo—HBD

(Croatian Lib. Assn.), *Pres.* Mira Mikačić; *Exec. Secy.* Mirjana Žugčić, National & Univ. Lib., Marulićev trg 21, YU-41000 Zagreb.

Savez Bibliotečkih Radnika Srbije (Union of Lib. Workers of Serbia), *Exec. Secy.* Branka Popović, Skerlićeva 1, YU-11000 Belgrade.

Savez Društava Bibliotekara Jugoslavije (Union of Libns. Assns. of Yugoslavia), 21000 Novi Sad. *Pres.* R. Vukoslavović; *Secy.* D. Bajić.

Sojuz na društvata na bibliotekarite na SR Makedonija (Union of Librarians Association of Macedonia), Bul. "Goce Delčev" br. 6, Box 566, YU-91000 Skopje.

Zaire

Association Zairoise des Archivistes, Bibliothecaires, et Documentalistes — AZABDO (Zairian Assn. of Archivists, Libns. & Documentalists), *Exec. Secy.* Mulamba Mukunya, Box 805, Kinshasa XI.

Zambia

Zambia Lib. Assn. (ZLA), Box 32839, Lusaka.

Zimbabwe

Zimbabwe Lib. Assn. — ZLA, *Hon. Secy.* R. Molam, Box 3133, Harare.

Directory of Book Trade and Related Organizations

Book Trade Associations, United States and Canada

For more extensive information on the associations listed in this section, see the annual issues of the *Literary Market Place* (Bowker).

Advertising Typographers Assn. of America, Inc., 461 Eighth Ave., New York, NY 10001. Tel: 212-594-0685. *Exec. Secy.* Walter A. Dew, Jr.

American Booksellers Assn., Inc., 122 E. 42 St., New York, NY 10168. Tel: 212-867-9060. *Past Pres.* Donald Laing.

American Institute of Graphic Arts, 1059 Third Ave., New York, NY 10021. Tel: 212-752-0813. *Pres.* David Brown; *Exec. Dir.* Caroline W. Hightower.

American Medical Publishers Assn. *Pres.* Albert E. Meier, W. B. Saunders, W. Washington Sq., Philadelphia, PA 19105. Tel: 215-574-4700; *Pres.-Elect.* Mercedes Bierman, Wiley Medical, John Wiley & Sons, Inc., 605 Third Ave., New York, NY 10158. Tel: 212-850-6000; *Secy.-Treas.* Lewis Reines, Churchill-Livingstone, Inc., 1560 Broadway, New York, NY 10036. Tel: 212-819-5400.

American Printing History Assn., Box 4922, Grand Central Sta., New York, NY 10163. *Pres.* E. H. (Pat) Taylor; *V.P. for Programs.* Alice Schreyer; *V.P. for Publications.* Stephen O. Saxe; *V.P. for Membership.* Ginna Johnson; *Secy.* Renee Weber; *Treas.* Philip Sperling; *Ed., Printing History.* Anna Lou Ashby; *Ed. & Asst. Ed., The Alpha Letter.* Catherine T. Brody, Philip Sperling.

American Society for Information Science (ASIS), 1010 16 St. N.W., Washington, DC 20036. Tel: 202-659-3644. *Exec. Dir.* Samuel B. Beatty.

American Society of Indexers, 235 Park Ave. S., 8th fl., New York, NY 10003. *Pres.* Dorothy Thomas, 123 W. 74 St., New York, NY 10023. Tel: 212-799-0970; *V.P.* Hans Wellisch, 5015 Berwyn Rd., College Park, MD 20740. Tel: 301-454-3785; *Secy.* Martha Spiegel, 85 Storer Ave., Pelham, NY 10803. Tel: 914-235-8738; *Treas.* Cynthia Weber, 195 Sunny Hill Rd., Northampton, PA 18067. Tel: 212-837-9615.

American Society of Journalists & Authors, 1501 Broadway, Suite 1907, New York, NY 10036. *Pres.* John H. Ingersoll; *Exec. V.P.* Evelyn Kaye; *V.Ps.* Dodi Schultz, Roberta Roesch; *Secy.* Suzanne Loebl; *Treas.* Alden Todd. Tel: 212-997-0947.

American Society of Magazine Photographers (ASMP), 205 Lexington Ave., New York, NY 10016. Tel: 212-889-9144. *Exec. Dir.* Stuart Kahan; *Pres.* Harvey Lloyd; *1st V.P.* Lou Jacobs, Jr.; *2nd V.P.* Helen Marcus; *Admin. Dir.* Sandra Peel.

American Society of Picture Professionals, Inc., Box 5283, Grand Central Sta., New York, NY 10163. *Natl. Pres.* Ben Michalski; *Natl. Secy.* Roberta Guerette.

American Translators Assn., 109 Croton Ave., Ossining, NY 10562. Tel:

914-941-1500. *Pres.* Virginia Eva Berry; *Pres.-Elect.* Patricia Newman; *Secy.* Deanna Hammond; *Treas.* Karl Kummer; *Staff Administrator.* Rosemary Malia.

Antiquarian Booksellers Assn. of America, Inc., 50 Rockefeller Plaza, New York, NY 10020. Tel: 212-757-9395. *Pres.* E. Woodburn; *V.P.* L. Weinstein; *Secy.* J. Lowe; *Treas.* R. Wapner; *Administrative Asst.* Janice M. Farina.

Assn. of American Publishers, One Park Ave., New York, NY 10016. Tel: 212-689-8920. *Pres.* Townsend Hoopes; *Sr. V.P.* Thomas D. McKee; *V.P. School Div.* Donald A. Eklund; *Dirs.* Phyllis L. Ball, Jane Lippe-Fine, Parker B. Ladd, Saundra L. Smith; *Washington Office.* 2005 Massachusetts Ave. N.W., Washington, DC 20036. Tel: 202-232-3335; *Sr. V.P.* Richard P. Kleeman; *Dirs.* Roy H. Millenson, Diane G. Rennert, Carol A. Risher; *Chpn.* Brooks Thomas, Harper & Row; *V. Chpn.* Donald A. Schaefer, Prentice-Hall; *Secy.* Andrew H. Neilly, Jr., John Wiley & Sons; *Treas.* Martin A. Tash, Plenum Publishing.

Assn. of American Univ. Presses, One Park Ave., New York, NY 10016. Tel: 212-889-6040. *Pres.* Arthur J. Rosenthal, Dir., Harvard Univ. Press; *Exec. Dir.* Richard Koffler. Address correspondence to the executive director, or to Andrea J. Teter, Dir., Membership Services.

Assn. of Book Travelers, c/o *Pres.* Edward Ponger, 21 Colingwood Rd., Marlboro, NJ 07746; *Treas.* Vicki Brooks, Cerberus Group; *Secy.* Conrad Heintzelman. Address correspondence to the president.

Assn. of Canadian Publishers, 70 The Esplanade, 3rd fl., Toronto, Ontario M5E 1R2 Canada. Tel: 416-361-1408. *Pres.* James J. Douglas; *V.P.* Catherine Wilson; *Treas.* Arden Ford; *Secy.* Karl Siegler; *Exec. Dir.* Phyllis Yaffe. Address correspondence to the executive director.

Assn. of Jewish Book Publishers, House of Living Judaism, 838 Fifth Ave., New York, NY 10021. *Pres.* Sol Scharfstein. Address correspondence to the president.

Bibliographical Society of America. *See* "National Library & Information-Industry Associations, United States and Canada," earlier in Part 6, for more detailed information — *Ed.*

Book Industry Study Group, Inc., 160 Fifth Ave., New York, NY 10010. Tel: 212-929-1393. *Chpn.* Leo Albert; *V. Chpn.* Martin P. Levin; *Treas.* John U. Wisotzkey; *Secy.* Robert W. Bell; *Managing Agent.* SKP Associates. Address correspondence to Sandra K. Paul.

Book League of New York. *Pres.* Alfred H. Lane, 19 Barrow St., New York, NY 10014. Tel: 212-243-6242.

Book Manufacturers Institute, 111 Prospect St., Stamford, CT 06901. Tel: 203-324-9670. *Pres.* B. Carl Jones, Pres., Haddon Craftsmen, Inc., Ash Street & Wyoming Ave., Scranton, PA 18509; *Exec. V.P.* Douglas E. Horner. Address correspondence to the executive vice president.

Book Publicists of Southern California, 6430 Sunset Blvd., Suite 503, Hollywood, CA 90028. Tel: 213-461-3921. *Pres.* Irwin Zucker; *V.P.* Sol Marshall; *Secy.* Elsie Rogers; *Treas.* Steven Jay Rubin.

Book Week Headquarters, Children's Book Council, Inc., 67 Irving Place, New York, NY 10003. Tel: 212-254-2666. *Exec. Dir.* John Donovan; *Chpn. 1984.* Ava Weiss, Greenwillow Books, 105 Madison Ave., New York, NY 10016. Tel: 212-889-3050.

The Bookbinders' Guild of New York, c/o *Secy.* Joel Moss, A. Horowitz and Sons, 300 Fairfield Rd., Fairfield, NJ 07006. Tel: 201-575-7070; *Pres.* Sam Green,

Murray Printing Co., 60 E. 42 St., New York, NY 10017; *V.P.* Thomas R. Snyder, Dikeman Laminating, 181 Sargeant Ave., Clifton, NJ 07013; *Treas.* Eugene Sanchez, William Morrow & Co., 105 Madison Ave., New York, NY 10016. *Asst. Secy.* Hank Perrine, John Wiley & Sons Inc., 605 Third Ave., New York, NY 10158.

Bookbuilders of Boston, Inc., c/o *Pres.* Martin B. Sweeney, Maple-Vail Book Manufacturing Group, 313 Washington St., Newton, MA 02158. Tel: 617-965-1120; *1st V.P.* Janis Capone, Janis Capone Designs, 383 Ferry St., Marshfield, MA 02050. Tel: 617-837-8429.

Bookbuilders West, 170 Ninth St., San Francisco, CA 94103. *Pres.* Pam Smith, Carpenter/Offutt Paper Co., 333 Oyster Point Blvd., S. San Francisco, CA 94080. Tel: 415-873-1383; *V.P.* Bob Odell, Univ. of California Press, 2223 Fulton St., Berkeley, CA 94720. Tel: 415-642-5394; *Secy.* Michelle Hogan, Mayfield Publishing Co., 285 Hamilton Ave., Palo Alto, CA 94301. Tel: 415-326-1640; *Treas.* Dave Delano, Webcrafters Inc., 6247 Paso Los Cerritos, San Jose, CA 95120. Tel: 408-268-7109. (Address correspondence to the secretary.)

Canadian Book Publishers' Council, 45 Charles St. E., 7th fl., Toronto, ON M4Y 1S2, Canada. Tel: 416-964-7231. *Pres.* Alan Cobham, Nelson, Canada; *1st V.P.* Peter Maik, Doubleday; *Exec. Dir.* Jacqueline Hushion; *Member Organizations.* The School Group, The College Group, The Trade Group, The Paperback Group.

Canadian Booksellers Assn., 49 Laing St., Toronto, ON M4L 2N4, Canada. Tel: 416-469-5976. *Convention Mgr.* Irene Read.

Chicago Book Clinic, 664 N. Michigan Ave., Suite 720, Chicago, IL 60611. Tel: 312-951-8254. *Pres.* Stuart J. Murphy, Ligature, Inc.; *Exec. V.P.* Trudi Jenny, Ligature, Inc.; *Treas.* Brad Heywood, The Lehigh Press, Inc.

Chicago Publishers Assn., c/o *Pres.* Robert J. R. Follett, Follett Corp., 1000 W. Washington Blvd., Chicago, IL 60607. Tel: 312-666-4300.

The Children's Book Council, 67 Irving Place, New York, NY 10003. Tel: 212-254-2666. *Exec. Dir.* John Donovan; *Assoc. Dir.* Paula Quint; *Asst. Dir.* Christine Stawicki; *Pres.* Richard W. Jackson, Bradbury Press, Inc., 2 Overhill Rd., Scarsdale, NY 10583. Tel: 914-472-5100.

Christian Booksellers Assn., Box 200, 2620 Venetucci Blvd., Colorado Springs, CO 80901. Tel: 303-576-7880. *Exec. V.P.* John T. Bass; *V.P. & Gen. Mgr.* Bill Anderson.

Connecticut Book Publishers Assn., c/o *Pres.* Alex M. Yudkin, Associated Booksellers, 147 McKinley Ave., Bridgeport, CT 06606; *Secy.* Barbara O'Brien; *Treas.* John Atkin.

The Copyright Society of the U.S.A., New York Univ. School of Law, 40 Washington Sq. S., New York, NY 10012. Tel: 212-598-2280/2210. *Pres.* Alan J. Hartnick; *Secy.* Raymond D. Weisbond; *Exec. Dir.* Alan Latman; *Asst.* Kate McKay.

Council on Interracial Books for Children, Inc., 1841 Broadway, New York, NY 10023. Tel: 212-757-5339. *Dir.* Bradford Chambers; *Pres.* Beryl Banfield; *V.Ps.* Albert V. Schwartz, Frieda Zames, Irma Garcia, Marylou Byler; *Managing Ed., Interracial Books for Children Bulletin.* Ruth Charnes; *Book Review Coord.* Lyla Hoffman; *Dir., CIBC Racism & Sexism Resource Center for Educators.* Robert B. Moore; *Secy.* Leonidas Guzman; *Workshop Coord.* Walteen Grady-Truely; *Textbooks and Social Justice Project.* Howard Dodson, Jr., Madelon Bedell; *Subscriptions Mgr.* Tom Bigornia.

Evangelical Christian Publishers Assn.,

Box 2439, Vista, CA 92083. Tel: 619-941-1636. *Exec. Dir.* C. E. (Ted) Andrew.

Graphic Artists Guild, 30 E. 20 St., Rm. 405, New York, NY 10003. Tel: 212-777-7353. *Pres.* Jeffrey Seaver.

Guild of Book Workers, 663 Fifth Ave., New York, NY 10022. Tel: 212-757-6454. *Pres.* Caroline F. Schimmel.

Information Industry Assn. *See* "National Library and Information-Industry Associations," earlier in Part 6 — *Ed.*

International Assn. of Book Publishing Consultants. *Pres.* Joseph Marks, 485 Fifth Ave., New York, NY 10017. Tel: 212-867-6341.

International Assn. of Printing House Craftsmen, Inc., 7599 Kenwood Rd., Cincinnati, OH 45236. Tel: 513-891-0611. *Pres.* Donald F. Bentz; *Exec. V.P.* John A. Davies.

International Copyright Information Center (INCINC), Assn. of American Publishers, 2005 Massachusetts Ave. N.W., Washington, DC 20036. Tel: 202-232-3335. *Dir.* Carol A. Risher.

International Standard Book Numbering Agency, 205 E. 42 St., New York, NY 10017. Tel: 212-916-1800, 1811, 1812. *Dir.* Emery I. Koltay; *Coord.* Beatrice Jacobson; *Officers.* Alina Hernandez, Scott MacFarland, Peter Simon, Leigh Yuster.

JWB Jewish Book Council, 15 E. 26 St., New York, NY 10010. Tel: 212-532-4949. *Pres.* Blu Greenberg; *Dir.* Ruth S. Frank.

Library Binding Institute, 1421 E. Wayzata Blvd., Suite 51, Wayzata, MN 55391. Tel: 612-475-2241. *Pres.* Albert L. Leitschuh, CAE; *General Counsel.* Dudley A. Weiss; *Technical Consultant.* Werner Rebsamen.

Magazine & Paperback Marketing Institute (MPMI), 344 Main St., Suite 205, Mount Kisco, NY 10549. Tel: 914-666-6788. *Exec. V.P.* Theodore A. Pleva.

Metropolitan Lithographers Assn., 21 E. 73 St., New York, NY 10021. Tel: 212-772-1027. *Pres.* Sherwood A. Barnhard; *Exec. Dir.* Kenneth I. Nowak.

Midwest Book Travelers Assn., c/o *Pres.* Ted Heinecken, Heinecken Assocs., 1733 N. Mohawk St., Chicago, IL 60614. Tel: 312-649-9181; *V.P.* Pat Friedlander; *Treas.* Robert Rainer; *Secy.* Michael Brennan.

Minnesota Book Publishers Roundtable. *Pres.* Chas. Wetherall, Wetherall Publishing, 510 N. First, Minneapolis, MN 55401; *V.P.* Eric Rohmann, Winston Press, 430 Oak Grove, Minneapolis, MN 55403; *Secy.-Treas.* Vicki Lansky, The Book Peddlers, 18326 Minnetonka Blvd., Deephaven, MN 55391. Tel: 612-475-1505. Address correspondence to Vicki Lansky.

National Assn. of College Stores, 528 E. Lorain St., Box 58, Oberlin, OH 44074. Tel: 216-775-7777. *Pres.* Wade Meadows, Student Book & Supply Store, Univ. of Tennessee, Knoxville, TN 37996; *Exec. Dir.* Garis F. Distelhorst.

National Council of Churches of Christ in the U.S.A., Div. of Education & Ministry, 475 Riverside Dr., New York, NY 10115. Tel: 212-870-2271/2272. *Assoc. Gen. Secy.* David Ng.

National Micographics Assn. *See* Association for Information and Image Management, under "National Library & Information-Industry Associations, United States and Canada," earlier in Part 6, for more detailed information — *Ed.*

New Mexico Book League, 8632 Horacio Place N.E., Albuquerque, NM 87111. Tel: 505-299-8940. *Exec. Dir.* Dwight A. Myers; *Pres.* Cecil Clotfelter; *V.P.* Harold Burnett; *Treas.* Frank N. Skinner; *Ed.* Carol A. Myers.

New York Rights & Permissions Group, c/o *Chpn.* Dorothy McKittrick Harris, Reader's Digest General Books, 750

Third Ave., New York, NY 10017. Tel: 212-850-7009.

Northern California Booksellers Assn., c/o *Pres.* Andy Ross, Cody's Books, 2454 Telegraph Ave., Berkeley, CA 94704.

Periodical & Book Assn. of America, Inc., 313 W. 53 St., New York, NY 10019. Tel: 212-307-6182. *Exec. Dir.* Joseph Greco; *Pres.* George Mavety; *V.P./Treas.* Gerald Rothberg.

Periodical Distributors of Canada, c/o *Pres.* Jim Neill, 120 Sinnot Rd., Scarborough, ON M1L 4NI, Canada. Tel: 416-752-8720; *V.P.* Cliff Connelly, 5 Kirkland St., Box 488, Kirland Lake, ON, Canada; *Secy.-Treas.* J. E. Stockdale, 417 Bagot St., Kingston, ON K7K 3C1, Canada; *Exec. Secy. & Mktg. Dir.* Ed McKim, 202 Hallett Ave., Whitby, ON L1N 5K8, Canada.

Philadelphia Book Clinic, *Secy.-Treas.* Thomas Colaiezzi, Lea & Febiger, 600 Washington Sq., Philadelphia, PA 19106. Tel: 215-925-8700.

Pi Beta Alpha (formerly Professional Bookmen of America, Inc.), 1215 Farwell Dr., Madison, WI 53704. *Pres.* Roland J. Stickney; *V.P.* Linda K. Schoeff; *Treas.* Steve Moline; *Pres.-Elect.* Dale E. Best; *Exec. Secy.* Charles L. Schmalbach.

Printing Industries of Metropolitan New York, Inc., 5 Penn Plaza, New York, NY 10001. Tel: 212-279-2100. *Pres.* James J. Conner III; *Dir., Industrial Relations.* James E. Horne; *Dir., Government Affairs.* Stuart L. Litvin; *Dir., Industry Activities.* Gary J. Miller.

Proofreaders Club of New York, c/o *Pres.* Allan Treshan, 38-15 149 St., Flushing, NY 11354. Tel: 212-461-8509.

Publishers' Ad Club, c/o *Secy.* Belle Carter Blanchard, 670 West End Ave., New York, NY 10025. Tel: 212-362-8926; *Pres.* Susan Ball, William Morrow & Co., 105 Madison Ave., New York, NY 10016. Tel: 212-889-3050; *V.P.*

Caroline Barnett, Denhard & Stewart, 122 E. 42 St., New York, NY 10017. Tel: 212-986-1900; *Treas.* Jack Draper, Time Magazine, 1271 Ave. of the Americas, New York, NY 10020. Tel: 212-841-3267.

Publishers' Alliance, c/o James W. Millar, Box 3, Glen Ridge, NJ 07028. Tel: 201-429-0169.

Publishers' Library Marketing Group, *Pres.* John Mason, Putnam Publishing Group, 51 Madison Ave., New York, NY 10010. Tel: 212-689-9200; *V.P.* Janet Seigel, Dell/Delacorte Publishing Co., 245 E. 47 St., New York, NY 10017. Tel: 212-605-3341; *Treas.* Sue Kalkbrenner, William Morrow & Co., 105 Madison Ave., New York, NY 10016. Tel: 212-889-3050; *Corres. Secy.* Jayne Willcock, Frederick Warne & Co., 2 Park Ave., New York, NY 10016. Tel: 212-686-9630; *Recording Secy.* Regina Dahlgren, Ganis & Harris, Inc., 119 W. 57 St., New York, NY 10019. Tel: 212-247-0172.

Publishers' Publicity Assn., c/o *Pres.* Harriet Blacker, Putnam Publishing Group, 200 Madison Ave., New York, NY 10016. Tel: 212-576-8850; *V.P.* Jill Danzig, Peter Bedrick Books, 125 E. 23 St., New York, NY 10010. Tel: 212-777-1187; *Secy.* Randall Warner, Alfred Knopf, 201 E. 50 St., New York, NY 10022. Tel: 212-572-2018; *Treas.* Marcia Burch, Penguin Books, 40 W. 23 St., New York, NY 10010. Tel: 212-807-7300.

The Religion Publishing Group, c/o *Secy.-Treas.* Dorothy M. Harris, Reader's Digest General Books, 750 Third Ave., New York, NY 10017. Tel: 212-850-7009; *Pres.* Brad Miiver, Bantam Books, 666 Fifth Ave., New York, NY 10103. Tel: 212-554-9663.

Research & Engineering Council of the Graphic Arts Industry, Inc., Box 2740, Landover Hills, MD 20784. Tel: 301-577-5400. *Pres.* William O. Krenkler;

1st V.P.-Secy. Frank E. Schaeffer; *2nd V.P.-Treas.* George Kaplan; *Managing Dir.* Harold A. Molz.

Société de Developpement du Livre et du Périodique, 1151 r. Alexandre-DeSeve, Montreal, PQ H2L 2T7, Canada. Tel: 514-524-7528. *Prés.* Guy Saint-Jean; *Directeur Général.* Louise Rochon, Association des Editeurs Canadiens, *Prés.* M. René Bonenfant; Association des Libraries du Québec, *Prés.* Hélène Chassé; Société Canadienne Française de Protection du Droit d'Auteur, *Prés.* Pierre Tisseyre; Société des Editeurs de Manuels Scolaires du Quebéc, *Prés.* Pierre Tisseyre.

Society of Author's Representatives, Inc., Box 650, Old Chelsea Sta., New York, NY 10113. Tel: 212-741-1356. *Pres.* Carl Brandt; *Exec. Secy.* Susan Bell.

Society of Photographer & Artist Representatives, Inc. (SPAR), 1123 Broadway, Rm. 914, New York, NY 10010. Tel: 212-924-6023. *Pres.* Anthony Andriulli.

Society of Photographers in Communication. *See* American Society of Magazine Photographers (ASMP).

Southern California Booksellers Assn., c/o *Pres.* Glenn Goldman, c/o Book Soup, 8868 Sunset Blvd., Los Angeles, CA 90069. Tel: 213-659-3110; *V.P.* Lori Flores, c/o Children's Book & Music Center, 2500 Santa Monica, CA 90404. Tel: 213-829-0215; *Secy.* Alan Kishbaugh, Publisher's Rep., 8136 Cornett Dr., Los Angeles, CA 90046; *Treas.* Larry Todd, Bookseller, 463 N. Rodeo, Los Angeles, CA 90210. Tel: 213-274-7301.

Technical Assn. of the Pulp & Paper Industry (TAPPI), Technology Park/Atlanta, Box 105113, Atlanta, GA 30348. Tel: 404-446-1400. *Pres.* Terry O. Norris; *V.P.* William H. Griggs; *Exec. Dir.* W. L. Cullison; *Vice Chpn. Bd. of Dirs.* Philip E. Nethercut.

West Coast Bookmen's Assn., 27 McNear

Dr., San Rafael, CA 94901. *Secy.* Frank G. Goodall.

Women's National Book Assn., c/o *National Pres.* Sylvia H. Cross, 19824 Septo St., Chatsworth, CA 91311. Tel: 213-886-8448 (home); *V.P./Pres.-Elect.* Sandra K. Paul, SKP Associates, 160 Fifth Ave., New York, NY 10010. Tel: 212-675-7804 (office); *Secy.* Cathy Rentschler, H. W. Wilson Co., 950 University Ave., Bronx, NY 10452. Tel: 212-588-8400 ext. 257 (office); *Treas.* Sandra J. Souza, 1606 Stafford Rd., Fall River, MA 02721. Tel: 617-678-4179 (home); *Past Pres.* Mary Glenn Hearne, Public Library of Nashville and Davidson Counties, Eighth Ave., North and Union, Nashville, TN 37203. Tel: 615-244-4700 ext. 68 (office); *National Committee Chairs: Pannell Chpn.* Ann Heidbreder Eastman, College of Arts and Sciences, Virginia Polytechnic Institute & State Univ., Blacksburg, VA 24061. Tel: 703-961-6390 (office); *Status of Women.* Claire Friedland, 36 E. 36 St., New York, NY 10016. Tel: 212-685-6205; *Ed. The Bookwoman.* Jean K. Crawford, Abingdon Press, 201 Eighth Ave. S., Nashville, TN 37202. Tel: 615-749-6422 (office); *Book Review Ed., The Bookwoman.* Mary V. Gaver, 300 Virginia Ave., Danville, VA 24541. Tel: 804-799-6746; *Membership Chpn.* Anne J. Richter, 55 N. Mountain Ave., A-2, Montclair, NJ 07042. Tel: 201-746-5166 (home); *UN/NGO Rep.* Sally Wecksler, 170 West End Ave., New York, NY 10023. Tel: 212-787-2239 (office); *Finance Chpn.* Sandra K. Paul, SKP Associates, 160 Fifth Ave., New York, NY 10010. Tel: 212-675-7804 (office); *Chapter Presidents: Binghamton.* Gilbert Williams, The Bellevue Press, 60 Schubert St., Binghamton, NY 13905. Tel: 607-729-0819; *Boston.* Cynthia Chapin, Little, Brown College Div., 18 Tremont St., Boston, MA 02106. Tel: 617-227-0730; *Cleveland.* Billie Joy Reinhart,

2856 Fairfax, Cleveland Heights, OH 44118. Tel: 216-371-0459; *Detroit.* Ruth Edberg, 924 S. Woodward #101, Royal Oak, MI 48067. Tel: 313-548-6783; *Los Angeles.* Lou Keay, 11684 Ventura Blvd., #309, Studio City, CA 91604. Tel: 213-789-9175 (office); *Nashville.* Margaret B. Burns, 6416 Harding Rd., Nashville, TN 37205. Tel: 615-356-9166 (home); *New York.* Lucy Hebard,

Times Books, 3 Park Ave., New York, NY 10016. Tel: 212-725-2050; *San Francisco.* Elizabeth Pomada, 1029 Jones St., San Francisco, CA 94109. Tel: 415-673-0939 (office); *Washington, DC/ Baltimore, MD.* Kevin Maricle, Office of the General Counsel, U.S. Copyright Office, Lib. of Congress, Washington, DC 20559. Tel: 202-287-8380.

International and Foreign Book Trade Associations

For Canadian book trade associations, see the preceding section, "Book Trade Associations, United States and Canada." For a more extensive list of book trade organizations outside the United States and Canada, with more detailed information, consult *International Literary Market Place* (R. R. Bowker), an annual publication, which also provides extensive lists of major bookstores and publishers in each country.

International

Antiquarian Booksellers Assn. (International), 45 E. Hill, London SW18 2QZ, England.

International Booksellers Federation (IBF), Grunangergasse 4, A-1010 Vienna 1, Austria. *Secy.-Gen.* Gerhard Prosser.

International League of Antiquarian Booksellers, c/o *Pres.* John Lawson, Kingsholm, East Hagbourne, Oxon OX11 9LN, England.

International Publishers Assn., 3 av. de Miremont, CH-1206 Geneva, Switzerland. *Secy.-Gen.* J. Alexis Koutchoumow.

National

Argentina

Cámara Argentina de Editores de Libros (Council of Argentine Book Publishers), Talcahuano 374, p. 3, Of. 7, Buenos Aires 1013.

Cámara Argentina de Publicaciones (Argentine Publications Assn.), Reconquista 1011, p. 6, 1003 Buenos Aires. *Pres.* Manuel Rodriguez.

Cámara Argentina del Libro (Argentine Book Assn.), Av. Belgrano 1580, p. 6, 1093 Buenos Aires. *Pres.* Jaime Rodriguez.

Federación Argentina de Librerías, Papelerías y Actividades Afines (Federation of Bookstores, Stationers and Related Activities), Balcarce 179/83, Rosario, Santa Fe. *Pres.* Isaac Kostzer.

Australia

Assn. of Australian Univ. Presses, c/o NSW University Press, Box 1, Kensington, N.S.W. 2033. *Pres.* Douglas S. Howie.

Australian Book Publishers Assn., 161

Clarence St., Sydney, N.S.W. 2000. *Dir.* Sandra Forbes.

Australian Booksellers Assn., Box 3254, Sydney, N.S.W. 2001. *Dir.* T.A.M. Cheshire.

Austria

Hauptverband der graphischen Unternehmungen Österreichs (Austrian Graphical Assn.), Grünangergasse 4, A-1010 Vienna 1. *Pres.* Komm.-Rat Dr. Dkfm. Willi Maiwald; *Gen. Secy.* Dr. Hans Inmann.

Hauptverband des österreichischen Buchhandels (Austrian Publishers and Booksellers Assn.), Grünangergasse 4, A-1010 Vienna. *Secy.* Gerhard Prosser.

Osterreichischer Verlegerverband (Assn. of Austrian Publishers), Grünangergasse 4, A-1010 Vienna. *Secy.* Gerhard Prosser.

Verband der Antiquare Österreichs (Austrian Antiquarian Booksellers Assn.), Grünangergasse 4, A-1010 Vienna. *Secy.* Gerhard Prosser.

Belgium

Association des Editeurs Belges (Belgian Publishers Assn.), 111 av. du Parc. B-1060 Brussels. *Dir.* J. De Raeymaeker.

Cercle Belge de la Librairie (Belgian Booksellers Assn.), r. du Luxembourg 5, bte. 1, B-1040 Brussels.

Syndicat Belge de la Librairie Ancienne et Moderne (Belgian Assn. of Antiquarian and Modern Booksellers), r. du Chêne 21, B-1000 Brussels.

Vereniging ter Bevordering van het Vlaamse Boekwezen (Assn. for the Promotion of Flemish Books), Frankrijklei 93, B-2000 Antwerp. *Secy.* A. Wouters. Member organizations: Algemene Vlaamse Boekverkopersbond; Uitgeversbond-Vereniging van Uitgevers van Nederlandstalige Boeken at the same address; and Bond-Alleenverko-

pers van Nederlandstalige Boeken (Book importers), Bijkoevelaan 12, B 2110 Wijnegem. *Pres.* M. Cornu.

Bolivia

Cámara Boliviana del Libro (Bolivian Booksellers Assn.), Box 682, La Paz. *Pres. Lic.* Javier Gisbert.

Brazil

Associação Brasileira de Livreiros Antiquarios (Brazilian Assn. of Antiquarian Booksellers), Rua do Rosario 155, 2° p., Rio de Janeiro RJ.

Associação Brasileira do Livro (Brazilian Booksellers Assn.), Av. 13 de Maio 23, andar 16, Rio de Janeiro. *Dir.* Alberjano Torres.

Cámara Brasileira do Livro (Brazilian Book Assn.), Av. Ipiranga 1267, andar 10, São Paulo. *Secy.* Jose Gorayeb.

Sindicato Nacional dos Editores de Livros (Brazilian Book Publishers Assn.), Av. Rio Branco 37, 15 andar, Salas 1503/6 e 1510/12, 20097 Rio de Janeiro. *Gen. Secy.* Berta Ribeiro.

Bulgaria

Darzhavno Sdruzhenie "Bulgarska Kniga i Pechat" (Bulgarian Book and Printing State Assn.), 11, Slaveykov Sq., Sofia 1000.

Soyuz Knigoizdatelite i Knizharite (Union of Publishers and Booksellers), vu Solum 4, Sofia.

Burma

Burmese Publishers Union, 146 Bogyoke Market, Rangoon.

Chile

Cámara Chilena del Libro, Av. Bulnes 188, Santiago. *Secy.* A. Newman.

Colombia

Cámara Colombiana de la Industria Editorial (Colombian Publishers Council), Cr. 7a, No. 17-51, Of. 409-410, Apdo. áereo 8998, Bogota. *Exec. Dir.* Hipólito Hincapié.

Czechoslovakia

Ministerstvo Kultury CSR, Odbor Knižni Kultury (Ministry of Culture CSR, Dept. for Publishing and Book Trade), Staré Mésto, námesti Perštyně 1, 117 65 Prague 1.

Denmark

Danske Antikvarboghandlerforening (Danish Antiquarian Booksellers Assn.), Box 2184, DK-1017 Copenhagen.

Danske Boghandlerforening (Danish Booksellers Assn.), Boghandlernes Hus, Siljangade 6, DK-2300 Copenhagen S. *Secy.* Elisabeth Brodersen.

Danske Forlaeggerforening (Danish Publishers Assn.), Kobmagergade 11, DK-1150 Copenhagen K. *Dir.* Erik V. Krustrup.

Ecuador

Sociedad de Libreros del Ecuador (Booksellers Society of Ecuador), C. Bolivar 268 y Venezuela, Of. 501, p. 5, Quito. *Secy.* Eduardo Ruiz G.

Finland

Kirja-ja Paperikauppojen Liitto ry (Finnish Booksellers & Stationers Assn.), Pieni Roobertinkatu 13 B 26, SF-00130 Helsinki 13. *Secy.* Olli Eräkivi.

Suomen Antikvariaattiyhdistys Finska Antikvariatforeningen (Finnish Antiquarian Booksellers Assn.), P. Makasiininkatu 6, Helsinki 13.

Suomen Kustannusyhdistys (Publishers Assn. of Finland), Merimiehenkatu 12 A6, SF-00150, Helsinki 15. *Secy.-Gen.* Unto Lappi.

France

Editions du Cercle de la Librairie (Circle of Professionals of the Book Trade), 35, rue Grégoire-de-Tours, F-75279 Paris, Cedex 06. *Dir.* Pierre Fredet.

Fédération française des Syndicats de Libraires (French Booksellers Assn.), 259 rue St.-Honoré, F-75001 Paris.

Office de Promotion de l'Edition Française (Promotion Office of French Publishing), 35, rue Grégoire-de-Tours, F-75279 Paris, Cedex 06. *Managing Dir.* Pierre-Dominique Parent; *Secy.-Gen.* Marc Franconie.

Syndicat National de la Librairie Ancienne et Moderne (SLAM), 47 rue St. André des Arts, F-75006, Paris. *Pres.* Jeanne Laffitte.

Syndicat National de l'Edition (French Publishers Assn.), 35, rue Grégoire de Tours, 75279 Paris, Cedex 06. *Secy.* Pierre Fredet.

Syndicat National des Importateurs et Exportateurs de Livres (National French Assn. of Book Importers and Exporters), 35, rue Grégoire de Tours 75279 Paris, Cedex 06.

German Democratic Republic

Börsenverein der Deutschen Buchhändler zu Leipzig (Assn. of GDR Publishers and Booksellers in Leipzig), Gerichtsweg 26, 7010 Leipzig.

Germany (Federal Republic of)

Börsenverein des Deutschen Buchhandels (German Publishers and Booksellers Assn.), Grosser Hirschgraben 17-21, Box 2404, D-6000 Frankfurt am Main 1. *Secy.* Dr. Hans-Karl von Kupsch.

Bundeverband der Deutschen Versand-
buchhändler e.V. (National Federation
of German Mail-Order Booksellers), An
der Ringkirche 6, D-6200 Wiesbaden.
Dirs. Dr. Stefan Rutkowsky; Kornelia
Wahl.

Landesverband der Buchhändler und
Verleger in Niedersachsen e.V. (Provincial Federation of Booksellers & Publishers in Lower Saxony), Hausmannstr.
2, D-3000 Hannover 1. *Manging Dir.*
Wolfgang Grimpe.

Presse-Grosso — Verband Deutscher
Buch-, Zeitungs-und Zeitschriften-
Grossisten e.V. (Federation of German
Wholesalers of Books, Newspapers &
Periodicals), Classen-Kappelmann-Str.
24, D-5000 Cologne 41.

Verband Bayerischer Verlage und Buch-
handlungen e.V. (Bavarian Publishers &
Booksellers Federation), Thierschstr.
17, D-8000 Munich 22. *Secy.* F. Nosske.

Verband Deutscher Antiquare e.V. (German Antiquarian Booksellers Assn.),
Unterer Anger 15, D-8000 Munich 40.

Verband Deutscher Bühnenverleger e.V.
(Federation of German Theatrical Publishers & Drama Agencies), Bismarckstr.
17, D-1000 Berlin 12.

Ghana

Ghana Booksellers Assn., Box 7869, Accra.

Great Britain

See United Kingdom.

Greece

Syllogos Ekdoton Vivliopolon (Greek
Publishers & Booksellers Assn.), 54
Themistocleus St., Athens 145.

Hong Kong

Hong Kong Booksellers & Stationers
Assn., Man Wah House, Kowloon.

Hungary

Magyar Könyvkiadók és Könyvterjesztök
Egyesülése (Hungarian Publishers &
Booksellers Assn.), Vörösmarty tér 1,
H-1051 Budapest. *Pres.* György Bernát;
Secy. Gen. Ferenc Zöld.

Iceland

Iceland Publishers Assn., Laufasvegi 12,
101 Reykjavik. *Pres.* Oliver Steinn Jó-
hannesson, Strandgötu, 31, 220 Haf-
narfjördur. *Gen. Mgr.* Björn Gíslason.

India

All-India Booksellers & Publishers Assn.,
17L Connaught Circus, Box 328, New
Delhi 110001. *Pres.* A. N. Varma.

Bombay Booksellers & Publishers Assn.,
c/o Bhadkamkar Marg, Navjivan Cooperative Housing Society, Bldg. 3, 6th fl.,
Office 25, Bombay 400 008.

Booksellers & Publishers Assn. of South
India, c/o Higginbothams, Ltd., 814,
Anna Salai, Mount Rd., Madras 600
002.

Delhi State Booksellers & Publishers
Assn., c/o The Students' Stores, Box
1511, 100 006 Delhi. *Pres.* Devendra
Sharma.

Federation of Indian Publishers, 18/I-C
Institutional Area, New Delhi 110 067.
Pres. O. P. Ghai; *Hon. Gen. Secy.*
Shakti Malik.

Indian Assn. of Univ. Presses, Calcutta
Univ. Press, Calcutta. *Secy.* Salil Kumar
Chakrabarti.

Indonesia

Ikatan Penerbit Indonesia (IKAPI) (Assn.
of Indonesian Book Publishers), Jalan
Kalipasir 32, Jakarta Pusat. *Pres.* Ismid
Hadad.

Ireland (Republic of)

CLE: The Irish Book Publishers' Assn., Book House Ireland, 65 Middle Abbey St., Dublin 1. *Secy.* Sheila Crowley.

Israel

Book & Printing Center of the Israel Export Institute, Box 29732, 29 Hamered St., 68 125 Tel Aviv. *Dir.* Baruch Schaefer.

Book Publishers Assn. of Israel, Box 20123, 29 Carlebach St., Tel Aviv. *Chpn.* Racheli Eidelman; *Exec. Dir.* Benjamin Sella; *International Promotion & Literary Rights Dept. Dir.* Lorna Soifer.

Italy

Associazione Italiana Editori (Italian Publishers Assn.), Via delle Erbe 2, I-20121 Milan. *Secy.* Achille Ormezzano.

Associazione Librai Antiquari d'Italia (Antiquarian Booksellers Assn. of Italy), Via Jacopo Nardi 6, I-50132 Florence. *Pres.* Renzo Rizzi.

Associazione Librai Italiani (Italian Booksellers Assn.), Piazza G. G. Belli 2, I-00153 Rome.

Jamaica

Booksellers Assn. of Jamaica, c/o B. A. Sangster, Sangster's Book Stores, Ltd., Box 366, 97 Harbour St., Kingston.

Japan

Antiquarian Booksellers Assn. of Japan, 29 San-ei-cho, Shinjuku-ku, Tokyo 160.

Books-on-Japan-in-English Club, Shinnichibo Bldg., 2-1 Sarugaku-cho 1-chome, Chiyoda-ku, Tokyo 101.

Japan Book Importers Assn., Rm. 603, Aizawa Bldg., 20-3, Nihonbashi 1-chome, Chuo-ku, Tokyo 103. *Secy.* Mitsuo Shibata.

Japan Book Publishers Assn., 6 Fukuro-machi, Shinjuku-ku, Tokyo 162. *Exec. Dir.* Sadaya Murayama; *Secy.* Masaaki Shigehisa.

Japan Booksellers Federation, 1-2 Surugadai, Kanda, Chiyoda-ku, Tokyo 101.

Textbook Publishers Assn. of Japan (Kyokasho Kyokai), 20-2 Honshiocho Shinjuku-ku, Tokyo 160. *Secy.* Masae Kusaka.

Kenya

Kenya Publishers Assn., Box 72532, Nairobi. *Secy.* G. P. Lewis.

Korea (Republic of)

Korean Publishers Assn., 105-2 Sagandong, Chongno-ku, Seoul 110. *Pres.* Young-Bin Min; *V.Ps.* Jong-Sung Moon, Yun-Hee Hong, Young-Hwan Kim; *Secy.* Doo-Young Lee.

Luxembourg

Confédération du Commerce Luxembourgeois-Groupement Papetiers-Libraires (Confederation of Retailers, Group for Stationers & Booksellers), 23, Centre Allée-Scheffer, Luxembourg. *Pres.* Pierre Ernster; *Secy.* Fernand Kass.

Malaysia

Malaysian Book Publishers Assn., 48A Jalan SS 2/67, Petaling Jaya. *Hon. Secy.* Johnny Ong.

Mexico

Instituto Mexicano del Libro A.C. (Mexican Book Institute), Paseo de la Reforma 95-603, Dept. 1024, México 4 D.F., C.P. 06030. *Secy.-Gen.* Isabel Ruiz González.

Morocco

Librairie-Papeterie, 344 Ave. Mohammed V, Rabat. *Contact* Kalila Wa Dimna.

Netherlands

Koninklijke Nederlandse Uitgeversbond (Royal Dutch Publishers Assn.), Keizersgracht 391, 1016 EJ Amsterdam. *Secy.* R. M. Vrij.

Nederlandsche Vereeniging van Antiquaren (Antiquarian Booksellers Assn. of the Netherlands), Nieuwe Spiegelstra. 33-35, 1017-DC Amsterdam. *Pres.* A. Gerits.

Nederlandse Boekverkopersbond (Booksellers Assn. of the Netherlands), Waalsdorperweg 119, 2597-HS The Hague. *Pres.* J. van der Plas; *Exec. Secy.* A. Coyajee.

Vereeniging ter bevordering van de belangen des Boekhandels (Dutch Book Trade Assn.), Lassusstraat 9, Box 5475, 1007 AL Amsterdam. *Secy.* M. van Vollenhoven-Nagel.

New Zealand

Book Publishers Assn. of New Zealand, Box 78071, Grey Lynn, Auckland 2. *Pres.* G. Beattie; *Dir.* Gerard Reid.

Booksellers Assn. of New Zealand, Inc., Box 11-377, Wellington. *Dir.* Kate Fortune.

Nigeria

Nigerian Booksellers Assn., Box 3168, Ibadan. *Pres.* W. Adegbonmire.

Nigerian Publishers Assn., c/o P.M.B. 5164, Ibadan. *Pres.* Bankole O. Bolodeoku.

Norway

Norsk Antikvarbokhandlerforening (Norwegian Antiquarian Booksellers Assn.), Ullevalsveien 1, Oslo 1.

Norske Bokhandlerforening (Norwegian Booksellers Assn.), Øvre Vollgate 15, Oslo 1.

Norsk Bokhandler-Medhjelper-Forening (Norwegian Book Trade Employees Assn.), Øvre Vollgate 15, Oslo 1.

Norske Forleggerforening (Norwegian Publishers Assn.), Øvre Vollgate 15, Oslo 1. *Dir.* Paul M. Rothe.

Norsk Musikkforleggerforening (Norwegian Music Publishers Assn.), Box 1499 Vika, Oslo 1.

Pakistan

Pakistan Publishers and Booksellers Assn., YMCA Bldg., Shahra-e-Quaide-Azam, Lahore.

Paraguay

Cámara Paraguaya del Libro (Paraguayan Publishers Assn.), Casilla de Correo 1705, Asunción.

Peru

Cámara Peruana del Libro (Peruvian Publishers Assn.), Jirón Washington 1206, of. 507-508, Lima 100. *Pres.* Andrés Carbone O.

Philippines

Philippine Book Dealers Assn., MCC Box 1103, Makati Commercial Centre, Makati, Metro Manila. *Pres.* Jose C. Benedicto.

Philippine Educational Publishers Assn., 927 Quezon Ave., Quezon City 3008, Metro Manila. *Pres.* Jesus Ernesto R. Sibal.

Poland

Polskie Towarzystwo Wydawców Książek (Polish Publishers Assn.), ul. Mazowiecka 2/4, 00-048 Warsaw.

Stowarzyszenie Ksiegarzy Polskich (Assn. of Polish Booksellers), ul. Mokotowska 4/6,00-641 Warsaw. *Pres.* Tadeusz Hussak.

Portugal

Associação Portuguesa de Editores e Livreiros (Portuguese Assn. of Publishers and Booksellers), Largo de Andaluz 16, 1, Esq., 1000 Lisbon. *Pres.* Fernando Guedes; *Gen. Secy.* Jorge Sá Borges; *Service Manager* José Narciso Vieira.

Romania

Centrala editorială (Romanian Publishing Center), Piata Scînteii 1, R-79715 Bucharest. *Gen. Dir.* Gheorghe Trandafir.

Singapore

Singapore Book Publishers Assn., Box 846, Colombo Court Post Office, Singapore 0617. *Secy.* Charles Cher.

South Africa (Republic of)

Associated Booksellers of Southern Africa, One Meerendal, Nightingale Way, Pinelands 7405. *Secy.* P. G. van Rooyen.
Book Trade Assn. of South Africa, Box 1144, Cape Town 8000. *Contact:* G. Struik.
South African Publishers Assn., One Meerendal, Nightingale Way, Pinelands 7405. *Secy.* P. G. van Rooyen.

Spain

Federacion de Gremios de Editores de España (Spanish Federation of Publishers Assn.), Paseo Castellana, 82 Madrid 6. *Pres.* Francisco Pérez González; *Secy.-Gen.* Jaime Brull.
Gremi d'Editors de Catalunya (Assn. of Catalonian Publishers), Mallorca, 272-274, Barcelona 37. *Pres.* Josep Lluis Monreal.
Gremi de Libreters de Barcelonia i Catalunya (Assn. of Barcelona and Catalunya Booksellers), c. Mallorca 272-276, Barcelona 37.

Instituto Nacional del Libro Español (Spanish Publishers & Booksellers Institute), Santiago Rusiñol 8-10, Madrid 3. *Dir.* Rafael Martinez Alés.

Sri Lanka

Booksellers Assn. of Sri Lanka, Box 244, Colombo 2. *Secy.* W. L. Mendis.
Sri Lanka Publishers Assn., 61 Sangaraja Mawatha, Colombo 10. *Secy.-Gen.* Eamon Kariyakarawana.

Sweden

Svenska Antikvariatföreningen, Box 22549, S-104 22 Stockholm.
Svenska Bokförläggareföreningen (Swedish Publishers Assn.), Sveavägen 52, S-111 34 Stockholm. *Managing Dir.* Lars Bergman.
Svenska Bokhandlareföreningen, Div. of Bok-, Pappers- och Kontorsvaruförbundet (Swedish Booksellers Assn., Div. of the Swedish Federation of Book, Stationery & Office Supplies Dealers), Skeppargatan 27, S-114 52 Stockholm. *Secy.* Per Nordenson.
Svenska Tryckeriföreningen (Swedish Printing Industries Federation), Blasieholmsgatan 4A, Box 16383, S-10327 Stockholm. *Managing Dir.* Per Galmark.

Switzerland

Schweizerischer Buchhändler-und Verleger-Verband (Swiss German-Language Booksellers & Publishers Assn.), Bellerivestr. 3, CH-8034 Zurich. *Managing Dir.* Peter Oprecht.
Società Editori della Svizzera Italiana (Publishers Assn. for the Italian-Speaking Part of Switzerland), Box 282, Viale Portone 4, CH-6501 Bellinzona.
Société des Libraires et Editeurs de la Suisse Romande (Assn. of Swiss French-Language Booksellers & Publishers), 2

av. Agassiz, CH-1001 Lausanne. *Secy.* Robert Junod.

Vereinigung der Buchantiquare und Kupferstichhändler der Schweiz (Assn. of Swiss Antiquarians & Print Dealers), c/o Walter Alicke, Schloss-Str. 6, FL 9490 Vaduz.

Thailand

Publishers and Booksellers Assn. of Thailand, 25 Sukhumvit Soi 56, Bangkok. *Secy.* W. Tantinirandr.

Tunisia

Syndicat des Libraires de Tunisie (Tunisian Booksellers Assn.), 10 av. de France, Tunis.

Turkey

Türk Editòrler Derneǧi (Turkish Publishers Assn.), Ankara Caddesi 60, Istanbul.

United Kingdom

Assn. of Learned & Professional Society Publishers, 30 Austenwood Close, Chalfont St., Peter Gerrards Cross, Bucks., SL9 9DE. *Secy.* R. J. Millson.

Booksellers Assn. of Great Britain & Ireland, 154 Buckingham Palace Rd., London SW1W 9TZ. *Dir.* T. E. Godfray.

Educational Publishers Council, 19 Bedford Sq., London WC1B 3HJ. *Dir.* John R. M. Davies.

National Book League, Book House, 45 E. Hill, London SW18 2QZ. *Dir.* Martyn Goff, O.B.E.

National Federation of Retail Newsagents, 2 Bridewell Place, London EC4V 6AR.

Publishers Assn., 19 Bedford Sq., London WC1B 3HJ. *Secy/Chief Exec.* Clive Bradley.

Uruguay

Cámara Uruguaya del Libro (Uruguayan Publishing Council), Carlos Roxlo 1446, p. 1, Apdo. 2, Montevideo. *Secy.* Arnaldo Medone.

Yugoslavia

Association of Yugoslav Publishers & Booksellers, Kneza Milosa str. 25, Box 883, Belgrade. *Pres.* Vidak Perić.

Zambia

Booksellers & Publishers Assn. of Zambia, Box 35961, Lusaka.

Zimbabwe

Booksellers Assn. of Zimbabwe, Box 1934, Salisbury. *Secy.* A. Muchaziwepi.

Calendar, 1984–1985

The list below contains information (as of February 1984) regarding place and date of association meetings or promotional events that are, for the most part, national or international in scope. State and regional library association meetings also are included. For those who wish to contact the association directly, addresses of library and book trade associations are listed in Part 6 of this *Bowker Annual*. For information on additional book trade and promotional events, see the *1983 Exhibits Directory*, published by the Association of American Publishers; *Chase's Calendar of Annual Events*, published by the Apple Tree Press, Box 1012, Flint, MI 49501; *Literary Market Place* and *International Literary Market Place*, published by R. R. Bowker; *Publishers Weekly* "Calendar," appearing in each issue; and *Library Journal's* "Calendar" feature, appearing in each semimonthly issue.

1984

May

1–6	Quebec International Book Fair	Quebec, P.Q., Canada
2–5	Mountain Plains Library Association	Cheyenne, Wyo.
2–5	Wyoming Association for Educational Communication and Technology	Cheyenne, Wyo.
2–5	Wyoming Library Association	Cheyenne, Wyo.
3–5	Minnesota Library Association	Rochester, Minn.
3–5	Montana Library Association	Helena, Mont.
4	Council of National Library and Information Associations	New York City
4–7	Council of Planning Librarians	Minneapolis, Minn.
6–8	Periodical Distributors of Canada	Vancouver, B.C., Canada
7–9	Associated Information Managers	Arlington, Va.
7–11	International Reading Association	Atlanta, Ga.
9–13	Illinois Association of Media in Education	Chicago, Ill.
9–13	Illinois Library Association	Chicago, Ill.
9–13	Illinois Library Trustee Association	Chicago, Ill.
10–13	Atlantic Provinces Library Association	Charlottetown, P.E.I., Canada
11–12	Saskatchewan Library Association	Saskatoon, Sask., Canada
14–15	Massachusetts Library Association	Springfield, Mass.
14–18	Florida Library Association	Orlando, Fla.
17–18	Maryland Library Association	Ocean City, Md.

May (*cont.*)

18–19	New York Library Association, School Library Media Section	Uniondale, N.Y.
18–21	Tokyo International Book Fair	Tokyo, Japan
20–25	American Society for Information Science	Bloomington, Ind.
23–24	Vermont Educational Media Association	Poultney, Vt.
23–24	Vermont Library Association	Poultney, Vt.
25–31	Medical Library Association	Denver, Colo.
5/28–6/2	Educational Film Library Association	New York City
26–29	American Booksellers Association	Washington, D.C.
*	Maine Educational Media Association	Orono, Maine
*	Maine Library Association	Orono, Maine
*	Association of Canadian University Presses	Toronto, Ont., Canada
*	Guild of Book Workers	New York City

June

7	International Feminist Book Fair	London, England
7–12	Canadian Library Association	Toronto, Ont., Canada
9–14	Special Libraries Association	New York City
10–12	Church and Synagogue Library Association	Indianapolis, Ind.
15–16	Council on Interracial Books for Children	New York City
17–20	Association of American University Presses	Spring Lake, N.J.
22–25	American Library Trustee Association	Dallas, Tex.
22–26	Canadian Booksellers Association	Toronto, Ont., Canada
23	Beta Phi Mu	Dallas, Tex.
23–28	American Library Association	Dallas, Tex.
25	Theatre Library Association	Dallas, Tex.
27	Chinese-American Librarians Association	Dallas, Tex.
*	Association of American University Presses	Spring Lake, N.J.
*	Association of Christian Librarians	Houghton, N.Y.
*	Association of Jewish Libraries	Atlanta, Ga.
*	Bibliographical Society of Canada	Toronto, Ont., Canada

July

1–4	American Association of Law Libraries	San Diego, Calif.
7–9	Canadian Booksellers Association	Toronto, Ont., Canada

*To be announced

July (*cont.*)

14–19	Christian Booksellers Association	Anaheim, Calif.
7/29–8/3	International Association of School Librarianship	Honolulu, Hawaii
*	International Reading Association	Hong Kong

August

5–8	International Association of Printing House Craftsmen	McAffee (Great Gorge), N.J.
22–25	Pacific Northwest Library Association	Billings, Mont.
8/30–9/3	Society of American Archivists	Washington, D.C.

September

20–22	Arizona Library Association	Phoenix, Ariz.
20–22	North Dakota Library Association	Williston, N. Dak.
20–23	Oral History Association	Lexington, Ky.
27–29	Evangelical Christian Publishers Association	St. Louis, Mo.
28–29	West Virginia Educational Media Association	Parkersburg, W. Va.
9/30–10/2	New England Library Association	Sturbridge, Mass.
*	International Federation for Documentation	The Hague, Netherlands
*	International League of Antiquarian Booksellers	London, England
*	International Antiquarian Book Fair	London, England

October

3–5	Missouri Library Association	Cape Girardeau, Mo.
3–5	North Carolina Association of School Librarians	Raleigh, N.C.
3–8	Frankfurt Book Fair	Frankfurt, Federal Republic of Germany
4–6	Michigan Library Association	Detroit, Mich.
4–7	Colorado Library Association	Copper Mountain, Colo.
7–9	Arkansas Library Association	Little Rock, Ark.
10–12	Kentucky Library Association	Louisville, Ky.
11–13	Ohio Educational Library Media Association (OELMA)	Columbus, Ohio
11–13	Oregon Educational Media Association (OEMA)	Corvallis, Oreg.

*To be announced

October (*cont.*)

11–13	Washington Library Media Association	Yakima, Wash.
11–14	Nevada Library Association	Ely, Nev.
15–20	Mississippi Library Association	Biloxi, Miss.
15–20	Southeastern Library Association	Biloxi, Miss.
16–20	International Board on Books for Young People	Nicosia, Cyprus
17–19	Iowa Library Association	Des Moines, Iowa
18–20	Ohio Library Association	Columbus, Ohio
19–21	Virginia Educational Media Association	Crystal City, Va.
20–24	Mid-Atlantic Regional Library Federation	Baltimore, Md.
21–26	American Society for Information Science	Philadelphia, Pa.
22–25	New York Library Association	Kiamesha Lake, N.Y.
23–26	Association of Research Libraries	Washington, D.C.
24–26	Nebraska Educational Media Association	Kearney, Nebr.
24–26	Wisconsin Library Association	La Crosse, Wis.
24–27	Florida Association for Media in Education	Miami Beach, Fla.
24–27	Ohio Educational Library/Media Association	Columbus, Ohio
25–28	Ontario Library Association	Ottawa, Ont., Canada
26–27	Nebraska Library Association	Kearney, Nebr.
26–28	Michigan Association for Media in Education (MAME)	Traverse City, Mich.
10/31–11/4	ALA American Association of School Librarians	Atlanta, Ga.
*	National Association of Book Manufacturers (PIA)	Chicago, Ill.

November

1–3	South Carolina Library Association	Columbia, S.C.
2	Council of National Library and Information Associations	New York City
4–7	Book Manufacturers Institute	Southhampton, Bermuda
8–9	New Jersey Education Association	Atlantic City, N.J.
9–11	Minnesota Educational Media Association	Brooklyn Park, Minn.
9–12	National Children's Book Week	U.S.A.
11–14	Information Industry Association	San Francisco, Calif.

*To be announced

November (*cont.*)

11–18	Advertising Typographers Association	Dorado Beach, P.R.
20–25	Montreal Book Fair	Montreal, P.Q., Canada
30	Association of Book Travelers	New York City
*	Virginia Library Association	Norfolk, Va.

December

1–5	California Library Association	Los Angeles, Calif.
27–30	Modern Language Association	Washington, D.C.

1985

January

18–23	Association for Educational Communication and Technology	Anaheim, Calif.
18–23	National Audio-Visual Association	Anaheim, Calif.
25	Bibliographical Society of America	New York City
1/31–2/2	Association for Library and Information Science Education	*
*	National Book Critics Circle	New York City

February

1–4	ALA American Library Trustee Association	Washington, D.C.
2–7	American Library Association	Washington, D.C.
10–13	Art Libraries Society of North America	Los Angeles, Calif.
1/30–2/1	Special Libraries Association	Philadelphia, Pa.

March

3–6	Association of American Publishers	Palm Springs, Calif.
3–9	Music Library Association	Louisville, Ky.
4–7	Technical Association of the Pulp and Paper Industry (TAPPI)	New Orleans, La.
15–23	Magazine and Paperback Marketing Institute (MPMI)	Acapulco, Mexico

April

2	International Children's Book Day	Worldwide
8–11	Catholic Library Association	St. Louis, Mo.
8–12	National Association of College Stores	San Antonio, Tex.

*To be announced

April (*cont.*)

10–13	London Book Fair	London, England
10–13	New Mexico Library Association	Clovis, N. Mex.
11–12	South Carolina Association of School Librarians	*
11–14	Oregon Library Association	Pendleton, Oreg.
14–20	National Library Week	U.S.A.
16–20	Texas Library Association	Dallas, Tex.
17–20	Washington Library Association	Sea-Tac, Wash.
18–20	Tennessee Library Association	Nashville, Tenn.
19–23	Council of Planning Librarians	Montreal, P.Q., Canada
23–28	Quebec International Book Fair	Quebec, P.Q., Canada
24–27	New Jersey Library Association	Atlantic City, N.J.
4/29–5/2	Association for Information and Image Management	Washington, D.C.

May

5–9	International Reading Association	New Orleans, La.
5–10	Association for Educational Communication and Technology	Minneapolis, Minn.
15–17	Maryland Library Association	Baltimore, Md.
24–30	Medical Library Association	New York, N.Y.
25–28	American Booksellers Association	San Francisco, Calif.
27–31	Florida Library Association	Orlando, Fla.
5/27–6/1	Educational Film Library Association	New York City
Mid-May	Maryland Library Association	Baltimore, Md.
Late May	Alaska Library Association	Anchorage, Alaska
*	Guild of Book Workers	New York City

June

8–13	Special Libraries Association	Winnipeg, Man., Canada
11–17	Canadian Library Association	Calgary, Alta., Canada
15–17	Periodical Distributors of Canada	St. John's, Nfld., Canada
21	American Theological Library Association	Madison, N.J.
23–25	Church and Synagogue Library Association	Washington, D.C. (tent.)
6/30–7/3	American Association of Law Libraries	New York City
*	Association of American University Presses	New Orleans, La.

July

5–8	ALA American Library Trustee Association	Chicago, Ill.

*To be announced

July (*cont.*)

6–11	American Library Association	Chicago, Ill.
9	Chinese-American Librarians Association	Chicago, Ill.
13–18	Christian Booksellers Association	Dallas, Tex.

August

4–7	International Association of Printing House Craftsmen	Chicago, Ill.
21–23	Pacific Northwest Library Association	Eugene, Oreg.
*	Children's Book Council	New York City

September

12–14	Minnesota Statewide Library Service **Forum, All-Association Conference II** (includes Minnesota Library Association and Minnesota chapters of all national library associations)	St. Paul, Minn.

October

1–5	North Carolina Library Association	Raleigh, N.C.
6–11	American Society for Information Science	Las Vegas, Nev.
9–14	Frankfurt Book Fair	Frankfurt, Federal Republic of Germany
13–19	Advertising Typographers Association	Carmel, Calif.
23–25	Wisconsin Library Association	Milwaukee, Wis.
10–12	South Carolina Library Association	Charleston, S.C.
10–12	Washington Library Media Association	Seattle, Wash.
10–12	West Virginia Library Association	Morgantown, W. Va.
11–12	Nebraska Library Association	Lincoln, Nebr.
16–18	Iowa Library Association	Davenport, Iowa
16–19	New York Library Association	Lake Placid, N.Y.
10/29–11/1	Society of American Archivists	Austin, Tex.
10/31–11/2	Ohio Library Association Ohio Educational Library/Media Association	Cincinnati, Ohio
*	Georgia Library Association	Augusta, Ga.
*	Mountain Plains Library Association	Las Vegas, Nev.
*	National Association of Book Manufacturers	Chicago, Ill.

*To be announced

October (*cont.*)

*	Nevada Library Association	Las Vegas, Nev.
*	Vermont Educational Media Association	Essex Junction, Vt.

November

3–6	Book Manufacturers Institute	Phoenix, Ariz.
14–16	Virginia Library Association	Hot Springs, Va.
16–20	California Library Association	Oakland, Calif.
18–24	National Children's Book Week	U.S.A.

December

27–30	Modern Language Association	Chicago, Ill.

*To be announced

Index

B